S0-BLV-687

THE PAPERS OF

THOMAS JEFFERSON

RETIREMENT SERIES

THE PAPERS OF
Thomas Jefferson

RETIREMENT SERIES

Volume 9
1 September 1815 to 30 April 1816

J. JEFFERSON LOONEY, EDITOR

ROBERT F. HAGGARD, SENIOR ASSOCIATE EDITOR

JULIE L. LAUTENSCHLAGER, ASSOCIATE EDITOR

ELLEN C. HICKMAN AND CHRISTINE STERNBERG PATRICK,
ASSISTANT EDITORS

LISA A. FRANCAVILLA, MANAGING EDITOR

ANDREA R. GRAY AND PAULA VITERBO, EDITORIAL ASSISTANTS

CATHERINE COINER CRITTENDEN AND SUSAN SPENGLER,
SENIOR DIGITAL TECHNICIANS

PRINCETON AND OXFORD

PRINCETON UNIVERSITY PRESS

2012

ARCHBISHOP ALEMANY LIBRARY
DOMINICAN UNIVERSITY
SAN RAFAEL, CALIFORNIA 94901

Copyright © 2012 by Princeton University Press

Published by Princeton University Press, 41 William Street,

Princeton, New Jersey 08540

IN THE UNITED KINGDOM:

Princeton University Press, 6 Oxford Street,

Woodford, Oxfordshire OX20 1TW

All Rights Reserved

Library of Congress Cataloging-in-Publication Data

Jefferson, Thomas, 1743–1826

The papers of Thomas Jefferson. Retirement series / J. Jefferson Looney, editor . . .

[et al.] p. cm.

Includes bibliographical references and index.

Contents: v. 1. 4 March to 15 November 1809—[etc.]—

v. 9. 1 September 1815 to 30 April 1816

ISBN 978-0-691-15670-5 (cloth: v. 9: alk. paper)

1. Jefferson, Thomas, 1743–1826—Archives. 2. Jefferson, Thomas, 1743–1826—

Correspondence. 3. Presidents—United States—Archives.

4. Presidents—United States—Correspondence. 5. United States—

Politics and government—1809–1817—Sources. 6. United States—Politics

and government—1817–1825—Sources. I. Looney, J. Jefferson.

II. Title. III. Title: Retirement series.

E302.J442 2004b

973.4'6'092—dc22   2004048327

This book has been composed in Monticello

Princeton University Press books are printed on
acid-free paper and meet the guidelines for permanence
and durability of the Committee on Production
Guidelines for Book Longevity of the
Council on Library Resources

Printed in the United States of America

DEDICATED TO THE MEMORY OF

ADOLPH S. OCHS

PUBLISHER OF THE NEW YORK TIMES

1896–1935

WHO BY THE EXAMPLE OF A RESPONSIBLE

PRESS ENLARGED AND FORTIFIED

THE JEFFERSONIAN CONCEPT

OF A FREE PRESS

ADVISORY COMMITTEE

LESLIE GREENE BOWMAN

CHARLES T. CULLEN

JAMES HORN

DANIEL P. JORDAN

PENELOPE J. KAISERLIAN

JOHN P. KAMINSKI

STANLEY N. KATZ

JOHN M. MURRIN

BARBARA B. OBERG

PETER S. ONUF

ANDREW J. O'SHAUGHNESSY

DAVID M. SEAMAN

JOHN C. A. STAGG

BRENT TARTER

THIS EDITION was made possible by a founding grant from The New York Times Company to Princeton University.

The Retirement Series is sponsored by the Thomas Jefferson Foundation, Inc., of Charlottesville, Virginia. It was created with a six-year founding grant from The Pew Charitable Trusts to the Foundation and to Princeton University, enabling the former to take over responsibility for the volumes associated with this period. Leading gifts from Richard Gilder, Mrs. Martin S. Davis, and Thomas A. Saunders III have assured the continuation of the Retirement Series. For these essential donations, and for other indispensable aid generously given by librarians, archivists, scholars, and collectors of manuscripts, the Editors record their sincere gratitude.

FOREWORD

THE 523 DOCUMENTS in this volume cover the period from 1 September 1815 to 30 April 1816. During these eight months Jefferson made three trips to Poplar Forest. On a visit early in autumn 1815, he had two important items on his agenda. The first was a stop in Buckingham County, where he presented evidence to the Superior Court in the lawsuit between the children and widow of Jefferson's late brother, Randolph. On 15 September Jefferson wrote out his own deposition in the case, which concerned the validity of competing versions of Randolph's will. The second project engaged Jefferson and two of his scientific colleagues, José Corrêa da Serra and Francis W. Gilmer, on an expedition to measure the elevation of the Peaks of Otter and study the botany of the region nearby. On this journey Jefferson made preliminary observations that he researched further on a trip later in the year, of which he wrote to his friend Charles Clay that "I was five days absent in my trip to the peaks of Otter, and have been five days engaged in calculating the observations made." During this second autumn visit Jefferson welcomed the returning war hero Andrew Jackson in a brief visit to Poplar Forest, accompanied him on a procession into Lynchburg, and offered a toast at a public dinner held in the general's honor.

With the War of 1812 over, Americans could once again freely order and receive shipments from Europe. Jefferson wrote the Norfolk wine importer John F. Oliveira Fernandes that "Disappointments in procuring supplies have at length left me without a drop of wine." In addition to restocking his wine cellar, Jefferson also sought books to begin replacing those he had sold to Congress. The young scholar George Ticknor, who had visited Jefferson at Monticello the previous spring, was now in Europe to undertake literary studies. He served as Jefferson's purchasing agent there and gave him his opinions on the merits of various editions of classical works.

Although Jefferson had not practiced law for several decades, he expended significant effort assisting his friend Joseph Miller, sometime brewmaster at Monticello, as Miller sought to gain possession of his own deceased brother's Virginia property. Jefferson's legal advice was also requested by Mary Blair Andrews, daughter of John Blair, a former associate justice of the United States Supreme Court. Jefferson found himself further embroiled in the settlement of the estates of his old friend Lucy Ludwell Paradise and of Charles Bellini, late professor of languages at the College of William and Mary. With the death of Philip Mazzei in March 1816, Jefferson was soon to be drawn into yet another series of legal concerns that would carry on for the rest of his lifetime and only be settled by his heirs.

Jefferson composed several pieces that were published in newspapers in this period. By early December his comments summarizing the conclusion of his calculations on the Peaks of Otter were reprinted in several newspapers. In drafting a letter to Horatio G. Spafford, Jefferson penned what he himself described as a "tirade" against a religious pamphlet written by the New England clergyman Lyman Beecher. Thinking better of expressing such strong views to a mere acquaintance, Jefferson revised the letter, but he retained the excised text and soon sent it to the *Richmond Enquirer* publisher Thomas Ritchie with permission to publish, so long as Ritchie kept Jefferson's authorship secret. An anonymous letter to the publishers of the Washington *Daily National Intelligencer* elicited a similarly anonymous response from Jefferson, who attempted to prevent an opinion he had written as George Washington's secretary of state from establishing a broad precedent.

Jefferson's incoming mail continued to span a wide array of correspondents and subjects. He received several updates on the debates in the Virginia General Assembly from Joseph C. Cabell, Thomas W. Maury, and Charles Yancey. In a letter to Yancey, Jefferson articulated his views of the importance of state funding for education, famously remarking that "if a nation expects to be ignorant & free, in a state of civilisation, it expects what never was & never will be." The passage of a resolution calling for a report on education and of a law calling for a resurvey and mapping of the state led Governor Wilson Cary Nicholas to seek Jefferson's advice on these issues, resulting in two detailed explanations from the retired statesman. Alden Partridge, a Vermont soldier and educator, sent Jefferson a series of geographical surveys and meteorological observations. An anonymous correspondent from Baltimore wrote a revealing description of the organization and personnel policies of a Baltimore cotton factory where young girls constituted the majority of the employees.

Jefferson's family circle continued to grow with the birth of a great-granddaughter, Margaret Smith Randolph, the first child of Thomas Jefferson Randolph and Jane H. Nicholas Randolph. Granddaughter Ellen spent time in Washington with the President and Mrs. Madison and provided Jefferson with some news from the nation's capital. A false report of his death having surfaced from an unidentified source, Jefferson reassured his old friend Elizabeth Trist that "I am here, my dear Madam alive and well, and notwithstanding the murderous histories of the winter, I have not had an hour's sickness for a twelvemonth past."

ACKNOWLEDGMENTS

MANY INDIVIDUALS and institutions provided aid and encouragement during the preparation of this volume. Those who helped us to locate and acquire primary and secondary sources and answered our research questions include our colleagues at the Thomas Jefferson Foundation, especially Anna Berkes, Jack Robertson, and Endrina Tay of the Jefferson Library; Robert H. Smith Director of Restoration William L. Beiswanger; Shannon Senior Research Historian Lucia C. Stanton; Elizabeth Chew, Diane Ehrenpreis, Justin Sarafin, and Carrie Taylor of the curatorial department; vice-president of visitor programs and services Gary Sandling; staff archaeologist Derek Wheeler; and Foundation historian Gaye Wilson. Also instrumental to our work were Cheryl Schnirring at the Abraham Lincoln Presidential Library, Springfield, Illinois; Andrew Bourque and Thomas Knoles at the American Antiquarian Society; Valerie-Anne Lutz and Charles Greifenstein at the American Philosophical Society; Sylvie Clair and Evelyne Borghiero at the Archives de Marseilles, Marseilles, France; François Wyn at the Bibliotheque Nationale de France, Paris; Seth Rockman at Brown University; Jim Gerencser at Dickinson College; Lucas R. Clawson at the Hagley Museum and Library; Stephen G. Hague of Philadelphia; David K. Frasier and Zach Downey at the Lilly Library, Indiana University, Bloomington; John Beekman at the Jersey City Free Public Library, New Jersey; Lewis Hobgood Averett at the Jones Memorial Library in Lynchburg; Linda August and Cornelia S. King at the Library Company of Philadelphia; Jeff Flannery, Megan Halsband, Bruce Kirby, and Julia Schifini at the Library of Congress; Brent Tarter and his coworkers at the Library of Virginia; Gregory R. Krueger of the Lynchburg Museum System; John McCusker, Trinity University, San Antonio, Texas; Eben Dennis at the Maryland Historical Society; Anna Cook, Elaine Grublin, Nancy Heywood, and Tracy Potter at the Massachusetts Historical Society; Molly Kodner at the Missouri History Museum Library and Research Center, Saint Louis; Patricia Anderson and Netisha Currie at the National Archives, College Park; Michael Wright at the National Archives, Southwest Region, Fort Worth, Texas; Alexandra M. Henri at the New York Public Library; Jennifer Payne and Gail E. Wiese at the Kreitzberg Library, Norwich University, Northfield, Vermont; Sandra Rebok at the Spanish National Research Council; Ted Delaney at the Southern Memorial Association, Old City Cemetery Museum & Arboretum, Lynchburg; Jacob Sandling of

ACKNOWLEDGMENTS

Williamsburg; Tillburg University, the Netherlands; Anne Causey, Edward Gaynor, Margaret Hrabe, and Regina Rush at the Albert and Shirley Small Special Collections Library, University of Virginia; Henry Wiencek of Charlottesville; and Joanne L. Yeck. As always, we received advice, assistance, and encouragement from a large number of our fellow documentary editors, including Margaret Hogan of the Adams Papers; Mary Hackett, Angela Kreider, David B. Mattern, and John C. A. Stagg of the James Madison Papers; Daniel Preston of the James Monroe Papers; and Martha J. King, John Little, James P. McClure, Linda Monaco, Barbara B. Oberg, and Elaine Weber Pascu of the Thomas Jefferson Papers in Princeton. Genevieve Moene and Roland H. Simon transcribed and translated the French letters included in this volume; Coulter George helped us with passages in Greek; Christina Ball, Jonathan T. Hine, Rosanna M. Giammanco Frongia, and Adrienne Ward provided aid with Italian; John F. Miller assisted us with Latin quotations; and David T. Gies and Jennifer McCune counseled us on a document in Spanish. Kevin B. Jones helped us to understand a large body of Jefferson's surveying calculations and related documents. The maps of Jefferson's Virginia and Albemarle County were created by Rick Britton. The other illustrations that appear in this volume were assembled with the assistance of Julie Miller and Bonnie Coles at the Library of Congress; Leah Stearns at the Thomas Jefferson Foundation; Christina Deane at the University of Virginia; Jamison Davis at the Virginia Historical Society; and Susan A. Riggs at the College of William and Mary's Special Collections Research Center. Stephen Perkins of IDM USA continued to assist us with all things digital. Finally, we would like to acknowledge the efforts of the able staff at Princeton University Press, including Dimitri Karetnikov and Jan Lilly, and our production editor and special friend, Linny Schenck.

EDITORIAL METHOD AND APPARATUS

1. RENDERING THE TEXT

From its inception *The Papers of Thomas Jefferson* has insisted on high standards of accuracy in rendering text, but modifications in textual policy and editorial apparatus have been implemented as different approaches have become accepted in the field or as a more faithful rendering has become technically feasible. Prior discussions of textual policy appeared in Vols. 1:xxix–xxxiv, 22:vii–xi, 24:vii–viii, and 30:xiii–xiv of the First Series.

The textual method of the Retirement Series will adhere to the more literal approach adopted in Volume 30 of the parent edition. Original spelling, capitalization, and punctuation are retained as written. Such idiosyncrasies as Jefferson's failure to capitalize the beginnings of most of his sentences and abbreviations like "mr" are preserved, as are his preference for "it's" to "its" and his characteristic spellings of "knolege," "paiment," and "recieve." Modern usage is adopted in cases where intent is impossible to determine, an issue that arises most often in the context of capitalization. Some so-called slips of the pen are corrected, but the original reading is recorded in a subjoined textual note. Jefferson and others sometimes signaled a change in thought within a paragraph with extra horizontal space, and this is rendered by a three-em space. Blanks left for words and not subsequently filled by the authors are represented by a space approximating the length of the blank. Gaps, doubtful readings of illegible or damaged text, and wording supplied from other versions or by editorial conjecture are explained in the source note or in numbered textual notes. Foreign-language documents, the vast majority of which are in French during the retirement period, are transcribed in full as faithfully as possible and followed by a full translation.

Two modifications from past practice bring this series still closer to the original manuscripts. Underscored text is presented as such rather than being converted to italics. Superscripts are also preserved rather than being lowered to the baseline. In most cases of superscripting, the punctuation that is below or next to the superscripted letters is dropped, since it is virtually impossible to determine what is a period or dash as opposed to a flourish under, over, or adjacent to superscripted letters.

Limits to the more literal method are still recognized, however, and readability and consistency with past volumes are prime considerations. In keeping with the basic design implemented in the first volume of the Papers, salutations and signatures continue to display in large and small capitals rather than upper- and lowercase letters. Expansion marks over abbreviations are silently omitted. With very rare exceptions, deleted text and information on which words were added during the process of composition is not displayed within the document transcription. Based on the Editors' judgment of their significance, such emendations are either described in numbered textual notes or ignored. Datelines for letters are consistently printed at the head of the text, with a comment in the descriptive note when they have been moved. Address information, endorsements, and dockets are quoted or described in the source note rather than reproduced in the document proper.

2. TEXTUAL DEVICES

The following devices are employed throughout the work to clarify the presentation of the text.

[...]	Text missing and not conjecturable. The size of gaps longer than a word or two is estimated in annotation.
[ ]	Number or part of number missing or illegible.
[roman]	Conjectural reading for missing or illegible matter. A question mark follows when the reading is doubtful.
[*italic*]	Editorial comment inserted in the text.
<*italic*>	Matter deleted in the manuscript but restored in our text.

3. DESCRIPTIVE SYMBOLS

The following symbols are employed throughout the work to describe the various kinds of manuscript originals. When a series of versions is included, the first to be recorded is the version used for the printed text.

Dft	draft (usually a composition or rough draft; multiple drafts, when identifiable as such, are designated "2d Dft," etc.)
Dupl	duplicate
MS	manuscript (arbitrarily applied to most documents other than letters)

PoC   polygraph copy
PrC   press copy
RC   recipient's copy
SC   stylograph copy

All manuscripts of the above types are assumed to be in the hand of the author of the document to which the descriptive symbol pertains. If not, that fact is stated. On the other hand, the following types of manuscripts are assumed not to be in the hand of the author, and exceptions will be noted:

FC   file copy (applied to all contemporary copies retained by the author or his agents)

Tr   transcript (applied to all contemporary and later copies except file copies; period of transcription, unless clear by implication, will be given when known)

4. LOCATION SYMBOLS

The locations of documents printed in this edition from originals in private hands and from printed sources are recorded in self-explanatory form in the descriptive note following each document. The locations of documents printed or referenced from originals held by public and private institutions in the United States are recorded by means of the symbols used in the *MARC Code List for Organizations* (2000) maintained by the Library of Congress. The symbols DLC and MHi by themselves stand for the collections of Jefferson Papers proper in these repositories. When texts are drawn from other collections held by these two institutions, the names of those collections are added. Location symbols for documents held by institutions outside the United States are given in a subjoined list. The lists of symbols are limited to the institutions represented by documents printed or referred to in this volume.

CLU-C   William Andrew Clark Library, University of California, Los Angeles
CSmH   Huntington Library, San Marino, California
        JF   Jefferson File
CSt   Stanford University, Stanford, California
CtY   Yale University, New Haven, Connecticut
CU-L   University of California, Law Library, Berkeley
DeGH   Hagley Museum and Library, Greenville, Delaware

DLC Library of Congress, Washington, D.C.
   TJ Papers Thomas Jefferson Papers (this is assumed if not stated, but also given as indicated to furnish the precise location of an undated, misdated, or otherwise problematic document, thus "DLC: TJ Papers, 213:38071–2" represents volume 213, folios 38071 and 38072 as the collection was arranged at the time the first microfilm edition was made in 1944–45. Access to the microfilm edition of the collection as it was rearranged under the Library's Presidential Papers Program is provided by the *Index to the Thomas Jefferson Papers* [1976])

DNA National Archives, Washington, D.C., with identifications of series (preceded by record group number) as follows:

   CD Consular Dispatches
   CRL Consular Records, Leghorn
   CS Census Schedules
   HFL History of the French in Louisiana
   LAR Letters of Application and Recommendation
   LRF Legation Records, France
   MLR Miscellaneous Letters Received
   MSA Miscellaneous Settled Accounts, Office of the Fifth Auditor
   PA Passport Applications
   PW1812 War of 1812 Papers
   ROSN Records of the Office of the Secretary of the Navy
   TP-F Territorial Papers, Florida

ICN Newberry Library, Chicago, Illinois
InU Indiana University, Bloomington
LNHiC Historic New Orleans Collection, New Orleans, Louisiana
MBCo Countway Library of Medicine, Boston, Massachusetts
MBPLi Boston Public Library, Boston, Massachusetts
MdHi Maryland Historical Society, Baltimore
MdU University of Maryland, College Park
MeHi Maine Historical Society, Portland
MH Harvard University, Cambridge, Massachusetts

MHi	Massachusetts Historical Society, Boston
MoSHi	Missouri History Museum, Saint Louis
	TJC-BC Thomas Jefferson Collection, text formerly in Bixby Collection
MoSW	Washington University, Saint Louis, Missouri
MWA	American Antiquarian Society, Worcester, Massachusetts
MWiCA	Sterling and Francine Clark Art Institute, Williamstown, Massachusetts
NBuHi	Buffalo and Erie County Historical Society, Buffalo, New York
Nc-Ar	North Carolina Office of Archives and History, Raleigh
NcU	University of North Carolina, Chapel Hill
	NPT Southern Historical Collection, Nicholas Philip Trist Papers
NhD	Dartmouth College, Hanover, New Hampshire
NHi	New-York Historical Society, New York City
NjHi	New Jersey Historical Society, Newark
NjMoHP	Morristown National Historical Park, Morristown, New Jersey
NjP	Princeton University, Princeton, New Jersey
NN	New York Public Library, New York City
NNGL	Gilder Lehrman Collection, New York City
NNPM	Pierpont Morgan Library, New York City
NNYSL	New York Society Library, New York City
PCarlD	Dickinson College, Carlisle, Pennsylvania
PHi	Historical Society of Pennsylvania, Philadelphia
PPAmP	American Philosophical Society, Philadelphia, Pennsylvania
PPL	Library Company of Philadelphia, Pennsylvania
PWacD	David Library of the American Revolution, Washington Crossing, Pennsylvania
TxFNA	National Archives, Southwest Region, Fort Worth, Texas
	RUSDCEDL Records of the United States District Court for the Eastern District of Louisiana
Vi	Library of Virginia, Richmond
ViHi	Virginia Historical Society, Richmond
ViLJML	Jones Memorial Library, Lynchburg, Virginia
ViRoHM	History Museum of Western Virginia, Roanoke

ViU	University of Virginia, Charlottesville	
	FWG	Frances Walker Gilmer Papers
	GT	George Tucker transcripts of Thomas Jefferson letters
	JCC	Joseph C. Cabell Papers
	JHC	John Hartwell Cocke Papers
	TJP	Thomas Jefferson Papers
	TJP-CC	Thomas Jefferson Papers, text formerly in Carr-Cary Papers
	TJP-ER	Thomas Jefferson Papers, text formerly in Edgehill-Randolph Papers
	TJP-LBJM	Thomas Jefferson Papers, Thomas Jefferson's Legal Brief in *Jefferson v. Michie*, 1804–15, deposited by Mrs. Augustina David Carr Mills
	TJP-MJ	Thomas Jefferson Papers, text formerly in Moyer-Jefferson Papers
	TJP-PC	Thomas Jefferson Papers, text formerly in Philip B. Campbell Deposit
ViW	College of William and Mary, Williamsburg, Virginia	
	TC-JP	Jefferson Papers, Tucker-Coleman Collection
	TJP	Thomas Jefferson Papers
VtMiM	Middlebury College, Middlebury, Vermont	
VtNN	Norwich University, Northfield, Vermont	

The following symbols represent repositories located outside of the United States:

FrM	Archives Municipales de Marseille, France
ItPiAFM	Archivio Filippo Mazzei, privately owned, Pisa, Italy
PlKMN	Muzeum Narodowe w Krakowie, Poland

5. OTHER ABBREVIATIONS AND SYMBOLS

The following abbreviations and symbols are commonly employed in the annotation throughout the work.

Lb   Letterbook (used to indicate texts copied or assembled into bound volumes)

RG   Record Group (used in designating the location of documents in the Library of Virginia and the National Archives)

SJL   Jefferson's "Summary Journal of Letters" written and received for the period 11 Nov. 1783 to 25 June 1826 (in DLC: TJ Papers). This epistolary record, kept in Jefferson's hand, has been checked against the TJ Editorial Files. It is to be assumed that all outgoing letters are recorded in SJL unless there is a note to the contrary. When the date of receipt of an incoming letter is recorded in SJL, it is incorporated in the notes. Information and discrepancies revealed in SJL but not found in the letter itself are also noted. Missing letters recorded in SJL are accounted for in the notes to documents mentioning them, in related documents, or in an appendix

TJ   Thomas Jefferson

TJ Editorial Files   Photoduplicates and other editorial materials in the office of the Papers of Thomas Jefferson: Retirement Series, Jefferson Library, Thomas Jefferson Foundation, Inc., Charlottesville

d   Penny or denier

f   Florin

£   Pound sterling or livre, depending upon context (in doubtful cases, a clarifying note will be given)

s   Shilling or sou (also expressed as /)

₶   Livre Tournois

℔   Per (occasionally used for pro, pre)

6. SHORT TITLES

The following list includes short titles of works cited frequently in this edition. Since it is impossible to anticipate all the works to be cited in abbreviated form, the list is revised from volume to volume.

Acts of Assembly   *Acts of the General Assembly of Virginia* (cited by session; title varies over time)

ANB   John A. Garraty and Mark C. Carnes, eds., *American National Biography*, 1999, 24 vols.

Annals   *Annals of the Congress of the United States: The Debates and Proceedings in the Congress of the United States . . . Compiled from Authentic Materials*, Washington, D.C., Gales & Seaton, 1834–56, 42 vols. (All editions are undependable and pagination varies from one printing to another. Citations given below are to the edition mounted on the American Memory website of the Library of Congress and give the date of the debate as well as page numbers)

APS American Philosophical Society

ASP *American State Papers: Documents, Legislative and Executive, of the Congress of the United States,* 1832–61, 38 vols.

Axelson, *Virginia Postmasters* Edith F. Axelson, *Virginia Postmasters and Post Offices, 1789–1832,* 1991

Betts, *Farm Book* Edwin M. Betts, ed., *Thomas Jefferson's Farm Book,* 1953 (in two separately paginated sections; unless otherwise specified, references are to the second section)

Betts, *Garden Book* Edwin M. Betts, ed., *Thomas Jefferson's Garden Book, 1766–1824,* 1944

Biddle, *Lewis and Clark Expedition* Nicholas Biddle, *History of the Expedition under the command of Captains Lewis and Clark to the Sources of the Missouri, thence across the Rocky Mountains and down the River Columbia to the Pacific Ocean. Performed during the years 1804–5–6. By order of the Government of the United States,* 2 vols., Philadelphia, 1814; Sowerby, no. 4168; Poor, *Jefferson's Library,* 7 (no. 370)

Biog. Dir. Cong. *Biographical Directory of the United States Congress, 1774–Present,* online resource, Office of the Clerk, United States House of Representatives

Biographie universelle *Biographie universelle, ancienne et moderne,* new ed., 1843–65, 45 vols.

Black's Law Dictionary Bryan A. Garner and others, eds., *Black's Law Dictionary,* 7th ed., 1999

Brigham, *American Newspapers* Clarence S. Brigham, *History and Bibliography of American Newspapers, 1690–1820,* 1947, 2 vols.

Bruce, *University* Philip Alexander Bruce, *History of the University of Virginia 1819–1919: The Lengthened Shadow of One Man,* 1920–22, 5 vols.

Burk, Jones, and Girardin, *History of Virginia* John Daly Burk, Skelton Jones, and Louis H. Girardin, *The History of Virginia, from its First Settlement to the Present Day,* 4 vols., Petersburg, 1804–16; Sowerby, no. 464; Poor, *Jefferson's Library,* 4 (no. 127)

Bush, *Life Portraits* Alfred L. Bush, *The Life Portraits of Thomas Jefferson,* rev. ed., 1987

Butler, *Virginia Militia*   Stuart Lee Butler, *A Guide to Virginia Militia Units in the War of 1812*, 1988

Callahan, *U.S. Navy*   Edward W. Callahan, *List of Officers of the Navy of the United States and of the Marine Corps from 1775 to 1900*, 1901, repr. 1969

Catalogue of U.S. Library   *Catalogue of the Library of the United States. To which is annexed, A Copious Index, alphabetically arranged*, Washington, 1815

Chambers, *Poplar Forest*   S. Allen Chambers, *Poplar Forest & Thomas Jefferson*, 1993

Clay, *Papers*   James F. Hopkins and others, eds., *The Papers of Henry Clay*, 1959–92, 11 vols.

Connelly, *Napoleonic France*   Owen Connelly and others, eds., *Historical Dictionary of Napoleonic France, 1799–1815*, 1985

CVSP   William P. Palmer and others, eds., *Calendar of Virginia State Papers . . . Preserved in the Capitol at Richmond*, 1875–93, 11 vols.

DAB   Allen Johnson and Dumas Malone, eds., *Dictionary of American Biography*, 1928–36, 20 vols.

DBF   *Dictionnaire de biographie française*, 1933– , 19 vols.

Delaplaine's Repository   Joseph Delaplaine, *Delaplaine's Repository of the Lives and Portraits of Distinguished Americans*, Philadelphia, 1816–18, 2 vols.; Poor, *Jefferson's Library*, 4 (no. 139)

Destutt de Tracy, *Commentary and Review of Montesquieu's Spirit of Laws*   Destutt de Tracy, *A Commentary and Review of Montesquieu's Spirit of Laws. prepared for press from the Original Manuscript, in the hands of the publisher. To which are annexed, Observations on the Thirty-First Book, by the late M. Condorcet: and Two Letters of Helvetius, on the merits of the same work*, Philadelphia, 1811; Sowerby, no. 2327; Poor, *Jefferson's Library*, 10 (no. 623)

Destutt de Tracy, *Treatise on Political Economy*   Destutt de Tracy, *A Treatise on Political Economy; to which is prefixed a supplement to a preceding work on the understanding, or Elements of Ideology*, Georgetown, 1817; Poor, *Jefferson's Library*, 11 (no. 700)

DNB   Leslie Stephen and Sidney Lee, eds., *Dictionary of National Biography*, 1885–1901, 22 vols.

DSB   Charles C. Gillispie, ed., *Dictionary of Scientific Biography*, 1970–80, 16 vols.

DVB   John T. Kneebone and others, eds., *Dictionary of Virginia Biography*, 1998– , 3 vols.

EG   Dickinson W. Adams and Ruth W. Lester, eds., *Jefferson's Extracts from the Gospels*, 1983, *The Papers of Thomas Jefferson*, Second Series

Fairclough, *Horace: Satires, Epistles and Ars Poetica*   H. Rushton Fairclough, trans., *Horace: Satires, Epistles and Ars Poetica*, Loeb Classical Library, 1926, repr. 2005

Fairclough, *Virgil*   H. Rushton Fairclough, trans., *Virgil*, Loeb Classical Library, 1916–18, rev. by G. P. Goold, 1999–2000, repr. 2002–06, 2 vols.

Ford   Paul Leicester Ford, ed., *The Writings of Thomas Jefferson*, Letterpress Edition, 1892–99, 10 vols.

Franklin, *Papers*   Leonard W. Labaree and others, eds., *The Papers of Benjamin Franklin*, 1959– , 40 vols.

HAW   Henry A. Washington, ed., *The Writings of Thomas Jefferson*, 1853–54, 9 vols.

Heitman, *Continental Army*   Francis B. Heitman, comp., *Historical Register of Officers of the Continental Army during the War of the Revolution, April, 1775, to December, 1783*, rev. ed., 1914

Heitman, *U.S. Army*   Francis B. Heitman, comp., *Historical Register and Dictionary of the United States Army*, 1903, 2 vols.

Hening   William Waller Hening, ed., *The Statutes at Large; being a Collection of all the Laws of Virginia*, Richmond, 1809–23, 13 vols.; Sowerby, no. 1863; Poor, *Jefferson's Library*, 10 (no. 573)

Hoefer, *Nouv. biog. générale*   J. C. F. Hoefer, *Nouvelle biographie générale depuis les temps les plus reculés jusqu'a nos jours*, 1852–83, 46 vols.

Hortus Third   Liberty Hyde Bailey, Ethel Zoe Bailey, and the staff of the Liberty Hyde Bailey Hortorium, Cornell University, *Hortus Third: A Concise Dictionary of Plants Cultivated in the United States and Canada*, 1976

Jackson, *Papers*   Sam B. Smith, Harold D. Moser, Daniel Feller, and others, eds., *The Papers of Andrew Jackson*, 1980– , 8 vols.

Jefferson Correspondence, Bixby   Worthington C. Ford, ed., *Thomas Jefferson Correspondence Printed from the Originals in the Collections of William K. Bixby*, 1916

JEP   *Journal of the Executive Proceedings of the Senate of the United States*

JHD   *Journal of the House of Delegates of the Commonwealth of Virginia*

JHR   *Journal of the House of Representatives of the United States*

JS   *Journal of the Senate of the United States*

JSV   *Journal of the Senate of Virginia*

Kimball, *Jefferson, Architect*   Fiske Kimball, *Thomas Jefferson, Architect*, 1916

L & B   Andrew A. Lipscomb and Albert E. Bergh, eds., *The Writings of Thomas Jefferson*, Library Edition, 1903–04, 20 vols.

Latrobe, *Papers*   John C. Van Horne and others, eds., *The Correspondence and Miscellaneous Papers of Benjamin Henry Latrobe*, 1984–88, 3 vols.

Lay, *Architecture*   K. Edward Lay, *The Architecture of Jefferson Country: Charlottesville and Albemarle County, Virginia*, 2000

LCB   Douglas L. Wilson, ed., *Jefferson's Literary Commonplace Book*, 1989, *The Papers of Thomas Jefferson*, Second Series

Leavitt, *Poplar Forest*   Messrs. Leavitt, *Catalogue of a Private Library . . . Also, The Remaining Portion of the Library of the Late Thomas Jefferson . . . offered by his grandson, Francis Eppes, of Poplar Forest, Va.*, 1873

Leonard, *General Assembly*   Cynthia Miller Leonard, comp., *The General Assembly of Virginia, July 30, 1619–January 11, 1978: A Bicentennial Register of Members*, 1978

List of Patents   *A List of Patents granted by the United States from April 10, 1790, to December 31, 1836*, 1872

Longworth's New York Directory   *Longworth's American Almanac, New-York Register, and City Directory*, New York, 1796–1842 (title varies; cited by year of publication)

MACH   *Magazine of Albemarle County History*, 1940– (title varies; issued until 1951 as *Papers of the Albemarle County Historical Society*)

Madison, *Papers*   William T. Hutchinson, Robert A. Rutland, John C. A. Stagg, and others, eds., *The Papers of James Madison*, 1962– , 33 vols.

   Congress. Ser., 17 vols.

   Pres. Ser., 6 vols.

   Retirement Ser., 1 vol.

   Sec. of State Ser., 9 vols.

Malcomson, *Historical Dictionary*   Robert Malcomson, *Historical Dictionary of the War of 1812*, 2006

Malone, *Jefferson*   Dumas Malone, *Jefferson and his Time*, 1948–81, 6 vols.

Marshall, *Papers*   Herbert A. Johnson, Charles T. Cullen, Charles F. Hobson, and others, eds., *The Papers of John Marshall*, 1974–2006, 12 vols.

Mazzei, *Writings*   Margherita Marchione and others, eds., *Philip Mazzei: Selected Writings and Correspondence*, 1983, 3 vols.

MB   James A. Bear Jr. and Lucia C. Stanton, eds., *Jefferson's Memorandum Books: Accounts, with Legal Records and Miscellany, 1767–1826*, 1997, *The Papers of Thomas Jefferson*, Second Series

Miller, *Treaties*   Hunter Miller, ed., *Treaties and other International Acts of the United States of America*, 1931–48, 8 vols.

Moulton, *Journals of Lewis & Clark*   Gary E. Moulton, ed., *The Journals of the Lewis & Clark Expedition*, 1983–2001, 13 vols.

Notes, ed. Peden   Thomas Jefferson, *Notes on the State of Virginia*, ed. William Peden, 1955

OCD   Simon Hornblower and Antony Spawforth, eds., *The Oxford Classical Dictionary*, 2003

ODNB   H. C. G. Matthew and Brian Harrison, eds., *Oxford Dictionary of National Biography*, 2004, 60 vols.

OED   James A. H. Murray, J. A. Simpson, E. S. C. Weiner, and others, eds., *The Oxford English Dictionary*, 2d ed., 1989, 20 vols.

Papenfuse, *Maryland Public Officials*   Edward C. Papenfuse and others, eds., *An Historical List of Public Officials of Maryland*, 1990– , 1 vol.

Peale, *Papers*   Lillian B. Miller and others, eds., *The Selected Papers of Charles Willson Peale and His Family*, 1983– , 5 vols. in 6

PMHB   *Pennsylvania Magazine of History and Biography*, 1877–

Poor, *Jefferson's Library*   Nathaniel P. Poor, *Catalogue. President Jefferson's Library*, 1829

Princetonians   James McLachlan and others, eds., *Princetonians: A Biographical Dictionary*, 1976–90, 5 vols.

PTJ   Julian P. Boyd, Charles T. Cullen, John Catanzariti, Barbara B. Oberg, and others, eds., *The Papers of Thomas Jefferson*, 1950– , 38 vols.

PW   Wilbur S. Howell, ed., *Jefferson's Parliamentary Writings*, 1988, *The Papers of Thomas Jefferson*, Second Series

Randall, *Life*   Henry S. Randall, *The Life of Thomas Jefferson*, 1858, 3 vols.

Randolph, *Domestic Life*   Sarah N. Randolph, *The Domestic Life of Thomas Jefferson, Compiled from Family Letters and Reminiscences by His Great-Granddaughter*, 1871

Shackelford, *Descendants*   George Green Shackelford, ed., *Col-*

lected Papers . . . of the Monticello Association of the Descendants of Thomas Jefferson, 1965–84, 2 vols.

Sowerby   E. Millicent Sowerby, comp., *Catalogue of the Library of Thomas Jefferson*, 1952–59, 5 vols.

Sprague, *American Pulpit*   William B. Sprague, *Annals of the American Pulpit*, 1857–69, 9 vols.

Stein, *Worlds*   Susan R. Stein, *The Worlds of Thomas Jefferson at Monticello*, 1993

Terr. Papers   Clarence E. Carter and John Porter Bloom, eds., *The Territorial Papers of the United States*, 1934–75, 28 vols.

TJR   Thomas Jefferson Randolph, ed., *Memoir, Correspondence, and Miscellanies, from the Papers of Thomas Jefferson*, 1829, 4 vols.

U.S. Reports   *Cases Argued and Decided in the Supreme Court of the United States*, 1790– (title varies; originally issued in distinct editions of separately numbered volumes with *U.S. Reports* volume numbers retroactively assigned; original volume numbers here given parenthetically)

U.S. Statutes at Large   Richard Peters, ed., *The Public Statutes at Large of the United States . . . 1789 to March 3, 1845*, 1845–67, 8 vols.

Va. Reports   *Reports of Cases Argued and Adjudged in the Court of Appeals of Virginia*, 1798– (title varies; originally issued in distinct editions of separately numbered volumes with Va. Reports volume numbers retroactively assigned; original volume numbers here given parenthetically)

VMHB   *Virginia Magazine of History and Biography*, 1893–

Washington, *Papers*   W. W. Abbot and others, eds., *The Papers of George Washington*, 1983– , 56 vols.

> *Colonial Ser.*, 10 vols.
> *Confederation Ser.*, 6 vols.
> *Pres. Ser.*, 16 vols.
> *Retirement Ser.*, 4 vols.
> *Rev. War Ser.*, 20 vols.

William and Mary Provisional List   *A Provisional List of Alumni, Grammar School Students, Members of the Faculty, and Members of the Board of Visitors of the College of William and Mary in Virginia. From 1693 to 1888*, 1941

WMQ   *William and Mary Quarterly*, 1892–

Woods, *Albemarle*   Edgar Woods, *Albemarle County in Virginia*, 1901, repr. 1991

CONTENTS

CONTENTS

CONTENTS

CONTENTS

CONTENTS

CONTENTS

CONTENTS

1816

CONTENTS

CONTENTS

CONTENTS

[xxxiv]

CONTENTS

CONTENTS

CONTENTS

CONTENTS

MAPS

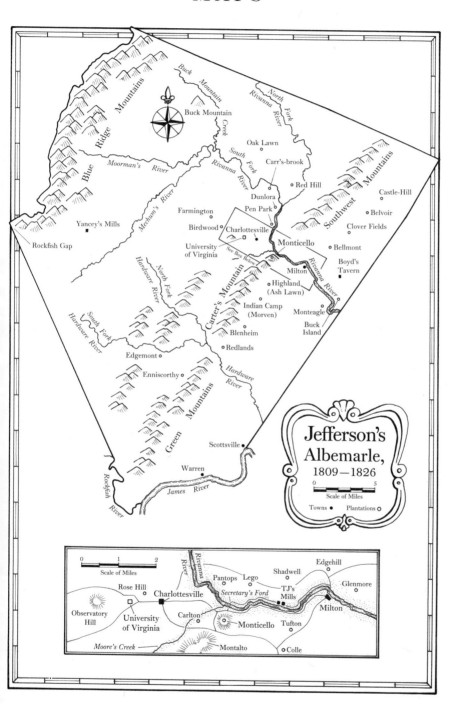

Jefferson's Albemarle, 1809–1826

Scale of Miles
0   5

Towns ●   Plantations ○

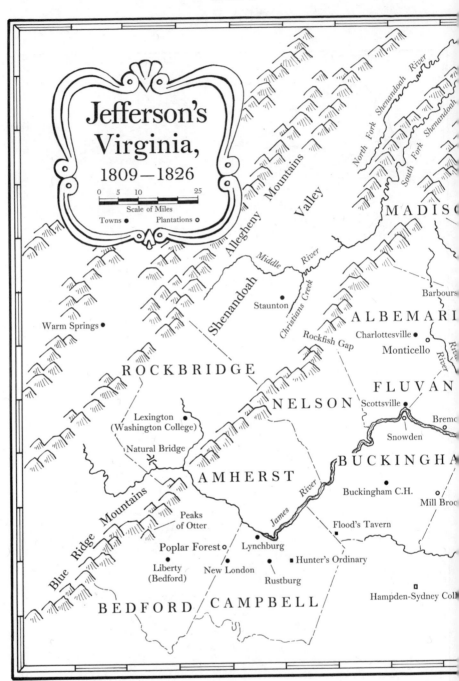

Jefferson's Virginia, 1809—1826

Scale of Miles

0 5 10 25

Towns ● Plantations ○

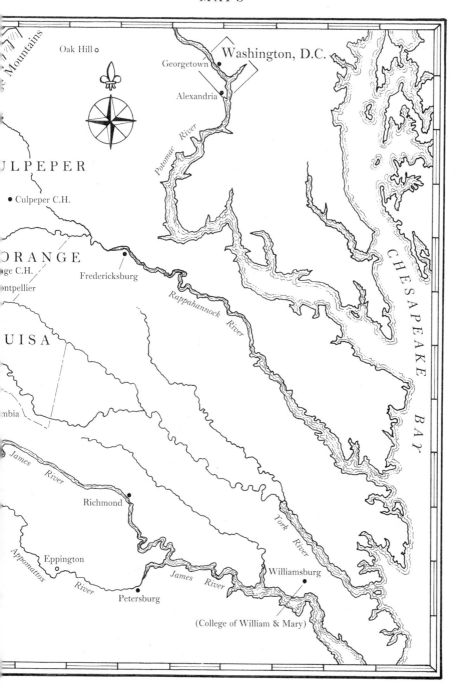

Oak Hill ○

Washington, D.C.

Georgetown

Alexandria

Mountains

Potomac River

ULPEPER

● Culpeper C.H.

CHESAPEAKE BAY

ORANGE

ge C.H.

Fredericksburg

ntpellier

Rappahannock River

UISA

nbia

James River

Richmond

York River

Appomattox River

Eppington

James River

Williamsburg

Petersburg

(College of William & Mary)

ILLUSTRATIONS

Following page 344

VIEW OF LIBERTY, NOW BEDFORD

Liberty (now the city of Bedford) became the county seat of Bedford County in 1782 and sits at the base of the Peaks of Otter. During his first expedition to survey the Peaks in the autumn of 1815, Jefferson had dinner in Liberty, and the town eventually became home to Peachy R. Gilmer and his wife, Elizabeth Trist's niece Mary House Gilmer. Trist's extended stays there allowed her to keep a watch on Jefferson and his family as they came and went from nearby Poplar Forest. Edward Beyer painted this oil-on-canvas landscape in 1855. A German artist who had studied at the Düsseldorf Academy before coming to the United States in 1848, Beyer published an *Album of Virginia* in 1858 that included forty lithographs of Virginia landmarks, including Natural Bridge (*MB*, 2:1313; Chambers, *Poplar Forest*, 93–4, 143; Peachy R. Gilmer to Nicholas P. Trist, 21 Mar. 1818 [NcU: NPT]; Barbara Crawford and Royster Lyle Jr., *Rockbridge County Artists & Artisans* [1995], 190; *DVB*, 1:479–80).

Courtesy of the Virginia Historical Society.

THOMAS JEFFERSON'S SURVEYING EQUIPMENT: THEODOLITE, WITH DETAIL OF THEODOLITE

Jefferson's interest in surveying may have been a legacy from his father, Peter Jefferson, who was highly accomplished in the field. Although Jefferson inherited some mathematical instruments from his father, he purchased this theodolite himself in 1778. The instrument came from Robert Andrews, a noted mathematician and later a professor at the College of William and Mary. It was crafted by Jesse Ramsden, a renowned British instrument maker. With this tool Jefferson could measure both horizontal and vertical angles, and its two telescopes made it useful for astronomical observations as well as surveying. Some months after he purchased the theodolite in Williamsburg, Jefferson recorded its use at Monticello, noting that he had placed it "on top of the house" and employed it to observe the neighboring mountains. Jefferson used this tool for his observations at the Peaks of Otter in November 1815 (Stein, *Worlds*, 357; *MB*, 1:456; *PTJ*, 2:202; Betts, *Garden Book*, 80; Silvio A. Bedini, *Jefferson and Science* [2002], 17–8).

Courtesy of the Thomas Jefferson Foundation, Inc.

THOMAS JEFFERSON'S SURVEYING EQUIPMENT: CIRCUMFERENTOR AND SURVEYOR'S CHAIN

The circumferentor, sometimes called a surveyor's compass, was Jefferson's primary surveying tool prior to his purchase of a theodolite. A theodolite has two sighting telescopes, while a circumferentor relies instead on two vertical sighting bars. Both tools include a compass for reading off angles, but in order to measure a distance to an object the surveyor needs a surveying or Gunter's chain. The English mathematician Edmund Gunter is credited with establishing four poles (sixty-six feet) as the standard length for land-surveying chains. The chains are composed of one hundred links (Stein, *Worlds*, 360; *OED*).

Courtesy of the Thomas Jefferson Foundation, Inc.

GUITAR

This English guitar, or cittern, is said to be the one purchased by Jefferson for his granddaughter Virginia J. Randolph (Trist) in March 1816. Jefferson bought the instrument for thirty dollars from Albemarle County resident Robert B. Sthreshly and his wife when the couple moved to Kentucky. The cittern has a flat back and a pear-shaped body resembling a lute and is played by plucking the metal strings (*MB*, 2:1319–20; Randolph, *Domestic Life*, 345, 348; Stein, *Worlds*, 422; TJ to Ellen W. Randolph [Coolidge], 14 Mar. 1816).

Courtesy of the Thomas Jefferson Foundation, Inc.

MONTICELLO PARLOR

The Monticello Parlor was among the principal public spaces of the house and was used for reading, the serving of tea, and amusements such as music and games. This room is the only space remaining from Jefferson's first construction of Monticello. It features a parquet floor, an elaborate entablature, and four triple-sash windows. Jefferson hung European works of art and portraits of American statesmen, explorers, and English intellectuals in this room. Two gilded pier mirrors adorn the walls. Jefferson's preferred campeachy chair is among the many chairs in this room, and a harpsichord and pianoforte were the most significant pieces of standing furniture. The parlor reflects a wide array of decorative arts styles indicative of Jefferson's evolving taste and financial means (Stein, *Worlds*, 71–9).

Courtesy of the Thomas Jefferson Foundation, Inc.

CATALOGUE OF THE LIBRARY OF THE UNITED STATES (WASHINGTON, 1815)

After the sale of Jefferson's library, George Watterston modified and published Jefferson's manuscript book inventory (which is no longer extant) as a *Catalogue of the Library of the United States. To Which is Annexed, A Copious Index, Alphabetically Arranged* (Washington, 1815). Watterston maintained Jefferson's general classification of the books, leaving them in the chapters in which Jefferson had organized them, but he alphabetized the entries within the chapters rather than retaining Jefferson's arrangement. When Watterston asked his opinion of the published version, Jefferson responded: "you ask how I like the arrangement within the chapters? of course, you know, not so well as my own; yet I think it possible the alphabetical arrangement may be more convenient to readers generally, than mine which was sometimes analytical, sometimes chronological, & sometimes a combination of both." Jefferson based the organization of his library on a table of "The Emanation of Sciences, from the Intellectual Faculties of Memory, Imagination, Reason," published on p. 41 of Francis Bacon, *Of the Advancement and Proficiencie of Learning: or the Partitions of Sciences* (London, 1674; Sowerby, no. 4916). This page from the printed catalogue shows the classification scheme Jefferson employed as it was translated into print by Watterston. The Library of Congress followed Jefferson's organizational system for much of the nineteenth century (TJ to Watterston, 7 May 1815, 2 Mar. 1816; Watterston to TJ, 13 Oct. 1815; James Gilreath and Douglas L. Wilson, eds., *Thomas Jefferson's Library: A Catalog with the Entries in His Own Order* [1989]).

Courtesy of the Albert and Shirley Small Special Collections Library, University of Virginia.

THOMAS JEFFERSON'S RETIREMENT LIBRARY CATALOGUE

When Jefferson began rebuilding his library at Monticello after the sale of his books to the Library of Congress, he also started a new catalogue, retaining his classification scheme as depicted here. With minor variations and omissions, the books were listed in the same order in the 1829 catalogue for the sale of Jefferson's library (Manuscript Catalogue, DLC: TJ Papers, Ser. 7; Poor, *Jefferson's Library*).

Courtesy of the Library of Congress.

PETER S. DU PONCEAU: PORTRAIT AND DAGUERREOTYPE

Thomas Sully painted this portrait of Peter S. Du Ponceau for the American Philosophical Society in March 1830. Du Ponceau, a native of France, came to the United States in 1777 to serve as secretary and aide to the Prussian army officer and Continental army general Friedrich Wilhelm von Steuben. Following the American Revolution, he settled in Philadelphia as an accomplished attorney and author. Du Ponceau became a member of the APS in 1791. After service as a councillor and vice president, he was elected president in 1828 and held that office until his death in 1844. The daguerreotype image of Du Ponceau was among the earliest made in the Philadelphia photographic portrait studio of Robert Cornelius late in 1839. It was donated to the APS the following year by Cornelius's silent partner and APS member, Paul Beck Goddard (Edward Biddle and Mantle Fielding, *The Life and Works of Thomas Sully (1783–1872)* [1921], 143; APS, *Proceedings* 1 [1840]: 213; *ANB*).

Courtesy of the American Philosophical Society.

Volume 9

1 September 1815 to 30 April 1816

JEFFERSON CHRONOLOGY

1743 · 1826

1743	Born at Shadwell, 13 April (New Style).
1760–1762	Studies at the College of William and Mary.
1762–1767	Self-education and preparation for law.
1769–1774	Albemarle delegate to House of Burgesses.
1772	Marries Martha Wayles Skelton, 1 January.
1775–1776	In Continental Congress.
1776	Drafts Declaration of Independence.
1776–1779	In Virginia House of Delegates.
1779	Submits Bill for Establishing Religious Freedom.
1779–1781	Governor of Virginia.
1782	Martha Wayles Skelton Jefferson dies, 6 September.
1783–1784	In Continental Congress.
1784–1789	In France on commission to negotiate commercial treaties and then as minister plenipotentiary at Versailles.
1790–1793	Secretary of State of the United States.
1797–1801	Vice President of the United States.
1801–1809	President of the United States.

RETIREMENT

1809	Attends James Madison's inauguration, 4 March.
	Arrives at Monticello, 15 March.
1810	Completes legal brief on New Orleans batture case, 31 July.
1811	Batture case dismissed, 5 December.
1812	Correspondence with John Adams resumed, 1 January.
	Batture pamphlet preface completed, 25 February; printed by 21 March.
1814	Named a trustee of Albemarle Academy, 25 March.
	Resigns presidency of American Philosophical Society, 23 November.
1815	Sells personal library to Congress.
1816	Writes introduction and revises translation of Destutt de Tracy, *A Treatise on Political Economy* [1818].
	Named a visitor of Central College, 18 October.
1818	Attends Rockfish Gap conference to choose location of proposed University of Virginia, 1–4 August.
	Visits Warm Springs, 7–27 August.
1819	University of Virginia chartered, 25 January; named to Board of Visitors, 13 February; elected rector, 29 March.
	Debts greatly increased by bankruptcy of Wilson Cary Nicholas.
1820	Likens debate over slavery and Missouri statehood to "a fire bell in the night," 22 April.
1821	Writes memoirs, 6 January–29 July.
1823	Visits Poplar Forest for last time, 16–25 May.
1824	Lafayette visits Monticello, 4–15 November.
1825	University of Virginia opens, 7 March.
1826	Writes will, 16–17 March.
	Last recorded letter, 25 June.
	Dies at Monticello, 4 July.

THE PAPERS OF
THOMAS JEFFERSON

·◦⟨══════⟩◦·

Deposition of James Lewis in
Jefferson v. Michie

[*Ed. Note*: On 1 Sept. 1815 James Lewis appeared at the house of Thomas Wells in Charlottesville and gave a deposition in the case of *Jefferson v. Michie* (Tr in ViU: TJP-LBJM; entirely in George Carr's hand) that was similar to the testimony he had given in the same case on 1 July 1812. This new statement was occasioned by a 7 Aug. 1815 ruling by the Albemarle County Court that, on a motion by TJ as complainant, Lewis's deposition be taken "in like manner, as those of the other witnesses named in said decree and for the same purpose" (MS in Albemarle Co. Order Book [1815–16], 74; Tr in ViU: TJP-LBJM; entirely in Carr's hand). The deposition of 1 Sept. 1815 differed most significantly from the earlier one in the omission of several sections of text. Portions that were dropped include questions asked by TJ and David Michie in 1812, the greater part of the testimony answering those questions, and a passage by Lewis stating that an unnamed attorney had advised him that, as a security for John Henderson's debts, it was improper for Lewis to have purchased the land in question. The later deposition ends with Lewis's summary that Henderson had never informed him that Michie or anyone else had a right to the land, but that Henderson had told him that Craven Peyton's claim to the contested mill seat at Milton was negligible.]

From Joseph Miller

Norfolk Sept 1ˢᵗ 1815.—

Honrᵈ Frind I now take the Liberty of informing you—this Day I have¹ shiped on Board the Sloop Canton Capt Willis Godwin one Cask of x I Do not Know What We Must call it, I think² Porter Brandy as it was Made from Soure Porter Like wise—I have Sent My Trunk along with it hopeng thay will Come Safe to hand—I have Drect them to Gibson &c Jefferson Richmond—I have been Detained Longer than I Wished Oweng to a Lott of Ground the

Contentes You¹ will heare—I will Sett off on the 4 or 5—wishing you to wright to Messer Gebeson Jefferson to forward the³

My Respt^s to all the Famuly

I Rem your Hunbe^l Servt   JOSEPH MILLER

NB I hope Peter and me will Do Better thes year than Last we will let the Wether be Coolder.

RC (DLC); at head of text: "Mr Jeffer-son"; mistakenly endorsed by TJ as a letter of 1 Aug. 1815 received 3 Oct. 1815 and so recorded in SJL.

PETER: Peter Hemmings.

¹ Manuscript: "I have <I informed> I have."
² Preceding two words interlined.
³ Thus in manuscript, at the end of a line.

From Benjamin Waterhouse

DEAR SIR,   Cambridge 1st Sepr 1815.

I cannot allow to pass this fair opportunity, by General & Mrs Dearborn, without sending, you some memorial of my gratitude & respect—

I have enclosed you two 4th of July Orations; one delivered in the District of Maine, to a people ripe for a seperation; and the other at Lexington, by a son in law of the late Vice President. They will shew you the sentiments and doctrines that are now maintained by a great portion of the yeomanry of Massachusetts. I have also enclosed a copy of Cobbett's Address to the Clergy of Massachusetts, with a prefatory Epistle by "Jonathan." Five thousand copies have been sold, in a State where Caleb Strong & William Phillips is Govr & Lieut Govr they being two rigid Calvinists of the deepest blue-dye. Having ceased to preach rebellion, & to utter treasonable doctrines in prayer, our restless Levites are now at open & bitter war among themselves, on account of the old, & tedious subject of the unity, trinity & atonement! The combatants are, however, all federalists. The Essex-Junto are the revivers & patrons of the imputed heresy of Unitarianism; but it unluckily happens that their two political champions, Strong & Phillips [are]¹ two of the most rigid calvinists in New England. When such a mixture is in high fermentation, we wicked Unitarian Republicans are waiting, with a sort of mischievous curiosity to see what the tertium quid will be. Both parties have diffused the Bible untill it has become as common as an Almanack; & are now quarreling about its meaning. Cambridge college is the grand fortress, or strong hold of federalism & Unitarianism, and the Boston clergy are fighting under the motto of "common sense," and "the Age of Reason," without daring to acknowledge it; while the Calvinists are absolutely[2] contending, tooth & nail, for the leading doctrines of the church of Rome; which they have cursed ever since I can remember! While the priesthood[3] are sharpely engaged in this unwise controversy, the common people are reading with avidity & relish William Cobbett's address to the "Cossack" clergy.

The Junto, or Faction have enlisted nearly every able & active young man of the three learned professions, in their service. They, like the Jesuits, fix upon all our brilliant young men, especially if they are poor, & mark them for their own. We have an almost incredible number of literary, religious, municipal, economical & political societies, associations, or clubs, which are filled by these young Jesuits. It is in this consists[4] their great influence. Draw out the militia, & we shall find two thirds of them Republicans. It is among the servile men of education that federalism utters its insolent voice. Their union is now threatened by an attack of the Calvinists, who have come suddenly upon them, with fire & brimstone. In this terrific contest, Morse the geographer leads the Orthodox troops of Mass[ts] & Pres[t] Dwight those of Connecticut while Rhode Island & Vermont are, literally speaking, neuter.

The faction have a numerous body of intriguers, writers, spies, & preachers throughout New England. In this rebellious corps I might have carried a pair of colours; but honor & conscience forbade it, and I threw myself into the lean & pinched up ranks of Republicans, and when very hard pressed by the college, & professional rivals, & their mercenaries, I retreated behind the press; from whence I have kept up a pretty constant fire,[5] & sometimes made cartridges for other posts. My venerable friend Adams early warned me of the danger of this procedure. "They will not, said he, hesitate to destroy, if they can, both you & your family."—But I felt the impulse operating like an irresistable instinct, so that, for more than seven years past, I have poured an incessant stream of republicanism on the wheels of government, through the medium of the press, while all about me were trying to impede them. Numerous as the federal writers have been, they were kept at bay; & their Hartford Convention has been made the laughing stock of the publick. Boston is already half ruined. Emigration is fast drawing off her best spirits. Those who can distinguish between business & bustle say, that she is rapidly on the decline. In the midst[6] of all this, their clergy are quarreling, their merchants discontented, their famous college trembling, their rich men uneasy, and the faction itself heartless & headless; & so it is with the republicans.

[5]

George Cabot cannot supply the place of Theophilus Parsons in the one, nor Samuel Dexter suit exactly with the other. We want a man of General Dearborn's system & energy for Governor.

Were I 20 years younger, I might be tempted to lead my children into a region more congenial to their education.—I have long wished to make a pilgrimage to Monticello; but must, I believe, relinquish it, or depute one of my sons to go a votary in my stead.   With a high degree of respect, I remain
your obliged humbl serv^t   BENJ^N WATERHOUSE

RC (DLC); endorsed by TJ as received 3 Oct. 1815 and so recorded in SJL. RC (Mrs. T. Wilber Chelf, Mrs. Virginius Dabney, and Mrs. Alexander W. Parker, Richmond, 1944; photocopy in ViU: TJP); address cover only, with PoC of TJ to Patrick Gibson, 28 Oct. 1815, on verso; addressed: "The Honorable Thos Jefferson Monticello By General & Mrs Dearborn." Enclosures: (1) John Holmes, *An Oration, Pronounced at Alfred, on the 4th of July, 1815* (Boston, 1815; Poor, *Jefferson's Library*, 13 [no. 826]; TJ's copy in ViU). (2) James T. Austin, *An Oration, Pronounced at Lexington, Mass. in commemoration of the Independence of the United States of America, and the Restoration of Peace. 4th July, 1815* (Boston, 1815; Poor, *Jefferson's Library*, 13 [no. 826]; TJ's copy in ViU). (3) William Cobbett, *An Address to the Clergy of Massachusetts. written in England, Nov. 13, 1814. with A Prefatory Epistle, to Certain Priests, by*

Jonathan (Boston, 1815; Poor, *Jefferson's Library*, 10 [no. 548]).

James T. Austin was the son-in-law of the LATE VICE PRESIDENT Elbridge Gerry. TERTIUM QUID: some indefinite thing that is related to, but distinct from, two known things (*OED*). CAMBRIDGE COLLEGE: Harvard University. In his address Cobbett called the clergy of Massachusetts a COSSACK priesthood for allegedly celebrating as a religious victory the arrival of Cossack forces in Paris in 1814 (Cobbett, *Address to the Clergy of Massachusetts*, 9–12). The THREE LEARNED PROFESSIONS are law, medicine, and divinity (*OED*).

¹ Omitted word editorially supplied.
² Manuscript: "absulotely."
³ Manuscript: "prieshood."
⁴ Manuscript: "consits."
⁵ Word interlined.
⁶ Manuscript: "midts."

From Edward Bancroft

MY DEAR SIR   London Septr 5th 1815.

Though some years, & many great events have intervened, since the date of your last letter to me, you will I flatter myself, pardon the liberty which I take in addressing you, to assure you of the continuance of my highest Esteem & best wishes, and also to introduce to the honor of your favourable notice, & Kind protection, the Viscount Barziza, who will become the Bearer of this Letter—He is the Youngest of the two Sons of the late Count Antonio Barziza, & of the two Grandsons of our deceased friend the late Mr Paradise; who was honored with so much of your friendship & Kindness, formerly at

Paris, that I am persuaded you will favourably recieve this child of his daughter, & afford him all convenient advice, countenance, & assistance, towards the attainment[1] of his principal object, in going to Virginia; which is that of Claiming & qualifying himself to inherit, the Estates lately possessed by his deceased grandmother M[rs] Paradise; which by her marriage Settlement & by subsequent acts, were Secured to the issue of her Daughter the late Lucy Countess Barziza, as you will doubtless recollect—Her eldest Son, the present Count Barziza, is now here, & intends in a few months also to proceed to Virginia to qualify himself according to the Laws of your State to partake of the inheritance in question; but being married & having left his Lady far advanced in Pregnancy at Venice, he wishes first to return to that City, which I hope he may do without putting his American rights into any Jeopardy; though in fact, we have not been able here to obtain any precise & authentic information of your Laws on that Subject: a circumstance which will I hope be allowed to have a favourable operation for the absent claimant, if there should be any precise time prescribed for his appearance in America, & if that time should prove to be shorter than is supposed.

I congratulate you sincerely on the prospect of a long continuance of Peace & high prosperity, which seems to be now opened to the United States; & beg you to be assured of the great respect & sincere devotion with which I have the honor to be My Dear Sir

Your most faithful & most Obedient Servant

EDW[D] BANCROFT

RC (DLC); dateline at foot of text; at foot of first page: "Thomas Jefferson Esq. &c. &c &c."; endorsed by TJ as received 15 Dec. 1815 and so recorded in SJL. Enclosed in Philip I. Barziza to TJ, 6 Dec. 1815.

Edward Bancroft (1744–1821), physician, chemist, and spy, was born in Westfield, Massachusetts, studied medicine in Connecticut, and worked as a doctor in Dutch Guiana before moving to London in 1767 to further his education. He practiced medicine in London and worked as a journal editor and author. Bancroft befriended Benjamin Franklin and Joseph Priestley, researched and wrote on vegetable dyes, and won election in 1773 to the Royal Society of London. During the American Revolution, Bancroft spent time in Paris and London employed as a spy by both the British and the Americans. While TJ resided in Europe, he corresponded extensively with Bancroft on the financial difficulties of John Paradise and Lucy Ludwell Paradise. Bancroft was awarded a British monopoly, 1785–99, on the importation of oak-bark dyes that he developed for calico printing, and the dye remained in use for more than a century. He died in Margate, England (ANB; DAB; ODNB; Franklin, Papers; PTJ, esp. 8:522, 9:41n; Julian P. Boyd, "Death by a Kindly Teacher of Treason?," WMQ, 3d ser., 16 [1959]: 165–87, 319–42, 515–50; London Morning Chronicle, 13 Sept. 1821).

Philip Ignatius Barziza (1796–1875) was a native of Venice. After arriving in the United States in 1815 to claim the estate of his grandmother Lucy Ludwell Paradise, he settled in Williamsburg.

Philip and his brother Giovanni (John L.), Count Barziza, petitioned the Virginia General Assembly in 1816 for title to their grandmother's land, but the request was denied the following year. In 1824 the Virginia Court of Appeals ruled that, because they were foreign-born, they could not inherit land in Virginia. Barziza enlisted TJ's aid and in 1817 visited him at Monticello. After abandoning the claim to his inheritance, Barziza was equally unsuccessful in attempts to be named the American consul at Tangiers in 1825 and a bearer of dispatches from the United States to Europe in 1826. He was the keeper of Williamsburg's Public Hospital (later the Eastern Asylum, and later still the Eastern State Hospital), 1837–41, and a steward in 1850. By 1847 Barziza was bankrupt. In 1854 he was confirmed as federal customs collector and revenue inspector for the port of Yorktown. Barziza eventually moved to Texas along with his wife and several of his children and died in Houston

(Archibald Bolling Shepperson, *John Paradise and Lucy Ludwell of London and Williamsburg* [1942], 446–8; R. Henderson Shuffler, "Decimus et Ultimus Barziza," *Southwestern Historical Quarterly* 66 [1963]: 501–12; petition of Barziza brothers, read 21 Nov. 1816, rejected 1 Jan. 1817 [Vi: RG 78, Legislative Petitions, Miscellaneous]; *Va. Reports*, 23 [2 Randolph], 302–8; TJ to Thomas Appleton, 1 Aug. 1817; Barziza to TJ, 10 Mar. 1824; Clay, *Papers*, 4:105–6, 5:373; Henry M. Hurd, ed., *The Institutional Care of the Insane in the United States and Canada* [1916], 3:711, 718; *Richmond Enquirer*, 29 Jan. 1847; DNA: RG 29, CS, Williamsburg, 1850; *JEP*, 9:192, 254 [11 Jan., 28 Feb. 1854]; *Galveston Daily News*, 26 Mar. 1875; gravestone inscription in Glenwood Cemetery, Houston).

TJ's LAST LETTER to Bancroft was dated 25 Sept. 1789 (*PTJ*, 15:476).

¹ Manuscript: "attaintment."

From Albert Gallatin

DEAR SIR   New York Sept^er 6th 1815

I enclose two letters from Europe, one from La Fayette, who desired that I should bear witness to his constant endeavours, under all circumstances, in support of the cause of liberty, and to his undiminished affection for his American friends & particularly for yourself.   I was much gratified by the receipt of your kind letter of March last brought by Mr Ticknor. Your usual partiality to me is evinced by the belief that our finances might have been better directed if I had remained in the Treasury. But I always thought, that our war expences were so great, perhaps necessarily so, in proportion to the ordinary resources of the country, and the opposition of the monied men so inveterate, that it was impossible to avoid falling into a paper system, if the war should be much longer protracted. I only regret that specie payments were not resumed on the return of peace. Whatever difficulties may be in the way, they cannot be insuperable, provided the object be immediately attended to. If delayed, private interest will operate here as in England and lay us under the curse of a depreciated & fluctuating currency. In every other respect, I must acknowledge that the war has been useful. The character of America stands now as high as ever on the European continent, and higher than ever it did in Great Britain. I may say that we are favourites every where except at Courts: and even there, although the Emperor of Russia is perhaps the only Sovereign who likes us, we are generally respected and considered as the Nation designed to check the naval despotism of England. France which alone can have a navy will, under her present dynasty, be for some years a vassal of her great rival; and the mission with which I have been honoured[1] is, in a political view, unimportant. The revolution has not however been altogether useless. There is a visible improvement in the agriculture of the country, and in the situation of the peasantry. The new generation belonging to that class, freed from the petty despotism of nobles and priests, & made more easy in their circumstances by the abolition of tithes, & by the equalisation of taxes have acquired an independent spirit & are far superior to their fathers in intellect and information. They are not republicans and are still too much dazzled by military glory: but I think that no monarch or ex-nobles can hereafter oppress them long with impunity. Accept, my dear Sir, the assurance of my constant & grateful attachment and respect.

Y^r ob^t Servt ALBERT GALLATIN

RC (DLC); at foot of text: "Mr Jefferson"; endorsed by TJ as received 3 Oct. 1815 and so recorded in SJL. FC (NHi: Gallatin Papers). Enclosures: David Bailie Warden to TJ, 9 Apr. 1815, and Louis Philippe Gallot de Lormerie to TJ, 22 Apr. 1815, incorrectly dated 22 Aug. 1815 by the Editors and printed under that date in Vol. 8:680–2.

No letter from LAFAYETTE was enclosed (see TJ to Gallatin, 16 Oct. 1815). Gallatin's MISSION was that of envoy extraordinary and minister plenipotentiary to France.

[1] Gallatin here canceled "may be."

From Alden Partridge

SIR   West Point (New york) Sept 6th 1815

Although I have not the honor of any personal acquaintance with you, yet a perfect conviction that nothing which can tend in the smallest degree to add to a knowledge of our Country would be unacceptable to you, emboldens me to address you. I accordingly take the liberty, Sir, to enclose you the Altitudes of the most elevated Mountains in the northern Section of the Country which I calculated several years ago from Barometrical observation. Of these, the white Mountains are probably the most elevated, of any this side the Missisippi. The Height of those mountains however I am convinced has been greatly overrated. Their real height I think is very little if any greater than I have found it. I would now take the liberty, Sir, to enquire of you whether any Actual measurement of the Altitude of the Alleghany mountains has ever been made, except that made by Col Williams in 1791, and published in the transactions of the American Philosophical Society at Philadelphia. Should any such measurement have been made, you would confer a great obligation on me, by informing me of the results. I am desirous of receiving the information, and[1] know of no one so able as yourself to give it. I have several tables, containing the results of a Series of meteorological observations[2] made by me during and subsequent to the year 1810. Should you consider those as worthy your attention, it will afford me great pleasure to send them to you. I must beg, Sir, you will excuse the liberty I have taken in writing to you. A desire to receive information upon the subject I have mentioned is perhaps the only reasonable apology I can offer—

I have the honor to be with the highest respect and esteem Sir your most obed[t] and humble Servant   A PARTRIDGE
Capt of Engs—

RC (DLC); at foot of text: "Thomas Jefferson Esquir Late President of the United States"; endorsed by TJ as received 3 Oct. 1815 and so recorded in SJL.

Alden Partridge (1785–1854), soldier and educator, was a native of Norwich, Vermont. He studied at Dartmouth College before being appointed a cadet at the United States Military Academy in 1805. The following year Partridge was commissioned a first lieutenant in the United States Army Corps of Engineers, and he remained at West Point as a faculty member, teaching mathematics and engineering. Early in 1815 he became acting superintendent, but he proved unpopular and, after an unsuccessful power struggle with his replacement, he resigned his commission in 1818. After working briefly surveying the northeastern boundary of the United States, Partridge founded the American Literary, Scientific and Military Academy (later Norwich University) in 1819 and spent the next twenty-four years as the institution's president. He started mostly short-lived military schools in a number of states and advocated a model of citizen-soldiery intended to avoid the evils of a standing

army and address the lack of training he observed during the War of 1812. In 1834–35 Partridge taught a subscription course on military science at the University of Virginia. In addition to his educational endeavors, he served as surveyor general of Vermont in 1822–23, lost three congressional elections, and was a Vermont state legislator in 1833, 1834, 1837, and 1839 (ANB; DAB; VtNN: Partridge Papers; General Catalogue of Dartmouth College and the Associated Schools, 1769–1925 [1925], 114; Heitman, U.S. Army, 1:773; JEP, 2:52, 53, 169, 173 [25, 27 Feb. 1807, 27 Feb., 1 Mar. 1811]; Lester A. Webb, Captain Alden Partridge and the United States Military Academy, 1806–1833 [1965]; Montpelier Vermont Patriot & State Gazette, 21 Jan. 1854; New York Independent, 26 Jan. 1854).

Jonathan WILLIAMS published his own observations, along with TJ's comments, as "Barometrical Measurement of the Blue-Ridge, Warm-Spring, and Alleghany Mountains, taken in Virginia, in the Summer of the year 1791," APS, Transactions 4 (1799): 216–23 (see also PTJ, 29:139–41).

[1] Manuscript: "an."
[2] Manuscript: "obsevations."

Alden Partridge's Table of Altitudes of Northern Mountains

[before 6 Sept. 1815]

A Table.

Containing the Altitudes of Mountains calculated from Barometrical Observation, by A Partridge Captain in the US. Corps of Engineers.

Names of the Ranges	Names of the different Peaks	Altitudes in feet.		Remarks.
		above their Bases	above the Sea.	
White Mountains	Mount Washington.	4885.—	6634 —	The White Mountains are situated in the northeast part of the State of New Hampshire, and are Probably the Highest on this side the Missisippi.
	1st Peak South of M.W.	3904.—	5653 —.	
	2d do do do	3584.	5333 —.	
	3d do do do	3430.—	5179.	
	4th do do do	3367 —	5116.	
	5th do do do	2881 —	4630 —	
	Base of the Mountains		1749.	
Catts-kill Mountains	Round Top.	3105.—	3804.—	These peaks lie west from Catts-kill town, and are probably as elevated as any in the range. The Turn-pike passes over the range of[2] Catts-kill Mts. from Catts-kill town to Delaware Rᣴ
	High Peak.	3019.—	3718.	
	Highest part of the turn-pike	1729 —	2425.[1]	
	Base of the mountains.		699.	
Green Mountains	Killington Peak.	2994 —	3924 —	Killington Peak is situated in the town of Killington, & is said to be the highest in the range
	Base of the Mountains		930 —	
New York High Lands.	Crows Nest.		1418.	These Mountains are situated on Hudson's River, below New Burgh, as most of them rise, immediately from the River, their altitudes above their Bases is not consider'd.
	Butter Hill		1529.	
	Bull Hill		1484.—	
	Old Beacon		1471.	
	New Beacon		1585 —	
	Bare Mountain.		1350 —	
	Break Neck		1187 —.	
	Anthony's Nose.		935 —.	
	Sugar Loaf		866 —.	
	Fort Putnam		598.	
	West Point Plain.		188.	

MS (DLC: TJ Papers, 80:13924); in an unidentified hand; undated; endorsed by TJ. MS (VtNN: Partridge Papers); in a bound volume of Partridge manuscripts; in an unidentified hand; undated. Printed in Washington *Daily National Intelligencer*, 10 Sept. 1816, with the addition of altitudes for Hempstead Harbor Hill in New York and three points in the Highlands of Navesink in New Jersey.

In February 1812 Jonathan Williams presented an earlier version of Partridge's calculations to the American Philosophical Society, and in that form they were subsequently published in APS, *Transactions*, new ser., 1 (1818): 147–50. Correspondence from Partridge to Williams and tables of these earlier calculations can be found in InU: Williams Papers.

TJ noted in a manuscript revision to the query on mountains in his *Notes on the State of Virginia* composed sometime after November 1815, that "The highest of the White mountains in N.H. by barometrical estimate made by Capt Partridge was found to be 4885.f. from it's base, and the highest of the Catskill mountains in N. York 3105. feet" (Jefferson, *Notes on the State of Virginia* [London, 1787; Sowerby, no. 4167; Poor, *Jefferson's Library*, 7 (no. 365); TJ's copy in ViU, with revisions, including this one, tipped in between pp. 28 and 29]).

[1] Thus in manuscript, but the correct figure should be either 2,428 for the altitude above sea level or 1,726 above the base.

[2] Manuscript: "from of."

From A. Baudon

SIR   Clinton Oneida Co New York [by 8 Sept. 1815]

Having heard your praises sounded by every tongue since I have been in this place I am induced to make known my situation to you in hopes of getting some relief: and I entreat you not to let the singularity of the address prompt you to throw aside the letter without giving it a candid perusal

In the First place, then sir I am what I believe Philosophers call an Albino. My hair is perfectly white and of a Pearl like appearance. My skin is fair and clear; My Eyes blue and very sensitive to the light and very near sighted. I am about of the middle size, well made, and naturally of a hardy constitution

The powers of my mind are (I think) of about the ordinary stamp a retentive memory being perhaps the only remarkable quality in it. I am not ignobly descended being able to trace my extraction from an illustrious family of the Old World My parents were poor expended thier little all in educating thier children as well as they could. At school I materially impaired my health which frustrated all the calculations I had made of[1] obtaining professional eminence I undertook merchandizing and was unsuccessful and in short honestly paid my debts and have not a Shilling left Now sir, as you are a philosopher a philanthropist and a gentleman I intreat you to consider my case, and devise if possible some way in which I can gain a living or at least to bestow on me a small pittance from the abundance with which providence in its smiles has blessed you my character both political and Moral is such as from your heart you would approve

May Heaven bless you

respectfully &c

A. BAUDON

A line addressed to A.B. Clinton Oneida will be thankfully rcd

RC (MHi); undated; addressed: "Thomas Jefferson Esquire late President of the United States Monticello Virginia"; franked; postmarked Clinton,

N.Y., 8 Sept.; endorsed by TJ as received 3 Oct. 1815 and so recorded in SJL.

[1] Manuscript: "I."

From Lafayette

MY DEAR FRIEND

Paris 7[ber] the 8[h] 1815

I do not know whether the Bearer of these Lines Has Had the Honour of Your Acquaintance while you were Visiting His family or friends—But I am Sure He Will Meet a kind Welcome at Monticelo and Shall only add the Expression of my Constant and Respectful affection

LAFAYETTE

RC (DLC); endorsed by TJ as received 27 Oct. 1817 and so recorded in SJL; with notation by TJ adjacent to endorsement: "(by Grouchy)." Enclosed in Emmanuel, marquis de Grouchy, to TJ, 20 Oct. 1817.

Emmanuel, marquis de Grouchy (1766–1847), military officer, was a native of Paris. In 1779 he entered the artillery corps and rose steadily in rank. A supporter of the French Revolution, he served under Lafayette in 1792, took part in a failed expedition to Ireland in 1796, fought under Jean Moreau in Italy in 1798, and spent a year as a prisoner of war. Grouchy served under Napoleon in numerous campaigns, and after the emperor returned from exile in March 1815, he rewarded Grouchy's loyalty by promoting him to marshal. Napoleon and others blamed him for the French defeat at Waterloo, because he neither marched his detached column to the sound of the guns nor prevented his Prussian adversaries from reinforcing their British allies. Following the restoration of Louis

XVIII, Grouchy went into exile in the United States. Spending his time in various American cities, in 1816 he met TJ's granddaughter Ellen W. Randolph (Coolidge) in Washington, D.C., and he lived in Philadelphia for several years. Grouchy was associated with the attempt of French emigrants to establish the Vine and Olive Colony in what is now Alabama, but he never settled there himself. In 1820 he returned to Europe, and a royal decree ended his exile from France the following year. Eventually Grouchy recovered his estates and army rank. For the remainder of his life he defended his role at Waterloo, ultimately writing several works on the subject (Connelly, *Napoleonic France*, 228–9; Hoefer, *Nouv. biog. générale*, 21:221–9; Philadelphia *Weekly Aurora*, 5 Sept. 1815; Ellen W. Randolph (Coolidge) to Martha Jefferson Randolph, 17 Feb. [1816] [ViU: Coolidge Correspondence]; Rafe Blaufarb, *Bonapartists in the Borderlands: French Exiles and Refugees on the Gulf Coast, 1815–1835* [2005]; ASP, *Public Lands*, 4:149, 151; John A. Paxton, *The*

Philadelphia Directory and Register, for 1818 [Philadelphia, 1818]; Paxton, *The Philadelphia Directory and Register, for 1819* [Philadelphia, 1819]; Philadelphia *Franklin Gazette,* 9 Aug. 1820; gravestone inscription in Cimetière du Père Lachaise, Paris).

TJ met several members of Grouchy's FAMILY in France, including his sister and brother-in-law, Sophie and Nicolas de Condorcet, and his brother-in-law Pierre Jean Georges Cabanis (*PTJ,* 22:98–9, 24:xliii, 34:441–2n, 38:524–5; George Ripley and Charles A. Dana, eds., *The New American Cyclopædia* [1858], 4:179).

From George W. Campbell

DEAR SIR,   Nashville 9ᵗʰ Sepbʳ 1815

I have long intended troubling you with a letter, but have been deterred for want of something that seemed worthy your perusal—I should have embraced the occasion presented by your friendly & esteemed favor of last summer handed me by Mʳ Barnes of George Town, of carrying my intention into execution, had not the very delicate state of my health, with the requisite attention to official duties imposed on me the necessity of omitting for the time every kind of correspondence that could be dispensed with.

The favorable sentiments you have been pleased to express in relation to the views with which I entered into public office are entitled to, & receive my sincere acknowledgments. The best reward we can receive in this life, & that which must prove most gratful to our feelings, for pure motives & sincere efforts to promote the public good is undoubtedly the good opinion of those we most esteem in society; & whose talents & virtues have distinguished them as the great Luminaries of the age that light up the way for their followers. The best evidence, perhaps that I could furnish in support of your opinion as to the views I carried into office, may be found in my retiring from that office, so soon as the impaired state of my health, was likely to prevent me, at least for a time, from rendering those services to the public that under other circumstances might have been expected.

Since retireing from public business, my health, though it continued some time imperfect, has very much improved, and been better for the last 6 months than for several preceeding years.

I should feel much gratified in learning the state of your health, which I trust remains unimpaired; and which I sincerely wish may long continue so in your passage down the stream of life, that is no doubt to you perfectly smooth & tranquil.

What have we here that could prove interesting to you? Our great national concerns, if you permit the passing events to intrude on your retirement are much better known to you than to us; & matters of a local nature can hardly lay claim to your particular notice. The return of peace was hailed in this quarter with the most lively & Sincere gratulations; & looked upon as an era from which to calculate a long period of prosperous & uninterrupted national repose; but the dreadful storm which has lately exploded[1] on the continent of Europe & threatens to deluge in blood, as indeed it has already in part done, the fairest portion of that quarter of the globe, which has scarcely had time to breathe from the ravages & convulsions of preceeding[2] wars; is calculated to incite some uneasiness for our future destiny. The prospect, however remote, of Seeing our beloved country again envolved[3] in war is an unwelcome, unpleasant reflection! It will however, press itself upon our notice, and is there not in the present state of the civilized world some ground for the apprehension?[4] May not the late extraordinary events in Europe, that baffle all calculations, & must astonish even the better informed of all parties, & countries result in the establishment of principles dangerous to <u>liberty</u>, & the <u>Independance</u> of nations? Interesting as this subject is I must not persue it further—

The rapid progress of this Section of the union[5] in population, wealth, & political importance cannot fail to prove satisfactory to you, who always appeared disposed to favor its rising[6] prosperity, by affording its natural advantages a fair opportunity of fully developing[7] themselves. The light of Science begins to dawn here; & several institutions for the education of youth are established by law in different parts of the state; the beneficiel effects of which are already experienced by the various classes[8] of Society.[9]

When I began to write, I did not intend to exhaust your patience; I fear however, I may have done so. I will therefore close, by tendering you assurances of the very high respect, & consideration,

with which I am, Sir, Your Sincere friend and most Obed[t]

G W. Campbell

RC (DLC); addressed: "Thomas Jefferson Late President of the United States—Monticello Virginia"; endorsed by TJ as received 3 Oct. 1815 and so recorded in SJL; with notation beneath endorsement by TJ: "his health." Dft (NjP: Andre deCoppet Collection).

Napoleon's March 1815 return from exile on Elba caused a storm in Europe (Connelly, *Napoleonic France*, 246–7).

[1] Word interlined in Dft in place of "burst."

[2] Word interlined in Dft in place of "former distructive."

[3] Reworked in Dft from "The prospect of being again involved."

[4] Remainder of paragraph added at foot of Dft, keyed to this point with an asterisk.

[5] Preceding four words interlined in Dft in place of "Western Country."

[6] Word interlined in Dft in place of "growing."

[7] Reworked in Dft from "opportunity to develope."

[8] Word interlined in Dft in place of "grades."

9 In Dft Campbell here canceled "The principles of Republicanism prevail in this quarter with as little nurture as in any portion of the union."

From James Maury

My dear Sir,   Liverpool 9 Sept 1815

On the 24th Ult^o I recieved your letters of the 15th & 16th of June & present you my thanks for them.

From what I have read in the public prints of the U.S.A. the peace appears generally to have been there hailed with a sincere welcome: here not; & so it continued until the Sovereign of Elba returned to France: then indeed the people of this country were truly pleased that peace had been made, even before the Yankees had had a confounded drubbing: and I believe they now really are still more satisficed on this point, since they have witnessed the immense influx of commerce poured into this country from our's in consequence of this happy event.

It is flattering to me to find your opinions on the good effects of a war mutually injurious so exactly concur with my own. I have frequently given it as mine that the experience each country lately has had of the great hurt they can do each other in war will produce mutual impressions favorable to a long continuance of peace,

How differently people here think to what you think! Here, probably, 49 out of 50 think; ay & really think we had not the smallest pretext for complaint;—the aggressions intirely ours & &c. And in truth they have acted accordingly; for, from what I have seen, I conclude that at no period has the war against France been more popular than that against our country: the opposition too in many, if not most, instances have unequivocally expressed the same sentiments as well within, as without, the house.+

After the return of peace with the U.S.A. the recommencement of war with France occasioned the recurrence to the usual mode of manning the Navy by impressment of seamen; when I had the singular satisfaction to observe that the utmost courtesy was used towards the crews of our ships & every disposition manifested by the officers of the Impress service[1] at this port to avoid all occasion of vexation.   I remember well that, during our revolutionary war,

+I should not however do justice to the administration of the country, were I not to say that, during the whole war, they have appeared more pacifically disposed than the nation at large.   J.M.

[16]

it was remarked that, in almost every trying case, there appeared a strong difference in the feelings of British born, and American born, emigrants from the U.S. During this late war I have been very attentive to what passed and could not help observing & observing too with singular pleasure that, almost, without exception, every American born, be he the <u>disciple of Mr Jefferson</u> or <u>of Mr Pickering</u> appeared to have the same feelings towards their country:—each equally transported with delight at any advantage obtained by the arms of the U.S.A. & each equally depressed by a reverse.

Give me leave to say something of myself: altho' I have lived in this country so long, have married a native of it, have children: &, besides all this, have experienced the most friendly attentions from the circles I have been in; yet, after all, I find I indeed am as <u>unqualified</u> an American in material points[2] as tho I never had resided out of the Land I am from; so true is it that, after a certain age, none of us can assimilate to a foreign country. This being so you well may say why not return to my own & <u>wind up there</u>? Answer, I cannot. I am too old to travel &c &c.

I do indeed read with delight what you say of the progressive increase of the inhabitants of our country: at first I thought your estimate beyond probability; but now I think not: let there be added to this boon a continuance of our happy union to keep us <u>United States</u>: and this will be enough.

Let me rejoice with you on the honorable[3] peace lately concluded with Algiers. I think it will be more lasting than many affect to consider it. About 28 or 27 years ago, Spain, after having been at war with that Country ever since 1496, made a truce with it for 30 years, & I do not recollect any complaints of infraction. perhaps indeed they are as much to be depended on in these matters as us Christians.

On the return of intercourse we all expected Tobacco would immediately have come down to about standard peace price, & this impression did lower it to nearly[4] that standard: however, since that, it has advanced & now is 12^d a 14 for stemed & 7 a 15^d for Leaf:—prices never thought of!

My eldest Son has not been blessed with good Stamina:—weak nerves & the consequences both as to body & mind. I have sent him to the land of his father to give him the chance of benefit from the voyage, change of climate, of Scene &c &c; hoping, tho' not confidently, that they may <u>mend</u> him: possibly he may give you a call. Accept my best wishes

most truly yours   J. Maury

RC (DLC); at foot of text: "Thomas Jefferson &c &c Monticello"; endorsed by TJ as received 15 Dec. 1815 and so recorded in SJL.

The United States had negotiated a peace treaty with ALGIERS in June and July following the Algerine War of 1815 (Miller, *Treaties*, 2:585–94; Frank Lambert, *The Barbary Wars: American Independence in the Atlantic World* [2005], 189–201).

[1] Manuscript: "servie."
[2] Preceding three words interlined.
[3] Manuscript: "honorabe."
[4] Manuscript: "nealy." Word interlined.

Jefferson's Travel Receipts

I. GUERRANT & STAPLES'S BILL FOR FOOD, [12 SEPT. 1815]

II. HENRY FLOOD'S BILL FOR FOOD AND LODGING, [13 SEPT. 1815]

III. ROBERT HUNTER'S BILL FOR FOOD, [13 SEPT. 1815]

IV. CHARLES HOYLE'S BILL FOR FOOD, [13 SEPT. 1815]

V. BILL FOR FOOD AT A TAVERN IN LIBERTY, VIRGINIA, [17 SEPT. 1815]

VI. ROBERT DOUTHAT'S BILL FOR FOOD AND LODGING, 21 SEPT. 1815

EDITORIAL NOTE

In the latter part of 1815 Jefferson made two lengthy visits to his Bedford County estate, Poplar Forest, a principal goal of which was observing and calculating the height and latitude of the nearby Peaks of Otter. This group of travel receipts documents a portion of the first of these trips. Jefferson had arrived at Poplar Forest on 21 Aug. 1815 for a prolonged stay. On about 10 Sept. he left on a brief journey to Buckingham Court House (later Buckingham) in order to testify on 12 Sept. regarding the disposition of his brother Randolph Jefferson's estate. The first four receipts in this group resulted from this trip. On 13 Sept. Jefferson's friends José Corrêa da Serra and Francis W. Gilmer joined him at Poplar Forest. The three men stayed from 17 to 19 Sept. 1815 at Mount Prospect, the Bedford County home of Jefferson's friend Christopher Clark, which was their base as they conducted observations in the surrounding countryside. The final two receipts record some of Jefferson's expenses during this scientific expedition. Local report described the trio as traveling "in a vehicle much resembling a mill hopper," with the goal of "taking the elevation of the Peaks of Otter and exploring the Sides of them for Subjects botanical." From Clark's residence they proceeded to Natural Bridge, where they concluded their studies. Corrêa da Serra and Gilmer departed together from there for further extended travels. Jefferson made additional measurements and calculations of the Peaks of Otter in November 1815 on a succeeding visit to Poplar Forest (*MB*, 2:1313–4, 1316; Peachy R. Gilmer to Francis W. Gilmer, 3 Oct. 1815 [ViU: Gilmer Family Papers]; Jefferson's Calculations of Altitude of the Peaks of Otter, editorial note and group of documents printed below at 10 Nov. 1815).

I. Guerrant & Staples's Bill for Food

[12 Sept. 1815]

Mʳ Jefferson

To Breakfast	2	3
3 Servants	4.	6
Dinner	3–0	
3 Servants	4–6	
5 Horses 30¹ hours	1.² 2–6	
3 Servants Breakfas	4–6	
3 Ditto Dinner	4–6	
	2³=5=9	

MS (MHi); written on a scrap in an unidentified hand; undated; endorsed by TJ: "Sep. 12. 15 Staples"; with TJ's calculations at foot of text converting the amount due Staples to $8.075; unrelated fragment of notes in an unidentified hand on verso.

Guerrant & Staples obtained a license to keep an ordinary in Buckingham County in August 1815 (Vi: RG 48, Personal Property Tax Returns, Buckingham Co., 1815; *MB*, 2:1313).

¹ Reworked from "24."
² Reworked from "2."
³ Reworked from "3."

II. Henry Flood's Bill for Food and Lodging

[13 Sept. 1815]

Colº Jefferson

1815

Sepᵗ 11ᵗʰ To 5 Horses feedᵍ 2/3	11.3	
" 1 Dinner	2.0	
" 3 Servᵗˢ Dinʳ 1/–	3.0	
" 1 Lodging	.9	
" Wine	2.6	
	19.6	
13ᵗʰ		
To 5 Horses feedᵍ 2/3	11.3	
" 1 Supʳ	2.0	
" 1 Lodging	.9	
" 1 Servᵗ	1.0	
" Wine	4.6	
	£1.19.0	

MS (MHi); undated; endorsed by TJ: "Sep. 13. 15. H. Flood"; with TJ's notation beneath sum that the amount owed was $6.50.

On 11 Sept. 1815 TJ recorded paying $.25 in tips at Flood's tavern. Two days later he paid a total of $6.75 for lodgings "&c. going & coming" (*MB*, 2:1313).

III. Robert Hunter's Bill for Food

[13 Sept. 1815]

Mʳ Jefferson—	Dʳ
Breakfast	2.0
3 Servants Dᵒ	4.6
5 Horses 1/–	5.0
	£0.11.6

MS (MHi); written on a scrap in an unidentified hand; undated; endorsed by TJ: "Sep. 13. 15. Hunter."

Robert Hunter (1766–1827), innkeeper and public official, was born at his family's home, Clover Green, in what is now Appomattox County. Between 1805 and 1823 TJ frequently patronized his ordinary near present-day Concord and Spout Spring as he traveled between Monticello and Poplar Forest. Hunter served as sheriff and justice of the peace for Campbell County. At the time of his death his personal estate was valued at $7,588.92 and included thirty slaves (Anna Maria Green

Cook, *History of Baldwin County, Georgia* [1925], 357–8; Ruth H. Early, *Campbell Chronicles and Family Sketches Embracing the History of Campbell County, Virginia, 1782–1926* [1927], 430–2; *MB*, esp. 2:1161; Chambers, *Poplar Forest*, 105, 141; Vi: RG 48, Personal Property Tax Returns, Campbell Co., 1815; Lynchburg *Virginian*, 10 Jan. 1828; Campbell Co. Will Book, 6:25–6, 29–33).

TJ recorded payment to Hunter of $1 for "oats &c." on his way to Buckingham Court House on 10 Sept. 1815. On his return trip to Poplar Forest three days later he paid him $2.06 for BREAKFAST "&c." (*MB*, 2:1313).

IV. Charles Hoyle's Bill for Food

[13 Sept. 1815]

Mr Jefferson

Dinner 3/– Club 2/–	5–0
2 Servts Dinners	3–0
4 Horses 1 feed ea	6–0
	14–0

MS (MHi); written on a small scrap in an unidentified hand; undated; endorsed by TJ at foot of text: "Lynchbg. Hoyle. Sep. 13. 15."; with TJ's subjoined calculation that the amount owed was $2.58, the sum of $2.33 and an apparent $0.25 tip.

Charles Hoyle (1753–1825), innkeeper, was a native of Ireland. By 1802 he leased and operated the Indian Queen tavern in Lynchburg. After the Franklin Hotel opened in that city in 1818, Hoyle acted as its manager (*MB*, 2:1313; Margaret Anthony Cabell, *Sketches and Recollections of Lynchburg by the Oldest Inhabitant (Mrs. Cabell) 1858* [1858; repr. with additional material by Louise A. Blunt, 1974],

296–7, suppl., 101–3; William Asbury Christian, *Lynchburg and Its People* [1900; repr. 1967], 25, 33–4, 64; Lynchburg Hustings and Corporation Court Deed Book, A:55–6; DNA: RG 29, CS, Lynchburg, 1810, 1820; Richmond *Enquirer*, 29 Sept. 1812; *Richmond Enquirer*, 23 Sept. 1825; gravestone inscription in Old City Cemetery, Lynchburg).

CLUB: a share in a joint expense, such as punch (*MB*, 1:39; *OED*). On 13 Sept. 1815 TJ recorded payment to Hoyle of $2.58 for "dinner" (*MB*, 2:1313).

V. Bill for Food at a Tavern in Liberty, Virginia

[17 Sept. 1815]

Mᴿ Jefersons Bill

To 2 horsefeeds	2–
" Dinner	2–
Servants Dinner	1–6
	5 6

MS (MHi); written on a small scrap in an unidentified hand; undated; endorsed by TJ at foot of text: "1815. Sep. 17. Liberty"; with unidentified map in pencil by TJ on verso.

On 17 Sept. 1815 TJ recorded spending $0.93 for DINNER in Liberty (*MB*, 2:1313).

VI. Robert Douthat's Bill for Food and Lodging

Natural Bridge Sepᴿ 21. 1815

2 dietts	37½	$0.75
1 Lodging		.12½
2 diets Servant		.50
2 Horses		.50
10 Gallˢ oats	12½	1.25
		$3.12½

R. DOUTHAT

[21]

MS (MHi); written on a scrap in Douthat's hand; endorsed by TJ: "Tavern bills. 1815."

Robert Douthat (ca. 1757–1818), innkeeper, merchant, and farmer, emigrated from his native Ireland to the United States about 1784 and eventually acquired land near Staunton. In 1787 he was granted a merchant's license in Augusta County, and by 1790 he was a county justice of the peace. Douthat was postmaster of Staunton, 1792–94. He also served as a major in the militia. By 1810 Douthat was living in Rockbridge County, where he operated a tavern near Natu-

ral Bridge. As of 1812 he was still a British citizen. At the time of his death Douthat owned a personal estate valued at $2,780.63 (Lyman Chalkley, *Chronicles of the Scotch-Irish Settlement in Virginia* [1912–13], 1:248, 252, 253, 481, 523; *CVSP*, 5:414, 6:51; Axelson, *Virginia Postmasters*, 16; *Alexandria Advertiser*, 27 Nov. 1798; DNA: RG 29, CS, Rockbridge Co., 1810; U.S. Marshal's Returns of Enemy Aliens, DNA: RG 59, PW1812; Rockbridge Co. Will Book, 4:383–6).

On 20 Sept. 1815 TJ recorded payment to Douthat of 3.37\frac{1}{2}$ for "lodgg. &c." (*MB*, 2:1314).

From Samuel K. Jennings

DEAR SIR,   *Lynchburg, Sepr 13th 1815*[1]

Your aid is solicited in bringing the Patent Steam Bath into general use in your neighborhood; and considerable calculations are made upon your influence.

Letters and recommendations will be exhibited for your inspection, intended to show you that the subject is not unworthy of your regard. Indeed, to lend assistance in staying the ravages of disease, which every where is prematurely sweeping away the lives of thousands, is a work which would do honor to the greatest man under the Sun.—The President of the United States has heard me patiently upon the subject, and favored me with his influence for the promotion of a benevolence so important to the good citizens of this commonwealth.

He wrote to Doctor Physic of Philadelphia and to Doctor Mitchell of New-York, to each in the following manner, viz.

Washington City, August, 1814.

DEAR SIR,

Doctor Jennings has a medical invention, in the value of which he feels so much confidence, that he is anxious to present it to the consideration of the most enlightened of the profession. Although a departure in some measure from an established rule, I cannot refuse a line which may promote an opportunity for the accurate explanations by which he wishes his invention to be tested. His benevolent character is a further apology for the liberty I take.

Accept assurances of my great esteem and friendly respects,

JAMES MADISON.

Doctor Physic.

Dr. Physic has been in ill health for twelve months past, and has not been able to attend to the practice.

Dr. Mitchell without having received his letter and without solicitation* enclosed under cover to the Physician General, the following letter to me, viz.

"*To Doctor Jennings,*   *New-York, March 25*, 1815.

I this day, excellent sir, wrote to the Physician General of the United States, my opinion on your mode of applying heat to the external surface of the human body; and on Portio's method of directing its action upon the stomach and internal parts.

I have caused several experiments to be made with the alkoholic vapour, on the patients of the New-York Hospital. I am inclined to believe it is an efficacious and valuable remedy. It is remarkably neat. Nothing can be more handy. And really it in some sort enables you to place your patient beyond the climates, where snow and frost exercise their chilling influence, to the regions where solar warmth is more uniform and elevated.

It is a most important part of your heated air, that it is free from all smoke, soot and ashes.

I have considered the spirituous decomposition chemically. I have examined the metallic apparatus mechanically. And I have witnessed the action of the rarefied vapours remedially.

Considering a torpor of the skin to be a cause or accompaniment of many diseases; and that heat is the best of all excitants; I am well satisfied that your method of applying calorie to stimulate the cuticular surface is happily calculated to give relief in such cases, and to produce extensive advantages to the sick and disabled, in many other maladies.   SAMUEL L. MITCHELL."

By a reference to my Pamphlet you will see a letter from the Physician General (Dr. Tilton written to me on the same subject last July) likewise a number of additional certificates from Physicians and other citizens of standing in this place. You will also perceive that together with my Bathing-apparatus, I offer a brief view of the mode of practice, which led to its invention.—A practice; simple, safe, and speedily effectual, and of course better adapted to family use, than any other heretofore attempted.

It is the more important, because it enables you in almost every

---

*I withheld the letter from the President to Doctor Mitchell intending to wait on him this season. It has been forwarded by mail, since the above honorable notice was received.

instance, to arrest sickness in its forming state.—And with a little experience, it will be highly useful in the following forms of disease:

IN COLDS, CATARRHS, COUGHS, PLEURISIES AND IN FEVER IN ITS VARIOUS SHAPES. In all these the application should always be *general and decisive*—taking care, to begin the treatment upon the first onset of the complaint.

IN LOCAL INFLAMATION, &c. such as SORE-BREAST in female cases—SWELLED-TESTICLE, ANTHRAX or carbuncle, SORE-THROAT, QUINSEY, EAR-ACHE, TOOTH-ACHE, when produced by cold, &c. In these instances, the application may be *general*, at night, and *topical* or directly upon the part affected, at any time in the day. Or if the one method prove ineffectual, let the other be tried also.

IN ST. ANTHONY'S-FIRE,[2] Nettle-Rash, Scald-head and such like affections,—In these the application may be made as in cases of local inflammation.

IN SUPPRESSION OF URINE, and other painful affections of the bladder.—IN COLIC and in cases of STRANGULATED HERNIA, &c. In these the application should be general and local, more or less decisive, and to be repeated as the exigency of the case may require.

IN FEMALE-COMPLAINTS of a certain description, including DIFFICULT LABORS, FLOODINGS, &c.—Here the application may be general, tho' sometimes it might be as well, to confine it to the lower extremities.

IN PILES, whether blind or protruded. Let the application be very hot, and direct it upon the part affected—to be repeated as often as the symptoms make it necessary

IN BLEEDING AT THE NOSE—or in HEMOPTOE or other recent case of HEMORRHAGE. The application should be general—repeating morning and evening—keeping the patient still and warm, and making a free use of table salt.—Say a teaspoonful three times a day or oftener. And if necessary, use the following pill, viz: take Acetate of lead, six grains, opium three grains: make six pills. Give one morning and evening. But let the salt also be continued.

IN EXCESSIVE FATNESS. Let the application be general at night—to be moderately repeated next morning, and to be used twice or three times in a week.

IN OLD AGE and other FEEBLE CASES. Here use the Bath instead of a warming-pan. Warm the patient in his bed night and morning, in all cold and damp weather, still remaining in bed till nine or ten o'clock, and then let him get up to a fire—whether in winter or summer.

IN GOUT, RHEUMATISM, &c. Sometimes the application should be local, sometimes general, as it may be found most effectual.

LYING-IN-WOMEN may be put to bed at once, in clean sheets and dry linnen. Only applying the Bath immediately, so as to produce a gentle perspiration. ☞ *See the Pamphlet, on after-pains.*

IN ALL CASES OF DEBILITY, where laudanum[3] and wine are necessary, the patient ought to be kept warm by this method.

☞ I would particularly request every individual who may use the Bath, to be careful to have a *suitable frame*; and in all recent cases to let the application be made as much as possible, *to the naked skin.* The more expeditiously the perspiration can be induced, the more effectual. And let it never be forgotten, that a tepid Bath in inflammatory cases, is imcomparatively[4] more dangerous than one which would commonly be thought extravagantly hot. Begin in time, therefore, and be decisive, and you have nothing to fear. Let it also be carefully remembered, that in any and every case of long standing, in which the powers of life are considerably exhausted, if this remedy be tried, it should always be directed by the hand of experience. And nothing can be more absurd than to expect an immediate recovery in cases, which necessarily require both time and good management for effecting their cure.

With due consideration, I have the honor to be yours, &c.[5]

SAM^L K JENNINGS

If Mr. Jefferson could conveniently take the time and trouble, necessary to give my pamphlet a careful reading, possibly it might afford him a partial remuneration, and put it in his power to promote a work involving considerations important to humanity.

In a few days, I send an Agent to the States of Ohio and Kentucky—and to the Missisippi territory—and possibly to Louisiana. A line or two favorable to my object, addressed to Citizens of Standing, under the signature of Mr Jefferson—or an open letter of appropriate shape, would extremely facilitate my object.

I am with high consideration His obed^t Sev^t

SAM^L K JENNINGS

RC (MHi); printed circular, with portions written in the hand of Jennings as noted below; addressed: "Hon¹ Thomas Jefferson Present"; endorsed by TJ as received 13 Sept. 1815 and so recorded in SJL.

In his PAMPHLET, *A Plain, Elementary*

Explanation of the Nature and Cure of Disease, predicated upon facts and experience; presenting a View of that Train of Thinking which led to the invention of the patent, portable Warm and Hot Bath (Washington, 1814; possibly Poor, *Jefferson's Library*, 5 [no. 199]), Jennings published a 16 July 1814 letter from physician and surgeon general James TILTON praising his bath (pp. 105–6). SCALD-HEAD: "ringworm infection of the scalp." FLOODINGS: "hemorrhages of the uterus." HEMOPTOE: "hemoptysis or spitting of blood" (*OED*).

[1] Month, day, and last digit of year filled in by Jennings.

[2] Printed circular: "ATHONY'S-FIRE."
[3] Printed circular: "laudmun."
[4] Thus in printed circular, with "incomparatively" or "incomparably" presumably intended.
[5] Remainder in Jennings's hand.

To William Steptoe

TH: JEFFERSON TO DOCT[R] STEPTOE.   Wednesday Sep. 13. 15.

M[r] Correa and mr Gilmer are here, and can stay three days only. these they wish to pass in Botanising the circumjacent country, & would be thankful for your advice and much more for your company. will you do us the favor to come and breakfast with us tomorrow; as they will set out on their peregrinations after an early breakfast.
on Sunday we all depart for the peaks of Otter & Natural bridge I salute you with friendship & respect.

RC (ViLJML); dateline at foot of text; with unrelated text in an unidentified hand on verso. Not recorded in SJL.

A 3 Aug. 1815 letter to TJ from Francis W. Gilmer, not found, is recorded in SJL as received the same day from Ridgway, Peter Minor's Albemarle County estate.

Gilmer later wrote a paper "On the Geological Formation of the Natural Bridge of Virginia," read at the American Philosophical Society on 16 Feb. 1816 and published in its *Transactions*, new ser., 1 (1818): 187–92. Based on the observations he made on this visit with TJ and José Corrêa da Serra, in the article Gilmer noted TJ's opinion that, although the Natural Bridge had "lost some of its embellishments in 50 years of invasion upon the trees which crowned its borders, and overhung its sides," it still retained enough beauty to validate the fulsome description of it in his *Notes on the State of Virginia*. Gilmer also gave the latitude of 37°–42′–44″ that TJ arrived at in his Calculations of Latitudes of the Sharp Peak of Otter and Natural Bridge, 18 Sept.–10 Nov. 1815.

To Christopher Clark

DEAR SIR   Poplar forest Sep. 14. 15

I have to acknolege the reciept of your kind letter and meant on Sunday next to have the pleasure of calling on you; alone, as I then expected: but I am joined here by a couple of friends who wish to go on also to the Natural bridge. one of them, a mr Correa is one of the most learned men of the age, and particularly fond of botany; one of the best & plainest, unassuming men in the world. the other is mr

Francis Gilmer, son of the late Dr Gilmer, who accompanies mr Correa for the benefit of the instruction he may get from him. they would be very glad to pass two days in exploring the botany of the peaks of Otter; and I have to ask your hospitality for them those two days. they will give you no trouble but of a morning & evening, as they will be out in their rambles all day. I shall go on to the bridge where they will join me. and from thence they go on Southwardly and I shall return by Petit's gap. in these proposed movements of ours, we beg not interfere with your necessary business. I know that this is the season of the courts and that you are obliged to attend them. we shall dine at Liberty on Sunday and be with you in the evening in time for me to examine the grounds for measuring the height of the mountain. if I find them suitable I should bring proper instruments with me in October[1] or November, and make the actual admeasurement then. I salute you with friendship & respect.   TH: JEFFERSON

PoC (DLC); at foot of text: "M^r [1] TJ here canceled "&."
Christopher Clarke"; endorsed by T.J.

To Mary Blair Andrews

DEAR MADAM   Poplar Forest Sep. 15. 15.
     It has been communicated to me through a friend that you wish my opinion on a paragraph of the will of the late venerated judge Blair, for which purpose a copy of the will has been transmitted to me. it is now more than 40. years since I have retired from the profession of the law, and during this long interval I have been occupied in pursuits which gave little occasion of retaining familiarity with it. I rarely therefore undertake to form law-opinions, and never to put them into competition with those whose present course of life keeps them in the daily exercise of it's speculations and practice. on the opinion therefore which I may now hazard I set no other value than that of proving my desire to gratify a wish of yours, and to manifest the sensibilities I retain towards a family with which I have had such affectionate friendships.
     The letter covering the copy of the will does not give me full information of the state of the family; but from a friend acquainted with it I learn that mrs Henderson died leaving a son, Thomas Hamilton Henderson, the only issue then living of either lady, and that he is since dead in infancy, intestate, and without issue.
     The interests given by the will of judge Blair in the Mountain

plains the negroes and stock appurtenant, are expressly life-estates only to each of his two daughters, taking as tenants in common, with contingent remainders in each moiety, to such of the children of both, per capita, as should be living at the death of either tenant for life. at the death of mrs Henderson then the remainder in her moiety became vested in Thomas H. Henderson in possession, and in fee; and being derived by purchase from his grandfather, and not from his mother, it passed, on his death, to his father, in fee also, as his sole heir.

The life-estate in mrs Andrews's moiety is still in being, and the remainder in contingency; and on her death it will vest in her children, if she shall have any; if none, the reversionary right (on failure of the contingency) which remained in the testator, undevised to any one, will be in his legal representative. but whether this reversionary right vested, immediately on his death, in his daughters, as his coheirs, (defeasible only on the happening of the contingency) or remains, as to this moiety, in abeyance, until the failure of the contingency is what I cannot now say with confidence, writing from a place where I have no books to consult to refresh my memory on subjects long absent from it. on this however depends the question whether mrs Andrews may (if she dies without a child) dispose of a moiety of the reversion by deed or will. gentlemen in daily familiarity with the law will readily solve this doubt.

Mrs Andrews and mr Henderson being understood to have held their estates in common, and undivided, have been entitled to divide the profits equally. but either may require an actual partition, and hold thenceforward in severalty.

Be so good, dear Madam, as to accept the offering of these imperfect views merely as a testimony of my friendly regard for your much esteemed father, and his family; and to be assured particularly yourself of my high respect and esteem.   TH: JEFFERSON

PoC (DLC); at foot of first page: "Mrs Andrews"; endorsed by TJ.

Mary Blair Andrews (ca. 1759–1820) was the daughter of John Blair, associate justice of the United States Supreme Court. In 1795 she married Robert Andrews (ca. 1748–1804), the mathematics professor at the College of William and Mary (father's and husband's biographies in *DVB*; *WMQ*, 1st ser., 5 [1896]: 143; will in Vi: RG 12, Wills from the Treasurer's Office; *American Beacon and Norfolk & Portsmouth Daily Advertiser*, 19 Jan. 1820; *Richmond Enquirer*, 20 Jan. 1820).

The FRIEND who provided TJ with a copy of John Blair's will was Thomas Eston Randolph, to whom it had been enclosed in a letter from David M. Randolph, writing from "Fighting Creek," 25 Aug. 1815: "Presumptuous as it certainly is, for me to hazard Law-opinions, yet am I induced to differ in my construction of the enclosed will of the Honourable John Blair deceased. From the sober exercise of my simple perceptions, my convictions are, that Mrs Andrews, the surviving daughter, is intitled to the Life-Estate in the Albemarle Lands, and every thing appertain[in]g thereto at the decree of the Testator, conjointly: and, from the decree of Mr Henderson, Mrs Andrews is equally intitled to the enjoyment of the whole of the said Estate, to her death—And if (since Thomas, the Son of Jane had never any defined rights) the rule of Law, is such as to bar Thomas; it would seem that the Husband of Jane and father of Thomas, can legally inherit nothing! For, as Mr Henderson now demands a division of the Albemarle Estate: since Mrs Andrews may produce heirs, to share 'per. Capita' how can a division be called for under the provisions of the will, until the decease of Mrs Andrews? Hence, I have grounded my opinion: and, from a serious consideration of the several items in the will, I am persuaded that your goodness, either seperately, or in union with T.M.R. [Thomas Mann Randolph] will <not only> parden me in taking upon me to hope, that you will obtain from Mr Jefferson his deliberate opinion; and a cheerful declaration of it to the Lady in question" (RC in MHi; addressed: "Thomas Eston Randolph Esqr. Milton near Monticello Albemarle"; stamped; postmarked Charlottesville, 6 Sept.; one word and one set of initials editorially expanded).

The portion of John Blair's will relating to the MOUNTAIN PLAINS THE NEGROES AND STOCK APPURTENANT provided that the "plantation, in Albemarle County, commonly called, The Mountain plane, together with the Slaves, and stock of every sort kept thereon, to my two dear daughters, that is to say, the one moiety thereof to Mary, the Wife of the said Robert Andrews, the other moiety thereof to Jane, the Wife of the said James Henderson, for and during their natural lives, remainder to their Children who shall be living at the time of the decease of either of my said Daughters or devisees for life, and the heirs of such children; which remainder to the Children to be per capita and not per stirpes; so that upon the death of either of my said daughters, her moiety shall go in remainder, not to her Children only but to them and the children of my surviving daughter in fee simple. Item, as by this disposition to the Children, the land, in case of many sharers, may come to be divided into such small parts, that it would be better for all parties, to sell the same and divide the money among them, I hereby authorize that to be done, even during the minority of some of the parties, if from circumstances it shall be thought adviseable" (will in Vi: RG 50, James River Company, Wills and Qualifications).

From Joseph Coppinger

SIR   New York 15th September 1815

Annexed you will find the Prospectus of the contemplated practical treatise on Brewing Malting[1] & Tanning which will Probably be ready for delivery in three weeks from this day. If you will be Kind enough to give me the name of your Bookseller at Washington I will take care that some Copy[s] be sent on to him for you and you[r] fr[iends] to whom I request you will h[ave] the goodness to recommend this little work[.] Assuring you I have used my best endeavour to make it generally useful, and I trust on perusal you will find it so—

I have the honor to be with great respect
Sir Your ob^t Servt   JOSEPH COPPINGER

[29]

RC (DLC); mutilated at seal; addressed: "The Hono^{ble} Thomas Jefferson Monté Cello Verginia"; stamp canceled; franked; postmarked New York, 16 Sept.; endorsed by TJ as received 3 Oct. 1815 and so recorded in SJL. Enclosure: prospectus for Coppinger, *The American Practical Brewer and Tanner*, noting that the author has twenty-five years of experience in brewing and malting; asserting that the work, which will cost $2.25 and include three illustrations, will be useful to gentlemen, merchants, farmers, brewers, and tanners; stating that "an extensive use of malt liquors is the natural, and, perhaps, the only, effectual remedy to the too great consumption of ardent spirits"; describing the tanning sections as "given from the Academy of Arts and Sciences at Paris"; indicating that improved methods will speed the process of tanning "Soal Leather" from at least twelve months to just twenty-one days, while calf skins can be tanned in three or four days rather than six to eight months, with corresponding increases in the return on capital; promising that the volume will include "the whole process of brewing Porter, Pale Ale, Table Beer, &c., of the best quality"; and concluding with a table of contents and a place to inscribe the name, residence, and number of copies ordered by subscribers (undated broadside in DLC: TJ Papers, 204:36436).

[1] Word interlined.

Deposition Regarding Randolph Jefferson's Estate

The deposition of Thomas Jefferson of Albemarle aged seventy two years, taken by consent of parties in a controversy depending in the Superior court of the district of Buckingham between M. B. Jefferson the widow of Randolph Jefferson of the county of Buckingham lately deceased of the one part, and Thomas Jefferson, Robert Lewis Jefferson, Field Jefferson, Randolph Jefferson and Lilburne Jefferson, sons of the said Randolph Jefferson dec^d on the other part.

This deponent being first sworn on the holy evangelists deposeth and saith that in the month of May 1808, being at his own house in Albemarle, his deceased brother Randolph Jefferson came to visit him and, while there, requested him to write his will, and stated to him the distribution he wished to make of his estate: that this deponent accordingly made a rough draught, read it to the testator, and, by some small corrections, made it conformable to his wish: that the testator, by the advice of this deponent, copied the same with his own hand, but on account of some small inaccuracies, copied it a second time, fairly and wholly with his own hand, had it moreover attested by three witnesses subscribing in his presence, and deposited the same with this deponent for safekeeping: that the testator was, at that date, a widower and married some time afterwards: that, after his marriage, one of the testator's sons came to see this deponent, and conversing on the subject of the marriage, expressed great uneasiness, on a report to which he gave credit, that his father had made a marriage settlement on his wife of the greater part of his estate: that the said Randolph Jefferson coming afterwards to see this deponent, he mentioned to the sd Randolph the uneasiness of his family on the report of a marriage settlement; whereupon the said Randolph declared to him it was entirely without foundation: that he never had had a thought of making a settlement, nor had his wife or any of her family or friends ever made such a proposition to him; that they knew she would be entitled to dower of his estate, and he supposed they deemed it a sufficient provision: that they proceeded to converse on the subject of the will, and both of them considering that in case of his death, the law would so far controul his will as to give his wife dower of his estate, and that the will would be valid as to all the rest, it was deemed by both unnecessary to make any alteration in it, and was still left with this deponent in it's original form: that the testator was always in the habit of consulting this deponent in all cases of importance respecting his[1] interests, and he knows of no such case in which he did not consult him, except that of his last marriage, of which he never spoke to him until after it's consummation: that being on a visit to him, at his house in Buckingham in May 1813 his wife spoke to this deponent concerning her husband's management of his affairs, and particularly the disadvantageous sales he made of his crops, and expressed a wish that this deponent would recommend to him to consult and advise with her on such transactions, and to consent to her generally taking a part in the direction of his affairs; which however he this deponent[2] did not do: that neither on the occasion of this visit nor of a second in September of the same year, which was the last he ever made to his brother, did he observe any appearance of extravagance in the economy of his house, or in any other article of his expences; that he considered his said brother as not possessing skill for the judicious management of his affairs, and that in all the occasions of life a diffidence in his own opinions, an extreme facility and kindness of temper, and an easy pliancy to the wishes and urgency of others made him very susceptible of influence from those who had any views upon him: that soon after the period of his last visit beforementioned, his sd brother, in the occasional conversations with him on the subject of his affairs, began to complain of his store debts at Scott's ferry and Warren, he thinks particularly with mr Moon and mr Johnson, & that these were accumulating chiefly by his wife: that these complaints became more and more serious, and at length, in the autumn of the last year, he stated that he should be under the necessity of selling some of his land: that he then spoke more pointedly of the agency of his wife in contracting these debts, he said that he had desired the merchants to furnish nothing but on an order written with his own hand; that after this orders were sent, not written by himself, but so like his hand as to decieve the merchants and produce the articles; that thereupon he used a secret mark in his orders, which had effect at first, but was soon after discovered & imitated: and these imitations he expressly said were by his wife: that as well before, as after his last marriage he expressed dissatisfaction with the undutiful and disrespectful conduct towards himself of some of his sons, particularly of Thomas and Field, but he does not remember his particularising any other of them: that nevertheless in all the conversations which this deponent had with his said brother on the subject of his affairs, altho' he cannot recollect the particular expressions, yet it was perfectly understood by both parties that the will in the possession of this deponent continued to be that which he meant to continue as his will, and that their conversations were founded on this basis; and he does verily believe that if the testator, in his sound & healthy state, had intended to change his will, he would have applied to this deponent to make the change: that on Tuesday the 1st of August he recieved a letter from the wife of the testator, addressed to himself and mrs Marks his sister, and on Friday the 4th one from mr Zach. Pryor, which are the two letters deposited in the court of Buckingham: that on Saturday the 5th Randolph Jefferson, son of the testator came to this deponent, informed him of the extreme danger of his father's situation, that he had expressed to him his uneasiness as to a will he had signed, which he did not understand, that his former will in possession of this deponent was the one he wished to stand, and his anxiety to see this deponent and have this effected: that this deponent assured the sd Randolph the younger that he would go to see his brother the moment his horses returned from carrying mrs Marks, who had gone that day to see him but that he would immediately prepare a short instrument for revoking the will recently made, and reestablishing the former one, which if his brother chose to sign would effect what was said to be his wish, whi[ch] instrument he did prepare and deliver to the said Randolph the young[er,] that he set out on Monday the 7th of August to visit his sd brother, but at Scott's ferry meeting information of his death, he returned home, and soon after inclosed the will of May 1808, deposited with him, to mr Perkins, who was named an executor in it, which is the same will which was presented to him in Buckingham court and was there recognised by him. and further this deponent saith not

Th: Jefferson
September 15. 1815.

PoC (ViU: TJP-CC); right edge of final page cut off due to polygraph misalignment, with several words rewritten by TJ; dateline added in a different ink.

TJ presented evidence in the SUPERIOR COURT OF THE DISTRICT OF BUCKINGHAM on 12 Sept. 1815 at a session in the town of Buckingham Court House (later Buckingham). He had returned to Poplar Forest by the date he gave to this deposition (*MB*, 2:1313).

For the letter of the 1ST OF AUGUST 1815 from Randolph Jefferson's wife to TJ and Anne Scott Marks, see note to TJ to

Mitchie B. Pryor Jefferson, 2 Aug. 1815. The 4 Aug. 1815 letter to TJ from Mitchie Jefferson's brother Zachariah B. PRYOR, not found, is recorded in SJL as received from Snowden that same day. A missing letter to TJ from his nephew Isham Randolph Jefferson (referred to above as RANDOLPH JEFFERSON, SON OF THE TESTATOR) is recorded in SJL as written and received on 6 Aug. 1815. For the WILL OF MAY 1808, see TJ to Hardin Perkins, 11 Aug. 1815, and note.

[1] TJ here canceled "affairs."

[2] Preceding two words interlined.

From Christopher Clark

DEAR SIR,   mount Prospect 17 sep 15
    your favor of the 14 (instant) was delivered to me as I [was][1] walking near the gate and could not prevail on the bearer to wait for an answer and observe now what I then intended to state to you that the satisfaction to us from your Visit will be encreased by the pleasure of Seeing your two friends mr Correa and Gilmer (the latter I think I have seen) they may as well as yourself be assured that nothing will be lacking on our part to make there time as agreeable as possable
    with Sentiments of Regard & estem I am Dr Sir your mo ob

CHRISTOPHER CLARK

RC (MHi); endorsed by TJ as received 17 Sept. 1815 and so recorded in SJL.

TJ, José Corrêa da Serra, and Francis W. Gilmer stayed with Clark at his

MOUNT PROSPECT estate while exploring the Peaks of Otter, arriving this day and departing 19 Sept. 1815 (*MB*, 2:1313–4).

[1] Omitted word editorially supplied.

To Thaddeus Norris

DEAR SIR   Sep. 17. 15.

Two persons of the name of Millar have offered themselves to me as overseers at farms which I have in Bedford, where we cultivate both wheat and tobacco. they say they are from the neighborhood of Fauquier C. H. & have been brought up there. but they are provided with no recommendations. their appearance bespeaks labor and industry, and their conversation intelligence. I have agreed with them, with a reserve of being off if on enquiry I find their characters amiss. they tell me they are known to you; and this makes me take the liberty of this letter to request of you such information about them as you possess yourself or can get without inconvenience, which, will come to me in time if sent by mail, addressed to me at Monticello near Milton. the inconvenience of employing men whose characters may be bad for ought I know will I hope apologise for the trouble I propose to you, with an assurance of my great esteem and respect.

TH: JEFFERSON

PoC (MHi); most line endings faint and enhanced by TJ; at foot of text: "Mr Norris"; endorsed by TJ on verso as a letter written to Thaddeus Norris from Poplar Forest, with canceled partial endorsement by TJ at head of recto.

Thaddeus Norris (d. 1823) operated a tavern in Fauquier Court House (later Warrenton) at which TJ occasionally stopped while traveling between Washington and Monticello during his presidency. By 1819 he had been declared insane, though Norris himself denied the categorization and was apparently of sound mind while writing his will in 1823. He left a personal estate valued at $3,826.50, including eight slaves (*MB*, 2:1148, 1201, 1203; James Edmonds Saunders and Elizabeth Saunders Blair Stubbs, *Early Settlers of Alabama* [1899], 364; Warrenton *Palladium of Liberty*, 26 Nov. 1819, 3 Nov. 1820; petitions of heirs of Septimus Norris, [presented 21 Dec. 1819], and of citizens of Warrenton, [presented 12 Dec. 1821] [Vi: RG 78, Legislative Petitions, Fauquier Co.]; *JHD* [1821–22 sess.], 113 [9 Jan. 1822]; Fauquier Co. Will Book, 8:462–3, 9:21; Nancy Chappelear Baird, *Fauquier County, Virginia, Tombstone Inscriptions* [1970], 183; Washington *Daily National Intelligencer*, 10 July 1827).

From 1816 to 1821 TJ employed Robert Miller (MILLAR) as overseer at his Bear Creek plantation in BEDFORD County, and he engaged William J. Miller at Tomahawk in 1816 and 1817. They each received £50 a year (*MB*, esp. 2:1332).

A missing and presumably misdated letter from Norris of 2 Sept. 1815 is recorded in SJL as received 15 Dec. 1815 from Fauquier Court House.

Notes on Distances between Poplar Forest and Natural Bridge

[ca. 17–21 Sept. 1815]

Roads

	Poplar Forest		
	Callaway's mill		
	bridge.	5.	soon after passing Callaw's
4	Leftwich's mill		mill a right hand is a better
	Liberty.	12	road, and saves 3. mi. to
2	Jenn's gap road		Clarke's.
10	Doneld's mill		
	Chr. Clarke's	6. miles	$41\frac{1}{2}$
	Jenning's gap.	5.	
	the river	8	
	Skidmore's	2[1]	
	Douthat's—	5	
	Nat^l bridge	$1\frac{1}{2}$	
	Greenlee's ferry	$3\frac{1}{2}$	8 hours ride, exclusive of
	W. foot of mount^n	$4\frac{1}{2}$	stoppages of which 2
	Petit's gap	2	hours are[2] for the 5 miles
	E. foot Mount^n	3	crossing the mountain
	Douglas's	3	32
	Tabernacle Meet^g H	8	
	Pop. For.	8	

MS (CSmH: JF); entirely in TJ's hand; undated; subjoined to TJ's MS pocket notes for his *MB* entries covering 17–21 Sept. 1815, with Dft of TJ's Calculations of Latitudes of the Sharp Peak of Otter and Natural Bridge, 18 Sept.–10 Nov. 1815, on verso.

[1] Numeral added in place of "ferry [...]?"
[2] Manuscript: "are are."

Calculations of Latitudes of the Sharp Peak of Otter and Natural Bridge

1815. Sep. 18. Sharp peak of Otter	° ′ ″		1815. Sep. 20. Natural bridge. ° ′ ″
Observed altitude of ☉.	109–21– 0		107–29– 0
– error of instrument	1–30		1–30
	109–19–30		107–27–30
true observed altitude	54–39–45		53–43–45
– refract^n 41″ + parallax 4″	37	– 42″ + 4″[1]	38
true altitude of ☉'s center	54–39– 8		53–43– 7
– ☉'s decln Greenwich 2–7–17		1°–20′–42″	
for 79°–45′–57.″ W 5– 8	2–12–25	5 – 9	1–25–51
true height of Æq.^{2} at Peak	52–26–43		52–17–16
	90–		90
Zenith distance of Æq. at Peak	37–33–17^3		37–42–44

1815. Nov. 10. Sharp peak of Otter	° ′ ″
Observed altitude	71– 8– 0
– error of instrument	1–30
corrected observn	71– 6–30
true observed altitude	35–33–15
– refract^n 1′–19″ + parallax 7″=	– 1–12
true Alt. of ☉'s center	35–32– 3
☉'s decln Greenwich 17°–0′– 1″	
for 79°–45′–57.″ W. + 3– 33	17– 3–33
height of Æq. at Peak	52–35–36
	90–
Zenith dist. or Lat.	37–24–24
observn of Sep. 18.	37–33–17
	74–57–41
mean of 2. observations	37–28–50

MS (MHi); filed with TJ's Weather Memorandum Book, 1802–16; on verso of TJ's Calculations of Latitude of Poplar Forest, 6 Aug.–10 Dec. 1815 (printed at the latter date); entirely in TJ's hand. Dft (CSmH: JF); on verso of TJ's Notes on Distances between Poplar Forest and Natural Bridge, [ca. 17–21 Sept. 1815], and TJ's MS pocket notes for his *MB* entries covering 17–21 Sept. 1815; entirely in TJ's hand; lacking calculations for 10 Nov. and textual explanation of calculations for 18 and 20 Sept.

TJ also created, but never used, a sheet with four additional blank versions of the chart employed here, two each on recto and verso (MS in MHi; filed with TJ's Weather Memorandum Book, 1802–16; entirely in TJ's hand; dated Sept. 1815).

TJ confirmed elsewhere that he observed the latitudes of the Sharp Peak of Otter and of Natural Bridge as 37°–33′–17″ and 37°–42′–44″ on SEP. 18 and SEP. 20, respectively (*MB*, 2:1313, 1314). He also noted in a handwritten revision to the query on mountains in his

Notes on the State of Virginia, composed sometime after November 1815, that "Two observns with an excellent pocket sextant gave a mean of 37°–28′–50″ for the Lat. of the sharp Peak of Otter" (Jefferson, *Notes on the State of Virginia* [London, 1787; Sowerby, no. 4167; Poor, *Jefferson's Library,* 7 (no. 365); TJ's copy with revisions in ViU, including this one tipped in between pp. 28 and 29]).

[1] Equation not in Dft.

[2] Abbreviation for "Equator," here and below.

[3] In Dft TJ canceled a preliminary version of his 18 Sept. calculation and replaced it with one that corrected a subtraction error in the first step.

From Patrick Gibson

SIR   Richmond 21st Septr 1815

In conformity to your instructions of the 19th Augt I directed on the 28th a letter to you at Poplar forest near Lynchburg of which the within is a Copy—I am disappointed at not receiving a reply to it as your note falls due tomorrow and your signature is wanting for a renewal—

With great respect I am Your obt Servt   PATRICK GIBSON

RC (ViU: TJP-ER); with Dupl of Gibson to TJ, 28 Aug. 1815, on verso; between dateline and salutation: "Thomas Jefferson Esqre"; endorsed by TJ as received 29 Sept. 1815 and so recorded in SJL.

To José Corrêa da Serra

DEAR SIR   Poplar Forest Sep. 22. 15.

I arrived here the morning after we parted, to wit, yesterday morning, and I have this day written by mail to mr Rhea and Govr Milledge: but I have thought it also safe to inclose in this letter a duplicate of that to Govr Milledge, and put both under cover to mr Rhea, lest any miscarriage should happen to that sent by mail. there is no person in Georgia who can be so useful to you as mr Milledge; & particularly as to plants, altho' not a regular botanist, he has been alway[s] uncommonly attentive to them. I shall leave this the 1st day of October, & be here again from the 1st to the middle of November, and shall hope to see you on your return either here or at Monticello, and to keep you as long as the science and society of Philadelphia will permit. I should envy mr Gilmer his botanical enjoyments with you had not long avocations of a different character first lessened my little stock in that science, and the decay of memory and decline of strength for rambling, forbidden me to think of renovating it. mr Gilmer while with you cannot be better employed. he will be enlarging the foundation on which his own fame and the hopes of his friends and country are to be raised. to the serious occupations which these will reserve for him his physical science will add ornament and comfort; but he must not expect that we shall permit him to devote to ornament & comfort alone the solid utilities we expect to derive from him. I salute you both with affectionate friendship and respect

TH: JEFFERSON

PoC (DLC); edge trimmed; at foot of text: "Mr Correa"; endorsed by TJ. Enclosure: TJ to John Milledge, 22 Sept. 1815. Enclosed in TJ to John Rhea, 22 Sept. 1815, Rhea to TJ, 20 Nov. 1815, and TJ to Corrêa da Serra, 1 Jan. 1816.

To John Milledge

DEAR SIR   Poplar Forest, near Lynchburg. Sep. 22. 15.

Two friends, who lately accompanied me to this place have proceeded on a tour through the Southern country. the one of these is mr Correa a gentleman from Portugal, of the first order of science, being without exception the most learned man I have ever met with in any country: modest, good-humored, familiar, plain as a country farmer, he becomes the favorite of every one with whom he becomes acquainted. he speaks English with ease. he is accompanied by mr Francis Gilmer, son of Doctor Gilmer formerly of my neighborhood, the best educated young man of our state, and of the most amiable dispositions. he travels with his friend Correa, as with a Mentor, for the benefit of his conversation and the information and improvement he may derive from it; and he will be in future whatever he pleases in either the State, or General government. at home in every science, botany is their favorite. as every plant of any singularity stays them, their progress will be slow, and this letter will reach you by mail long before they will reach your residence. pray recieve them as strangers, as men of science, of worth, and as my friends. they are persons of whom every country should ambition the good opinion. I know the value they will set on the information you can give them as to the vegetables of your state, and whatever else they wish to learn concerning it, and that which you will set on their esteem when they shall be known to you. I am the more gratified in being instrumental to this, as it furnishes me a new occasion of assuring you of my great friendship and respect.   TH: JEFFERSON

[38]

RC (Rosa Milledge Pattillo, Atlanta, 1971); at foot of text: "Govr Milledge." PoC (DLC); endorsed by TJ. Enclosed in TJ to José Corrêa da Serra, 22 Sept. 1815, TJ to John Rhea, 22 Sept. 1815, Rhea to TJ, 20 Nov. 1815, and TJ to Corrêa da Serra, 1 Jan. 1816.

To John Rhea

DEAR SIR   Poplar Forest near Lynchburg. Sep. 22. 15

Two friends of mine, who lately accompanied me to this place, have proceeded on a tour through the Southern country. the one of these is mr Correa, a gentleman from Portugal, of the first order of science, being without exception the most learned man I have ever met with in any country. modest, good humored, familiar, plain as a country farmer, he becomes the favorite of every one with whom he becomes acquainted. he speaks English with ease. he is accompanied by mr Francis Gilmer, son of Doct^r Gilmer formerly of my neighborhood, the best educated young man of our state, and of the most amiable dispositions. he travels with his friend Correa merely for the benefit of his conversation and the information & improvement he may derive from it. at home in every science, botany is their favorite. as every plant of any singularity stops them, their progress is of course slow, and this letter will reach you by mail, before they will reach Knoxville the first place of their destination. pray recieve them as strangers, as men of science, as my friends, and as they merit, and engage your friends to honour themselves and their state by their attentions to such men, and the facilities they can give to their enquiries. we have a character to establish with the European world. it will be a high one if we can be made known to them as we really are: and this must be through the report of such of their good men as come among us. for their honor and our reputation too few of their good men come to see us. of libellers they send us plenty, and especially England.[1] ever and with sincerity

your friend   TH: JEFFERSON

PoC (ViW: TC-JP); at foot of text: "Jacob Rhea Member of Congress"; endorsed by TJ as a letter to "Rhea honble mr." Enclosure: TJ to José Corrêa da Serra, 22 Sept. 1815, and enclosure.

[1] Sentence interlined.

Account with William Steptoe

1815   Thos Jefferson Esquire to Will: Steptoe—   D[r]
           To ballance ℔ acc[t] render'd—

Jany 21st	To Visit & Prescription Script[m] to 3 negroes	£0:17:0
	" Emplastrum Epispasticum	5:
27th	Visit to Edy 8/— Rad. Polygola Seneka	11:0.
	Prescription Scriptum	6
Feb[y] 20th	" Visit & Prescript[n] Verb[l] for Aggy's child	12:6
26th	D[o] to negroe child in the night. &c	15:
Apl—	Prescriptions script to Maria & a negroe man }	12:0
		£3:18:6[1]

       C[r]

By shop acctt
By 8 bushells wheat   £2:[2] 8:0
By Cash—$5:   1:10:0[3]

	£	s	d
Balance of acc[t] of 1813. 1814.	6	16	10
amount of acc[t] for 1815. as within	3	18	6
35.89 =	10.	15.	4

Sep. 22. 15. pd by order on A. Robertson

MS (ViU: TJP-MJ); undated section in Steptoe's hand, with concluding line in TJ's hand; written on both sides of a single sheet.

SCRIPT[M]: "written." An EMPLASTRUM EPISPASTICUM is a blistering plaster (Nicholas Culpeper, *Culpeper's Complete Herbal* [London, 1816], 371; James Rennie, *A New Supplement to the latest Pharmacopœias*, 4th ed. [1837], 136). RAD. POLYGOLA SENEKA is the root of *Polygala senega*, commonly Seneca snakeroot (*Hortus Third*, 894). AGGY'S CHILD was Sally Goodman. The figure of £6–16–10 was carried over from TJ's Account with Steptoe, 1 June 1814. On SEP. 22. 15. TJ recorded payment of $35.89 to Steptoe for "Medical services after deducting smith's acct." (*MB*, 2:1314).

[1] Recto ends here.
[2] Reworked from "1."
[3] Remainder in TJ's hand.

From Mathew Carey

SIR   Philad[a] Sept. 23. 1815.

By this day's mail I send, & request Your acceptance of, a copy of the last Edition of the Olive Branch, greatly enlarged.

Absence from Philadelphia & long continued indisposition have tarnished the work with some most egregious blunders, of which I feel deeply ashamed.

I hope & trust the 72^d Chapter will be found a complete & unanswerable refutation of some most pernicious & deleterious errors. I remain, sir, respectfully

Your ob^t h^{ble} serv^t
MATHEW CAREY

RC (MHi); dateline at foot of text; endorsed by TJ as received 3 Oct. 1815 and so recorded in SJL. RC (MoSHi: TJC-BC); address cover only; with PoC of TJ to John Manesca and Victor Value, 26 Oct. 1815, on verso; addressed: "Hon Thomas Jefferson, Expresident U.S Monticello V^a"; franked; postmarked Philadelphia, 23 Sept. Enclosure: Carey, *The Olive Branch: or, Faults on Both Sides, Federal and Democratic. A Serious Appeal on the Necessity of Mutual Forgiveness and Harmony*, 6th ed. (Philadelphia, 1815).

In the 72^D CHAPTER of the enclosure (pp. 418–35), Carey refutes the idea that the United States suffered economically during the administrations of TJ and James Madison.

To John Holmes

SIR   Poplar Forest near Lynchburg Sep. 23. 15.

I have now been absent from home upwards of a month, and write from a place 90. miles Southwardly. this must apologise for my late answer to your esteemed favor covering a copy of your oration on the 4th of July. I have read it with great satisfaction; at least with as much as the spectacle of wickedness under flagellation admits. I am glad too it recieves the stripes from a domestic hand; wishing that all others would hold off, and leave to the sound in each state the treatment of it's own unsound members. our gazettes however do not observe this caution, every paper teeming with invective against the fratricides of the East. repentance and conciliation are not to be thus produced. and indeed these seem to be distant and desperate, when we advert to the estimate which, from the five Eastern states, gives but 3. republicans out of 41. members elected for the 14th Congress. knowing that the leaders were monarchists and Anglomen in principle, I had still always hoped that a great majority of the <u>people</u> of those states were Unionists and republican, led astray only by an infatuated devotion to England. on what principles, political or commercial, they can calculate advantage in a subordination to England, and separation from their co-states, and consequent exclusion from their harbors even in time of peace is, to my arithmetic, incomprehensible. however you have so often made this plain and palpable to them in your excellent speeches that I conclude they would not, on this subject, listen to one even from the dead.

Your oration has the more value from the example it has set of abandoning the hackneyed state of things of 1776. and seeking, in the times present, subjects profitable and proper for our anniversary themes. I hope the example will be followed and make the 4th of July a day of revision of our conduct, and of recall to the principles which made it our birth-day.

Accept the assurance of my distinguished respect and esteem.

Th: Jefferson

RC (MeHi: Autograph Collection); torn at crease, with missing text supplied from PoC; addressed: "John Holmes esquire Alfred District of Maine"; franked; postmarked. PoC (DLC); mutilated at crease; endorsed by TJ.

On 6 Sept. 1815 the Washington *Daily National Intelligencer* published an ESTIMATE that three of the representatives from Massachusetts to the Fourteenth Congress would be Republicans. Of the forty-one representatives originally elected to that congress from the FIVE EAST-ERN STATES of Connecticut, Massachusetts, New Hampshire, Rhode Island, and Vermont, only Samuel Shepard Conner and Albion Keith Parris were Republicans (*Biog. Dir. Cong.*; Washington *Daily National Intelligencer*, 4 Dec. 1815). In response to the Hartford Convention, John Randolph of Roanoke stated that if the New England states seceded, their ships and goods would be excluded from the HARBORS of the remaining states (Georgetown *Federal Republican*, 28 Dec. 1814).

From John Jefferson

Dear Sir   Pittsylvaina C° Septr 23rd 1815

I have the pleasure of informing that I am in good health, and hope you enjoy the same, Mr Arthur Hopkins Grand Son of my Sister Judiths, Will be glad to be Acquainted with you, He is a young Gentleman of the Bar believed of great Talents, the favor you have done for me lays me under the greatest Obligation, Tho, my suit ag^t Col° James being of so long a date that, my Lawyers, & disinterested Gentlemen of the Bar, after an offer of One thousand Dollars, insisted on me to acceed to it, and that the law was pointedly against me, which I did, but am as much Obliged to you, as if I had gained the whole amount

I am With the greatest Sincerity[1] Dr Sir y^r Mo. Affec^t Friend

Jn° Jefferson

RC (ViU: TJP-CC); addressed: "Col° Thomas Jefferson Bedford Co^{ty} Favored by Mr Hopkins"; endorsed by TJ as received 6 Nov. 1815 and so recorded in SJL.

John Jefferson was a son of TJ's uncle Field Jefferson. He lived in Cumberland and Pittsylvania counties. TJ occasionally offered Jefferson legal advice, and in 1790 he gave him financial support in his lawsuit against Richard James for payment of a forfeited bond. In 1772 a John Jefferson was appointed collector for Southam Parish in Cumberland County (*Tyler's Quarterly Historical and Genealogical Magazine* 7 [1925]: 49–50, 121, 124; Mecklenberg Co. Will Book, 1:4; *MB*, 1:6–7, 49–50; *PTJ*, 16:87–8, 181, 20:419; Ann K. Blomquist, *The Vestry Book of Southam Parish, Cumberland County, Virginia, 1745–1792* [2002], 227, 271; *Lynchburg Weekly Gazette*, 13 Oct. 1798).

Arthur Francis Hopkins (1794–1865), attorney, was the grandson of TJ's first cousin Judith Jefferson Hopkins, a sister of John Jefferson. He was born in Pittsylvania County and studied at the New London Academy, at an academy in Caswell County, North Carolina, and at the University of North Carolina before reading law with William Leigh in Halifax County, Virginia. Hopkins qualified at the bar of Bedford County in 1814 and moved to Alabama in 1816. There he practiced law and was a member of Alabama's first constitutional convention in 1819 and a state senator, 1822–24. Hopkins was elected to the Alabama supreme court in 1834 and briefly served as chief justice before resigning the judgeship in 1837 to resume his legal practice. He ran unsuccessfully as a Whig candidate for the United States Senate in 1844 and 1849, and in 1861 he represented Alabama's interests in Virginia in order to coordinate secession. Hopkins served for several years as president of the Mobile & Ohio Railroad and accumulated large landholdings in Alabama and Mississippi (*DAB*; Walter Lee Hopkins, *Hopkins of Virginia and Related Families* [1931], 36–8; James Edmonds Saunders and Elizabeth Saunders Blair Stubbs, *Early Settlers of Alabama* [1899], 87–93; Bedford Co. Order Book, 16:245; William Garrett, *Reminiscences of Public Men in Alabama, for thirty years* [1872], 377–80, 754, 773, 775, 791; gravestone inscription in Magnolia Cemetery, Mobile).

[1] Manuscript: "Sincrity."

To Samuel K. Jennings

D[EA]R SIR   Poplar Forest Sep. 23. 15.

I thank you for the pamphlet you have been so kind as to send me, and I have read it with great pleasure. but when you request an opinion on it, it is more than I am able to give or to form. I am not sufficiently intimate with the structure of our frame, nor yet with the medical agents which may change it's condition from bad to good, or the converse, to decide between systems on which the learned in the healing art have been divided. these studies have fallen[1] but incidentally within my attention. your theory is ingenious, well developed, and worthy of an acute observer. but when I consider the many theories which within the last century or two have succeeded each other, all plausible, all rested on facts ingeniously applied, I am obliged to remain in indecision between them, and to say 'Non nostrum, inter vos, tantas componere lites.' I have little doubt of the great potency of your steam-bath; and that it will be found capable of marked efficacy in human diseases. more time and observation may however be necessary to discriminate between the particular cases wherein it will be useful or otherwise. for in medecine experience is the sovereign guide. this discrimination once settled, the steam-bath will probably become, as the Kinkina, mercury, opium and other real medicaments, one of the means given us by providence for soothing our sufferings, while he permits [us]² to stay here. Accept my share of the public acknolegements due to your efforts for solacing our condition, and the assurance of my great esteem & respect.   TH: JEFFERSON

PoC (MoSHi: TJC-BC); salutation faint; at foot of text: "Doctʳ Jennings"; endorsed by TJ. Printed in *Richmond Enquirer*, 13 Jan. 1816, and elsewhere, and (as a letter of 28 Sept. 1815) in Jennings, *Letters and Certificates, recommending the Patent Portable Warm and Hot Bath* (Norfolk, 1816), 11.

NON NOSTRUM, INTER VOS, TANTAS COMPONERE LITES: "It is not for me to settle so close a contest between you," in Virgil, *Eclogues*, 3.108 (Fairclough, *Virgil*, 1:48–9). Quinquina (KINKINA) is the bark of the cinchona tree, also known as Peruvian bark (*OED*; note to TJ to John Barnes, 29 June 1811).

¹ Word interlined in place of "come."
² Omitted word supplied from *Richmond Enquirer* and Jennings, *Letters and Certificates*.

From James Monroe

DEAR SIR   Albemarle sepr 23. 1815

Judge Roane committed to my charge his opinion on the question whether the congress had power to regulate an appeal from the superior courts of the States individually, and of course from any of their courts, in cases relating to treaties & laws of the U states, with a view that I might submit it to you. He remarked that his opinion had not been deliver'd, the cause tho' argued, being still undecided. Aware of the importance of the subject, he is desirous of knowing your sentiments on it, from the respect he entertains for them. He would not ask them, if he supposed you had any objection to making them known, the contrary of which he infers from the freedom with which you have always expressd your opinions on great national questions. I expected to have handed you this in person, but find that I must depart without having the pleasure of seeing¹ & conferring with you on this & other interesting topics. In case you think proper to communicate your sentiments on the question invok'd in Judge Roane's paper, it will I presume be best that you should address them to him, with the paper itself, tho' it will give me pleasure to be the organ, if you should prefer that mode.

I return you your own remarks on the subject² of finance, tho' I should have been much gratified to have taken them with me to washington, as that subject must be disposed of at the next session of Congress, and the plan which is so ably advocated by them, presents the only alternative to that of a national bank [for the State banks offer none] for providing a circulating medium, that I know of. I will gladly receive this paper there, to be used under such injunctions as you may prescribe.

It appears that France is subdued, and likely to be dismemberd, all her armies having surrender'd, & the whole country being in possession of the allies. Bonaparte has terminated his career ingloriously, by any criterion by which his conduct can be examind. To say nothing of his having overthrown, or at least participated in the overthrow of the liberties of his country, we had a right to expect in a military chief looking to power & renown, consistent proofs or examples, of gallantry & even heroism, with a defiance of his adversaries, & a scorn of life, in his last acts. we are told by his enemies that he fought the battle well, but now this is denied by marshall Ney, and with great force, if we may believe his statment of facts. From the moment of his defeat, he appears to have lost all command of himself. His retreat from the army, thereby depriving it of a head when it most wanted a great leader; his abdication, whereby all efficient gov^t was dissolved, when the enemy were approaching Paris, and no other person could be relied on, to rally the army, in consequence of which it was dispersed, with many other acts as reported, indicate a feebleness which was not expected of him. He seems to have had in view the preservation of his own life only, after he lost the power, for which he had contended, in one battle, & to have sunk under the defeat. The Bourbons are reduc'd to the most wretched condition. no means present themselves whereby they may support the independance of their country, or their own honor. The creatures of the allies, they must be their instruments. Even if they should place the gov^t in the hands of the revolutionary party, the case would Still, for a while, and perhaps a long one, be desperate. I do not think, that they can be, leaders, of that party, and of course I do not see how they can, contribute to the independance of France.

Our gentlemen have formd a treaty with England under powers given them when they left home, and when it was hoped that every thing would be settled at the same time. altho' it leaves much for future arrangm^t, yet it may be useful, at the present time, and satisfactory to the country. The complete overthrow of France, has excited much apprehension for the safety of our political institutions, & system. A treaty with the power most hostile to us, at a moment when that danger was to be most[3] dreaded, may dissipate that fear, even with the most timid, which may be of considerable utility. It is important that its operation is limited to 4. years.

very respectfully your friend & servant   JAˢ MONROE

RC (DLC); brackets in original; endorsed by TJ as received 3 Oct. 1815 and so recorded in SJL.

Spencer ROANE'S PAPER, not found, was a draft version of his opinion in the case of *Martin v. Hunter's Lessee*, which was nearing final decision after more than two decades of litigation in Virginia state courts and the United States Supreme Court. Roane delivered his opinion when the case came before the Virginia Court of Appeals in the spring of 1814. At its most basic level, the case pitted the state appeals court and the nation's Supreme Court against each other, with the latter maintaining its constitutional authority to overturn the decision of a state tribunal. Roane argued that the federal authority was not that of a "sole and consolidated government. The governments of the several states, in all their parts, remain in full force, except as they are impaired, by grants of power, to the general government." He ultimately concluded that the Constitution had not in fact granted the Supreme Court the power to "meddle with the judgments of this court, in the case before us; that this case does not come within the actual provisions, of the twenty-fifth section of the judicial act; and that this court is both at liberty, and is bound, to follow its own convictions on

the subject, any thing in the decisions, or supposed decisions, of any other court, to the contrary notwithstanding." Roane's opinion, which was printed in full in the 1 Feb. 1816 issue of the *Richmond Enquirer*, was overturned by the United States Supreme Court in March 1816. This ruling was the first example of the highest federal court asserting its authority over state courts in matters of federal law (*Va. Reports*, 18 [4 Munford]: 25–54, esp. 30, 54; *U.S. Reports*, 14 [1 Wheaton]: 304–82; Marshall, *Papers*, 8:108–21).

The enclosed REMARKS ON THE SUBJECT OF FINANCE by TJ have not been identified. For earlier correspondence he had shared on this subject, see note to Monroe to TJ, 10 Oct. 1814, and TJ to Monroe, 16 Oct. 1814. John Quincy Adams, Henry Clay, and Albert Gallatin (OUR GENTLEMEN) signed a convention of commerce with Great Britain on 3 July 1815. The agreement, which the United States Senate ratified on 19 Dec. 1815, regulated the imposition of trade duties for 4. YEARS. President James Madison signed enabling legislation on 1 Mar. 1816 (Miller, *Treaties*, 2:595–600; *JEP*, 3:6; *U.S. Statutes at Large*, 3:255).

[1] Manuscript: "seing."
[2] Manuscript: "subjet."
[3] Word interlined.

From Henry Dearborn

DEAR SIR,   Washington Septʳ 26ᵗʰ 1815

If no new causes of delay occur we[1] shall set out tomorrow morning for Monticello. I wrote to Mʳ Rodney immediately after I was honored with your friendly letter, and expected on my arrival at Wilmington that he would have Joined me at this place & proceeded on with us, but his official, or professional, ingagements disappointed me of the pleasure of his company. I now fear that my visit will be so late as to interefere with your usual visits to your distant plantations, but I cannot deny myself the pleasure I have so long contemplated.—

yours with the highest respect
& esteem,

H. DEARBORN

RC (DLC); endorsed by TJ as received 3 Oct. 1815 and so recorded in SJL. RC (MHi); address cover only; with PoC of TJ to Richard Rush, 26 Oct. 1815, on verso; addressed: "Hon^bl Thomas Jefferson Monticello"; franked; postmarked Washington City, 27 Sept.

Caesar A. RODNEY was at this time a Delaware state senator (*ANB*).

¹ Reworked from "I."

From Charles Yancey

D^R SIR   Hopefull Mills 26th September 1815

I think it's due from me to you to state to you the Reason why the petition to establish a College in Albemarle & appropriate Certain Monies belonging to Said county to promote Said establishment did not pass through our house I Saw the petition was in your hand writing & Something like a project also which Made me ansious to have a hearing as I espected Notwithstanding your advanced age If a law was made on the proprosed plan it wou'd Receive your aid as to government &^c the Gentleman to whom the petition was entrusted gave it to Mr Watson a representative from Louisa County to use his Judgment as to presenting it whose better Judgment was not to present it at So late an hour & finding he was principally relied on I gave way to his Judgment. Should you think proper to present or Send enclosed to me & my colleague a bill &^c to establish Said College it Shall receive my particular Support I have Seen with Mortification the Neglect of education & have Severely felt the want of it. in hopes that you will again Send forward a project &^c I avail myself of this opportunity to assure you I have not nor never Shall forget the debt we owe you for our political standing accept my dear Sir of the assuranc[e] of my Sincere wish for your pre[sent] & future happiness Your Mo Ob Ser^t

CHARLES YANCEY

RC (DLC); edge trimmed; endorsed by TJ as received 3 Oct. 1815 and so recorded in SJL. RC (DLC); address cover only; with Dft of TJ to Joseph Milligan, 27 Oct. 1815, on verso; addressed: "Thomas Jefferson Esqr late president of the U. States" by "Mail"; franked; postmarked Yancey's Mills, by postmaster Joel Yancey Jr., and Charlottesville, 28 Sept.

For the history and passage of the PETITION TO ESTABLISH A COLLEGE IN ALBEMARLE, see the Minutes of the

Albemarle Academy Board of Trustees, 25 Mar. 1814, with editorial headnote on The Founding of the University of Virginia: Albemarle Academy, 1803–1816. The GENTLEMAN to whom TJ had given the petition was Peter Carr.

From John Glendy

BELOVED SIR   Charlottesville Sept[r] 28th 1815.

I bitterly regret your absence from home, as I promised myself[1] on leaving Baltimore a cordial interview with you at Monticello; perhaps, the last oppertunity with which I could hope to be favored by Heaven, whether the thread of my existence may be spun out to a lengthened period, or snapped in a few revolving Moons.

Yesterday, I dined at the peaceful and hospitable board, of President Madison—Great and Just cause has he, to congratulate his Country, and felicitate himself on its Glory and prosperity—The secretary of State and his family connexions were there, on their way to the seat of Government.

Monroe! what moral worth, primitive simplicity, profound intelligence, and undeviating patriotism, center and shine, in that upright, downright Republican?

I am on my way to Staunton, and purpose returning to Baltimore by the way of Charlottesville—were I to Occupy the bench in the Court-House of this town, as an itinerant preacher on sunday week, the 8th day of Oct[r] next, pray, could I have the honor of your sitting under my ministry on the Occasion?

If you could promise me a Congregation on that day (and that the stated pastor would not be jealous) I would pledge myself to deliver a discourse at that period. At all events, I will hazard the appointment; and Deo volente, you may rely on my attendance.

With grateful affection, and devout wishes, for your temporal and eternal felicity, believe me Beloved Sir, faithfully your's

JOHN GLENDY

RC (DLC); dateline beneath signature; endorsed by TJ as received 3 Oct. 1815 and so recorded in SJL. RC (MHi); address cover only; with PoC of TJ to Henry Sheaff, 26 Oct. 1815, on verso; addressed: "Tho[s] Jefferson Esquire Present."

John Glendy (1755–1832), a native of Londonderry, Ireland, attended the University of Glasgow and was ordained as a

Presbyterian clergyman. Arrested for protesting British policy in Ireland and forced to immigrate to America, he arrived in Norfolk in 1799. Glendy served as a minister for about two years in Staunton and the surrounding area before moving to Baltimore by 1804 to become pastor of the newly formed Second Presbyterian Church, where he remained for the rest of his career. He declined appointments as chaplain of the United

States House of Representatives in 1805 and of the Senate in 1816. Glendy moved to Philadelphia to be with family members after 1830 and lived there until his death. TJ met him during his time in Staunton and later praised him as one of the best preachers he had ever heard, a man as "distinguished for his eloquence in the pulpit as for liberality of principles & amiableness of manners" (Sprague, *American Pulpit*, 4:229–37; *PTJ*, esp. 35:350–1, 36:25–7; Glendy, *An Oration*, *on the death of Lieut. Gen. George Washington* [Staunton, 1800]; TJ to Thomas McKean, 3 Mar. 1805 [PHi: McKean Papers]; *JHR*, 5:188, 198 [4, 13 Dec. 1805]; TJ to James Ogilvie, 21 June 1808 [DLC]; *JS*, 6:34, 50 [6, 16 Dec. 1816]; DNA: RG 29, CS, Md., Baltimore City, 1830; Washington *Daily National Intelligencer*, 8 Oct. 1832).

[1] Word interlined.

To Randolph Harrison

DEAR SIR   Poplar Forest, Sep. 28. 15.

During a long visit to this place I have had leisure to think of your house. you seemed to require 6. rooms, neither more nor less, and a good entrance or passage of communication. the inclosed is drawn on that plan. the ground plat is in detail, and exact; the elevation is merely a sketch to give a general idea. the workman, if he is any thing of an Architect will be able to draw the particulars. affectionately yours   TH: JEFFERSON

PoC (MHi); at foot of text: "Mr Harrison"; endorsed by TJ.

Randolph Harrison (1769–1839), planter and first cousin of TJ, married another first cousin, Mary Randolph, in 1790, and one of their sons, William Mortimer Harrison, was buried in the graveyard at Monticello in 1812. He managed a portion of the Cumberland County plantation of his father, Carter Henry Harrison, for a number of years and was given a parcel of this land. Harrison eventually bought out his brothers' shares in their father's property, relocated his family in about 1800 to the parental home of Clifton, and prospered. He contributed to the subscription for Central College and represented Cumberland County in the Virginia House of Delegates, 1826–27.

After his death at the White Sulphur Springs, Harrison's estate was valued at close to $90,000 (*VMHB* 35 [1927]: 207–11, 302–9, 451–5; *MB*, 2:1248, 1249, 1279; Cynthia A. Kierner, *Scandal at Bizarre* [2004], 33–6, 66–7, 154, 163; TJ to Harrison, 23 Mar. 1807 [DLC]; Harrison to TJ, 17 Feb. 1818; Shackelford, *Descendants*, 1:253; Leonard, *General Assembly*, 328, 333; Cumberland Co. Will Book, 10:164–5, 310–14; *Richmond Enquirer*, 1, 11 Oct. 1839).

The enclosed GROUND PLAT and ELEVATION have not been identified. An undated architectural drawing by TJ has sometimes been linked to this letter and to an addition Harrison made about 1835 to an existing structure on his Ampthill property near Clifton (Kimball, *Jefferson, Architect*, nos. 203–4, p. 185).

From Nicolas G. Dufief

MONSIEUR,   A Philadelphie ce 29 Septembre 1815

Vous trouverez ci-Inclus, un avis au sujet d'un ouvrage Américain qui peut être repondrait à vos vues aussi-bien que celui pour lequel vous m'avez écrit il y a longtemps & qui je crois n'a jamais paru. Si cela était faites-moi l'honneur de me le mander afin que je vous l'adresse aussi-tôt qu'il Sera imprimé

Je Suis, Monsieur, avec les sentimens qui vous Sont dus,

Votre très-dévoué & très-respectueux Ser^r   N. G DUFIEF

EDITORS' TRANSLATION

SIR,   Philadelphia 29 September 1815

You will find enclosed a notice regarding an American work about which you wrote me a long time ago and which, I believe, was never published. It might still meet your needs. If so, do me the honor of asking for it, so that I may send it to you as soon as it is printed

I am, Sir, with all due sentiments,

Your most devoted and most respectful servant   N. G DUFIEF

RC (DLC: TJ Papers, 199:35468); endorsed by TJ as received 6 Oct. 1815 and so recorded in SJL; with TJ's Book List, [after 6 Oct. 1815], on verso. RC (MHi); address cover only; with PoC of TJ to Horatio G. Spafford, 22 Dec. 1815, on verso; addressed: "Thomas Jefferson, Esquire Monticello V^a"; franked; postmarked Philadelphia, 29 Sept. Translation by Dr. Roland H. Simon.

The enclosed notice (AVIS) may have concerned Joseph Coppinger's recently published work, *The American Practical Brewer and Tanner* (New York, 1815), which Dufief had been attempting to obtain for TJ since 1813 (TJ to Dufief, [18] Sept. 1813; Dufief to TJ, 6 Apr. 1814; *New York Evening Post*, 22 Sept. 1815).

To Patrick Gibson

DEAR SIR   Poplar Forest Sep 29. 15

I have been here since the 20th of the last month, and am now within two or three days of my departure for Monticello. during this time no letters addressed to me have been transmitted on account of the slowness and uncertainty of the cross mail between the two places. I do not exactly know how I stand on your books, but my impression is that when I left Monticello I had nearly or quite exhausted my funds with you. the sheriff of this county now applying for my taxes here, and some other plantation calls have obliged me to draw on you this day in favor of mr Archibald Robertson for 387.D. and on my return home I shall meet a similar call for taxes, and some other demands there. the season not admitting the grinding of our wheat, nor the state of the rivers it's being boated down, I must ask the indulgence of the bank for another thousand dollars: and for that purpose I now inclose a note which I leave blank, that it may be filled up either with 1000.D. the sum now asked, separately or with 2000.D. including the former note when renewable. our crops of wheat are very deficient in quantity but equal in quality to any I have ever seen. tobacco was considerably bruised and torn by the storm which has injured it's appearance more than it's quality. I salute you with friendship & respect.   TH: JEFFERSON

PoC (DLC: TJ Papers, ser. 10); at foot of text: "Mr Gibson"; endorsed by TJ. Enclosure not found.

To Archibald Robertson

DEAR SIR   Poplar Forest Sep. 29. 15

Being now within a day or two of my departure from this place, I inclose you a draught on Messrs Gibson & Jefferson to reimburse the advances of cash you have been so good as to make for me while here. they stand I believe as follows

to Richard Chilton for corn on mr Yancey application	100. D
to Dr William Steptoe on my ord of Sep. 22	35.89
Wm Salmons sheriff Bedford: on order of same date	165.62
Morgan & McDaniel, assees of May on my ord. of Sep. 24. 60.	
Michael Adkinson on an order still to be given	25.47
	368.98[1]

to cover this I inclose an order as abovementioned for 387.D. should there be any error in my statement I shall be here again towards the end of the ensuing month and will correct it.   be pleased to send me by the bearer 3000. nails of the length of the longest sample sent & 3000. of the shortest. wrought nails would be preferred, but cut ones will do.

Accept the assurance of my esteem & respect   TH: JEFFERSON

P.S. be so good as to send also 1. ℔ tea.

PoC (MHi); adjacent to signature: "Mr Robertson"; endorsed by TJ. Enclosure not found.

The payment to William Salmon (SALMONS) for state taxes included $51.74 assessed on TJ's personal property in Bedford County, following TJ's Statement of Bedford and Campbell County Property Subject to State Tax, 11 Feb. 1815, but counting only five slaves between the ages of nine and twelve; and $80.03 assessed on TJ's Bedford County landholdings, totaling 3,790 acres (Vi:

RG 48, Personal Property Tax Returns and Land Tax Returns, both Bedford Co.). That to MORGAN & MᶜDANIEL, assignees (ASSEES) of John May, covered the purchase of a mare. TJ recorded giving Michael Atkinson (ADKINSON) an order on Robertson on this date as payment for sawing that Atkinson had finished the same day (*MB*, 2:1314).

[1] TJ wrote "<u>386</u>" in the left margin of this line to correct an addition error.

From James Penn
(for Archibald Robertson)

SIR,   Lynchburg, september 29th, 1815

I have received yours of this date enclosing a draft on Gibson & Jefferson for $387.   You will find, by examining your statement, a Small error in the addition The different orders mentioned, only two of which have been yet[1] presented, amount to $386.98 instead of $368.98; the other three will be attended to with pleasure upon application.   Wrought nails of the description you wanted, could not be precured, I have therefore sent cuts.

Verey respectfully, Yr mo Obt srvt

J PENN for A ROBERTSON

RC (MHi); in Penn's hand; at foot of text: "Mr Thomas Jefferson"; endorsed by TJ as a letter from Robertson received 29 Sept. 1815 and so recorded in SJL.

[1] Word interlined.

Deposition of Elizabeth Henderson in
Jefferson v. Michie

Shelby County[1] Kentucky

The deposition of Eliza Henderson taken before us two of the justices of the peace in and for the County aforesaid to be read as evidence in a suit in Chancery now depending and undetermined in the County Court of Albemarle & State of Virginia wherein Thomas Jefferson is Complainant and David Michie is Defendant taken at the house of Matthew Nelson of said County the present place of residence of her the said Eliza Henderson—This deponent being duly sworn deposeth to the following Interrogatories

Question by Lewis F Stephens by authority of Christopher Greenup agent for said Thomas Jefferson—Did you not sell your dower right of Certain lands in Albemarle County Virginia against the town of

Milton to Craven Peyton and[2] was there any reserve made written or verbal at the time to the knowledge of the said Peyton, or was he then informed that John Henderson had permission to Cut a Canal through it, Answer—I did sell my dower right of lands in Albemarle County to Craven Peyton and there was a reserve made by me to the knowledge of said Peyton but whether verbal or written I dont recollect[3]

Question by the same—Did not John Henderson obtain a written permission from you in the year 1803. for leave to Cut a Canal through your dower land aforesaid and did you give him that power? Answer he did obtain a permission from me to run a Canal through my dower land, but whether verbal or written I do not recollect, neither do I recollect the date of the year.

Question by the same—Did not the said John Henderson give you a writing at the same time that the said permission granted him should not interfere with your Contract with said Peyton and please to State or insert the same verbatim in your Answer? Answer I do not recollect of any writing passing between Jno Henderson and myself, but that I was not to be involved in the permission granted him.

Question by the same. Did the said John Henderson give or bind himself to pay you any Consideration for such Canal, and if he did, at what time?

Answer no he did not as I recollect

Question by Jno Henderson agent for David Michie.

Question 1st Did you not receive a Considerable annual income from the old mill?

Answer I did.

Question by the same—When m[r] Jefferson sent subpoenas for the purpose of pulling down the old dam, did he not let you know that you should never be injured during your life?

Answer yes he did.

Question by the same—Have not you and your family been greatly distressed by his pulling down the dam?

Answer we have.

Question by Same—Whether you and M[r] Jefferson being nearly related was not the Cause of your not Contesting with him in law to prevent him from pulling it down having had his promises not to do so.? Ans[r] it was.

Question by same. Whether the Courts of Justice were not stopped at the time Bennett Henderson erected that mill which prevented his getting an order according to law.?

Answer I believe they were.

[53]

Question by Lewis F Stephens. In what way did M[r] Jefferson inform you or by whom that you should not be injured dureing your life? Answer I received my information from the sheriff John Key & Jno R Carr and further this deponent saith not

ELIZABETH HENDERSON

Shelby County sc[t]

The above deposition was taken and subscribed & sworn to before us on the 30[h] day of September 1815 in Conformity to a notice to us directed

PHILLIP W. TAYLOR JP[4]
PETER TICHINOR JP.
A Copy
Test
Ira Garrett CC

Tr (ViU: TJP-LBJM); in George Carr's hand; docketed in an unidentified hand: "Jefferson vs Michie} Copy Record," and, along with Garrett's attestation, probably applying to the entire case record. Enclosed in Christopher Greenup to TJ, 9 Oct. 1815.

Lewis F. Stephens was a resident of Frankfort, Kentucky. In the 1820s he served on the board of trustees of the town of South Frankfort (*Proceedings of the Grand Lodge of Kentucky* [1814]: 22; [1815]: 29; [1816]: 32; DNA: RG 29, CS, Ky., Frankfort, 1820; *Frankfort Roundabout*, 12, 19 Jan. 1895).

SC[T]: abbreviation for "scilicet." IRA GARRETT was appointed deputy clerk of court for Albemarle County on 15 Oct. 1819 and clerk on 18 Oct. 1831 (Albemarle Co. Law Order Book [1809–21], 374; [1831–37], 28).

[1] Manuscript: "Counety."
[2] Manuscript: "as."
[3] The manuscript closes this sentence with a question mark.
[4] Adjacent to this and the next name are written indications that the signers had added their seals.

From James Mease

DEAR SIR   Philadelphia Oct: 1: 1815.

I wish to preserve an account of the various medals which were struck by order of Congress during the War of the revolution and have been able to see and describe, those for the evacuation of Boston.—Burgoyne's Capture;—Battle of Eutaw: D° Cowpens presented to General Morgan.—D° to Col: Howard on the same occasion.—The one presented to Col: Washington for his gallantry at the same battle: Those presented to Colo: Fleury for his bravery in the Storming West Point, and to Paul Jones for capturing the Serapis, I have not seen. one was also struck on the declaration of Independence, and another on the Capture of Andrei:—but I have not Seen them.

If you have any of the medals which I have not met with, and will favour me with a description of them, I shall esteem myself much indebted to you.—I would not trouble you, was my own gratification concerned, but I wish to present the account to the historical Society of New York—.

I rejoice to find that you continue to enjoy good health.—May it long Continue.

Accept the assurances of my Sincere respect.—

JAMES MEASE

RC (DLC); at foot of text: "Thomas Jefferson Esqr Monticello"; endorsed by TJ as received 6 Oct. 1815 and so recorded in SJL.

The French officer François Louis Teissèdre de FLEURY was awarded a silver medal by the Continental Congress for his actions in 1779 at Stony Point, near WEST POINT, New York (Heitman, *Continental Army*, 230; R. W. Julian, *Medals of the United States Mint: The First Century, 1792–1892*, ed. N. Neil Harris [1977], 118). Mease communicated his research on medals issued by the United States to the New-York HISTORICAL SOCIETY in 1818 and published his initial findings as "Description of some of the Medals, Struck in relation to Important Events in North America, before and since the Declaration of Independence by the United States," in New-York Historical Society, *Collections* 3 (1821): 387–404. He published an expanded version of this article under the same title in Massachusetts Historical Society, *Collections*, 3d ser., 4 (1834): 297–320.

From Thomas Addis Emmet

SIR   New York Octr 2nd 1813 [1815]

The solicitation of a friend whom I wish to serve & to oblige, is leading me to a measure which I fear will scarcely be considered pardonable. However your past experience must have long since made you feel, that distinguished eminence of character & public Estimation necessarily Expose the man who enjoys them, to be solicited for favors by persons, whose only pretensions arise from their participating in the common sentiments of respect & affection. I shall never forget the condescension & kindness with which you received me, when I presented myself to you at Washington, shortly after my arrival in America: and that remembrance so frequently present to my mind, emboldens me to hope that I may be excused, when I seek to procure a similar gratification for one whom I esteem. Mr Dumoulin the bearer of this letter is an Irish Gentleman, bred to the bar & of very considerable talents & acquirements—His love for the institutions of this Country & feeling for the fate of his own have decided him to become a Member of Our Community—& he is travelling thro' the

Country to acquire a more intimate knowledge of it before he fixes a permanent residence. He could not possibly be in the vicinity of Mr Jefferson, without anxiously wishing to offer his own respects to him & to enjoy the happiness of having seen him. May I flatter myself with being so far remembered & esteemed as that my introduction will procure for him the gratification he desires?

I have the Honor to be

Sir with the sincerest respect & esteem Your very Obliged & Obedient Servant

THO^s ADDIS EMMET

RC (DLC: TJ Papers, 199:35475); misdated; at foot of text: "Thos Jefferson Esqr"; endorsed by TJ as received 25 Oct. 1815 and so recorded in SJL.

Thomas Addis Emmet (1764–1827), attorney and Irish patriot, was born in County Cork, Ireland. He received a B.A. in 1783 from Trinity College, Dublin, and he took a medical degree the following year at the University of Edinburgh. After practicing medicine for a few years, Emmet decided to become a lawyer. Called to the Irish bar in 1790, he quickly earned a reputation as a formidable barrister and an ardent Irish nationalist. Emmet joined the United Irishmen, soon became the society's secretary, and was one of its directors by 1797. He was imprisoned by the British authorities, 1798–1802, and then exiled in consequence of his support for Irish independence. Having spent a short time on the European mainland, Emmet immigrated to New York in 1804. With important initial assistance from George Clinton and DeWitt Clinton, he made a name for himself within the American legal establishment. During his long career Emmet argued a number of cases before the United States Supreme Court, most famously *Gibbons v. Ogden* (1824), in which he unsuccessfully maintained the constitutionality of a New York law granting Robert Fulton and Robert R. Livingston a thirty-year monopoly on steamboat traffic in the state. Although Emmet largely eschewed politics after his arrival in the United States, he lost a bid as a Republican for a seat in the New York legislature in 1812, and he served as state attorney general, 1812–13. Emmet met TJ in Washington shortly after his arrival in America (*ANB*;

DAB; *DNB*; *ODNB*; Charles Glidden Haines, *Memoir of Thomas Addis Emmet* [1829]; George Dames Burtchaell and Thomas Ulick Sadleir, eds., *Alumni Dublinenses: A Register of the Students, Graduates, Professors and Provosts of Trinity College in the University of Dublin (1593–1860)* [1935], 264; Joel Barlow to TJ, 20 Aug. 1804 [DLC]; John Hollins to TJ, 14 Dec. 1804 [MHi]; New York *Mercantile Advertiser*, 16 Apr. 1805; New York *Columbian*, 18 Apr. 1812; New York *Commercial Advertiser*, 15 Aug. 1812; New York *Public Advertiser*, 19 Feb. 1813; Marshall, *Papers*, 8:67, 10:7, 10–1; *New-York Spectator*, 16, 20 Nov. 1827).

John Franklin Dumoulin (ca. 1792–1825), attorney, was a native of Dublin who attended school in Portarlington, Queen's County (later County Laoighis), Ireland, before earning a B.A. in 1810 from Trinity College, Dublin. He qualified for the bar in Ireland before immigrating to the United States in 1815. By 1817 Dumoulin had settled in New Orleans, where he practiced law and befriended the extended Trist family. A member of the Hibernian Society of New-Orleans who served as that organization's secretary in 1819, Dumoulin became a naturalized American citizen in 1821. He died in New Orleans (John Cook Wyllie, "The Jefferson-Randolph Copies of an Anonymous Work Entered Three Ways by Sabin," *VMHB* 56 [1948]: 80–3; Burtchaell and Sadleir, *Alumni Dublinenses*, 249; NcU: NPT; *Orleans Gazette and Commercial Advertiser*, 4 Mar. 1819; Louis Moreau Lislet, *A General Digest of the Acts of the Legislature of Louisiana: Passed from the Year 1804, to 1827, Inclusive* [1828], 2:408–9;

Dumoulin's naturalization record, 30 July 1821 [TxFNA: RG 21, RUSDCEDL, Minute Book, 5:148–9]; New Orleans *Louisiana Gazette*, 5 Aug. 1825; New Orleans *Louisiana State Gazette*, 16 Nov. 1825; New Orleans *Louisiana Advertiser*, 17 Oct. 1826).

From Richard S. Hackley

SIR   Cadiz 3rd Octobr 1815.

Samuel Curson esq^r who lately arr^d at this port from Lima, left in my charge, with a request that it might be forwarded to you, a Loaf of Sugar made by the natives at Cusco, S^o America,

I execute the commission with much pleasure by the Ship Imogine, Capt Wheeler to the Care of the collector at Richmond. with much respect

Sir Your Ob^t Ser^t

RICH^D S: HACKLEY

RC (MHi); at foot of text: "Thos Jefferson Esqr late President of the U States, Virginia"; endorsed by TJ as received 15 Dec. 1815 and so recorded in SJL. RC (MHi); address cover only; with PoC of TJ to David Higginbotham, 25 Dec. 1815, on verso; addressed: "Thomas Jefferson esq^r late President of the united States Monticello Virginia"; franked; postmarked Hampton, 23 Nov. Enclosed in TJ to James Gibbon, 24 Dec. 1815, and Gibbon to TJ, 5 Jan. 1816.

Richard Shippey Hackley (ca. 1771–1843), merchant and public official, was a native of Fredericksburg. Trained in commerce from his youth, by 1800 he was working as a merchant in New York City. In 1806 Hackley married his second wife, Harriet Randolph, the sister of TJ's son-in-law Thomas Mann Randolph. Later that same year TJ appointed him consul at Sanlúcar de Barrameda, Spain, and Hackley soon thereafter reached an agreement with Josef Yznardy, consul at nearby Cádiz, whereby Hackley would act as his vice-consul there. This agreement began to fall apart in 1813, and by 1816 Hackley was back in Sanlúcar de Barrameda. In 1820 he returned to the United States and rejoined his family in Richmond. Hackley worked unsuccessfully for many years to prove his claim to Florida land granted to him by the Duke of Alagon, and his frequent financial crises often caused him to relocate. He died in Norfolk (DNA: RG 59, LAR, 1801–25; New York *Mercantile Advertiser*, 28 May 1800; *New-York Evening Post*, 30 Jan. 1802; Richmond *Enquirer*, 18 Jan. 1806; *JEP*, 2:45 [15, 17 Dec. 1806]; Martha Jefferson Randolph to TJ, 16 Jan. 1808 [MHi]; TJ to Martha Jefferson Randolph, 2 Feb. 1808 [NNPM]; TJ to Thomas Mann Randolph, 2 Jan. 1809 [MHi]; James Madison to TJ, 9 Apr. 1809; TJ to Madison, 19 Apr. 1809; Madison, *Papers, Pres. Ser.*, 6:323–4; *ASP, Miscellaneous*, 2:315; DNA: RG 59, CD, Cádiz; Ellen W. Randolph [Coolidge] to Martha Jefferson Randolph, 31 May 1820 [ViU: Coolidge Correspondence]; Thomas Mann Randolph to Mary J. Randolph, 25 Feb. 1827 [NcU: NPT]; Harriet Hackley and Jane B. Cary Smith to Virginia Randolph Cary, 2 May 1828 [NcU: NPT]; *Terr. Papers*, esp. 26:593–9; DNA: RG 59, PA; New York *Evening Post*, 1 Mar. 1843).

Promissory Note from Joel Yancey to Charles Clay on Behalf of Thomas Jefferson

FOR VALUE RECEIVED *I* promise to pay or cause to be paid unto *Charles Clay* his executors, administrators or assigns, on or before the *first* day of *Dec.* 1815 the just and full sum of *Ninety Seven Doll. Seventy five Cents* current money of *U. States*[1] for which payment well and truly to be made *I* bind *myself*[2] *My*[3] heirs Executors and administrators firmly by these presents in the penal sum of *one hundred & ninty dollars & fifty cents* like money, given under *my* hand and seal this *3rd* day of *October* 1815 attested by *for Thomas Jefferson*

JOEL YANC[EY]

MS (ViU: TJP-ER); printed form, with blanks filled in by Yancey indicated in italics; signature partially torn away, presumably to cancel the note; endorsed by Clay: "Th. Jeferson $97.75"; with Clay's notation at head of text that the correct figures were $97.75 and $195.50; notation by TJ on verso: "Clay Charles. pd Apr. 29. 16. by ord. on Archib. Robertson 100.20. for corn"; additional notation by TJ in pencil on verso: "John Depriest 70.D. June 1," with this notation relating to the purchase of a horse for which TJ contracted on 29 Apr. 1816 (*MB*, 2:1322).

In a brief note he signed and dated 27 Apr. 1816, Yancey reminded TJ that the $97.75 for corn had been due since 1 Dec. 1815 and that "the Rye Mr Clay is willing may Stand vs his Shop account" (RC in ViU: TJP-ER; written on a small scrap; addressed: "Mr Jefferson"; with calculation by TJ that with 5 months interest the sum due to Clay was $100.20).

[1] Yancey here canceled printed text reading "with interest from the date."
[2] Yancey here canceled printed text reading "jointly, and severally."
[3] Yancey here canceled printed text reading "joint and several."

From Mathew Carey

SIR,   *Philadelphia, October 4, 1815.*

The rapid sale of the sixth edition of the Olive Branch, recently published, places it beyond doubt, that a new edition will be indispensably necessary. I am, therefore, making all the necessary preparations to put one to press about the first of November, which I hope to publish early in December.

The pressure of business—the utter want of that degree of leisure and abstraction of mind, which literary exertions indispensably require—the deficiency of materials and documents under which I laboured—and the very great variety of subjects embraced in the work, have conspired to tarnish it with defects and errors; which I strove to avoid;

which I deeply regret; and which I am sincerely disposed to correct in the edition now contemplated.

I therefore earnestly and respectfully solicit the aid of every citizen, who is possessed of any documents connected with, or bearing upon the topics embraced in the work, or who is capable of pointing out errors, or suggesting improvements in it. From whatever quarter they may come, federal or democratic, Anglican or Gallican, American or anti-American, they shall be thankfully received, and duly attended to.

Tros Tyriusque mihi nullo discrimine agetur.

I wish, however, to be clearly and distinctly understood. I promise no man, however dignified or exalted, that I will implicitly adopt his opinions or follow his suggestions. I pledge myself, nevertheless, to weigh them well, and not to reject them without strong reasons. But as I alone am responsible for the work, to cotemporaries, and (should it have the good fortune to survive me) to posterity, I must, I will decide on every circumstance to the best of my judgment, according to the evidence that I may be able to procure.

I am, respectfully, Your obedient humble servant,

MATHEW CAREY.

P. S. An early attention to this application is requested, should you have any communications to make. Otherwise it may be passed over in silence.

RC (MHi); printed circular; endorsed by TJ as a "(circular)" received 11 Oct. 1815 and so recorded in SJL. RC (DLC); address cover only; with PoC of TJ to Patrick Gibson, 17 Oct. 1815, on verso; addressed: "Thomas Jefferson, Esq' Ex president U. S Washington"; franked; postmarked Philadelphia, 4 Oct.

TROS TYRIUSQUE MIHI NULLO DISCRIMINE AGETUR: "Trojan and Tyrian I shall treat alike," in Virgil, *Aeneid*, 1.574 (Fairclough, *Virgil*, 1:302–3).

To Joseph Milligan

DEAR SIR   Monticello Oct. 5. 15.

I am just now returned from a 7. weeks visit to Bedford, to which place I went immediately on writing you my letter of Aug. 17. on my return I find here your two letters of Aug. 16. and 20. the former covering my account amounting to 264.75 from which deducting the 92.D. remitted a balance remains of 172.75 I knew there had been other books furnished me of which I had no account; but it runs much in my mind that I have paid for the early vols of Wilson which makes the principal mass of this balance. I think I paid for some of them either at Washington or very soon after, however I have no strength of confidence in my memory, and the less as it does not suggest thro' what channel I paid. I will search into it [the] moment the letters accumulated during my absence will permit, and will immediately remit the balance whatever it may be. in the mean time I greatly want the two books mentioned in my letter of Aug. 17. which I sent to be cut and bound, the one into 3. vols and the other into two. to wit Hutton's tables and the Requisite tables. if you will do up two vols together they might come in the mail without too much burthening it, if sent one package only of two vols[1] each week; or perhaps you could send the whole by the stage to mr Gray with a request to forward it immediately by the mail tumbrel.—you shall hear from me again in a few days. Accept my friendly salutations.   Th: Jefferson

PoC (DLC); on verso of reused address cover of John Vaughan to TJ, 31 July 1815; mutilated at seal; at foot of text: "Mr Millegan"; endorsed by TJ.

[1] Preceding three words interlined.

Book List

[after 6 Oct. 1815]

Enfield
Mackay on Longitude
<Nautical almanac for 1816. by Blunt N.Y.>
<d° by Garnet>
<Garnet's Requisite tables>
<La Croix wants> 2^d vol.
a Fr. dict. of about 1550–1600
Antoninus. 12mo
Playfair's statistical Breviary. 8vo
McMahon's gardening. 8vo
Chronologist of the war 1789–96 12mo
Hardie's Remembrancer. 12mo
Dufief's dict.

MS (DLC: TJ Papers, 199:35468); on verso of Nicolas G. Dufief to TJ, 29 Sept. 1815; entirely in TJ's hand; undated, but composed after 6 Oct. 1815 receipt of Dufief's letter.

This document appears to be a partial list of books TJ hoped to acquire, with many of the titles mentioned in subsequent correspondence and eventually finding their way into his final library.

From Peter Stephen Chazotte

SIR.   Philadelphia 6th oct^{ber} 1815

Author of, A New System of Banking To establish, either a Merchants' or A Grand National Bank, a subject intimately connected with the wellfare of this republic, the honour, prosperity and liberties of which you have long been the exalted and faithful guardian and are deservedly considered as the most illustrious of its citizens; I make it a duty for me, to present you with a copy of it, and to accompany it with a request that you would so far extend your[1] kindness to me as to give it a perusal.

Accept my sincere wishes for your health and happiness;

Sir, Your humble & obed^t Servant;   P^R STEPHEN CHAZOTTE

RC (DLC); at foot of text: "Th^s Jefferson, Esqre: Virginia"; endorsed by TJ as a letter from "Charotte P. Stephen" received 11 Oct. 1815 and so recorded in SJL. RC (DLC); address cover only; with PoC of TJ to Robert Patterson, 22 Dec. 1815, on verso; addressed: "Thomas Jefferson Esquire, Virginia." Enclosure: Chazotte, *A New System of Banking, Developed and Exemplified, in a New Scheme to establish A Merchants Bank of General Deposits. and also, in a Scheme to Establish A Grand National Bank* (Philadelphia, 1815; Poor, *Jefferson's Library* 12 [no. 710]).

Peter Stephen Chazotte (ca. 1775–1846), teacher and author, was a planter in Saint Domingue until slave rebellions there forced him to leave. He spent two years in Charleston, South Carolina, before returning to Saint Domingue in 1800. Chazotte fled again in 1804, this time arriving in Baltimore. By 1808 he was living in Philadelphia, where he intermittently ran schools and taught French between 1811 and 1822. In 1821–22 Chazotte served as the director of the East Florida Coffee Land Association, which unsuccessfully sought permission from the United States government to purchase land for agricultural purposes in East Florida. His books covered a variety of topics including languages, banking, and agriculture, and he sent several of them to TJ during the latter's retirement.

In 1830 Chazotte was living in Brooklyn. Ten years later he was in Jersey City, New Jersey, where he died (Canter Brown Jr., "The East Florida Coffee Land Expedition of 1821: Plantations or a Bonapartist Kingdom of the Indies?," *Tequesta: The Journal of the Historical Association of Southern Florida* 51 [1991]: 7–28; Philadelphia *Poulson's American Daily Advertiser*, 30 Sept. 1808, 21 Sept. 1811, 18 Apr. 1815, 30 May 1818; James Robinson, *The Philadelphia Directory for 1811* [Philadelphia, 1811], 68; *Richmond Enquirer*, 31 Aug. 1821; Chazotte, *Facts and Observations on the Culture of Vines, Olives, Capers, Almonds, &c. in the Southern States, and of Coffee, Cocoa, and Cochineal, in East Florida* [Philadelphia, 1821]; *JHR*, 15:155, 281–2, 393, 16:78 [17 Jan., 20 Feb., 26 Mar., 27 Dec. 1822]; *ASP, Public Lands*, 3:457–67; *The Philadelphia Directory and Register, for 1822* [Philadelphia, 1822]; DNA: RG 29, CS, N.Y., Brooklyn, 1830, N.J., Hudson Co., 1840; Chazotte, *Historical Sketches of the Revolutions, and the Foreign and Civil Wars in the Island of St. Domingo* [1840]; *Jersey City Advertiser and Hudson County Republican*, 27 Jan. 1846).

Writing from Philadelphia on 26 Sept. 1815, Chazotte sent a similar letter and the same enclosure to President James Madison (DLC: Madison Papers).

[1] Manuscript: "you."

To Patrick Gibson

[DEA]R SIR   Monticello Oct. 6. 15.

I wrote you from Poplar Forest on the 29th Ult. covering a blank note for the renewal of my former note in bank with an addition: the messenger which carried that letter to Lynchburg brought me your two favors of Aug. 28. & Sep. 21. I am persuaded the former had laid long in the post office, altho I had never failed once or twice a week to have enquiry made there for letters. I very much regret indeed the failure of sending my note in time. I had no paper with me which could warn me of the date for renewal, & counted on recieving notice. I will in future guard against this by never leaving home without furnishing you with a note for renewal. I mentioned in my letter of the 29th that I should have to meet here the call of the sheriff for taxes, and some other occurring demands. I will therefore thank you for a line of information on the acceptance of my note at bank with the addition asked. ever yours with friendship and respect.

TH: JEFFERSON

PoC (Mrs. T. Wilber Chelf, Mrs. Virginius Dabney, and Mrs. Alexander W. Parker, Richmond, 1944; photocopy in ViU: TJP); on verso of reused address cover to TJ; salutation incomplete, probably due to polygraph malfunction; at foot of text: "Mr Gibson"; endorsed by TJ.

Notes on a Conversation with Henry Dearborn

1815. Oct. 7. Genl Dearborne informs me that the plaister of Paris is brought from the head of the Bay of Funday, where it extends all along the coast Windsor is the nearest town. the price pd to the proprietor for the stone is a quarter dollar a ton; and it is quarried & brought to the water edge for three quarter dollars a ton, so that it costs at the water edge a dollar a ton.

MS (DLC); entirely in TJ's hand; on verso of reused address cover of Thomas Paine McMahon to TJ, 12 Aug. 1815; with PoC of TJ to Dearborn, 7 Oct. 1815, subjoined.

To Henry Dearborn

DEAR SIR   Monticello Oct. 07. 15.

I ask the favor of you when at Boston to engage for me fourteen tons of plaister of Paris to be delivered at Richmond to mess[rs] Gibson and Jefferson, my correspondents there, who will on my account pay for the same on delivery whatever sum you shall have agreed on for all costs and charges, the party presenting to them this paper with the sum endorsed by yourself. I will in the mean time apprise mess[rs] Gibson and Jefferson that such application will be made to them. ever affectionately yours   TH: JEFFERSON

PoC (DLC); on verso of reused address cover of Thomas Paine McMahon to TJ, 12 Aug. 1815; subjoined to TJ's Notes on a Conversation with Dearborn, 7 Oct. 1815; at foot of text: "Gen[l] Dearborne"; endorsed by TJ.

From Christopher Greenup

SIR   Frankfort K. Oct[o] 9th 1815

Being unable to ride either on Horseback or in a Carriage (by an obstinate Rheumatic) the distance M[rs] Henderson lives from this (35 miles) I engaged a M[r] Stephens to attend the taking her deposition, for fear of another failure—I furnished interrogatories and also forwarded the Copy of James Henderson's aff[idavit?] with your letters of explanation, which were laid before the Commissioners,[1] and also read to her. The Dep[o] was taken at her present place of dwelling, she keeping no house of her own, and is herewith inclosed. John Henderson attended—I understand she [is] very old and appeared forgetful—I write in pain so conclude with assurances of my
High respect and consideration   CHRIST[R] GREENUP

RC (MHi); damaged at seal; addressed: "Thomas Jefferson Esq[r] late President of the United States Charlottesville Virginia"; franked; postmarked Frankfort, 13 Oct., and Charlottesville, 26 Oct.; endorsed by TJ as received 27 Oct. 1815 and so recorded in SJL. Enclosure: Deposition of Elizabeth Henderson in *Jefferson v. Michie*, 30 Sept. 1815.

Christopher Greenup (ca. 1750–1818), attorney and public official, was a native of Loudoun County. He studied law before serving during the American Revolu-

tion as a first lieutenant in the Continental army, 1777–78. Greenup was later a colonel in the Virginia militia. In 1781 he moved to Frankfort in what was then the Kentucky district of Virginia. Greenup was admitted to the local bar and represented Fayette County in the House of Delegates, 1785–86. He sat in the Kentucky conventions of 1784, 1785, and 1788, where he supported statehood. Greenup was a member of the first congressional delegation from Kentucky, serving in the United States House of Representatives, 1792–97. In 1804 he was elected governor as a Jeffersonian

Republican and completed one four-year term. He then resumed his legal career while continuing to be politically active in Frankfort. TJ apparently met Greenup in the 1790s while both men were serving in the federal government at Philadelphia, and they corresponded sporadically on business thereafter (*ANB*; *DAB*; *PTJ*, esp. 25:99–100; Heitman, *Continental Army*, 261; Leonard, *General Assembly*, 156; Frankfort *Argus of Western America*, 1 May 1818; Washington *Daily National Intelligencer*, 16, 20 May 1818).

A missing letter from TJ to Greenup of 30 July 1815 is recorded in SJL.

[1] Manuscript: "Commissiors."

From Caspar Wistar

My Dear Sir,   Philad[a] Octob[r1] 9–1815—

My last letter was So long & multifarious that M[r] Correa would Say it was "de Omnibus Rebus, & quibusdam aliis." I ought not to intrude upon you So Soon with another epistle, but I have lately returned from a journey, during which I thought of you very frequently, & determined to write as Soon as I had leisure—I spent a few days in Centre County in this State, where Logan once resided— His name remains to designate a Gap, a Path, & a stream, a branch of the Bald Eagle Creek—A Few white persons resided in that district while he lived there; almost all of them are gone, but those who knew him were accustomed to mention him often, & very respectfully— A M[r] Boggs, one of the Judges of the Inferior Court, was well acquainted with him & regarded him as a very Superior man—Logan was So expert a hunter that M[r] Boggs Supposed he derived about $600 P[r] Ann: from the Sales of the skins &[c.] to the whites—These negociations Some times Compelled him to have recourse to law, to recover what was justly due to him—His first application to a Magistrate was in these words—

Are you a Justice? yes, was the reply—

Are you a strong Justice? Yes was also replied—Then you Can make A.B. pay me what he owes me. The magistrate Satisfied that the Claim was just, & the Debtor able to pay—answered he shall pay you in three or four months—

Tell me rejoined Logan when I shall Come for it. The Magistrate Soon understood his[2] man, & as he often did business for Logan, when he found it necessary to grant a further delay to the Debtor, he advanced the money to Logan at the time appointed—

They mention, as an instance of Superstition, a practice of this interesting Savage which was very intelligible—When he had determined to hunt—On the morning of the day appointed, he used to shoot at a mark, after making the requisite preparation of his gun—If it was a good shot, he would proceed immediately to the hunting ground. If it was a bad shot, he gave up his design for that day—If it was an indifferent shot, he used to fire a Second time, & unless he then did very well, he also postponed it—

Logan was still So much of the Indian, that he often used Spirits to excess—

I wished very much to hear more of him, & have obtained a promise from Dr Dobbins, an ingenious & respectable young Physician at Bellefont, the Capital of Centre County, that he would Collect the materials, & give us a Biographical account of him—

During this tour I met with a very amiable & interesting man, M^r Jn° Heckewelder of Bethlehem. This Gentleman has passed many years of his life with the Lenni Lenapi or Delaware Indians as a Missionary from the Moravian Society. He appears to be very intimately acquainted with their language & habits, & I hope we Shall be able to procure from him an account of them for the Historical department of our Society. Dr Barton has directed Mr Heckewelder's mind to the Contemplation of the Indian Subject generally, & I therefore will be Cautious not to interfere with the Doctors views of publication; but the Account of the Lenni Lenapi Seems necessary to our history of Pennsylvania—Their Language is very interesting. The long words in it, which I have wondered at indolen[t] Savages for adopting, seem to be compounds derived from many primitive words—thus Monongahela Signifies the "river with high banks that often fall in." Mr Heckewelders Conversations lead me to a belief that a great deal of intellectual talent has been exerted upon their language—

The Moravians have more knowledge of the Indians of this[3] part of N. America than any persons I have met, with—Mr H. tells me that in the Archives of Bethlehem in Pennsylvania there is a memorandum (by a Mr Pyleus one of their former missionaries) which states that the Confederacy of the Six Nations was formed about[4] forty or fifty years before the foundation of Albany.

Their Federal Constitution was agreed upon by five or Six Delegates whose names are also mentioned. Mr Heckewelder Says one fundamental regulation was that the road or path to the great Council House should always be Sacred, & no one molested upon it, whatever was his crime.

The Word Tyoga which you [know][5] is the name of a point at the forks of the north branch of Susquehannah, near the line which divides N. York from Pennsylvania implies "the Gate of the Path to the great Council House."[6]   He deplores the corruption of Indian names; many words as pronounced by him are very pleasing that are the reverse in our present pronunciation. Some of the readings of Indian Words are very whimsical—Yellow Breeches the name of a creek that flows I believe into the Potowmack is the pronunciation of an Indian name which when pronounced by him Sounds as much like any other Garment.

Coquannock we are told was the name of the Spot occupied by Philadelphia—according to Mr H. it is Qué qué ná ku the Grove of lofty Pines.

Menahachtang, the word from which Manhattan is derived, originates from Menathey an Island & another term which implies drinking, the Signification is "The Island on which we got drunk."

I hope our Country will forgive the recent aggressions of the Indians—They may be Considered in Some measure as Children, who are not aware of the[7] Consequences of their own actions; & they have been much misinformed & deceived by foreign Agents. Will not your benevolent plans of civilizing them be again taken up I hope Col: Hawkins is not discouraged.

Our Country is So happy that we ought to be good natured—I had no idea that the improvement of the old Settlements of Pennsylvania were what they are, although I have been constantly hearing of them. In the great limestone valley between the Blue Ridge & the South Mountains, or as we call them, the Lehi, the Oley & the Conewago Hills the price of limestone land is from $150 to $200 Pr Acre—I think that in sight of the great road which passes through this valley, from the Delaware to the Schuyllkill, there are at least 50 Stone Barns, from 80 to 120 feet long; most of them recently built. I believe there are two Causes for this—The long continued high price of grain, and the effects of Gypsum. I have made many inquiries of intelligent farmers in different parts respecting the amount of benefit derived from Gypsum and they agree that the agricultural product of Pennsylvania below the Blue Ridge has been doubled by it.

The primary effect of Gypsum in this important process is exciting the Growth of Clover & Indian Corn[8] & from these all the other consequences result.

I pleased my self with the idea of paying my respects to you at Monticello about the middle of this month & returning with Mr Correa— My health was So much impaired by the heat of summer that I was forced to go immediately to our nearest mountains, & as I improved Slowly in Consequence, it Seemed most prudent to continue riding in that region, until my health was reestablished, accordingly I spent five weeks in that manner & am So happy as to have derived Considerable benefit from it, but it will deprive me of the immense gratification of visiting you—

Please to Communicate this to our very good friend. I hope my failure in this respect will not incommode him & that at any rate he will forgive it

Adieu my Dear Sir—

With the best wishes for your family as well as yourself I remain your most obliged friend   C WISTAR

P.S. With my last I sent 2 Volumes of Anatomy did they Come to hand—

RC (DLC); edge chipped; endorsed by TJ as received 17 Oct. 1815 and so recorded in SJL.

DE OMNIBUS REBUS, & QUIBUSDAM ALIIS: "concerning all things, and certain others." The memorandum written by Moravian missionary Johann Christoph Pyrläus (PYLEUS) in the 1740s reported that the League of the Iroquois had been formed one generation previously by the Mohawks, Oneidas, Onondagas, Cayugas, and Senecas (Pyrläus, "Lexicon der Macquaischen Sprachen" [MS in PPAmP]; William A. Starna, "Retrospecting the Origins of the League of the Iroquois," APS, *Proceedings* 152 [2008]: 282–7). As agent to the Creeks in Georgia, Benjamin HAWKINS encouraged them to rely on farming for their livelihood, change their gender roles so that men owned and cultivated the land, and restructure their tribal government (*ANB*).

[1] Reworked from "Septr."
[2] Wistar here canceled "client."
[3] Wistar here canceled "neighbourhood."
[4] Word interlined in place of "within."
[5] Omitted word editorially supplied.
[6] Omitted closing quotation mark editorially supplied.
[7] Wistar here canceled what appears to be "nature."
[8] Preceding three words interlined.

From Lafayette

MY DEAR FRIEND   La Grange October 10[h] 1815

A Long while Has Elapsed Since I Had the pleasure to Hear from you—I might Say a Century Was I to Reckon upon the Succession of Revolutions and dynasties—But as Royal and imperial Cycles are to you and me very Secondary objects, I only mean the true time during which I Have Been deprived of your Correspondance

In your Letters of Last year, anterior to the first Abdication of Bonaparte, you Had Expressed a due Sense of that Character who Having it in His Power to Be a Blessing did prefer to Become a Curse to Mankind. His despotism and His follies Had made the Restoration of the Bourbons, notwithstanding[1] foreign invasion,[2] a popular Event—They Returned the Compliment. Their prejudiced mismanagement, the more Glaring improprieties of Privilege-men Gave Napoleon the Opportunity to Reappear as a Representative of the Revolution. Whatever may Have Been a few Subaltern Intrigues, the Great, the Efficacious Conspiracy in His Behalf may Be attributed to the Counter Revl[uti]onary party.

in those transactions I took No part altho' I would Have Readily assisted in Opposing Napoleon Had Not the patriotic System me[t] the Same objections which Had Ruined the Constitutional throne of 92.

We then Have Seen the Imperial destroyer of french Liberty Reassuming a Republican Language, Bowing to [na]tional Sovereignty, allowing a free press, and altho' Vindictive or Arbitrary acts too often Betray'd old Habits, persuading many patriots to Rejoice at His Conversion—Not So did I—But While I Shunned personal Communication with Him, I declared that, if a free Representation was Convened, I would Stand a Candidate—we were, my Son and myself elected.

at the Same time a million of foreign invaders were, in Concert with Lewis the 18ᵗ and the elder Branch of His family, Led Against Bonaparte, was it Said, against what and whom the Event Has proved—the defense of national independance and territory Became, of Course, our principal object. it was my opinion that Unanimity and vigor Could Better Be Roused By a popular than By the Imperial Government—The Majority of the Assembly and Army depended more on the General Ship of Napoleon altho' His whole troops did little Exceed two Hundred thousand. So we all joined on that Line of Resistance. No impediment was thrown, Every Assistance was Given. Never did our Heroïc Army fight Better than at waterloo. a Stubborn Mistake of Bonaparte Lost the day. He deserted His Soldiers, and Determined to dissolve our Assembly, usurp dictatorial powers, prefering the chances of Confusion and involving destruction to those of firmness and patriotism. That part of the impending Evils was timely prevented. it might Have Been the Case with the other part, altho' Coming upon us in a Storm, Had Not the old diplomacy in poland, Napoleon's policy in Spain, the Spirit of pilnitz in 91, and of the Last Congress at vienna Been far Surpassed By the present Coalition.

inclosed you will find a few pieces Relative to our Late House of Representatives. their declaration of the 5ᵗ July 1815 Congenial with the principles of 1789 are an additional proof that if the french people Have deplorably Erred in the means they Have Steadily persevered in the primary object of the Revolution.

I am Returned to my Retirements of La Grange where I Shall Remain with my family provided no foreigners are to Be quartered Here—My eleventh Grand child, George's Son, Has in addition to the family Name of Gilbert Received the friendly Name of Thomas— He is Born to freedom—the Cause of french, of European liberty is far from Being Lost.

M. de tracy' Health is much altered—His Sight forsakes Him—He However Attends the House of Peers—He Shares in my anxiety to Hear from you.

Adieu, my dear friend, Be pleased to present my Best Respects to Mrs Randolph—I Have Been Lately very Happy in the Acquaintance of our young general Scott, and Colonel Mercer's Son who travels with Him. I am Sure You often Remember your Affectionate Grateful friend   LAFAYETTE

RC (DLC); holes in manuscript; endorsed by TJ as received 16 Dec. 1815 and so recorded in SJL. Enclosures not found.

Lafayette and his SON, George Washington Lafayette, were elected to the lower house of the French parliament in 1815 (*Mémoires, correspondance et manuscrits du général Lafayette, publiés par sa Famille* [1838], 5:434–5, 444). For the SPIRIT OF PILNITZ, see note to Thomas Leiper to TJ, 17 Apr. 1814. The PIECES RELATIVE TO OUR LATE HOUSE OF REPRESENTATIVES may have included the "Déclaration des droits des Français et des principes fondamentaux de leur constitution" ("Declaration of the rights of the French people and the fundamental principles of their constitution") and "Déclaration de la Chambre des Représentants" ("Declaration of the House of Representatives") (*Archives Parlementaires de 1787 a 1860*, 2d ser., 14 [1869]: 609–10).

[1] Manuscript: "notwistanding."
[2] Reworked from "intrusion."

To George Watterston

SIR   Monticello Oct. 10. 15.

It was sometimes my practice, when reading on a subject to make notes on a separate paper, and to stick the paper loosely into the book to which it related, as the most convenient place for finding it again. in one of the volumes of Bezout's Cours de mathematiques, you will find such a note on the method of taking inaccessible heights and of reducing the planes of the triangles, when inclined, to the plane of the horison. I believe it is in Bezout's course for the artillery, tho possibly in that for the Marine, for they are distinct works. it is in one or two leaves of 8vo size. proposing soon to undertake an operation of this kind on the ground, I should be very glad to recover that paper of notes, to refresh my memory on the subject. You would greatly oblige me by turning to the book and withdrawing the paper, which is loose, and inclosing it to me by <u>return</u> of the mail.—I am anxious to learn that they are printing the catalogue, being desirous to get a copy of it. it will need a most careful revisal of the proof sheets. Accept the tender of my esteem and respect. TH: JEFFERSON

PoC (DLC); on verso of reused address cover of Nicolas G. Dufief to TJ, 5 Aug. 1815; at foot of text: "Mʳ P. Watterson"; endorsed by TJ.

Observations at Monticello
Related to Calculation of Latitude

date	Merid. Alt. by circle	same halved	merid. Alt. from horizon	difference	⊕error of instrum.	
	° ′ ″	° ′ ″	° ′ ″	° ′ ″	′ ″	*satisfactory
1815.						† not satisfactory
*Oct. 11	90–18– 0	45– 9– 0	45–26–0	0–17–0	6– 0	
13	88–29– 0	44–13–30¹			7–30	
					5–	⊕ the line of colli-
18	85– 2–30				*3–30	mation (or point of
					*6	coincidence of the
19	84–22– 0	42–11– 0	42–34–0	0–23′–0	*6	2 images) which
*25	80– 6– 0	40– 3– 0	40–23	0–20 –0	*6	ought to be at the
1816.						zero inscribed on
Jan. 21	64– 0– 0	32– 0– 0			1–30	the instrument is
29	*67–58– 0				2–30	found to be really
30	B. 68–28–30 / p 68–26				4– / 3–30	so many minutes below it. the mea-
31	B 68–56 / p 68–25				3–30 / 4	sure of the vertical angle therefore

commencing so much below it, the difference must be added if the upper graduation is used or subtracted if the lower.²

MS (MHi); filed with TJ's Weather Memorandum Book, 1802–16; written entirely in TJ's hand on one side of a single sheet.

¹ Thus in manuscript, but the correct figure is 44°–14′–30″.

² Above this paragraph TJ canceled "⊕ the error to be subtracted where the count is on the lower graduan [i.e., graduation]; but to be added if on the upper."

To Alden Partridge

I thank you for the statement of Altitudes, which you have been so kind as to send me of our Northern mountains. it came opportunely, as I was about making enquiries for the height of the White mountains, of N. Hampshire, which have the reputation of being the highest in our Maritime states, and purpose shortly to measure geometrically the height of the Peaks of Otter, which I suppose the highest <u>from their base</u>, of any on the East side of the Missisipi, except the White mountains, and not far short of their height if they are but of 4885. feet.   The method of estimating heights by the barometer is convenient and useful, as being ready, and furnishing an approximation to truth. of what degree of accuracy it is susceptible we know not as yet; no certain theory being established for ascertaining the density and weight of that portion of the column of atmosphere contiguous to the mountain; from the weight of which nevertheless we are to infer the height of the mountain. the most plausible seems to be that which supposes the mercury of the barometer divided into horizontal lamina of equal <u>thicknesses</u>. and a similar column of the atmosphere into lamina of equal <u>weights</u>. the former divisions give a set of Arithmetical, the latter of geometrical progressionals, which being the character of Logarithms and their numbers, the tables of these furnish ready computations, needing however the corrections which the state of the thermometer calls for. it is probable that in taking heights in the vicinity of each other in this way, there may be no considerable error, because the passage between them may be quick and repeated. the height of a mountain from it's base, thus taken, merits therefore a very different degree of credit from that of it's height above the level of the sea, where that is distant. according, for example, to the theory abovementioned, the height of Monticello from it's base is 580. feet, and it's base 610 f–6 I above the level of the ocean. the former, from other facts, I judge to be near the truth: but a knolege of the different falls of water from hence to the tide-water at Richmond, a distance of 75. miles, enables us to say that the whole descent to that place is but 170. or 180. feet. from thence to the ocean may be a distance of 100. miles. it is all tidewater, and thro' a level country. I know not what to conjecture as the amount of descent, but certainly not 435. feet, as that theory would suppose, nor the quarter part of it. I do not know by what rule Genl Williams made his computations. he reckons the foot of the Blue ridge, 20 miles from hence, but 100 feet above the tide water at Richmond. we know the descent, as before observed, to be at least 170. feet from hence, to which is to be added that from the Blue ridge to this place, a very hilly country, with constant and great waterfalls. his estimate therefore must be much below truth. results so different[1] prove that for distant comparisons of height, the barometer is not to be relied on according to any theory yet known. while therefore we give a good degree of credit to the results of operations between the summit of a mountain and it's base, we must give less to those between it's summit and the level of the ocean.

I will do myself the pleasure of sending you my estimate of the Peaks of Otter, which I count on undertaking in the course of the next month. in the mean time accept the assurance of my great respect.

TH: JEFFERSON

RC (VtNN: Partridge Papers); lacking address cover. RC (photocopy in ViU: Partridge Papers); including address cover; addressed: "Capt A. Partridge of the Corps of Engineers West point New York"; franked; postmarked Charlottesville, 18 Oct. PoC (DLC). Tr (MHi); posthumous copy.

In the meteorological notes he sent TJ in 1796, Jonathan WILLIAMS listed "Woods" as 100 feet higher than Richmond (*PTJ*, 28:597).

[1] Tr: "distant."

To Spencer Roane

DEAR SIR   Monticello Oct. 12. 15.

I recieved, in a letter from Col° Monroe the inclosed paper communicated, as he said, with your permission, and even with a wish to know my sentiments on the important question it discusses. it is now more than 40. years since I have ceased to be habitually conversant with legal questions; and my pursuits thro' that period have seldom required or permitted a renewal of my former familiarity with them. my ideas at present therefore, on such questions, have no claim to respect but such as might be yielded to the common auditors of a law argument.

I well knew that in certain federal cases the laws of the US. had given to a foreign party, whether pl. or def. a right to carry his cause into the federal courts; but I did not know that where he had himself elected the state judicature, he could, after an unfavorable decision there,[1] remove his case to the federal court, and thus take the benefit of two chances where others have but one: nor that the right of entertaining the question in this case had been exercised or claimed by the federal judiciary after it had been postponed on the party's first election. his failure too to place on the record the particular ground which might give jurisdiction to the federal court, appears to me an additional objection of great weight. the question is of the first importance. the removal of it seems to be out of the analogies which guide the two governments on their separate tracts, and claims the solemn attention of both judicatures, & of the nation itself. I should fear to make up a final opinion on it, until I could see[2] as able a developement of the grounds of the federal claim as that which I have now read against it. I confess myself unable to foresee what those grounds would be. the paper inclosed must call them forth, and silence them too, unless they are beyond my ken. I am glad therefore that the claim is arrested, and made the subject of special and mature deliberation. I hope our courts will never countenance the sweeping pretensions which have been set up under the words 'general defence and public welfare.' these words only express the motives which induced the Convention to give to the ordinary legislature certain specified powers which they enumerate, and which they thought might be trusted to the ordinary legislature, and not to give them the unspecified also; or why any specification? they could not be so awkward in language as to mean, as we say, 'all and some.' and should this construction prevail, all limits to the federal government are done away. this opinion, formed on the first rise of the question, I have never seen reason to change, whether in or out of power; but on the contrary find it strengthened and confirmed by five & twenty years of additional reflection and experience: and any countenance given to it by any regular organ of the government, I should consider more ominous than any thing which has yet occurred.

I am sensible how much these slight observations, on a question which you have so profoundly considered, need apology. they must find this in my zeal for the administration of our government according to it's true spirit, federal as well as republican, and in my respect for any wish which you might be supposed to entertain for opinions of so little value. I salute you with sincere & high respect and esteem.

TH: JEFFERSON

RC (CU-L). PoC (DLC); at foot of first page: "Judge Roane." Tr (MHi); posthumous copy.

Spencer Roane (1762–1822), public official and author, attended the College of William and Mary and read law under George Wythe before his admission to the bar in 1782. He represented Essex County for two terms in the Virginia House of Delegates, 1783–85, and he sat on the Virginia Council of State, 1785–86. In 1786 Roane married Patrick Henry's eldest daughter. The following year he joined Henry in the antifederalist camp by writing a pseudonymous newspaper letter arguing against ratification of the United States Constitution until a bill of rights was added. Later in life Roane wrote pseudonymous newspaper essays challenging decisions handed down by United States chief justice John Marshall. After serving for one session and part of a second in the state senate, 1788–89, in the latter year the legislature appointed Roane to the Virginia General Court. In 1794 he received a new appointment to the Court of Appeals, the state's highest tribunal, on which he served until his death. Roane was a prominent Virginia Republican described successively as a member of two informal leadership groups, the Richmond Essex Junto and the Richmond Party. He backed the presidential candidacy of James Madison in 1808 and supported the War of 1812. Roane subsequently advised TJ on

his financial and legal burdens after the bankruptcy and death of Wilson Cary Nicholas (*ANB*; *DAB*; Margaret Horsnell, *Spencer Roane: Judicial Advocate of Jeffersonian Principles* [1986]; Leonard, *General Assembly*, 149, 153, 171, 178; Washington *National Intelligencer*, 8 July 1807; TJ to Roane, 31 May 1822; Roane to TJ, 8 July 1822; Richmond City Hustings Court Will Book, 3:239–43; *Richmond Enquirer*, 13, 17 Sept. 1822).

For the INCLOSED PAPER, see James Monroe to TJ, 23 Sept. 1815, and note. GENERAL DEFENCE AND PUBLIC WELFARE paraphrases the United States Constitution, article 1, section 8.

[1] Word interlined.
[2] Word not in Tr.

To Mathew Carey

DEAR SIR   Monticello Oct. 13. 15.

I thank you for the copy of the 6th edition of your Olive branch, which you have been so good as to send me. I am glad to see that it grows in size and demand: and in compliance with the invitation of your printed letter of the 4th inst. which is also recieved, I will notice a circumstance in your Appendix which may be worthy of correction in the new edition proposed. in page 400. the introduction of the conscription into France is ascribed to Bonaparte. this however is not correct. it was instituted there by the republican government before Bonaparte's name was known. the exact date of it I do not recollect, whether under the Committee of safety or their successors the Directory. this however you can ascertain by turning to histories which I have not an opportunity of doing. he found the conscription ready established to his hand, and conquered the world with it. and his ultimate failure was from the abuse of it, the whole of the youth of France being killed up, and the defence of the country left to their old men, who being inadequate to it, they are now suffering under the yoke of conquest. convinced myself that the classification of our militia according to ages, the ascribing to each class it's proper sphere of duty, and giving the government compleat command of it's service, with the addition proposed by Secretary[1] Monroe of sectional divisions, each to keep a man constantly in the regular lines, as was the law of this state in the revolutionary war, is the only means by which a country, with our constitution, can ever be defended in war, I think it all important to remove every prejudice which stands in it's way. among other federal artifices in the same style, the ascription of this institution to Bonaparte (whose name is so justly detested by every friend to the liberty of man, and independance of nations) has been too successfully used to prevent this only measure of salvation to our country, and it's republican constitution. I salute you with esteem and respect   TH: JEFFERSON

RC (NjMoHP: Lloyd W. Smith Collection); addressed: "Mʳ Matthew Cary Philadelphia"; frank clipped; postmarked Charlottesville, 18 Oct.; endorsed by Carey as received 21 Oct. PoC (DLC); on verso of reused address cover of George P. Stevenson to TJ, 10 Aug. 1815; endorsed by TJ.

On PAGE 400 of the sixth edition of his publication, Carey argues that the system of military conscription that drew soldiers from set divisions was used during the American Revolution and that "This relieves the system of classification from the odium attached to it as a discovery of the prolific brain of Bonaparte. His inventive powers have had more credit in this respect than they deserve. He has taken the plan at second hand from the sages and heroes of the revolution" (Carey, *The Olive Branch: or, Faults on Both Sides, Federal and Democratic. A Serious Appeal on the Necessity of Mutual Forgiveness and Harmony*, 6th ed. [Philadelphia, 1815]). In the seventh edition of the same work, published on 20 Dec. of the same year, Carey revised the beginning of this passage to read "This relieves the system of classification from the odium attached to it as a discovery of the French republic"

(Carey, *Olive Branch*, 7th ed. [Philadelphia, 1815], 404).

The levée en masse of 1793 was the first large-scale conscription of the French Revolution. The DIRECTORY followed it in 1798 with the Jourdan-Delbrel Law, which mandated the drafting of all single men between the ages of twenty and twenty-five. It remained in effect until 1814 (Connelly, *Napoleonic France*, 126–7, 270–1). In October 1814 Secretary of War James MONROE had proposed several different plans of conscription, under the first of which men aged between eighteen and forty-five would be grouped into classes of one hundred men, with each class to provide four soldiers at all times (*ASP, Military Affairs*, 1:515; John H. Cocke to TJ, 6 Nov. 1814, and note). During the REVOLUTIONARY WAR Virginia ordered several drafts. One such call in October 1780, during TJ's service as governor, divided militia units into classes, each of which was to provide a recruit for the Continental army (Hening, 10:326–37; John R. Van Atta, "Conscription in Revolutionary Virginia: The Case of Culpeper County, 1780–1781," *VMHB* 92 [1984]: 263–7).

[1] Word interlined in place of "Colº."

To Tristram Dalton

DEAR SIR   Monticello Oct. 13. 15.

I thank you for the two agricultural pamphlets you were so kind as to send me by the hands of General & mrs Dearborne; with which I was the more pleased as they gave me the sincere gratification of learning that you were well and situated to your own satisfaction. always sensible of your merit, I am equally so to your well-being. I have read mr Dexter's publication on peat with great pleasure. it gives more information on that subject than we have before recieved from any other source; and I tender my portion of the public[1] obligation to him for it. I found many other interesting pieces in the magazine. I have had the happiness of possessing Gen[l] & mrs Dearborne here a few days, but quite too few. these revivals of antient feelings are peculiarly grateful to old age: for I find that our friendships, like our wines, improve with time. I hope mrs Dalton & yourself enjoy health and contentment, and that she as well as yourself will be so good as to accept the tender of my sincere esteem and respect.

TH: JEFFERSON

RC (CtY: Franklin Collection); addressed: "Tristram Dalton esq. Boston"; franked; postmarked Charlottesville, 18 Oct.; endorsed by Dalton as received 25 Oct. 1815. PoC (DLC); on verso of reused address cover of Dabney Carr to TJ, 9 Aug. 1815; endorsed by TJ.

[1] TJ here canceled "thanks."

To Robert Patterson

DEAR SIR   Monticello Oct. 13. 15.
A long absence from home must apologise for my delay in acknoleging your favor of Aug. 25. and thanking you for your attention to the time piece. the best method of packing it would be to wrap it in one or more coarse striped woollen blankets (commonly called Dutch blankets) place it in a well jointed case, and if the case could be covered with oil cloth it would be still safer from moisture; for it will come up the river I live on in an open boat. the blankets and oil cloth will be worth their cost when here. mr Vaughan has a small balance of mine in his hands, and will be so good, on sight of this letter, as to pay all expences of package, drayage E[t]c. it is to be sent by sea to Richmond, addressed to Mess[rs] Gibson & Jefferson my correspondents there, who will pay freight and charges and forward it to me.—you once mentioned to me an artificial horison of your invention, for the use of the Sextant, or Borda's Circular instrument. that of the fluid quicksilver is so troublesome both to carry, and use that if any workman in Philadelphia makes yours, I should be glad to get one, and will remit the cost thro' mr Vaughan.   I should think a convenient and correct one might be made of a piece of polished metal platina, for instance, or the mixt metal of the telescopic specula, or even of common glass mirror, with cross spirit levels bedded at the sides thus

such an one would admit very ready adjustment when de-ranged, would be easily portable and used. however this is one of the things appearing easy in theory but all but impracticable in fact. I have no doubt but yours is best. I salute you with affection and respect.   TH: JEFFERSON

RC (PPAmP: Thomas Jefferson Papers); at foot of text: "Doct^r R. Patterson"; address leaf torn, with only the word "Philadelphia" remaining in TJ's hand; with partial Dft of Patterson to TJ, 24 Oct. 1815, on verso of remnant of address leaf, partial Dft of Patterson to TJ, 28 Nov. 1815, on recto of address leaf and verso of letter, and evidently unrelated notes and diagrams by Patterson on verso of letter. PoC (photocopy in ViU: TJP).

Patterson mentioned his ARTIFICIAL HORISON in a 12 Mar. 1811 letter to TJ. BORDA'S CIRCULAR INSTRUMENT was a reflecting circle invented by Jean Charles Borda that was used for surveying. French scientists also used it to measure the length of the meridional arc, the standard on which they based the metric system (*DSB*). SPECULA are metallic mirrors forming part of a reflecting telescope (*OED*).

To Henry Sheaff

SIR   Monticello Oct. 13. 15.

I took the liberty of writing to you on the 11th of August & of requesting you to send me a quarter cask of dry Sherry or dry Lisbon whichever you had most recommendable. being out of wine and not hearing from you, I trouble you with a repetition of the request, lest any accident should have happened to my letter or your answer. I mentioned that on noting to me the cost, it should be remitted within 90. days after shipment; but if this is out of your course of dealing it shall be remitted as soon as the cost is known. I desired it to be in a double cask,[1] sent to Richmond by sea, addressed to Messrs Gibson and Jefferson, my correspondents [t]here, who would pay freight & charges and forward it to me. asking the favor of a speedy answer I repeat to you the assurances of my great respect and esteem

TH: JEFFERSON

PoC (MHi); on verso of reused address cover to TJ; mutilated at seal; at foot of text: "Mr Henry Sheaff"; endorsed by TJ.

[1] Reworked from "case."

To Benjamin Waterhouse

DEAR SIR   Monticello Oct. 13. 15.

I was highly gratified with the receipt of your letter of Sep. 1. by Gen[l] and mrs Dearborne; and by the evidence it furnished me of your bearing up with firmness and perseverance against the persecutions of your enemies, religious, political and professional. these last I suppose have not yet forgiven you the introduction of vaccination, and annihilation of the great variolous field of profit to them: and none of them pardon the proof you have established that the condition of man may be ameliorated, if not <u>infinitely</u>, as enthusiasm alone pretends, yet <u>indefinitely</u>, as bigots alone can doubt. in lieu of these enmities you have the blessings of all the friends of human happiness, for this great peril from which they are rescued.

I have read with pleasure the orations of mr Holmes & mr Austin. from the former we always expect what is good; and the latter has by this specimen taught us to expect the same in future from him. both have set the valuable example of quitting the beaten ground of the revolutionary war, and making the present state of things the subject of annual animadversion and instruction. a copious one it will be and highly useful if properly improved.   Cobbet's address would of itself have mortified and humbled the Cossac priests; but brother Jonathan has pointed his arrow to the hearts of the worst of them. these reverend leaders of the Hartford[1] nation it seems then are now[2] falling[3] together about religion, of which they have not one real principle in their hearts. like bawds, religion becomes to them a refuge from the despair of their loathsome vices.[4] they seek in it only an oblivion of the disgrace with which they have loaded themselves, in their political ravings, and of[5] their mortification at the ridiculous issue of their Hartford convention.   no event, more than this, has shewn the placid character of our constitution. under any other their treasons would have been punished by the halter. we let them live as laughing stocks for the world, and punish them by the torment of eternal contempt.[6]—the emigrations you mention from the Eastern states are what I have long counted on. the religious & political tyranny of those in power with you, cannot fail to drive the oppressed to milder associations of men, where freedom of mind is allowed in fact as well as in pretence. the subject of their present clawings and caterwaulings is not without it's interest to rational men. the priests have so disfigured the simple religion of Jesus that no one who reads the sophistications they have engrafted on it, from the jargon of Plato, of Aristotle & other mystics, would conceive these could have been fathered on the sublime preacher of the sermon on the mount. yet, knowing the importance of names they have assumed that of Christians, while they are mere Platonists, or any thing rather than disciples of Jesus.   one of these parties beginning now to strip off these meretricious trappings; their followers may take courage to make thorough work, and restore to us the figure in it's original simplicity and beauty. the effects of this squabble therefore, whether religious or political, cannot fail to be[7] good in some way.

   The visit to Monticello, of which you hold up an idea, would be a favor indeed of the first order: I know however the obstacles of age & distance, and should therefore set due value on it's vicarious execution, should business or curiosity lead a son of yours to visit this Sodom and Gomorrah of parsons Osgood, Parish, & Gardener.   Accept my wishes for your health and happiness, and the assurance of my great esteem & respect.

Th: Jefferson

RC (MBCo: Waterhouse Letterbook); torn at seal, with missing text supplied from PoC; three words interlined by Waterhouse. PoC (DLC); on reused cover sheet of TJ's Account with Joseph Milligan, [ca. 16 Aug. 1815]; at foot of first page: "Doctr Benj. Waterhouse." Tr (MHi); posthumous copy; incomplete. Tr (ViU: TJP); posthumous copy in Nicholas P. Trist's hand; incomplete.

   For William Cobbett's address aimed at cossac priests and the epistle of brother jonathan, see note to Waterhouse to TJ, 1 Sept. 1815.

[1] Waterhouse here interlined "Convention."
[2] MHi Tr: "not."
[3] Waterhouse here interlined "out."
[4] ViU Tr begins here.
[5] MHi Tr ends here.
[6] ViU Tr ends here.
[7] Waterhouse here interlined "do."

From George Watterston

Sir,   City of Washington Octr 13th 1815
   I had the honor to receive your letter of the 10th inst: yesterday evening, requesting the transmission of your M.S notes, contained in Bezout—& am happy to have it in my power to comply with your request, by enclosing & forwarding them to you—In the book refered to I find three half sheets carefully fastened between the printed pages, one of which (—the one I presume, you require) I have taken out—& enclose; the other two relate to plane & spherical trigonometry & the solution of oblique angled triangles & that of right angled spherical triangles.—If you should desire either of these two, by making known to me that desire, I will cheerfully transmit them to you.

[79]

The three folio vol^s of the Laws of Virginia which you state in your former letter, to be in known hands, have not yet been received—& Mr Milligan has said nothing to me on the subject—

I am happy to inform you that the catalogue is now in press—& that, in a few weeks, it will be published—I have preserved your arrangement, as one that I think excellent & that I had previously thought of adopting—I have introduced but[1] one alteration & that is in arrangeing each chap: alphabetically—Having pasted printed labels on each vol—it gives them a uniformity of appearance quite agreable to the eye & having put them up in a very beautiful & comodious appartment, the display is really beautiful—& seems to meet with the approbation of all—The proof sheet of the catalogue is examined several times & by several persons, so that it is as accurate as it can well be made—I have, from the very scant & limited appropriation made by Congress; (only 800 dollars) been obliged to exercise some ingenuity to get the catalogue printed before the session of congress—As soon as it is compleated I will send you a copy—

I have the honor to be Sir very resp^y yr ob^t servt

GEORGE WATTERSTON

RC (DLC); adjacent to closing: "Thos Jefferson Esq^e"; endorsed by TJ as received 19 Oct. 1815 and so recorded in SJL.

For TJ's notes on the SOLUTION OF OBLIQUE ANGLED TRIANGLES & THAT OF RIGHT ANGLED SPHERICAL TRIANGLES, see Notes on Napier's Theorem, printed above at 18 Mar. 1814. Of the initial 800

DOLLARS appropriated to Watterston for the Library of Congress, $190 had been paid to William Elliot for printing services. In 1815–16 Elliot received additional payments totaling $1,519.50 for the printing of the library catalogue and related expenses (*ASP, Miscellaneous*, 2:281–2).

[1] Manuscript: "by."

Notes on Étienne Bézout's *Cours de Mathématiques*

[before Apr. 1815]

To reduce angles observed on an inclined plane to that of the horison. Bezout. trigonom 320. cours d'Artillerie.

let d.g.i be the plane of the base of a hill, and a.b.c. points on it's side at different height

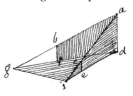

suppose the ∠b.a.c. found by observation to be   62–3°
the ∠ of inclination b.a.d (a.d. being vertical)   88–
the ∠ of inclination of c.a. to wit c.a.d.   78–1
it is required to find the ∠g.d.i. in the plane of the horizon.
let a.b. and a.c be prolonged until they meet the horizontal plane d.g.i. at g. & i.

consider a.d. as the radius of the tables, then d.g. & d.i. become tangents of the tables, and a.g. & a.i. their secants; turn to the tables.

the ∠g.a.d. = 88°–5′ has for it's tabular secant 29.90   neglecting subseqᵗ fractions
it's tangent 29.88

the ∠i.a.d. = 78–17 has for it's tabular secant 4.92
tangent 4.82

1ˢᵗ operation

in the △ a.g.i. given a.g. = 29.9
a.i = 4.92 $\Big\}$ required g.i
∠a = 62°37′¹

$ag + ai : ag - ai :: t\,\frac{i+g}{2} : t\,\frac{i-g}{2} = t\ 49°–43'$
then Si. ∠g : ai :: Si. ∠a. : gi = 28.

2ᵈ opernᵈ

in the right angled △ a.i.d. given the ∠a. = 78°–17′
the hypoth. a.i = 4.92. reqᵈ d.i.
Rad. : 4.92 :: Si. 78°–17′ : d.i. = 4.8175

---

in the right angled △ a.g.d. given the ∠a = 88°–5′
the hypoth. a.g = 29.9. reqᵈ d.g.
Rad : 29.9 :: Si. 88°–5′ : d.g. = 29.883

3ᵈ opernᵈ

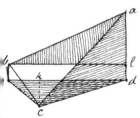

in the △ g.d.i. given   d.g = 29.883 $\Big\}$ required the
d.i = 4.92   ∠g.d.i.
g.i = 28

dg : gi + di :: gi – di : gk – dk = 25.456
and di : Rad. :: kd : Si. ∠dik which is complement to the
∠gdi = 62°–39′–20″²

Suppose a the summit of a mountain: ad it's height, b & c points at it's foot, c being in the level of it's base, or of the common horison, & b above that level.

	o	′	″
that the ∠aCb is observed to be	63	20	40
aBc	66	39	20
aCd	7	59	36
aBl	7	48	0
bCg	0	28	39

& that bc is by admeasuremᵗ 6000. feet.

Required ad the height of mountⁿ bg the height of station b.³ & the whole △ cdg, being the reduction of the points abc to the plane of the horizon.

△ acd			
or ac.	Si. bAc = 50°	: bc 6000	:: Si. aBc = 66–39–20 : ac = 7191.27
or cd	Rad.	: ac = 7191.27	:: S. cAd = 82– 0–24 : cd = 7121.4
or ad	Rad.	: ac.	:: S. aCd = 7–59–36 : ad = 1000.
△ abc			
or ab	S. bAc = 50°	: bc = 6000	:: S. aCb = 63–20–40 : ab = 7000.
△ abl			
or bl	Rad.	: ab = 7000	:: S bAl = 82–12– 0 : bl = 6935.23

for al	Rad.	: ab.	:: S. aBl = 7–48– 0 : al = 950.

△ bcg

for cg	Rad.	: bc = 6000	:: S. cBg = 89–31–21 : cg = 5999.8
for bg	Rad.	: bc.	:: S. bCg = 0–28–39 : bg = 50.

△ cdg

	dg	: cd + cg	:: cd – cg : dk – gk.
	6935.23	: 13121.2	:: 1121.6 : 2122.04

then dk = 4528.63 and gk = 2406.59

△ cdk

°   ′   ″

for dCk	cd	: Rad.	:: dk.	: S. dCk = 39–29–17
				then cDg = 50–30–43

△ cGk

for gCk	cg	: Rad.	:: gk	: S. gCk = 23–38–52
				then cGd = 66–21– 8

then the ∠dCg = dCk + gCk   = 63– 8– 9

we have then the height of the mountain ad = 1000.f
height of the station b. = 50.f.

and the whole △ cdg, to wit
cd = 7121.4
cg = 5999.8
dg = bl = 6935.23

°   ′   ″

∠cDg = 50–30–43
∠cGd = 66–21– 8
∠dCg = 63– 8– 9

Note. the plane of the theodolite being adjusted to that of the horizon, will render truly (and without needing reduction) the horizontal angles at the two stations, whether they be in the same, or different horizontal planes; because, if different, as b. and c. their planes being parallel, the degrees on them will be coincident. but in this case the base measured on the inclined plane b.c. must be reduced to the horizontal one g.c.

The above diagram supposes the plane of the theodolite adjusted to the inclined plane a.b.c. which renders necessary the reduction of it's angles as well as lines to the horizontal plane d.g.c.

MS (MHi); filed with TJ's Weather Memorandum Book, 1802–16; written entirely in TJ's hand on both sides of a small sheet; undated, but composed prior to, and probably much earlier than, shipment of TJ's library to Washington.

TJ based these notes in part on section 320 of Étienne Bézout, *Cours de Mathématiques, a l'Usage du Corps Royal de l'Artillerie* (Paris, 1788; Sowerby, no. 3681) 1:334–6.

[1] Equation interlined.
[2] Page ends here.
[3] Preceding six words interlined.

From George Ticknor

DEAR SIR,   Göttingen (Germany) Oct. 14. 1815.

I had yesterday the pleasure of receiving a line from you dated Aug. 6. enclosing the copy of a letter of credit on Paris for 350.D. and containing an intimation of a previous letter of July 4. covering your catalogue which my father informs me he has sent for greater safety through the hands of my banker in London, & which I may, therefore, expect to receive in the course of this month. In June I wrote to you from London and informed you, as soon as I had myself determined upon it, that the disturbances in France had made it necessary for me to come first to Holland and Germany. This letter I sent by our commissioner Mr. Clay, as I was very anxious that you should soon & surely[1] receive it in order that you might govern yourself accordingly. The same circumstances, which first brought me here have induced me to determine on remaining here until the spring opens, when I shall hasten to France and make it my first employment to execute your commission. I am happy to find that my disappointment and delay will be none to you, for if I had gone directly from London to Paris your list would not have overtaken me in season to allow me to send them out this fall, and I should not have trusted them to a winter's voyage without your especial direction.

Your letters to your friends in this quarter of the world I am sorry to say are—with the exception of that to the Baron de Moll which I forwarded to him by one of the Professors of this University—still in my hands. One opportunity only occurred while I was in England by which I could have sent them to France but for the reasons which I gave you and also from my want of full confidence in the person going, I did not risque them; and since I have been on the continent, there has been nothing like a regular communication with Paris. The post has been suspended and the roads unsafe. Should an opportunity occur to which I think you would yourself trust them, I shall not fail to forward them.—otherwise they will remain with me until the roads become passable in the spring and then I shall deliver them in person.

You were kind enough, I recollect, in one of the letters I had the honour to receive from you in America to ask me to write to you. If I have not as yet fully availed myself of this privilege it is not because I did not feel it to be such but because I knew not what to send that would interest you. I saw England, indeed, at the heighth of her power and pride—I saw Holland, too, a fallen and ruined nation—but, even at so great a distance, I was sure that you would estimate the probable consequences of the ominous ripeness of the one and the dotage and decripitude of the other much better than I could, present as I was to the circumstances of both. Of their literature, I could of course say nothing, for England's is our own and in Holland, though I saw a collection of nearly four hundred volumes of their poets and as much more of other belle-lettre writing, yet I believe their literature is still to appear. In Germany, however, I may be more fortunate. With its political organization and consequence, I believe we are sufficiently familiar in America, but its literature is a kind of <u>terra in cognita</u> to us. Its language is so strangely different from all the foreign dialects we have been accustomed to learn, and their classical authors are all so recent, that it does not enter into the system of our education nor, until Mad. de Stael's book came among us, was its history or condition talked about or thought of. Yet I find it a very interesting literature. It has all the freshness and faithfulness of poetry of the early ages, while words are the representatives of sensible objects and simple feelings, rather than of abstractions and generalities, and yet being written so late has enough of modern refinement & regularity. Göthe, who is still alive, is their most popular and successful writer—and Werther, which we know in English only by a miserable imitation of a garbled French translation, made by someone, who understood neither of the languages, is their most popular book. Klopstock—except for his odes—is out of fashion—Wieland, too, is less respected than he was in his life-time—but Bürger, Voss, Lessing and Schiller have become classicks. The flexibility[2] of their language,—which arises in a considerable degree from its being unsettled—enables them to make better translations than any other nation. This gives them a great advantage. The Greek tragedians and orators are rendered to them with a fidelity and purity and grace, of which in English we have no idea ever from Potter & Sir Wm. Jones.[3] Voss's Homer in the hexameter and line for line is an extraordinary approximation to the solitary greatness of the original and Schlegel's Shakespeare seems to me every time I open it to be a new miracle. From what I had read of their literature in America I was satisfied it was very extraordinary but my expectations have been much exceeded.— In ancient learning they are unrivalled. D[r] Parr, the best scholar alive in England, and certainly quite as vain of his own reputation and quite as proud of that of his country as a scholar need to be, bore to me a reluctant but decisive testimony to the superiority of Germany, which he justly attributed to a spirit of liberality & philosophy in their learning, which makes but slow progress in England. Winkelmann, who has long been the first authority in France & Italy on all subjects relating to the arts of the ancients and Heyne & his school in ancient criticism have placed yr.[4] country at the head of classical learning in Europe. Indeed, I found from the english scholars & bibliographers, that there is hardly a single <u>editio</u> <u>optima</u> of a Greek or Roman author received among them, that was not elaborated in Germany.—In science, I know nothing of them as yet but by reputation. In mineralogy, botany & entomology, I find what the Abbé Correa told me, to be true, that they lead the rest of Europe. Professor

Gauss—still a very young man—has recently acquired extraordinary reputation by his astronomical calculations. In the estimation of England and Germany he is already the rival of la Place and if the accounts I have received of the early developement and present compass of his talents are true, must soon stand before him, if farther discoveries remain to be made.—But, it is in vain to speak of particular persons or even particular branches of learning and science, for it is not from solitary and independent examples that the spirit of a nation can be measured. The σχολαςικος in Hierocles carried a brick in his pocket as a specimen of the house he offered at sale and the name of a single author is an item no less inconsiderable in the account of national greatness. But no man can go far into the body of German literature—above all no man can come into their country & see their men of letters & professors, without feeling that there is an enthusiasm among them, which has brought them forward in forty years as far as other nations have been three centuries in advancing & which will yet carry them much farther—without seeing that there is an unwearied & universal diligence among their scholars—a <u>general</u> habit of labouring from fourteen to sixteen hours a day—which will finally give their country an extent and amount of learning of which the world has before had no example.

The first result of this enthusiasm & learning, which immediately[5] broke through all the barriers that opposed it, was an universal toleration in all matters of opinion. No matter what a man thinks, he may teach it & print it, not only without molestation from the government but also without molestation from publick opinion which is so often more oppressive than ye arm of authority. I know not that any thing like it exists in any other country. The same freedom in france produced the revolution and the same freedom in England would now shake the deep foundations of the British throne—but here it passes as a matter of course and produces no effect but that of stimulating the talents of their thinking men. Every day books appear on government and religion which in ye rest of Europe would be suppressed by the state and in America would be put into the great <u>catalogus expurgatorius</u> of publick opinion but which here are read as any other books and judged according to their literary & philosophical merit. They get, perhaps, a severe review or a severe answer, but these are weapons which both parties can use and unfairness is very uncommon. Indeed every thing in Germany seems to me to be measured by the genius or acuteness or learning it discovers without reference to previous opinion or future consequences to an astonishing and sometimes to an alarming degree. Some of the examples of this are quite remarkable. This university, for instance, where there are now above nine hundred & fifty students to be instructed for Germany and Europe, is under the immediate protection & influence of the British crown. Its professors—forty in number—are paid from the treasury of Hannover and appointed by its regency. Yet the principal theologian & most popular professor here (Eichhorn) has written a very learned and eloquent book and delivers to a crowded audience lectures no less learned & eloquent to prove that the New Testament was written in ye latter end of the second century—and another professor of much reputation (Schultz) teaches that "a miracle is a natural and a revelation a metaphysical impossibility"—If truth is to be attained by freedom of inquiry, as I doubt not it is, the German professors & literati are certainly in the high road, and have the way quietly open before them.

This freedom and scepticism sometimes takes a singular direction. In classical literature it has been very busy and what Father Hardouin so clumsily maintained a century ago in relation to some of the Roman writers has been made amusing and in some instances popular in relation to the Greek by the acuteness and eloquence and learning of some of the most distinguished German scholars. It received its first considerable impulse from Wolf of Berlin, the Porson of Germany, who in 1795 published his prolegomena to Homer, in which he maintained that there probably never was a man of that name and age, and, if there were, that it was impossible so long poems should have been transmitted from him by tradition—that the Iliad and Odyssey were originally practical accounts of the war of Troy &c which were sung and recited in separate fragments by their respective authors before writing had come into use—that during the early ages of Greece additions were continually made to them & these additions gradually incorporated into the poems by collectors & poets & transcribers who arranged them in order, divided them into books &c—and that, at last, by the successive accretions of centuries they becam[e] the great models they are now. This he supported with much learn[ing] & skill. His principal arguments were drawn 1. from the barbarism of the age in which the alledged Homer lived, which, he maintained, <u>could</u> not have produced such perfection in arrangement, style, versification &c—2 From the absolute impossibility of transmitting two heroick poems of such length by tradition—& 3. From the internal evidence of several different mythologies indicating several different ages and states of society. This work excited a great sensation. Wieland in his "German mercury" and St. Croix in France were the principal opponents of the innovation. The old school, however, made but a feeble defence and publick opinion went very soon over to the side of Wolf, where Heyne, the Vosses & the Schlegels had already ranged themselves. The only question was as to the right of discovery, which Heyne (in his review for '95) claimed for himself as having taught it in his lectures when Wolf was his scholar but which Wolf denied in some angry & learned letters which he published in '97. The general impression, I think, seems to be, that the discovery or, as I still fondly believe it, the <u>invention</u> was Heynes but as to the <u>doctrine</u>,[6] in a year it came into the rubricks of all the Universities & Gymnasia of Germany.—Many similar but not equally successful attempts have been made. The authenticity of the three tragedians has been called in question—An attempt has been made to prove that the odes of Pindar had originally something of a dramatick form &c &c but I suspect the boldest assault on antiquity was one made by Wolf on Cicero. In 1802 he published the Oratio pro Marcello with a commentary full of learning & eloquence & enthusiasm to prove it spurious. This was too gross an outrage. Wormius replied in 1803 so as to detain publick opinion which here always leans to the side of scepticism & in 1804 Weiske came out with a "commentarius perpetuus et plenus" which decided it against wolf & prevented him from laying his unconsecrated hands on any thing else of Cicero's.—The effect of all this, however, is very good. It brings the classical authors into notice & makes them ye. subjects of a much more thorough investigation than they would otherwise receive. It has compelled all the young men to become familiar with them at the Universities and has contributed essentially to form the learned professors with which Germany now abounds.

It is time for me, however, to close my letter, which after all I fear, has told you nothing you did not know much better before. It has fulfilled my intentions, however, if it has in any way served to convince you of the respect and regard with which I am your obliged and obedient servant,   Geo: Ticknor.

Perhaps you may wish to make some alterations in your catalogue, so that I may have the pleasure of receiving a line from you in Paris or, perhaps, you will write to me with no more important motive than that of doing me a favour, and giving me some account of my country, which was never seen by me in a proper point of view, until I saw it from amidst the miseries & crimes of Europe.—   I pray you to do me the favour to remember me to Colo. Randolph & Mrs. Randolph, who together with the rest of your family have not, I hope, forgotten me.—If Mr. Gilmer is still in America, you will do me a favour by thanking him for his letter, which I received in England, & which I shall answer as soon as I know where to address him.

RC (DLC); edge trimmed; endorsed by TJ as received 12 June 1816 and so recorded in SJL.

TJ's letter to Ticknor was dated 16 Aug. 1815, not AUG. 6. MAD. DE STAEL'S BOOK was *De l'Allemagne*, 2 vols. (Paris, 1810). The MISERABLE IMITATION OF A GARBLED FRENCH TRANSLATION was probably Johann Wolfgang von Goethe, *The Sorrows of Werter: A German Story* (London, 1779). WINKELMANN: Johann Joachim Winckelmann. σχολαςικος: "pedant."

Samuel Johnson, in the preface to his edition of *The Plays of William Shakespeare*, 8 vols. (London, 1765), commented that Shakespeare's "real power is not shewn in the splendour of particular passages, but by the progress of his fable, and the tenour of his dialogue; and he that tries to recommend him by select quotations, will succeed like the pedant in *Hierocles*, who, when he offered his house to sale, carried a brick in his pocket as a specimen." A version of the tale also appeared in Adamantios Coray, ed., Ἱεροκλέους Φιλοσόφου Ἀστεῖα. *Facéties. D'Hiéroclès Le Philosophe* (Paris, 1812),

6. CATALOGUS EXPURGATORIUS: "catalogue of prohibited books."

THIS UNIVERSITY: the University of Göttingen. Excepting Napoleonic interruptions, holders of the BRITISH CROWN also ruled the German state of HANNOVER from 1714 until 1837. SCHULTZ: Gottlob Ernst Schulze. Christoph Martin Wieland founded and edited *Der Teutsche Merkur* (the GERMAN MERCURY), a quarterly literary magazine. Christian Gottlob Heyne's REVIEW FOR '95 appeared in the serial *Göttingische gelehrte Anzeigen*, 21 Nov., 19 Dec. 1795. Friedrich August Wolf's response, in the form of a letter to Heyne, was printed as a pamphlet, *Briefe an Hernn Hofrath Heyne von Professor Wolf* (Berlin, 1797). Benjamin WEISKE published *Commentarius Perpetuus et Plenus in Orationem M. Tullii Ciceronis pro M. Marcello* (Leipzig, 1805).

[1] Preceding two words added in margin and interlined.
[2] Manuscript: "flexibity."
[3] Preceding four words interlined.
[4] Abbreviation for "their."
[5] Manuscript: "immediatel."
[6] Word interlined in place of "fact."

To George W. Campbell

DEAR SIR   Monticello Oct. 15. 15.

Your kind favor of Sep. 9. was recieved here on my return after a long absence. it gives me the pleasing information of the improvement of your health, and I hope it will continue to improve so as to restore you again to the public councils. we have always need of the talents and integrity of our best citizens, and I believe as much so now as at any time. we call it indeed peace: but it is but a truce until the impressment of our seamen is properly guarded against. the late war has indeed terminated most honorably, for which we are most indebted to the Western states: yet it has sufficiently proved that our military system is not in a form adequate to our safety in a state of war. now then is the moment of giving it a proper form while nobody will be so immediately affected by it as to produce clamor. now too is the moment for laying the foundation of a financial system which may pay off the debts contracted, and place the resources of our country more under our future controul. the basis of this can only be by taking the circulating medium into the hands of the nation to whom it belongs, out of that of private adventurers, who have so managed it for their own profit as to leave us without any common measure of the value of property, and to subject all[1] private fortunes to the fluctuations of their swindling projects. the coining of paper money by private authority is a higher degree of treason than the coining the precious metals. the present volcanic state of Europe should warn us to prepare for it's explosion. if it does not blow up under the feet of the combination of robbers now plundering and dividing the spoils of the world, we may[2] become the next subject of division. we were safe from the enterprises of Bonaparte because he had not the fleets of Britain to bring him here, and from those of Britain because she had Bonaparte on her back. but we have now, the conquerors of Bonaparte to fear, with the fleets of Britain at their willing command. the productions and metals of Spanish America are a tempting subject of partition, and our republican government a hated and mischievous example of what every nation might be under similar rule. I hope therefore our ensuing Congress will avail themselves of the present moment to put our house in order; and especially to place in the hands of the national government the means of enforcing constitutional obedience to the laws. the Hartford nation is humbled but not conciliated. something indeed is done by the disgrace of Massachusets and the reduction of her insolent pretensions to the government of the Union. but altho' embers only now appear, they cover unextinguished fire. I think I may congratulate you on the success of the steam boats. no part of the world can be more benefited by them than our Western states, and no river more than that of Tenissee. I salute you with great esteem and respect.   TH: JEFFERSON

RC (NjP: Andre deCoppet Collection); addressed: "George W. Campbell esquire Nashville Tenissee"; franked; postmarked Milton, 20 Oct., and Nashville, 31 Oct.; with postmaster's note to "forw[d]" and address altered to "Washington City"; endorsed by Campbell. PoC (DLC); on reused address cover of Robert Patterson to TJ, 25 Aug. 1815; endorsed by TJ.

Earlier in 1815 the *Enterprise* was the first steamboat to ascend the Mississippi and Ohio rivers from New Orleans to Pittsburgh, expanding commercial possibilities for the WESTERN STATES (Norfolk *American Beacon and Commercial Diary*, 3 Oct. 1815; Louis C. Hunter, *Steamboats on the Western Rivers: An Economic and Technological History* [1949], 17–8).

[1] Preceding two words interlined in place of "place."
[2] Word interlined in RC and overwritten in PoC in place of "shall."

To Peter Stephen Chazotte

Monticello. Oct. 15. 15.

Th: Jefferson presents his compliments and his thanks to M[r] Chorotte for the pamphlet on the plan of a bank which he has been so kind as to send him, and which he shall read with pleasure. it is a subject with which he is not intimate, and particularly as practised in the United States, where it has had the effect of depriving us of any common measure of the value of property, being itself more uncertain in value than any thing to which it can be applied. he is particularly sensible of the kind sentiments which mr Charotte is so good as to express towards himself, and salutes him with great respect.

RC (Mrs. Richard D. Nelson, Short Hills, New Jersey, 1949); dateline at foot of text. PoC (DLC); on verso of reused address cover of John Vaughan to TJ, 12 Aug. 1815; endorsed by TJ as a letter to "Charotte P. Stephen" and so recorded in SJL.

To George Logan

DEAR SIR   Monticello Oct. 15. 15.

I thank you for the extract in your's of Aug. 16. respecting the emperor Alexander. it arrived here a day or two after I had left this place, from which I have been absent 7. or 8.[1] weeks. I had from other information formed the most favorable opinion of the virtues of Alexander and considered his partiality to this country as a prominent proof of them. the magnanimity of his conduct on the first capture of Paris still magnified every thing we had believed of him; but how he will come out of his present trial remains to be seen. that the sufferings[2] which France had inflicted on other countries justified severe reprisals, cannot be questioned. but I have not yet learned what crimes of Poland, Saxony Belgium, Venice, Lombardy and Genoa had merited for the[m] not merely a temporary punishment but that of permanent subjugati[on] & a destitution of independance and self government. the fable of Aesop of the lion dividing the spoils is I fear[3] becoming true history, an[d] the moral code of Napoleon and the English government, a substitute for that of Grotius, of Puffendorf, and even of the pure doctri[ne] of the great author of our own religion. we were safe ourselves from Bonaparte because he had not the British fleets at his command. we were safe from the British fleets, because they had Bonaparte at their back. but the British fleets and the conquerors of Bonapar[te] being now combined, and the Hartford nation drawn off to them we have uncommon reason to look to our own affairs. this however I leave to others, offering prayers to heaven[4] the only contribution of old age, for the safety of our country. be so good as to present me affectionately to mrs Logan, and to accept yourself the assurance of my esteem and respect.

Th: Jefferson

PoC (DLC); on verso of reused address cover to TJ; mutilated at seal, with some missing text rewritten by TJ; edge trimmed; at foot of text: "Doct[r] Logan." Printed in Philadelphia *Poulson's American Daily Advertiser*, 2 May 1816.

In Aesop's fable of "The Lion's Share," the lion claims all four quarters of a stag captured during a hunt with the fox, the jackal, and the wolf. The SPOILS of Eu-rope were divided at the Congress of Vienna by the principal allied powers: Austria, Great Britain, Prussia, and Russia (Connelly, *Napoleonic France*, 486–8).

[1] Reworked from "6. or 7."
[2] Word interlined in place of "injuries."
[3] Preceding two words interlined.
[4] Preceding two words interlined in place of a comma.

To James Mease

Dear Sir   Monticello Oct. 15. 15

I am sorry it is not in my power to give you descriptions of the medals mentioned in your letter of the 1st instant. those to Col° Washington, Fleury, & Paul Jones were made under the direction of Col° Humphreys, and according to devices which he obtained. he can probably give you the descriptions you desire. duplicates of all these medals were struck for Gen[l] Washington in silver, and delivered to him by myself, & they must now be in the possession of his representatives. there was a medal struck under the direction of Dr Franklin on the alliance with France. those you suppose to have been struck on the declaration of Independance and the capture of André, I never saw nor heard of, and unless your information be certain, I would express my belief that none such were ever struck <u>by public authority</u>. the journals of the old Congress however would settle this, as every medal voted by them is there entered. Accept the assurance of my great respect & esteem.

Th: Jefferson

RC (PPAmP: Thomas Jefferson Papers); addressed: "Doct[r] James Maese Philadelphia"; franked; postmarked Milton, 18 Oct.; endorsed by Mease. PoC (DLC); on verso of a reused address cover from John George Baxter to TJ; endorsed by TJ.

George W. Erving presented TJ with restrikes of the medals honoring Colonel William WASHINGTON, John PAUL JONES, and others in 1823 (TJ to Erving, 12 Apr. 1823; Stein, *Worlds*, 245–7). While in France, TJ oversaw the production of some commemorative medals, and on arriving in New York in 1790 he DE-LIVERED a set to George Washington (*PTJ*, 16:53–79). Benjamin FRANKLIN began designing the Libertas Americana medal in 1782 and commissioned it the following year to celebrate the American alliance with France (Franklin, *Papers*, 36:lviii–lix, 644; Mease, "Description of some of the Medals, Struck in relation to Important Events in North America, before and since the Declaration of Independence by the United States," in Massachusetts Historical Society, *Collections*, 3d ser., 4 [1834]: 307). On 3 Nov. 1780 the Continental Congress resolved that New York militiamen John Paulding, David Williams, and Isaac Van Wart should receive silver medals for their role in the capture of Major John ANDRÉ, a British spy (Worthington C. Ford and others, eds., *Journals of the Continental Congress, 1774–1789* [1904–37], 18:1009–10; Mease, "Description of some of the Medals," 303–5).

To Charles Yancey

DEAR SIR   Monticello Oct. 15. 15.

A long absence from home must apologise for this late acknolegement of your favor of Sep. 26.—I was desired by the late mr Peter Carr and some of the Commissioners for the academy proposed to be established in Albemarle to furnish them with a plan for the institution. I accordingly communicated to them the best I could devise, after an enquiry of many years into the nature of similar establishments, and forming from the whole what I thought adapted to our situation. I also prepared a petition for them to the general assembly and the form of such an act as I thought should be past. these papers I gave to mr Carr, and have never seen them since, nor do I know in whose hands they are. indeed I had apprehended that the proposition was not attended to since his death, until I saw an advertisement that a petition would be presented to the assembly to authorize the purchase of a house for it in Charlottesville. [If] this has been authorised by the board of Commissioners, it is more [th]an I know; and if not authorised by them it is a predetermination of a question which in my judgment decides for ever the fate of the institution.—Capt Joseph Miller, a resident of Norfolk, but who has staid a good deal in this county, and with me particularly, & who I believe is known to you, will have a petition before the assembly for carrying into effect the will of his brother, which we hope will meet with your patronage. Accept the assurance of my esteem and respect.   TH: JEFFERSON

PoC (DLC); on verso of a reused address cover from Joseph Milligan to TJ; torn at seal; at foot of text: "Col° Charles Yancey"; endorsed by TJ.

TJ included his PLAN for the Albemarle Academy in a 7 Sept. 1814 letter to Peter Carr. For the petition he PREPARED, see Minutes of the Albemarle Academy Board of Trustees, 25 Mar. 1814, with editorial headnote on The Founding of the University of Virginia:

Albemarle Academy, 1803–1816. His draft of AN ACT is printed above at 18 Nov. 1814.

An ADVERTISMENT in the Richmond *Enquirer*, 19 Aug. 1815, gave notice that a petition would be presented to the Virginia General Assembly requesting a law authorizing Triplett T. Estes to hold a lottery and dedicate its proceeds to the purchase of his own house and lot in Charlottesville for use as an academy. Joseph Miller's BROTHER was Thomas Reed.

From Mary Blair Andrews

Wilton Octr 16th 1815

Your Favor Sir of the 15th Ul^t has follow'd me to this place—most gratefully do I feel my Obligation to you, for the Trouble you have taken on my Behalf My Father's Estate in Albemarle was the only part of his property that he attempted to gaurd for the use of his own offspring, of which I am unhappily sole Survivor—the possibility of my being so, never occur'd to him, for he left two infant Grandsons by my Sister; one of them lived only a few months after his Grandfather & Mother's Death; the other just compleated his 16th year, & in the time twined round my Heart; for I beheld in him every Quality to form him a virtuous Representative of his Grandfather. This fair Hope was[1] suddenly cut down & withered: sharer in woe with his Father I determined he should share with me in this Estate (for himself had suggested what had never before enterd my Head) that it would be mine did I survive my Nephew; I soon however found he had got other Ideas of the Succession; yet, I wishing to slip from Life as I had lived, without Contention, I satisfied myself with bequeathing this property to a near Relation of my Father's, but from this peacefull System I was drawn by Mr Henderson's declaring himself Heir to th[e] whole at my Death:—I then consulted Mr Wickham, he, I found, had previously been consulted by Mr Henderson but he sent me the Opinion he had given him, "that Mr Henderson was entitled to one half, of the Estate now, as Heir to his Son, & at my Death to half of the Negros, & a fourth of the Land of the part I posses"[2]— [a]nother Gentleman eminent in Law was of Opinion that M^r H: was Heir to one half of the Estate on ye Death of his Son, & on mine, to a third of the property I posses & several other Opinions given on the Case, by Gentlemen of the Law, were more various; but it was lately suggested to me by a Freind of my Father's, who look'd at his will, that as his Grandchildren by either Daughter, were to be equal Sharers in the Estate, he thought till my Death no determined proportion c^d belong in Fee to my Sister's Children—This induced the

Application to you, on whose Opinion I could rely; but I Trespass again on your time, by thus accounting for the Trouble I have already ventured to give you—tho' I must see those posses the Inheritance of my Father, who have not a drop of his Blood in their Veins, & who are already enrich'd by his Bounty, far beyond what his Daughter posseses, the Sentiments of your Esteem & Affection to his memory, & the Kindness you have shewn me Sir on his Account is highly gratifying to me

Your obliged Serv & Friend   MARY BLAIR ANDREWS

RC (MHi); edge chipped and trimmed; endorsed by TJ as received 24 Oct. 1815 and so recorded in SJL. RC (DLC); address cover only; with PoC of TJ to James Madison, 22 Dec. 1815, on verso; addressed: "Tho⁹ Jefferson Esq' Monticello near Charlottesville"; stamp canceled; franked; postmarked Charlottesville, 22 Oct.

Jane Blair Henderson's TWO INFANT sons were Blair Munro Henderson (1800–01) and Thomas Hamilton Henderson (1798–1814) (gravestones in Bruton Parish Cemetery, Williamsburg). Their father, James Henderson, who had declared HIMSELF HEIR to a portion of John Blair's estate, died in 1818. In his will he left his interest in the Blair estate to his three children by his second wife. The dispute remained unsettled at Andrews's death in 1820. In her will she disposed of the estate according to her understanding of her father's will, stating that "Mʳ Henderson kept possession of half the estate after the death of his son, and has left the whole to his son James by another wife on my death, as I am so ad-

vanced in life, I have forborne to contest his asumed rights, but I leave all my right in that estate either as heir to my Father, or by his will to said John Blair Peachy and his heirs." Andrews further stipulated that if it be found "that I had a right to the whole during my life from the death of Thomas, Mʳ Henderson's heirs will have to refund to my estate the proffits of half the estate during that time which if recovered I leave to Doctor Thomas Griffin Peachy" (will in Vi: RG 12, Wills from the Treasurer's Office). A chancery court eventually found that John Blair Peachy was "entitled to one moiety of the real estate in question, and to one fourth part of the slaves and other personal estate." It called for "accounts of the slaves and their increase, and of the profits of the whole subject accrued since Mrs. Andrews's death." The chancery decision was upheld in 1831 on appeal by James Henderson's executors (*Va. Reports*, 74 [33 Grattan]: 557–62).

¹ Reworked from "These Hopes were."
² Editorially corrected from closing single quotation mark.

To Albert Gallatin

DEAR SIR   Monticello Oct. 16. 15.

A long absence from home must apologize for my so late acknolegement of your welcome favor of Sep. 6. our storm of the 4ᵗʰ of that month gave me great uneasiness for you; for I was certain you must be on the coast, and your actual arrival was unknown to me. it was such a wind as I have not witnessed since the year 1769. it did however little damage with us, only prostrating our corn, and tearing tobacco, without essential injury to either. it could have been nothing compared with that of the 23ᵈ on the coast of N. England, of which we had not a breath, but on the contrary, fine, fair weather. is this the judgment of god between us?   I congratulate you sincerely on your safe return to your own country, and, without knowing your own wishes, mine are that you would never leave it again. I know you would be useful to us at Paris: and so you would any where; but no where so useful as here. we are undone, my dear Sir, if this banking mania be not suppressed. aut Carthago, aut Roma delenda est. the war, had it proceeded, would have upset our government: and a new one, whenever tried, will do it. and so it must be while our money, the nerve of war, is much or little, real, or imaginary, as our bitterest enemies chuse to make it. put down the banks, and if this country could not be carried thro' the longest war against her most powerful enemy, without ever knowing the want of a dollar, without dependance on the traitorous classes of her citizens, without bearing hard on the resources of the people, or loading the public with an indefinite burthen of debt, I know nothing of my countrymen. not by any novel project, not by any charlatanerie, but by ordinary and well experienced means; by the total prohibition of all private paper at all times, by reasonable taxes in war aided by the necessary emissions of public paper of circulating size, this bottomed on special taxes, redeemable annually as this special tax comes in, & finally within a moderate period. even with the flood of private paper by which we were deluged, would the treasury have ventured it's credit in bills of circulating size, as of 5. or 10.D. Eᵗc. they would have been greedily recieved by the people in preference to bank paper. but unhappily the towns of America were considered as the nation of America, the dispositions of the inhabitants of the former as those of the latter, and the treasury for want of confidence in the country delivered itself bound hand and foot to bold and bankrupt adventurers & pretenders to be money holders, whom it could have crushed at any moment. even the late half-bold, half-timid threat of the treasury shewed at once that these jugglers were at the feet of the government. for it never was, and is not, any confidence in their frothy bubbles, but the want of all other medium, which induced, or now induces the <u>country</u> people to take their paper. and at this moment, when nothing else is to be had, no man will recieve it but to pass it away instantly; none for distant purposes. we are now without any common measure of the value of property, and private fortunes are up or down at the will of the worst of our citizens. yet there is no hope of relief from the legislatures who have immediate controul over this subject. as little seems to be known of the principles of political economy as if nothing had ever been written or practised on the subject, or as was known in old times, when the Jews had their rulers under the hammer. it is an evil therefore which we must make up our minds to meet and to endure as those of hurricanes, earthquakes and other casualties. let us turn over therefore another leaf.[1]

I grieve for France: altho' it cannot be denied that by the afflictions with which she so wantonly and wickedly overwhelmed other[2] nations, she has merited severe reprisals. for it is no excuse to lay these enormities on the wretch who led to them, and who has been the author of more misery & suffering to the world than any being who ever lived before him. after destroying the liberties of his country, he has exhausted all it's resources, physical and moral, to indulge his own maniac ambition, his own tyrannical and overbearing spirit. his sufferings cannot be too great. but theirs I sincerely deplore. and what is to be their term? the will of the allies? there is no more moderation, forbearance, or even honesty in theirs than in that of Bonaparte. they have proved that their object, like his, is plunder. they, like him, are shuffling nations together, or into their own hands, as if all were right which they feel a power to do. in the exhausted state in which Bonaparte has left France I see no period to her sufferings until this combination of robbers fall together by the ears. the French may then rise up and chuse their side. and I trust they will finally establish for themselves a government of rational and well tempered liberty. so much science cannot be lost; so much light shed over them can never fail to produce to them some good, in the end. till then we may ourselves fervently pray, with the liturgy a little parodied, 'give peace till that time, oh lord, because there is none other that will fight for us but only they, oh God.'—it is rare that I indulge myself in these political effusions: but your former and latter relations with both subjects have associated you with them in my mind, and led me beyond the limits of attention I ordinarily give to them. whether you go, or stay with us, you have always the prayers of your's affectionately

TH: JEFFERSON

P.S. the two letters you inclosed me were from Warden & De Lormerie, and neither from La Fayette as you supposed.

RC (NHi: Gallatin Papers); addressed: "Albert Gallatin New York"; franked; postmarked Milton, 18 Oct.; with additional unrelated calculations on address leaf in an unidentified hand. PoC (DLC). Tr (MHi); incomplete, consisting of final page; posthumous copy.

On 8 Sept. 1769 a hurricane passed near Williamsburg and caused much destruction throughout the Chesapeake Bay area. The major hurricane that struck on THE 23ᴰ Sept. 1815 was the so-called "Great September Gale" that made landfall at Long Island and continued through New England (David M. Ludlum, *Early American Hurricanes, 1492–1870* [1963], 24–5, 77–81). AUT CARTHAGO, AUT ROMA DELENDA EST ("either Carthage or Rome must be destroyed") echoes Roman senator Marcus Cato's supposed statement that Carthage must be destroyed (see note to TJ to John Wayles Eppes, 11 Sept. 1813). The treasury notes authorized by Congress in February 1815 constituted a THREAT to the dominance of privately issued paper money because they were small enough to circulate (Donald H. Kagin, "Monetary Aspects of the Treasury Notes of the War of 1812,"

Journal of Economic History 44 [1984]: 81–3, 86; *JHR*, 9:723 [11 Feb. 1815]; *JS*, 5:657, 661, 665 [21, 22, 24 Feb. 1815]).

To FALL TOGETHER BY THE EARS is to fight or scuffle (John Walker, *A Critical Pronouncing Dictionary, and Expositor of the English Language*, 3d American ed. [New York, 1807; for a different ed. see Sowerby, no. 4876], 269). The LITURGY correctly reads "Give peace in our time, O Lord"; "Because there is none other that fighteth for us, but only thou, O God" (*The Book of Common-Prayer* [London, 1662; Sowerby, no. 1507], unpaginated section on "The order for Evening Prayer daily throughout the year").

¹ Page 2 ends short at this point.
² Tr begins here, with some textual loss in first line due to chipped edge.

From John Manesca and Victor Value

MONSIEUR,   Philadⁱᵉ 16 Octobre 1815.
Nous avons cru que l'offrande de cette modeste production de notre plume, le premier ouvrage de ce genre publié, en français, dans les Etats-Unis, ne Serait pas dédaignée par le Philantrope, ami des lettres.
Nous avons l'honneur d'être,
Monsieur, avec la plus parfaite considération, Vos très humbles Serviteurs,   J. MANESCA & V. VALUE

EDITORS' TRANSLATION

SIR,   Philadelphia 16 October 1815.
We thought that the offering of this modest production of our pen, the first work of this kind published in French in the United States, would not be disregarded by the Philanthropist, friend of the humanities.
We have the honor to be,
Sir, with the most perfect respect, your very humble servants,
J. MANESCA & V. VALUE

RC (MoSHi: TJC-BC); in an unidentified hand; at foot of text: "The Honᵇˡᵉ Thomas Jefferson Esqʳ Monticello"; endorsed by TJ as received 25 Oct. 1815 and so recorded in SJL. Translation by Dr. Genevieve Moene. Enclosure: Manesca

and Value, *Historiettes Nouvelles, a l'Usage de la Jeunesse des Deux Sexes et des Ecoles* (Philadelphia, 1815).

John Manesca (d. 1838), teacher, translator, and author, immigrated to the

United States from Saint Domingue. From at least 1816 until his death he taught French in New York City. Manesca created an oral method of language instruction and authored works on that subject as well as on phrenology. In 1837 he was a founder of a New York society that promoted the beliefs of the French utopian philosopher Charles Fourier in the United States (Louis Manesca, *The Serial and Oral Method of Teaching Languages; Adapted to the French* [1856], xxii–xxiv; *New-York Evening Post*, 23 Oct. 1816; *Longworth's New York Directory* [1817]: 300; [1819]: 269; [1838]: 427; DNA: RG 29, CS, N.Y., New York, 1820; Carl J. Guarneri, *The Utopian Alternative: Fourierism in Nineteenth-Century America* [1991], 31–2; New York *Evening Post*, 3 Sept. 1838; New York *Morning Herald*, 4 Sept. 1838).

Victor Value (ca. 1792–ca. 1859), teacher and author, was a native of Saint Domingue who studied at the Collège de Sorèze in France. By 1819 he was teaching French in Mantua, near Philadelphia, and in the 1820s he served as principal of the Mantua Academy. Value continued to teach and administer schools at various locations in Philadelphia for the remainder of his life. He wrote books on mathematics and on language education, and in 1835 he was elected a curator of the newly formed Pennsylvania Lyceum of Teachers. In 1844–45 Value was a teacher of French at the University of Pennsylvania. He was living in Philadelphia at the time of his death (Nicholas B. Wainwright, "The Diary of Samuel Breck, 1814–1822," *PMHB* 102 [1978]: 503; Phyllis Kihn, "The Value Family in Connecticut," *Connecticut Historical Society Bulletin* 34, no. 3 [1969]: 79–93; John Adems Paxton, *The Philadelphia Directory and Register, for 1819* [Philadelphia, 1819]; New York *National Advocate*, 30 Apr. 1823; DNA: RG 29, CS, Pa., Philadelphia, 1830–50; Charles H. Pennypacker, *History of Downington, Chester County, Pa.* [1909], 56, 58–9; *Catalogue of the Trustees, Officers, & Students of the University of Pennsylvania. 1844–45* [1845], 7; *McElroy's Philadelphia City Directory* [1859]: 726; [1860]: 1014).

From J. Sheaff (for Henry Sheaff)

SIR   Philad^a October 16^t 1815

Yours of the 11^t August I duly received, and untill this day it was not in my Power to answer it owing to indisposition, I have retir'd from all kinds of Business, I can procure you a Quarter Cask of Sherry Wine the price will be $2.75 Per Gallon And Lisbon 2.50 & 2.60 of a Superior Quality if that will answer by letting me know I will Send you a Quarter Cask. I have had a Pareletic stroke which has deprived me of the use of my right side Entirely

I remain sincerly Your friend   for HENRY SHEAFF

J, SHEAFF

RC (MHi); in J. Sheaff's hand; at foot of text: "Thomas Jefferson Esqr"; endorsed by TJ as a letter from Henry Sheaff received 25 Oct. 1815 and so recorded in SJL.

To Patrick Gibson

Dear Sir   Monticello Oct. 17. 15.

I wrote you from Bedford on the 29th of Sep. and again on the 6th inst. on my arrival here. since that date 35. barrels of flour have been shipped from my mill on my account by T. M. & T. E. Randolph's for rent, being instead of so much of 55. Bar. formerly shipped for me, but their destination changed as noted in a former letter. in my last I requested to hear from you on the discount of the additional 1000.D. I asked of the bank. I am anxious on this subject because I shall have to draw on you about the close of this month for 309.82 D in favor of the sheriff of Albemarle for my taxes in that county, the discharge of some overseers also in order to get my affairs into better hands subjects me to an immediate & unexpected payment of their wages, not otherwise due till the spring; to which will be added some other urgent calls which will absorb the additional thousand dollars. [sh]ould it be necessary you will at your discretion sell the 35. Barels [o]f flour for what ever they will bring. I will have my tobacco sent down as soon as it can be prepared because I know no reason to expect higher prices than are going. as to the year's crop of flour I shall only aim to get that down in Dec. & January, believing that the present state of things in Europe, and what may be expected for some time to come give a prospect of a good demand for that market, which may not be felt however till the spring. hoping to hear from you in relief of my anxieties on the subject of the additional discount I salute you with friendship & respect.   Th: Jefferson

PoC (DLC: TJ Papers, ser. 10); on verso of reused address cover of Mathew Carey to TJ, 4 Oct. 1815; mutilated at seal; at foot of text: "Mr Gibson"; endorsed by TJ.

On 30 Nov. 1815 TJ made a payment of $50 to his discharged overseer Jeremiah A. Goodman, and he also assumed a $78.35 debt owed by Goodman. TJ made final payments totaling $180.96 to the other recently dismissed overseer, Nimrod Darnil, in May 1816 and April 1817 (MB, 2:1316, 1323, 1332). On 26 Oct. 1815 TJ recorded drawing on Gibson & Jefferson for $309.82 to pay Albemarle County sheriff Clifton Harris for "taxes, levies & tickets now due" (MB, 2:1315). This sum included $203.23 assessed on TJ's personal property, largely following his Statement of Albemarle County Property Subject to State Tax, Mar. 1815, and $60.86 levied on TJ's Albemarle County landholdings, including 5,374¾ acres described as "Rivanna River & Buck Island" and 266⅔ acres held jointly and described as "Hardware River" (Vi: RG 48, Personal Property Tax Returns and Land Tax Returns, both Albemarle Co.).

From David M. Randolph

SIR, Richmond 17th October 1815

The ruin of my family and the consequent wretchedness of my declining years, produced by an exercise of arbitrary power in your hands, together with the active malignity of certain advocates of your infallibility, shoud have been born with consistent resignation, were it not that an unoffending hapless offspring are likely to be deprived of their only inheritance,—their fathers unsullied reputation. Hence Sir, I take leave, in the unfeigned spirit of affectionate regard for former recollections and family intimacies, to apprise you of my intention (in due season) to effect an issue between us through the medium of the public press. Mindful of the maxim "that no man's character is the better for handling"; and, at the same time, the exalted station you equivocally hold in the community, I am equally sensible, that monstruous fame like the monstruous mamoth, when tainted, will generate greater nausea than simple report, or, the putrescence of a Dormouse—And, however impervious to the shafts of Truth, you may conceive your party-panoply of fraud and faction to be, yet will I not shrink from any process of fact and reason, however tortuous, or doubt of a favorable issue to my purpose. Order upon this forced-occasion, is especially requisite to my conclusions. You therefore Sir, will be pleased to recall the factitious Scenes open'd by the Secretary of State to the Marshal of Virginia: the peculiar favour, and the insidious conversations advanced in August 1793, as well in your Cabinet, as at your Country residence: when from distinguished privileges granted the Marshal, and the fervid observations addressed to him, the most profound respect was converted into jealous indignation! When the Secretary of the Treasury, more particularly, furnished the fertile topics of the most unworthy animadversions: when characters of minor consideration, and, even the president too, were introduced as the prescious objects, on whom to lavish your illiberal innuendos, even to the excitement of congenial responses from the other four chosen members of your festive board on the banks of the Schiulkill. There it is Sir, I wou'd fain stimulate your reminiscence. And, whilst no one more truely laments the death of my personal and esteemed friend Dr Rush than myself, or, can be more indifferent to the fame of the deceased Governor of Tennessee, I wou'd, with every degree of justice to the honorable characters of Pierce Butler Esqur. (and, I believe) Colo. Thos Blount, challenge your appeal to their memories for the correctness of these few hints, to shew the source of those details, among others, which I shall hereafter unfold. And, believe me Sir, I woud "nothing extenuate, or set down aught in <u>malice</u>," in the progress of an odious task imposed on me as an indispensable duty.

I beg leave to assure you more over, that this communication will remain wholly unknown to others, until the final result of a similar Affair at Law, instituted for an equally necessary purpose.

I am Sir, with appropriate Sensibility,

Your Hum¹ Ser^t   D M RANDOLPH

RC (ViW: TC-JP); at foot of text: "Thomas Jefferson Esqr."; endorsed by TJ as received 24 Oct. 1815 and so recorded in SJL.

David Meade Randolph (ca. 1759–1830), planter, public official, and inventor, served in the American Revolution as captain of a Virginia regiment in 1777, and two years later he studied at the College of William and Mary. He married his cousin Mary Randolph, the sister of TJ's son-in-law Thomas Mann Randolph. They lived first at his James River plantation, Presqu'ile, and later in a house called Moldavia that they built in Richmond. At TJ's recommendation Randolph was appointed marshal of Virginia in 1791. Shortly after he became president in 1801, TJ removed Randolph from his post for jury packing. Randolph then became an outspoken Federalist and vocal critic of TJ. The loss of his position forced Randolph to sell his property. He attempted to repair the family fortunes by becoming a partner in a coal mine and patenting various inventions. By 1808 Randolph was living in England and seeking investors for his inventions while his wife ran a boardinghouse in Richmond. He returned to Richmond by 1815. TJ and Randolph ended their estrangement in 1823, when Randolph testified for TJ in a legal case. Randolph died at his son's home near Yorktown (Fillmore Norfleet, *Saint-Mémin in Virginia: Portraits and Biographies* [1942], 121, 201; Jonathan Daniels, *The Randolphs of Vir-*

ginia [1972]; *ANB*, 18:132–3; William G. Stanard, "Randolph Family," *WMQ*, 1st ser., 9 [1901]: 183, 250; *PTJ*, esp. 16:509, 22:189, 219–20, 33:260; Heitman, *Continental Army*, 458; *William and Mary Provisional List*, 33; *JEP*, 1:86, 88, 194–5, 325–6 [1, 7 Nov. 1791, 10, 15 Dec. 1795, 5, 6 Dec. 1799]; Martha Jefferson Randolph to TJ, 2 Jan. 1808 [ViU: TJP-ER]; *MB*, 2:1399, 1400; *Repertory of Arts, Manufactures, and Agriculture*, 2d ser., 16 [1810]: 193–207; 18 [1811]: 80–2; *List of Patents*, 154, 226; Thomas Mann Randolph to Peachy R. Gilmer, 30 May 1812 [Vi: Personal Papers Collection, Randolph Papers]; Washington *Daily National Intelligencer*, 14 Apr. 1820; *Richmond Enquirer*, 28 Sept. 1830; gravestone inscription in Bruton Parish Cemetery, Williamsburg).

As SECRETARY OF STATE and MARSHAL OF VIRGINIA respectively, TJ and Randolph were both in Philadelphia in August 1793 (*PTJ*, 26:617, 675). Randolph had been shocked by INSIDIOUS CONVERSATIONS he evidently heard at TJ's dinner table subjecting SECRETARY OF THE TREASURY Alexander Hamilton, PRESIDENT George Washington, and others to ILLIBERAL INNUENDOS. The OTHER FOUR he recalled as being at this meeting were Benjamin RUSH, GOVERNOR William Blount, Pierce BUTLER, and Thomas BLOUNT. NOTHING EXTENUATE, OR SET DOWN AUGHT IN MALICE comes from William Shakespeare, *Othello*, act 5, scene 2.

From John Martin Baker

Sir,   Malaga, october 18th 1815.

I have the Honor most Respectfully to address You, and hope You enjoy the Blessing of health.

I returned in March last to my Consulate, after my Recovery from very Serious illness, while in France, Our Trade has not as yet taken any course that way, very unfortunate for me, for the support of an amiable Wife, and five infant children: my family are at Montpellier, I left them all well thank Divine Providence on the ninth ultimo, and hope to see them soon again; I shall return to Tarragona in a few days.

I pray you Sir, to do myself and family the kindness to Represent to the President of the United States of America, our great sufferings during our late wars, owing to my peculiar situation in office, and entreat your goodness Sir, with the President of the United States, to be appointed Consul for Tripoly, in the event of said office becoming vacant: I pray your feeling consideration in my favor: permit me Sir, to say Tripoly, or any other consulate to afford me support for my family.—I have the Honor to remit by the American Schooner Murray of Charleston, Captain Miner,—bound for New york, to the care of the United States Collector at said port, a Small Box, addressed to you, containing Italian Garden seeds, flowers, and other seeds, selected at Mrs Bakers request for you, by M. Edward Caffarena, acting as Vice Consul at Genoa—I have also the Satisfaction to inclose a letter from Mr Mazzei of Pisa, at whose residence my family passed one day, when we were on our way to Paris: Mr Mazzei, is now very aged, and had great pleasure to renew his memory with the Honor and satisfaction he had in being well known to you: Mrs Baker had the pleasing satisfaction to discourse lengthy with M. Mazzei, on the Happiness of her beloved Country.—

Myself and family Sir pray for your Life, Health and Happiness.—
I have the Honor to be with the Highest Respect, and Gratitude—
Sir Your most humble obedient faithful Servant.

JOHN MARTIN BAKER

RC (MHi); at foot of text: "To The Most Honorable Thomas Jefferson. Monti-cello"; endorsed by TJ as received 13 Jan. 1816 and so recorded in SJL.

The COLLECTOR at New York was David Gelston. For the enclosed LETTER FROM MR MAZZEI, see note to Philip Mazzei to TJ, 24 Sept. 1814.

From Arsène Lacarrière Latour

S<small>IR</small>,   Philadelphia October the 18th 1815

Permit me to Enclose you the Prospectus of an historical Memoir of the War in West florida and Louisiana, which I have written and which is now in the Press—

I have the honor to be with great respect,

Sir,

Your most obedient and Most humble Servant

A. L<small>ACARRIERE</small> L<small>ATOUR</small>

RC (MoSHi: TJC-BC); at foot of text: "Thomas Jefferson Esqre late president of the United States"; endorsed by TJ as received 25 Oct. 1815 and so recorded in SJL. Enclosure: *Proposals, for Publishing by Subscription, The History of the War in Louisiana & West Florida*; describing the author as the "principal engineer in the late seventh military district," whose book has been translated by Henry P. Nugent; summarizing the work as comprising "every event of importance" that occurred in Louisiana and West Florida from 1 Sept. 1814 to the close of the War of 1812; describing each of the nine plates, consisting of a portrait of Andrew Jackson and maps and diagrams of military actions, to be included in the quarto atlas accompanying the single octavo volume of the work; advertising a price of $5 for subscribers and $6 for nonsubscribers; and concluding with a blank subscription list (undated broadside in MoSHi: TJC-BC).

Géraud Calixte Jean Baptiste Arsène Lacarrière Latour (1778–1837), architect and engineer, was born in Aurillac, France, where he apprenticed with a local architect beginning in 1799. He continued his studies in architecture and engineering at the Académie des Beaux Arts in Paris in 1801. The following year Latour departed for Saint Domingue in an unsuccessful attempt to lay claim to property that was part of his wife's dowry. He served briefly in the French army's Corps

of Engineers before fleeing from Saint Domingue to the United States by 1804. The following year Latour was in New York City, working first as a trader and then as an architect. Early in 1806 he was in Louisiana, where he created a plan for the city of Baton Rouge, worked as a surveyor, and eventually started an architecture firm in New Orleans. In 1812 Latour became a United States citizen. After his business failed in 1813, he became a military engineer for Andrew Jackson in 1814 and made important contributions to the American victory at the Battle of New Orleans. Latour embarked with Jean Lafitte on a surveying and mapping expedition of the Southwest in 1816 as an agent of Spain, but he turned down an offer to serve as Spanish consul at New Orleans. From 1818 to 1834 he worked as an architect in Havana. Latour subsequently returned to France, where he died (Latour, *Historical Memoir of the War in West Florida and Louisiana in 1814–15. With an Atlas. Expanded Edition*, ed. Gene A. Smith [1999], ix–xlii; George W. Cullum, *Campaigns of the War of 1812–15 . . . with Brief Biographies of the American Engineers* [1879], 309–41; LNHiC: Latour Archive; *New-York Evening Post*, 8 Aug. 1805; *Hispanic American Historical Review* 18 [1938]: 221–7; Thomas L. Hodges and Charlotte Hodges, "Jean Lafitte and Major L. Latour in Arkansas Territory," *Arkansas Historical Quarterly* 7 [1948]: 237–56; Jackson, *Papers*, vol. 3).

From Noah Worcester

Sir,   Brighton Octo. 18. 1815

Although a stranger to you I take the liberty of addressing you on a subject deeply interesting to humanity. I am encouraged to do this by a recollection of some things in your state papers which I then regarded as indications that you had become convinced of the impolicy of war, and that you wished to avoid a rupture with foreign nations.

Near the close of the late war, I was some how excited to examine the subject of war in general; and I became fully convinced that the custom of settling national disputes by war, is perfectly needless, unjust and inhuman, as well as antichristian; and that the custom is supported by delusion and a barbarous fanaticism. Under these impressions and convictions, I have published three pamphlets on the subject—a copy of each I send with this, soliciting you to accept and peruse them.

Having some knowledge of your advanced age, your talents and your weight of character, I am desirous that you should attend to the subject of the pamphlets according to their importance, and that you should favor me with the result of your reflexions, that if your opinion shall accord with mine, your testimony may be employed for the good of our country and the peace of the world.

Near the close of the 2nd No.[1] you may find some encouraging facts.

As you may wish to know more of the stranger who addresses you with so much freedom, I will say, that[2] I have been employed for 25 years in the work of the ministry in the state of New-Hampshire. Upwards of two years I have been in the vicinity of Boston, employed as Editor of a periodical work called the Christian Disciple. A principle object of the work is to cultivate friendly affections Among the various sects of Christians, and to promote peace and harmony.[3]

Should I meet with encouragement, the Friend of Peace will be continued quarterly. Any information or hints which you may give in favor of the glorious object, will be gratefully accepted by Your

Sincere friend   Noah Worcester—

P.S Dec. 23d—I have delayed sending till a 3d No of the Friend of Peace is published, which I also send for your perusal.

RC (DLC); between signature and postscript: "Honble T. Jefferson Esq."; endorsed by TJ as received 27 Jan. 1816 and so recorded in SJL. Dft (MHi: Worcester Papers); containing emenda- tions during composition and additional markings connected to subsequent publication, with place of composition, one paragraph as noted below, signature, and postscript circled and omitted in published version; endorsed by Worcester: "Copy of a Letter to T. Jefferson." Printed in Worcester, *The Friend of Peace, No. IV. reasons for believing that efforts for the abolition of war will not be in vain* (Cambridge, Mass., [1816]; Poor, *Jefferson's Library*, 9 [no. 488]), 21–2. Enclosures: (1) Worcester, *A Solemn Review of the Custom of War* (Cambridge, 1815). (2) Worcester, *The Friend of Peace: containing a Special Interview* (Cambridge, 1815). (3) Worcester, *The Friend of Peace, No. II. containing a review of the arguments of Lord Kames in favor of war* (Cambridge, 1815). (4) Worcester, *The Friend of Peace. No. III. The Horrors of Napoleon's Campaign in Russia* (Cambridge, 1815). Enclosures 2–4 in Poor, *Jefferson's Library*, 9 (no. 488).

Noah Worcester (1758–1837), clergyman and peace advocate, was a native of Hollis, New Hampshire. He served as a fifer during the American Revolution and taught and farmed in Thornton, Grafton County, New Hampshire. He became a Congregational minister there in 1786. Worcester also was an agent of the New Hampshire Missionary Society, 1802–10, before leaving Thornton to serve as a minister in Salisbury, in what was then Hillsborough County, New Hampshire, 1810–13. After publishing several tracts on his changing view of the Trinity, he split with the Congregational Church and moved in 1813 to Brighton, Massachusetts (later annexed by Boston), to edit the Unitarian *Christian Disciple*. The War of 1812 inspired Worcester to take up the cause of peace, and in 1815 he became a founder of the Massachusetts Peace Society and the editor of the society's serial publication, the *Friend of Peace*. He retired in 1828 but continued writing. Worcester died in Brighton (*ANB*; *DAB*; Henry Ware, *Memoirs of the Rev. Noah Worcester, D.D.* [1844]; Sprague, *American Pulpit*, 8:191–9; Boston *Atlas*, 3 Nov. 1837; *Christian Register and Boston Observer*, 16 Dec. 1837).

On pp. 37–40 of the second number of his *Friend of Peace*, Worcester published ENCOURAGING FACTS on the increasing numbers of peace-promoting sects and organizations in Great Britain and the United States.

[1] Dft and *Friend of Peace, No. IV*, here add "of The Friend of Peace."

[2] In Dft Worcester here canceled "I was a soldier two campaigns in the revolutionary war."

[3] Paragraph circled in Dft, with marginal note by Worcester: "This paragraph to be omitted." Paragraph not in *Friend of Peace, No. IV*.

Account with William Ballard

[ca. 20 Oct. 1815]

Wm Ballard in account with Th: Jefferson

	D
1815. Aug. 16. To cash of Th:J.	100.
Oct. 5. To order favor E. Bacon	16.50
To cash from Th: J. Randolph	50.
20. To d°	200
Cr.	
1814. By service for this year 1814. £65	216.67
By a lock 1.50 D by 17. turkies 8.5 D	10.
By service for this year 1815	216.66
	443.33

MS (MHi); entirely in TJ's hand; undated; subjoined to MS of Agreement with William Ballard, 18 July 1813.

In addition to the $200 that Thomas Jefferson RANDOLPH paid Ballard on 20 Oct. on TJ's behalf, between then and 28 Oct. 1815 Randolph paid Ballard the $76.83 still due to him. TJ reimbursed Randolph for his payments to Ballard on the latter date (*MB*, 2:1315).

To Patrick Gibson

DEAR SIR   Monticello. Oct. 20. 15

Our late letters have happened to cross one another by the way, the messenger which carried mine of the 17ᵗʰ to the Post office having brought on his return yours of the 10ᵗʰ. I regret much the accident which prevented my note for the bank being in time for the term of renewal, and am very thankful for your having supplied it with your own. this shall not happen again. the object of the present is to mention that my affairs in Bedford call me urgently there, but I cannot go until I know that I may safely draw for my taxes and other demands for which the additional thousand dollars were asked from the bank, as stated in my last letter. if this is effected, be so good as to inform me by return of mail, and state at the same time the date of the note that I may know to provide in time for renewals. Accept my friendly and respectful salutations.   TH: JEFFERSON

PoC (Mrs. T. Wilber Chelf, Mrs. Virginius Dabney, and Mrs. Alexander W. Parker, Richmond, 1944; photocopy in ViU: TJP); on verso of reused address cover of Nicolas G. Dufief to TJ, 25 Aug. 1815; at foot of text: "Mʳ Gibson."

Gibson's letter OF THE 10ᵀʰ, not found, is recorded in SJL as received 17 Oct. from Richmond.

To Thomas Ritchie

Monticello Oct. 20. 15.

Th: Jefferson asks the favor of mr Ritchie to insert in his paper the underwritten Notice as often as the rules of the assembly require it to be done; and to place the cost in Th:J's account for newspapers which mr Ritchie recieves at such epochs as he pleases from mr Gibson. it is on behalf of a friend who is not in the way to have it done for himself. he salutes mr Ritchie with constant friendship and respect.

Notice is hereby given that a petition will be presented to the General assembly at their ensuing session for authority to have carried into execution the last will and testament of Thomas Reed, late of the borough of Norfolk relative to the disposal of his property in that borough and elsewhere.

PoC (MHi); on verso of reused address cover of Tristram Dalton to TJ, 21 Aug. 1815; dateline beneath closing; endorsed by TJ.

The NOTICE ran in the *Richmond Enquirer* between 4 Nov. and 5 Dec. 1815. The FRIEND was Joseph Miller.

From Richard Rush

Washington October 20. 1815.

R. Rush presents his compliments to Mr Jefferson, and begs he will do him the honor to accept the little pamphlet herewith sent.

RC (MHi); dateline at foot of text; addressed: "Mr Jefferson"; endorsed by TJ as received 25 Oct. 1815 and so recorded in SJL. Enclosure: Rush, *American Jurisprudence, written and published at*

Washington, being a few reflections suggested on reading "Wheaton on Captures" (Washington, 1815; Poor, *Jefferson's Library*, 10 [no. 593]).

To George Watterston

Monticello Oct. 20. 15.

I thank you, Sir, for the paper you have been so kind as to return me from Bezout. it was nothing more than an exemplification of the process prescribed in his book. the other leaf or leaves inserted therein are not desired. they were inserted as a supplement to his spherical trigonometry, because he omits (as nearly all French Mathematicians do) Ld Napier's[1] catholic canon, which is of great value, as supplying the many rules in that branch by a single one, easily retained in the memory. I inserted the same in Potter's mathematics, because he has given Ld Napier's canon unintelligibly & incorrectly.

With respect to the 3. vols of Virginia laws, 2 of them are in my own possession, but at a distant place from which no conveyance has yet occurred; but there will be one about the last of next month. the other is a MS. volume of laws never yet printed. mr Hening had borrowed it, being the only copy now existing. he is engaged in having the inedited acts in it printed, and as soon as that is done, it will be forwarded to you. Accept the assurance of my esteem and respect.

TH: JEFFERSON

RC (NN: T. H. Morrell Collection); at foot of text: "Mʳ George Watterston." PoC (DLC); on verso of reused address cover to TJ, postmarked Philadelphia; endorsed by TJ; with foot of recto containing an unrelated salutation, dateline, and internal address of a letter to James Lloyd dated Philadelphia, 22 Aug. 1815, in an unidentified hand.

For the MS. VOLUME OF LAWS NEVER YET PRINTED, see TJ to Watterston, 7 May 1815, and note. INEDITED: "unpublished" (*OED*).

[1] Manuscript: "Nepier's."

To Louis H. Girardin

DEAR SIR   Monticello Oct. 21. 15.

Your favor of the 7ᵗʰ has been recieved, and I now send you the letter of mr Page which you requested, and will subjoin to this letter the comparative view of some of Longman's prices with what Congress paid me for the same books. Longman's book itself shall go by the same mail—I thank you for your attention to the Microscope. it was well repaired and safely recieved. to your Weekly remembrancer I shall gladly become a subscriber; but I know of nobody here who is likely to contribute any aid of essays Eᵗc. we have good neighbors, but not scientific. I parted, on the Natural bridge, a month ago with mr Correa and F. Gilmer, in good health. they set out on a tour through Tenissee, Georgia Eᵗc and were doubtful whether they would return to Philadelphia by sea or land. the state of France is really deplorable, and I do not see what will be it's term. that it will have one is certain, and a bloody one to be feared. if they can bear with their sufferings until the allies withdraw and disband their armies, it will be wise. every day of their continuance in France extends the circle of irritation till it will comprehend every individual, and woe be to Louis for whom all this is supposed to be done. they will rise in their strength, find a Sᵗ Helena for him, and establish a government of rational liberty. so much science, and so much experience cannot be lost. I salute you with great friendship and respect

TH: JEFFERSON

		London prices		prices paid by Congress for the same book in Dollars
		in Sterlᵍ money	in Dollars	
		£ s d		
Catesby's Nat. hist.	2. v. folio	26– 0–0	115.44	20.
Suidas	3. v. folio	21– 0–0	93.24	30.
Dugdale's Monasticon	3. v. folio	42– 0–0	186.48	30.

Dugdale's Baronage	2. v. fol.	21– 0–0	93.24	20.
Hakluyt's voyages	3. v. fol.	31–10–0	139.86	30.
Horseley's Britannia.	1. v. fol	15–15–0	70.	10.
Rapin with Tindal's continuation	7. v. fol.	150– 0–0	666.	70.
Milton's works	3. v. fol	18–18–0	84.	30.
Johnson's Dictionary	2. v. fol.	8– 8–0	37.30	12.
Polybius Gr. Lat.	3. v. 8ᵛᵒ	4– 4–0	18.64	9.
Dionysius Halicarn. Reiskii.	6. v. 8ᵛᵒ	5–10–0	24.42	18.
Clarendon's history	6. v. 8ᵛᵒ	5– 5–0	23.31	18.
		349–10–0	1552.00[1]	297

RC (PPAmP: Thomas Jefferson Papers); postscript on verso; addressed: "Mʳ L. H. Girardin Richmond"; franked; postmarked Milton, 22 Oct.

Girardin's FAVOR OF THE 7ᵀᴴ, not found, is recorded in SJL as received 17 Oct. 1815 from Richmond. The enclosed LETTER OF MR PAGE may have been John Page to TJ, 11 Nov. 1775, describing skirmishes between British and colonial forces in Norfolk and Hampton late in

October 1775 (*PTJ*, 1:256–9). LONG-MAN'S BOOK was *A General Catalogue of Valuable and Rare Old Books, in the Ancient and Modern Languages, and Various Classes of Literature; which are now on sale at the prices affixed to each, by Longman, Hurst, Rees, Orme, & Brown, Paternoster-Row, London*, 4 parts (London, 1814).

[1] The exact sum is $1,551.93.

From George Logan

DEAR SIR   Stenton Oct: 21:[1] 1815

I am much pleased with your late Letter, because it manifests a sincere desire for the prosperity and honor of our beloved country, distracted by local factions

The love of honest fame, predominant during the revolutionary war, is changed into cupidity, disinterestedness into selfishness; and the public good, is sacrificed to personal views of ambition. In this disgraceful situation, it becomes the duty of every genuine citizen, not only "to offer up prayers to heaven for the safety of our country," but personally to exert himself, for its prosperity.

I trust we have a sufficient fund of good sense and prudence in the United States, to preserve internal tranquility; but it must be brought forward, with activity, and solely influenced by the sublime views of enlightened patriotism, discerning and preferring nothing but the public good.

I view with greater anxiety the aspect of European affairs; and the probable effect they will have upon us: which if we were armed with perfect[2] innocence, I think we might defy. But we have not been so scrupulously just to our neighbours, as to avoid the suspicion, if not the accusation that republicans too can be ambitious: and can avail themselves of the troubles of others, to their own mistaken advantage—For I hold it as a sound political principle—that nothing is permanently beneficial to a nation, either in self government, or in its foreign relations, that is not founded on the broad basis of honesty; utterly disclaiming every species of intrigue. Adopting this correct maxim in our public councils, would save us the trouble of resorting to those diplomatic subtleties, which constitute too frequently the machiavelian[3] policy of petty Princes—or of employing men versed in such arts.

Sir Francis Bacon's advice to Sir George Villiers, afterwards Duke of Buckingham, is well worthy the attention of all who have the disposal of office[4]—When he says "I recommend to you principally, that you countenance and advance able men in all kinds degrees and professions; and in places of moment rather make able and honest men yours, than advance those that are otherwise because they are yours."

History is the school of statesmen; it is their duty to inform themselves of the errors of past ages, in order to shun them. I do not accuse the President of a want of this highly important knowledge— But I apprehend he has too frequently given up his correct judgment to parasites and clamorous[5] demagogues. He and not them will be accountable for his official conduct.

The extent of territory of the United States, its increasing population, and resources, will create a spirit of jealousy in foreign governments. I am assured from undoubted authority, that a feeling of this nature, already exists in some of the European cabinets. To obviate such injurious sentiments—Let us act towards all nations, with impartiality, justice and even forbearance; to prevent a state of war; by which our republican manners, and institutions may be destroyed. Let us have concise, friendly and reciprocal treaties with all nations with whom we have commercial intercourse: particularly with Great Britain, and Russia. From the former we have not much of real injury to apprehend. For however blind and corrupt the ministry, the spirit of liberty diffused among the people; supported[6] by many of the most enlightened men in that nation; will secure us from any wanton attack.

Russia is yet in embrio. The astonishing success which some of her Sovereigns have had in civilising her immense population, gives reason to expect that under the paternal care of Alexander, she will become the arbiter of Europe. La Harp says the Emperor is a republican. I know he is partial to the United States—Let us therefore cherish his Friendship; it may under many points of view be of essential service to us.

Mrs Logan unites with me in best respects to yourself and amiable family.[7] accept assurances of my esteem   GEO LOGAN

PS

Pray what route is most direct from Philad^e to Monticello. I am anxious for one days free conversation with you.

If I can make it convenient I will see you early in December

GL

RC (DLC); at foot of text: "Thos Jefferson Esqr"; endorsed by TJ as received 15 Dec. 1815 and so recorded in SJL. Dft (PHi: Logan Papers); at head of text: "Copy"; lacks postscript. Printed without postscript in Philadelphia *Poulson's American Daily Advertiser*, 2 May 1816.

SIR FRANCIS BACON'S ADVICE was communicated to SIR GEORGE VILLIERS in a letter dated 12 Aug. 1616 (*The Works of Francis Bacon, Baron of Verulam, Viscount St. Alban, and Lord High Chancellor*

of England [London, 1740; Sowerby, no. 4915], 4:650).

[1] Dft: "20th:"; *Daily Advertiser*: "20."
[2] Word added in margin in Dft.
[3] Word interlined in Dft.
[4] Dft and *Daily Advertiser*: "offices."
[5] RC: "clamarous." Dft and *Daily Advertiser*: "clamorous."
[6] RC: "suported." Dft and *Daily Advertiser*: "supported."
[7] Sentence not in Dft or *Daily Advertiser*.

To Martin Dawson, with Jesse Abell's Receipt

DEAR SIR   Monticello Oct. 22. 15.

I have bought a mule of the bearer mr Jesse Abell for eighty Dollars, and not having the money by me, I ask the favor of you to pay it for me, and it shall be repaid in cash in the course of the week, or by an order on Gibson & Jefferson at your choice which will oblige your humble servant   TH: JEFFERSON

P.S. should mr Dawson be from home I ask the same favor of mr Watson, and will call on him in a day or two & replace the money

TH:J.

Milton October 23rd 1815 Recieved of Watson & Dawson eighty dollars in full for above mule   JESSE ABELL

Teste

JAMES WOOD

RC (MHi); in TJ's hand, with receipt, on address leaf, in Wood's hand, signed by Abell and Wood; addressed: "Mr Dawson Milton"; endorsed by TJ: "Abell Jesse." Not recorded in SJL.

On this date TJ recorded buying a four-year-old MULE from Jesse Abell, of Kentucky, the funds for which he repaid to Watson & Dawson three days later (*MB*, 2:1315).

To John Glendy

DEAR SIR   Monticello Oct. 22. 15.

I was absent on a journey at the date of your favor of Sep. 28. and arrived here a day or two only before that on which you gave us to hope we might attend you at Charlottesville. I should have much regretted the want of time to give notice; but that my family assured me that your intentions had been known and notified generally. the change in the weather was a great disappointment; and the morning itself so threatening as to deter all distant persons from coming.

I set out from home myself at 11. aclock in expectation momently of rain; but before I reached Charlottesville, it cleared away. you had left the place about an hour. about twelve aclock many came, all indeed who were near enough to get there in time after the weather cleared up. the loss of the pleasure of hearing you is the more regretted, as it can rarely if ever be expected to be renewed. yet we will not despair of it. I hope you enjoy good health, and I know you have the happiness of being amidst the affections & respect of those around you, and of none more than of

Your friend & serv^t   TH: JEFFERSON

PoC (DLC); on verso of reused address cover of Robert Brent to TJ, 18 Aug. 1815; at foot of text: "rev^d mr <*Glendie*> Glendye"; endorsed by TJ as a letter to "Glendy rev^d John" and so recorded in SJL.

TJ ARRIVED at Monticello from Poplar Forest on 3 Oct. 1815 (*MB*, 2:1315; SJL).

From Philip Mazzei

DEGNISSIMO E CARISSIMO AMICO,   Pisa, 5 [22] 8bre, 1815

Alla grata, e amorevolissima sua del 29 xbre, 1813, pe[r]venutami per mezzo del Sig^r David Bailey Wandeny nostro Console[1] a Parigi, feci subito una breve risposta, e la mandai al Sig^r Guglielmo Enrico Crawford nostro Ministro Plenipotenziario in Francia, per mezzo del nostro Console all'Isole Boreali, il quale (venendo da Livorno per andare a Parigi, e di là tornarsene al suo posto) ebbe la bontà di trattenersi un giorno e una notte in casa mia colla sua numerosa e angelica famiglia.

Ò tradotto la sua lettera per comunicarla agli Amici qui, a Livorno, a Lucca, e a Firenze. Il tutto è stato letto con sommo piacere, a riserva del tradimento del nostro primo Generale, e del massacro alle Frontiere, che ànno eccitato lo sdegno e l'ira universale.

Il Sig.^r Bernardo Lessi, Legale sommo, stato Auditore qui e a Livorno, Avvocato regio in Firenze, poi Auditore nel Supremo Tribunal di Giustizia, ed è ora Membro della Real Consulta (la quale rappresenta il Sovrano) mi ci rispose come segue. "Ò letto l'interessantissima lettera di Jefferson con sommo piacere, ed ò ammirato l'uomo di stato, l'amico dei suoi simili, il vero Amico vostro. Non lasciai trascorrere un momento per comunicarla al Fabbroni ed eccovi la sua risposta." (son veramente grato all'amico Filippo e a voi per la comunicazione dell'interessante lettera. Il candore che vi regna, e il carattere di chi la scrive, danno la più alta autenticità ai fatti, che stanno in constrasto con i fatti riferiti dai novisti venali.² Avrei curiosità di sapere quel che è seguito dal Gennaio a questa parte.)

N. B. Continovazione della lettera di Lessi:

"Intanto ritorno nelle vostre mani l'interessantissima lettera di Jefferson, ed unisco al plico i recapiti riguardanti l'eredità del Bellini. Le sorelle morirono, e l'Erede è un certo Prete Fancelli che sta al Pignone,³ in correspettività dei soccorsi caritatevoli dati alle medesime quando erano in vita. La Luisa, che fa testamento, stava e morì in casa sua, ed era trattata, ed assistita come se fosse stata sua sorella. I recapiti che vi mando non ànno firma di mercanti, per quanto abbiano tutte le altre legalizzazioni. Non vorrei che fossero infruttuosi, giacchè ànno costato mille impazzamenti." (Ella si ricorderà, che mandai al Signor Bracken la Procura delle sorelle del Bellini per autorizzarlo a vendere il Moro, la Mora e i mobili che lasciò il fratello.)⁴ Le sopraddette carte di Procura (che Lessi⁵ dice aver costato mille impazzamenti)⁶ sono voluminose, e avrebbe costato molto il mandarle a Parigi per la Posta, onde ò aspettato che vengano a Livorno i nostri Bastimenti Americani⁷ dei quali si spera che ne venranno molti, e presto; ma intanto La prego d'informarsi di quel che à fatto Bracken, onde poter' agire subito che riceverà le sopraddette carte.

Ella mi dice "Il messaggio del Presidente all'apertura del Congresso vi darà un dettaglio esatto della nostra condotta. Conoscendo il vostro affetto per questo paese, e il vostro desiderio della sua prosperità, ò creduto che la relazione dei suoi eventi vi avrebbe fatto piacere."

Desidero di vederla, ma se non me la manda presto, non la vedrò. Si ricordi che ò 11 anni più di Lei, come ne à Ella più di Madison; e oltre il peso degli 84 anni (terminati il 25 del passato xbre)[8] ò le gambe molto molto[9] enfiate, non ò appetito,[10] e soffro molto a motivo d'una fasciatura con un piombo, che pigia fortemente sul Pube, onde impedire all'intestino colon il transito nello scroto, dove inevitabilmente formerebbe un'ernia incarcerata.

Le son molto grato della vendita della mia casa e Lot in Richmond, il cui prodotto à[11] superato la mia aspettativa; ma gradirei che mi fosse rimesso immediatamente per più motivi. Ella probabilmente saprà, che l'insaziabil tirannia dell'iniquo Napoleone à rovinato tutti i Paesi che à potuto invadere, e che gl'individui più angariati sono stati i conosciuti, o supposti nemici del Potere arbitrario. Conseguentemente io sono stato uno dei più perseguitati, onde le mie finanze ànno sofferto molto, e mi sarebbe di gran sollievo il poter ritirare immediatamente il prodotto del mio stabile in Richmond, poi chè la grande scarsezza del denaro fà sì, che può impiegarsi adesso con mallevadoria territoriale a uno per 100 il mese. Io dunque rilascierei volentieri al compratore una somma discreta, piuttosto che aspettare a incassare il capitale uno, o 2 anni. La prego di farmene ottener l'intento, poichè (oltre il maggior frutto che attualmente produrrebbe qui) difficilmente si ottiene dagli Esecutori testamentarj l'attenzione e circospezione d'un marito e d'un padre. E quanto alla somma da rilasciarsi al compratore, mi rimetto intieramente alla sua discretezza.

Per darle un'idea della presente[12] scarsezza del denaro in questo paese, Le dirò, che il Granduca à chiesto ai suoi sudditi l'imprestito d'un milioni di scudi per un'anno, al frutto d'8 per 100.

Il Pacchetto contenente i fogli relativi alla piccola eredità del Bellini fù consegnato dal nostro Console Appleton al Capitano Jenkins, che il 7 Agosto, partì da Livorno per Baltimore col suo Bastimento l'Adeline[13]

Quanto a Derieux, che à 10, o 12 figli, e l'à[14] pregato di raccomandarmelo, e dirmi, che "any crumbs from my property would help him to subsist"[15] La prego di dargli per conto mio[16] 18, o 20[17] dollars, rammemorandogli che[18] io non diedi mai il mio consenso per il suo imprudente matrimonio colla mia figliastra, (causato dalle loro scellerate madri.) e abbia la bontà di rammemorargli ancora, che (senza mia saputa)[19] quando venne[20] di francia, a[21] Charles town, e mi notificò la sua trista situazione (la moglie aveva abortito, ed non avendo un soldo),[22] e gli mandai una somma non indifferente, che dopo glie ne diedi un'altra alla mia partenza, oltre la libertà di abitar nella mia casa a Colle, far uso dei prodotti, e[23] farvi un piccol commercio, e che la cambiale che mi diede[24] per le 2 d^e somme l'ò bruciata

Quando[25] Ella era in Parigi Ministro degli Stati Uniti, e vi ero anch'io (essendo[26] Incaricato d'Affari dl Rè e della Repubblica di Pollonia, a quella Corte)[27] Ella partì per andar' a veder l'Italia; ma il contenuto in[28] una lettera del Presidente del Congresso[29] l'obbligò a ritornare al suo posto quando non aveva neppur veduta tutta la Lombardia, e gli affari non Le permessero mai di ritornarvi. Se ne avesse tuttavia il desiderio, potrebbe venir qua in un bastimento da guerra, ed io (non ostante la mia decrepita età e i sopraddetti incomodi) l'accompagnerei non solo nel giro dell'Italia, ma ritornerei probabilmente seco per seco terminare i miei giorni in Patria libera.[30] Il Granduca Leopoldo mi permesse, come Ella si ricorderà, di condur meco degli uomini e un'intiera famiglia per introdurvi l'arte di coltivar delle vigne; e il presente Sovrano suo Figlio mi à detto, che se avesse il piacere di veder La qua,[31] Le lascierà condurre anche una[32] dozzina. Ella saprà che fù obbligato d'abbandonare il suo stato, mediante la preponderanza dell'iniquo Napoleone, che è finalmente annichilato. Al suo ritorno, essendo venuto a Pisa con un suo Segretario privato, che è mio amico, gli feci sapere, che desideravo ardentemente d'andare a rendergli il mio omaggio; ma che m'era impedito dal non potermi vestir decentemente, mediante le necessarie precauzioni contro la minaccia d'un'ernia incarcerata ed egli mi fece sapere che mi avrebbe veduto volentieri[33] anche in veste da camera. Aveva saputo che avevo ricevuto una lettera da Lei, che l'avevo tradotta per farla conoscere agli Amici, e me ne chiese una copia. Quel che mi disse di Lei dopo che l'ebbe letta, m'autorizza a dirle, che venendo Ella qua per vedere il resto dell'Italia, son persuaso che ne deriverebbero conseguenze molto utili per la mia cara adottiva Patria[34] e altrettanto piacevoli.^× In tal caso potrebbe portarmi il denaro; e se mi risolvassi ritornar con Lei in Virginia, potrò riportarvelo, farne qui l'uso che le mie circostanze richiederanno. Intanto mi confermo Suo vero, e affezionato[35] Amico,   FILIPPO MAZZEI.[36]

Intanto, pregandola nuovamente di darmi la consolazione di vedercela (prevedendo che la sua venuta produrrebbe ottime conseguenze per codesta mia cara Patria adottiva,) mi confermo qual sempre fui dal momento che ebbi la fortuna di conoscerla, Suo affezionato e costante amico,   FILIPPO MAZZEI

×Il sopraddetto suo segretario privato

⊖ Spero, che all'arrivo di questa le avrà ricevute, poichè partirono da Livorno per Baltimore il 7 Agosto nel Bastimento l'Adeline, Capitan Jenkins, al quale furon consegnate dan nostro Console Appleton.[37]

E D I T O R S '   T R A N S L A T I O N

MOST WORTHY AND DEAREST FRIEND,   Pisa, 5 [22] October, 1815

To your welcome and very fond letter of 29 December 1813, which reached me through Mr. David Bailie Warden our consul at Paris, I immediately wrote a brief reply, and I sent it to Mr. William Harris Crawford our minister plenipotentiary in France, by way of our consul in the Balearic Islands, who (coming from Leghorn to Paris and from there returning to his post) had the goodness to stay a day and a night in my house with his numerous and angelic family.

I translated your letter so as to communicate it to friends here, in Leghorn, Lucca, and Florence. The contents were read with great pleasure except for the sections on the betrayal of our foremost general and the massacre on the border, both of which have roused universal disdain and anger.

Mr. Bernardo Lessi, an excellent lawyer and formerly auditor here and in Leghorn, royal advocate in Florence, later auditor of the supreme court of justice, and now a member of the royal council (which represents the sovereign) answered me as follows: "I read Jefferson's very interesting letter with great pleasure and admire him as a statesman, a friend to his fellow man, and a true friend to you. I did not let a moment pass before communicating it to Fabbroni and here is his response." (I am truly grateful to our friend Philip and to you for communicating this interesting letter. Its pervasive candor and its author's character lend the utmost authenticity to the facts it contains, which contrast with those reported by writers for hire. I would be curious to know what has happened since January.)

N.B. Lessi's letter continues:

"In the meantime I am returning Jefferson's most interesting letter to you, and I am including in the package the documents regarding Bellini's estate. His sisters have died, and the heir is a certain Father Fancelli who lives in Pignone and is being compensated for the care he gave the sisters during their lifetime. Luisa, who wrote the will, lived and died in his home and was treated and cared for as if she were his sister. The papers I am sending you do not have the merchants' signature, although they have all the other legal authentications. I hope that these papers will not prove useless, especially as they have already caused a thousand headaches." (You will recall that I sent the Bellini sisters' power-of-attorney to Mr. Bracken to allow him to sell the negro, the negress, and the furniture left by their brother.) The abovementioned proxy papers (which Lessi said cost a thousand headaches) are voluminous, and it would have cost a great deal to send them to Paris by mail. I have waited for our American ships to come to Leghorn. I hope many will come soon, but in the meantime I would ask you to find out please what Bracken did, so as to be able to act quickly as soon as you receive the above papers.

You say to me, "The President's message at the opening of Congress will give you an exact account of our actions. Knowing your affection for this country and your wishes for its prosperity, I thought that a report on its events would please you." I want to see it, but if you do not send it to me soon, I will not. Remember, I am eleven years your senior, just as you are older than Madison. And, in addition to the weight of my eighty-four years (completed on the 25th of last December) my legs are very, very swollen, I have no appetite, and I am in great pain as I have to wear a support belt with a lead seal that presses heavily against my groin, in order to prevent my colon from entering into my scrotum, which would inevitably lead to a strangulated hernia.

I am very grateful to you for the sale of my house and lot in Richmond, the proceeds of which surpassed my expectation. But for a number of reasons I would prefer that they be remitted to me immediately. You probably know that the insatiable tyranny of the iniquitous Napoleon has ruined all the countries that he managed to dominate, and that the known, or alleged, enemies of arbitrary power have been the most oppressed. Consequently, I have been one of the most persecuted, and as a result my finances have suffered greatly. I would be greatly relieved if I could collect the income from my estate in Richmond immediately, especially as the great scarcity of money is such that one can now invest in landed securities at a rate of 1 percent per month. Therefore I would willingly discount the sale to the buyer rather than wait one or two years to receive the principal. Please help me accomplish this, because (besides the greater profit that it would currently produce here) it is difficult to get the same kind of care and attention from estate executors that one gets from a husband or a father. As for the amount of the buyer's discount, I confide myself entirely to your discretion.

To give you an idea of the present scarcity of money in this country, I will tell you that the grand duke has asked his subjects for the loan of a million scudi for one year, yielding 8 percent.

The packet containing the papers concerning the small estate of Bellini was delivered by our consul Appleton to Captain Jenkins, who left Leghorn for Baltimore on his ship, the Adeline, on 7 August.

As for Derieux, who has ten or twelve children, and who begged you to recommend him to me and tell me that "any crumbs from my property would help him to subsist," please give him on my behalf 18 or 20 dollars, reminding him that I never gave my consent for his imprudent marriage to my stepdaughter (which was brought about by their wicked mothers), and please be so good as also to remind him again, that when (without my knowledge) they came from France to Charleston, and he notified me of his sad situation (his wife having miscarried and he being penniless), I sent him a not inconsequential sum, and then I gave him another on my departure, as well as the freedom to use my house at Colle and its revenue and to make a small business, and that I burned his promissory note for the two aforementioned sums.

When you were United States minister in Paris, and I was also there (being the chargé d'affaires of the king and of the republic of Poland to that court), you left to tour Italy, but the contents of a letter from the president of the congress obliged you to return to your post when you had not yet even seen all of Lombardy, and events have never permitted you to return there. If you still have the desire, you could come here in a warship and (notwithstanding my decrepit age and the abovementioned discomforts) I would accompany you not only on a tour of Italy, but I would probably return with you to end my days in a free country. As you will remember, Grand Duke Leopold allowed me to bring some men and an entire family with me to introduce there the art of vineyard cultivation. The present sovereign, his son, told me that if he had the pleasure of seeing you here he would let me take as many as a dozen men there. You know that he was obliged to abandon his state when he was overpowered by the iniquitous Napoleon, who has finally been annihilated. On his return, having come to Pisa with his private secretary, who is my friend, I let him know that I ardently wished to go and pay him my respects, but that I was prevented by being unable to dress decently, because of the necessary precautions I have to take against the threat of a strangulated hernia, and he let me know that he would willingly see me even in my dressing gown. He had learned that I had received a letter from you, which I had translated to share with friends, and he asked me for a copy of it. What he told me about you after he read it, authorizes me to tell you, that should you come here to see the rest of Italy, I am convinced that my dear adoptive country would derive very profitable and pleasant consequences from it.[×] In that case you could bring me the money; and if I resolved to return with you to Virginia, I could bring it back there and make use of it as my circumstances would require. Meanwhile I confirm myself your true and affectionate friend,

PHILIP MAZZEI

Meanwhile, begging you again to give me the consolation of seeing you (expecting that your arrival would produce excellent consequences for my dear adoptive country) I confirm myself as being what I have been from the moment that I had the fortune of meeting you, your affectionate and constant friend,   PHILIP MAZZEI

⊖ I hope that by the time this arrives you will have received them, because they left from Leghorn for Baltimore on 7 August in the vessel Adeline, Captain Jenkins, to whom they were delivered by our consul Appleton.

[×]The aforesaid private secretary.

FC (ItPiAFM); dated 5 Oct. 1815, with date corrected to 22 Oct. 1815 based on SJL and TJ's use of the later date in the Tr listed below; incomplete; corner torn; at head of text: "Copia (a Mʳ Jefferson)." Dft (NhD); dated 5 Oct. 1815. Tr (DLC); extract in TJ's hand in his 24 Jan. 1816 letter to Peter Derieux; dated 22 Oct. 1815; consisting only of the paragraph on Derieux. Dft (ItPiAFM); undated and unsigned; incomplete; of similar purport to other texts, but using a different order and substantially different phrasing; relating the previous transmissions of Mazzei's response to TJ's letter of 29 Dec. 1813, inquiring about the funds from the sale of Mazzei's property in Richmond, telling of his past dealings with Derieux, mentioning the Bellini estate, outlining the state of Mazzei's health, and expressing a wish that TJ would visit Italy. Dft (ItPiAFM); undated fragment consisting only of partial paragraph on Mazzei's dealings with Derieux and a sentence stating that the letter would depart Leghorn for Baltimore on about the 20th of the month on board the Schooner *General Jackson*; with note on verso in an unidentified hand stating that the *Adeline*, commanded by Captain Jenkins, "took the letter for Jefferson & Sail'd about the 7ᵗʰ of August for Baltimore," and adding that "The merchant-vessel now in Leghorn, is the Schooner

General Jackson, bound to Baltimore & will Sail about the 20ᵗʰ of October." Translation by Dr. Jonathan T. Hine. Recorded in SJL as a letter of 22 Oct. 1815 received 16 Dec. 1815. Enclosed in Thomas Appleton to TJ, 25 Oct. 1815.

Mazzei apparently composed multiple versions of this letter under different dates for transmission to TJ. The initial paragraphs of this letter were themselves reworked from Mazzei's 24 Sept. 1814 letter to TJ. Based on TJ's partial Tr listed above, the missing RC was dated 22 Oct. 1815 and differed significantly from the text reconstructed above.

On 3 Jan. 1816 Mazzei composed yet another letter to TJ, asking that, for the reasons stated above, TJ forward the proceeds from the sale of Mazzei's house and lot in Richmond, as well as the interest accrued since 14 July 1813 (Dft [It-PiAFM]; unsigned; written as if dictated to Elisabetta Mazzei [Pini], but in Philip Mazzei's hand; with a postscript indicating that Mazzei had asked his daughter to prepare three copies and transmit them through Appleton; on recto of a reused address cover to Mazzei; not recorded in SJL and probably never seen by TJ).

GUGLIELMO ENRICO CRAWFORD: William Harris Crawford. The CONSOLE ALL'ISOLE BOREALI was John Martin Baker. TJ told Mazzei in his letter of 29 Dec. 1813 that ANY CRUMBS from his property would help Derieux's family. For TJ's April 1787 visit to Italy while he was MINISTRO DEGLI STATI UNITI, see *PTJ*, 11:354, 432–42. News reached TJ that Arthur St. Clair had been elected PRESIDENTE DEL CONGRESSO while he was en route to Italy early in April 1787, but official communications and instructions from St. Clair did not reach TJ until December, long after his return to Paris (*PTJ*, 11:129–30, 627–9).

¹ NhD Dft here adds "degli Stati Uniti" ("of the United States").
² FC ends here, with remainder of transcription based on NhD Dft.
³ Preceding four words interlined.
⁴ Omitted closing parenthesis editorially supplied.

⁵ Reworked from "che Jefferson" ("which Jefferson").
⁶ Parenthetical phrase interlined.
⁷ Word interlined.
⁸ Sentence from "degli" to this point reworked from "degli anni (che terminaranno il 25 del prossimo xbre)" ("of the years [which will be completed on the 25th of next December]").
⁹ Preceding two words interlined.
¹⁰ Preceding three words interlined.
¹¹ Mazzei here interlined and then canceled "(essendo 6342 dolleri e 21 centesimi)" ("[being $6,342.21]"), which refers to the sale price of Mazzei's house and lot in Richmond as reported in TJ to Mazzei, 29 Dec. 1813.
¹² Word interlined.
¹³ Preceding nine words interlined in place of a heavily reworked phrase reading, in part, "il 20 del corrente partirà parimente per Baltimore e questa sarà consegnata al capitano dello Schooner General Jackson" ("the 20th of the current month will also depart for Baltimore and this will be given to the captain of the Schooner General Jackson").
¹⁴ Preceding seven words interlined.
¹⁵ Preceding thirteen words not in Tr.
¹⁶ Preceding five words interlined in place of phrase reading in part "carità" ("charity"). Tr reads "carità 18. o 20. dollars"
¹⁷ Preceding five words interlined.
¹⁸ For remainder of paragraph, Tr substitutes "quando venne inaspettatamente di Francia a Charlestown colla moglie (che aveva abortito nel viaggio) gli mandai il denaro per pagare il Capitano, e per venire in Virginia; che gli diedi un'altra somma rispettabile alla mia partenza di costà, e che la cambiale (che mi diede per le 2. dette somme) la bruciai subito che seppi l'infelice stato delle sue finanze" ("that when he came unexpectedly from France to Charleston with his wife [who had miscarried during the voyage] I sent him money to pay the captain and to come to Virginia; that I gave him another considerable sum on my departure, and that I burned the promissory note [which he gave me for these two sums] as soon as I learned of the unhappy state of his finances").
¹⁹ Parenthetical phrase interlined.

[20] Word interlined.

[21] Preceding two words interlined.

[22] Parenthetical phrase interlined.

[23] Preceding five words interlined.

[24] Preceding seven words interlined.

[25] An unmatched opening bracket preceding this word is editorially omitted.

[26] Preceding three words interlined.

[27] Preceding three words interlined.

[28] Preceding three words interlined.

[29] Preceding two words interlined.

[30] Mazzei here canceled "anche in tal caso non sarebbe necessario di rimetter qua il prodotto del mio stabile, che farei fruttare costo forse anche più che qua in questo paese" ("however in that case it will be unnecessary to send the profit from my building, which will earn interest, perhaps even more than it would in this country").

[31] Sentence from "se avesse" to this point heavily reworked, with the redundant phrase "venendo Ella qua; Le" added in addition to "di veder La qua," with neither canceled.

[32] Preceding two words interlined in place of "mezza" ("half").

[33] Preceding four words interlined.

[34] Preceding six words interlined.

[35] Word interlined in place of "obbligato" ("obliged").

[36] Mazzei here canceled a postscript reading "P.S. Determinandosi a venir qua, siccome io ritornerei costà con Lei, non sarebbe necessario che mi portasse il prodotto del mio stabile, mi basterebbe il frutto, ma non venendo Ella qua, Le prego di mandarmi anche il capitale il più presto possibile poi chè qua potrei farlo fruttare adesso [...] forse più [...] di qualche frutto" ("P.S. Should you decide to come here, inasmuch as I would return there with you, it would not be necessary that you bring me the principal from my property, the interest would be enough for me, but if you are not coming here, please send me the principal also as soon as possible, because I could now make it yield some more interest here").

[37] Mazzei may have intended that this sentence replace the reworked text above on the transmission of the Bellini estate documents, but if so he failed to indicate where it should be inserted.

From Spencer Roane

DEAR SIR. Richmond, Oct° 22ᵈ 1815.

I received, a few days ago, your favour of 12ᵗʰ instant, enclosing[1] the scheme of my opinion, in the case of Martin v Hunter. I am very much flattered and gratified by the receipt of that letter.

Going up to the springs, about the last of August, I had intended to avail myself of that opportunity, to pay the homage of my respects, to our first Citizen: Your absence from home, both as I went and came, deprived me of that pleasure, which was to me a source of real regret. Beleiving the question discussed in that paper to be of the first importance, and that your willingness to aid the Cause of truth and public utility, was only equalled by your ability to serve[2] it, I had designed, had it fallen in my way, to ask your opinion upon it. With my present impressions on that subject, I am not sure that the opinion (merely,) of any man, could have produced a change:[3] but if there be such an opinion, I am frank[4] to say it would be that of Mʳ Jefferson.—Finding my friend Col° Monroe at the Springs, I submitted the

paper to his perusal, and as he seemed entirely to concur in my conclusions, it strengthened the Claim of this paper to your Inspection. I
was therefore highly[5] gratified, when, on my return, he offered[6] to
Send it to you.

I am much flattered and gratified by the receipt of your letter: flattered, by the very civil manner in which you are pleased to speak of
my humble labours; and gratified to find, that I have not erred, in the
great principles at least, on which the question seems to turn. Your
opinion, as far as it goes, is a great authority, both for the considerations before alluded to, and because you are beleived to be equally
friendly to the just claim of both governments.

with sentiments of the highest Consideration respect, and Esteem,
I am, Dear Sir,

y^r mo: ob^t serv^t   SPENCER ROANE

RC (DLC); at foot of text: "Thomas
Jefferson Esqr."; endorsed by TJ as received 27 Oct. 1815 and so recorded in
SJL. Dft (ViU: TJP); endorsed by
Roane as a letter "in answer to one Enclosing & approving SR's op^n in the Case
of Hunter v Fairfax."

[1] Dft: "accompanying."
[2] Word interlined in Dft in place of
"effect."

[3] Reworked in Dft from "induced me to
change them."
[4] Preceding two words interlined in
Dft in place of "have not to flatter."
[5] Word interlined in Dft in place of
"much."
[6] Preceding two words interlined in
Dft in place of "proposed."

To Caspar Wistar

DEAR SIR   Monticello Oct. 22. 15.

Your favor of the 9th is received, and I am much amused with the
anecdotes of Logan, and other circumstances relative to the Indians.
it is a great pity, and indeed a scandal that we let that race of men dis-
appear without preserving scarcely any trace of their history. what an
opportunity Hawkins has had to have given us the history of the
Creeks during the period he has been with them: to have related their
councils, debates, political views, wars, and to have followed them
into their houses families fields and huntings. one such history would
have given us a specimen of the whole. Heckewelder too, whom I
knew very well, what could he do better than to give us the life of
Logan, as a warrior, a statesman, an orator, a hunter, a father, son, &
husband. I wish mr Dobbins may pursue this subje[ct.]

I have been more gratified by reading Birckbec[k's ac]count of his tour thro' France than by any publication for a long time. what a contrast with the dinners and suppers of Shepherd. in the former not a word to spare; not an observation which is not marked with sound sense. how precisely too he has seised the exact character of Bonaparte. altho' much more of detail might have been given, and you wish for more, yet the solidity of what he does give counts for much.   I should have been infinitely gratified had your rides in pursuit of health led you in this direction, where too you would have found as much of it as any where. the counties next below the blue ridge are deemed more healthy and of a much finer climate than those above it. you would have probably fallen in with Correa, Gilmer and myself in time to have gone with us to the Peaks of Otter and Natural bridge I parted with them the 20ᵗʰ of Sep. on the bridge, from which they set out for Tenissee, S. Carolina & Georgia, uncertain whether they should return by sea or land. if the latter they will call on me either here or in Bedford where I informed them I should pass the month of November. however the French have a proverb which may stand me in stead. 'tout-ce qui est differé n'est pas perdu.' in your future rides and retirements from business you may perhaps try this route, where I shall always be most happy to see you. should I be in Bedford, where I stay much, you will find mr Randolph here & Jefferson who always speaks of you with a high sense of gratitude. he is married & become an industrious and skilful farmer. I salute you with great affection and respect.   TH: JEFFERSON

PoC (DLC); on verso of reused address cover of George Ticknor to TJ, 18 June 1815; mutilated at seal; at foot of first page: "Doctor Wistar"; endorsed by TJ.

Morris Birkbeck (BIRCKBECK) observed during his travels in France that Napoleon was successful in matters of internal improvement and government, but that his foreign policy had sacrificed French lives, commerce, and manufacture (Birkbeck, *Notes on a Journey through France . . . in July, August, and September, 1814, Describing the Habits of the People, and the Agriculture of the Country*, 1st American ed. [Philadelphia, 1815; Poor, *Jefferson's Library*, 7 (no. 324)], 106). TOUT-CE QUI EST DIFFERÉ N'EST PAS PERDU: "not all that is postponed is lost."

To John Bracken

SIR   Monticello Oct. 23. 15.
    In a late letter from mr Mazzei I have recieved inclosed a power of Attorney from the representatives of th[e][1] late mr Bellini for the settlement of the administration of his affairs and remitment of the

proceeds. my distance rendering it impracticable for myself, I have thought it would be for your convenience also to engage some person in your neighborhood to attend to this. I have therefore requested of mr Robert Saunders to undertake it which if he consents to do, I will fill up the power of attorney [wit]h his name so that you may be placed on sure ground in what is done by him, by this regular sanction. Accept the assura[nces] of my esteem and respect.

Th: Jefferson

PoC (DLC); on verso of reused address cover of Louis Philippe Gallot de Lormerie to TJ, 22 Aug. 1815; torn at seal, with one missing word rewritten by TJ; at foot of text: "The rev[d] mr Bracken"; endorsed by TJ.

[1] Word faint.

To Robert Saunders

Sir   Monticello Oct. 23. 15.

You probably knew the late mr Bellini, one of the professors of William and Mary college, who died at that place. mr Bracken took out administration of his effects. his representatives in Italy have lately sent me a power of attorney for the settlement of the administration account and to have the proceeds remitted to them.   understanding that the execution of this power is within your line of business, I request the favor of you to undertake the settlement, to collect the proceeds, and place them in the bank of Virginia in Richmond, where I will engage some merchant to effect the remittance. if you will be so good as to drop me a line informing me you will undertake it, I will fill up the power of attorney with your name, and transmit it to you. it is very voluminous as is the foreign custom. interest I suppose is a thing of course where money has laid so long in hand. your compensation you will I presume retain out of the sum recieved. Accept the assurance of my great respect

Th: Jefferson

PoC (DLC); on verso of a reused address cover from John Vaughan to TJ; torn at seal, with missing word rewritten by TJ; at foot of text: "M[r] Robert Saunders"; endorsed by TJ.

Robert Saunders (1761–1835), attorney, attended the College of William and Mary in about 1775 and was a notary public in Williamsburg between 1789 and 1799. He also served as deputy commonwealth's attorney for James City County, and he represented a district consisting of Elizabeth City, Warwick, and York counties in the Senate of Virginia, 1800–05. In 1813 Saunders declined a judgeship on the Virginia General Court, in part because he was serving in the militia as captain of a Williamsburg cavalry unit. He also sat on the board of visitors of the

College of William and Mary and was a director of the Public Hospital in Williamsburg. Saunders died in Williamsburg (*WMQ*, 1st ser., 7 [1899]: 155; 14 [1906]: 147; *William and Mary Provisional List*, 35; *CVSP*, 4:627, 5:384, 6:463, 656, 9:70, 10:214; Leonard, *General Assembly*; Butler, *Virginia Militia*, 113, 247; *The Officers, Statutes and Charter of the College of William and Mary* [Philadelphia, 1817]; *American Beacon and Norfolk and Portsmouth Daily Advertiser*, 19 May 1835; will in Vi: RG 50, James River Company, Wills and Qualifications).

From Patrick Gibson

SIR   Richmond 24ᵗʰ Octʳ 1815

I have received your favor of the 20ᵗʰ Insᵗ. The note forwarded to me in yours of the 29ᵗʰ Ultº was offer'd at bank on Friday last and rejected, in consequence of a determination which had been made to curtail—This circumstance however need not prevent your drawing as I shall, as heretofore substitute the inclosed note, in lieu of my own, which I can withdraw without inconvenience,—none of your flour has yet arrived, the price asked by our millers is $9 on 60 ᵈ/– very little sold at that—Tobacco brisk—John Harris crop sold today at 27½$ the leaf and 25$ the stemm'd, the little new that has come in altho only middling has been sold at from 17 to 21½$ for the New York market—With great regard Your obᵗ Servᵗ

PATRICK GIBSON

RC (MHi); between dateline and salutation: "Thomas Jefferson Esqʳᵉ"; endorsed by TJ as received 27 Oct. 1815 and so recorded in SJL. Enclosure not found.

To Charles Massie

SIR   Monticello Aug. [Oct.] 24. 15.

I formerly had some good cyder of you, & I understand you generally make it. if you can furnish me 100. gallˢ of what you can recommend I shall be glad to take it, and will send the money and a cart for it any day you will name in December, because I shall be from home all the month of November. Accept my best wishes and respects

TH: JEFFERSON

PoC (MHi); misdated; on verso of reused address cover to TJ; at foot of text: "Mʳ Massie"; endorsed by TJ: "Massie Charles." Recorded in SJL as a letter of 24 Oct. 1815 and presumably written then, as TJ was not at Monticello on 24 Aug.

Charles Massie (1765–1830), farmer, worked with his father, Charles Massie

(1727–1817), on the family's extensive apple orchard at Spring Valley in southwestern Albemarle County, which he later inherited. The Massie family first supplied cider to TJ in the spring of 1812 and continued to do so until the spring of 1826 (Woods, *Albemarle*, 266; DNA: RG 29, CS, Albemarle Co., 1810, 1820; *MB*, esp. 2:1275, 1417; Albemarle Co. Will Book, 6:288–9, 10:141–3; *Richmond Enquirer*, 4 May 1830; gravestone inscriptions in Spring Valley Cemetery).

From John Minor

DEAR SIR   Fredericksbg. Oct 24ᵗʰ 15.

The young Gentleman who will deliver this Letter (Mʳ Dumolin) is from Ireland, his native Country, which he has left for the purpose of not[1] witnessing the cruel lacerations, which are daily inflicted on her, and of courting Fortune where she may be kinder; he has fixed on our Country as the last asylum of Liberty; but before he adopts the place of his final settlement wishes to traverse the Country, and become acquainted with the People—his motive for visiting Montecello, is to become acquainted with a Man whose well earned fame has procured him the Thanks of his Country, and intitled him to the approbation of the Wise of all nations. his introduction to me is from a Gentleman of high respectability, lately of the American Army: I have been in his company only a few Hours, and have been much pleased with his Conversation and Manners: These with his Letter from Mʳ Emmett, will be his best recommendation to your Hospitality and attention—

I am with high respect & Esteem
Dear Sir yr. mo. ob. serv   J MINOR

RC (MoSHi: TJC-BC); endorsed by TJ as a letter from John Minor received 25 Oct. 1815 and so recorded in SJL.

[1] Word interlined in place of "avoid."

From Robert Patterson

SIR   Philadelphia 24ʰ Octʳ 1815

I have been favoured with your letter of the 13ᵗʰ & shall immediately take measures to send on your Time-piece as you have directed.

I have had, for some years an <u>artificial horizon</u>, which, by means of a reflecting sextant, answers the purpose of measuring all altitudes of the sun, or any other visible object, from 0 to 90° as well as all depressions not exceeding 50° with great ease & accuracy; & shall, Sir, have one made for you, on the same principles, to be sent on with the Time-piece; tho this may possibly occasion a delay of one or two weeks.

Mr Hassler has just arrived here from England, with a complete apparatus of mathematical & astronomical instruments, for the use of the Government; in taking a survey of the coast &c The pendulum of his astronomical clocks is on the same construction with that used in the Observatory of Greenwich. I expect to obtain from him one of the same kind for your Time-piece.

I am, Sir, with the greatest respect & esteem, your most obed^t Servt   R^T PATTERSON

RC (DLC); endorsed by TJ as received 15 Dec. 1815 and so recorded in SJL. RC (DLC); address cover only; with PoC of TJ to Jean David, 25 Dec. 1815, on verso; addressed: "Thomas Jefferson Monticello V^a"; franked; postmarked Philadelphia, 24 Oct. Dft (PPAmP: Thomas Jefferson Papers); on verso of remnant of address leaf of TJ to Patterson, 13 Oct. 1815; right half of page torn away, resulting in substantial loss of text; in heavily abbreviated form; with concluding section apparently differing significantly from RC but unrecoverable due to damage and illegibility.

From Thomas Appleton

Leghorn 25th October 1815.

You will recieve, Sir, by this conveyance, a letter from m^r mazzei, relating to the money which arose from the sale of his house in Richmond, by which you will percieve, he is still very desirous, to have in his possession this amount, alledging the advantageous purchases which might be made in Tuscany, or the still more lucrative mode of lending it a great interest.—It is from such erroneous ideas that he has already diminish'd his estate more than one third, in the short space of a few years; and as the faculties of his mind seem rapidly retiring, he would certainly add this Sum to the number of his losses, were it to fall into his hands.—The real truth is, that there is not a spot of ground in all Tuscany, which produces 4 per c^t, and it is with great difficulty, that money can be securely plac'd at Six.—In the letter which I had the honor of addressing you, Sir, in date of the 28th of August, I have very fully related to you, how totally incapable, is m^r mazzei of administring his pecuniary affairs, and the very earnest request of his wife & daughter, that the capital should remain for the present, in the Secure Situation in which it now is, and that only the interest which arises thereon, should be forwarded to them, as it becomes due.—

There is, Sir, in florence, an artist of the very highest rank in sculpture; indeed, there is but one in all Italy who is thought to excel him, and who is the fam'd Canova. from a very intimate knowledge of m^r Bartolini, (the name of the person of whom I am now writing) I have conciev'd for him the greatest esteem for his sublime talents! and from the ardent passion he discovers for our government & our Country, I confess there are few men, for whom I bear, So Sincere a friendship. He is only 30 Years of age; of the most engaging aspect; and manners; and speaks the french language with great facility.—His residence for the last Six years, has been in Carrara, where he presided over the accademy of sculpture, modelling, and drawing, with universal approbation.—The number of his élèves were about one hundred, but the recent changes which have taken place in Europe, have intirely dispers'd them; and Bartolini became the principal object of the fury of these diabolical fanatics, who finding he had escap'd thier stilettos, took thier vengeance on his divine works.—He was charg'd by the late Grand Dutchess of Tuscany, to copy in marble, the colossal Statue of Napoleon, by Canova; he did more, for he far surpass'd the original.—He form'd a vase, of nearly eight feet in diameter, and sculptur'd on the exterior, in demi bosso figures, representing the corronation of Napoleon; his marriage; and the birth of the King of Rome. this work was nearly compleated, and was destin'd for the museum of paris, when the assassins of Carrara, compell'd him to fly from thier territory. of all the works now remaining of grecian or roman artists, there are none of superior merit. In drawing & modelling he stands unrivall'd in Italy, as he certainly will in sculpture, at a period not far distant. I have been thus particular, Sir, in the great and numerous qualities of m^r Bartolini, because, he is ardently inflam'd with a desire of fixing himself in the U: States, for never did there exist a man, whose passion for freedom, rose higher than his; and as he often assures me, to repeat his own words, "Could I but once breathe the air of a free Country every Stroke of my chizzel or my pencil, would evince the change of my Situation."—but where he ought to place himself in America, or what probable encouragement he would find, that would be, in any-wise, on a level with his merit, are circumstances not in my power to inform him.—I have thought, Sir, that an acquisition of this Kind to our country, would be extreemely agreeable to you, and it is for this reason, I have ventur'd to address you in his behalf; for as he cannot sett forward for the U: States, before the ensuing spring or summer, your advice would be reciev'd with the most grateful Sentiments; for your virtues, Sir, were familiar to him, long before I form'd his acquaintance.

Pardon me, Sir, if I have thus trespass'd on your time, or if the request I have made, shou'd seem to you indiscrete, for I have hasarded both! presuming that the great utility which our Country may derive from the possession of m^r Bartolini, would Serve as an apology for the one and for the other.—Accept, Sir, the sincere expressions of my highest respect & esteem.—   TH: APPLETON

P:S—I Know not, Sir if the letter I wrote you, many years Since, reach'd you, in which I inform'd you, that I am the possessor of the original plaister model of General Washington, and made by Cerrachi.—I have very lately sent to Baltimore, to my nephews N & C. Appleton merchants there, two fine Copies in marble; as likewise two copies of Vespucius & Columbus, copied from the original busts in the gallery of florence.—[1]
Iterum—   T: A.

RC (DLC); at head of text: "Thomas Jefferson esq Virginia"; endorsed by TJ as received 16 Dec. 1815 and so recorded in SJL. FC (Lb in DNA: RG 84, CRL); in Appleton's hand. Enclosure: Philip Mazzei to TJ, 22 Oct. 1815.

Appleton's previous letter to TJ was dated the 26th, not the 28TH OF AUGUST 1815. ÉLÈVES: "students."
Elisa Bonaparte, the GRAND DUTCH-ESS OF TUSCANY and sister of Napoleon, promoted the career of the sculptor Lorenzo Bartolini. Bartolini produced numerous sculptures of Napoleon and his family, including an eighteen-foot-tall likeness and an alabaster vase depicting the apotheosis of Napoleon. The vase and other works by Bartolini were destroyed when Napoleon fell from power and the sculptor fled to Leghorn (Douglas K. S. Hyland, *Lorenzo Bartolini and Italian Influences on American Sculptors in Florence, 1825–1850* [1985], 23–30).
A sculpture generally in low relief is styled demi-basso (DEMI BOSSO) when "there are parts that stand clear out, detached from the rest" (William Nicholson, *American Edition of the British Encyclopedia, or Dictionary of Arts and Sciences* [Philadelphia, 1816–17; Poor, *Jefferson's Library*, 14 (no. 931)], vol. 5, cf. "Relievo").
The KING OF ROME was Napoleon's son, Napoleon François Joseph Charles Bonaparte. Appleton's two NEPHEWS in Baltimore were Nathaniel W. Appleton and Charles H. Appleton (Philipp Fehl, "The Account Book of Thomas Appleton of Livorno: A Document in the History of American Art, 1802–1825," *Winterthur Portfolio* 9 [1974]: 132, 140; Isaac Appleton Jewett, comp., *Memorial of Samuel Appleton, of Ipswich, Massachusetts* [1850], 36, 40). ITERUM: "once again."

[1] FC ends here with a second postscript: "N:B. The foregoing Sent by the Sch° Genl Jackson—Capt Chaytor."

To Arsène Lacarrière Latour

Monticello Oct. 26. 15.

Th: Jefferson presents his compliments to Major Carriere La Tour, acknoleges the receipt of the Prospectus of his history of the war of Louisiana & West Florida, and asks leave to subscribe for a copy. should it be published in the original language, he would prefer that. he salutes him with respect

RC (LNHiC: Latour Archive); dateline at foot of text; addressed: "Maj^r A. Carriere Latour Philadelphia"; franked; postmarked Charlottesville, 1 Nov. PoC (MoSHi: TJC-BC); on verso of a reused address cover from Joseph Milligan to TJ; endorsed by TJ.

Latour's work was published only in English, as *Historical Memoir of the War in West Florida and Louisiana in 1814–15. With an Atlas* (Philadelphia, 1816), and not in its ORIGINAL French.

To John Manesca and Victor Value

Monticello Oct. 26. 15.

Th: Jefferson presents his compliments to Messrs Manesca and Value, and thanks them for the copy of the Historiettes nouvelles which they have been so kind as to send him. it seems well calculated for it's object by a happy combination of amusement and instruction and hopes that the success with the American public of this first example in that stile will encourage others to follow it. he salutes them with great respect.

PoC (MoSHi: TJC-BC); on verso of reused address cover of Mathew Carey to TJ, 23 Sept. 1815; dateline at foot of text; endorsed by TJ.

To Richard Rush

Monticello Oct. 26. 15.

Th: Jefferson presents his compliments to mr Rush and his thanks for the pamphlet he has been so kind as to send him. he takes it with him on a journey on which he is setting out, and has no doubt of finding it an amusing and instructive companion. he salutes mr Rush with great esteem & respect.

PoC (MHi); on verso of reused address cover of Henry Dearborn to TJ, 26 Sept. 1815; dateline at foot of text; endorsed by TJ.

To Henry Sheaff

DEAR SIR   Monticello Oct. 26. 15.

Your favor of the 16th is recieved, and I regret that I troubled you with an application so improper. it had been long since I had had correspondence with you, and I was led to suppose your continuance in business by the Philadelphia Directory in which I found your name, as still a wine-merchant, and at the old stand. I still learn with more regret the bodily affliction under which you labor, and hope it will add to the examples we have seen of entire recovery from so distressing a disease. Accept my best wishes for it and the assurance of my great esteem & respect   TH: JEFFERSON

P.S. I conclude it better to get a supply of wine from Richmond as being nearer, and my stock out.

PoC (MHi); on verso of reused address cover of John Glendy to TJ, 28 Sept. 1815; postscript adjacent to signature; at foot of text: "M[r] Henry Sheaff"; endorsed by TJ.

To Joseph Milligan

D[R] SIR   Monticello Oct. 27. 15.

The answers to letters which had accumulated during a seven weeks[1] absence in Bedford, and the daily calls of my affairs here have delayed longer than I expected the examination promised in my letter of the 5th into the paiment I beleived I had made for the early volumes of Wilson's ornithology. I was led astray too in my researches by an idea that that paiment had been made while I lived at Wash[n] or soon after, and I bewildered myself in the old[2] accounts of Dufief, Conrad, Duane, Rapine E[t]c and at length finding it in none of these I recurred[3] to yours where I at length found it. in an account rendered by you embracing from 1809. June 17. to 1811. May 14. you will find the last article to be 'To 3. vols American Ornithology 36.D.' the amount of the acc[t] including that is 65. D $12\frac{1}{2}$. C and in my letter of Mar. 16. 12. to you you will find it stated that I had desired Gibson & Jefferson to remit a sum to mr Barnes, out of which I had requested mr Barnes to pay you 65. D $12\frac{1}{2}$ C which you will certainly find to have been done. these 36.D. with the 92. D last remitted, making 128.D being deducted from the 264.75 amount of your last account leave a balance of 136.75 D which sum by a letter of this day I desire mess[rs] Gibson & Jefferson to remit you.

I set out for Bedford the day after tomorrow, shall be back the last week in[4] November, and will then immediately begin the revisal of the translation of Tracy & forward[5] it to you faster than you can print it. I shall be engaged in Bedford in making a geometrical admeasurement of the Peaks of Otter which has never been done yet, altho deemed the highest mountains of our ranges.[6] for this work Hutton's tables were extremely necessary; but they are not come and I shall be much distressed by the want of them. I blame you for this but still remain

Your friend & serv[t]   TH: JEFFERSON

Dft (DLC); on verso of reused address cover of Charles Yancey to TJ, 26 Sept. 1815; at foot of text: "M[r] Joseph Millegen"; endorsed by TJ.

The ACCOUNT RENDERED by Milligan is printed above at 2 Dec. 1811, where it was enclosed to TJ. TJ's letter to Patrick GIBSON requesting that $200 be remitted to John BARNES and his letter directing Barnes to pay Milligan out of those funds are both dated 15 Mar. 1812. TJ wrote

Gibson authorizing the payment to Milligan of $136.75 in a letter of 28 Oct. 1815 rather than in one OF THIS DAY.

[1] Preceding two words interlined in place of "two months."
[2] Word interlined.
[3] Word interlined in place of "turned."
[4] TJ here canceled "December."
[5] Manuscript: "foward."
[6] Preceding nine words interlined.

To John Bankhead

DEAR SIR   Monticello Oct. 28. 15.

Considering our young friend (who arrived here last night) as a medical subject under your care, I deem it indispensable that every point in his case should be known to you. nothing less than his good, and the hope of restoring happiness to his family and friends & to yourself particularly could have induced me to the pain of this communication. on his arrival here on the occasion of his former visit we were all delighted with the change in his appearance and the hope which that inspired of his being restored a rational and valued member to the society of his friends. an early visit however to Charlottesville damped these hopes, and this repeated and repeated till it became daily put an end to them: he returned usually in the evening, and in a state approaching insanity. among other acts indicating it he committed an assault on his wife of great violence, ordered[1] her out of the room, forbidding her to enter it again,[2] & she was obliged to take refuge for the night[3] in her mother's room. nor was this a new thing. in the morning, when cooled, he would become repentant, and sincerely distressed, but recur again to the same excesses. at his farm he destroyed all subordination of his negroes to their overseer, went to buying and bargaining again as if not sensible of having surrendered his [a]uthority there. when sober he spoke perseveringly of selling his farm here and moving elsewhere. said he had lost all consideration in this neighborhood & could never be happy here. but his habits would follow him wherever he went, except under your roof, and we had too many proofs that his family would be safe no where else. there, his respect for you overcomes them, but not here or any where else. a state of abstinence continued for some time may we hope, recover him; but considerable time will be requisite. these details are very much unknown to mr Randolph and my daughter has communicated such of them as happened under her eye to me for counsel. I should have stated them to you when we had the pleasure of possessing you here, but she undertook to take an opportunity of doing it, and I thought she could do it more fully. but on my return from Bedford after a two months absence she told me no such opportunity had occurred: and nothing in the universe could have induced me to give either to you or myself the pain of this letter but a conviction of it's necessity; inasmuch as it may enable you to judge of the course you think it best to pursue for his reclamation and restoration to himself, his family & friends. if some occupation could be devised to which he could attach himself, it would be a great auxiliary to his cure. he was very fond of his farm at first, but became tired of it at length. the gun is a very enticing occupation if once a fondness for it is acquired. it is a very healthy one, and I should suppose as likely to engage him as any other. but of all this you are the best judge and will best know how to lead him to it. to this letter nobody is privy but my daughter and myself; it might increase Anne's uneasiness were she to know of it, and if known to mr Bankhead himself, might alienate him from us, which would add to the distresses of the case. accept the sincerest assurances of sentiments of high respect and esteem for yourself and mrs Bankhead from Dear Sir

Your's affectionately   TH: JEFFERSON

PoC (ViU: TJP-ER); on reused paper labeled "Letter" in an unidentified hand; one word faint; at foot of first page: "Dr John Bankhead"; endorsed by TJ, with his additional notation: "Spring grove near Vielle boro'" (Villboro, Caroline County).

The YOUNG FRIEND was John Bankhead's son Charles L. Bankhead, whose WIFE was TJ's granddaughter Ann C. Bankhead.

[1] Word interlined in place of "thrust."
[2] Preceding six words interlined in place of "locked her out."
[3] Preceding three words interlined.

To Patrick Gibson

DEAR SIR   Monticello Oct. 28. 15

Your favor of the 24ᵗʰ was recieved yesterday. I did not know that the bank had determined to curtail their discounts, which lays me under the greater obligations to you, for indeed I should have been much distressed without the accomodation. my taxes here and some demands not regularly payable till the spring were so urged as to embarras me. being to set out for Bedford tomorrow; I have drawn 660. D 25 c of the money[1] from my grandson and given him an order on you, as also to the sheriff, Clifton Harris I have given an order for 309.82 D for my taxes here, and I must pray you to remit for me to Joseph Millegan bookseller at Georgetown (Columbia) 136.75 D my grandson is also desired to procure for me in Richmond a quarter cask of Lisbon which he will desire you to pay, about 75.D. this will render necessary the sale of the 35. barrels of flour mentioned in my last letter, which I trust is delivered before this time, as mr T. M. & T. E. Randolph, tenants of my mill, both assured me it was sent off on my account, and both are now in Richmond. on my arrival in Bedford I will hurry the getting my tobᵒ ready (about 15,000. ℔) as fast as the weather will admit it to be handled, & forwarded to Richmond for immediate sale, as I see no reason for declining present prices in expectation of better. from hence I shall have about 200. barrels of flour now on hand, 150. barrels more for rent of my mill[2] due or to become due between this and March, and from Bedford somewhere between 100. and 150. barrels. I think that before the spring the demand for that must produce a good price. I inclose the note for 2000.D. with my signature and if you will let me know the date it shall be renewed in time. I must request you to send me a bale of cotton by Johnson, or by Gilmer's boats which may be trusted. Accept the assurances of my esteem & respect.   TH: JEFFERSON

PoC (Mrs. T. Wilber Chelf, Mrs. Virginius Dabney, and Mrs. Alexander W. Parker, Richmond, 1944; photocopy in ViU: TJP); on verso of reused address cover of Benjamin Waterhouse to TJ, 1 Sept. 1815; at foot of text: "Mʳ Gibson"; endorsed by TJ. Enclosure not found.

On this date TJ recorded compensating his GRANDSON Thomas Jefferson Randolph with an order on Gibson & Jefferson in repayment of $672.25 that TJ had borrowed throughout the month of October to cover his cash needs, payments made to plantation employees, shoes, and household expenses (*MB*, 2:1315–6). For the 35. BARRELS OF FLOUR, see TJ to Gibson, 17 Oct. 1815.

[1] Preceding three words interlined.
[2] Preceding three words interlined.

From John Guillemard

SIR   Bordeaux. 28th. October. 1815.

If you are surprized at receiving a letter from me I hope you will excuse me for my motives sake. It is to render service to an intelligent young Man of Florence, who is desirous of a botanical and chemical correspondent in America, that I take the liberty of addressing you. With your influence and in the large circle of your friends you may possibly engage some Man of Science, or possibly more than one, to enter into such a correspondance. The young Man in question is a noble Florentine called Il Marchese Cosimo Ridolfi. American Vessells go often, I imagine to Leghorn, and thence to Florence the distance is not great.

At Pisa I paid a visit to Signor Mazzinghi who read to me part of a letter he had lately received from you. Tho' very far advanced in years he has not lost his powers of intellect, and he speaks with fire when he speaks of you. It was in the month of February that I called on him with a letter of introduction from a Gentleman of Lucca and I hoped to have seen him again in the course of the Summer, but the Revolution at naples detained me there so long that I was obliged to give up my plan of returning to Pisa and Genoa and of paying my respects to an intelligent and kind hearted Old Man for whom I feel great respect.

I am going directly to Paris whence, after about a month passed with my old friends the Rochefoucaulds &c. I shall make my way to London. I shall have been absent from England about a year and a half and I begin to hanker after my English friends among whom I still number a former American Traveller Sir William Strickland who generally makes a visit to me Every Spring.

At Geneva I met another American Traveller Weld who had lately made a Voyage from Dublin to London in a large Vessell which came from the Clyde to Ireland propelled by the new method of water wheels moved by a steam Engine. This mode of navigation will soon be extended over the Occean and what will be its results can be scarcely calculated.

I have seen within the compass of a few months the lavas of Vesuvius and the Basalts of the extinguished Volcanos of the Puy de Dome. You know that the Hebrides and a great part of Scotland are basaltic. When I contemplate the traces of the great Revolutions of the Earth my Imagination sometimes overpowers me. I do not recollect having observed any basalt in the United States.

I must not intrude further upon your leisure and I hasten to subscribe my self

Your obliged & respectful humble servan[t]

J. GUILLEMARD

RC (DLC); edge chipped; at foot of text: "Thos Jefferson &c. &c. &c."; endorsed by TJ as received 21 Jan. 1816 and so recorded in SJL.

John Lewis Guillemard (1764–1844) was born in England to a Huguenot family. In 1786 he received a B.A. degree from Saint John's College, Oxford University. Guillemard traveled to the United States in the 1790s, and in 1796 he visited Monticello with the Duc de La Rochefoucauld-Liancourt. While in Philadelphia in 1797, Guillemard served on a commission established under the Jay Treaty to help settle British creditors' pre-Revolutionary claims. He was a member or officeholder in numerous American and British learned societies, including the American Philosophical Society, the Linnean Society of London, the Royal Asiatic Society, the Royal Geographical Society, the Royal Institution, and the Royal Society of London (*PTJ*, 29:149n, 154–5; Joseph Jackson Howard, ed., *Miscellanea Genealogica et Heraldica*, new ser., 3 [1880]: 388; *Notes and Records of the Royal Society* 3 [1940–41]: 95–6; John Bassett Moore, *History and Digest of the International Arbitrations to which the United States has been a Party* [1898], 1:271–94; APS, Minutes, 21 July 1797 [MS in PPAmP]; *Annals of Natural History; or, Magazine of Zoology, Botany and Geology* 1 [1838]: 412; *Journal of the Royal Asiatic Society* 5 [1839]: xxii; *Journal of the Royal Geographical Society of London* 1 [1832]: xvi; Royal Institution of Great Britain, *A List of the Members,*

Officers, and Professors [1863], iv; *Jackson's Oxford Journal*, 30 Nov. 1844).

Cosimo Ridolfi (1794–1865), agriculturist and politician, was a native of Florence. In the 1820s he traveled in Europe studying farming practices, and he eventually established an agricultural school on his estate at Meleto. Ridolfi later taught agricultural courses at the University of Pisa. He served in 1849 as a minister of Leopold II, grand duke of Tuscany, and later he was a senator of the unified country of Italy. In 1860 he was elected director of the Museum of Physics and Natural History in Florence (Raffaello Lambruschini, *Elogio del presidente March. Cosimo Ridolfi letto alla R. Accademia dei Georgofili* [1866]).

By SIGNOR MAZZINGHI Guillemard apparently meant Philip Mazzei. REVOLUTION AT NAPLES: Napoleon's brother-in-law Joachim Murat, king of Naples, kept his throne by joining the allied powers early in 1814. After Napoleon's return from Elba, however, Murat attacked the Austrian forces in northern Italy and was defeated. Naples returned to Bourbon rule thereafter, and Murat was executed after a final rebellion failed (Connelly, *Napoleonic France*, 346–7, 352). In May 1815 Isaac WELD took the steamboat *Thames* from Dún Laoghaire, Ireland, to London (*ODNB*; George Dodd, *An Historical and Explanatory Dissertation on Steam-Engines . . . concluding with A Narrative, by Isaac Weld, Esq., of the Interesting Voyage of the Thames Steam-Yacht* [London, 1818], 253–80).

From Robert Saunders

S<small>IR</small>, Williamsburg 29th Octr 1815.

I have received your favor of the 22^d inst. on the subject of the Property left by the late m^r Bellini—In order that I might understand this subject; I applied yesterday to m^r Bracken to be informed what remained in his hands, before I should determine to act under the Authority you have been pleased to say you will confide to me. From m^r Bracken I learn that he has in his hands, perhaps, five hundred dollars; no settlement of his administration having been made whereby the precise Sum can be ascertained. On the subject of interest Mr Bracken remarks, that, under a Power given by the Representatives of m^r Bellini to Mr Mazzeï, and at the solicitation of the latter, he remitted to London several years since a Bill which was accepted in his name to be demanded by him—That the money lay upwards of two years in London, and not being demanded by Mr Mazzei, was redrawn by him. That this circumstance, as well as being always ready to pay over the balance, ought to exempt him from the Payment of interest.

I will accept the offer of the Power, and proceed to obtain a settlement of the estate with as little delay as possible—So soon as the money is received I will cause it, after the customary deductions, to be placed to your credit in the Bank of Virginia.

with every consideration of respect,

I am, Sir, your obed^t Servant R<small>O</small>: S<small>AUNDERS</small>.

RC (DLC); dateline at foot of text; endorsed by TJ as received 15 Dec. 1815 and so recorded in SJL. RC (Mrs. T. Wilber Chelf, Mrs. Virginius Dabney, and Mrs. Alexander W. Parker, Richmond, 1944; photocopy in ViU: TJP); address cover only; with PoC of TJ to Patrick Gibson, 27 Jan. 1816, on verso; addressed: "Thomas Jefferson Esquire Monticello. Albemarle"; franked; postmarked Williamsburg, 30 Oct., and Charlottesville, 5 Nov.

TJ's letter to Saunders was dated 23 Oct. 1815, not T<small>HE</small> 22^D <small>INST</small>.

From William Bentley

SIR   Salem Mass. USA. Oct 30. 1815.

I received from my Aged friend & Correspondent Professor C D. Ebeling his Letter of 22 of May last. In it I find the following paragraph, which as I believe was dictated by profound respect & from a man who once said, I wish all [...] could produce such a man! I take the liberty to transcribe at length, that you might see the whole history of it.

At present my description of Virginia is printing. About 20 sheets are finished. I hope to send it soon. The Manuscript was ready for the press long ago, but I would not submit it to the French pretention to send it to Paris, to be examined by a Censor, or perhaps be suppressed by him. Since we have been in great want of Composers, & I could not send it elsewhere to be printed, as the many nomina propria required my own care in correcting the proof sheets. I have a mind to dedicate this Volume to Mr Jefferson, as some copies will be printed with the particular title of Description of Virginia. Perhaps it would be possible to give a translation of this part to your countrymen, corrected & improved, as also enlarged as to what belongs to the last 4 or 5 years. Mr Morse will not perhaps much approve it, as I could not make great use of his Geography of this State, which is mostly copied verbatim from Mr Jefferson's Notes. As to the history of Virginia I regret much not to have at hand the 2d & 3d part of Burke's history. The first I owe to your kindness. Your literary history of the last five years is almost unknown to me &c.[1]

The high obligations I am under, in behalf of my learned friend have encouraged the hope, Sir, that you would at your leisure, just give me an outline of such materials, as might finish the work of this good man, whose Geography already finished, in the manner of Busching, has reached six large volumes, & some parts in a second edition & has been kindly received wherever the German language is known.

This Letter has been accompanied with the history[2] of Hamburg for private use. One article, written in May, & received while N. was in Paris, I take the liberty to transcribe, as nothing[3] could then have been known, of what has happened since N. joined the Army.

It is hoped the war will be short. N & his former friends distrust each other. You have no idea of the spirit of Germany, particularly of

Prussia. Only a part of Saxony is behind the rest, because they dislike the partition of their Country, which the Congress of Vienna found necessary (I know not with what right) to sever.[4]

As the outline given by an eyewitness, & for the use of a friend, may be pleasing to you, & will exhibit the real [sense?] of one of the greatest Commercial Cities, at some future opportunity I will transmit to you. No praise I can utter, can equal the gratitude I feel, as a Citizen[5] of the United States, my own highest praise is, in the worst of times, not to have been ungrateful to our greatest national benefactor.

with all respect your devoted Servant,   WILLIAM BENTLEY.

RC (DLC); two words illegible; at foot of text (first word illegible): "[...]: Thomas Jefferson, Ex President of the US.A. Monticello"; endorsed by TJ as received 15 Dec. 1815 and so recorded in SJL.

Bentley loosely quotes from Christoph Daniel Ebeling's LETTER OF 22 OF MAY 1815, which describes Ebeling's work on the seventh and final volume of his history of the United States, *Erdbeschreibung und Geschichte von Amerika. Die vereinten Staaten von Nordamerika* (Hamburg, 1793–1816; Poor, *Jefferson's Library*, 7 [no. 368]; TJ's copy of vol. 7 in PPL, inscribed: "To His Excellency Thomas Jefferson most respectfully offered by the author"), and which gives an extensive history of recent events in Hamburg (MS in MH: Ebeling letters to Bentley). NOM-

INA PROPRIA: "personal names." Ebeling chose not to DEDICATE the seventh volume of his work to TJ and honored Bentley and others instead (*PTJ*, 28:427n). Anton Friedrich Büsching (BUSCHING) published his geographical work, *Neue Erdbeschreibung*, in Hamburg in eleven volumes, 1754–92 (Charles W. J. Wither, *Placing the Enlightenment: Thinking Geographically about the Age of Reason* [2007], 183).

[1] Paragraph written in a different hand or possibly by Bentley in a disguised hand.
[2] Manuscript: "hisory."
[3] Manuscript: "nothig."
[4] Paragraph written in a different hand or possibly by Bentley in a disguised hand.
[5] Manuscript: "Citzen."

From George Fleming

SIR   Louisa Healing Springs Octo 30th 1815

The papers I have taken the liberty of sending to you contain the description of a new theory on the application of Steam, I sent a copy to Doc[r] Thornton (patent office) some weeks past, who has done me the honor to notice my communication in a manner that gives me much encouragement, I wished for some months past to send them to you, & only hesitated because I never had the happyness of your acquaintance, nor the pleasure of seeing you, if under these circumstances I have made too free I still hope you will excuse me, & that you will believe there is no one I should be more unwilling to offend than yourself

I have a small Mill whose profits are yet very important to me & which often wants water & "duris urgens in rebus egestas" has led to this imagination & some others, but none terminating in results like this, for if this can perform but one fourth only what the philosophy & figures promise, I shall be satisfied,

I can scarcely tell you how much I should be gratified if you will have the goodness & can spare the time to look at this thing, & in that case a line directed to me at Goochland C. House would reach me sooner than from the office of this county.—I am Sir wth the highest respect

your[1] obedient &[ca]   GEO. FLEMING

RC (DLC); endorsed by TJ as received 15 Dec. 1815 and so recorded in SJL.

George Fleming, miller, emigrated as a young man from his native Ireland before 1781, when he was living in Maryland. He worked as a merchant before turning to farming. By 1799 Fleming owned a 1,300-acre tract of Louisa County land known as Healing Springs. He unsuccessfully sought a consular position in Europe in 1809. Due to his expertise in milling, in 1820 Fleming was appointed a commissioner at TJ's suggestion in the latter's lawsuit against the Rivanna Company. In 1827 Fleming patented his improvement in "the application of steam power in raising water, &c." (Louise Pecquet du Bellet, *Some Prominent Virginia Families* [1907; repr. 1976], 1:406; William Hand Browne and others, eds., *Archives of Maryland* [1883–1972], 47:533; Fleming to Samuel Overton, 3 Feb. 1799 [ViW: Overton Family Papers]; Richmond *Enquirer*, 14 Oct. 1808; Edmund Winston to James Madison, 9 Nov. 1809, and Spencer Roane to Madison, 30 Nov. 1809 [both in DNA: RG 59, LAR, 1809–17]; TJ to John H. Peyton, 22 Jan. 1820, and enclosure; Peyton to TJ, 24 Feb. 1820; *List of Patents*, 334).

DURIS URGENS IN REBUS EGESTAS: "Want that pinches when life is hard," from Virgil, *Georgics*, 1.146 (Fairclough, *Virgil*, 1:108–9).

[1] Manuscript: "you."

I

George Fleming's Drawing of a Steam Engine

[ca. 30 Oct. 1815]

Draught of an Hydraulic engine to work from Steam & Atmospheric Pressure.—

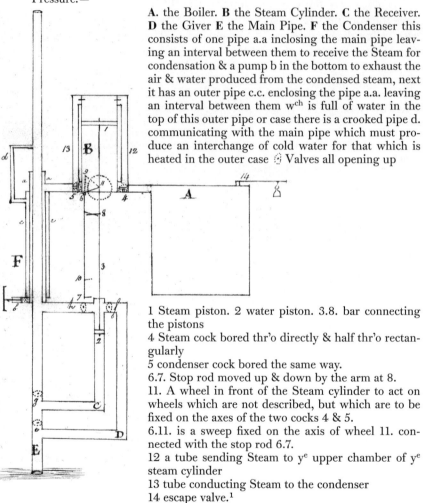

A. the Boiler. **B** the Steam Cylinder. **C** the Receiver. **D** the Giver **E** the Main Pipe. **F** the Condenser this consists of one pipe a.a inclosing the main pipe leaving an interval between them to receive the Steam for condensation & a pump b in the bottom to exhaust the air & water produced from the condensed steam, next it has an outer pipe c.c. enclosing the pipe a.a. leaving an interval between them wch is full of water in the top of this outer pipe or case there is a crooked pipe d. communicating with the main pipe which must produce an interchange of cold water for that which is heated in the outer case ⊙ Valves all opening up

1 Steam piston. 2 water piston. 3.8. bar connecting the pistons

4 Steam cock bored thr'o directly & half thr'o rectangularly

5 condenser cock bored the same way.

6.7. Stop rod moved up & down by the arm at 8.

11. A wheel in front of the Steam cylinder to act on wheels which are not described, but which are to be fixed on the axes of the two cocks 4 & 5.

6.11. is a sweep fixed on the axis of wheel 11. connected with the stop rod 6.7.

12 a tube sending Steam to ye upper chamber of ye steam cylinder

13 tube conducting Steam to the condenser

14 escape valve.[1]

MS (DLC: TJ Papers, 205:36686); written entirely in Fleming's hand on one side of a single sheet; undated.

[1] At foot of text, beneath drawing, Fleming canceled "Sin 60°" and "Tan 3° 14'."

II

George Fleming's Description of a Steam Engine

[ca. 30 Oct. 1815]

Mod. operandi.

pour in the top of ye mainpipe water enough to cover the valves, from the position of cock 4 the steam now passes directly into the lower chamber of ye steam cylinder, & from ye position of cock 5. the steam previously collected over pistons is at ye same time passing to ye condenser, under these circumstances the pistons 1 & 2 & the bar 3.8. connecting them must rise, when they have reached the top, the arm at 8. will have raised the stop rod 6.7. the sweep 6.11 will be at 9.11. the arm 7. will be at 10. & the cocks 4 & 5. will be turned in ye other direction, the cock 4 must then direct the steam to the upper chamber of ye steam cylinder & cock 5. will at same time convey the steam from the lower chamber of the steam cylinder to the condenser, the pistons 1 & 2 must then descend with ye bar 3.8 connecting them, & while descending the arm 8. will force down the arm 7 now at 10. to its former place & the wheel & cocks will be turned as at first. A few strokes up & down expels from all the pipes the Atmos^c air; on the principle of the common pump the water must then rise to the upper valves in pipes **E** & **D**. & in pipe **C**. it will rise up to piston 2, while piston 2 descends the water it forces down cannot escape thr'o valve. e. but must rise thr'o valve. g. & discharge an equal column from ye top of pipe **E** & while piston 2 descends[1] it is followed by a stream of water from pipe **D**. by Atmos^c pressure wch cooperates with the steam pressing on piston. 1. when piston 2 ascends it forces up the water now above it which cannot escape thr'o valve. f. but must go by valve. h. into pipe **E** & discharge an equal quantity from the top, the water now follows piston 2 ascending from the same cause & contributes the aid of Atmos^c pressure to the piston 2 both ascending & descending. —

Rationale —

The power of an engine thus constructed must then be compounded of two forces viz. Steam & Atmos^c pressure, the power of Steam is again in the compound ratio of its temperature & the surface pressed on, while Atmos^c pressure is simply as ye surface —

It has been ascertained that Atmos^c pressure is nearly equal to 15 lbs on every square inch, & that steam at 212° Fahrenheit presses also 15 lbs on every inch, as long as it is unnecessary to raise the steam much over 212° F. there can be no danger of explosion, for any vessel can confine steam while its elasticity is but equal to the pressure without the boiler.

On these principles we can calculate the power of such an engine, let the boiler be of a moderate size with an escape valve one inch square & a Thermometer so placed as to indicate the temperature let the steam cylinder & piston 1 be 18 inches diameter let the receiver, piston 2. & all the other pipes be 6 inch^s diam^r & the steam at 212° Fa^e it is required what weight & what height it will heave a column of water —

We may first count 34 feet gained by Atmos^c pressure on the well, upon ye principle of the common pump, this needs no demonstration for if piston 2 worked within 34 feet of the wells surface the water would follow to that height, & if piston 2. worked at the wells surface, it would be pressed up by a force equal to y^e weight of 34 feet of water on the same principle.

As every circle is equal to a triangle whose base is equal to y^e circumference & perpendicular equal to Radius, we have the area of piston 1. $\frac{3.1416 \times 18 \times 9}{2} =$ 254.4696 inches the area of piston 1. which multiplied by 15 the force of Steam at 212° Fa. gives 3817.0440 lbs for the Steam pressure on piston. 1. The pipes being all equal and 6 inch^s diamt^r we find the number of cubic inch^s in one foot $\frac{6 \times 3.1416 \times 3}{2} \times 12 = 339.2928$ cubic inches in each foot of this pipe, measuring 1.4688 Gal^n & weighing 12.4848 lbs in every foot; divide 3817.0440 lbs steam pressure by 12.4848 the weight of each foot of water & you have the number of feet in height to which this engine will heave the water & multiplying the number of feet so obtained by 12.4848 you have the weight.

the Log^m for y^e steam pressure is 　　　　　3.5817271
the Log^m for y^e weight of 1 foot of water is 1.0963812
　　　　　　　　　　　　　　　　　　2.4853459 = 305.73 feet the
height to which the water is raised by this force of Steam, but there presses also on the upper end of pipe **E** a column of air equal to the weight of 34 feet of water, which must be subtracted from the steam & Atmos^c pressure below, its power may be expressed 34 + 305.73 − 34 = 305.73 feet in height contain^g 449 G^{ns} and weighing 3816.77 lbs the power & resistance being thus nearly ballanced just as you increase the tempera^e of y^e Steam so may you accelerate the motion of the pistons up & down; a weight of 5 lbs on a valve 1 Sq^e inch is as much I think as can ever be wanting; making a pressure equal only to one Atmosphere & one third; if the receiver is 4 feet long & 6 inch^s diameter every time piston 2. goes up or down an equal quantity of water must be discharged from the top of pipe **E** equal to 5.8752 G^{ns} at 20 double strokes to the minute it will discharge[2] 235 G^{ns} in that time.—

It is easily seen by calculation how the proportions of the parts composing such an engine may be altered or modified so as to suit the different quantities of water or heights to which it may be necessary to heave it. for example, what height would this same steam power raise water in pipes of 4 inch^s instead of 6 circles are to each other as the squares of their diam^{tr} therefore $\overline{4}]^2 : \overline{6}]^2 : : 305.73 : 687.89$ feet in height raised by same Steam pressure in pipes of 4 inch^s. Or let it be necessary to raise the water only 20 feet for a Mill or other mechanical purpose requiring much power. Let the Steam cylinder & piston 1, be 18 inch^s diam^r let the receiver, piston 2 & all the other pipes be 18 inches diam^r let the lower end of ye receiver be 6 feet above the well, let piston 2 be at the bottom of the receiver, & let all the pipes be full of water; it is asked what force of steam to the inch is sufficient to raise the water to this height.—

There is then 6 feet of water in the pipe below piston 2. sustained by the Atmos^c pressure below. & 14 feet of water above pressing on piston 2 with a like Atmos^c pressure on top of pipe **E**. the difference between what we gain from Atmos^c pressure below piston 2 & weight we must encounter of water & Atmos^c pressure above piston 2 is the resistance the Steam must counteract.—

each foot of those pipes contains 13.2187 G^{ns} weighing 112.3589 lbs that multiplied by 6 the height of piston 2 above the well gives 674.1534 lbs of water already sustained below piston 2 by Atmo^c pressure on the well, & we have 14 feet water above piston 2 equal to 185.0618 G^{ns} weighing 1573.0246 lbs: the atmos^c pressure on pipes of 18 inches diam^r at 15 lbs the inch is 3817.0440 and it is equal at the top & bottom therefore $\overline{3817.0440} + 1573.0246 - \overline{3817.0440} - 674.1534 = 2247.3280^3$ lbs the resistance the steam must counteract; divide the resistance so found by 254.4696 the area in inch^s of piston 1, quotient 8.8314 lbs is w^t p^r square inch the steam must press to counterpoise this resistance, this is a low degree of temperature little more than half the Atmo^c pressure without; if y^e Steam pressure be raised 2 or 3 lbs to the inch this engine may make 20 double strokes to the minute, & if the receiver is 4 feet long it will discharge 105.7496 × 20 = 2114.9920 Gall^{ns} in one minute—

Corollary—

If the diam^r of the pipes be lessened (cæteris paribus) the same quantity of water will be discharged in same time, for [when]^4 the power is the same the resistance is diminished. When the water is raised any height less than 34 feet the difference between what you gain from Atmo^c pressure below piston 2. & the weight of water & Atmos^c pressure above piston 2. is the resistance. When the water is to be raised exactly 34 feet the whole resistance is the Atmos^c pressure on top of the pipe. When the water is to be raised any height above 34 the Atmos^c pressure above & below being equal calculate the weight of water in all pipe **F**. & you have the resistance.—

MS (DLC: TJ Papers, 205:36684–5); written entirely in Fleming's hand on four numbered pages; undated.

[1] Manuscript: "desends."
[2] Manuscript: "discharg."
[3] The correct figure is 2247.178.
[4] Omitted word editorially supplied.

From Sir John Sinclair

DEAR SIR, 32. Sackville Street London. 1. November–1815.

After a long interruption, I am happy to renew our correspondence, and to have another opportunity of expressing my sincere wishes for your health and happiness.

I have of late been engaged in a work which I hope will be of use both to my own country, and to America; and the circulation of which, I am persuaded you will be happy to promote on the other side of the atlantic.

The inclosed paper, which explains the contents of the work; and a sketch of the Chapter on those customs and habits which influence Health, will enable you to form an idea of the nature of the plan, and the mode of its execution.

I rejoice that the two countries are again at peace, which I hope will long continue; and; if possible shall never again be interrupted.

With much esteem & regard Believe me,

Dear Sir, Your faithful & obedient Servant   JOHN SINCLAIR

RC (MHi); dateline adjacent to signature; at foot of text: "Thomas Jefferson Esqr &c—&c—&c"; endorsed by TJ as received 3 May 1816 and so recorded, as a letter of 21 Nov. 1815, in SJL. RC (MHi); part of address cover only; with PoC of TJ to David Gelston, 3 Aug. 1816, on verso; addressed: "Thom[...]"; postmarked Charlottesville, 1 May. Enclosure: circular concerning a new, single-volume, octavo edition of Sinclair's *Code of Health and Longevity* (originally published in 4 vols. in Edinburgh, 1807), consisting of an introductory paragraph asking for comments and additional information on the material included herein from "those respectable characters, to whom copies of this paper shall be transmitted"; and an extract consisting of chapter five of part two, treating "Of the Customs and Habits which Influence Health, and Rules therewith Connected," which elaborates rules of health and hygiene recommended by Sinclair, summarizes similar recommendations from a variety of authors, and warns against the use of tobacco, opium, and a morning dram of spirits ([Edinburgh, 1815?]; TJ's copy in ViU, with Sinclair's handwritten inscription at head of text: "Thomas Jefferson Esqʳ From the author"). The extract was published as chapter four of part two in Sinclair, *The Code of Health and Longevity; or, A Gen-*eral *View of the Rules and Principles Calculated for the Preservation of Health, and the Attainment of Long Life* (London, 1816), 453–71.

Sir John Sinclair (1754–1835), public official, author, and agricultural reformer, was born in Caithness, Scotland, educated at the universities of Edinburgh, Glasgow, and Oxford, and became a baronet in 1786. He was a member of parliament intermittently from 1780 to 1811 and served as president of the newly formed Board of Agriculture in the 1790s and again from 1806–13. Sinclair conducted agricultural experiments on his Scottish estates and wrote extensively on a wide range of topics, including agriculture, current events, political economy, and public health. His special interest was the compilation of data, and his lasting achievement was the *Statistical Account of Scotland*, 21 vols. (Edinburgh, 1791–99; repr. 1977–83). TJ and Sinclair met in France about 1786 and afterwards exchanged numerous pamphlets and corresponded on agriculture and politics, including a lengthy letter in which TJ described his moldboard plow. Sinclair died in Edinburgh (*DNB*; *ODNB*; Rosalind Mitchison, *Agricultural Sir John: The Life of Sir John Sinclair of Ulbster, 1754–1835* [1962]; *PTJ*, esp. 9:405–6, 30:197–209; Sowerby).

To Christopher Clark

DEAR SIR   Poplar Forest Nov. 2. 15

I arrived here two days ago, and have brought with me instruments for our project at the peaks. as I presume you would like to see something of the proceedings, you must be so good as to say when your business will permit you to be at home for three or four days; for I think it will take that time. to me, after tomorrow, all days will be equal; and the sooner the better while we have such fair and moderate weather. your earliest convenience therefore will suit me best, and you will be good enough to make it known to me by the bearer. I think I shall be obliged again to clamber to the top of the sharp peak. present me respectfully to mrs Clarke and accept the assurance of my great esteem and respect.   TH: JEFFERSON

PoC (MHi); at foot of text: "Christopher Clarke esq."; with PoC of TJ to Martha Jefferson Randolph, 4 Nov. 1815, on verso.

From Christopher Clark

DEAR SIR,   Mount Prospect 2 of Nov[r] 1815

your favor of this morning was just now delivered by the servant I am glad to hear of your Return to Bedford and if convenient to you shall be glad to see you here on next sunday to dinner, this will give us the advantage of the early part of next week, and by which time the smoke will have probably disapated so as to afford a fair View of the summit of the mountain

I have discovered a much better situation to asertain the altitude of the sharp than the one we Viewed and by the time you arrive will endeavour to have the Necessary poles prepared for measurement according to your discription

In coming up you will Remember to take the Right hand Road about two miles this side of the Otter Bridge that will bring you streight here we shall be glad to see any acquaintance of yours that may accompany you

Very Respectfully

D[r] Sir your mo ob st   CHRISTOPHER CLARK

RC (MHi); endorsed by TJ as received 2 Nov. 1815 and so recorded in SJL.

From the Citizens of Lynchburg

SIR;   Lynchburg 4th November 1815

We are directed by the Citizen's of Lynchburg to Solicit the favor of your Company and that of your Companion's or Visitor's at a public Dinner which will be given, in the Town of Lynchburg, to Maj[r] Gen[l] Andrew Jackson on Tuesday next—The Citizen's of Lynchburg are happy to have it in their power to entertain at the Same time two such distinguish'd Citizen's—

T A HOLCOMBE
JOHN H SMITH
JAMES B RISQUE
RICH. POLLARD
JOHN ROBINSON.

On behalf of the Citizen's of Lynchburg—

RC (MHi); in Smith's hand, signed by Holcombe, Smith, Risque, Pollard, and Robinson; endorsed by TJ as a letter from "Holcombe et al." received 4 Nov. 1815 and so recorded in SJL.

John Hill Smith (ca. 1783–1843), attorney, studied at the College of William and Mary and represented King and Queen County in the Virginia House of Delegates, 1806–09. He practiced law in Williamsburg, and during the War of 1812 he served in the militia as a captain of riflemen at Yorktown. Smith soon moved to Lynchburg and qualified at the bar of Bedford County late in 1814. He subsequently moved with his family first to Hanover County and then in 1820 to Richmond, where he practiced law, sat on the Virginia Council of State, 1827–31, and served as commissioner of Revolutionary War claims, 1834–36. Smith later moved to Dinwiddie County, where he died (Louise Pecquet du Bellet, *Some Prominent Virginia Families* [1907; repr. 1976], 1:56–8; *William and Mary Provisional List*, 37; Leonard, *General Assembly*, 244, 248, 252; Butler, *Virginia Militia*, 113; Bedford Co. Order Book, 16:345; *JHD* [1826–27 sess.], 33 [16 Dec. 1826]; [1830–31 sess.], 161 [11 Feb. 1831]; [1835–36 sess.], 204–5, 257 [10, 21 Mar. 1836]; *Resolutions, Laws, and Ordinances, relating to the pay, half pay, commutation of half pay, bounty lands, and other promises made by Congress to the Officers and Soldiers of the Revolution* [1838], 331–2; *Richmond Whig and Public Advertiser*, 7 Apr. 1843; gravestone inscription in Village View Cemetery, Dinwiddie).

James Beverly Risque (1767–1843), attorney, was a native of Fincastle. He studied at Liberty Hall Academy (later Washington and Lee University) in the 1780s, and by 1808 he was practicing law in Botetourt County. Risque later moved to Lynchburg, continuing his legal work there. He was a frequent visitor to Nashville and was an associate and political supporter of Andrew Jackson. In 1821 Risque unsuccessfully sought a federal appointment in the Florida Territory. He died in Lynchburg, leaving a personal estate valued at over $3,700, including nine slaves (Margaret Anthony Cabell, *Sketches and Recollections of Lynchburg by the Oldest Inhabitant (Mrs. Cabell)* 1858 [1858; repr. with additional material by Louise A. Blunt, 1974], 64–5; Stella M. Drumm, comp., "The Kennerlys of Virginia," *Missouri Historical Society Collections* 6 [1928]: 107; *Catalogue of the Officers and Alumni of Washington and Lee University, Lexington, Virginia, 1749–1888* [1888], 52; *Richmond Enquirer*, 9 Sept. 1808; Jackson, *Papers*, 2:244–5, 553, 557, 561; DNA: RG 29, CS, Lynchburg, 1820–40; DNA: RG 59, LAR, 1817–25; *Richmond Enquirer*, 27 Nov. 1827; Campbell Co. Will Book, 9:295, 317–9, 425–6).

Richard Pollard (ca. 1790–1851), attorney, was a native of King and Queen County who studied at the College of William and Mary, 1808–09. By 1812 he was licensed to practice law, and he unsuccessfully sought a position as secretary of the Mississippi Territory. Pollard served in the United States Army, 1812–14, starting as a captain in the 20th Infantry Regiment and rising to major in the 21st Infantry. After leaving the army he worked as a merchant and lawyer in Lynchburg. By 1820 Pollard moved to Nelson County and practiced law in the surrounding counties. He was serving on the board of visitors of the United States Military Academy in 1833. President Andrew Jackson appointed Pollard chargé d'affaires to Chile, a position he held from 1834 to 1841. On his return to the United States, he settled in Albemarle County, where he farmed and resumed his legal career. In 1850 Pollard's real estate was valued at $15,000. He died in Washington (Alexander Brown, *The Cabells and their Kin*, 2d ed., rev. [1939; repr. 1994], 473; *William and Mary Provisional List*, 32; Heitman, *U.S. Army*, 1:796; Madison, *Papers, Pres. Ser.*, 4:118; DNA: RG 29, CS, Nelson Co., 1820, Albemarle Co., 1850; *Richmond Enquirer*, 14 Mar. 1828, 19 Nov. 1850; Washington *Globe*, 15 June 1833; *JEP*, 4:427, 430, 434, 5:407 [24, 27 June 1834, 16 July 1841]; Albemarle Co. Will Book, 20:315–6; Washington *Daily National Intelligencer*, 22 Feb. 1851; gravestone inscription at Oak Ridge estate cemetery, Nelson Co.).

On the following TUESDAY, 7 Nov. 1815, TJ attended the Lynchburg festivities in honor of Andrew Jackson, who was passing through on his way to Washington. The same five-man Committee of Arrangement that had written TJ composed an address inviting Jackson. TJ rode with Jackson in the procession into town. He reportedly declared the event to be "the most extravagant dinner ever he saw." TJ offered the second volunteer toast (the first being Jackson's), calling for "Honor and gratitude to those, who have filled the measure of their country's honor" (*Richmond Enquirer*, 15 Nov. 1815; Pocahontas Bolling Cabell to Susan Wilcox Hubard, 23 Dec. 1815 [NcU: Southern Historical Collection, Hubard Family Papers]).

To Martha Jefferson Randolph

MY DEAREST MARTHA   Poplar Forest Nov. 4. 15.

We arrived here on the third day of our journey, without any accident; but I suffered very much both mornings by cold. I must therefore pray you to send my wolf-skin pelisse and fur-boots by Moses's Billy, when he comes to bring the two mules to move the Carpenters back. he is to be here on the 27th by my directions to mr Bacon. In the closet over my bed you will find a bag tied up, and labelled 'Wolf-skin pelisse,' and another labelled 'fur-boots,' wherein those articles will be found. the pelisse had better be sowed up in a striped[1] blanket to keep it clean and uninjured; the boots in any coarse wrapper.

mr Baker called on me yesterday, and tells me Francis is gone to Monticello. I am in hopes Ellen will give him close employment. mr Baker is come to look for land in this quarter, and will return here this evening and start with me tomorrow morning to mr Clark's to examine his land which is for sale. it will place his family exactly under the sharp peak of Otter, 20. miles only from hence, and along a good road. lands of 2d quality are selling here now for 25. Dollars.—I am this moment interrupted by a croud of curious people come to see the house. Adieu my Dear Martha, kiss all the young ones for me; present me affectionately to mr Randolph, and be assured of my tenderest love.   TH: JEFFERSON

P.S. I was most agreeably surprised to find that the party whom I thought to be merely curious visitants were General Jackson and his suite, who passing on to Lynchburg did me the favor to call.

RC (NNPM); endorsed by Randolph. PoC (MHi); on verso of PoC of TJ to Christopher Clark, 2 Nov. 1815; endorsed by TJ.

TJ's WOLF-SKIN PELISSE was most likely the "fur" given to him by Tadeusz Kosciuszko in 1798 (*PTJ*, 30:331; Gaye Wilson, "Recording History: The

Thomas Sully Portrait of Thomas Jefferson," in Robert M. S. McDonald, ed., *Light and Liberty: Thomas Jefferson and the Power of Knowledge* [2012], 194–8). MOSES'S BILLY was William Hern, son of Moses Hern. The Monticello CARPEN-TERS had been at Poplar Forest working on the balustrade (Chambers, *Poplar Forest*, 91–5).

[1] Word interlined.

To Christopher Clark

DEAR SIR   Poplar Forest Nov. 5. 15.

I had every thing packed and prepared yesterday to set out this morning for Mount Prospe[c]t; but Gen[l] Jackson called on me in the forenoon, and a committ[e]e from the citizens of Lynchbg in the afternoon to invite me to partake of a dinner they give the General on Tuesday. respect to the citizens of Lynchburg as well as the hero of N. Orleans forbade a refusal. I will however be with you to dinner on Wednesday. should you conclude to join the party in Lynchburg in their respect to the general, we may return here in the evening of Tuesday, and set off together on Wednesday morning for our operations at the peak. be so good as to accept this apology for my failure to our appointment & the assurance of my great esteem & respect.

TH: JEFFERSON

PoC (MHi); on verso of reused address cover to TJ; two words faint; at foot of text: "M[r] Clarke"; endorsed by TJ.

TJ left for Mount Prospect on or about WEDNESDAY, 8 Nov., and stayed until 12 Nov. 1815 (*MB*, 2:1316; TJ to Charles Clay, 18 Nov. 1815).

From Christopher Clark

DEAR SIR,   Mount Prospect 5 Nov[r] 1815

I not only accept your Apology for not coming up to day but am pleased at the circumstance that has produced the failure I should Rejoice to join the Citizens of Lynchburg in their civility to the "hero of Orleans"[1] but fear it will be out of my power we shall be glad to see you on wednesday

accept the Renewed assurances of my high esteem

CHRIS CLARK

RC (MHi); endorsed by TJ as received 5 Nov. 1815 and so recorded in SJL.

[1] Closing single quotation mark editorially changed to double.

From Claude Alexandre Ruelle

MONSIEUR   Paris, le 5. 9bre 1815

Je m'empresse de vous offrir trois des premiers exemplaires imprimés de la Constitution dont vous avés eû la bonté de déposer le Manuscrit à la Bibliothèque du Congrès, j'en envoïe aussi à M. Madison, comme vous le verrés dans la copie ci-jointe de la lettre que je lui écris à cette occasion et dont je vous prie de seconder les voeux de tout votre pouvoir.

J'ai eû bien de la joye en apprenant l'offre que vous avés faite de votre Bibliothèque pour remplaçer celle qui a été détruite par le Sac de Washington, car c'était pour moi un certificat de votre existence pour la prolongation de la quelle je forme constamment des voeux bien ardens.

Agréés, je vous prie, Monsieur, une nouvelle assurance de ma plus haute et plus respectueuse considération.   RUELLE

Rue Trainée, N° 15.

EDITORS' TRANSLATION

SIR   Paris, 5. November 1815

I am eager to offer you three of the first printed copies of the constitution, the manuscript of which you kindly deposited in the Library of Congress. I am also sending some copies of it to Mr. Madison, as you will see in the enclosed copy of the letter I am writing him on this occasion, and I entreat you to support with all your power the wishes expressed in this letter.

I felt very happy when I learned that you had offered your library to replace the one that was destroyed in the sack of Washington, as it reminds me of your existence, for the prolongation of which I constantly have very warm wishes.

Please accept, Sir, a renewed expression of my highest and most respectful regards.   RUELLE

Rue Trainée, Number 15.

RC (ViW: TC-JP); between dateline and salutation: "Ruelle, ancien Agent diplomatique; A Monsieur Jefferson, ancien Président des Etats-Unis de l'Amérique"; endorsed by TJ as received 27 Jan. 1816 and so recorded in SJL. Translation by Dr. Genevieve Moene. Enclosure: Ruelle, *Constitution de la République Beninienne, ou Modèle d'une*

Constitution Républicaine (Paris, 1815; Poor, *Jefferson's Library*, 11 [no. 680]), three copies. Other enclosure printed below.

For the MANUSCRIT of Ruelle's work, which TJ deposited in the Library of Congress, see note to Ruelle to TJ, 24 May 1809.

Claude Alexandre Ruelle to James Madison

MONSIEUR, Paris, 5. 9bre 1815

Puis que la Bibliothèque du Congrès, où M. Jefferson avait déposé le Manuscrit d'une Constitution de ma composition, a été détruite, j'ai l'honneur de vous en envoïer six Exemplaires imprimés, en vous priant de vouloir bien en faire mettre trois au même dépot, et d'agréer l'hommage des trois autres.

J'ai lû, Monsieur, dans un Message que vous adressâtes au Congrès, le 4. 9bre 1812, que les gouverneurs de Massachuset et de Connecticut avaient refusé de fournir les détachemens de Milices qui leur avaient été demandés pour la defense de vos frontieres maritimes; mais je ne vois pas encore que ce premier exemple des inconvéniens sans nombre du Système fédératif ait assés généralement éclairé vos Compatriotes pour y renonçer.

J'en souffre réellement beaucoup, car le genre humain est grandement intéressé à ce que votre République se perpétue, et elle ne saurait y parvenir sans l'unité et l'indivisibilité dont ma Constitution donne le Modèle.

En attendant qu'elle sorte des ténebres du fédéralisme, je désirerais, du moins, que ma Constitution fût traduite et imprimée en Espagnol pour être envoïée au Mexique et autres Colonies de cette Nation; même qu'elle fût réimprimée en francais pour être également envoïée à Saint-Domingue, comme étant absolument décisive pour arrêter les Torrens de sang qui se répandent dans ces Contrées, et couronner tout-à-coup leurs révolutions.

Certes, on ne saurait jamais faire un plus grand acte d'humanité, mais ce serait en même tems la spéculation la plus lucrative possible pour des Libraires de votre Pays.

Au reste, Monsieur, je soumets ces vües au Plan que vous vous êtes sans doute formé sur des événemens qui intéressent si fort les Etats-Unis, puis qu'ils fournissent evidemment l'occasion d'expulser successivement la Roïauté de toutes les parties de l'amérique.

Agréez &^{ca}

SIR, Paris, 5. November 1815

Since the Library of Congress, where Mr. Jefferson had deposited the manuscript of a constitution I had composed, has been destroyed, I have the honor of sending you six printed copies of it, and I am asking you to be so kind as to have three of them put in that same place and to accept the other three as a token of my esteem.

I have read, Sir, in a message you addressed to Congress on 4 November 1812, that the governors of Massachusetts and Connecticut had refused to supply the militia detachments that had been requested from them for the defense of your seacoast; but I do not yet see that this prime example of the innumerable disadvantages of the federative system has in general enlightened your fellow citizens sufficiently to cause them to give it up.

This gives me much real pain, because mankind is greatly interested in the perpetuation of your republic, and it cannot survive without the unity and in-divisibility exemplified in my constitution.

While waiting for your republic to emerge from the darkness of federal-ism, I would like, at the least, for my constitution to be translated and printed in Spanish. If it could be sent to Mexico and the other colonies of Spain, and even be reprinted in French and sent also to Saint Domingue, it would be ab-solutely decisive in stopping the torrents of blood being shed in these regions and in bringing their revolutions to an immediate conclusion.

Indeed, one could not commit a greater act of humanity, and at the same time it would be the most lucrative speculation for your country's book-sellers.

In any case, Sir, I submit these views to supplement the plan you have probably formed regarding events that are of such great interest to the United States, inasmuch as they obviously provide the opportunity to expel monarchy successively from all parts of America.

Please accept etc.

Tr (ViW: TC-JP); entirely in Ruelle's hand; at head of text: "Lettre de M. Ru-elle à M. madison." Translation by Dr. Genevieve Moene.

Madison's annual MESSAGE to Con-gress of 4 Nov. 1812 discussed the refusal of the GOUVERNEURS of Massachusetts and Connecticut, Caleb Strong and Roger Griswold, to allow state militia units to serve under federal command during the War of 1812 (Madison, *Papers, Pres. Ser.*, 5:429; *ANB*).

From Edmund Bacon

DEAR SIR.   Monticello 8ᵗʰ November. 1815.

a few days ago the inclosed note came to me from the contents I presume you pobably made application for cider. my not Knowing any thing Positive about it I consider it most Proper to inclose the note so that you may compleatly understand the matter. I sent in an-swer to the inclosed that I expected you would send according to the day appointed. I apprehend the cart will be down before that time to send for the cider.

I am disappinted in geting corn at 15./ I cannot find but very little to be bought even @ 18/. twenty shillings is commonly asked. as many ask 21/. as do 18/—I have Purchased none yet. my expectation was to have found a compleat supply at court 3 days ago. but the price at Richmond being so high seems to Keep up the price here. sharp sold his for 18/– cash the same day I recieved his message to send for his corn. the sale or perchase Mʳ Craven made at 15/. was not upon such terms as to establish a fair Price his wifes brother was comeing to live at his mill Craven agreed to give him such or certain Prices for all his

Property and to give him a certain price for his serviceis the yeare lumping all together. by which means his corn of 25 bar^ls cost about 15/. I never saw yet the day but I could Perchase what I wanted at some thing under what most of People gave and I have spaired no pains in inquireing for the cheapest corn and at Present am fully Purswaded it will put me fully up to my best exirtions to get supplyed at 18/. Mr Randolph advises me to get all I can at that Price but I shall be moderate untill I hear from you

I find the falled in dirt in the canal genrally 3 feet deep. we shall hardly get it out this week 3 or 4 day to come I am done sowing wheat a full month sooner than ever has been on tufton before sowed there 215. bus^ls at my Place 50. Mr Ham will get done in 8 or 10 days. there will not be a very good supply of corn made at tufton to last I dont think enough. with sincere respect. your Humble St   E: BACON

RC (ViU: TJP-ER); idiosyncratic punctuation editorially omitted; at foot of text: "Mr Jefferson"; endorsed by TJ as received 30 Jan. 1816 and so recorded in SJL.

For the INCLOSED NOTE from Charles Massie, see note to TJ to Massie, 18 Dec. 1815. Instead of purchasing CORN from John H. CRAVEN, on 4 Mar. 1816 TJ gave Bacon funds to buy ninety-nine barrels at a price of 18/6 each from Craven Peyton (*MB*, 2:1319).

From Henry Jackson

SIR   Paris Novr 9th 1815

Your note covering the letter for Mr Cathalan has been received,[1] and the request it contained immediately complied with. — Mr Cathalan has not yet had time to acknowledge its receipt. —

From the tenor of the note it would appear to be the second time you had requested my Services — This however is the first application that has reached me. — suffer me, sir, to assure you that during my stay[2] in Europe, nothing will give me greater pleasure, — nothing will so much gratify the best feelings of my heart, than to be enabled, by any service in my power, to give even a feeble testimony of my sincere & respectful esteem. —

There has been in my possession for five or six weeks an order on Lafitte of this city in favour of Mr Tickinor, drawn by Mr Girard of Philadelphia — I have not yet seen or heard of Mr Tickinor — should he not arrive,[3] I shall attend your orders, either directly from yourself, or mediately through Mr Vaughan, as to its ultimate disposition. —

With the most sincere & respectful attachment
I remain sir Your obed serv[t]   HENRY JACKSON

RC (DLC); at foot of text: "Thomas Jefferson—Late president of The United States"; endorsed by TJ as received 27 Jan. 1816 and so recorded in SJL. FC (DNA: RG 84, LRF, Miscellaneous Letters Sent); dated 8 Nov. 1815.

For the order on Perregaux, Laffitte (LAFITTE) & Company in favor of George Ticknor (TICKINOR), see note to John Vaughan to TJ, 31 July 1815.

[1] FC here adds "some days Since."
[2] FC here adds "in France or."
[3] FC: "not visit Paris."

Jefferson's Calculations of Altitude of the Peaks of Otter

I. LABELED DIAGRAMS RELATED TO CALCULATIONS OF ALTITUDE OF THE PEAKS OF OTTER, [BEFORE 10 NOV. 1815]

II. FIELD NOTES AND CALCULATIONS OF ALTITUDE OF THE PEAKS OF OTTER, [10–CA. 17 NOV. 1815]

III. SUMMARY COMMENTS ON THE PEAKS OF OTTER, [BEFORE 2 DEC. 1815]

EDITORIAL NOTE

Following his September visit to Bedford County and surrounding areas with José Corrêa da Serra and Francis W. Gilmer, Jefferson returned in November 1815 to expand on his earlier scientific observations and make more extensive geometrical calculations of the altitude of the Peaks of Otter. For this purpose he brought surveying tools from Monticello, including a theodolite made by the British instrument-maker Jesse Ramsden (a photograph of which is reproduced elsewhere in this volume). Jefferson stayed with his friend Christopher Clark at Mount Prospect, the latter's plantation, from about 8 to 12 Nov. 1815. Jefferson wrote that he devoted five days to making observations followed by five days of calculations based on this data. He probably began the Labeled Diagrams printed below before making his field observations in order to plan the calculations he would make. A summary of Jefferson's findings, which revealed that the Peaks were not as high as had been anticipated, soon found its way into the *Lynchburg Press*. The version reprinted in the *Richmond Enquirer* is given below (*MB*, 2:1313, 1316; TJ to Clark, 2, 5 Nov. 1815; Clark to TJ, 2, 5 Nov. 1815; TJ to Charles Clay, 18 Nov. 1815).

I. Labeled Diagrams Related to Calculations of Altitude of the Peaks of Otter

[before 10 Nov. 1815]

to obtain the altitude a.b. from 2. stations c. & d. each in the plane of the axis of a mountain a.b. and themselves on an inclined plane.

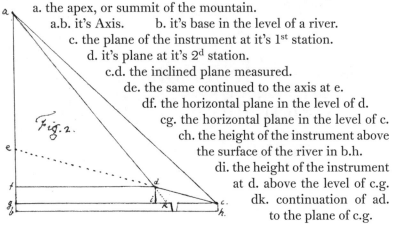

a. the apex, or summit of the mountain.
a.b. it's Axis.   b. it's base in the level of a river.
c. the plane of the instrument at it's 1st station.
d. it's plane at it's 2^d station.
c.d. the inclined plane measured.
de. the same continued to the axis at e.
df. the horizontal plane in the level of d.
cg. the horizontal plane in the level of c.
ch. the height of the instrument above the surface of the river in b.h.
di. the height of the instrument at d. above the level of c.g.
dk. continuation of ad. to the plane of c.g.

at c. observe the vertical ∠ acg. and rhumb of c.g.
and the height of the instrument above the water, to wit, ch.
the vertical ∠ icd[1]
measure c.d.
at d. observe the ∠ of altitude a.d.f.

In the △ cdi. to reduce cd. to ci. to find di. and c.i.
given cd and all the angles
in the △ dik. to find i.k. in order to reduce c.i. to ck. (given di. & all the ∠^s)
in the △ ack. to find ak. (given ck. and all the ∠^s)
in the △ akg. to find ag. and gk. (given ak. and all the ∠^s)
to ag. add ch. or gb. for the whole altitude ab.

To ascertain the height and distance of an inaccessible object (e.g. the summit of the sharp, or South peak of Otter) by a measured base

between two stations on an inclined plane, nearly parallel
with the mountain.

let l. be the apex, or summit of the mountain.

q. a point in it's axis in the level of it's base q.r.s &
of the surface of Otter river

m. the plane in which the instrument is
placed at it's 2^d and highet[2] station.

n. it's plane at the 1st[3] or lowest station.

m.n. the inclined plane measured
from station to station.

m.o.u. the horizontal plane
of m.

n.t.p. the horizontal plane of n.

m.t. the difference of level between these two planes

m.r. the height of m. above the base, or water of the river.

l.o.p.q.
m.t.r   } are vertically coincident. then
u.n.s

m.u.o
t.n.p. } are 3. horizontal $\triangle$^{s} vertically coincident, & consequently
r.s.q.   similar & equal.

in this figure the line p.n. is assumed longer than o.m. that it may
project in the profile, & shew in perspective the parallelograms
m.u.s.r. & m.u.n.t. the diagonal m.n. & $\triangle$ l.m.n.

at m. observe the vertical $\angle$^{s} l.m.o. & u.m.n.

the horizontal $\angle$ o.m.u. & rhumbs of m.o. & m.u.

the height of m.r.

[the altitude, horizontal $\angle$ & rhumb of the summit of
the North peak **L.** for another object]

measure the inclined plane m.n.

at n. observe the vertical $\angle$ l.n.p.

the horizont^l $\angle$ t.n.p. & rhumb of n.p.

[the altitude, horizontal $\angle$ & rhumb of the summit of
the North peak **L.**]

with these data proceed as follows.

to reduce n.m. to n.t. = u.m. & to find m.t. in the $\triangle$ m.n.t. given m.n.
& all the $\angle$^{s}

to find t:p = m.o. and n.p. in the horizont^l $\triangle$ n.p.t. given n.t. & all the $\angle$^{s}

to find l.o.   in the vertical $\triangle$ l.m.o. given m.o. & all the $\angle$^{s}.

to find l.p.   in the vertical $\triangle$ l.n.p. given n.p. & all the $\angle$^{s}.

add l.o. to o.q. and l.p. to p.q. and take the mean for the true height l.q.

The observations of the North peak from m. and n. may be used to obtain the distance between the two peaks, according to the diagram & method of Fig. 1. page 1. by reducing m.n. to t.n. which will then correspond with a.b. there, as c.d. there will correspond with l. and **L.** in these observations.

MS (MHi); filed with TJ's Weather Memorandum Book, 1802–16; written entirely in TJ's hand on two sheets of paper, with recto of unnumbered first page containing related theoretical mathematical exercises and two unnumbered figures in TJ's hand (omitted here) for ascertaining the distance and altitude of inaccessible objects from known points and calculating the bearing and distance from each other of inaccessible objects; undated; brackets in original.

[1] Reworked from "acd."
[2] Thus in manuscript.
[3] Reworked from "2^{d}."

II. Field Notes and Calculations of Altitude of the Peaks of Otter

[10–ca. 17 Nov. 1815]

Field Notes.   1st operation.

1815. Nov. 10. went on the top of the sharp or South peak of Otter, & from thence made these observations.

	o	′
the meridian altitude of the sun by sextant	71–	8
– error of instrument		1–30
	71–	6–30
	35 33	15[1]

---

magnetic rhumb of North or flat peak N. 35.° 50′ E.
(the varian[2] of needle had been before observed to be 2° East of N. i.e. 2° to the right of the true rhumb in all points)[3]
∠ of elevation of N. peak from apex of S. peak 52.′

---

from the apex of the sharp peak
the highest point of the main ridge of Willis's mountains makes an ∠ with the course of[4] the summit of N.[5] peak of 43°–37′
magnetic rhumb of same point in Willis's mount N. 80. E making the error of the needle 33′
∠ of depression of the same point in Willis's ridge from the apex of the S. peak is 46′

6

1815. Nov. 11. 2^d opern

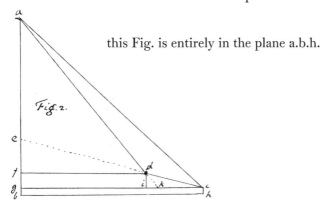

this Fig. is entirely in the plane a.b.h.

Fig. 2.

at c. observe it's position
> the vertical ∠ acg. + 7°–15′
>> magn. rhumb c.g. N. 46. W
>> height of instr. above water. ch 8.f
>> vertical ∠^{s} icd + 21′^{7}

ch   l

measure c.d. to bank of Otter 25–52
to publick road   17–
42–52 = 2806.32 f

at d. observe
> the vertical ∠ adf 8°–12′^{8}

both vertical & horizontal angles refer to the horizon.[9]
the rhumb is magnetical. varian 2.° E. of North.
measures in chains of 4. po.[10] & 100. links, except where otherwise
mentioned[11]
Notes for corrections
> Fig. 2.   in the vertical ∠ i.c.d. the elevn of 21.′ pointed 18 I. above
>> the true parallel to the inclined plane. c.d.
>> note that in all the operns the plane of the theodolite was
>> 3 f 8 I. above the ground.
> Fig. 3.   in the vertical ∠ t.n.m. the elevn of 27′ pointed 11.f. above
>> the true parallel of the inclined plane n.m.
> Fig. 2.   where the measured line c.d. crossed the main Otter river
>> the plane of the theodolite was 3 f–8 I + 4 f–4 I = 8. f
>> above the surface of the water.
> Fig. 3.   at the close of the measured line n.m. of 399.33 po. the
>> main Otter crossed it at 8. po. from m. and twice more
>> in the 12. po. preceding the last crossing.[12]

1815. Nov. 11. 3^d opern

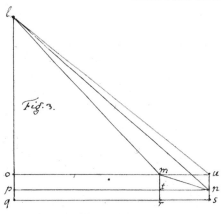

at n. observe it's position

the | vertical ∠   l.n.p. 8°–20′ |

    horiz^l ∠   t.n.p. 90°–13[13]

    magn. rhumb. n.p.   N. 56. W

    vert^{l14} ∠   tnm   27′

    rhumb   nmS 32° 25′ W

    height of instrum. above the water NS. 3 f–8 I + 4 f–4 I = 8 f

    the altitude of summit of N. peak **L** 8°–27′

       it horiz^l ∠ with n.p. 27°–11′[15]

               with n.m 117°–24′[16]

      it's magn. rhumb. N 29°–52½′ W

measure n.m. 399.33 po. = 6589.f

at m. observe

    the vertical ∠ lmo 8°–2′[17]

       horiz^l ∠ omu 70°–41

       rhumb of mo N. 37–45 W

    alt. of summit of N[18] peak **L** 7°–13′[19]

       it's horiz^l ∠ with mo 21°–53′

              mu 48°–48′[20]

    it's magnetic rhumb. N. 15°–45′ W[21]

Nov. 12. a repetition of the observns from the station m.

the ∠ between mn. & the N. peak. 48°–48′   u.m.**L.**

    rhumb of the N. peak N. 15°–45′ W.   m.**L.**

    vertic^l ∠ of altitude of N. peak 7°–13′

    horiz^l ∠ between that & S. peak 21°–53′   o.m.**L.**

    rhumb of S. peak. N. 37°–45′ W.   m.o.

    vertic^l ∠ of altitude of S. peak 8°–2′

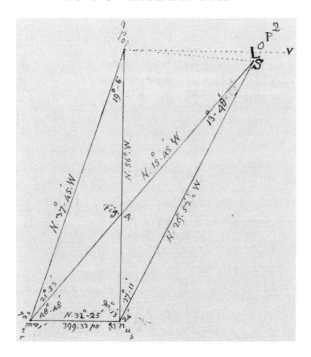

Fig.[22] 2.

in the vertical[23] $\triangle$ cdi. to reduce cd. to ci

         R : cd :: d : ci

         R. : 2806.32 :: S. 89°–39′ : ci = 2806.261

         Log. 2806.32 = 3.4481372

         L.S. 89°–39′   9.9999910

– Rad.   3.4481291.   = 2806.261

         req^d d.i.

         R   : cd   :: c   : di

         Rad : 2806.32 :: S. 21′ : di   = 17.1427

         Log 2806.32 = 3.4481372

         L.S. 21′   = 7.7859427

– Rad.   1.2340799   = 17.1427

but this is to be corrected by subtracting   1.5   see page 3.

gives the true length of di. =   15.6427

now to reduce the $\angle$ icd. to the corrected length of d.i.

in the $\triangle$ cdi. given ci = 2806.261

               di = 15.6427

      req^d $\angle$ icd

ci : di :: Rad : T. dci
2806.261 : 15.6427 :: Rad : T. dci = 19′–9″
  Log. 15.6427 =   1.1943118
+ Rad   10.
               11.1943118
– Log 2806.261   3.4481279
               7.7461839 = 19′–9″
then in the △ cdi as reduced & corrected
  the ∠ icd = 19′–9″
      ci = 2806.261
      di =   15.6427[24]

---

in the vertical[25] △ dik, to find i.k. in order to reduce ci. to ck.
    given di. and all the angles
  S. k :   di ::   S d   : ik
S. 8°–12′ : 15.6427 :: S. 81°–48′ : ik = 108.5521
  Log. 15.6427   1.1943118
  L.S. 81°–48′   9.9955370
             11.1898488
– L.S. 8°–12′   9.1542076
            2.0356412 = 108.552
then ck = ci – ik = 2806.261 – 108.552 = 2697.709

in the vertical[26] △ ack to find ak.
        given ck = 2697.709
            ∠ c = 7°–15′
            ∠ k = 180° – 8°–12′ = 171°–48′
            ∠ a = 180° – c[27] – k =   57′
          req^d ak.
S. a :   ck ::   S. c.   : ak
S. 57′ : 2697.709 :: S. 7°–15′ : ak = 20533.8
  Log. 2697.709 3.4309952
  L.S. 7°–15′   9.1010558
            12.5320510
– L.S. 57′   8.2195811
           4.3124699 = 20533.8

in the right ∠^{d} vertical[28] △ akg. given ak = 20533.8
                ∠ k = 8°–12′
                ∠ a = 81–48
            req^d ag. and gk.

Rad : ak :: S. k : ag.
Rad : 20533.8 :: S. 8°–12′ : ag. = 2928.711
Log. 20533.8 4.3124699   + 4.333
L.S. 8°–12′ 9.1542076   2933.044 = ab
– Rad. 3.4666775[29]   = 2928.711

Rad : ak :: S. a : gk.
Rad : 20533.8 :: S. 81°–48′ : gk. = 20323.9
Log. 20533.8 4.3124699
L.S. 81°–48′ 9.9955370
– Rad. 4.3080069[30]   = 20323.9
                      + 2697.709 = ck
                    23021.609 = cg[31]

Fig. 3.

in the r. $\angle^d$ vertical[32] $\triangle$ mnt to reduce nm. to nt
        and to find mt.
    given nm = 6589. feet.
        $\angle$ n = 27′
        $\angle$ m = 89°–33′
    req^d nt. and mt.
Rad.: nm :: S. m : nt
Rad : 6589 :: S. 89°–33′ : nt. = 6588.8
  Log. 6589 3.8188195
  L.S. 89°–33′ 9.9999866
– Rad. 3.8188061[33]   = 6588.8

for mt. say Rad.: nm :: S. n. : mt
        Rad : 6589 :: S. 27′ : mt = 51.7493
  Log. 6589. 3.8188195
  L.S. 27′ 7.8950854
– Rad. 1.7139049[34]   = 51.7493
to be corrected by subtracting 11.   see page 3.
    true length of mt = 40.7493

next reduce the $\angle$ n. to the corrected length of mt.
in the r. $\angle^d$ $\triangle$ mnt. given nt = 6588.8
                  mt = 40.7493
              req^d $\angle$ n.
  nt : mt :: Rad. : T. n
6588.8 : 40.7493 :: Rad. : T. n = 21′–11″
  Log. 40.7493 + Rad. = 11.6101202
– Log. 6588.8   3.8188061
              7.7913141. = T. 21′–11″

in the horizontal $\triangle$ npt. given nt. = 6588.8

$$\overset{\text{o}\qquad\prime}{}$$
$$\angle\text{ tnp} = 90\text{--}13$$
$$\angle\text{ ptn} = 70\text{--}41$$
$$\angle\text{ npt} = 19\text{--}6$$

req^d pt. and pn.

for pt. say S. p. :   nt   ::   S. n   : pt

    S. 19°–6′ : 6588.8 :: S. 90°–13′ : pt. = 20135.61

    Log. 6588.8   3.8188061

    L.S. 90°–13′ = 89°–47′ 9.9999969

                          13.8188030

– L.S. 19°–6′   9.5148371

                        4.3039659 = 20135.61 = pt[35]

for pn. say S. p :   nt   ::   S. t.   : pn.

    S. 19°–6′ : 6588.8 :: S. 70°–41′ : pn. = 19002.2

    Log. 6588.8   3.8188061

    L.S. 70°–41′   9.9748361

                          13.7936422

– L.S. 19°–6′   9.5148371

                        4.2788051 = 19002.2 = pn

in the r. $\angle^d$ vertic^l $\triangle$ lmo given mo. = 20135.61

$$\angle\text{ m.} = 8°\text{--}2′$$
$$\angle\text{ l} = 81\text{--}58$$

req^d lo.

    S. l. :   mo   ::   S. m.   : lo.

S. 81°–58′ : 20135.61 :: S. 8°–2′ : lo. = 2841.83

                                oq. =   48.7493

    Log. 20135.61   4.3039659 lq = 2890.5793

    L.S. 8°–2′   9.1453493 | op = mt = 40.7493

                    13.4493152 | pq = tr =   8.

– L.S. 81°–58′   9.9957172 | oq. = 48.7493

                    3.4535980 = 2841.83[36]

let **LOPQ.** be points in the axis of the North peak corresponding horizontally with l.o.p.q. in y^t of the S. peak; and S. the summit of the
North peak.

we have still to find the horizont^l distance of the two Axes

                    the height of S. by the observns at l.

                                              at m.

                                              at n.

reduce the inclined[37] trapezium lmn**L**. fig. 4. to it's corresponding horisontal[38] one p.t.n.**P**. in the horizontal plane of n

In the horizontal[39] △ **Ptn**.

given nt = 6588.8

$$\angle \text{Pnt} = 117.\ 24\ \text{or}\ 62\text{--}36$$
$$\angle \text{Ptn} = \quad 48\text{--}48$$
$$\angle \text{tPn} = \quad 13\text{--}48$$

req^d **Pn**.

Pt.

to find **Pt. S. P.** : nt :: S. **Pnt** : **Pt**

S. 13°–48′ : 6588.8 :: S. 62°–36′ : **Pt**. = 24523.3

Log. 6588.8	3.8188061
L.S. 62°–36′	9.9483227
	13.7671288
– L.S. 13°–48′	9.3775493
	4.3895795 = 24523.3

to find **Pn. S. P** : nt :: S. **Ptn** : **Pn**.

S. 13°–48′ : 6588.8 :: S. 48°–48′ : **Pn** = 20783.21

Log. 6588.8	3.8188061
L.S. 48°–48′	9.8764574
	13.6952635
– L.S. 13°–48′	9.3775493
	4.3177142 = 20783.21

In the horiz^l[40] △ **Ptp**. given **Pt** = 24523.3

pt = 20135.61

$$\angle \text{Ptp} = 21°\text{--}53'$$

req^d p**P**.[41]

Pt + pt : **Pt** – pt :: T. $\frac{\text{tpP. + pPt}}{2}$: T. $\frac{\text{tpP} - \text{pPt}}{2}$

44658.91 : 4387.69 :: T. 79–3–30 : T. 26–55–26

Log. 4387.69	3.6422278	79– 3–30
L.T. 79°–3′–30″	10.7134430	105–58–56 = tp**P**.
	14.3556708	52– 8– 4 = t**P**p.
– Log. 44658.91	4.6499081	
	9.7057627	= 26°–55′–26″ = T $\frac{d}{2}$

for p**P**. S. t**P**p : pt :: S. **Ptp** : p**P**

S. 52°–8′–4″ : 20135.61 :: S. 21°–53′ : p**P**. = 9506.451

Log. 20135.61   4.3039648
L.S. 21°–53'   9.5713802
                  13.8753450
– L.S. 52°–8'–4" 9.8973264
                  3.9780186 = 9506.451

In the horiz[142] $\triangle$ Pnp. given **Pn** = 20783.21
                        pn = 19002.2
                   $\angle$ **Pnp** = 27°–11'   req^d p**P**.

$$\textbf{Pn} + \text{pn}: \textbf{Pn} - \text{pn} :: \text{T.} \frac{n\text{p}\textbf{P} + n\textbf{P}\text{p}}{2} : \text{T.} \frac{n.\text{p}\textbf{P} - n\textbf{P}\text{p}}{2}$$

           o   /   "   o   /   "
39785.41 : 1781. :: T. 76–24–30 : T. 10–28–23[43]
Log. 1781.   3.2506639   76–24–30
L.T. 76°–24'–30"   10.6165949   86–52–53 = np**P**.
                    13.8672588   65–56– 7 = n**P**p.
– Log. 39785.41   4.5997239
                    9.2675349 = T. $\frac{d}{2}$ = 10°–28'–23"

---

for p**P**. S. n**P**p   :   pn   ::   S. **Pnp**   : p**P**.
   S. 65°–56'–7" : 19002.2 :: S. 27°–11' : p**P**. 9507.27
Log. 19002.2   4.2788039
L.S. 27°–11'   9.6597633
                    13.9385672
– L.S. 65°–56'–7"   9.9605114
                    3.9780558 = 9507.27
                                 9506.451
                                 19013.721
by mean of 2. operns   p**P**. =   9506.86 f. = 1.8 mile
                                 9506.45
                                 19013.31
              mean length of p.**P**.   9506.65[44]

By way of proof of these operations, we may at this stage collate the magnetic rhumb of m.n. or t.n.[45] observed Nov. 11. and transferred by calculation to p.**P**. fig. 5. with the rhumb of l.S. or p.**P**. observed from l. Nov. 10.

from p. in the horizontal trapezium ptn**P**. Fig. 5. draw pv. parallel with tn. this parallelism makes the $\angle$ tpv the supplement to ptn.

		° ′
we found the	∠ ptn =	70–41
then is	tpv =	109–19
but	tp**P** =	105–58–56
and consequently	**P**.pv =	3–20– 4
by observn Nov. 11. tn = pv	is N.	32–25– 0 E
add the	∠ **P**pv	3–20– 4
gives by calculn	p**P**	N. 35–45– 4
by observn of Nov. 10	p**P**.	N. 35–50– 0
difference		0– 4–56

altho' the needle is not to be relied on for exact precision, the magnetic rhumbs of the lines were taken as general checks on the other observations, and particularly to indicate whether the corresponding angles observed were to the right or left. the rhumbs now collated are so far a confirmation of the correctness of the intermediate work.

---

for the height **S**. above l. that is, the height of the North peak above the South, by the observns at l.
in the right ∠^{d} vertical △ l**LS**. Fig. 1.

$$\text{given } ∠ \text{ SlL.} = 52'$$
$$\text{lL } = \text{p}\mathbf{P}. = 9506.86$$
$$\text{req}^d \text{ LS}$$

Rad :   lL   :: T. SlL : LS
Rad : 9506.86 :: T. 52′ : LS = 143.482

Log. 9506.86	3.9770371
L.T. 52′	8.1797626
– Rad.	2.1567997^{46} = 143.482

---

for lS Si. of l**SL** :   lL   :: Rad : lS
S. 89–8′ : 9506.65 :: Rad : lS = 9507.73

Log. 9506.65 + Rad.	13.9780275
L.S. 89°–8′	9.9999503
	3.9780772 = 9507.73 = lS.^{47}

for the height of **S**. the summit of the N. peak by the observations
from m.
in the horizontal △ **O**mu. Fig. 4.

$$\text{given mu} = 6588.8$$

$$\angle\, umO = \overset{\circ\quad\prime}{48\text{--}48}$$

$$muO = 117\text{--}24 \text{ or } 62°\text{--}36'$$

$$mOu = 13\text{--}48$$

req^d mO

uO.

S. O :   mu   ::   S. u   :   mO.

S. 13°–48′ : 6588.8 :: S. 62°–36′ : mO. = 24523.3

Log. 6588.8   3.8188061

L.S. 62°–36′   9.9483227

                     13.7671288

– L.S. 13°–48′   9.3775493

                     4.3895795 = 24523.3

for uO, S. O :   mu   ::   S. m   : uO

S. 13°–48′ : 6588.8 :: S. 48°–48′ : uO = 20783.21

Log. 6588.8   3.8188061

L.S. 48°–48′   9.8764574

                     13.6952635

– L.S. 13°–48′   9.3775493

                     4.3177142 = 20783.21[48]

In the right $\angle^d$ vertical $\triangle$ $Sm O$

given mO. = 24523.3

$$\overset{\circ\quad\prime}{\angle\, m = 7\text{--}13}$$

$$\angle\, S = 82\text{--}47$$

req^d SO

S. S :   mO ::   S. m   : SO

S. 82°–47′   : 24523.3 :: S. 7°–13′ : SO. = 3105.261

Log. 24523.3   4.3895795   + oq =   48.749

L.S. 7°–13′   9.0990651   SQ = 3154.01

                   13.4886446

– L.S. 82°–47′   9.9965459

                  3.4920987 = 3105.261

In the right $\angle^d$ vertical $\triangle$ SnP.

given nP $= $ uO $= 20783.21$

$$
\begin{array}{rl}
& \text{o} \qquad \prime \\
\angle n = & 8\text{--}27 \\
\angle S = & 81\text{--}33 \\
\end{array}
$$

req^d SP

S. S :   nP   ::   S n.   : SP

S. 81°–33′ : 20783.21 :: S. 8°–27′ : SP. = 3087.54

Log. 20783.21	4.3177142	+ pq = _8._
L.S. 8°–27′	9.1671586	SQ = 3095.54
	13.4848728	
– L.S. 81–33	9.9952597	
	3.4896131 = 3087.54^{49}	

Proceeding to the result of the observations of altitude, they do not come out so fortunately correct as the horizontal angles did. for, taking a mean of the two altitudes of the S. peak, and of the two of the North peak, that of 143 f resulting from the observation at l. will not fill up the whole space of their difference. to bring them together we must distribute the whole error equally among the several vertical angles which enter into the operations.

3. of these are in Fig. 2. viz. acg. dci. & adf.

2. are in Fig. 3. mnt & lmo.

1. in Fig. 1. SlL.

<u>2.</u> in the altitudes of the N. peak, the one taken

8.   from m. the other from n.

the following equation gives the portion of error in altitude to be ascribed to each of these vertical angles.

$$\frac{2933 + 3x + 2890 + 2x}{2} + 143 + x = \frac{3154 - 2x + 3095 - x}{2.}$$

$$3054.5 + 3.5x = 3124.5 - 1.5x$$

$$5x = 70$$

$$x = 14$$

there must be a correction then of 14.f in altitude for every vertical angle entering into each result, as follows.

the height of S. peak

from Fig. 2. is 2933. add 14 × 3. y^e error for 3 $\angle^s$ gives   2975

from station m. 2890 + 14 × 2.   for 2. $\angle^s$ 2918

                                                       5893

the mean may be consid^d the height of S. peak   2946.5

the height of N. peak

from station m. 3154. subtract 14×2. error for 2. $\angle^s$			3126.
from station n. 3095.	-14	error of 1. $\angle$	3081
			6207

the mean height of the N. peak   3103.5

to the height of S. peak 2946.5 add $143 + 14 = 157$
     for 1. $\angle$ 3103.5

from the height of N. peak 3103.5 subtract   157   2946.5

this error of 14.f. in altitude on every vertical observn amounts to about $2\frac{1}{4}'$ which with an instrument whose Nonius indicates to 3.' only, is perhaps as near as we may generally count on coming; at least as near as eyes of 72. may come. add to y^s too the diameter of the crosshair which, magnified as it is produces sensible uncertainty.[50]

To recapitulate

the mean height of the sharp or S. peak	f
above the surface of Otter river is	2946.5
of the North peak	3103.5
their difference of height	157.

the distance of the 2 summits nearly 1.8. mile exactly 9507.73

the magnetic bearing of the summit of the North from that of the S. peak is N. 35–50. E from which 2.° must be subtracted for the present variation of the needle.

the base lines measured, the one of 2806.33 feet or .55 of a mile, the other of 6589 f. or $1\frac{1}{4}$ mile, were on the plains of Otter river[51] belonging to Christopher Clarke esq. & to Donald's heirs, near the mill of the latter; the former line in exact direction to the axis of the S. peak, the latter nearly parallel with the bearing of the one peak from the other.

the distance of the base lines measured, from the points in the bases of the mountains vertically under their summits was, the nearest 19002.2 f. the farthest 24523.3 f. or about 4. miles generally.

supposing the radius of the earth 3965. miles and the height of the[52] N. Peak 3103.5 feet = .5876893 mile then it may be seen over a level country to the distance of 68.2083 miles, which will include the whole or a part of the counties of Amherst, Nelson, Albem. Fluvanna, Buckingh. Cumbl^d Franklin, Bedf^d Campb^{ll} Pr. Edwd Charlotte Patrick, Henry, Pittsylva, Halifax and over the tops of the intervening mountains in Rockbridge & Botetourt, the following is the proof.

in a right $\angle^d$ $\triangle$ given the hypoth. b.c. = 3965.588 miles a leg. ac = 3965. required the other leg. ab.

bc : Rad :: ac : S. b.

3965.588 : Rad. :: 3965 : S. b = 89°–0′–52″

Rad. + Log. 3965   13.5982432

– Log. 3965.588   3.5983075   °   ′   ″

    9.9999357 = 89– 0–52 = $\angle$ b

and   59– 8 = $\angle$ c[53]

Rad : bc   ::   S c   : ab

Rad : 3965.588 :: S. 59′–8″ : ab 68.2083

Log. 3965.588   3.5983075

L.S. 59′–8″   8.2355299

– Rad.   1.8338374[54] = 68.2083

vertical angles		corresponding bases		corresponding perpendiculars	
	° ′				
SlL.	0–52	lL	9506.86	SL.	143.482
icd.	21	ci	2806.261	di	17.1427
akg	8–12	gk.	20323.9	ag.	2928.711
acg.	7–15	cg	23021.609	ag.	2928.711
tnm.	27	nt.	6588.8	mt.	51.7493
lmo	8– 2	mo.	20135.61	lo.	2841.83
S.mO	7–13	tP.	24523.3	SO.	3105.261
SnP.	8–27	nP.	20783.21	SP.	3087.54

to estimate loosely the average of error in the vertical observations the average of the perpendiculars is 1888. of which 14 f. is the $\frac{1}{135}$ part the average of the vert^l angles is 5°–6′–7$\frac{1}{2}$″ = 18360.″ 135th part is 136″ = 2′–16″[55]

Map of the ground. scale 1000. f = ¼ inch

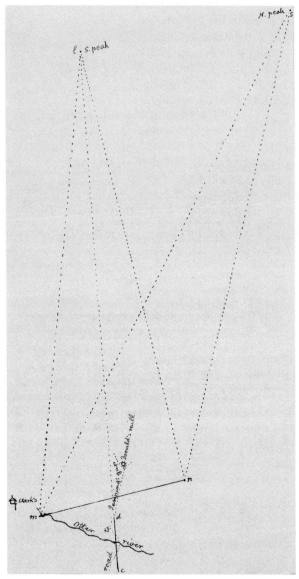

The[56] form of the Peaks
as seen from mr Clark's

MS (MHi); filed with TJ's Weather Memorandum Book, 1802–16; written entirely in TJ's hand on rectos and versos of several long sheets, folded and stitched together; partially dated, with terminal date conjectured from TJ to Charles Clay, 18 Nov. 1815.

A NONIUS is "a device consisting of a series of concentric arcs engraved on a quadrant, used for the accurate measurement of angles, altitudes, and heights" (*OED*).

In addition to the sketched map of the ground that he included here, TJ created a similar sketch on a separate sheet that depicts the same points of reference, but shows the Peaks of Otter at two different sizes, with the smaller sketch superimposed on the larger (MS in MHi; filed with TJ's Weather Memorandum Book, 1802–16; written entirely in TJ's hand on one side of a single sheet; undated; endorsed by TJ on verso: "Mountains.

Peaks of Otter. their heights measured. Nov. 10. 11. 12. 1815.").

TJ summarized these calculations in a manuscript revision to the query on mountains in his *Notes on the State of Virginia*, stating that "In Nov. 1815. with a Ramsden's theodolite of $3\frac{1}{2}$ I. radius with Nonius divisions to 3' and a base of $1\frac{1}{4}$ mile on the low grounds of Otter river, distant 4. miles from the summits of the two peaks of Otter I measured geometrically their heights above the <*bed*> water of the river at it's base and found

	f
that of the sharp or S. peak	$2946\frac{1}{4}$
that of the flat or N. peak	$3103\frac{1}{2}$

as we may with confidence say that the base of the Peaks is at least as high above the tidewater at Richm^d as that of the Blue ridge at Rockfish gap (being 40. miles farther Westward) and their highest summit of course $3203\frac{1}{2}$ f above that tidewater, it <*shews*> follows that the summit of the highest peak is $343\frac{1}{2}$ f.

higher than <*the top summit*> that of the Allegany" as measured by Gen[l] Williams" (Jefferson, *Notes on the State of Virginia* [London, 1787; Sowerby, no. 4167; Poor, *Jefferson's Library*, 7 (no. 365); TJ's copy in ViU, with revisions, including this one, tipped in between pp. 28 and 29]).

[1] Row of numbers interlined.

[2] Abbreviation for "variation," here and below.

[3] Omitted closing parenthesis editorially supplied.

[4] Preceding three words interlined.

[5] Reworked from "S."

[6] Page ends here.

[7] Reworked from "8°–12′."

[8] Page ends here.

[9] TJ here canceled

"in vertical ∠[s] + or x ⅃. means elevation
o means the horizon
– means depression

in horizont[l] + or [. . .] means inflection to y[e] right
– or [. . .] inflection to the left
and always refers to the last course unless otherwise mentioned."

[10] Abbreviation for "poles," here and below.

[11] TJ here canceled a drawing of a triangle and its explanation.

[12] Page ends here.

[13] Number added in place of "89–36," with "117°–24′" canceled afterwards.

[14] Reworked from "horiz[l]."

[15] Number added in place of "26°–34′."

[16] Number added in place of "118°."

[17] Number added in place of "7°–57′."

[18] Reworked from "S."

[19] Number added in place of "7°–9′."

[20] Number added in place of "70–42," with a question-mark canceled.

[21] Figure added in place of "N 16. W." Page ends here.

[22] New page begins with this word.

[23] Preceding three words interlined.

[24] Page ends after horizontal rule.

[25] Word interlined.

[26] Word interlined.

[27] Reworked from "i."

[28] Word interlined.

[29] Reworked from "13.4666775."

[30] Reworked from "14.3080069."

[31] Page ends here.

[32] Word interlined.

[33] Reworked from "13.8188061."

[34] Reworked from "11.7139049."

[35] Page ends here.

[36] TJ here canceled a set of calculations by enclosing them in a box that struck through the first and last lines. The original reading was "in the r. ∠[d] vert[l] △

$$\text{lnp. given p.n} = 19002$$
$$\angle n = 8°–20$$
$$\angle l = 81–40$$
$$\text{req}^d \text{ lp}$$

S. l.	:	pn.	::	S. n.	: lp.

S. 81°–40′ : 19002.2 :: S. 8°–20′ : lp. = 2783
Log. 19002.2   4.2788051   pq =   8
L.S. 8°–20′   9.1611639   lq = 279
– L.S. 81°–40′   13.4399690
                            9.9953902
                            3.4445788 = 2783.42."

Beneath these calculations and the horizontal rule depicted here, the page ends with five heavily canceled and partly illegible lines.

[37] Word interlined.

[38] Word interlined.

[39] Word interlined.

[40] Word interlined.

[41] Page ends here.

[42] Word interlined.

[43] Reworked from "10–28–33."

[44] Page ends here.

[45] Preceding two words interlined.

[46] Reworked from "12.1567997."

[47] Page ends here.

[48] Page ends here.

[49] Page ends here.

[50] Page ends here.

[51] Word interlined.

[52] Preceding three words interlined.

[53] Page ends here.

[54] Reworked from "11.8338374."

[55] Page ends here.

[56] New page begins with this word. Drawing and heading are oriented perpendicularly to preceding text.

III. Summary Comments on the Peaks of Otter

[before 2 Dec. 1815]

PEAKS OF OTTER.

We are indebted to an obliging friend in Bedford for the following nice Geometrical calculations. We believe they were made by Mr. Jefferson, who is now at his seat in Poplar Forest.—[*Lynchburg Press.*][1]

The height of the Peaks of Otter deemed the highest mountains (from their base) of this state,[2] and amongst the highest in the United States, which has hitherto been a subject of uncertain conjecture, has lately been taken by geometrical operations with an excellent instrument and great care. They are found to be much short of the conjecture which has prevailed.

The following are the particulars most worthy of notice.

The Latitude of the sharp Peak (which is the south one) taken by a single observation made on its apex, is 37 deg. 33 min. 17 sec.[3] North.

By a mean of the observations,[4] the height of the north Peak, above the surface of Otter River is—3103 1-2[5] feet of the south or Sharp Peak—2946 1-2 feet. Their difference of height—157 feet.

The distance of the two summits is nearly 1 & 8-10 of a mile, but exactly 9507 3-4 feet.

The magnetic bearing of the summit of the North from that of the South Peak is, N. 35 deg. 50 min. east—from which two deg. must be subtracted for the present variation of the needle.

The base lines measured, the one of 2806 feet or 55-100 of a mile; the other of 6589 feet or 1 1-4 mile, were on the plains of Otter River, belonging to Christopher Clarke, Esq. and the heirs of Andrew Donald, near the mill of the latter; the former line in exact direction to the axis of the south Peak; the latter nearly parallel with the bearing of the one Peak from the other.

The distance of the base lines measured from the points in the bases[6] of the mountains, vertically, under their summits, was, the nearest, 19002[7] feet; the farthest 24523 feet or about 4 miles generally.

Supposing the radius of the earth 3965 miles, the north Peak may be seen over a level country to the distance of sixty-two and a quarter miles; this will include the whole or a part of the counties of Amherst, Nelson, Albemarle, Fluvanna, Buckingham, Cumberland, Franklin,

Bedford, Campbell, Prince Edward, Charlotte, Patrick, Henry, Pittsylvania and Halifax, and it may be seen over the summit of the Blue Ridge, in Rockbridge and Botetourt.

Printed in *Richmond Enquirer* and Washington *Daily National Intelligencer*, both 2 Dec. 1815. Text based on *Richmond Enquirer*, with the most significant variations accounted for below.

[1] Omitted closing bracket editorially supplied. In place of this paragraph *Daily National Intelligencer* substitutes "We copy from the Lynchburg Press the following nice Geometrical calculations, which are the result of the unweared [unwearied] industry and scientific character of the venerable JEFFERSON, who is now on a visit to his farm at Poplar Forest, in that neighborhood. It is delightful to witness the serenity and elasticity of the eve of a well-spent life, as exemplified in the present pursuits and habits of this illustrious Republican philosopher."

[2] For preceding two words *Daily National Intelligencer* substitutes "Virginia."

[3] *Richmond Enquirer*: "87 deg. 38 min. 17 sec." *Daily National Intelligencer*: "87° 33' 17"." Corrected figure comes from TJ's Calculations of Latitudes of the Sharp Peak of Otter and Natural Bridge, 18 Sept.–10 Nov. 1815

[4] *Richmond Enquirer*: "observations of." *Daily National Intelligencer*: "observations," followed by a comma.

[5] *Daily National Intelligencer*: "3108¼."

[6] Both printed texts: "basis."

[7] *Richmond Enquirer*: "1600." *Daily National Intelligencer*: "19002."

From John Adams

DEAR SIR   Quincy Nov. 13 1815

The fundamental[1] Article of my political Creed is, that Despotism, or unlimited Sovereignty, or absolute Power is the Same in a Majority of a popular Assembly, an Aristocratical Counsel, an Oligarchical Junto and a Single Emperor. Equally arbitrary cruel bloody and in every respect, diabolical.

Accordingly arbitrary Power, wherever it has resided, has never failed to destroy all the records Memorials and Histories of former times which it did not like and to corrupt and interpolate Such as it was cunning enough to preserve or to tolerate. We cannot therefore Say with much confidence, what Knowledge or what Virtues may have prevailed in Some former Ages in Some quarters of the World.

Nevertheless, according to the few lights that remain to Us, We may Say that the Eighteenth Century, notwithstanding all its Errors and Vices[2] has been, of all that are past, the most honourable to human Nature. Knowledge and Virtues were increased and diffused, Arts, Sciences useful to Men, ameliorating their condition, were improved, more than in any former equal Period.

But, what are We to Say now? Is the Nineteenth Century to be a Contrast to the Eighteenth? Is it to extinguish all the Lights of its

Predecessor? Are the Sorbonne, the Inquisition, the Index expurgatorius, and the Knights Errant of St Ignatius Loyola to be revived and restored to all their Salutary Powers of Supporting and propagating the mild Spirit of Christianity? The Proceedings of the Allies and their Congress at Vienna, the Accounts from Spain France &c the Chateaubriands and the Genlis, indicate which Way the Wind blows. The Priests are at their Old Work again. The Protestants are denounced and another St Bartholomew's[3] day, threatened.

This however, will probably, 25 years hence, be honoured with the Character of "The effusions of a Splenetic mind, rather than as the Sober reflections of an unbiassed Understanding."

I have rec[d] "Memoirs of the Life of D[r] Price"[4] by William Morgan F.R.S. In pages 157 and 158 M[r] Morgan Says. "So well assured was D[r] Price of the establishment of a free constitution in France, and of the Subsequent Overthrow of Despotism throughout Europe as the consequence of it, that he never failed to express his Gratitude to Heaven for having extended his life to the present happy Period in which 'after Sharing the Benefits of one Revolution, he had been Spared to be a Witness to two other[5] Revolutions both glorious.'[6] But Some of his Correspondents were not quite So Sanguine in their expectations from the last of these Revolutions; and among these, the late American ambassador, M[r] John Adams. In a long letter which he wrote to D[r] Price at this time, So far from congratulating him, on the occasion, he expresses himself in terms of contempt, in regard to the French revolution; and after asking rather too Severely what good was to be expected from a Nation of Atheists,[7] he concludes with foretelling the destruction[8] of a million of human Beings as the probable consequence of it. These harsh censures and gloomy Predictions were particularly ungratefull to D[r] Price; nor can it be denied that they must have then appeared as the effusions of a Splenetic mind, rather than as the Sober reflections of an unbiassed Understanding."

I know not what a candid Public will think of this practice of M[r] Morgan after the Example of M[r] Belsham, who finding private Letters in the Cabinet of a great and good Man after his decease, written in the Utmost freedom[9] and confidence of intimate friendship, by Persons Still living, though after the lapse of a quarter of a Century produces them, before the World.[10] D[r] Disney had different Feelings, and a different Judgment. Finding Some cursory Letters among the Papers of M[r] Hollis he would not[11] publish them without my consent. In answer to his request I Submitted them to his discretion and might have done the same to M[r] Morgan. Indeed had M[r] Morgan published my Letter entire I Should not have given him nor myself any concern about it. But as in his Summary he has not done the Letter Justice, I Shall give it with all its faults.

M[r] Morgan has been more discrete and complaisant to you than to me. He has mentioned respectfully your Letters from Paris to D[r] Price, but has given Us none of them. As I would give more for those Letters than[12] for all the rest of book,[13] I am more angry with him for disappointing me, than for all he Says of me and my Letter, which, Scambling as it is, contains nothing but the Sure Words of Prophecy.

I am as usual yours   JOHN ADAMS.

RC (DLC); addressed by Susan B. Adams: "Thomas Jefferson Esq[re] Monticello Virginia"; postmarked Quincy, 17 Nov.; endorsed by TJ as received 15 Dec. 1815 and so recorded in SJL. FC (Lb in MHi: Adams Papers); dated 18 Nov. 1815.

The SORBONNE was originally the faculty of theology of the University of Paris. INDEX EXPURGATORIUS: official list of passages to be changed or omitted in order for works to be authorized by the Catholic church. KNIGHTS ERRANT OF ST IGNATIUS LOYOLA: Jesuits (*OED*). William Morgan based his assertion that Adams had a SPLENETIC MIND on the latter's LONG LETTER of 19 Apr. 1790 to Richard Price (RC in MHi: R. C. Waterston Autograph Collection; Morgan, *Memoirs of the Life of the Rev. Richard Price, D.D. F.R.S.* [London, 1815], 157–8).

Thomas BELSHAM had published letters written by TJ to Joseph Priestley later owned by the GREAT AND GOOD Theophilus Lindsey in his *Memoirs of the Late Reverend Theophilus Lindsey, M.A.* (London, 1812), 443–4, 535–7, 538–9. In 1807 John Adams and Abigail Adams both authorized John DISNEY to publish their letters to Thomas Brand HOLLIS in his biography of the latter (Disney

to John Adams, 24 Aug. 1807 [MHi: Adams Papers]; John Adams to Disney, 9 Nov. 1807 [Lb in MHi: Adams Papers]; Disney, *Memoirs of Thomas Brand-Hollis, Esq.* [London, 1808], 30–40). Morgan declined printing TJ's LETTERS FROM PARIS TO D[R] PRICE because the events of the French Revolution that they had predicted were "long ago either fulfilled or falsified" (*Memoirs of Richard Price*, 152). SCAMBLING: "rambling" or "scattered" (*OED*).

[1] RC: "fundmental." FC: "fundamental."

[2] Preceding six words interlined.

[3] RC: "Bartholomeu's." FC: "Bartholomew's."

[4] Omitted closing quotation mark editorially supplied.

[5] RC: "others." FC and *Memoirs of Richard Price*: "other."

[6] Set of double quotation marks editorially altered to single.

[7] RC: "Atheits." FC and *Memoirs of Richard Price*: "Atheists."

[8] RC: "destrution." FC and *Memoirs of Richard Price*: "destruction."

[9] RC: "fredom." FC: "freedom."

[10] Preceding five words interlined.

[11] Word interlined.

[12] RC: "that." FC: "than."

[13] FC: "the Book."

From Peter S. Du Ponceau

It is a duty no less pleasing than honorable to me, to address you on behalf of the Historical & literary Committee of the American Philosophical Society, in the Capacity of their Corresponding Secretary. You have, no doubt, been informed of the recent establishment of this Committee, & of the views & objects for which it has been instituted. If not, you will receive full information on the Subject from the printed notice which I have the honor to enclose, together with an official Copy of the Resolution pointing out the duty in the execution of which I am now for the first time engaged. To you, Sir, the first thoughts of a friend to American Science & literature are naturally turned, & independent of my individual feelings, I am Satisfied that I am acting in conformity with the wishes of the Committee by paying you this first tribute of respect.

You will See by the enclosed papers that one of the principal objects of the Committee is to rescue from oblivion a great multitude of interesting tracts of the early history of our Country, which at present lie scattered in private hands, trusted only to perishable memorials or to the more perishable memory of man. The Historical Societies of Massachusetts & New York have preserved many important facts & documents of this description, in their valuable collections which will be of great use to the future historians of their respective states; the American Philosophical Society, faithful to the original comprehensive design of their institution have not limited the researches of their Committee by State boundaries, but have left them free to avail themselves of the Communications of patriotic & literary characters in every part of the Union, among whom, Sir, the conspicuous place which you fill has induced the Committee to hope that you will not refuse them your powerful Co-operation, which I have been ordered particularly to Solicit in their name. It is not their wish to trespass more on your time & leisure than you will yourself find perfectly Convenient, yet they flatter themselves that you will occasionally draw in their favor from those stores of knowledge which you have acquired thro' a long & active life, & that your influence on the literary Characters & well informed Citizens of the state in which you reside will be Sometimes exerted to procure for them & enable them to preserve a variety of interesting Historical & statistical facts & documents which would otherwise be lost to posterity. I need not point out to you the advantage which the future Historian of Virginia will derive from these records, & as there is not yet in that state any establishment or institution professing the same objects with those of the Committee, it is to be hoped that those who are possessed of interesting public papers or private letters calculated to throw light on the History of the Country, or whose knowledge of the localities of their district enables them to describe with accuracy, their past history or their present state, will be disposed to avail themselves of the opportunity which now offers of rendering the papers or knowledge which they possess permanently useful to Society.

Having Said thus much with respect to the general objects of the Committee, I beg leave to request, if in your power, Some information respecting an interesting manuscript which has lately fallen into their hands. It is an oblong Volume, which originally contained 219 pages of Small neat writing, the first 24 pages, & about a dozen more pages in the middle of the work have unfortunately been torn off; from the context it appears to be the Journal of certain Commissioners appointed by the Colony of Virginia to run together with other Commissioners appointed by North Carolina, the boundary line between the two Colonies. The Historians inform us that those Commissioners were appointed in the Year 1728. On the part of Virginia, they were Col. Bird, (I presume of Westover) Richard Fitzwilliam & Wm Dandridge—On the part of North Carolina, John Lovick, Christopher Gale, Edwd Moseley & William Little—The question is who wrote this Journal? All that appears from the manuscript is that it was not Fitzwilliam, as it is stated that he left the Commissioners before they had gone thro' their operation. It is therefore either Col. Bird or Mr Dandridge—The style of the work is lively, fraught with a vein of humour, much like two letters of the same Commissioners printed at the end of Williamson's history of North Carolina. If you can give any information to the Committee respecting who was the author of this Journal they will be peculiarly obliged to you for it. If you wish to read the work, it shall immediately be Sent to you, it will well repay the trouble of perusal. At least I can Say that I have gone thro' it with very great interest & pleasure. It contains a lively picture of the manners & mode of life of the North Carolina borderers of that day

I have the honor to be with the greatest respect

Sir Your most obedient humble Servant

PETER S. DU PONCEAU

RC (DLC); at head of text: "Thomas Jefferson, Esqr"; endorsed by TJ as received 15 Dec. 1815 and so recorded in SJL. FC (PPAmP: APS Historical and Literary Committee Letterbook); endorsed as "read 21 nov^r." Enclosure: "Literary Notice" dated Philadelphia, 14 Aug. 1815, and signed by William

Tilghman, chairman, Du Ponceau, corresponding secretary, and John Vaughan, recording secretary, announcing that the American Philosophical Society has formed a "committee for history, moral science, and general literature"; soliciting donations or loans of documents related to United States or Pennsylvania history; proposing to publish these documents; and expressing a particular interest in information on American Indians, immigrants to and religious sects of Pennsylvania, and William Penn and his associates (MS in PPAmP: APS Archives; printed in *Port Folio*, 3d ser., 6 [1815]: 295–6; reprinted in APS, *Transactions of the Historical & Literary Committee* 1 [1819]: viii–x). Other enclosure printed below.

Peter Stephen Du Ponceau (1760–1844), attorney and author, was a native of France. He studied for the priesthood before accompanying Baron von Steuben to the United States in 1777 as his secretary and, soon after, his aide-de-camp. Du Ponceau served both Steuben and Nathanael Greene as an aide while also studying law. After his military service ended he settled in Philadelphia, where he became a citizen in 1781, worked under Robert R. Livingston in the United States Department of Foreign Affairs, 1781–83, opened a legal practice, and became an authority on civil and foreign law. Du Ponceau was elected to the American Philosophical Society in 1791 and served as a councillor, 1801–16, a vice president, 1816–28, and president of the organization from 1828 until his death. He was also a founding member of the Law Academy of Philadelphia in 1821, and he was president of the Historical Society of Pennsylvania at the time of his death. Du Ponceau translated and authored works on law, history, and philology, achieving international recognition for his work on Native American languages. In 1808 and 1809 he wrote pamphlets that supported Edward Livingston's legal right to the Batture Sainte Marie and undermined TJ's contention

that French law favored public ownership of that property. Du Ponceau and TJ corresponded frequently during TJ's retirement on the subjects of history, American Indians, and American Philosophical Society business (*ANB*; *DAB*; APS, Minutes, 15 July 1791, 2 Jan. 1801, 5 Jan. 1816, 4 Jan. 1828 [MS in PPAmP]; George Dargo, *Jefferson's Louisiana: Politics and the Clash of Legal Traditions* [1975], 79–80, 83, 87, 91; Sowerby, nos. 3494, 3497, 3506; Philadelphia *North American and Daily Advertiser*, 2 Apr. 1844; Robley Dunglison, "Biographical Sketch of Peter S. Du Ponceau," *American Law Magazine* 5 [Apr. 1845]: 1–33). Likenesses of Du Ponceau are reproduced elsewhere in this volume.

The Historical and Literary Committee of the American Philosophical Society was founded as its seventh committee on 17 Mar. 1815 under the original name of Committee of History, Moral Science, and General Literature. Its goal was gathering, preserving, and publishing historic documents (APS, Minutes, 17 Mar., 7 Apr., 21 July 1815 [MS in PPAmP]; APS, *Transactions of the Historical & Literary Committee* 1 [1819]: v–xiii; Gilbert Chinard, "Jefferson and the American Philosophical Society," APS, *Proceedings* 87 [1943]: 269–71).

The American Philosophical Society had recently acquired a manuscript VOLUME of "The History of the Dividing Line" by William Byrd (BIRD) (1674–1744), of Westover (Maude H. Woodfin, "Thomas Jefferson and William Byrd's Manuscript Histories of the Dividing Line," *WMQ*, 3d ser., 1 [1944]: 363–73; Kathleen L. Leonard, "Notes on the Text and Provenance of the Byrd Manuscripts," in Louis B. Wright, ed., *The Prose Works of William Byrd of Westover: Narratives of a Colonial Virginian* [1966], 417–23). TWO LETTERS between the Virginia and North Carolina boundary commissioners can be found in Hugh Williamson, *The History of North Carolina* (Philadelphia, 1812), 2:234–6.

Resolution by the Historical and Literary Committee of the American Philosophical Society

American Philosophical Society
   In Committee of History, the moral Sciences & general Literature.
                             Monday October 30th 1815.
   Resolved: That the Corresponding Secretary[1] be authorized to correspond with and invite [Com^s from][2] such persons either in or out of the State, that[3] may be capable and disposed to forward the views of the Committee, and that he communicate [the] Correspondence from time to time to the Committee.
   Extract from the Minutes   JN VAUGHAN
                                       Recording Sec^y P.T

Tr (DLC); torn, with missing word supplied from MS; in an unidentified hand, signed by Vaughan. MS (PPAmP: APS Archives, Minutes of the Historical and Literary Committee); lacking heading; in John Vaughan's hand; with membership attendance listed as Caspar Wistar, Peter S. Du Ponceau, and Vaughan.

[1] In MS Vaughan here canceled: "P S Du Ponceau."
[2] Preceding two words, not in Tr, supplied from MS.
[3] In MS Vaughan here canceled "from information rec^d."

From James Madison

DEAR SIR   [Washington, 15 Nov. 1815]
   Mr Gray, son of Mr William Gray so distinguished for his wealth & his patriotism, wishing with his lady to pay their respects at Monticello, I can not do less than favor the opportunity by a line of introduction. I am unacquainted with him, otherwise than by his introduction thro' a friend here; but doubt not that he will be found worthy of your civilities which will be acceptable to his father as well as himself. They are on a visit to Georgia, where Mrs Gray's father resides. It may not be amiss to intimate that M^r G's political connections may not altogether correspond with the sentiments of his father. On this point however I am not certain. His view in desiring the present letter[1]

RC (DLC: Madison Papers); clipped, with loss at foot of text of conclusion of letter, signature, and, presumably, the dateline (supplied from TJ's endorsement and SJL); endorsed by TJ as received 15 Dec. 1815 and so recorded in SJL. Enclosed in William R. Gray to TJ, 22 Nov. 1815.

William Rufus Gray (1783–1831), merchant, was the son of William Gray, a prominent Massachusetts merchant and public official, and the brother of Francis C. Gray, who visited TJ earlier in 1815. Gray was a native of Salem, Massachusetts, and graduated from Harvard University in 1800. In 1802 he successfully petitioned the Massachusetts legislature to change his name from William Gray to William Rufus Gray. Moving to Boston about 1803 and acting as his father's agent, Gray became a merchant in his own right by 1805. In 1820 he became a director of the Boston office of discount and deposit for the Bank of the United States. Gray died in Boston (Thomas L. V. Wilson, *The Aristocracy of Boston; who they are, and what they were* [1848], 17–8; *Harvard University Quinquennial Catalogue of the Officers and Graduates, 1636–1925* [1925], 182; *Laws of the Commonwealth of Massachusetts, passed at Several Sessions of the General Court* [Boston, 1802], 12 [23 June 1802]; Edward Gray, *William Gray of Salem, Merchant* [1914], 9, 19, 33; Boston *Repertory*, 15 Oct. 1805; *The Boston Directory* [1805]: 58; [1830]: 158; *Providence Patriot*, 6 Dec. 1820; *Salem Gazette*, 2 Aug. 1831).

Mary Clay Gray (1790–1867) was raised in Savannah. She moved with her family to Boston when her father, Joseph Clay, accepted a position as pastor of the First Baptist Church there in 1807. She married William R. Gray in 1809 in Newark, New Jersey, and lived thereafter in Boston (Montgomery Cumming, comp., *Table of the Descendants of Joseph Clay of Savannah, Ga., 1741 to 1804* [1897]; Sprague, *American Pulpit*,

6:487–8; Newark *Sentinel of Freedom*, 24 Oct. 1809; DNA: RG 29, CS, Mass., Boston, 1860; *Boston Daily Advertiser*, 18 Nov. 1867).

The elder William Gray's POLITICAL CONNECTIONS were originally to the Federalists, but he broke with the party over the Embargo of 1807 and was elected lieutenant governor of Massachusetts on a Republican ticket in 1810 (*DAB*).

William R. Gray also obtained a letter of introduction to TJ from James Monroe, Washington, 16 Nov. 1813 [1815], in which Monroe indicated that "Mr. Gray & his lady of Boston" very much wished to meet TJ during their southern tour, and that "Mr. Gray is the son of the late Lt. Governor of Mass. who is so well known to you for his PATRIOTISM, & ATTACHMENT TO THE REPUBLICAN CAUSE" (Tr in Ben Bloomfield auction catalogue, List DI–3 [ca. Apr. 1950], item 108; printed extracts only; original described as being in Monroe's hand, signed by him, and addressed to "Thomas Jefferson, Monticello"; not recorded in SJL and probably never received by TJ). Monroe's letter to Gray of the same date offering to supply him with letters of introduction is in CSt.

[1] Remainder of letter clipped and missing.

From John Barnes

DEAR SIR—   George Town Co^a 18th Novr 1815.

It is long since, I had the Honor of receiving any of your fav^{rs} (the last of 25th May.)—situated as the good Genl then was and unhappy state of public Affairs in Paris, my Anxiety increased on Acco^t of my Remittance to him 26th April via Messrs Baring Brothers & Co from whom, I am at length releived—by the inclosed recd. the 16th Ins^t—

the Genl by the public papers I perceive left Paris, ab^t 9^h July. for Soleuer among the Alps. intending to Remain in Switzerland till circumstances renderd it convenient for him to Return to Paris.

but why not Keep you Advised[1] of his movements? (presume you may expect daily advices) and particular—the most certain place for Remitting him a further supply—without loss of time.—The extra

Advance of ex. on London from 15 to $17\frac{1}{2}$ pct as well on Amsterdam equally—so—

most Respectfully—with sentim[ts] of the highest Esteem I am Dear Sir—your most Obed[t] serv[t]   JOHN BARNES,

RC (ViU: TJP-ER); notation by Barnes at foot of text: "with London price Curr[t] 14th Sep 1815" (see enclosure printed below); endorsed by TJ as received 15 Dec. 1815 and so recorded in SJL. RC (DLC); address cover only; with PoC of TJ to John F. Oliveira Fernandes, 24 Jan. 1816, on verso; addressed: "Thomas Jefferson Esquire Monticello—Virginia"; franked; postmarked.

25TH MAY 1815 was the date of Barnes's previous letter to TJ. The most recent letter from TJ to Barnes was that of 12 May 1815. THE GOOD GEN[L]: Tadeusz Kosciuszko. Barnes had written to Baring Brothers & Company on Kosciuszko's behalf on 28 Apr. 1815, not the 26TH.

[1] Manuscript: "Advsed."

ENCLOSURE

Baring Brothers & Company to John Barnes

SIR   London 14 September 1815

We have duly received your esteemed letter of 28 April, in reply to our respects of 20 Oct advicing you remittance of £400.   a 60% on W[m] Murdock on Account & for the Use of General Kosciusko at Paris which has been accepted—and we have placed the same at the disposition of the General forwarding him at the same time your letter to his address—

We beg your reference to our quotations at foot & Remain very Truly Sir Your Ob[t] Servants—   BARING BROTHERS & Co[1]

Tobacco	Virginia	fine	18	@	20			
		good	$15\frac{3}{4}$	"	17			
		Midl[g]	14	"	$15\frac{1}{2}$			
		Ord[y] & low	10	"	14			
		fat P B / Sweet Scented	16	"	18	@	20	
		[. . .] O.	13	"	16			
	Maryland	fine	14	"	18	"	22	
		Coloury	$11\frac{1}{4}$	"	14			
		O. Brown	9	"	11			
		Brown	$7\frac{3}{4}$	"	9			
		low & Ord[y]	5	"	$7\frac{1}{2}$			
	Kentucky		$11\frac{1}{2}$	"	14			
Cotton	Sea Island		2/9	"	3/8			
	New Orleans		2/.	"	2/3		Market Steady	
	Bowed		$21\frac{1}{2}$	"	$23\frac{1}{2}$			
Rice	in Bond		30/	"	34/.			

RC (ViU: TJP-ER); one abbreviation illegible; letter and price list each in a different, unidentified hand, with signature in yet another unidentified hand, identical to the signature to Baring Brothers & Company to TJ, 13 May 1815; at head of text: "John Barnes Esqʳ George-Town Columbia."

P B: "part black." O.: "ordinary." COLOURY: with a color indicative of high quality (*OED*). BOWED cotton was short-staple cotton from which the seeds had been removed by the vibrations of a bow (*Manufactures of the United States in 1860; Compiled from the Original Returns of the Eighth Census* [1865], ccxv).

[1] Recto ends here with "P.T.O" ("Please Turn Over").

To Charles Clay

TH:J. TO MR CLAY   Pop. For. Nov. 18. 15.

I was five days absent in my trip to the peaks of Otter, and have been five days engaged[1] in calculating the observations made. this brings me down to yesterday evening when I finished them. I am going to-day to see mr Clarke at his new habitation, and tomorrow, weather permitting, will pay you a morning visit. in the mean time I send you a note of the result of my ten days labor and some Otaheite or Paper mulberries, valuable for the regularity of their form, velvet leaf & for being fruitless. they are charming near a porch for densely shading it.

RC (ViRoHM); dateline at foot of text; addressed: "Mʳ Clay"; endorsed by Clay as a letter from "Tho. Jefferson About the Peaks &ᶜ Nov. 10—15." Tr (ViU: TJP; posthumous copy). Not recorded in SJL. Enclosure not found.

Christopher Clark (CLARKE) had recently purchased a Campbell County estate called the Grove, which was adjacent to TJ's Bedford County lands (*DVB*). TJ had planted sixty-four OTAHEITE OR PAPER MULBERRIES in the nursery at Poplar Forest on 2 Nov. He planted nineteen of these apiece on each side of the house, between the privies and the fence, on 25 Nov. 1815 (TJ's Notes on Poplar Forest Plantings and Geography, 1 Feb. 1811–6 Oct. 1821, printed above at the earlier date).

[1] Word not in Tr.

From Horatio G. Spafford

ESTEEMED FRIEND—   Albany, 11 Mo. 18, 1815.

A few weeks of ill health have confined me to the house, & prevented my correcting the proofs for the Magazine. Thou wilt find an interesting Biography of Baron Steuben, written by General William North, one of the Baron's Aids. The General does not wish to be publicly known as the writer. He is a distinguished Federalist,[†] & was

[†]I mention this circumstance, because that in doing justice to thyself, & some others, he has not followed the fashion of his party.

lately Speaker of our Assembly. I have a Letter from Count Volney, from which I shall publish an extract. It is dated at Paris, Aug. 21. Poor France!

May I entreat of thee a favor? The Post Master in this city, who was appointed about a year Since, is just gone of a consumption. I never had an Office, & I am very anxious to get this, which will Soon be vacated by death. I am poor, having lately lost several thousand dollars, by the failure of a house in this city. It would be in thy power to aid me very much, by only intimating thy wishes. May I entreat of thee to ask for me a favor of the P.M. General? or of the President? I really think myself entitled to consideration, & I know how to be grateful. I should like, particularly, to be indebted to Col. Monroe, for his aid in obtaining for me this office. I flatter myself that I have been a useful Citizen, & that I could serve the Republic in some office that might aid in the support of a numerous family. Pray favor me with thy consideration, & as much of thy interest in my behalf, as may Seem to thee proper. Pardon this freedom, urged by the pressure of adverse events, & believe me to be, with the highest esteem, thy friend,   H. G. SPAFFORD.

RC (DLC: James Madison Papers); endorsed by TJ as received 15 Dec. 1815 and so recorded in SJL. Enclosed in TJ to James Madison, 22 Dec. 1815. Enclosure: *American Magazine, a monthly miscellany*, vol. 1, no. 5 (Oct. 1815).

The POST MASTER of Albany was Peter P. Dox, who died on 21 Nov. 1815 (*Albany Daily Advertiser*, 23 Nov. 1815). The postmaster GENERAL was Return J. Meigs (*ANB*).

From John Rhea

DEAR SIR   Sullivan Court House 20th November 1815

I had proceeded to the Westward beyond Knoxville, and previous to my return came, to the post office there, Your letter of the 22d of September last inclosing one to Mr Correa—Your letter had been some time in the office, and there is reason to believe that Mr Correa, if he passed through Knoxville, had gone through, during my absence from that place—I would have wrote to You from Knoxville but thinking Mr Correa might still have been to the Eastward and that I might meet him between that place and this, I refrained writting to You untill now—and believing that I will not see him, I have inclosed and sent to You Your letter to him, deeming it more proper so to do than to retain the letter with Expectation of seeing him. Very much indeed do I regret that I had not the pleasure of seeing Mr Correa and his fellow traveller, and of manifesting to them Every friendly attention in my power—.

Inclosed I send to You the flower of an herb which grows wild in the woods of Tennessee—the root of which is said to be a sovereign and certain remedy, in Cases of the Dysentery or flux of any kind— the root consists of several fibres—about the length and thickness of the little finger of the hand, [one][1] of them is taken, put into a Cup, with about a pint of Water, set on some coals or Embers, Warmed slowly untill it becomes blood warm, and continued so untill the strength of the root is extracted or the Water impregnated with it. a Small table spoonfull may be taken at a time—I have not Experienced the Efficacy, but such is the information Given, of it—

With Great satisfaction I have read in the Lynchburg newspaper that You were present when General Jackson arrived at that place. Under Your auspices and direction the Extensive Louisiana was purchased and annexed to the United States of America: General Jackson with the Tennessee Militia and other forces—gallantly defended it and repulsed with terrible overthrow the daring invasion of a powerfull Enemy.

You will have seen by the newspapers that my fellow Citizens of Tennessee have not thought proper to continue me a member of Congress, I have however the consolation humbly[2] to believe that, during the time I had that honor, my efforts were exerted to maintain the independence—and to promote the Welfare and happiness of our beloved country. For reasons of a public nature I wished to be a member of the fourteenth Congress—. but the will of the majority being, in such case, the law, to bow with respectfull submission to that will is a duty, but, notwithstanding that, there is some difficulty in withdrawing the mind from the contemplation of subjects with which it had been engaged for a considerable time. Except attending to my own little affairs, I am now disengaged from all public business, and cannot avoid expressing to You a wish that it was otherwise,—for my earnest desire is to be usefull as long as I am able.

I received Your letter with Emotions of satisfaction—it recalled to my mind times and circumstances which have passed over, and will not return; times in which I had the pleasure of seeing You, and circumstances which tended to smooth the path of life. at all times to know You are well, will be highly gratifying to me, and if at any time hereafter You will honor me with a letter please to direct to me at Sullivan Courthouse Tennessee—with sentiments of sincere and friendly Esteem—I have the honor

to be Your ob^t serv^t JOHN RHEA

Will you please to write and inform me whether You receive this with the inclosed to Mʳ Correa—

RC (ViW: TC-JP); between signature and postscript: "Thomas Jefferson Esqʳ Late President of the United States"; endorsed by TJ as received 16 Dec. 1815 and so recorded in SJL. Enclosures: TJ to José Corrêa da Serra, 22 Sept. 1815, and enclosure.

Corrêa da Serra's FELLOW TRAVELLER was Francis W. Gilmer. Samuel Powell had recently defeated Rhea in his bid to represent Tennessee in the FOURTEENTH CONGRESS (Washington *Daily National Intelligencer*, 15 Aug. 1815).

¹ Omitted word editorially supplied.
² Word interlined.

From John Vaughan

D SIR   Philadᵃ Nov. 21ˢᵗ 1815

I have recᵈ a letter from Cathalan 8 Sep. & 2 Octʳ Mess Peregaux had remitted to Mʳ C. 1056 fˢ being $5\frac{28}{100}$ per Dollar for Mr Girards credit of 200$ which sum is passed to your credit by Mʳ S. Cathalan—He had receieved no letter from you, but referring to what he had Sent you from 7 to 9 Years ago he was preparing to Send you a Small Stock of wines by the first American Vessel bound to the Cheseapeak, Phil. or New York, of which he requests I would advise You & Mʳ Girard—I forwarded a Catalogue¹ of Books Selected by Mʳ Ticknor & Mʳ Everett on the Continent & sent to Boston, where they are to be Sold the 20 Decʳ—They were at Gœtingen 4 Sep. Studying German & feeling Confident that in a few weeks they should be able to attend the German Lectures—

I remain Your obᵗ serv &c   JN VAUGHAN

RC (MHi); at head of text: "Thomas Jefferson Monticello"; endorsed by TJ as received 15 Dec. 1815 and so recorded in SJL; with TJ's additional notation on verso listing the subjects of his response: "books Cathalan Leghorn."

The catalogue of BOOKS selected for sale by George Ticknor and Edward

Everett was *Books, Rare, Curious, Elegant and Valuable, in the departments of the Classicks, Civil Law, History, Criticism, Belles Lettres and Theology, for sale at auction, in Boston, 20 December, 1815* (Boston, 1815).

¹ Manuscript: "Catalogoue."

From William R. Gray

SIR,   Richmond 22 Nov 1815.

I anticipated the honor of delivering to you, a letter from the President of the United States; but recent information that you were absent from Monticello, and the advanced state of the season, have induced Mrs Gray and myself to defer paying our respects to you, until our return from charleston. as the letter may not be merely one of introduction, I have taken the liberty of enclosing it

With great respect Your obed serv   W^M R GRAY

RC (DLC); dateline at foot of text; endorsed by TJ as received 15 Dec. 1815 and so recorded in SJL. Enclosure: James Madison to TJ, 15 Nov. 1815.

From Alden Partridge

SIR   West Point, Novr 23^d 1815

I had the honor duly to receive your letter of the 12th of october. I now take the liberty Sir, to enclose you an Extract from some observations which I made in 1811. (shortly after my return from the white Mountains,)[1] upon the Method of calculating Heights by means of the Barometer—together with the Rule I used for that purpose. This will shew you the manner in which my calculations were made, and may, perhaps assist you in determining what degree of credit ought to be attached to them. I hope therefore it will not be unacceptable to you. The calculations of Genl. Williams were made from a table, constructed by himself and Mr Patterson. This table The Genl was afterwards convinced, was incorrect—he accordingly in 1810 requested me to take his data, and make the calculations over again by the Rule I had used. This I did, and obtained Results considerably different, from those he had previously obtained. These were published,[2] by his direction, in a periodical[3] work, Edited in New york. A Copy of those Altitudes is enclosed, as they stand corrected by my calculation, and also as they were first published in the 4th volume of the American Philosophical Transactions. I shall feel myself much obliged to you for your calculations of the Heights of the Peaks of Otter as I wish to compare them with the Altitudes of our Northern[4] Mountains. I shall take the liberty Sir, in the course of a few days to enclose you some tables containing Meteorological observations[5] which I have made during, and Subsequent to the year 1810, and

[187]

which I trust will not be unacceptable to you— I have the honor to be with

the highest Respect and Esteem Sir your Obedient Servant

A PARTRIDGE
Capt. of Engs

RC (DLC); at foot of text: "Thomas Jefferson Esquire Late President of the United States"; endorsed by TJ as received 15 Dec. 1815 and so recorded in SJL.

[1] Omitted closing parenthesis editorially supplied.
[2] Manuscript: "publishe."
[3] Manuscript: "peridical."
[4] Manuscript: "Northeron."
[5] Manuscript: "obsevations."

ENCLOSURES

I

Alden Partridge's Observations on the Use of Barometers to Compute Altitudes

Extract.[1]

The rule for computing altitudes from Barometrical observation is as mathematically demonstrable as those for trigonometrical calculation; the accuracy of the results deduced from either method of calculation must therefore depend wholly upon the accuracy of the data obtained. In order to calculate the altitude of a mountain by trigonometry (where the angle of ascent is not a right one) we must have two stations, which two stations and the part to be calculated must be in the same perpendicular plane; that is, the first station must be exactly between the mountain & the second Station. the distance between the two Stations must be known. also the angle of elevation of the top of the mountain from each of the Stations and, (in case the two stations are not upon the Same level) the angle of ascent or descent of the base of the mountain above or below the first station. these things being obtained, by the solution of one oblique & one right angled triangle, in each of which a side & its opposite angle are two of the given parts, we obtain the altitude required. the only difficulty here (& this I am inclined to think, will be rather a serious one) is to ascertain correctly the length of the base, (the distance between the two stations.) and the dimensions of the several angles, for either of these being incorrect it is evident the results will be erroneous; The difficulty of accurately measuring a line of any considerable length even on good ground, is I presume, evident to every one who has made the experiment; but when instead of plain open ground the operation is to be performed on ground somewhat uneven, & perhaps covered with bushes, (such as we generally find near the foot of mountains) the difficulty will be greatly increased, so much so as to render an accurate measurement almost impossible; the measuring of the angles is also a very nice operation, and one, in which the most accurate observers owing to a variety of circumstances too numerous to mention, but which I presume are generally known, are very liable to err.

I shall now proceed to make some observations upon the Barometrical method of computation. Torricelli the Disciple of the famous Galileo first proved by experiment that the Atmosphere had weight, this ingenious Philosopher having filled a glass tube closed at one end with Mercury, and then inverting it with the open end downwards in a bason of Mercury, he found that a column of Mercury of a certain height remained suspended in the tube, he therefore very rationally concluded that the weight of the column of Mercury in the tube must be balanced by the pressure of the air upon the surface of the Mercury in the bason, this experiment gave rise to the Barometer, an Instrument for measuring the weight of the atmosphere; by repeated experiments, it has been found that at the mean temperature of $55°$ a column of air of any given base and of the height of the atmosphere is equal in weight to a column of Mercury of an equal base, & $29\frac{1}{2}$ inches high. This property of the atmosphere, (its gravity) being fully established as well as its elasticity, it follows that the air nearest the surface of the earth being pressed by the weight of the superincumbent atmosphere, must be more dense than the air above it, having a greater weight to sustain; & consequently the air must continually decrease in density & of course in weight in proportion as we ascend above the common surface of the earth.

From what has been said it would seem natural to conclude that, if at the common surface of the earth the air by its pressure will support a column of Mercury in the Barometer $29\frac{1}{2}$ inches high; that at any altitude above the common surface, where the air is less dense, it must support a column less than $29\frac{1}{2}$ inches high, and consequently that in proportion as we ascend the mercury in the Barometer must descend;

The truth of the above conclusion was first experimentally proved by the celebrated Pascal, who thereby substantiated the correctness of the conclusion deduced from the experiment of Torricelli.

Philosophers have demonstrated that the density of the air (at different heights above the earth) decreases in such a manner that when these heights are taken in Arithmetical Progression the corresponding densities decrease in a geometrical progression; and[2] since the terms of an arithmetical progression are proportional to the log.s of the terms of a geometrical one, it follows that different altitudes above the earths surface are as the logarithms of the densities, or weights of the air at those altitudes,[3] and consequently the difference between the altitudes of any two places is as the difference of the logarithms of the densities of the air at those places. so that if d. denote the density at the altitude $\mathbf{A}$. and (∂) the density at the altitude (a). then by what has been said $\mathbf{A}$ is as the log. of d, and (a) is as the log. of ∂. Also the difference of altitude $\mathbf{A} - a$, is as the difference of log. d – log. ∂ or log.$\frac{d}{\partial}$. and if $\mathbf{A} = 0$ or d = the density at the surface of the earth, then it is evident that any altitude as (a) above the surface of the earth is as the log $\frac{d}{\partial}$;[4]

from what has just been said is derived the method of calculating the heights of mountains or other eminences by means of the Barometer,[5] for if by means of this instrument the pressure or density of the air be taken at the foot of any mountain, and again at the top of it, the difference of the logarithms of these two pressures or densities, or the log. of their quotient (which is the same thing) will be as the[6] difference of altitudes or as the height of the mountain, supposing the temperature of the air to be the same at both places.[7] but since this formula expresses only the relation between different altitudes with respect to their densities it will be necessary to obtain the real altitude which corresponds to any given density, or the density which corresponds to a given altitude,[8] and since it has been proved that (a) is as the log.$\frac{d}{\partial}$, assume (h) so that a = h × log.$\frac{d}{\partial}$ where (h) will be of one constant value for all altitudes. Now to determine the value of (h) let a case be taken in which we know the altitude (a) corresponding to a known density ∂; as for instance let (a) be taken equal to one foot or some such small altitude, then because the density (d) may be measured by the pressure of the atmosphere or the uniform column of 27600 feet (which is the altitude of a column of air of the same density throughout as the air at the surface of the earth at the temperature of 55°, that would balance a column of Mercury of equal base with it, and $29\frac{1}{2}$ inches high)[9] when the temperature is 55°.

Therefore 27600 feet will denote the density d at the lower place and 27599 the less density ∂ at one foot above it; consequently $1 = h \times \log.\frac{27600}{27599}$ [10] $= h \times ,0000158 = h \times ,0000158 \times \frac{27600}{27600} = h \times \frac{.43429448}{27600}$ nearly, $= h \times \frac{.43429448}{27600}$ $\times \frac{2,3025850929940}{2,3025850929940} = \frac{h \times 1}{63551}$ ft.[11] (see the accompanying demonstration) therefore for any altitude we have this general theorem vizt a $= 63551 \times \log.\frac{d}{\partial}$ or $= 63551 \times \log.\frac{M}{m}$ or $=$ to $10592 \times \log.\frac{M}{m}$ fathoms where M is the column of mercury at the bottom, and consequently equal to the weight of the[12] atmosphere at that place, and (m) that at the top of the altitude (a).[13] This formula is adapted to the mean temperature of 55° but since it has been found by experiment that air expands about the 435th part of its whole bulk for every degree of heat; it follows, that[14] for every degree that the mean temperature between the temperatures at the top & bottom of the altitude a, exceeds 55° that altitude must be increased by its 435th part & diminished in the same ratio for every degree the mean is below 55° —

It is also found that Mercury expands about the $\frac{1}{9600}$ th part of its whole bulk for every degree of heat, and since it often happens that there is a considerable difference between the temperature at the top & bottom of a mountain, it would follow that the Mercury in the Barometer, would be more expanded by heat in the one case than the other, and consequently if not rectified would introduce an error into the calculation. in cases of this kind the mercury may be reduced to the same temperature by increasing the column in the coldest temperature or diminishing that in the warmest by its $\frac{1}{9600}$ part for every degree of difference between the temperatures at the top & bottom of the altitude a,[15] but the formula may be rendered much more convenient for practice, by reducing the factor 10592 to 10,000 which we may do provided we change the temperature proportionally from 55°. thus since the difference 592 is the 18th part of the whole factor 10592 and also since 18 is the 24th part [of][16] 435, therefore the corresponding change of temperature is 24° which reduces the 55° to 31° & therefore the formula becomes a $=$ 10,000 × log $\frac{M}{m}$ where the temperature is 31°, & therefore for every degree above that, the result is to be increased by so many times its 435th part.[17]

From the foregoing observations I think it is evident that the Barometric mode of calculation is true in theory; & I can discover but one objection that can be urged against it in practice. Every Person accustomed to make observations with a Barometer knows that it is much affected by different currents of air, the Mercury uniformly (with very few exceptions) rising with westerly or northerly winds, and falling when southerly or easterly ones prevail. If then, in making observations different winds should prevail at the upper & lower stations (which may often happen when those stations are at a consid- erable distance from each other) it would follow that the Mercury in the Barometer being from this cause elevated at one station and depressed at the other more than it ought, the results deduced would be erroneous. In order to remedy this my method has been (in cases where the stations were a con- siderable distance apart) to have a regular journal kept at the lower one, in which were inserted daily the altitude of the Mercury in the Barometer, the temperature of the air, and the prevailing winds, together with the state of the weather generally, & then by comparing the observations made upon the top of the height to be calculated, I could select therefrom one that agreed with it as it respects the prevailing winds, and state of the weather and from those make out the calculations required. From the preceding observa- tions the following easy rule for the calculation of heights generally (by the Barometer) is deduced. — [18]

1st Observe the height of the Barometer at the Bottom of any height or depth to be measured; with the temperature of the Mercury by means of a Ther- mometer attached to the Barometer and also the temperature of the air in the Shade by means of a detached Thermometer.

2d Let the same thing be done at the top of the said height or depth, and at the same time, or as near the same time as may be. And let those Altitudes of the Barometer be reduced to the same temperature, if it be thought neces- sary, by correcting either the one or the other, that is, augment the height of the Mercury in the colder temperature, or diminish that in the warmer by its $\frac{1}{9600}$ part for every degree of difference of the two.

3d Take the difference of the common Logarithms of the two heights of the Barometer, corrected as above if necessary, cutting off three figures next the right hand for decimals,[19] where the Log. tables go to seven places of figures, or cut off only two figures when the tables go to six places, and so on; or in general remove the decimal point four places, more towards the right hand those on the left hand being fathoms in whole numbers.

4th Correct the number last found for the difference of the temperature of the air, as follows, take half the sum of the two[20] temperatures, for the mean one; & for every degree which this differs from the temperature 31.° take so many times the $\frac{1}{435}$ part of the fathoms above found, & add them if the mean tem- perature be above 31.° but subtract them if the mean temperature be below 31.° and the sum or difference will be the true altitude in fathoms. or being multiplied by six, it will be the altitude in feet.[21]

Norwich Vt Augst 20th 1811.[22]

Demonstration

that h × log. $\frac{27600}{27599}$ is nearly = to h × $\frac{.43429448}{27600}$. The number ,43429448 is the modulus of the common system of Logarithms, and is equal to the quotient which arises from dividing 1 by 2,3025850929940. but for the purpose of more clearly investigating the matter, I shall have recourse to the logarithmic curve, the principal property of which is, that the abscisses being taken in arithmetical progression the corresponding Ordinates will be in Geometrical Progression—that is, the Abscisses are the log.s of their corresponding ordi- nates. Let x represent any abscissa, y its ordinates; & let (a) represent the subtangent[23] of the curve, Moreover let the fluxion of x be denoted thus, (ẋ) and the fluxion of y thus, (ẏ). then by similar triangles (the figure being constructed) it will be as, $\dot{y} : \dot{x} :: y : a$, and if instead of $\dot{x}$ & $\dot{y}$ be substituted their increments marked, thus $(\dot{x})(\dot{y})$ which may be done (see simpsons Fluxions, page 109, Scholium) the above proportion will stand thus, as, $\dot{y} : \dot{x}$ :: y : a; now it is evident from the property of the Curve abovementioned, that if y represent any number x will represent its log. it is also evident that the small quantity, $\dot{y}$, may express the difference between any two numbers very nearly equal, and also that the other small quantity, $\dot{x}$, may denote the difference between the log.s of those numbers. the last proportion therefore, $\dot{y} : \dot{x} :: y : a$, being put into words, will be, as the difference between any two numbers, nearly equal, is to the dif. of their log.s. so is either of those numbers, to the modulus of the system of logarithms. to apply this to the case under consideration, here are two numbers 27600 & 27599 nearly equal to each other, their difference being 1, and the log. of their ratio, .0000158; therefore from what has been said, as 1 : 27600 :: .0000158 : ,43429448 nearly, therefore h × log. $\frac{27600}{27599}$ is = h × .0000158 = h × .0000158 × $\frac{27600}{27600}$ = h × $\frac{.43429448}{27600}$ nearly, = h × $\frac{.43429448}{27600}$ × $\frac{2,3025850929940}{2,3025850929940}$ = $\frac{h \times 1}{63551}$, nearly which is = $\frac{h}{63551}$.—

MS (DLC); in an unidentified hand. MS (VtNN: Partridge Papers); in a bound volume of Partridge manuscripts; in an unidentified hand. Excerpt printed (with covering letter from Partridge dated West Point, 31 Aug. 1816), in Washington *Daily National Intelligencer*, 10 Sept. 1816. Portions of Partridge's text paraphrased Charles Hutton, *A Course of Mathematics* (London, 1798; Sowerby, no. 3683), 2:234–5, 244–5, as indicated below, with only the most significant changes noted.

Later in 1811 Partridge sent an expanded version of this document to his colleague Jonathan Williams for the attention of the United States Military Philosophical Society (MS in InU: Williams Papers; in an unidentified hand; undated; endorsed by Williams: "30 Octo[r] 1811 Cap[n] Partridge on the mode of calculating Barometrical heights for the Society"; covering letter dated Norwich, 30 Oct. 1811, in same).

[1] Unmatched opening double quotation mark preceding next word editorially omitted. VtNN MS here adds "From some observations relative to the calculation of the Altitudes of mountains and other heights by means of the Barometer—By Alden Partridge captain in the United States corps of Engineers."
[2] Extract from *Course of Mathematics* (2:234–5) begins here.

[3] Sentence ends here in *Course of Mathematics*.
[4] *Course of Mathematics* here adds "Or, in general, the log of $\frac{D}{d}$ [$\frac{d}{9}$ in MS] is as the altitude of the one place above the other, whether the lower place be at the surface of the earth, or any where else."
[5] *Course of Mathematics* here adds "which is an instrument that measures the pressure or density of the air at any place."
[6] Manuscript: "the the."
[7] *Course of Mathematics* here adds "and the gravity of air not altered by the different distances from the earth's centre."
[8] *Course of Mathematics* here adds "And there are various experiments by which this may be done. The first, and most natural, is that which results from the known specific gravity of air, with respect to the whole pressure of the atmosphere on the surface of the earth."
[9] Parenthetical phrase not in *Course of Mathematics*.
[10] For remainder of sentence *Course of Mathematics* substitutes "which, by the nature of logarithms, is nearly = h × $\frac{.43429448}{27600}$ = $\frac{h}{63551}$ nearly; and hence h − 63551 feet."
[11] For preceding letters "ft.," VtNN MS substitutes "nearly, which is $\frac{h}{63551}$, therefore l = $\frac{h}{63551}$, and consequently h = 63551 feet."
[12] Preceding three words not in VtNN MS.
[13] *Course of Mathematics* here adds

"and where M and *m* [M and m in MS] may be taken in any measure, either feet, or inches, &c."

[14] Text from "since it has been found" to this point not in *Course of Mathematics*.

[15] In place of paragraph to this point, *Course of Mathematics* reads "Note also, that a column of 30 inches of mercury varies its length by about the $\frac{1}{320}$ part of an inch for every degree of heat, or rather $\frac{1}{9600}$ of the whole volume."

[16] Omitted word supplied from *Course of Mathematics*.

[17] Extract from *Course of Mathematics* ends here.

[18] Extract from *Course of Mathematics* (2:244–5) and text in *Daily National Intelligencer* both begin here with variants of this sentence. *Course of Mathematics*: "FROM the principles laid down in the

Scholium to prop. 66, concerning the measuring of altitudes by the barometer, and the foregoing descriptions of the barometer and thermometer, we may now collect together the precepts for the practice of such measurements, which are as follow." *Daily National Intelligencer*: "*The rules for calculating heights generally, by means of the barometer and thermometer.*"

[19] For remainder of sentence, *Course of Mathematics* substitutes "the rest being fathoms in whole numbers."

[20] Preceding four words not in *Daily National Intelligencer*.

[21] *Daily National Intelligencer* and extract from *Course of Mathematics* end here.

[22] Remainder on a separate sheet.

[23] Manuscript: "subtanget."

II

Alden Partridge's Table of Altitudes of the Blue Ridge and Allegheny Mountains

[by 5 Nov. 1810]

Altitudes of the Blue Ridge & Alleghany Mountains, in feet above the level of tide water, in virginia, calculated from Barometrical[1] Observation, by Gen[l] Jonathan Williams. (corrected).

1.	The Highest point of the Blue Ridge, near Rock fish Gap	1908.
2.	The foot of the Blue Ridge, on the western side	895
3.	The summit of the first mountain, near the warm springs	2018.
4.	The summit of the second mountain near the warm springs	2380
5	The summit of the Alleghany Ridge, about six miles west of the Sweet Springs	2988.

The foregoing Altitudes as published in the 4th Volume of the American Philosophical Transactions.

1.	The Highest point of the Blue Ridge near Rock fish Gap	1822.
2.	The foot of the Blue Ridge on the western Side	863.
3.	The summit of the first mountain near the warm Springs	1898.
4.	The summit of the second mountain near the warm Springs	2247.
5.	The summit of the Alleghany Ridge, about six miles west of the Sweet Springs	2760.

MS (DLC: TJ Papers, 193:34414); in an unidentified hand; undated.

Partridge had communicated the COR-RECTED altitudes to Jonathan Williams, who included them in a paper read at a meeting of the United States Military Philosophical Society on 5 Nov. 1810 (*American Medical and Philosophical Register*, 2d ed., 1 [1814]: 337; Poor,

Jefferson's Library, 5 [no. 190]). Williams PUBLISHED the figures from the second table in APS, *Transactions* 4 (1799): 219–20.

¹ Manuscript: "Baronometrical."

From Horatio G. Spafford

ESTEEMED FRIEND—   Albany, 11 Mo. 23, 1815.

The event which I expected, has terminated the life of my friend Dox, & vacated the office of Post Master in this City. May I now solicit thy aid in obtaining that office for me? I need some kindness very much, having a numerous family to support, & having lately lost a good deal of property. Thy aid would be very grateful to my feelings, & an intimation from thee would ensure me success. I write by this mail, to the Post Master General, & perhaps to the President. Pray have the goodness to take this into consideration, & to apprize me of thy conclusion. With very great esteem & respect, thy friend,

H. G. SPAFFORD.

RC (DLC); at foot of text: "Hon. Thomas Jefferson"; endorsed by TJ as received 15 Dec. 1815 and so recorded in SJL.

From Robert Patterson

SIR   Nov. 24. 15

The Author of this Synopsis (formerly Secretary of Congress) desires me to send you, by this opportunity, a copy of the work, of which he begs your acceptance; & Requests that you would please to favour him with your remarks on the same

I am, Sir, most respectfully, your obed^t serv^t R^T PATTERSON

RC (MHi); dateline beneath signature; addressed: "Thomas Jefferson"; endorsed by TJ as received 27 Dec. 1815 "with the clock" and so recorded in SJL; with TJ's notation beneath endorsement: "Ch^s Thompson." Enclosure: Charles Thomson, *A Synopsis of the Four Evan-* *gelists: or, a Regular History of the Conception, Birth, Doctrine, Miracles, Death, Resurrection, and Ascension of Jesus Christ, in the Words of the Evangelists* (Philadelphia, 1815; Poor, *Jefferson's Library*, 9 [no. 509]).

From George Ticknor

DEAR SIR,   Göttingen Nov. 25. 1815.

Besides the letter, which I had the honour of sending you by our commissioner Mr. Clay from London, I wrote you a long one from this place Oct. 14 giving you the reasons which induce me to spend the winter here and some slight notices of German literature—and Oct. 30. on hearing of the emigration of your friend Mons. Dupont de Nemours to the U.S. I enclosed to you the letter of introduction your kindness furnished me to him. To day I have received your favour of July 4. inclosing your catalogue of books. If I had been in France I should have received it a month earlier but even that would have been too late to send out your books this fall and I rejoice by this comparison of dates to find that, though you will not receive them till the spring, you will receive them as early as it would have been possible even under the plan I originally contemplated. Whenever they go, may they have a more fortunate fate than an hundred pounds worth of choice and curious classicks, which I shipped to my father from Holland, and which I have too much reason to believe were lost in some of those tremendous storms which in August and September seem to have covered the Atlantick with wrecks.

In the mean time, as I have had access to the great library here, and seen there all the editions of the classicks extant, I can, wherever you have left a choice open to my decision, first consult you with all the knowledge I could get at Paris, & mention to you, perhaps, some editions that will be more to your taste, as you have expressed it in your letter, even in some cases, where you have left me no alternative.—

1. Herodotus. 3. 8vo. Oxon. there is a german edit. of this in the same form & size, which will be cheaper & quite as good.

2. Thucydides. You express some doubts of the Bip. in 6. 8vo. Perhaps you were not aware that it is a reimpression of Duker's with emendations & decidedly the ed. opt.

3. Diog. Laertius. The edit. of Meibomius in two small thin quartos is one of the best edited Greek classicks extant.—

4. Plutarchi Vitæ. There is a curious & beautiful edition of the lives published in 8vo. at Paris by Coray[1] the modern Greek from Scios (Χίος). He has published, also, a specimen of an edit. of Homer, a Hierocles, & two or three other small Greek works with Greek Prefaces, & notes written with great purity & taste & a selection of scholia, which I think would please you very much.

5. I know of no decent edit. of Dion Cassius but that by the famous

Reimarus in 2. fol. which is one of the best edited Greek classicks extant.

6. <u>Tacitus</u>. The edition of Oberlinus in 4. 8vo. is the optime.

7. <u>Homeri Op</u>. I know of no edition of Homer (except Didymus 1689) cum scholiis. If, however, you add to this Heyne's Iliad in 8. 8vo. you will have a complete corpus of everything relating to the criticism of Homer. The running commentary of Heyne is beautiful—and his excursi admirable. His scholia, too, are more curious & ample than those of any other edit. His Iliad, his Pindar[2] 3. 8vo., his Tibullus 1. 8vo, and his Virgil 6. 8vo are unrivalled as editions of the classicks.

8. The best <u>Theocritus</u> is by Valkenaer 1. 8vo. with very few notes.

9. <u>Juvenal</u> by Ruperti 2. 8vo. gives a better explanation of this difficult author than was ever before given &, indeed, as good as is to be expected. Gifford, in London, spoke of it to me with unmeasured praise, & I am satisfied that I never understood it till I read it with this admirable commentary.

10. The optime of <u>Hesiod</u> is now by Loesner, 1. 8vo with scholia & Le clerc's notes.

11. Aeschylus 3. 8vo. <u>German</u> edit. by Schultz is the best.

12. Reiske's Orators in 12. 8vo, now that the apparatus criticus and scholia &c are complete is very much sought. It cost me in Holland 80 florins = $.32.—

I mention these items to you merely as bibliographical hints. In many instances you undoubtedly have personal & peculiar reasons for preferring the elder editions to the optimes, for an old edition or copy in which we have been accustomed to read is like an old friend, who is not to be put aside for a younger one, even though he should be of more promise.—If, therefore, I receive no further direction from you, I shall fulfil your orders as expressed in your list, immediately on my arrival at Paris, which will be as soon as the roads are comfortable in the spring.—

A letter addressed to our legation in France—to Francis Williams Esq. Paris—or to my father Boston will reach & govern me.—

I am, with much respect,

Your obedient servant,   GEO: TICKNOR.—

I had forgotten to mention that your's of Aug. 16 was received Oct. 13. with Mr. Vaughan's enclosure. My father mentioned that he had received a very kind & polite letter from you for which I pray you to accept my thanks as you have doubtless before received his.—

G. T.

RC (DLC); addressed: "To His Excellency, Thomas Jefferson Esquire, late President of the United States Monticello, Albermarle county, Virginia"; stamped "SHIP"; with notation: "Received & forwarded Rotterdam 5 Decr 1815 by y mo H Servants Collings & Maingy"; franked; postmarked Boston, 28 Jan.; endorsed by TJ as received 7 Feb. 1816 and so recorded in SJL; with two marginal notes by TJ described below; and with Ticknor's numbered list annotated in pencil, probably by TJ in preparation for his 8 Feb. 1816 reply, with plus-signs next to nos. 1–4, 6–7, and 9–11, and minus-signs next to nos. 5, 8, and 12.

Ticknor's letter to TJ of OCT. 30. is not recorded in SJL and has not been found. Adamantios Coray's edition of Plutarch's

LIVES was Πλουτάρχου Βίοι Παράλληλοι (Ploutarchou bioi parallēloi), 6 vols. (Paris, 1809–14; TJ's copy in MoSW).

TJ's marginal notes described below reference a book review of William Martin Leake's *Researches in Greece* (London, 1814), in which the scholarship of Adamantios CORAY is mentioned several times, and a list of new publications that included an edition of PINDAR, Christian Gottlob Heyne's *Pindari Carmina* (*Edinburgh Review* 47 [1814]: 266; 48 [1815]: 353–69; either TJ's pagination is erroneous or he used a different edition).

[1] To the left of this word TJ keyed a note with an asterisk: "see Edinb. Rev. 1815. Feb. pa. 350."
[2] To the left of this word TJ keyed a note with a dagger: "see Edin. Rev. Nov. 1814. Monthly catalogue pa. 266."

From Jean David

MONSIEUR   Richmond le 26 novembre 1815—
Je ne me Serois pas permis de vous ecrire pour vous offrir mes Services, (ce dont vous auriez été instruit comme tout le monde par la voie des journaux,) Si je n'y avois été encouragé par Mr Girardin; c'est donc Sous Ses auspices que je prends cette liberté.
il S'agit de la culture de la vigne et de la maniére de faire le vin, choses que je connois parfaitement. Je pense que cette culture Seroit plus avantageuse à la haute virginie, qu'aucune de celles auxquelles on S'y livre. Je Sais que divers essais ont eu lieu, qui n'ont pas repondu aux esperances des entrepreneurs; mais je ne puis penser que ce Soit à cause du Sol ou du climat, je Serois bien plutôt porté à croire que ceux qui dirigeoient ces entreprises n'avoient pas toutes les connoissances necessaires—
  Les vignes Se plaisent beaucoup plus Sur les coteaux que dans les plaines, ce n'est pas qu'elles ne viennent quelquefois très bien dans celles ci; lorsque la qualité du terrain, pierreux ou Sabloneux, permet aux eaux de S'ecouler; car la vigne ne craint rien tant que d'avoir Ses racines dans un terrain trop humide; elle y perit. et tant par cette consideration, que parceque Sur un coteau, le raisin y murit mieux, on doit preferer cette derniére exposition.
une autre observation de la plus grande importance, c'est la taille de la Vigne.—

En toscane, par exemple, on fait du très bon et du très mauvais Vin, et cette difference provient essentiellement de la maniére de tailler la Vigne

Beaucoup de cultivateurs font grimper leurs Vignes Sur des arbres ou Sur des grands echalas, ils en etendent les Sarments au loin, ce qui forme des espéces de guirlandes garnies de grapes de raisin, et une Seule vigne en produira quelquefois 50 livres et même davantage. Le vin que l'on retire de ces grappes est presque toujours detestable; tant parceque la vigne portant trop de fruit, ce fruit est aqueux et Sans goût, que parcequ'etant Suspendu à une trop grande elevation de la terre il n'y murit jamais bien; car la reverberation du sol, qui fait plus que doubler la chaleur, ne s'y fait presque pas sentir.

Les cultivateurs, au contraire; qui preferent la qualité à la quantité, tiennent leurs vignes basses à environ deux pieds du Sol, les taillant de maniére à ce que chaque ceps ne produise communement que 4 a 5 livres de raisin, lequel Se trouvant alors Succulent et Suffisamment mur, fait de l'excellent vin—

La fabrication du vin est encore un objet très essentiel, soit pour le degré de maturité que doit avoir le raisin, le temps qu'il faut donner à la fermentation, la forme et la proprete des usines et des tonneaux &c&ª &cª—il me faudroit ecrire un livre, Si je voulois entrer dans le detail de tout ce qu'il est necessaire de connoitre pour reussir dans une pareille entreprise; mais je crois vous en avoir dit assez pour que vous puissiez juger Si je connois ou non cette partie—

Je connois parfaitement aussi la plantation et la culture de l'olivier, ainsi que la maniére de fabriquer l'huile de première qualité; mais je ne Sais Si l'olivier pourroit resister aux froids de la virginie. il Se trouve des oliviers en Europe, jusqu'au 44ᵉᵐᵉ degré de latitude, il Seroit bien extraordinaire qu'ils ne puissent[1] pas exister en Amerique au 37ᵉᵐᵉ. L'olivier peut Supporter un froid très fort lorsque l'arbre Se trouve Sec. j'ai vu souvent perir des oliviers par le froid, mais c'est toujours lorsqu'une forte gelée Survient après la pluie, et que l'arbre n'a pas eu le temps de Secher, alors l'ecorce Se gerce et il meurt, ou du moins il faut le couronner, ce qui le retarde de plusieurs années. une autre observation qui n'auroit lieu que pour la haute Virginie, c'est que l'olivier aime le voisinage de la mer; on n'en trouve plus, même en Espagne, à trente lieues des côtes. d'après celá quoique je pense qu'il reussirait très bien dans la basse Virginie, il Se pourroit qu'il ne put reussir dans votre proprieté.

Je vous offre Monsieur mes Services dans toutes les choses auxquelles je puis être propre. vous pensez bien que connoissant à fond la culture de la Vigne et de l'olivier, je dois avoir des notions Sur toutes Sortes de cultures en general et même Sous ce Seul point de vue, je ne vous Serois pas inutile

Je termine cette longue lettre en vous disant que je desire beaucoup qu'il vous convienne de memployer auprés de vous; permettez moi d'ajouter que l'interet pecuniaire n'est pas le Seul motif de ce desir.

Je vous Salue respectueusement   J. DAVID

care of Doctor Lemosy.—

Si vous vous determiniez à planter la vigne, le mois de fevrier prochain, me paroitroit l'epoque la plus convenable dans ce climat, il faudroit alors renoncer pour cette année à faire venir des provins d'Europe, et S'en procurer de quelques unes des plantations existantes, Soit en virginie, dans le Kentuki, en pensilvanie &c^a—

on pourroit ensuite ecrire à temps pour en faire venir de france, de divers bons pays de vignoble, tels que la Bourgogne, le Bordelais, le Languedoc, et la provence, pour les planter lannée d'aprés. je vous conseillerois même d'employer de ces divers plants, pour donner ensuite la preference à ceux qui reussiroient le mieux et donneroient le meilleur vin. peut être Sera ceux que vous aurez pris en Amerique, attendu qu'ils Sont dejá acclimatés &c^c—

quant à mon traitement; mes pretentions Sont bien loin d'etre elevées, vous le regleriez vous même Suivant l'utilité que vous retireriez de moi.—

EDITORS' TRANSLATION

SIR   Richmond 26 November 1815—
I would not have permitted myself to write you to offer my services (of which you would have been informed like everybody else through the newspapers), if I had not been encouraged by Mr. Girardin; it is therefore under his auspices that I take this liberty.

My offer concerns the cultivation of vineyards and the making of wine, topics that I know perfectly well. I think this cultivation would be more beneficial to upper Virginia than any other practiced there. I know that several attempts that have been made did not rise to the expectations of the entrepreneurs, but I cannot believe that the soil or climate are to blame. I would tend rather to believe that the people who were in charge of these enterprises did not have all the necessary knowledge—

Vineyards do much better on hillsides than in lowlands, although they can do well in the latter, provided that the quality of the terrain, be it rocky or sandy, allows water to drain. Vines fear nothing more than having their roots in overly wet soil; they die there. For this reason, and also because grapes ripen better on a slope, one should opt for this exposure.

Another observation of the greatest importance is the pruning of the vine.—

In Tuscany, for example, they make both very good and very bad wine, and this difference derives in essence from the manner in which one prunes the vines

Many cultivators make their vines climb up trees or large stakes. They spread the vine shoots far apart, forming a sort of garland garnished with clusters of grapes, and a single vine will sometimes produce 50 pounds of grapes or even more. The wine produced from these grapes is almost always detestable, because the vine carries too much fruit, which causes the grapes to be watery and tasteless, and also because, being suspended too high above the ground, they never ripen properly, since the reflection from the ground, which almost doubles the warmth, is hardly felt at all.

Cultivators who, on the contrary, prefer quality to quantity, keep their vines at about two feet from the ground, pruning them in such a way that each vine usually produces only 4 or 5 pounds of grapes, which are accordingly delicious, sufficiently ripe, and make an excellent wine—

The production of wine is also an essential topic, either because of the degree of maturity grapes must reach or because of the time one must allow for fermentation, the shape and cleanliness of the equipment and barrels, etc., etc. I would have to write a book if I wanted to detail everything one must know to succeed in such an enterprise; but I believe I have said enough for you to judge whether or not I know what I am talking about—

I am also perfectly knowledgeable about the planting and cultivation of olive trees, as well as the way to manufacture high-quality olive oil; but I do not know whether olive trees could withstand the cold temperatures in Virginia. Olive trees are found in Europe up to the 44th degree of latitude, and it would be surprising if they could not exist in America on the 37th degree. Olive trees can withstand intense cold when they are dry. I have often seen olive trees die from the cold, but it always happens when a strong frost comes after it rains. When the tree has had no chance to dry, the bark cracks and the tree dies, or at least it must be pruned, which sets it back several years. Another observation applicable only to upper Virginia is that olive trees like to be close to the sea. They are not found, even in Spain, thirty leagues from the coast. Because of this, even though I think they would do very well in lower Virginia, they may not succeed on your property.

Sir, I offer you my services for everything for which I am qualified. You may imagine that since I know vineyards and olive trees so well, I must have ideas on all kinds of cultivation in general, and even from this point of view alone, I would not be useless to you.

I finish this long letter by telling you that I very much hope that it suits you to employ me, and allow me to add that pecuniary concerns are not the only motivation for this desire.

I send you my respectful regards   J. DAVID
                                           care of Doctor Lemosy.—

If you decided to plant vineyards, it seems to me that next February would be the most suitable time in this climate. One would then need to give up on sending for stocks from Europe this year and get them instead from some of the existing plantations, either in Virginia, or in Kentucky, Pennsylvania, etc.—

Afterwards we could write in time to have some sent from France, from various good vine-growing areas, such as Burgundy, the Bordeaux region, Languedoc, and Provence, to plant the following year. I would even advise you to use these various plants to determine the preference you will later give to the ones that excel and produce the best wine. They will perhaps be the ones you have gotten in America, since they are already acclimated, etc.—

My pretensions as to salary are far from being high; you can adjust it on the basis of my usefulness to you.—

RC (DLC); at head of text: "L'honnorable Th⁵ Jefferson Ecuyer ["Esquire"] Monticello"; endorsed by TJ as received 15 Dec. 1815 and so recorded in SJL. Translation by Dr. Genevieve Moene. Enclosed in Louis H. Girardin to TJ, 26 Nov. 1815, not found, but recorded in SJL as received 15 Dec. 1815 from Richmond.

¹ Manuscript: "pussent."

From Albert Gallatin

DEAR SIR   New York Nov⁽ᵉʳ⁾ 27ᵗʰ 1815

On my return from Washington, I found your welcome letter of Oct⁽ᵉʳ⁾ 16ᵗʰ which my friends here, daily expecting my return, had kept instead of forwarding it.

Our opinion of Bonaparte is precisely the same. In that, La Fayette's and every friend's of rational liberty in France did coincide. The return of that man was generally considered by them as a curse. Notwithstanding the blunders & rooted prejudices of the Bourbons, the alienation of the army and the absolute want of physical force had made them upon the whole harmless; and as soon as the termination of the Congress at Vienna & the dissolution of the coalition would have left France independent of foreign interference, they must, in the course of things, either have been overset or have governed according to public opinion. After Bonaparte's restoration, it was hoped by some that his weakness would compel him to pursue a similar course; others placing confidence in the declarations of the allies, hoped to get rid both of him and of the Bourbons; all saw the necessity of defending the country against foreign invasion; but the fatal catastrophe was not, to its full extent, anticipated by any. I call it a catastrophe with an eye only to the present; for, exhausted, degraded and oppressed as France now is, I do not despair of her ultimate success in establishing her independence, and a free form of Government: The people are too enlightened to submit long to any but a military despotism: what has lately passed was a scene in the drama, perhaps necessary to effect a radical cure of that love of conquest which had corrupted the nation &

[201]

made the French oppressors abroad & slaves at home. As to independence, we have the recent instance of Prussia, which with far inferior population, resources, or intellect, arose in two years from almost annihilation to the rank of a preponderating power. But, to return to Bonaparte, I lament to see our republican editors, so much dazzled by extraordinary actions or carried away by natural aversion to our only dangerous enemy, as to take up the cause of that despot & conqueror, and to represent him, as the champion of liberty, who has been her most mortal enemy, whose hatred to republican systems was founded on the most unbounded selfishness and on the most hearty contempt for mankind. I really wish that you would permit me to publish, or rather that you would publish your opinions on that subject. This might have a tendency to correct those which are daily published and which do injury to our cause at home, to our country abroad.

Under different circumstances, without having any wish for a foreign mission or a residence in France, I might have accepted the appointment of minister there. But satisfied that nothing can at this moment be effected in that country, and it being very reluctant to my feelings to be on a mission to a degraded monarch & to a nation under the yoke of foreign armies, I thought that I might without any breach of public duty or of private gratitude consult my own convenience; and I have accordingly officially informed our Government, that I declined altogether the appointment.

On the lamentable state to which the Banks have reduced the circulating medium of the country, there ought to be but one opinion. Yet I fear with you that there will be no legislative effectual interference. The remedy becomes also more difficult every day it is delayed. Specie for which there is no use but for exportation is hoarded up, or exported. The number of borrowers & of pretended lenders, equally interested in continuing and extending the present system at the expence of the community daily encreases. What might have been done last April with perfect facility, cannot now be effected without causing much clamour & some distress; and if delayed much longer, will not be done at all & will place us in a situation similar to that of Great Britain. I have no patience on that subject. The war has been successfully & honorably terminated; a debt of no more than 80 millions incurred, which, as we had paid more than 40 during your administ[n], & till the war began, makes that debt only 40 millions or 50 p% more than it was in March 1801; and Louisiana paid for, and an incipient navy created in the bargain; our population encreased in the same & our resources in a much greater proportion; our revenue greater than ever: and yet we are guilty of a continued[1] breach of faith towards our creditors, our soldiers, our seamen, our civil officers; public credit, heretofore supported simply by common honesty, declining at home & abroad; private credit placed on a still more uncertain basis; the value of property, and the nature of every person's engagements equally uncertain; a baseless currency varying every fifty miles & fluctuating every where: all this done or at least continued[2] contrary to common sense & to common integrity, not only without necessity or law, but in the face of positive laws & of the provisions of the Constitution itself. Yet a majority of the republican papers already leans to that system. The seat of Government is the worst focus of the evil, there being not less than 14 banks already organised in the district of Columbia, and some more preparing. The language of several of the Bank directors is similar to that of Peter to his brothers in the tale of the tub. They insist that their bread (God grant it was even bread) is good, substantial, mutton, that their rags are true solid silver; and some of them do already damn to all eternity every unbeliever. I have however some hope that the magnitude of the evil will produce a corrective; and I cannot help thinking that the Treasury will now be so rich that its will would alone be sufficient to prostrate at once that paper fabric. I have also indulged, with more warmth than is usual to me, in a political effusion; but I have been so long wedded to the national credit & integrity, that any stain which attaches to them touches me in a very tender point.

Ever respectfully and affectionately Your's,

ALBERT GALLATIN

RC (DLC); at foot of text: "Mr Jefferson"; endorsed by TJ as received 15 Dec. 1815 and so recorded in SJL. FC (NHi: Gallatin Papers).

On 23 Nov. 1815 Gallatin OFFICIALLY INFORMED President James Madison and Secretary of State James Monroe that he was declining appointment as minister to France (DLC: Madison Papers and Monroe Papers, respectively). Jonathan Swift wrote an allegorical work, *A Tale of a Tub*, in which PETER represents Roman Catholicism while HIS BROTHERS Jack and Martin personify Calvinism and Anglicanism (*ODNB*).

[1] Word interlined.
[2] Preceding four words interlined.

From Robert Patterson

SIR Philadᵃ Novʳ 28ᵗʰ 1815

A pretty severe attack of the prevailing epidemic, with a good deal of sickness in the family, must be my excuse for not sending on your Time-piece somewhat sooner. It was, however, last saturday shipped on board the Guinea Hen, &, according to your directions, consigned to messʳˢ Gibson & Jefferson of Richmond.[1]

On examining the pendulum mentioned in my last, & which I proposed to substitute for the one now in use, I find that it would be attended with too much difficulty & danger in transportation, & be very unmanageable in the adjustment. It consists of a large glass cylinder attached to the lower extremity of an iron rod, which is filled to the height of over 7 inches with mercury, (about 10 pounds) & serves as the bob of the pendulum. This pendulum possesses the principle of compensation, on account of the change of temperature in the air. For, on the increase of temperature, which would <u>lower</u> the center of oscillation, by lengthening the rod of the pendulum, the expansion of the mercury, from the same cause, would <u>raise</u> the center of oscillation. But the pendulum now attached to the clock is more simple in its construction, or at least much less expensive, & from a trial of some years, in all states of temperature, appears to preserve a very uniform rate. It is, I believe, (as I mentioned formerly) the invention of David Rittenhouse, & is sufficiently described in the Memoirs of his life by Wᵐ Barton, p. 584–5.

I have not very much confidence in the cylindrical pendulum as a standard of lineal measure, ☞when suspended by a spring[2]☜ for, according to a series of experiments made by mʳ Adrain of N.Y. a difference in the length or strength of the spring, produces an incalculable difference in the time of oscillation. But Mʳ Hassler suggests a manner of suspension which would be free from this sourse of error; namely, to suspend the cylindrical rod on what is termed <u>a knife-edge</u>, passing thro a perforation made at the distance of $\frac{1}{3}$ of its length from the upper extremity. A small cylindrical pendulum, thus suspended, would make its oscillations very nearly isochronous with a bob pendulum of the same length, & would furnish a true universal standard of lineal measure. For, having given—the latitude of the place, the elevation above the surface of the sea, the mean temperature of the air, the metal of the pendulum, the proportion between its length & thickness, the proportion between the length of the parts above & below the center of suspension, the number of oscillations in a sidereal day[3] and what proportional part of the Length is to be considered as the unit of measure (an English foot for instance) then it could be found by calculation, from data well enough ascertained, what proportional part of <u>any</u> other <u>pendulum</u> of the same form, where all the above data should be different, would be the same unit of measure.

You will find in a small tin box, along with the clock, the artificial reflecting horizon which I formerly mentioned, with a very accurate spirit level, made by m^r Hassler. He has determined, in a very simple manner, which I may hereafter describe, & with the utmost accuracy, the two oblique angles of the inclined plane, which you will find engraved on the same.

The manner of using this apparatus, for measuring any altitude of a celestial or terrestrial object, is as follows.—

1. Place the horizontal reflecting plane on any convenient stand, as the cill of a window, a table, or the like. On this plane, & parallel to the longer side, lay the spirit level, &, by turning one or other of the screws, bring the bubble to the middle of the glass tube.

2 Lay the spirit level accross the plane, &, by turning the side screw, bring the bubble again to the middle of the tube The plane will then be level, or horizontal, in all directions.

3. If the altitude to be measured be not less than 15° nor greater than half the graduated limb of the reflecting sector, then the altitude may be measured, in the common way, by means of the reflecting horizontal plane.

4. If the altitude be less than 15° then, on the horizontal plane, place the inclined plane, with its lesser angle <u>directly</u> <u>towards</u> the object, & measure the altitude above this plane, & then the real altitude above the horizon will be this measured altitude, <u>diminished</u> by the quantity of the lesser angle of the plane, (29° 40′)

5. If the altitude exceeds the limits of the sector—place the lesser angle of the inclined plane directly <u>opposite</u> to the object, & then the true altitude of the object will be its measured altitude above this plane, <u>increased</u> by the lesser angle of the plane.

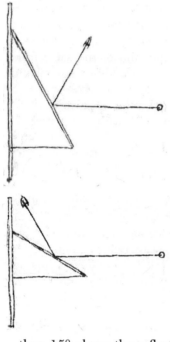

If a <u>sextant</u> be used, then all possible altitudes, from 0 to 90° may be measured as above; but if an <u>octant</u> be used, then to measure altitudes from 45° to 75° you must place the lesser angle of the inclined plane <u>opposite</u> to the object; & to measure altitudes exceeding 75° you must place the greater angle of the inclined plane <u>on</u> the horizontal plane, & opposite to the object; for then the true altitude will be the measured altitude above the inclined plane <u>increased</u> by the greater angle (60° 53′ 17″)

Remarks

1. In taking the altitudes of objects, by means of a reflecting surface, it is found very difficult, & in some cases impracticable, to measure small altitudes; but, by following the above directions, no angle less than 15° above the reflecting plane, will ever be required to be measured, whether the sextant or the octant be used.

2. With respect to terrestrial objects, it is frequently necessary not only to measure altitudes but <u>depressions</u>; Now, with the above described apparatus, any depression not exceeding 45° may be readily measured by turning the reflecting surface of the inclined plane <u>towards</u> the object.

3. The reflecting surfaces are made of a piece of good [broken] looking-glass, with the polish ground off from one surface, & attached to the brass plane by black sealing-wax. The reflection is then made from the upper surface of the glass, & gives a very perfect image; nearly of the same degree of brightness with that made by a double reflection from the specula of the sector.

4. The use of this apparatus may be very readily extended to the measurement of all possible angular distances, even up to 180° & will thus render the reflecting sector the most complete & accurate surveying instrument that can be made use of

But not to put your patience to any further trial, I shall, for the present, conclude

I am, Sir, with the greatest respect & esteem, Your most obed^t serv^t

R^T PATTERSON

☞ The small appendages mentioned above, you will please, Sir, to accept, without charge, as it would be too trifling to make.

RC (DLC); brackets in original; adjacent to closing: "Thomas Jefferson"; endorsed by TJ as received 15 Dec. 1815 and so recorded in SJL. Dft (PPAmP: Thomas Jefferson Papers); incomplete; dated 22 Nov. 1815; on recto of remnant of address leaf of RC of TJ to Patterson, 13 Oct. 1815, and on verso of that letter; heavily abbreviated and partially illegible, with related, heavily abbreviated instructions on the use of octants and sextants on verso of the text of that letter.

[1] Sentence interlined in Dft.
[2] Dft ends here.
[3] Preceding eight words interlined.

From Carlo Botta

Monsieur   Paris 29 Novembre 1815 Rue de la Tixanderie N° 41.

le Dr Valli, mon ami, et mon compatriote, se rend en amérique pour se procurer l'occasion d'y observer la fievre jaune. Je n'ai pas voulu laisser echapper cette occasion sans me rappeler á votre souvenir, et sans vous rémercier de l'accueil favorable que vous avez bien voulu faire á mon histoire de la guerre d'amérique. J'imprime dans ce moment-ci un poème epique intitulé, il Camillo, o Vejo conquistata; aussitôt qu'il sera imprimé, je me ferai un empressement de vous en faire passer un exemplaire. Heureux, si vous pouvez trouver que j'aie rempli, du moins en partie, les loix et le but de l'Epopée.

le Dr Valli qui aura l'honneur de vous remettre la présente, est un des médecins les plus distingués de l'Europe. Il a vu la peste á Smyrne et á Constantinople; il a eu le courage de faire sur lui meme des expériences aussi dangereuses qu'intéressantes. Il veut maintenant essayer de la fievre jaune. l'amour de l'humanité que personne n'a jamais poussé plus loin que lui, lui fait braver toute espèce de fatigues et de dangers. Il joint les sentiments les plus élévés aux connaissances les plus profondes.

Je n'ai pas le droit de vous le recommander. Je prends seulement la liberté de vous l'adresser. l'amour de l'humanité qui vous distingue si eminement l'un et l'autre, fera le reste.

veuillez, Monsieur, agréer les nouveaux souhais que je fais, pour votre bonheur, et me conserver toujours une place dans votre bon souvenir.

votre très humble Serviteur   Charles Botta

SIR   Paris 29 November 1815 Rue de la Tixanderie Number 41.
Dr. Valli, my friend and compatriot, is going to America to observe cases of yellow fever. I did not want to let this occasion pass without remembering myself to you and thanking you for the favorable welcome you were pleased to give to my history of the American war. I am just now printing an epic poem entitled *Il Camillo, o Vejo Conquistata.* As soon as it is published, I will hasten to send you a copy. I will be happy if you find that I have fulfilled, at least in part, the rules and objects of the epic genre.

Dr. Valli, who will have the honor of delivering this letter to you, is one of the most distinguished physicians in Europe. He witnessed the plague at Smyrna and Constantinople; he has had the courage to perform experiments on himself that were as dangerous as they were interesting. He now wants to try out yellow fever. The love of humanity, which no one has ever pursued farther, allows him to brave every kind of fatigue and danger. He combines the most elevated sentiments with the most profound knowledge.

I have no right to recommend him to you. I only take the liberty of sending him to you. The love of humanity that so eminently distinguishes you both will do the rest.

Please accept, Sir, my renewed wishes for your happiness and always preserve for me a place in your kind memory.

Your very humble servant   CHARLES BOTTA

RC (DLC); dateline above signature; at foot of text: "Mr. Thomas Jefferson en amérique"; endorsed by TJ as received 3 May 1816 and so recorded in SJL. Translation by Dr. Amy Ogden. Enclosed in Eusebio Valli to TJ, 26 Apr. 1816.

Eusebio Giacinto Valli (1755–1816), physician, was born in what is now Casciana Alta, Italy. In 1776 he enrolled at the University of Pisa, where he studied medicine and philosophy for two years before obtaining a scholarship to the university's Collegio di Sapienza, eventually earning a dual doctorate in philosophy and medicine in 1783. Valli then embarked on a trip that took him to Smyrna in what is now Turkey, where he observed and wrote about cases of bubonic plague. From Smyrna he traveled successively to Greece and France. After obtaining a position as a doctor in the French army, Valli and his regiment departed for Pondicherry, in what is now India. During his military service he traveled extensively in southern Asia before returning to Italy in 1789. In 1802 Valli journeyed to Constantinople (later Istanbul) to ob-serve cases of plague, and in 1809 he so-licited a medical post with the French army in Spain in order to study yellow fever there. His interest in that disease brought him to New York City by March 1816 and later that year to Havana, where he died of the malady after attempting to inoculate himself. Throughout his career Valli published his observations on a wide array of medical topics, including disease, rabies vaccination, and animal electricity (Giuseppe Valli, *Cenni Biografici sul dottore Eusebio Valli* [1886]; Giovanni de Bernardis, "Eusebio Valli," *Rivista di Storia delle Scienze Mediche e Naturali* 29 [1938]: 249–56; *Eclectic Repertory and Analytical Review* 7 [1817]: 413–8; *Medical Repository,* new ser., 3 [1817]: 362–75; 4 [1818]: 104; Georgetown *Daily Federal Republican,* 2 Mar. 1816; New York *Commercial Advertiser,* 9 Mar. 1816; Valli to TJ, 3 June 1816; *New-York Evening Post,* 9 Nov. 1816; Tomas Romay, *Elogio de Eusebio Valli, Leida en junta ordinaria de la Sociedad económica el 22 de Noviembre de 1816* [Havana, 1816; Poor, *Jefferson's Library,* 5 (no. 163)]).

From Stephen Cathalan

My Dear sir & most
Respected Friend! Marseilles the 29th november 1815—

Before this may Reach you, you will have been Informed by Mr John Vaughan of Phil^a that I acknowledged him by my Letters of the 8th Sep^ber Last & the 2^d Oct^ber Receipt of his Letter of the 31st July Inclosing one of the 30th d^o of Mr Stephen Girard of Said City bearing a Credit by your order & for y^r acc^t on Messrs Perregaux Laffitte & c^o of Paris in my favor for Two hundred Dollars, which they had honored by their Remitance on Marseilles unto my order p^r F 1056— being the amount of Said D 200—at F 5.28 Centimes p^r D^ar which Sum in Francs, I had Encashed & passed on your Credit;—I Begged him of Informing you of it, & that I had not Received any Letters from you, with your orders, how I was to Invest that money for your Said Account.—

it is only on the 5th Ins^t that your kind favour of the 16th august Reached me, but the Letter you Inform me of your having—wrote me on the 3^d July Requesting me to Send one[1] Some wines,—I have not as yet Received; I Regret very much you did not Sent me a Duplicata of it as I could have executed your orders & Sent you by this vessel bound for new york all what you wish to Receive from this Country;—while tho' I have perused your Letter of the 29th June 1807, (which is the Last I Received from you before yours of the 16th august Last) in which it was the list of the articles you wanted, which I Sent you, I am at a Loss whether you was Satisfied of their qualities, or not, & if you want the Same qualities of wines, with the other articles, or wines only, you mentioning only—Some Wines,—

I observed in yours of 1807. that you did not wish any wine of Mr Jourdan, when it would be Dry and hard, Resembling Sauterne or Barsac, that you want only Such wine when it is Soft or Silky, which we Call here doux & Liquoreux—

on the Contrary Mr P. Butler of Philad^a who appears to be a Grand Connoisseur in Wines, by his Letter to me of the 11th april last, asking me Some virgin hermitage Says—he do not Like that which has a Sweet taste, & wishes for that of a light Colour, with much fixed air in it Sparkling Somewhat like Champaigne, he do not wish for any of the Sweet kind.—

on Receipt of his Letter on the 22^d may I transmitted that Parag[raph] to Mr Jourdan of Tain, who answered me—he would Supply Mr Butler[2] with wine, hermitage Blanc mousseux et non Doux adding—Ce ne peut etre du vin de Paille qu'il desire, Car celui ci est toujours Liquoreux plus ou moins, tout celui que nous avons est plus ou moins doux et trés Bon—nous Remplirons Sa Commission Sur nous l ordre &c—I Sent him a Copy of this on the 27th July last, & am waiting for his answer. Mr Jourdan by his Letter of the 16th Sepber Last Informed me that the Crop of wine had fine Prospect as to it's quality, but that as to it's <u>quantity</u>, it would be but very Short & Lessening dayly by the Soldiers (austrians) whereof they hope however to gett Soon Rid of!—

as to the wine of nice which I Sent you, I don't know if you was Satisfied of that one I Sent you;—Mr Sasserno died Some years ago, however I might procure you Some from his Successors; it is a Pity that your Letter of the 3d July remains Still [beliered?]³ or is miscarried, as I wished to fullfill your orders with the Greatest attention & exactitude, and at your entire satisfon Since the moment I Received the Letter of Mr Vaughan & I hope Still to Receive it or a Copy very Soon.

There is not any american Vessels Bound direct for the Cheasapeak, Those Sailed out from this Port Since Last Spring or Preparing for their Return home, are for Massachusset, New york, Philada & new orleans; of the Seven vessels in Port now, Two will Sail for Phila in about one month hence, & I wish I may be able to Send you Some wines &ca by one of them;—

about Political Intelligences, I must Reffer you my Dear sir to the news Papers from Paris, which I hope you receive quicker via or Thro' the northern Ports than they Could Reach you from Marseilles, in which you will have observed, that this City after having So much Suffered, by the Republican tyrany of Roberspierre, of the Directory; & by the foolish Gigantesque ambition of Bonaparte, & of his own tyrany, was So happy, by the Return on the Throne of France in 1814, & by a Gal Peace, that they have Remained faithfull to the king tho' it Runned the danger of the greatest Evils by the French Troops who on the Return of Bonaparte from the Isle of Elbe, had forfeited their oath, & turned on his Side, if the Energy of the national Guard, even of the women had not forced them to Repair into Toulon; we were even threatened by them after Bonaparte's 2d abdication, which forc'd the autorities of this Department to Seek for the Immediate assistance of the British and other foreign Troops, this has been an Evil, but it prevented perhaps the destruction of this City!—which Since last July enjoys of Peace, Tranquility and of a maritime Intercourse, which had been interupted Since 25 years but allmost Shut up Since the orders in Council & the Berlin & Milan decrées, which had reduced to misery the most Respble houses as well as the lowest Classes of People; while but very few had made much money during that dreadfull period; —

it will Require indeed very long time before France may Recover it's Rank and welth amongst the other nations. Even as it enjoyed while you remained in France, but if She has lost So much of her Preponderance, it is owed to Bonaparte's ambition while he was on the Throne, & Since Great deal more, when he Landed from Elbe on this Coast, & was Joined by the French army, which Caused the Gen^al Invasion of the Coalised Powers, who have taken Since too Great advantages over France, which She cannot at Least for the Present avoid, they being masters to dictate too hard Laws, or a shamefull Peace, but they are this time Less Generous & more Interested than they were in the year 1814 & we must Resign to our fate; & the fault is not to be attributed to Louis the XVIII who Suffers of it as much; as all his Faithfull People!

I am very Gratefull for the kind Interest you take on my Self; I have Lost Great deal of my Property & by annual Income during the French Revolution, but Thank God, I am enjoying of a Good health, Spirit,[4] & am Still active, and able to Continue to perform my Duties as Consul of the united states as Long as I may Continue to be agreable in that Capacity to the President & the Senate; on that Subject I claim your kind Protection near them; —The President will have Received by the cartel <u>Transit</u> a Petition I adressed to him on the 25th Sep^ber 1814—claiming my being reimburced of the Interests on my advances for the distressed Seamen, which Interests had been Rejected by the Secr^y of State J^es Monroe Esqr when he ordered the minister Plen^y at Paris W. h. Crawford Esqr to pay me only the Capital—I claimed for the Same towards Mr Monroe, before and at the Same time, Stating my Father & my own Past Services, & using your own Expressions—that—when I will be by age or infirmity disabled to continue in Service—Retire Poorer than when I entered in it, —&^a &^a &^a I would wish you could be able to peruse all what I mentioned in it, not only for my Self but for the am^an Consuls who after So many years Service, at full Satisf^on are to Retreat; but I hoping to be able to continue Still for many years. —

I have not hitherto Received any answers, and not been Favored of <u>a Line</u> from Mr Monroe (whom I may Call my old Friend) Since he is in office, & many of my Colleague Consuls, have not been more fortunate than I, no Doubt owing to more Important business! but I perceive that I will detain you to Long if you will have patience to read my Bad hand writing.

I am Convinced of the deep Interest you feel for France & this City,

& I would be very happy if you Should visit it next year, as it would Give me an opportunity to Reiterate to you verbally the assurance of the Great Respect with which I have the honor to be very Sincerely
my Dear sir
your obed^t & most devoted Servant & well wisher—

STEPHEN CATHALAN.

RC (DLC); edge chipped; at foot of text: "Thos Jefferson Esqr Monticello united States"; endorsed by TJ as received 31 Jan. 1816 and so recorded in SJL.

DUPLICATA: "duplicate." HERMITAGE BLANC MOUSSEUX ET NON DOUX: "white hermitage, sparkling, and not sweet." CE NE PEUT ETRE ... NOUS L ORDRE: "vin de paille cannot be what he wants, because this is always more or less liqueur-like, all that we have is more or less sweet and very good—we will fill his order as instructed when we receive it." Vin de paille or straw wine is a sweet white wine made from grapes that have been dried on straw mats (Jancis Robinson, ed., *The Oxford Companion to Wine* [1994], 1024–5). Cathalan's PETITION to James

Madison of 25 Sept. 1814 was enclosed in Cathalan to TJ, 19 Mar. 1816. His letter to James Monroe asking for a settlement of his consular accounts, written AT THE SAME TIME as his petition to Madison, as well as numerous letters written before and after on the same topic, can be found in DNA: RG 217, MSA, no. 125. In his letter to Cathalan of 29 June 1807 (DLC), TJ remarked that after forty years of service to his country, he was about to RETIRE POORER than when he had entered office.

[1] Thus in manuscript. Cathalan may have meant "on."
[2] Manuscript: "Botler."
[3] Word illegible.
[4] Manuscript: "Sprit."

From Alexander Murray

SIR;   Nassau N. P. Bahamas Novr 29th 1815—

The annexed Letter will I hope prove my apology for addressing you; particularly as I am given to understand, that you are almost the only acquaintance now left; which my Deceased Father (The late Earl of Dunmore) had, when Govr of Virginia—

As such, and from the High Situations you have held in that State (as well as in the Union) I cannot have a doubt but that you are fully informed respecting the promise alluded to; and consequent claim stated in my Sister's letter—In support of which, I have a full conviction of your doing all in your power to further her views, that your acknowledged rectitude of principle, and worth of Character will warrant, if not from her afinity to your old acquaintance; yet from her afinity to the State of which you are so distinguished a Member, and on whose Protection as such, she has her claims:—indeed your kindness to my Brother Capt Murray some years ago, when on a Visit in

Virginia, gives me the most sanguine hope, that you will extend it to his Sister; by taking the trouble of making known her claims to that Body which is to decide on them, and of furthering them with your powerful interest.—

I shall only further intrude on your time, to inform you, that I have had the annexed for a considerable time by me;—but that the times were not favorable for its presentation—

Trusting that you will forgive my so long intruding on your leisure—I shall only add that I am Sir with great respect your Humble Servant—   A MURRAY

RC (DLC); at foot of first page: "Tho⁵ Jefferson Esqʳ &ᶜ &ᶜ &ᶜ"; endorsed by TJ as received 5 Jan. 1817 and so recorded in SJL. Enclosure: Lady Virginia Murray to TJ, [before 29 Nov. 1815].

Alexander Murray (1764–1842), British soldier and public official, was born in Edinburgh, the son of John Murray, 4th Earl of Dunmore. In 1774 Murray, his siblings, and their mother joined Lord Dunmore at Williamsburg, where the latter was serving as governor of Virginia. Murray promptly enrolled at the College of William and Mary, but colonial unrest the following spring precipitated his return to Great Britain in 1775. He entered the British army as an ensign in 1778 and eventually rose to the rank of lieutenant colonel. In 1788 Dunmore, now governor of the Bahamas, granted his son over 1,000 acres of land there. The following year Murray lost an election for a seat in the colonial assembly, but Dunmore appointed him king's agent and collector of customs at Turks Islands. Murray be-

came customs collector at Nassau by 1815. He died in Frimley, England, where he had been living (Sir James Balfour Paul, ed., *The Scots Peerage* [1904–14], 3:389–90; Williamsburg *Virginia Gazette* [Purdie & Dixon], 3 Mar. 1774, and [Purdie], 30 June 1775, supplement; *WMQ*, 2d ser., 1 [1921]: 120, 124; Sandra Riley, *Homeward Bound: A History of the Bahama Islands to 1850* [1983], 171, 181; London *Diary; or, Woodfall's Register*, 1 Oct. 1789; *Federal Gazette and Philadelphia Advertiser*, 7 Aug. 1793; New York *Daily Advertiser*, 29 Dec. 1804; Rosanne Marion Adderley, *"New Negroes from Africa": Slave Trade Abolition and Free African Settlement in the Nineteenth-Century Caribbean* [2006], 138–9, 218; *United Service Magazine and Naval and Military Journal* [1842]: 600).

N. P.: New Providence Island. Murray's BROTHER, John Murray, visited Monticello about 19 Apr. 1803 (James Currie to TJ, 16 Mar. 1803 [MHi]; John Page to TJ, 16 Mar. 1803 [DLC]).

From Lady Virginia Murray

[before 29 Nov. 1815] Trafalgar Place
SIR—   Opposite Cumberland gate Oxford Road London

I am at a loss how to begin a Letter in the which I am desirous of stating claims that may long since have been forgotten—but which I think no time can really annihilate until fufilment has followed the promise—I imagine you must have heard that during my Father the late Earl of Dunmore's residence in America—I was born—& that the Assembly then sitting at Williamsburg requested I might be their God Daughter, & christened by the name of Virginia—which request being complied with—they purposed providing for me in a manner suitable to the honor they conferred upon me—& to the responsibility; they had taken upon themselves—I was accordingly christened as the God Daughter of that Assembly & named after the State— Events have since occurred which in some measure may have altered the intentions then expressed—in my favour,—these were (so I have understood) that a Sum of money should be settled upon me, which by accumulating during my minority would make up the Sum of one hundred thousand pounds when I became of age—it is true many changes may have taken place in America—but that fact still remains the same,—I am still the God Daughter of the Virginians—by being that,—may I not flatter myself I have some claims upon their benevolence—if not upon their justice? may I not ask the Gentlemen of that State—Especially you Sir their Governor—to fulfil in some respects the Engagements entered into by their Predecessors? Your Father's promised mine, that I should become their charge;—& I am totally unprovided for—my Father died without making a Will,—my Brothers are married—having families of their own, & not being bound to do any thing for me—they regard with indifference my unprotected & neglected situation—perhaps I ought not to mention this circumstance, as a proper inducement for you to act upon, nor would I—were it not my Excuse for wishing to remind you of the claims I now advance—I hope you will feel my right to your favour & protection, to be founded on the promises made by your own Fathers, & on the situation in which I stand with regard to the State of Virginia; You will ask Sir,—Why my appeal to your Generosity & justice have been so tardy?—While my Father lived—I lived under his protection & guidance,—he had incurred the displeasure of the Virginians—& he feared an application from me then,—would have seemed like one from him—& to him you were bound by no ties,—as his subsequent conduct had broken them:—not so with me—at his decease I became a free Agent,—I had taken no part which could displease my God Fathers—& myself remaincd what the Assembly had made me— their God Daughter—consequently their Charge—I wish particularly to [enforce?] my dependence on your bounty for I feel hopes revive which owe their birth to your known generosity & to that of the State—whose representative I now address.—Now that my Father is no more, I am certain you will remember what merited your Esteem in his Character & conduct & forget that which Estranged your hearts from so honourable a man,—but sh^d you not—you are too Just to visit what you may deem the Sins of the Father upon his luckless Daughter—

I am Sir Your Obedient &c &c VIRGINIA MURRAY

RC (DLC: TJ Papers, 205:37224–6); undated; one word illegible; place of composition at foot of text; addressed, in Alexander Murray's hand: "Thos Jefferson Esqr late President of the United States Monticello Virginia"; endorsed by TJ as received 5 Jan. 1817 and so recorded in SJL. Tr (Vi: Personal Papers Collection, Murray Family Papers); endorsed as a "Copy of L^y Virginia Murray's Address to Thos Jefferson Esqr late President of the United States—Original given in Charge to Genl H Lee Decr 3rd 1815." Enclosed in Alexander Murray to TJ, 29 Nov. 1815.

Lady Virginia Murray (b. 1774), daughter of John Murray, 4th Earl of Dunmore and last royal governor of Virginia, was born in Williamsburg and left Virginia permanently with her mother and siblings in 1775. She was granted an English civil-list pension of £184 beginning in 1784. In 1792–93 Murray was living in Rome with her sister and their mother, Charlotte Stewart Murray, Countess of Dunmore. Following the 1818 death of her mother, Murray inherited a house in Twickenham, England, that she sold in 1841. By this time she had been living in France for an extended period. Murray helped raise her siblings' children and opened an asylum in Paris to assist young female converts to Catholicism. In 1844 she traveled to England to testify in support of an unsuccessful claim to the dukedom of Sussex by her nephew Sir Augustus Frederick D'Este (Williamsburg *Virginia Gazette* [Purdie & Dixon], 8 Dec. 1774, suppl.; Williamsburg *Virginia Gazette* [Dixon & Hunter], 21 Jan. 1775; *The Extraordinary Black Book* [1831], 468; *Gentleman's Magazine: and Historical Chronicle* 88 [1818]: 640; Richard S. Cobbett, *Memorials of Twickenham* [1872], 342–3; Elizabeth Grant Smith, *Memoirs of a Highland Lady*, ed. Jane Maria Grant Strachey [1899], 151; Thomas Raikes, *A Portion of the Journal kept by Thomas Raikes, Esq. from 1831 to 1847* [1856–57], 1:273; *The Annual Register, or a view of the History and Politics of the year 1844* [1845]: 345; Henri Raymond Casgrain, *La Société des Filles du Cœur de Marie* [1899–1905], 3:62, 74).

In 1820 Murray's representative, John Stevens, visited TJ at Monticello. At TJ's suggestion he commissioned a search of the records of the House of Burgesses, but it failed to confirm the supposed promise of a large SUM OF MONEY for Murray by the legislature. Murray sought redress in a petition to the General Assembly in 1824, but nothing came of it ("Lady Virginia Murray and Her Alleged Claim Against the State of Virginia," *WMQ*, 1st ser., 24 [1915]: 85–101).

Conveyance of Sally Goodman to Jeremiah A. Goodman

Know all men by these presents that I Thomas Jefferson of the county of Albemarle do hereby sell and convey to Jeremiah A. Goodman now of the county of Bedford a certain negro girl slave named Sally, being the daughter of Aggy one of the slaves of the sd Thomas, which said Girl Sally is about three years of age in consideration of the sum of one hundred and fifty Dollars to me the sd Thomas, by the sd Jeremiah in hand paid: to hold & to own the sd girl Sally in absolute property free of all uses, trusts, or other incumbrances: and the said slave Sally I do hereby warrant to the sd Jeremiah A. Goodman his executors, administrators & assigns for ever. Witness my hand this 30ᵗʰ day of November one thousand eight hundred and fifteen.

TH: JEFFERSON

Witness
ROLIN GOODMAN

The sd girl Sally remains in my possession by agreement in the care of her mother until either the sd Jeremiah Goodman or myself chuses that she shall be taken into his possession

TH: JEFFERSON

MS (DLC); in TJ's hand, signed by TJ and Rolin Goodman.

Sally Goodman (b. 1812) was the daughter of the Poplar Forest slave Aggy and the granddaughter of Dick and Dinah. Almost two years after his 1815 purchase of Sally from TJ, Jeremiah A. Goodman reconsidered and TJ agreed to cancel the sale. According to a list of Poplar Forest slaves composed sometime late in December 1823 (ViU: Randolph Family Papers), at that time she was still at Poplar Forest (Betts, *Farm Book*, pt. 1,

131, 167; *MB*, 2:1316, 1372; Goodman to TJ, 19 July 1817; TJ to Goodman, 20, 30 July 1817). A fifty-five-year-old mulatto woman named Sallie Goodman was listed in the 1870 census for Albemarle County, in which Jeremiah A. Goodman resided at his death in 1857 (DNA: RG 29, CS, 1870, Albemarle Co., Fredericksville Parish).

On this date TJ settled his account with Jeremiah A. Goodman and recorded that after this and other transactions, he owed him $413 plus $200 in final wages (*MB*, 2:1316).

From Thomas Leiper

DEAR SIR   Philadᵃ November 30ᵗʰ 1815

Your very interesting letter of the 12ᵗʰ June came duly to hand and I have again and again since put my opinions on record with a view of forwarding to you but I have been so completely mistaken in my conjectures respecting the issue of Bonaparte and the French nation that what I wrote one day I was obliged to blot out the next—But now my mind is made up respecting the people of that nation they consist of the best and worst men on earth and it is a melancholy truth that the Scum and Scurf have got uppermost but I Trust in a kind Providence he will soon make it otherwise—

You and I agree in every thing but in the character of Bonaparte It is clearly established wherever Bonaparte Conquered he established a better Government than they had before and he did more for the honor or interest of France than all the Kings of that nation ever did you complain of Bonaparte Turn^g his Back on us for my part I do not wonder at it when we consider at that time we had Fifteen Thousand sailers in the British Fleet fighting against France—

The French nation are now suffering in the extreme for their injustice and ingratitude to Bonaparte from that circumstance many here do not pity them—

Last Congress a majority of which were republicans too past an Excise Law which you know is the Horror of all free states—This Law was Copied from a British Statute by Samuel Harrison Smith and delivered to Mr Eppes the Chairman of the Committee of Ways and Means who give it a currency and past both Houses as it stands on Record in the British Code—Had this Law been brought forward by Mr Otis it would have been in Character but I think Mr Eppes will never be able to forgive himself for he certainly most known any sum could have been collected in a direct way on our Estates Indeed the Tobacconist proposed to have it on the Leaf but Mr Eppes answer was it then would be a Tax on the Planters—my answer was what difference could it make whether it was on the Leaf before it was manufactured or after—Mr Eppes saw a difference The Tobacconists submitted to the Law not with pleasure but with pain expecting the next Congress would Repeal the Law and I am certain from your former opinions you will help us to obtain a Repeal I shall send by this days Mail the Excise Law you will see the subject of it on slaves and his House is not his Castle—I shall also send you a short History on the nature and consequences[1] of Excise Laws—Mr Madison said their was no answering the Book in 1795[2]—Mr Madison in Congress again and again spoke against the system but if he had reason to complain of the Law of 1795 he had Ten times more reason to complain of the Law of 1815—

I shall also send you the proceeding of the Town Meeting of the City of New York—I have also sent you Mr Matthew Carey's character of the last Congress which in my opinion is perfectly correct—I have also consigned to Edward Trent Esqr of Richmond a Box directed to you—It contains Two Prints of Napolean Le Grand One of which is Allegorical which you will please to accept from me As I did not expect we should have a second Edition soon I purchased Four Prints Two I retained for myself—

I find all the Tories Hate Napolean that is a sufficient reason for me to like He is now wanted in France and we shall feel the want of him there in less than eighteen months for we shall have a War with England by that time and I should not be surprized to see Alexander with all his Virtue sending 20,000 of his slaves to enable Britain to make slaves of us for I take it for granted he was one of the legitimates that agreed to the doctrines of the 25th of March last When a News Paper under the direction of the British Goverment will call M[r] Madison our President a Scoundrel it is time to prepare for War—

I observe you have always been[3] dragged from your[4] studies from the times you happened to live in—You must be dragged again for their never was a time when more Wistom was required than the present for we shall have the whole Legitimates of Europe to contend with— May God bless you is the prayer of Your
 Most Obedient Servant   Thomas Leiper

RC (DLC); endorsed by TJ as received 15 Dec. 1815 and so recorded in SJL. RC (MHi); address cover only; with PoC of TJ to Bernard Peyton, 20 Jan. 1816, on verso; addressed: "Thomas Jefferson Late President of the United States Virginia"; franked; postmarked Philadelphia, 1 Dec. Enclosed or sent separately in the same mail were: (1) James T. Callender, *A Short History of the Nature and Consequences of Excise Laws* (Philadelphia, 1795; Sowerby, no. 3183). (2) Mathew Carey, *The Olive Branch: or Faults on Both Sides, Federal and Democratic* (Philadelphia, 1814, and later eds.; Sowerby, no. 3539). Other enclosure not found.

SCURF is another term for "scum" (*OED*). The laws passed by the LAST CONGRESS and enclosed here included "An Act to provide additional revenues for defraying the expenses of government, and maintaining the public credit, by laying a direct tax upon the United States, and to provide for assessing and collecting the same," 9 Jan. 1815, which taxed the locally assessed value of land, houses, and slaves, and "An Act to provide additional revenues for defraying the expenses of government, and maintaining the public credit, by laying duties on various goods, wares, and merchandise, manufactured within the United States," 18 Jan. 1815, which included a 20 percent value-added tax on tobacco, manufactured ci-

gars, and snuff. The first statute was repealed 5 Mar. 1816, and the second was repealed on 22 Feb. 1816 (*U.S. Statutes at Large*, 3:164–80, 180–6, 254, 255–6). For James Madison's 1794–95 speeches AGAINST THE SYSTEM of excise taxes, see Madison, *Papers, Congress. Ser.*, vol. 15.

A print of Napoleon, based on a painting by Jacques Louis David, was advertised for sale at Nathaniel P. Poor's 1829 dispersal sale of TJ's library: "a splendid Portrait of Napoleon, sent to Mr. J. from France, large as life in frame, from the celebrated painting by David" (Washington *Daily National Intelligencer*, 5 Mar. 1829). DOCTRINES OF THE 25TH OF MARCH LAST: Austria, Great Britain, Prussia, and Russia concluded an alliance against Napoleon at Vienna on 25 Mar. 1815 (*British and Foreign State Papers* 2 [1814/15]: 443–50; Connelly, *Napoleonic France*, 382). A NEWS PAPER editorial in the London *Times*, 28 Aug. 1815, asked of former Bonapartists: "Why are these scoundrels tolerated in civilized countries? If they must be sent out of France, instead of being hanged there, as the law would have them to be, why not confide them to the paternal care of Mr. President MADISON? Birds of a feather should flock together."

[1] Manuscript: "consequeces."
[2] Preceding two words interlined.
[3] Manuscript: "be."
[4] Manuscript: "you."

From Dabney Carr

My Dear Sir.   Winchester. Dec'r 1ˢᵗ 1815.

When I last saw my lamented brother Peter (then on his death bed) we were conversing about our father, & particularly of the motion made by him in the Virginia Assembly, for appointing Committees of correspondence—I remarked, that I thought it, but justice to his memory, & a duty on his Sons, to make this fact, known to the world—& suggested, that the life of P Henry, which Mr Wirt was then writing, would furnish an appropriate vehicle—my brother was very much struck with the idea, & earnestly begged me, to attend to it, & have it done; adding that you were particularly acquainted with the circumstances, & he was sure, would with pleasure, give a statement of them—a few days after this conversation I was at Monticello, & you may recollect Sir, mentioned the subject to you. You detailed to me the particulars, shewed me the inscription you had prepared, for my father's tomb=stone; & also Mazzei's book, in which the motion is mentioned as having been made, by him. I then took the liberty of requesting you to give me a statement of the facts, which you readily promised to do, after refreshing your memory by a recurrence to the documents. Will you pardon me Sir, for now recalling this subject to your recollection, & asking, that you will, at your first leisure hour, forward me the, statement accompanied, by a brief sketch of my father's[1] character? I have written to Mr Wirt, & he replies, that he will with much pleasure give it a place in his book.

In the 2ᵈ Vol of Marshall's life of Washington, I find him giving the whole credit of originating this measure, of appointing Committees of correspondence, to massachussetts—as you may not have the book, I will transcribe the passage—in pa. 149 under date of 1770. Sept: he says "From the commencement of the contest, Massachussetts appears to have deeply felt, the importance of uniting all the colonies, in one system of measures & in pursuance of this favorite idea, a committee of correspondence, was at this session elected, to communicate, with such committees, as might be appointed, by other Colonies." after a few intervening remarks he adds "The example was afterwards followed by other Colonies, & the utility of this institution, became apparent, when a more active opposition, was rendered necessary."

Is not this incorrect Sir? I think I understood you to Say, that Virginia & Massachussetts acted about the same time; & that the messengers bearing the propositions of the two States met each other—if so, we ought not to suffer the Old Dominion, to be robbed of her fame, & made to follow in the wake of Massachussetts.

I should not beg your immediate attention to this affair, if I were not apprehensive, that Mr Wirt's book is so far advanced, as to render an early communication to him, necessary.

with every sentiment of affectionate respect. yrs &C   D CARR

RC (DLC); endorsed by TJ as received 15 Dec. 1815 and so recorded in SJL. RC (DLC); address cover only; with PoC of TJ to Marc Auguste Pictet, 31 Jan. 1816, on verso; addressed: "Thomas Jefferson Esqr. Monticello Albemarle County for the Milton post office"; franked; postmarked Winchester, 3 Dec.

For the INSCRIPTION TJ prepared for the gravestone of his friend and brother-in-law Dabney Carr (1743–73) in the cemetery at Monticello, see *PTJ*, 27:673–5. In Philip MAZZEI'S BOOK, *Recherches historiques et politiques sur les États-Unis de l'Amérique Septentrionale* (Paris, 1788; Sowerby, no. 3005), 1:140–1, Mazzei credited Carr with initiating the proposal in the Virginia General Assembly for the establishment of a Committee of Correspondence. Mazzei described Carr as an "homme recommandable par les qualités les plus rares"

("commendable man with the rarest of qualities"). He also noted that a relative of Carr's to whom Carr was "tendrement attaché" ("tenderly attached"), presumably TJ, had "consacré la mémoire par une inscription qu'il a fait graver sur son tombeau" ("consecrated his memory with an inscription that he caused to be engraved on his tomb").

William Wirt gave Carr A PLACE IN HIS BOOK, stating that the measure proposing a Committee of Correspondence had been "brought forward by Mr. Dabney Carr, a new member from the county of Louisa, in a committee of the whole house, on the 12th of March, 1773" (*Sketches of the Life and Character of Patrick Henry* [Philadelphia, 1817; Poor, *Jefferson's Library*, 4 (no. 131)], 87).

[1] Manuscript: "fathers" followed by a comma.

From Robert Patterson

SIR   Philadᵃ Decʳ 2ᵈ 1815

Mʳ Hassler has just transmitted to the Sec'y of the Treasury, a descriptive list of the instruments which, in execution of his appointment for that purpose, he had procured in Europe, & has lately brought with him to this city.

Presuming that you might be pleased to have a copy of this list, I herewith send you one, for your acceptance.

Mʳ Hasslcr's circumstances are, at present, somewhat imbarrassing. Congress have not, for some time past, made any appropriation for his stipulated compensation. The Sec'y of the Treasury, however, writes, that he has no doubt, that Congress will, at their ensuing session, make the necessary appropriation for that purpose.

From the long & intimate acquaintance which I have had with this gentlemans extraordinary abilities, I am confident, that Government could find no person better qualified than he is, to exercise a principal agency in the business for which these instruments have been procured, or in which they may hereafter be employed.

He is not only perfectly acquainted with the construction & use of all the instruments, & all the necessary calculations connected therewith, but can keep the same in order, & even make,[1] with his own hands & instruments, most of the repairs or additions that may be wanted.

I would, therefore, Sir, take the liberty of requesting, that you would have the goodness, to use your interest with the Government, to procure for him some temporary or permanent employment; either in the contemplated survey of the coast, the running of boundary lines, or the superintendance of a national observatory.

I ask this favour, not merely from the regard I have for this gentleman, but also from the conviction that his talents would be a useful acquisition to the Government.

I am, Sir, with the greatest respect & esteem Your Most obed[t] serv[t]

R[T] PATTERSON

RC (DLC: James Madison Papers); at foot of text: "Thomas Jefferson"; endorsed by TJ as received 15 Dec. 1815 and so recorded in SJL. Enclosed in TJ to James Madison, 22 Dec. 1815.

The Secretary of the TREASURY was Alexander J. Dallas. After returning to the United States with the instruments and books he had been authorized to purchase for the United States Coast Survey, Ferdinand R. Hassler presented his accounts on 20 Nov. 1815, according to which the government owed him a balance of £13.13.6½ in COMPENSATION (*ASP, Commerce and Navigation*, 2:30). He officially became superintendent of the SURVEY OF THE COAST in August 1816 (Hassler, *Principal Documents relating to the Survey of the Coast of the United States, since 1816* [1834], 9–11).

[1] Word interlined in place of "supply."

ENCLOSURE

Ferdinand R. Hassler's List of Scientific Instruments Procured for the United States Coast Survey

General List of Mathematical Instruments and Books, destined for the survey of the Coast of the United States, delivered into the custody of Robert Patterson Esq[e] Director of the Mint in Philadelphia, by F. R. Hassler, after his return from the mission for this object; in November 1815.—

N° 1.   One Theodolite of two feet diameter, of very improved construction, silver arch readings by three micrometer microscopes, wire micrometers in the Telescopes &[c] made by M[r] Edward Troughton.[1]

2. Two double repeating Theodolites of twelve inches diametre, on principles suggested by F. R. Hassler, with full vertical circle, double repeating, made by the same.

3. Two double repeating Circles, on the principles of Borda, of improved construction, vertical & horizontal circles, both of eighteen inches diameter, readings to the back telescope &c made by the same.

4. Four double repeating reflecting circles of ten inches diameter, on principles suggested by F. R. Hassler.—Spirit level for small angles of elevation,[2] made by the same.

5. Four Stands to the above with artificial horizons of mercury; covered with a glass hat.

6. Two double repeating Reflecting circles, in all respects exactly equal to those in N° 4. except no levels.—made by the same.

7. Two artificial horizons to the above, of mercury; covered with a glass hat.

8. Two artificial horizons of plane glass with ground spirit levels; the one of dark glass, the other of plate glass, blackened on the lower plane.

9. Two surveying Theodolites of nine inches diameter, of common construction.

10. Two surveying Compasses of one foot needle in length:—construction directed by F. R. Hassler.—Silvered plate—needles inverting—telescope describing a full vertical; spirit levels: center work for the stand, made by Thomas Jones.

11. Two Alhidades for plane tables.—construction invented by F. R. Hassler. Telescopes arranged like transit instruments. made by the same.

12. Two center works to the plane tables; to be used with the above two sets of brass spring clamps, to hold the paper on the plane table.

13. Two sets of apparatus for measuring base lines, by an arrangement invented by F. R. Hassler, giving an optical determination of the end-points of the bars—each consisting of the following parts. viz[t]

   a. Four iron bars, upwards of seven[3] feet in length; not yet standarded, because they were intended to be cut to a proper standard on the most authentic measures, by F. R. H.—

   b. Various screw works & rollers for the motion of these bars; and [the boxes][4] they must be put in when in use.

   c. A sector with a spirit level, to measure the inclination of[5] these bars, screwed on the part making the motion in the direction of the length of the bars.[6]

   d. Four Thermometers with Farenheit & Centigrade scales mounted to be fixed to the bars; the balls sheltered with brass cups.[7]

   e. A Telescope arrangement to direct the boxes of the bars in the direction of[8] three rectangular ordinates, carrying microscopes, in which the object lenses consist of two halves of different foci; by which the image of cross lines on these stands is brought in the same focus with that of the ends of the bars, which are cut out to admit a cobweb to spread over the ends: the optical contact of which two images determines the place of the ends of the bars, in like manner as Hadleys instrument does the image from the great mirror and the object viewed directly.

14. One Standard English measure of 82 inches in length, divided on Silver in tenths of inches; microscopes and micrometers for comparisons, and an arrangement with a cutting tool, to divide scales from it. made by M[r] Edward Troughton.[9]

16. One brass metre standarded by Lenoir in Paris from his brass metre, which was made at the same time, and standarded at the temperature of melting ice, together with those distributed by the Committee of weights & measures in Paris, to all the deputies of different nations; compared also at the observatory of Paris, with their standards.

N.B, this brass meter of M[r] Lenoir being the only one in this metal made by the Committee of weights & measures in Paris; gives therefore also the only means to a direct comparison of french and english measures, without reductions for expansion of different metals; the latter having their standards in brass, and the former in iron.

A Certificate of the comparisons of N° 15 & 16 accompanying them, signed Arrago & Bouvard, & sealed by the seal of the observatory.

N° 15— One Iron toise standarded by Lenoir in Paris, and compared with the standards of the observatory there.

17. One Iron metre, standarded by Lenoir.

18. One Iron tool, to file bars off perpendicularly, in standarding measures.

19 An Iron plane, to use on metals & on wood.

20. One strong scale with accurate standarded english weights; made by M[r] Edw[d] Troughton.

21. Two standard subdivided Kylogrames, of parallelopipedon form, made by Fortin, in Paris.

22 Two Litres modeles, with ground glass plate covers, standard. by Fortin, in Paris.

23. Two transit instruments of very improved construction; telescopes of five feet, illumination through the axis, shades to the object-glasses, silver arched semicircles with levels at the eye ends to point by; spring counterpoises &[c] &[c] made by M[r] E. Troughton.

24. Two astronomical Clocks, of the same improved construction as those lately made by the same artist and inventor, M[r] W[m] Hardy, for the observatories of Greenwich & Glasgow.[10] spring scapement, silver plated dial, compensation by a glass cylinder with mercury, acting as [lens of][11] the pendulum.

25. Two one day box chronometers with silver dial plates, compensation of the balance and for short and long vibration the invention of the maker, the said M[r] Hardy.

26. One box chronometer of Brockbanks, of two days going, for the case of accidental omission of winding.

27. Two one-day box chronometers, of the same.
28. One one-day box chronometer, of extraordinary good performance, of Messrs Grimaldi & Johnson.
29. Two one-day silver pocket chronometers, of Brockbanks.
30 One time piece shewing the $\frac{1}{300}$ of a second; going only when in use; for determinations of velocities of sound, falling bodies &^{c} made by Mr William Hardy, at the suggestion of F. R. Hassler
31. One six feet achromatic telescope, of Dollond: four inches aperture of the object-glass; six astronomical and one terrestrial eye-tubes. a finder, the tube unscrewing in three pieces. Mahogany stand of two parts, securing the telescope in two places, for greater steadiness.
32. One five feet achromatic Telescope of Dollond; $3\frac{3}{4}$ inches aperture of object glass; one terrestrial & six astronomical eye-tubes: lantern illumination by a small mirror in the center; a finder, brass equatorial motion, shifting brasses, mahogany folding stand and steadying rods.
33. One five feet achromatic Telescope; four inches aperture of object glass, tube in two parts; four astronomical and one terrestrial eye-tube; level on the tube; a finder, equatorial mahogany folding stand with steadying rods. Made by Tulley.
34. One four feet eight inches achromatic Telescope; three inches aperture of the object-glass; four astronomical & two terrestrial eye-tubes; tube in two parts; a finder; equatorial mahogany folding stand with steadying rods. Made by Tulley.—
35. One three and a half feet achromatic Telescope; $2\frac{3}{4}$ inches aperture; simple brass tube, without stand or finder; six astronomical & one terrestrial eye-tube. Made by Dollond.
36. One three & a half feet achromatic Telescope, of $2\frac{3}{4}$ inches aperture of object glass; two terrestrial & three astronomical eye-pieces; brass stand with mahogany steadying rods. Made by Mr Troughton.[12]
37. Three double wire micrometers, of Dollond, on Mr Troughton's construction, with prisms before the eye-piece, for objects near the zenith;—two of them fitting the Telescopes N° 31 & 32, and one fitting those under N° 33, 34, 35 & 36.
38. One top joint and socket for a Telescope, for easy transportation in the fields, to fit any telescope.
39. Six mountain-Barometers mounted in brass tubes; made by Mr Troughton on his improved construction.
40. Two Thermometers, Farenheits & Reaumurs divisions on silvered scales, going to boiling water; Glass face & mahogany case; for the use of observatories within doors. made by Mr Edward Troughton.
41. Two Thermometers on box wood scales, brass shelter to the balls; for the use of observatories before the windows. made by mr E. Troughton.
42. Four detached Spirit-levels mounted in brass, of two different sizes, for various purposes; made by the same
43. Two sets of Magnets; one of two large bars & one of four bars.

44. One Dynameter, or instrument to measure the magnifying power of[13] Telescopes; of M[r] Ramsdens invention; made by M[r] Dollond.[14]

45. Two beam Compasses, with double rods of different lengths, change of points, & one sett to work on metals.—One made by Will[m] Cary; the other by R[t] Fidler.

46. Three proportional Compasses, with perpendicular legs; made by Fidler.[15]

47. Two steel Rulers, five feet long. made by Fidler.

48. Four steel right angled triangles, of two different sizes, to fit the forementioned rulers. made by Fidler.

49. One Cabestan head screw key, pins in various[16] directions.

The following Articles were added to the Collection, to supply accidental losses on breaking; and for various accessary uses.

1. Four[17] setts of detached dark glasses.

2. Nine simple & double reading magnifiers.

NB. of these two articles there have been some[18] used already, to replace such as had been forgotten in various boxes of instruments.[19]

3 Six spare glass tubes, of proper size for the Barometers.

4 Twelve spirit levels, in sizes for the instruments; tried by M[r] Troughton.

5 Three plates of parallel Glass.

6 Two rolls of metal wire, for the plumblines.[20]

7 Two bottles of Varnish.

8. Twelve turn screws, in sizes two of each size.[21]

☞ The catalogue of books contains 87[22] volumes, all calculated for the use of fixed observatories.—

The above instruments are sufficient to furnish two sets of surveyors—& two national observatories.—

Tr (ViU: TJP); in a clerk's hand, with text after final numbered list in Robert Patterson's hand; partially dated; endorsed by TJ: "Mathematical Instruments procured by mr Hassler for the US." MS (PPAmP: Robert M. Patterson Papers); in Hassler's hand; docketed in an unidentified hand: "List of U.S. Astronomical Instruments—dep[d] with R. Patterson, by Mr. Hassler." Printed in *Message from the President of the United States transmitting a Report of Secretary of the Treasury, relative to the Measures which have been Taken to Complete an Accurate Survey of the Coast of the United States* (Washington, 1816), 6–10, and in *ASP, Commerce and Navigation*, 2:27–9; both printed texts following the PPAmP MS more closely, with only the most significant differences noted below.

WIRE MICROMETERS are used in telescopes that have cross wires at the focus of the eyepiece. A single thread from a spider's COBWEB was used in optical instruments (*OED*). HADLEYS INSTRUMENT: an octant invented by John Hadley for measuring angles by reflection (Gerard L'Estrange Turner, *Nineteenth-Century Scientific Instruments* [1983], 264–5). A TOISE is a French unit of lineal measure roughly equal to 1.949 meters or 6.4 feet (*OED*). OBJECT-GLASSES are the objective lenses, those closest to the item under observation. SCAPEMENT: "escapement." MOUNTAIN-BAROMETERS are modified for use as altimeters. CABESTAN: "capstan" (*OED*).

[1] ViU Tr: "Throughton." All other texts: "Troughton," and this spelling is also used later in ViU Tr.

[2] For preceding three words, printed texts substitute "vertical angles, &c."

³ Printed texts give this figure as seventy.

⁴ Preceding two words, omitted, supplied from PPAmP MS. Printed texts: "the boxes which."

⁵ ViU Tr: "of of."

⁶ Printed texts omit this item and assign number 13c to next item on list, with the number 13d skipped in *Message from the President*.

⁷ In place of preceding three words PPAmP MS substitutes "by projecting brass sides on the scales."

⁸ Sentence in PPAmP MS and printed texts ends here by adding "the base line." Remainder of item 13e is then broken into an additional item 13f (PPAmP MS and *Message from the President*) and 13e (*ASP*), with new opening: "Three brass stands, with motion work in the direction of."

⁹ In left margin next to this entry in ViU Tr is written "Nº 15 vide forward." Items 15 and 16 are in correct order in PPAmP MS and printed texts.

¹⁰ ViU Tr: "Glascow." All other texts: "Glasgow."

¹¹ Preceding two words, omitted, supplied from PPAmP MS. Printed texts: "the lens of."

¹² Descriptions of items here labeled 35 and 36 are reversed in printed texts.

¹³ ViU Tr: "of of."

¹⁴ Printed texts list this item as number 38, with manuscript items 38–44 renumbered accordingly.

¹⁵ PPAmP MS here interlines "and divided and adjusted by Mʳ Troughton."

¹⁶ Reworked to read "three" in PPAmP MS.

¹⁷ Printed texts: "Two."

¹⁸ Word interlined in ViU Tr and not included in other texts.

¹⁹ PPAmP MS here interlines "the above being the remaining ones."

²⁰ Instrument list ends here in *Message from the President*.

²¹ Remainder of ViU Tr in Patterson's hand. Other texts instead include two itemized lists of books purchased by Hassler for use by observatories and the United States Coast Survey, with the first list consisting of books already received and the second those "contained in a Box which was forwarded from France to Guernesey in 1813, on peace being made returned to Sᵗ Malo, & Mʳ Michaud in Paris undertook to forward them to Philadelphia, but they have not yet arived" (PPAmP MS).

²² Reworked by Patterson from "78."

From Henry Dearborn

DEAR SIR   Boston Decemʳ 3ᵈ 1815

on my arrival at Washington from Virginia I enclosed your note to your friends at Richmond concerning the pay for plaster, to my Son in Boston, with a request that he would procure the plaster & have it sent to Richmond, provided he could agree for its being delivered for ten or eleven dollars pʳ ton, on my return to Boston he informed me that he had not been able to make any agrement on any other termes than what would amount to the currant price at Richmond. but as I found the quantity of Plaster increasing at this place I thought it probable that I could find some opportunity for forwarding the quantity you desired on reasonable termes, but after many trial[s] I have failed, I had, as I thought, made an agrement yesterday for having 13 or 14 Tons delivered at Richmond for eleven dollares pʳ Ton but finding other extra bills were to be added I gave it up, and I have since been informed that the present price at Richmond does not probably exceed 11 or 12$ — I have therefore concluded at last, not to make any more attempts to send any on. — Mr^s Dearborn & myself had a pleasand Journey home and found our friends well. —

Mr^s Dearborn unites with me in requesting you to accept our most respectfull regards, to present our best respects to Col & Mr^s Randolph and your Grand Children. H. DEARBORN

RC (DLC); edge chipped; endorsed by TJ as received 16 Dec. 1815 and so recorded in SJL.

Trigonometry Exercise

1815.
Dec. 4.

The 2. cases of all the ∠^{s} or all the sides of a spheric. △ being given. tried by the formula supplement^y to Nepier's

a = 49–54

d = 37–19

e = 62–25

? ae = 14–45–42

see N° 91. de

ag

dg

suppose ag. & aeg the greater segments

$T\frac{a}{2} \times T\frac{d}{2}$ of segm. of mid. p. = $T\frac{e}{2} \times T\frac{d}{2}$ of oppos. parts.

t 31°–12′–30″ × t $\frac{aeg - deg}{2}$ = t 43°–36′–30″ × t 6°–17′–30″

t. 43–36–30	9.9788944	31–12–30	
+t 6–17–30	9.0423948	± 9–50–43	
	19.0212892	41– 3–13 = aeg	
– t 31–12–30	9.7822155	21–21–47 = deg.	
= t $\frac{aeg - deg}{2}$ =	9.2390737	= 9°–50′–43″	

for ae. $\boxed{Rad \times}$ Cos. ae = $\dfrac{Cot. a \times Cot\ aeg}{Rad}$

		o , ″	
Cot. a	=	49–54– 0	9.9253524
+ Cot. aeg	=	41– 3–13	10.0600716
– R = Cos. ae			<1>9.9854240 = 14°–45′–42″

for de. $\boxed{Rad \times}$ Cos de = $\dfrac{Cot. d \times Cot\ deg}{Rad}$

	o , ″	
Cot. d	37–19– 0	10.1178993
+ Cot. deg	21–21–47	10.4076544
– R. = Cos de		10.5255537. impracticable.

[227]

suppose dg & deg the greater segments

then (as above) $t\frac{deg-aeg}{2}$ = 9°–50′–43″ and 41– 3–13 = deg
21–21–47 = aeg

for ae. $\boxed{Rad \times}$ Cos. ae = $\dfrac{Cot.\ a \times Cot.\ aeg}{Rad}$

	o ′ ″	
Cot a	49–54– 0	9.9253524
+ Cot aeg	21–21–47	10.4076544
– R. = Cos. ae		10.3330068 impracticable.

N° 89.

	given	found o ′ ″	
	d = 63–45	dfg = 56–26–37	df = 70–53–30
	e = 71–49	efg = 38–25–23	ef = 65–32–21. or 63°–7′–30″
	f = 94–52		de = 82–17
		dg = 51–56–34	51–56–34
		eg = 34–27 or	33–40
		86. 23. 34 or	85–36–34 or 82°–17′

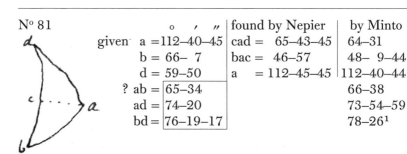

N° 80

	given	o ′	by Nepier	by Minto
		a = 59–47	abc = 42–12–30	44– 2–19
		b = 77–39–23	cbd = 35–26–53	33–37– 3
		d = 64–15.	ab = 50– 3	52–58– 0
	found		bd = 47–21	43–29–22
			ad = 56–15	

N° 81

	given	o ′ ″	found by Nepier	by Minto
		a =112–40–45	cad = 65–43–45	64–31
		b = 66– 7	bac = 46–57	48– 9–44
		d = 59–50	a = 112–45–45	112–40–44
	? ab =	$\boxed{65–34}$		66–38
	ad =	$\boxed{74–20}$		73–54–59
	bd =	$\boxed{76–19–17}$		78–26[1]

N° 86.

		originally given	by Bezout	by Minto
req^d	d =	62–40	62–39– 6	62–39–47
	e =	33– 2	33– 1–42	33– 1–46
	f =	72–32– 6	72–30–39	107–28–41 ?
	ae =	61– 1– 0		

given de = 79–56

ef = 66–29

df = 34–14–27

found in y^e opern

af = 34–37–54″

ad = 68–52–21

aef = 38–17–58

aed = 71–19–40

eg = 62–34– 8

dg = 17–21–52

fg = 29–59–24

$\begin{cases} 32-\ 0-56 = \text{dfg ?} \\ 75-27-45 = \text{efg ?} \end{cases}$

give d. e. & f. as above ⎫
to find de, ef, df ⎬ by Minto, the results are of ef = 16– 1–34 by Bez.
⎭ & Nepier

df = 59–53–30

eg = 13–33–37

dg. impossible

there must be something vicious in the data.

MS (CSmH: JF); written entirely in TJ's hand on both sides of a single sheet.

In setting up these problems, TJ drew on examples published in John Potter, *A System of Practical Mathematics* (London, 1753; Sowerby, no. 3667), 277–8, 284–6, 289–90, 293. What TJ here calls the supplementary FORMULA for solving spherical triangles when either all of the angles or all of the sides are known comes from David Steuart Erskine and Walter Minto, *An Account of the Life, Writings, and Inventions of John Napier, of Merchis-* ton (Perth, 1787), 97–103. For TJ's explanation of Napier's (NEPIER's) Theorem, see TJ to Louis H. Girardin, 18 Mar. 1814, and Notes on Napier's Theorem, printed above at 18 Mar. 1814. Étienne BEZOUT discussed methods for solving spherical triangles given the values for the three sides in his *Cours de Mathématiques, a l'usage Des Gardes du Pavillon et de la marine* (Paris, 1764–69; Sowerby, no. 3680) pt. 2, 345–6, 349–50.

¹ Recto ends here.

From Charles Clay

C. CLAY TO M^R TH. JEFFERSON   Dec. 5.—15

as you appeard pleased with the sample of Potatoes the Servant brought the Other Day Mrs Clay by Bob Sends you a few more for seed, She Says her mode of Cultivating them in the Garden, is to plant a fine large Single potatoe, uncut in a hill, that by doing so, she has had the finest large potatoes & greatest in Number, of all the Modes she has tryed, that by Cuting, she thinks the Vigor of the plant is lessened, the produce Smaller in size & fewer in Number, that by planting the Small Ones the produce is similar to that from Cutings, & constantly decline from year to year if persisted in, until a fine potatoe is not to be expected.—please except our friendly Salutations.

RC (MHi); dateline at foot of text; endorsed by TJ as received 5 Dec. 1815.

From Philip I. Barziza

HONORABLE SIR   Richmond the 6 of December 1815
Having had the honor to recive a Lettre of introduction to yuor protection, as a son of the Late Count Antonio Barziza; and Grandson of Mr and Mrs Paradise deceased. I' take the Liberty to included for the moment, and in the meanwhile[1] that I' reserv myself, for another occation the honor to cam in person to pay my respects, and dutty, I' dare bege from your goodness to honour me with an answer on the folowing quesits, or to instruct me in whatever conserns the object of my coming in thes country.

Whether the Marriage settlement of Mr & Mrs Paradise has ever been admited to record in any of the Courts of Virginia, and whether the Original instrument be not in this Country.—It is believed that during your Embassy at Paris was consulted by Mr & Mrs Paradise on the subject; and it is possible that you may have the settlement in your possession, or give information conserning it.—They may perhaps have executed some writings at that period under the powers reserved to them by the Marriage Agreement.—Whatever may have been done in relation to this subject under your direction. This is, most honorable, Sir, that the orphan of yours beloved Friends dares petition you for it. I' hope you will pardon the liberty I' have taken, and that you will honour me with an answer directed to Mr William Wickham of this Town. I have the honor to be with the Greatest respect

Your Must humble & Obidient Servant

FILIPPO I. BARZIZA

RC (DLC); endorsed by TJ as a letter from "Barziza Visct Philip S." RC (DLC); address cover only; with PoC of TJ to Henry Jackson, 31 Jan. 1816, on verso; addressed: "Thomas Jefferson Esqr Monticello near Charlottesville"; stamped; postmarked Richmond, 6 Dec., and Charlottesville, 10 Dec. Recorded in SJL as received 15 Dec. 1815. Enclosure: Edward Bancroft to TJ, 5 Sept. 1815.

[1] Manuscript: "menwill."

From Pierre Samuel Du Pont
de Nemours

Très respectable Ami,   Mounticello: 7 X^bre 1815.

je viens de passer trois jours dans votre Maison, comblé des bontés de Madame Randolph,[1] et du plaisir de voir vos grandes et Belles Petites Filles ainsi que la toute charmante très petite Fille.

Corréa dit qu'il faut absolument que je parte, Si je ne veux pas être arrêté par la rigueur de l'Hyver, et forcé de vous importuner de moi pendant trois mois.

Il est parti lui même avant-hier. Je Suis resté deux jours de plus dans l'esperance de vous voir arriver d'heure en heure.

J'aurais volontiers bravé l'hyver. J'ai voyagé en Pologne dans les neiges.[2] Mais mon Fils, qui a quitté Sa manufacture pour m'accompagner, est obligé d'y retourner, et je suis tellement ignorant de la Langue anglaise, quand il faut la parler ou l'écouter, qu'il [3] m'est en voyage d'une utilité presque indispensable.

Je me Suis cependant déterminé pour apprendre un peu de cette langue, dont un Ami de l'Amérique ne peut ici Se passer, à commencer le travail que vous m'aviez ordonné de traduire moi même[4] en anglais mon ouvrage Sur l'éducation.

Je vous en laisse les premieres Pages. Vous me direz Si je dois continuer, ou abandonner cette entreprise.—Je n'oublie point que, Si j'y persiste, vous m'avez promis votre Plume excellente pour corriger mon mauvais anglais avant l'impression.

Je vous laisse aussi deux autres ouvrages, dont je désire beaucoup que le plus considérable vous paraisse digne de votre attention et obtienne votre approbation.

Les trois Républiques unies de la nouvelle Grenade, de Carthagène et de Caraccas m'ont fait demander mes idées Sur la Constitution à laquelle elles voudraient S'arrêter, ne regardant leur etat actuel que comme révolutionnaire et provisoire.

Je crois qu'il pourra y avoir douze grandes Républiques espagnoles en Amerique, et quelles devront Se confederer tant entre elles qu'avec vos Etats unis.—Et je tâche de leur appliquer autant que leurs circonstances locales pourront le permettre les Projets que mes Amis et moi avions formés pour le rétablissement de la République Française, Si nous avions pu comme nous le voulions renverser[5] Buonaparte Sans recevoir ni accepter d'autres Rois.

Le troisieme ouvrage dont je vous prie d'accepter une copie a été fait en mer, et ne traite que de choses qui vous Sont très connues ainsi que l'estimable Ecrivain auquel je les ai adressées. Mais vous y trouverez (Pages 36 à 44) une très[6] longue note qui contient ce que je pensais de Buonaparte en quittant la France, avec une addition Sur ce que je pense aujourd'hui de Sa conduite ulterieure et des malheurs de ma Patrie.—Hélas elle périra, et entrainera l'Europe dans Sa chute.

Celle[7] de l'Allemagne, celle de l'Italie et celle de l'Angleterre ne tarderont point à Suivre la nôtre.

S'il arrivait cependant qu'elles fussent un peu[8] retardées, il est certain que l'Angleterre vous fera encore une guerre Sanglante dont elle ne dissimule pas les préparatifs:—Elle fera cette guerre tant par haine qu'afin d'avoir un prétexte pour conserver Sa <u>Standing Army</u>, qu'elle n'a nulle intention de réformer, et qui par les Places à donner et les marchés à faire est pour Son Ministère d'un grand interêt.

Si cette Guerre a lieu, je désire que mes Enfans, mes Petits Enfans et moi même, malgré mon age, nous y fassions remarquer comme de fidelles Américains et de vaillans Républicains.

C'est une des raisons qui me font appuyer auprès de vous, et vous prier d'appuyer de toute votre influence[9] auprès de Monsieur le Président, la demande que fait mon Fils ainé d'un Warrant de Midshipman pour un de Ses enfans qui est d'une grande esperance.

Les Du Pont, à commencer par Pontius Cominius qui porta les lettres de Camille au Capitole, et passa le Tibre Sans bateau ne Sachant pas nager, ont toujours êté des Hommes[10] de résolution et de ressource. Je ne veux pas qu'ils soient une richesse nulle, ni une mauvaise acquisition pour aucun Pays, moins encore pour le Vôtre.

Mon Fils et moi ne vous aurions pas tourmenté pour Son Enfant, Si nous ne Savions que les demandes Sont très multipliées et que celles qui Seront fortement recommandées pourront Seules esperer de réussir.—nous joignons une Note Sur ce qui peut militer pour mon Petit Fils, né en Amerique longtems depuis que Son Pere a êté citoyen des Etats-Unis, et qui par conséquent n'est pas du tout <u>foreigner</u>.

Vous connaissez le tendre et respectueux attachement que je vous ai voué.   DuPont (de Nemours)

EDITORS' TRANSLATION

Very respectable Friend,   Monticello: 7 December 1815.
    I just spent three days in your house, showered with Mrs. Randolph's acts of kindness and filled with the pleasure of seeing your beautiful grown-up granddaughters as well as your very charming, very young granddaughter.

Corrêa says that I must leave if I do not want to be detained by the harshness of winter and forced to be a nuisance to you for three months.

He left the day before yesterday. I stayed two more days in the hope of seeing you arrive at any moment.

I would have braved winter gladly. I have traveled in Poland through the snow. But my son, who left his factory to accompany me, is obliged to return to it, and I am so ignorant of the English language when I have to speak or listen to it, that he is almost indispensable to me on a trip.

However, in order to learn some of this language, which is essential to a friend of America in this country, I have decided to start on the task you had requested of me, to translate my work on education into English.

I leave you the first pages of it. You will tell me whether I should continue or abandon this enterprise.—If I persist, I do not forget that you promised to use your excellent pen to correct my bad English before it is printed.

I also leave two other works for you, and I very much hope that you will find the longest one deserving of your attention and that it receives your approbation.

The three united republics of New Granada, Cartagena and Caracas have asked me for my ideas on a constitution on which they can agree, as they consider their current state to be revolutionary and provisional.

Twelve large Spanish republics will probably emerge in America, and I believe they should unite into a confederation among themselves and with your United States.—And I am trying to apply to them, as much as their local circumstances will allow, the projects that my friends and I had formed for the reestablishment of the French republic if, as we wanted, we could have overthrown Bonaparte without receiving or accepting any other kings.

The third work of which I ask you to accept a copy was composed at sea and deals only with things that are very well known to you as well as to the worthy writer to whom I have addressed them. But you will find in it (pages 36 to 44) a very long note that contains what I thought about Bonaparte when I left France, with an addition dealing with what I think today of his subsequent behavior and the misfortunes of my country.—Alas, it will perish and drag Europe down with it.

The collapse of Germany, of Italy, and of England will soon follow ours.

However, if it happened that these downfalls were a little delayed, England would certainly wage a bloody war against you, for which she does not hide her preparations:—She will wage this war out of hatred as much as to have a pretext for keeping her standing army, which she has no intention of discharging, and which greatly supports its government because through it positions can be bestowed and deals can be made.

Should this war take place I desire that my children, my grandchildren, and myself, despite my age, will distinguish ourselves in it as faithful Americans and brave republicans.

This is one reason I rely on you and ask you to support with all your influence my eldest son's request to the president that a midshipman's warrant go to a very promising child of his own.

The Du Ponts, starting with Pontius Cominus, who carried Camillus's letters to the capitol and, not knowing how to swim, crossed the Tiber without a boat, have always been resolute and resourceful men. I want them to be neither rich idlers nor a bad acquisition to any country, and especially not to yours.

My son and I would not have bothered you about his child if we had not known that the requests are many and that only those who are strongly recommended have a chance of succeeding.—We enclose a note that may bolster the chances of my grandson, who was born in America long after his father became a citizen of the United States and who therefore is not at all a foreigner.

You know my tender and respectful attachment for you.

DuPont (de Nemours)

RC (DLC); at head of text: "au Philosophe Thomas Jefferson"; endorsed by TJ as received 15 Dec. 1815 and so recorded in SJL. Dft (DeGH: Pierre Samuel Du Pont de Nemours Papers, Winterthur Manuscripts); unsigned; with substantial variations from RC, only the most important of which are noted below. Translation by Dr. Genevieve Moene. Enclosures: (1) Partial manuscript English translation, not found, of Du Pont, *Sur l'éducation nationale dans les États-Unis d'Amérique* (2d ed., Paris, 1812; Poor, *Jefferson's Library*, 5 [nos. 207 (described as "MS. 4to."), 209 (described as a piece by Du Pont in a volume of "Tracts on Education"), and 210 (described as a piece by Du Pont in a volume of "Pamphlets on Education")]). (2) Manuscript, not found, of Du Pont's missing "Mémoire aux républiques équinoxiales." (3) Manuscript, not found, of Du Pont's *Lettre a M. Jean Baptiste Say, ex-membre du tribunat, sur son Traité d'Économie Politique* (Poor, *Jefferson's Library*, 11 [no. 698 (described as an "MS.")]; published with its own title page in Du Pont, *Examen du Livre de M. Malthus sur le Principe de Population; auquel on a joint La Traduction de quatre chapitres de ce livre supprimés dans l'edition française; et une Lettre a M. Say sur son Traité d'Economie Politique* [Philadelphia, 1817], 118–59). Other enclosure printed below.

Du Pont and his son Victor visited Martha Jefferson RANDOLPH and her family at Monticello from 4–7 Dec. 1815. In a letter to his wife, Du Pont described their stay, beginning with an entry dated from Monticello, 4 Dec.: "Nous dinions chez le Président qui nous a dit que la meilleure route pour Mounticello etait celle de Fredericsburg, et quil fallait etre au Steam boat à Sept heures du Soir, à quoi nous avons eu bien de la peine. Nous y avons passé la nuit, assez bien couchés, ce qui est une autre grande commodite des Steam-boats; et de Fredericsburg nous n'avons pas arriver que ce Soir à Mounticello, où Mr Jefferson n'est pas, mais où il est attendu d'heure en heure   Mr de Corréa qui voulait faire le voyage avec moi l'Eté dernier, y était ce matin et doit y revenir demain J'avais laissé partir Mr de Correa seul, parceque j'attendais de tes lettres et ne pouvois ni vivre Sans elles, ni m'excuser à retarder d'un mois leur réception   Je n'ai pas l'honneur d'être connu de Madame Randolph, quoique l'aie vue à Paris, mais toute jeunesse chez Son Pere Mr Jefferson.—Elle tient la maison et lhabite avec Ses dix enfans, dont une petite fille de deux ans.   Elle nous a reçus avec quelque Surprise, mais nous traite avec la plus grande bonté.—Seule de la maison elle entend le Français: et en Anglais je Suis réduit au Silence.   6 Xbre. Mr Jefferson n'est point revenu. Mr de Corréa est arrivé hier, et reparti ce matin. Nous avions tant de choses à nous dire, particulierement Sur Son voyages et les Cherokées, et aussi Sur les affaires de l'Europe, qu'il ne m'a laissé que peu de loisir" ("We had dinner at the President's house, and he told us that the best route to Monticello was by way of Fredericksburg, and that it was necessary to be at the steamboat at seven in the evening, which was very hard for us to do. We spent the night there, lodged rather well, which is another great convenience of steamboats; and from Fredericksburg we did not arrive until this evening at Monticello, where Mr. Jefferson is not present, but is expected at any time. Mr. Corrêa, who wanted to take the trip with me last summer, was here this morning and is supposed to come back tomorrow. I had allowed Mr. Corrêa to leave by himself because I was waiting for your letters and could barely live without them, nor forgive myself if I delayed their reception by a month. I do not have the honor of being known to Mrs. Randolph, although I saw her in Paris, but that was at the residence of her father, Mr. Jefferson, when she was all youth.—She keeps the house and lives in it with her ten children, including a two-year-old little girl. She received us with some surprise, but is treating us with the greatest kindness.—She is the only one in the house who understands French: and in English I am reduced to silence. 6 Dec. Mr. Jefferson did not return. Mr. Corrêa arrived yesterday and left this morning. We had so many things to tell each other, especially regarding his trips and the Cherokee and also about European affairs, that he left me little leisure time") (extracted from Du Pont to Françoise Poivre Du Pont de Nemours, 30 Nov.–15 Dec. 1815 [RC in DeGH: Pierre S. du Pont Papers, Longwood Manuscripts]; translation by Dr. Genevieve Moene).

The TRÈS PETITE FILLE was TJ's youngest granddaughter, Septimia A. Randolph (Meikleham). Du Pont said that the 1815 return of Napoleon Bonaparte (BUONAPARTE) to France had been supported by only a small portion of the army; that his reappearance at a time when France was beginning an economic and political recovery served only to plunge a weakened army and nation into renewed war; and that he was a despot who had never been concerned for the good of the French people, but only with the satisfaction at any cost of his personal ambitions (*Examen du Livre de M. Malthus*, 150–3). According to Plutarch, PONTIUS COMINIUS carried a message from Marcus Furius Camillus across enemy lines to the besieged senate in Rome and returned with news of Camillus's appointment as dictator (Plutarch, *Camillus*, book 24, in *Plutarch's Lives*, trans. Bernadotte Perrin, Loeb Classical Library [1914–26; repr. 1985], 2:154–7).

[1] Word interlined in Dft.
[2] Sentence interlined in Dft.
[3] Preceding eight words interlined in Dft.
[4] Preceding two words interlined in Dft.
[5] Preceding nine words interlined in Dft in place of "lorsque nous esperions nous delivrer de" ("when we hoped we would free ourselves from").
[6] Word interlined in Dft.
[7] Reworked in Dft from "Je crois que celles" ("I believe that those").
[8] Preceding seven words interlined in Dft in place of "Si elles etaient" ("If they were").
[9] Preceding four words interlined in Dft.
[10] Dft: "gens" ("people").

ENCLOSURE

Victor du Pont's Notes on Samuel F. Du Pont

[ca. 7 Dec. 1815]

A Few Facts[1] in Support of the request made by Victor du Pont of a Warrant of Midshipman for his son Samuel Francis—
    Two objections will probably[2] be made
1° Mr du Pont is a foreigner
2° What has M^r d. P. done to obtain a preference from the Government
    The first of these objections can be answered in stating that V. d. P. came over to the U.S. upwards of twenty eight years ago and has been naturalised about sixteen years—That when living in the State of New york he has held

two Commissions under Governors Lewis & Tompkins, one of 1ᵗ major of militia, the other for an office of trust & profit, Clerk of a County—Since V. d. P. lives in the State of Delaware he has been elected twice and is now a member of the State Legislature, So in point of Citizenship he is equal to any naturalised Citizen in the union.[3]

In answer to the Second objection, it will be easy to prove that the Messʳ du Pont who are naturalised have been usefull & active Citizens, and that their father who is not naturalised But who was employed by the french government in the confection of the treaty of 1783 has since that time been a constant friend and a zealous supporter & advocate of the rights & interests of the United States in france—V. d. P just before his naturalisation was Several years consul of the French Republic and his conduct in that capacity contrary to that of some of[4] his predecessors has been as he was informed perfectly satisfactory to the State & to the general Government—

The Messʳˢ du Pont have imported the first Merino Ram in the U.S.

They have established some of the first and of the most extensive Factories in this Country, and which are Certainly among the most perfect of their kind—

During the late War the Messʳ du Pont have at their own expence (except the muskets which were loaned to them by the Commisary general) raised & equiped three Companies of Volunteers called the Brandywine Rangers making a respectable force of 280 effective men, well uniformed and disciplined—the men were drilled once a week and excercised to sham battles in the woods and among the Rocks of the Brandywine,[5] of these 280 men about 200 were in the employ of the Messʳ du Pont, consequently every afternoon drill did cost them somewhere about $100 in wagges—the amount of these wagges, of the ammunition and other attending expences, was a voluntary War tax of considerable magnitude, and will they hope place them in the ranks of those who have well deserved of their Country[6]

All they ask is the chance of placing in the Navy a very promising youth, who will probably do honor to the Service & follow the steps of our Brave commanders

MS (DLC: James Madison Papers); filed at 18 Jan. 1816; entirely in Victor du Pont's hand; undated; edge trimmed. FC (DeGH: Victor du Pont Papers, Winterthur Manuscripts); endorsed by Victor du Pont: "Letter & Memorial to the President requesting a Warrant of Midshipman for Francis—Washington December 14ᵗʰ 1815." Also enclosed in TJ to James Madison, 22 Dec. 1815.

Samuel Francis Du Pont (1803–65), naval officer, was born at Bergen Point, New Jersey, and attended school in Germantown, Pennsylvania. President Madison appointed him a midshipman on 19 Dec. 1815, and he first went to sea in 1817. Du Pont was promoted to lieutenant in 1826, commander in 1843 (with the commission to date from 1842), captain in 1855, and rear admiral in 1862. He served on the California coast during the Mexican War, sat on the Naval Efficiency Board in 1855, and participated in an 1857–59 expedition to China and Japan. During the Civil War, Du Pont was charged with blockading the South Atlantic, captured Port Royal, South Carolina, in 1861, and led an unsuccessful 1863 attack on Charleston, South Carolina. He died in Philadelphia (ANB; DAB; Kevin J. Weddle, Lincoln's Tragic Admiral: The Life of Samuel Francis Du Pont [2005]; Callahan, U.S. Navy, 174; JEP, 3:530, 534, 6:150, 161, 10:17, 125, 12:67, 154, 155, 13:2, 29 [17, 28 Apr. 1826, 14 Dec. 1842, 5 Jan. 1843, 16 Jan., 17 July 1856, 6 Jan., 6 Mar., 5 Dec. 1862, 9 Jan. 1863];

John D. Hayes, ed., *Samuel Francis Du Pont: A Selection from his Civil War Letters*, 3 vols. [1969]; *Philadelphia Inquirer*, 24 June 1865; gravestone in Du Pont de Nemours Cemetery, Wilmington, Del.).

The FC is subjoined to an FC of Victor du Pont to Madison, Washington City, 14 Dec. 1815, in which he asks that the enclosed memorial be thrown in the fire immediately after perusal; remarks that Madison may be unacquainted with some of the circumstances favoring the application and that "we are very serious to obtain & merit your approbation"; and states that "The recommendation will be left in the office of the Minister of the Navy" (DeGH: Samuel Francis Du Pont Papers, Winterthur Manuscripts). In 1801 Victor du Pont's brother, Eleuthère I. du Pont de Nemours, helped to import Don Pedro, one of the first MERINO sheep in the United States (*Agricultural History* 33 [1959]: 86–8).

[1] FC here adds "humbly Submitted to his Ex^y Mr Madison Pre^dt of the U.S."

[2] FC: "perhaps."

[3] FC here adds "and all his children are born in this country."

[4] Preceding two words interlined.

[5] Preceding fifteen words not in FC.

[6] Remainder of FC reads "From their long residence and numerous acquaintances Mess. d. P. could certainly add a long list of respectable names to the recommendations in favor of the appointment of Samuel Francis in the Navy, they have only and for form Sake collected few in Wilmington, trusting alltogether in the Wisdom & justice of his Excellency who if he does not think proper to grant the favor, will only discover in the application a new proof of the zeal & devotion of a family which will always be proud & anxious to Serve the Country in every Generation & on every occasion."

From George Watterston

SIR,   City of Washington Decr 7th 1815.

I have requested Mr Millegan to bind one of the printed catalogues in calf & transmit it to you—There are some errors in it which could not be avoided. I trust, however, you will, on the whole, be pleased with its execution—The alphabetical arrangement under each chapter is not so correct as I wished it, but it could not without great trouble, be improved; as it would have required a new copy of your M.S. The numbers you suggested, as necessary to the completion of the Index, were unavoidably omitted as they would have had a tendency to swell it to too great a size & as that necessity is in some degree obviated, by the alphabetical order of the chapters—I find, on reexamining the book, that there are two works which have not been received viz—"Rays American Tars in Tripoli & Morris' Accounts"—These are the only defeciencies I know of, except the M,S Laws of Virginia of which you have already apprised me.

I have the honor to be With great respect Sir, Yr obt serv^t

GEO, WATTERSTON

RC (DLC); adjacent to closing: "Thos Jefferson Esq^e"; endorsed by TJ as received 21 Jan. 1816 and so recorded in SJL; with notation by TJ beneath signature: "Morris. C. 24. 439. Ray's Tripoli. C. 2. 82. marked."

At some time between this date and that of TJ's letter to Watterston of 2 Mar. 1816, Joseph Milligan (MILLEGAN) sent TJ three copies of the published version of TJ's catalogue of the library he sold to Congress, *Catalogue of U.S. Library.*

Robert Morris's ACCOUNTS were published in *A Statement of the Accounts of the United States of America, during the Administration of the Superintendant of Finance* (Philadelphia, 1785; Sowerby, no. 3165).

To William Steptoe

D[EA]R SIR   Poplar Forest Dec. 8. 15

I have not troubled you with frequent calls to see the boy who has been so long sick here, because his case seemed to be that of a continued fever in which I have always understood from my medical friends that nothing could be done of any effect but to keep the body open and support the strength of the patient by proper food. expecting to leave this place on Sunday I should be glad to have your better judgment on the boy before I go away. any time to-day or tomorrow that suits you I shall be glad to see you. I generally ride out about the middle of the day, but am at home in the forenoon & afternoon. Accept the assurance of my great esteem and respect

TH: JEFFERSON

PoC (ViU: TJP-ER); one word faint; at foot of text: "Doct^r Steptoe"; endorsed by TJ.

The sick BOY was TJ's slave Lovilo Hern.

From Alden Partridge

SIR   West Point. Decembr. 9th 1815

Agreeably to promise I now take the liberty to enclose you the Meteorological Tables mentioned in my last letter, and hope they will not be unacceptable to you. I expect to leave here in a few days to go to the state of Vermont, where I shall spend the winter. Should you have any communication to make to me I will thank you to direct to Norwich, County of Windsor State of Vermont—

I have the honor to be with the highest respect and Esteem, Sir, your Obed^t Servt   A PARTRIDGE

Capt. of Engs

RC (DLC); at foot of text: "Thomas Jefferson. Esquir late President of the United States"; endorsed by TJ as received 21 Dec. 1815 and so recorded in SJL.

E N C L O S U R E

Summary of Meteorological Observations by Alden Partridge

[ca. 9 Dec. 1815]

Meteorological Table

Containing the Results of a Series of Observations made at West Point, State of New York,
from April 5th to October 31st 1810

Months	No of Observations	Thermometer					Barometer						No of Pleasant Days	No of Days on which rain fell.	No of Cloudy Days without Rain	No of Days partly clear and partly Cloudy.
		Greatest degree of Cold	Greatest degree of heat	Mean Temperature	Greatest Variations	Diff. of Temperature between each succeeding month	Greatest Altitude	Least Altitude	Mean Altitude	Greatest Variations	Date of the greatest degree of Cold in each month	Date of the greatest degree of heat in each month				
April	73	33°	80°	60°	47°	6 1/10	30.00	29.16	29.60	.80¹	11h sunrise	27th PM	12	7		6
May	86	37	94	66 1/10	57	6 13/20	29.83	28.94	29.59	.89	8h do	29h 4² PM	18	8	1	4
June	85	52	86	72 3/4	34	3 1/4	29.85	29.40	29.61	.45	8h do	16h & 17h PM	13	13	1	3
July	70	65	88	76	23	1 1/2	29.80	29.38	29.59	.42	2d do	12th PM	15	13	1	2
August	90	49	90	74 1/4	41	8 1/6	29.80	29.30	29.58	.50	31st AM	12th do	13	15		3
Septemr	90	46	84	66 2/3	38	11 3/12	30.08	29.53	29.76	.55			14	9	2	5
October	73	29	79	55 1/4	50		30.16	29.04	29.70 1/2	1.12			16	9	2	4
From the 5th April, to 31st Octr 1810	567⁵	29°	94°	67 2/7°	65°		30.16	28.94	29.63	1.22			101	74	7	27

Meteorological Table

Containing the Results of a Series of Observations made at West Point, State of New York from the 1st April to 31st May 1811, & also from the 11th May to the 30th Nov.r 1812

Months	N.o of Observations	Thermometer					Barometer				Date of the greatest Degree of Cold.	Date of the greatest Degree of heat.	Depth of Snow in inches	N.o of Clear Days.	N.o of Days on which rain fell.	N.o of Days on which Snow fell.	N.o of Cloudy Days.	N.o of Days partly Clear and partly Cloudy.
		Greatest degree of Cold	Greatest Degree of heat	Mean Temperature	Greatest variations	Diff. of temperature between each succeeding month.	Greatest Altitude	Least Altitude	Mean Altitude	Greatest variations								
AD. 1811																		
April.	90	27°	82°	52°	55°		30.10	29.10	29.44	1.00	2^{d}	18^{h}		14.	8	2	1	6
May.	75	40	77	60	37		30.06	29.10	29.66	.96	3^{d}	7^{h}		17	11.	2	1	2
From April 1st to May 31st	165	27°	82°	56°	55°	8°	30.10	29.10	29.55	1.00	Apr^{l} 2^{d}	A^{rl} 18.		31	19	2	1	8.
AD. 1812																		
May	59	46	79	61	33	$10\tfrac{1}{2}$	29.91	29.23	29.60	.68	17th	31		3	9		1	7
June	77	57	86	$71\tfrac{1}{3}$	29	$4\tfrac{2}{6}$	29.76	29.20	29.49	.56	5th	9^{h}		3	18			9
July	92	56	91	76	35	$2\tfrac{3}{5}$	29.80	29.40	29.59	.40	1st	7^{h}		8	11		1	12
August	78	63	87	$73\tfrac{1}{3}$	24	$7\tfrac{2}{15}$	29.85	29.40	29.60	.45	13th	25th		5	13		3	12
Septemb^{r}	89	48	81	$66\tfrac{3}{5}$	33	$10\tfrac{8}{15}$	29.98	29.27	29.72	.71	21st	2^{d}		6	11		1	10
Oct^{r}	57	40	78	$55\tfrac{2}{3}$	38	$10\tfrac{15}{15}$	30.00	29.20	29.66	.80	24^{h}	2^{d}		5	9	2	3	16
Novem^{r}	89	22	67	44	45	$11\tfrac{1}{3}$	30.16	29.08	29.57	1.08	25^{h}	5^{h}		5	7		3	13
From may 11th to Novr 30th	541	22°	91°	66°	69°		30.16	29.08	29.60	1.08	Novr 25^{h}	July 7th		35	78	2	9	79

Meteorological Table.

Containing the Results of a Series of Observations made at Norwich, State of Vermont from the 1st July 1811 to the 1st May 1812.

Months	N⁰ of observations	Greatest degree of Cold	Greatest degree of heat	Thermometer — Mean Temperature	Greatest Variations	Diff. of temperature between each succeeding month	Barometer — Greatest Altitude	Least Altitude	Mean Altitude	Greatest variations	Date of the greatest degree of Cold	Date of the greatest degree of heat	Depth of Snow in inches	N⁰ of Clear Days	N⁰ of Days, on which rain fell.	N⁰ of Cloudy Days.	N⁰ of Days on which snow fell.	N⁰ of Days partly Clear & partly Cloudy.
July	40	50°	92°	70 2/3°	42°		29.19[9]	28.71	28.91	.46[10]	27th	18th		14	16	1		1
August	90	45	92	70	47	2/3	29.30	28.75	28.67	.54[11]	9th	20h		18	9	2		3
September	84	31	85	65	54	5	29.24	28.55	28.94	.69	27th	4h		17	7	3		4
October	83	17	75	47	58	18	29.42	28.50	28.99	.92	27th	12h	3 5/10	13	12	3	2	1
November	82	12	51	32 1/2	39	14 1/2	29.44	28.40	28.95	1.04	26h	9h	5	7	13	9	3	4
December	87	-16	48	19 1/2	64	13	29.20	28.09	28.74	1.11			23 9/10	3	2	6	8	9
January	88	-24	36	14	60	5 1/2	29.23	28.09	28.60	1.14	18h	26h	23 4/10	3		2	16	6
February	75	-31	35	15	66	1 1/2	29.14	28.15	28.77	.99	25	4.	38	7	1	4	13	6.
March	86	- 4	51	24 2/3	47[12]	9 1/3	29.25	28.45	28.90	.80	2d	27h	14 1/10	10	3	2	7	7
April	79	23	65	40	42	15 2/3	29.26	28.38	28.89	.88	12.	25	5	5	7		3	13
From the 1st July 1811 to 1st May 1812	794	-31°	92°	39 9/10°	123°		29.44	28.09	28.83	1.35	Feb. 25.	July 18.	112 9/10	97	70	32	52	54

Note: The Town of Norwich is situated in the East part, of the State of Vermont, adjoining Connecticut River, & opposite Dartmouth College, in the State of New Hampshire, in north Lat. 43.° 33.′[14]—The Altitude of that part of the Town, where the Observations were made, above tide-water, I found, by Barometrical Calculation, to be 917 feet & 629 feet above Connecticut River. In the 2d Column, of the above Table, whenever the sign –Cypher, thus –16° denotes that the Thermometer was 16 degrees below Cypher.

Meteorological Table

Containing the Results of a Series of Observations made at West Point, State of New York, from April 1st to Dec[r] 1st 1813.

Months	N[o] of Observations	Thermometer					Barometer.				Date of the greatest degree of Cold	Date of the greatest degree of heat	N[o] of Clear Days	N[o] of Days on which rain fell.	N[o] of Days on which [snow] fell.	N[o] of Cloudy Days.	N[o] of Days partly clear & partly Cloudy.
		Greatest degree of cold	Greatest degree of heat	Mean Temperature	Greatest Variations	Diff. of Temperature between each succ[ing] month	Greatest Altitude	Least Altitude	Mean Altitude	Greatest Variations							
April	90	37°	76°	56$\frac{2}{3}$°	14$\frac{1}{3}$° ^{016}		30.06	29.14	29.68	.82[17]	1st	20th	3	11		1	16
May	87	46	80	61$\frac{1}{3}$	34	4$\frac{2}{3}$	29.90	29.37	29.63	.53	7[h]	24[h]	2	18			10
June	90	53	90	75	37	13$\frac{2}{3}$	30.03	29.34	29.63	.69	1st	18[h]	2	12			16
July	92	62	93	75$\frac{1}{4}$	31	$\frac{1}{4}$	29.97	29.29	29.61	.68	6[h]	9th	2	13			16
August	91	61	91	78	30	2$\frac{3}{4}$	29.97	29.29	29.66	.69[18]	19[h]	7[h]	8	11			12
Sep[r]	88	52	92	69$\frac{3}{4}$	40	8$\frac{1}{4}$	29.94	29.27	29.68	.67	30[h]	13[h]	6	8			16
October	93	32	68	55$\frac{1}{2}$	36	14$\frac{1}{4}$	30.05	29.00	29.45	1.05	22[d]	17th	4	11	2	3	11
Novemb[r]	87	25	69	46$\frac{1}{2}$	22$\frac{1}{2}$[19]	9	30.10	29.23	29.66	.81[20]	15[h]	10th	8	6	2	1	13
From April 1st to Dec[r] 1st	718	25°	93°	64$\frac{3}{4}$°	68°		30.10	29.00	29.62	1.10	Nov[r] 15th	July 9th	35	90	4	5	110.

Meteorological Table

Containing the Results of a Series of Observations, made at West Point, State of New York, from the 1st March to the 30th Nov' 1814, inclusive.

Months.	No of Observations	Thermometer					Barometer				Date of the greatest Degree of Cold	Date of the greatest Degree of Heat.	Depth of Snow in inches	No of clear Days.	No of Days on which rain fell	No of Cloudy Days.	No of Days on which snow fell.	No of Days partly Clear, & partly cloudy.
		Greatest degree of cold	Greatest degree of heat	Mean Temperature	Greatest Variations	Diff. of temperature between each succeeding month.	Greatest Altitude	Least Altitude	Mean Altitude	Greatest Variations								
March	92°	8°	65°	39°	$31°21$	$15\frac{1}{6}$	29.98	28.83	29.46	1.15	5th	30h		6	4	1	6	14
April	89	35	84	$54\frac{1}{6}$	49	$14\frac{1}{2}$[22]	30.04	29.11	29.65	00.93	12th	27h		2	9	2	00	17
May	90	41	89	$68\frac{1}{4}$	48	$3\frac{1}{12}$	29.81	29.20	29.49	00.61	2d	4h		00	14	00	00	17
June	87	54	90	$71\frac{1}{3}$	36	$3\frac{11}{12}$	29.93	29.34	29.64	00.59	24th	29h		2	9	00	00	19
July	92	53	92	$75\frac{1}{4}$	39	$3\frac{7}{12}$	29.80	29.19	29.59	00.61	13h	16h		6	10	3	00	12
August	56	55	94	$72\frac{2}{9}$	39	$3\frac{7}{9}$	29.98	29.30	29.68	00.68	22d	2d		5	7	2	00	17
September	87	40	90	$66\frac{1}{4}$	50	$5\frac{6}{9}$	29.97	29.28	29.59	00.69	26d	3d		3	9	2	00	16
October	91	31	75	$53\frac{3}{4}$	44	$12\frac{1}{2}$	30.08	29.24	29.53	00.84	24th	14h		5	5	00	00	21
November	88	21	64	$42\frac{1}{7}$	43	$11\frac{2}{3}$	30.25	29.16	29.74	1.09	29h	14h	3	4	13	1	2	10
From March 1st to Nov' 30th 1814[23]	772	8°	94°	$60\frac{1}{4}°$	86°		30.25	28.83	29.60	1.42	March 5h	Aug st 2d	3	33	80	11	8	143

MS (DLC: TJ Papers, 205:36532–7); written in an unidentified hand, with each table on a separate sheet; undated. MS (VtNN: Partridge Papers); in a bound volume of Partridge manuscripts; written in an unidentified hand; undated.

[1] The correct figure is .84.
[2] Word not in VtNN MS.
[3] VtNN MS: "$6\frac{1}{20}$."
[4] VtNN MS: "7."
[5] DLC MS: "576." VtNN MS: "567," which is correct.
[6] VtNN MS: "$4\frac{2}{3}$."
[7] Preceding six words not in VtNN MS.
[8] This and preceding column reversed in VtNN MS.
[9] VtNN MS: "29.17."
[10] VtNN MS: ".40." The correct figure is .48.
[11] The correct figure is .55.
[12] The correct figure is 55.
[13] Phrase not in VtNN MS.
[14] Reworked from: "33.° 33.'"
[15] Manuscript: "rain."
[16] The correct figure is 39°.
[17] The correct figure is .92.
[18] The correct figure is .68.
[19] The correct figure is 44.
[20] The correct figure is .87.
[21] The correct figure is 57°.
[22] VtNN MS: "$14\frac{1}{12}$."
[23] Preceding seven words not in VtNN MS.

Calculations of Latitude of Poplar Forest

1815 observns not all[1] carefully made. the good & satisfactory are marked with an *

	Aug. 30.	Sep. 1.	Sep. 2. *
	° ′ ″	°	° ′ ″
observed altitude	123–46	122–21	121–35– 0
error of instrument	5	5	5
true observed altitude	123–41	122–16	121–30– 0
	61–50–30	61– 8– 0	60–45– 0
– refraction 31″ + paral. 3″	28	28	29
true altitude of ☉'s center:	61–50– 2	61– 7–32	60–44–31
	90–	90– 0– 0	90–
☉'s true Zenith distance	28– 9–58	28–52–28[2]	29–15–29
☉'s declinn at Greenw. 9°–15′		8–31–51	8–10– 3
Pop. For. –	– 5	– 4–55	– 4–56
	9–10	8–26–56	8– 5– 7
Lat. Pop. For	37–19–58	37–19–24[3]	37–21–36
corrected to error instrum.	37–18–13	37–17–39	37–19–51

		Sep. 3. *	Sep. 6. *	Sep. 7. *	Sep. 15. *
		° ′ ″			
1	observed altitude.	120–51– 0	118–36– 0	117–55– 0	111°–50– 0
2	– error of instrument	1–30	1–30	1–30	1–30
3	true observed altitude	120–49–30	118–34–30	117–53–30	111– 48–30
		60–24–45	59–17–15	58–56–45	55– 54–15
4	– refraction + parallax	29	29	30	34
5	true altitude of ☉'s center	60–24–16	59–16–46	58–56–15	55– 53–41

⊙'s declinn Greenwich	6	7-48- 8	6-41-37	6-19-13	3-16-49
– Pop. Forest	7	– 4-57 7-43-11	5- 1 6-36-36	5- 2 6-14-11	5- 8 3- 11-41
true height Equator at P.F	8	52-41- 5	52-40-10	52-42- 4	52-42- 0
		90	90–	90–	90–
Zenith distance of equator⁴ = Lat. P.F.	9.	37-18-55	37-19-50	37-17-56	37- 18- 0

	Sep. 16.	Sep. 24	Sep. 25.	Oct. 4.	Nov. 13
1.	111°- 3'- 0	104°-50'- 0	104°- 2'- 0	74°- 55'- 0	69°- 37'- 0
2. –	1-30				
3.	111- 1-30 / 55- 30-45				
4. – +	35				
5.	55- 30-10				
6.	2-53-42				
7.	– 5- 8 2- 48-34				
8.	52- 41-36 / 90				
9	37- 18-24				

		Sep. 24		Oct. 4.	Dec. 2.
Nov. 14.	69- 4- 0	17.	21	23	
		67-33- 0	65-42- 0	64-45- 0	61-27- 0
Dec 10					
	59- 33- 0				

1815. Aug. 6. the average of 14. satisfactory observns makes the error of the instrument 1'½ to be deducted from altitude

MS (MHi); filed with TJ's Weather Memorandum Book, 1802–16; with TJ's Calculations of Latitude of the Sharp Peak of Otter and Natural Bridge, 18 Sept.–10 Nov. 1815, on verso; written entirely in TJ's hand on recto of a single sheet of paper, with text through the end of the 2 Sept. entry perpendicular to remainder of text.

[1] Word interlined.

[2] Calculation to this point for September 1 reworked by TJ to correct error of subtracting 28′ from 61°–08′, rather than 28″; with duplicate uncanceled figures for refraction plus parallax and for the true altitude of the sun's center editorially omitted.

[3] Number inserted by TJ in place of "37–46–56."

[4] Preceding two words interlined.

From Benjamin Austin

SIR   Boston Dec[r] 11 1815

Since the return of General Dearborne from his visit to monticello, I am highly gratify'd in hearing that you enjoy your health & that you are so happily situated in your domestic retirement.—During the convulsions of Europe, & the events which have taken place in our own Country, a person of your accurate observation must have experienced the most anxious solicitude for the result of those important controverceis.—As to France we are all disapointed in a termination of a revolution, which promised a releif from the tyranny of establishments,[1] which are advocated (even in America) as <u>legitimate</u>.— But the "ways of heaven are dark & intricate," & we are oblig'd to submit to the decrees of providence, however contrary to what we may think, are productive of the general happiness of Mankind.—As France has fallen by an Alliance of Tyrants, America must expect to rise by a Union of freemen acting in their Constitutional capacity— Their destiny is a lesson of admonition to Us.—

It must afford you the highest consolation to find, that the honor & Glory of our Country, have been promoted, by the very means which our enemies had predicted would be ruinous & destructive—nothing but the interposition of providence could have produced so much good, from what was consider'd by many, as productive of so much Evil.—The united states were compel'd into a controvercy in defence of their maritime[2] rights, which if they had faild in vindicating, would probably have check'd, if not eventually have terminated their future prosperity as a nation.—at the beginning of the conflict, the prospect was gloomy & perilous: repeated disasters almost appal'd us[3] in the prosecution, while the[4] internal Enemy were dayly becoming formidable, by every insidious management which faction could generate—amidst these complicated difficulteis, we have succeeded in our Appeal to Heaven, & every American must feel a pride, that the energeis of an administration beset with such a Phalanx of opposition, have triumph'd, not only over the forign Enemy, but baffled the efforts of a more dangerous combination of domestic Foes.[5]—As the present state of our Country demands some extraordinary efforts in Congress to bring forward the <u>Agricultural & manufacturing Interests</u> of the united States, I am induced to mention the plea often used by the freinds of England, <u>that the Work Shops of Europe are recommended by you, as the most proper to furnish Articles of manufactures to America.</u>—By which they infer, that it is Your opinion, the manufactures of this Country are not proper objects for Congressional pursuits.—They frequently enlarge on this Idea, as corresponding with your sentiments, & endeavor to weaken our efforts in this particular, by quoting you as the advocate of foreign manufactures,[6] to the exclusion of our own.—not that these persons are influenced by any generous or freindly motive towards you, but they think it will answer their purposes, if such sentiments can be promulgated with any appearance of respect to your opinion—I am sensible that they mean to misrepresent your real intentions, being convinced, that the latitude which these persons take with your <u>abstract remarks</u> on manufactures is far beyond what you orginally contemplated.[7]—A Nation whose feilds are abundantly covern'd with merino Sheep Flax & Cotton, it is hoped, will not long depend on Looms at 3000 miles distance, to furnish them with Cloathing, provided their ingenuity & enterprize are adequate to produce such necessary Articles from their internal resources, & industry.—

you will pardon my remarks, & excuse my writing you on this subject—but it would be an essential service at this Crizis, when the question of manufactures will come so powerfully before Congress by petitions from various important establishments, if you would condescend to explain more minutely your Idea of the Work Shops of Europe, in the supply of such articles as can be manufactur'd among ourselves.—As it could not be your intention to discourage all domestic manufactures, & render useless our raw materials,[8] an explanation from you on this subject would greatly contribute to the advancement of those manufactures, which have <u>now</u> riscn to a rcspectable state of maturity & improvement.[9]—If the general Idea sh^d prevail, that you prefer foreign Work Shops to domestic, the high Character you sustain among the freinds of our Country, may lead them to a discouragment of that enterprize, which is vewed by many as an essential object of our Independance—I should not have taken the freedom to suggest my Ideas, but being convinc'd of your patriotism & devotedness to the good of your Country, have urged me to make these observations.—your candor will pardon if they are incorrect.—

I should be happy in receiving a reply, for in the present state of political controvercy & intrigue, the real republicans must rely on our "<u>long tried patriots</u>" (among which you stand foremost) to guide & direct in the future pursuits of Goverment—Though retir'd from public life, yet your private Council is essential, & we must solicit your aid,[10] to substantiate[11] in Peace, what we obtain in War.—The patriot is always call'd on Duty, while the exigencies of his Country need his advice, & his exertions are requird to carry it into operation.—We are limited but to a few years to discharge our trust as Citizens, & we must become the more active as the period shortens.[12]—The old patriots if not employd in navigating the Ship, yet they are vew'd as Beacons by which the helmsmen must steer to the Haven of Safety—

Your freinds in this quarter would be highly gratify'd if it s^d be in your power to visit them in these "ends of the Earth"—Massachusetts once stood high, & was powerfull, but out of the <u>Strong</u> came forth weakness[13]—   I remain Sir

with the highest sentiments of Respect, Your undeviating freind
BENJ^N AUSTIN

PS—As I have been honord by your acceptance of a Volume of Old South, permit me to present you with the enclos'd pamphelt for your candid perusal a few corrections of the print are necessary—[14]

RC (DLC); at foot of text: "Honble Thomas Jefferson Monticello"; endorsed by TJ as received 21 Dec. 1815 and so recorded in SJL. Printed in Boston *Independent Chronicle*, 19 Feb. 1816, as a letter of 9 Dec. 1815, with only the most significant variations noted below; widely reprinted from this source in other newspapers and at least one broadside, *National Utility, in opposition to Political Controversy: Addressed to the Friends of American Manufactures* (Boston, [1816]). Enclosure: "Honestus" [Austin], *Observations on the Pernicious Practice of the Law* (Boston, 1814; Poor, *Jefferson's Library*, 10 [no. 593]).

Benjamin Austin (1752–1820), public official and author, was a native of Boston, where he became a merchant. He served as a Massachusetts state senator in 1787, 1789–94, and 1796. TJ appointed him commissioner of loans for Massachusetts in 1804, and he served until 1817. An ardent Republican, Austin was an advocate of a simplified legal system and had a strong following among Boston's artisans. He wrote under a variety of pseudonyms and corresponded occasionally with TJ on political topics (*ANB*; *DAB*; TJ to Austin, 28 June 1803 [DLC]; *JEP*, 1:475–6, 477 [30 Nov., 11 Dec. 1804]; Boston *New-England Palladium*, 11 Dec. 1804; *ASP, Finance*, 3:249; *Independent Chronicle and Boston Patriot*, 6 May 1820).

The character Portius declares that the WAYS OF HEAVEN ARE DARK & INTRICATE in act 1 of Joseph Addison, *Cato. A Tragedy* (London, 1713), 2. TJ argued in his *Notes on the State of Virginia* that WORK SHOPS and manufacturing were better suited to Europe than the United States (*Notes*, ed. Peden, 164–5). As governor of Massachusetts, Caleb STRONG supported the 1814 Hartford Convention (*ANB*). In the Bible, sweetness came forth out of the strong, not WEAKNESS (Judges 14.14). OLD SOUTH was Austin's *Constitutional Republicanism, in opposition to Fallacious Federalism; as published occasionally in the Independent Chronicle, under the Signature of Old-South* (Boston, 1803; Sowerby, no. 3534).

[1] Remainder of sentence in *Independent Chronicle* reads "which have been inconsiderately advocated in the federal papers as 'legitimate.'"

[2] Manuscript: "maritine."

[3] *Independent Chronicle*: "the timid."

[4] Remainder of sentence in *Independent Chronicle* reads "disaffected were daily attempting to counteract our national efforts, by systematic combinations, and illegitimate conventions."

[5] *Independent Chronicle* here adds "I would not wish to be censorious, but the fact is too evident to be denied. Not that we consider every *nominal* federalist was thus inimical, but the artful proceedings of certain leaders urged many *honest men* to adopt those resolutions which have produced numberless serious evils. We can easily distinguish between the *enticers* and the *enticed*."

[6] Word interlined in place of "importations."

[7] Manuscript: "contenplated." Remainder of paragraph in *Independent Chronicle* reads "The purity of your mind conld [could] not lead you to anticipate the perfidy of foreign nations, which has since taken place—If you had, it is impossible that you would have discouraged the manufactures of a nation, whose fields have since been abundantly covered with merino sheep, flax and cotton, or depended on looms at 3000 miles distance, to furnish the citizens with clothing, when their internal resources were adequate to produce such necessaries by their domestic industry."

[8] Sentence to this point not in *Independent Chronicle*.

[9] *Independent Chronicle* here adds "*Domestic* manufacture is the object contemplated; instead of establishments under the sole controul of capitalists, our children may be educated under the inspection of their parents, while the habits of industry may be duly inculcated."

[10] *Independent Chronicle* here adds "to help the administration."

[11] *Independent Chronicle* here adds "by wise measures."

[12] *Independent Chronicle* here adds "The real patriot never sacrificed principles to policy—Washington, Adams, Hancock, Madison, and yourself rose superior to such a degradation."

[13] Paragraph to this point not in *Independent Chronicle*.

[14] Preceding eight words interlined. Postscript not in *Independent Chronicle*.

From John Wayles Eppes

DEAR SIR,   Mill Brook Dec[r] 11. 1815.

Francis arrived at warren the day after you passed on your last visit to Bedford. on learning there that you had passed on instead of proceeding to Monticcllo hc rcturncd home—I was seized a few days afterwards with a violent attack of the Rheumatism and he has been detained in consequence of my indisposition much longer than I could have wished—

You can keep him at Monticello as long as you think his time can be more profitably employed there than at school—The Spring session of the school to which I propose sending him will commence in april and unless you direct otherwise I shall send for him about the first of april. This will allow four months for his French in which time I hope he will acquire an accurate pronunciation and a sufficient knowledge of the language to read it with ease—It will then only be necessary to furnish him with books in that language adopted to his capacity and Taste. With these I can easily supply him. If it would not interfere too much with your time I could wish him to keep up his latin in which indeed I fear he is not sufficiently advanced to enter the school to which I propose sending him—I fear you have undertaken a troublesome task—It is one I should certainly not have imposed on you and from which I shall feel great pleasure in relieving you whenever it becomes[1] too weighty or whenever you suppose Franciss time can be as well bestowed elsewhere—

Present my best wishes to the family and accept your self assurances of attattchment and respect—

Yours sincerely   JNO: W: EPPES

RC (ViU: TJP-ER); at foot of text: "Th: Jefferson Esqʳ"; endorsed by TJ as received 15 Dec. 1815 and so recorded in SJL.

[1] Eppes here canceled "too burthensome."

From Peter Derieux

MONSIEUR   Richmond ce 12. Decʳ 1815

N'ayant pas eu l'honneur de vous ecrire depuis plus de deux ans, par la crainte de vous importuner J'ose esperer que vous me pardonnerés de prendre aujourd'hui cette liberté, pour vous Supplier de me marquer Si les promesses que vous eutes la bonté de me faire par votre Lettre de juillet 1813. de voulloir bien user votre influence auprés de mon beau pere en ma faveur, ont eu le Succés que votre pouvoir Sur Son esprit et les grandes richesses dont on dit quil jouit maintenant me donnoient lieu d'en esperer.   Il y a tant d années, Monsieur que J'expie par mes malheurs L'erreur fatale que je commis de n'avoir pas Suivi vos conseils dans l'emploi de mon argent que j'ose esperer quen consideration des souffrances et des meaux continuels qui en sont la Suite, que vous vous dissuaderés de Lidée que vous pouvés entretenir, que je ne ferois peut etre pas un meilleur emploi des Secours qui pouroient me venir, Soyes au contraire je vous prie bien persuadé que la plus modique et permanente aisance me Seroit a present du plus grand prix, et que je n'eus jamais fait une telle fautte, Sans le motif d'ambition qui me porta a preferer le commerce, dans les Vues de pouvoir Sur les Benefices faire honneur aux engagements que j'avois, et differer jusquà lors L'etablissement d'agriculture que j'avois toujours eu contemplation. non Seulement jai perdu par la tout ce que je possedois d'effectif, mais encore par une Suite de malheurs sans exemple toutte la fortune de M^de Bellange[r] Sur laquelle mes esperances paroissoient ne pouvoir etre mieux fondées, et pour combler ma ruine Le Col Bell de Charlotte ville aprés avoir recu le montant des propriétés que j'avois laissé entre Ses mains, est mort a ce quon ma dit insolvable, Sans avoir payé un seul de mes creanciers dont le claim est de beaucoup au dessous de ce quil a touché, de maniere que de tous les cotés j'ai été malheureux et je regarderais desormais ma situation sans le moindre espoir Si la confiance que j'ose encore prendre dans vos bontés ne me per-suadoient que Si vous n'avés pu reussir dans vos premier[es] tenta-tives auprés de Mr Mazzei, vous le poures peut etre par la suite si vous voullés bien continuer de vous montre[r] desirer d'en obtenir pour nous quelques moyens qui pouroient mettre notre Vieillesse a Labri du Besoin.

quoiquil y ait prés de trois ans que nous habitons Richmond, je ne puis encore avoir la satisfaction Monsieu[r] de vous apprendre que nos exertions ayent changé notre Situation, et je vois avec regret que nous ne pouvons nous flatter d'aucune amelioration, tant que les moyens nous manqueront pour nous loger meubler et paroitre comm[e] il le faudroit dans cette ville pour obtenir une bonne Ecolle ajoutés a cela que les rentes de maisons Sont encore augmentées de ce quelles etoient Lannée dernière et que la vie est d'une Chereté exor-bitante Sans que cela occasionne la moindre augmentation dans Les prix de L'Education.

M^de Derieux a L'honneur de vous presenter Son respect et j'ai celui dêtre dans les sentiments du plus respectueux attachement, et reconnoissance.

Monsieur

Votre très humble et très obéisst Serviteur

PETER DERIEUX

EDITORS' TRANSLATION

SIR   Richmond 12. December 1815

Not having had the honor of writing to you for more than two years for fear of pestering you, I dare hope that you will forgive me for the liberty I take today in begging you to let me know if your kind promises in your let-ter of July 1813 to intercede in my favor with my father-in-law have had the success which your influence with him and the great wealth he is now said to enjoy had given me reason to expect.   Sir, I have been atoning for so many years for my fatal error in not following your advice regarding the use of my money that I dare hope that you will consider the continuous pain and suffering that resulted and reject any notion you may have that I would perhaps make no better use of the help that might now come my way. On the contrary, please be persuaded that at this time I would greatly value the most modest permanent security and that I would have never made my previous mistake had I not been motivated by an ambition that led me to prefer commerce, in the hope of using the profits to honor my engagements, and postpone the agricultural establishment I had always contemplated. In this manner I lost not only everything I owned but, through a succession of unprecedented misfortunes, I also lost the entire fortune of Madame Bellanger on which my hopes seemed to be well founded. To complete my ruin, Colonel Bell, of Charlottesville, after having received all of my remaining property, died insolvent, I have been told, without having paid a single one of my creditors, whose total claims are far less than what he received. I have thus been unfortunate all the way around and would regard my situation henceforward as hopeless if my continued trust in your kindness did not persuade me that, if you failed in your first attempts with Mr. Mazzei, you might perhaps succeed hereafter if you are willing to continue to seek some way to shelter us from want in our old age.

Although we have been living in Richmond for almost three years, I regret to inform you, Sir, that our exertions have not changed our situation. I see with regret that we cannot achieve any kind of improvement so long as we lack the means to house, furnish, and present ourselves as we should in this city in order to obtain a good school. Furthermore, the expense of renting a house has gone up again this year and the cost of living is outrageously expensive, but this has not been accompanied by the slightest rise in the price of education.

Mrs. Derieux has the honor of sending her regards, and I add mine with the most respectful attachment and gratitude.

Sir

Your very humble and very obedient servant   PETER DERIEUX

RC (DLC); edge trimmed and chipped; endorsed by TJ as received 16 Dec. 1815 and so recorded in SJL. RC (NjMoHP: Lloyd W. Smith Collection); address cover only; with PoC of TJ to Patrick Gibson, 2 Jan. 1816, on verso; addressed: "The Honble Th^s Jefferson Monticello Near Milton Albemarle Cty. Virginia"; stamp canceled; franked; postmarked Richmond, 13 Dec. Translation by Dr. Genevieve Moene.

For the bequest of Marie Françoise Plumard de BELLANGER, see note to Plumard to TJ, 12 Sept. 1810. In 1795 Derieux conveyed his Charlottesville house, land, and other assets to Thomas BELL, Robert Jouett, and Cornelius Schenk, who were to act as trustees to pay his debts. Bell died in 1800, and years later his creditors remained unpaid (Woods, *Albemarle*, 398; Albemarle Co. Deed Book, 11:360–2; Albemarle Co. Will Book, 4:146–8).

To Patrick Gibson

Dear Sir   Poplar Forest Dec. 12. 15

I shall leave this place tomorrow on my return to Monticello from which I have been absent ever since the date of mine of Oct. 28. so that if you have favored me with any line since that time it will be unrecieved until I get back. some plantation demands oblige me to draw on you this day in fav^r of A. Robertson[1] for 112.65 which I do with reluctance but of necessity.[2] within a week from this time a boat load of flour will be sent off from hence, and instantly on my return to Albemarle what I have there will go off, as it was ready for delivery when I came away, but the river too low. the weather has been so favble for handling tob° that mr Yancey who now superintends my affairs here thinks our crop will be ready to send off soon after Christmas. it is not a half one. I have great hopes that under his direction, I shall hereafter have a very different turn-out here from what I have had the last 3 or 4 y.[3] the tob° I would wish sold on it's arrival, as I know of no reason to count on a continued rise of price. the flour I would rather keep back except so far as my calls on you may render immediate sales necessary. accept assurances of my great esteem & respect

Th: Jefferson

PoC (DLC: TJ Papers, ser. 10); at foot of text: "Mr Gibson"; endorsed by TJ as a letter to Gibson & Jefferson; with part of an unrelated sketch of a geometrical figure in an unidentified hand on verso, apparently separated from remainder of this drawing on verso of PoC of TJ to Archibald Robertson, 12 Dec. 1815. Recorded in SJL as a letter to Gibson.

[1] Preceding five words interlined.
[2] Preceding three words interlined, with "necessary" deleted earlier in sentence, before "plantation demands."
[3] Preceding eleven words interlined in place of "hereafter," which TJ interlined earlier in sentence.

To Archibald Robertson

Dear Sir   Poplar Forest. Dec. 12. 15.

I now inclose you an order on Messrs Gibs. & Jeff. for 112.65 to reimburse the 45. D.   paid to mr Yancey

50. D.	cash to Jer. A. Goodman
17.65	my ord. in fav^r Cooney
112.65	

the assumpsit of Goodman's store debt to you shall be paid in the same way at the time promised, and at the same time the further sum of 69.35 for leather purchased for us at the request of mr Yancey. I expect to leave this tomorrow, and now present you the assurance of my great esteem & respect   TH: JEFFERSON

PoC (ViU: TJP); at foot of text: "Mr Archib^d Robertson"; endorsed by TJ; with part of an unrelated sketch of a geometrical figure in an unidentified hand on verso, apparently separated from remainder of this drawing on verso of PoC of TJ to Patrick Gibson, 12 Dec. 1815. Enclosure not found.

On this date TJ recorded that the enclosed order on Gibson & Jefferson covered $45 paid to Joel YANCEY for corn and that the other sums related to orders on Robertson given to Jeremiah A. GOODMAN, on 30 Nov., and to James COONEY in partial payment for a horse, on 2 Dec. (*MB*, 2:1316–7).

From Benjamin Waterhouse

DEAR SIR   Cambridge 14th Decr 1815

I received your letter of 13th Octr with pleasure, and read it with great satisfaction.—I here enclose a curious publication, printed first in Connecticut, & reprinted at Andover, 20 miles from this place, where is a new & well endowed theological college, being a splinter struck off from Cambridge, at the time when we elected an unitarian professor of divinity. Dwight of the Connecticut-College;—Morse the geographer, & Pearson, late Professor of Hebrew & oriental languages here; are the three most distinguished Cardinals; but the first has the most external, if not internal marks of being our Pope Bonaface the first. The last named gentleman has just published a sermon, bottomed on the calculations & reasonings of the Tract N° 70. here enclosed, which taken collectively, is the largest & boldest stride towards the establishment of calvinistical-popery we have yet seen.—

By this Tract you will percieve that your native State is but poorly represented in Heaven, there being "914,000^1 of her population destitute of the means of grace!"—whence we infer that "Virginia influence" scarcely extends to the New-Jerusalem:—we are also as certain, that in miserable Louisiana the people "sit in darkness, and the shadow of death^2—there being not one protestant minister within its limits."—

In the sermon above referred to, the preacher says—"I shudder when I think that the constitution of the U.S. does not recognize the being of a God, nor ever once mentions His name!"—and he might have encreased his shuddering by adding—"while every Bill of lading does."

I hope some able hand in the south will reply to this Tract N° 70. You will see by the poetry in the enclosed news-paper, that we attack this rant with other weapons beside those of serious argument. The Hartford Convention has fallen flat before the unceasing streams of ridicule, which swelled, at last, into a torrent. But it is to be lamented that those who assume the pen in the cause of truth, liberality & common sense do not exceed[3] three in number We need the aid of some of the fine spirits of the South.

The venerable Adams, who is "—a stout polemic, stubborn as a rock," has several times in years past, expressed to me his very serious apprehension of the movements of these restless, & aspiring priests. This calvinistic-junto have paid great court to the sage of Quincy, till at length he wrote Dr Morse a letter with leave to publish it, which he never will do: the substance of it has however got abroad: he tells the geographical divine that he knows more of this old controversy of trinitarianism, & of the corruptions of christianity than he does, or all his party; that he himself has always been an Unitarian. Since this letter they have ceased to burn incense under the nose of our God. <u>Terminus</u>.

This controversy has produced a strange state of things, and a queer jumble of opinions in this our American Canaan The Essex-Junto & this University are boasting of Adams & Jefferson, while their political idol Caleb Strong is a gloomy calvinist of the deepest blue connecticut dye; and it bids fair to break up their political covenant. Strong will retire; and his party will support the Republican candidate of last year, Mr S. Dexter, while the Republicans will try to carry Gen. Dearborn.—But the religious dispute is obliterating the political one; and some think the calvinists will rally under the banners of the general government. They already[4] speak of Mr Madison & Monroe with decency, while they shudder at the anti-terrific doctrines of the Junto.—It is strange, but we have a vast number of both sexes, who love to be agitated by the horrid doctrine of the eternal punishment of fire & brimstone. I however found out, while guarding Vaccination, in its disputed march through an host of enemies, that a man need not dispair making a certain class of people believe any thing but truth.—

You will find by the enclosed newspaper, that our fanaticks are attacked by other weapons than that of serious argument.

I remain with a high degree of respect your steady admirer

BENJ^N WATERHOUSE

P.S. By letters I have recently received from Mr J. Q. Adams, he says—"I do not think there is an immediate prospect of tranquility in Europe. The Allies appear to think that the dismemberment & ruin of France is indispensable for the security of the world against universal monarchy; and that to put down the Jacobins, all the Protestants in France must be St Bartholomewed; they think that to consummate the holy triumph of lawful monarchy, Religion & social order,[5] rivers of Jacobin blood must be poured forth from the scaffold. All this is the orthodox doctrine consecrated by the victory of La Belle Alliance.[6] Their alternatives are all of a nature which will require the rod of iron, the sharp pointed-rod, to carry them into effect."

RC (DLC); addressed: "Honorable Thomas Jefferson"; endorsed by TJ as received 23 Dec. 1815 and so recorded in SJL. Enclosure: Lyman Beecher, *On the Importance of Assisting Young Men of Piety and Talents in Obtaining an Education for the Gospel Ministry* (1st ed., New Haven, [1814]; 2d. ed., Andover, [1815], at head of text: "No. 70."). Other enclosure not found.

Andover Theological Seminary was a SPLINTER STRUCK OFF from Harvard University as a result of a controversy ignited when the latter institution appointed a Unitarian minister, Henry Ware, as professor of divinity in 1805 (Edwards A. Park, *The Associate Creed of Andover Theological Seminary* [1883], 13). CONNECTICUT-COLLEGE: Yale College (later Yale University). Waterhouse paraphrased quotations from pages 7 and 8 of the TRACT . . . ENCLOSED. The SERMON ABOVE REFERRED TO was Eliphalet Pearson, *A Sermon delivered in Boston before The American Society for Educating Pious Youth for the Gospel Ministry. Oct. 26, 1815* (Andover, 1815; paraphrased quotation from p. 23). As Waterhouse observed, at this time printed forms for a ship's BILL OF LADING routinely began "Shipped by the grace of God" (examples that reached TJ, dated 30 May 1816 and 24 Sept. 1819, in MHi). A STOUT POLEMIC, STUBBORN AS A ROCK paraphrases book 4, line 195, of Alexander Pope, *The Dunciad, in Four Books* (London, 1743), 172: "Each staunch Polemic, stubborn as a rock."

John Adams responded to Jedidiah Morse's *Review of American Unitarianism* (Boston, 1815) in a letter to Morse dated 15 May 1815, at the head of which Adams wrote "This letter must not be printed." Morse later explained that "a copy of your letter (not from me) has found its way on Change in Boston, and copies have been multiplied and sent into different parts of the country" (both letters transcribed in William B. Sprague, *The Life of Jedidiah Morse* [1874], 125–6). The letter Waterhouse had RECENTLY RECEIVED from John Quincy Adams was written 27 Aug. 1815 (Lb in MHi: Adams Papers; printed from this text in Worthington Chauncey Ford, ed., *Writings of John Quincy Adams* [1913–17], 5:353–7; varying substantially in organization from text as quoted by Waterhouse). Napoleon's defeat at the hamlet known as LA BELLE ALLIANCE is more commonly known as the Battle of Waterloo.

[1] Omitted opening quotation mark editorially supplied.
[2] Superfluous closing quotation mark editorially omitted.
[3] Manuscript: "exceeed," reworked from "exceed."
[4] Manuscript: "alread."
[5] Manuscript here contains an ampersand, not in the Adams letter as cited above and editorially omitted.
[6] Superfluous closing quotation mark editorially omitted.

Petition of Joseph Miller to the
Virginia General Assembly

[presented 15 Dec. 1815]

To the General assembly of the Commonwealth of Virginia the petition of Joseph Miller of the borough of Norfolk in the sd commonwealth humbly sheweth

That Frances Reed, mother of your Petitioner, having had issue by a former marriage Anne and Thomas Reed, intermarried with John Miller, father of your petitioner, and had issue Elizabeth, Aldersea, and Daniel Miller: that the said John and Frances Miller emigrated in the year[1] 1775 to Maryland, and established themselves at the town of Chester therein, with an intention of permanently remaining there, which, by the laws then existing made them citizens of Maryland:[2] that your petitioner was born in the said town of Chester, as he has ever been informed and believes, in the month of July 1776. but that his said father dying a little before or after his birth, his mother, unwilling[3] to remain alone at so great a distance from all her connections, returned with your petitioner, an infant at the breast to the place of her former residence in England: that your petitioner was brought up to the seafaring business, which he followed some years,[4] and afterwards procured himself to be instructed in the art of brewing, and carried on the business of brewing for some time in England.

That in the year 1783. his half brother Thomas Reed beforenamed emigrated to this state, became in due form a naturalized citizen thereof, and established himself in the borough of Norfolk, where he exercised for many years the trade[5] of a carpenter, and acquired by his industry and skill considerable property in lots and lands,[6] negroes, and other articles in the sd borough and it's vicinity: that being seised and possessed thereof he departed this life on the 10th day of November 1809. having first made his last will & testament, wherein he devised all his property to his[7] brothers and sisters aforesaid of the whole and half blood, and to a certain Mary Longcake his god-daughter, assigning to each a specific and definite portion thereof: and of the sd will he made Findlay Ferguson and Joseph Hays executors, as by the same,[8] duly proved and recorded in the Hustings court of the said borough will fully appear: that on recieving information of his death, your petitioner determined to return to this country permanently to reside therein, and the other devisees not being so disposed, he purchased from them their portions of his said brother's property, to wit, from his sisters and brothers[9] Anne,[10]

Elizabeth, Aldersea, and Daniel, and from the said Mary Longcake, paying them for the same the sum of 450. pounds sterling, which with the costs of conveyance[11] and other charges and expences was raised in the end to[12] nearly 600. pounds sterling, as by their deeds, duly executed and proved, and by other documents[13] will appear: that your petitioner took his passage, in the Lydia, an American vessel, bound to Norfolk, a rumor then prevailing indeed, but not fully credited,[14] that war had been declared by the United States against England: that he sailed on the 21st of October 1812. in the said ship Lydia, was taken first by a French privateer, and after long detention discharged; a second time by the Plantagenet, and a third time by the Juno, British ships of war, and in like manner, after long detentions by them, permitted to proceed, insomuch that the Lydia did not arrive in the bay of[15] Chesapeak until February 1813. where she was immediately brought to by the British blockading squadron, prohibited from going into port, and ordered again to sea: that they left the capes of Chesapeak and endeavored to make a Northern port, but being overtaken by a storm they were cast away near Lewis town, and their ship totally lost: that your petitioner thence made his way, sometimes by land, sometimes by water, and reached Norfolk on[16] the 4th or 5th of April: that on the day of his[17] arrival there he was warned by the deputy marshal to leave the place immediately and to repair to Fluvanna court house, in the interior of the country: that having obtained leave to remain only[18] until he could get some[19] linen washed, but without permission to quit the house, or to look after his property, he departed at the end of three days for Fluvanna court house, and being refused reception, on account of the sickness of the family residing there,[20] he went to Charlottesville in the county of Albemarle, where he continued under the approbation and orders of the Marshal of the state: that he then applied to the Marshal claiming his rights as a native citizen under the law which declares all free persons born within the state to be citizens, and the constitution of the United states, which gives to the citizens of each state the rights & privileges of citizens in the several states, and claiming the said rights moreover[21] as the son of one who had been a citizen, under the law of the US. of 1802. which declares that the children of persons who have been citizens of the US. shall be considered as citizens, tho' born out of their limits: that by the kind indulgence of the Marshal he was permitted to go to Norfolk to take order respecting his property, and to remain there until further orders, and also to proceed to Chester town in Maryland to procure testimony of the residence of his father, and of his own birth in that place: that on proceeding thither, he found that his parents having resided there but a short time before the death of his father and removal of his mother,[22] they had probably become known to few, that of these some had died, some had removed away, and in fact that in the course of the 38. years which had elapsed, and of the two wars which had intervened,[23] a new generation had taken place of the former, insomuch that no certain[24] vestiges of his family could be traced: that as soon therefore as the Proclamation of peace appeared, he took the regular measures for his own re-naturalisation by taking, on the 13th of March 1815. before the county court of Nansemond, the oath of fidelity to the US. and abjuration of all other allegiances as directed by law, and has continued to exercise in the sd borough of Norfolk[25] his calling of a brewer, which he had before begun there: that some of the buildings which had belonged to his said brother the testator being in imminent danger of ruin for want of repairs, your petitioner, at great expence, has had them repaired, and put into a state of preservation.

That notwithstanding the just claims of your petitioner, as before stated, to the inheritance of his brother, it has been suggested by some that these may be questioned and disturbed, and that it is advisable to apply to this honorable body to quiet and assure the same: in consideration therefore of all the premisses, and particularly of the citizenship acquired by the residence and death of his father in the United states, of your petitioner's own right either as a native citizen, or as the child of one who had been a resident; of the naturalisation of his brother the testator, and his just right of bequeathing the fruits of his industry among his nearest relations, of the misfortune of the loss of testimony by the lapse of time, the accidents of war,[26] by deaths, removals and other human casualties, of the great sum of money paid by your petitioner for the rights of the other devisees, and for repairs and preservation of the property, a great sum indeed for your petitioner, the earnings of his own industry, as being poor, and without other resources than the labor of his hands, and that the property passing to him from his brother is but the ordinary and daily[27] case of a transfer from one citizen to another, and to one too, in this case, who by the exercise of an useful and wholesome art hopes to be not altogether unprofitable to the country of his birth and choice; your petitioner consequently[28] prays that the General assembly will be pleased to confirm by a law the will of his said brother the testator, to confirm and quiet the rights of your petitioner regularly derived therefrom, and generally authorising the executors and all others to carry the same into full effect, and giving validity to all acts done or to be done for that purpose; and your petitioner, as in duty bound, shall ever pray E[t]c.

JOSEPH MILLER

MS (Vi: RG 78, Legislative Petitions, Norfolk Borough); in TJ's hand, signed by Miller; undated; endorsed in a clerk's hand: "<Thomas> Joseph Miller's Petition.—Dec[r] 15th 1815. ref[d] to C[ts] of J. [the Committee for Courts of Justice]" and in another hand: "Reasonable   to confirm a title to land purchased of aliens." Dft (DLC: TJ Papers, 209:37336); in TJ's hand; on reused address cover to TJ; un- ·dated; endorsed by TJ: "Miller Joseph."

Thomas Reed's LAST WILL & TESTA- MENT was recorded on 28 Dec. 1809 (Norfolk City Hustings and Corporation Court Will Book, 2:452–3). The DEEDS of lease and release conveying Reed's property from Miller's half sibling Anne Reed Irving; his siblings Aldersea Miller, Elizabeth Miller, and Daniel Miller; and Reed's goddaughter Mary Longcake were signed in September and October 1812, prior to Miller's departure from England for the United States. They were produced, proved, and recorded in Nor- folk on 26 May 1817 (Norfolk City Hus- tings and Corporation Court Deed Book, 14:41–55).

Andrew Moore was the MARSHAL OF THE STATE, and the DEPUTY MARSHAL was William Mann.

For the LAW WHICH DECLARES ALL FREE PERSONS BORN WITHIN THE STATE TO BE CITIZENS, see Acts of As- sembly (1786–87 sess.), 12–4. For TJ's role in drafting this legislation, see PTJ, 2:476–9. Article 4, section 2 of the CON- STITUTION OF THE UNITED STATES states that "The citizens of each state shall be entitled to all privileges and immuni- ties of citizens in the several states." The LAW OF THE US. OF 1802, passed 14 Apr. 1802, was "An Act to establish an uni- form rule of Naturalization, and to repeal the acts heretofore passed on that subject" (U.S. Statutes at Large, 2:153–5). On 9 Feb. 1816 the General Assembly did CONFIRM BY A LAW Miller's rights by passing "An Act vesting in Joseph Miller the Commonwealth's right to the real and personal estate of which Thomas Reed

died seised and possessed" (Acts of As- sembly [1815–16 sess.], 251).

[1] Paragraph to this point heavily re- worked in Dft, with clean version rewrit- ten in margin, differing mainly from MS in describing John Miller as "then of Carlisle in the kdom of England" at the time of his emigration.

[2] Preceding eleven words interlined in Dft.

[3] Word interlined in Dft in place of "fearing."

[4] Dft here adds "in the commerce be- tween Gr. Britain & these US. and other countries."

[5] Preceding five words interlined in Dft in place of "the business."

[6] Dft here adds "houses."

[7] In Dft TJ here canceled "sister Anne of the whole blood."

[8] Preceding seventeen words interlined in Dft in place of "his property, as by the sd will."

[9] Preceding three words interlined in Dft in place of "the sd."

[10] In Dft TJ here canceled "Mary."

[11] Word interlined in Dft in place of "deeds."

[12] Reworked in Dft from "other nes- sary [necessary] expenses amounted to."

[13] Phrase to this point interlined in Dft, with "by" omitted.

[14] Preceding four words interlined in Dft, as "but <which was> not generally <believed> credited."

[15] Preceding two words interlined in Dft.

[16] Word interlined in Dft in place of "about."

[17] Reworked in Dft from "that instant- ly on his."

[18] Word interlined in Dft.

[19] Word interlined in Dft in place of "his."

[20] Preceding two words interlined in Dft.

[21] Preceding six words not in Dft, in which text from this point to "out of their limits" is interlined earlier, after "within the state to be citizens."

22 Preceding five words interlined in Dft.

23 Preceding eight words interlined in Dft.

24 Word interlined in Dft.

25 Preceding six words interlined in Dft.

26 Preceding four words interlined in Dft.

27 Preceding two words interlined in Dft.

28 Word interlined in Dft.

To Fanny Brand

MADAM   Monticello Dec. 16. 15

I was unfortunately from home when you were so kind as to send information of your having cyder to spare. I returned yesterday only, and now send the bearer to ask the favor of some samples of your best casks of cyder. he carries 6. phials with numbers on their corks, and if you will be so good as to give a sample from each good cask, and number the cask correspondingly with the number on the vial into which it's sample is put, I can chuse with certainty what I prefer. if your cyder is as good as what I had before I shall willingly take two or three hundred gallons. [the] quantity will depend on the quality   I am Madam

Your most obed^t serv^t   TH: JEFFERSON

PoC (MHi); on verso of reused address cover to TJ; mutilated at seal; at foot of text: "Mrs Brand"; endorsed by TJ as a letter to "Brand Fanny" and so recorded in SJL.

Fanny (Frances) Whitlock Brand (1755–1832) was born in Hanover County. She married Joseph Brand and lived at Findowrie, between Cismont and Campbell in Albemarle County. At the time of her death Brand owned personal property valued at $3,650, including nine slaves (Mabel Thacher Rosemary Washburn, *The Virginia Brand-Meriwether*

Genealogy [1948], 10–1, 24; Brand family Bible record [photocopy of transcript in TJ Editorial Files]; Marcia Joseph, "Findowrie, Albemarle County" [1994], unpublished research paper in ViU; Brand to TJ, 23 Feb. 1818; DNA: RG 29, CS, Albemarle Co., 1820, 1830; *Richmond Enquirer*, 30 Nov. 1832; Albemarle Co. Will Book, 11:118–20, 334–5, 14:469–70).

On 24 Dec. 1815 TJ sent Brand $28.50 for CYDER. Although the amount purchased in this instance is uncertain, two days earlier Charles Massie sold TJ 143 gallons of cider for $25 (*MB*, 2:1317).

From Sarah Bowdoin Dearborn

Boston 16 Decr 1815.

Mrs Dearborn's respectful Compliments to Mr Jefferson, recollecting his wish to have some of the seed of the winter Squash—She requested her Son Brigadier General Dearborn to procure some for him—he has put up some of several sorts which he says are very good. M^rs D— hopes Mr Jefferson will be successful in raising them, and that they will be agreable to him—the <u>winter</u> Squash must <u>not</u> be <u>gathered</u> <u>until</u> they are <u>ripe</u>.

M^rs D— encloses a letter for Mrs Randolph—She hopes she need not assure Mr Jefferson that it would afford her Husband, & herself much pleasure to see him, & their Monticello friends in Boston.

RC (MHi); dateline at foot of text; endorsed by TJ; unrelated calculations by TJ on verso. Recorded in SJL as received 2 Jan. 1816. Enclosure not found.

To John F. Oliveira Fernandes

DEAR SIR   Monticello Dec. 16. 15.

Disappointments in procuring supplies have at length left me without a drop of wine. I must therefore request you to send me a quarter cask of the best you have. Termo is what I would prefer; and next to that good port. besides the exorbitance of price to which Madeira has got, it is a wine which I do not drink, being entirely too powerful. wine from long habit has become an indispensable for my health, which is now suffering by it's disuse. this urges me to request the immediate forwarding what is now desired to Messrs Gibson and Jefferson of Richmond to whom I now write to pay your draught for the amount at sight. should you have no sound wine of the characters I have named, my necessity obliges me to ask the favor of you to get any person in Norfolk who has such as you can recommend to forward me the supply, whose draught on your letter of advice to Gibson & Jefferson will be instantly paid. the wine should be in a double cask to prevent adulteration.

I have had the happiness of possessing here two or three times your most learned and amiable[1] countryman Correa di Serra. he left us a few days ago; but I hope to have him here again in the spring. it would double the pleasure were curiosity or any other motive to induce you to visit this part of the country & meet him here. I think you should see something of the interior of our country.

I salute you with assurances of great esteem & respect.

TH: JEFFERSON

PoC (DLC); on verso of reused address cover of a letter to TJ addressed by James Ligon; at foot of text: "Dr Fernandes"; endorsed by TJ.

John Francisco Oliveira Fernandes (1761–1829), physician, wine merchant, and diplomat, was a native of the Madeira Islands. He earned a medical degree from the University of Coimbra in 1785 and practiced medicine in Lisbon. After an 1803 gift of lands from the prince regent of Portugal (later King John VI), he added Fernandes to his name. Soon thereafter, to help his friend the prince regent avoid a scandal, Oliveira Fernandes ostensibly kidnapped the prince's supposed mistress and was duly sentenced to death. Oliveira Fernandes fled to the United States in 1803, settled in Norfolk, and established himself as a physician and a wine importer, operating first under the name Oliveira Fernandes & Company and by 1810 as Oliveira & Sons. He was active in the Catholic church in Norfolk, where he lobbied for greater lay authority. TJ met Oliveira Fernandes in November 1803 and began buying wine from him two years later. The two corresponded on the subject of wine, and Oliveira Fernandes sent TJ a walking stick in 1805.

His death sentence was overturned in 1820, and he served successively as Portuguese minister plenipotentiary to England, as ambassador to France, and as a representative of the Madeira Islands in the Portuguese parliament. Oliveira Fernandes died in Lisbon (*Grande Enciclopédia Portuguesa e Brasileira* [1935–60], 19:374–5; Patrick W. Carey, "John F. O. Fernandez: Enlightened Lay Catholic Reformer, 1815–1820," *Review of Politics* 43 [1981]: 112–29; *MB*; TJ to Oliveira Fernandes, 4 Jan. 1805 [DLC]; Stein, *Worlds*, 428; *The Norfolk Directory* [Norfolk, 1806], 15, 25; Madison, *Papers, Pres. Ser.*, 2:594, 3:1; Oliveira Fernandes, *Letter, Addressed to the Most Reverend Leonard Neale, Arch Bishop of Baltimore* [Norfolk?, 1816]; DNA: RG 29, CS, Norfolk Borough, 1820).

[1] Reworked from "able."

From Amos J. Cook

Sɪʀ,   Fryeburg, December 18. 1815.

It is customary in this northern section of our country to connect with the more important seminaries of learning a Museum of natural and artificial curiosities. Such a connexion is deemed both pleasing and useful.—We have an Academy in this town, endowed with a capital, which affords an annual interest of about $800. out of which a Preceptor (and a Preceptress, during the summer quarters) is supported. An apartment is reserved for a Library, and whatever may be rare and gratify the virtuoso.—We have already obtained by benefactions 150 Vols. of books; a variety of minerals from the Derbyshire mines in England; and some, which are peculiar to America; pipes of different qualities and sizes, detached parts of dress from many tribes of Indians, &c.—We are now availing ourselves of a specimen of the hand-writing of a number of our most eminent Characters. Mr. Adams of Quincy, Mass. a former President of the United States, has complied with our wishes in sending for the above purpose, the following Latin verses, copied by his own hand from over the door of a Monk in Spain.

Si tibi pulcra domus, Si splendida mensa, quid inde?
Si species auri atque argenti massa, quid inde?

Si tibi sponsa decens, si sit generosa; quid inde?
Si tibi sint nati, si praedia magna, quid inde?
Si fueris pulcher, fortis, divesve, quid inde?
Longus Servorum, si serviat ordo; quid inde?
Si doceas alios in qualibet arte; quid inde?
Si rideat mundus; si prospera cuncta; quid inde?
Si Prior, aut Abbas; si Rex, si Papa; quid inde?
Si rota fortunae, te tollat ad astra; quid inde?
Annis si foelix regnes mille, quid inde?
Tam cito praetereunt, haec omnia, quae nihil inde?
Sola manet virtus, quâ glorificabimur inde:
Ergo De[o][1] servi; quia sat tibi provenit inde,
Quod fecisse volens in tempore quo morieris
Hoc facias juvenis, dum corpore sanus haberis.
Quod nobis concedas Deus noster. Amen.—

Although, in our English tongue, it may appear difficult to give an elegant and literal translation of this piece "of purer morality than elegant Latinity," a gentleman of our village has favored me with the following imitation.

> Tho' pleasure may your steps attend
> And love and wine their joys may blend
> And fortune add a faithful friend;
> _____What then?
>
> Thievish time may cease his stealth,
> Age may bloom in rosy health
> And avarice wallow in his wealth;
> _____What then?
>
> While laurel wreaths his brows surround,
> Ambition is with empire crown'd,
> Time its space and earth its bound;
> _____What then?
>
> Should death relenting, cease to doom
> Youth and beauty to the tomb,
> In all the pride of early bloom;
> _____What then?
>
> All nothing;—Power is but a name,
> Pleasure is a taper's flame,
> Dirt is wealth, and breath is fame;
> _____What then?

O then, in truth's delightful bowers,
Deck'd with amaranthine flowers,
Strive as joy wings all the hours
> To live.

O then, in virtue seek the charm,
Life's goods to crown and ills disarm,
And teach, at last, without alarm,
> To die.

I am aware, Sir, that the scene of our Instituti[on] [...] from you, but not beyond the reach of your fostering hand. The influence of the benevolent mind is not confined within the bounds of a single State or kingdom, but will be extended to promote the interest of the great family of man.—Whatever you may have to bestow on us, in behalf of science and literature will be gratefully received and acknowledged.— A piece of your hand-writing (and in Latin for our translation, if you think proper) I hope you will be pleased to grant; and in the meantime to accept the friendly salutations of respect from your obedient humble servant, AMOS J. COOK,
Preceptor of Fryeburg Academy
in the District of Maine.—

P.S. Perhaps you may be able to furnish us a piece of the late George Washington's hand-writing

RC (MHi); mutilated at seal; postscript adjacent to signature; addressed: "Thomas Jefferson, L.L.D. Late Pres^t of the U. States—Monticello. Virginia"; franked; postmarked Fryeburg, Me., 8 Jan.; endorsed by TJ as received 17 Jan. 1816 and so recorded in SJL.

Amos Jones Cook (1778–1836), educator, was a native of Westminster, Massachusetts. He studied divinity and earned an A.B. at Dartmouth College in 1802. Cook succeeded Daniel Webster as preceptor of Fryeburg Academy in the district (later state) of Maine, serving for most of the years 1802–33. He was a missionary for the Bible Society of Massachusetts, a Mason, and the author of a textbook. Cook died in Fryeburg (*Vital Records of Templeton, Massachusetts, To the end of the year 1849* [1907], 19; George T. Chapman, *Sketches of the Alumni of Dartmouth College, from the first graduation in 1771 to the present time,* with a brief history of the institution [1867], 107; Boston *Mercury and New-England Palladium,* 3 Sept. 1802; Portland, Me., *Eastern Argus,* 13 Sept. 1804; Walpole, N.H., *Political Observatory,* 7 Sept. 1805; *Fryeburg Webster Centennial, Celebrating the coming of Daniel Webster to Fryeburg, 100 years ago* [1902], 46, 58–62, 70; James T. Champlin, "Educational Institutions in Maine, While a District of Massachusetts," in Maine Historical Society, *Collections* 8 [1881]: 163; Jedidiah Morse, *Signs of the Times. a Sermon* [Charlestown, Mass., 1810], 70; Cook, *The Student's Companion* [Portland, 1812]; Concord *New-Hampshire Statesman and State Journal,* 23 Apr. 1836).

John Adams copied the LATIN VERSES in December 1779 while in Corunna, Spain, and he sent them to Cook in 1807 (Lyman H. Butterfield and others, eds., *Diary and Autobiography of John Adams* [1961], 2:411–2; Adams to Cook, 30 Nov.

1807 [Lb in MHi: Adams Papers]). Adams commented that the verses were characterized by PURER MORALITY THAN ELEGANT LATINITY in a letter to Cook of 4 Jan. 1809 in which Adams also praised the loose, poetic English translation by the then eighteen-year-old Thomas Fes-

senden given above (*Fryeburg Webster Centennial*, 59). The FRYEBURG ACADE-MY was incorporated in 1792 (*Acts and Laws, Passed by the General Court of Massachusetts* [Boston, 1792], 132–4).

[1] Word obscured by ink stain.

To Charles Massie

SIR   Monticello Dec. 18. 15.

I had left home when your answer to my letter came and altho mr Bacon forwarded it, I have never got it. he says however that he engaged what cyder you had left and that you would either deliver it at your own house or at Charlottesville. the latter will suit me best and on notice of it's being there I can send for it immediately or it may be delivered there to mr James Leitch for me whom I will desire to pay you the cost of it. Accept my best wishes and respects

TH: JE[FFERSON]

PoC (MHi); on verso of reused address cover of Thomas Appleton to TJ, 26 Aug. 1815; torn at seal; endorsed by TJ as a letter to "Massie Charles."

Massie's ANSWER to TJ's letter of 24 [Oct.] 1815 is not recorded in SJL and has not been found.

From André Thoüin

MONSIEUR ET VÉNÉRABLE COLLÈGUE,   Paris le 18. X^bre 1815.

Permettez-moi de vous présenter un de nos Savans confrères, Mr Lakanal, membre dela classe d'histoire et de Littérature Ancienne de notre institut; homme recommandable par Sa moralité autant que par ses connaissances et aux quels nos institutions Scientifiques ont de grandes obligations. Il quitte notre vieille Europe, dans laquelle la civilisation va en retrogradant, pour Se fixer lui et plusieurs de ses amis dans la jeune Amérique, appellée à de si hautes destinées et où déjà l'organisation sociale offre à Ses heureux habitans la liberté, la tranquillité et le bonheur. Il emporte avec lui des capitaux asséz considérables pour établir Sa fortune et la rendre indépendante; mais ce qui vaut mieux pour Ses nouveaux concitoyens, Sont le grand nombre de connaissances et le fonds de philosophie dont il est en possession.

Veuillez, je vous prie, accueillir Mr Lakanal, lui donner les conseils dont il a besoin dans Sa nouvelle carrière et lui rendre les Services dont il pourra avoir besoin. Vous obligerez un galant homme qui vous en aura ainsi que moi la plus Sincère et la plus durable obligation.

Recevez je vous prie Monsieur et vénérable collègue L'expression de mon très respectueux attachement   THOÜIN

SIR AND VENERABLE COLLEAGUE,   Paris 18. December 1815.
Allow me to introduce to you one of our learned fellow members, Mr. Lakanal, a member of the class of history and ancient literature at our institute; this man is recommended for his morality as well as for his knowledge, and our scientific institutions owe much to him. He is leaving our old Europe, where civilization is regressing, to settle with several of his friends in young America, which is destined for great things, and where the organization of society offers its fortunate inhabitants liberty, tranquility, and happiness. He is taking with him a rather considerable capital, enough to establish his fortune and become financially independent, but what will be most valuable to his new fellow citizens is the great variety of knowledge and understanding of philosophy he has mastered.

Please be so kind as to welcome Mr. Lakanal, give him the advice he will need in his new career, and help him in whatever way he might need. You will thereby oblige a gentleman who will join me in most sincere and lasting gratitude.

Please accept, Sir and venerable colleague, the expression of my respectful attachment   THOÜIN

RC (DLC); on printed letterhead of the "Administration du Muséum d'Histoire Naturelle, au Jardin du Roi"; endorsed by TJ as received 1 July 1816, but probably received with its covering letter on 10 July. Translation by Dr. Genevieve Moene. Enclosed in Joseph Lakanal to TJ, 1 June 1816.

Joseph Lakanal (1762–1845) was a native of southern France who changed his name from Lacanal to distinguish himself from his royalist relatives. He trained for the Catholic priesthood and served as a teacher of rhetoric and philosophy at various schools before he became involved in revolutionary politics. Elected to the National Convention in 1792, Lakanal voted for the execution of Louis XVI the following year. He worked for educational reform in France and was elected president of the Committee of Public Instruction in 1794. After Napoleon came to power, Lakanal held a series of minor teaching and administrative positions. As inspector of weights and measures, 1809–15, he was charged with implementing the metric system. Lakanal immigrated to America in 1816 following the restoration of Louis XVIII and lived in Kentucky for six years. In 1817 he was involved in a plot to free Napoleon from exile. Lakanal moved to New Orleans in 1822 and served as president of Orleans College for about a year before moving to Mobile, Alabama. In 1837 he returned to France, where he died. Lakanal was a member of both the Institut de France and the Légion d'honneur (John Charles Dawson, *Lakanal the Regicide: A Biographical and Historical Study of the Career of Joseph Lakanal* [1948]; Hoefer, *Nouv. biog. générale*, 27:931–5; *ASP, Public Lands*, 4:149–50; Lakanal, *Exposé Sommaire des Travaux de Joseph Lakanal* [1838]; gravestone inscription in Cimetière du Père Lachaise, Paris).

From James Gibbon

SIR   Custom House Richmond Decr 19. 1815

a Small bundle has been sent to the Custom house directed for you, to my care;

I learn from the Capt of the Ship Imogen which arve'd recently from Cadiz that it contains a specimen of refin'd sugar put in his Charge by the Consull Mr Hackley—

It appearing[1] on the Ships manifest makes it necessary, I shou'd render some acc[t] of it but as I am unwilling to open it; it is left subject to y[r] order: with a request that you will state y[e] contents; if sugar it will only be necessary to say so, as the quantity, from its size, must be too inconsiderable as an object of duty, were it admissible. which it is not, by law—

I have the honor to be very Resp[c] Y[o] M[o] Ob[t]

J GIBBON Cole[r]

I know of no means of forwarding it or I wou'd do so—

RC (DLC); dateline adjacent to signature; endorsed by TJ as received 23 Dec. 1815 and so recorded in SJL.

[1] Manuscript: "appeaing."

From Charles Massie

DEAR SIR   Albemarle 19 De[r] 15

I do not recollect makeing any other arangment with M[r] Bacon then a complyance with your first which would have been most convenient for me on account of the Casks—However it will be a great pleasure to me, to furnish you with the best Cider that I have got. And will endeavour to deliver it at M[r] Leatch,s on friday next. this I may fail to do in consequence of two of my Wagon horses being Verry lame at present. at any rate it will be there in a few days shall be obligd to send it in two tirces which will contain two kinds[1] which will contain more then you first wrote for I must enjoin upon you to return my Casks when empty in the course of next spring or summer to the care of M[r] J. Winn. Ch[e]—I am Sir with the highest[2] esteem Respectfully Yours &c.   CHARLES MASSIE—

RC (MHi); addressed: "M[r] T. Jefferson Esq[r] Monticello"; endorsed by TJ as received 19 Dec. 1815 and so recorded in SJL.

TJ paid Massie $25 for cider and delivery on 22 Dec. 1815, which was the next FRIDAY (*MB*, 2:1317). Tierces (TIRCES) are equal to one-third of a pipe (*OED*). CHᴱ: Charlottesville.

[1] Preceding five words interlined.
[2] Manuscript: "highes."

From Joseph Delaplaine

DEAR SIR,   Philadelphia December 20ʰ 1815
I have taken the liberty of enclosing the last edition of the prospectus of my work. By it you will perceive that the Repository will be soon published. The Biography of each character is preparing. My principal object in writing now, is to request your opinion respecting the extent of the biography. Should a Biography be a concise statement of facts and nothing more, or should it be embellished?—
One other thing. Is it your opinion that living characters (particularly selected) may be given?—
Ve[spu]cius from the engraving you did me the ho[nor to] send to me, is nearly finished, & will be exquisitely executed.—
Hoping to be favoured with a letter soon, I remain
Dʳ sir, with perfect respect & esteem your obedᵗ sᵗ
JOSEPH DELAPLAINE

RC (DLC); mutilated at seal; addressed: "Thomas Jefferson Esqʳ Monticello Virginia"; franked; postmarked Philadelphia, 21 Dec.; endorsed by TJ. Recorded in SJL as received 2 Jan. 1816.

The enclosed PROSPECTUS for *Delaplaine's Repository* may have been identical to that enclosed in Delaplaine's letters to TJ of 14 and 27 Jan. 1816.

From Pierre Samuel Du Pont de Nemours

TRÈS RESPECTABLE AMI,   Washington city 20 Xᵇʳᵉ 1815.
vous aurez compris à quel point, malgré les bontés dont Madame votre Fille nous a comblés, j'ai regretté de ne vous avoir pas vu dans votre Palais de Mounticello.
Si vous y avez lu le mémoire pour les Républiques Equinoxiales, je vous Serais obligé de me le renvoyer, ou directement Si votre franchise de ports de lettre S'étend à ce pouvoir, ou par l'intermédiaire

Soit de Monsieur le Président, soit de Monsieur le Secretaire d'Etat, qui me le feraient passer Sous leur Contreseing.

Je vous en renverrai un autre[1] exemplaire que je fais copier Sur la minute.

mais j'aurais besoin de donner celui là à don Pedro Gual[2] envoyé au Etats Unis par les Républiques[3] qui m'ont consulté et qui Sont réunies Sous le nom de la nouvelle Grenade. Il est possible que le Général Palacios n'ait pas reçu un Seul des deux Exemplaires que je lui ai adressés; et l'occasion d'en remettre un troisieme en main propre à un agent civil de ces Républiques n'est pas à negliger.

Je présente mon respect à Madame Randolph, à toutes Ses belles et grandes dames et demoiselles, et même à Miss Septimia, qu'il faut que j'appelle aussi dans votre étrange et dèraisonnable langue anglaise your great-daughter, quoiqu'elle Soit une très petite fille et meme une des plus jolies petites filles que dieu ait créés.

Je vous embrasse avec respect et tendresse

Du Pont (de Nemours)

nous partirons demain de Washington. Correa Sera chez nous a Eleutherian Mill le 1er Janvier. Nous y boirons à votre Santé avec autant de veneration que d'attachement.

21 Xbre Monsieur le President, et Monsieur le Ministre de la Marine viennent d'accorder à mon Petit Fils la place de Midshipman que nous désirions pour lui

Il devient donc inutile que vous employiez pour cela votre bonté, et nous n'en Sommes pas moins reconnaissans.

EDITORS' TRANSLATION

VERY RESPECTABLE FRIEND,   Washington city 20 December 1815.
You will have understood how much, despite the acts of kindness showered on us by Madame your daughter, I have regretted not seeing you at your palace of Monticello.

If you have read the "Mémoire aux républiques équinoxiales," I would be grateful if you could send it back to me, either directly if your franking privilege allows it, or through either the president or the secretary of state, who could get it to me under their countersignatures.

I will send you another copy of it which I am having prepared right now.

But I need to give the former one to Don Pedro Gual, who has been sent to the United States by the republics that consulted me and that are united as New Granada. It may be that General Palacio has not received either of the two copies I sent him; and the opportunity of transmitting one personally to a civil officer of these republics is not to be neglected.

I send my regards to Mrs. Randolph, to all her beautiful grown-up and young ladies, and even to Miss Septimia, whom in your strange and unreasonable English language I have to call your <u>great-daughter</u>, even though she is <u>a very little girl</u> and <u>one of the prettiest little girls</u> God has created.

I embrace you with respect and tenderness

Du Pont (de Nemours)

We will leave Washington tomorrow. Corrêa will be at our house at <u>Eleutherian Mill</u> on 1 January. We will drink your health there with much veneration and attachment.

21 December. The president and the secretary of the navy just granted my grandson the position of midshipman that we wished him to have.

You need not therefore exert yourself on this account, but we are no less grateful.

RC (DLC); at head of text: "a Monsieur Jefferson"; endorsed by TJ. Tr (DeGH: H. A. Du Pont Papers, Winterthur Manuscripts); posthumous copy. Translation by Dr. Genevieve Moene. Recorded in SJL as received 2 Jan. 1816.

after the Spanish recaptured Cartagena and Bogotá in 1815–16 (Harold A. Bierck Jr., "Pedro Gual and the Patriot Effort to Capture a Mexican Port, 1816," *Hispanic American Historical Review* 27 [1947]: 456–7).

PEDRO GUAL had arrived in Washington in August 1815 as a representative to the United States from the Confederation of New Granada. He lost his standing

[1] Manuscript: "autr."

[2] Preceding four words interlined.

[3] Preceding two words interlined in place of "celles" ("those").

From James Gibbon

SIR   Richmond Decr 22. 1815

Coll. T. Randolph will convey to you ye small parcell spoke of to you in my letter a few days past;

The Cap^tn who brought it, says it is sugar made by the Indians of Venezula and is intended as a subject of information—   I am very Resp^ly

Y^o M^o Ob   J Gibbon

RC (DLC); dateline at foot of text; endorsed by TJ as received 27 Dec. 1815 and so recorded in SJL.

From Patrick Gibson

SIR   Richmond 22nd Decem^r 1815

I have received your favor of the 12th Inst and shall attend to your draft in favor of A. Robertson In your letters of the 20 & 28th Octr you mention a boat load of flour having been sent off on your account

on that head I have only to say that I have not yet received one barrel—about that time I sold at $9\frac{1}{4}$$, now it is offering at 8$, altho not
by myself as I think it must be higher towards Spring, if my accounts
from Spain be correct—Altho your note in bank is not due until the
19th of next month, yet as a precautionary measure I now inclose you
one for your signature—Tobacco is surely beyond all reasonable calculation, from 15 to 30$ according to quality—

    With great esteem & respect I am Your ob Servt

PATRICK GIBSON

R Patterson of Philada has sent to my care an Astronomical timepiece
in two boxes, as great care is necessary in the transportation of it, you
will be pleased to direct by whom it must be sent—I have just seen
Mr Randolph who has advised their being sent up by his boatman
Harry, who has charge of them

RC (MHi); between dateline and salutation: "Thomas Jefferson Esqre"; endorsed by TJ as received 27 Dec. 1815
and so recorded in SJL. Enclosure not
found.

TJ had mentioned the boatload of flour
shipped to his account by Thomas Eston
Randolph and Thomas Mann Randolph
in his letters to Gibson of 17 and 28TH
OCTR but not in his letter of 20 Oct. 1815.

To James Madison

DEAR SIR   Monticello Dec. 22. 15.

    Declining in every possible case to harrass you with sollicitations
for office, I yet venture to do it in cases of science and of great merit,
because in so doing I am sure I consult your partialities as well as my
own. mr Hassler furnishes an occasion of doing this. you will find his
character, his situation and claims stated in the inclosed letter from
Rob. Patterson, whose integrity & qualifications to judge of mr Hassler's merit cannot need any additional testimony from me, altho' I
conscientiously join my opinions & wishes to his.

    The case of Dupont, the grandson I have warmly at heart. the fa-
ther has merit for his establishments of gunpowder & of broadcloth.
but no foreigner stands more prominently for us than the grandfather. he has been intimately known to me 30. years, and during that
time I can testify that there has been no more zealous American out
of America. from 1784. to 1789. while at the head of a bureau of commerce in France I was under infinite obligations to him for patronis-
ing in every way in his power[1] our commercial intercourse with
France. I considered him as among the ablest and most honest men
in France, & in the foremost rank of their science: but all this is so

well known to yourself, as he is also personally, that my dwelling on it is merely to gratify my own affections.

I inclose a letter from mr Spafford who being personally known to you, and not to myself I forward it merely ut valeat quantum valere debet. God bless you and aid you in the numerous good things you have brought under the notice of the present legislature

TH: JEFFERSON

RC (DLC: Madison Papers); at foot of text: "The President of the US."; endorsed by Madison. PoC (DLC); on verso of reused address cover of Mary Blair Andrews to TJ, 16 Oct. 1815; mutilated at seal; endorsed by TJ. Enclosures: (1) Robert Patterson to TJ, 2 Dec. 1815. (2) Victor du Pont's Notes on Samuel F. Du Pont, [ca. 7 Dec. 1815] (see Pierre

Samuel Du Pont de Nemours to TJ, 7 Dec. 1815). (3) Horatio G. Spafford to TJ, 18 Nov. 1815.

UT VALEAT QUANTUM VALERE DEBET: "so that it may have as much effect as it should."

[1] Preceding six words interlined.

To Joseph Milligan

DEAR SIR   Monticello Dec. 22. 15.

On my return here from Bedford a few days ago, I found the Hutton and Requisite tables, bound to my mind. by this mail I send you an Ovid's metamorphoses almost entirely worne out & defaced, yet of so valuable and rare an edition that I wish you to put it into as good a state of repair as it is susceptible of. by the next mail I will forward a Cornelius Nepos to be bound. be so good as to procure and forward to me by stage the underwritten books. I salute you with friendship & esteem

TH: JEFFERSON

Garnett's Requisite Tables   ⎫
Garnett's Nautical Almanac for 1816. ⎭ printed in Phila.
Ainsworth's Lat. & Eng. dict. abridged. to be bound [...]
    the Lat. & Eng in one, & the Eng. & Lat. [...]
Ovid's metamorphoses. the Delphin edn in 8vo
Cornelius Nepos. the Delphin edn if to be had; if not some other
    good one.
Virgil. the Delphin edn lately printed in Phil. with English notes.
Mair's Tyro's dictionary.
I observe a mr Richardson advertises in the National Intelligencer
    the Scientific dialogues: if the edition be compleat comprehending
    the Chemical part, I should be glad to have it

PoC (DLC); on verso of reused address cover to TJ; torn at seal, with loss of some text and one missing word rewritten by TJ; adjacent to signature: "Mr Millegan"; endorsed by TJ.

The VALUABLE AND RARE edition of Ovid's *Metamorphoses* that TJ wanted Milligan to rebind may have been *Pub. Ouidii Nasonis Metamorphoseon*, ed. Jakob Pontanus (Antwerp, 1657; TJ's copy in ViU, with partial binding slip tipped in, reading "Calf gilt—for Mr Ran[dolph?]").

George Richards (RICHARDSON) advertised in the Washington *Daily National Intelligencer*, 7 Dec. 1815, that he had lately received an eight-volume edition of Jeremiah Joyce, *Scientific Dia-logues, intended for the Instruction and Entertainment of Young People*. While in Washington in the spring of 1816, TJ's granddaughter Ellen W. Randolph (Coolidge) purchased the 1815 Philadelphia edition of *Scientific Dialogues*, consisting of six volumes in three, for $3 (Ellen W. Randolph [Coolidge] to Martha Jefferson Randolph, 17 Feb. [1816] and [ca. 26 Mar. 1816] [ViU: Coolidge Correspondence]). The CHEMICAL PART of Joyce's work that TJ had been attempting to acquire since at least 1809 was issued separately as *Dialogues in Chemistry, intended for the Instruction and Entertainment of Young People*, 2 vols. (London, 1807) (TJ to Milligan, 7 July 1809).

To Robert Patterson

DEAR SIR   Monticello Dec. 22. 15.

Of the last 5 months, I have passed 4. at a possession I have 90. or 100. miles S.W. from this. this must apologise for my having to acknolege your three favors of Oct. 24. Nov. 28. & Dec. 2. all at the same time. on my return, I make it my first duty to comply with your request of Dec. 2. by writing to the President on behalf of mr Hassler, which I have done by this mail. I am sure he will do for him whatever he can with propriety. the collection of instruments he has brought us is really superb, and it gives me great pleasure that they are placed under your care. pressed by the numerous letters accumulated during my absence, I have only had time to read your favors of Oct. 24. & Nov. 28. & to be sensible how much I am indebted to you for them, for your trouble with my timepiece, for the artificial horizon & the fulness of your explanations of the manner of using it. with my thanks for all these kindnesses Accept the assurances of my affectionate & friendly esteem and respect   TH: JEFFERSON

RC (PPAmP: Thomas Jefferson Papers); at foot of text: "Doct^r Robert Patterson." PoC (DLC); on verso of reused address cover of Peter Stephen Chazotte to TJ, 6 Oct. 1815; endorsed by TJ.

To Horatio G. Spafford

DEAR SIR   Monticello Dec. 22. 15.

Of the last 5. months I have past 4 at a possession 90. or 100 miles S.W. from hence. this must apologise for my answering and acting at this late date on your letters of Nov. 18. & 23. I have written by this mail to the President on the subject of your request, altho more as evidence of my wish to be useful to you than with the hope of it's effect, as the occasion I fear has past away while your letters were un-recieved by me. pressed by the numerous letters accumulated during my absence I have time only to add my wishes for your success and assurances of my esteem and respect.   TH: JEFFERSON

RC (NjMoHP: Lloyd W. Smith Collection); addressed: "Horatio G. Spafford esq. Albany"; franked; postmarked Charlottesville, 27 Dec.; endorsed by Spafford as received 4 Jan. and answered 9 Jan. 1816. PoC (MHi); on verso of reused address cover of Nicolas G. Dufief to TJ, 29 Sept. 1815; endorsed by TJ.

To John Vaughan

DEAR SIR   Monticello Dec. 22. 15.

One of my long and frequent absences at a possession about 100. miles S.W. of this has occasioned this tardy acknolegement of your favor of Nov. 21. I rejoice to learn that mr Cathalan was proceeding to send me some wines without awaiting the reciept of my letter, altho, having sent duplicates by different & sure channels he ought to have recieved one before Oct. 2. I thank you for the Communication of Ticknor's catalogue. most of what I find in it interesting to me had been inserted in the catalogue I had inclosed to him, and are as I suppose now on their way to me. there are in it indeed two volumes which I should be much gratified to obtain. having no correspondent there I thankfully accept your kind offer of procuring them for me; tho it may be too late unless they have been bought at the auction by a bookseller to be resold. they are the following

No 131. Hederici Lexicon manuale Gr. Lat. Ernesti. 8vo I wish it
        only in the case of it's being really in 8vo

No 271. Timaei Sophistae lexicon vocum Platonicarum, Ruhnkenii.
their cost will be too inconsiderable to be worth limiting. I shall have occasion soon to remit 50.D. to Leghorn. can this be done by a draught directly on the place. I salute you affectionately
                                              TH: JEFFERSON

RC (PWacD: Sol Feinstone Collection, on deposit PPAmP); at foot of text: "John Vaughan esq."; endorsed in an unidentified hand as received 31 Dec. PoC (MHi); on verso of reused address cover to TJ; endorsed by TJ.

The two works that TJ requested were Benjamin Hederich (HEDERICI), *Graecum Lexicon Manuale*, ed. Johann August Ernesti (Leipzig, 1788; for an earlier edition owned by TJ, see Sowerby, no. 4762), and an edition by David Ruhnken (RUHNKENII) of Timaeus's lexicon of words from Plato, Λεξικὸν περὶ τῶν παρὰ Πλάτωνι Λέξεων . . . *Lexicon Vocum Platonicarum* (Leiden, 1754) (*Books, Rare, Curious, Elegant and Valuable, in the departments of the Classicks, Civil Law, History, Criticism, Belles Lettres and Theology, for sale at auction, in Boston, 20 December, 1815* [Boston, 1815]). TJ eventually acquired later editions of both works (Poor, *Jefferson's Library*, 13 [no. 847]; 8 [no. 422]).

To Jerman Baker

DEAR SIR   Monticello Dec. 23 15

My grandson Jefferson tells me he wrote to sollicit your patronage of the petition of Capt Joseph Miller now before the legislature praying the confirmation of the will of Thos Reed his half-brother, under which he claims his property. that letter, with the petition will have fully possessed you of the facts and principles on which his claim is founded, and I add my sollicitations that you will be so good as to support his claim. I am told that the commissioners of the literary fund habitually oppose these applications. no one wishes more than I do to see the literary fund increase: but not by the plunder of individuals. the testator in this case had a fair claim to the privilege of every citizen of disposing of the property which he had made by his own industry, to those dearest to him, and especially where the donee[1] wishes to become a citizen and to succeed to the duties & services as well as to the property of his brother. I believe I should be justified in saying that England is the only country in Europe which lays her hands on the property in such a case. I speak from a knolege of the fact as to several countries on the continent, because I have known many individuals there who held lands under different powers & allegiances. the Duke of Richmond is a remarkable instance. he is of French descent, and held, when I left that country in 1789. & has held from time immemorial, a great Ducal estate there, and was one of the hereditary dukes & peers of France. this you will see in the Almanac Royal of France of that year. if his estate has been since confiscated, of which I am not informed, it is not as a foreigner, but in the mass of the Seigneurial property in that country confiscated during the revolution. we have copied this predatory proceeding from England in our general law; but the legislature justly and wisely retains the power & practice of dispensation with it in reasonable cases, as I hope & believe they will in this, wh[en a?] property is to change hands from one citizen to another [one?] as in ordinary cases, and not desired to be retained by the subject of a foreign allegiance. you will see moreover in the petition it's further grounds on the establishment of the parents here at the time of the revolution, & of the birth of the petitioner in the US. an acquaintance with Capt Miller from his arrival here, observation of the honest worth and sincere Americanism of his character, and proofs of his great skill in the art he means to follow, & which is so important to be encoraged in this state, has attached me to hi[m] and make me feel a lively interest in his success. he has been our guest now about 2. months & a welcome one to all. you will much oblige me therefore by espousing his claim in aid of the representatives of our county who have his petition particularly in hand. Accept the assurances of my great esteem [an]d respect.

TH: JEFFERSON

PoC (DLC); on portion of a reused address cover from James Monroe to TJ; edge trimmed; damaged at seal; at foot of first page: "Jerman Baker esq."; endorsed by TJ.

Jerman Baker (1776–1828), legislator and treasurer of Virginia, was a native of Chesterfield County. He attended the College of William and Mary in 1795. Baker's son John Wayles Baker, a first cousin of TJ's grandson Francis Eppes, was a frequent guest at Poplar Forest and Monticello. Baker began his career in the Virginia House of Delegates as a representative from Cumberland County, serving in nine sessions, 1803–07, 1808–09, and 1813–17. The General Assembly then elected him to the Council of State in 1818, a position he held until he took office as state treasurer in 1820. Baker's penchant for land speculation left him plagued by debt. To keep up his mortgage payments, he embezzled a total of nearly $25,000 from the state treasury. After a committee of the Council of State launched an audit, Baker committed suicide. Litigation ensued, and eventually his heirs and sureties repaid most of the funds (*DVB*; *William and Mary Provi-*

sional List, 6; Leonard, *General Assembly*; *PTJ*, 30:587; Richmond City Hustings Court Will Book, 4:408–9, 423–5, 5:5–7; *Richmond Enquirer*, 1 Apr. 1828).

MY GRANDSON JEFFERSON: Thomas Jefferson Randolph.

The French property of the 3d DUKE OF RICHMOND, Charles Lennox (1735–1806), was sequestered just prior to his death. A secret provision in the 1814 Treaty of Paris returned it to his eldest nephew, Charles Lennox (1764–1819), 4th Duke of Richmond. The sisters of the third duke subsequently brought suit in the French courts arguing for a division of the property according to French laws of succession, which would have split the estate among the third duke's heirs. In 1839 the French Cour de Cassation ruled in favor of the heirs of the third duke (*ODNB*; Eric E. Bergsten, *Community Law in the French Courts: The Law of Treaties in Modern Attire* [1973], 56–9; *Journal du Palais, recueil le plus complet de la Jurisprudence Française* [1839], 24 June 1839).

[1] Word interlined in place of "claimant."

To Joseph C. Cabell

DEAR SIR   Monticello Dec. 23. 15.

A petition has been presented to our present legislature by a Capt
Joseph Miller, praying a confirmation of the will of his half brother
Thomas Reed who died not long since at Norfolk possessed of lands
and slaves which he devised to his half brothers and sisters then living in England. this one bought up the shares of the whole and came
over to reside here as a citizen. he arrived after the declaration of war,
and was instantly ordered up to Charlottesville. we of course became
acquainted with him and were soon attached to him by the honest
simplicity of his character, so that he was soon at home in every
house. we found him as zealous an American as any of ourselves and
I interceded with the Marshal to let him go to Norfolk to look to his
property, making myself responsible for the fidelity of his conduct. he
set up a brewery there in partnership with a mr Hays, which he still
carries on with great success; being, I verily believe the most skilful
brewer that has ever come to the country. but during his stay here he
has become attached to the neighbors & neighborhood and is looking
out for a farm to carry on the business of farming & brewing jointly
& on a moderate scale. he has now been with me two months a very
welcome guest to all the family,[1] and this may explain the interest I
take in his case. considering him too as becoming one of your constituents I have thought I might without impropriety sollicit your patronage of his claim. his petition was put into the hands of mr Maury
one of our representatives, and I now write to mr Baker to ask his aid
in that house. the facts and principles of his claim are so fully stated
in the petition that I need add nothing to them. I have been told the
Commrs of the literary fund habitually oppose these petitions. No
one wishes more than I do to see the literary fund increase; but not
by the plunder of individuals. the testator in this case had a fair claim
to the privilege of every citizen of disposing of the property which he
had made by his own industry to those dearest to him. I believe I
should be correct in saying that England is the only country in Europe which seizes the property in such a case. I speak from a knolege
of the fact as to several countries on the continent of Europe, and a
full belief of it in others. France exhibits a remarkable instance. the
Duke of Richmond is of French extraction, held when I left that
country in 1789. a great Ducal estate there, and was one of the hereditary[2] dukes and peers of France. this you will see in the Almanac
Royal of that year, and in the Court Calendar of England of every
year. his estate may have been confiscated in the mass of Seigneural

property there during the revolution; but of this I am not informed. we have[3] copied this barbarism from England in our general law, but the legislature properly relaxes it in all reasonable cases, as I hope & believe they will in this, where the claimant desires to become a resident citizen as his brother was. I say nothing of the fact that his parents were established in the US. at the time of the revolution, and himself born in them, because you will find the details of that specially stated in the petition. pray obtain justice for him and accept my respectful & affectionate salutations.   TH: JEFFERSON

RC (ViU: TJP); addressed: "Joseph C. Cabell esq. of the Senate of Virginia now at Richmond"; franked; postmarked Milton, 24 Dec.; endorsed by Cabell as a letter about "Capt: Miller" answered 23 Jan. 1816. PoC (DLC); on reused address cover to TJ; damaged at seal; endorsed by TJ.

The MARSHAL was Andrew Moore. Duke of Aubigny, France, is among the additional titles of the DUKE OF RICHMOND listed in *The Royal Kalendar; or complete and correct Annual Register for England, Scotland, Ireland, and America* (London, 1792; Poor, *Jefferson's Library*, 7 [no. 328]; TJ's copy in ViU), 2.

[1] Preceding four words interlined.
[2] Manuscript: "heredita."
[3] TJ here canceled "unfortunately."

From Charles Willson Peale

DEAR SIR   Belfield Dec[r] 23[d] 1815
    It is my wish to communicate to you whatever I think has a chance of being novel and interresting. I have just seen a Machine for sowing grain in drills, of the most simple construction of any I have seen before—A mechanic was making it from one which he had seen at Doct[r] Logans lately brought from England. Like the Perambulator it has a Wheel and a handle to push it along. but as I mean to give you a tolerable description of it. I begin with saying that the Wheel is 2 f. 7 I diameter, the Handles are framed thus[1] (a) is the hob on which

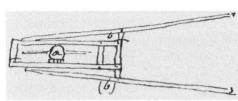

is a bevel wheel. at (b) is a notch to receive a trough of 12 feet long, this trough is made of two boards forming a gutter, each end closed. holes are[2] made near the bottom of this trough 6½ Inches from each other and in the bottom of the trough between each of the holes are blocks   to slide towards the holes the grain put into the trough, and on the outside of the trough covering the holes are plates. or rather 2 plates, the first plate fastened to

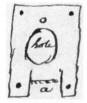

the trough by nails at the dots, & the hole oppening with the hole in the trough, the 2ᵈ Plate is rivited to this at (o) is circular, each made of sheet copper the notch (a) after being slit is turned over to imbrace the edge of the circular plate, and the hole in it cor-

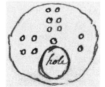

risponds to that of the under plate this plate is about 3 Inches diame-ter, & the holes round this plate are for small grain, the large hole for Wheat or other large grain, & the opening is made small or large at pleasure by turn-ing the Circular plate. a greater or lesser number of the small holes are said to be for different sizes of Grain, i,e, for Turnep seed, the two holes are placed opposite the hole of the under plate, The last thing I have to explain are Brushes within the trough against the holes in order to drive the seed through the holes in the copper plates—I mentioned on the other side a bevel wheel on the hob of the large or rolling wheel. In the center of the trough to hold the grain is a small box that contains a bevel wheel of the same di-ameter[3] of that on the hob, each end of the axis of this wheel is square to recieve a socket of wire rods[4] (of Nᵒ 3 or smaller) extending to each end of the trough, on it are fixed brushes of 2 Inches diameter,[5] say one Inch thickness of turned blocks in which bristles are sett projecting $\frac{1}{2}$ an Inch, a staple between each brush to keep them steady to their work of pushing the grain through the holes— a rod with wheels about half the diameter of that on the hob com-municates the motion from the Roling wheel to the rod containing the brushes.

I think the boards forming the trough is about 7 Inches wide and has a cover to it. The length of the handles I suppose are about 7 feet, including the frame work—The whole so light that a Boy of 12 or 14 Years old could moove it with little exertion.   I hope that I have explained this Machine intelli-gently, yet I do not much doubt that you are acquainted with the Ma-chine, if not my Scrole will be more amusing to you. on resuming my Pensil I find that I can paint better Portraits then when I was in the prime of life—this will scarcely be beleived when my age and long absence from practice is considered, but thus I can account for it, my Judgment is ripened, my knowledge of colours by the aid of my Son Rembrandt with my remembrance of the colours I have formerly made use of[6] considered, and also having now practiced in some new modes of painting my Idea's of the proper tints are much to my advantage—I have lately painted a number of Pictures, and every one who has seen them verifie by their observation what I have said above, Doct^r Wistar urges me to return to my labours in Natural History. I say that I have mispent great part of my life in the practice of Mechanicks, I ought to have paid others to do my work, much better than I could do it myself, and my Pensil would have produced me greater profit with increased reputation. my labours gave me happiness, for I never thought further while at work—I now find pleasure with my Brushes & I hope my health will enable me to pursue it.

I mean to make tryal of wire fences, it is very probable that they will be found cheaper than Posts & railes and if managed properly more durable, in my next I shall be able to give you further notice of them

I am as ever with much esteem your friend   C W PEALE

RC (DLC); at foot of text: "To Thomas Jefferson Esqre"; torn at seal, with missing text supplied from PoC; endorsed by TJ. PoC (PPAmP: Peale Letterbook). Recorded in SJL as received 2 Jan. 1816.

A PERAMBULATOR is a wheel with a handle that is used in surveying to measure distance by rolling the wheel over the ground and counting the number of revolutions. A BEVEL WHEEL is a toothed wheel in the shape of the base of a cone, generally used in conjunction with another bevel wheel positioned at a right angle to the first. The ROLLING WHEEL here is the one designed to roll on the ground (*OED*).

[1] To the left of this drawing Peale canceled another version of it as shown below.

[2] Manuscript: "a."
[3] Manuscript: "diamertor."
[4] RC: "rods." PoC: "rod."
[5] Manuscript: "Incles diamerter."
[6] Manuscript: "off."

To Philip I. Barziza

DEAR SIR   Monticello Dec. 24. 15.

A long absence from home must apologize for this late acknolegement of your favor of the 6th. accept in the first place my congratulations on your safe arrival here, my best wishes for your obtaining whatever is your right in this country, and the assurance of any aid I can give towards it. of counsel you will have no need as I conclude with pleasure from your letter that you arc in thc hands of mr Wickham, than whom you could have engaged no better counsel. in answer to your enquiries I will observe that there can be no doubt that the marriage articles between mr & mrs Paradise must have been recorded in the General court, or in the court of James city. mr & mrs Paradise were in possession of one of the original copies, and either in London or Paris put it into my hands in order to enable me to draw a deed of compromise between them & their creditors. while in my hands I made a full abstract from it that I might be enabled to advise them occasionally, without the risk of it's being sent to me. of this abstract I inclose you a copy as also of one made by Sr William Jones. knowing, as I do, the importance which mrs Paradise attached to the original of this instrument in their hands, I have not a doubt it was among her papers at her death. I do not believe that any appointments were ever made by her & her husband under the authority of this instrument, during his life. of what she may have done by deed or will after her return to this country I am uninformed.

Dr Bancroft writes me that your brother the count Barziza was in England at the date of his letter, meant to return to Venice, and thence come to this country. if a letter could reach him from hence before he will have left Venice, I would presume to trouble him with the bringing me some particular editions of books printed there and rarely to be got elsewhere. it might be to him a convenient mode of transferring the sum they would cost to this country. I will request your advice on this subject.

The visit to me at this place, which your letter kindly intimates will be a very welcome one, as it will give me pleasure to assure you personally of the friendship I have borne your family, and of my desire to testify to yourself my sentiments of friendly esteem & respect.

TH: JEFFERSON

RC (CSmH: JF); at foot of first page: "Viscount Barziza." PoC (DLC); on verso of reused address cover to TJ; torn at seal, with missing text rewritten by TJ; endorsed by TJ.

ENCLOSURES

I

Abstract of Marriage Settlement of John Paradise and Lucy Ludwell Paradise

[after 10 May 1769]

Extracts from marriage settlement.
Date.   May 10. 1769.
Parties   John Paradise esq. son of Peter Paradise 1st part.
        Peter Paradise 2^d part.
        Lucy Ludwell 3^d part.
        Wm Dampier 4th part
        James Lee 5th part.
Recites   will of Philip Ludwell dated Feb. 28. 1767. & devising to Richard Corbin E^t others in trust, for use of his 3. daurs towit, $\frac{1}{3}$ (which he

[283]

specifies) to each & her heirs for ever if either died before age or marriage, her part to be equally divided between survivors & their heirs. appointing Peter Paradise John Paradise & Wm Dampier their guardians, and that Wm Dampier alone took guardnshp on himself. that the testr died Mar. 25. 1767. Frances Ludwell died Sep. 7. 1768. under age & unmarr^d—that marrge intend^{d1} e^{t}c that Peter Paradise will give John Paradise 4000£ immed^{ly} and 4000£ more on his death, the latter to be put into hands of James Lee & Rob. Cary for trusts hereaft. mnt^d

Limitns of Real estate & hereditam^{ts}

1. to J. P. for life with^t impeachm^t waste[2] with pow^r of leas^g 21. years reserv^g best ren[t]
2. after his death to L. P. for life with^t imp^t e^{t}c with pow^r to lease e^{t}c
3. to James Lee & Rob. Cary dur^g lives of J. P. & L. P. to supp^t Conting^t remrs[3]
4. to child or chdrn of J. & L. P. for such estates (not exceed^g an estate tail) and in such shares & proportns, with or with^t power of revocn, and with such remrs & limitns over '(but such limns over to be for the benefit of some or one of the sd children)' as the sd J. P. & L. L. or the survivor by deed or will duly exd shall appoint
5. (if no app^{mt} made) to all the chdr^n as ten. in com.[4] in tail wth cross rem^{rs} in tai[l]
6. rem^r to such person as L. L. shall app^t by deed or will
7. in default of app^{mt} to survivor of sd J. & L. in fee.

Power, with consent of trustees, to exchange for lands in Engl^d or to sell, & buy others to be settl^d e^{t}c

Personal estate of sd L. L. the use of it

1. to J. P. for life. 2. afterwds to L. P.[5] for life. 3. to chdr, on such proportns and such limns (sd limns ever to be for benefit of some of ye chdr^n) as the sd J. & L. o[r] the survivor by deed or will shall app^t 4. if no app^{mt} then to chdr equally and under many intricate limns. 5.[6] if no chdr^n then to such person as L. shall by deed or will app^t 6.[7] if no such app^{mt} then to survivor.

The 4000£ paiable at death of P. Paradise to be placed in public funds or on landed security, with consent of truste[es] and of J. & L. interest to be received

1. by J. P. for life 2. aftwds L. for life. 3. to chdr^n as before provid^d for Person^l est. of sd^d L. with power, with consent of Trustees & of J. & L. to lay out the 4000 £ in lands in Engl^d to be limite[d] as the real estate of sd L. before described

MS (DLC: TJ Papers, 53:9038); entirely in TJ's hand; undated; edge trimmed; with Tr of following enclosure on verso. Tr (Stephen Phillips Jr., Salem, Mass., 1961); entirely in TJ's hand; undated; at head of text: "An Extract of the marriage settlement of John & Lucy Paradise by Th Jefferson"; presumably being the clean copy TJ made for Philip I. Barziza.

John Paradise (1743–95), linguist, was born in Thessaloníki and studied at the University of Padua and at Oxford University. He and his father, Peter Paradise, acted as executors for Philip Ludwell, and on 18 May 1769 John married Ludwell's daughter Lucy. Paradise knew eight languages, devoted himself to scholarly pursuits, became a fellow of the Royal Society of London, and enjoyed the friendship of Edmund Burke, David Garrick, Samuel Johnson, and Sir Joshua Reynolds. He managed his wife's Virginia lands from afar, with the assistance of TJ and others. The Paradises visited Virginia in 1788 but soon returned to London, where John died (*ODNB*; Archibald Bolling Shepperson, *John Paradise and Lucy Ludwell of London and Williamsburg* [1942]).

Lucy Ludwell Paradise (1751–1814) was born at Green Spring plantation, near Williamsburg. She moved with her family to London in 1760, where she met and married John Paradise. Paradise and her surviving sister, Hannah Philippa Ludwell Lee, split their father's estate following the death of their sister Frances Ludwell in 1768. A decade after the death of her husband, Paradise returned to Williamsburg to live. She was declared

insane in 1812 and died in Williamsburg two years later (Shepperson, *John Paradise and Lucy Ludwell*).

TJ had met John Paradise by 1786. Beginning with the couple's May 1788 visit to Paris, TJ became heavily involved in helping them sort out their tangled affairs. TJ had seen the original marriage settlement from which this extract was made by 6 Sept. 1788. On that date he sent a copy of it to Nathaniel Burwell, who was managing the Paradises' Virginia estates (*PTJ*, esp. 9:434–5, 11:242–3, 13:472–3, 543–5, 570–1, 14:418–20).

[1] Tr: "that a marriage was intended to be had."

[2] Tr: "without impeachment of waste."

[3] Tr: "to support Contingent remainders."

[4] Tr: "tenants in common."

[5] Reworked from "2. to L. P. for life."

[6] MS: "4." Tr: "5."

[7] MS: "5." Tr: "6."

II

Sir William Jones's Notes on Marriage Settlement of John Paradise and Lucy Ludwell Paradise

[after 10 May 1769]

<u>Limitations of the real estate.</u>

1. to the husband for life, without impeachment of waste, and with power of leasing for 21. years reserving the best rent.

2. remr to the wife for life, with^t E^{t}c. & with the like power

3. remr to trustees to preserve contingent remrs.

4. remr to such child or children of the marriage (in tail or for a less estate) as the husband & wife or the survivor shall appoint.

5. remr (in default of an appointment) to the children of the marriage in tail, as tenants in common.

6. Remr (in default of issue) to such <u>person as the wife alone shall appoint</u>.

7. remr (in default of such appointment) to the survivor in fee.

The above is a copy of Sr Wm Jones's state of the limitns of the real estate in the marriage contract of mr & mrs Paradise.

Tr (DLC: TJ Papers, 53:9038); entirely in TJ's hand; undated; on verso of MS of preceding enclosure.

Sir William Jones (1746–94), judge and linguist, was born in London and studied Arabic and Persian at University

College, Oxford, where he earned a B.A. in 1768. He entered the Middle Temple to study law in 1770 and was called to the bar in 1774. Jones practiced law in Wales from 1775 until his appointment in 1783 to the Bengal supreme court. He pub- lished a variety of works on law and linguistics and numerous translations, including digests of Hindu and Muslim law. Jones died near Calcutta (*ODNB*).

Jones presumably made his notes some time before his 1783 departure for India.

To James Gibbon

S<small>IR</small>   Monticello Dec. 24. 15.

I recieved last night your favor of the 19th and now inclose you a letter from mr Hackley our Consul at Cadiz which will give you all the information I possess relative to the small bundle which is the subject of your letter. if you will be so good as to deliver it to mr Gibson he will pay any duties or other expences to which it is liable and will forward it to me. with thanks for the trouble this has given you, I pray you to accept the assurance of my great esteem & respect

T<small>H</small>: J<small>EFFERSON</small>

PoC (DLC); on verso of reused address cover to TJ; at foot of text: "Maj^r Gibbon"; endorsed by TJ. Enclosure: Richard S. Hackley to TJ, 3 Oct. 1815.

From Charles Yancey

D<small>R</small> S<small>IR</small>.   Richmond 24th dec^r 1815

we have been as yet principly engaged in Receiving petitions, Making appointments, &^c a few bills have been reported, & have passed our house, & some of Considerable Importance depending. One of which, has for its object the call of a Convention. on which there appears to be a Considerable degree of difference in Opinion; but I am inclined to think, it will pass our house in Some Shape or other, & be negatived in the senate, as they are a little further from the people. I confess, when I reflect on the danger of Innovation, I am at a loss what to do. Another of great importance, of which we shall have many respecting the establishment of another Banking association. in this I feel also considerable Imbarrasment. Seeing other states grant Charters to almost every association of the kind. & hearing people of good standing Charge the directors, of being engaged in what is commonly called Shaving of paper, & improperly Curtailing to emberass the man who is much in debt in bank, to make a way to Shave him close, & seeing that by the laws, & usages, respecting banks, Some persons Must ultimately Suffer, is Serious Cause of Alarm. every Measure which would tend to prevent Such evil ought Now to be Adopted, If possible. we have a Committee, appointed to Report on this part of the Governors Communication, Respecting Roads, & internal Navigation, out of which I hope Some Common benefit will result. a petition has been presented, praying the passage of a law, to come at Damages in a Sumary way, from those who have locks On the Rivanna River. & to prevent Dams in future[1] across said river, or Any other obstruction, unless granted by the Legislature. Should this by Any probable Means, effect Your Interest, or that of Col° Randolphs, & not benefit this public. Any Communication You, or he, may feel dispossd to Make, would be cheerfully Rec^d And attended to by Your friend & Mo. Ob. Ser^t CHARLES YANCEY

RC (DLC); addressed: "Thomas Jefferson Esqr late president of the United States"; franked; postmarked Richmond, 27 Dec.; endorsed by TJ; with notes by TJ on verso relating to his 6 Jan. 1816 response: "banks   roads & canals ✓Rivanna ✓college ✓Miller." Recorded in SJL as received 2 Jan. 1816.

On 12, 13, and 15 Dec., ten Virginia counties petitioned the House of Delegates for a CONVENTION to amend the state constitution in order to expand suffrage to all (presumably white) males who either paid taxes or served in the militia. The select committee to which the petitions were referred presented a bill on 21 Dec. "Requiring the Sheriffs of the different counties and corporations within this Commonwealth, to take the sense of the people upon the propriety of calling a Convention." The bill was rejected on 9 Feb. 1816 (Vi: RG 78, Legislative Petitions; JHD [1815–16 sess.], 33, 37, 43, 60, 167).
On 14 Dec. 1815 the House appointed a

select committee chaired by Charles Fenton Mercer and charged with investigating unchartered BANKING associations. The committee's 5 Jan. 1816 report recommended the passage of a law to protect chartered banks from the "abuses of unauthorised Private Banking" (JHD [1815–16 sess.], 39, 97–103, 160, 207). "An Act more effectually to prevent the circulation of notes emitted by unchartered banks" became law on 24 Feb. 1816 (Acts of Assembly [1815–16 sess.], 46–50).
Yancey and twenty-one other Albemarle County residents presented a PETITION to the House of Delegates on 21 Dec. calling for a law mandating payment of damages to people detained on the Rivanna River by faulty locks. The Committee on Roads and Internal Navigation ruled the petition to be reasonable on 27 Dec., and the House ordered that a bill be written to that effect (Vi: RG 78, Legislative Petitions, Albemarle Co.; JHD [1815–16 sess.], 62, 73).

[1] Manuscript: "futer."

To Jean David

SIR   Monticello Dec. 25. 15.
    A long absence from home[, a]nd but a late return to it must apologise for the delay in ackno[le]ging the reciept of your letter of Nov.

26. on the subject of the vine & wine. in the earlier part of my life I have been ardent for the introduction of new objects of culture suited to our climate. but at the age of 72. it is too late. I must leave it to younger persons who have enough of life left to pursue the object and to enjoy it's attainment. should I be able to meet with such a person I should recommend strongly to him[1] the undertaking, and to avail themselves of your qualifications to conduct it. I am disposed to think the trial had better be made with one or two kinds of grape only, & these of the wines known to be preferred in this country, as the Madeira Bordeaux Champagne. once establish that any one good wine can be made here, and the varieties will be attempted in profusion. there is in our woods a native grape which of my own knolege produces a wine so nearly[2] of the quality of the Caumartin of Burgundy, that I have seen at my own table a large company acknolege they could not distinguish between them. I do not know myself how this particular grape could be known in our woods, altho' I believe it abounds: but there is a gentleman on Potomak who cultivates it. this may be worth your attention. should you think it worth while to examine the aptitude of this part of the country for the vine, I shall be very happy to receive you at Monticello. Accept my respectful salutations   TH: JEFFERSON

PoC (DLC); on verso of reused address cover of Robert Patterson to TJ, 24 Oct. 1815; torn at seal, with missing text rewritten by TJ; portions faint; at foot of text: "Mʳ John David"; endorsed by TJ as a letter to "Jean" David. Enclosed in TJ to Louis H. Girardin, 25 Dec. 1815.

John Adlum had produced a wine that TJ considered similar to the burgundy of Chambertin (CAUMARTIN) at his previous home near Havre de Grace, Maryland, at the mouth of the Susquehanna River, not on the Potomac (POTOMAK).

[1] Word reworked from "them" by TJ, who neglected later in sentence to revise "themselves" similarly.
[2] Preceding two words interlined.

To Louis H. Girardin

DEAR SIR   Monticello Dec. 25. 15.
   I have thought it safest to put my answer to mr David under your cover. I have formerly been eager to introduce the culture of the vine and sunk a good deal of money in the endeavor. altho' unsuccesful, I would still persevere were I younger. but I would do it on a small scale. I would engage a laboring vigneron from France, skilled in the culture of the vine & manipulation of the wine. by only so much ground as he with one or two common laborers could cultivate in or-

dinary, having occasional assistance when there was great pressure. let them raise their own provisions of every kind, and to meet the other expences proceed at once to making wine from the wild grape. I have seen too many instances of good wine made from the woods to doubt it's success. there is a wild grape so remarkable for the quality of it's wine that it ought to be tried. the vigneron should have a liberal interest in the success of the vineyard. such an experiment would expose one to little loss, and admit of enlargement according to it's success. but this would be too small a scale for the talents of mr David. he should if possible be engaged on a larger one; and should the opportunity occur I should not fail to recommend his employment. but after so many unsuccesful attempts, without a single instance of success, he must not wonder if he finds great backwardness in a new effort. any of us could spare him the use of land, a house E^tc. but few will be willing to take off their laborers from a known & prosperous culture to employ them in one which experience makes them consider as unpromising. I salute you with great esteem & respect

Th: Jefferson

P.S. I gave you once a statement of the agency that mr Dabney Carr had in the establishment of a committee of correspondence in the beginning of the revolution. this I made out while I had the journals, acts E^tc of the times in my possession. his sons have lately requested such a statement of me; but I no longer possess the same materials. will you be so good as to send me the one I gave you, which shall be speedily returned.

RC (PPAmP: Thomas Jefferson Papers); at foot of first page, beneath signature: "turn over"; addressed: "Mr L. H. Girardin Richmond"; franked; postmarked Milton, 27 Dec. Enclosure: TJ to Jean David, 25 Dec. 1815.

A letter from Girardin to TJ of 8 Jan. 1816, not found, is recorded in SJL as received 13 Jan. from Richmond.

TJ discussed the role of DABNEY CARR (1743–73) in the creation in 1773 of a Virginia committee of correspondence in his 15 Jan. 1815 letter to Girardin.

To David Higginbotham

DEAR SIR   Monticello Dec. 25. 15.

Before a day is fixed for settling the question between Col^o Monroe we must be sure that mr Price will attend; that done I will get a day settled with mr Dawson, Col^o Coles and the county surveyor. you are so convenient to mr Price that I wish you would ascertain the point with him. I think the old gentleman should be paid for his attendance past and to come. whether by the one or the other party, or both, the Arbitrators must settle. you had better so state it to mr Price

friendly salutations to mrs H. and yourself   TH: JEFFERSON

PoC (MHi); on verso of reused address cover of Richard S. Hackley to TJ, 3 Oct. 1815; at foot of text: "Mr Higginbotham"; endorsed by TJ.

A missing letter from Higginbotham to

TJ of 21 Nov. 1815, not found, is recorded in SJL as received 15 Dec. from Milton. SJL also records a missing letter from TJ to Higginbotham of 22 Dec. 1815.

The COUNTY SURVEYOR was William Woods.

To Robert Saunders

SIR   Monticello Dec. 25. 15.

An absence of two months from home has occasioned this very late acknolegement of your favor of Oct. 29. I now inclose the following documents for the settlement of Bellini's affairs, all duly authenticated by the local authorities.

N° 1. a Certificate that Charles Bellini was son of Leon Girolamo Bellini with his pedigree

   2. d^o that Aurora Bellini was daughter of the same. same pedigree

   3. d^o that Luisa Bellini was daughter of the same. same pedigree.

   4. d^o that Aurora died Mar. 7. 1808. aged 66.

   5. d^o that Luisa died May 21. 1813. aged seventy some[1] odd.[2]

   6. Notarial copy of the will of Luisa, dated 1811. Jan. 6. constituting Giovan Batista Fancelli an Ecclesiastic of Florence her universal heir and legatary.

   7. Power of Attorney from Giovan Batista Fancelli to myself to settle, recieve, recover E^{t}c the effects of the sd Charles Bellini brother of Luisa & Aurora, the latter dead intestate the former dead also having instituted him heir.

I add also a power of Attorney from myself to you, and the letters which have heretofore passed between mr Bracken the admr & myself, except any which I may have written in 1805.6.7. which, in the mass of my papers of that period I cannot readily lay my hands on. mr Bracken's claim of the suspension of interest from the date of his remittance until he redrew it, and on that sum whatever it was, seems just: your letter supposes this was about 2. years; I think from his letters to me it would seem to have been 3. or 4. years. but during the rest of the period, he certainly would not think it just. because during all that time he has had the balance[3] in use, he has not kept it constantly locked up & untouched in his desk. the letters I inclose you

will shew that he was not always ready to pay that I would have recieved and remitted it at any time, and his letters prove he was not
afraid to trust that channel. indeed Mazzei's power of Attorney to
me would have made any payment to me a legal payment to him—
however on this subject of interest you are a better judge than myself;
you are recent in the practice & know best the present rules of the
courts. I leave it to yourself therefore to settle every thing as you
think right without further appeal to me, and to lodge the sum in the
Virginia bank in Richmond[4] to the credit of John Baptist Fancelli by
Tho⁵ Jeff[erson, h]is attorney. be so good as to return me the papers
whe[n done?] with, with a copy of the whole administration account
as finally settled. I was desired to make particular enquiry as to two
negroes Bellini had at his death.

Accept the tender of my great esteem & respect.

TH: JEFFERSON

PoC (DLC); on reused address cover
to TJ; damaged at seal; at foot of first
page: "Robert Saunders esq."; endorsed
by TJ. Enclosures: (1) Birth record for
Charles Bellini, from the baptismal register of the Church of San Giovanni Battista, Florence, extracted 29 Aug. 1814;
providing birth date of 6 Nov. 1732; giving full name as Carlo Maria Marchionne
Bellini; and listing parents as Leon Girolamo Bellini and Maria Vittoria Luchini
Bellini, paternal grandfather as Carlo
Maria Niccola Bellini, and maternal
grandfather as Giuseppe Luchini (MS in
DLC: TJ Papers, 202:35929; printed
form completed by the archivist Giuseppe
Formigli; in Italian; with attestations
dated 30 Aug. 1814; notation by TJ at
head of text: "Nº 1."). (2) Birth record for
Aurora Bellini, from the baptismal register of the Church of San Giovanni Battista, Florence, extracted 29 Aug. 1814;
providing birth date of 25 Apr. 1741; giving full name as Maria Aurora Gaspera
Bellini; and listing same lineage as above
(MS in DLC: TJ Papers, 202:35930;
printed form completed by Formigli; in
Italian; with attestations dated 30 Aug.
1814; notation by TJ at head of text: "Nº
2."). (3) Birth record for Luisa Bellini,
from the baptismal register of the Church
of San Giovanni Battista, Florence, extracted 29 Aug. 1814; providing birth
date of 4 Apr. 1738; giving full name as

Maria Luisa Eleonora Bellini; and listing
same lineage as above (MS in DLC: TJ
Papers, 202:35928; printed form completed by Formigli; in Italian; with attestations dated 30 Aug. 1814; notation by
TJ at head of text: "Nº 3."). (4) Death
record for Aurora Bellini, from the death
register of the Church of Santa Felicita,
Florence, extracted 23 Aug. 1814; stating
that Bellini died suddenly on 7 Mar.
1808, aged sixty-six and unmarried, and
was buried in the churchyard (MS in
DLC: TJ Papers, 202:35916; printed
form completed by the archivist Giulio
Ferdinando Pucci; in Italian; with attestation dated 25 Aug. 1814; notation by TJ
at head of text: "Nº 4."). (5) Death record
for Luisa Bellini, from the death register
of the Church of Santa Maria al Pignone,
Diocese of Florence, extracted 29 Aug.
1814; stating that Bellini died suddenly
on 22 May 1814 and was buried there
(MS in DLC: TJ Papers, 202:35931;
in the hand of the parish priest Luigi
Chelazzi; in Italian; with attestations
dated 30 Aug. 1814; notation by TJ at
head of text: "Nº 5."). (6) Will of Luisa
Bellini, dictated to the notary Carlo Antonio Topi, Florence, 6 Jan. 1811, stating
that, as she had no living ancestors or descendants, her sole heir after the payment
of taxes and the celebration of funeral
masses was to be the priest Giovanni Battista Fancelli; and indicating that Bellini

had been living in Fancelli's home in Pignone, in the canton of Galluzzo (Tr in DLC: TJ Papers, 202:35932–3; notarized copy made on 24 Aug. 1814, with attestations dated 25 and 26 Aug. 1814; in Italian; with notations by TJ, at head of text: "Nº 6."; in margin of p. 2: "the will of Luisa Bellini Jan. 6. 1811," and his penciled translation of final attestation). Other enclosures printed below.

SEVENTY SOME ODD: in enclosure 5 above, the second digit of Luisa Bellini's age at death is unclear. Based on her birth and death dates above, she died aged

seventy-six. The correspondence between TJ and John BRACKEN enclosed here probably included TJ to Bracken, 2 Aug. and 9 Oct. 1811, and Bracken to TJ, 13 Aug. and 25 Oct. 1811. Bracken conveyed funds to London for Charles Bellini's heirs some time after January 1807, and REDREW the unclaimed funds by August 1811 (Bracken to TJ, 13 Aug. 1811).

[1] Word interlined.
[2] TJ here canceled "(I cannot."
[3] Preceding two words interlined in place of "it."
[4] Preceding two words interlined.

ENCLOSURES

I

Power of Attorney from Giovanni Battista Fancelli

Al Nome di Dio Amen—L'Anno del Nostro Signore Gesù Cristo milleotto-centoquattordici—Indizione Romana Seconda, e questo dì Ventinove del mese di Agosto in Firenze, sotto il Pontificato dì sua Santità Pio Settimo Sommo Pontefice Romano, e sua Altezza Imperiale, e Reale il Serenissimo Ferdinando Terzo, Principe Reale d'Ungheria, e di Boemia, Arciduca d'Austria, e Granduca dì Toscana, nostro amatissimo Sovrano felicemente dominante.—
Avanti di Noi dottr. Carlo Antonio Topi Notaro Regio, Residente a Firenze, ed abitante in Via del Leone al Nº 32., e alla presenza dei sottoscritti due Testimoni si è personalmente presentato, il Sigʳ Canonico Giovan Batista del fù Pietro Fancelli Possidente, e Sacerdote, domiciliato al Pignone Cantone del Galluzzo Circondario di Firenze il quale come Erede universale della fù Sigʳᵃ Luisa del fù Leon Girolamo Bellini, nativo della Città di Firenze, di Condizione ex Monaca da essa instituita col suo Testamento dl dì 6 Gennaio 1811, celebrato avanti di me Notaro suddetto, e sottoscritto, spontaneamente, liberamente in forza del presente Atto Costituì, e Costituisce, elesse, ed elegge per suo Procuratore, Attore, e Mandatarjo S. E. il Sigʳ Tommaso Jefferson stato Presidente degli Stati Uniti d'America, affinchè in Nome, e per interesse del medesimo Sigʳ Costituente Adisca ed Accetti L'Eredità lasciata dal Sigʳ Carlo del fù Leon Girolamo Bellini, Fratello della suddetta Sigʳᵃ Luisa Bellini, già Oriundo Italiano, e Professore nel Collegio di Guglielmo e Maria in Virginia, morto ℞ quanto è a notizia del Sigʳ Costituente fine del mese di Settembre 1802, negli Stati uniti dì America, e nella parte Settentrionale dei medesimi senza aver fatta nuova disposizione Testamentaria, ℞ lo chè al medᵒ essendo sacerdote le Signore Luisa suddetta, ed Aurora Bellini di lui Sorelle Germane, ed attesa la morte accaduta in Firenze nella cura di S. Felicita sotto di 7 Marzo 1808, della Sigᵃ Aurora una dì dᵉ Sorelle Bellini, conforme Risulta dalla Fede del dì 23. Agosto corrente Rilasciata dal Sigʳ Giulio Ferdinando

Pucci Archivista della Curia Arcivescovile Fiorentina opportun^e Registrata senza aver disposto in modo alcuno delle cose sue, essendo succeduta nella dì lei Eredità la detta sua sorella Sig^a Luisa Bellini così in forza del Testamento da questa come sopra fatto il dì 6. Gennaio <u>1811.</u> ℔ il ministero dì me Notaro predetto, e sottoscritto è venuta a convalidarsi l'intiera Eredità Intestata dl sud° Sig^r Carlo Bellini nel surriferito Sig^r Canonico Fancelli Costituente, ed in conseguenza il suddetto Sig^r Tommaso Jefferson suo Procuratore come sopra costituito faccia tutti gl'atti opportuni, tanto giudiciali che estragiudiciali che occorressero ℔ la detta Porzione d'Eredità sempre chè questi non fossero stati fin quì fatti in forza d'altri mandati Rilasciati in Vita dalla suddetta Sig^ra Luisa Bellini Autrice del Sig^r Costituente.—

Obj. a potere procedere alla Vendita tanto privata che pubblica, e per quel prezzo Maggiore che sarà possibile di ricavare dei due Mori supposti esistenti nell'Eredità dl sud° Sig^r Carlo Bellini non meno che di tutti gl'altri Beni tanto Immobili, che mobili componenti l'Eredità medesima, e ℔ conseguenza, esigere, ritirare, e risquotere dal Compratore, o Compratori dei detti Beni il prezzo dei medesimi, come pure esigere quasivoglia Credito, ed assegnamento spettante all'Eredità sud^a con fare in nome, e ℔ interesse dl Sig^r Costituente nella qualità suddetta ogni opportuna Ricevuta tanto in Conto che di Saldo delle Somme il surriferito Sig^r Tommaso Jefferson sarà a riscuotere nei modi, e forme che sono di Ragione, secondo l'uso del Paese—

Obj. a poter transigere, e stralciare qualunque Credito diritto, ed azioni spettanti al Sig^r Costituente, come Erede sudetto in quel modo, e forma che sembrerà, ad esso più utile, e conveniente all'interese del Sig^r Costituente medesimo.—

Obj. a poter adire qualunque Tribunale, tanto dì Giustizia che di Grazia che si rende necessario ℔ conseguire l'intera sodisfazione dì qualunque Credito, o diritto spettante al Sig^r Costituente, come pure dare interrogatorj, deferire giuramento, prender questo sopra l'Anima dl Sig^r Costituente tutte le volte, e quante volte occorrerà secondo ì congrui, e Respettivi Casi.—

Obj. a potere Rapporto alle Vendite, libretti e Risoluzioni da farsi come sopra degli assegnamenti, Beni, e Capitali della suddetta Eredità, fare, e poter fare ogni, e qualunque dichiarazione, quietanza e obbligazione che secondo l'uso dl Paese occorresse, con obbligare non tanto gl'assegnamenti, e Beni dell'Eredità medesima, quant'ancora gl'assegnamenti, e Beni proprj del Sig^r Costituente.—

Obj. a potere rimettere tutto il libretto che sarà fatto dal Sig^r Mandatario della suddetta Eredità Bellini, o dì mano in mano di quelle Somme che averà esatte, nella Città di Firenze all'istesso Sig^r Canonico Fancelli Costituente, o [ovvero?] nella Città, e Porto di Livorno, all'Indirizzo del Sig^r Gio^i Santi Bargellini Pubblico Negoziante di Colà,.—

E generalmente a fare, e poter fare intorno alle cose suddette e ciascheduna d'esse tutto quello, e quanto farebbe il Sig^r Costituente se fosse presente ancora che fossero cose tali che Richiedessero un più Speciale Mandato, colla Clausula come libera, et ut alter Ego promettendo sotto le più estese, e valide obbligazioni permesse dal vegliante Codice Civile, di avere il tutto ℔ grato, e fermo, e di Rilevare indenne da ogni spesa, danno, e pregiudizio, il suddetto Sig^r Tommaso Jefferson suo Procuratore, come sopra Costituito nei modi e forme che sono di Ragione.—

Fatto, Letto, e Rogato il presente Atto in Brevet, nello Studio del Sig^r Dottore Antonio Manzani posto in Via degl'Accenni. quivi presenti i Sg^i Jacopo di Pietro Bianchi e Luigi del fù Francesco Brunacci di Professione Scrivani ambidue domiciliati in Firenze, che il primo in Via chiara, e l'altro in Via Ardiglione, Testimonj a noi cogniti, ed aventi i Requisiti voluti dalla Legge, i quali unitamente al suddetto Sig^r Canonico Fancelli, e noi Notaro hanno firmato il presente Atto dopo fatta Lettura del medesimo, a loro chiava, e piena intelligenza, questo dì, ed anno suddetto in Firenze.—

Il Canonico Gio: Batta: Fancelli

Jacopo Bianchi. Testimone

Luigi Brunacci Testimone

DR Carlo Antonio Topi Notaro Pubblico a Firenze

Reg^r a firenze Li 29–Agosto 1814. Publ. 16. fol^o 174.
R. C 7. Ricev. un franco

[. . .]

Visto da noi Presidente del Tribunale dì Prima Istanza dì Firenze ✝ Legalizzazione della firma dl Sig^{re} Antonio Topi Notaro in d^a Città, che hà firmato l'atto sud^o dal Trible Li 30: Agosto 1814.

GHERARDINI Cav.   CARDUCCI

Visto da Noi Cavalier Bartolomeo Raffaelli Primo Presidente della Regia Corte suprema di firenze ✝ legalizzazione della firma, e qualità prese dai Signori Carducci, e Gherardini, il primo Presidente ed il secondo Cancelliere del Tribunale di prima Istanza di detta Città.

Dal Palazzo di nostra Residenza
    firenze 30: Agosto 1814.
        BART: RAFFAELLI
        [. . .]

EDITORS' TRANSLATION

In the name of God amen—In the year of Our Lord Jesus Christ one thousand eight hundred and fourteen—second Roman indiction, and this 29th day of the month of August in Florence, under the pontificate of His Holiness Pius the Seventh supreme Roman pontiff, and His Imperial and Royal Highness the Most Serene Ferdinand the Third, royal prince of Hungary and Bohemia, archduke of Austria and grand duke of Tuscany, our most beloved sovereign happily ruling.—

Before us, Dr. Carlo Antonio Topi, royal notary, resident of Florence, and living at number 32 Via del Leone, and in the presence of the two undersigned witnesses, did personally present himself, Mr. Canon Giovanni Batista, priest, son of the late Pietro Fancelli, property owner, resident of Pignone, canton of Galluzzo, district of Florence, who as the sole heir of the late Mrs. Luisa Bellini, former nun, daughter of the late Leon Girolamo Bellini, a native of the city of Florence, appointed by her in her will of 6 January 1811, formalized before me, the aforesaid and undersigned notary, voluntarily and freely pursuant to this deed did and does constitute, did and does elect as his power of attorney, agent, and manda-tory, his excellency Mr. Thomas Jefferson former president of the United States of America, in order that, in the name and interest of the same sig-natory, he may proceed and accept the inheritance left by Mr. Charles Bellini, son of the late Leon Girolamo Bellini, brother of the aforesaid Mrs. Luisa Bellini, formerly a native of Italy, and a professor at the Col-lege of William and Mary in Virginia, who, as far as the signatory knows, died at the end of the month of September 1802, in the United States of America, and in the northern part of the same, without having changed his will, under which will the same priest was appointed by the aforesaid Mrs. Luisa and Aurora Bellini his full sisters, and in view of the death in Florence, while in the care of Santa Felicita, on 7 March 1808, of Mrs. Aurora, one of the aforesaid Bellini sisters, as is recorded in the cer-tificate of 23 August of this year issued by Mr. Giulio Ferdinando Pucci, archivist of the curia of the archdiocese of Florence, duly recorded, with-out having provided in any way for her things, the said sister of hers, Mrs. Luisa Bellini, thus entering into her inheritance pursuant to the will above, made on 6 January 1811 through the offices of myself, the afore-said and undersigned notary, the entire inheritance of the late Mr. Charles Bellini has come to be vested in the aforementioned Mr. Canon Fancelli the signatory, and as a consequence the aforesaid Mr. Thomas Jefferson, his power of attorney, as above appointed may do all such acts, judicial and extrajudicial as may be necessary for said portion of the inheritance as long as these have not already been done pursuant to other mandates issued while still living by the aforesaid Mrs. Luisa Bellini the principal of the said signatory.—

With the objective of being able to proceed with the sale, either private or public, and for the highest price possible, of the two slaves supposed to exist under the inheritance of the aforesaid Mr. Charles Bellini, as well as all the other goods, whether immovable or movable, that comprise the in-heritance itself, and thus demand, withdraw, and collect from the buyer or buyers of said goods the price of the same, as well as to exact any credit and assignment owing to the aforesaid inheritance, making in the name and interest of the signatory, in the aforesaid capacity, any appropriate re-ceipt whether on account or in settlement of the sums the aforementioned Mr. Thomas Jefferson may collect in the correct ways and forms, accord-ing to the custom of the country—

With the objective of being able to transact and to liquidate any rightful credit and shares owed to the signatory, as aforesaid heir, in whatever mode and form shall seem to him more useful and profitable to the inter-ests of the same signatory.—

With the objective of being able to petition any court, whether at law or in equity, as may be necessary to obtain the entire satisfaction of any credit or right owed to the signatory, as well as to respond to interrogatories, to tes-tify under oath, representing the aforesaid signatory every time, and as many times as may be necessary according to the suitable and respective cases.—

With the objective of being able to report the sales, records, and resolutions to be done as above of assignments, goods, and capital of the aforesaid inheritance, to make, and to be able to make, any and all declarations, releases, and obligations that may be necessary according to the usage of the country, obligating the assignments and goods of the inheritance itself as well as the very assignments and goods of the signatory.—

With the objective of being able to remit all of the sums recorded, which will be done by the mandatory, of the aforesaid Bellini inheritance, or piecemeal of those sums which he will have exacted, to the city of Florence on behalf of the same Mr. Canon Fancelli, the grantor, or in the city and port of Leghorn to the address of Mr. Giovanni Santi Bargellini, public merchant of that place.

And generally to do, and to be able to do concerning the aforesaid things, and each and every one of them, all that which the signatory would do if he were present even should such things require a more special mandate, with the clause as libera et ut alter ego, promising under the most extensive and valid obligations according to the civil code in effect, to have all as granted, and firm, and to hold indemnified from any expense, damage, and prejudice, the aforesaid Mr. Thomas Jefferson, his power of attorney, as established above in the correct manners and forms.—

Done, read, and notarized, the present official deed, in the office of Doctor Antonio Manzoni in Via degl'Accenni, there being present Messrs. Jacopo Bianchi, son of Pietro Bianchi, and Luigi Brunacci, son of the late Francesco Brunacci, clerks by profession, both residents of Florence, the former in Via Chiara, and the other in Via Ardiglione, witnesses known to us, and possessing the qualifications required by law, who together with the aforesaid Mr. Canon Fancelli, and ourselves the notary, have signed the present deed after having read the same with full and clear intelligence, this day and aforesaid year in Florence.—

CANON GIO: BATTA: FANCELLI
JACOPO BIANCHI, witness
LUIGI BRUNACCI, witness
D ᴿ CARLO ANTONIO TOPI notary public in Florence

Registered in Florence on 29 August 1814. Pub. 16 Fol° 174.
R. C 7. Received. one franc

[. . .]

Endorsed by us, the president of the tribunal of the first instance of Florence, authenticated by the signature of Mr. Antonio Topi, notary in said city, who has signed the aforesaid deed. At the tribunal this 30 August 1814.

GHERARDINI Knight   CARDUCCI

Endorsed by us, Sir Bartolomeo Raffaelli, first president of the Royal Supreme Court of Florence, for authentication of the signatures and capacities of Messrs. Carducci and Gherardini, the first president and the second clerk of the tribunal of the first instance of said city.

At the palace our residence
Florence, 30 August 1814.
BART: RAFFAELLI
[. . .]

MS (DLC); in an unidentified hand, signed by Fancelli, his witnesses, and Topi; signed attestations in different hands; bearing four stamps, including Topi's notarial stamp; three words illegible; docketed in an unidentified hand on first page, reading, in part: "Procura in Brevetto" ("Official Power of Attorney"); with notation "Nᵒ 7" by TJ at head of text. Translation by Dr. Jonathan T. Hine.

Charles Bellini died in Williamsburg in 1804, not 1802 (*ANB*). LIBERA ET UT ALTER EGO: "freely and as a second self."

II

Transfer of Power of Attorney for Giovanni Battista Fancelli from Thomas Jefferson to Robert Saunders

To Robert Saunders esq. Attorney at law. William[sburg]

By virtue of the power and authority vested in me by Giovan Batista Fancelli of the city of Florence in Tuscan[y] for the settlement and reciept of the goods chattels and effects whereof Charles Bellini late of the College of Wᵐ & Mary died possessed, the right to which having passed to Luisa Bellini, only surviving sister of the sd Charles but now deceased[1] were by her bequeat[h]ed to the sd Giovan Batista Fancelli, I hereby appoint you Attorney with full powers[2] to settle the administration accounts of the goods & chattels of the sd Charles and to recover and recieve the same or their proceeds in money, and for the same to give full and valid reciepts and discharges,[3] hereby confirming whatever you shall do in that behalf. Witness my hand this 25ᵗʰ day of December 1815.   TH: JEFFERSON

PoC (DLC); on verso of reused address cover to TJ; with some text along right margin missing due to polygraph misalignment.

[1] Preceding three words interlined.
[2] Preceding three words interlined.
[3] Preceding two words interlined.

From Horatio G. Spafford

ESTEEMED FRIEND—   Albany, 12 Mo. 25, 1815.

I enclose to thee a long Paper, which I wish to have thee read, & to favor me with thy suggestions on any amendment or alteration. I wish to learn thy opinion of the propriety of the sentiments, & whether or not it may be well to publish them now. It was intended for the Dec. & Jan. Nos. of my Magazine, but I have concluded to delay it till January. Please have the goodness to enclose the Paper to President Madison, for his perusal, as soon as thou hast had time to read it;—& to favor me with thy remarks. The people in the S. are not sufficiently aware of that despotism of theological opinion that threatens us in this quarter. Its influence must be counteracted. The history of our principal Schools of literature, would make the alarming progress of this influence plain. The man I allude to in p. 19, is Dʳ

Mason, Pres. Columbia College, New York. This paragraph alone, would make quite a bustle in the nests of young theologians.

I want to dedicate this Paper to thee, & ask thy permission. Thy name is a host—& the man who has braved danger through life, in discharge of duty, will certainly not fear the Priests. If thou wilt point out any improvements, I shall be glad to avail myself of thy great knowledge: & could wish to make the Paper worthy of the Man to whom I would dedicate it.

The life of Baron S. is concluded in the No of the Magazine I now send thee—& in my next I shall publish Count Volney's Letter, which I probably mentioned when I wrote thee before.

The ill state of my health must be my apology for the unfinished state of the Paper on the School, as well as for this hasty & illegible scrawl.

With esteem, thy friend,   H. G. SPAFFORD.

RC (MHi); at foot of text: "Th: Jefferson"; endorsed by TJ as received 3 Jan. 1816 and so recorded in SJL. Enclosures: (1) MS (not found) of Spafford's essay on establishing a national school of science and the mechanical arts and reforming the patent system, the published version of which subsequently appeared in the *American Magazine, a monthly miscellany*, vol. 1, nos. 8–9 (Jan.–Feb. 1816): 289–97, 313–26. (2) *American Magazine, a monthly miscellany*, vol. 1, no. 6 (Nov. 1815).

Spafford also wrote a letter this day to James MADISON on the subject of his essay, advising the president that he had asked TJ to forward the manuscript to him (DLC: Madison Papers). John Mitchell MASON was the provost, not the president, of Columbia College (later Columbia University) (*DAB*, 4:326, 6:369).

From Charles Yancey

Dʀ SIR   Richmond 27 decʳ 1815

enclosed is a bill which has for its object an alteration of our state Constitution any Information You may feel disposed to give after Reading it will be thankfully Recᵈ I expect You See the public prints & can be informed of our proceedings. accept of my good wishes for Your health & happiness with Sentiments of esteem I am Your friend & Mo. Ob Serᵗ   CHARLES YANCEY

RC (DLC); endorsed by TJ as received 9 Jan. 1816 and so recorded in SJL.

Yancey probably here enclosed a copy, not found, of a BILL "Requiring the Sheriffs of the different counties and corporations within this Commonwealth, to take the sense of the people upon the propriety of calling a Convention," of which the Virginia House of Delegates ordered 250 copies to be printed on 22 Dec. 1815 (*JHD* [1815–16 sess.], 63).

To William Bentley

DEAR SIR   Monticello Dec.[1] 28. 15

At the date of your letter of Oct. 30. I had just left home on a journey from which I am recently returned. I had many years ago understood that Professor Ebeling was engaged in a geographical work which would comprehend the US. and indeed I expected it was finished and published. I am glad to learn that his candor and discrimination have been sufficient to guard him against trusting the libel of D[r] Morse on this state. I wish it were in my power to give him the aid you ask. but it is not. the whole forenoon with me is engrossed by a correspondence too extensive and laborious for my age. health, habit, and necessary attention to my farms require me then to be on horseback until a late dinner, and the society of my family and friends, with some reading furnish the necessary relaxations of the rest of the day. add to this that the cession of my library to Congress has left me without materials for such an undertaking. I wish the part of his work which gives the geography of this country may be translated and published, that ourselves and the world may at length have something like a dispassionate account of these states. poor human nature! when we are obliged to appeal for the truth of mere facts from an eye-witness to one whose faculties for discovering it are only an honest candor and caution in sifting the grain from it's chaff!

The Professor's history of Hamburg is doubtless interesting and instructive, and valuable as a corrective of the false information we derive from newspapers. I should read it with pleasure; but I fear it's transportation and return would expose it to too much risk. notwithstanding all the French and British atrocities, which will for ever disgrace the present aera of history; their shameless[2] prostration of all the laws of morality which constitute the security, the peace and comfort of man, notwithstanding the waste of human life, and measure of human suffering which they have inflicted on the world, nations hitherto in slavery, have descried, thro' all this bloody mist, a glimmering of their own rights have dared to open their eyes, and to see that their own power & their own will suffice for their emancipation. their tyrants must now give them more moderate forms of government, and they seem now to be sensible of this themselves. instead of the parricide treason of Bonaparte in employing the means confided to him as a republican magistrate to the overthrow of that republic, and establishment of a military despotism in himself & his descendants, to the subversion of the neighboring governments, and erection of thrones for his brothers, his sisters and sycophants, had he honestly employed that power in the establishment & support of the freedom of his own country, there is not a nation in Europe which would not at this day have had a more rational government, one in which the will of the people should have had a moderating and salutary influence. the work will now be longer, will swell more rivers with blood, produce more sufferings & more crimes. but it will be consummated. and that it may be, will be the theme of my constant prayers, while I shall remain in the earth beneath, or in the heavens above. to these I add sincere wishes for your own health & happiness.

TH: JEFFERSON

RC (MWA: Thomas Jefferson Papers); addressed: "Mr William Bentley Salem Massachusets"; franked; postmarked Milton, 3 Jan. PoC (DLC). Tr (MHi); posthumous copy; frayed at top, with loss of dateline; incomplete. Recorded in SJL as a letter of 28 Dec. 1815.

Christoph Daniel Ebeling had consulted TJ on his work MANY YEARS AGO, in 1795. In composing his thoughts on Ebeling's queries at that time (*PTJ*, 28:423–9,

506–10), TJ wrote that Jedidiah MORSE and Noah Webster were "Good authorities for whatever relates to the Eastern states, and perhaps as far South as the Delaware. But South of that, their information is worse than none at all; except as far as they quote good authorities" (p. 506).

[1] RC: "Jan." Corrected to "Dec." in PoC.
[2] Tr ends here.

From Lafayette

MY DEAR FRIEND   La Grange Xber 28h 1815

The Bearer of these Lines is Mr Lakanal Member of the french institut, officer of the University and inspector General of the New Metrical System who abandons those functions and a Handsome treatment to Become a Settler in the State of Kentucky. He Has for Several years been in the Representative Assemblies of france, and is Going to Seeck in the U.S. Liberty, Security, and Happiness. I Cannot procure for Him a Greater Gratification than by introducing Him to you, and I know you will find a pleasure in favouring Him with your Advices and Recommendations for the part of the Country Where He means to Settle Himself and family.

after a short excursion into public life I am Returned to my Rural Retirement in a Situation not unlike that which prevented my Accepting your kind invitation. I Have not for a very long while Heard from you and eagerly Beg you to write were it only for a line.

Most Affectionately forever Your friend   LAFAYETTE

RC (DLC); endorsed by TJ as received 10 July 1816 and so recorded in SJL. Enclosed in Joseph Lakanal to TJ, 1 June 1816.

In this context, TREATMENT means "salary" or "emolument," from the French "traitement" (*OED*). In an 1804 letter to TJ, Lafayette declined to settle on Louisiana lands given to him by the United States government, choosing to remain in RURAL RETIREMENT in France (Lafayette to TJ, 8 Oct. 1804 [PHi]).

From Martin Dawson

DEAR SIR   Milton 29th December 1815

I have not as yet herd from John Bacon, and I expect he is dead, I have concluded to receive the Money due him, a[nd take?] the Necessary Steps to pay it to him, or his Heirs, above you [...] the Amounts, also your Accot with me to the first of August last If Convenient you will please to send me the Money to Court on Monday next by Mr Edmund Bacon, a Dft on Richmond will be the same to me as Money, a part of the bond belongs to Mr Edmund Bacon, he can give me in my Recpt for his part and take in the bond,

Mr John Watson & my Self have been in partnership in the Mercantile Business in this place since the first of August last—we have yet remaining on hand, Plains, Coarse Cloths, Kerzeys Blanketts Kendal Cottons German Oznas &C of our Fall Supply of goods, Shoud you require any of those Articles, we will be Glad to Supply you with any Other goods we have on hand—   Yo. Ob. Hu, Sevts   MARTIN DAWSON

Thomas Jefferson esqre

1815	In Account with Martin Dawson			
June 13	To 6 lbs Shot ℔ Note		@ 1/6	$1.50
July 7	" 8 Loaves Sugar [Wt?]1 46¾ lbs		3/	23.37
				$24.87
Decr 31	" part of your Bond to Edmund Bacon Assigned by him to John Bacon due 1 Augt 1813	$327.12		
	Interest on Same from 1 Augt 1813 to 31 Decr 1815	47.48		374.60
				$399.47

RC (ViU: TJP-ER); account at head of text; mutilated at seal; addressed: "Thomas Jefferson esqre } Monticello"; endorsed by TJ. Recorded in SJL as received 2 Jan. 1816.

The BOND assigned by Edmund Bacon to John Bacon was TJ's Promissory Note to Edmund Bacon, 7 Apr. 1813.

1 Word illegible.

To George Fleming

At the date of your favor of Oct. 30. I had just left home on a journey to a distant possession of mine, from which I am but recently returned: and I wish that the matter of my answer could compensate for it's delay. but, Sir, it happens that of all the machines which have been employed to aid human labor, I have made my self the least acquainted with (that which is certainly the most powerful of all) the steam engine. in it's original & simple form indeed, as first constructed by Newcomen & Savary, it had been a subject of my early studies: but once possessed of the principle, I ceased to follow up the numerous modifications of the machinery for employing it, of which I do not know whether England or our own country has produced the greatest number. hence I am entirely incompetent to form a judgment of the comparative merit of yours with those preceding it; and the cession of my library to Congress has left me without any examples to turn to. I see indeed in yours the valuable properties of simplicity, cheapness, & accomodation to the small and more numerous calls of life; and the calculations of it's power appear sound & correct. yet experience & frequent disappointment have taught me not to be over-confident in theories or calculations, until actual trial of the whole combination has stamped it with approbation. should this sanction be added, the importance of your construction will be enhanced by the consideration that a smaller agent, applicable to our daily concerns, is infinitely more valuable than the greatest which can be used only for great objects. for these interest the few alone, the former the many. I once had an idea that it might perhaps be possible to economize the steam of a common pot, kept boiling on the kitchen fire until it's accumulation should be sufficient to give a stroke, and altho the strokes might not be rapid, there would be enough of them in the day to raise from an adjacent well the water necessary for daily use; to wash the linen, knead the bread, beat the homony, churn the butter, turn the spit, and to do all other houshold offices which require only a regular mechanical motion. the unproductive hands now necessarily employed in these, might then increase the produce of our fields. I proposed it to mr Rumsey, one of our greatest mechanics, who believed in it's possibility, and promised to turn his mind to it. but his death soon after disappointed this hope. of how much more value would this be to ordinary life than Watt's & Bolton's 30. pr of millstones to be turned by one engine, of which I saw 7 pr in actual operation. it is an interesting part of your question, how much fuel would be requisite for your machine?

Your letter being evidence of your attention to Mechanical things, and to their application to matters of daily interest, I will mention a trifle in this way, which yet is not without value. I presume, like the rest of us in the country, you are in the habit of houshold manufacture, and that you will not, like too many, abandon it on the return of peace, to enrich our late enemy, and to nourish foreign agents in our bosom, whose baneful influence & intrigues cost us so much embarrasment & dissension.   the shirting for our laborers has been an object of some difficulty. flax is so injurious to our lands, and of so scanty produce, that I have never attempted it. hemp, on the other hand, is abundantly productive and will grow for ever on the same spot. but the breaking and beating it, which has been always done by hand, is so slow, so laborious, and so much complained of by our laborers, that I had given it up, and purchased & manufactured cotton for their shirting. the advanced price of this however now makes it a serious item of expence; and in the mean time a method of removing the difficulty of preparing hemp occurred to me, so simple & so cheap, that I return to it's culture and manufacture. to a person having a threshing machine, the addition of a hemp break will not cost more than 12. or 15.D. you know that the first mover in that machine is a horizontal horsewheel with cogs on it's upper face. on these is placed a wallower and shaft which give motion to the threshing apparatus. on the opposite side of this same wheel I place another wallower and shaft, thro' which, and near it's outer end, I pass a cross-arm of sufficient strength, projecting on each side 15.I. in this form. nearly under the cross arm is placed a very strong hemp-break, much stronger & heavier than those for the hand. it's head block particularly is massive, and 4.f. high, and near it's upper end, in front, is fixed a strong pin (which we may call it's horn). by this the cross arm lifts & lets fall the break twice in every revolution of the wallower. a man feeds the break with hemp stalks, and a little person holds under the head block a large twist of the hemp which has been broken, resembling a twist of tobacco but larger, where it is more perfectly beaten than I have ever seen done by hand. if the horse wheel has 144. cogs, the wallower 11. rounds, and the horse goes 3 times round in a minute, it will give about 80. strokes in a minute. I had fixed a break to be moved by the gate of my sawmill, which broke & beat at the rate of 200 ℔. a day. but the inconveniences of interrupting that induced me to try the power of a horse, and I have found it answer perfectly. the power being less, so also probably will be the effect, of which I cannot make a fair trial until I commence on my new crop. I expect that a single horse will do the breaking & beating of 10 men. something of this kind has been so long wanted by the cultivaters of hemp, that as soon as I can speak of it's effect with certainty, I shall probably describe it anonymously in the public papers, in order to forestall the prevention of it's use by some interloping patentee.   I shall be happy to learn that on actual experiment your steam engine fulfil's the expectations we form of it, and I pray you to accept the assurances of my esteem & respect.

TH: JEFFERSON

PoC (DLC); at foot of first page: "Mr George Fleming."

SAVARY: Thomas Savery (*ODNB*). TJ presumably proposed his ideas on the use of steam power to American inventor James RUMSEY when the two men met in France in 1789 (*ANB*; *PTJ*, 15:39–40, 145–6). TJ visited James WATT's and Matthew Boulton's (BOLTON'S) steam mill in London in 1786 (*PTJ*, 9:400–1). A WALLOWER is a trundle, or lantern-wheel (*OED*).

To Pierre Samuel Du Pont de Nemours

Monticello. Dec. 31. 15.

Nothing, my very dear and antient friend, could have equalled the mortification I felt on my arrival at home, and receipt of the information that I had lost the happiness of your visit. the season had so far advanced, and the weather become so severe, that together with the information given me by mr Correa, so early as September, that your friends even then were dissuading the journey I had set it down as certain it would be postponed to a milder season of the ensuing year. I had yielded therefore with the less reluctance to a detention in Bedford by a slower progress of my workmen than had been counted on. I have never more desired any thing than a full and free conversation with you. I have not understood the transactions in France during the years 14. and 15. from the newspapers we cannot even conjecture the secret and real history: and I had looked for it to your visit. a pamphlet (Le Conciliateur) received from M. Jullien had given me some idea of the obliquities & imbecilities of the Bourbons, during their first restoration. some maneuvres of both parties I had learnt from La Fayette, and more recently from Gallatin. but the note you referred me to at page 360. of your letter to Say has possessed me more intimately of the views, the conduct and consequences of the last apparition of Napoleon. still much is wanting. I wish to know what were the intrigues which brought him back, and what those which finally crushed him? what parts were acted by A. B. C. D. E.ᵗc. some of whom I know, & some I do not? how did the body of the nation stand affectioned, comparatively, between the fool and the tyrant? Eᵗc. Eᵗc. Eᵗc.   from the account my family gives me of your sound health, and of the vivacity & vigor of your mind, I will still hope we shall meet again, and that the fine temperature of our early summer, to wit of May and June, may suggest to you the salutary effects of exercise, and change of air & scene. en attendant we will turn to other subjects.

That your opinion of the hostile intentions of Great Britain towards us is sound, I am satisfied, from her movements North & South of us, as well as from her temper. she feels the gloriole of her late golden atchievements tarnished by our successes against her by sea and land; and will not be contented until she has wiped it off by triumphs over us also. I rely however on the Volcanic state of Europe to present other objects for her arms and her apprehensions: and am not without hope we shall be permitted to proceed peaceably in making children, and maturing and moulding our strength & resources.[1] it is impossible that France should rest under her present oppressions and humiliations. she will rise in that gigantic strength which cannot be annihilated, and will fatten her fields with the blood of her enemies. I only wish she may exercise patience and forbearance until divisions among them may give her a choice of sides.   to the overwhelming power of England I see but two chances of limit. the first in her bankruptcy, which will deprive her of the golden instrument of all her successes. the other in that ascendancy which nature destines for us by immutable laws. but to hasten this last consummation, we too must exercise patience & forbearance. for 20. years to come we should consider peace as the summum bonum of our country. at the end of that period we shall be 20. millions in number, and 40. in energy, when encountering the starved & rickety paupers and dwarfs of English workshops. by that time I hope your grandson will have become one of our High-admirals, and bear distinguished part in retorting the wrongs of both his countries on the most implacable and cruel of their enemies.   in this hope, & because I love you, and all who are dear to you, I wrote to the President in the instant of reading your letter of the 7ᵗʰ on the subject of his adoption into our navy. I did it because I was gratified in doing it, while I knew it was unnecessary. the sincere respect and high estimation in which the

President holds you, is such that there is no gratification, within the regular exercise of his functions, which he would withhold from you. be assured then that, if within that compass, this business is safe.

Were you any other than whom you are, I should shrink from the task you have proposed to me, of undertaking to judge of the merit of your own translation of the excellent letter on education. after having done all which good sense & eloquence could do on the original, you must not ambition the double meed of English eloquence also. did you ever know an instance of one who could write in a foreign language with the elegance[2] of a native? Cicero wrote Commentaries of his own Consulship in Greek. they perished unknown, while his native compositions have immortalised him with themselves. No, my dear friend; you must not risk the success of your letter on foreignisms of style which may weaken it's effect. some native pen must give it to our countrymen in a native dress, faithful to it's original. you will find such with the aid of our friend Correa, who knows every body, and will readily think of some one who has time and talent for this work. I have neither. till noon I am daily engaged in a correspondence much too extensive and laborious for my age. from noon to dinner health, habit and business require me to be on horseback; and render the society of my family & friends a necessary relaxation for the rest of the day. these occupations scarcely leave time for the papers of the day; and to renounce entirely the sciences and belles-lettres is impossible. had not mr Gilmer just taken his place in the ranks of the bar, I think we could have engaged him in this work. but I am persuaded that mr Correa's intimacy with the persons of promise in our country will leave you without difficulty in laying this work of instruction open to our citizens at large.

I have not yet had time to read your Equinoctial republics, nor the letter to Say; because I am still engrossed by the letters which had accumulated during my absence. the latter I accept with thankfulness, and will speedily read and return the former. God bless you, and maintain you in strength of body, and mind, until your own wishes shall be to resign both.   TH: JEFFERSON

RC (DeGH: Pierre Samuel Du Pont de Nemours Papers, Winterthur Manuscripts). PoC (DLC); at foot of first page: "M. Dupont de Nemours."

EN ATTENDANT: "in the meantime"; GLORIOLE: "halo" (OED). Du Pont's GRANDSON was Samuel Francis Du Pont.

[1] Preceding three words interlined in place of "strength."
[2] Word interlined in place of "eloquence."

From Hosea Humphrey

R<small>ESPECTED</small> <small>SIR</small>   Johnston near Providence R.I. Decr 31st 1815

Although you enjoy in retirement the warmest approbation and esteem of every honest American yet it is not to be supposed that your mind is not occupied with carefull attention to the concerns of our country and if notwithstanding the abilities and integrity of our cheif Magistrate and the administration in general occasion requires your usefull advice is not with held yet sir it cannot be doubted but you find leasure to attend to those Philosophical investigations which have Occupied your mind from childhood which is incontestably evident from those comprehensive views of human concerns that you have so frequently exhibited and which could not be disconnected with a knowledge of almost all attainable[1] natural causes and effects

Having published many new Ideas concerning natural opperations and novelty being considered by a great part of mankind as conclusive evidence of error and being sensible of the probability thereof from prejudice in favour of my own productions—but still having confidence in the correctness of what I have advanced and wishing the work to be perused by the ablest Philosophers not doubting they will do strict justice in the premises I have taken the liberty to present you a volume which tho small in extent may be much Smaller in consequence and permit me sir earnestly to request that if upon perusal you Shall find it unworthy of attention you will consider yourself under not the least obligation to read it through—and if at any future time when at Leasure you Shall consider it So far worthy attention as to induce you to write me any observations concerning it, you will be at least as candid in notifying me of its errors as any matters you may approve of therein

The accompanying pamphlet is worth your reading no further than to discover my political Sentiments as respects parties

The hand Bill contains an attempted appology for the want of systematic arrangement in the work a part of which ought to have been bound with the Sheets

Accept sir the assurance of my Cordial respects for your merit and unfeigned wishes for your happiness   H<small>OSEA</small> H<small>UMPHREY</small>

RC (DLC); addressed: "Thomas Jefferson Esqr late Presiden of the United States"; endorsed by TJ as received 8 June 1816 and so recorded in SJL. Enclosures: (1) Humphrey, *A Dissertation on Fire, or Miscellaneous Inquiries and Reflections concerning the Operations of the Laws of Nature; with An Appendix, containing Thoughts on Memory, Reflection, Decision, Muscular Motion, &c.* (Providence, 1814; Poor, *Jefferson's Library*, 7 [no. 302]). (2) Humphrey, *Long Talk, spoken at Seekhonk, on the Fourth of July, 1812; before the Tammany Society,*

Panther Tribe, Number 1—Massachusetts (Newport, R.I., 1813; Poor, *Jefferson's Library*, 13 [no. 826]; TJ's copy in ViU). (3) Advertisement for Humphrey's *Dissertation on Fire*, indicating that Humphrey began the work for his own entertainment when illness and severe weather prevented him from working; describing his lifelong interest in observing and considering natural phenomena; expressing his surprise that what he had originally planned as a short, anonymous pamphlet had swollen to double its intended length plus an appendix; attributing any errors in the book to the limited time he could devote to writing, owing to his need to work to pay off the debt he incurred when his cotton mill burned; and asserting that the work is entirely the product of "his own reflection and reasoning" (broadside in ViU, bound with TJ's copy of Humphrey's *Long Talk*). Probably enclosed in Hugh Nelson to TJ, 7 June 1816.

Hosea Humphrey (1757–1816), physician and textile manufacturer, was a native of Norfolk, Connecticut. Early in his career he worked as a saddle and harness maker in Providence, Rhode Island. Humphrey represented Norfolk in Connecticut's House of Representatives in 1787, and he served in the state's 1788 ratification convention, where he voted against adopting the new United States Constitution. By 1800 he was living in Rhode Island, where he served as justice of the peace for North Providence, 1801–06. Humphrey was running a wool-carding business by 1805, and he opened a cotton mill in North Providence the following year. He died in Johnston, Rhode Island (Frederick Humphreys, *The Humphreys Family in America* [1883], 144–5; Merrill Jensen, John P. Kaminski, and others, eds., *The Documentary History of the Ratification of the Constitution* [1976–], 3:343, 436–7, 539, 547; DNA: RG 29, CS, R.I., Providence, 1800; Joseph Jencks Smith, comp., *Civil and Military List of Rhode Island. 1800–1850* [1901], 19, 33, 50, 65, 79, 92; *Providence Phœnix*, 21 Sept. 1805, 14 Feb. 1807; *Letter from the Secretary of the Treasury, transmitting a Report, in Part, on the Subject of American Manufactures* [Washington, 1810]; John Warner Barber, *Historical Collections, being a general collection of interesting facts, traditions, biographical sketches, anecdotes, &c., relating to the History and Antiquities of Every Town in Massachusetts* [1839], 138; *Boston Weekly Messenger*, 11 July 1816).

On this date Humphrey sent a similar letter and set of enclosures to President James Madison (DLC: Madison Papers).

[1] Word interlined.

To José Corrêa da Serra

Monticello Jan. 1. 16.

I learnt, my dear Sir, with inexpressible concern, on my arrival at home, that my detention in Bedford had lost me the pleasure of your visit here. having heard nothing from you since our parting on the Natural bridge, I had supposed your return longer delayed than you had expected, and that even possibly your course might be so shaped as to take Poplar Forest in your way. I hungered for your observations on the country you had passed over, and should not probably have been mistaken in your estimate of it. it was additionally unlucky that when you were at Monticello my family did not observe the letters for you lying on my table. some of them had been recieved a considerable time before, but not knowing your exact trajectory, or in what part of it they might light on you, I was afraid to risk them in the attempt. I now inclose them, and add a letter I wrote you under cover to mr Rhea, expecting it would get to Knoxville by mail before your arrival there, as it probably did: but mr Rhea being unfortunately absent on a journey to the Westward, you failed in the receipt of it, as in the benefit you might have derived from his friendly attentions. he lately returned it to me with expressions of his regret at having lost the opportunity of being useful to you; and I now inclose it only to shew that the failure did not proceed from want of attention in me. not knowing whether you may have arrived at Philadelphia when this gets there, I put the whole under cover to mr Vaughan.

The death of Dr Barton revives my anxiety to recover the MS. journals of Capt Lewis, for the satisfaction of his family; and may at the same time facilitate it. he had promised me sacredly that he would see to it's restoration; and as you were so kind as to say you would attend to it on your return to Philadelphia, I now earnestly entreat your aid for this object. knowing nothing of what is doing, or intended to be done as to the publication of the papers respecting the natural history & geography of the country, you will oblige me by any information you can obtain on this subject. the right to these papers is in the government, as may be seen by the instructions to Capt Lewis. they were left in his hands that he might derive to himself the pecuniary benefits of their publication, on the presumption they would certainly be published. if that presumption is to fail, the government must reclaim them; and it is to put this object into an effective course that I wish for information what is doing, or likely to be done. I know I should have the concurrence of Genl Clarke in this, were he within the timely reach of consultation; and I shall not fail to advise with him as soon as I can do it understandingly.

I am ashamed to ask whether your observation or information as to the Cisterns of Charleston can facilitate the perfecting those I have constructed: because by some accident which I cannot ascertain, I lost the paper you were so kind as to give me at Dowthwaite's. you recollect our situation there. I was shaving, changing linen, opening and doing up my baggage on the bed, when you put that paper into my hands. I thought it certain that I put it into my pocket; but when I got back to Poplar Forest I could not find it. whether it was lost out of my pocket, or laid & left on the bed, I cannot say; but being lost, I am thrown again on your goodness to replace it if you can.

What effect will the apparent restoration of the Bourbons have on your movements? will it tempt your return? I do not see in this a restoration of quiet. on the contrary I consider France as in a more Volcanic state than at any preceding time. there must be an explosion, and one of the most destructive character. I look forward to crimes more fierce and pitiless than those which have already distinguished that bloody revolution. these are not scenes, my dear friend, for you to be thrown into. they have no analogies with the tranquility of your character. true we cannot offer you the scientific society of Paris. but who can enjoy science, or who think of it, in the midst of insurrection, madness and massacre? besides, you possess all science within yourself. from others you can get nothing new, and the pleasure of communicating it should be greatest where it is most wanting. stay then with us. become our instructor. help us on in the paths of that science which is wanting to our ripening character. you know how much you are beloved and desired every where, welcome every where, but no where so cordially as at Monticello. come and make it your home then, the place of rest & tranquility, from which, as your piè-des-tal, you can make what excursions you please. you will find it's summers as moderate as those of Philadelphia, and it's winters more so. had I arrived before your departure, I should have pressed your trial of it the present winter. a comfortable room, in a country of fuel, for retirement when you chose it, and a sociable family, full of affection & respect for you, when tired of being alone, would have made you forget the suspension[1] of the season for botanical rambling. turn this subject in your mind, my good friend, and let us have as much of the benefit of the result as shall be consistent with your own happiness, and in all cases be assured of my warm affection & respect.   TH: JEFFERSON

PoC (DLC); at foot of first page: "M. Correa"; endorsed by TJ. Enclosures: TJ to Corrêa da Serra and to John Milledge, both 22 Sept. 1815. Other enclosures not found.

No covering letter from TJ to John VAUGHAN is recorded in SJL, and none has been found. Benjamin Smith BARTON died of tuberculosis in Philadelphia on 19 Dec. 1815 (ANB; Philadelphia Poulson's American Daily Advertiser, 20 Dec. 1815). He had been assigned the task of preparing the scientific journals of Meri-

wether LEWIS for publication in 1810, but he never completed this work (Moulton, Journals of Lewis & Clark, 2:530–1). Barton had PROMISED that he would return the journals in a letter to TJ of 16 Oct. 1810. TJ's INSTRUCTIONS to Lewis included directions on creating a written record of the expedition (TJ to Lewis, 20 June 1803 [DLC]). Robert Douthat's (DOWTHWAITE'S) tavern was at Natural Bridge. PIÈ-DES-TAL: "pedestal" (OED).

[1] Word interlined in place of "absence."

From Jean David

J'ai reçu la lettre que vous avez pris la peine de m'ecrire le 25 Decembre dernier, et vous remercie beaucoup de votre intention à me recommander auprès des personnes qui pourroient être dans le cas de m'employer.

Je Sens que d'après les essais inutiles qui ont été tentés pour introduire la culture de la vigne en Virginie, on ne doit s'y livrer aujourd'hui qu'avec beaucoup de reserve Je dis plus, quand même aucun essai n'auroit eu lieu, je n'oserois pas conseiller à un particulier Seul de faire en commençant une depense considerable à ce sujet, quoique je Sois intimement persuadé que cette culture ne peut manquer de reussir et qu'on parviendroit à faire du très bon vin. Ce que vous me dites des vignes Sauvages que l'on trouve dans vos bois, me confirme dans mon opinion, car Si ces vignes donnent d'elles mêmes du raisin propre à faire du bon vin, que ne doit on pas attendre de celles qui Seroient cultivées. Cette même vigne etant greffée Seroit peut être le meilleur plant à employer

Si j'avois des facultés pecuniaires j'entreprendrois cet essai pour mon propre compte, mais la chose m'est impossible, il faudroit pour cela que je pusse me procurer ma Subsistance de quelqu'autre maniére, et alors le peu d'epargnes que je pourrois faire, je l'emploierois à cette entreprise, et en même temps j'offrirois mes Services à ceux qui voudroient essayer de cette culture Soit en grand Soit en petit. mes conditions leur conviendroient certainement, car je ne leur demanderois pour le moment aucun Salaire, mais Seulement une portion en nature du nouveau produit que je leur aurois procuré.

Si je trouvois à m'occuper à Richmond, la rive gauche de <u>james River</u> dans les environs de cette ville me paroitroit une position excellente à cet effet; je n'y craindrois qu'une chose, cest qu'on me[1] vint voler les raisins Sur la vigne—

Au cas que je ne trouve pas à travailler dans ce pays, mon dessein est de le quitter dans le mois de mars prochain; je me rendrai peut être dans le Kentuky ou l'on m'a dit que beaucoup de gens cultivent la vigne et aux quels je pourrois être utile soit pour Sa culture même Soit pour la maniére de faire le vin; mais avant de le quitter (Si la depense n'est pas trop forte pour moi,) je tacherai d'aller voir sur le Potomak la plantation dont vous me parlez, et proffiterai alors de l'offre que vous me faites dans votre lettre, pour me procurer l'avantage de votre connoissanc[e] personnelle—

Je vous Salue respectueuse[ment]   J David

S<small>IR</small>   Richmond 1 January 1816.

I have received the letter you took the trouble of writing on 25 December, and I thank you very much for your intention to recommend me to persons who might employ me.

From the fruitless attempts that have been made to introduce the cultivation of vineyards into Virginia, I feel that it must now be attempted only with a great deal of caution. Even if no attempt had taken place, I would not dare advise an individual acting alone to spend a considerable sum getting started, even though I am absolutely convinced that it cannot fail to succeed and that good wine can be produced. Your account of the wild grapes found in your woods confirms my opinion, because if, on their own, these vines produce grapes suitable for making good wine, what cannot be expected from those that would be cultivated? This same wild vine, once grafted, would perhaps be the best plant to use

If I had the financial means, I would undertake this experiment on my own account, but that is impossible. I would need to find other ways of making a living and then use the small amount of money I could save to finance the enterprise. I would however offer my services to those interested in trying this culture on either a large or a small scale. My terms would certainly suit them, as for the time being I would ask them for no salary, but only for a share of the new produce I procured for them.

If I could find employment in Richmond, the left bank of the <u>James River</u> in the vicinity of this city would seem to me to be excellent for this purpose, and my only fear would be someone stealing the grapes off the vine—

In case I do not find work in this country, I plan to depart next March. I will perhaps head for Kentucky, where I am told that a lot of people cultivate grapevines. I might be useful to them either in growing grapes or making wine; but before leaving (if the expense is within my means), I will try to visit the plantation on the Potomac that you mention to me and take advantage of the offer in your letter of giving me the advantage of your personal acquaintance.

I salute you respectfully   J D<small>AVID</small>

RC (DLC); torn at seal; addressed: "The honourable Th^s Jefferson Esqr Monticello"; franked; postmarked Richmond, 3 Jan.; endorsed by TJ as received 9 Jan. 1816 and so recorded in SJL. Translation by Dr. Genevieve Moene.

¹ Manuscript: "ne."

To Patrick Gibson

D<small>EAR</small> S<small>IR</small>   Monticello Jan. 2. 16.

Your favor of Dec. 22. is recieved, and I now return the note with my signature. what you mention of the boat load of 35. barrels of flour mentioned in mine of Oct. 28. not having been delivered; is the first notice I have of that failure, and the 2^d time I have been misinformed in the same manner. the tenants of my mill are bound to de-

liver their rent of fifty odd barrels a quarter at Richmond, and assured me on the former occasion that 55. and on the latter that 35.
barrels had actually gone from there to be delivered in Richmond
on my account. it seems however that their destination has been
changed by the way. my crop flour here has been waiting a rise of the
river. [m]r Gilmer is engaged to carry it down, and promises if there
is not a rise in a few days he will take it by half loads to Columbia &
whole loads from there. this increases the expence of transportation[.] my crop here has been an indifferent one, & that in Bedford
worse. should it not enable me to take my whole note out of the bank,
it will furnish enough to pay up all the curtailments which the bank
may require for the year.   being entirely out of wine, I have
written to Dr Fernandes of Norfolk for a quarter cask of Lisbon or
Port, or Sherry, and have desired him to draw on you for the cost.
accept the assurance of my great esteem & respect.

TH: JEFFERSON

P.S. having got 800. bushels of wheat into the ground here & in Bedford, and aiming at a tolerable crop of tob° there, I hope at length to
get freed from the difficulties which embargoes, war, heavy taxes &
short crops have kept me laboring under for the last three years. the
wine when it comes to your hands must be trusted only to Johnson or
Gilmer <u>personally.</u>

PoC (NjMoHP: Lloyd W. Smith Collection); on verso of reused address cover
of Peter Derieux to TJ, 12 Dec. 1815; mutilated at seal, with several words rewritten by TJ; adjacent to signature: "mr
Gibson"; endorsed by TJ. Enclosure not
found.

TJ had previously been MISINFORMED
by the TENANTS of his mill, Thomas
Eston Randolph and Thomas Mann Randolph, when they told him that they were
sending 213 barrels of flour to Gibson to
pay for rent of TJ's mill. In fact, 67 of the
barrels had been delivered elsewhere
(Gibson to TJ, 5 July 1815; TJ to Gibson,
28 July 1815; *MB*, 2:1310).

To Alden Partridge

SIR   Monticello Jan. 2. 16.[1]
I am but recently returned from my journey to the neighborhood
of the Peaks of Otter, and find here your favors of Nov. 23 & Dec. 9.
I have therefore to thank you for your meteorological table and the
Corrections of Col° Williams's altitudes of the mountains of Virginia, which I had not before seen; but especially for the very able
extract on Barometrical measures. the precision of the calculations,
and soundness of the principles on which they are founded furnish,

I am satisfied, a great approximation towards truth, and raise that method of estimating heights to a considerable degree of rivalship with the trigonometrical. the last is not without some sources of inaccuracy, as you have truly stated. the admeasurement of the base is liable to errors which can be rendered insensible only by such degrees of care as have been exhibited by the Mathematicians who have been employed in measuring degrees, on the surface of the earth. the measure of the angles, by the wonderful perfection to which the graduation of instruments has been brought by a Bird, a Ramsden, a Troughton, removes nearly all distrust from that operation; and we may add that the effect of refraction, rarely worth notice in short distances, admits of correction by[2] well established laws. these sources of error once reduced to be insensible, their geometrical employment is certainty itself. no two men can differ on a principle of trigonometry. not so, as to the theories of Barometrical mensuration. on these have been great differences of opinion, and among characters of just celebrity.

Dr Halley reckoned $\frac{1}{10}$ I. of mercury equal to 90.f. altitude of the atmosphere:

Derham thought it equal to something less than 90.f.

Cassini's tables to 24° of the Barometer allowed 676. toises of altitude;

Mariote's   to the same   544. toises

Scheuchzer's   to the same   559. toises

Nettleton's tables applied to a difference of .5975 of mercury, in a particular instance gave 512.17 f. of altitude, and Bouguer's & DeLuc's rules, to the same difference gave 579.5 f   Sr Isaac Newton had established that at heights in Arithmetrical progression the ratio of rarity in the air would be geometrical; and this being the character of the Natural numbers and their Logarithms, Bouguer adopted the ratio in his mensuration of the mountains of S. America, and, stating in French lignes the height of the mercury at different stations, took their Logarithms to 5 places only, including the index, and considered the resulting difference as expressing that of the altitudes in French toises. he then applied corrections required by the effect of the temperature of the moment on the air and mercury. his process, on the whole, agrees very exactly with that established in your excellent extract. in 1776. I observed the height of the mercury at the base and summit of the mountain I live on, and, by Nettleton's tables, estimated the height at 512.17 f. and called it about 500.f. in the Notes on Virginia. but calculating it since, on the same observations, according to Bouguer's method with De Luc's improvements, the result was 579.5 f. and lately I measured the same height trigonometrically, with the aid of a base of 1175.f in a vertical plane with the summit, and at the distance of about 1500. yards from the axis of the mountain, and made it 599.35 f. I consider this as testing the advance of the barometrical process towards truth by the adoption of the Logarithmic ratio of heights and densities; and continued observations and experiments will continue to advance it still more. but the first character of a common measure of things being that of invariability, I can never suppose that a substance so heterogeneous & variable as the atmospheric fluid, changing daily and hourly it's weight & dimensions to the amount sometimes of one tenth of the whole, can be applied as a standard of measure to any thing with as much Mathematical exactness as a trigonometrical process. it is still however a resource of great value for these purposes, because it's use is so easy, in comparison with the other, and especially where the grounds are unfavorable for a base; and it's results are so near the truth as to answer all the common purposes of information. indeed I should in all cases prefer the use of both, to warn us against gross error, and to put us, when that is suspected, on a repetition of our process. when lately measuring trigonometrically the height of the peaks of Otter (as my letter of Oct. 12. informed you I was about to do) I very much wished for a barometer, to try the height by that also. but it was too far and too hazardous to carry my own, and there was not one in that neighborhood.   On the subject of that admeasurement, I must premise that my object was only to gratify a common curiosity as to the height of those mountains, which we deem our highest, and to furnish an à peu près, sufficient to satisfy us in a comparison of them with the other mountains of our own, or of other countries. I therefore neither provided such instruments, nor aimed at such extraordinary accuracy in the measures of my base, as abler operators would have employed in the more important object of measuring a degree, or of ascertaining the relative position of different places for astronomical or geographical purposes. my instrument was a theodolite by Ramsden, whose horisontal and vertical circles were of $3\frac{1}{2}$ I. radius it's graduation subdivided by Noniuses to 3.′ admitting however by it's intervals, a further subdivision by the eye to a single minute, with two telescopes, the one fixed, the other moveable, and a Gunter's chain of 4. poles, accurately adjusted in it's length, and carefully attended on it's application to the base line. the Sharp, or Southern peak was first measured by a base of 2806.32 f. in the vertical plane of the axis of the mountain. a base then nearly parallel with the two mountains of 6589 f. was measured, and observations taken at each end, of the altitudes and horizontal angles of each[3] apex, and such other auxiliary observations made as to the stations, inclination of the base E^{t}c as a good degree of correctness in the result would require. the ground of our bases was favorable, being an open plain of close grazed meadow, on both sides of the Otter river, declining so uniformly with the descent of the river as to give no other trouble than an observation of it's angle of inclination, in order to reduce the base to the plane of the horizon. from the summit of the sharp peak I took also the angle of altitude of the flat or Northern one above it, my other observations sufficing to give their distance from one another. the result was, the mean height of the Sharp peak above   f

ye surface of Otter R.   2946.5

                  of the flat peak   3103.5

      the distance between the two summits   9507.73

      their rhumb N. 33° 50′ E. the distance of the stations of observation from the points in the bases of the mountains vertically under their summits was the shortest 19002.2 f. the longest 24523.3 f. these mountains are computed to be visible to 15. counties of the state, without the advantage of counter-elevations, and to several more with that advantage.   I must add that I have gone over my calculations but once, and nothing is more possible than the mistake of a figure, now and then, in calculating so many triangles, which may occasion some variation in the result. I mean therefore, when I have leisure, to go again over the whole.   The ridge of mountains of which Monticello is one, is generally low. there is one in it however, called Peter's mountain, considerably higher than the general ridge. this being within a dozen miles of me North Eastwardly, I think, in the spring of the year, to measure it by both processes, which may serve as another trial of the Logarithmic theory. should I do this you shall know the result. in the mean time accept assurances of my great respect & esteem   TH: JEFFERSON

RC (NN); addressed: "Capt A. Partridge Norwich Windsor county Vermont"; franked; postmarked Milton, 3 Jan. PoC (DLC).

Edmond HALLEY published his findings on the relationship between the height of mercury and altitude in "A Discourse of the Rule of the Decrease of the Height of the Mercury in the Barometer, according as Places are elevated above the Surface of the Earth," Royal Society of London, *Philosophical Transactions* 16 (1686/92): 104–16. William DERHAM found in his experiments that mercury in a barometer would drop $\frac{1}{10}$ of an inch at an elevation of either 80 or 82 feet ("Part of a Letter of Mr. William Derham . . . Giving an Account of some Experiments about the Heighth of the Mercury in the Barometer, at Top and Bottom of the Monument," *Philosophical Transactions* 20 [1698]: 2–4). For one version of the TABLES of Jacques Cassini, Edme Mariotte, and Johann J. Scheuchzer, see John G. Scheuchzer, "The Barometrical Method of measuring the Height of Mountains, with two new Tables shewing the Height of the Atmosphere at given Altitudes of Mercury," *Philosophical Transactions* 35 (1727/28): 537–47. Thomas NETTLETON'S TABLES were published as "Observations concerning the Height of the Barometer, at different Elevations above the Surface of the Earth," *Philosophical Transactions* 33 (1724/25): 308–12.

TJ obtained the RULES of Pierre Bouguer and Jean André Deluc for estimating heights barometrically from the entry on barometers in the *Dictionnaire de Physique* (Paris, 1793; forming part of the *Encyclopédie Méthodique* [Paris, 1782–1832; Sowerby, no. 4889]), and he copied his resulting notes into his Weather Memorandum Book, 1776–1821 (DLC). Sir ISAAC NEWTON discussed the relationship between height and air density in *The Mathematical Principles of Natural Philosophy*, trans. Andrew Motte (London, 1729; repr. London,

1803; Sowerby, no. 3721), 2:57–60. Bouguer published his MENSURATION OF THE MOUNTAINS of South America in *La Figure de la Terre, Déterminée par les Observations de Messieurs Bouguer, & de la Condamine* (Paris, 1749; Sowerby, no. 3804).

LIGNES are equal to a twelfth of an inch (*OED*). TJ's 15 Sept. 1776 calculation that Monticello was 512.17 feet in height can be found in his Weather Memorandum Book, 1776–1821 (DLC). In his *Notes on the State of Virginia*, TJ described Monticello's summit as being 500.F in "perpendicular height above the river which washes its base" (*Notes*, ed. Peden, 76). À PEU PRÈS: "approximation."

[1] Reworked from "15."
[2] TJ here canceled "known laws."
[3] TJ here canceled "peak."

To Pierre Samuel Du Pont de Nemours

MY DEAR FRIEND   Monticello Jan. 3. 16.

A mail left us this morning which carried my letter of Dec. 31. the messenger returning from the post office brings me yours of Dec. 20. requesting the immediate return of your letter to the equinoctial republics. I had just entered on the reading of it, & got to the 10th page: but on the receipt of your letter, as another mail goes out tomorrow morning, and no other under a week, I now inclose it, in the hope you will be able to lend me another copy which shall be safely and speedily returned to you. if mr Correa be with you, be so good as to tell him that I wrote to him by the mail of this morning, covering several letters to him, and not knowing whether he would be in Philadelphia I directed my letter to the care of mr Vaughan, from whom he can have it brought in one day to the Eleutherian mills. the papers by this mail tell us thro' Fouche that the daughter of Louis XVI is aiming at the crown, the Salic law notwithstanding. the empty acclamations of the populace have turned her head, which I suspect is modelled more in the form of the mother's than the reputed father's. our family all join in affection to you, including even the little Septimia, who retains the recollection and name of the bons-bons & their giver. I salute you as ever with cordial affection & respect.   TH: JEFFERSON

RC (DeGH: Pierre Samuel Du Pont de Nemours Papers, Winterthur Manuscripts); at foot of text: "M. Dupont de Nemours." PoC (DLC); on verso of reused address cover to TJ; endorsed by TJ. Enclosure: second enclosure to Du Pont to TJ, 7 Dec. 1815.

A widely reprinted report from Joseph Fouché, duc of Otranto and outgoing minister of police, warned the French king Louis XVIII that support was growing for Marie Thérèse, duchesse d'Angoulême, the DAUGHTER of Louis XVI and Marie Antoinette. Earlier reports from Europe suggested that Marie Thérèse's personality most closely resembled her MOTHER's (*Richmond Enquirer*, 11 Nov., 30 Dec. 1815).

To George Watterston

SIR   Monticello Jan. 3. 16.

My grandaughter Ellen Randolph has just set out for Richmond from whence she will go on to Washington in about ten days. she has in charge the two vols of Virginia laws which were not at home when the library went on, which she will have delivered to you. the only volume now remaining undelivered is the MS. one of laws in the hands of mr Hening as formerly stated. as soon as he has extracted from it what is necessary for his publication, he will send it on to you.—I remain in the hope of receiving from you a copy of my catalogue when printed, being very necessary in enabling me to replace many of the same editions of books. Accept the assurance of my esteem and respect.   TH: JEFFERSON

RC (ICN); addressed: "Mr George Watterston librarian to Congress Washington"; franked; postmarked Milton, 10 Jan. PoC (DLC); on verso of reused address cover to TJ; endorsed by TJ.

TJ's GRANDAUGHTER Ellen W. Randolph (Coolidge) took an extended trip to Richmond, Washington, Philadelphia, and Baltimore, returning to Monticello about the end of May 1816 (Ellen W. Randolph [Coolidge] to Martha Jefferson Randolph, letters between 5 Jan. and 12 May 1816 [ViU: Coolidge Correspondence]).

From James Gibbon

SIR   Richd Jany 5. 1815 [1816]

By Coll. Randolps servant I take occasion to return, the letter you were at the trouble to send in relation to the Lima Sugar
with much respect Im Yo Mo Ob   J GIBBON

RC (DLC: TJ Papers, 203:36111); misdated; dateline at foot of text; endorsed by TJ as a letter of 5 Jan. 1816 received 7 Jan. 1816 and so recorded in SJL. Enclosure: Richard S. Hackley to TJ, 3 Oct. 1815.

Thomas Mann Randolph's (RAN-DOLPS) slave may have been Harry (*MB*, 2:1317).

From William Short

DEAR SIR   Philad^a Jan: 5.—16.

In the course of the last summer I had the pleasure of recieving a letter from you in which you were so good as to mark the progress that the land affair had made towards a final termination. You then thought it was inevitable in the course of the autumn succeeding. And although appearances so far were not favorable to me, yet I wished the point to be settled on several accounts.   Having not heard from you, when I learned from a sister of Mrs Carter, who resides here, that she was then expecting a visit from M^r & Mrs Carter, I was particularly anxious to know if possible, the result before Mr Carter should leave Philadelphia. I therefore took the liberty of writing to you on the 21st of Novr last. I have not since had the pleasure of hearing from you—I at first thought you might be in Bedford—but so much time has now elapsed, that I am inclined to think either that my letter must have miscarried on the way, or that that lot has fallen on yours.   In the meantime fortunately Mr Carter's arrival has been postponed. Mrs Izard is still expecting[1] him daily as she tells me, though she has not heard from him or her sister for a very long time, which does not surprize her as they seldom write—It is this aversion to writing of our countymen which makes me anxious to be able to treat of this affair with Mr Carter <u>viva voce</u>, & if possible settle it with him.   As relates to Mr Higginbotham also it is important for me to know how I stand—his last payment became due on the 25th ult^o but he has said nothing to me respecting it. When he does it will be necessary for me to know what sum precisely I am to deduct, on the principle wch you mentioned to me.

Notwithstanding this urgency of the case I do not believe I should have again troubled you at this moment but for a letter I have lately recieved from a person in France of whom I think you formerly entertained a very favorable opinion, & who I am sure still deserves it. It is M. de la Motte formerly our Vice-consul at Havre. It has been a very long time since I have had sign of life from him—and his letter explains this by informing me he had purchased a farm in the country, to which he had retired for many years as a gentleman farmer. He has now returned to Havre in consequence of the peace & resumed his commercial pursuits. He is anxious to have his former appointment & has written to M. Monroe, on the subject, but has had no answer from him. This he attributes to a person at Paris who he thinks is opposed to him & may have counteracted him, wishing the place himself. I should doubt this, & I impute Monroe's silence to his multifarious occupations in which this <u>minimum</u> of de la Motte has been lost sight of. If you think with me that in consequence of de la Motte's long & honest services in this place, there would be a degree of injustice in pushing him out of it, & if you think, as I do, that he would really be more useful there than any other, & if moreover, as I hope, you have not any repugnance to give your opinion either to Monroe, or Mr Madison, I wish indeed you would do so & procure this act of justice for a man who was always really devoted to you & to the country^2 wch employed him. If you do not wish it he shall never know that you took this step, nor shall any other know. I am sure that in a case of this nature one word from you would suffice to secure a measure of good policy, & rigorous justice to a man whom you have long known & valued as I believe.

In looking over some papers a few days ago I was surprized to find that I was still in possession of your bonds & mortgage. I had quite forgotten them. I find that I had taken occasion to obliterate their signature, so that no inconvenience could have ensued if I had died—but still I had rather they should be returned into your hands where they ought in regularity to have been some time ago. It was certainly my intention to have written to you to ask your authorization to send them by mail, or dispose of them in any other way so that you should have them—& I think I must have written to that effect at the time,—but if I did I have not rec^d an answer as to that article. I will thank you now to say how I may comply with your wishes on this head.

I am glad to hear that the price of one of the staples of Virginia has so risen as to introduce much prosperity into that State—& I hope Mr Higginbotham will be still more pleased with his purchase—Being satisfied myself I am always glad when those with whom I deal find themselves satisfied also.

I was extremely anxious, as you may have percieved, as to the state of things in this country during the war. According to my view still, we were on a precipice, or rather near a rock wch was the more dangerous to the vessel of State, that the Pilots, ignorant in most respects of this kind of navigation, were absolutely blind as to this particular danger. I own that my indignation as to their ignorance & stupidity was often raised to a degree that was very near making me break my resolution long ago made of never entering the public papers as an anonymous author—Things have now passed over—I should probably have done no good & should have vexed & mortified myself to no purpose—I can now say, & have no doubt I shall be able to say at the day of my death, that I have never inserted or contributed in any way to an anonymous article in the vile & dirty nuisances of public newspapers. I am now reconciled in heart & spirit to those whom we have put in authority over us & who have done us so much mischief, but who finally have at least not opposed the greatest good, peace; & indeed may be said to have given it to us;[3] as we have it, & they could certainly have witheld it.— Our great danger now lies in the Treasury—Every thing is unsound, & without experience or knowlege there—How is it possible to place confidence there under its present director—We, the profane vulgar know only that he left a most lucrative practise here—that he was always a needy man from his expensive habits—hospitable & apparently generous in the extreme, his house was by far the most expensive in this City—& notwithstanding he had a numerous family & was a fond & excellent father, he could not [resist?] his inducements to expence, in order to save a part of his earnings for this family, who w^d have been destitute had they lost him—at least this was the general opinion. Now vanity as well as hospitality will combine to add to all his expenses, & I have no doubt it will be seen that his expenses far exceed any Minister who has resided at Washington, & probably those of the President himself. I judge so from the character of the man. Now where are these expenses to come from, unless it be from the want of fixity in our finances, which is the best state for enabling one behind the curtain to speculate to great & mammoth advantage, as they now are & are likely to be under proper management to this effect, for some time to come. The income of this gentleman was here from 15 to 20,000 doll^s p ann—This is abandoned by a man qui à ùn besoin de depense, for ostensibly 5000 dol^{ls} p. ann, with additional excitements to expense. But he is a thorough going Republican, he is a perfect democrat. This is the saving mantle for everything—This ought to inspire confidence—for sure no politician at Rome or at Paris who professed this religion, ever did it without remaining always true to the love of country, the purity of principle & an absolute "abnegation de soi-meme." I have no doubt with this lever he will find the means of moving his party, who certainly form the majority & of course can do no wrong. It is a strange perversion wch should have made Mr M. get rid of Gallatin & send him abroad, where most particularly our national pride, if not our national character should have prohibited our sending him; & thus lose his talents, after he had acquired a sufficient degree of wealth to enable him to think alone of the public good, & substitute a man of inferior talents unquestionably, & one who could not, from his circumstances, if he were so disposed, confine himself to study this good alone.   God bless you my dear sir; & believe me ever your friend & servant   W SHORT

RC (MHi); one word illegible; endorsed by TJ as received 13 Jan. 1816 and so recorded in SJL; with additional notation by TJ beneath endorsement: "his land my bond la Motte finances."

Short's letter of the 21ST OF NOV^R 1815, not found, was recorded in SJL as received from Philadelphia at Monticello on 15 Dec. 1815. TJ rendered the BONDS moot by repaying his debt to Short following the sale of his library to Congress

(*MB*, 2:1286, 1307). The Secretary of the TREASURY was Alexander J. Dallas. QUI À ÙN BESOIN DE DEPENSE: "who has expenses to cover." ABNEGATION DE SOI-MEME: "self-denial."

[1] Manuscript: "expectig."
[2] Word interlined in place of "government."
[3] Preceding three words interlined in place of "us."

From Philip I. Barziza

HONORABLE SIR   Williamsburg 6th January 1816
Its with truly sentiments of gratitude that I Knowledge your must graciuse lettre annexd with the instructions that you had the goodness to forward me upon my affairs. I have the satisfaction to participate you that the contract of Marriage, of which I was in want to complete my documents, I founded here in the hands of Mr William McCandlish, the same Gentleman whom was named by Governement to be Curator of the Estate of my deceased Grand Mother Mrs Paradise, and under the assistance of whom I am at present acting for the purpose of reccovering boths my and my Brother Proprety; as to your Kind invitation I' Certenely shall call myself very hapy, as soon as my busines permits me to come in person to pay my respects and to enjoy the honour of your friendship.
My Brother not being necessary, will not come over to America, but if you will be pleased to send me the Catalogue of the Books that you wish to have sent from that part of the world, you will do infinite pleasure, and I' assure you Sir, that I would endeawour to do my utmost to satisfy your wish. In case that you would honour me with your Comands, have the goodness to directed to M^r

William McCandlish, in the house of which Gentleman I now Live. Permit me Sir to have the honor to subscribe myself with the greatest respect

Sir Your Most Humble and Ob^te Servant

PHILIPP I. BARZIZA

RC (DLC); endorsed by TJ as received 13 Jan. 1816 and so recorded in SJL. RC (DLC); address cover only; with PoC of TJ to John Barnes, 7 Feb. 1816, on verso; addressed: "Thomas Jefferson Esqre Monticello near Charlottesville"; franked; postmarked Williamsburg, 5 Jan., and Charlottesville, 10 Jan.

From Stephen Cathalan

MY DEAR SIR &
RESPECTED FRIEND!   Marseilles the 6th January 1816—

I answered on the 29th nov^ber last to your Favor of the 16th august, & at Last your's of the 3 July Last reached me Thro' Bordeaux under Cover of Col. Fenwick, on the 26th D^ber ult^o—it being S^nt Stephen's Day I Received it with Great pleasure, and as a nosegay—I am very gratefull for your kind expressions towards me & family, Begging you to Rely on the Sincerity of my Best wishes for you & yours;—The Ship Eagle[1] being under sails for Philad^a I cannot write you as fully as I would wish, it will be very Soon;—

in the meantime I Inform you that I have ordered to Mr Jourdan of Tains the white hermitage wine, to Messrs P^re Mages &^co of nice (Successors, to Mr Sasserno who died about 18 months ago of an appoplexy) the old of wine of nice, & to M^r f^ois Durand de Perpignan the Red wine de Roussillon, that you have ordered to me, transmitting Respectively to Each of them a litteral traduction of or about the exact quality, taste & flavour of those wines as mentioned in your Letter to me, & I hope, that Soon I will be Able to Send you the whole with the Maccarony, by Some Am^an vessel Bound for New york—Boston or Philad^a, being none now into this Port for the cheasapeack.

if I could have found here fresh & Good Maccarony of Naples, or Sestri on the River of Genoa, I would have Sent it by this opportunity but there is none such in this moment in Town & Soon expected;

Please to excuse me for Such a Short Letter, but I apprehend to miss this opportunity, I having been much busied to dispatch this & other am^an vessels Since the Receipt of your kind Favour—

I have the honor to be with a Great Respect
my Dear sir your most obedient & Devoted Servant

STEPHEN CATHALAN.

[323]

RC (MHi); at foot of first page: "Tho⁵ Jefferson Esqʳ"; endorsed by TJ as received 30 Mar. 1816 and so recorded in SJL. RC (MoSHi: TJC-BC); address cover only; with PoC of TJ to James Warrell, 2 June 1816, on verso; addressed: "Tho⁵ Jefferson Esqʳ Late President of the united States Monticello Virginia"; stamped "SHIP"; franked; postmarked Philadelphia, 25 Mar.

TRADUCTION: "translation." The RIVER OF GENOA is the Italian Riviera (*OED*).

¹ Word interlined in place of "Cupid."

To James Gibbon

SIR   Monticello Jan. 6. 16.

The stage calling at our door three days a[go] I sent by it a part of the South American loaf of sug[ar] to be deposited in your office. the merchants having often occasion to call there will have opportunities of seeing it, which I presume was the object in sending it to me. but neither price, place, nor person have been mentioned, it is but a blind indication.

I salute you with esteem and respect.   TH: JEFFERS[ON]

PoC (DLC); on verso of reused address cover to TJ; with several line endings cut off due to polygraph misalignment; at foot of text: "Major Gibbon"; endorsed by TJ.

From John F. Oliveira Fernandes

Sᴿ   Norfolk 6ᵗʰ January 1816

Your letter of the 16ᵗʰ ultº came to hand on the 23ʳ dº   I am sorry to state to you, that here is not to be found in this place, a Single Quarter Cask of Lisbon wine   Tenerife and Sherry, are of a very indiefferent Kind.

Rob. E. Steed, who keeps a tolerable Grocery, has Some Port wine; but I could not, in sincerity, recomend & Still Less, purchase it for you.

In this Situation, having attention to your present defficiency of wine, & to my wishes to oblige you, in every respect, I resolved to Send up to you, the only quart Cask of Port wine in my power, of the Superior quality (Factory-wine)—which I received Lately for my own use—by the Brig—General Silveira—Bound to Baltimore: for which you will pay—@ $2.75. gallon R. E Steed's price, for his common Port wine (whole Sale)¹—for which I paid at Oporto at the rate of 250. milreis—to $312.50—pʳ pipe—

I beg Leave to inform you that in consequence of the holly²—(or rather Lazy) days—and the time necessary for my inquiries, It was only in my power to Ship the Q. Cask yesterday, to Messrs Gibson & Jefferson of Richmond to whom, I enclosed Bills of Lading, and custom House Entry—on the Same Gentlemen I will draw, for the amm^t—as p^r acc^t below—$83.08.

I am extremelly sensible and gratefull, to your Kind offer, to pay to you a visit in the Spring, and to meet, at Monticello, my Country Man Joseph Correa da Serra;   I will chearfully accept of the offer; if, ever^3 in my power, to leave town, at that time: A physician (even in a free Country) is always a political Slave—however, such is the honour, & the pleasure, I promise myself, in So interesting & Learned society, as yours and of M^r L'Abbè Corrêa—that I will endeavour, to take that Trip—Should the circumstances permit me to do so—   It was really a Surprise to me, to Know that L'Abbè Corréa, was in this Country; being informed by Litterary Correspondences, that he was engaged in one of the recent, French, Litterary-periodical Publications viz—

"Nouveau Buletin des Sciences; par La Societé Philomatique;
    redigé par—Brongniard—Descostels—Cuvier—Corrêa & & &—"^{4}
which began to be published 1st oct. 1807—monthly
Nor do I know, why, being Secretary of the Royal Accademy of the Sciences—of Lisbon—he Left the Place; in the epoch of the French Invasion into Portugal—

Wise men do not always adopt the best political <u>Measures</u>—amidst the hasardous, political revolutions, & Calamaties—in general—all <u>is</u> <u>well</u>, that <u>ends well</u>

Please to accept of, the assurances of the great respect; and Sincere regard with which I beg Leave to Subscribe My Self

Sir your ob^t Servant   JOHN F. OLIVEIRA FERNANDES^5

a quart cask Port wine containing
29½ gall. Port wine @ $2.75. $81.13
    Case & Casing—p^r Bill   1.50
    Drayage & warfage   45
                                  $83,08

J F. O. FERNANDES

RC (DLC); addressed: "Thomaz Jefferson Esquire Monticello Milton Virginia"; franked; postmarked Norfolk, 6 Jan.; endorsed by TJ as received 13 Jan. 1816 and so recorded in SJL.

Portuguese wine was classed as either FACTORY-WINE or wine for home consumption, the former being generally of finer quality and reserved for export (*Tradesman; or Commercial Magazine* 13 [1814]: 121–2). The BRIG General Silveira had departed Baltimore for Porto on 18 Nov. 1815 (*Baltimore Price Current*, 25

Nov. 1815). José Corrêa da Serra became a member of the Société Philomathique in 1806. In October 1807, along with Alexandre Brongniart (BRONGNIARD), Hippolyte Victor Collet Descotils (DES-COTELS) and others, he restarted the society's dormant publication as *Nouveau Bulletin des Sciences, par la Société Philomatique de Paris*, with the stated goal of publishing new discoveries in science submitted by correspondents from all countries. By the printing of the first issue of the second volume in 1810,

Frédéric CUVIER had been added as an editor.

[1] Omitted closing parenthesis editorially supplied.
[2] Thus in manuscript, presumably alluding to "holidays."
[3] Manuscript: "ev."
[4] Omitted closing quotation mark editorially supplied.
[5] Beneath the signature Oliveira Fernandes wrote "P.T.O." ("Please turn over"), with account on next page.

From Madame de Staël Holstein

MY DEAR SIR.   pise ce 6 janvier 1816.

je n'exagererai point mes Sentiments pour vous quand je vous dirai que la lettre que vous avez bien voulu m'adresser en suède est Serrèe dans une caisse de fer où le testament de mon père est renfermé—je la relirai Souvent cette belle prophètie de la chute de bonaparte par l'esprit de liberté—dans ce moment où notre Europe n'éntend plus rien qui ressemble à ce language. le plus grand mal qu'ait fait bonaparte au monde c'est d'avoir confondu la tyrannie avec la liberté de telle manière qu'on le prètend libèral en rètablissant le vieux despotisme—j'ai de la peine à croire à Sa durèe cependant mais comme j'avais dix neuf ans il y a 26 ans en 1789 je commence à craindre de ne pas vivre assez pour voir la Statue de mon père à l'hòtel de ville—elle ne peut y étre placèe que le jour où un vèritable gouvernement représentatif sera reconnu comme l'ègide et la gloire de la france—on fait renaitre de touts parts des superstitions aux quelles personne ne croit plus—ainsi don pèdro Roi de portugal faisait dèterrer inès de Castro pour la couronner après Sa mort—je ne Sais Si les journaux vous ont dit que j'avéz soutenu contre un bien noble adversaire le duc de wellington la cause de votre amèrique—Si vous parvenez à dètruire l'esclavage dans le midi il y aurait au moins dans le monde un gouvernement aussi parfait que la raison humaine peut le concevoir—je suis en italie où votre lettre du mois de juillet m'est parvenue j'ai <u>fui</u> la france <u>au moment</u> où bonaparte y a dèbarqué rien ne m'aurait fait pactiser avec lui! je n'ai pu me rèsoudre encore à retourner en france tant que les ètrangers en Sont les maitres—cependant c'est à paris chez M^r de lessert que je vous prie de m'adresser une lettre Si vous m'en trouvez encore digne—j'ai été hier à livourne vous Saluer à travers la mer il me Semblait que je pouvais vous entendre à travers les flots—mon fils a toujours le projet d'aller vous voir c'est un pèlerinage vers la raison et la liberté qu'il veut faire et vous aurez Ses premiers voeux—il est le digne petit fils de m^r necker ma fille lui et moi nous l'avons tous pour notre Saint Sur la terre—je vais marier ma fille qui à 18 ans avec le duc de broglie c'est un pair de france d'autrefois et de maintenant petit fils du marèchal et de plus un ami de m^r de la fayette et cela dit tout en fait d'opinions politiques—

notre famille est encore une petite isle intellectuelle où franklin, washington et jefferson Sont rèvèrès comme dans leur patrie—

daignez agréer tous les respects de mon coeur et que mes lumières, Si vous m'en croyez, vous rèpondent de mon attachement pour vous.

NECKER DE STAËL H—

soyez assez bon pour me donner des nouvelles du midi de l'amèrique je souhaite bien leur indèpendance—

EDITORS' TRANSLATION

MY DEAR SIR.   Pisa 6 January 1816.
I will not be exaggerating my feelings toward you when I tell you that the letter you were so kind as to send me in Sweden is put away in an iron box with my father's will—I will often reread this beautiful prophecy of Bonaparte's defeat by the spirit of liberty—at a time when our Europe no longer hears anything that resembles this discourse. The greatest evil Bonaparte did to the world was to have so confused tyranny with liberty that he is considered liberal for having reestablished the former despotism—I have a hard time believing that it will last, but as I was nineteen in 1789, twenty-six years ago, I am starting to fear that I will not live long enough to see the statue of my father at the Hôtel de Ville—It cannot be placed there until the day that a truly representative government is recognized as the aegis and glory of France—Superstitions in which people no longer believe have been revived everywhere—thus as Peter I, the king of Portugal, had Inês de Castro exhumed in order to crown her after her death—I do not know if the newspapers have informed you that I supported the American cause against a truly noble adversary, the Duke of Wellington—If you succeed in destroying slavery in the South at least one government in the world will be as perfect as can be conceived by human reason—I am in Italy where your letter of the month of July came to me. I <u>fled</u> France <u>at the moment</u> Bonaparte disembarked there. Nothing could convince me to make a pact with him! I could not persuade myself to return to France as long as foreigners are masters of it—However, I am asking you to send me a letter via Mr. Delessert in Paris if you still deem me worthy of it—Yesterday I was in Leghorn to salute you from across the sea. It seemed to me that I could hear you across the waves—My son still intends to go and see you; he wants to make a pilgrimage toward reason and freedom, and you will have his first wishes—He is the worthy grandson of Mr. Necker; to my daughter, son, and myself, he is our earthly saint—I am going to marry my 18-year-old

daughter to the duc de Broglie. He is a former and current peer of France, the grandson of the marshal, and moreover a friend of Mr. de Lafayette, and this speaks volumes about his political opinions—

Our family is still a small intellectual island where Franklin, Washington, and Jefferson are as revered as they are in their own country—

Please accept all the respects of my heart, and may my wisdom, if you believe in it, vouch for my attachment to you.   NECKER DE STAËL H—

Be good enough to give me some news from South America. I really desire its independence—

RC (DLC); endorsed by TJ as received 10 Mar. 1816 and so recorded in SJL. Another copy of this letter, not found, is recorded in SJL as received 10 Apr. 1816 from Pisa. Translation by Dr. Genevieve Moene.

A bust by Jean Antoine Houdon of Madame de Staël Holstein's father, Jacques Necker, was removed from display at the HÔTEL DE VILLE in Paris in 1792 and reportedly destroyed (Anne L. Poulet and others, *Jean-Antoine Houdon: Sculptor of the Enlightenment* [2003], 351). After he became king of Portugal in 1357, Peter I (DON PÈDRO) exhumed his murdered mistress, Inês de Castro, and reputedly crowned her queen before reburying her (E. Michael Gerli and others, eds., *Medieval Iberia: An Encyclopedia* [2003], 212–3). De Staël Holstein defended the American cause in a conversation with the Duke of WELLINGTON in October 1814, after the British burning of the public buildings in Washington (London *Times*, 14 Oct. 1814; Philadelphia *Poulson's American Daily Advertiser*, 2 Jan. 1815). De Staël Holstein's daughter Albertine married Victor, 3d duc de BROGLIE, later in 1816. He was the grandson of the 2d duc and MARÈCHAL, Victor François de Broglie (Madame de Staël Holstein, *Ten Years of Exile*, trans. Avriel H. Goldberger [2000], liv).

To Charles Yancey

DEAR SIR   Monticello Jan. 6. 16.

I am favored with yours of Dec. 24. and perceive you have many matters before you of great moment. I have no fear but that the legislature will do on all of them what is wise & just. on the particular subject of our river, in the navigation of which our county has so great an interest, I think the power of permitting dams to be erected across it ought to be taken from the courts so far as the stream has water enough for navigation. the value of our property is sensibly lessened by the dam which the court of Fluvanna authorised not long since to be erected, but a little above it's mouth. this power over the value & convenience of our lands is of much too high a character to be placed at the will of a county court, and that of a county too which has not a common interest in the preservation of the navigation for those above them. as to the existing dams, if any conditions are proposed more than those to which they were subjected on their original erection, I think they should be allowed the alternative of opening a sluice for the passage of navigation, so as to put the river into as good a condition for navigation as it was before the erection of their dam, or as it would be if their dam were away. those interested in the navigataion might then use the sluices or make locks as should be thought best. nature and reason, as well as all our constitutions condemn retrospective conditions as mere acts of power against right.

I recommend to your patronage our Central college. I look to it as a germ from which a great tree may spread itself.

There is before the assembly a petition of a Capt Miller which I have at heart, because I have great esteem for the petitioner as an honest and useful man. he is about to settle in our county, and to establish a brewery, in which art I think him as skilful a man as has ever come to America. I wish to see this beverage become common instead of the whiskey which kills one third of our citizens and ruins their families. he is staying with me until he can fix himself, and I should be thankful for information from time to time of the progress of his petition.

Like a dropsical man calling out for water, water, our deluded citizens are clamoring[1] for more banks, more banks. the American mind is now in that state of fever which the world has so often seen in the history of other nations. we are, under the bank-bubble, as England was under the South sea bubble, France under the Misisipi bubble, and as every nation is liable to be, under whatever bubble design or delusion may puff up in moments when off their guard. we are now taught to believe that legerdemain tricks upon paper can produce as solid wealth as hard labor in the earth. it is vain for common sense to urge that <u>nothing</u> can produce but <u>nothing</u>: that it is an idle dream to believe in a philosopher's stone which is to turn every thing into gold, and to redeem man from the original sentence of his maker that 'in the sweat of his brow shall he eat his bread.' not Quixot enough however to attempt to reason Bedlam to rights, my anxieties are turned to the most practicable means of withdrawing us from the ruin into which we have run. 200. Millions of paper in the hands of the people (and less cannot be from the employment of a banking capital known to exceed 100. millons) is a fearful tax to fall at hap-hazard on their heads. the debt which purchased our independance was but of 80. millions, of which 20. years of taxation had in 1809. paid but the one half. and what have we purchased with this tax of 200. millions which we are to pay[2] by wholesale but usury, swindling, & new forms of demoralisation: revolutionary history has warned us of the probable moment when this baseless trash is to recieve it's fiat. whenever so much of the precious metals shall have returned into the circulation as that every one can get some in exchange for his produce, paper as in the revolutionary war[3] will experience at once an universal rejection. when public opinion changes it is with the rapidity of thought. confidence is already on the totter; and every one now handles this paper as if playing at Robin's alive. that in the present state of the circulation the banks should resume payments in specie would require their vaults to be like the widow's cruise. the thing to be aimed at is that the excesses of their emissions should be withdrawn as gradually, but as speedily too, as is practicable without so much alarm as to bring on the crisis dreaded. some banks are said to be calling in their paper. but ought we to let this depend on their discretion? is it not the duty of the legislature to endeavor to avert from their constituents such a catastrophe as the extinguishment of 200. millions of paper in their hands? the difficulty is indeed great; and the greater because the patient revolts against all medecine. I am far from presuming to say that any plan can be relied on with certainty, because the bubble may burst from one moment to another; but if it fails we shall be but where we should have been without any effort to save ourselves. different persons doubtless will devise different schemes of relief. one would be to suppress instantly the currency of all paper not issued under the authority of our own state or of the general government: to interdict after a few months the circulation of all bills of 5.D. & under; after a few months more all of 10.D. & under; after other terms those of 20, 50, & so on to 100.D. which last, if any must be left in circulation, should be the lowest denomination. these might be a convenience in mercantile transactions & transmissions, and would be excluded by their size from ordinary circulation. but the disease may be too pressing to await such a remedy. with the legislature I chearfully leave it to apply this medecine, or that medecine, or no medecine at all. I am sure their intentions are faithful, and embarked in the same bottom, I am willing to swim or sink with my fellow citizens. if the latter is their choice, I will go down with them without a murmur. but my exhortation would rather be 'not to give up the ship.'

I am a great friend to the improvements of roads, canals & schools. but I wish I could see some provision for the former as solid as for the latter, something better than fog. the literary fund is a solid provision, unless lost in the impending bankruptcy. if the legislature would add to that a perpetual tax of a cent a head on the population of the state, it would set agoing at once, and for ever maintain a system of primary or ward schools, and an university where might be taught in it's highest degree every branch of science useful in our time & country:

and it would rescue us from the tax of toryism, fanaticism, & indifferentism to their own state which we now send our youth to bring from those of New England. if a[4] nation expects to be ignorant & free, in a state of civilisation, it expects what never was & never will be. the functionaries of every government have propensities to command at will the liberty & property of their constituents. there is no safe deposit for these but with the people themselves; nor can they be safe with them without information. where the press is free and every man able to read, all is safe.—the frankness of this communication will, I am sure, suggest to you a discreet use of it. I wish to avoid all collisions of opinion with all mankind. shew it to mr Maury with expressions of my great esteem. it pretends to convey no more than the opinions of one of your thousand constituents, and to claim no more attention than every other of that thousand.

I will ask you once more to take care of Miller & our college, and to accept assurances of my esteem & respect.   TH: JEFFERSON

PoC (DLC); at foot of first page: "Col° Yancey." Tr (MHi); posthumous copy; torn at foot of each page.

The SOUTH SEA BUBBLE occurred in 1720 when speculation in shares in the British South Sea Company resulted in its catastrophic failure. The Mississippi bubble in France happened between 1717 and 1720, when the value of the shares of the French company that controlled trade and colonization in North America rose dramatically and then collapsed (OED). In the Bible, God tells Adam that IN THE SWEAT OF HIS BROW SHALL HE EAT HIS BREAD (Genesis 3.19). The biblical story of the WIDOW's cruse, a vessel that never ran out of oil, can be found in 1 Kings 17.8–16. TJ's EXHORTATION recalls the words of the mortally wounded United States naval captain James Lawrence, "Don't give up the ship," during the defeat of the USS Chesapeake by HMS Shannon, 1 June 1813 (ANB).

[1] Tr: "calling."
[2] Preceding eight words interlined.
[3] Preceding five words interlined, with "in" reworked from "after."
[4] TJ here interlined and canceled "civilised."

From Jerman Baker

DEAR SIR,   Richmond 7 Jan[y] 1816

Having left this place on the 17th Ult° in consequence of a severe attack of the Influenza, I had not the pleasure of receiving your favor untill the 2 Ins[t] previous to which the Committee for Courts of Justice had made a favorable report on the Petition of Cap[t] Miller. The subject is now before the House in the shape of a bill & of its final passage I entertain no doubt—I shall take pleasure in giving it my feeble support, as well on account of the Justice of the Application, as that you have said, it will be gratifying to you—

A subject of considerable importance (the increase of the Banking Capital of the State) is at this time submited to the Legislature, The Committee to whom several petitions on that subject were referred have made a lengthy report recommending the establishment of fifteen new and independant Banks. This is a subject with which I suspect that a very great majority of the Legislature are but little acquainted, & but few among them if any more anxious than myself to acquire information

May I my good Sir, beg the favor of you to make such communication to me on this highly interesting subject as your leisure will permit

I shall at all times be as desirous of opposing those measures injurious to the interest of my Country as of supporting those which may promote its welfare & happiness

Be pleased Sir to present my affectionate regards to Mrs Randolph & family & to accept assurances of my sincere esteem & high respect for yourself JERMAN BAKER

RC (MHi); endorsed by TJ as received 8 Jan. 1816 and so recorded in SJL. RC (MHi); address cover only; with PoC of TJ to William Marshall, 7 Feb. 1816, on verso; addressed: "Thomas Jefferson Esquire Monticello" and "Attention of Mr Jefferson Randolph."

The COMMITTEE FOR COURTS OF JUS-TICE reported to the Virginia House of Delegates on 21 Dec. 1815 that Joseph Miller's petition was reasonable. A committee led by Charles Fenton Mercer reported its recommendations for the ESTABLISHMENT OF FIFTEEN NEW AND INDEPENDANT BANKS to the House of Delegates on 5 Jan. 1816 (*JHD* [1815–16 sess.], 39, 60, 97–104).

From Nathaniel Macon

SIR Washington 7 Jany 1816

The Legislature of North Carolina has ordered a full size statue of General Washington of the best marble and workmanship to be procured and put up in the Capitol of the state; The Governor who is authorized to carry the order into execution, has requested me to ascertain whether one worthy the Character [it][1] is to represent & the state which erects it, can be made in the United states, and the sum that it will probably cost, if it cannot be got in this country; The best means of getting one from Italy, the time it may require and the probable cost there

Relying[2] on your known and uniform willingness to give information, whenever it has been asked, I have ventured to trouble you on this subject, with which I am entirely unacquainted, It is proper that

I should state to you, that it is my intention, to transmit the answer you may give to the Governor

That the evening of your life may be as happy as the Meridian has been usefull, is the[3] sincere prayer of

Sir Your unfeigned friend & H[ble] ser[t]   NATH[L] MACON

RC (DLC); endorsed by TJ as received 21 Jan. 1816 and so recorded in SJL.

The LEGISLATURE OF NORTH CAROLINA voted to procure a statue of George Washington in December 1815 (*Journal of the House of Commons* [Raleigh, 1816],

52; *Journal of the Senate* [Raleigh, 1816], 47). The GOVERNOR was William Miller.

[1] Omitted word editorially supplied.
[2] Manuscript: "Rlying."
[3] Manuscript: "the the."

From David Gelston

SIR,   New York January 8th 1816—

I have received a letter from M[r] Baker, consul at Tarragona, with a box for you said to contain "flower garden seeds"—the box may be too large to put in the mail (about 12 inches by 6) and as no use can be made of the seeds until the spring,[1] I shall wait your instructions,

With great respect and esteem,

I am, Sir, your obedient servant,   DAVID GELSTON

RC (MHi); endorsed by TJ as received 17 Jan. 1816 and so recorded in SJL. RC (DLC); address cover only; with PoC of TJ to LeRoy, Bayard & McEvers, 7 Apr. 1816, on verso; addressed: "Thomas

Jefferson Esquire Monticello"; franked; postmarked New York, 9 Jan.

[1] Manuscript: "sping."

To Benjamin Austin

DEAR SIR   Monticello Jan. 9. 16.

Your favor of Dec. 21. has been recieved, and I am first to thank you for the pamphlet it covered. the same description of persons which is the subject of that is so much multiplied here too as to be almost a grievance, and, by their numbers in the public councils, have wrested from the public hand the direction of the pruning knife. but with us, as a body, they are republican, and mostly moderate in their views: so far therefore less objects of jealousy than with you.[1]   Your opinions on the events which have taken place in France are entirely just so far as these events are yet developed. but[2] they have not reached their ultimate termination: there is still an awful void between the present and, what is to be, the last chapter of that history; and I fear it is to be filled with abominations as frightful as those which have already disgraced it. that nation is too high minded, has too much innate force, intelligence and elasticity, to remain under it's present compression. Samson will arise in his strength, as of old, and, as of old, will[3] burst asunder the withes, and[4] the cords, and the webs of the Philistines. but what are to be the scenes of havoc and horror, and how widely they may spread between brethren of the same house,[5] our ignorance of the interior feuds and antipathies of the country places beyond our ken.[6] it[7] will end nevertheless in[8] a representative government, in a government in which the will of the people will be an effective ingredient. this important element has taken root in the European mind, and will have it's growth. their despots,[9] sensible of this, are already offering this modification of their governments, as if of their own accord.[10] instead of the parricide treason of Bonaparte, in perverting the means confided to him as a republican magistrate, to the subversion of that republic, and erection of a military despotism for himself & his family,[11] had he used it[12] honestly for the establishment & support of a free government in his own country,[13] France would now have been in freedom[14] and rest, and her example operating in a contrary direction,[15] every nation in Europe would have had[16] a government over which the will of the people would have had some[17] controul. his atrocious egoism[18] has checked the salutary progress of principle,[19] and deluged it with rivers of blood, which are not yet run out. to the vast sum of devastation and of human misery, of which he has been the guilty cause, much is still to be added. but the object is fixed in the eye of nations, and they will press on to it's accomplishment, and to the general amelioration of the condition of man.   What a germ have we[20] planted, and how faithfully should we[21] cherish the parent tree at home![22]

You tell me I am quoted by those who wish to continue our dependance on England for manufactures. there was a time when I might have been so quoted with more candor, but within the 30. years which have since elapsed, how are circumstances changed! we were then in peace. our independant place among nations was acknoleged. a commerce which offered the raw material in exchange for the same material after receiving the last touch of industry was worthy of welcome to[23] all nations. it was expected that those especially to whom manufacturing industry was important would cherish the friendship of such customers by every favor, by every inducement,[24] and particularly cultivate their peace by every act of justice & friendship.

under this prospect the question seemed legitimate, whether, with such an immensity of unimproved land, courting the hand of husbandry, the industry of agriculture, or that of manufactures, would add most to the national wealth? and the doubt was entertained on this consideration chiefly, that to the labor of the husbandman a vast addition is made by the spontaneous energies of the earth on which it is employed. for one grain of wheat committed to the earth, she renders 20. 30. & even 50. fold. whereas to the labor of the manufacturer nothing is added.[25] pounds of flax, in his hands, yield on the contrary, but penny weights of lace.   this exchange too, laborious as it might seem, what a field did it promise for the occupations of the ocean; what a nursery for that class of citizens who were to exercise and maintain our equal rights on that element. this was the state of things in 1785. when the Notes on Virginia were first printed;[26] when, the ocean being open to all nations, and their common right in it acknoleged & exercised under regulations sanctioned by the assent & usage of all, it was thought that the doubt might claim some consideration. but who in 1785 could foresee the rapid depravity which was to render the close of that century the disgrace of the history of man?[27] who could have imagined that the two most distinguished in the rank of nations, for science and civilisation, would have suddenly descended from that honorable eminence and setting at defiance all those moral laws established by the author of nature between nation and nation as between man and man, would cover earth and sea with robberies & piracies, merely because strong enough to do it with temporal impunity, & that under this disbandment of nations from social order, we should have been despoiled of a thousand ships, and have thousands of our citizens reduced to Algerine slavery. yet[28] all this has taken place. one of these nations[29] interdicted to our vessels all harbors of the globe without having first proceeded to some one of hers, there paid a tribute proportioned to the cargo, and obtained her licence to proceed to the port of destination. the other[30] declared them to be lawful prize if they had touched at the port, or been visited by a ship of the enemy nation. thus were we completely excluded from the ocean. compare this state of things with that of 85. and say whether an opinion founded in the circumstances of that day can be fairly applied to those of the present. we have experienced what we did not then believe, that there exists both profligacy and power enough to exclude us from the field of interchange with other nations. that to be independant for the comforts of life we must fabricate them ourselves. we must now place the manufacturer by the side of the agriculturist. the former question is suppressed; or rather assumes a new form:[31] shall we make our own comforts, or go without them, at the will of a foreign nation? he therefore who is now against domestic manufacture must be for reducing us either to dependance on that foreign nation, or to be clothed in skins, & to live like wild beasts in dens & caverns.[32] I am not one of these. experience has taught me that manufactures are now as necessary to our independance as to our comfort: and if those who quote me as of a different opinion will keep pace with me in purchasing nothing foreign where an equivalent of domestic fabric can be obtained, without regard to difference of price, it will not be our fault if we do not soon have a supply at home equal to our demand, and wrest that weapon of distress from the hand which has[33] wielded it. if it shall be proposed to go beyond our own supply, the question of 85. will then recur, Will our <u>surplus</u> labor be then most beneficially employed in the culture of the earth, or in the fabrications of art? we have time yet for consideration, before that question will press upon us; & the maxim to be applied will depend on the circumstances which shall then exist. for in so complicated a science as political economy, no one axiom can be laid down as wise and expedient for all times and circumstances, & for their contraries[34] inattention to this is what has called for this explanation, which reflection would have rendered unnecessary with the candid, while nothing will do it with those who use the[35] former opinion only as a stalking horse to cover their disloyal propensities[36] to keep us in eternal vassalage to a foreign & unfriendly people.

I salute you with assurances of great respect & esteem

TH: JEFFERSON

PoC (DLC); at foot of first page: "Benjamin Austin esq." Printed in Boston *Independent Chronicle,* 19 Feb. 1816, and widely reprinted from this source in other newspapers and in at least one broadside, *National Utility, in opposition to Political Controversy: Addressed to the Friends of American Manufactures* (Boston, 1816).

Austin's FAVOR OF DEC. 21. was actually a letter of 11 Dec., received 21 Dec. 1815. The SAME DESCRIPTION OF PERSONS: lawyers. The extraordinary strength of SAMSON is chronicled in the Bible, Judges 13–6. TJ's *Notes on the State of Virginia* was FIRST PRINTED in Paris in 1785 in a small edition not intended for public consumption. The first public release authorized by TJ came out in London two years later (Malone,

Jefferson, 2:94–5, 104–5). Query 19 in TJ's *Notes,* the QUESTION OF 85., describes "Manufactures" as to be "resorted to of necessity not of choice" and asks "Is it best then that all our citizens should be employed in its [the land's] improvement, or that one half should be called off from that to exercise manufactures and handicraft arts for the other?" (*Notes,* ed. Peden, 164).

[1] For preceding paragraph *Independent Chronicle* substitutes "I acknowledge with pleasure your letter of the 9th Dec. last."

[2] *Independent Chronicle* adds "we have reason to suppose that."

[3] *Independent Chronicle* substitutes "and probably will ere long" for preceding eight words.

4 Preceding three words not in *Independent Chronicle*.

5 *Independent Chronicle*: "of one family."

6 *National Utility*: "view."

7 For this word *Independent Chronicle* substitutes "Whatever may be the convulsions, we cannot but indulge the pleasing hope, they."

8 *Independent Chronicle*: "will end in the permanent establishment of."

9 *Independent Chronicle*: "rulers."

10 *Independent Chronicle* substitutes "under the plausible pretence, that it is a voluntary cession on their part" for preceding six words.

11 Sentence to this point not in *Independent Chronicle*.

12 *Independent Chronicle*: "had Bonaparte used his legitimate power."

13 Preceding four words not in *Independent Chronicle*.

14 *Independent Chronicle*: "prosperity."

15 *Independent Chronicle*: "operating for the benefit of mankind."

16 *Independent Chronicle*: "would eventually have founded."

17 *Independent Chronicle*: "had a powerful."

18 *Independent Chronicle*: "his improper conduct however."

19 Remainder of sentence not in *Independent Chronicle*.

20 *Independent Chronicle*: "the Freemen of the United States."

21 *Independent Chronicle*: "they."

22 *Independent Chronicle* adds "Chagrine and mortification are the punishments our enemies receive."

23 *Independent Chronicle*: "worthy the attention of."

24 Preceding three words not in *Independent Chronicle*.

25 *Independent Chronicle* substitutes "the labour of the manufacturer falls in most instances vastly below this profit" for preceding nine words.

26 *Independent Chronicle*: "published."

27 *Independent Chronicle*: "a disgrace to the history of civilized society?"

28 *Independent Chronicle*: "And."

29 *Independent Chronicle*: "The British."

30 *Independent Chronicle*: "The French."

31 *Independent Chronicle* adds "The grand enquiry now is."

32 *Independent Chronicle* adds "I am proud to say."

33 *Independent Chronicle* adds "so long wantonly."

34 Preceding four words not in *Independent Chronicle*.

35 *Independent Chronicle* substitutes "to answer the cavils of the uncandid, who use my" for text from "which reflection" to this point.

36 Preceding five words not in *Independent Chronicle*.

From John Bradbury

SIR   Wards bridge N.Y. 9 Ja[n.] 1816

In my Tour up the Missouri I was deeply impressed with the belief that the region South of that River was extremely rich in Mineralogical as well as Botanic Treasures, and returned with a decided intention to explore the Arkansas and Red Rivers with a view to collect (at least) the materials for the Nat. History of that country.

This design I communicated to Doc^r Smith PL.S. now Sir James Edward, I received from him the most friendly promises of assistance in the Nomenclature &c &c I came to the Eastern States in order to raise the means by a Sedulous attention to business or to obtain a Situation in which such an undertaking should become a duty. I have tried the former alternative and am disappointed, partly by the present state of Manufactures in this country but more by the turpitude of the man with whom I am connected in business as Partner:

The consideration that the period of Vigour with us has other limits than Death now urges me to look round for the most Speedy means of accomplishing my darling object. This wish has received an additional impulse on be[in]g lately informed that a person is now on his way to explore those regions sent from England with the intent that his discoveries shall be published in that country. If impelled by these feelings I make an improper appeal to you Sir impute it I beg to the true motive, <u>Zeal</u> for <u>Science</u>

I notice in the reports of the proceedings of congress that a Road is in contemplation from St Louis to the Northern boundary of Louisiana for the laying out of which commissioners are to be appointed. I am well acquainted with a considerable portion of the country from St Louis to the Arkansas, have recived a Mathematical education and have a competen[t] knowledge of Surveying. In the Geological par[t] of Mineralogy & the external characters of fossils I am not less versed than in Botany. As the Road will assuredly pass through a mineral country, if a Mineralogical report would be desirable in addition to the Survey I might if employed furnish it

should I be honored with an appointment in this business, or farther in the interior (which [I] should prefer) I pledge myself that the result shall be published in the United States

I must apologize for obtruding myself [on] you and plead as my excuse that I am unacquainte[d] with and unknown to those in power. If the application is improper you will of course suppress it.

I am Sir Your most obedient & obliged   JOHN BRADBURY

PS. My discoveries in Botany have be[en] published in England and are considered as Valuable

RC (DLC); hole in manuscript, edge chipped and trimmed, torn at seal; addressed: "Thos Jefferson Esqr Monticello Virginia"; franked; postmarked Ward's Bridge, 13 Jan.; endorsed by TJ as received 27 Jan. 1816 and so recorded in SJL; with additional notation by TJ on verso giving the dates of William H. Crawford to TJ, 16 June 1814, and TJ to Crawford, 14 Feb. 1815, which TJ referenced when quoting a portion of Bradbury's letter to Crawford on 29 Feb. 1816.

Sir James Edward Smith was elected the first president of the Linnean Society of London (PL.S.) in 1788 (*ODNB*). Bradbury had been CONNECTED IN BUSINESS with Jacob T. Walden in a factory at the falls of the Walkill River in Orange County, New York (New York *Columbian*, 14 Feb. 1816). On 22 Dec. 1815 the United States House of Representatives ordered its Committee on Roads and Canals to research the expediency of opening and improving roads between Saint Louis, Arkansas Post, and the NORTHERN BOUNDARY OF LOUISIANA. Missouri Territory delegate

Rufus Easton proposed that the president "appoint a suitable number of commissioners to survey, mark, and lay out the said roads" (*JHR*, 10:86; Baltimore *Niles' Weekly Register*, 30 Dec. 1815). Frederick Pursh PUBLISHED descriptions of botanical specimens collected by Bradbury in the supplement to his *Flora Americæ Septentrionalis; or, A Systematic Arrangement and Description of the Plants of North America* (London, 1814), 2:727–43 (Rodney H. True, "A Sketch of the Life of John Bradbury, Including his Unpublished Correspondence with Thomas Jefferson," APS, *Proceedings* 68 [1929]: 145–6).

From Horatio G. Spafford

ESTEEMED FRIEND—   Albany, 1 Mo. 9, 1816.

I am very thankful for thy attention, nor was it yet too late 'to be useful to me,' nor is it still.

My long Essay on establishing a School of Science, &c. had not, probably, reached thee, at the date of thy Letter, Dec. 27, '15. I hope thou wilt have time to examine it, & to favor me with thy opinion, & advice. It has been read by several of our most eminent Literary characters, & some 4 or 5 theologians, who say they approve the sentiments, & should be glad to see it in print. I am anxious to dedicate the Essay to thee, though I shall publish it in my Magazine. Under thy auspices, it might do much good; & the very authority of thy Name, known as the most distinguished patron of liberal opinions, would keep the little theologians in awe. I am also anxious that the Essay should be so published during thy life, that <u>all</u> the effect may be secured to it which every circumstance can conspire to give.

During the next Summer, (should I not see thee before that time,[1] for I intend going to Washington this Winter,) I purpose to Send thee a Paper on the Art of making Iron & Steel, from our native Ores. This Paper is now in the hands of my friend David Parish, at Philadelphia, for perusal. The invention will make a saving of one half the expense in making Cast-Steel, & from $\frac{1}{4}$ to $\frac{1}{3}$ in making Iron. I dare not entrust it to our Patent Office, nor shall I make it public, until a better system prevails. My Cast-Steel is as ductile & weldable & malleable as the best German bar, or English blister steel. Would the Government give me the chance that I ought to have for introducing my improvements, I would soon make a fortune for myself, & greatly benefit the public. Could I obtain some office that would aid me in my need, I should be glad—but whenever the law of the land shall secure to original inventors the safe possession of their rights, & extend the period to 30 years, I will ask nothing more of the government. Thou couldst do much, by thy opinion, toward promoting this great object, as just as necessary for the public good. I am perfectly astonished that Dr Thornton should be retained in the Patent Office, when there are so many complaints against him. For myself, I can only say that I would not entrust any important invention to him, if ever so anxious to secure a right by Patent. He is, in my opinion, (but thou must know him much better than I can,) a very dishonest man, & dishonorable; & I know that he is a deadly foe to Col. Monroe, & the President, & in short the whole Administration.

With offering an apology for so long a Letter, I close with assurances of my esteem.   H. G. SPAFFORD.

RC (MHi); endorsed by TJ as received 17 Jan. 1816 and so recorded in SJL. RC (MHi); address cover only; with PoC of TJ to George Ticknor, 31 Jan. 1816, on verso; addressed: "Thomas Jefferson, LL.D. Monticello, Va."; franked; postmarked Albany, 9 Jan.

TJ's letter, which included his wish TO BE USEFUL TO Spafford, was actually dated 22 DEC. 1815. MY MAGAZINE was the *American Magazine, a monthly miscellany.* Spafford submitted his PAPER, entitled "Cursory Observations on the Art of Making Iron and Steel, from Native Ores of the United States" (not

found), to the American Philosophical Society in the spring of 1816. An APS committee studied the paper for four months before returning it to Spafford with recommendations for further experimentation and rewriting (Julian P. Boyd, "Horatio Gates Spafford, Precursor of Bessemer," APS, *Proceedings* 87 [1943]: 47–50). Spafford received two patents on 30 Oct. 1822, one for improvements in the art of making wrought or CAST-STEEL and another for advances in the manufacture of iron or steel (*List of Patents*, 242).

[1] Extraneous closing parenthesis here editorially omittted.

To Charles Thomson

MY DEAR AND ANTIENT FRIEND   Monticello Jan. 9. 16.[1]

An acquaintance of 52. years, for I think ours dates from 1764. calls for an interchange of notice now & then that we remain in existence, the monuments of another age, and examples of a friendship unaffected by the jarring elements, by which we have been surrounded, of revolutions, of government, of party & of opinion. I am reminded of this duty by the receipt, thro' our friend Dr Patterson, of your Synopsis of the four Evangelists. I had procured it as soon as I saw it advertized, and had become familiar with it's use. but this copy is the more valued as it comes from your hand. this work bears the stamp of that accuracy which marks every thing from you, and will be useful to those who, not taking things on trust, recur for themselves to the fountain of pure morals. I too have made a wee little book, from the same materials, which I call the Philosophy of Jesus. it is a paradigma of his doctrines, made by cutting the texts out of the book, and arranging them on the pages of a blank book, in a certain order of time or subject. a more beautiful or precious morsel of ethics I have never seen. it is a document in proof that I am a <u>real Christian</u>, that is to say, a disciple of the doctrines of Jesus, very different from the Platonists, who call <u>me</u> infidel, and <u>themselves</u> Christians and preachers of the gospel, while they draw all their characteristic dogmas from what it's Author never said nor saw. they have compounded from the heathen mysteries a system beyond the comprehension of man, of which the great reformer of the vicious ethics and deism of the Jews, were he to return on earth, would not recognise one feature. if I had time I would add to my little book the Greek, Latin and French texts, in columns side by side, and I wish I could subjoin a translation of Gassendi's Syntagma of the doctrines of Epicurus, which, notwithstanding the calumnies of the Stoics, and caricatures of Cicero, is the most rational system remaining of the philosophy of the ancients, as frugal of vicious indulgence, and fruitful of virtue as the hyperbolical extravagancies of his rival sects.

I retain good health, am rather feeble to walk much, but ride with ease, passing two or three hours a day on horseback, and every three or four months taking, in a carriage, a journey of 90. miles to a distant possession, where I pass a good deal of my time. my eyes need the aid of glasses by night, and with small print in the day also; my hearing not quite so sensible as it used to be; no tooth shaking yet, but shivering and shrinking in body from the cold we now experience, my thermometer having been as low as 12.° this morning. my greatest oppression is a correspondence afflictingly laborious, the extent of which I have been long endeavoring to curtail. this keeps me at the drudgery of the writing table all the prime hours of the day, leaving for the gratification of my appetite for reading only what I can steal from the hours of sleep. could I reduce this epistolary corvée within the limits of my friends, and affairs, and give the time redeemed from it to reading and reflection, to history, ethics, mathematics, my life would be as happy as the infirmities of age would admit, and I should look to it's consummation with the composure of one 'qui summum nec metuit diem nec optat.'

So much as to myself; and I have given you this string of egotisms in the hope of drawing a similar one from yourself. I have heard from others that you retain your health, a good degree of activity, and all the vivacity & chearfulness of your mind. but I wish to learn it more minutely from yourself. how has time affected your health, your strength, your faculties & spirits? what are your amusements literary & social? tell me every thing about yourself, because all will be interesting to one who retains for you ever the same constant & affectionate friendship & respect.   TH: JEFFERSON

RC (DLC: Thomson Papers); hole in manuscript and edge torn away, with missing text supplied from PoC; addressed: "Charles Thompson esq. near Philadelphia"; franked; postmarked Milton, 16 Jan. PoC (DLC).

Charles Thomson (1729–1824), secretary of the Continental Congress and revolutionary leader, emigrated from Ireland with his family about 1739. Following the death of his father during the voyage, he was placed in the care of a blacksmith in Delaware. By 1743 Thomson began classical studies under Rev. Francis Alison, and in 1750 he became a Latin tutor at Benjamin Franklin's Philadelphia Academy, later the University of Pennsylvania. Thomson was a member and later a leader of Benjamin Franklin's "Junto," the forerunner of the American Philosophical Society. He served as one of the founding secretaries of the latter organization. Having served as a liaison between the local Native Americans and colonial officials, Thomson published *An Enquiry into the Causes of the Alienation of the Delaware and Shawanese Indians from the British Interest* (London, 1759). In the years prior to the American Revolution, he became a leader of the Philadelphia Sons of Liberty. After a few largely unsuccessful business endeavors, Thomson served successively as secretary of the First Continental Congress in 1774, the Second Continental Congress, 1775–83, and the Confederation Congress, 1783–89. He was noted for his active role in conducting foreign affairs during his tenure as congressional secretary, but his outspokenness gained him numerous enemies, including John Adams and Richard Henry Lee. Thomson retired from public life when he received no post under the new federal government in 1789. He spent the remainder of his years at Harriton, his estate near Philadelphia, where he worked on translations of the Septuagint and the New Testament, published as *The Holy Bible, containing the Old and New Covenant, commonly called the Old and New Testament: translated from the Greek*, 4 vols. (Philadelphia, 1808–09; Sowerby, no. 1474). (*ANB*; *DAB*; Boyd Stanley Schlenther, *Charles Thomson: A Patriot's Pursuit* [1990]; *Catalogue of the Alumni of the University of Pennsylvania . . . 1749–1877* [1877], 14; *PTJ*, 3:196; *An Historical Account of the Origin and Formation of the American Philosophical Society* [1914], 17, 19, 24, 34, 43; Paul H. Smith and others, eds., *Letters of Delegates to Congress, 1774–1789* [1976–2000]; Eugene R. Sheridan and John M. Murrin, eds., *Congress at Princeton: Being the Letters of Charles Thomson to Hannah Thomson, June–October 1783* [1985]; Robert Patterson to TJ, 24 Nov. 1815; Philadelphia *Aurora General Advertiser*, 18 Aug. 1824).

For TJ's PHILOSOPHY OF JESUS, see *EG*, 45–122. GASSENDI'S SYNTAGMA: Pierre Gassendi, *Syntagma Epicuri Philosophiae* (The Hague, 1659). TJ owned a six-volume collected edition of the works of Gassendi, a French philosopher and mathematician (Sowerby, no. 4914). QUI SUMMUM NEC METUIT DIEM NEC OPTAT: "who neither fears the last day nor prays for it." TJ here adapted the final line of an epigram by the Latin poet Martial, *Epigrammata*, book 10, poem 47 (Martial, *Epigrams*, ed. and trans. David R. Shackleton Bailey, Loeb Classical Library [1993; later printing with variant pagination], 2:360–1). TJ owned two editions of Martial's works (Sowerby, nos. 4496–7).

¹ RC: "15." Reworked to "16." on PoC.

From Carlo Botta

SIGNOR JEFFERSON ONORANDO. Di Parigi 10 Gennaio 1816 Place St. Sulpice N. 8 au coin de la Rue des Canettes.

Io non so, se nella sua solitudine di Monticello ello si sia qualche volta ricordato di me. Ma so bene, che a me non uscí mai di mente la benignitá, con la quale Vostra Signoría ricevé la mia Storia della guerra d'america. Io le mando quí alligato un mio nuovo Lavoro, che di fresco ho dato alla luce, intitolato il Camillo, o Veio Conquistata. Io lo prego di farle buon viso, non per alcun merito mio, né dell'opera, ma pel reverendo nome di Camillo, e per esser tutta cosa, che tratta di civiltá, e d'indipendenza.

Io lo prego di avermi nel numero de' suoi piú devoti servitori.

CARLO BOTTA

EDITORS' TRANSLATION

HONORABLE MR. JEFFERSON. Paris 10 January 1816 Place St. Sulpice Number 8 at the corner of the Rue des Canettes.

I do not know if sometimes, in your solitude at Monticello, you have remembered me. But I know very well that the kindness with which you received my history of the American war has never left my mind. I am enclosing here a new work of mine, which I just finished, entitled *Il Camillo, o Vejo Conquistata*. I ask you to look on it kindly, not because of any merit of mine, or of the work, but on account of Camillo's revered name, and because it is wholly dedicated to civilization and independence.

Please count me amongst your most devoted servants.

CARLO BOTTA

RC (DLC); dateline at foot of text; endorsed by TJ as received 21 Nov. 1816 and so recorded in SJL. Translation by Dr. Adrienne Ward. Enclosure: Botta, *Il Camillo, o Vejo Conquistata* (Paris, 1815; Poor, *Jefferson's Library*, 12 [no. 742]).

Enclosed in David Bailie Warden to TJ, 9 Aug. 1816.

Marcus Furius Camillus (CAMILLO) was made dictator of Rome in 396 B.C. in order to conquer the Etruscan city of Veii (*OCD*, 615–6, 1584).

To Horatio G. Spafford

DEAR SIR   Monticello Jan. 10. 16.

Of the last 5 months, 4 have been passed at my distant possession, to which no letters are carried to me, because the cross post is too circuitous and unsafe to be trusted. on my return I find an immense accumulation of them calling for answers, & among these your favor of the 25th ult. in this you request me to examine the MS. tract it covered, to suggest amendments or alterations, give my remarks & opinion of the propriety of the sentiments, point out improvements, and say whether it should be published now. from this undertaking, my good Sir, I must pray you to excuse me. in the first place I really have not the time to spare. my other occupations are incessant and indispensable, within doors and without, there is something ever pressing, insomuch that I often have not a moment to read the papers of the day, and if to read any thing else, it must be in hours stolen from those of sleep. in the next place I have made it a point not to meddle with the writings of others. it is unpleasant to one's self, and generally injurious to the composition reviewed. the train in which a man commits his own thoughts to paper has in it generally a certain method and order. if this be altered, interrupted, chequered by the ideas of another, the composition becomes a medley of different views of the same subject, incoherent & deformed. so few are my spare moments that I have not been able even to read it through: because the MS. is in a handwriting extremely difficult to me; and I shall read it with more pleasure, and more understandingly in print. I concur with you in it's design; and as far as I have penetrated, I find the matter good, and am sure it will be useful. I hope therefore to see it in your next magazine to be followed by many others having the same object.¹ I have not sent it to the President, as you desired, fearing that if further delay be added to that already incurred, it will be too late for your purpose of inserting it in the January magazine. from contest of every kind I withdraw myself entirely. I have served my tour,² and a long one it has been. tranquility is the object of my remaining years; and I willingly leave to younger & more vigorous hands & minds the direction which has lawfully devolved on them in succession. Accept the assurances of my great esteem & respect

TH: JEFFERSON

RC (NjMoHP: Lloyd W. Smith Collection); at foot of first page: "Horatio G. Spafford esq."; endorsed by Spafford as received 26 Jan. 1816 and answered 22 [23] Nov. 1816, with the notation: "& sent No. 7 American Magazine. Wrote for his opinion concerning a Gazetteer of Virginia; & also for permission to publish extract from a former Letter." FC (DLC); consisting of PoC of first page and Dft of concluding two pages. Tr (ViU: GT and MHi); posthumous copy; text based on FC; first two pages in ViU: GT and third page in MHi. Enclosure: first enclosure to Spafford to TJ, 25 Dec. 1815.

¹ Second page of FC and Tr begin with this word, followed by a section bracketed by TJ and not in RC, printed below at 21 Jan. 1816 as document 2 in a group of documents on Jefferson's Essay on New England Religious Intolerance.
² Tr (portion at MHi): "hour."

View of Liberty, now Bedford

Thomas Jefferson's Surveying Equipment:
Theodolite, with Detail

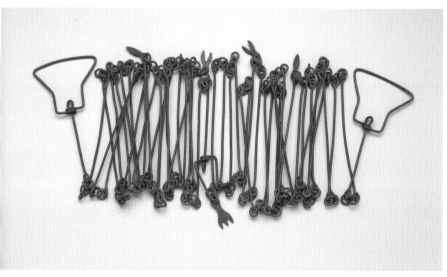

Thomas Jefferson's Surveying Equipment:
Circumferentor and Surveyor's Chain

Guitar

Monticello Parlor

BOOKS may be classed according to the faculties of the mind employed on them: these are—

I. MEMORY.   II. REASON.   III. IMAGINATION.

Which are applied respectively to—

I. HISTORY.   II. PHILOSOPHY.   III. FINE ARTS.

					Chapt.
I. HISTORY	Civil	Civil Proper	Antient	Antient History	1
			Modern	Foreign	2
				British	3
				American	4
		Ecclesiastical		Ecclesiastical	5
	Natural	Physics		Natural Philosophy	6
				Agriculture	7
				Chemistry	8
				Surgery	9
				Medicine	10
		Nat. Hist. Proper	Animals	Anatomy	11
				Zoology	12
			Vegetables	Botany	13
			Minerals	Mineralogy	14
		Occupations of Man		Technical Arts	15
II. PHILOSOPHY	Moral	Ethics		Moral Philosophy / L. of Nature & Nations	16
		Jurisprudence	Religious	Religion	17
			Municipal — Domestic	Equity	18
				Common Law	19
				Law Merchant	20
				Law Maritime	21
				Law Ecclesiastical	22
			Foreign	Foreign Law	23
		Oeconomical		Politics / Commerce	24
	Mathematical	Pure		Arithmetic	25
				Geometry	26
		Physico-Mathematical		Mechanics / Statics / Dynamics / Pneumatics / Phonics / Optics	27
				Astronomy	28
				Geography	29

Catalogue of the Library of the United States (Washington, 1815)

The Faculties of the Human Mind

Memory ... History
- Civil ...
  - antient .... Antient Hist. 1
  - modern .... Modern. Hist. 10
- Natural
  - Nat. Hist. Gen. .... Nat. Hist. Gener.
  - Animals
    - Brutes .... Zoology. 22
    - Man. his
      - Structure .... Anatomy. 24
      - Physiology .... Surgery. / Medicine.
      - Occupations .... Technics. 28 / Agriculture 32
  - Vegetables .... Botany. 36
  - minerals .... Mineralogy
  - Physics .... Chemistry / Physics. 38.
  - the Earth .... Geography 40
  - the Heavens .... Astronomy 48

Reason ... Philosophy
- Mathematics
  - the science of Quantity .... Mathematics 50
  - the science of Space .... Geometry. 54.
- Ethical
  - Morality .... Ethics. 56.
  - Moral Supplements .... Religion 68. / Law. 76.
  - Social organisation .... Politics. 86.

Imagination ... Fine Arts
- Beaux Arts. sc. Architecture. Garden. Paint. Sculpture. Music. .... Design. 96.
- Belles Lettres
  - Poetry
    - Narrative
      - Metrical .... Epic. 98
      - Prosaic .... Romance 100
    - Dialogue .... Dramatic.
    - Moral
      - metrical / Prosaic .... Didactic 102
    - Levities. sc. Pastoral. Amatory. Lyric &c. 104.
  - Oratory .... Rhetoric. / Oratory. 106.
  - Criticism .... Criticism. 110 / Philology. 112 / Bibliography

the Faculties Promiscuously .... Polygraphical 122.

Thomas Jefferson's Retirement Library Catalogue

Peter S. Du Ponceau: Portrait and Daguerreotype

To John Adams

Dear Sir   Monticello Jan. 11. 16.

Of the last five months I have past four at my other domicil, for such it is in a considerable degree. no letters are forwarded to me there, because the cross post to that place is circuitous and uncertain. during my absence therefore they are accumulating here, & awaiting acknolegements. this has been the fate of your favor of Nov. 13.

I agree with you in all it's eulogies on the 18th century. it certainly witnessed the sciences and arts, manners and morals, advanced to a higher degree than the world had ever before seen. and might we not go back to the aera of the Borgias, by which time the barbarous ages had reduced national morality to it's lowest point of depravity, & observe that the arts and sciences, rising from that point, advanced gradually thro' all the 16th 17th and 18th centuries, softening & correcting the manners and morals of man? I think too we may add, to the great honor of science & the arts, that their natural effect is, by illuminating public opinion, to erect it into a Censor, before which the most exalted tremble for their future, as well as present fame. with some exceptions only, through the 17th and 18th centuries morality occupied an honorable chapter in the political code of nations. you must have observed while in Europe, as I thought I did, that those who administered the governments of the greater powers at least, had a respect to faith, and considered the dignity of their government as involved in it's integrity. a wound indeed was inflicted on this character of honor in the 18th century by the partition of Poland. but this was the atrocity of a barbarous government chiefly, in conjunction with a smaller one still scrambling to become great, while one only of those already great, and having character to lose, descended to the baseness of an accomplice in the crime. France, England, Spain shared in it only inasmuch as they stood aloof and permitted it's perpetration. how then has it happened that these nations, France especially & England, so great, so dignified, so distinguished by science & the arts, plunged[1] at once into all the depths of human enormity, threw off suddenly & openly all the restraints of morality, all sensation to character, & unblushingly avowed and acted on the principle that power was right? can this sudden apostacy from national rectitude be accounted for? the treaty of Pilnitz seems to have begun it, suggested perhaps by the baneful precedent[2] of Poland. was it from the terror of monarchs, alarmed at the light returning on them from the West, and kindling a Volcano under their thrones? was it a combination to extinguish that light, and to bring back, as their best auxiliaries, those enumerated by you, the Sorbonne, the Inquisition, the Index expurgatorius, & the knights of Loyola? whatever it was, the close of the century saw the moral world thrown back again to the age of the Borgias, to the point from which it had departed 300. years before. France, after crushing and punishing the conspiracy of Pilnitz, went herself deeper and deeper into the crimes she had been chastising. I say France, & not Bonaparte; for altho' he was the head and mouth, the nation furnished the hands which executed his enormities. England, altho' in opposition, kept full pace with France, not indeed by the manly force of her own arms, but by oppressing the weak, & bribing the strong. at length the whole choir joined and divided the weaker nations among them. your prophecies to Dr Price proved truer than mine; and yet fell short of the fact, for instead of a million, the destruction of 8. or 10. millions of human beings has probably been the effect of these convulsions. I did not, in 89. believe they would have lasted so long, nor have cost so much blood. but altho' your prophecy has proved true so far, I hope it does not preclude a better final result. that same light from our West seems to have spread and illuminated the very engines employed to extinguish it. it has given them a glimmering of their rights and their power. the idea of representative government has taken root and growth among them. their masters feel it, and are saving themselves by timely offers of this modification of their own powers. Belgium, Prussia, Poland, Lombardy E^{t}c. are now offered a representative[3] organisation: illusive probably at first, but it will grow into power in the end. opinion is power, & that opinion will come. even France will yet attain representative government. you observe it makes the basis of every constitution which has been demanded or offered: of that demanded by their Senate; of that offered by Bonaparte; & of that granted by Louis XVIII. the idea then is rooted, and will be established, altho' rivers of blood may yet flow between them and their object. the allied armies now couching upon them are first to be destroyed, and destroyed they will surely be. a nation united can never be conquered. we have[4] seen what the ignorant bigotted and unarmed Spaniards could do against the disciplined veterans of their invaders. what then may we not expect from the power & character of the French nation? the oppressors may cut off heads after heads, but like those of the Hydra, they multiply at every stroke. the recruits within a nation's own limits are prompt and without number; while those of their invaders from a distance are slow, limited, and must come to an end. I think too we percieve that all these allies do not see the same interest in the annihilation of the power of France. there are certainly some symptoms of foresight in Alexander that France might produce a salutary diversion of force were Austria and Prussia to become her enemies. France too is the natural ally of the Turk, as having no[5] interfering interests, and might be useful in neutralising and perhaps turning that power on Austria. that a re-acting jealousy too exists with Austria & Prussia I think their late strict alliance indicates; and I should not wonder if Spain should discover a sympathy with them. Italy is so divided as to be nothing. here then we see new coalitions in embryo[6] which after France shall in turn have suffered a just punishment for her crimes, will not only raise her from the earth on which she is prostrate, but give her an opportunity to establish a government of as much liberty as she[7] can bear, enough to ensure her happiness and prosperity. when insurrection begins, be it where it will, all the partitioned countries will rush to arms, and Europe again become an Arena of gladiators. and what is the definite object they will propose? a restoration certainly of the status quo prius, of the state of possession of 89. I see no other principle on which Europe can ever again settle down in lasting peace.   I hope your prophecies will go thus far, as my wishes do, and that they, like the former, will prove to have been the sober dictates of a superior understanding, and a sound calculation of effects from causes well understood. some future Morgan will then have an opportunity of doing you justice, and of counterbalancing the breach of confidence of which you so justly complain, and in which no one has had more frequent occasion of fellow-feeling than myself. permit me to place here my affectionate respects to mrs Adams, and to add for yourself the assurances of cordial friendship and esteem.   TH: JEFFERSON

RC (MHi: Adams Papers); endorsed by Adams as answered 2 Feb.; docketed by Charles Francis Adams. PoC (DLC); at foot of first page: "John Adams." Tr (MHi); posthumous copy; incomplete.

The BORGIAS were members of a family influential in papal and Italian politics during the fifteenth and sixteenth centuries. In TJ's estimation, the nations participating in the eighteenth-century partitions of Poland were A BARBAROUS GOVERNMENT (Russia), A SMALLER ONE STILL SCRAMBLING TO BECOME GREAT (Prussia), and one ALREADY GREAT, AND HAVING CHARACTER TO LOSE (Austria). STATUS QUO PRIUS: "previous state of affairs."

[1] PoC and Tr here add "all," with word presumably added to the former by TJ when rewriting a line due to a polygraph fault.

[2] Tr: "precept."

[3] TJ here canceled "government."

[4] Tr here adds "never."

[5] Tr ends here.

[6] RC: "embrio." PoC corrected by TJ to "embryo."

[7] Word interlined in place of "they."

To John Adlum

DEAR SIR   Monticello Jan. 13. 16.

While I lived in Washington you were so kind as to send me 2. bottles of wine made by yourself, the one from currans, the other from a native grape, called with you a fox-grape, discovered by mr Penn's gardiner. the wine of this was as good as the best Burgundy and resembling it. in 1810. you added the great favor of sending me many cuttings. these were committed to the stage Mar. 13. on the 27ᵗʰ of that month I set out on a journey. the cuttings arrived at our post office a day or two after, & were detained there till my return. they were recieved Apr. 19. and immediately planted, but having been 6. weeks in a dry situation not a single one lived. disheartened by this failure and not having any person skilled in the culture, I never troubled you again on the subject. but I have now an opportunity of renewing the trial under a person brought up to the culture of the vine & making wine from his nativity. am I too unreasonable in asking once more a few cuttings of the same vine? I am so convinced that our first success will be from a native grape, that I would try no other. a few cuttings, as short as you think will do, put into a light box, & mixed well with wet moss, if addressed to me by the stage, to the care of mr William F. Gray in Fredericksbg, will be forwarded by him to Milton without delay, where I shall be on the watch for them. I must find my apology in this repeated trouble in your own patriotic dispositions to promote an useful culture and I pray you to accept the assurance of my great esteem & respect.   TH: JEFFERSON

RC (ViU: TJP); addressed: "Majʳ John Adlum at Wilton farm near Havre de grace Maryland"; address canceled and redirected in an unidentified hand to "near Geo. Town D C−"; franked; postmarked Milton, 16 Jan. 1816; endorsed by Adlum, with his additional notation: "To request Mʳ Jefferson to send me some hicory nuts." PoC (DLC); on verso of reused address cover to TJ; endorsed by TJ.

The NATIVE GRAPE grown by Adlum was the Alexander grape, discovered by Thomas PENN's gardener, James Alexander (TJ to Adlum, 7 Oct. 1809; Adlum to TJ, 15 Feb. 1810; Peter J. Hatch, *The Fruit and Fruit Trees of Monticello* [1998], 152–4). Jean David was A PERSON TJ hoped would aid him in renewed efforts at viticulture (TJ to James Monroe, 16 Jan. 1816).

To Jean David

SIR   Monticello Jan. 13. 16

Your favor of Jan. 1. is recieved. you intimate in that a thought of going to the Patomac to examine the vines I mentioned to you. it was a Maj^r Adlam near the mouth of that river who sent me the wine, made from his own vineyard. but this was 7. or 8. years ago, and whether he still pursues the culture or is even still living I do not know. I should be sorry you should take such a journey on such an uncertainty. I will write to him by the next mail, and will even ask him to send me some cuttings of the vines.

I have heard with great pleasure that you have had some conversation with Genl Cocke of the county adjoining this on the subject of his undertaking a vineyard under your direction. there is no person in the US. in whose success I should have so much confidence. he is rich, liberal, patriotic, judicious & persevering. I understand however that all his arrangements for the present year being made, he cannot begin on the vineyard till the next. but should you go to Kentucky in the spring as you suggest, it will be too late for this year, & no certainty when you get there. should you not be engaging in any thing about Richmond, I wish you could come and see this part of the country. I shall be glad of your company here until you can come to a final determination. Col^o Monroe, our Secretary of state, whose seat is within 2 or 3. miles of me, has a fine collection of vines which he had selected & brought with him[1] from France with a view to the making wine. perhaps that might furnish something for you. you will here too be within a few hours ride of Genl Cocke, should any communications with him be desired. we must endeavor some how to get over the difficulty of the present year, which if you favor us with a visit, may perhaps be contrived. Accept my best wishes for it & assurances of respect   Th Jef[ferson]

PoC (DLC); signature incomplete; on verso of reused address cover to TJ; at foot of text: "M. David"; endorsed by TJ as a letter to "John" David.

[1] Preceding two words interlined.

To Thomas Appleton

Dear Sir   Monticello Jan. 14. 16.

Your letters of Aug. 26. and Oct. 25. have been both recieved. the condition of my friend Mazzei, both of body and mind, is really afflicting. of the former he had given me some account himself, of the latter I was unapprised, altho' his very advanced age, with such bodily infirmities, might have given room to expect it. it is unfortunate too that persons in that situation are themselves the least & last sensible of it, and injure their affairs and family by not knowing when to give them up. under the circumstances you state, friendship to himself requires a cooperation with his family in keeping him and them from injury. it is what himself would have approved in the sounder state of his mind. it is unlucky that a little before the date and two months before the receipt of your first letter, I had written to him assurances that he should recieve a third of his principal with it's interest in the ensuing spring, and the remaining two thirds at two annual instalments after. of course some excuse must be framed to him when, according to the request of his family, I remit the interest only in the spring without the portion of principal. this may be found perhaps in the expediency of his keeping something as a forlorn hope for himself and his family in a country where all is secure, until the affairs of Europe are more settled, or in some motives of inconvenience to myself, which his friendship may admit. I will remit the year's interest therefore in the spring thro' your hands, and you will act on it for him and his family, as you and they shall find most practicable and for the best. in this and whatever else may be best for his family, I beg you to assure them they may rely on me, conscious that in serving them, I shall do for him what I would expect my friends to do for me in a like situation.

I wish it were in my power to hold up to mr Bartholini a prospect of employment and emolument here worthy of his talents. our early and prolific marriages, and the justice of our laws dividing the property of the parents equally among all the children, place the body of our people in ease and happiness in the mass, but occasion rare instances of great individual wealth. you know how unusual these instances are, and how few, even among them, have a taste for the fine arts. there is at this time an Italian artist of the name of Andiriani [or Franzoni, I do not know which][1] lately gone from this country to Florence, Rome E^{t}c. in quest of artists to assist in repairing the Capitol at Washington, burnt by the British. he is one of two, who were procured by mr Mazzei, and forwarded over by yourself about 8. or 10. years ago. his object there at present is to obtain architects only, and I name him merely because, having resided here so long, he would be able to give to mr Bartolini information of the country the best adapted to his views.

I note what you say of the bust of Genl Washington by Ciracchi, and those of Columbus and Vespucius. but I am done with dealing in marble. an humble copy in plaister of Ciracchi's Washington[2] would be my limit in that way. perhaps if you can tell me what such an one will cost, I may include it in some future remittance. for the present I confine myself to the physical want of some good Montepulciano; and your friendship has heretofore supplied me with that which was so good that I naturally address my want to you. in your letter of May 1. 05. you mention that what you then sent me was produced on grounds formerly belonging to the order of Jesuits and sold for the benefit of the government in 1773. at the time that that institution was abolished. I hope it has preserved it's reputation, & the quality of it's wines. I send this letter to my friend John Vaughan of Philadelphia and inclose with it to him 50.D. to be remitted to you and I pray you to send me it's amount in Montepulciano, in black bottles, well corked & cemented, and in strong boxes, addressed to the Collector of any port from Boston to the Chesapeak, to which the first opportunity occurs: Norfolk & Richmond being always to be preferred, if a conveyance equally early offers. but the warm season will be so fast advancing, when you recieve this, that no time will be to be lost. perhaps I may trouble you annually to about the same amount, this being a very favorite wine, and habit having rendered the light and high flavored wines a necessary of life with me. I salute you with assurances of my constant esteem & respect.   TH: JEFFERSON

PoC (DLC); brackets in original; at foot of first page: "Thomas Appleton esq."; notation in TJ's hand at foot of text: "the original thro' mr Vaughan. Duplicate thro' the Secretary of State"; endorsed by TJ. Enclosed in TJ to John Vaughan, 15 Jan. 1816, and TJ to James Monroe, 16 Jan. 1816.

Giovanni Andrei (ANDIRIANI) was commissioned to travel to Italy to hire craftsmen for the United States Capitol in August 1815. He sailed from Norfolk on 8 Sept. (Charles E. Fairman, *Works of Art in the United States Capitol Building* [1913], 7–8; Washington *Daily National Intelligencer*, 13 Sept. 1815). Philip Mazzei recruited Andrei and his fellow sculptor Giuseppe Antonio FRANZONI in 1805 to work on the Capitol. With assistance from Appleton, they arrived in the United States the following year (Latrobe, *Papers*, 2:141–4). According to Appleton's letter of MAY 1. 05 (DLC), he had recently sent TJ ten cases of Montepulciano wine that had been seized and sold in 1773 after the suppression of the ORDER OF JESUITS.

[1] Bracketed phrase interlined.
[2] Preceding three words interlined.

From Joseph Delaplaine

DEAR SIR,   Philadelphia Jany 14^h 1816

A few days ago I took the liberty of requesting your opinion respecting a subject in relation to the work whose prospectus is annexed. If convenient & agreable I shall be extremely happy to receive it.—

It appears that Mr Stewart evinces no disposition to yield the portrait of yourself.

Two or three days ago Mr Wood our distinguished miniature painter, in speaking of your portrait, observed, that he had seen at Mr Madison's one of the finest portraits of you that Stewart perhaps ever painted, & advised me by all means to have my engraving taken from that.—Mr Wood will leave this in 2 or 3 days for Washington, purposely to paint the following portraits for me—Mr Madison.—Mr Munroe's—Chief Justice Marshall—Mr Crawford &c &c—I do wish sir, Mr Wood could find the means & opportunity of visiting you; he says he has never seen you. I have asked him to visit you & paint a portrait of you for me. He says he positively has not the means, & I feel as if I have not, because this work that I am projecting absorbs all my Capital. I would much rather have a portrait of you by Mr Wood, than by any other man in the world, because it is a universal opinion, that no man has ever had the ability to take such striking likenesses. I wish I could send him. If there can be no means devised, I shall beg you sir hereafter to give me your influence in procuring your portrait from Mr Madison. If Mr Madison however declines letting the picture be sent to me, I will request our distinguished young Countryman Mr Morse of Boston lately arrived from London, to prevail on Mr Stuart to permit him to Copy your portrait now in his possession.—

I am with much respect Your obed^t s^t JOSEPH DELAPLAINE

RC (DLC); on verso of enclosed prospectus; addressed: "Thomas Jefferson Esqr Monticello Virginia"; franked; postmarked Philadelphia, 15 Jan.; endorsed by TJ as received 27 Jan. 1816 and so recorded in SJL. Enclosure: prospectus for *Delaplaine's Repository*, stating that publication of the work has been delayed due to imperfect engraving, but that Delaplaine expects to issue the first half-volume in January 1816; noting that this issue will contain the lives and portraits of George Washington, Alexander Hamilton, Fisher Ames, Benjamin Rush, Christopher Columbus, and Amerigo Vespucci, as well as "an elegant vignette Title page by Fairman, and Frontispiece by Lawson"; advising subscribers that they may withdraw their names after completion of any individual volume; indicating that the work will be printed in quarto and issued in half-volumes, and that each full volume will consist of twelve portraits and accompanying biographies; listing the price as $4 per half-volume for subscribers and $6 for nonsubscribers; explaining that because likenesses of George Washington by Gilbert Stuart and Jean Antoine Houdon are both popular, each image will be included; and supplying a list of agents taking subscriptions, including George Richards in Georgetown, D.C., and Fitzwhylsonn & Potter in Richmond (broadside in DLC: TJ Papers, 205:36611, on verso of covering letter, undated, mutilated at fold; broadside in DLC: TJ Papers, 206:36638, on verso of Delaplaine to TJ, 27 Jan. 1816, undated, mutilated; see also note to Delaplaine to TJ, 16 Apr. 1814).

Delaplaine wanted James Monroe's (MUNROE'S) portrait.

To George Ticknor

DEAR SIR   Monticello Jan. 14. 16.

Your letter from London of June 18. was not recieved until the 3ᵈ of Oct. in the mean time I had written you mine of July 4. & Aug. 16 the former conveyed my formidable catalogue of the books desired, and informed you that mr Girard would give an order on his correspondent at Paris to hold 350.D. subject to your call; & the latter inclosed a copy of his letter to messʳˢ Perrigaux, La fitte & co. to pay to your order that sum, and even more, should my catalogue require more. in yours of June 18. you inform me of your intention to proceed first to Gottingen, and not to Paris until the autumn. as my letters went by duplicates, one copy thro' your father, the other to Doctʳ Jackson, our Chargè at Paris to await your arrival there, I am in hopes that from your father followed you to Gottingen; where very possibly some part of my wants might be better supplied than at Paris. the postponement of your visit to this last place would of course postpone the forwarding the books, which is attended with no inconvenience, and gives me time to make the little addition to my catalogue, of translations of some of Cicero's works, which you will find at the end of this letter. you know in how defective and deformed a state his philosophical writings especially have come down to us. in every page his annotators are challenging the text with 'glossema interpretum' 'emblema librariorum,' 'a sciolis intrusa,' 'ab homine stolido barbaroque profectum' Eᵗc. and in truth the corruptions of the text render the sentiment often indecypherable. translations aid us with the conjectures of those who have made it a particular business to study the subject and it's text.   The return of Louis XVIII. the removal of Bonaparte, and presence of the allied troops in Paris, will for some time keep that place in quiet & safety, for the literati at least, who will have no inducement to enter into the passions of either party. I suppose indeed Paris will be quieter for a while than after the nation has had time to unite in sentiments of sufferance under the pressure of the allied troops, and to ripen for insurrection. when this takes place, I expect that Europe will again be in a state of general conflagration. what a divine contrast is the calm of our condition to the Volcanic state of that! how do our little party bickerings and squabbles shrink to nothing compared with the fire and sword, havoc and desolation of that Arena of gladiators!   our greatest present evil is the bank-mania which has siesed all our state legislatures especially. unversed in political economy, they are now under all the delusions of the English South-sea scheme, the French Misisipi scheme, and, unjustified by the same necessities, are running into the excesses of the old Continental money, & of the French assignats: and even the National legislature seem to be carried away with the tide: for they are proposing a bank of 35 millions in addition to more than 100. millions of private capital already in banking employment, and millions & millions more now brewing in the state legislatures. this too when all these institutions refuse to pay cash for their own notes. necessity obliges every one to take this trash for the present, because there is no other medium of payment or exchange. but the moment that the course of commerce shall bring among us so much specie as will scantily perform these functions, there will be an universal rejection of this baseless paper. nor can the banks give it base unless they shall call in such a proportion of it as may place the remainder within the compass of their resources for cash payment. and this call will make sad havoc among the ephemeral merchants.—these are our difficulties. I wish those of Europe were of as bloodless a character. for it is a kind law of nature that every nation prospers by the prosperity of others.

I tender you my best wishes that your literary pursuits may meet no obstructions from the insurrectionary state of the people among whom you are, and assurances of my friendly esteem and respect.

TH: JEFFERSON

Oeuvres Philosophiques de Ciceron. 10. vols. in 16° Paris 1796. [this contains the translations of Durand, Demarais, d'Olivet, Bouhier, Morabin, & Barrett.]

Lettres familieres de Ciceron par Prevost, avec le texte Latin. edition de Goujon. 5. v. 8vo Paris 1800. or 1801.

Lettres de Ciceron et de Brutus. Lat. Fr. par Prevost.

Lettres de Ciceron à Atticus. Lat. Fr. par Mongault.

} Flescher in his Annuaire de la librairie of about 8. or 10. years ago, in announcing Goujon's edition of Prevost's Lettres familieres de Ciceron says that a like edition of all the other letters was then in hand, which have doubtless appeared long since.

PoC (DLC); brackets in original; at foot of first page: "Mr George Tickner"; endorsed by TJ. Enclosed in TJ to Elisha Ticknor, 15 Jan. 1816, and TJ to Henry Jackson, 16 Jan. 1816.

GLOSSEMA INTERPRETUM: "a gloss of interpreters." EMBLEMA LIBRARIORUM: "editions by copyists." A SCIOLIS INTRUSA: "intrusions by dabblers." AB HOMINE STOLIDO BARBAROQUE PROFECTUM: "carried out by a dull and uncultivated man." Congress enacted legislation establishing the Second Bank of the United States on 10 Apr. 1816. The capital investment of 35 MILLIONS of dollars included $7 million from the federal government and $28 million "subscribed and paid for by individuals, companies, or corporations" (*U.S. Statutes at Large*, 3:266–77). The *Annuaire de La Librairie* (Paris, 1802) by Guillaume Fleischer (FLESCHER) announced the publication of Antoine François Prévost's 5-volume edition of Cicero's letters and also noted (p. 100) the availability of a 3-volume edition: "La même traduction, sans le texte original (disposée pour faire suite, si l'on veut, aux *Œuvres choisies de l'abbé Prévost*, en 39 volumes)" ("The same translation, without the original text [arranged to follow suit, if one desires, with *Œuvres choisies de l'abbé Prévost*, in 39 volumes]").

From Joseph Fox

HONOR'D SIR—   No. 323 Spruce Street[1] Philad: [ca. 15] Jan. 1816—

For a number of years with much difficulty and expense I have employed myself in discovering dyes, &c. suitable to the manufacture of various articles in the United States, and finding them of advantage to many throughout our country, and having been requested by persons interested to make them public, by publishing a work containing from one to two hundred pages, as my circumstances may permit, I have in the event concluded to dedicate it to you in the following manner:—

This

Original Work

Is most respectfully[2] dedicated

by the Author

To the Hon. Thomas Jefferson, Esq[r]

For the many attentions bestowed by him
on his fellow citizens

In promoting the sciences

and
For the general welfare
of his Country.

D[r] sir, your patronage and assent would be gratefully received—
Yours, very respectfully   J. Fox

RC (DLC: TJ Papers, 206:36650); partially dated; endorsed by TJ as a letter from Joseph Fox received 27 Jan. 1816 and so recorded in SJL. RC (MHi); address cover only; with PoC of TJ to Isaac A. Coles, 18 Feb. 1816, on verso; addressed: "Hon. Thomas Jefferson Esqr Virginia"; franked; postmarked Philadelphia, 15 Jan. Enclosure not found.

Joseph Fox was listed intermittently in Philadelphia directories as a teacher and printer from 1808 until 1833. He issued a proposal for printing *The Friends Monthly Magazine* in 1799 and published its only issue that April (H. Glenn Brown and Maude O. Brown, *A Directory of the Book-Arts and Book Trade in Philadelphia to 1820, Including Painters and Engravers* [1950], 50; *Philadelphia Gazette & Universal Daily Advertiser*, 21 Mar. 1799;

James Robinson, *The Philadelphia Directory, for 1808* [Philadelphia, 1808]; Robert Desilver, *Desilver's Philadelphia Directory and Stranger's Guide, for 1833* [1833], 72).

[1] Address to this point given perpendicularly in margin at foot of text.
[2] Manuscript: "respectfull."

From Joshua Norvell

DEAR SIR,   St Louis, Missouri Territory Jan. 15. 1816.

Remotely situated from the seat of political information, relating to the interests of the gov^t of the U.S. the people in this Quarter at all times feel much at a loss on subjects of general concernment.

There is, however, a topic (in which considerable feeling is expressed) lately come into discussion; and about the policy or impolicy of the provisions of government concerning much contrariety of sentiment exists. I mean, the establishment and extension of factories and trading houses with the different tribes of Indians. How far it operates to the prejudice of the settlers in the countries bordering those nations—and whether or not it advances the permanent interest of the U.S.—and may not some better plan than the present be devised.

If you will obtain Leisure enough to remark upon these several subjects it will be esteemed a great favor, pledging myself that no improper use shall be made of your suggestions

This liberty is taken, on account of a proper knowledge of your disposition and kindness—and from a supreme reverence for your opinions.

With distinguished esteem,[1] Yr: ob: Servt

JOSHUA NORVELL

RC (MHi); endorsed by TJ as received 16 Feb. 1816 and so recorded in SJL. RC (MHi); address cover only; with PoC of TJ to Ellen W. Randolph (Coolidge), 14 Mar. 1816, on verso; addressed: "Thomas Jefferson Esqr Monticello Virginia" by "mail"; franked; postmarked Saint Louis, 15 Jan.

Joshua Norvell (1791–1821), attorney and journalist, edited the Lancaster, Kentucky, *Political Theatre*, 1808–09, the

Kaskaskia *Illinois Herald*, ca. 1814, the Saint Louis *Western Journal*, 1815–17, and the Lexington *Kentucky Gazette*, 1819–20. He also practiced law in Kentucky and in Missouri Territory, where he served as a prosecuting attorney for Arkansas County, 1817–18. During the War of 1812 Norvell was a second lieutenant in an infantry regiment in the United States Army in 1812 and served in the Kentucky militia the following year. After he unsuccessfully solicited a judgeship in Arkansas Territory in 1819, he received an appointment from President James Monroe as United States consul on the island of Saint-Barthélemy in 1821. Norvell died in Havana en route to this post (Brigham, *American Newspapers,* 1:135, 161, 163, 434; Norvell to TJ, 30 Nov. 1808 [MoSHi: TJC-BC]; Heitman, *U.S. Army,* 1:753; A. C. Quisenberry, "Kentucky Troops in the War of 1812,"

Register of the Kentucky State Historical Society 10 [1912]: 52, 61; David Kaser, *Joseph Charless: Printer in the Western Country* [1963], 100; *Terr. Papers,* 15:48–9, 76, 112–3, 275, 277, 373; DNA: RG 59, LAR, 1817–25; *JEP,* 3:236, 240 [23 Jan., 7 Feb. 1821]; Arkansas Post *Arkansas Gazette,* 20 Oct. 1821).

[1] Manuscript: "esteeem."

To William Short

Dear Sir   Monticello Jan. 15. 16.

Of the last 5 months, 4 have been past at Poplar Forest where I am engaged in improvements requiring much of my presence. while there no letters are forwarded to me, the cross post being very circuitous. they are accumulating here during my absence, and on my return are pressing for answers. as soon after my last return as my progress in this corvée afforded me the prospect of a day to spare, I wrote to mr Higgenbotham (being next door neighbor to Price) to ascertain whether we might count on Price's attendance, without which nothing could be done, and I did not know in what dispositions the hurt he recieved on the last occasion might have left him. this was on the 25th of Dec. on the 30th fell a snow, and since that three others, which have rendered the survey and arbitration impracticable, as all must be on foot, the operation being near the top of one of our highest mountains, and on it's rockiest and steepest part. I believe I am the only person who ever clambered it on horseback, and that was because I had not strength to walk. nothing can be done until the snow disappears. as soon as it does I will get a day fixed & send out and collect the arbitrators & surveyors who live in different & distant parts of the county. we cannot expect the former, to undertake it but in reasonable weather, as their acting is a favor. I had not answered your letter of Nov. 21. which I found here on my return, because I had the daily hope of being able to inform you of it's settlement, and thus make one letter do for two, which is an economy not to be neglected by one who is confined to the writing table from 4. to 6. hours of every day answering letters. but the unpromising appearance of the weather and reciept of yours of the 5th inst. renders this earlier information a duty, altho' but interlocutory.—my bonds Etc in your hands may either be burnt or returned to me by the mail.

I retain a great esteem for mr La Motte, and entire confidence in the integrity and worth of his character, and will certainly interest myself for him with the Secretary of State, with whom the selection effectually rests. but perhaps the place is already full. it is possible also that it may be the rule of the government to give a preference to native competitors. if neither of these obstacles be in the way, I shall not despair of obtaining it for him. in a question between a native & foreigner I believe the Senate is immoveable.—I concur with you in considering the retirement of mr Gallatin from the Treasury as a great misfortune. had he remained he would have shielded us from the <u>faux frais</u> of the War & Navy departments which constituted a great portion of our expenditures, he would have sooner recurred to the resource of substantial taxation, have devised more economical & effectual means of using the public credit, and altho' not without good will to some banking establishment, he would have crushed that mob of banks which it was so entirely in the power of the government to have done. I see no issue now but in their bankruptcy, in that of a great portion of our merchants, and a total loss of the whole mass of circulating paper in the hands of the people, except the paper of the government. I think our taxes from the general & state governments this year have been half a crown in the pound on land, as much Excise, & as much Impost, or perhaps the last has been equal to both the former. this is from 7/6 to 10/ in the pound of income. I still wish it to continue till we pay our debt, as I consider a permanent public debt as a canker inevitably fatal. I am informed by one who speaks from experience that of the 15^{d} or 18^{d} a day recieved by an English laborer, he pays 10^{d} or 12^{d} to government, the remaining 5^{d} or 6^{d} barely sufficing to keep body & soul together. government in this case costs certainly more than it is worth, and the laboring class would be happier as the Indians are, without government. for I imagine there can be no comparison between the happiness of an Indian & an English laborer. ever and affectionately yours

TH: JEFFERSON

RC (ViW: TJP); at foot of first page: "Mr Short"; endorsed by Short as received 22 Jan.

The SECRETARY OF STATE was James Monroe. Regarding the appointment of consuls and vice-consuls and A QUESTION BETWEEN A NATIVE & FOREIGNER, see PTJ, 17:244–9. FAUX FRAIS: "incidental expenses."

To Elisha Ticknor

SIR   Monticello Jan. 15. 16.

I avail myself of your kind permission to obtain a safe conveyance
of the inclosed letter to your son. I presume he keeps you informed
where his letters will find him. in one to me from London dated in
June, he informed me he should go first to Gottingen and thence to
Paris in the autumn. but as I have not heard of his actual departure
for Paris, and have no channel of conveyance to Gottenburg, I think
it safest to resort to your goodness for the conveyance. Accept the
assurance of my great respect and esteem.   TH: JEFFERSON

PoC (MHi); on verso of reused address
cover to TJ; at foot of text: "Mr Elisha
Ticknor"; endorsed by TJ. Enclosure: TJ
to George Ticknor, 14 Jan. 1816.

By GOTTENBURG TJ presumably
meant Göttingen.

To John Vaughan

DEAR SIR   Monticello Jan. 15. 16.

In a letter of Dec. 22. I asked whether a remittance of a small sum
could be directly made from Philada to Leghorn; and not doubting
that it may I take the liberty of inclosing to you 70.D. bills of the
US. and of asking the favor of you to remit 50. Dollars to Thomas
Appleton Consul of the US. at that place.

I have done it without waiting an answer to my enquiry, because the
remittance is for some Florence wine, which if not sent off by the 1st
of April will hardly bear the passage. were there no direct opportunity from Philadelphia mr Appleton has two nephews in business at
Baltimore thro' whom perhaps it could be made.

the balance of the inclosed I wish to remain in your hand as a small
fund on which I can draw for trifling charges sometimes occurring,
as lately in the case of Dr Patterson for the package of a clock. for the
same reason I had sometime ago desired mr Short to pay to you a
small balance in his hands. I will request you to forward the inclosed
letter with the remittance to mr Appleton.

The papers tell us that Chaptal & La Cepede are to take refuge
with us from the persecutions of their new old masters. Oh! for a National University to avail ourselves of such talents. Affectionately
yours   TH: JEFFERSON

RC (Robert T. L. Patterson, Garden
City, N.Y., 1948); at foot of text: "Mr

Vaughan"; endorsed by Vaughan as received 24 Jan. and answered 26 Feb.

1816, with the further notation that the letter had contained $70 in treasury notes to be sold, of which $50 was to be remitted to Thomas Appleton in Leghorn. PoC (MHi); on verso of reused address cover to TJ; endorsed by TJ. Enclosure: TJ to Appleton, 14 Jan. 1816.

On 17 Jan. 1816 the Washington *Daily*

National Intelligencer reprinted an inaccurate report that the French scientists Jean Antoine CHAPTAL and Lacépède (LA CEPEDE) were preparing to come to the United States because of the return to power of their NEW OLD MASTERS, the Bourbons (*DSB*, 7:546–8; Connelly, *Napoleonic France*, 105–6).

From Joseph C. Cabell

DEAR SIR,   Richmond. 16ᵗʰ Jan: 1816.

I received in due time by the mail, your favor respecting Mʳ Miller's[1] petition: and I have deferred writing to you, till the fate of that bill, & of the bill respecting the Central College, could be ascertained, so far as it depended on the House of Delegates. Both these bills arrived in the Senate this day: and I have had them committed, and shall take all the care of them in the compass of my feeble abilities. I should have preferred a delay of some days longer before I should write to you: but the mail leaving town this evening, & being desirous to avoid the effect of too long a delay, I must not postpone my communication any longer. As to Mʳ Miller's[2] bill, I am not as yet aware of any opposition. In regard to the bill respecting the Central College; there is some little danger. The clause respecting the literary fund, was stricken out in the lower House. The actual destination which that fund will hereafter receive, is not decided. I think my letter to you from Warminster apprized you that I apprehended some opposition to that part of the bill respecting that fund: and I advised mʳ maury, not to press that subject, if opposition should arise to such an appropriation at this time. Opposition was made to it, & that part of the bill was stricken out. The bill has passed quietly thro' the House of Delegates, with that single exception. After it had passed that House, & before it had reached the Senate Col: yancey came to me & requested me to oppose that part of the bill which gives to the trustees the power to fix the time for commencing on the plan of general instruction in the county of Albemarle. I endeavored to satisfy his mind. He appeared to be afraid of giving offence to the people of the county; by putting them on a different footing from the people in other counties of the State. My resolution was formed to endeavor to get the bill thro' the Senate without any change whatsoever; but I find some objection among some of the principal members of the

Senate, to that part of the bill giving to the Professors the power of imprisoning the students. In this state of things I have determined to write you, & request the favor of you to inform me whether your Letter to Mr Carr, contains all that you have written upon the subject of this seminary; and if it does not, to ask the kindness of you to transmit to me by the return of the mail, any other communications which in any shape, you may have made upon the subject. I beg also that you will enter into as full a statement, as your convenience will permit, of the reasons that induced you to give to the Professors the power of imprisoning students. My object would be to shew your letter to the leading members of the Senate. If there should be no particular objection, you would confer a favor by stating your reasons for taking from the Court of Albemarle, & giving to the Trustees the power of fixing a period for the establishment of schools in Albemarle. The petition respecting the House in Charlottesville[3] M^r maury & myself have determined not to press into view till the College bill gets well under way: because its fate should be made dependant on the latter. A Mr Braidwood teacher of the deaf & dumb, now established at some point on this River below the falls, would come to Charlottesville, & establish himself there provided he could get such a House as Mr Estis's. How would it answer your purpose, to get an act passed, for a lottery, to purchase that House, for an establishment for the deaf & dumb as a wing of the Central College. In your answer, it would be well to separate any thing you may have to say of a private nature, from what it might be well to communicate to certain members.[4] Permit to suggest the propriety of your requesting the co-operatio[n of M^r] Johnson, Mr Poindexter, Mr Watts, & Genl Greene of the Sena[te. S]uch aid would be [of][5] infinite use, at future stages of this enterprize: & a request from you to these valuable men, would have very great influence, upon its ultimate destiny. I write in great haste: But beg you to rest assured of my constant attachment & great respect.

Jos: C: Cabell

RC (ViU: TJP-PC); torn at seal; addressed: "Thomas Jefferson esq. Monticello"; franked; postmarked Richmond, 20 Jan.; endorsed by TJ as received 23 Jan. 1816 and so recorded in SJL.

For the legislative history of the BILL RESPECTING THE CENTRAL COLLEGE, see editorial headnote on The Founding of the University of Virginia: Albemarle Academy, 1803–1816 (printed at 25 Mar. 1814) and TJ's Draft Bill to Create Central College and Amend the 1796 Public Schools Act, [ca. 18 Nov. 1814]. Cabell's letter to TJ FROM WARMINSTER was dated 5 Mar. 1815, and TJ's LETTER TO MR CARR was dated 7 Sept. 1814. For the PETITION RESPECTING THE HOUSE, see TJ to Charles Yancey, 15 Oct. 1815, and note.

[1] Word interlined in place of "Read's."

² Word interlined in place of "Read's."
³ Word interlined in place of "Albemarle, we have determi."

To Henry Jackson

SIR   Montice[llo] Jan. 16. 16.

In July last I took the liberty of availing my self of the protection of
your cover for a letter to mr George Ticknor a young gentleman from
Masschusets, with a request that you would retain it until he should
arrive in Paris. I learned afterwards that this would not be till autumn: nor have I as yet heard of his actual arrival there. under this
uncertainty I again take the benefit of your cover, with a like request,
if he be not in Paris, to retain the inclosed letter until he arrives there,
before which time his reciept of it is not very material. again praying
your indulgence of this liberty I repeat the assurances of my great
esteem & consideration.   TH: JEFFERSON

PoC (DLC); on verso of reused address cover to TJ; dateline faint; at foot of text:
"Doctʳ Henry Jackson"; endorsed by TJ. Enclosure: TJ to George Ticknor, 14 Jan.
1816. Enclosed in TJ to James Monroe, 16 Jan. 1816.

To James Monroe

DEAR SIR   Monticello Jan. 16. 16.

It being interesting to me that the inclosed letters should get safely
to their destination, I pray you to give them a passage under the protection of your cover by your first dispatches to Paris & Leghorn. On
my return from Bedford I had proposed a meeting of the arbitrators
& surveyor to settle finally the question between you & mr Short. but
successive snows which have kept the ground constantly covered
since that have prevented. the surveyor guided by Price will measure
the quantity, and I suppose the arbitrators, already understanding
the question, will settle it together without going on the ground. I
shall attend neither operation. I have an opportunity of getting some
vines planted next month under the direction of M. David, brought
up to the business from his infancy. will you permit me to take
the trimmings of your vines, such I mean as ought to be taken from
them the next month? it shall be done by him so as to ensure no injury to them.

A M. La Motte of Havre wishing the consulate of that place, I have been requested to state to you what I know of him. during the revolution war D[r] Franklin appointed a M. Limouzin Consul there, & I think he appointed La Motte vice consul. Limozin died & La Motte succeeded to the duties of the office, but whether appointed Consul in full, I do not remember. on the French revoln & decline of commerce he retired into the country & Cutting was appointed Consul. who since[1] I know not. La Motte has now returned and wishes the office. what I know of him is that he is a very honest man, of great worth, very much respected there & very diligent. I knew him well while I was in France, & esteemed him highly. who are the competitors I know not; but you will judge of their comparative merit. ever & affectionately yours

TH: JEFFERSON

RC (NNYSL); torn at seal, with missing text supplied from PoC; addressed: "James Monroe Secretary of State Washington"; franked; postmarked Milton, 16 Jan.; endorsed by Monroe as answered 22 Jan. 1816. PoC (DLC); on verso of reused address cover to TJ; endorsed by TJ. Enclosures: (1) TJ to Thomas Appleton, 14 Jan. 1816. (2) TJ to Henry Jackson, 16 Jan. 1816, and enclosure.

The SURVEYOR was William Woods. American commissioner Benjamin FRANKLIN left no comment on William Lee's unofficial appointment of André Limozin (LIMOUZIN) as commercial agent at Le Havre in 1778. Limozin, who

had performed some of the functions of a consul, died in 1789. The following year Delamotte was appointed United States vice-consul at Le Havre and served in that capacity until the 1793 appointment and confirmation of Nathaniel CUTTING as consul. Cutting was succeeded the following year by Thomas Waters Griffith (Franklin, *Papers*, 25:639, 26:60–2, 27:128–9; *PTJ*, 11:99, 12:244, 13:388, 14:60, 62n, 537, 15:237, 16:206, 207n, 575; *JEP*, 1:48, 52, 129, 131, 166 [4, 22 June 1790, 19, 20 Feb. 1793, 17, 18 Dec. 1794]).

[1] Manuscript: "sine."

From Philip Doddridge

DEAR SIR   [Richmond 17] Jan[y] 1816

Although I have not the pleasure of a personal acquaintance with you, I take the liberty of asking your information upon the following points

1st At what time the Convention of this State first resolved to give a bounty in lands to their officers and Soldiers?

2[d] whether you are in possession of a full journal of the proceedings of the convention of this State of 1776, and if you are not, any information you may possess, which may aid me in the pursuit of that journal—

I find in the Council Chamber a printed volume Containing a part of that journal—The desire appears to be general to have that volume printed and distributed—If the whole Could any where be obtained, the utility of printing and distributing would be greatly increased

Will you be So good Sir as to give me by the return of mail, addressed to me here, any information you may possess upon the foregoing subjects

I would cheerfuly pay whatever might be the postage upon any document in your possession, which you may enclose to me here, or to the Clerk or Speaker of the H. of Delegates, calculated to throw light upon those Subjects—The originals shall be returned and without doubt a vote will pass for their printing and distribution

respectfuly

P DODDRIDGE

RC (DLC: TJ Papers, 205:36593); top edge trimmed, with loss of endorsement and part of dateline. Recorded in SJL as a letter of 17 Jan. received 27 Jan. 1816 from Richmond.

Philip Doddridge (1773–1832), attorney and public official, was born in Bedford County, Pennsylvania, and received his formal education in Charlestown, Virginia (now Wellsburg, West Virginia). Self-educated in law, he was admitted to the Virginia bar in 1797 and quickly rose to prominence in the legal community. In 1804 Doddridge was elected to the Senate of Virginia, representing the counties of Brooke, Harrison, Monongalia, Ohio, Randolph, and Wood. In 1808 he resigned his senate seat to accept a position as commonwealth's attorney. Doddridge represented Brooke County for five terms in the House of Delegates, 1815–17, 1820–21, 1822–23, and 1828–29. He was an advocate for the western part of the state and supported a reform agenda that included universal white male suffrage and direct election of governors. A delegate to the 1829–30 state constitutional convention, Doddridge was a leader of an unsuccessful movement to institute apportionment changes that would have decreased the influence of the long-settled Tidewater region and strengthened the underrepresented western districts. He won a seat in the United States House of Representatives in 1828 and was reelected in 1830. As a congressman, Doddridge supported protective tariffs and federally funded internal improvements. He became ill while working on a new legal code for Washington, D.C., and died there (ANB; DAB; Leonard, General Assembly; Waitman T. Willey, A Sketch of the Life of Philip Doddridge [1875]; Washington Daily National Intelligencer, 20 Nov. 1832; Washington Globe, 20 Nov. 1832).

By an act passed in the General Assembly on 22 June 1779, the state of Virginia FIRST RESOLVED TO GIVE A BOUNTY IN LANDS TO THEIR OFFICERS AND SOLDIERS (JSV [1779 sess.], 52; Acts of Assembly [1779 sess.], 21–8). After the state senate's rejection on 24 Feb. 1816 of "An Act directing the publication and distribution of the Journals of the Conventions which assembled in Virginia in the years 1775 and 1776," Doddridge successfully moved two days later that the clerk of the House be ordered to have five hundred copies printed of the PROCEEDINGS "of the Conventions which assembled in Virginia in the years 1775 and 1776," with the additional instructions that he "transmit one copy of each of the said Journals to Thomas Jefferson Esq. late President of the United States, as a mark of respect from this House: and that the remaining copies thereof be deposited with the Executive, subject to the future order of the House of Delegates." On 20 Feb. 1817 the legislature approved "An Act providing for the distribution of the printed edition of the Journals of the Conventions of one thousand seven hundred and seventy-five, and one thousand seven hundred and seventy-six," retaining the House's earlier proviso that a copy be sent to TJ while others were to go to "the librarian of the public library at the city of Washington," the offices of the clerks of the Virginia House and Senate, the "Council Chamber," and various public officials. The remainder were to be "disposed of by the public printer, in such manner as to him shall seem most advisable, and the proceeds thereof, after deducting a commission of ten per centum thereon, be paid by him into the treasury" (*JHD* [1815–16 sess.], 201, 203 [misprinted "230"]; [1816–17 sess.], 219; *Acts of Assembly* [1816–17 sess.], 24; *The Proceedings of* *the Convention of Delegates for . . . the Colony of Virginia, Held at Richmond . . . on the 20th of March, 1775* [Richmond, 1816; Poor, *Jefferson's Library*, 10 (no. 576), described as "Proceedings of Convention, 1776(5)–6, 4to," and "Copy given by the Gen. Assem."; TJ's copy in Vi, inscribed by him (trimmed): "To Thomas Jefferson by resolution of the Genera(l Assembly) of Virgini(a)," and bound with the reprinted proceedings of the other revolutionary conventions]).

From Thomas W. Maury

DEAR SIR.   Richmond 17ᵗʰ January 1816

I at length have the pleasure to announce to you the passage thro the House of Delegates of our Bill for the establishment of the College, and of the Bill for the relief of Capᵗ Millar The last will make it's way thro the Senate with much ease; But as to the first, I much doubt whether it will be passed in it's present shape. It has lost in the H. of D. the section providing for aid from the Literary Fund. I found the H of D. so sensitive on that subject as to create a persuasion (in which my friends concurred) that insisting on that section might put the whole bill to hazard.—The probable objection in the Senate is founded on that feature in the bill which invests one of the Officers of the institution with the powers of a justice of the peace I have this day had conversations with some of the Members of the Senate & have referred them to the history of some other colleges for precedents, but fear it will be lost. As to the substance of the bill there can be no difficulty.

There are three very important subjects before the Legislature, the calling of a Convention, a large addition to the banking capital of the Commonwealth, and roads & internal improvement—The mania which has raged in relation to the two first, will (I trust) find a salutary check in the wisdom of the Legislature. In relation to the last, I think I have well founded hopes that a beginning may at least be made, which will lead to great & happy results.

I am very respectfully Sir.

yʳ mo: obᵗ   THOˢ W. MAURY

RC (DLC); addressed: "Thomas Jefferson Esqʳ Monticello near Charlottesville"; franked; postmarked Richmond, 20 Jan., and Charlottesville, 24 Jan.; endorsed by TJ as received 27 Jan. 1816 and so recorded in SJL.

From Charles Yancey

Dᴿ SIR   Richmond Janʸ 17ᵗʰ 1816
the petition of Mʳ Miller has passed our body agreeable to the
prayer & I have Spoken to Mʳ Cabell to Support it in the Senate.
the petition for the central college has also passed our body & the one
concerning the obstruction of the Navigation &ᶜ excuse hurry with
esteem I am Dʳ Sir Your friend & Hble Serᵗ
                                        CHARLES YANCEY

RC (DLC); endorsed by TJ as received 21 Jan. 1816 and so recorded in SJL.

From John F. Oliveira Fernandes

DEAR SIR: Norfolk 18ᵗʰ January 1816
I had this honor on the 6ᵗʰ instant, informing you, to have Shipped
on board the Rolley (Blennett master) a quart Cask of the best Port
Wine—cased; directed (as per order) to the care of Messʳˢ Gibson
& Jefferson of Richmond—which, I hope, has, by this time, arrived
Safe—
Judging, after your information, that you prefer, for your own
common use, a Sound genuine, old, but not brandyed, wine; and hav-
ing received on the 16ʰ per the, Jane Couts, from Tenerife, a Small
parcell of Teneriffe wine of which 2 [hhs?]¹ & 4 quart Casks—are
very old & of the best quality, I thought proper, to inform you, of—
that I may Send to you Some of it, if you Say So—
Waiting for your orders, I will not dispose of it—for this 15 days—
With the greatest respect & a very Sincere Esteem
I remain Dʳ Sir Your Mo: obᵗ Servᵗ
                              JOHN F. OLIVEIRA FERNANDES

RC (DLC); endorsed by TJ as a letter
of 15 Jan. received 23 Jan. 1816 and so
recorded in SJL. RC (DLC); address
cover only; with PoC of TJ to Benjamin
W. Crowninshield, 30 Jan. 1816, on
verso; addressed: "Thomas Jefferson
Esqʳ Monticello Milton Virgᵃ"; franked;
postmarked Norfolk, 18 Jan.

The brig *Rolla* (ROLLEY), Captain
Bennett (BLENNETT), stopped briefly in
Norfolk on 4 Jan. 1816 on its way from
Providence to Richmond (Norfolk *Ameri-
can Beacon and Commercial Diary*, 4 Jan.
1816).

¹ Illegible abbreviation for "hogsheads" or the equivalent "half-pipes."

From John Barnes

Dear Sir—   George Town 19th Jany 1816—

My last inquiry respecting the good Genl K. was of the 18th Novr last. since when, nothing has transpired with me, to direct, in what mode I should proceed, in Order to transmit him Via London, or Amsterdam—a further Remittance in Course of a M° or two—I have already Interest on hand, to the Amo^t of 1130\frac{65}{}$ exclusive of his Principal $4.500 in Treasury Notes. bearing 5$\frac{2}{3}$ Int. due & payable 16th April next. of Course my Anxiety for information increases. Nevertheless, Messrs Baring Brothers & C° in London, no doubt Corrispond with the Genl—nor should I hesitate, to remit him thro those Gent^s—mean while Request the fav^r of you to advise and direct me, thereupon—as well respecting—the Treasury Notes—

I am Dear Sir

Most Respectfully and truly—Your obed^t servant

JOHN BARNES.

RC (ViU: TJP-ER); at foot of text: "Thomas Jefferson Esqr Monticello"; endorsed by TJ as received 27 Jan. 1816 and so recorded in SJL.

GEN^L K.: Tadeusz Kosciuszko.

To Dabney Carr

Dear Sir   Monticello Jan. 19. 16.

At the date of your letter of Dec. 1. I was in Bedford, & since my return so many letters, accumulated during my absence, have been pressing for answers, that this is the first moment I have been able to attend to the subject of yours. while mr Girardin was in this neighborhood writing his continuation of Burke's history, I had suggested to him a proper notice of the establishment of the committee of correspondence[1] here in 1773. and of mr Carr, your father, who introduced it. he has doubtless done this, and his work is now in the press. my books, journals of the times, E^tc being all gone, I have nothing now but an impaired memory to resort to for the more particular statement you wish. but I give it with the more confidence as I find that I remember old things better than new. the transaction took place in the session of assembly of Mar. 73. Patrick Henry, Richard H. Lee, Frank Lee, your father and my self met, by agreement one evening, about the close of the session, at the Raleigh tavern, to consult on the measures which the circumstances of the times seemed to call for. we agreed in result that concert in the operations of the several colonies was indispensable—and that to produce this some channel of correspondence between them must be opened: that therefore we would propose to our House the appointment of a Committee of correspondence which should be authorised & instructed to write to the Speaker of the Houses of Representatives of the several colonies, recommending the appointment of similar committees on their part, who, by a communication of sentiment on the transactions threatening us all, might promote a harmony of action salutary to all. this was the substance, not pretending to remember words. we prepared the resolution, & your father was agreed on to make the motion. he did it the next day, March 12. with great ability, reconciling all to it, not only by the reasonings, but by the temper and moderation with which it was developed. it was adopted by a very general vote. Peyton Randolph, some of us who proposed it, and who else I do not remember, were appointed of the Committee. we immediately dispatched letters by expresses, to the Speakers of all the other assemblies. I remember that mr Carr and myself, returning home together & conversing on the subject by the way, concurred in the conclusion that that measure must inevitably beget the meeting of a Congress of deputies from all the colonies, for the purpose of uniting all in the same principles and measures for the maintenance of our rights. my memory cannot deceive me when I affirm that we did it in consequence of no such proposition from any other colony. no doubt the resolution itself, & the Journals of the day will shew that ours was original, and not merely responsive to one from any other quarter. yet, I am certain I remember also that a similar proposition, & nearly cotemporary, was made by Massachusets, & that our Northern messenger passed theirs on the road. this too may be settled by recurrence to the records of Massachusets. the proposition was generally acceded to by the other colonies, & the first effect, as expected, was the meeting of a Congress at New York the ensuing year. the committee of correspondence appointed by Massachusets, as quoted by you from Marshal under the date of 1770. must have been for a special purpose, and functus officio before the date of 1773. or Massachusets herself would not then have proposed another. records should be examined to settle this accurately.   I well remember the pleasure expressed in the countenance & conversation of [the] members generally on this debut of mr Carr, & the hopes they conceived as well from the talents as the patriotism it manifested. but he died within two months after; & in him we lost a powerful fellow laborer. his character was of a high order. a spotless integrity, sound judgment handsome imagination, enriched by education & reading, quick & clear in his conceptions, of correct & ready elocution, impressing every hearer with the sincerity of the heart from which it flowed. his firmness was inflexible in whatever he thought was right: but when no moral principle stood in the way, never had man more of the milk of human kindness, of indulgence, of softness, of pleasantry in conversation & conduct. the number of his friends, & the warmth of their affection were proofs of his worth, & of their estimate of it. to give to those now living an idea of the affliction produced by his death in the minds of all who knew him, I liken it to that lately felt by themselves, on the death of his eldest son, Peter Carr, so like him in all his endowments and moral qualities, and whose recollection can never recur without a deep-drawn sigh from the bosom of anyone who knew him.   You mention that I shewed you an inscription I had proposed for the tombstone of your father. did I leave it in your hands to be copied? I ask the question, not that I have any such recollection, bu[t] that I find it no longer in the place of it's deposit, and think I never took it out but on that occasion. ever and affectionately yours   TH: JEFFERSON

PoC (DLC); edge chipped; at foot of first page: "Dabney Carr."

Without crediting the elder Dabney Carr as indicated above, John Daly Burk (BURKE) discussed the 1773 session of the House of Burgesses in Burk, Jones, and Girardin, *History of Virginia*, vol. 3. The fourth and final volume did not mention Carr. The Virginia resolution to establish a standing Committee of Correspondence is recorded under MARCH 12. 1773 in the *Journal of the House of Burgesses* (Williamsburg, 1773), 23. In addition to PEYTON RANDOLPH, TJ, and Carr, the committee's members were Robert Carter Nicholas, Richard Bland, Richard Henry Lee, Benjamin Harrison, Edmund Pendleton, Patrick Henry, Dudley Digges, and Archibald Cary. The earliest formal committee of correspondence in Massachusetts was established in 1772 under the leadership of Samuel Adams to foster cooperation within that colony (Adams to James Warren, 4 Nov. 1772 [MHi: Warren-Adams Papers]). Virginia and Massachusetts were NEARLY COTEMPORARY in urging the creation of an intercolonial network of correspondence committees (Circular Letter from the Boston Committee of Correspondence, 9 Apr. 1773 [printed broadside, Boston, 1773]). FUNCTUS OFFICIO: "without further authority or legal competence because the duties and functions of the original commission have been fully accomplished" (*Black's Law Dictionary*).

[1] TJ here canceled "in this state."

To David Gelston

DEAR SIR   Monticello Jan. 20. 16.
    Your favor of the 8[th] is just now recieved, informing me of the reciept of a box of garden & flower seeds from mr Baker of Tarragona

for me. I do not think I can better dispose of them than by asking from the Botanical garden of New York their a[ccept]ance of them. perhaps there may be among them something worthy their notice and I am happy in an occasion of shewing my willingness to be useful to them. you do not say if there has been any duty, freight or other expence on them. if there has, have the goodness to note it to me and however small I will find the means of remitting it.

On the return of peace I have written to Marseilles, Leghorn E^{t}c. for some wines, and as their opportunities do not give them a choice of ports, I have taken the liberty of desiring them to be addressed to the Collector of whatever port a vessel may be coming to. the extensive commerce of New York will probably subject you at times to some of these addresses. in this case I must throw myself on your friendship for notice of the case, with an assurance that all expences shall be remitted by my self or my correspondents at Richmond (Gibson & Jefferson) by return of mail with much thankfulness, to which permit me to add assurances of my constant esteem and respect.   TH: JEFFERSON

PoC (MHi); on verso of a reused address cover from George Logan to TJ; torn at seal, with some text rewritten by TJ; at foot of text: "Mr Gelston"; endorsed by TJ.

To Patrick Gibson

DEAR SIR   Monticello Jan. 20. 16.

The ice of our river has at length broke up, which enables us to get off this day 3. or 4. loads of flour, which, the tide being good, will be with you nearly as soon as this letter. the boatmen will call on you for their pay @ 3/6 per barrel. mr Yancey some weeks ago informed me that such was the press of tob° going from Lynchburg, that flour could not then be got down under 15/ a barrel, & of course that he must defer sending mine off till the price of carriage should fall. I do not know whether he has sent off the tob° as yet. if he has, the immediate sale of that, which I wish, will^1 cover my draughts & permit the flour to be held up for the spring demand. if not, it must be sold for the price going. Gilmer is in one of these boats, and may be trusted with the cask of wine from Dr Fernandes, which having been shipped at Norfolk on the 5th inst. will I hope be with you in time for Gilmer.—an old acquaintance of mine Capt Peyton, having settled in Richmond in the mercantile line, instead of troubling you with the purchase of little special articles, as I have too often been obliged to do, I shall address those little commissions to him hereafter, and only ask the favor of you to pay the bills for which he will call on you. I have now written to him to procure for me 4. gross of bottles, 12 gross of corks & some anchovies, the bills for which I must ask you to pay, and to be so good as to direct Gilmer to call on him for the articles, as I have not directed him to call on Capt Peyton. Accept the assurance of my great esteem and respect.   TH: JEFFERSON

PoC (ViHi: Adrienne D. Maxwell Papers); on verso of a reused address cover from Horatio G. Spafford to TJ; torn at seal, with missing text rewritten by TJ; at foot of text: "Mr Gibson"; endorsed by TJ.

¹ TJ here canceled "enable."

To Bernard Peyton

DEAR SIR   Monticello Jan. 20. 16.

I was much pleased to learn you had set up business in Richmond in the mercantile way, and I sincerely wish you success in it. it will be an easier life than that of a camp, and a happier one. my dealings are chiefly of course in this place, yet there have been often occasions in which I have wished for some mercantile connection in Richmond, for supplies of things not to be had here, or at prices too unreasonable. your establishment furnishes me with this accomodation, and certainly I would rather have it with an acquaintance & friend, than with a stranger. of such articles as you deal in yourself, whatever I may have occasion to call for, your account rendered quarterly, or half yearly, or at what intervals you please, shall be always paid by an order on mr Gibson my correspondent in Richmond. but I shall sometimes trouble you for things not in your line, & requiring cash payment. these bills mr Gibson will always pay for me at sight, on which subject I now write to him. of this nature is the trouble I now propose to give you; which is to request you to procure for me 4. gross of bottles, the strong kind preferred & 12. gross of corks, the best, as bad ones is throwing away our liquor. there are two only of the Milton watermen who can be trusted with any thing which can be plundered or adulterated, Gilmer & Johnson. Gilmer starts this day, and will call on mr Gibson, from whom you may know how to get the bottles & corks delivered to him; for he has no notice to apply to you. I shall be glad to have them on his return as the season for bottling beer & cyder is approaching. if there are any good anchovies to be had I should be glad to recieve half a dozen bottles. I write to mr Gibson to pay for these things. Accept the assurance of my great esteem and respect   TH: JEFFERSON

PoC (MHi); on verso of reused address cover of Thomas Leiper to TJ, 30 Nov. 1815; at foot of text: "<*M^r*> Capt Bernard Peyton, of the firm of Green & Peyton"; torn at seal, with missing text rewritten by TJ; endorsed by TJ.

To Peter Wilson

SIR   Monticello Jan. 20. 16.

Of the last five months I have been absent four from home which must apologise for so very late an acknolegement of your favor of Nov. 22. and I wish the delay could be compensated by the matter of the answer. but an unfortunate accident puts that out of my power. during the course of my public life, and from a very early period of it, I omitted no opportunity of procuring vocabularies of the Indian languages; and for that purpose formed a model expressing such objects in nature as must be familiar to every people savage or civilized. this being made the standard to which all were brought, would exhibit readily whatever affinities of language there might be between the several tribes. it was my intention, on retiring from public business, to have digested these into some order, so as to shew, not only what relations of language existed among our own aborigines, but, by a collation with the great Russian Vocabulary[1] of the languages of Europe and Asia, whether there were any between them and the other nations of the continent. on my removal from Washington the package, in which this collection was coming by water, was stolen & destroyed. it consisted of between 30. and 40. vocabularies, of which I can, from memory, say nothing particular; but that I am certain more than half of them differred as radically, each from every other, as the Greek, the Latin & Islandic. and even of those which seemed to be derived from the same Radix, the departure was such that the tribes speaking them could not probably understand one another. single words, or two or three together, might perhaps be understood: but not a whole sentence of any extent of construction. I think therefore the pious missionaries, who shall go to the several tribes to instruct them in the Christian religion, will have to learn a language for every tribe they go to; nay more, that they will have to create a new language for every one, that is to say, to add to theirs new words for the new ideas they will have to communicate. law, medecine, chemistry, mathematics, every science has a language of it's own, and Divinity not less than others. their barren vocabularies cannot be vehicles for ideas of the fall of man, his redemption, the triune composition of the god head, and other mystical doctrines, considered by most Christians of the present date as essential elements of faith. the enterprize is therefore arduous, but the more inviting perhaps to missionary zeal, in proportion as the merit of surmounting it will be greater.　　　Again repeating my regrets that I am able to give so little satisfaction on the subject of your enquiry, I pray you to accept the assurance of my great consideration and esteem.

TH: JEFFERSON

PoC (DLC); at foot of first page: "Dr Peter Wilson, Professor of languages. Columbia college. N. York."

Peter Wilson (1746–1825), educator, classicist, and public official, was born in Ordiquhill, Banffshire, Scotland, and studied at the University of Aberdeen. After moving to New York City in 1763, he worked as a teacher and then as principal of the Hackensack Academy before becoming professor of Greek and Latin at Columbia College (later Columbia University), 1789–92 and 1797–1820. During the latter stint he was also professor of Grecian and Roman antiquities. Wilson's service at Columbia was interrupted by a principalship at Erasmus Hall Academy in Flatbush, New York. He received honorary degrees of A.M. from the College of Rhode Island (later Brown University) in 1786 and LL.D. from Union College in 1798. Wilson represented Bergen County in the New Jersey General Assembly, 1778–81 and 1787. In 1783 he helped prepare a revision and codification of the laws of the state. Wilson's other publications included textbooks and edited volumes of classical works (*DAB*; Ward W. Briggs Jr., ed., *Biographical Dictionary of North American Classicists* [1994], 715–6; NjHi: Wilson Papers; Milton Halsey Thomas, *Columbia University Officers and Alumni 1754–1857* [1936], 92; *Historical Catalogue of Brown University, Providence, Rhode Island, 1764–*

1894 [1895], 334; John P. Dullard, comp., *Manual of the Legislature of New Jersey* [1921], 175; Willis Boughton and Eugene W. Harter, *Chronicles of Erasmus Hall* [1906], 52–4; Boston *Columbian Centinel*, 6 Aug. 1825).

Only the address cover of Wilson's FAVOR OF NOV. 22. has been found (RC in MHi; with PoC of postscript of TJ to Nathaniel Macon, 22 Jan. 1816, on verso; addressed: "His Excellency Thomas Jefferson Esqr Monticello Virginia"; franked; postmarked New York, 22 Nov.; recorded in SJL as received 15 Dec. 1815 from New York). For TJ's collection of VOCABULARIES OF THE INDIAN LANGUAGES, see TJ to Benjamin Smith Barton, 21 Sept. 1809, and note.

Catherine the Great initiated a linguistic project to compile a comparative VOCABULARY of two hundred languages. Her research was published as *Linguarum Totius Orbis Vocabularia comparativa*, ed. Peter Simon Pallas, 2 vols. (Saint Petersburg, 1786–89; Sowerby, no. 4736). With assistance from Lafayette, Catherine obtained American Indian vocabularies from George Washington (Mary Ritchie Key, *Catherine the Great's Linguistic Contribution* [1980], esp. 47, 49; Washington, *Papers, Confederation Ser.*, 3:555, 6:30, 31).

¹ Word interlined in place of "catalogue."

To Amos J. Cook

Sir   Monticello Jan. 21. 16.

Your favor of Dec. 18. was exactly a month on it's way to this place; and I have to thank you for the elegant and philosophical lines communicated by the Nestor of our revolution. whether the style or sentiment be considered, they were well worthy the trouble of being copied and communicated by his pen. nor am I less thankful for the happy translation of them. it adds another to the rare instances of a rival to it's original: superior indeed in one respect, as the same outline of sentiment is brought within a compass of better proportion. for if the original be liable to any criticism, it is that of giving too great extension to the same general idea. yet it has a great authority to support it, that of a wiser man than all of us. 'I sought in my heart to give myself unto wine; I made me great works; I builded me houses; I planted me vineyards; I made me gardens and orchards, and pools to water them; I got me servants and maidens, and great possessions of cattle; I gathered me also silver and gold, and men singers, and women singers, and the delights of the sons of men, and musical instruments of all sorts; and whatsoever mine eyes desired I kept not from them; I witheld not my heart from any joy. then I looked on all the works that my hands had wrought, and behold! all was vanity and vexation of spirit! I saw that Wisdom excelleth folly, as far as light excelleth darkness.' the Preacher, whom I abridge, has indulged in a much larger amplification of his subject. I am not so happy as my friend and antient colleague, mr Adams, in possessing any thing original, <u>inedited</u>, and worthy of comparison with the epigraph of the Spanish monk. I can offer but humble prose; from the hand indeed of the father of eloquence, and philosophy; a moral morsel, which our young friends under your tuition should keep ever in their eye, as the ultimate term of your instructions and of their labors. 'Hic, quisquis est, qui moderatione et constantia quietus animo est, sibique ipse placatus; ut nec tabescat molestiis, nec frangatur timore, nec sitienter quid expetens ardeat desiderio, nec alacritate futili gestiens deliquescat; is est **Sapiens**, quem quaerimus; is est beatus; cui nihil humanarum rerum aut intolerabile ad dimittendum animum, aut nimis laetabile ad efferendum, videri potest.'

Or, if a poetical dress will be more acceptable to the fancy of the Juvenile student;

'Quisnam igitur liber? **Sapiens**, sibique imperiosus:
Quem neque pauperies, neque mors, neque vincula terrent:

Responsare cupidinibus, contemnere honores
Fortis, et in seipso totus teres, atque rotundus;
Externi ne quid valeat per laeve morari:
In quem manca ruit semper Fortuna.'

And if the **Wise**, be the happy man, as these sages say, he must be virtuous too; for, without virtue, happiness cannot be. this then is the true scope of all academical emulation.

You request something in the handwriting of General Washington. I inclose you a letter which I received from him, while in Paris, covering a copy of the new constitution. it is offered merely as what you ask,[1] a specimen of his handwriting.

On the subject of your Museum, I fear I cannot flatter myself with being useful to it. were the obstacle of distance out of the way, age and retirement have withdrawn me from the opportunities of procuring objects in that line.

With every wish for the prosperity of your institution, accept the assurances of my great respect and esteem.   TH: JEFFERSON

RC (Christie's, New York City, 2006); chipped along folds, with faint and damaged text supplied from FC. FC (DLC); entirely in TJ's hand; at foot of first page: "Mʳ Amos J. Cook, Preceptor of Frye-burg academy in the district of Maine." Enclosure: George Washington to TJ, 18 Sept. 1787 (*PTJ*, 12:149–50).

The NESTOR OF OUR REVOLUTION: John Adams. The biblical quotation, I SOUGHT ... EXCELLETH DARKNESS, is from Ecclesiastes 2.3–13.

HIC, QUISQUIS ... VIDERI POTEST: "Therefore the man, whoever he is, whose soul is tranquillized by restraint and consistency and who is at peace with himself, so that he neither pines away in distress, nor is broken down by fear, nor consumed with a thirst of longing in pursuit of some ambition, nor maudlin in the exuberance of meaningless eagerness— he is the wise man of whom we are in quest, he is the happy man who can think no human occurrence insupportable to the point of dispiriting him, or unduly delightful to the point of rousing him to ecstasy" (Cicero, *Tusculan Disputations*, 4.17, in *Cicero: Tusculan Disputations*, trans. John E. King, Loeb Classical Library [1927; rev. ed., 1945], 366–7).

QUISNAM IGITUR ... SEMPER FORTU-NA: "Who then is free? The wise man, who is lord over himself, whom neither poverty nor death nor bonds affright, who bravely defies his passions, and scorns ambition, who in himself is a whole, smoothed and rounded, so that nothing from outside can rest on the polished surface, and against whom Fortune in her onset is ever maimed" (Horace, *Satires*, 2.7.83–8, in Fairclough, *Horace: Satires, Epistles and Ars Poetica*, 230–3).

[1] Preceding three words interlined in FC.

From Lafayette

My dear friend La grange January 21ˢᵗ 1816

I Have Been for a Long While Anxiously Expecting Answers to Several Letters of Mine Which I principaly Atribute to the distance from Monticelo to the Sea port places where opportunities are to Be found—But as the departure of Mʳ Gallatin Cannot fail to Be known to You I Hope He May Be the Bearer of Your dispatches.

the Situation of Europe is too Comprehensive, the Events of Last Year Have Been too Complicated and Numerous for me to pretend making that History of twelve months the Subject of a Letter. You will Have, in the papers, shackled as they now are in france partial as they Have Been elsewhere, found materials Enough to form a Correct judgement. Let me only firmly assert that the Cause of European Liberty far from Being Lost in france Has Never Been So well Understood By the mass of the people and that the Reactionnary Spirit of the day is doing more for it than Either the Conventional or the imperial System. the Medicine is Bitter and to obnoxious Characters Not Very Safe. Yet to the party of privileges and to the party of Rights, the Result Not only in this But in other Countries Cannot fail to prove what for upwards of forty Years You and I Have Wished it to Be.

A Series of unfortunate Circumstances, the Effect of Recent despotism, as the Excesses of the Revolution Had Sprung from the education of the <u>Ancien Regime</u>, Had Roused Against Us Not only our Natural adversaries of <u>Coblentz</u> and <u>pilnitz</u> But all the population of Europe. it Remained for Us either to shake off[1] the Expeller of the Bourbons, and Appeal to the nation who Could No more trust Him or them, or to Let Him, with a standing army and His Eminent talents, face an Enemy[2] five times their Numbers. in the Hurry of defense, the Later Ressource was prefered By an active majority. we thought it imprudent to dissent, and Were Unanimous in Giving Napoleon Every Means of defense. But when, Having Lost His principal forces, and Left His Gallant Soldiers to their fate, He turned to the Representative of the people to dissolve them, and Resume Arbitrary power, He Was Stopped in the mad Attempt. Had We got a little time, popular measures might Have Saved us. on my Return from An Embassy to the allies which I Could not decline, We found the Capitulation of paris Had Been Signed. the Executive and the peers dissolved themselves. president fouché Became a minister to the king. We Were shut out of our House But Not Before a manifesto

Had Been published, July the 5ʰ, Very Similar to what Had Been declared in July 1789. I inclose it. You know How the Royal Government Has Become an instrument[3] in the Hands of the Allies to disarm first, then to oppress the Country. Under these Circumstances two Houses Have Been framed. Their produce You may See from the news papers. Both majorities and minorities You Would think much alike. among a few individual Exceptions, I Send You the printed Opinion of My Young friend, Victor Broglie, Grand Son to the marechal, Son to the one You Have Seen in the Constituent Assembly. He Seats as a duke in the House of peers, and Has Called Yesterday at La Grange on His Way to Marry the Charming daughter of our friend mde de Staël.

for my part, my dear friend, I am Returned to my old Agricultural Post With a determination not to Quit it. many french Citizens, Several of them of distinguished talents, are Going to the U.S. either to obey or to Avoid proscription. How Happy I Would Be to find myself Under the Hospitable friendly Roof of Monticelo You Well know, But Cannot Blame me for Staying.

Our Worthy friend tracy who Holds His peerage, is Almost Blind. a letter from You would Be a Great Comfort to Him. if You Can Send me two Copies of a Certain Anonymous Work on montesquieu's writings I Will Be obliged to You Be pleased to present my Best Respects to Mʳˢ Randolph, to Receive those of my family. Most affectionately forever

Your old Loving friend   LAFAYETTE

RC (DLC); at foot of first page: "Mʳ Jefferson"; endorsed by TJ as received 16 May 1816 and so recorded in SJL.

The MANIFESTO, not found as enclosed by Lafayette, was the 5 July 1815 declaration of the French Chamber of Representatives. Translated into English and published in the *New York Evening Post*, 24 Aug. 1815, and other newspapers, it emphasized the continued independence of the French nation, asserted the status of the chamber as a delegation of the people, and restated its commitment to liberty,

equality, and the rights expressed in the 1789 Declaration of the Rights of Man. The enclosed opinion, not definitely identified, may have been the *Opinion de M. de Broglie Sur la Loi d'amnistie portée par les Ministres de Sa Majesté à la Chambre des Pairs le 9 janvier 1816* (Paris, [1816]; listed as "Broglie" in Poor, *Jefferson's Library*, 11 [no. 681], with other foreign political pamphlets).

[1] Manuscript: "of."
[2] Manuscript: "Enmemy."
[3] Manuscript: "intrument."

Jefferson's Essay on New England Religious Intolerance

I. THOMAS JEFFERSON TO THOMAS RITCHIE, 21 JAN. 1816

II. ESSAY ON NEW ENGLAND RELIGIOUS INTOLERANCE (DRAFT),
[CA. 10 JAN. 1816]

III. ESSAY ON NEW ENGLAND RELIGIOUS INTOLERANCE
(AS PUBLISHED), [27 JAN. 1816]

EDITORIAL NOTE

While drafting his 10 Jan. 1816 response to Horatio G. Spafford's letter of 25 Dec. 1815, Jefferson digressed from comments on Spafford's enclosed manuscript to what he here describes to Thomas Ritchie as a "tirade" on a religious publication sent to him by Benjamin Waterhouse on 14 Dec. 1815. The work in question, Lyman Beecher's pamphlet *On the Importance of Assisting Young Men of Piety and Talents in Obtaining an Education for the Gospel Ministry* (1st ed., New Haven, [1814]; 2d. ed., Andover, [1815]), was in Jefferson's view an obnoxious instance of religious intolerance. He hoped that by bringing Beecher's arguments to the attention of the public, he would lessen the damage these views might otherwise inflict. On reflection, Jefferson dropped the section on attempts to spread New England's religious influence from his letter to Spafford. Instead, he passed the text on to the newspaper editor Thomas Ritchie along with his permission to print the essay as an anonymous contribution to the *Richmond Enquirer*. The copy sent to Ritchie has not been found, but Jefferson's retained draft and the version adapted and published by Ritchie are printed in full below.

I. Thomas Jefferson to Thomas Ritchie

DEAR SIR   Monticello Jan. 21. 16.

In answering the letter of a Northern correspondent lately, I indulged in a tirade against a pamphlet recently published in his quarter. on revising my letter however, I thought it unsafe to commit my self so far to a stranger. I struck out the passage therefore, yet I think the pamphlet of such a character as ought not to be unknown, or unnoticed by the people of the United States. it is the most bold and impudent stride New England has ever made in arrogating an ascendancy over the rest of the Union. the first form of the pamphlet was an Address from the rev^d Lyman Beecher chairman of the Connecticut society for the education of <u>pious</u> young men for the ministry. it's matter was then adopted and published in a sermon by a rev^d mr Pearson of Andover in Massachusets, where they have a <u>theological</u> college; and where the Address 'with circumstantial variations to adapt it to more general use' is reprinted, on a sheet and a half of paper, in so cheap a form as to be distributed, I imagine, gratis. for it has a final note indicating 6000. copies of the 1st edition printed. so far as it respects Virginia the extract of my letter gives the outline. I therefore send it to you to publish or burn, abridge or alter as you think best. you understand the public palate better than I do. only give it such a title as may lead to no suspicion from whom you receive it. I am the more induced to offer it to you because it is possible mine may be the only copy in the state, and because too it may be à propos for the petition for the establishment of <u>a theological society</u> now before the legislature, and to which they have shewn the unusual respect of hearing an advocate for it at their bar. from what quarter this theological society comes forward I know not. perhaps from our own tramontaine clergy, of New England religion and politics. perhaps it is the entering wedge from it's <u>theological</u> sister in Andover, for the body of 'qualified religious instructors' proposed by their pious brethren of the East 'to evangelize, and catechise,' to edify our daughters by 'weekly lectures' and our wives by 'family visits' from these pious young monks of Harvard and Yale.　　　　However do with this what you please and be assured of my friendship & respect.

TH: JEFFERSON

PoC (DLC); at foot of first page: "Mr Thomas Ritchie."

The second edition of the work by Lyman Beecher cited above was the one issued in 6000. COPIES. A PETITION FOR THE ESTABLISHMENT OF A THEOLOGICAL SOCIETY was presented and read in the Virginia House of Delegates on 7 Dec. 1815. Although the Committee of Propositions and Grievances concluded on 13 Dec. 1815 that the request was reasonable, on 2 Jan. 1816 Jerman Baker moved that the resolution to incorporate a Theological Seminary of Virginia be rejected. Rev. John H. Rice, a trustee of the seminary, was then "admitted to the Bar of this House, and heard in opposition to the said motion, and in support of the said resolution of the Committee; after which he withdrew." On 1 Feb. 1816 the resolution was considered again, and "The Reverend William Hill, the Reverend John H. Rice, and William Wirt, Esq. the Committee of the Trustees aforesaid, were then admitted to the bar of this House, and heard in support of the said petition." Despite their efforts, the House struck down the bill by a vote of 119 to 48 (*JHD* [1815–16 sess.], 23, 35, 88–9, 153; Vi: RG 78, Legislative Petitions, Prince Edward Co.). Notwithstanding this refusal to incorporate the Presbyterian seminary located at Hampden-Sydney College, it survived and eventually moved to Richmond as the Union Theological Seminary in Virginia (John Luster Brinkley, *On This Hill: A Narrative History of Hampden-Sydney College, 1774–1994* [1994], esp. 137–42, 379–89).

OUR OWN TRAMONTAINE CLERGY: in this context, by tramontane TJ means the Presbyterian clergy of the Shenandoah Valley of Virginia.

II. Essay on New England Religious Intolerance (Draft)

[ca. 10 Jan. 1816]

you judge truly that I am not afraid of the priests. they have tried upon me all their various batteries, of pious whining, hypocritical canting, lying & slandering, without being able to give me one moment of pain. I have contemplated their order from the Magi of the East to the Saints of the West, and I have found no difference of character, but of more or less caution, in proportion to the information or ignorance of those on whom their interested duperies were to be plaid off. their sway in New England is indeed formidable. no mind beyond mediocrity dares there to develope itself. if it does, they excite against it the public opinion which they command, & by little, but incessant and teazing persecutions, drive it from among them. their present great emigrations to the Western country are real flights from persecution, religious & political. but the abandonment of the country by those who wish to enjoy freedom of opinion leaves the despotism over the residue more intense, more oppressive. they are now looking to the fleshpots of the South, and aiming at foothold there by their missionary teachers. they have lately come forward boldly with their plan to establish '<u>a qualified religious instructor</u> over every thousand souls in the US.' and they seem to[1] consider none as qualified but their own sect. thus, in Virginia, they say there are but 60. qualified, and that 914. are still wanting of the full quota. all besides the 60. are 'mere nominal ministers unacquainted with theology.' now the 60. they allude to are exactly in the string of counties at the Western foot of the Blue ridge, settled originally by Irish presbyterians, and composing precisely the tory district of the state. there indeed is found, in full vigor, the hypocrisy, the despotism, and anti-civism of the New England <u>qualified religious instructors</u>. the country below the mountains, inhabited by Episcopalians,[2] Methodists & Baptists (under[3] mere nominal ministers unacquainted with theology) are pronounced 'destitute of the means of grace, and as sitting in darkness and under the shadow of death.' they are quite in despair too at the insufficient means of New England to fill this fearful void 'with Evangelical light, with catechetical instructions, weekly lectures, & family visiting. that Yale cannot furnish above 80. graduates annually, and Harvard perhaps not more. that there must therefore be an immediate, universal, vigorous & systematic effort made to evangelize the nation to see that there is a bible for every family, a school for every district, and a qualifi[ed'] (i.e. Presbyterian) 'pastor for every thousand souls; that newspapers, tracts, magazines, must be employed; the press be made to groan, & every pulpit in the land to sound it's trumpet long and loud. a more homogeneous' (i.e. New-England) 'character must be produced thro' the nation.' that section then of our union having lost it's political influence by disloyalty to it's country is now to recover it under the mask of religion. it is to send among us their Gardiners, their Osgoods, their Parishes & Pearsons, as apostles to teach us their orthodoxy. this is the outline of the plan as published by mess^{rs} Beecher, Pearson & co. it has uttered however one truth. 'that the nation must be awaked to save itself by it's own exertions, or we are undone.' and I trust that this publication will do not a little to awaken it; and that in aid of it newspapers, tracts and magazines must sound the trumpet. yours I hope will make itself heard. and the louder as yours is the nearest house in the course of conflagration

Dft (DLC: TJ Papers, 206:36599–600), extracted by Editors from FC of TJ to Horatio G. Spafford, 10 Jan. 1816; undated; torn. Tr (ViU: GT and MHi); posthumous copy, with the first two pages in ViU: GT and third page in MHi, consisting of text of entire original FC to Spafford and thus containing the same extracted material. TJ bracketed the text printed above to indicate that it was omitted from the RC to Spafford, and these brackets are also in the Tr.

TJ here quotes and paraphrases from the PLAN AS PUBLISHED BY MESS^{RS} BEECHER, PEARSON & CO., enclosed in Benjamin Waterhouse to TJ, 14 Dec. 1815.

[1] Preceding two words interlined.
[2] Tr (portion at MHi) begins with this word.
[3] Word interlined.

III. Essay on New England Religious Intolerance (As Published)

[27 Jan. 1816]

To the Editor of the Enquirer.

A pamphlet[1] has lately been published to the North, of such a character, as ought not to be unknown, or unnoticed by the people of the United States. It is the boldest and most impudent stride New England has ever made in arrogating an ascendency over the rest of the Union. The first form of the pamphlet was an Address from the rev. Lyman Beecher, Chairman of the Connecticut Society for the education of *pious* young men for the ministry. Its matter was then adopted and published in a sermon by a Rev'd. Mr. Pearson of Andover, in Massachusetts, where they have a *Theological* College; and where the Address "with circumstantial variations to adapt it to more general use" is re-printed on a sheet and a half of paper in so cheap a form as to be distributed, I imagine, gratis; for it has a final note indicating 6000 copies of the 1st edition printed. So far as it respects Virginia, the following extract of a letter furnishes the outline:—This Extract is now offered, because it may be apropos for the Petition for the establishment of a *Theological Society* now before the Legislature, and to which they have shewn the unusual respect of hearing an Advocate for it at their bar. From what quarter this Theological Society comes forward, I know not. I will not say it is *intended;* but who will say that it is not *calculated* as the entering-wedge with its *theological* sister in Andover, for the body of "qualified religious instructors" proposed by their pious brethren of the East, "to evangelize, and catechise," to edify our daughters by "weekly lectures" and our wives by "family visits" from these pious young Monks of Harvard and Yale?

EXTRACT—*of a letter.*

"The sway of the New-England priests is indeed formidable. No mind beyond mediocrity dares there to develope itself; if it does, they excite against it the public opinion which they command, and by little, but incessant and teazing persecutions, drive it from among them. Their present great emigrations to the western country are real flights from persecution, religious and political. But the abandonment of the country by those who wish to enjoy freedom of opinion, leaves the despotism over the residue more intense, more oppressive. They are now looking to the flesh-pots of the South, and aiming at foothold there by their missionary teachers; they have lately come forward boldly with their plan to establish 'a *qualified religious instructor* over every thousand souls in the United States;' and they seem to consider none as qualified, but their own sect. Thus, in Virginia, they say there are but 60 qualified, and that 914 are still wanting of the full quota. All besides the 60 are "mere nominal ministers, unacquainted with theology." The 60 here alluded to are understood to be the Presbyterian ministers on the western side of the Blue-ridge. The country below the mountains, inhabited by Episcopalians, Methodists & Baptists (under "mere nominal ministers, unacquainted with theology") are pronounced "destitute of the means of grace, and as sitting in darkness and under the shadow of death." They are quite in despair too at the insufficient means of New-England to fill this fearful void "with Evangelical light, with catechetical instructions, weekly lectures, and family visiting. That Yale cannot furnish above 80 graduates annually, and Harvard perhaps not more. That there must therefore be an immediate, universal, vigorous[2] and systematic effort made to evangelize the nation, to see that there is a bible for every family, a school for every district, and a qualified" i. e. Presbyterian[3] "pastor for every thousand souls; that newspapers, tracts, magazines, must be employed, the press be made to groan, and every pulpit in the land to sound its trumpet long and loud. A more homogeneous" i. e. New-England "character must be produced through the nation." That section then of our union having lost it's political influence by disloyalty to it's country, is now to recover it under the mask of religion: it is to send among us their Gardiners, their Osgoods, their Parishes and Pearsons, as apostles to teach us their orthodoxy, their patriotism. This is the outline of the plan, as published by Messrs. Beecher, Pearson, & Co. It has uttered, however, one truth, "that the nation must be awakened, to save itself by its own exertions, or we are undone." And I trust that this publication will do not a little to awaken it; and that in aid of it, "news-papers, tracts and magazines, will sound the trumpet long and loud."

Printed in the *Richmond Enquirer*, 27 Jan. 1816; undated.

[1] *Richmond Enquirer*: "phamphlet."
[2] *Richmond Enquirer*: "vigorons."
[3] *Richmond Enquirer*: "Presbyserian."

To Peter S. Du Ponceau

DEAR SIR   Monticello Jan. 22. 16.

I have been 4. of the last 5. months absent from home, which must apologise for this very tardy acknolegement of your favor of Nov. 14. I learn with much satisfaction the enlargement by the Philosophical society of the scope of their institution, by the establishment of a standing committee for History, the moral sciences and general literature. I have always thought that we were too much confined <u>in practice</u> to the Natural and Mathematical departments. this Committee will become a depository for many original MS. many loose sheets, of no use by themselves and in the hands of the holder; but of great value when brought into a general depot, open to the use of the future historian or literary enquirer.   I shall be very happy in contributing to the usefulness of your establishment by any thing in my possession, or within the reach of my endeavors; and I begin by inclosing you a geographical and statistical account in MS. of the Creek or Muscogee Indians and country, as it was in the years 98. and 99. this was written by Col° Hawkins who has lived among them as agent now upwards of 20. years. besides a general interspersion of observations on the state of society, manners and opinions among them, there is in the latter part an interesting account of their government, & ceremonies, civil and religious; the more valuable as we have so little information of the civil regimen of the Indian nations. I think it probable I may find other things on my shelves, or among my papers, worth preserving with you, and will with pleasure forward them from time to time, as I lay my hands on them.

Of the MS. journal of the Commissioners of 1728. on the North Carolina boundary, I cannot give you positive information. it has always been understood that the Westover family possessed such a journal, written by their ancestor Doct^r Byrd, who was one of the Commissioners; was the father of the late Col° William Byrd, a member of our Council, who died soon after the beginning of our revolution. Doct^r Byrd was the founder of the Westover library, and of the princely estate which was dissipated by his son; & has left behind him the reputation of being a man of learning and understanding. within these two or three years I was offered the reading of this MS. by some one whom I cannot now recollect, but a connection of the Westover family. I will make enquiry into this and communicate to you the result. Accept the assurance of my great respect and esteem

TH: JEFFERSON

RC (PPAmP: Thomas Jefferson Papers); at foot of first page: "M. Du Ponceau"; endorsed by Du Ponceau as received 27 Jan.; docketed at APS in an unidentified hand as "read 2 Feby 1816 refered to Historical Commee." PoC (DLC); on verso of a reused address cover from Robert Patterson to TJ; endorsed by TJ.

The enclosed GEOGRAPHICAL AND STATISTICAL ACCOUNT was a manuscript version (PPAmP) of a work later printed as Benjamin Hawkins, "A Sketch of the Creek Country, in the years 1798 and 1799," Georgia Historical Society, *Collections* 3 (1848), pt. 1.

To Nathaniel Macon

DEAR SIR   Monticello Jan. 22. 16.

Your favor of the 7th after being a fortnight on the road, reached this the last night. on the subject of the statue of Genl Washington which the legislature of N. Carolina has ordered to be procured, and set up in their capitol, I shall willingly give you my best information and opinions.

1. Your first enquiry is whether one worthy the character it is to represent, and the state which erects it, can be made in the US.? certainly it cannot. I do not know that there is a single marble statuary in the US. but I am sure there cannot be one who would offer himself as qualified to undertake this monument of gratitude and taste.— besides no quarry of Statuary marble has yet, I believe, been opened in the US. that is to say of a marble pure white, and in blocks of sufficient size, without vein or flaw. the quarry of Carara in Italy is the only one in the accessible parts of Europe which furnishes such blocks. it was from thence we brought to Paris that for the statue of Genl Washington made there on account of this state, and it is from thence alone that all the Southern & maritime parts of Europe are supplied with that character of marble.

2. Who should make it? there can be but one answer to this. Old Canove of Rome. no artist in Europe would place himself in a line with him; and for 30. years, within my own knolege, he has been considered by all Europe, as without a rival. he draws his blocks from Carara, and delivers the statue compleat & packed for transportation at Rome. from thence it descends the Tyber; but whether it must go on to Leghorn or some other shipping port, I do not know.

3. Price, time, size and style? it will probably take a couple of years to be ready. I am not able to be exact as to the price. we gave Houdon at Paris 1000. guineas for the one he made for this state; but he solemnly & feelingly protested against the inadequacy of the price, & evidently undertook it on motives of reputation alone. he was the first artist in France, & being willing to come over to take the model of the General, which we could not have got[1] Canove to have done, that circumstance decided on his employment. we paid him additionally for coming over about 500 guineas, and when the statue was done we paid the expences of one of his underworkmen to come over and set it up, which might perhaps be 100. guineas more. I suppose therefore it cost us in the whole 8000.D. but this was only of the size of the life. yours should be something larger. the difference it makes in the impression can scarcely be conceived. as to the style or costume, I am sure the artist, and every person of taste in Europe would be for the Roman, the effect of which is undoubtedly of a different order. our boots & regimentals have a very puny effect. works of this kind are about one third cheaper at Rome than Paris; but Canove's eminence will be a sensible ingredient in price. I think that for such a statue,

with a plain pedestal, you would have a good bargain from Canove at 7. or 8000.D. and should not be surprised were he to require 10,000.D. to which you would have to add the charges of bringing over, and setting up. the one half of the[2] price would probably be to be advanced, & the other half paid on delivery.

4. from what model? Ciracchi made the bust of Gen[l] Washington in plaister. it was the finest which came from his hand, & my own opinion of Ciracchi was that he was second to no Sculptor living, except Canove, and if he had lived, would have rivalled him. his style had been formed on the fine models of antiquity in Italy, and he had caught their ineffable majesty of expression. on his return to Rome, he made the bust of the General in marble, from that in plaister, it was sent over here, was universally considered as the best effigy of him ever executed, was bought by the Spanish minister for the king of Spain, and sent to Madrid. after the death of Ciracchi, mr Appleton, our Consul at Leghorn, a man of worth and taste, purchased of his widow the original plaister, with a view to profit by copies of marble and plaister from it. he still has it at Leghorn, and it is the only original from which the statue can be formed. but the exterior of the figure will also be wanting, that is to say the outward lineaments of the body & members to enable the artist to give to them also their true forms and proportions. there are, I believe, in Philadelphia, whole length paintings of Gen[l] Washington, from which, I presume, old mr Peale or his son would sketch on canvas the mere outlines at no great charge. this sketch, with Ciracchi's bust would suffice.

5. Through whose agency? none so ready, or so competent as mr Appleton himself. he has had relations with Canove, is a judge of price, convenient to engage the work, to attend to it's progress, to recieve & forward it to N. Carolina.   besides the accomodation of the original bust to be asked from him, he will probably have to go to Rome himself to make the contract, and will incur a great deal of trouble besides from that time to the delivery in N. Carolina; and it should therefore be made a matter of interest with him, to act in it, as his time and trouble is his support. I imagine his agency from beginning to end would not be worth less than from 1. to 200 guineas. I particularise all these things, that you may not be surprised with after-claps of expence, not counted on beforehand. mr Appleton has two nephews at Baltimore in the mercantile line, & in correspondence with him. should the Governor adopt this channel of execution, he will have no other trouble than that of sending to them his communications for mr Appleton and making the remittances agreed

on as shall be convenient to himself. a letter from the Secretary of state to mr Appleton informing him that any service he can render the state of N. Carolina in this business, would be gratifying to his government, would not be without effect.

Accept the assurance of my great esteem & respect.

TH: JEFFERSON

P.S. you mention that you shall communicate my letter to the Governor. to this I have no objections, provided it be kept out of newspapers. but as I do not know to how many he may have to communicate it, I add this P.S. for your & his consideration only. Appleton has a friend and great favorite in a sculptor of the name of Bartholini, whom he thinks equal to Canove, & his friendship may lead him to find difficulties with Canove and draw the job to Bartolini, of whose name I never heard but from mr Appleton. but I could not yield to his opinion alone against that of all Europe. he should understand (without mentioning Bartolini) that it is particularly to the hand of Canove, & no other that they chuse to confide this work.—
another private circumstance. I know nothing of mr Appleton's nephews in Baltimore, not even their names. that of course must be looked into. ever, constantly and affectionately you[rs]   TH:J.

PoC (DLC); lacking postscript; at foot of first page: "Macon Nathaniel." PoC (MHi); postscript only; on verso of reused address cover of Peter Wilson to TJ, 22 Nov. 1815 (see note to TJ to Wilson, 20 Jan. 1816); mutilated at seal, with two words rewritten by TJ, and torn at bottom right corner; endorsed by TJ: "Macon Nathaniel. P.S. to lre of Jan. 22. 16." Tr (Nc-Ar: William Miller Letterbook); lacking postscript.

TJ negotiated the agreement and made the arrangements to bring Jean Antoine HOUDON to Virginia to TAKE THE MODEL OF THE GENERAL (*PTJ*, esp. 7:378–9, 566–7, 8:282–3, 31:304). Although the sculptor Giuseppe Ceracchi sold his marble bust of George Washington to the Spanish commissioner Josef de Jaudenes, the piece was never given to King Charles IV. It was eventually acquired by the Metropolitan Museum of Art in New York City (Washington, *Papers, Pres. Ser.*, 9:133). For Thomas Appleton's ownership of Ceracchi's ORIGINAL PLAISTER of Washington, see Appleton to TJ, 26 Dec. 1814.

The statue of Washington by Antonio Canova (CANOVE) arrived in North Carolina in 1822 and was installed in the state capitol, where it was destroyed by fire in 1831 (Washington *Daily National Intelligencer*, 2 Jan. 1822; *Richmond Enquirer*, 28 June 1831). The original plaster model is at the Canova Museum, Possagno, Italy (Francis Davis Whittemore, *George Washington in Sculpture* [1933], 39). The GOVERNOR of North Carolina at this time was William Miller.

[1] Manuscript: "get."
[2] TJ here canceled "money."

From James Monroe

washington Jany. [22] 1816

The letters to Dr Jackson & mr Appleton received with yours of the 16th shall be forwarded by the first opportunity, of which, many, frequently offer. you will settle the question between m^r Short and me, whenever it may be most convenient to yourself & the arbitrators. my attendance is altogether unnecessary. I will instruct a m^r York who has succeeded m^r Byrd in the managment of my farm, to allow your agent, to trim my vines, & take from them whatever he thinks fit. If he will perform that office, on all of them, I will make him a just compensation, as old Richard, I fear, does not understand it, and Byrd is otherwise engaged. m^r Lamotte has very strong claims to the consulate at Havre. I experienc'd in my intercourse with him while in France, a conduct deserving in all respects great confidence & esteem. A mr I. C. Barnett, has been consul at that port many years, tho' as the port was blockaded, he resided at Paris, & was under the Louisiana convention a commiss^r. He is I presume not unknown to you. The late war has thrown on the gov^t, from the army & flotilla service, many applicants, some of great merit, who are destitute of all resource, and willing to make experiments in any line to gain a living. Altho' they are not, in many instances, qualified for such a trust, and there is a strong sentiment, that they ought to pursue in private life industrious occupations, yet their claim is felt in all cases when put in competition with foreigners. There is not in truth a single consulate held by one of the latter description, no matter how long, that there are not many applications for, supported too by members of Congress, who have uniformly supported the government.

I send you a letter, which I have just receivd from Genl Scott at Paris, which gives a correct view, as I presume, of the state of that wretched country. By a letter of the 3^d of Decr. from our consul at Bordeaux, I find that in behalf of the allies, by way of indemnity for restoring order in France & Europe generally, by the suppression of the late mov'ment of Boniparte, comprizing a vast additional sum to England on acc^t of spoliations since 1793., there is to be paid by her gov^t about 400.000.000. of dol^rs, in 5 years. A copy of the treaty as publish'd is receiv'd, and will be republished here without delay. Return me gen^l Scotts letter after perusing it.

On the return of Ferdinand to Spain, the President appointed m^r Erving minister to him, & instructed Mr Erving to state that he had objections to the recognition of Mr Onis of a personal nature, which induc'd a preference to the reception of another, but that if he asked it as a personal favor, Mr Onis would be receiv'd. This was finally done, in the Spanish mode, of doing business involving sentiment, rather adding, to preceding insults, than makin[g] reparation for them. There being however no justifiable reason for declining longer to restore the diplomatic intercourse, Onis was receiv'd. To this measure there were other considerations of weight. without it, no accomodation could be made with Spain, nor could any step of any kind, be taken with advantage, untill a fair experiment to obtain an accomodation was made. Shortly after his reception he demanded 1st the restitution of west Florida, 2. the apprehention of Toledo, Humbert & others, leaders of the spanish patriots, their trial & punishment. 3^d the exclusion of the flags of Bunoz Ayres Carthagena &ca from the ports of the U States. There were two modes of replying to his letters, one by confining the answer strictly to a defense of the conduct of the gov^t, the other by tak[ing] a review of the conduct of Spain for many years past, shewing that by spoliations, the suppression of the deposit at N Orleans, &ca, she had merited & invited war, which, had not this gov^t, indulged feelings of moderation, would probably have been adopted. The latter was preferr'd, in [executing?][1] which, the surrender of W. Florida has been refused; the punishment of Toledo & others, their acts occurring beyond our jurisdiction, stated to be a case to which our laws do not extend; & that orders have been sometime since given to admit the vessels of all countries without regard to their flags, pirates excepted. The groun[d] taken in each instance, is believd to be solid, in regard to spain, and such as will be approved here, & satisfactory to the colonists; while a door is opend to the spanish gov^t, to settle our differences, by mutual cessions, amicably, to which, it is invited.

I am very respectfully & sincerely your friend   JA^s MONROE

RC (DLC: TJ Papers, 206:36651); partially dated, with day of composition supplied from postmark and from Monroe's endorsement of TJ's 16 Jan. letter to him; edge chipped; endorsed by TJ as received 27 Jan. 1816 and so recorded in SJL. RC (MHi); address cover only; with PoC of TJ to David Higginbotham, 28 Feb. 1816, on verso; addressed: "Thomas Jefferson Monticello Virg^a"; franked; postmarked Washington, 22 Jan.

Isaac Cox Barnet was a member of a three-person commission appointed in 1803 by Monroe and Robert R. Livingston and charged with the liquidation of claims related to the LOUISIANA Purchase (Madison, Papers, Sec. of State Ser., 4:569–70). The LETTER OF THE 3^D OF DECR. from William Lee to Monroe (DNA: RG 59, CD, Bordeaux) enclosed a copy of the TREATY of Paris, signed 20 Nov. 1815 (Connelly, Napoleonic France, 382). A translation of the treaty appeared in the New York *Commercial Advertiser*, 18 Jan. 1816, and subsequently in other newspapers. For the RECOGNITION of Luis de Onís as Spanish minister plenipotentiary and the negotiations between the United States and Spain, see John C. A.

Stagg, *Borderlines in Borderlands: James Madison and the Spanish-American Frontier, 1776–1821* (2009), esp. 180–3.

[1] Word illegible.

ENCLOSURE

Winfield Scott to James Monroe

MY DEAR SIR, Paris Nov. 18th, 1815.

I had the honour of addressing a letter to you by my friend Mr. Robertson who left Paris some six weeks since on his return to the U. States and who will be better able to give an account of the wonderful <u>devolopements</u> of the few preceding months than, perhaps, any other American then in Europe.

France is at present in that precise condition which was foreseen by every friend to her independence. The Allies continue to exhaust and degrade her in the name of the King, who, in return holds his throne by the number of their bayonets. The neighbouring powers aggrandize themselves in territory at the expense of their military rival; the English guard against the revival of French manufactures and a French marine—all are paid and endemnified by this country, and the wretched Louis is happy to find in the misery of his people the best guarantee of his dynasty, for he well knows that whilst there shall exist in France a sentiment of independence or one spark of military pride, his name and family will be spurned & detested.

The officers who served in the late short campaign are excluded from the new army and are not even permitted to reside in Paris. Many thousands have lately been ordered away. One of them, a general, who had neglected to obey the mandate was arrested and brought before the Police. Where am I to go?—said he. I have no particular place of abode For twenty years a bivouac has been my home, and I am now come to the capital of my country to seek a shelter. It is true that I have not fought for the Bourbons, but I have fought for the glory and the independence of France and bear about me the records of my services. He was told that the order was irrevocable—and so is my determination, said the veteran, as he plunged a dagger into his breast. Similar instances of desperation have not been unfrequent of late, but the French papers dare not even announce them. Indeed nothing can be more abject than the present state of the French Press. The journal I take has been three times suppressed within the last two months. It is required that every political article should be submitted to the Censor before publication and of course he sanctions nothing that tends in the remotest degree to reflect on the conduct of the court or the Allies. A neglect of this precaution is fatal to the Editor. The journal in question has been renewed under different titles. It was at first called <u>The Independant Courier</u>, but the Editor knowing me to [be][1] a citizen of a country in which the press is free in fact as well as in name was in the habit of running his pen thro' the word "Independent" in the particular papers sent to my address. The following is the paragraph which caused its last suppression, and which I give in order that you may perceive what are the ruling fears of the court.

"Nous apprenons [from Vienna Octr 11th][2] que S. M. l'empereur a accordé au jeune Napoléon le régiment d'hulans, qui est vacant par la mort comte de Meerfeldt. Dimanche passé le jeune prince parut, pour la première fois, avec l'uniforme de major de ce régiment, accompagné de S. M. l'emperatrice d'autriche. On remarque que ce prince est toujours appelé François-Charles dans les ordonnances de la cour qui ont rapport à lui."

The struggle of the S° Americans for independence excites a high degree of interest in Europe, and the general expectation is, that the U.S. will openly declare for them. Indeed it is supposed that the contest will be between us & England to see which shall first extend to them the required assistance. Commercial cupidity is the only aim of the British, but proximity, political principle,—every thing seems to point out the course we should adopt. I trust in God that Congress may make the declaration. We have nothing to apprehend from the infamous Ferdinand and every thing to hope from our continental brethren. The Baron Humboldt thinks with me on this subject and the feelings [of][3] our most venerable countryman, General La Fayette, are the same which crown'd him with glory and us with independence thirty five years ago.

A declaration in behalf of the patriots would not necessarily involve us in a War with Ferdinand, or if it should the war would be merely nominal so far as it respects the injuries we should suffer. Spain has no naval force, or but a very small number of indifferent[4] ships, more indifferently manned. We might easily exclude her from America or[5] even from the Atlantic ocean; and I see no prospect of having our claims upon the Spanish government discharged except by the occupation of East Florida. Our peace establishment would be adequate to this object. But a certain class of our citizens, would no doubt first like to enquire, What would be the probable conduct of England if we should oppose ourselves to the holy march Ferdinand is now making on two continents at once towards the destruction of every feeling & principle most dear to mankind?—I have taken some pains to ascertain the temper of Englishmen on this question and am decidedly of the opinion that no ministry could sustain itself in that country, Six months after making common cause with Ferdinand against the American patriots.

The Council of War assembled for the trial of Marshal Ney decided a few days since against its competency. He is now before the Chamber of Peers and will no doubt be condemned, for the Duke de Richelieu, has in an official Speech, told the chamber that nothing less will satisfy his majesty, or his allies. All the ministers & generals of the allies attend the trial, to overawe the accused, & the better to ensure his conviction To witness the execution, tickets for places are already granted

You no doubt will have seen the new law against seditious cries &c. Its publication has excited a strong sensation among the people, but supported as it is by 150,000 foreign bayonets, the French are obliged to yield. Yesterday six or seven young men put seals upon their lips & in this situation, supposing themselves safe from sedition & the Police, walked arm in arm thro' the garden of the Tuilleries. But the significant concert did not escape notice. They have been committed for transportation.

Marshal Ney has taken a new ground in his defence before the Peers, and demands the protection of the Allies on the faith of the late capitulation of Paris. His two several notes to the foreign ministers have been transmitted to

London for the opinion of the British cabinet and if there be faith or honour remaining in Europe he is safe. The 12th article of that convention embraces his case in the strongest terms, and according to which the execution of Labédoyere was a most barbarous murder. Maj. Mercer is endeavouring to procure the notes in question & if he succeeds they will be enclosed.

The Americans in Paris experience many inconveniences from the want of a minister here. Mr. Jackson is extremely civil to us all, & does every thing in his power to serve us, but I beleive he has not been acknowledged by the present government. The expectation at present is, that Mr. Dallas will be substituted in the place of Mr. Gallatin. May I take the liberty of suggesting that if it should be agreeable to the government & the particular gentleman appointed to this court, that Major Mercer would be very happy to receive the appointment of Secretary of Legation? He is already well acquainted with the language of the country and wishes to spend some years in this capital: and I may add, that there is no American in Paris whose manners & principles do greater honour to our country. He does not expect to be substituted in the place of any gentleman already in the view of the government, & much less to be thought of in opposition to Mr. Jackson, who has laid him under many obligations of civility.

Mrs. Pattison arrived here a few days since and begins to be the subject of no little curiosity.

I still adhere to the resolution of returning to my duty early next spring, by which period I hope I shall have accomplished the objects I had in view in coming to Europe, & when I shall be very well content to remain at home, for the remainder of my life—unless I should be required to march out at the head of an army. Indeed it is in Europe, that a citizen of the U.S., learns, by comparison, to place the highest value on his own country & government. I have not met with an American abroad who was not proud of the name, and who did not concur in the general policy we have pursued in our foreign relations. The Soundness of that policy no longer admits of dispute.

I must not omit to mention, that the Baron Humboldt, who takes a lively interest in our affairs, intimated in the course of a conversation the other day, that certain letters of his to some members of our government, had remained a long time unanswered. His influence in the moral & literary world is greater than that of any other man in Europe. France owes to him the preservation of the garden of plants (in which the Prussian army was, at one time, about to bivouac) and the few objects of the arts which remain to her, out of the general wreck of the Louvre.

I must again apologize for this trespass on your time, & assure you of the continued respect & esteem, in which

I have the honour to remain, Yr most obedient Servant,   W. Scott.

RC (DNA: RG 59, MLR); at foot of text: "The honb^le J. Monroe, &^c &^c &^c"; at head of text: "Private"; endorsed by Monroe. Also enclosed in TJ to Monroe, 4 Feb. 1816.

Winfield Scott (1786–1866), soldier, was born near Petersburg, studied briefly at the College of William and Mary in 1804–05, departed to read law, and was admitted to the Virginia bar in 1806. His military career began in 1808 when TJ appointed him a light artillery captain in the United States Army. During the War of 1812 Scott was involved in several actions along the Niagara frontier, and in 1814 he was made a brigadier general. A severe injury at the Battle of Lundy's

Lane later that year took him out of combat for the remainder of the war. Scott's military successes won him a brevet promotion to major general and a congressional medal. Following the war he traveled in Europe, headed the board of inquiry into the conduct of General William H. Winder, published a military field manual, revised a work on tactics that was frequently reissued thereafter, and worked in the War Department to enhance military tactics and training. In 1832 Scott served in the Black Hawk War, and in 1836 he traveled to Florida to conduct a campaign against the Seminole Indians. Late in the 1830s he took the lead in several successful peacekeeping negotiations along the United States–Canadian border. By the outbreak of the Mexican War in 1846, Scott had become general-in-chief of the army, and despite severe logistical difficulties, he personally led the American forces to victory. After being considered as a presidential candidate several times, he headed the unsuccessful Whig ticket in 1852. In the period leading up to the Civil War, Scott supported President Abraham Lincoln and the Union. He was discouraged by the actions of younger military leaders and those who discounted his advice. By the end of 1861 poor health combined with frustration led him to retire from military service. Scott spent several of his remaining years in West Point, New York, where he died (*ANB*; *DAB*; Scott, *Memoirs of Lieut.-General Scott, LL.D., Written by Himself* [1864]; *William and Mary Provisional List*, 36; *JEP*, 2:99, 107 [25 Jan., 2 Feb. 1809]; Malcomson, *Historical Dictionary*, 507–9; *New York Herald*, 30 May 1866).

NOUS APPRENONS . . . À LUI: "We learn [from Vienna Octr 11th] that his highness the emperor has assigned to the young Napoleon the leadership of the Uhlan regiment, which has been vacant since Count Meerfeldt's death. Last Sunday the young prince appeared for the first time in the uniform of a major of this regiment, accompanied by her highness the empress of Austria. One notices that this prince is always called François

Charles in the ordinances of the court concerning him."

On 11 Nov. 1815 the DUKE DE RICHELIEU presented King Louis XVIII's ordinance calling for the trial of Marshal Michel Ney, who, after promising to capture Napoleon when he landed in France in 1815, had instead joined forces with him to overthrow the Bourbon monarchy. Richelieu then gave his own speech to the chamber of peers (Hewson Clarke, *The History of the War, from the Commencement of the French Revolution to the Present Time* [London, 1816], 3:430–1). Louis XVIII signed the NEW LAW AGAINST SEDITIOUS CRIES on 9 Nov. 1815 (France, *Bulletin des Lois*, 7th ser., 1 [1816]: 415–9).

On 13 Nov. 1815 Ney wrote to Sir Charles Stuart and Arthur Wellesley, the Duke of Wellington, contending that under the 12TH ARTICLE of the capitulation of Paris, he deserved clemency. Wellington, in a communication first sent to Ney and later to the ministers of the allied powers, commented that "The object of the XIIth Article was to prevent the adoption of any measure of severity, under the Military Authority of those who made it, towards any Persons in Paris, on account of the Offices which they had filled, or their conduct or their political opinions; but it was never intended, and could not be intended, to prevent either the existing French Government, under whose authority the French Commander-in-Chief must have acted, or any French Government which should succeed to it, from acting in this respect as it might deem fit" (*British and Foreign State Papers* 2 [1815/16]: 194, 260–3, 267). A court of peers ultimately condemned Ney to death (Connelly, *Napoleonic France*, 368).

MRS. PATTISON: Elizabeth Patterson Bonaparte.

[1] Omitted word editorially supplied.
[2] Brackets in original.
[3] Omitted word editorially supplied.
[4] Word interlined.
[5] Reworked from "&."

To Philip I. Barziza

DEAR SIR   Monticello Jan. 23. 16.

It was from D[r] Bancroft's letter I understood that your brother would come to this country in the Spring, and that suggested the idea that the little commission I mentioned might not be inconvenient to him. but as you are so kind as to undertake the having it executed, I will avail my self of your goodness to procure for me the two or three works, which having been originally printed at Venice & Rome, can probably be had at Venice, while I know from trial they are not to be had from Paris or London. I should guess their cost in Venice to be about 20 Dollars, which shall be remitted you either at that guess or when their cost shall be exactly known as may be most convenient to you. I doubt if we have any direct commercial voyages to Venice; but abundance to Leghorn, to which place I presume there must be regular land conveyances from Venice. if this package therefore can be sent to the hands of mr Thomas Appleton, our Consul at Leghorn, he will convey it speedily & safely to me. I subjoin the titles of the books and add the assurances of my great respect and esteem.

TH: JEFFERSON

Il Vocabolario della Crusca. Venice 1741. 5. vols. 4to. it is this particular edition I wish, on account of it's small size. I would not chuse to have the folio edition.

Opere di Platone di Dardi Bembo. Venice. 1601. 5. vols 12mo

Euclidis Elementorum libri XV. à Caiano. Greek & Italian. Romae. 1545. 8vo

RC (R. Sturgis Ingersoll, Philadelphia, 1946); addressed: "Viscount Philip S. Barziza to the care of mr W[m] M[c]Candlish Williamsburg. Virga"; franked; post- marked Milton, 24 Jan. PoC (DLC); on verso of reused address cover to TJ; torn at seal, with missing words rewritten by TJ; endorsed by TJ.

From Joseph C. Cabell

DEAR SIR,   Richmond. 23 Jan: 1816.

I wrote you by the last mail, that the bills respecting the Central College, and Capt: Miller's claim, had just reached the Senate: and that the former was objected to in two points: 1st because it gives to the Trustees of the College the power of determining the time at which the act of 22[d] Dec[r] 1796. shall be carried into execution in albemarle, and 2[dly] because it confers on the Proctor of the college the powers and authorities of a Justice of the peace within the precincts of the institution. Since my letter was committed to the mail, I have conversed with the Governor, who considers the first objection of great weight, as it would probably place the people of the county in hostility to the College. Whilst I am awaiting your answer to my last letter, it becomes proper that I should address you on two other subjects before the Senate, in which you take an Interest. I cannot find among the papers in Capt: Miller's case, the evidences of the conveyance made to him by the other devisees of their portions of Thomas Reed's estate. I should infer from the manner in which they are referred to in the petition that they would appear among the accompanying documents: accordingly I immediately enquired for them. but they neither are to be found, nor can either of the Delegates from albemarle give any account of them. Those papers are essential to the success of the bill in the Senate: and with their aid, I trust I can get it thro' the house; altho' Mr Johnson, and, perhaps others, may oppose it. I beg the favor of you to request Capt: Miller to furnish me with these documents with as little delay as possible. Whilst I await their arrival, I will by all means in my power endeavor to smooth the way to the passage of the bill.

From a letter you recently wrote Col: yancey, I perceive you consider the Bill to prevent obstructions in the navigable watercourses of the commonwealth, of importance to the people on the banks of the Rivanna. I enclose you a copy of the Bill, and of some amendments hastily sketched by Col: Green: and would thank you to send me such corrections as you deem proper. These subjects may be suspended till I can get your answer, without injury to the parties concerned.

I regard the passage of the bill respecting the Central College as pretty certain, provided the modifications suggested in the points objected to shall be made: and perhaps without those changes, its passage may be secured by your explanations. I believe the Bill for internal improvement will pass, and that if the Genl assembly should be disposed to give any thing to education it will be to the Literary fund for the establishment of free schools. It is barely possible that they may give some thing to the Central College for teaching the deaf & dumb. I am endeavoring to prepare the more liberal part for an attempt at an endowment of a professorship of the deaf & dumb. Thus far it is well received: but I may be baffled. I have thought that such a plan might engage the affections of the coldest members. Any suggestions from you on this subject would be thankfully received.

I beg you to pardon the trouble I give you: & to be assured it re-sults from my wish to afford[1] you satisfaction, in the business en-trusted to my care.

I am d[r] Sir most sincerely yours   JOSEPH C. CABELL

P.S. Doct[r] Smith, President of W[m] & Mary, has desired me to ask the favor of you to recommend a Text book on the principles of Govern-ment for the use of the Students at that College. He is not satisfied with either Locke or Rousseau.

Can you inform me whether De Say on Political Economy has been translated into our Language?

RC (ViU: TJP-PC); postscript on verso of address leaf; addressed: "Thom-as Jefferson esq. Monticello"; endorsed by TJ as received 30 Jan. 1816 and so recorded in SJL; with additional notation by TJ on address leaf: "✓College Deaf & Dumb   ✓Navigable waters   D[r] Smith   ✓Miller   my catalogue." En-closed in Cabell to TJ, 24 Jan. 1816.

The Virginia statute OF 22[D] DEC[R] 1796 was "An Act to establish Public Schools" (*Acts of Assembly* [1796 sess.], 3–4). Wil-son Cary Nicholas was THE GOVERNOR of Virginia. TJ to Charles Yancey, 6 Jan. 1816, was the LETTER YOU RECENTLY WROTE. The enclosed COPY OF THE BILL was an unidentified draft version of "An Act to prevent obstructions in the naviga-ble water courses within the Common-wealth," which, with the AMENDMENTS proposed by John W. Green, became law on 13 Feb. 1816 (Cabell to TJ, 14 Feb. 1816; *Acts of Assembly* [1815–16 sess.], 67–9). "An Act to create a Fund for IN-TERNAL IMPROVEMENT" passed into law on 5 Feb. 1816 (*Acts of Assembly* [1815–16 sess.], 35–9). John Augustine SMITH was elected president of the Col-lege of William and Mary in 1814 (*DAB*). DE SAY: Jean Baptiste Say.

[1] Word interlined in place of "give."

To Joseph C. Cabell

DEAR SIR   Monticello Jan. 24. 16.

Your favor of the 16th experienced great delay on the road and to avoid that of another mail I must answer very briefly.

My letter to Peter Carr contains all I ever wrote on the subject of the College, a plan for the institution being the only thing the trustees asked or expected from me. were it to go into execution, I should certainly interest myself further & strongly in procuring proper professors.

The establishment of a Proctor is taken from the practice of Europe where an equivalent officer is made a part, and is a very es-sential one, of every such institution: and as the nature of his func-tions requires that he should always be a man of discretion, understanding & integrity, above the common level, it was thought that he would never be less worthy of being trusted with the powers of a justice, within the limits of the institution here, than the neighboring justices generally are; and the vesting him with the conservation of the peace within that limit was intended, while it should equally secure it's object, to sheild the young and unguarded student from the disgrace of the common prison, except where the case was an aggravated one. a confinement to his own room was meant as an act of tenderness to him, his parents and friends. in fine, it was to give them a compleat police of their own, tempered by the paternal attentions of their tutors. and certainly in no country is such a provision more called for than in this, as has been proved from times of old, from the regular[1] annual riots & battles between the students of William & Mary, with the town boys, before the revolution, quorum pars fui, and the many and more serious affrays of later times.— Observe too that our bill proposes no exclusion of the ordinary magistrate, if the one attached to the institution is thought to execute his power either partially or remissly.

The transfer of the power to give commencement to the Ward or Elementary schools from the court and Aldermen to the Visitors, was proposed because the experience of 20. years has proved that no court will ever begin it. the reason is obvious. the members of the courts are the wealthy members of the counties; and as the expences of the schools are to be defrayed by a contribution proportioned to the aggregate of other taxes which every one pays, they consider it as a plan to educate the poor at the expence of the rich. it proceeded too from a hope that the example and good effects being exhibited in one county, they would spread from county to county and become general. the modification of the law, by authorising the Aldermen to require the expence of tutorage from such parents as are able would render trifling, if not wholly prevent, any call on the county for pecuniary aid. you know that nothing better than a log-house is required for these schools, and there is not a neighborhood which would not meet and build this themselves for the sake of having a school near them.

I know of no peculiar advantage which Charlottesville offers for mr Braidwood's school of deaf and dumb. on the contrary I should think the vicinity of the seat of government most favorable to it. I should not like to have it made a member of our college. the objects of the two institutions are fundamentally distinct. the one is science, the other mere charity. it would be gratuitously taking a boat in tow, which may impede, but cannot aid the motion of the principal institution. ever and affectionately yours.   TH: JEFFERSON

P.S. I detach the postscript of my letter for the reasons suggested in yours. you wish me to write to several gentlemen on the subject of our college. I could write to mr Johnson, with whom I am acquainted, & for whom I have a sincere esteem and respect. but I have no acquaintance with the others you name. and indeed, my friend, I am no longer equal to the labor. I pass from 4. to 6. hours of every day of my life at my writing table, in the drudgery of answering letters in which I have no personal concern or pleasure. it is weighing and wearing down my life with an oppression of body and mind I am not able to bear up against. I must throw it off, and intrench myself within the limits of my friends and my own affairs. I want too to have some time for reading.[2]

P.P.S. shew the P.S. to mr Johnson. it will apologise for my not writing to him; for indeed I consider the writing to you as to him also.

RC (ViU: TJP); addressed: "Joseph C. Cabell of the Senate of Virginia now in Richmond"; franked; postmarked Milton, 28 Jan.; endorsed by Cabell, with his additional notation that the subject was "(Central College)"; first postscript on detached small sheet, separately endorsed by Cabell; second postscript on slip glued to verso of address leaf. PoC (DLC); lacking second postscript.

TJ's LETTER TO PETER CARR was dated 7 Sept. 1814. TJ described the role of the PROCTOR as well as the organization of ward schools in his Draft Bill to Create Central College and Amend the 1796 Public Schools Act, [ca. 18 Nov. 1814]. While TJ was a student at the College of William and Mary, he commented on the disciplining of several of his comrades following an altercation with TOWN residents (PTJ, 1:12). QUORUM PARS FUI: "of which I was a part." MORE SERIOUS AFFRAYS involving William and Mary students occurred during the winter of 1799–1800 and in 1802 (VMHB 29 [1921]: 267–71; New-York Evening Post, 3, 24 Apr. 1802).

[1] Word interlined.
[2] In PoC TJ here added the date "Jan. 24. 16."

From Joseph C. Cabell

DEAR SIR,   Richmond. 24 Jan: 1816.

Since writing the enclosed letter, I have conversed with m[r] Mercer of the House of Delegates, to whom I had lent your Letter to m[r] Carr, upon being informed by him that he had it in contemplation to endeavor to get a considerable part of the debt due from us by the Gen[l] Gov[t] to the State of Virginia, appropriated to the establishment of a grand scheme of education. He appears much pleased with your view of the subject, and as he proposes to make a report to the Lower House, concurs with me in the propriety of availing the country of the light you have shed upon this great interest of the community.

Would you object to the publication of your Letter to Mr Carr? Indeed, Sir, I may take the liberty to have your Letter printed before I can get your answer. I do not believe the Genl Assembly will make so great an appropriation at this time as the one proposed by m^r mercer: but I will do any thing in my power to promote it. And should the measure succeed, my object w^d be to make your plan the basis of our measures. The location of the principal Seminary would be a secondary consideration; & it might happen that the people beyond the mountains would not come into the measure unless Staunton or Lexington should be made the principal scite. This would be a disagreeable result to me: but I see a scheme already formed to carry the seat of Gov^t sooner or later to Staunton, and powerful private interests silently preparing & expecting that event. Should a great State Seminary be established at Charlottesville, it might touch the interests of this party. This suggestion I beg you to consider as confidential. My intention is, as soon as I hear from you to secure the passage of the bill respecting the Central college, nearly or entirely in its present shape. Then or previously I will, if not prevented, publish your Letter to m^r Carr, so as to prevent this game from being easily taken out of the hands of those who are entitled to it.

In haste, I am, D^r sir, most truly yours Jos: C: Cabell.

RC (ViU: TJP-PC); endorsed by TJ as received 30 Jan. 1816 and so recorded in SJL; with additional notation by TJ: "College location. lre to P. Carr." RC (DLC); address cover only; with PoC of TJ to Cabell, 28 Feb. 1816, on verso; addressed: "Thomas Jefferson esq. Monticello"; franked; postmarked Richmond, 24 Jan. Enclosure: Cabell to TJ, 23 Jan. 1816.

TJ's LETTER TO MR CARR was dated 7 Sept. 1814. Loudoun County delegate Charles Fenton Mercer, chairman of the Committee on Finance, presented a RE-PORT TO THE LOWER HOUSE on 13 Feb. 1816 in which the panel observed that "Should it be the pleasure of the General Assembly, to lay the foundation of a comprehensive system of public education, ample means for the accomplishment of this laudable purpose, may be found in the residue of the debt due to the Commonwealth from the Government of the United States, and the provision which the Committee have presumed to recommend for gradually extinguishing the debts of the Commonwealth to the Banks of Virginia" (*JHD* [1815–16 sess.], 177).

To Peter Derieux

Sir   Monticello Jan. 24. 16.

Since the receipt of your favor of the 12th ult. one has come to hand from mr Mazzei in answer to mine, in which I had sollicited from him some attention and aid to your wants. I must give you the answer in his own words. it is dated Pisa. Oct. 22. 1815. 'Quanto a Derieux che à 10. o 12. figli, che l'à pregato di raccomendarmelo, la prego di dargli per carità 18. o 20. dollars, e di rammemorargli che quando venne inaspettatamente di Francia a Charlestown colla moglie (che aveva abortito nel viaggio) gli mandai il denaro per pagare il Capitano, e per venire in Virginia; che gli diedi un'altra somma rispettabile alla mia partenza di costà, e che la cambiale (che mi diede par le 2. dette somme) la bruciai subito che seppi l'infelice stato delle sue finanze.' in compliance with this request I now inclose you an order on mess^{rs} Gibson and Jefferson of Richmond, for twenty dollars. I sincerely wish he had authorised a much larger sum; but, after my former urgency to him, his answer shews that no further applications to him from me can be useful to you. indeed his age (85. years) and the total demolition of his health both of body and mind render his continuance in life uncertain from day to day. I will thank you for a little scrip of a receipt which I may inclose to him in proof that I have executed his authority. Accept the assurance of my esteem & respect

TH: JEFFERSON

PoC (DLC); on verso of reused address cover of otherwise unlocated letter from Lacépède to TJ, 19 July 1815 (addressed: "à Monsieur Th. Jefferson à Monticello en virginie"; franked; postmarked New York City, 12 Nov.; recorded in SJL as received 15 Dec. 1815 from Paris); mutilated at seal, with missing text rewritten by TJ; at foot of text: "Mr Derieux"; endorsed by TJ. Enclosure not found.

TJ's letter of 29 Dec. 1813 to Philip Mazzei SOLLICITED FROM HIM SOME ATTENTION to Derieux's plight.

From Thomas W. Maury

DEAR SIR   Richmond 24th January 1816

I have been requested by several members of the House of Delegates to ask your attention to the following memorandum & enquiries, and to ask that you will (as soon as convenient,) reply to them, inasmuch as the business before the house depends upon the information they ask.

The House of Delegates has created a committee with leave to bring in a bill "to provide an accurate chart of each County and a general map of the territory of the Commonwealth. The map of the County is intended to be upon a large scale. It will be important to direct the attention of the several Counties to the proper objects to be embraced by such a map. In their enumeration assistance might be derived from an intelligent naturalist. Quere should not a mineralo-gist be engaged to describe the character of the Country by reference to the substratum of its soil, or the fossils which appear above it? How far may the progress of science be otherwise aided by the pro-posed labour?

It may be the intention of the committee of finance, to substitute for the commissioner's returns of a variety of taxable property, on which the taxes may be repealed, the formation & return of statistical tables. Quere. what objects should those tables embrace?—"

A bill proposing the creation of fifteen additional banks was yes-terday read in the H. of D. It passed to a second reading with fifty or sixty votes against it. This is considered as prophetic of its fate. It will certainly be lost—

The bill concerning Capt Miller has met with some opposition in the Senate, for want of evidence of the fact of a transfer from his brothers & sisters of the Half blood, of their interest in the property of which Ths. Reed died seized. Documents to this effect ought im-mediately to be forwarded, if to be procured. I hope you will excuse the trouble I give you, and beleive me

most respectfully y^r mo: ob^t THO^s W. MAURY

RC (DLC); addressed: "Thomas Jeffer-son Esqr Monticello near Charlottes-ville"; franked; postmarked Richmond, 24 Jan.; endorsed by TJ as received 30 Jan. 1816 and so recorded in SJL; with additional notations by TJ on address leaf: "Maps
Mineralogy
Statistical
Miller."

For the bill to PROVIDE AN ACCURATE CHART OF EACH COUNTY AND A GENER-AL MAP OF THE TERRITORY OF THE COM-MONWEALTH, see Wilson Cary Nicholas to TJ, 22 Mar. 1816, and note. The bill proposing the creation of ADDITIONAL BANKS was read in the Virginia House of Delegates on 22 Jan., and after consider-ation by the Committee of the Whole House, further action on it was postponed until the next legislative session (*JHD* [1815–16 sess.], 131, 159–60 [22 Jan., 6 Feb. 1816]).

To John F. Oliveira Fernandes

DEAR SIR   Monticello Jan. 24. 16.

I this moment receive your favor of the 15th and have but another left to get this into the mail of the neighboring village before it's de-parture, so as to be with you within the time of grace given me by your letter. I thank you for thinking of me on the receipt of your Teneriffe, which tho of a place whose wines are not generally of high estimation, yet I know there are some crops of it of excellent quality. you mention that yours is sound, unbrandied, and old. the two first of these qualities are indispensable, and the last a high recommendation. I will therefore gladly take a quarter cask & request you to send it to Richmond to the care of Gibson & Jefferson, but either in a double cask or box, to prevent watering by the rascally boatmen of our river. be pleased to send me a note of the cost which shall be remitted you by a draught on the same gentlemen.

I am much indebted to you for the Port you have been so kind as to spare me. if it were at Richmond on the 22^d it will be here in a few days by a boat which would call for it then. I am in daily expectation of light wines (which I mostly use myself) from France and Italy, for which I wrote some time ago, and hope not again to be left entirely without as lately. and yet I think it better to be without than to buy the poisonous breweries of our ordinary wine-sellers. Accept the assurance of my great esteem & respect.   TH: JEFFERSON

PoC (DLC); on verso of reused address cover of John Barnes to TJ, 18 Nov. 1815; at foot of text: "Doct^r Fernandes"; endorsed by TJ.

Oliveira Fernandes's FAVOR OF THE 15TH was actually dated 18 Jan. 1816.

From Philip Thornton

D^R SIR   Richmond January 24th 1816

I will pay to your order in Town, or remit $150 the sum due you, on account of the Bridge, as you may direct. Your friends here evinced a high degree of affliction at a report of your death, by way of Lynchburg, stated in an extract of a letter from some merchant in that place

fortunately a letter of yours, to a house in this Town, of the same date was conclusive evidence to the contrary—It oftener happens that men suffer the pain of many deaths; than their friends, the pain of lamenting it. May you die but once, and that period be a protracted one is the Sincere wish of your

Friend and Humble Servant   PHILIP THORNTON

RC (MHi); endorsed by TJ as received 30 Jan. 1816 and so recorded in SJL. RC (DLC); address cover only; with PoC of TJ to Alexander J. Dallas, 26 Feb. 1816, on verso; addressed: "Thomas Jefferson esq^r Montichello Charlottsville"; stamp canceled; franked; postmarked Rich-mond, 24 Jan., and Charlottesville, 28 Jan.

On 6 Feb. 1816 TJ recorded that he had sent Patrick Gibson an ORDER "on Philip Thornton for 150.D. rent for the Natural bridge" (*MB*, 2:1319).

From Benjamin Austin

SIR   Boston Jany 25 1816

I have the honor of acknowledging your Letter of Jany 9th & have taken the liberty to read it to many of our republican friends—Its contents are consider'd so valuable, that I induc'd to request your permission to have it inserted in the Chronicle.—There are many observations which are highly interesting, not only as they respect the manufacturs of our Country, but as they relate to Europe.—your opinions on the great events in france, & your disapprobation of the ambitious veiws of Boanparte, will serve to confound your enemeis, who have been assiduous to misrepresent your conduct towards Him—It w^d be highly gratifying to our Republicans in the Northern states, if such a document could appear at this period—My request is not altogether founded on my desire, but is urged by many of your most sincere friends—

I subscribe myself Your undeviating friend   BENJ^N AUSTIN

Would thank you for as early an answer as may be convenient, previous to the 1st of April—

RC (DLC); at foot of text: "Hon^l Thomas Jefferson"; endorsed by TJ as received 7 Feb. 1816 and so recorded in SJL.

From Elisha Ticknor

SIR,   Boston, 26th Jany 1816.

Yours of the 15th ins. came to hand yesterday, inclosing a letter to my son, which I hope to forward to him in a few days by a Vessel, bound to Hamburg. He is now I suppose in Gottingen, Germany. I have received and heard nothing from him, since the 24th Sept. last, at which time he writes, that he was in fine health—that he had arrived at a place, which he had long wish'd to visit, and where "every thing seems to be exactly arranged to suit the [nee]ds and wants of a scholar, and to be absolutely incapable of improvement." Thus in a word he is situated. He found, however, after his arrival, that they (the Rev. Mr Everett of Boston is with him) could enjoy none of the benefits and advantages of the University, except they became members; of course they were immediately matriculated and admitted to all the privileges of the University, for which he paid 3 dollars. He now has free access to a Library of 200 000 Vol. the choice of 40 Professors, paid by Government, and 40 others, who lecture occasionally on different subjects, many of whom can better qualify him for travelling through France, Italy and Greece, than any other, with whom he had before had the pleasure of being acquainted. He writes, therefore, that as he is at a place about which he has so often dreamt, that he shall probably remain in Gottingen, 'till April. I think it more probable, he <u>will</u>, 'till May as the roads will then be good and the country will show its state of cultivation and improvement. After which he will proceed on for Paris, and Rome and Athens. If you have any communications, sir, which you wish to have forwarded to my son, I will take charge of them with pleasure and send them on to him as soon [as] possible.

I am, sir, With the highest consideration, Your most obedient and Very humble servant, ELISHA TICKNOR.

RC (DLC); torn at seal; endorsed by TJ as received 7 Feb. 1816 and so recorded in SJL. RC (DLC); address cover only; on verso of PoC of TJ to William H. Crawford, 29 Feb. 1816; addressed: "Thomas Jefferson, Esquire Late President of the United States, Monticello, Virginia"; postmarked Boston, 28 Jan.

To Sarah Bowdoin Dearborn

Monticello Jan. 27. 16.

Th: Jefferson presents his compliments to mrs Dearborn and his thanks for the very acceptable seeds she has been so kind as to send him and which will occupy his care & attention in the season now beginning to invite the labors of the garden. he cannot omit this first occasion of expressing to mrs Dearborn the uneasiness which the unpleasant weather in which she left Monticello gave to the family. they sympathized in all the inconveniences she must have felt on the road.   with the hope that the residue of the journey was more agreeable, that she found her friends well, and their city less desolated by the storm than the papers had announced he begs leave to salute herself & Genl Dearborn with assurances of his affectionate attachment and respect

PoC (MHi); on verso of reused address cover to TJ bearing the frank of James Monroe; dateline at foot of text; endorsed by TJ.

A strong hurricane struck the Boston area in the early hours of 23 Sept. 1815. PAPERS around the nation carried reports of the resulting damage and destruction (Washington *Daily National Intelligencer*, 1 Oct. 1815; Richmond *Enquirer*, 4 Oct. 1815).

From Joseph Delaplaine

DEAR SIR,   Philadelphia January 27ʰ 1816

I have taken the liberty twice lately of addressing you, and have not been favoured with a reply.—

If Mʳ Wood cannot conveniently visit you for the purpose of painting your portrait, I shall request him to make me a copy of your picture in the possession of Mʳ Madison. If, unfortunately this portrait is at Mʳ Madisons' country seat, I know not what I shall do. I want much to hear from you on the subject for my government.

I have pleasure in enclosing for your acceptance, a portrait of the late Robert Fulton, which I believe I did not before send to you.—

Vespucius is nearly finished. It will be very beautiful. In a few days I shall send you one, with the original which you furnished me. Your name will appear on the plate. Mʳ Jay, and the late President Adams have been kind enough to send me very recently a sketch of their lives. I beg you sir, to have the goodness to give to me the facts of your life. Birth, parentage, profession times of going to Europe, returns to this Country—offices &c &c. Politicks & panegyric will form no part of my work.

I am very respectfully your obedᵗ sᵗ   JOSEPH DELAPLAINE

RC (DLC); on verso of prospectus for *Delaplaine's Repository*, described above at Delaplaine to TJ, 14 Jan. 1816; addressed: "Thomas Jefferson Esqʳ Monticello Virginia"; franked; postmarked Philadelphia, 29 Jan.; endorsed by TJ as received 7 Feb. 1816 and so recorded in SJL.

Benjamin West's portrait of ROBERT FULTON was engraved by William S. Leney and included in *Delaplaine's Repository*, vol. 1, plate opp. p. 201.

To Philip Doddridge

SIR   Monticello Jan. 27. 16.

I have no recollection when the bounty of lands was first given to the soldiers of the revolutionary war; yet I know it was so early that it cannot be a long research into the ordinances and acts to find it. I inclose you a copy of the journals and Ordinances of the Convention of 1776. and as you mention that the public offices are without a compleat copy, be so good as to deposit it in the office either of the Council or House of Representatives with whom it will be of more important use than on my shelves.   Accept the assurances of my respect.   TH: JEFFERSON

PoC (DLC); on verso of portion of a reused address cover to TJ; at foot of text: "Mr P. Doddridge." Enclosures: (1) *The Proceedings of the Convention of Delegates, Held at the Capitol, in the City of Williamsburg, in the Colony of Virginia, on Monday the 6th of May, 1776* (Williamsburg, [1776]). (2) *Ordinances Passed at a General Convention of Delegates and Representatives, From the several Counties and Corporations of Virginia, Held at the Capitol, in the City of Williamsburg, on Monday the 6th of May, Anno Dom: 1776* (Williamsburg, [1776]; Sowerby, no. 1844).

By the HOUSE OF REPRESENTATIVES TJ meant the Virginia House of Delegates.

To Patrick Gibson

DEAR SIR   Monticello Jan. 27. 16.

My calls for money being here, and my grandson having to transfer the monies of his collection to Richmond[1] it is a mutual convenience to give him my draughts on you in exchange for cash here, inasmuch as it saves to us both the hazards of the road. I have accordingly this day drawn on you in his favor for 446. D 25 c which (if my tob° should not be arrived) be so good as to cover by a sale of so much of the flour on hand. I am desirous of delaying for better prices the sale of whatever portion of that is not necessary to meet my draughts.

Accept the assurance of my great esteem & respect.

TH: JEFFERSON

PoC (Mrs. T. Wilber Chelf, Mrs. Virginius Dabney, and Mrs. Alexander W. Parker, Richmond, 1944; photocopy in ViU: TJP); on verso of reused address cover of Robert Saunders to TJ, 29 Oct. 1815; at foot of text: "Mr Gibson"; endorsed by TJ.

MY GRANDSON: Thomas Jefferson Randolph.

[1] Preceding two words interlined.

To Thomas W. Maury

DEAR SIR   Monticello Jan. 27. 16.

I am favored with yours of the 17th. mr Cabell had apprised me of the objections to the power of imprisonment given to a functionary of our College; and having explained to him the reason of it I must refer you to him for a sight of my letter. the object seems to have been totally mistaken, and what was intended in tenderness to the pupil has been misconstrued into an act of severity, for every one knows they may now be sent by a common magistrate to the common prison for a breach of the peace.　　　With respect to the bank-mania, I foresaw it in 1791. and then opposed the establishment of the Bank of the US. which I knew was only an inoculation. I have marked the progress of the disease and seen that it was incurable, and to end in death. there will be a vast crush of private fortunes as on the death of the old Continental paper, as of the Assignats of France, the Misipi paper of Law, the South-sea paper of England E^{t}c the most pitiable of it's victims now as before[1] will be the helpless widow & orphan. prudent men will mitigate it's effects by caution. they will protect themselves as they do their fences when the woods are afire, by firing against it. what is most blameable is the cruelty of your process, roasting us before a slow fire like the martyrs in the days of persecution. instead of your 15. banks, be merciful, and give us the coup de grace, make it a thousand. however I am perfectly content with the 15. and to meet all hazards and trials with my fellow citizens. if we keep together we shall be safe, and when error is so apparent as to become visible to the majority, they will correct it, and what we suffer during the error must be carried to account with the losses by tempests, earthquakes E^{t}c　　　Your's with great friendship

TH: JEFFERSON

RC (ICN); addressed: "Thomas Walker Maury esq. of the legislature in Richmond"; postmarked Milton, 4 Feb. PoC (MHi); on verso of portion of a reused address cover from Robert Patterson to TJ; endorsed by TJ.

MY LETTER: TJ to Joseph C. Cabell, 24 Jan. 1816. For TJ's 1791 opinion on the ESTABLISHMENT OF THE BANK OF THE US., see *PTJ*, 19:275–82.

[1] Preceding three words interlined.

From Dabney Carr

DEAR SIR.　　　　　　　　　Winchester. Jan'ry 29th 1816.

I rec^d last evening your letter of the 19th ins^t. Accept I pray you, my best thanks, for it's contents—they are perfectly satisfactory—If I could ascertain with certainty, that Girardin in his continuation, of Burks history, has taken that notice of my father, which you suggested to him; I should doubt, whether it ought to be repeated, in Mr Wirt's book—in conveying to him, the information received from you; I will mention this circumstance: he can probably ascertain the fact. If the statement you give me, shall be used by Mr Wirt, your name will not appear.

You ask me whether you left in my hands, the inscription you had proposed for my father's tombstone? I am very certain that you did not—I have a pretty distinct recollection, of seeing you, when about to close Mazzei's book, (from which you had read, the notice he takes of my father) put the paper, containing the inscription, (which was a small one), into the book, & shut it; & I think it very probable, that the paper is now in the book in Washington.

With sincerest wishes for your health believe me most affectionately yrs &C   D Ca[rr]

RC (ViU: TJP-CC); edge chipped; endorsed by TJ as received 13 Feb. 1816 and so recorded in SJL.

From Thomas Eston Randolph

Dear Sir   Ashton 29th Jany 1816

The last Mail brought me a letter from my Son Mann, which has given me considerable uneasiness—he informs me, that he has ever had an aversion to Mercantile pursuits, and although he has endeavour'd to conquer it, he finds it impossible, and that his mind is possitively bent on entering the Navy—The object of this address, is to ask the favor of you to give him a letter to the President to obtain for him a Midshipman's warrant, he is extreemly desirous to be attach'd to the Washington 74, commanded by Commodore Chauncey, as he earnestly wishes to be in active service, and he is inform'd that she goes to the Mediterranean to be station'd there for eighteen months, or two years—

I should have waited on you to make this application in person, but I am suffering under a severe attack of Rheumatism, and I dread wetting my feet in crossing the river—With sentiments of great respect and esteem I am Dr sir

Your mo: Obdt Servt   Thos Eston Randolph

It has occurr'd to me Sir, that an application to Mr Madison for a warrant, and if obtained—if it was forwarded to him at Baltimore, it will save him the expence of a trip to Washington, and also considerable expence in his equipment, which I apprehend he can effect much better at Baltimore than the City—As I am unacquainted with Etiquette in such cases, I must depend on your friendly offices—and the only apology I can offer for thus troubling you, is the great anxiety I feel for my Son's future welfare—

(address Thos Mann Randolph Baltimore)   T.E.R

RC (MHi); dateline between signature and postscript; endorsed by TJ as received 29 Jan. 1816 and so recorded in SJL.

Thomas Mann Randolph (1798–1835), naval officer, was the son of TJ's cousin Thomas Eston Randolph. He entered the United States Navy as a midshipman on 30 May 1816, resigned on 28 May 1822, and subsequently served in the merchant marine and in the United States Revenue Marine. Randolph moved to Florida in 1833 and was appointed inspector of the federal land office for Florida and Alabama. He died in Key West (Robert Isham Randolph, *The Randolphs of Virginia* [1936], 107; Callahan, *U.S. Navy*, 452; Randolph Whitfield and John Chipman, *The Florida Randolphs, 1829–1978* [2d ed., 1987], 58, 59; Shackelford, *Descendants*, 1:177; *American Beacon and Norfolk and Portsmouth Daily Advertiser*, 29 Sept. 1835).

From George Watterston

DEAR SIR,   City of Washington Jany 29th 1816.

I have received your letter of the 10th; but have not yet received the books you mention. Have you gotten the catalogue I requested Mr Milligan to forward you? And if you have, will you be so good as to let me know how it pleases you? You will, no doubt discover some errors in it; but those were unavoidable in the printing of so large a work—The Library Committee are dissatisfied with me for having the Catalogue printed, without having waited to consult their <u>superior judgment</u>; but the members generally speak very highly of your arrangement & disposition of the books & I suppose will have no hesitation in allowing for its printing—the report of the Committee to the contrary notwithstanding—

I have the honor to be Very respectfully Yr ob^t serv^t

GEO, WATTERSTON

RC (DLC); addressed: "Thos Jefferson Esq^e Montecello—Virginia"; franked; postmarked Washington City, 29 Jan.; endorsed by TJ as received 5 Feb. 1816 and so recorded in SJL; with additional notation by TJ: "Catalogue from Millegan. arrgemt L. Virga   C. 24. N° 246."

TJ's most recent letter to Watterston was dated 3 Jan. 1816, not THE 10TH.

On 15 Dec. 1815 the United States House of Representatives referred a resolution seeking in part "additional compensation to the librarian for services performed since the last session of Congress" to the joint LIBRARY COMMITTEE (*JHR*, 10:62). In their REPORT presented to the Senate on 26 Jan. 1816, the committee determined that the "only evidence of the literary services of the librarian within the knowledge of your committee is, the publication of the catalogue with which we were presented at the beginning of the session; and the merit of this work is altogether due to Mr. Jefferson, and not to the librarian of Congress. Your committee are persuaded that, however ingenious, scientific, philosophical, and useful such a catalogue may be in the possession of a gentleman who (as was the case with the former proprietor of this, now the library of Congress) has classed his books himself, who alone has access to them, and has become, from long habit and experience, as perfectly familiar with every book in his library as a man who has long lived in a city is familiar with every street, square, lane, and alley in it, still this form of catalogue is much less useful in the present state of our library, consisting chiefly of miscellanies not always to be classed correctly under any particular head, than a plain catalogue in the form which had been adopted for the formation of the catalogue of the old library, which probably might not have cost more than $100 (if that much) whilst the catalogue with which we were presented, including three copies of it bound, calf gilt, costs the United States $1,360 50, one-third more than the annual appropriation made heretofore by Congress for the additional increase of the library, and more than one-twentieth of the actual cost of our whole library" (*ASP, Miscellaneous*, 2:280).

To Noah Worcester

SIR   Monticello. Jan. 29. 16.

Your letter bearing date Oct 18. 1815. came only to hand the day before yesterday, which is mentioned to explain the date of mine. I have to thank you for the pamphlets accompanying it, to wit, the Solemn review, the Friend of peace or Special interview, & the Friend of peace N⁰ 2. the first of these I had received thro' another channel some months ago. I have not read the two last steadily thro', because where one assents to propositions as soon as enounced,[1] it is loss of time to read the arguments in support of them. these numbers discuss the 1ˢᵗ branch of the causes of War, that is to say Wars undertaken for the <u>point of honor</u>. which you aptly analogise with the act of duelling between individuals, and reason with justice from the one to the other. undoubtedly this class of wars is in the general what you state them to be, 'needless, unjust, and inhuman, as well as anti Christian.'   The 2ᵈ branch of this subject, to wit, Wars undertaken on account of <u>wrong done</u>, and which may be likened to the act of robbery in private life, I presume will be treated of in your future numbers. I observe this class mentioned in the Solemn review p. 10. and the question asked 'Is it common for a nation to obtain a <u>redress</u> of wrongs by war?' the answer to this question you will of course draw from history. in the mean time reason will answer it on grounds of probability, that where the wrong has been done by a weaker nation, the stronger one has generally been able to enforce redress; but where by a stronger nation, redress by war has been neither obtained nor expected by the weaker. on the contrary the loss has been increased by the expences of the war in blood and treasure. yet it may have obtained another object equally securing itself from future wrong. it may have retaliated on the aggressor losses of blood and treasure far beyond the value to him of the wrong he had committed, and thus have made the advantage of that too dear a purchase to leave him in a disposition to renew the wrong in future. in this way the loss by the war may have secured the weaker nation from loss by[2] future wrong. the case you state of two boxers both of whom get a 'terrible bruising' is apposite to this. he of the two who committed the aggression on the other, altho' victor in the scuffle, yet probably finds his aggression not worth the bruising it has cost him.   to explain this by numbers. it is alledged that Great Britain took from us before the late war near 1000. vessels, and that during the war we took from her 1400. that before the war she seized and made slaves of 6000. of our citizens, and that in the war we killed more than 6000 of her subjects, and caused her to expend such a sum as amounted to 4. or 5,000. guineas a head for every slave she made. she might have purchased the vessels she took for less than the value of those she lost, and have used the 6000. of her men killed for the purposes to which she applied ours, have saved the 4. or 5000 guineas a head, and obtained a character of justice, which is valuable to a nation as to an individual, these considerations therefore leave her without inducement to plunder property and take men in future on such dear terms. I neither affirm nor deny the truth of these allegations, nor is their truth material to the question. they are possible, and therefore present a case which will claim your consideration in a discussion of the general question whether any degree of injury can render a recourse to war expedient? still less do I propose to draw to myself any part in this discussion. age and it's effects both on body and mind, has weaned my attentions from public subjects, and left me unequal to the labors of correspondence beyond the limits of my personal concerns. I retire therefore from the question with a sincere wish that your writing may have effect in lessening this greatest of human evils, and that you may retain life and health to enjoy the contemplation of this happy spectacle, and pray you to be assured of my great respect.

Th: Jefferson

PoC (DLC); at foot of first page: "Rev[d] mr Worcester." Printed in Worcester, *The Friend of Peace, No. IV. reasons for believing that efforts for the abolition of war will not be in vain* (Cambridge, Mass., [1816]; Poor, *Jefferson's Library,* 9 [no. 488]), 22–4, and Washington *Daily National Intelligencer,* 12 July 1816.

Worcester's analogy between war and

duelling appears in his *A Solemn Review of the Custom of War* (Cambridge, Mass., 1815), 9. The quote needless ... anti christian comes from Worcester to TJ, 18 Oct. 1815. The case of two boxers is cited in *Solemn Review,* 10.

[1] *Friend of Peace* and *Daily National Intelligencer:* "announced."
[2] *Daily National Intelligencer:* "of."

To Benjamin W. Crowninshield

SIR   Monticello Jan. 30. 16.

Mr Thomas Mann Randolph, the son of a neighbor and relation of mine is desirous of entering the naval service, and I am requested by his father to sollicit a midshipman's warrant for him. I have known the young gentleman from his birth and can assure you he is of perfectly correct morals and demeanor, and of an amiable disposition. he is about 18. years of age, and had made some proficiency in classical education, when an offer of employment in a counting house at Baltimore carried him to that place where he now is. should he be so fortunate as to obtain his wish I will request the favor of you to send his warrant to himself, addressed to Thomas Mann Randolph at Baltimore, to the care of George Stevenson esq. merchant at that place.

Having had the happiness of an intimate acquaintance with your deceased brother and a great and affectionate esteem for him, I avail myself with pleasure of this occasion of expressing it, and of adding assurances to yourself of my high respect and consideration.

TH: JEFFERSON

RC (on deposit NcU: Maurice Family Papers); addressed: "The honble Mr Crownenshield Secretary of the Navy Washington"; postmarked Milton, 31 Jan.; endorsed by a clerk: "1229 Thomas M. Randolph Midsⁿ File." PoC (DLC); on verso of reused address cover of John F. Oliveira Fernandes to TJ, 18 Jan. 1816; mutilated at seal, with missing text rewritten by TJ; endorsed by TJ.

Benjamin Williams Crowninshield (1772–1851), businessman and public official, belonged to a family of merchant-seamen in his native Salem, Massachusetts. He was a partner in his father's firm, George Crowninshield & Sons and its successors, a business that prospered during the War of 1812 but dissolved in 1817. Crowninshield was elected to the Massachusetts House of Representatives in 1811 and to the state senate the following year. President James Madison appointed him secretary of the navy late in 1814. Although at first declining the position, Crowninshield soon consented and remained in office until his resignation in

1818. Thereafter he returned to his business pursuits, having been elected president of the Merchants Bank of Salem in 1811. Crowninshield became a director of the Second Bank of the United States in 1822 and remained connected to that institution until its charter expired in 1836. He reentered the political arena with election to the Massachusetts House in 1821, and he sat in the United States House of Representatives, 1823–31, where he aligned himself politically with John Quincy Adams. In 1833 Crowninshield served one final term in the Massachusetts House before retiring to Boston, where he died (*ANB*; *DAB*; *JEP*, 2:595, 597, 3:142 [16, 19 Dec. 1814, 27 Nov. 1818]; Boston *New-England Palladium*, 26 July 1811; *Salem Gazette*, 22 Jan. 1822; *New-Bedford Mercury*, 26 Feb. 1836; *Boston Daily Atlas*, 4 Feb. 1851).

In a letter written to Martha Jefferson Randolph from Washington, 17 Feb. [1816], Ellen W. Randolph (Coolidge) commented on seeing Thomas Mann Randolph (1798–1835), the SON of Thomas Eston Randolph, who had come to that city seeking a MIDSHIPMAN'S WARRANT. She noted that although Randolph had other letters of recommendation, Crowninshield told him that "M[r] Jefferson's is sufficient" and promised to award the young man the next vacancy (RC in ViU: Coolidge Correspondence; partially dated).

Crowninshield's DECEASED BROTHER Jacob Crowninshield, who declined TJ's nomination in 1805 to serve as secretary of the navy, sat in the United States House of Representatives from 1803 until his death in 1808 (*DAB*).

To Albert Gallatin

DEAR SIR   Monticello Jan. 30. 16.

M[r] Dabney Terril, a relation of mine (the grandson of my sister) wishing to finish his education in Europe, I have advised him to go to Geneva preferably to any other place. his foundation is a moderate progress in Latin French[1] and Mathematics. he is 17. years of age, perfectly correct in his morals and deportment, amiable in his dispositions, and thirsty after knolege. his circumstances admit an expence of about 1000.D. a year. in a foreign country one wishes to be known as being somebody in their own country and to have access to some society of his own standing, as well for present enjoyment as to form some estimate of the state of society out of his own country. can you give him a letter or two to friends in Geneva which may answer these views? you will greatly oblige me by doing it, and by inclosing them to himself under the address of 'Dabney Terril of Kentucky. to the care of George Stevenson esq. merchant at Baltimore,' and put that if you please under an outer cover addressed to mr Stevenson himself. mr Terril will be in Baltimore within 10. days from this date to go on board[2] the first vessel bound to any port of France, or Holland; so that no time will be to be lost in writing & forwarding the letters I ask. ever and affectionately

your friend & serv[t]   TH: JEFFERSON

RC (NHi: Gallatin Papers); addressed: "Albert Gallatin esq New York"; franked; postmarked Milton, 31 Jan.; endorsed by Gallatin. PoC (DLC); on verso of reused address cover to TJ; endorsed by TJ.

Dabney C. Terrell was the GRANDSON of TJ's sister Martha Jefferson Carr.

[1] Word interlined.
[2] TJ here canceled "any."

From Gilbert J. Hunt

RESPECTED SIR,   New York Jan.ʸ 30 1816

The honor of your signature to the enclosed paper will confer a particular obligation on the author.

The hope of this favor being granted would not have been indulged, nor this trouble intruded upon one in your dignified retirement, but for the liberality which is known to dwell in the bosoms of the friends and Supporters of <u>Columbian Liberty</u>.

Your most obt St.   G. J. HUNT

N.B. A return of the enclosed will be attended with my thanks, & you have my best wishes for your health & happiness.—

RC (MHi); endorsed by TJ as received 14 Feb. 1816 and so recorded in SJL; with additional notation by TJ on verso: " 1½ D.

1.	Oram
12½	Watson
15."	

RC (DLC); address cover only; with PoC of TJ to Robert Ould, 2 Mar. 1816, on verso; addressed: "Hon. Thomas Jefferson Late President of the U. States Monticello State of Virginia"; franked; postmarked New York, 30 Jan.

Gilbert John Hunt, manufacturer and author, was making blank cards, calling cards, and playing cards in New York City by 1808. He supplemented his card business by making sandpaper, and in 1818 he advertised his American Vermillion Manufactory. In 1816 Hunt published *The History of the Late War between the United States and Great Britain. Written in the ancient historical style* (New York, 1816; Poor, *Jefferson's Library*, 5 [no. 144]), several variant editions of which, including a textbook, appeared from 1816–19. He also wrote poetry and issued a prospectus for a work in that genre. Hunt operated his New York shop until at least 1821 (*Longworth's New York Directory* [1808]: 182; [1819]: 12, 213 [misprinted as 113]; [1821]: 236; *New-York Evening Post*, 23 Mar. 1812; New York *Columbian*, 16 June 1812; New York *Commercial Advertiser*, 4 Mar. 1813; New York *Mercantile Advertiser*, 1 Aug. 1818; *Proposal for Publishing by Subscription, the Poetical Works of Gilbert John Hunt* [undated prospectus in DLC: Printed Ephemera Collection]; DNA: RG 29, CS, N.Y., New York, 1820).

The ENCLOSED PAPER, not found, was a prospectus for Hunt's *History of the Late War*.

For the payments described by TJ on the letter's verso, see TJ to Hunt, to James Oram, and to John F. Watson, all 29 Feb. 1816.

Observations for Calculating the Latitude of Monticello

1816.	Jan. 30	Jan. 31.	Feb. 3	⊙'s semidiam. here & hereafter	Feb. 4.
Observed altitude	68–28–30	68–56– 0	70–39–30		70–39–30
error of instrum^t					
true observ^d alt.					
– refr^n + parallax					
true alt. of ⊙'s center					
⊙'s decln Greenwich					
– Monticello					
true height of					
Equator					
Zenith dist. = Lat.					
pocket sextant[1]	68–24–30.	68–23–30			70–39– 0

MS (MHi); filed with TJ's Weather Memorandum Book, 1802–16; written entirely in TJ's hand on one side of a single sheet of paper, forming a grid with four rows and six columns.

[1] TJ repeated these headings in the second row, but he left the remainder of the last three rows blank.

To Thomas Eston Randolph

DEAR SIR   Monticello Jan. 30. 16.

I have this morning written to the Secretary of the navy, to sollicit a midshipman's warrant for Mann. the bearer of this letter carries that to the post office so that it may go by tomorrow's mail. it was more direct and certain to address it at once to the Secretary of the navy, and I have requested him to inclose the warrant to Mann, at Baltimore to the care of George Stevenson.

I desired mr Bacon to ask the favor of a copy of my mill account, the season being now arrived to which my important demands are generally fixed for settlement. I am sorry to hear of your rheumatism and hope the return of mild weather will bring relief

Affectionately Yours   TH: JEFFERSON

PoC (MHi); on verso of reused address cover to TJ; at foot of text: "Thoˢ E. Randolph esq."; endorsed by TJ.

[415]

To Thomas Appleton

DEAR SIR   Monticello Jan. 31. 16.

I wrote you a long letter on the 14th inst. and as it went by Duplicates one thro' mr Vaughan of Philada, the other thro' the Sec^y of
States office, I do not doubt you will receive them. but a gentleman
now setting out direct for Paris, you may recieve this before either of
the others. I will repeat therefore from that letter only a single article.
it informed you that 'I had put into the hands of mr Vaughan 50.
Dollars to be remitted to you, and it requested you to send me the
amount of it in Montepulciano wine, in black bottles well corked and
cemented, and in strong boxes, addressed to the Collector of any port
from Boston to Chesapeak, to which the first opportunity should
occur; Norfolk and Richmond being always to be preferred, if a conveyance equally early offers. but the warm season will be so fast advancing that no time will be to be lost.' it is on account of the pressure
of the season that I catch at the present conveyance, as, confident you
will receive the remittance immediately thro' mr Vaughan, you may
in the mean time procure and send off the wine. I requested it to be
of the quality you formerly furnished me, & which, in a letter of May
1. 1805. you mentioned to be of the growth of grounds formerly belonging to the order of Jesuits and sold for the benefit of the government in 1773 at the time that that institution was abolished. referring
for other things to that letter, I repeat here the assurance of my
friendly esteem & great respect.   TH: JEFFERSON

PoC (DLC); on verso of reused address cover of otherwise unlocated letter
from Lancelot Minor to TJ, 8 Dec. 1815
(addressed: "Thomas Jefferson Esquire
Monticello" in care of "Mr S. O. Minor";
franked; postmarked Charlottesville, 10
Dec.; recorded in SJL as received 15
Dec. 1815 from Louisa); at foot of text:

"Thomas Appleton esq."; endorsed by
TJ, with his added notation: "by D. Ter-
ril & Dr Jackson." Enclosed in TJ to
Henry Jackson, 31 Jan. 1816.

The GENTLEMAN NOW SETTING OUT
DIRECT FOR PARIS was Dabney C.
Terrell.

To Joseph C. Cabell

TH:J. TO MR CABELL   Mont° Jan. 31. 16.

Your letters of the 23^d and 24th come to hand just in the moment of
the return of our mail. I have only therefore time to inclose the Conveyances for which Miller's bill is hung up. I had no doubt but that he
had deposited them with the other papers. friendly salutations.

RC (ViU: TJP); dateline at foot of text; endorsed by Cabell.

For the enclosed CONVEYANCES, see note to Petition of Joseph Miller to the Virginia General Assembly, [presented 15 Dec. 1815].

To Henry Jackson

DEAR SIR   Monticello Jan. 31. 16.

On the 16th inst. I took the liberty, thro' the office of the Secretary of State, of asking a second time your care of a letter to mr Ticknor. ten days after that I received your favor of Nov. 9. I am very thankful for the kind dispositions it expresses towards myself, and can assure you that the approbation of the wise and worthy is truly a pillow of down to an aged head.   a direct conveyance occurring by a gentleman going immediately to Paris, I have thought a line to mr Ticknor by him might probably get to his hands sooner than that thro' the office of the Secretary of State; and I therefore trespass on you again with one for him, as also one for mr Appleton our Consul at Leghorn. this last I presume can find it's destination by the common mail, or perhaps thro' the diplomatic agent of Tuscany at Paris. my correspondence with Europe, of which Paris, under all it's afflictions, is still the center, will, I fear, but too often oblige me to avail myself of your kind attentions.

This will be handed you by mr Dabney Terril of Kentucky, a relation of mine, being the grandson of my sister, who is proceeding to Geneva for the purposes of education. he is a youth of perfect correctness of morals and manners, and of amiable dispositions. he will stop a few days only in Paris, and asks me to procure him the honor of presenting himself to you. he will probably need the protection of your passport on his journey, and perhaps indeed of a permanent one to cover his residence at Geneva.

I avail myself with pleasure of the occasion which the request of these favors furnishes of tendering you the assurance of my high consideration and esteem.   TH: JEFFERSON

RC (ViU: TJP); addressed: "The honorable Doct^r Henry Jackson Chargé des affaires of the US. of America at Paris" to be carried "by mr Terril a citizen of the US. of America. Th: Jefferson"; endorsed by Jackson. PoC (DLC); on verso of reused address cover of Philip I. Barziza to TJ, 6 Dec. 1815; endorsed by TJ. Enclosures: (1) TJ to Thomas Appleton, 31 Jan. 1816. (2) TJ to George Ticknor, 31 Jan. 1816.

Dabney C. Terrell was the grandson of TJ's SISTER Martha Jefferson Carr.

From Bernard Peyton

DEAR SIR,   Rich^d 31st Janu^y 1816

Immediately on the rec^t of your esteem^d favo'r of the 20th Current I proceeded to search for the Articles you wish^d and am sorry to say I could neither meet with Bottles or Corks of the description mentioned—I was desirous to have the Bottles picked, and packed in a Hogshead to prevent their being injured by removing, but, this the gentleman (and the only one who had them in the City) would by no means consent too—I was permitted to take them in the situation they are sent only, which I concluded it was best to do—

The Corks are infamous, but I assure you the very best Rich^d affords, after dilligent enquiry and inspection I found those sent preferable, I selected them with my own hands and in consequence of their being so indifferent determin'd to forward only eight Gross, should you find them to ans^r I can procure any quantity of the same quality—

The Anchovies are said to be of excellent quality by those who have tried them, for this however I can't answer as I am not a judge of the Article—I hope they may turn out well—

I regret exceedingly it was not in my power to fill your memorandum agreeable to the direction; it is owing alone to the situation of this Market which is very badly assorted indeed; of some articles we have an over portion and none of a great many others, time tho' will regulate this—

I feel gratified that you should have thot' proper to confide the execution of your commissions in this place to Green & Peyton, we will with the utmost pleasure sir comply with any order you may please to forward us, and in the way most likely to meet your aprobation either in the Dry Good or any other line—

You will find herewith annex^d a statement of the cost of each Article which Bills we have discharged and shall agreeable to your wish call on Mr Gibson for payment—the Boatmans rec^t I also forward—   Should you wish any Articles in our line we will take pleasure in opening an accompt with you—payment once or twice a year (whicheer will be most agreeable to you) will be entirely satisfactorry to us—

For your good wishes be pleased to accept my thanks—with perfect respect

Your Very Obd: Hub: Servt: BERNARD PEYTON

RC (MHi); endorsed by TJ as received 2 Feb. 1816 and so recorded in SJL. RC (MHi); address cover only; with PoC of TJ to James Oram, 29 Feb. 1816, on verso; addressed: "Thomas Jefferson Esqʳ Monticello near Milton Virgᵃ" by "Mail"; franked; postmarked Richmond, 31 Jan. Enclosures not found.

To Marc Auguste Pictet

Sir   Monticello in Virginia. Jan. 31. 1816.

Mʳ Dabney Terril, of the state of Kentucky, a relation of mine being desirous to go to Europe for his education, I have advised him to give to the College of Geneva the preference which I consider it as deserving over any other Seminary of Europe. he accordingly has decided to proceed thither, and will have the honor of delivering you this letter. he is about 17. years of age, perfectly correct in his principles and deportment, amiable in his disposition, and thirsting after knowledge. young, distant as he will be from his friends, and insulated among strangers, he cannot but be anxious to see some protecting hand under which he may feel himself safe from injury. the interchange of some letters between us many years ago, the place you fill in the college, and the distinguished estimation in which you are held in the world, encourage me to address my young friend to you, with a request that you will extend to him the benefit of your patronage, and of your counsel in all cases where either his conduct or his course of education may need it. he has laid as yet but a moderate foundation in Latin, French and Mathematics. I can assure you he will prove himself worthy of your kind attentions; and to his gratitude will be added the obligations under which I shall acknowledge myself your debtor for them. Permit me at the same time to assure you of my high consideration and esteem.   Th: Jefferson

RC (Frédéric Rilliet, Geneva, Switzerland, 1947); addressed: "Mʳ Pictet Professor of the College of Geneva Member of the National Institute of France at Geneva" to be carried "by mr Terril a citizen of the US. of America. Th: Jefferson"; endorsed by Pictet. PoC (DLC); on verso of reused address cover of Dabney Carr to TJ, 1 Dec. 1815; endorsed by TJ.

To George Ticknor

DEAR SIR   Monticello Jan. 31. 16.

I wrote you a long letter on the 14th inst. and as it went by duplicates thro good channels, I am sure you will get it. but a gentleman
going from hence to Paris direct, which he will probably reach before
either of the other channels of conveyance I will repeat from that letter but a single article, the request to add to the catalogue I formerly
troubled you with, the underwritten books. referring therefore to that
letter, I repeat the assurances of my friendly esteem and respect.

                                            TH: JEFFERSON

Oeuvres Philosophiques de Ciceron. 10. vols. in 16° Paris. 1796. this
    contains the translations of Durand, Desmarais, d'Olivet, Bouhier,
    Morabin & Barrett.
Lettres familieres de Ciceron par Prevost. Lat. Fr. edition de Goujon
    5. v. 8vo Paris 1800. 1.

Lettres de Ciceron et de Bru-   ⎫ Fleschier in his Annuaire de la
    tus. Lat. Fr. par Prevost   ⎬ librairie of about 8. or 10. years
Lettres de Ciceron à Atticus.   ⎪ ago, in announcing Goujon's edition
    Lat. Fr. par Mongault   ⎭ of Prevost's Lettres familieres de
                                      Ciceron, says that a like edition of
                                      all the other letters was then in
                                      hand, which have doubtless
                                      appeared long since.

RC (Catherine Barnes Historical Autographs and Documents, Philadelphia, 2007); addressed: "M[r] George Ticknor Paris"; endorsed by Ticknor. PoC (MHi); on verso of reused address cover of Horatio G. Spafford to TJ, 9 Jan. 1816; with additional notation in TJ's hand at foot of text: "by Dabney Terril"; endorsed by TJ.

To Stephen Cathalan

MY DEAR SIR AND FRIEND   Monticello Feb. 1. 1816.

I recieved yesterday your favor of Nov. 29. from which I learn, with
much mortification (of the palate at least) that my letter of the 3[d] of
July has never got to your hands. it was confided to the Secretary of
state's office. regrets are now useless, and the proper object to supply
it's place. it related generally to things friendly, to things political E[t]c
but the material part was a request of some particular wines which
were therein specified.

1. white Hermitage of the growth of M. Jourdan; not of the dry kind, but what we call silky, which in your letter just recieved you say are called doux. but by our term silky we do not mean sweet, but sweetish in the smallest degree only. my taste in this is the reverse of mr Butler's, who you say likes the dry and sparkling, I the non mousseux & un peu doucereux.

2. Vin de Nice, as nearly as possible of the quality of that sent me by mr Sasserno, formerly; whose death, by the bye, I had not before heard of, and much regret.

3. Vin de Roussilon. I used to meet with this at the best tables of Paris, where it was drank after the repast, as a vin de liqueur. it was a little higher colored than Madeira near as strong, and dry, and of fine flavor. I am not certain of the particular name, but that of Rivesalte runs in my head. if, from what you know of the Rivesalte it should answer this description nearly, then we may be sure this was the wine: if it does not, you will probably be able to know what wine of Roussilon corresponds with the qualities I describe.

I requested that after paying for 50. ℔ of Maccaroni out of the 200. Dollars, and reserving what would pay all charges till shipped about a fifth of the residue should be laid out in Hermitage, and the remaining four fifths in Vins de Nice [and] de Roussillon equally. send them to any port, from Boston to the Chesapeak inclusive, but to Norfolk or Richmond of preference, if a conveyance occurs. if addressed to the Collector of the port, he will receive & forward them to Richmond, which is at the head of the tidewater of James river on which I live, and from whence it comes by boat navigation. I suppose you can never be long without vessels at Marseilles bound to some of our ports above described. were it to be otherwise the wines might come thro' the Canal of Languedoc to mr Lee our Consul at Bordeaux. but this would increase risk and expence & is only mentioned as a pis-aller, and left entirely to your judgment.

The political speculations of my letter of July 3. are not worth repeating because the events on which they were hazarded have changed backwards & forwards, two or three times since that. my wishes are for the happiness of France, without caring what executive magistrate makes her happy. I must confess however I did not wish it to be Bonaparte. I considered him as the very worst of all human beings, & as having inflicted more misery on mankind than any other who had ever[1] lived. I was very unwilling that the example of his parricide usurpation should finally stand approved by success. he is now off the scene, I hope never to return on it: but whether you are much more at your ease in the hands of the allies; you know better than I do.   On the subject of your continuance in the Consulate, I hope you will never have any thing to fear; never, certainly whilst any effort of mine can have any weight with the government: and in a late[2] letter to the Secretary of state wherein I had occasion to speak of you I have placed your merits on ground which I think will never be assailed. God bless you and preserve you many years in health and prosperity   Th: Jefferson

PoC (MHi); on reused address cover to TJ; torn at seal; at foot of first page: "M. Cathalan"; endorsed by TJ, with his added notation: "by D. Terril & Dr Jackson." Enclosed in TJ to Henry Jackson, 1 Feb. 1816.

NON MOUSSEUX ET UN PEU DOUCEREUX: "not sparkling and a little sweet." PIS-ALLER: "last resource." TJ's LETTER to James Monroe, the SECRETARY OF STATE, was dated 4 Feb. 1816.

[1] Word interlined.
[2] Word interlined.

From Jean David

MONSIEUR   Richmond le 1er fevrier 1816.

    La bienveillance que vous m'avez temoignée dans les deux lettres que vous avez eu la bonté de m'ecrire, et notamment dans celle du 13 Janvier, m'enhardit a vous entretenir de nouveau de mes projets et même a vous demander des conseils.

    Persuadé que la culture de la vigne deviendroit une Source de richesses pour les Etats unis, et en particulier pour la Virginie, j'avois fait a ce sujet un memoire très court que je comptois presenter ou faire presenter à la Legislature de l'Etat de Virginie actuellement assemblée à Richmond. Mr Girardin avoit eu la bonté de le traduire en Anglais, mais avant de le presenter il me conseilla de le communiquer à Mr Wilson Carey Nicholas Gouverneur de Virginie, il me donna une lettre d'introduction auprès de lui, et ensuite m'y accompagna Mr Nicholas en paroissant persuadé de l'utilité de cette culture, et même de Sa reussite, me dit que très certainement la Legislature ne voudroit faire aucune depense pour cet objet, et qu'etant surchargée d'affaires, il doutoit qu'elle mit en deliberation ce qui fesoit le Sujet de mon memoire; que tout ce qu'on pourroit en obtenir de plus favorable Seroit une prime de tant—Sur chaque barrique de Vin, et tant Sur chaque barrique d'eau de vie provenant de mes plantations, ce qu'il regardoit comme tres incertain, et qu'il croyoit que pour former une pareille entreprise il me conviendroit mieux de tacher de reunir quelques riches proprietaires ou bien de la faire par actions.

Ce ne fut pas du tout mon avis attendu qu'il est tres difficile de re-unir plusieurs personnes pour une entreprise quelconque, et qu'il est impossible de la faire par actions Si l'on n'est auparavant assuré d'un certain nombre d'actionaires. de Sorte que mon memoire na pas été presenté.

Mais ce qui a arreté toutes mes demarches, c'est un scrupule qui m'est Survenu et dont j'ai fait part à Mr Girardin, le voici—

C'est qu'en introduisant dans l'amerique Septentrionale la culture de la Vigne je porte un prejudice considerable à ma patrie. Car je Suis persuadé que Si j'entreprends cette culture avec quelques moyens; et que je puisse la Suivre Seulement cinq ou Six ans je mettrai ce pays dans le cas de Se passer des vins et des eaux de vie de france, et d'exporter de ces denrées dans touts les pays de l'amerique ou la france les fournit aujourd'hui. je ne veux pas dire que tout celá aura lieu dans cinq ou Six ans; mais que dans cinq ou Six ans j'aurai fait connoitre cette culture de maniére que tout le monde pourra S'y livrer Sans avoir besoin de moi

Cette idée a fait une telle impression Sur moi que Si j'etois assuré que les francais continuassent a exister en corps de nation j'abandonnerois toute tentative à ce Sujet. Mais qui Sait Si j'aurai encore une patrie! cette question est au moins tres problematique

Cependant je Suppose que l'on put me convaincre que mon scrupule n'est pas fondé, Soit par ce qu'on pourroit employer pour cette entreprise quel qu'autre personne aussi experte et même plus experte que moi, (ce qui cependant ne me paroitroit pas une raison Suffisante) Soit par tout autre moyen; il ne S'en Suivroit pas que le gouvernement des Etats unis ne me dut une recompense, pour y avoir introduit une branche de production aussi importante, car quoique l'on y fasse du vin dans quelques cantons, il S'en faut de beaucoup que je regarde celá comme une reussite assurée, il me Semble que ce Sont des gens qui essayent et Si ce n'etoit ainsi depuis le temps qu'on S'occupe de cet objet, la moitié de la Caroline du nord, du Kentucky, de la Virginie, du Maryland, de la Pensilvanie et du Jersey devroient être complantés en Vignes

Imaginant donc de reussir plus complettement et Surtout plus rapidement que ceux qui m'ont precedé, je me crois en droit de demander une recompense proportionnée au Service que j'aurois rendu à l'etat, et Si on me la refusait je ferois comme ce statuaire qui brisa Sa statue plutôt que de la donner au dessous de Sa valeur

Vous voyez donc Monsieur qu'avec de pareilles pretentions il est difficile que je puisse m'arranger avec de Simples particuliers, à moins que ceux ci n'eussent les moyens d'obtenir du Gouvernement un privilége une prime, une recompense quelconque, dont ils m'attribueroient une juste portion.

J'avois fait une Petition ou memoire à ce sujet, pour être presenté au Congrés Soit en mon nom Soit au nom d'un ou plusieurs particuliers avec qui jaurois pris des arrangements. je vous la transmets cy joint. mais je vous prie de la regarder pour le moment, comme une chose à laquelle je Suis bien loin dêtre determiné. je ne crois pas même dans quelque position pressante que je pusse me trouver, que je voulusse employer un pareil moyen tant que je pourrai penser que j'ai une patrie. Mais Si la france etoit envahie de nouveau et partagée, alors je ferois bon marché de mes connoissances en ce genre

Excusez je vous prie cette longue lettre dans laquelle j'ai cedé à l'impulsion de mon cœur; je ne parlerois pas ainsi à tout le monde, car aujourd'hui on Se moque de celui qui ne fait pas passer Son interêt particulier avant tout—

Je vous Salue bien respectueusement   J. DAVID

EDITORS' TRANSLATION

SIR   Richmond 1 February 1816.

The kindness you have shown me in the two letters you were so good as to write me, and especially in the one dated January 13, emboldens me to discuss with you again my projects and even to ask for your advice.

Convinced that the cultivation of vineyards would become a source of wealth for the United States and particularly for Virginia, I had written a very short report on this topic that I intended to present or have someone present for me to the Virginia legislature currently assembled in Richmond. Mr. Girardin was kind enough to translate it into English, but before submitting it, he advised me to communicate it to Mr. Wilson Cary Nicholas, governor of Virginia. He gave me a letter of introduction for the governor and then accompanied me there. Mr. Nicholas seemed convinced of the usefulness of this cultivation and even of its success. He told me, however, that the legislature would quite certainly be unwilling to spend any money for this purpose, and he doubted that it would deliberate on the subject of my report, as it was overburdened with other affairs; that the most favorable thing that could be obtained from it would be a subsidy of so much on each barrel of wine and brandy produced on my plantations, but that he considered this a very uncertain prospect. He believed that in order to start such an enterprise it would suit me better to try to unite a few wealthy landowners or do it as a joint stock venture.

This was not at all my opinion, considering that it is very difficult to bring together several persons for any enterprise and that it is impossible to succeed with stock unless a certain number of shareholders has already been secured. As a result of all this, my report was not presented.

But what stopped me in my tracks was a doubt that came over me and of which I informed Mr. Girardin. Here it is—

My concern is that my introduction of the cultivation of vineyards to North America might be detrimental to my native land. I am convinced that if I undertake this project with some means, and if I am able to follow it up, even for as little as five or six years, I will enable this country to do without wines and brandies from France and to export these products to all the countries of America where France exports them now. I do not mean to say that all this will take place in five or six years, but that in five or six years I will have made this culture known in such a way that anyone will be able to dedicate himself to it without needing me

This idea made such an impression on me that if I had any guarantee that the French will continue to exist as a nation, I would give up all my attempts on this matter. But who knows whether I will still have a homeland! This question is, to say the least, very problematic

However, I suppose that I could be convinced that my doubts are not well founded, either because another person, with as much or even more expertise than I, could be employed in this enterprise (this however does not seem to me to be a sufficient reason) or through any other means. It would follow that the government of the United States would owe me a reward for having introduced such an important line of production, because although wine is produced in a few counties, I am far from considering their success to be secure. It seems to me that people are still only making a trial of it. If this were not the case, half of North Carolina, Kentucky, Virginia, Maryland, Pennsylvania, and New Jersey would now be covered in vineyards

Consequently, imagining that I would succeed more completely and above all more rapidly than those who have preceded me, I believe I have a right to ask for a reward in proportion to the services I would render to the state, and if it were refused, I would do like the sculptor who smashed his statue rather than give it up at a price below its value

Therefore, Sir, you can see that with such pretensions it is difficult for me to deal with mere individuals, unless they have the means of obtaining from the government a privilege, grant, or some kind of reward, of which they would allot me a just portion.

I had composed a petition or report about this to be presented to Congress either in my name or in the name of one or several individuals with whom I would have made arrangements. I enclose it herein. But I ask you to regard it for the moment as a project that I am far from being determined to undertake. I even doubt that, no matter how pressing my situation might become, I would do it so long as I believed I had a homeland. But if France were to be invaded again and partitioned, then I would sell my expertise cheaply

Please forgive this long letter in which I gave in to the impulse of my heart. I would not speak thus to just anybody, because today people who do not value personal profit above all else are mocked—

I send you my respectful regards J. David

RC (DLC); at head of text: "The honorable Th[s] Jefferson Monticello"; endorsed by TJ as received 7 Feb. 1816 and so recorded in SJL. Translation by Dr. Genevieve Moene.

Jean David's Petition and Memorial
to Congress on American Viticulture

[ca. 1 Feb. 1816]

Projet de Petition et Memoire Sur l'utilité de la culture de la vigne.
Par J. D——

Les avantages que les Etats Unis d'Amerique retireroient de la culture de la vigne Sont immenses: il n'est aucunne personne un peu versée dans les principes de l'economie politique et du commerce, qui ne comprenne combien il Seroit precieux pour ce pays, de pouvoir, non seulement Se passer des vins et des eaux-de-vie d'Europe; ce qui changeroit en Sa faveur la balance de Son commerce avec cette partie du monde; mais encore de pouvoir en exporter dans les isles antilles, et dans les colonies Espagnoles qui ont Secoué le joug de leur Metropole, et dont le produit serviroit à payer le Sucre, le Café, le cacao et autres marchandises que l'on retire de ces contrées.

En outre le luxe qui S'est prodigieusement accru dans les Etats Unis, est une des principales causes que Son change avec l'Europe est constamment à Son desavantage; ce qui prouve que les Etats Unis retirent plus de l'Europe qu'ils ne lui donnent; inconvenient majeur qui tend à ruiner ce pays.

une administration Sage et prevoyante doit donc prendre touts les moyens qui Sont en Son pouvoir pour diminuer la Somme des importations etrangéres; et un des meilleurs Sans doute est l'introduction de la nouvelle branche de produit que je propose, puisque, ainsi que je l'ai dit non seulement elle allegeroit les etats unis du tribut qu'ils payent à l'Europe pour les vins et les eaux-de-vie; mais encore les mettroit dans quelques années en état d'en exporter dans le Sud de l'amerique.

Il n'y auroit donc d'autre raison pour que le Gouvernement ne S'empressât pas de favoriser cette culture, que l'incertitude de Sa reussite; mais ceci n'est plus un problême, puisque on est parvenu à faire du vin, quoique en petite quantité dans quelques contrées des Etats Unis, et puisqu'on trouve dans les forêts de la virginie, et Sans doute ailleurs aussi, des vignes Sauvages qui produisent des raisins agreables au goût et avec lesquels on a fait du bon vin.

D'après ces considerations Le S^r D—— Se proposant de Se livrer à la culture de la vigne qu'il entend parfaitement ainsi que la maniére de faire le vin, demande à la Legislature des Etats Unis une prime de   Dollars par chaque barrique de vin et une prime de   Dollars pour chaque barrique d'eau-de-vie, provenant de Ses plantations.

Cette Prime est juste et necessaire.—

Juste, parceque celui qui enrichira ce pays d'un pareil produit merite une recompense.—

Necessaire, parceque le S^r D—— n'ayant pas des facultés pecuniaires suffisantes pour une pareille entreprise; ce n'est que l'appui d'un benefice analogue aux avances qu'il faudra faire, qui pourra lui procurer des interessés.

Il S'attend a ce qu'on lui dise:—que pour prouver qu'on peut faire du vin dans les Etats Unis, il S'est etayé sur ce qu'on en fait dans quelques contrées.

Si donc on y fait du vin sans qu'il ait été pour cela necessaire d'accorder une prime; Sa demande aujourd'hui paroit n'être pas fondée.—

il repond—Que Si les etablissements existants en ce genre prouvent qu'on peut faire du vin dans les Etats-unis; attendu le peu de Succés qu'ils ont eu jusqu'à ce jour, ils prouvent egalement une de ces deux choses:

Ou que des obstacles que le S^r D—— ne sauroit deviner S'opposent à cette culture.

ou que ceux qui l'ont entreprise ne prennent pas touts les moyens convenables a Son entière reussite et dans ces deux cas il croit être fondé a demander une prime, Soit comme encouragement, Soit comme une recompense; ainsi qu'on accorde un brevet d'invention à celui qui fait la decouverte d'une machine nouvelle; et Si l'on pouvoit obtenir un brevet d'invention pour le Sujet dont il S'agit, Le S^r D—— borneroit la Ses pretentions, mais comme la chose ne peut pas être, il Se croit fondé a demander une prime Sans laquelle il lui est impossible d'entreprendre cette culture—

Cependant Si le Gouvernement jugeoit à propos de le recompenser de toute autre maniére, ou qu'il preferât que cet etablissement Se fit pour Son propre compte Sous la Direction du Sr David, celui ci y accederoit avec plaisir persuadé qu'on lui accorderoit une recompense proportionnée aux avantages qu'il auroit procuré aux Etats unis d'Amerique

Le Sr David a entendu dire qu'un pareil etablissement pour compte du Gouvernement, avoit eu lieu dans la Caroline du nord, mais que le Directeur etant mort on avoit été obligé de l'abandonner. Si la chose est ainsi, il n'y auroit alors qu'a continuer ce qui est commencé, en corrigeant les erreurs dans lesquelles l'ancien directeur pourroit être tombé.—

E D I T O R S '   T R A N S L A T I O N

[ca. 1 Feb. 1816]

Draft Petition and Memorial on the usefulness of cultivating vineyards.
By J. D——

The advantages to the United States of America from the cultivation of vineyards are immense. No one even slightly knowledgeable about the principles of political economy and commerce fails to understand how valuable it would be if this country could not only do without wines and brandies from Europe, which would change in its favor the balance of its commerce with that part of the world, but also allow for the export of some of it to the Antilles and to the Spanish colonies that have shaken off the yoke of their mother country, the profit of which would be used to pay for sugar, coffee, cocoa, and other merchandise that is obtained from these regions.

Moreover, the luxury that has prodigiously increased in the United States is one of the main reasons why its exchange with Europe is constantly at a disadvantage, which proves that the United States receives more from Europe than it gives back. This major shortcoming tends to ruin this country.

A wise and farsighted administration must therefore use all the means in its power to decrease foreign imports, and one of the best ways to do so is no doubt the introduction of the new branch of product I am proposing, since, as I have mentioned, it would not only reduce the tribute the United States pays to Europe for wines and brandies, but, in a few years, it would also give the United States the ability to export some of them to South America.

Only the uncertainty of success would prevent the government from hastening to favor this cultivation, but this is no longer a problem, since in some regions of the United States wine has been successfully produced, though in small quantities, and because in the forests of Virginia, and probably elsewhere also, one can find wild vines that produce tasty grapes from which good wine has been made.

From these considerations, Mr. D—— proposes to dedicate himself to viticulture, which he understands perfectly, as well as he comprehends the making of wine, and he is asking the legislature of the United States for a subsidy of   dollars per barrel of wine and   dollars per barrel of brandy produced on his plantations.

This subsidy is just and necessary.—

Just, because the person who will enrich this country with such a product deserves a reward.—

Necessary because, Mr. D—— lacking sufficient financial means for such an enterprise, only the prospect of a profit similar to the necessary advances will attract interested people to him.

He expects to be reminded that he argued that wine is being produced in some regions in order to prove that wine can be made in the United States.

Therefore, if wine is produced without the need for a subsidy, his request today does not seem to be well-founded.

He replies that if the existing establishments of this kind prove that wine can be made in the United States, considering what little success they have had until now, they also prove one of the following two things:

Either that obstacles that Mr. D—— cannot predict hamper this cultivation.

Or that those who undertake it are not taking all of the appropriate measures to achieve complete success; and in both cases, he believes himself justified in requesting a subsidy, either as an encouragement or as a reward, just as a patent of invention is granted to a person who discovers a new machine; and if one could obtain a patent for the matter at hand, Mr. D—— would limit his claims then and there, but since this cannot be, he feels justified in asking for a subsidy, without which it would be impossible for him to undertake this work—

However, if the government deems it appropriate to reward him in any other manner or if it would prefer this enterprise to be undertaken on its own account under the direction of Mr. David, he would oblige with pleasure, convinced that he would be granted a reward in proportion to the advantages he would have procured to the United States of America.

Mr. David heard that such an enterprise on behalf of the government had been undertaken in North Carolina, but that the director having died, it had been abandoned. If this is the case, one would only have to continue what has been started and correct any errors into which the former director may have fallen.—

MS (DLC: TJ Papers, 206:36656–7); entirely in David's hand; undated. Translation by Dr. Genevieve Moene.

To Henry Jackson

DEAR SIR   Monticello Feb. 1. 16.

After I had sealed my letter of yesterday, a mail arrived, bringing me one from mr Cathalan, which informs me that mine to him of July 3. had never got to his hands. as this went thro' the same channel (the Sec^y of state's office) with mine to you of July 5. it shews that the doubt expressed in your favor of Nov. 9. was real, and that that letter had not then got to hand. it covered one to M^de de Staël, and another to mr Ticknor, and I hope has since got to your hands. mr Terril's immediate departure for Paris furnishes so happy an opportunity of replacing that to mr Cathalan, that I take the liberty of giving it the protection of your cover and of repeating here the assurances of my great esteem & respect   TH: JEFFERSON

PoC (DLC); on verso of reused address cover to TJ; at foot of text: "Dr Henry Jackson"; endorsed by TJ as a letter to be carried "by D. Terril" and so recorded in SJL. Enclosure: TJ to Stephen Cathalan, 1 Feb. 1816.

From Jeremiah Platt

DEAR SIR   Albany 1st Feb 1816

with out the privilege of a personal acquantance with you and being at the same time sory, to trouble you in your retirement on a subject that is not interesting to you, I hope you will pardon my digression when I inform you that I have not been able to inform myself through any other Channel as Geography does not give any particulaur account or description of the timber in the state of Virginia, I have consulted your Notes on that State but as they were written in Seventeen hundred & Eighty One if there[1] had been at that time, large quantities[2] it might have been Destroyed before this time I therefore beg you to have the Goodness to inform me by letter as soon as opportunity may permit concerning the timber of the state according to your acquaintance with it but more particulaurly on the James River if there should be any particulaur lots or parcels of Land of White or yellow pine timber if you should be accquainted with the price or quality of timbered land you would do me a very great favour[3] by Stateing that in your letter I should[4] be pleased to have it above Richmond if timber is plenty in that quarter or if there Should be any other place in Virginia that you would recommend in prefference to Richmond for the establishing of Saw mills as that Country has been very highly recommended to me for business of that kind and I am inform that there is but few saw mills in that Part of the State of Virginia likewise that the inhabitance do not under[stand] making lumber as well as they do in this state & the Destrict of Main finally Sir if you should think any place Calculated to Carry on Lumbering on a large or an advantageous Scale for industrious men pleas to recommend it as soon as convenient and if you Should not think of a place proper for Such an undertaking please to state the same to your most Obedient &ᶜ Humble Servant

Yours with much respect   JEREMIAH⁵ PLATT

N B if you Should think it probable that I could sucseed in lumbering in that State I should be Glad to come on in the spring with a company of men that understand it and endeovour to carry it on to advantag if you should Recommend any place for that purpose

RC (MHi); edge trimmed; endorsed by TJ as received 9 Feb. 1816 and so recorded in SJL. RC (DLC); address cover only; with PoC of TJ to Wilson Cary Nicholas, 29 Feb. 1816, on verso; addressed: "Mʳ Thomas Jefferson Late president of the US Monticello Albemarl County State of Virginia"; stamp canceled; franked.

Jeremiah Platt joined Albany's First Presbyterian Church in 1813. In 1814 he was the proprietor of a grocery store. Platt entered into a partnership with lumber merchant Aaron Hand in 1816, but the firm was dissolved the same year (J. McClusky Blayney, *History of the First Presbyterian Church of Albany, N.Y.* [1877], 95; Joseph Fry, *The Albany Directory, for the Year 1814* [Albany, 1814], 31, 47; Fry, *The Annual Register, and Albany Directory, for the year 1816* [Albany, 1816], 37; *Albany Daily Advertiser*, 29 Nov. 1816).

[1] Manuscript: "therere."
[2] Manuscript: "quantiies."
[3] Manuscript: "favovour."
[4] Manuscript: "shoul."
[5] Manuscript: "Jereremiah."

Statement of Taxable Property in Albemarle County

A list of the taxable property of the subscriber in Albemarle Feb. 1. 1816.

5. white tythes.
74. slaves of 16. years old and upwards.
14. dᵒ of 12. years & not 16.
33. horses, mules, mares & colts.
1. gig.
1. four wheeled carriage, a Landau.   TH: JEFFERSON

MS (MHi); written entirely in TJ's hand on verso of a portion of a reused address cover to TJ; endorsed by TJ: "Sheriff Albem. taxable property 1816."

The Virginia General Assembly set PROPERTY tax rates for 1816 in a law enacted on 22 Feb. of that year (*Acts of Assembly* [1815–16 sess.], 3–4). TYTHES: "tithables."

To David Bailie Warden

DEAR SIR   Monticello Feb. 1. 16.

It is long since I have written to you. the reason has been that from one of your letters I concluded you were returning to the US. by yours of Apr. 9. 15. I found you were still at Paris. I can assure you that I did every thing in your case which could be done, as far as decency or effect permitted: but I found that nothing would avail; & ceased under the hope that your presence here might remove obstacles whatever they were. I should very gladly have recommended to your attentions mr Ticknor, a very learned young gentleman of Boston who I imagine got to Paris in autumn. I should have even taken the liberty of asking your friendly aid to him in a commission for the purchase of some books for me which he was so kind as to undertake. if you have made his acquaintance, I am sure you have found him worthy of it in every respect moral, and literary. this will be handed you by mr Terril a young gentleman of Kentucky, a relation of mine, who will stop a few days only in Paris on his way to Geneva for his education. he is a youth of perfect correctness of morals & manner, of good dispositions and of great appetite for science. I have desired him to wait on you, as well to make his own bow as to deliver you this letter which bears to you the expressions of my great and sincere esteem and respect.   TH: JEFFERSON

RC (MdHi: Warden Papers); addressed: "David Baillie Warden esq. Paris by mr Terril"; endorsed by Warden. PoC (DLC); on verso of a reused address cover from John Wayles Eppes to TJ; endorsed by TJ.

From John Adams, with Postscript by Abigail Adams

DEAR SIR   Quincy Feb. 2. 1816

I know not what to Say of your Letter of the 11th of Jan. but that it is one of the most consolatory, I ever received.

To trace the Commencement of the Reformation I Suspect We must go farther back than Borgia, or even than Huss or Wickliff, and

I want the Acta Sanctorum to assist me in this Research. That Stupendous Monument of human Hypocricy and Fanaticism the Church of St. Peter at Rome, which was a Century and an Half in Building; excited the Ambition of Leo the tenth, who believed no more of the Christian Religion than Diderot, to finish it: And finding St. Peters Pence insufficient, he deluged all Europe with Indulgences for Sale, and excited Luther to contravert his Authority to grant them. Luther and his Associates and Followers, went less than half way in detecting the Corruptions of Christianity; but they acquired Reverence and Authority among their Followers almost as absolute as that of the Popes had been, To enter into details would be endless. But I agree with you, that the natural Effect of Science and Arts is to erect public opinion into a Censor, which must in Some degree be respected by all.

There is no difference[1] of Opinion or Feeling between Us, concerning the Partition of Poland, the intended Partitions of Pilnitz or[2] the more daring Partitions of Vienna.

your Question "How the Apostacy from National Rectitude can be Accounted for"[3] is too deep and wide for my capacity to answer. I leave Fisher Ames to dogmatize up the Affairs of Europe and Mankind. I have done too much in this Way. A burned Child dreads the Fire. I can only say at present, that it Should Seem that human Reason and human Conscience, though I beleive there are such things, are not a Match, for human Passions, human Imaginations and human Enthusiasm. You however I believe have hit one Mark, "The Fires the Governments of Europe felt kindling under their Seats":[4] and I will hazard a shot at another, The Priests of all Nations imagined they felt approaching Such Flames as they had So often kindled about the Bodies of honest Men. Priests and Politicians, never before, So Suddenly and So unanimously concurred in Reestablishing Darkness and Ignorance[5] Superstition and Despotism.

The Morality of Tacitus, is the Morality of Patriotism, and Britain & France have adopted his Creed; i.e. that all things were made for Rome. Jura negat Sibi lata, nihil non arrogat Armis, Said Achilles. Laws were not made for me, Said the Regent of France and his Cardinal Minister Du Bois. The Universe was made for me, Says Man. Jesus despized and condemned this Patriotism:[6] But what Nation or What Christian has adopted his System? He was, as you Say "the most benevolent Being, that ever appeard on Earth." France and England, Bourbons and Bonaparte, and all the Sovereigns at Vienna, have acted on the same Principle "All things were made for my Use." "Lo! Man for mine, replies a Pampered Goose." The Philosophers of the 18th Century have acted on the Same Principle. "When[7] it is to combat Evil, 'tis lawful to employ the Devil." Bonus Populus vult de-cipi; decipiatur. They have employed the Same Falsehood[8] the Same deceit, which Philosophers and Priests of all ages have employed for their own Selfish Purposes. We now know how their Efforts have Succeeded. The old Deceivers have tryumphed over the New. Truth, must be more respected than it ever has been, before, any great Improvement can be expected in the Condition of Mankind. As Rochfaucault his "Maxims drew, from" history and from Practice, "I believe them true" From the whole Nature of Man, moral intellectual and physical he did not draw them.

We must come to the Principles of Jesus. But, when will all Men and all Nations do as they would be done by? Forgive all Injuries and love their Enemies as themselves? I leave those profound Phylosophers whose Sagacity perceives the Perfectibility of Humane[9] Nature, and those illuminated Theologians who expect the Apocalyptic Reign, to enjoy their transporting hopes; provided always that they will not engage us in Crusades and French Revolutions, nor burn us for doubting. My Spirit of Prophecy reaches no farther than, New England Guesses.

you ask, how it has happened that all Europe, has acted on the Principle "that Power was Right."[10] I know not what answer to give you, but this, that Power always Sincerely, conscientiously, de tres bon Foi, believes itself Right. Power always thinks it has a great Soul, and vast Views, beyond the Comprehension of the Weak; and that[11] it is doing God Service, when it is violating all his Laws. Our Passions, Ambition, Avarice, Love, Resentment &c possess so much metaphysical[12] Subtilty and so much overpowering Eloquence, that they insinuate themselves into the Understanding and the Conscience and convert both to their Party. And I may be deceived as much as any of them, when I Say, that Power must never be trusted without a Check.

Morgan has misrepresented my Guess. There is not a Word in my Letters about "a Million of human Beings." Civil Wars, of an hundred years, throughout Europe, were guest at, and this is broad enough for your Ideas; for Eighteen or twenty Million would be a moderate Computation for a Century of civil Wars, throughout Europe. I Still pray that a Century of civil Wars, may not desolate Europe and America too South, and North.

Your Speculations into Futurity in Europe are So probable that I can Suggest no doubts to their disadvantage. All will depend on the Progress of Knowledge. But how Shall Knowledge Advance? Independant of Temporal and Spiritual Power, the Course of

Science and Litterature is obstructed and discouraged by So many Causes that it is to be feared, their[13] motions will be Slow I have just finished reading four Volumes of D'Israeli, two on the Calamities and two on the Quarrels of Authors. These would be Sufficient to Shew that, Slow rises Genius by Poverty and Envy oppressed. Even Newton and Lock and Grotius could not escape. France could furnish four other Volumes of the Woes and Wars of Authors,

My Compliments to M[rs] Randolph, her Daughter Ellen and all her other Children, and believe me, as ever,   JOHN ADAMS

To which mrs Adams adds her affectionate reegards—and a wish that distance did not Seperate Souls congenial—

RC (DLC); with postscript in the hand of Abigail Adams; mistakenly endorsed by TJ as a letter of 16 Feb. received 14 Feb. 1816 and so recorded in SJL. RC (MHi); address cover only; with PoC of TJ to James Barbour, 5 Mar. 1816, on verso; addressed by Susan B. Adams: "Thomas Jefferson Esq[re] Late President of the US. Monticello Virginia"; postmarked Quincy, 5 Feb. FC (Lb in MHi: Adams Papers); lacks postscript by Abigail Adams.

JURA NEGAT SIBI LATA, NIHIL NON ARROGAT ARMIS: "he denies that laws were enacted for him, he makes all his claims by warring," from a variant text of Horace, Ars Poetica, 122 (Fairclough, Horace: Satires, Epistles and Ars Poetica, 460–1). The French prelate Guillaume Dubois (DU BOIS) was the close advisor of the regent Philippe II, duc of Orléans. ALL THINGS WERE MADE FOR MY USE . . . PAMPERED GOOSE comes from line 45 of Alexander Pope, An Essay on Man. In Epistles to a Friend. Epistle III (London, 1733), 7. TO COMBAT EVIL, 'TIS LAWFUL TO EMPLOY THE DEVIL appears in Matthew Prior's poem "Hans Carvel" in his Poems on Several Occasions (London, 1707), 36. BONUS POPULUS VULT DECIPI; DECIPIATUR: "The good people wish to be deceived; let them be deceived." The reference to the MAXIMS of François de La Rochefoucauld paraphrases the opening line of Jonathan Swift, Verses on the Death of Dr. S—, D.S.P.D. occasioned By reading a Maxim

in Rochefoulcault (London, 1739): "As Rochefoucault his Maxims drew From Nature, I believe 'em true: They argue no corrupted Mind In him; the Fault is in Mankind." DE TRES BON FOI: "very candidly." Adams had JUST FINISHED READING two works by Isaac D'Israeli: Calamities of Authors; including Some Inquiries respecting their moral and literary characters, 2 vols. (New York, 1812), and Quarrels of Authors; or, Some Memoirs for our Literary History, including Specimens of Controversy to the Reign of Elizabeth, 2 vols. (New York, 1814). SLOW RISES GENIUS BY POVERTY AND ENVY OPPRESSED paraphrases Samuel Johnson, London: A Poem, In Imitation of the Third Satire of Juvenal, 2d ed. (London, 1738), 14: "Slow rises Worth, by Poverty deprest."

[1] RC: "differnce." FC: "difference."
[2] RC: "or or." FC: "or."
[3] Adams here quotes from TJ's 11 Jan. 1816 letter.
[4] Adams here paraphrases TJ's 11 Jan. 1816 letter.
[5] RC: "Ignoranc." FC: "Ignorance."
[6] RC: "Patrotism." FC: "Patriotism."
[7] Omitted opening quotation mark supplied from FC.
[8] RC: "Falshod." FC: "falsehood."
[9] FC: "human."
[10] Adams here quotes from TJ's 11 Jan. 1816 letter.
[11] RC: "thait." FC: "that."
[12] RC: "metaphysial." FC: "metaphysical."
[13] Word interlined in RC above an uncanceled "its." FC: "their."

To Joseph C. Cabell

DEAR SIR   Monticello Feb. 2. 16.

Your favors of the 23ᵈ & 24ᵗʰ ult. were a week coming to us. I instantly inclosed to you the deeds of Capᵗ Miller; but I understand that the Post-master, having locked his mail before they got to the office, would not unlock it to give them a passage.

Having been prevented from retaining my collection of the acts & Journals of our legislature by the lumping manner in which the Committee of Congress chose to take my library, it may be useful to our public bodies to know what acts and journals I had, and where they can now have access to them. I therefore inclose you a copy of my catalogue which I pray you to deposit in the council office for public use. it is in the 18ᵗʰ & 24ᵗʰ chapters they will find what is interesting to them. the form of the catalogue has been much injured in the publication: for altho they have preserved my division into chapters, they have reduced the books in each chapter to Alphabetical order, instead of the Chronological or Analytical arrangements I had given them. you will see sketches of what were my arrangements at the heads of some of the chapters.[1]

The bill on the obstructions in our navigable waters appears to me proper; as do also the amendments proposed. I think the state should reserve a right to the use of the waters for navigation, and that where an individual landholder impedes that use, he should remove the impediment, and leave the subject in as good a state as nature formed it. this I hold to be the true principle; and to this Colᵒ Green's amendments go. all I ask in my own case is that the legislature will not take from me <u>my own works</u>: I am ready to cut my dam in any place, and at any moment requisite, so as to remove that impediment if it be thought one[2] and to leave those interested to make the most of the natural circumstances of the place. but I hope they will never take from me my canal, made thro' the body of my own lands, at an expence of twenty thousand Dollars, and which is no impediment to the navigation of the river. I have permitted the riparian proprietors above (and they are not more than a dozen or twenty) to use it gratis, and shall not withdraw the permission unless they so use it as to obstruct too much the operations of my mills, of which there is some likelihood.

Doctʳ Smith, you say, asks what is the best elementary book on the principles of government? none in the world equal to the Review of Montesquieu printed at Philadelphia a few years ago. it has the advantage too of being equally sound and corrective of the principles of

Political economy: and all within the compass of a thin 8vo. Chipman's and Priestley's Principles of government, & the Federalist are excellent in many respects, but for fundamental principles not comparable to the Review.　　I have no objections to the printing my letter to mr Carr, if it will promote the interests of science; altho' it was not written with a view to it's publication.

My letter of the 24th ult. conveyed to you the grounds of the two articles objected to in the College bill. your last presents one of them in a new point of view, that of the commencement of the Ward schools as likely to render the law unpopular to the county. it must be a very inconsiderate and rough process of execution that would do this. my idea of the mode of carrying it into execution would be this. declare the county ipso facto divided into wards, for the present by the boundaries of the militia captaincies: somebody attend the ordinary muster of each company, having first desired the Captain to call together a full one. there explain the object of the law to the people of the company, put to their vote whether they will have a school established, and the most central and convenient place for it; get them to meet & build a log school house, have a roll taken of the children who would attend it, and of those of them able to pay: these would probably be sufficient to support a common teacher, instructing gratis the few unable to pay. if there should be a deficiency, it would require too trifling a contribution from the county to be complained of; and especially as the whole county would participate, where necessary, in the same resource. should the company, by it's vote, decide that it would have no school, let them remain without one. the advantages of this proceeding would be that it would become the duty of the Wardens[3] elected by the county to take an active part in pressing the introduction of schools, and to look out for tutors.[4]　　If however it is intended that the State government shall take this business into it's own hands, and provide schools for every county,[5] then by all means strike out this provision of our bill. I would never wish that it[6] should be placed on a worse footing than the rest of the state. but if it is beleived that these elementary schools will be better managed by the Governor & council, the Commissioners of the literary fund, or any other general authority of the government, than by the parents within each ward, it is a belief against all experience. try the principle one step further, and amend the bill so as to commit to the Governor & Council the management of all our farms, our mills, & merchants' stores.　　No, my friend, the way to have good and safe government, is not to trust it all to one; but to divide it among the many, distributing to every one exactly the functions he is competent to. let the National government be entrusted with the defence of the nation, and it's foreign & federal relations; the State governments with the civil rights, laws, police & administration of what concerns the state generally; the Counties with the local concerns of the counties; and each Ward direct the interests within itself.[7] it is by dividing and subdividing these republics from the great National one down thro' all it's subordinations, until it ends in the administration of every man's farm and affairs by himself; by placing under every one what his own eye may superintend, that all will be done for the best. what has destroyed liberty and the rights of man in every government which has ever existed under the sun? the generalising & concentrating all cares and powers into one body, no matter whether of the Autocrats of Russia or France, or of the Aristocrats of a Venetian Senate. and I do believe that if the Almighty has not decreed that Man shall never be free, (and it is blasphemy to believe it) that the secret will be found to be in the making himself the depository of the powers respecting himself, so far as he is competent to them, and delegating only what is beyond his competence by a synthetical process, to higher & higher orders of functionaries, so as to trust fewer and fewer powers, in proportion as the trustees become more and more oligarchical. the elementary republics of the wards, the county republics, the State republics, and the republic of the Union, would form a gradation of authorities, standing each on the basis of law, holding every one it's delegated share of powers, and constituting truly a system of fundamental balances and checks for the government. where every man is a sharer in the direction of his ward-republic, or of some of the higher ones, and feels that he is a participator in the government of affairs not merely at an election, one day in the year, but every day; when there shall not be a man in the state who will not be a member of some one of it's councils, great or small, he will let the heart be torn out of his body sooner than his power be wrested from him by a Caesar or a Bonaparte. how powerfully did we feel the energy of this organisation in the case of the Embargo? I felt the foundations of the government shaken under my feet by the New England townships. there was not an individual in their states whose body was not thrown, with all it's momentum, into action, and altho' the whole of the other states were known to be in favor of the measure, yet the organisation of this little selfish minority enabled it to overrule the Union. what could the unwieldy counties of the middle, the South and the West do? call a county meeting, and the drunken loungers at and about the Court houses would have collected, the distances being too great for the good people and the industrious generally to attend. the character of those who really met would have been the measure of the weight they would have had in the scale of public opinion. as Cato then concluded every speech with the words 'Carthago delenda est,' so do I every opinion with the injunction 'divide the counties into wards.' begin them only for a single purpose; they will soon shew for what others they are the best instruments.[8] God bless you, and all our rulers, and give them the wisdom, as I am sure they have the will, to fortify us against the degeneracy of our government, and the concentration of all it's powers in the hands of the one, the few, the well-born or but the many.

Th: Jefferson

RC (ViU: TJP); addressed: "Joseph C. Cabell esquire Richmond"; franked; postmarked Milton, 4 Feb.; endorsed by Cabell. PoC (DLC). PoC of Tr (DLC: TJ Papers, 199:35492–3); extract entirely in TJ's hand; at head of text: "Extract of a letter from Th: Jefferson to Joseph C. Cabell esq. Feb. 2. 1816"; conjoined with PoC of Tr of TJ to John Adams, 28 Oct. 1813, and PoC of TJ's Notes on Popular Election of Juries, [ca. 2 Apr. 1816]; enclosed in TJ to Wilson Cary Nicholas, 2 Apr. 1816. Tr (ViU: TJP); extract by Nicholas P. Trist. Tr (Vi: RG 3, Wilson Cary Nicholas Executive Papers); extract in Cabell's hand; at head of text: "Extract of a Letter from Mr Jefferson to a member of the Senate Feb: 2. 1816."

The 18TH & 24TH CHAPTERS of the enclosed *Catalogue of U.S. Library* listed works on "Jurisprudence. Equity" and "Politics" respectively. The latter (p. 93) included one of the SKETCHES OF WHAT WERE MY ARRANGEMENTS, breaking the category down into "General Theories of Government" and "Special Governments, Antient" and "Modern," followed by sections on France, England, the United States, and "Political Oeconomy," with the last four broken down further still.

MY LETTER TO MR CARR: TJ to Peter Carr, 7 Sept. 1814. CARTHAGO DELENDA EST: "Carthage must be destroyed" (see note to TJ to John Wayles Eppes, 11 Sept. 1813).

[1] Vi Tr consists solely of this paragraph.

[2] Preceding five words interlined.

[3] In PoC TJ interlined "Aldermen" in place of this word.

[4] PoC of Tr to this point consists of the following revision of this paragraph: "the proposition to give to the Visitors of our Albemarle College the power of dividing the county into wards, and of establishing a school in each was with a view to exhibit an example of that salutary measure. I expected that the Aldermen when elected by the county would declare it ipso facto divided into wards, for the present, by the boundaries of the militia Captaincies; that one of them would have attended a meeting of each company on a muster day, would have referred to their election the most eligible site for their school, would have engaged them to join force and build log houses for the school and dwelling of the master, would have taken a roll of the children who would attend, and of the parents able to pay, the unable alone being to be instructed gratis. such buildings, good enough at all times, would certainly have been sufficient, until there should be time and occasion for making a more regular designation of the wards, the variations of which might call for a change of site. the Aldermen would then have had to provide a schoolmaster for every ward, and to induct him." ViU Tr begins with the opening sentence only of this revision and continues at this point.

⁵ Preceding six words not in ViU Tr.
⁶ PoC of Tr and ViU Tr substitute "our county" for this word.
⁷ PoC of Tr and ViU Tr delete the

"and" at the beginning of this clause and here add "and each man manage his own farm and concerns."
⁸ PoC of Tr and ViU Tr end here.

From John B. Smyth
(for William Duane)

SIR   Aurora Office Philad^a 2^d Feby 1816
    At head you will be pleased to find your account which I hope may be found correct—if so would be very much obliged to you for a remittance of the amount; I should not have taken the liberty of sending it on so early but am much in want of money.
    Yours very respectfully   JOHN B SMYTH
                                           for WILLIAM DUANE.

RC (DLC); subjoined to enclosure; dateline at foot of text; addressed: "Thomas Jefferson Esqr Monticello Virginia" by "(Mail)"; franked; postmarked; endorsed by TJ as a letter from Duane received 9 Feb. 1816 and so recorded in SJL. Enclosed in TJ to Joseph Milligan, 11 Feb. 1816.

ENCLOSURE

Account with William Duane

                                                    [ca. 2 Feb. 1816]
Thomas Jefferson Esqr   To Wm Duane D^r
1815 March   To Translation of a Work of Destutt Tracy $60.00
1816 May 1st   " 1 y^r Subscr to Country Aurora due this day—   5.00
                                                           $65.00

MS (DLC); in John B. Smyth's hand; undated; with RC of covering letter subjoined. Also enclosed in TJ to Joseph Milligan, 11 Feb. 1816.

To Thomas W. Maury

DEAR SIR   Monticello Feb. 3. 16.
    Your favor of the 24th Ult. was a week on it's way to me, and this is our first subsequent mail day. mr Cabell had written to me also on the want of the deeds in Capt Miller's case, and as the bill was in that house, I inclosed them immediately to him. I forgot however to desire

that they might be returned when done with, and must therefore ask this friendly attention of you.

You ask me for observations on the memorandum you transcribe,[1] relating to a map of the states, a mineralogical survey and statistical tables. the feild is very broad, and new to me. I have never turned my mind to this combination of objects, nor am I at all prepared to give an opinion on it. on what principles the association of objects may go that far and not farther, whether we could find a character who would undertake the mineralogical survey, and who is qualified for it, whether there would be room for it's designations on a well filled geographical map, and also for the statistical details, I cannot say. the best mineralogical charts I have seen have had nothing geographical but the watercourses, ranges of hills, and most remarkable places, and have been colored so as to present to the eye at once the mineralogical ranges.   for the articles of a statistical table I think the last Census of Congress presented what was proper, as far as it went, but did not go far enough. it required detailed accounts of our manufactures, and an enumeration of our people, according to ages, sexes & colors. but to this should be added an enumeration according to their occupations. we should know what proportion of our people are employed in agriculture what proportion are carpenters, smiths, shoemakers, Taylors, bricklayers, merchants, seamen E^{t}c. no question is more curious than that of the distribution of society into occupations, & none more wanting. I have never heard of such tables being effected but in the instance of Spain, where it was first done under the administration, I believe, of Count d'Aranda, and a second time under the count de Florida Blanca. and these have been considered as the most curious & valuable tables in the world. the combination of callings with us would occasion some difficulty, many of our tradesmen being, for instance agricolists also. but they might be classed under their principal occupation.   On the geographical branch I have reflected occasionally. I suppose a person would be employed in every county to put together the private surveys, either taken from the Surveyor's books or borrowed from the proprietors, to connect them by supplementary surveys, and to survey the public roads, noting towns, habitations & remarkable places, by which means a special delineation of watercourses, roads E^{t}c will be obtained. but it will be further indispensable to obtain the Latitudes and Longitudes of principal points in every county, in order to correct the errors of the topographical surveys, to bring them together, and to assign to each county it's exact space on the map. these observations of Latitude and Longitude might be taken for the whole state, by a single person well qualified, in the course of a couple of years. I could offer some ideas on that subject to abridge and facilitate the subject,[2] and as to the instruments to be used; but such details are probably not within the scope of your enquiries. they would be in time if communicated to those who will have the direction of the work. I am sorry I am so little prepared to offer any thing more satisfactory to your enquiries than these extempore hints. but I have no doubt that what is best will occur to those gentlemen of the legislature who have had the subject under their contemplation, and who, impressed with it's importance, are exerting themselves to procure it's execution. Accept the assurance of my great esteem & respect.

Th: Jefferson

RC (NNGL, on deposit NHi). PoC (DLC); at foot of first page: "Thos W. Maury."

The LAST CENSUS OF CONGRESS had been taken in 1810. Article 1, section 2, of the United States Constitution mandates a decennial census. In 1768 Pedro Pablo Abarca de Bolea, conde de Aranda, ordered a census in SPAIN in which individuals were enumerated rather than house-holds. José Moñino y Redondo, conde de Floridablanca, repeated the process in 1787 employing improved methodology (Massimo Livi Bacci, "Fertility and Nuptiality Changes in Spain from the Late 18th to the Early 20th Century," *Population Studies* 22 [1968]: 86).

[1] Manuscript: "transscribe."
[2] Word canceled in PoC, with "operations" interlined in its place.

From Destutt de Tracy

MONSIEUR   Paris, 4 fevrier, 1816.

J'ai reçu le 4 mai 1814, par Mr Warden, votre trés aimable lettre du 29 9bre 1813; j'y ai répondu le 14 juillet 1814, par le fils de Mr Madison, et je vous ai exprimé, autant qu'il m'était possible, Combien j'en étais charmé et reconnaissant.

Vous aviez la bonté de me dire dans Cette lettre que vous aviez été assez Content de mon ouvrage Sur l'Economie politique pour le faire traduire et que je devais recevoir en même temps, que votre lettre, au moins un éxemplaire de Cette traduction; je l'ai attendu vainement jusqu'à aujourd'hui et Vous ne Sauriez[1] douter Combien il en a Couté à mon impatience; Enfin il ne m'est jamais arrivé et je n'ai plus reçu de vos nouvelles.

Aujourd'hui par une Singuliére Circonstance, on vient d'imprimer, presque Sans mon aveu, l'original de Cet ouvrage qui forme la quatrième partie de mes Elémens d'Idéologie; il est précédé d'un Supplément à la troisième partie et Suivi d'un Commencement de la Cinquième. je m'emprèsse de vous en faire hommage, ainsi qu'à la

Société Philosophique de Philadelphie, par le moyen de Mr Warden, qui veut bien se charger de cette lettre; Mais vous Croyez bien, Monsieur, que je n'en tiens pas moins à l'honneur d'être traduit dans votre langue et sous vos auspices. Vous m'avez flatté quelque part que les trois premiers volumes de mes Elemens d'idéologie avaient le même honneur; Et avec le Commentaire Sur Montesquieu que vous avez bien voulu approuver et le morceau Sur l'instruction publique que je vous ai envoyé aussi, lesquels réunis pourraient tenir lieu de Sixième volume de mes Elémens que je ne puis plus Composer; Cela forme un Ensemble Complet.

Je Serais bien heureux Si vous aviez la bonté de me faire parvenir quelques éxemplaires anglais ou français des differentes parties de tout cela que vous avez eu la bonté de faire publier et plus heureux, Encore, si vous daignez agréer toujours ma respectueuse reconnaissance.

Ceci est mon testament; je Suis devenu aveugle et infirme; je ne puis plus rien faire; je regrette de laisser imparfait un ouvrage dont l'idée me parait importante; mais encore une fois, le Commentaire sur Montesquieu et le morceau sur l'instruction publique renferment le germe de toutes mes idées sur la législation et votre indulgence extrême me Confirme dans mes opinions.

Recevez je vous prie, Monsieur, l'assurance de mon plus inviolable attachement et de mon profond Respect.　　　DESTUTT DE TRACY

EDITORS' TRANSLATION

SIR　　　　　　　　　　　　　　　　Paris, 4 February, 1816.
On 4 May 1814 I received through Mr. Warden your very friendly letter of 29 November 1813. In my reply of 14 July 1814 through Mr. Madison's son I expressed to you, as much as I was able, how delighted and grateful I was.

You were so kind as to tell me in this letter that you had been pleased enough by my work on political economy to have it translated and that I would receive at the same time as your letter at least one copy of this translation. I have been waiting for it in vain until this day, and you cannot imagine how my patience has been taxed. In short, it never arrived, and I received no more news from you.

Today, by a peculiar circumstance, the original version of this work, which forms the fourth part of my *Élémens d'Idéologie*, has just been printed, almost without my permission. It is preceded by a supplement to the third part and followed by a beginning of the fifth. I am eager to offer it to you as a token of my esteem and also to the American Philosophical Society, through Mr. Warden, who is willing to take charge of this letter. But believe me, Sir, I still value just as much the honor of being translated into your language and under your auspices. You flattered me by mentioning somewhere that the first three volumes of my *Élémens d'Idéologie* would be similarly honored. The *Commentary and Review of Montesquieu's Spirit of Laws*, which you were kind enough to approve, and the piece on public instruction I also sent you, could take the place of the sixth volume of my *Élémens* that I can no longer write, and the whole would form a complete set.

I would be very happy should you be so kind as to send me a few French or English copies of the various parts of all these works, which you have had the kindness to have published, and I would be even happier if you always condescended to receive my respectful gratitude.

This is my testament. I have become blind and infirm and can no longer do anything. I regret leaving in an imperfect state a work which seemed important to me, but again, the *Commentary and Review of Montesquieu's Spirit of Laws* and the piece on public instruction contain the seed of all my ideas on legislation, and your extreme indulgence confirms me in my opinions.

Please accept, Sir, the assurance of my most inviolable attachment and deepest respect. DESTUTT DE TRACY

RC (DLC); in an unidentified hand, signed by Destutt de Tracy; endorsed by TJ as received 21 Nov. 1816 and so recorded in SJL. Translation by Dr. Genevieve Moene. Enclosed in David Bailie Warden to TJ, 9 Aug. 1816.

TJ's letter to Destutt de Tracy was dated 28 Nov. 1813, not 29 Nov. LE FILS DE Mʀ MADISON was his stepson, John Payne Todd. For the QUATRIÈME PARTIE DE MES ELÉMENS D'IDÉOLOGIE, see

enclosure to Lafayette to TJ, 17 Feb. 1816, and note. TJ had Destutt de Tracy's MORCEAU SUR L'INSTRUCTION PUBLIQUE, *Observations sur le Systême Actuel d'Instruction Publique* (Paris, 1801), bound with other tracts on education by James Ogilvie, Joseph Lancaster, and Pierre Samuel Du Pont de Nemours (Sowerby, no. 1109; Poor, *Jefferson's Library*, 5 [no. 209]).

¹ Manuscript: "Scauriez."

To Christopher Greenup

DEAR SIR Monticello Feb. 4. 16.

Your favor of Oct. 9. arrived here during a two months absence from home, to which I returned a little before Christmas only. I have thought it best to detain the answer thro' the month of January to lessen the risks of bad weather. indeed we have never known a month of more snow and constant bad weather. I now inclose 8. Dollars, the amount of mr Stevens's bill in notes of the Virginia bank which we are told are current with you. with these I have to return you very sincere thanks for the trouble you have been so kind as to take, and hope [i]t is now closed. mr Mickie's claim is laid to rest by the other [de]positions and will not be benefited by what the presence¹ of [J]ohn Henderson seems to have made the old lady either remember or forget. the interests too of the younger branches of the family in the lands adjoining Milton, are with my own sunk to nothing by the extension of the navigation many miles above it, and abandonment of the town where there will never be another house built or repaired. I have long offered the lands for what I gave, but nobody will give the half. the body of their former mill house has been entirely taken away by the negro inhabitants of the place, & the warehouses, formerly profitable, have been given up as not worth repairing, and neither recieve any thing, nor could cover it. when I offered therefore to those members of the family to pay over again one half of what I had already paid once, I offered certainly more than they will ever get for their interests. with a repetition of my thanks for your kindness, accept the assurance of my great esteem & respect.

TH: JEFFFERSON

PoC (MHi); on verso of a reused address cover from James Gibbon to TJ; torn at seal; at foot of text: "Govern^r Greenup"; endorsed by TJ.

The OLD LADY was Elizabeth Henderson.

[1] Manuscript: "prence."

To James Monroe

DEAR SIR   Monticello Feb. 4. 16.

Your letter covering that of Genl Scott is recieved, and his is now returned. I am very thankful for these communications. from 40. years experience of the wretched guesswork of the newspapers of what is not done in open day light, and of their falsehood even as to that, I rarely think them worth reading, & almost never worth notice. a ray therefore now & then from the fountain of light is like sight restored to the blind. it tells me where I am; and that to a mariner who has long been without sight of land or sun, is a rallying of reckoning which places him at ease. the ground you have taken with Spain is sound in every part. it is the true ground especially, as to the South Americans. when subjects are able to maintain themselves in the field they are then an independant power, as to all neutral nations, are entitled to their commerce, and to protection within their limits. every kindness which can be shewn the South-Americans, every friendly office and aid within the limits of the law of nations, I would extend to them, without fearing Spain or her Swiss auxiliaries. for this is but an assertion of our own independance. but to join in their war, as Genl Scott proposes, and to which even some members of Congress seem to squint is what we ought not to do as yet. on the question of our interest in their independance, were that alone a sufficient motive of action, much may be said on both sides. when they are free, they will drive every article of our produce from every market by underselling it, and change the condition of our existence, forcing us into other habits and pursuits.   we shall have indeed in exchange some commerce with them, but in what I know not, for we shall have nothing to offer which they cannot raise cheaper; and their separation from Spain seals our everlasting peace with her. on the other hand, so long as they are dependant, Spain, from her jealousy,[1] is our natural enemy, and always in either open or secret hostility with us. these countries too, in war, will be a powerful weight in her scale, and, in peace, totally shut to us. interest then, on the whole, would wish their independance, and justice makes the wish a duty. they have a right to be free, and we a right to aid them, as a strong man has a right to assist a weak one assailed by a robber or murderer. that a war is brewing between us and Spain cannot be doubted. when that disposition is matured on both sides, and open rupture can no longer be deferred, then will be the time for our joining the South Americans, and entering into treaties of alliance with them. there will then be but one opinion, at home or abroad, that we shall be justifiable in chusing to have them with us, rather than against us. in the mean time they will have organised regular governments, and perhaps have formed themselves into one or more confederacies: more than one, I hope, as in single mass they would be a very formidable neighbor. the geography of their country seems to indicate three; 1. what is North of the isthmus. 2. what is South of it on the Atlantic: and 3. the Southern part on the Pacific. in this form we might be the balancing power.   à propos of the dispute with Spain, as to the boundary of Louisiana. on our acquisition of that country, there was found in possession of the family of the late Govr Messier a most valuable and original MS. history of the settlement of Louisiana by the French, written by Bernard de la Harpe, a principal agent thro' the whole of it. it commences with the first permanent settlement of 1699. (that by de la Sale in 1684. having been broken up) and continues to 1723. and shews clearly the continual claim of France to the province of Texas as far as the Rio Bravo, and to all the waters running into the Missisipi, and how, by the roguery of St Denis, an agent of Crozat the merchant to whom the colony was granted for 10. years the settlements of the Spaniards at Nacogdoches, Adaïs, Assinaÿs and Natchitoches were fraudulently invited & connived at. Crozat's object was commerce, and especially Contraband with the Spaniards, and these posts were settled as convenient smuggling stages on the way to

Mexico. the history bears such marks of authenticity as place it beyond question. Govr Claiborne obtained the MS. for us, and thinking it too hazardous to risk it's loss by the way, unless a copy were retained, he had a copy taken. the original having arrived safe at Washington, he sent me the copy, which I now have. is the original still in your office? or was it among the papers burnt by the British? if lost, I will send you my copy; if preserved, it is my wish to deposit the copy for safe keeping with the Philosophical society at Philadelphia, where it will be safer than on my shelves. I do not mean that any part of this letter shall give to yourself the trouble of an answer; only desire mr Graham to see if the original still exists in your office, and to drop me a line saying yea, or nay; and I shall know what to do. indeed the MS. ought to be printed, and I see a note to my copy which shews it has been in contemplation, & that it was computed to be of 20. sheets @ 16.D. a sheet for 320. copies, which would sell at 1.D. a piece and reimburse the expence.

On the question of giving to La Motte the Consulship of Havre, I know the obstacle of the Senate. their determination to appoint natives only is generally proper, but not always. these places are for the most part of little consequence to the public; and if they can be made resources of profit to our ex-military worthies, they are so far advantageous. you and I however know that one of these raw novices, knowing nothing of the laws or authorities of his port, nor speaking a word of it's language, is of no more account than the 5th wheel of a coach. had the Senate a power of removing as well as of rejecting, I should have fears, from their foreign antipathies for my old friend Cathalan, Consul at Marseilles. his father was appointed by Dr Franklin, early in the revolutionary war, but being old, the business was done by the son. on the establishment of our present government, the commission was given by Genl Washington to the son, at the request of the father. he has been the Consul now 26. years, and has done it's duties nearly 40. years. he is a man of understanding, integrity, zeal, of high mercantile standing, an early citizen of the US. and speaks & writes our language as fluently as French. his conduct in office has been without a fault. I have known him personally and intimately for 30. years, have a great and affectionate esteem for him, and should feel as much hurt were he to be removed, as if removed myself from an office. but I trust he is out of the reach of the Senate, and secure under the wings of the Executive government. let me recommend him to your particular care and patronage, as well deserving it, and end the trouble of reading a long letter with assurances of my constant & affectionate friendship.   Th: Jefferson

RC (CLU-C); torn and edge trimmed, with missing text supplied from PoC; endorsed by Monroe. PoC (DLC); at foot of first page: "Monroe James." Enclosure: enclosure to Monroe to TJ, [22] Jan. 1816.

GOV^R MESSIER: Athanase de Mézières. The ORIGINAL MS. HISTORY, which TJ

sent to Monroe on 9 Apr. 1816, is described at that date. For Stephen Cathalan's namesake FATHER as consul at Marseilles, see Franklin, *Papers*, 26:454, 27:447, 39:447, 456; *PTJ*, 14:59, 62n, 16:554.

[1] TJ here canceled "of us."

From John F. Watson

SIR   Germantown 5 Feby 1816—

By this days mail, I Send you the 7 & 8 Vol^s of the Edinb^g Review—since our last settlement^x I have sent you the Vol^s 4, 5 & 6th ℞ mail—for which five Vol^s—(12½ Dollrs–), you may either remit me ℞ mail, or in such manner as may be most convenient to you—If notes of your State I will prefer those of Richmond state Bank—

I have within a year past become Cashier of the Bank here in Germantown, your future Vol^s will therefore be sent to you by E Earle, bookseller of Philad^a as fast as they are printed—

I am Sir Very respectfully   JOHN F WATSON

P.S.—I conclude to retain vol 8—3 or 4 days so as not to put too much in one mail at a time—

^x p^d me by N G Dufief—

RC (DLC); dateline beneath signature; endorsed by TJ as received 14 Feb. 1816 and so recorded in SJL. RC (DLC); address cover only; with PoC of

TJ to Robert Saunders, 2 Mar. 1816, on verso; addressed: "Thomas Jefferson Esqre Monticello V^a"; franked; postmarked Philadelphia, 6 Feb.

To Joseph Fox

SIR   Monticello Feb. 6. 16.

I have duly recieved your favor of Jan. ___ informing me of your intention to publish the result of your experience in the art of dying and coloring various substances used in common life; and the prospectus specifying the objects particularly. whatever doubt may have heretofore existed it must now be apparent to all that we must become a manufacturing nation, to the extent of our own wants. the aggressions of England and France on our use of the ocean for twenty years past are in proof that we must fabricate within ourselves those comforts from the use of which we are not willing to be cut off, or we must fight for their free conveyance, at the risk and expence of success. the former alternative is shortest. every endeavor therefore to instruct our citizens in the necessary processes is patriotic, and merits their encouragement and to none are these more important than to our household manufacturers, who have all to learn. to them the arts you propose to explain are peculiarly interesting.

The notice you are pleased to take of my dispositions to promote whatever may be useful to our country, is beyond the merit of the occasions I have had of manifesting them. with my best wishes for a general extension of the benefits of your work, and a just remuneration to yourself, accept the tender of my great respect.

TH: JEFFERSON

PoC (DLC); on verso of a reused address cover from James Gibbon to TJ; mutilated at seal, with missing text rewritten by TJ; at foot of text: "Mr Joseph Fox"; endorsed by TJ.

To John Barnes

DEAR SIR   Monticello Feb. 7. 16.

Your favor of Jan. 19. requests my advice as to the 4500. Dollars Treasury notes of Genl Kosciuzko's payable the 16th of April next, which of course ought to be invested in time in some other form bearing interest. I am unacquainted with the different kinds and prices of US. stock, and I would trust no other; but I think we had better as soon as it can be done advantageously, exchange it into some other stock, whatever can be obtained on the best terms. I have heard that the Treasury notes are something above par, and some US. stock below par; if so we may increase the capital by both operations. I am not certain whether the US. are not still borrowing, and on a bonus. I must therefore leave to yourself entirely the most advantageous conversion of these funds for the General. in the mean time it would be well to make his annual remittance of interest, which could not be done more safely than through the Barings. I hope you enjoy good health, as I do, altho I have been killed lately by report of very general circulation. I suppose they have a mind to be in time for what must happen ere long. ever and affectionately yours

TH: JEFFERSON

PoC (DLC); on verso of reused address cover of Philip I. Barziza to TJ, 6 Jan. 1816; at foot of text: "Mr Barnes"; endorsed by TJ.

To Patrick Gibson

Dear Sir   [Mon]ticello Feb. 7. 16.

I inclose you an order on Dr Thornton for 150. Dollars which he informed me he was ready to pay on demand as also mr John Harvie's bond for 104.56 D due on the 1st prox. which Dr Brockenborough will I suppose pay as usual when due. I have this day given an order in favor of Wm Marshall for 13.91 D and something additional for clerks tickets which the order will explain. I shall have occasion the 1st of next month for about 500.D. due some days ago, but which I have got put off in the hope of hearing that my tob^o was in Richmond. Gilmer failed to bring me either of my casks of wine from Dr Fernandez altho one of them, I think at least must have arrived as it[1] was shipt at Norfolk the 6th of January. he is gone down again and I hope will call for it. I am in hopes to recieve from you soon my quarterly account. Accept the assurance of my friendly esteem & respect

Th: Jefferson

PoC (DLC: TJ Papers, ser. 10); on verso of reused address cover of an otherwise unlocated letter from DeWitt Clinton to TJ, 8 Jan. 1816 (addressed: "Thomas Jefferson Esqr Monticello"; franked; postmarked New York, 9 Jan.; recorded in SJL as received from New York, 17 Jan. 1816); dateline faint; at foot of text: "Mr Gibson"; endorsed by TJ. Enclosures not found.

[1] Preceding five words interlined and added in margin.

To William Marshall

Sir   Monticello Feb. 7. 16.

Mr Higgenbotham presented me on your part 2 tickets in the suit of Livingston v. myself for 13.91 D for which I inclose you an order on mr Gibson. I shall be glad to recieve from you a copy of the decree, and if costs were allowed me (as I believe they were) process for their recovery against whomsoever was made responsible for them. you will percieve that provision is made in the inclosed order for the charges for these articles also. accept the assurance of my respect.

Th: Jefferson

PoC (MHi); on verso of a reused address cover from Jerman Baker to TJ, 7 Jan. 1816; at foot of text: "Mr Wm Marshall"; endorsed by TJ.

The 2 tickets were bills for costs in the suit of *Livingston v. Jefferson*, to be paid to Marshall in his capacity as clerk of the United States Circuit Court for the Virginia District. The first ticket included a charge of forty-eight cents from May 1810 for "Atto: ads [attorney at the suit of] Livingston 24. order for secy. [security] for costs 24," along with a $6.72

charge from June 1810 for "2 Copies of declaration ads Livingston" and another from December 1810 of $1.18 for "filing plea 47. order 24 filing secy: for costs 47," for a total of $8.38 (MS in DLC: TJ Papers, 190:33811; in an unidentified hand; undated; docketed on verso: "Mr Jefferson $8.38 C^ts" and "albemarle"; with TJ's calculation on verso that he owed a total of $13.91). The second ticket consisted of charges from January 1811 of $1.88 for "filing 4 additional pleas ads Livingston," forty-seven cents for "filing demurrer to his rep^l [replication] to plea of Jurisdiction," and $2.35 for "filing 5 demurrers to 5 Counts in declaration." A final charge of eighty-three cents from November 1811 covered "Judgment & Copy ads Livingston 48. filing papers 35," bringing the total for the ticket to $5.53 (MS in DLC: TJ Papers, 192:34149; in an unidentified hand; un-

dated; docketed on verso: "$5:53 Costs" and "albemarle"; with TJ's notations on verso again calculating that he owed a total of $13.91 and indicating that this sum was "pd by ord. of Feb. 7. 16 on Gibson & Jefferson").

The enclosed ORDER ON MR GIBSON for Marshall, not found, is recorded by TJ at 6 Feb. 1816: "13.91 for 2 tickets in Livingston's suit + his charge for a copy of the decree & exn." (MB, 2:1319).

When the United States Circuit Court decided the case of *Livingston v. Jefferson* on 5 Dec. 1811, COSTS WERE ALLOWED to TJ, with John Wickham serving as security. For a different charge of defendant's costs, see Decision of United States Circuit Court in *Livingston v. Jefferson*, 5 Dec. 1811, one of a group of documents on the dismissal of *Livingston v. Jefferson*; and TJ to Marshall, 13 July 1812.

To Philip Thornton

DEAR SIR   M[ontice]llo Feb. 7. 16.

I have duly received your favor of Jan. 24. and according to request have inclosed to mr Gibson of Richmond an ord[er] on you for one hundred and fifty Dollars. I was disappoint[ed] in not meeting with you at the bridge on my visit to it the l[ast] fall, however 'tout ce qui est differé n'est pas perdu,' and I found the ride between that & Poplar forest so trifling that I believe I shall be tempted to take it annually in autumn. it is but about 30. miles of good road & a passable gap. the story of my dea[th] which you mention has I suppose given a momentary pleasure to the inventor, and some political partisans who think it ought to have happened 20. years ago. however it has not affected my health which has been uninterruptedly good, nor was I in Bedford where the death happened for a month before it's period. with my best wishes for your health & happiness accept the assurance of my great esteem and respect.   TH: JEFFERSON

PoC (MHi); on verso of a reused address cover from Philip Mazzei to TJ; dateline faint; several line endings missing due to a polygraph malfunction; at foot of text: "Dr Philip Thornton"; endorsed by TJ.

TOUT CE QUI EST DIFFERÉ N'EST PAS PERDU: "not all that is postponed is lost."

From Peter Derieux

Monsieur   Richmond 8. Fev^r 1816

J'ai recu la Lettre que vous m'avés fait L'honneur de m'ecrire, et vous prie d'agreer mes remerciments des efforts que vous avés eu la bonté de faire pour m'obliger, J'en Suis aussi reconnaissant que sils m'eussent procuré le bien que j'avois lieu d'en esperer.

D'aprés ce que Mr Mazzei vous marque de la grande Surprise que lui causa notre arrivée en amerique, je dois conclure que sa memoire est une des autres facultés qui paroissent l'avoir abandonné, ou il pourroit aisement se rappeller que nous n'y vinmes pas sans son consentement, et que nous n'eussions pas quitté La France, si au lieu d'authoriser Mr Blancan Neg^t a Bordeaux de nous procurer un passage a son compte, il nous eut un bon pere ouvert les yeux Sur la nature de nos esperances a son egard en nous disant "Mes Enfants; La terre que je vous ay donné en Virginie, n'est pas bonne il sen faut de beaucoup, et quoique dans votre contrat je m'en Sois reservé L'usufruit jusquau tems que vous iriés en prendre possession, elle n'est d'aucun rapport a personne, puisquelle est en friche et n'a n'y maisons n'y fénses; comme aussi vous ne devés faire aucun fondement Sur la promesse de vous laisser les Biens qui resteront a ma mort puisque je me suis reservé la liberté den disposer autrement; et pour esperer que je fournisse aux fraix de votre etablissement en V^a, ce n'est pas mon intention; ainsi comme vous n'estes ny artisan n'y Laboureur, je vous conseille de rester dans votre patrie ou vous avés des parents riches qui pourront un jour vous mettre a L'aise, plutot que d'aller dans un pays etranger ou vous n'avés en realité d'autre ressource que la possession d'un morceau de Terre qui ne se vendroit pas pour ce que votre passage couteroit; ainsi je vous declare que je ne faciliterai point les moyens d'une Emigration dont même L'idee est reprehensible en pareille circonstance."[1]

S'il nous eut parlé dans ces termes que j'ai reconnu depuis eussent eté ceux de La verité, et quil ne se fut pas rendu caution de notre passage, et agi de maniére a nous faire croire que son intention etoit de nous traiter comme ses enfants, nous n'eussions jamais fait la folie de nous aventurer Sur de telles prospectives.—Quant au Billet dont il parle, il ne L'avoit obtenu que sous la condition expresse de n'en faire jamais usage Sinon dans le cas ou il tomberoit un jour dans la misere, et que je refuserois de le Secourir Lorsque je serois peut etre devenu Riche; Car il eut toujours cette manie de plaider pauvreté, même au sein des plus grandes superfluités de la vie.

Vous m'excuserés je vous prie, Monsieur de ne pas vous envoyer quittance de sa donation, il n'en peut attendre aucune puisque Sa grande générosité la lui a fait convertir dans un acte de Charité; et quant a la certitude que vous desirés Lui donner que cette derniére mortiffication de sa part m'est parvenue, votre assurance lui en Sera plus que Suffisante.

j'ai L'honneur d'être dans Les Sentiments les plus Respectueux Monsieur Votre très humble Sert   P. DERIEUX

EDITORS' TRANSLATION

SIR   Richmond 8. February 1816

I have received the letter you did me the honor of writing me, and I thank you for the efforts you were so kind as to make on my behalf. I am as grateful for them as if they had procured for me the benefit I had reason to expect from them.

From what Mr. Mazzei tells us of the great surprise that our arrival in America caused him, I must conclude that his memory is another of his faculties that seems to have abandoned him. Otherwise he could easily remember that we did not come without his consent and that we would not have left France if, instead of having authorized Mr. Blancan, merchant in Bordeaux, to procure us a passage and send him the bill, he would, like a good father, have opened our eyes to the nature of our expectations regarding his intentions by telling us: "My children, the land I have given you in Virginia is far from being any good, and even though in your contract I have reserved for myself the usufruct of it until you take possession, it is unprofitable to anyone, since it lies fallow and has neither houses nor fences; you must also not trust my promise to leave you my property after my death, since I have reserved the right to dispose of it otherwise; and as regards your hope that I will pay the cost of your establishment in Virginia, I have no such intention; thus, as you are neither an artisan nor a farmer, I advise you to stay in your own country, where you have rich relatives who will be able to make you comfortable someday, rather than go to a foreign country where you really have no other resources than the possession of a piece of land that is not worth the cost of your passage; therefore I declare to you that I will not facilitate an emigration, the idea of which is reprehensible under such circumstances."

If he had spoken to us in these words, the truth of which I have subsequently recognized, and if he had not provided security for our passage and acted so as to make us believe that he intended to treat us as his children, we would never have made the foolish decision to venture out with such prospects.—As for the note he mentions, he obtained it only under the express condition of never using it unless he fell into poverty and I refused to help him when I might perhaps have become rich, because he has always had this odd habit of pleading poverty, even while living in the lap of luxury.

Please excuse me, Sir, for sending you no receipt for his donation, which he cannot expect, since his great generosity has caused him to convert his gift into an act of charity; and with respect to the assurance you would like to give him that his latest mortification has reached me, your confirmation will more than suffice for him.

I have the honor of being with the most respectful sentiments Sir your very humble servant   P. DERIEUX

RC (DLC): dateline at foot of text; endorsed by TJ as received 13 Feb. 1816 and so recorded in SJL. Translation by Dr. Genevieve Moene.

[1] Omitted closing quotation mark editorially supplied.

From Peter S. Du Ponceau

SIR   Philadelphia 8th Feb. 1816

The letter which you did me the honor to write to me on the 22[d] ult° was duly laid before the Philosophical Society & the Historical Committee at their Successive meetings. The Committee met last night, & I have it in charge to return you thanks in their name for the very acceptable present of M[r] Hawkins's Sketch of the Creek Country, & the generous offer which you have made of Such other papers of an interesting nature as you may find among Your Collections from time to time, for which they feel particularly grateful.

The Committee are pleased to find from the facts which you have stated respecting the Westover Manuscript that there is Some hope that the imperfect Copy in their possession is but a transcript from the Original, which may yet be found, & in pursuing the enquiries which you have proposed to make on the Subject, you will add to the obligations which they are already under to you. They will take no order respecting the MSS. in their possession until they hear further from you.

You will hear with pleasure that our Collection of interesting papers encreases from day to day, that the Committee proceed in their work with great activity, & that we hope Soon to be able to publish a Volume. We have also the promise of Communications for the general Transactions of the Society, which, I hope, will enable us in the Course of the Year to appear once more before the world in the proper Character of a learned Society.

As there are no doubt many persons in your state who could contribute interesting Documents for our Historical Collections, the Committee would be very much obliged to you if you would take the trouble to point out to them thro' me Some of those who might be written to with success. The Committee are determined to Spare no pains to attain the object which they have in view, and as their faithful

Servant, I shall aid the good Cause with my personal exertions to the utmost of my power. I am already amply rewarded for my labours, by the opportunity which my Situation gives me of enjoying the honor of your Correspondence.

I have the honor to be
with the greatest respect
Sir Your most obed^t humble servant

PETER S. DU PONCEAU

RC (DLC); addressed: "Thomas Jefferson, Esqr Monticello Virginia"; franked; postmarked Philadelphia, 9 Feb.; endorsed by TJ as received 14 Feb. 1816 and so recorded in SJL. FC (PPAmP: APS Historical and Literary Committee Letterbook); dated 9 Feb. 1816.

To Henry Jackson

Monticello Feb. 8. 16.

I am really ashamed, Sir, to repeat at such short intervals the liberties I take with your cover. but I recieved last night a letter from mr Ticknor from Gottingen, two days after mr Terril had left us, and my anxiety that an answer should overtake him induces me to attempt it.

mr Ticknor writes me he will be in Paris in the spring as early as the roads will permit, by which time I am in hopes this letter may be there also. I ask of your goodness to retain it for him, and repeat the assurance of my great obligns & respect. TH: JEFFERSON

PoC (DLC); on verso of a reused address cover from William Short to TJ; at foot of text: "Dr Henry Jackson," with additional notation by TJ beneath that: "put under cover to Geo. Stevenson with a request to deliver it to mr Terril if not gone, & if gone, to give it the first safe conveyance he could"; endorsed by TJ. Enclosure: TJ to George Ticknor, 8 Feb. 1816. Enclosed in TJ to George P. Stevenson, [ca. 8 Feb. 1816], not found and not recorded in SJL.

To George Ticknor

DEAR SIR Monticello Feb. 8. 16.

I had written you on the 14th of Jan. by duplicates through your father and the Secretary of state, when a mr Terril, a young friend and relation of mine visited us, on his way, viâ Paris to Geneva for his education. this direct conveyance tempted me to write you a short letter by him on the 31st. he left us two days ago, & yesterday I recieved your favor of Nov. 25. the hope that this may still overtake him at Baltimore where he will embark, induces me to hazard it.

I am much gratified by the information you give me of the improvements in the editions of the Classics which you find in Germany. my knolege of them is such only as could be acquired in Paris 30. years ago, since which I have had little opportunity of information; and even at that time and place the Northern editions were but partially known to me. I must pray you therefore to avail me of your better opportunities of selecting, and to use your own judgment where you find that there is a better edition than that noted by me. and indeed many of these were not known to me, but taken on credit from their titles as stated in printed catalogues, and I have no doubt I should have been disappointed in some of them by the obsoleteness of type, it's minuteness, or other circumstance, which could not be learnt from the enunciation in the catalogue. only be so good as to remember my aversion to folios & 4^{tos} & that it overweighs a good deal of merit in the edition. the nerveless hand of a more than Septuagenaire wields a folio or 4to with fatigue, and a fixed position to read it on a table is equally fatiguing. I value explanatory notes; but verbal criticisms and various readings, not much. I am attached to the Scholia of the Greek classics because they give us the language of another age: and with the Greek classics prefer translations as convenient aids to the understanding of the author. with these recollections be so good as to exercise your own judgment & knolege freely; the value of which I can estimate from the specimens of editions noted in your letter, of which I prefer at least two thirds to those I had noticed myself. for example

Herodotus. I prefer the German edition noted by you to the Oxford of my own catalogue, because as good and cheaper.

the Plutarch's lives of Caray, I shall be delighted with as curious as well as excellent, & I shall be glad if you will add to it his specimen of Homer, his Hierocles & smaller things.

Oberlin's Tacitus to Gronovius's noted by me.

the Homer's Iliad of Heyne, in addition to that of Didymus; & I shall also be glad of his Virgil.

the Juvenal Ruperti instead of that of Schrevelius.

the Hesiod of Loesner to that noted in my catalogue.

and the German edition of Schultz' Aeschylus.

---

you confirm my choice of the Bipont Thucydides, which however I had never seen.

[455]

there being several 8vo editions of Diogenes Laertius, I leave to your judgment whether their difference of size, compared with the 2. 4^{tos} of Meibomius, are an equivalent for the differ^{ce} of merit.

the Theocritus cum scholiis of Oxford & London noted by me, I should prefer to Volknaer's because you say this has very few notes. the other edns I know to be excellent.

the edition of the Grecian orators of 2^d grade of Hanover 1699. noted by me, was chosen because cheap. it did not comprehend Gorgias, Alcidamas, & Antisthenes; but they are not material, altho' desirable, if to be had separately. Lysias & Isocrates I possess. and I suppose good separate editions of Demosthenes & Aeschylus can be had. Reiske's is too expensive, and without translations. it was among my books ceded to Congress. I paid for the 22. vols neatly bound, 150^{tt} in Paris 30. years ago.

These brief notes will shew how willingly I resign my self to your choice of editions. Your favors of Oct. 14. & 30. have not come to hand, but are not yet to be despaired of. that from London is the only one I have recieved from you since in Europe. after troubling you twice so lately, I will add to the present only a repetition of my great thankfulness for the trouble you give yourself for me, and the assurance of my friendly esteem and respect.   TH: JEFFERSON

RC (NN: Pforzheimer Collection); addressed: "George Ticknor esq. Gottingen"; endorsed by Ticknor as received 19 Apr. 1816. PoC (DLC); with additional notation by TJ at foot of text: "1st by mr Terril thro' Stevenson & Jackson. 2^d thro' mr E. Ticknor"; endorsed by TJ. Enclosed in TJ to Henry Jackson, 8 Feb. 1816, and TJ to Elisha Ticknor, 9 Feb. 1816.

Ticknor's letter of 30. Oct. 1815 is not recorded in SJL and has not been found.

From Elizabeth Trist

MY DR FRIEND   Henry 8th Feby 1816

I have heard with much concern that you were very Ill, so much so, that your life was despaird of, and your being so far from your dear connections fills my mind with Sorrow least you may not be properly attended, often have I wish'd that it was in my power to administer to your comfort—but alas it is my fate to be of little servise to my friends, severely hath my immagination figur'd that you may have stood in need of Mrs Randolphs attention, altho Burwell wou'd do every thing that he cou'd to render your situation comfortable, yet it requires more than one person to attend properly to a Person in extreme Illness—The prevailing cold like a pestilence has carried off[1] many in a few days even in this Neighbourhood I presume it is that, which has attack'd you I am uneasy and shall be, till I hear that you are well or in a fare way of recovering God grant that may be the case, at present but let me recommend it to you not to expose your self or set out on your journey home till you are quite well if you have sufficient strength to set up, and can use a pen with out fatigue to your self, I will thank you to let me hear from you, if only to say I am better It will give all at Bird wood the greatest pleasure—May Heaven spare you many years to your Country and friends among the most sincere is your old and obliged friend   E, TRIST

RC (MHi); endorsed by TJ as received   ¹ Manuscript: "of."
12 Mar. 1816 from a location "near Mar-
tinsville" and so recorded in SJL.

To Benjamin Austin

SIR   Monticello Feb. 9. 16.

Your favor of Jan. 25. is just now recieved. I am in general extremely unwilling to be carried into the newspapers. no matter what the subject; the whole pack of the Essex kennel open upon me. with respect however to so much of my letter of Jan. 9. as relates to manufactures, I have less repugnance, because there is perhaps a degree of duty to avow a change of opinion called for by a change of circumstances, and especially on a point now become peculiarly interesting.

What relates to Bonaparte stands on different ground. you think it will silence the misrepresentations of my enemies, as to my opinions of him. No Sir; it will not silence them. they had no ground, either in my words or actions, for these misrepresentations before, and cannot have less afterwards; nor will they calumniate less. there is however a consideration, respecting our own friends, which may merit attention. I have grieved to see even good republicans so infatuated as to this man, as to consider his downfall as calamitous to the cause of liberty. in their indignation against England, which is just, they seem to consider all <u>her</u> enemies as <u>our</u> friends; when it is well known there was not a being on earth who bore us so deadly a hatred. in fact he saw nothing in this world but himself; and looked on the people under him as his cattle, beasts for burthen and slaughter. promises cost him nothing when they could serve his purpose. on his return from Elba, what did he not promise? but those who had credited them a little, soon saw their total insignificance, and, satisfied they could not fall under worse hands, refused every effort after the defeat of Waterloo. their present sufferings will have a term; his iron despotism would have had none. France has now a family of fools at it's head, from whom, whenever it can shake off it's foreign riders, it will extort a free constitution, or dismount them, & establish some other on the solid basis of national right. to whine after this exorcised demon is a disgrace to republicans, and must have arisen either from want of reflection, or the indulgence of passion against principle. if any thing I have said could lead them to take correcter views, to rally to the polar principles of genuine republicanism, I could consent that that part of my letter also should go into a newspaper. this I leave to yourself and such candid friends as you may consult. there is one word in the letter however which decency towards the allied sovereigns requires should be softened. instead of <u>despots</u>, call them <u>rulers</u>. the first paragraph too of 7. or 8. lines must be wholly omitted. trusting all the rest to your discretion, I salute you with great esteem and respect.   Th: Jefferson

PoC (DLC); at foot of first page: "Benjamin Austin esq."

From Benjamin W. Crowninshield

Sir,   Navy Department February 9th 1816.

I am honoured by your letter of the 30th ultimo, in behalf of Mr Thomas M. Randolph, who is desirous of engaging in the Naval Service of the United States.

The application is filed and recorded, and his Appointment will be attended to, with deference to your request in his favour, so soon as a Resignation, or what may be considered a vacancy, shall permit.

I appreciate, with grateful sensibility, the expression of your sentiments in regard to my late Brother; and assure you, of the high estimation in which I consider you, as one of the first benefactors of our common Country.   B W Crowninshield

RC (DLC); in a clerk's hand, signed by Crowninshield; endorsed by TJ as received 14 Feb. 1816 and so recorded in SJL. RC (MHi); address cover only; with PoC of TJ to Garrit Storm, 2 Mar. 1816, on verso; addressed: "Thomas Jefferson Late President of the U. States Monticello Va"; franked; postmarked Washington, 11 Feb. FC (DNA: RG 45, ROSN, General Letterbook, 12:399).

To Joseph Delaplaine

SIR   Monticello Feb. 9. 16.

Before the receipt of your letter of Jan. 27. I had received those of Dec. 20. & Jan. 14. which remained unacknoleged. this I am certain you will pardon when I assure you that I pass from four to six hours of every day of my life at the writing table, answering letters in nine tenths of which neither my interests nor inclinations are engaged. this mass of labor obliges me to marshal it's calls, and to answer first what presses most. your two preceding letters related to a portrait on which I had, in one or more former ones,[1] given you all the information I possessed, and having nothing new to add, I thought you would excuse my not repeating the old.

I have to thank you for the print of mr Fulton. it is a good likeness and elegantly executed.   you request me, in your last letter, to give you 'the[2] facts of my life, birth, parentage, profession, time of going to Europe, returning, offices Etc.' I really have not time to do it, and still less inclination. to become my own biographer is the last thing in the world I would undertake. No. if there has been any thing in my course worth the public attention, they are better judges of it than I can be myself, and to them it is my duty to leave it.   there was a work published in England under the title of 'Public characters' in which they honored me with a place. I never knew, nor could suspect, who wrote what related to myself; but it must have been some one who had been in a situation to obtain tolerably exact and minute information. I do not now possess the book, and therefore cannot say whether there were inaccuracies in it. with my excuse for thinking I ought not to meddle with this subject, accept the tender of my respects.   TH: JEFFERSON

RC (PHi: Dreer Collection); at foot of text: "Mr Delaplaine." PoC (DLC).

PUBLIC CHARACTERS was an annual publication. TJ's biography appeared in the volume covering 1800–01 and issued the latter year in London. Although TJ owned two volumes of that work (Sowerby, no. 402) and they were listed in *Catalogue of U.S. Library*, they were not among the books TJ sent to Washington in 1815. Subsequently canceled in the library's own copy of its catalogue, they were omitted from later versions.

[1] Reworked from "in a former one."
[2] Omitted opening quotation mark editorially supplied.

To Elisha Ticknor

Monticello Feb. 9. 16.

Your favor of Jan. 26. is at hand, and I had the happiness by the same mail to recieve a letter from your son dated Gottingen Nov. 25. this requiring an immediate answer, I avail myself of your kindness, and now inclose it with a request that you will be so good as to forward it. I am much pleased to learn that he is so well satisfied with his situation at Gottingen. but Paris and Rome will please and profit him more. he will return fraught with treasures of science which he could not have found in a country so engrossed by industrious pursuits as ours. but he will be a sample to our youth of what they ought to be, and a model for imitation in pursuits so honorable, so improving and so friendly to good morals. Accept the assurance of my great esteem and respect.   T<small>H</small>: J<small>EFFERSON</small>

RC (MBPLi); at foot of text in an unidentified hand: "The above inclosed letter was forwarded pr the Brig Independence on the 17 Feby, 1816, bound to Amsterdam." PoC (MHi); on verso of a reused address cover from Horatio G. Spafford to TJ; at foot of text: "Mr Elish Ticknor"; endorsed by TJ. Recorded in SJL as a letter to Elisha Ticknor enclosing a "dupl to G. T." Enclosure: TJ to George Ticknor, 8 Feb. 1816.

From Joseph Delaplaine

D<small>EAR SIR</small>,   Philadelphia February 10th 1816.

I have taken the liberty of writing to you several times lately, & have not been favoured with a reply.—

I am desirous to place your portrait & a biographical sketch of your life in the second half volume of my work, & shall do so if it is possible to get an <u>approved</u> portrait of you. Mr Wood one of the most extraordinary portrait painters of the present day has been sent by me to Washington to paint the portraits of President Madison Mr Munroe, Mr Clay &c. He is now busily engaged in painting those characters.

I regret exceedingly that I cannot afford to send Mr Wood to your house for the purpose of painting your portrait. If sir, any means for effecting this very desirable object, should present to you, do have the goodness to inform me & Mr Wood shall proceed accordingly thither.—I will venture to affirm, that for <u>truth of likeness,</u> Mr Wood has no rival in this, or any other country.

I beg sir, you will have the goodness to furnish me with a sketch of your life. Birth, parentage—Education—profession—times of going abroad—offices &c &c &c. The late President Adams & Mr Jay as well as other characters have readily complied with my requests on the subject. I pledge my honor, that nothing of politics, religion, or any other subject, which can possibly offend, shall appear in the Repository.—

In the second half volume of my work the portrait & life of the late Peyton Randolph will be given.—The Honble Judge Tucker of Williamsburg refers me for a small sketch of his life to you in these words "Mr Jefferson is probably the only man now alive that can do justice to the character of this truly great and good man." Can I trouble you sir for a few facts.

I enclose for your acceptance a portrait of Mr Jay.—

With great respect I am your obed^t s^t   JOSEPH DELAPLAINE

RC (DLC); at foot of text: "Thomas Jefferson Esqr"; endorsed by TJ as received 16 Feb. 1816 and so recorded in SJL. RC (DLC); address cover only; with PoC of TJ to George Watterston, 2 Mar. 1816, on verso; glued to backing sheet, with address illegible; postmarked Philadelphia, 11 Feb.

Gilbert Stuart's portrait of John JAY was engraved by William S. Leney and included in *Delaplaine's Repository*, vol. 1, plate opp. p. 157.

From George Fleming

SIR   Healing Springs Louisa Feby 10. 1816

On the subject [of]¹ your hempbreak a thought occurr'd to me since I received your letter which I submit to your judgement. On the axis of the wallower instead of arms 15 in long, suppose a cast iron wheel 15 in diam^r with cogs only half way round   & on the face of the head block instead of a horn, a curved   piece of cast iron 30 in long & 4 broad, with cogs corresponding in number &^c with those on the cast wheel, the upper cog on this curved iron should be one half inch longer than the one next it, for it will then more certainly be taken by the upper cog on the wheel, this will facilitate the introduction of the following cogs to their respective places & prevent butting, There would be some danger when the head block recoils, that the long cog in the upper part of the curved iron would strike the lower cogs of the wheel, to prevent which, the cogs of the wheel should gradually shorten till the last cog should be half an inch shorter than the first, a corresponding shape must be given to the cogs of the curved iron, that is, if the first cog is $3\frac{1}{2}$ inches, the 2nd will be 3 i, & every following cog must be gradually longer till the last cog is

$3\frac{1}{2}$ in. The wheel & head must then run free, great exactness is necessary in the forms for the castings they should be made at home & experimented on till they are exactly adjusted, a Mill wright would make them in 2 days & the irons would cost 5 or 6$.

The arms at first view appear to have one advantage over a Wheel, they give 2 strokes for one revolution of the wallower, this but one, but the power of this wheel 15 i dia^r is to the power of an arm 15 i long, inversely as the semi dia^r of the wheel is to the length of the arm, ie. as 15 is to $7\frac{1}{2}$ or 2 to 1. or presenting but half the resistance the velocity doubles. It will also raise the weight much higher & as the velocities of falling bodies are uniformly accelerated thr'o their whole descent, the effect of the stroke must be augmented by that cause, to show this, The arm of 15 i long cannot I think with advantage take the horn at an angle greater than 30° below the horizontal plane passing thr'o the axis, if so, it must drop the horn at the same angle above that plane, the arm must then have described an arc of 60° & while doing so it must have raised the head block to a height equal to the chord of that arc, but the chord of 60° is equal to Radius, therefore the break will be raised 15 i high by an arm 15 i long.—The whole circumference of the cog wheel 47.124 [i] the half or part with cogs is 23.562 i this acting on the curved iron must make the head block describe an arc exactly the same length, let the moving part of the break be 12 feet, this arc 23.562 is the measure of an angle whose quantity may be found a Rad 12 f gives a circumf^e 904.7808 i then say as the circle is to this arc so is 360° to 9.°22. The chord of this arc is the measure of the breaks ascent, but as the chord of every arc is double the sine of half the angle it measures, the length of that chord (ie) the perpendicular ascent of the break may be found, bisect that angle 4.°41 & say as Rad is to the sine 4.°41 so is the length of the break 12 f. to half its ascent 11.7 × 2 = 23.4 in. I once projected a thing for this use 2 fluted cast iron cylinders deriving motion from a small water wheel spur cog & trundle, the dispatch would have been rapid, the hemp well broke but this is better I think.—

Nothing can be more simple than the construction of a steam engine for all, perhaps more domestic purposes than your letter requires, recollect the figure I sent to you, a strong iron bar connects the steam & water pistons, an arm is fixed in that bar for the purpose of turning the cocks, let a horizontal shaft be connected with that arm, let this shaft go thr'o the kitchen, & let the other end play on a hinge in the wall 7 or 8 feet from the floor, let a hominy pestle a dough pestle & a churn staff be appendant to that shaft with a small contrivance to turn the spit, it [is]^2 obvious as the piston bar goes up

& down the whole machinery is at work, pipes for raising the water need not be larger in the bore than a musket, the power of steam necessary to do all this is trifling, the boiler may be worked into & even with the back of the fireplace or it may be of a rectangular form the perpendicular in the fire back the horizontal into & even with the hearth, thus a greater surface is exposed to the heat, no room is lost, nor an atom more of fuel consumed than without it,—In 2 or 3 Months if I can I shall go to Phil[a] to have the model of my projet executed. Be pleased to accept my gratefull acknowlegements for your polite attention to my last & believe me to be as I have ever been most respectfully & sincerely Y[rs]   GEO. FLEMING

PS On further reflection I think it probable this construction of y[e] hempbreak may be subject to this hasard that the cog wheel when freed from the weight may revolve too quick & meet the head block too soon, one cog less would remedy this, or I would rather recommend two more rounds in the wallower which will answer the same end & at same time increase the levatic power; but after all we shall be best instructed by trials.—

RC (DLC); edge chipped; addressed: "Thomas Jefferson Esq[re] Monticello Albemarle"; franked; postmarked Goochland Courthouse, 19 Feb. 1816, and Charlottesville, 21 Feb.; endorsed by TJ

as received 21 Feb. 1816 and so recorded in SJL.

[1] Omitted word editorially supplied.
[2] Omitted word editorially supplied.

To Joseph Milligan

DEAR SIR   Monticello Feb. 11. 16.

The last letter recieved from you was of Aug. 20. on the 27th Oct. I wrote you a statement of our balance 136.75 D and that I should that day write to mr Gibson to remit it to you. I wrote to him the next day, and the day following set out for Bedford and was absent two months, so that I never heard from mr Gibson of the actual remittance. yet[1] I have no reason to doubt it, and the less as I think you would have been so kind as to note it to me had it not been made. mr Gibson's account for our last quarter, which would shew this is not yet recieved. being thus without positive information, I do not feel easy, and therefore pray your information on the subject.

I inclose you the copy of a letter just recieved from Gen[l] Duane on the subject of the translation of Tracy's book. he has improperly headed his account with my name; because he was to have the book translated & printed at his own expense, & for his own sole benefit. I had no interest in it & engaged nothing more than to let him have the original to translate. you ment^d when here his offer of it to you for 60.D. the expense of translat^g and that you would accept it, and on that I promised you to revise and correct the translation, which, with the original, came to me some time after, from you as I suppose, for no letter came with it. I shall be glad, if you will permit me, to pay the 60.D. to Genl Duane, and place it in account between you and me. I can conveniently give him an order to receive the money on the spot: and I pray you to write me on this subject by the first mail, as I must give some answer to Genl Duane.

the vast accumulation of letters, during my absence in Bedford, has kept me employed in writing answers till within a few days. I have now entered on the revisal of the translation. it is a most laborious business, and will engage me 4. or 5. hours a day for a month. nothing but my promise to you could engage me to go through such a piece of drudgery. but I will do it, and the translation shall be an exact one, now dreadfully otherwise. I had nearly as lieve translate it anew. I have got through about a fourth; in about a fortnight I shall be half through, and will then forward that much to you, confident that with that ahead, I shall be able to keep up with the printing. I have heretofore asked several books of you which I have not recieved. I will state below such of them as I still request you to send, with as little delay as you can, and with them the cost, which shall be remitted the next month being my annual epoch for paying up the accounts of the year. with a repetition of my prayer to hear from you immediately I tender you the assurance of my esteem and respect.

Th: Jefferson

Moore's Greek grammar translated by Ewen.
Ainsworth's Dict. abridged in 2. v. 8vo
Virgil Delphini, the notes in English. lately printed in Phila.
Bailey's Ovid (not the Delphin one as first requested)
Mair's Tyro's dictionary.
Cornelius Nepos.
A Cornelius Nepos & Ovid were also sent you to be bound

PoC (DLC); on verso of a reused address cover from Claude Alexandre Ruelle to TJ; at foot of first page: "Mr Millegan"; endorsed by TJ. Enclosure: John B. Smyth (for William Duane) to TJ, 2 Feb. 1816, and enclosure.

LIEVE is a variant of "lief" (*OED*). TJ sought a copy of the GREEK GRAMMAR by

Samuel Blatchford, *Elements of the Greek Language, Exhibited, for the most part, in New Rules, made easy to the memory by their brevity: being a Translation of Dr. Moor's Celebrated Greek Grammar. To which are added, Greville Ewing's Continuation and Syntax* (New York, 1807).

[1] Word reworked from "so that."

From John Barnes

DEAR SIR—   George Town Co^a 12th Febuary 1816—

The long wished for letter from the good Genl has at length Arrived and I hasten herewith to inclose you Duplicate—you will perceive by my letter of the 19 Ult^o the app^t Balance of his a/c in my hands was \$1130.$\frac{69}{100}$ exclusive of his Treasury Notes \$4.500—bearing 5$\frac{2}{5}$ Int. due 16 April—to be then funded—I may therefore count on remitting him £200 Ster^g on the best terms going—will I presume—Amo^t to somewhere ab^t \$950—to \$1000—with the expectation of another & like Remittance to follow in the fall—will I trust—be satisfactory to the General

I am quite Anxious to be favor'd with a line from you, lest indisposition may have been the cause of my not receiving One—

yours most Respectfully, with the greatest Esteem,

JOHN BARNES.

RC (ViU: TJP-ER); at foot of text: "Thomas Jefferson Esqr Monticello—Virg^a"; with enclosure on verso; endorsed by TJ as received 16 Feb. 1816 and so recorded in SJL.

The GOOD GEN^L was Tadeusz Kosciuszko.

RC (ViU: TJP-ER); at foot of text: "Thomas Jefferson Esqr Monticello—Virg^a"; with enclosure on verso; endorsed by TJ as received 16 Feb. 1816 and so recorded in SJL.

ENCLOSURE

Tadeusz Kosciuszko to John Barnes

SIR—   Soleure in Switzerland 26^h Novr 1815.

I had the honor to receive your letter dated the 22^d June 1814. by which you have sent me, a Memorand^m containing, a detail, of the recovery, that you have made—on my Acco^t and the Notice of two remittances each of £400—which you have made to Messrs Barring Brothers & Co equally on my Acco^t—I shall be obliged to you,—to send me Copy—of my Acco^t settled—at your House—at the End of the year—in this expectation—

I have the honor to assure you Sir:—of my Esteem & Consideration the most distinguished   (signed) KOSCUSZKO—

I Embrace, my Dear & Respectable Mr Jefferson,—

Tr (ViU: TJP-ER); entirely in Barnes's hand; on verso of covering letter; at head of text: "Duplicate"; at foot of text: "Mr John Barnes, George Town—in America."

For Barnes's LETTER DATED THE 22^D JUNE 1814 and the MEMORAND^M, see note to Barnes to TJ, 22 June 1814, and enclosed account printed there.

From José Corrêa da Serra

DEAR SIR   Philadelphia 12. Feby 1816

I have found at my return in Philadelphia near a month ago, your kind letter for which i would have immediately returned my most grateful thanks, if it did not contain two articles to which it was my duty to answer, viz. the cements for cisterns, and the papers of Captain Lewis. As to the first, the books containing the prescriptions were not at hand, and i could attain them with some difficulty, but having after unavoidable delays had sight of them, i am able to send you the contents.

1. Cendrèe de Tournay, ciment qui a La proprieté de se consolider dans L'eau et de devenir au bout de quelques annèes plus dur que Les pierres auxquelles il sert de Liaison.

Melez de la chaux pure avec La cendre du charbon de terre, jusques a ce que Le melange pese $\frac{1}{4}$ de plus qu'un egal volume de chaux pure—Il est necessaire d'ecraser La cendrèe jusques a ce qu'elle fasse une pâte unie et douce, et par La seule force du frottement, et sans y mettre plus d'eau qu'il n'en faut pour L'eteindre

2° Imitation de pouzzolane dont L'efficace est prouvèe—Prenez une moitiè chaux, un quart brique pilée bien pulverisée et passée au tamis, un quart machefer egalement bien pulverisé.

3° Ciment pour Les jointures des citernes particulierement de celles destinèes a garder du vin—Prenez une pierre de chaux, que vous Laisserez et etendre[1] a L'air prenez du sang de boeuf, avant qu'il ait caillè, c'est a dire encore chaud; melez ces deux substances, en Les fouettant Longtems ensemble, jusques a ce qu'elles aient La consistance d'une colle epaisse, enduisez en toutes Les jointures.

General observations for the construction of good cisterns—1° to avoid any gravel or stony nucleus of any size whatever in the cement—2° to spread the cement which must cover all the inside (l'enduit) in thin strata successively and equally. It is a work of patience and attention, which is well repaid by the excellence of the cistern.

I am sorry the cisterns of Charleston did not occupy my attention, but i have strong reasons to suspect, they are not well constructed. The water of Charleston is far from being so good as rain water generally is, and differs from it so much in taste and in salubrity, that it is more than probable that in so low a situation and so surrounded by water as Charleston is, the cisterns admit by filtration other waters Now what they take in there, would be Let out if they were situated in a high and dry ground.

Now for Captain Lewis's papers, i have found it a difficult work, but you may rely on my zeal and assiduity to fulfil your wishes. Several times have i called on Mrs Barton and twice on Mr Pennington her brother, who has great influence on her, and assists her in the arrangement of her affairs, but i am not more advanced than in the beginning. The D^r has Left such an immense heap of papers, and in such disorder; the reclamations for papers and books are so many, that i conceive how the poor Lady is embarrassed how to do. It seems that for a great number of years the Drs Library and cabinet followed the same Law that Dante has inscribed on the gate of hell

Uscite di speranza o voi che entrate.

But i hope there will be an end to this suspence; you will know the result.

The Letters you directed to Knoxville i have also received here, and cannot but blush at the excessive praises, which your goodness bestows on me, but as to the danger of Mr Gilmer catching from me an immoderate taste for ornamental Knowledge, you may well change your opinion, and he will tell it himself—Curious and strange as it may seem, he has received from me during all the voyage more hints and dissertations about what i conceive to be the real interests of his country and the means of her reaching the high destinies to which it seems destined by nature, than even about the plants we were meeting. He must have wished to find many of his countrymen so zealous on that subject as his european companion; as i Love the country and Like his mind and his heart, my grand point was to help him with whatever was in my power to do that good which i myself would have attempted, and fit him to se mergire civilibus undis with glory to himself and his country.

I come Lastly to the Kindness you show to me, in the interest you take in the future steps of my Life. As Long as i Live will i feel your goodness, and keep a grateful sense of so much kindness. Your judgement of European present and future affairs, is what myself think; but i see Little chance of escaping the necessity of returning there. What i can do is not rashly to chuse Paris for my residence, till i see the turn things take. As Long as i shall remain on this continent i will perform with devotion and gratitude my annual pilgrimage to Monticello, and when in Europe i will turn very often my eyes to the West and think of the real greatness and dignity of the man who has Laid such a claim to my respect and heartfelt gratitude.

I am most feelingly and sincerely yours

J. Corrèa de Serra

[467]

RC (DLC); dateline at foot of text; addressed: "Thomas Jefferson Esq Monticello Albemarle County Virginia"; franked; postmarked Philadelphia, 13 Feb.; endorsed by TJ as received 21 Feb. 1816 and so recorded in SJL; with TJ's notation: "Cement." Translation by Dr. Genevieve Moene.

1. CENDRÈE DE TOURNAY . . . ENDUISEZ EN TOUTES LES JOINTURES: "1. Tournay ashes, cement that has the property of solidifying in water and becoming after a few years harder than the stones it bonds. Mix pure quicklime with coal ashes until the mixture weighs $\frac{1}{4}$ more than an equal volume of pure lime. It is necessary to crush the cinders until they form a smooth and soft paste, only by rubbing it, and without adding any more water than necessary. 2. Imitation pozzolana whose efficiency is proven. Take a half measure of lime, a quarter of crushed brick, well ground and put through a sieve, and a quarter of clinker also well ground. 3. Cement for joints in cisterns, particularly for those made to hold wine. Take limestone that you will spread out in the open air; take some ox blood, before it coagulates, that is to say while it is still warm; mix these two substances by whipping them together for a long time, until they have the consistency of a thick glue, and smear over all the joints."

At some point Corrêa also sent TJ a similar note containing directions for cistern cement, which states that "In the Cours complet d'Agriculture edited by the Abbé Rozier and written by the Frenchmen the more deeply versed in each of the branches, in the second edition, in the article Citerne, and in the articles Tonneau and Foudre, in which all the details are given for building the cisterns for the keeping and conservation of wine, the following cements are described: 1º Brique pilée et tamisée fine melée a la chaux vive au lieu de gravier 2º What they call 'Cendrèe de Tournay' ciment de chaux et cendres de charbon de terre, bien melees ensemble jusques a ce que le ciment pese un quart de plus que la chaux simple — Il durcit sous l'eau et devient plus dur que les pierres qu'il lie 3. Dans les angles et dans les jointures du mur, ou les crevasses sont plus aisement faites, on employe pour les lier davantage et les rendre impermeables, le ciment suivant — Eteignez une pierre de chaux vive, avec du sang de boeuf chaud, avant d'avoir caillè, melez et fouettez longtems jusques a consistance de colle epaisse ['1. Pounded and finely sifted brick, mixed with quicklime instead of gravel 2. What they call "Tournay ashes," cement made of lime and coal ashes, mixed together well until the cement weighs a quarter more than the plain lime. It hardens under water and becomes harder than the stones it holds together 3. In the angles and joints of the wall, where cracks are more easily made, the following cement is used to connect them better and make them waterproof. Turn some quicklime into slaked lime, add warm ox blood, before it coagulates, mix and whip for a long time until it has the consistency of thick glue']. By all the details given in this book, it seems that every cement employed in cisterns must be employed in slight layers successively patiently and carefully applied with the aim of making them a solid and tight body without any the slightest vacuity" (MS in DLC: TJ Papers, 206:36691; in Corrêa's hand; undated and unsigned; endorsed by TJ: "Recipe. Cement." Translation of French section by Dr. Genevieve Moene). François Rozier edited the *Cours Complet d'Agriculture* until his death in 1793. The first volume of the series, which consisted of an alphabetically arranged collection of essays by different authors, was published in Paris in 1781, with a total of twelve volumes published by 1805. The articles "Citerne" ("Tank"), "Foudre" ("Cask"), and "Tonneau" ("Barrel") appear in vols. 3:366–73, 5:16–8, and 9:419–36, respectively.

L'ENDUIT: "the coating." The text inscribed above the GATE OF HELL in Canto 3 of Dante's *Inferno* includes the phrase "Lasciate ogne speranza, ch'entrate" ("Abandon every hope, you who enter") (Maria Picchio Simonelli, ed., *Inferno III* [1993], 10, 17). For the LETTERS YOU DIRECTED TO KNOXVILLE, see

TJ to Corrêa, 1 Jan. 1816. SE MERGIRE CIVILIBUS UNDIS: "Now I become all action, and plunge into the tide of civil life" (Horace, *Epistles*, 1.1.16, in Fair-clough, *Horace: Satires, Epistles and Ars Poetica*, 252–3).

[1] Manuscript: "eteindre."

From George P. Stevenson

SIR   Baltimore February 12th 1816

Your's covering a letter for Paris is this moment received—; the gentleman who is expected to take charge of it for you has not yet presented himself to me—There is no opportunity hence to France and should none occur in a few days I will forward your letter to my house in New York, who will send it forward immediately, as there are daily conveyances thence—I need not repeat, how much pleasure I take in always fulfilling your wishes—

Very Respectfully   GEO: P. STEVENSON

RC (DLC); endorsed by TJ as received 16 Feb. 1816 and so recorded in SJL. RC (Mrs. Henry Howe Richards, Groton, Mass., 1947); address cover only; with PoC of TJ to John Barnes, 14 Mar. 1816, on verso; addressed: "Thomas Jefferson Esq[r] Monticello near Milton V[a]"; stamped; postmarked Baltimore, 12 Feb.

For TJ's letter COVERING one FOR PARIS, see note to TJ to Henry Jackson, 8 Feb. 1816. Dabney C. Terrell was EXPECTED TO TAKE CHARGE OF IT.

From Joseph C. Cabell

DEAR SIR,   Senate Chamber. 14 Feb: 1816.

M[r] Miller's bill has passed. The Bill respecting the central college has also passed—but with modifications. The bill respecting the navigable waters of the commonwealth, with Col: Greene's amendments, has also passed. your various letters of late have been gratefully received: and your copy of the books in the national Library has been deposited in the Council chamber. I am compelled to write you in great haste: but will give you further particulars by the next mail.

With sentiments of the greatest regard, I remain d[r] Sir, y[r] ob[t] serv[t]

JOSEPH C. CABELL

RC (ViU: TJP-PC); endorsed by TJ as received 16 Feb. 1816 and so recorded in SJL. RC (DLC); address cover only; with PoC of TJ to Richard Peters, 6 Mar. 1816, on recto and verso; addressed: "M[r] Jefferson Monticello"; franked; postmarked Richmond, 14 Feb.

From Stephen Cathalan

Marseilles the 15th February 1816
by my Last of the 6th January ult° I acknowledged you Receipt of
your kind favour of the 3^d July;

    This is to Inclose you, Bill of Loading and Invoice of one case Containing 50 Bottles hermitage white wine & one case Maccarony Shipped on the Brig Pilot of Phil^a [M^l?] Dixon Master, bound for Philad^a & consigned to the Colector of that district, amounting to F248–02 which Please to pass on my Credit; Messrs Jourdan & Fils (who have Lost their old Father 83 years age at that epoqua) assures me that the quality of this wine will Satisfy your Taste;—they have Sent me 240 Bottles <u>vin</u> <u>Sec</u> for Mr P^{ce} Butler of Phil^a which they Say is what is the most natural quality to that Territory, & which Mr Butler as well as the English in General Preffer, whilst the Liquoreux is produced from few vineyards, Reaped at perfect maturity; as to the maccarony, there is Two qualities, this article, Tho' we appear to enjoy the Free Port, pays as well as all the Imports, the duty of Consumption, when not declared for Réexportation, & not under the keys of the Custom, which been on this article not Important enough for Such formality at ƒ20 ℔ 100K or 200 Cw. & 10 ℔c^t above Duty, renders it Dear & Scarce on acc^t of the Short Crop of wheat at naples & Sicily; it for that motive I have not Sent you As much as you asked; but I will order a Small parcel at naples which on arival I will declare for Réexportation, by which you have Soon from me a fresh Supply & I hope at Lower Price;—

    as to the wine of nice, & to our old Friend Mr Sasserno, I beg your Refference to the herein Copy of the house who Succeeded to his Commerce long before he Died, in answer to mine of the 3^d ult° in which I Sent them a Copy of your Paragraph Relative to him & Said wine;—and as Since, I have not heard of them, I wrote them on the 19th Ins^t to entreat a quick dispatch of their expected Invoice;

    Mr F^{ois} Durand of Perpignan by his Letter of the 7th Ins^t Informs me that by the description I Transmitted him of the wine of Roussillon you wish to procure, he is acquainted with the exact quality you want, & that he was preparing to Send it to me;—I Then hope Both parcels will reach me in time to embrace the opportunity of an american vessel which will Sail for the cheasapeack about the end of this month; as the Pilot will Sail on Tomorow; about the Inconveniencies of the actual Freedom of the Port & Territory of Marseilles I am as well as the Greatest part of the Merchants of this city, of the opinion of a Printed Memorial, I Send it to you herein Inclosed, Confident of the Kind Interest you Bear for Marseilles & it's prosperity; The Intercourse with the united States is active, but the Benefits are hitherto Small, which is not Suprising after what has happened;—however it is hoped that This Place & France will Soon recover from what we Suffered by the Revolution of March Last, & enjoy of the Benefit of a Lasting Peace, which if it Costed So Dear, is not the fault of the king, but of the ones who Parjured of their oath of allegiance; Reffering you to the news Papers, meantime I may write you in not Such a Great haste, & wishing you Should once more visit France & Marseilles, as I despair to ever visit The united States, & Monticello!!! I have the honor to be with a Great Respect & I dare to add with a Constant & Sincere Friendship

Dear sir

your most obed^t & Devoted serv^t STEPHEN CATHALAN.

Mr C. D. Coxe our Late Consul at Tunis who Left this on the 1st January for Philad^a told me he will visit you Soon & has Promised me to Give you Details on me & family with whom he resided for a Little while in my house;

RC (MHi); one word illegible; at foot of text: "Thos Jefferson Esq^e"; endorsed by TJ as received 16 May 1816 and so recorded in SJL, which mistakenly dates the letter 25 Feb. Enclosures: (1) bill of lading and invoice, not found. (2) *Mémoire sur les Inconvéniens de la Franchise du Port de Marseille, Sur la nécessité de supprimer les barrières intérieures, et sur les moyens de faire jouir le commerce de cette ville de la plus grande liberté possible* (Marseille, 1816; possibly Poor, *Jefferson's Library*, 11 [no. 681]). Other enclosure printed below.

VIN SEC: "dry wine." LIQUOREUX: "sweet." The PARAGRAPH RELATIVE TO HIM & SAID WINE was probably taken from TJ to Cathalan, 3 July 1815. The REVOLUTION OF MARCH LAST was Napoleon's brief return to power.

ENCLOSURE

Amant Spreafico to Stephen Cathalan

Nice 9 Janvier 1816

Nous nous empressons de repondre à la lettre que vous nous avez fait l'honneur de nous écrire le 3 Courant, et de vous témoigner combien nous sommes sensible et reconnaissant à la part que vous avez pris à la perte de M^r V Sasserno,[1] Sa veuve qui Se trouve dans ce moment à Paris en Sera instruite et en nos qualité de Son fondé de pouvoir nous vous prions en agréer toute Sa reconnaissance; Si elle passe à son retour dans votre ville elle Se fera un devoir de vous Saluer.

Bonne note est prise de la commission que vous nous donnez de 200 B^{lles} bon vin vieux de Bellet; c'est une liqueur rare et chere dans ce moment, cependant nous nous obligeons de vous le fournir Sous 15me au même prix de f 165 les 100 Bout^{lles} caisses & port a bord compris:[2] Si nous vous demandons un delai de 15 jours pour vous faire cet envoi, c'est que desirant servir Mr Jefferson comme il le mérite, nous allons mettre en perce une Barrique qui a cinq ans, vin que nous avons fait nous même et qui est três bon; vous en jugerez par une B^{lle} que nous remetterons au Capitaine qui sera chargé des 2 caisses. quant au montant nous en prévaudrons Sur vous, Monsieur, conformément à votre ordre.

nous avons l'honneur d'être avec estime et consideration &^{ca}

Par P^{RE} DE MAGES & Co — (Signé) AMANT SPREAFICO.

Monsieur le consul, L'amitié qui me liait avec Mr Sasserno et celle que lui portait Mr Jefferson m'engage à repondre à l'article de votre lettre, concernant le consulat de Nice; j'ose M^r Le Consul réclamer en ma faveur, ce titre d'honneur, avec l'obligation de céder cette honnorable place au fils de mon ancien ami, dans l'espace de deux ans époque à la quelle il aura acquit L'expérience nécessaire pour la remplir dignement; il se trouve dans ce moment auprês d'un oncle qui reside à Paris, et qui doit venir se fixer dans notre ville en may prochain; il laisse[3] Son neveu chez M Mr D^{que} André & Cottier Banquier pour S'y former au commerce, dela il l'enverra en Angleterre pour S'y perfection[ner] dans la langue anglaise, qu'il connait déja. Cet oncle nommé Mr Arson, possede une fortune assez consequente, il a acquit dans notre ville pour 300 Mille francs de bien-fonds; il aime beaucoup Son neveu qui merite bien Son affection, ainsi M^r le consul, Si je reclame votre protection auprês de votre gouvernement ce n'est absolument que pour être utile au fils d'un ami qui mettait toute Sa confiance en moi, et auquel je Serais bien aise de procurer une place, aussi honnorable et qui le rendrait indépendant du gouvernement Sous lequel il doit vivre.

Veuillez je vous prie M^r Le Consul, m'honnorer d'une réponse & Si vous entrevoyez que je puisse obtenir la place que je reclame pour ne la remplir que pendant deux ans, m'obligeant de la céder au fils de mon ami, qui parlera & écrira l'anglais; quant à moi je vous avoue que je ne comprends pas du tout cette Langue — J'ai l'honneur d'être &c &c

(Signé) AMANT[4] SPREAFICO

E D I T O R S '   T R A N S L A T I O N

Nice 9 January 1816

We hasten to reply to the letter you did us the honor of writing on the third of this month and to let you know how appreciative and grateful we are for the interest you have taken on the occasion of the loss of Mr. Victor Sasserno. His widow, who is in Paris at the moment, will be informed of this, and in our capacity as her authorized representatives, we ask you to accept her gratitude. If, upon her return, she passes through your city, she will consider it her duty to visit you.

We take note of your order for 200 bottles of good, aged, Bellet wine. This liqueur is rare and expensive at the moment. However, we are determined to obtain it for you in the next two weeks at the same price of 165 francs per 100 bottles, boxes and shipping included. If we ask you for a 15-day delay before making this shipment, it is because, in order to serve Mr. Jefferson as he should be, we are going to tap a barrel, aged 5 years, of a very good wine that we made ourselves. You will judge of it by a bottle that we will deliver to the captain who will be entrusted with the 2 boxes. As for the payment, we will charge it to you, Sir, according to your orders.

We have the honor to be, with respect and consideration etc.

By Pierre de Mages & Company—(Signed) Amant Spreafico.

Mr. Consul, my friendship with Mr. Sasserno and his with Mr. Jefferson induces me to reply to the portion of your letter regarding the consulate at Nice. Mr. Consul, I dare request in my favor this title of honor, with the obligation of relinquishing this honorable position to the son of my old friend, in the space of two years time, when he will have acquired the experience necessary to fill it properly. He is at the moment staying with an uncle who lives in Paris and is supposed to come and settle in our city next May. He will leave his nephew at the firm of Messieurs Dominique André & Cottier, bankers, to be trained in commerce. From there he will send him to England to perfect his knowledge of the English language, which he already knows. This uncle, named Mr. Arson, has a rather large fortune. He has acquired 300 thousand francs worth of property in our city. He is very fond of his nephew, who well deserves his uncle's affection. Hence, Mr. Consul, if I request your protection in dealing with your government, it is absolutely only to be useful to the son of a friend, who has placed all his trust in me and for whom I would be happy to procure a position as honorable as this one, which would make him independent of the government under which he must live.

Please, Mr. Consul, be so kind as to honor me with a reply, if you feel that there is the slightest chance I might obtain the position I am requesting to occupy for only two years, obliging myself then to relinquish it to my friend's son, who will speak and write English. As for myself, I confess that I do not understand that language at all—I have the honor to be etc. etc.

(Signed) Amant Spreafico

Tr (MHi); edge trimmed; in an unidentified hand, with attestation in Cathalan's hand: "⚘ Copy Stephen Cathalan"; notation, adjacent to dateline and repeated beneath first signature: "Copie" ("Copy"); at head of text: "Mr Etnne Cathalan Consul Gl des Etats Unis d'Amerique Marseille." Translation by Dr. Genevieve Moene.

The fils de mon ancien ami was Victor Adolphus Sasserno.

[1] Manuscript: "S. Sassereno."
[2] Near this point, in left margin, TJ noted: "1.65 = <.32> .31 cents = 22d a bottle."
[3] Manuscript: "il aisse."
[4] Manuscript: "Amand."

Notes on Wine Consumption

1816.   Wines
Feb. 15. rec^d quarter
   cask Port wine
July 21. it is out

} 120. bottles have lasted 156. days which is 3. bottles in 4. days. it is probable the other wine used in same time makes it up 1. bottle a day, or 400. bottles a year.

MS (MHi); entirely in TJ's hand.

From Isaac Briggs

MY DEAR FRIEND,   Washington City, 2 mo 16–1816.

May I intrude on that retirement where from a dignified elevation the mind looks over the extensive scene of a well spent life, and nothing meets the vision but the placid images of an approving conscience? Yes, there the voice of friendship will be heard—the incidents of former days will be remembered—and the faultering tongue of humility will not plead in vain.

I have again petitioned Congress. The petition has been referred to a Committee of the Senate, and by that Committee to the Secretary of the Treasury—who, I expect, has ere this time written to thee on the subject. My petition prays, for relief from obstacles, growing out of the late invasion by the British, to the settlement of my accompts as Surveyor of the lands of the United States South of Tennessee—and for compensation for exploring and ascertaining the topography of a Post-route from Washington City to New Orleans, at the special request of the executive. 2000 dollars <u>now</u> for this service, would, in consequence of the delays, expenses and embarrassments, incident to a 10 years prosecution of this claim, be a compensation far less adequate, than $1000 when first proposed.

Thou knowest the circumstances of my last departure from the Mississippi Territory. I departed suddenly and without previous arrangement,[1] & brought with me no papers, except those relating to the enterprise of Burr. I directed Gideon Fitz, my principal deputy, and Samuel L. Winston, my clerk, to make up my accompts and send them on with the vouchers. In the years 1807 and 1808, accompts were sent on by my clerk, containing only the items of salary and clerk-hire—and a credit for $750 was obtained for me by Seth Pease, my successor. A balance, to the amount of $9,217$\frac{67}{100}$, then remained on the Treasury-books against me. Authorised and instructed by the

Secretary of the Treasury, I advanced, to my deputies before the commencement of their work, money which was charged against me at the Treasury, from which charges I could be released only when the work was completed and returned, often a long time afterwards. A good deal of work was in progress when I left that station, & probably much impeded by the confusion consequent on Burr's attempt.

Accompts and detached vouchers were, by Gideon Fitz and Samuel L. Winston, sent to me at various times, after 1808, for disbursements acctually made previous to the time of my resignation, 4th of the 3rd mo—1807—Still hoping to receive them in more satisfactory form—I delayed perhaps too long to present them such as they were. For this delay, I must plead in excuse, the necessity of my utmost exertions to support a numerous and helpless family, requiring the exercise of all my powers of mind and body, and that continually.

In the year 1809, after many earnest efforts, I prevailed on two of my friends, to engage in a plan proposed by me for manufacturing Cotton, and to furnish the Capital. The establishment was conducted and managed by me, for no other compensation than a share of the profits. This compensation, at the conclusion of the year 1814, was nothing—and my family had been enabled to live but just decently, by the absorption of most of my wife's little property, made independently hers before our marriage. I looked forward, however, with considerable expectation of prosperity. In the spring of last year, I was awakened from this dream of Hope, by the service of a writ at the suit of the United States for $9,217\frac{67}{100}$. This Arrest, operating strongly on the fears of my worthy, but timid patrons, I was again thrown out of business. I gave bail—and presented at the Treasury my accompts which, if allowed, would reduce the balance against me to $888\frac{29}{100}$. The accompting Officers of the Treasury say they cannot ascertain, in consequence of the loss of papers in the late invasion, that these accompts have not been heretofore admitted to my credit. I allege that I ought not to suffer by, as I could not prevent, the loss of their papers. They also say they can find no law authorising the ascertainment of Latitude 33°, running the line on that parallel of latitude, from the Mississippi to Red River; and for the survey of the Mississippi river, and bayous Chafalaya & Têche, from Latitude 33° to the Sea. For this item, I disbursed more than $5000, in obedience to written instructions of the Secretary of the Treasury. I think a work of the same magnitude has very rarely been performed for double that amount. It was a service of great exposure and hardship.

Respecting compensation for exploring and ascertaining the

topography of the Post-route; As it was a service performed at the special request of the Executive, I petition Congress to refer it entirely to the Executive—to authorise him to enquire into it—and to grant such compensation as to him may appear just and reasonable. Should $2000 be allowed, and my accompts suffered to pass at the Treasury; after paying 888\frac{29}{100}$, the balance of those accompts, there would remain in my favor 1111\frac{71}{100}$—out of which, repaying thy generous loan without interest, I should retain 711\frac{71}{100}$. With this I would cheerfully consent even now to begin the world. In Wilmington, state of Delaware, where I now reside, I enjoy a fair fame; and it is to me an inexpressible satisfaction that I have enjoyed the esteem of good men wherever I have been well known.

I am here before Congress, in two very different characters, one a petitioner for relief—and the other a Delegate from the Manufacturers of Wilmington and Brandywine and their vicinity. I inclose for thy perusal and criticism, if it be worth so much, a little pamphlet, being an Address delivered to the Committee of Commerce and Manufactures, after several argumentative and eloquent speeches from my fellow-delegates.

Now, my dear friend, if thou canst with propriety say any thing or do any thing to assist me in extricating myself from these severe embarrassments, I think I am sure of thy benevolence and friendly disposition.

Accept assurances of my veneration and love; and my respectful salutations.   ISAAC BRIGGS.

RC (DLC); addressed: "Thomas Jefferson, Monticello, Virginia"; endorsed by TJ as received 23 Feb. 1816 and so recorded in SJL. Enclosure: Briggs, *Statements and Remarks, addressed to Thomas Newton, Chairman of the Committee of Commerce and Manufactures, on the subject of Agriculture, Ma[n]ufactures, and Commerce* (Washington, 1816; Poor, *Jefferson's Library* 12 [no. 710]), discussing the consequences of agricultural surplusses for the national economy; stating that the demand for goods has been met by a combination of domestic and foreign sources, with the former providing for the majority of needs while the latter supplies "*surplus wants,*" including "clothing, sugar, tea, coffee, spices, &c."; calculating the population increase for the United States at just over 3 percent per year and suggesting that "surplus wants will increase in the same ratio of course" (p. 4); analyzing the rates of importation, exportation, and production, and determining that the nation "must, per force, circumscribe the amount of our purchases of foreign articles within the limits of the amount of surplus produce which foreign nations will choose to buy of us, *for we have no other means of purchasing either merchandise or bullion, or of paying, for the support of government, the impost laid thereon*" (p. 9); and concluding that a new market for manufactured cotton and woolen goods will emerge in Mexico and South America.

Isaac Briggs (1763–1825), astronomer, surveyor, and mathematician, was born to a Quaker family at Haverford, Pennsylvania, and received an A.B. from the University of the State of Pennsylvania in 1783. He was elected to the American Philosophical Society in 1796, published and edited almanacs from late in the 1790s until at least 1802, and worked with Andrew Ellicott to survey and lay out Washington, D.C. Briggs also taught for a time at a Quaker school in Maryland and partnered with two brothers-in-law to establish a cotton mill. TJ appointed him surveyor of the lands south of Tennessee in 1803 and followed that up the next year by asking him to lay out a post road between Washington, D.C., and New Orleans. Because Congress made no authorization for that survey, TJ paid Briggs's expenses himself. The legislature did not vote to settle his federal accounts until 1818. Briggs resigned his federal surveyorship in 1807 and returned to other business ventures. He worked as an engineer on a section of the Erie Canal, and when that was completed in 1819 he moved to Richmond, where he was chief engineer of the James River and Kanawha Canal. Early in November 1820 Briggs visited TJ at Monticello. In 1823 he surveyed a projected canal from Baltimore to the Potomac, but it was not constructed. Briggs died of a malarial fever at his home in Sandy Springs, Maryland (Ella Kent Barnard, "Isaac Briggs, A.M., F.A.P.S.," *Maryland Historical Magazine* 7 [1912]: 409–19; MdHi: Briggs-Stabler Papers; *General Alumni Catalogue of the University of Pennsylvania* [1917], 21; APS, Minutes, 15 Jan. 1796 [MS in PPAmP]; *Briggs's Maryland, Pennsylvania & Virginia Almanac; or, Baltimore Ephemeris: for the Year of our Lord, 1798* [Baltimore, 1798]; *Palladium of Knowledge: or, the Carolina and Georgia Almanac, for the Year of our Lord, 1803* [Charleston, 1802]; *JEP*, 1:453, 455 [11, 15 Nov. 1803]; *PTJ*, esp. 32:501–3; *MB*, 2:1130, 1205–6; Briggs's Account of a Visit to Monticello, 2–4 Nov. 1820; Washington *Daily National Intelligencer*, 10 Jan. 1825).

Briggs PETITIONED CONGRESS unsuccessfully in 1807. His second petition was presented to the Senate on 30 Jan. 1816 by William H. Wells. On that date the Senate referred the petition to a select committee composed of Wells, Nathaniel Macon, and Dudley Chase. On 24 Feb. 1817 Wells once again presented the petition, which was then referred to the Committee of Claims. On 3 Mar. 1817 a bill mandating the settlement of Briggs's account with the United States and the termination of related litigation passed and moved to the House. After a failed attempt to amend the bill in that body, it passed both houses in its final form and on 9 Apr. 1818 was signed by President James Monroe (*JHR*, 5:569, 643, 10:553, 11:457, 465, 494 [6 Feb., 3 Mar. 1807, 3 Mar. 1817, 13, 15, 20 Apr. 1818]; *JS*, 6:127, 301, 389, 7:388 [30 Jan. 1816, 24 Feb., 3 Mar. 1817, 18 Apr. 1818]; *U.S. Statutes at Large*, 6:209).

¹ Word interlined in place of "preparation."

From Alexander J. Dallas

SIR   Treasury Department 16. February 1816.

At the request of Mr Isaac Briggs, I take the liberty of asking you to state your reccollection of the facts represented by that gentleman in the inclosed letter, relative to the subject of his Petition, referred by the Senate to this Department.

I have the honor to be, with every Sentiment of respect and attachment, Sir, Y^r mo. obed Sev^t   A. J. DALLAS

RC (DLC); at foot of text: "The Honble Thomas Jefferson. Monticello"; endorsed by TJ as received 21 Feb. 1816 and so recorded in SJL, where the letter is mistakenly dated 12 Feb. 1816. Enclosure not found.

From Francis W. Gilmer

DEAR SIR.   Winchester 16th Feb. 1816

During the sickness which has confined me to my room a great part of the winter, and from which I am still but slowly convalescent, I have occasionally turned my mind to the Florida question which the late demand of the Chevalier Onis has revived. When in Philadelphia last winter, I obtained from his secretary Mr. Heredia, the whole strength of their cause, which I found so weak, that I promised myself an easy victory over all its partizans in this country. It was not until I heard with regret, & astonishment, that Judge Cooper was one of the most zealous, as he is certainly the most able of them, that I dreaded an opposition more formidable than that of the Spanish Embassy. I have not yet seen Judge Coopers essay in the 'Democratic Press' of Philadelphia, and am therefore unable to say whether it be as profound as his known learning would lead us to expect. But as the case still appears to me a plain one, I will not abandon its defence, from a natural reluctance to enter the lists with such an adversary, accoutred at all points with various & elegant learning.

As I have none of these advantages, but rely entirely upon the simplicity of the question, I will beg Sir, briefly to state to you the order in which I shall view the subject, & to ask of you some information which your knowledge of the public law will no doubt enable you to give me.

1. The first proposition upon which the Spanish minister relies, tho' not stated in his letter to Mr monroe is, that the treaty of St Ildefonso was to take effect upon the performance of a condition precedent, relative to the duke of Parma, which the French Government failed to perform, & that therefore the treaty of St Ildefonso is void.

I do not know how the fact was, as to the non-compliance with this condition. But the treaties of St. Ildefonso & of Paris by which Louisiana was ceded to the U.S., having been published & acted on without any protest on the part of Spain, became a part of the public law which all nations are bound to respect.

Besides, the failure of the condition upon which the treaty of St Ildefonso was to be binding upon Spain, applies with equal force to the acquisition of that part of Louisiana to the west, as to that on the East of the mississippi, & as Spain does not contest our claim pro tanto it is a waiver of the objection to the whole.

2. They contend that the treaty of St Ildefonso conveyed Louisiana to France under the same boundaries with which she held it, after all East of the mississippi except the isle of orleans had been ceded to England by the treaty of 1763. But the words of the treaty 'et qu'elle avoit lorsque la France la possedait' cannot by any fair interpretation be confined to the period when France held it with the narrowest limits, more especially as France was at the time of the treaty of St. Ildefonso [1800] the dominant power in Europe, & from its known address in diplomacy would never have suffered such an evasion when it was able to resist it. The obvious[1] meaning of the clause is, that Spain ceded to France, every thing which she then held, & that France had at any time held as Louisiana. Now the journal of the Chevalier la Salle shews that the first settlements of the French in Louisiana were on the Ilinois, & then at St. Joseph near the lakes. The first settlements in the south [as will appear from the journal of Messrs. Bienville & Iberville] were at Biloxi & Mobile, both far to the East of the mississippi. They had also a settlement at Alabama at Toulouse, & indeed according to the European usage they claimed all the waters both of the mississippi & of the Alabama.

3. The whole extent of this vast country then, was conveyed to France by the treaty of St. Ildefonso, with the exception of such portions as had been taken from it by previous conventions, which were

1. all East of Rio Perdido by the treaty of Cambray between France & Spain [1714 or 1719.]

2. all which fell within the boundaries of the U.S. at the recognition by Spain of our Independence, which was all north of the 31° N. Lat. between the mississippi and the chatahouchy, & thence all north of the junction of Flint River with the chatahouchy, & the sources of St: Marys.

If this interpretation of the treaty of St. Ildefonso be correct, and these facts be true, the conclusion is irresistible, that all which was ever Louisiana, now belongs to the U.S. except that portion which lies between the Perdido & the sources of St. Marys, south, constituting the present East Florida.

I will beg of you the favor Sir, if it be not giving you too much trouble, to give me any information that may be necessary to support these positions but especially as to the boundary between Louisiana & Florida as fixed by the treaty of Cambray.

I am sorry that others much more capable than I am, from facility of access to all the repositories of public law, are too indifferent to a question of such national concern to employ their time in a work which could not fail to be useful to their country. I have already offered this scheme of defence to George Dallas of Philadelphia, but he shuns the contest. I shall only engage in it, upon the condition that I can draw from your quiver, some better weapons than any that I find in my own.

I beg to be presented with sentiments of regard to Mrs Randolph, and

that you will accept the homage of my admiration and esteem

F. W. GILMER

RC (MoSHi: Gilmer Papers); brackets in original; addressed: "Thomas Jefferson esquire Monticello Albemarle county. via Washington. mail"; franked; postmarked Winchester, 16 Feb.; endorsed by TJ as a letter from "Gilmer Francis H." received 21 Feb. 1816 and so recorded in SJL.

A diplomatic exchange including a 30 Dec. 1815 letter from Luis de ONIS to James Monroe, with a 2 Jan. 1816 postscript, and Monroe's 19 Jan. 1816 reply was printed in the Richmond *Virginia Argus*, 3 Feb. 1816, and also appears in *ASP, Foreign Relations*, 4:422–6. Thomas Cooper's ESSAY IN THE 'DEMOCRATIC PRESS' OF PHILADELPHIA may have been the pseudonymous article by "Viator" that was reprinted in the *Virginia Argus*, 14 Feb. 1816, and which TJ enclosed in a letter to Monroe, 17 Feb. 1816. The FRENCH GOVERNMENT did in fact PERFORM the provision of the Treaty of San Ildefonso (1800) under which the Spanish king Charles IV's son-in-law Louis, son of the duke of Parma, received a kingdom in Italy (Frances Gardiner Davenport and Charles Oscar Paullin, eds., *Eu-*ropean Treaties bearing on the History of the United States and its Dependencies* [1917–37], 4:181–2, 183). PRO TANTO: "to that extent" (*Black's Law Dictionary*).

The phrase ET QU'ELLE AVOIT LORSQUE LA FRANCE LA POSSEDAIT ("and that it had when France possessed it") was included in both the Treaty of San Ildefonso and the 1803 Louisiana Purchase Treaty (Davenport and Paullin, *European Treaties*, 4:181; Miller, *Treaties*, 2:499). Jean Baptiste Le Moyne, sieur de BIENVILLE, and his brother Pierre Le Moyne, sieur d'IBERVILLE, each served as French colonial governor of Louisiana (*ANB*). In 1719 French forces captured Pensacola from the Spanish, initiating a boundary dispute that was settled by the secret terms of the Treaty of Madrid (1721) and discussed not long thereafter at the Congress of Cambrai (CAMBRAY), France (Herbert Eugene Bolton and Thomas Maitland Marshall, *The Colonization of North America, 1492–1783* [1921], 279, 295; Davenport and Paullin, *European Treaties*, 4:20–4).

[1] Manuscript: "obious."

From Wilson Cary Nicholas

MY DEAR SIR   Richmond Feby 16. 1816

Large appropriations have been made for internal improvements & I expect the literary fund will be increased several hundred thousand dollars. I am sure the application of public money to these objects will meet your approbation. You are made one of the Directors of public works. I took the liberty (thinking it cou'd not be agreeable to you to serve) to suggest it was unreasonable to impose such a burthen upon you at your time of life and after so long and arduous a devotion to the public service. It was replied that it was of the utmost importance to gain the confidence of the State that you shou'd be one of the directors, that the money wou'd [be]¹ diverted to some other use if this cou'd not be secured & that it was all important that the first measures of the board shou'd be of a character to command that confidence, it was stated too that Gen¹ Washington served as president of the potomac company to his death. your name being once mentioned it was impossible to prevent your being elected. I cannot presume to give any advice to you upon the subject; many reasons suggest themselves why you shou'd not among others the unpleasantness of the accommodations in the taverns in this City. I hope it is in my power to remove that by requesting you will do us the favour of accepting a room at our house during your continuance in Richmond I am sure your acceptance of the appointment wou'd give great satisfaction, and that it wou'd be in your power to render essential service, if you only held it until the meeting of the next assembly. I cordially congratulate you upon the prospect of the great advantages that will result to our country from the proceedings of this assembly; no such spirit has been manifested since we had the power of self government.

I am My Dear Sir with the greatest respect your hum. Serv.

W. C. NICHOLAS

RC (DLC); endorsed by TJ as received 28 Feb. 1816 and so recorded in SJL. RC (DLC: TJ Papers, ser. 10); address cover only; with PoC of TJ to Patrick Gibson, 18 Mar. 1816, on verso and Tr of Account of Flour Shipped by Thomas M. Randolph & Company, [ca. 12 Mar. 1816], on recto.

On 14 Feb. 1816 TJ was elected one of ten DIRECTORS OF PUBLIC WORKS by a joint vote of the two houses of the Virginia General Assembly (*JHD* [1815–16 sess.], 184).

¹ Omitted word editorially supplied.

From Dabney C. Terrell

DEAR SIR   Baltimore. Feby 16th 1816

I arrived here two days ago and have seen Mr Stevenson. No vessel is sailing at this time to any French port; indeed there are very few departures at all. The basin has been frozen for six weeks. I have procured a passage to Amsterdam in a vessel which is to sail on the 22nd. I hope to hear from you before that time. Mr Gallatin's letters have not yet arrived; they will probably come by tomorrow's mail. I understand that Mann Randolph has a promise from the Secretary of the Navy, of obtaining a Midshipman's warrant on the vacancy. Present my respects to Mrs Randolph and believe me to be with sentiments of the highest consideration and esteem,

Yours &^{c} DABNEY. C. TERRELL.

P.S. The Governor of Pennsylvania does not intend demanding me: probably because he expects that I am not to be found.   DCT.

RC (ViU: TJP-CC); endorsed by TJ as received 21 Feb. 1816 and so recorded in SJL. RC (MHi); address cover only; with PoC of TJ to Bernard Peyton, 8 Mar. 1816, on verso; addressed: "Thomas Jefferson. Esqr Monticello Near Charlottesville Virginia" by "Mail"; stamp canceled; franked; postmarked Baltimore, 16 Feb.

Dabney Carr Terrell (d. 1827), attorney and poet, was a grandson of TJ's sister Martha Jefferson Carr and a native of Kentucky. He studied at Dickinson College in Carlisle, Pennsylvania, where he killed his fellow student John T. Corbin in a duel in 1815 and was expelled. With TJ's help Terrell continued his education in Geneva, Switzerland, where he came under the tutelage of Marc Auguste Pictet. After Terrell's return to the United States, TJ assisted him in a course of legal studies. When searching for the first law professor for the University of Virginia, TJ submitted Terrell's name for consideration, but he was not chosen. He subsequently moved to New Orleans, where he died of yellow fever. A small collection of Terrell's poems was published posthumously (Robert Isham Randolph, *The Randolphs of Virginia* [1936], 122; *VMHB* 2 [1895]: 223; Trustees Minutes, Dickinson College, 18 Dec. 1815 [PCarlD]; Charles Coleman Sellers, *Dickinson College: A History* [1973], 440–1; Edward Govan to Terrell, Carlisle, 4 Feb. 1816, and Terrell to Martha J. Terrell, brig *Rolla*, 1 Mar. 1816, both in ViU: Papers of the Carr and Terrell Families; Pictet to TJ, 1 Nov. 1819; TJ to Terrell, 26 Feb. 1821; TJ to University of Virginia Board of Visitors, 20 Jan. 1826; *Richmond Enquirer*, 28 Sept. 1827; *Virginia Literary Museum and Journal of Belles Lettres, Arts, &c.* 1 [1829]: 40–1, 51, 59, 196, 223, 361).

Terrell was concerned that Simon Snyder, the GOVERNOR OF PENNSYLVANIA, might seek to prosecute him for killing Corbin. His friend Edward Govan advised him that he would send him his diploma but that Terrell should stay in Virginia or Kentucky, because a coroner's or grand jury had brought in a "verdict" of "murder in the first degree." Govan concluded, however, that there was "no danger at present to be apprehended" (Govan to Terrell, 4 Feb. 1816).

Notes for a Settlement with William D. Fitch

Notes for a settlement with mr Fitz.   Feb. 17. 16.

There are 3. subjects of account between us.
1. the Warehouse 2. Rent for his tenemt. 3. firewood.

The Warehouse. this account was settled with Craven Peyton to the end of the year 1808.

1809. I settled the account for this year on the
6th Aug. 1813

thus. 1810. Aug. 6.	By paim^t of Oglesby &	£
	Fitz to J. H. Craven	5–12–[6]
	By my order on them in	
	fav^r of J. H. Craven	19–12–1
1813. Aug. 6.	By balance for 1809. now	
	rec^d in cash	16–13–8
		41–18–3 [= 139.71]

for 1810. & downwards there has been neither settlem^t nor paiment

---

Firewood and rent. mr Fitz. pd Craven Peyton for firewood for
1807–1808 [12.D.]

1811. Oct. 1. a regular lease in writing @ 11.D. a year for firewood
was signed

1813. Apr. 6. mr Fitz pd me for wood & rent	20.D.
Sep. 6. he pd to E. Bacon for d°	20.D.
1814. Apr. 5. he pd for firewood	7.D.

these acc^{ts} for rent & firewood for 1809. & downwards are unsettled,
& no payments on them but the above 47.D

1815 June. we bot of him 31. gall^s whiskey @ .85. & pd him by an
order on Gibson & Jefferson for 26.35.   TH: JEFFERSON

MS (MHi); entirely in TJ's hand; edge trimmed, with bracketed material supplied from Dft; endorsed by TJ: "Fitz. Wm Feb 17. 16." Dft (MHi); written entirely in TJ's hand on both sides of a single sheet; undated; consisting of two versions, both repeating the information in MS, with one side, headed "Wm Fitz," organized in separate sections on warehouse, firewood and rent, and whiskey, and the other side, headed "Wm Fitz in acc^t with Th:J," arranged as an account.

William D. Fitch (ca. 1792–1848) was the son of William Daniel Fitch, a woodworker and wheelwright with whom TJ first transacted business in 1771. The younger Fitch worked as a tobacco inspector, leased space in TJ's Milton warehouses as early as 1808, and was active in the local Masonic lodge. He ran a tavern in Milton before relocating by 1831 to Charlottesville, where he operated various taverns and public houses. Fitch died at the University of Virginia (*MB*, esp.

1:261, 2:1135, 1259; TJ's Account with Craven Peyton for Rents and Profits from Henderson Lands, 1801–7 Jan. 1811, enclosed in TJ to Peyton, 28 Oct. 1812; Woods, *Albemarle*, 58, 194–5, 400, 403; Richmond *Enquirer*, 19 Feb. 1814; *Proceedings of a Grand Annual Communication of the Grand Lodge of Virginia* [Richmond, 1817]; *Richmond Enquirer*, 18 July 1823, 22 July 1831; Lay, *Architecture*, 87, 148; *Richmond Whig and Public Advertiser*, 10 Oct. 1848).

In undated notes on his account WITH MR FITZ, TJ recalled that "Mr Fitz's lease for firewood was dated June 1. 1812. 11.D. a year. in my acc^t with him which I gave mr Bacon are 2. paim^{ts} for wood   I gave Th: J. Randolph an order for the wood rents one year   I do not remember the year exactly, but it was about 1815" (MS in MHi; on verso of a reused address cover to TJ; entirely in TJ's hand).

A missing letter of 20 Feb. 1816 from CRAVEN PEYTON to TJ is recorded in SJL as received the same day from Monteagle. The REGULAR LEASE for firewood was probably similar to the agreement with James Marr printed above at 6 Feb. 1813.

From Lafayette

MY DEAR FRIEND   La grange february 17ʰ 1816
I Have not, Since a very Long while, Received An Answer from You. a Letter of Mine will probably Go By the opportunity which Carries these Lines. I shall Therefore only inclose a Copy of the Letter writen to our friend dupont de Nemours By Another friend of ours. it Relates more to you than to Him and if you Can Give the informations and Send the Books Herein Requested You will greatly oblige us. The Situation of His Health and Eyes is very painfull.

while the Spirit of pilnitz and Coblentz is pursuing its Counter Revolutionary System I Hold my Agricultural Retirement of La grange, Surrounded By my family and Entertaining myself with the fond Hope That the Cause of french and European Liberty is far from Being Lost.

Most Affectionately forever
Your old friend   LAFAYETTE

RC (DLC); endorsed by TJ as received 1 Aug. 1816 and so recorded in SJL. RC (DLC); address cover only; with PoC of TJ to Wilson Cary Nicholas, 9 Oct. 1816, on verso; addressed: "Thomas Jefferson Esq. Monticelo Virginia"; franked; postmarked Washington City, 28 July.

ENCLOSURE

Destutt de Tracy to Pierre Samuel Du Pont de Nemours

MON CHER MAÎTRE   Paris Ce 30. Janvier 1816.
je ne vous ai pas ecrit plutôt parceque je croyais toujours que vous alliez nous revenir; mais aujourd'hui quoique j'espere vous revoir bientôt, je Suis obligé de m'adresser à vous et je le fais avec confiance, vous connaissant trop pour ne pas espérer de vous trouver toujours le même pour moi et pour le Sujet de mes etudes

Comme vous êtes dans un autre monde il doit etre celui des lumieres et de la Vérité Car celui que j'habite est assurement celui du mensonge et de l'aveuglement. J'ai plus que ma part de l'aveuglement général; car j'ai presque perdu les yeux, et Sans mon petit Secretaire Augustin je ne pourrais Communiquer avec vous, mais pour le mensonge je n'en Suis pas quoique j'aie été quelque fois mystérieux par necessité

En votre qualité d'habitant du pays de la lumiere vous Savez aujourd'hui de qui est certain Commentaire, imprimé en Anglais à Philadelphie en 1811. maintenant je vous dirai de plus que M. Jefferson me l'annonçait par une lettre infiniment aimable du 16 Janvier 1811. laquelle je n'ai reçuë avec un Seul exemplaire de ce commentaire que le 27. 7bre suivant Je lui ai repondu le 21. 8bre et 15. nov^{bre} même année pour le remercier et lui ai envoyé en même tems mes trois Volumes imprimés et le manuscrit de mon quatrième; J'ai été très long tems sans entendre parler de lui. Enfin le 14 Mai 1814 J'ai recu de lui une lettre du 28. 9bre 1813. en reponse à celle là dans laquelle il me dit 1° qu'il espère faire publier bientôt le Commentaire en français. 2° qu'il fait traduire en anglais le manuscrit de mon quatrième Volume et que je le recevrai avec Sa lettre; rien de tout cela ne m'est arrivé encore; je ne Sais Si la reponse que je lui ai faite le 14 Juillet 1814 a été plus heureuse; je le remerciais à ce Sujet et aussi pour les Soins obligeants que Mes Gallatin et Adams Avaient eus de mon fils en Russie; depuis ce tems, je n'ai plus eu de nouvelles de lui ni de mon diplôme de la Société Philosophique qu'il devait m'envoyer. Je crois bien qu'on m'a retenu ou perdu quelque lettre et quelque paquet

Maintenant, mon cher maitre, mon maudit imprimeur vient, malgré ma répugnance, de publier mon quatrième Volume et un Commencement du cinquième dont j'avais déposé le manuscrit chez lui avec une note finale, parceque c'est tout ce que j'ai fait et ferai jamais. Seulement j'ai obtenu qu'il n'en fut pas parlé dans aucuns journaux, voulant vivre et mourir en paix désormais.

Je vous envoye cy-joint, un exemplaire de ce tome pour M. Jefferson, un pour la Societé philosophique et deux pour vous; je mets le tout Sous votre protection, je vous prie de me faire Savoir Si cela Vous est parvenu; Vous me feriez en outre, un extréme plaisir de me faire passer quelques exemplaires du Montesquieu, tant en Anglais qu'en francais, plus de la traduction Anglaise de ce quatrième Volume et aussi de celle de mes trois premiers, Si toutefois, cette derniere existe Comme on m'en a flatté je reconnaitrai là vos anciennes bontés et elles me Seront toujours plus chères. Je vous demande exprêssement la permission de remettre à Mad^e Dupont ce que tout ce fatras aura pu vous couter

Recevez mon cher maître, les nouvelles assurances de mon ancien et inviolable attachement

Mettez-moi je vous prie aux pieds de m. Jefferson; un pauvre aveugle n'ose plus lui ecrire

EDITORS' TRANSLATION

MY DEAR MASTER   Paris 30. January 1816.
I did not write to you earlier because I always believed that you would come back to us, but today, though I hope to see you again soon, I am forced to contact you and I do it confidently, knowing you too well to doubt your constancy toward me and the subject of my studies

Since you are in another world, it must be the world of enlightenment and truth, because the one in which I live is assuredly that of lies and blindness. I have more than my share of the general blindness, because I have almost lost my vision and could not communicate with you without my little secretary Augustin. But I do not favor lies, although I have at times been mysterious out of necessity

As an inhabitant of the enlightened country, you know today who wrote a certain commentary, printed in English in Philadelphia in 1811. Moreover, I will now tell you that Mr. Jefferson had announced it to me in an infinitely kind letter dated 16 January 1811. I did not receive that letter, which contained a single copy of this commentary, until the following 27 September. I replied on 21 October and 15 November of the same year to thank him, and I sent him at the same time my three printed volumes and the manuscript of my fourth one. Much time elapsed before I heard from him. Finally, on 14 May 1814 I received his letter dated 28 November 1813 in response to my 21 October letter, in which he tells me first, that he hopes soon to have the commentary published in French, and second, that he has had the manuscript of my fourth volume translated into English and that I will receive it with his letter. None of these things has yet reached me. I do not know whether better luck has attended the reply I wrote him on 14 July 1814 thanking him for them and for the kind care Mr. Gallatin and Mr. Adams had taken of my son in Russia. Since then, I have had no news from him nor of my American Philosophical Society diploma that he was supposed to send me. I believe that some letter or package must have been detained or lost

Now, my dear master, despite my repugnance, my cursed printer has just published my fourth volume and the beginning of the fifth, the manuscript of which I had deposited at his house with a final note, because this is all I have done and all I will ever do. I only made certain that it would not be mentioned in any newspaper, as henceforth I want to live and die in peace.

Enclosed please find one copy of this volume for Mr. Jefferson, one for the philosophical society, and two for you. I am placing everything under your protection, and I ask you to let me know if they all reach you. Furthermore, you would give me much pleasure by sending me a few copies of the Montesquieu, in English as well as in French, along with more of the English translation of the fourth volume and also of my first three volumes, if it exists as I have been told. I would recognize in this your previous acts of kindness, and it will be even dearer to me. I expressly request your permission to remit to Mrs. Du Pont whatever this whole jumble will have cost you

My dear master, please accept renewed assurances of my old and inviolable attachment

Please lay me at the feet of Mr. Jefferson; a poor blind man no longer dares to write him

---

Tr (DLC). Translation by Dr. Genevieve Moene.

The COMMENTAIRE, IMPRIMÉ EN ANGLAIS À PHILADELPHIE EN 1811 was Destutt de Tracy, *Commentary and Review of Montesquieu's Spirit of Laws.* TJ's LETTRE INFINIMENT AIMABLE to Destutt de Tracy was dated 26 Jan. 1811, not 16 Jan. The recently published QUATRIÈME VOLUME ET UN COMMENCEMENT DU CINQUIÈME enclosed here was Destutt de Tracy, *Traité de la volonté et de ses effets* (1st ed. Paris, 1815; 2d ed. Paris, 1818; Poor, *Jefferson's Library*, 8 [no. 454]).

To Joseph Miller

DEAR CAPTAIN   Monticello Feb. 17. 16.

I have the pleasure to announce to you that your bill is passed; so
that you may now take possession of your property, and sell and do
with it what you please. I recieved the information last night in a letter of the 14th from mr Cabell, our Senator, who undertook the care
of the bill. you would do well to write to the clerk of the House of
Representatives for a copy of the law, paying the postage of your letter, and procuring some friend in Richmond[1] to pay for the copy. in
the mean time however you may safely be taking any measures respecting the estate. Accept the assurances of my friendly esteem and
respect   TH: JEFFERSON

PoC (DLC); on verso of a reused address cover from John Barnes to TJ; at
foot of text: "Capt Joseph Miller"; endorsed by TJ.

The CLERK of the Virginia House of
Delegates was William Munford.

[1] Preceding two words interlined in
place of "there."

To James Monroe

TH: JEFFERSON TO COLº MONROE.   Monticello Feb. 17. 16.

It is impossible for you to note and preserve every thing as it passes
in newspapers. I have therefore cut out of the Virginia Argus of Feb.
14. the inclosed paper. have it filed with the papers on the Louisiana
title, and when you have to take up that subject it will suggest to you
facts for enquiry. it is from some hand acquainted well with the subject, & contains some facts not in the MS. on which I wrote to you the
other day, nor in my memoir & Chronological statement which is in
your office, and was I believe furnished to our Commrs at Madrid. fac
valeas, meque mutuo diligas.

RC (DNA: RG 59, TP-F); dateline at
foot of text; addressed: "James Monroe
Secretary of State Washington"; franked;
postmarked Milton, 21 Feb.; endorsed in
an unidentified hand, with the additional
notation: "Covers an Extract from a
newspaper containing a chronological
statement of the principal facts in relation
to the Settlement & boundaries of
Louisiana." PoC (DLC); endorsed by TJ.

The INCLOSED PAPER, a letter by

"VIATOR" clipped from the 14 Feb.
1816 issue of the Richmond *Virginia
Argus*, dated 7 Feb. from Philadelphia
and originally addressed "*To the Editor of
the Democratic Press*," commented that
"As the boundary question relating to
Louisiana, is likely to become an interest-
ing object of public attention, I send you a
brief statement of the title of the United
States to the country from Rio Perdido, in
East Florida, to Rio Bravo, west of the
Bay of St. Bernard—Perhaps I may by

and bye, send you the title now set up by the court of Spain to the country east of the Ibberville, and west of the Mississippi, should the present essay appear to you worth attention"; asserted that the American right to Louisiana derived from the French title; gave the history of the French claims from 1673 to 1803; and concluded that the current disagreement between the United States and Spain grew out of the 1803 treaty between the United States and France in which the latter sold its Louisiana lands to the United States, including those ceded by Spain to France under the Treaty of San Ildefonso.

TJ's MEMOIR & CHRONOLOGICAL STATEMENT included his "Chronological Series of Facts relative to Louisiana," [ca. 15 Jan. 1804] (DLC: TJ Papers, 137:23690–1; ViU: TJP; PPAmP), and "An examination into the boundaries of Louisiana," 7 Sept. 1803, with 15 Jan. 1804 postscript (DLC: TJ Papers, 135:23267–71; ViU: TJP; PPAmP). Monroe and Charles Pinckney negotiated with the Spanish government at MADRID in an effort to settle the Louisiana boundary dispute (*ASP, Foreign Relations*, 2:627–33). FAC VALEAS, MEQUE MUTUO DILIGAS: "Goodbye, and cherish me as I do you."

To Isaac A. Coles

DEAR SIR   Monticello Feb. 18. 16.

At our last court it was settled with the county surveyor that he should attend to make the survey in the case of Col° Monroe & mr Short on Wednesday next the 21st inst. he will come here the overnight, so as to be ready to begin it early the next day, that he may finish it in the day. I must ask the favor of you to come and let us make a close of this business. I wish you could come the overnight also, to which it may be some induce[me]nt that they have a ball in Charlottesville that evening (Tuesday) at which you can attend if you please. ever and affectionately yours   TH: JEFFERSON

PoC (MHi); on verso of reused address cover of Joseph Fox to TJ, [ca. 15] Jan. 1816; torn at seal; at foot of text: "Col° Coles"; endorsed by TJ.

The COUNTY SURVEYOR was William Woods.

To James L. Jefferson

DEAR LILBURNE   Monticello Feb. 18. 16.

My sister Marks tells me you are in want of clothes and other necessaries, and are living at the tavern at the ferry until the question is decided about my brother's will. I wish you would come and stay with us. I have proposed this on one or two former occasions, and would now press it. you shall employ your time as you please, and as usefully to yourself as you please, in which, and in any thing else I can I will render you my best services. but come particularly and let me have you furnished at Charlottesville with all proper and comfortable clothing. in the hope of seeing you I remain affectionately [your]s.   TH: JEFFERSON

PoC (MoSHi: TJC-BC); on verso of reused address cover to TJ; mutilated at seal; at foot of text: "Mr Lilburne Jefferson"; endorsed by TJ.

A missing letter of 30 Jan. 1816 from TJ to his SISTER Anne Scott Marks is recorded in SJL.

Although Jefferson never accepted TJ's repeated invitations to live at Monticello, TJ's account books show that he gave his nephew ten dollars in April 1816 and bought him a pair of shoes the following year (*MB*, 2:1322, 1330).

From James L. Jefferson

DEAR UNCLE   Scotts Ferry Feb^r 18th 1816—
I received your letter by Guilley you advice[1] in respect to my situation I thank you kindly for your advice. I went to Buckingham C. H on monday last and spoke to the Curator in respect to my situation and he refused to let me have money out of the estate; I then appealed to the Court for justice the court would not authorise the Curator to let me have money out of the estate unless I would choose[2] a guardian I then choosed a guardian and he will no doubt do justice by me. I have not been in want of clothing but I thought that I was entitled to funds out of the estate I should be verry happy to come and live with you but I have rented the ferry and the man that I rented it of wont I am affraid compromise with me but if he will I will come over. My anxiety is to travel and that westardly The plantation snowden is to be rented out next week and I had a thought of renting a part of it. the widow has moved to her mothers She had not moved there more then two days before the house caught on fire and bournt everything into ashes. I will let you know in a few days is soon as I can see Mr Thomas the gentleman that I rented the ferry of he is gone to Ricmond.
    I am Sir your affectionate nephew   JAMES L. JEFFERSON—

RC (ViU: TJP); at foot of text: "M^r Th Jefferson"; endorsed by TJ as received 18 Feb. 1816 and so recorded in SJL.

GUILLEY may have been TJ's slave Gill Gillette. Although Jefferson claimed he had no WANT OF CLOTHING, a 25 Mar. 1816 receipt to TJ from the

Charlottesville firm of Bramham & Jones documents his purchase of "5 p stockings" for his nephew at a cost of 9 shillings per pair, for a total of £2.5 (MS in ViU: TJP; in an unidentified hand; endorsed by TJ: "Jefferson J. Lilburne").

THE WIDOW Mitchie B. Pryor Jefferson had moved in with her mother, Susan

B. Pryor, just before fire claimed THE HOUSE at Snowden she had shared with her deceased husband, TJ's brother Randolph Jefferson (Edythe Rucker Whitley,

Genealogical Records of Buckingham County, Virginia [1984], 106).

[1] Manuscript: "advic."
[2] Manuscript: "shoose."

From Robert Saunders

SIR,   Williamsburg Vª 20th feb'ry 1816.

Having made an Examination and Settlement with M[r] Bracken as the Admor of the late Charles Bellini under the Authority granted to me by your Letter of Attorney of the 25th of december last, I now cover to you a statement of the account, an exact Copy of that left in M[r] Bracken's possession, annexing thereto my account shewing the balance to be received by your Constituent, together with a certificate from the Cashier of the Bank of Virginia shewing that I had placed to your credit the sum of $635:48—corresponding with my account.

From a view of the Papers and vouchers respecting M[r] Bracken's transactions on this estate:—the Powers granted to him by the Sisters of M[r] Bellini, and his efforts to remit the sum due from him, I thought it right not to insist on Interest for a longer period than is allowed; being of opinion, that these circumstances would shelter him therefrom in a Court of Chancery—I found that no other property, as far as I could obtain information, came into M[r] Bracken's hands than the slaves: which, indeed, M[r] Bellini purchased from College, and, as I understand, were not entirely paid for at his death:—M[r] Andrews, the late Bursar of College having taken a pledge of his Household furniture, very inconsiderable in itself, for the purpose of satisfying this debt—

I also return the several Papers transmitted to me as you request. Be pleased to acknowledge the credit thro' the Bank for the amount placed there by me, as well as the receipt of the Papers returned.

with every consideration of the highest respect,

I am, D[r] sir, Your obed[t] Serv[t]   RO: SAUNDERS.

RC (DLC); dateline adjacent to signature; at foot of text: "To Thomas Jefferson Esq[r] Monticello"; endorsed by TJ as received 1 Mar. 1816 and so recorded in SJL.

The enclosed STATEMENT OF THE ACCOUNT is printed below. The CERTIFICATE FROM THE CASHIER OF THE BANK OF VIRGINIA has not been found. For the SEVERAL PAPERS also enclosed here, see TJ to Saunders, 25 Dec. 1815.

Charles Bellini Estate Account

The Estate of Charles Bellini decd in acc^t with
John Bracken admor

			D^r &		C^r	
1806						
Jan'ry	By hire of Mars 1805 rec^d in 1806	£20: 0:0= $			66	66
April	By sale of ditto	£80: 0:0=			266	66
	To Amount of Doct^r Galt's Judgment & Costs	£88:13:2=	295	53		
	To paid estate of Doctor James Carter claim	£5: 8:0=	18			
	To paid Robert Saunders his acc^t for fees		6	25		
decemb^r	By Sale of Slave Lucy and child £120: 0:0=				400	
			319	78	733	32
	To 5 ⅌Cent Com^s on Receipts		36	65		
		$	356	43	733	32.
					356	43
	By this balance due the Estate Jan'ry 1st 1807				$ 376	89
1810						
Jan'ry	By Sale of Lucy's youngest child £60: 0:0=				200	
	To 5 ⅌C^t Com^n on this receipt		10			
		$	10		200	
					10	
	By this balance of last Sale Jan'ry 1810	$			190	

In february 1807 The Administrator remitted a Bill of Exchange on London for £100—sterling, which was accepted thro' the aid of James Monroe Esqr in favor of Mr Mazzei for and on behalf of Aurora and Louisa Bellini Sisters of his intestate Charles Bellini; That the Admor acted under a Power of Attorney from the said Aurora and Louisa Bellini. From the State of Europe at that time the money was not received by them; and it remained unredeemed in London 'till some time in 1810 when it was redrawn by the aid of Mr Rutherfoord at Richmond, Mr Gist of London becoming security to the acceptor against the claim of Mr Mazzei.—From this period 'till October 1811, no opportunity occurred by which the Admor could attempt a remittance.

In October 1811 The Admor by the advice and assistance of Thomas Jefferson Esqr, made a remittance of the whole fund in his hands by Mr George Jefferson then going to Lisbon as American Consul. This Payment Mr Jefferson was unable to effect from the disturbed State of Italy:—and Mr Jefferson having died before his return to the U. States, the administrator did not receive the amount from his Estate 'till January 1813, when it was paid into the hands of Mr Robert Greenhow of Richmond for him. Under these circumstances the administrator believes he is not justly chargeable with Interest from 1807 to January 1813.—[1]

The following will be the result from the Statement rendered, and the remarks of the Administrator;

Dr Mr John Bracken Administrator

<u>To Aurora and Louisa Bellini.</u>

To balance due on the account of Administration Jan'ry 1807. $376:89

To ditto   ditto   Jan'ry 1810.   190:00

$566:89

To interest on the whole from Jan'ry 1813 to   }   102: 3.
Jan'ry 1816

$668:92

JOHN BRACKEN

Under the Authority granted to me by Thomas Jefferson esq^r of Monticello in Virginia acting for and on behalf of John Baptist Fancelli of Florence in Italy, I have settled the within Administration account of John Bracken on Charles Bellini's estate, and have received from him the Sum of Six hundred and sixty eight dollars and ninety two Cents the balance due from him as above stated. having signed a duplicate.   Williamsburg January 30th 1816.   RO: SAUNDERS.[2]

Dr John Baptist Fancelli, by Thomas Jefferson his attorney,
   in acc^t with Robert Saunders—

1816.

Jan'ry 30.   To Commission @ 5 ℔C^t for settling and   }
                receiving balance due from John Bracken   } $33:44
                admor of Charles Bellini $668:92 as ℔ acc^t }
                rendered herewith

Feb'y 3^d & 14th To this sum deposited in the Bank of Virginia
                to your credit by Thomas Jefferson Esqr $635:48

$668:92

1816   C^r

Jan'ry 30th By Amount received from John Bracken   }
                Admor of Charles Bellini for Aurora and   } $668:92
                Louisa Bellini his Hrs as ℔ acc^t—   }

Williamsburg Virginia
feb'ry 20th 1816.
RO: SAUNDERS.

MS (DLC); in the hand of Saunders, signed by Bracken and Saunders.

For Bracken's BILL OF EXCHANGE remitted to TJ in 1807, see note to TJ to Bracken, 2 Aug. 1811.

[1] First page ends here.

[2] Second page ends here, in middle of page.

From David Bailie Warden

DEAR SIR,   Paris 20. febr. 1816.

The object of this note is to inform you, that I have recieved from mr. Ticknor of Boston, now at Gottingen, a list of Books, which he wishes me to purchase for you, with a draft on the house of Perregaux for the amount. It will give me great pleasure to execute this Commission; and I shall have them forwarded as soon as possible by the way of Havre.   mr. Tracy has this day presented me a volume for you on Subjects connected with political economy—which I shall send you with a poem by Botta, and a Description of the District of washington which I have just published—

I am, dear Sir, with great respect, your most obedt Sert

D B. WARDEN.

RC (DLC); at foot of text: "Thomas Jefferson Esquire"; endorsed by TJ as received 16 May 1816 and so recorded in SJL; with notes by TJ on verso relating to his 17 May 1816 reply to Warden: "Ticknor Opere di Plantone di Dardi Bembo Venice 1601. 5. v. 12ᵐᵒ certif Talleyrand Monroe our taxes tob° wheat. weather family."

For the VOLUME by Destutt de Tracy and the POEM by Carlo Botta, see Tracy to TJ, 4 Feb. 1816, and Botta to TJ, 10 Jan. 1816, both of which were enclosed in Warden to TJ, 9 Aug. 1816. Warden's JUST PUBLISHED work was *A Chorographical and Statistical Description of the District of Columbia, the seat of the general Government of the United States* (Paris, 1816; Poor, *Jefferson's Library*, 7 [no. 362]).

To Joel Yancey

DEAR SIR   Monticello Feb. 20. 16.

A letter of the 14ᵗʰ from mr Gibson informs me my tob° was not then down. this occasions me to send the bearer express, our cross mail being too dilatory to be depended on. my anxiety on this subject is occasioned by my having money engagements due at our last and next court which depend for fulfilment on the tob° getting to mr Gibson's hands, until which I cannot draw on him. I imagine the delay is occasioned by the high demands probably of the boatmen. but these we must yield to, and give what others do. we may lose more by a fall of price than the difference of transportation. I wish it therefore to be hurried down. if by delaying the bearer a day or two you can get it's departure engaged for a fixed day so as to inform me of that by his return, it will enable me to speak with precision to those with whom I am under engagements. mr Gibson will pay the Boatage on your order & delivery of the tob°   with respect to the flour, it's transportation may wait more reasonable prices; but it should be down in all March. I learn from Richmond that the Lynchburg boatmen refuse to take up plaister under 22½ D the ton[1] this puts the use of it there with us out of question for the present year: I have not bought therefore for that place. if there should be danger of this exorbitance continuing, we must adopt other means for carrying it up hereafter either by people of our own, or the Milton boatmen who bring it here for 8.D. but of this we will talk when I see you which will probably be about mid-April. I am in hopes you have got clover seed. I have given 12.D. for what we use here. I shall be glad to learn how Lovilo is, and how likely to be. I have some thought of sending up a waggon about the close of the month with some trees & necessaries for my use there: but this is uncertain. I should be much pleased should there be a prospect of Lovilo's being able to return in it. I salute you with great [es]teem and friendship.

PoC (MHi); on verso of a reused address cover from the "B.A.S." (probably the Berkshire Agricultural Society) to TJ; torn, with some text rewritten by TJ; at foot of text: "Mr Joel Yancey"; endorsed by TJ.

Patrick Gibson's LETTER OF THE 14TH, not found, is recorded in SJL as received 16 Feb. 1816 from Richmond.

Missing letters from Yancey dated 14 Oct. and 31 Dec. 1815 are listed in SJL as received from Bedford on 24 Oct. 1815 and 5 Jan. 1816, respectively.

[1] Preceding two words interlined.

Auditor's Report on the Purchase of Thomas Jefferson's Library

Treasury Department Auditors Office February 21st[1] 1816

N° 31.537.[2]

I have examined and adjusted an Account between the United States and Thomas Jefferson in relation to the Sale of his Library, and find that he is chargeable on said account

To Treasury Warrants for amount of the following issued in his favor   Viz

N° 8584 dated 21 April 1815 √	8580
8585 " " " " √	4870
8611 " 4 May " √	10500
Dollars √	23950

I also find that he is entitled to Credit on said account

By Amount of the Purchase of his Library as Authorised by Act of Congress of the 30th of Jany 1815   Dollars √ 23950

As appears from the Statement and Vouchers herewith transmitted for the decision of the Comptroller of the Treasury thereon

R. HARRISON Auditor

MS (DLC: TJ Papers, 206:36700B); in Patrick Ferrall's hand, signed by Richard Harrison, with check marks in an unidentified hand; adjacent to signature: "To Joseph Anderson Esq Comptroller of the Treasury"; with subjoined note signed by Anderson at the Comptroller's Office, 21 Feb. 1816: "Admitted & Certified"; redirected beneath that "To Jos: Nourse Esqr Register"; stamped on verso: "REGISTERED"; docketed on verso, in Ferrall's hand: "Auditors Report On the Account of Thomas Jefferson," and in one or more unidentified hands: "31.537" and "Reg^d Entered 23^d Feby 1816 blotter Page 55"; initialed on verso by Andrew Ross, clerk in the Comptroller's Office.

TREASURY WARRANTS numbers 8584, 8585, and 8611, in the sums and with the dates given above and totaling $23,950, were certified in the Register's Office by John D. Barclay on 20 Feb. 1816 (MS in DLC: TJ Papers, 206:36700A; in Barclay's hand and signed by him; docketed on verso: "Registers Certificate Thomas Jefferson relative to the Sale of his Library").

On 20 Feb. 1816 Patrick Ferrall, principal clerk in the Auditor's Office, drew up a statement of TJ's account with the United States Treasury corresponding in its particulars with the report above (MS in DLC: TJ Papers, 206:36700C–D; in Ferrall's hand; with subjoined certification by Ross, 21 Feb. 1816; docketed on verso by Ferrall: "Statement of the Acco^{ts} of Thomas Jefferson" and in one or more unidentified hands: "31.537" and "Entered 23 Feby 1816 blotter Page 55"; initialed on verso by Ross).

^{1} Word added in an unidentified hand.
^{2} Word added in an unidentified hand.

From Joseph C. Cabell

DEAR SIR,   Richmond. 21st Feb: 1816.

I wrote you hastily by a late mail a short letter containing the substance of our proceedings respecting those Bills in which you felt a particular interest. A more particular statement may not be unacceptable to you. Capt: Miller's Bill passed in the Senate by a vote of 12 to ab^t 5. after an elaborate discussion, in which not only the merits of the particular claim, but the general law of escheats, was brought into view. The style of the petition and the support you gave Capt: Miller, were no doubt, the cause of so large a majority in his favor. It was well that the title papers arrived when they did: otherwise the Bill would have been lost: and Capt: Miller would have been driven to the sale of the Real estate under the 3^d section of the Act of 8th Feb: 1813: on which m^r Johnson thought he ought to be suffered to rely. The honest but droll exultation of the worthy Captain, when he was informed of the passage of the Bill, was a source of great satisfaction & merriment to m^r maury & myself. I am well persuaded he will always justify the statements you have made on his behalf, and that his gratitude to you will cease only with his life. His papers were returned to him, and were carried to Norfolk, to which place he hastened, as soon as the Bill passed.

I communicated to the Senate that part of your Letter containing your motives for giving to the Proctor of the Central College the powers of a Justice of the peace. Finding notwithstanding many members opposed to that part of the Bill, and we deeming it not very important to carry it at this time, I consented to strike it out. I moved also to strike out those sections relative to schools in the county of Albemarle. This motion, however, was not made till I had fully consulted with Governor Nicholas, my brother William, and several other friends. It is unquestionably in the contemplation of the Assembly, to establish a general system of education throughout the state; and for that purpose augmentations are made from time to time to the Literary fund. A resolution has recently passed the House of Delegates the object of which is to give to the Literary fund, the whole of the Surplus of the debt due to this state from the U. States, over & above the sum of six hundred thousand dollars. Whether this resolution will finally grow into a Law or not, the passage of it demonstrates the existence of a favorable temper, in regard to a speedy amelioration in the existing state of education in this state. As the revenue bill is now on the table of the Senate, and the estimated amount of the taxes embraces a sinking fund for paying gradually our debt of $750,000, to the Banks, I presume the Assembly will give the surplus of the debt over $600,000, to the Literary fund. As the people of Albemarle will be taxed to pay the debts of the state, or in other words, to form the Literary fund, they probably would have very great objections to a power in the Trustees of the Central College to impose additional taxes on them.[1] Under these views of the subject, & supported by the unanimous advice of the abovenamed friends, I made the motion to amend the Bill in the part alluded to. Previous to its arrival in the senate, the part respecting the Literary fund was stricken out in the Lower House.—Mr Poindexter had been very friendly in regard to this Bill, and when he made a motion at a late stage of the proceedings to amend it, in such manner as to save to the counties of Louisa, and Fluvanna, their respective interests in the Glebes of St Anne, & Fredericksville, I could but yield to it, the more especially as I am confident the Senate would have overuled me had I opposed him on that point. I was the more inclined to this conciliatory course, because m^r maury informed me, that only a very small part of the two Glebes could be claimed by Fluvanna & Louisa: and for this further reason, that the policy of the friends of the Central College, must be, to rely on funds to be here after obtained from the Legislature, rather than on the very limited means contemplated by the Bill. With these modifications the Bill has passed into a Law. The Bill respecting M^r

Estis's Lottery was rejected in the Senate. As it came to this House, it was a bill for a Lottery—the proceeds of which were to be applied to the purchase of Estis's buildings, provided the trustees should consider them the best scite for the Central College. I proposed in the Senate, to amend the Bill by directing the proceeds of the Lottery to be applied to the use & benefit of the Central College, provided they should not wish to establish the College in Estis's houses, or provided they should not be able to purchase them on such terms as they should deem just & reasonable. It was suggested by a member of the Senate that such a Bill as this would be giving the Petitioners "a stone when they asked for bread." I admitted the departure in the Bill as it came from the House of Delegates, from the Petition: and the still further departure contemplated by the amendments I proposed: But informed the House of the conflict that might arise between Mr Estis's Academy & the Central College, if his petition should be granted; & urged such possible conflict as a sufficient reason for rejecting the application of the petitioners in the form in which it appeared before the House of Delegates. If however the views of the petitioners could be reconciled with the interests of the College, I could have no objections: and as an additional Lottery for the benefit of the Central College might possibly succeed, I should vote for the Bill, & proposed the amendments merely to clear up all doubts as to the destination of the proceeds of the Lottery. The Senate rejected the Bill: nor was I much grieved by the decision.—You will have seen your Letter to Mr Carr in the Enquirer. It came out on the morning of the day that the Resolution passed the House of Delegates appropriating the surplus of our U. States debt to the Literary Fund, and I have reasons to believe, had a considerable effect in promoting the passage of that Resolution. I fear, however, no measure will be founded on it. The manner in which it is generally spoken of, induces me to believe that its publication will produce a very happy effect on the interests of science in this state.—I should be pleased to see in print[2] your remarks on the division of the counties into wards, as preparatory to the future introduction of that measure into the Assembly. The proper point of time for making the attempt I presume would be, when the Literary fund shall be applied to the establishment of schools.—The Bill respecting the navigable waters of this commonwealth, with Col: Green's amendments, has passed into a Law. No retrospective provision is embraced in the Law. Having now given such information as I thought might be agreeable to you, I have to beg the kindness of you at any leisure moment, to drop me a line, informing me whether De Say's work on political Economy has ever been translated, I have some idea of making the attempt, sh^d it not already have been done by some other person. I feel myself infinitely obliged by the several letters you have had the goodness to write me during this session. I know the extent of your correspondence, & the drudgery it imposes on you: and all I ask is a line about De say.

Most respectfully & truly yours   JOSEPH C. CABELL

RC (ViU: TJP-PC); endorsed by TJ as received 23 Feb. 1816 and so recorded in SJL.

The Virginia statute OF 8TH FEB: 1813 was "An Act, releasing the Commonwealth's right to lands, in certain cases, and vesting in the Commonwealth, in certain cases, the title to the undisposed of residuum of personal estates." Its third section provided that an alien who held or claimed Virginia land could sell it to American citizens if proceedings for escheating the property to the state had not commenced (*Acts of Assembly* [1812–13 sess.], 35–6).

The BILL RESPECTING MR ESTIS'S LOTTERY resulted from a Petition of Albemarle County Inhabitants to the Virginia House of Delegates (MS in Vi: RG 78, Legislative Petitions, Albemarle Co., in an unidentified hand, signed by John Harris and 155 other petitioners, docketed: "Albemarle Petition. Decr 15th 1815.

ref^d to C^t of J.   Reasonable   Bill drawn January 24th 1816"; Tr in ViU: JCC, in an unidentified hand, lacking nine names, endorsed by Cabell: "Petition of 147 Inhabitants of Albemarle. 1815"). Presented to the House of Delegates on 15 Dec. 1815 (*JHD* [1815–16 sess.], 43), it urged the General Assembly to pass a law "authorising a sufficient sum to be raised by lottery, adequate to the purchase of the house at present occupied by T: T. Estes in the village of Charlottesville, to be used & established as an Academy, & to raise such other sums, & make such other provisions, as to your Honorable Body may appear adequate to the object."

YOUR LETTER TO MR CARR: TJ to Peter Carr, 7 Sept. 1814. DE SAY: Jean Baptiste Say.

[1] Cabell here canceled "for the same object."
[2] Preceding two words interlined.

From Thomas Eston Randolph

DEAR SIR   Ashton 21st Feby 1816

I shall always acknowledge with grateful sensibility my obligations to you for your very friendly application to the secretary of the navy in favor of my son Mann—

Mann waited on him in Washington, was very kindly received by him, and assured of obtaining a warrant so soon as there is a vacancy—The profession he has chosen, I confess, is not perfectly agreable to me, but he has a right to chuse for himself, and I most fervently pray that if an opportunity is afforded him, his conduct may reflect honor on himself, and do credit to your recommendation—

Your Mill account for the last year, you will perceive was made out last August, under the impression that all your flour had been deliver'd, nor did I know until very lately that any mistake had occurr'd respecting it—it has given M[r] Randolph and myself much uneasiness; expecting to receive a letter from him by this days Mail, explaining the matter, I was induced to delay answering your favor of the 30th Jan[y]—the simple fact is, that 67 barrels of Flour were shipp'd on M[r] Randolphs boat for you, but by some mistake it was deliverd to Mess[rs] Warwicks—the business shall immediately be adjusted to your satisfaction—and mean while, as fast as boats can be procured, I will send flour to your Agent to pay off the present years Rent—52 barrels were sent down on Monday for your account—I pray you to accept assurance of great respect and very affectionate regards

THO[S] ESTON RANDOLPH

RC (MHi); endorsed by TJ as received 22 Feb. 1816 and so recorded in SJL.

M[R] RANDOLPH: Thomas Mann Randolph (1768–1828). TJ's AGENT was Patrick Gibson.

From John G. Robert
(for Patrick Gibson)

SIR   Richmond February 22[d] 1816

I send you by Gilmers boat a Cask Teneriffe Wine rec[d] of D[r] Fernandes through Fox & Richardson & have by your directions inclosed it in a rough cask to secure it from the Watermen—

The Gauger's[1] mark (as you will observe at the head of the cask) is twenty nine Gallons, one Gall out Maj[r] Gibbon has judged of the wine & M[r] Richard[n] informs me that the maj[r] says[2] it is the best Teneriffe he has ever tasted—

I am Sir
Y[rs] Respectfuly

PATRICK GIBSON
By JOHN. G. ROBERT

ps Inclosed is Maj[r] Gibbons Certificate

RC (ViU: TJP-ER); between dateline and salutation: "Tho[s] Jefferson Esq[r]"; endorsed by TJ as a letter from Gibson received 29 Feb. 1816 and so recorded in SJL. Enclosure not found.

John Gibson Robert (1799–1830) was a lieutenant in 1814 in the Richmond Junior Blues, a group of boys aged about fifteen who had "embodied themselves as volunteers" to defend the city. He served as a clerk for Gibson until at least 1820

and was the master of a Richmond Masonic lodge in 1825 (CVSP, 10:381; Robert [for Gibson] to TJ, 13 Apr. 1820; David K. Walthall, History of Richmond Lodge, No. 10, A. F. & A. M. [1909], 195; Clay, Papers, 5:312; Daily Richmond Whig, 18 Sept. 1830; gravestone inscription in Shockoe Hill Cemetery, Richmond).

[1] Manuscript: "Guager's."
[2] Preceding three words interlined.

From John Barnes

DEAR SIR—   George Town Co^a 23^d feb^y 1816.

Your Esteemed fav^r 7^h recd 21st Relieved me from the Vague Rumour, which indeed, I paid little regard to—the Stock—intended for these treasury notes, are the funded 7 ₱Cents. which I shall attend to—with reference to a Bill on London the Most extravagant exchanges in paper, both to the Northw^d and S^{o}w^d has so deranged, the exchanges on Europe, that the Shipping Mercht^s here and at Balt^o will not, draw, at this present Under 17$\frac{1}{2}$ a 20 per C^t advance—whilst at NYork, you may purchase a 5 a 7$\frac{1}{2}$ and at Boston a 2$\frac{1}{2}$ to pay in their paper—not Ours. neither can I, remit my friend Mr Griffin at York Town under 6 ₱Cent. disc^t for this paper—flour here is a 9$\frac{1}{2}$ dolls tho not in demand at Boston I am told Under \$8—owning to there Various Vexasious Exchanges—how long it may Continue is very Uncertain—at least I shall wait, a while, in the hope of a more favorable Crisis—

that you may Continue to disappoint—your disappointed Enemies and suffer them—quietly—to take the lead of you on so momentious—a Crisis—is the ardent[1] Wish—

of Dear Sir Your most Obed^t & very hum^l serv^t

JOHN BARNES,

RC (ViU: TJP-ER); at foot of text: "Thomas Jefferson Esqr Monticello Virg^a"; endorsed by TJ as received 28 Feb. 1816 and so recorded in SJL.

[1] Manuscript: "adent."

Isaac A. Coles's Account of a Conversation with Thomas Jefferson

[before 23 Feb. 1816]

With Mr Jefferson I conversed at length on the subject of architecture—Palladio he said "was the Bible"—. You should get it & stick close to it—. He had sent all his Books &c. &c. to Washington, or he would have drawn y^r House for you—it would have been a pleasure to him—but now he could not undertake to do it before the fall when he expected other Books from Paris—He disapproved of parapet walls—no House could be made perfectly tight with them—there must be a gutter along the wall which in heavy falls of rain &c. would sometimes overflow—[1] as was the case with the Presidents House in

Washington & every other House similarly constructed that he had ever seen—the roof should cover the walls & the Balustrade could be raised above it as at Monticello which tho not handsome was safe— The flat roof He thought very practicable—the sort he most approved of was the one I described to you of sheet Iron with a rise of half an inch in each foot—viz of $12\frac{1}{2}$ Inches to your House $50^{f.}$ wide—your cross gutters &c &. would never do, & ought not to be thought of— He lays it down as a rule never to be departed from "That a gutter over a wall can never be safe"—Your South Portico would be very handsome & should be supported on arches as you proposed—the height not to be less than 16^f.—The rule was that the height of a room should be equal to its width—20^f therefore would not be too much but 16^f would do—his was 18^f which gave chambers over all the smaller rooms on the north of his House which you might have in yours.—The tuscan order was too plain—it would do for your Barns &c. but was not fit for a dwelling House—the Doric would not cost much more & would be vastly handsomer—his was doric—you could get drawing[2] of the Columns, cornice &c &c. &c. from him—Dinsmore who is now in Petersburg he recommends to you as a good & faithful workman or Oldham who is (I think) in Richmond—either of them would build you a House without any false architecture, so much the rage at present—The Italian rule for windows is a third of the whole space—viz—7 feet of light to every 21. feet of wall—He is a great advocate for light and air—as you predicted he was for giving you Octagons—they were charming—they gave you a semicircle of air & light—He thought the[3] window you proposed would be very handsome for a passage or Hall &c. but seemed not to know that they were in use & fashionable for rooms.—In a word the old Gentleman entered as he always does in to every thing, with great Zeal into your building scheme, and I now regret more than ever that you did not see him

I cannot recollect, much less write the one half of what he said to me; but when we meet which will be very soon I will repeat much more of our Conversation—

RC (ViU: JHC); extract by the Editors from Coles to John H. Cocke, 23 Feb. [1816]; partially dated "Saturday Night Feb: 23ᵈ," with year assigned based on endorsement and internal evidence, although 23 Feb. 1816 was a Friday; signed: "I. A. Coles"; addressed: "Genˡ John H. Cocke. Bremo"; endorsed by Cocke: "Colº I A Coles Feby 23ᵈ 1816."

In the unextracted portions of this letter, Coles explained that he could not accompany his brother the next day because his planting was not yet complete and could not be trusted to agents for another week, and he described negotiations he conducted with a workman on Cocke's behalf while "On my way to Monticello."

John H. Cocke set plans in motion in

1815 for the construction of several new buildings at his Bremo estate in Fluvanna County. He did not begin building his new house until 1818 (Fiske Kimball, "The Building of Bremo," *VMHB* 57 [1949]: 5–6, 11). Andrea PALLADIO was a sixteenth-century Italian architect and writer who interpreted and popularized ancient Roman architectural ideas for an early modern European audience. For editions of his works owned by TJ, see Sowerby, nos. 4174–5, 4181, and 4215, and Poor, *Jefferson's Library*, 12 (no. 723).

Writing from Bremo on 14 Jan. 1816, Cocke's first wife, Ann Blaws Barraud Cocke (d. 1816), described the architectural plan under discussion here in a letter to her mother, Ann B. Barraud: "My husband has amused himself all the bad weather in drawing a plan for our house—he is full of it and we hold long consultations about it—I have here given you a sketch of the result of his last Labours—I have given you the basement story the 4 front rooms of which will be situated like Mr Ambler dining but the north rooms will be several feet below the surface the conveniencies of this story are many but there are some objections to the story above—The room over the dining room would be my Chamber—That over the Servants hall The Nursery—over the store room a private room for myself—Over the Lodging room a drawing room—Over the Library and Nancy store-room—Lodging rooms—The house you must understand is but one story and the basement—The back passage which is cut in small cellar-room below—would on the second floor be similar to Mr Tuckers My husband thinks it will be the most convenient plan and that he can make it very handsome—Let us know what you think of it—Our minds are not at all made up" (RC with sketch of floor plan in ViU: JHC).

[1] Coles here canceled "a Balustrade was best."

[2] Manuscript: "grawing."

[3] Manuscript: "to."

From Robert Ould

SIR   Lancasterian School Georgetown D.C. Feb 23rd 1816

Permit me to offer you for perusal an Epitome of Lancasters system of Education

Symptoms of a desire to promote general instruction seem to pervade a considerable number of individuals in the United States, but they are at a loss for a plan to direct their energies

Nothing more than a Teacher of the above establishment I have ventured to address[1] you hoping that you will examine the enclosed little volume and tell me what opinion you have of it, and whether you think it best[2] calculated for an elementary school for the inhabitants of this country

I am (as the enclosed will shew) an Englishman have been in this place more than four years, and have qualified Thirty Teachers who have gone to various parts of the United States to dispense a knowledge of the same

not[w]ithstanding these exertions a sanction is required to promote the object *

* Any views of your own on this matter would be received and duly appreciated.

I feel somewhat more zeal for the system and its founder from my being a pupil of his, therefore if I have in any way spoken of myself more than I ought I beg you will attribute it to a desire for the promotion of general instruction than for anything else.

I should have troubled you much earlier on this subject had I not remembered that a moment like the present would better suit the promotion of a philanthropic system of Education than any other.

I remain with great respect Sir Your obed[t] servant

ROB[T] OULD

RC (DLC); corner chipped; endorsed by TJ as received 28 Feb. 1816 and so recorded in SJL. Enclosure: Joseph Lancaster, *The British System of Education: being A Complete Epitome of the Improvements and Inventions practised By Joseph Lancaster: to which is added, A Report of the Trustees of the Lancaster School at Georgetown, Col.* (Washington, D.C., 1812; Poor, *Jefferson's Library,* 5 [no. 209]).

Robert Ould (1788–1840), educator, was born in London and educated there by Joseph Lancaster. A proponent of the Lancasterian model of instruction, which relied heavily on older students teaching younger ones, Ould was tapped late in 1811 by Lancaster himself to be the first of his protégés to relocate to the United States as a teacher. Ould agreed to the move provided that he could bring along Henry Ould, his younger brother and fellow teacher. Robert stayed at the Georgetown Lancaster school while Henry was soon running an academy of his own in

Washington, also in the District of Columbia. The elder Ould was employed by the Georgetown school until at least 1821. In 1828 he introduced the Lancasterian system to an academy for Choctaw Indians in Kentucky. Ould died in Georgetown (Edson B. Olds and Susan S. Gascoyne Old, *The Olds (Old, Ould) Family in England and America* [1915], 318–9; Lancaster, *British System of Education,* 124–5, 128–30; John Clagett Proctor, "Joseph Lancaster and the Lancasterian Schools in the District of Columbia, with Incidental School Notes," *Records of the Columbia Historical Society* 25 [1923]: 6–7, 18–20; Ronald Rayman, "Joseph Lancaster's Monitorial System of Instruction and American Indian Education, 1815–1838," *History of Education Quarterly* 21 [1981]: 403; Washington *Daily National Intelligencer,* 11 Apr. 1821, 24 July 1840).

[1] Extraneous comma editorially omitted.
[2] Word interlined.

From Garrit Storm

DEAR SIR   Newyork February. 23[d] 1816

The enclosed Paragraph was Some time Since taken from the National Intelligencer and must be my apology for the great liberty I am taking in addressing this Letter to you Sir with the view of making enquiry respecting this M[r] Quarrier—You will confer a very great obligation by informing me if the Gentleman alluded to in the advertisement is a Frenchman, and whether he was in this City about the year 1800.—If these questions are answered in the affirmative—You will most materially serve me by informing me of his Situation as to pecuniary matters.—Offering Dear Sir my very sincere apologies for all this trouble, and with a wish to have the pleasure to fulfil any commands you may have in this place.   I am with the very highest respect

Your Mo assured & obedient[1] humble servant

GARRIT STORM

RC (MHi); between dateline and salutation: "Honble Thomas Jefferson Esqr"; endorsed by TJ as received 1 Mar. 1816 and so recorded in SJL. RC (DLC); address cover only; with PoC of TJ to Benjamin J. Campbell, 26 Mar. 1816, on verso; glued to backing sheet, with address illegible; postmarked New York, [23?] Feb.

Garrit Storm (1778–1851), merchant in New York City, went into partnership with his father in 1796 and assumed control of the latter's grocery about 1808. He retired in 1824, turning the store over to his stepson. Storm was a founding director of the Globe Insurance Company in 1814 and continued to serve on its board until at least 1819. He was also a founding trustee of the New-York Life Insurance and Trust Company, and from 1820 until at least 1840 he was a director of the Phenix Bank. A member of the city's chamber of commerce, Storm was a successful businessman who subscribed $10,000 to federal war loans during the War of 1812. He paid taxes on an estate valued at $50,000 in 1815 and $22,000 in 1820. Storm amassed large tracts of New York City real estate, including a Wall Street lot and a city block at Forty-second Street and Fifth Avenue (Eugene A. Hoffman, *Genealogy of the Hoffman Family* [1899], 514, 515; "Walter Barrett" [Joseph Alfred Scoville], *The Old Merchants of New York City* [1863–69; repr. 1968], 3:323–9; *New-York Gazette & General Advertiser*, 7 Feb. 1809, 4 May 1811, 8 July 1820; *Laws of the State of New-York, passed at the Thirty-Seventh Session of the Legislature . . . January, 1814* [Albany, 1814], 54; *Charter and By-Laws of the New-York Chamber of Commerce* [New York, 1818], 28; *New-York Daily Advertiser*, 2 Feb. 1819; *Rates and Proposals of the New-York Life Insurance and Trust Company* [1830], 4, 18; Edwin Williams, *The New-York Annual Register* [1840], 265; David Thomas Valentine, *Manual of the Corporation of the City of New-York* [1864], 764; *New York Times*, 10 June 1917; Thomas E. V. Smith, *The City of New York in the year of Washington's Inauguration, 1789* [1889], 50; Geoffrey P. Miller, "Meinhard v. Salmon," *New York University Law and Economics Working Papers* 105 [2007]: 1–2).

The ENCLOSED PARAGRAPH, clipped from the Washington *Daily National Intelligencer*, 17 Dec. 1814, and still filed with the RC, states that "Information Is hereby given to the person advertising for and wishing to know whether a certain ALEXANDER QUARRIER be alive, &c. that the said Alexander Quarrier is alive and living in Kenhawa county, Virginia, and that he can be identified to the satisfaction of said advertiser, by applying to the Hon. Thomas Jefferson, the Hon. James Monroe, or to Wm. Burns, living in the city of Richmond, Virginia." For TJ's relationship with Quarrier, see Quarrier to TJ, 24 May 1812, and TJ's 7 June 1812 certificate of acquaintance with Quarrier, enclosed in his letter of that date to William Burns.

[1] Manuscript: "obeident."

From Joel Yancey

DR SIR   Poplar Forrest Feby 24.^h 16

Your favour of the 20^h by Billy I reeceivd early in the day on thursday last and immediately I rode to Lynchburg to engage a Boat to carry down your To^bo. I could get none, they were mostly down, and what few was empty were engaged, however I made an engagement with Doct^r Cabell to take it in his Boats so soon as they return, which they ought to do by the last of next week, I think you may safely Say, that your To^bo will take its departure from Lynchburg on, or before 10th March, I am truly Sorry that it is not in Richmond at this time, I have some Reasons and excuses to offer for the delay, but it is needless now to trouble you with them, I assure you I have done the best I could The wheat is all delivered, early in Jany. at Mitchels, mills, but we cant spare it our corn will not last until Harvest I, am almost certain, and there's none to be had for less than six dollars, and thirty miles off I should be greatly relieved if you consent for us to hold the flour, until there is a certainty that we can do without it, we are as careful of the corn as possible, I believe there is not year goes out, without its being, counted or measured should we be compell^d to use the flour for Bread, the <u>fine</u> might I suppose be easily exchanged for midlings or coarrse and the difference, we have sown about thirty acres in clover[1] (in the chaff) and have engaged as much more as I shall want at 10 dollars it is not yet come to hand but I hourly expect^d it, should I be disappoint[ed] in that, there is plenty in Lynchburg at 12.D Poor Lovilo, never will leave the Forest, he has been gradually waisting away ever since you left here and at times appears to be in great pain, he may live several months but I think it is impossible he can recover Doc^r Steptoe has declined his visits to him and says that <u>he</u> cannot relieve him, I sent stocks to the mill, and believe they are nearly all saw,d for the Saw mill. I have got also the plank from Depriest for the House, but I find in putting it on, that we shall lack 10 or fift[een] plank I sent too for 100 feet more than Goodman said it would require, as soon as I can possibly get the To^bo off (and I shall use every exerten,) Ill write you again, I shall be very glad to see you at the Forest, but I shall dread your Horses until after Harvest, Accept my best wishes for your welfare   JOEL YANCEY

RC (MHi); edge trimmed; endorsed by TJ as received 27 Feb. 1816 and so recorded in SJL. RC (MHi); address cover only; with PoC of TJ to Yancey, 15 Mar. 1816, on recto and verso; addressed:

"Thomas Jefferson Esqr Monticello— Virginia"; franked; postmarked.

[1] Yancey here canceled "seed."

From Joseph C. Cabell

DEAR SIR, Richmond. 26 Feb: 1816.

I have at length procured from the Editor of the Enquirer & now return your original Letter to Mr Carr. Its publication, in my opinion, was well timed, and has produced a happy effect on the measures of the assembly. We have appropriated all our U. States' debt, except $600,000, to the purposes of education, and have required the President & Directors of the Literary Fund, to report to the next assembly the best plan of an university, colleges, academies & schools. The passage of both these measures is unquestionably to be ascribed in a great degree to your Letter. But, it may be asked, why enquire of the President & Directors of the Literary Fund, for plans, when one so satisfactory is already before the public? I will tell you. Appropriations abstracted from their location are most easily obtained. Should the next Assembly sanction the scheme of an university, you will see the Presbyterians about Lexington, and the Scotch Irish about Staunton, striving to draw it away from Albemarle, and the whole western delegation, according to custom, will threaten to divide the state unless this institution should be placed beyond the Ridge. Staunton wants the seat of government, and considers the day near at hand when she will be the metropolis of the state. Any brilliant establishment at the eastern foot of the Ridge will shake those claims, and disturb speculations founded upon them. Mr Mercer of the House of Delegates will be an advocate for a western scite. The Washington College at Lexington will be the bantling of the Federalists. But I think the Central College will triumph over them all. I am pleased to think that Governor Nicholas will be in office at the commencement of the next session of assembly. In the interim, the friends of science will be able to form the necessary plans to promote the general weal.—We have had some singular proceedings in the Caucuses at this place which were held for the purpose of making an electoral ticket. I had hoped never again to be involved in trouble about Col: monroe, and on this occasion, have been most reluctantly dragged into the business. This is the second instance in which a ruffian of a party of pretenders, fools & knaves, in our district, has taken the trouble to come all the way down to the assembly, to injure me in the public estimation: but I have the satisfaction to reflect, that in this, as in the former instance, the aggressor is exposed on the spot, & the injury aimed at myself, recoils upon his own head.

I am, d^r Sir, y^{rs} most faithfully & truly   JOSEPH C. CABELL

RC (ViU: TJP-PC); endorsed by TJ as received 5 Mar. 1816 and so recorded in SJL. Enclosure: TJ to Peter Carr, 7 Sept. 1814.

Thomas Ritchie was the EDITOR of the *Richmond Enquirer*. In section 5 of "An Act appropriating the Public Revenue," which passed into law on 24 Feb. 1816, the Virginia General Assembly APPROPRIATED ALL OUR U. STATES' DEBT, EXCEPT $600,000, TO THE PURPOSES OF EDUCATION (*Acts of Assembly* [1815–16 sess.], 5–7).

The legislature also agreed to a joint resolution "on the subject of a system of Public Education," in which it was "resolved, by the General Assembly, that the President and Directors of the Literary fund be requested to digest, and report to the next General Assembly, a system of public Education, calculated to give effect to the appropriations made to that object by the Legislature, heretofore, and during it's present session; and to compre-hend in such system the establishment of one University, to be called, 'The University of Virginia,' and such additional Colleges, Academies, and Schools, as shall diffuse the benefits of education through-out the Commonwealth, and such rules, for the government of such University, Colleges, Academies and Schools, as shall produce economy in the expenditures for the establishment and maintenance, and good order and discipline in the manage-ment, thereof—Agreed to by both Houses of the General Assembly of Virginia.—Feby 24th 1816" (Tr in DLC; entirely in William Munford's hand; printed in *Acts of Assembly* [1815–16 sess.], 266–7).

The former Washington Academy in Lexington became WASHINGTON COLLEGE (later Washington and Lee University) by a 2 Jan. 1813 act of the General Assembly (*Acts of Assembly* [1812–13 sess.], 90). Cabell was nominated a presidential elector during CAUCUSES held in Richmond (*Richmond Enquirer*, 20 Feb. 1816).

To Alexander J. Dallas

DEAR SIR   Monticello Feb. 26. 16.

According to request in your's of the 12th I will give the best statement I can of Isaac Briggs's case with the joint aid of memory and the papers to which I have recourse.

After the acquisition of Louisiana it became extremely interesting to the government of the US. that the communication between Washington & New Orleans should be made as short and rapid as possible. it seemed to me very absurd that the road between these two places, in the maritime country, not 1000. miles apart, should take a circuit of 12. or 1500. miles, over all the ridges of mountains, crossing and recrossing them, and passing thro' Indian deserts as destitute and dangerous as those below the mountains. Mr Isaac Briggs one of the Surveyors general of the US. being, in the summer of 1804. about to set out on his journey from Washington to his station, I explained to him, in a conversation, my ideas of finding a new and direct route by Franklin C.H. in Georgia, Tuckabatchee E^tc to N. Orleans; that, considering how much less the distance was, he could not lose much time were he to proceed by that rather than by the mountainous &

ordinary route; and that with a pocket sextant he might, by daily observations of latitude and longitude, of the places he passed by, give us a more accurate draught of the course the road should pursue, than could be obtained by chain & compass. he came into the proposition at once, and undertook it chearfully. as neither of us believed that either the labor or the expence of the journey would be sensibly increased, I do not think a word was said between us about any compensation; but that the impression of both was that the difference would not merit consideration. it turned out very differently indeed. I procured him an excellent sextant, & he set out from Washington, I think, in July 1804. and did not reach N. Orleans till the end of November; after a journey of labor & suffering scarcely to be equalled; of which some account will be found in his letters of 1804. Sep. 2. Oct. 2. Nov. 26. & Dec. 31. herewith inclosed. on his arrival in N. Orleans he was taken with a fever, the consequence probably of his long detention among the bogs and slashes of the country he had past thro' in the Autumnal season, an account of which will be found in the same letters. he forwarded from N. Orleans a Report & Map of the country; which I recieved Feb. 20. 1805.   in the mean time, Congress, by a resolution of Dec. 31. 04. had expressed some wish to me on the subject, which I cannot now specify, because I have no copy of the journals of that date. but it was something to which the messages of which copies are inclosed, were an answer. this resolution of the house will of course be turned to. the Map being delivered to Congress, for the information of the members, & deposited among their papers, they made an appropriation for opening the road, which was repeated at subsequent sessions, as the work proceeded, and it would have been completed in 1808. had we not been disappointed in an undertaking of the late Daniel Clarke who promised to have an actual examination made of the best route (I think from Pascagoola or Pearl river) to N. Orleans, and especially of that which should reduce to a minimum the water passage thro' the Rigolets. towards this, his possessions on that route, and his local knolege of the best agents, gave him facilities. he failed in effecting it. in this state of the enterprise I left it: and it was afterwards abandoned for reasons which I never learned. as to every thing respecting the opening of the road, and the actual & rapid transmission of some mails along it, using water carriage for the last unopened portion, the late P. M. G. mr Granger, and his deputies mr Bradley & mr Pease can give full information.

Mr Briggs's expences, his labors & sufferings having greatly exceeded expectations, he thought, and so did I, that they would now become a fair subject of compensation by the public. it was first attempted by the way suggested in my letter to mr Holland, a member, of which I inclose a copy, but was not effected. at the succeeding session of 1805. 6. it was proposed to insert a compensation in the appropriation bill, but to this it was objected that nothing should be inserted in that but what had been sanctioned by a previous law, and that the regular way would be for mr Briggs to petition the House, in which case a law would pass authorising a proper compensation. accordingly he came on to the next session of 1806. 7. and preferred a petition for compensation, which was referred to the committee of claims. some difficulties being made there, I think they did not act on it, and I learnt privately from a member that some thought I ought not to have engaged a service without a previous approbation and appropriation by Congress, and that the sanction of it would be of bad example. as soon as I understood this, I informed mr Briggs I could no further meddle in the case publicly or privately, that altho' there had never been any engagement, yet I held myself in equity bound to divide with him the inconveniences incurred, that I would reimburse his actual expences, as the time and labor would be burthen enough for him. this I accordingly did, on his own statement that they were about 400. Dollars. subsequent experience has proved the necessity of the President's sometimes risking himself in contracts not previously authorised, where Congress is not in session, the occasion urgent, and likely to pass by, subject always to the approbation or rejection of Congress. the purchase of sulphur, salt petre, arms & ordnance on the capture of the Chesapeake and imminent expectation of war, to the amount of hundreds of thousands of Dollars was an instance. in the case of the road, the opportunity offered of having a survey made by the accurate and easy process of observations of latitude and longitude for which the accident of[1] a qualified person, passing might never again occur, and the necessity otherwise of doing this by the more expensive tedious and incorrect process of chain and compass, ought not to have been lost, even had expence been foreseen: but none being expected, no scruple was entertained. however, as it turned out contrary to expectation, the acceptance of the result of mr Briggs's labors by Congress, the adopting the plan, the executing the road, nearly to completion on that plan, and thus availing the public of the whole benefit of Briggs's losses, labors and sufferings was a sufficient confirmation & sanction of what had been done. but it was not for me to decide on this, & as to myself, I preferred the little pecuniary sacrifice to having any question made about it. mr Briggs also, I believe, withdrew from further applications until lately, as I learn, that some difficulties make it desirable for him to be allowed this set-off in his public accounts. Congress are in possession of the original map of mr Briggs, if not lost in the conflagration of the Capitol, and if lost, they will still find a copy of it in one of the Atlasses of the library they possess. I do not think that Congress ever passed a decision directly on the question of compensation, nor do I know that any committee ever did. I am inclined to believe it passed off under the frowns of particular members, rather than by any formal decision. but I hazard this on memory only; the records may correct me.   Should this case be reviewed, and a compensation be allowed mr Briggs for the use the public made of his labors, I will request that his claims may be considered without regard to what he has recieved from me, which I would wish him to retain as a further retribution for his sufferings and difficulties, which I am glad to contribute, believing him to be an honest and good man, and knowing that he is a very able one.   Be pleased to accept the assurance of my great esteem and respect

TH: JEFFERSON

PoC (DLC); at foot of first page: "The honble the Secretary of the Treasury." Tr (MdHi: Briggs-Stabler Papers); in Isaac Briggs's hand.

Dallas's letter to TJ was dated 16 Feb. 1816, not THE 12TH. The enclosed letters from Briggs gave SOME ACCOUNT of his journey from Washington to New Orleans (Briggs to TJ, 2 Sept., 2 Oct., 31 Dec. 1804 [MdHi: Briggs-Stabler Papers]; Briggs to TJ, 26 Nov. 1804 [DLC]). Briggs's 22 Dec. 1804 letter from New Orleans forwarding A REPORT & MAP was printed in a *Message from the President of the United States, communicating Further Information in relation to a Public Road from the City of Washington to New-Orleans* (Washington, 1805).

On DEC. 31. 04. the United States House of Representatives resolved that "a post road ought to be established from the City of Washington, on the most convenient and direct route, to pass through or near the Tuckabachee settlement to the Tombigby settlement, in the Mississippi Territory, and from thence to the City of New Orleans," and that "the President of the United States be requested to cause to be laid before this House, any documents, and give such other information as he

may think proper, relative to opening a post road from the City of Washington to the City of New Orleans." TJ complied with messages to the House dated 1 and 23 Feb. 1805 (*JHR,* 5:71–2, 115, 149).

RIGOLETS: streams, rivulets, or straits (*OED*). TJ wrote on Briggs's behalf to James HOLLAND on 22 Feb. 1805 (DLC). In the 1805. 6. session of Congress, a proposed House resolution that "there be allowed to Isaac Briggs, and his assistant, ——— dollars, as a full compensation for their services in exploring and describing the most eligible route for the transportation of the mail from the city of Washington to New Orleans" was referred to the Committee of Ways and Means (*JHR,* 5:153 [28 Feb. 1805]). TJ later informed Briggs that the compensation had been denied as a part of the appropriations bill because the payment had not been sanctioned by a previous law. He added that if Briggs submitted a regular petition to Congress, a law might be passed to authorize a proper amount, but he concluded that "delay is next to a denial" and bound himself to pay Briggs's expenses (TJ to Briggs, 26 Apr. 1806 [DLC]).

[1] Preceding three words interlined.

To Alexander J. Dallas

DEAR SIR   Monticello Feb. 26. 16.

When the law past laying a direct tax, & established the offices of Assessor & Collector, as it appeared that the first of these officers would be of extreme importance to the landholders, whose property would be taxed very much at his will, I consulted such principal men of our district as I was able to see, and there was but one opinion on the subject. all agreed they would rather trust to the good sense, practical knolege of values, and immoveable integrity of mr Peter Minor of this county than to any other person. I sollicited his appointment therefore; but the President & Secretary of the Treasury had before fixed on my son in law Thomas M. Randolph for Collector, and the principle of geographical distribution then required the Assessor to be named in another county. of this their intention [in] favor of mr Randolph I had not had the least intimation. my grand[son] [Th: J.] Randolph, who succeeded his father as Collector is about to resign the office; and as I raised the expectations of mr Minor to the other office before (for he had never thought of it, nor knew of my solliciting it until I had done it) I feel the obligation, now that there is an opportunity of an equivalent appointment, of asking it for him. the geographical argument is now in his favor, and I am perfectly safe in affirming there is not a man who knows him, and who will say there is in the whole district one fitter for it in every qualification of ability, morals, or public confidence. he is personally known to the Secretary of state, and by character, if not personally to the President. if I believed there wa[s] a safer or fitter man in the district to recieve this public trust, nothi[ng] would have induced me to make this unsollicited proposition.

I salute you with friendship and respect.   TH: JEFFERSON

PoC (DLC); on verso of reused address cover of Philip Thornton to TJ, 24 Jan. 1816; mutilated and edge chipped; at foot of text: "The Secretary of the treasury"; endorsed by TJ.

Instead of PETER MINOR, President James Madison appointed Valentine W. Southall to succeed Thomas Jefferson Randolph as collector of direct tax and internal duties for Albemarle, Amherst, Fluvanna, and Nelson counties (*JEP*, 3:68 [2, 3 Jan. 1817]).

To Alexander J. Dallas

Dear Sir   Monticello Feb. 26. 16.

My other two letters being on distinct subjects, and to go perhaps into other hands, I write this separately. will you pardon a criticism on your tariff which the public papers have given us compleat, but as yet without the report explaining it's principles? having written to Europe for some wines, I was led by curiosity to look at that part of the tariff to see what duties I should have to pay, and found it in the follow^g articles.

'Claret & other wines not enumerated, imported
     in bottles, per gallon   70. cents.
    when imported otherwise than in bottles   25. cents,
  black bottles, glass, quart,   per gross 144 cents'

the duty on the wine then being $6\frac{1}{4}$ cents per quart, & on the bottle 1. cent = $7\frac{1}{4}$ cents the act of putting it into the bottle where made (and where it is so much better that it should be done) is dutied at $11\frac{1}{2}$ cents the bottle. this wants proportion an essential principle in just taxation; and if considered morally, is a premium for encoraging in the higher classes of society the same drunkenness which whiskey has introduced into the lower, by giving the monopoly of our tables to the strong wines. these will be always imported in the cask, and the bottle come empty, so as never to pay the additional $11\frac{1}{2}$ cents per bottle for bottling. the light wines on the contrary which will not bear transportation in the cask, as Florence for instance, must pay the prohibitory duty, or stand prohibited. it will really be a proscription of them. yet it is much for the comfort and temperance of society to encourage them. there are abundance of good wines in Europe (called ordinary, or country wines, and sometimes having appropriate names), such as one would be willing to drink every day, which are sold there at 2. cents the quart, and would not bear transportation in the cask. these, with an ad valorem duty proportioned to that of the others, would cost here less than cyder, and would extend the comfort of that liquor, now enjoyed by the few wealthy only to a vast circle of our citizens to the expulsion of that loathsomeness and death they now drink in the form of whisky. would it not be better, my dear Sir, to let the bottled wine stand on it's former ground? we have always paid duty for the wine by the gallon, whether brought in cask or bottles, and, if in the latter, the duty on that was added. in the case above particularised, 25. cents would be paid for the gallon of wine, and 4. cents for the bottles containing it. excuse this suggestion. it is not to give you the trouble of an answer, but merely to draw your attention,

if it should have been an accident of inadvertence. I subjoin the copy
of a Tariff for wines which I prepared for mr Gallatin when we were
in office together, and which was to have been proposed instead of the
tariff then existing, if that law had come under consideration in our
time. it may enable you to be more specific in your enumeration if
you think that desirable. the classification and prices are on my own
knolege. I salute you with great and friendly respect.

TH: JEFFERSON

	cost p.gall[n]	25 pc duty
Tokay, Cape, Malmesey, Hock	4.00	1.00
Champagne, Burgundy, Hermitage, *Claret	2.75	.68$\frac{3}{4}$
† Medoc, Grave, Palus, Coterotie, Condrieu, Moselle	1.25	.31$\frac{1}{4}$
Madeira, London particular	2.20	.55
Madeira, all other	1.80	.45
Pacharetti, Sherry	1.50	.37$\frac{1}{2}$
St Lucar, and all wines of Portugal	.80	.20
Sicily, Teneriffe, Fayal, Malaga & other Western islands	.67	.16$\frac{3}{4}$

all non-enumerated wines 25. p.c. ad valorem.

---

*the term Claret should be expunged, there being no definite wine of that name, and in-
stead of it should be enumerated the 4. crops, Lafitte, Latour, Margaux & Hautbrion,
the only wines of that family of distinguished price.
  †Medoc includes Blanquefort, Calon, Leoville, Cantenac E^{t}c
  Grave includes Barsac, Sauterne, Beaume, Preignac, St Bris, Carbonien, Langon,
  Podenac E^{t}c

PoC (DLC); at foot of first page: "M^r
Dallas"; endorsed by TJ.

The Washington *Daily National Intelligencer* of 20 Feb. 1816 and other PUBLIC
PAPERS printed Dallas's REPORT along
with a schedule of articles on which duties were to be levied. Dallas presented
his "report on the subject of a general
tariff of duties proper to be imposed on
imported goods, wares, and merchandise" to the United States House of Representatives on 13 Feb. 1816 (*ASP, Finance,* 3:85–99). The proposed tariff
became law on 27 Apr. 1816 with no
changes to the portion TJ transcribed
above (*U.S. Statutes at Large,* 3:310–4).
On 1 June 1807 TJ wrote to Albert GAL-
LATIN, then the secretary of the treasury,
suggesting the alternative tariff given in
the postscript above (DLC). The text
originally sent to Gallatin varies slightly
in semantics, provides additional calculations, and includes "St George" among
the wines enumerated from SICILY, TEN-
ERIFFE, FAYAL, MALAGA & OTHER WEST-
ERN ISLANDS.

From John Vaughan

D SIR.   Philad. Feby 26. 1816

Your Letter for Aspinwall[1] was forwarded from New York via Gibraltar—I could get no Bill here—My friend Robert Dickey procured a Bill of 50$ which has gone by two opp^s—It might be well to forward Duplicates of your letter to Aspinwall[2]—Cost of remitting to New York to pay the 50$ & postages $54\frac{24}{100}$—I rec^d from Mr Short $34\frac{34}{100}$ & when I have sold the T^y notes will transmit the account—Mr Correa is with us—& well—Mr Walsh removed to Baltimore whom we all miss. I remain Yours sincerely[3]

JN VAUGHAN

RC (MHi); at head of text: "Thomas Jefferson Esqr Monticello"; endorsed by TJ as received 6 Mar. 1816 and so recorded in SJL.

The LETTER FOR ASPINWALL was actually a letter from TJ to Thomas Appleton, 14 Jan. 1816. OPP^s: "opportunities." T^y: "Treasury."

[1] Word underscored by TJ and corrected in left margin to "Appleton."
[2] Word underscored by TJ and corrected in left margin to "Appleton."
[3] Manuscript: "sincely."

From John Adlum

DEAR SIR   George Town District of Columbia Feby. 27th 1816—

I did not receive your favour of the 16th U^lt untill yesterday. I now reside in the neighbourhood of this Town, and have lived here near two years, I heard by accident of your letter being in the Post office of Havre degrace, and wrote to the Post master for it, it was very neglectful of him not to forward it to me, as he knew I resided in this vicinity,

As I suppose the person to whom I sold my farm at Havre degrace had grubbed up all the grape vines I left there, I have written to Levin Gale Esquire son to my late friend Mr George Gale who got the grape from me to forward you a number of the cuttings of the grape you want, which I am very sure he will do with a great deal of pleasure, and I have requested him that when he forwards them to you to write you that no time may be lost, in planting them &^c. I have also written him some time since to save a number of cuttings for me, and expect to be at his house some time next month. and if it is not too late, I will send you an additional number of cuttings, I hope you will believe that I do not think it any trouble, where I can be in any manner useful in promoting the culture of any thing useful in my country— I am Dear Sir

with sentiments of respect & esteem your most Obed^t Servt

JOHN ADLUM

RC (DLC); at foot of text: "The Honble Thomas Jefferson"; endorsed by TJ as received 1 Mar. 1816 and so recorded in SJL.

TJ's letter to Adlum was dated 13 Jan., not the 16TH U^{LT}. The POST MASTER of Havre de Grace, Maryland, was John Dutton (*Table of Post-Offices in The United States, with the Names of the Post-Masters, the Counties and States in which they are situated, and the Distances from the City of Washington* [Washington, 1817], 33).

To Isaac Briggs

DEAR SIR   Monticello Feb. 27. 16.

I am to thank you for your pamphlet on manufactures. you have availed a question of political economy of the sound process of Mathematical reasoning, and proved very solidly the expediency of our encoraging manufactures to the extent of <u>our own wants</u>. when we shall have reached that point, should there still be surplus labor, whether that should be employed in agriculture or manufactures will depend on the circumstances and opinions of the day: and very much on the condition of S. America. they will be our rivals in agriculture, and our market for manufactures. but in manufactures we shall have rivals in all the nations of Europe. how their freedom will affect us I do not foresee: but I wish them free because they have a right to be so.

In a letter to the Sec^y of the Treas^y I have made such a statement of your case as my memory and papers together enabled me to do: & I have requested that if on a review of it a compensation shall be allowed you it may be made without regard to what you recieved from me, which I wish you to retain as a further retribution for your sufferings & difficulties, which I am glad to contribute. I have inclosed to the Secretary of the Treas^y copies of two messages of mine to the H. of Repres^s on the subject and of a letter to mr Holland. also your original letters of 1804. Sep. 2. Oct. 2. Nov. 26. & Dec. 31. these last I shall be glad to recieve again when done with. I have not asked this of the Sec^y of the Treas^y because such a request to a man in office would be unreasonable. but you can think of it and ask & return them to me, for which I shall be obliged to you. I salute you with friendship and respect.

TH: JEFFERSON

RC (NjP: Andre deCoppet Collection); at foot of text: "Mr Isaac Briggs." PoC (DLC); on verso of reused address cover to TJ; endorsed by TJ.

From James Monroe

DEAR SIR   washington Febry 27th 1816

I was much gratified to find that you approved the ground taken with the Spanish minister, respecting the sp^h colonies & in our affairs with Spain generally. the minister left this shortly after the correspondence for Phil^a, on account of the ill health of his family, not in disgust as has been represented. He has since arrival there written me another letter, adhering to his former claims, but in a tone of moderation, intimating a desire that a negotiation may be opend for the arrangment of every difference at madrid. This is under consideration, and a special mission may be the result—He suggested in conference, his wish, that East Florida &a might be ceded to the US., in consideration of territory on the western side of the mississippi, & in satisfaction of any well founded claims. He intimated also that it was probable that Buenos ayres, montevideo, &a, might be exchanged for Portugal with the Portuguese gov^t. This seems to be more probable, from a late account that 6000. troops are going from   to Buenos Ayres. The policy of G. Britain has been to govern the Spanish provinces thro' the Pen'Insula. While therefore she governs the pen'insula, she is opposd to the independance of the provinces. at present she governs France Spain & Portugal, as well as Holland, and may be concluded to be opposed to any change of that kind[1] in this hemisphere. Having gain'd such an ascendancy in Europe, I should not be surprised to see a regular plan pursued in concert, by several of the powers, under her direction for the subjugation of the Spanish colonies, with ulterior objects bearing on us. The event is so probable, that all movments in that quarter ought to be watched attentively by this government

It is very important to obtain the manuscript which you rec^d from Govr Claiborne. It is possible that the copy deposited in the dep^t of state may still be there. The papers preserv'd, and by far the greater part were, are still packed in boxes, which will not be opend till the office is in a state to receive them, which will not happen in less than a month. If you will be so good as to send me the document in your possession I will have a copy taken, & then forward it, as you may direct. The cutting from the Argus is receivd.

Mr Pinkney of maryland will be nominated to Russia, with a special mission to Naples, respecting claims. He relinquishes a practice said to be worth 25000 dolrs a year.

Mr Gallatin goes to France. He hesitated some time, but at last decided to accept the mission.

with great respect & esteem your friend & servant

JA^s MONROE

RC (DLC); endorsed by TJ as received 1 Mar. 1816 and so recorded in SJL.

Luis de Onís, the SPANISH MINISTER, wrote Monroe from PHIL^A on 22 Feb. 1816 (*ASP, Foreign Relations*, 4:426–9). Federalist newspapers reported that he had left Washington on 9 Feb. 1816 IN DISGUST at "the treatment he had received in his official capacity; declaring his determination not to return" (George-

town *Daily Federal Republican*, 12 Feb. 1816). William PINKNEY was nominated as "Envoy Extraordinary and Minister Plenipotentiary to Russia, with a special mission to the King of the Two Sicilies," but the Senate confirmed only his Russian appointment (*JEP*, 3:32, 33, 34–5 [28 Feb., 2, 7 Mar. 1816]).

[1] Preceding three words interlined.

To Joseph C. Cabell

DEAR SIR   Monticello Feb. 28. 16

You enquire whether Say has ever been translated into English? I am certain he never has in America, nor do I believe he has in England. I have never seen his work named in their catalogues or advertisements nor do I believe it has been noticed by the Edinburgh reviewers. nor have they noticed the Review of Montesquieu, altho Duane sent them a copy. you will render this country a great service in translating it; for there is no branch of science of which our countrymen seem so ignorant as Political economy. the bulk & prolixity of Smith forbid venturing on him. I salute you always with affection

TH: JEFFERSON

RC (ViU: TJP); addressed: "Joseph C. Cabell esq. of the Virginia Senate now in Richmond"; franked; postmarked Milton, 2 Mar.; endorsed by Cabell. PoC (DLC); on verso of reused address cover of Cabell to TJ, 24 Jan. 1816; endorsed by TJ.

Jean Baptiste Say's *Traité d'Économie Politique* was not published in English translation until 1821 (Say, *A Treatise on*

Political Economy; or the Production, Distribution, and Consumption of Wealth, trans. Charles R. Prinsep, 2 vols. [Boston, 1821]; Robert R. Palmer, *J.-B. Say: An Economist in Troubled Times* [1997], 125). For William Duane's effort to have Destutt de Tracy's work on MONTESQUIEU reviewed in the *Edinburgh Review*, see Duane to TJ, 14 Feb. 1813, and TJ to Duane, 4 Apr. 1813.

To Francis W. Gilmer

DEAR SIR   Monticello Feb. 28. 16.

I am sorry it is not in my power to furnish you any documents on the subject of the Louisiana boundary. all these went with my library. soon after the acquisition of that country, I investigated it's history & boundaries minutely, made out a Chronological series of it's historical events, and formed a memoir establishing it's boundaries from Perdido to the Rio Bravo. these were sent to our Comm^{rs} at Madrid who had that negotiation in hand, but copies remain in the Sec^y of State's office. afterwards there was found in possession of the family of the late Govr Messier an original MS. history of the settlemt of that country from 1699. to 1723. written by Bernard de la Harpe in the form of almost a daily journal, he being on the spot. this contained much interesting matter. it proved the constant claim of France to the Bravo, and that the settlements of the Spaniards at Nacogdoches, Adaïs, Assinaÿs, Natchitoches, were corruptly contrived between M. St Denys an agent of Crozat the merchant & patentee, and a Spanish priest. Crozat's object was commerce alone, and chiefly contraband with Mexico,[1] and these were contrived as smuggling posts: and before the expiration of his patent and return of the govmt to the crown, they had become established firmly. this MS. is in the Sec^y of State's office. in the Virginia Argus of about a month ago was an excellent Chronological statement, which appeared so much like an extract from mine & from La Harpe's MS. that I almost suspected it came from some one in the Sec^y of State's office. it had few omissions & no errors. you may safely trust it. Cooper will make the most of his materials; but they must be very scanty.

Your's affectionately   TH: JEFFERSON

RC (ViU: TJP); at foot of text: "Francis W. Gilmer esq." PoC (DLC); endorsed by TJ.

For the CHRONOLOGICAL SERIES and the article from the Richmond *Virginia Argus*, see TJ to James Monroe, 17 Feb.

1816, and note. GOV^R MESSIER: Athanase de Mézières. For the MS. HISTORY by Benard de La Harpe, see TJ to Monroe, 9 Apr. 1816, and note. S^T DENYS: Louis Juchereau de Saint Denis.

[1] Manuscript: "Nexico."

To David Higginbotham

DEAR SIR   Monticello Feb. 28. 16

The Surveyor left [wi]th me your plat and deed which I now inclose. he foun[d the] disputed bounds to contain 68. a^s so that you deduct 680.D. from your last payment to mr Short, of which I this day give him notice.

affectionately yours.   TH: JEFFERSON

PoC (MHi); on verso of reused address cover of James Monroe to TJ, [22] Jan. 1816; torn at seal, with one word rewritten by TJ; at foot of text: "Mr Higgenbothem"; endorsed by TJ.

The SURVEYOR was William Woods.

For the DEED, see TJ to William Short, 10 Feb. 1813, and note. Other enclosure not found.

A missing letter of 6 Apr. 1816 from Higginbotham to TJ is recorded in SJL as received 3 May 1816.

To James Monroe

DEAR SIR   Monticello Feb. 28. 16.

The arbitrators, surveyor E^{t}c met on the 21st. they decided the line in your favor, but divided costs as a tax on you for so careless a designation of the line as to entrap a subsequent purchaser. the disputed lines were found to contain 68. acres. the costs will be 6. or 7.D. a piece to you. I inclose you the original award & the plat you inclosed to me.

ever & affectionately yours.   TH: JEFFERSON

RC (MWiCA: Robert Sterling Clark Collection of Rare Books); addressed: "James Monroe Secretary <at War> of State Washington"; franked; postmarked Milton, 6 Mar.; endorsed by Monroe. PoC (MHi); on verso of reused address cover to TJ; endorsed by TJ.

The SURVEYOR was William Woods. Monroe enclosed the PLAT in his letter to TJ of 10 July 1815. Other enclosure not found.

To William Short

DEAR SIR   Monticello Feb. 28. 16.

Having procured an appointment for the 21st inst. the Surveyor, arbitrators, parties (by their agents) and witnesses met. the forenoon was showery but the difficulty & uncertainty of all collecting again from different parts of the county induced all to go thro' the work. the Surveyor run the lines,

and instead of something less than 30. a^s as had been conjectured, he found them to contain 68. a^s. this proceeded from a great bend of Dick's branch as it went up the mountain which had been expected to be nearly strait. mr Carter had considered the place (a) in the[1] diagram of the margin as the head of the branch, & had run your line from a. to b. he might have been decieved by the sinking of the branch as it does in several places, but reappears again, so that it exists distinctly up to the spring at c. near the gap of the mountain. the arbitrators decided that to be the head of Dick's branch, and the branch itself to be the line. mr Higgenbotham therefore will deduct 680.D. from his last payment. according to former opinions and some decisions, mr Carter would be bound to pay you that sum. but I understand that according to the law as now established, he is liable only for the original sum he recieved, 23/6 per acre, and interest on that to the present day. this brings it to about 8. Dollars an acre so that you will recieve 2.D. an acre less on the whole for these 68. acres than for the rest. mr Carter, who conducted us himself along the line to which he said he had sold to Col° Monroe had certainly been too careless in examining the ground before. the first time we went on it to examine, it was evident that Dick's branch formed the main division between the two mountains. every person present concurred in the opinion of the arbitrators. they divided costs, which will be about 6. or 7. Dollars apiece to you. I salute you with constant & affect^{te} respect.

Th: Jefferson

RC (ViW: TJP); at foot of text: "Mr Short"; endorsed by Short as received 9 Mar.

The SURVEYOR was William Woods. A 25 Jan. 1816 letter from Short to TJ, not found, is recorded in SJL as received 31 Jan. 1816 from Philadelphia.

[1] TJ here canceled "plat."

To John Bradbury

Dear Sir   Monticello Feb. 29. 16.

Your letter has laid by me a month unacknoleged and unacted on; which should not have happened, had not an engagement in a business of peculiar pressure obliged me to suspend all correspondence till I got thro' it. I have now written to the Secretary at war, expressing to him your wish and your fitness for the appointment of a Commissioner on the Arkansa road. I should be very glad indeed if either in a public or private capacity you should be able to give us an account of the natural history of the Arkansa & Red river country. should your friends have sent you spare copies of the publication of your Western discoveries, I should be gratified by a sight of one of them. Accept the assurance of my great esteem and respect

                                                                    Th: Jefferson

RC (DLC); addressed: "Mr John Bradbury New York"; franked; postmarked Charlottesville, 2 Mar.; with penciled notation in an unidentified hand (mutilated at seal): "Charles Bra[...] Esqr Boston"; endorsed by TJ, with his notation: "retd from N.Y. because not found." PoC (DLC); on verso of a reused address cover from Dabney Carr to TJ; endorsed by TJ.

The SECRETARY AT WAR was William H. Crawford.

To William H. Crawford

Dear Sir   Monticello Feb. 29. 16.

I take the liberty of quoting to you the passage of a letter I have recieved from a mr John Bradbury of New York, as follows. 'I notice in the reports of the proceedings of Congress that a road is in contemplation from St Louis to the Northern boundary of Louisiana; for the laying out of which Commrs are to be appointed. I am well acquainted with a considerable portion of the country from St Louis to the Arkansas, have recieved a Mathematical education, and have a competent knowledge of surveying. in the geological part of mineralogy and the external characters of fossils, I am not less versed than in botany. as the road will assuredly pass thro' a mineral country, if a mineralogical report would be desirable in addition to the survey, I might, if employed, furnish [it. s]hould I be honored with an appointment, in this business, or farther in the interior (which I should prefer) I pledge my self Etc.' and he adds a request that I would state to the government what I know of him. mr Bradbury is an Englishman, a man of science particularly in Botany & natural history. he

[521]

was at the head of a great weaving establishment in Liverpool, which the pressure of their taxes obliged him to break up. desirous of coming to this country to seek an establishment, he got an appointment from the Linnean society of Liverpool to botanize for them in Louisiana. he came over in 1809. or 1810. brought me a letter of strong recommendation from mr Roscoe, staid with me about 3. weeks and went to the Westward, ascended the Missouri with a trading party, on researches in botany & natural history. latterly he has been engaged with a manufacturing company to the Eastward. he is a very modest and learned man, and I believe of great worth. in stating to you what I know of him you will be so good as to consider me merely as a witness without interest or desire, & to do in it what is best for the public.

While at Paris you honored me with a letter of June 16. 1814. which I answered Feb. 14. 1815. and sent to the office of the Sec^y of state with a request to mr Graham, as we had expectations of your return, to forward, or retain & deliver it here, according to his knolege of your movements. I hope you recieved it; and I now mention it lest any miscarriage which might have happened to it should be imputed to me as an inattention of which my esteem for you renders me incapable; and I pray you now to accept the assurance of my great respect

Th: Jefferson

PoC (DLC); on verso of reused address cover of Elisha Ticknor to TJ, 26 Jan. 1816; torn at seal, with missing text supplied from John Bradbury to TJ, 9 Jan. 1816; at foot of first page: "Mr Crawford Sec^y at War"; endorsed by TJ.

The STRONG RECOMMENDATION was William Roscoe to TJ, 25 Apr. 1809.

To Gilbert J. Hunt

Sir   Monticello Feb. 29. 16.

Your favor of Jan. 30. was recieved on the 14th inst. and I now return you the Prospectus with my signature, and 2. Dollars for the copy subscribed for in a Richmond bank bill which I understand is recievable with you at par. the volume when published may be forwarded by mail. I salute you with respect   Th: Jefferson

PoC (MHi); on verso of reused address cover to TJ; at foot of text: "Mr G. J. Hunt. N. York"; endorsed by TJ. Enclosure not found.

From Joseph Miller

HON: FRIND   Norfolk Feb^{ry} 29th 1816—

yours of the 17 I Rec^d yesterday with Pleasure—Mr Murry has Sent me a Copey of the Law Mr Hayes has Taken me in but Not So Much as I thought of it will be from 1600 1700¹ Doll^{rs} the Deeds of Every thing I have Got Safe but he had the Goodness to offer the houses for Saile Privitely for Cash the Week before he Left he Baught a very fine Sch^r and a Cargo of Tobaco with Others Articles Cleared her out for New york a Frinch Captain on Board no one in Norfolk had the Least Idea on him, is Famuly and him went on Board he Told people is Famuly was Going to New york and he was Going Down the Bay he Sent a Gigg to Bring him Back the, Pillot Went out of the Capes with them and the Pillot Left he Said He woold Go on and See how the Scho^r sailed—it was 3 Days before the Newes Cam[e] but where thay have Gon no Person Knows but he Left 120000 Doll^{rs} to Pay and nothing to Pay it with I have Got Sum Corks from New york Very Good ones I will Send them by the first Vesoll that Comes to Richmond—I will Offer Sume Part of the Property for Sale Next Week—But thes Place is Verry Dull Nothing Dowing but Merchents Stoping Every Other Day and I am afraid It Will be Sume Time before thes Place Recover its Selfe—

I Rem your Ob^{nt} st   JOSEPH MILLER

RC (DLC); corner torn; at head of text: "Mr Jefferson"; endorsement by TJ torn. RC (MHi); address cover only; with PoC of TJ to John Vaughan, 7 Apr. 1816, on verso; addressed: "Thos Jefferson Esqr Monticello Milton Albemarle County"; stamped; postmarked Norfolk,

1 Mar. Recorded in SJL as received 5 Mar. 1816.

MR MURRY: Thomas W. Maury.

¹ Word interlined.

To Wilson Cary Nicholas

DEAR SIR   Monticello Feb. 29. 16.

I received yesterday your favor of the 16th inst. informing me that the General assembly had been pleased to appoint me one of the Directors of the board of public works recently instituted by them. the spirit with which they have entered on the great works of improvement and public instruction will form an honorable epoch in the history of our country, and I sincerely wish the effects of age permitted me to assist in the execution of their wise and salutary purposes. but I feel it a duty to leave to younger bodies and minds services which require activity of either. journies which should call me from home at fixed times would often find me unable to undertake them, and the absence of a member of such a board would give uneasiness to that portion of country with whose interests he would be supposed particularly acquainted & charged. I am very thankful to the legislature for this proof of their confidence and hope my declining it will be imputed to it's true motive, and not to a want of zeal which will never cease to pray for the advancement and prosperity of our country. Accept the assurances of my high consideration and respect.

Th: Jefferson

PoC (DLC); on verso of reused address cover of Jeremiah Platt to TJ, 1 Feb. 1816; at foot of text: "H. E. Governor Nicholas"; endorsed by TJ. Enclosure: TJ to Nicholas, 29 Feb. 1816, second letter. Printed in *Richmond Enquirer*, 6 Mar. 1816 (with mistaken date of 19 Feb. 1816).

To Wilson Cary Nicholas

Dear Sir   Monticello Feb. 29. 16.

As the outer letter may be to go into different hands I place in a separate one my thanks for your kind offer of the comfortable quarters of your house in the event of my acting as a Director of the public works. but at the age of 73. volunteer journies are out of the question. those to Bedford are of necessity. for them however I chuse my own time, am there with one or two nights only intervening, and the cavalcade now necessary for moving me is there also at home. whatever the young & robust may think, I am sure the old will excuse me. ever affectionately

Yours   Th: Jefferson

RC (CSmH: JF); endorsed by Nicholas. PoC (DLC); on verso of reused address cover to TJ; at foot of text: "Govr Nicholas"; endorsed by TJ. Enclosed in TJ to Nicholas, 29 Feb. 1816, first letter.

To James Oram

Monticello Feb. 29. 16.

Th Jefferson returns to mr Oram the prospectus of Ware's English grammar with his signature and a Dollar Richmond bank note, which he understands is recievable at par at N. York, the price of a copy which when published may be forwarded by mail, and tenders him his respectful salutations.

PoC (MHi); on verso of reused address cover of Bernard Peyton to TJ, 31 Jan. 1816; dateline following body of letter; at foot of text: "James Oram New York 102. Water street"; endorsed by TJ. Recorded in SJL with the additional notation: "1.D."

James Oram (ca. 1760–1826), printer, publisher, and bookseller, divided his career between New York City and Trenton, New Jersey. From 1796–1804 he published the weekly *New-York Price Current*, a paper to which TJ subscribed in 1798. In 1805 Oram relocated his business to Trenton, where he published the weekly *Miscellany*. He returned to New York City in 1806, but by 1810 he was again running his print shop and bookstore in Trenton. By 1812 Oram was back in New York City, where he took over the publication of the *New-York Weekly Museum*. He changed that journal's title to the *Ladies' Weekly Museum* in 1817.

When Oram took part in an 1825 New York City parade celebrating the completion of the Erie Canal, he was described as "the oldest printer in the city" (John Flavel Mines, *Walks in Our Churchyards: Old New York, Trinity Parish* [1896], 95–6; DNA: RG 29, CS, N.Y., New York, 1790, 1800, 1820; Brigham, *American Newspapers*, 1:519, 660, 680, 701–2; *MB*, 2:983, 1319; *PTJ*, 30:217; New York *Commercial Advertiser*, 23 Oct. 1799; *New-York Price-Current*, 2 Aug. 1800; New York *Mercantile Advertiser*, 15 Nov. 1806; *Trenton Federalist*, 23 July 1810; *New-York Weekly Museum*, 9 May 1812; *Longworth's New York Directory* [1816]: 338; *New-York Evening Post*, 5 Nov. 1825, 27 Oct. 1826).

The enclosed PROSPECTUS, not found, was for Jonathan Ware, *A New Introduction to the English Grammar, composed on the principles of the English language, exclusively* (Windsor, Vt., 1814).

To John F. Watson

SIR   Monticello Feb. 29. 16.

Your favor of the 5th inst. has been recieved, as are also the 7th and 8th volumes of the Review, and I now inclose you 13. Dollars, the amount of the last 5. volumes as nearly as I can come, there being no fractions of Dollars in our bank bills. those inclosed are of Richmond as desired. I shall be glad to recieve from mr Earle the other volumes as fast as they come out: Accept the assurance of my respects

TH: JEFFERSON

PoC (DLC); on verso of reused address cover to TJ; mutilated at seal, with missing text rewritten by TJ; at foot of text: "M[r] John F. Watson Germantown"; endorsed by TJ.

From Josiah Meigs

SIR   Washington City March 1. 1816

My friend, Doctor Daniel Drake of Cincinnati, Ohio, has requested me to transmit to you a Copy of his work, entitled "Picture of Cincinnati"—I presume it will gratify you, as an elegant and valuable work—

The Author is a native of New Jersey, from which state his Father, after having served in the Revolutionary War, emigrated to Kentucky—he has acquired a valuable fund of Literature & Sceience—proprio Marte—without the aid of Schools or Colleges—he is a sincere and faithful friend of our free Institutions. It is pleasant to know that the best disciplined minds are supporters of those Institutions.—

I have the honour to be with sincere esteem, respect and veneration Yours.   JOSIAH MEIGS

RC (DLC); at foot of text: "Thomas Jefferson Esquire"; endorsed by TJ as received 6 Mar. 1816 and so recorded in SJL. Enclosure: Daniel Drake, *Natural and Statistical View, or Picture of Cincinnati and the Miami Country, Illustrated by Maps* (Cincinnati, 1815; TJ's copy in William Reese Company, *American Presidents* [2011; catalogue 283], item no. 43, inscribed: "For the honorable Thomas Jefferson—with the respects of his Very obed.ᵗ Serv.ᵗ Dan Drake").

Daniel Drake (1785–1852), physician, naturalist, educator, and author, was born near Bound Brook, New Jersey, and received a medical degree from the University of Pennsylvania in 1816. He was most frequently in Cincinnati but taught medicine successively at schools in Kentucky, Ohio, and Pennsylvania. Drake was a member of both the American Antiquarian and American Philosophical societies and established a medical college and hospital in Cincinnati, where he died (*ANB*; *DAB*; Henry D. Shapiro and Zane L. Miller, eds., *Physician to the West: Selected Writings of Daniel Drake on Science & Society* [1970]; APS, Minutes, 17 Apr. 1818 [MS in PPAmP]; Washington *Daily National Intelligencer*, 16 Nov. 1852).

PROPRIO MARTE: "by his own prowess."

From John Adams

DEAR SIR   Quincy March 2. 16

I cannot be Serious! I am about to write You, the most frivolous letter, you ever read.

Would you go back to your Cradle and live over again your 70 years? I believe you would return me a New England Answer, by asking me another question "Would you live your 80 Years over again"?

If I am prepared to give you an explicit Answer, the question involves So many considerations of Metaphysicks and Physicks, of Theology and Ethicks of Phylosophy and History, of Experience and Romance, of Tragedy Comedy and Farce; that I would not give my opinion without writing a volume to justify it.

I have lately lived over again, in part, from 1753, when I was junior Sophister at Colledge till 1769 when I was digging in the Mines, as a Barrister at Law, for Silvor and gold, in the Town of Boston: and got as much of the Shining dross[1] for my labour as my Utmost Avarice, at that time craved.

At the hazard of all the little Vision that is left me, I have read the History of that Period of 16 Years, in the Six first Volumes of the Baron de Grimm. In a late Letter to you, I expressed a wish to See an History of Quarrels and Calamities of Authors in France, like that of D'Israeli in England, I did not expect it So Soon: but now I have it in a manner more masterly than I ever hoped to See it

It is not only a Narration of the incessant great Wars between the Ecclesiasticks and the Phylosophers, but of the little Skirmishes and Squabbles of Poets, Musicians, Sculptors Painters Architects Tragedians, Comediens, Opera Singers and Dancers, Chansons, Vaudevilles Epigrams, Madrigals[2] Epitaphs, Anagrams Sonnets &c

No Man is more Sensible than I am, of the Service to Science and Letters, Humanity, Fraternity, and Liberty, that would have been rendered by the Encyclopedists and Œconomists, By Voltaire, D'Alembert,[3] Buffon Diderot, Rouseau La Lande, Frederick and Catharine, if they had posessed Common Sense. But they were all totally destitute of it. They all Seemed to think that all Christendom was convinced as they were, that all Religion was "Visions Judaicques" and that their effulgent Lights had illuminated all the World. They Seemed to believe, that whole Nations and Continents had been changed in their Principles Opinions Habits[4] and Feelings by the Sovereign Grace of their Almighty Philosophy, almost as Suddenly as Catholicks and Calvinists believe in instantaneous conversion. They had not considered the force of early Education on the Millions of Minds who had never heared of their Philosophy.

And what was their Phylosophy? Atheism; pure unadulterated Atheism. Diderot, D'Alembert, Frederick, De Lalande and Grimm were indubitable Atheists. The Universe[5] was Matter only and eternal; Spirit was a word without a meaning; Liberty was a word without a Meaning. There was no Liberty in the Universe; Liberty was a word void of Sense. Every thought word Passion Sentiment

Feeling, all Motion and Action was necessary. All Beings and Attributes were of eternal Necessity

Conscience, Morality were all nothing but Fate.

This was their Creed and this was to perfect human Nature and convert the Earth into a Paradise of Pleasure,

Who, and what is this Fate? He must be a Sensible Fellow. He must be a Master of Science. He must be Master of Spherical Trigonometry and Great Circle Sailing. He must calculate Eclipses in his head by Intuition. He must be Master of the Science of Infinitessimal "Le Science des infiniment petits," He must involve and extract all the Roots by Intuition and be familiar with all possible or imaginable Sections of the Cone. He must be a Master of Arts Mechanical and imitative. He must have more Eloquence than Demosthenes, more Wit than Swift or Voltaire,[6] more humour than Butler or Trumbull. And what is more comfortable than all the rest, he must be good natured, for this is upon the whole a good World. There is ten times as much pleasure as pain in it.

Why then Should We abhor the Word God, and fall in Love with the Word Fate? We know there exists Energy and Intellect enough to produce Such a World as this, which is a Sublime and beautiful one, and a very benevolent one, notwithstanding[7] all our Snarling, and a happy one, if it is not made otherwise by our own fault.

Ask a Mite, in the Center of your Mammoth Cheese, what he thinks of the "το παν."

I Should prefer the Philosophy of Tymæus of Locris, before that of Grimm and Diderot, Frederick and D'Alembert, I Should even prefer the Shastra[8] of Indostan, or the Chaldean Egyptian, Indian, Greek, Christian Mahometan Tubonic or Celtic Theology.

Timæus and Ocellus[9] taught that three Principles were eternal. God, Matter and Form. God was good, and had Ideas. Matter was Necessity, Fate, dead, without Ideas, without form without Feeling, perverse, untractible. capable however of being cutt into Forms of Spheres Circles, Triangles, Squares cubes Cones &c. The Ideas of the good God laboured upon matter to bring it into Form: but Matter was Fate Necessity, Dulness obstinacy and would not always conform to the Ideas of the good God who desired to make the best of all possible Worlds but Matter, Fate Necessity resisted and would not let him compleat his Idea. Hence all the Evil and disorder, Paine Misery and Imperfection of the Universe.

We all curse Robespierre and Bonaparte; but were they not both Such restless vain extravagant Animals as Diderot and Voltaire?

Voltaire was the greatest Litterary Character and Bona the greatest Millitary Character of the 18 Century. There is all the difference between them. Both equally Heros and equally Cowards.

When you asked my Opinion of a University, it would have been easy to advise Mathematicks Experimental Phylosophy, Natural History Chemistry and Astronomy Geography and the Fine Arts, to the Exclusion of ontology Metaphysicks and Theology. But knowing the eager Impatience of the human Mind to Search into Eternity and Infinity, the first cause and last End of all Things I thought best to leave it, its Liberty to enquire till it is convinced as I have been these 50 years that there is but one Being in the Universe, who comprehends it; and our last Resource is Resignation.

This Grimm must have been in Paris when you was there, Did You know him or hear of him?

I have this moment rec^d two volumes more, but these are from 1777 to 1782. leaving the Chaine broken from 1769 to 1777. I hope hereafter to get the two intervening Volumes

I am your old Friend   JOHN ADAMS

RC (DLC); at foot of text: "President Jefferson"; endorsed by TJ as received 15 Mar. 1816 and so recorded in SJL. FC (Lb in MHi: Adams Papers).

VISIONS JUDAICQUES: "Judaical visions." LE SCIENCE DES INFINIMENT PETITS: "the science of the infinitely small" (calculus). For the MAMMOTH CHEESE, see *PTJ*, 36:246–52. το παν: "totality; all." TJ asked Adams's OPINION OF A UNIVERSITY in his letter of 5 July 1814.

[1] Preceding four words interlined.
[2] Word interlined.
[3] RC: "Dolembert." FC: "D'Alembert."
[4] Word interlined.
[5] RC: "Univere." FC: "Universe."
[6] RC: "Volltaire." FC: "Voltaire."
[7] RC: "notwithanding." FC: "notwithstanding."
[8] RC: "Shasta." FC: "Shastice."
[9] FC: "Piellus."

To Robert Ould

SIR   Monticello Mar. 2. 16.

I have to thank you for the copy of the Abridgment of the Lancastrian method of education which you were so good as to send me. when that method was first introduced I was too much engaged in business to pay more than a very limited attention to it; altho' it was the subject of considerable discussion before the public; and since my retirement no circumstance has led my enquiries towards it. of course I am too much a stranger to the method to have formed any judgment concerning it. but it's value must now have been sufficiently tested by experience, and those who have had sufficient opportunities of observing its effects are the proper witnesses to ascertain it's merits. being become a mere matter of fact, a theoretical opinion of it's probable effect formed on reading a description only of the process would have no weight[.] this must be my apology for not hazarding one, for which I am moreover quite unqualified. I presume it's advantages must be confined to cities where great numbers of pupils can be collected together. in the country our schools are from a dozen to 20. generally, which being too few to be divided into classes according to the progress each has made, I suppose that method would be impracticable. with this apology for my giving no opinion o[n] the subject, accept my wishes for your success in the use of it and the assurances of my respect.   TH: JEFFERSON

PoC (DLC); edge trimmed; on verso of reused address cover of Gilbert J. Hunt to TJ, 30 Jan. 1816; at foot of text: "Mr Robert Ould George town."

Joseph Lancaster FIRST INTRODUCED his method in his *Improvements in Education, as it respects the Industrious Classes of the Community* (London, 1803). TJ owned the third edition of that work (London, 1805; Sowerby, no. 1113).

To Robert Saunders

[SI]R   Monticello Mar. 2. 16.
I recieved yesterday your favor of Feb. 20. covering an acknolegement of the Cashier of the bank of Virginia at Richmond that you had deposited there the sum of six hundred and thirty five Dollars 48 cents to my [c]redit for the use of John Baptist Fancelli: and I recieved under the same cover a return of Fancelli's letters of At[tor]ney to me which had been forwarded to you for the settle[m]ent of his claims on mr Bracken as admr of the late Charles Bellini. with an expression of my entire satisfaction with your agency in this business & thanks for your diligence in it be pleased to accept the assura[nce] of my great respect and esteem.
                                    TH: JEFFERSON

PoC (DLC); on verso of reused address cover of John F. Watson to TJ, 5 Feb. 1816; edge trimmed, with some text rewritten by TJ; mutilated at seal; at foot of text: "Mr Robert Saunders"; with TJ's Notes on the Administration of Charles Bellini's Estate, 4 Apr. 1818, on verso; endorsed by TJ.

To Garrit Storm

SIR   Monticello Mar. 2. 16.

In answer to the enquiries of your letter of Feb. 23. concerning Alexander Quarrier I can inform you that I have known a person of that name ever since the year 1783. he was then a coachmaker in Philadelphia in partnership with Hunter. he removed to Richmond where I knew him well many years as a very worthy citizen. he was a captain in the militia of the city, in the artillery I believe, and deemed a good officer. it is several years I believe since he left Richmond, but whither he went, I know not, nor whether he is still living. of course I know nothing of his pecuniary circumstances. Accept my respectful salutations.   TH: JEFFERSON

P. S. mr Quarrier was either a Scotchman or Irishman.

PoC (MHi); on verso of reused address cover of Benjamin W. Crowninshield to TJ, 9 Feb. 1816; between signature and postscript: "Mr Garrit Storm N. York"; endorsed by TJ.

To George Watterston

DEAR SIR   Monticello Mar. 2. 16.

I am afraid that for some time I shall be occasionally troublesome to you. I suspect that I stuck a paper containing an epitaph intended for Dabney Carr into the Recherches historiques of Mazzei where they speak of that gentleman. this work is Ch. 24. N° 246. if there, will you be so good as to inclose it to me? I sent the 2. vols of Virginia laws by my grandaughter Ellen Randolph, now at the President's but she left them at Richmond, the stage being too much loaded to take them in. I shall recall them here and see to their safe transportation. I think you may be assured you have Morris's acc^{ts} C. 24. N° 439. and that they are accidentally out of place. I remember that Ray's Tripoli C. 2. N° 82. was missing.   I recieved three copies of the Catalogue from mr Millegan for which I thank you. the typography is handsome, and, the execution generally pleasing to the eye. there are some errors of the press, but such a number of titles in so many different languages could not be expected to be otherwise. you ask how I like the arrangement within the chapters? of course, you know, not so well as my own; yet I think it possible the alphabetical arrangement may be more convenient to readers generally, than mine which was sometimes analytical, sometimes chronological, & sometimes a combination of both. I salute you with esteem and respect.

TH: JEFFERSON

RC (DLC: Watterston Papers); addressed: "Mʳ George Watterston Librarian of Congress Washington"; frank clipped; postmarked Milton, 6 Mar. PoC (DLC); on verso of reused address cover of Joseph Delaplaine to TJ, 10 Feb. 1816; torn at seal; endorsed by TJ.

From James Barbour

SIR   Barboursville March 4ᵗʰ 16—

Being anxious to add, to my new establishment, whatever, is rare or desirable of the fruit, shrub, or tree kind; and knowing with a like inclination, you have had an ample opportunity to gratify it, I have taken the liberty to request of you, any little thing you can spare, without inconvenience, adapted to the garden, or pleasure grounds—

I tender you my best respects   JAˢ BARBOUR

RC (MHi); endorsed by TJ as received 5 Mar. 1816 and so recorded in SJL.

Barbour's NEW ESTABLISHMENT was Barboursville, his Orange County plantation.

To James Barbour

DEAR SIR   Monticello Mar. 5. 16.

If I knew what you possessed, or what you particularly wished my attention more especially applied to the latter might better have fulfilled them. sending at random I fear I may add little to your actual possessions. but I do the best I can by sending those things which are not absolutely possessed by every body.

for the garden. Sprout Kale. which no body in the US. has but those to whom I have given it. sow & transplant as cabbage. let it stand out all winter. it needs no protection. in the beginning of December it begins to furnish sprouts, & will give 3 crops of them before spring. a very delicate green.

———

Long haricots, a species of bean or snap brought me from Georgia by Genˡ Sumpter. plant in rows 3.f. apart, & 12 I. asunder in the row. stick the plants with flat prongy bushes, which will let you go between the rows. early in July it gives beans from 2. to

6.f. long accdg to the ground, & continues[1] till frost. dress them as snaps or in all the ways of asparagus. they are cut into lengths.

———

Trees & shrubs. 2. pods of Kentucky locust.
> seeds of Spanish broom. they come up best in cart ruts or[2] bottoms of gullies.
> lilac.
> Althaea.
> Balsam poplar, a branch for cuttings.
> Calycanthus.
> the Monticello Aspen, entirely peculiar & superior to all others.
> Paper mulberry from Otaheite. the most beautiful & best shading tree
>> to be near the house, entirely clean, bearing no fruit. scarcely yet known in America.

My collection of fruits went to entire decay in my absence and has not been renewed, so that it is in my power to send you but little in that way. I send however cuttings of the Carnation cherry so superior to all others that no other deserves the name of cherry; and cuttings of the Taliafferro apple, the best cyder apple existing, discovered by old Maj[r] Taliaferro near Williamsburg. wishing you good success with them I salute you with esteem & respect.   TH: JEFFERSON

M[rs] Randolph adds a collection of flower seeds for mrs Barber with her respects.

RC (NN: Barbour Papers); addressed: "The honble James Barbour esq Barbourville Orange." PoC (MHi); on verso of reused address cover of John Adams to TJ, with Postscript by Abigail Adams, 2 Feb. 1816; endorsed by TJ.

OTAHEITE: Tahiti.

[1] Manuscript: "continus."
[2] PoC: "and."

From Anonymous

SIR   [ca. 6 Mar. 1816]

The hope of giving you some information that my experience and pursuits in life enable me to furnish; and that in your posession may be usefull to the nation, has prompted me to an act of indecorum, in addressing you, without either acquaintance, or business to authorise it.

I have read your letter of the 9th January last to Benjamin Austin

Esquire; and am much pleased with your explanation of the notes on virginia, in what relates to american manufactures. This explanation is seasonable, the wieght of your name; and the latitude given to your expressions on this Subject, was operating injuriously on the public mind; and producing effects hostile to the public Interest.

On the Subject of manufacturing our own Supplies, to the extent of our absolute wants, <u>whether for Peace or war</u>. after the experience we have had, there Can be but one opinion, however interest may operate on individuals; and influence their Conduct. it is Scarcely possible that any one can think it wise, to rest the security and defence of the Country, on Supplies to be derived from abroad, Subject to the pleasure of foreign nations, to losses on the ocean; and to delays that may be productive of the most fatal evils to the nation. The policy of manufacturing to this extent, rests on Considerations purely national and it becomes a question, whether the government will leave these essential Supplies, to the unprotected efforts of individuals, or give the individuals who have embarked their fortunes in it, Such protection against foreign Competition, as will insure their Success. I will wait the answer to this question from those whose duty it is to decide it.

toward the Close of your letter, you State a question to be hereafter decided, viz, "will our Surplus labour be then more beneficially employed in the Culture of the earth, or in the fabrication of art" that is in manufacturing beyond the Supply of our own wants. There will no doubt be time enough to deliberate on this Subject, but we Cannot be too early in Collecting the facts and Circumstances necessary to a Sound decission. such as the particular Species of labour employed in these Several pursuits. their effects on the morals and Habits of Society. their tendancy to promote or depress each other &c. here I will give you the result of my experience and observation on the Subject, I am a practical manufacturer, not bred to the business. but I have an interest in a Cotton factory, where I Spend Some Hours daily to Superintend the Business. we employ in this work about one hundred hands, in Carding & Spining, <u>we weave none</u>. we have one man to manage the Carding; and one to manage the Spinning, one machinist to Keep the machinery in repair; and one porter. in all four men, nine women; and eighty or ninety female Childern, from nine to thirteen years of age. Hence it will appear that we draw no labour from the agricultural[1] field; and that the labour we employ, Could not be applied to the Culture of the earth. our works are in a Town where we Can have a Choice of hands; and where much larger works

Could be Carried on by the Same Kind of labour we employ; and we have Selected them, not from necissity, but as the most Suitable. These Children live with their parents, they come to work at Sun rise, have time allowed to get their meals; and at Sun Set return to their respective families to pass the night. on Saturday evening we brake off work a little earlier than usual, to clean up the mill; and pay the weekly wages. The first application of their Small weekly earnings, is generally to procure neat, Comfortable Cloathing. when this object is accomplished, their Surplus earnings generally goe to procure Schooling, in which Cases they leave us for a time. Here it may be proper to notice, that the terms of the employ are, that they may leave it at pleasure without any previous notice, and we may dismiss them in like manner; and this right of dismission is the only deciplin we employ. I have touched on the interior economy of mill, to obviate frivolous objections raised against mannufacturing, that in this Country have no foundation in fact, Such as that it is injurious to health, to morals; and incompatible with the necessary instruction of the mind. The fact is, that in all these respects the Condition of[2] the Children we employ is greatly improved; and while the results of their labour, is adding to the wealth, Comfort and Security of the nation, they are individually deriving Comfort & Subsistance from it; and acquiring habits of industry that will be permanently benificial to themselves & to the Country.

you will notice from this Sketch That we not only, draw no labour from Culture of the ground, but we give beneficial employ to a Species of labour, that hitherto has not been brought into requisition[3] among us. This is not merely making two blades of Grass grow, where only one had grown before, it is Causing many blades to Spring up, in Soil that had been altogether unproductive.

It is probable our works are Carried on by a greater proportion of Childerns labour than is usual, — in about the proportion we employ, we prefer it to any other, and our works being in a Town, abounding in this Species of population, as well as every other, we are enabled to make our Selection to our liking, while in Country Situations, they may be obliged from necessity to employ a greater proportion of men. but generally it may be averred in truth, that the manufacture of wool, and of Cotton may be Carried on in this Country to a great extent, without any material Subduction from the labour of the feild; and in a great measure by labour that would not otherwise be beneficially employed.

To this view of the Subject may be added many important benefits, that will result from an extention of our domestic manufactures, <u>at least, to the Supply of our wants</u>, Such as employing the Capital at home, where it will be in Constant Circulation thro the Community, defusing life and activity, thro every branch of our industry. the Spring it will give to agriculture by an encreased demand for the raw materials; and a market therefor at home, free from Spoliation; and the expence and dangers incident to all foreign markets. The feild of industry opened to our labouring poor; and the wholsome tone it will give to our Society, by its tendancy to concentrate[4] the interests, prospects; and affections of our population within the[5] Country. the manufacturer has no hopes or wishes beyond our teritorial limits. and much good will probably flow from the intercourse it will promote between the different Sections of the Country; and their mutual dependance on each other for necessary Supplies, tending to Suppress Jealousies & animosities,[6] to promote harmony and good will in our Community, and between the different States; and to Cement and Strengthen the bonds of our political union. —in every light, in which I have been able to view the Subject, I See a benefit to the public from manufacturing our own Supplies; and when I recur to the experience of the late war; and of the revolutionary war, I am forcibly impressed, <u>by the hardships we then Suffered; and the hazards to which we were then exposed</u>, with the necessity of protecting the ground they have recently gained; and of affording them Such Support against foreign Competition, as will in a reasonable time free us from foreign dependance for necessary Supplies, whether for peace or war; and to this point all my observations are limited. It may perhaps be profitable to extend our manufactures beyond the point of internal Supply, but that may very Safely be left to individual interprise; and is a Subject no way necessary to be acted on now: But to the extent of our wants, I deem it insaperably Connected with the public Interest & Security, that they Should be Supplied from our own industry and ingenuity. This will make us in reality an independant nation; and enable us to present a formidable front to an enemy, if any Should be disposed to disturb our tranquility & happiness. It would give to the united States a point of elivation and Security, truely desirable; and which I beleive no other nation Can attain So fully,

I have been led to the indiscretion of[7] addressing you this letter, principally, from your Idea of applying manufacturing labour to agricultural[8] pursuits; and it is true that the labour of the miller. the black Smith, the wheel wright. the Taylor, the Ship Carpenter &c, might be So applied: But only a Small portion of the labour employed in the manufacture of wool and Cotton, <u>the principal articles</u> <u>of Cloathing</u>, Could be brought into the feild, if these manufactures were wholly laid aside. I am aware that very little respect is due to my Statement of facts Connected with this Subject, under the particular Circumstances in which they are brought to your notice,[9] I do not wish them to be taken on my authority: I wish them to pass for what they may be worth, under all the Circumstances of disadvantage in which they appear. They are written by one who has great respect for your Charracter; and who takes great Interest in your happiness; and who deems it proper to Cover his indiscretion in addressing you, by withholding his name.

RC (DLC: TJ Papers, 206:36729–34); at foot of text: "Thomas Jefferson Esquire"; endorsed by TJ (brackets in original) as a letter from "Anon. [manufactures] post mark Baltimore Mar. 6. rec[d] Mar. 13." and so recorded in SJL.

The Maryland state legislature issued its first corporate charter for a textile plant to the Union Manufacturing Company in Baltimore in 1808. In 1814 Robert & Alexander McKim opened the city's first steam-powered mill, the Hamilton COTTON FACTORY. By 1810 five textile mills were in operation in Baltimore, and the factories continued to thrive in spite of an 1815 textile depression and the growing pressure of British competiton following the War of 1812 (Edward Matchett, *The Baltimore Directory and Register, For the Year 1816* [Baltimore, 1816], 222; *Commercial Directory* [Philadelphia, 1823], 76; Seth Rockman, *Scraping By: Wage Labor, Slavery, and Survival in Early Baltimore* [2009]; Richard W. Griffin, "An Origin of the Industrial Revolution in Maryland: The Textile Industry, 1789–1826," *Maryland Historical Magazine* 61 [1966]: 24–36).

MAKING TWO BLADES OF GRASS GROW, WHERE ONLY ONE HAD GROWN BEFORE paraphrases a passage from Jonathan Swift's *Gulliver's Travels*: "that whoever could make two Ears of Corn, or two Blades of Grass, to grow upon a spot of Ground where only one grew before, would deserve better of Mankind, and do more essential Service to his Country than the whole Race of Politicians put together" (*Travels into several Remote Nations of the World . . . by Lemuel Gulliver* [London, 1726], 1:129).

[1] Manuscript: "agricutural."
[2] Manuscript: "of of."
[3] Manuscript: "requsition."
[4] Manuscript: "concanterate."
[5] Manuscript: "the the."
[6] Manuscript: "animsities."
[7] Manuscript: "of of."
[8] Manuscript: "agrcultural."
[9] Author here canceled "But."

From Joseph Milligan

DEAR SIR   Georgetown March 6th 1816
I received the balance $136 75 from M[r] Gibson and on due examination find it all correct—on my return from Monticello I wrote to Gen[l] Duane requesting him to send the translation and original of Tracy,s manuscript to M[r] R C Weightman of Washington and I would pay

him the $60 which he demanded of me the preceding winter for it. but I heard nothing more of it until you advised me you had received it why he sent it to you rather than to my direction I cannot say unless he knew that you were to revise it before publication but that he should have tho^t fit to charge it In your account rather than receive his money through Mr Weightmans hands which was the way that he at first proposed to receive it I cannot tell but as he has charged it in your account and you have had the goodness to say that you will pay it I will place it to your credit and close the business

I have had the Type & paper ready a long time to print the work   when you send on the first part of the Manuscript have the goodness to furnish The title of the book with it that I may anounce the work as soon as I put it to press—

I have sent you by the way of Fredericksburg to the care of Mr William F. Gray a parcel as follows

Ainsworth's

Dictionary 2 vols	$5 50 ⎫		
Virgil Delphini	4 00 ⎪ Moors Greek Grammar ⎫		have not yet got
Baileys ovid	2 75 ⎬ Mairs Tyro Dictionary ⎭		
Cornelius nepos	1 00 ⎭		
	$13–25[1]		

Your books are now in the hands of the binders and as soon as bound say three weeks I will send them

    Yours with Esteem and respect   JOSEPH MILLIGAN

RC (DLC); endorsed by TJ as received   [1] First page ends here with "turn over."
15 Mar. 1816 and so recorded in SJL.

To Richard Peters

DEAR SIR   Monticello Mar. 6. 16.

I have to thank you for the copy of your Discourse on agriculture which you have been so kind as to send me. I participate in all your love for the art,[1] and wish I did also in your skill. but I was never but an amateur, and have been kept from it's practice until I am too old to learn it. we are indebted to you for much of our knolege as to the use of the plaister, which is become a principal article of our improvements, no soil profiting more from it than that of the country around this place. the return of peace will enable us now to resume it's use. my son in law, Col^o Randolph is perhaps the best farmer of the state, and by the introduction of the horizontal method of ploughing, instead of straight furrows, has really saved this hilly country. it was running off into the vallies with every rain; but by this process we now scarcely lose an ounce of our soil.

a rafter level traces a horizontal line around the curve of the hil[l] or valley at distances of 30. or 40. yards, which is followed by the plough; & by these guide-lines the ploughman finishes the interval by his eye, throwing the earth into beds of 6.f. wide, with large water-furrows between them. when more rain falls than can be instantly absorbed, the horizontal furrows retain the surplus until it is all soaked up, scarcely a drop ever reaching the valley below. some 2. or 3. years ago, I mentioned to mr Peale this method of ploughing, and I think he has informed me of his having since practised it with satisfaction. it is probable therefore you may have heard of it from him, if not thro' some other channel.

Mr Randolph has contrived also, for our steepest hill sides, a simple plough which throws the furrow always down hill. it is made with two wings welded to the same bar, with their planes at a right angle with each other. the point and heel of the bar are formed into pivots, & the bar becomes an axis, by turning which, either wing may be laid on the ground, and the other then standing vertically, acts as a mould board. the right angle between them however is filled with a sloping piece of wood, leaving only a cutting margin of each wing naked, & aiding in the office of raising the sod gradually, while the declivity of the hill facilitates it's falling over. the change of the position of the share at the end of each furrow is effected in a moment by with-drawing and replacing a pin. the little paper model inclosed may help out my description of the share.

I must now ask whether time has not commenced it's inroads on you? whether your farming activity does not abate, and the bodily faculties begin to blunt a little? these decays however are less to be regarded if the blessing of health continues: and that it may long continue with you is the prayer of one who has never ceased to respect and esteem you affectionately.[2]   TH: JEFFERSON

PoC (DLC); on reused address cover of Joseph C. Cabell to TJ, 14 Feb. 1816; damaged at seal, with most of the affected text rewritten by TJ; at foot of first page: "Richard Peters"; endorsed by TJ. Printed in Philadelphia Society for Promoting Agriculture, *Memoirs* 4 (1818): 16–7.

Richard Peters (1744–1828), public official, judge, and experimental farmer, graduated from the College of Philadelphia (later the University of Pennsylvania) in 1761. He was admitted to the bar in 1763 and began practicing law. Prior to the commencement of the Revolutionary War, Peters acted as Pennsylvania's register of admiralty. After serving briefly as a militia officer, in 1776 the Continental Congress elected him secretary of the board of war, and he served until late in 1781. The following year Peters was elected to the Continental Congress for a one-year term. After a period of European travel, he returned to Pennsylvania, where he was a member of the unicameral General Assembly, 1787–90 (concluding with service as Speaker), and he served as the first Speaker of the state senate, 1791–92. In 1792 Peters was appointed judge of the United States district court of Pennsylvania, an office he retained for the rest of his life. He made significant contributions to maritime law and was the author of *Admiralty Decisions in the District Court of the United States, for the Pennsylvania District*, 2 vols. (Philadelphia, 1807). Peters was keenly interested in agricultural research and engaged in experiments at Belmont, his Philadelphia estate. He served as president of the Philadelphia Society for Promoting Agriculture, contributed many papers to its *Memoirs*, and wrote *Agricultural Enquiries on Plaister of Paris* (Philadelphia, 1797; Sowerby, no. 745) and *A Discourse on Agriculture* (Philadelphia, 1816; Poor, *Jefferson's Library*, 6 [no. 270]) (*DAB*;

Washington, *Papers, Confederation Ser.*, 6:142–3, and *Pres. Ser.*, 9:426, 11:451–2; *PTJ*, 5:239–40, 10:416–7; Simon Baatz, *"Venerate the Plough": A History of the Philadelphia Society for Promoting Agriculture, 1785–1985* [1985]; Philadelphia *Poulson's American Daily Advertiser*, 23, 25 Aug. 1828).

A RAFTER LEVEL is a "levelling instrument consisting of an A-frame made of long spars of wood with a pendulum suspended from the apex, used to ascertain the differences of level in a piece of land" (*OED*). TJ described THIS METHOD OF PLOUGHING in a letter to Charles Willson Peale, 17 Apr. 1813. Peale wrote of his SATISFACTION with the technique in a letter to TJ of 28 Dec. 1813. The enclosed LITTLE PAPER MODEL of Thomas Mann Randolph's "Hill-side Plough" has not been found, but see Peters to TJ, 28 June 1817, and note.

[1] Remainder of sentence and succeeding sentence not in *Memoirs*.
[2] Paragraph not in *Memoirs*.

From Mary B. Briggs

Wilmington Del: 3rd moth 7th 1816

Although personally unacquainted,—I have, from my infancy, been taught to love and revere Thomas Jefferson!—those sentiments were early implanted in my mind by, my father, who <u>ever</u> felt for him the most high respect and affectionate esteem—and now—when I hear, from that beloved & excellent father, of the renewed instances of the generous goodness, we have admired—and when every grateful feeling is excited to enthusiasm in my mind—I cannot deny myself the pleasure of offering, with my father's; <u>my</u> thanks;—Wilt, thou accept, dear, <u>kind</u>, friend, the artless but sincere offering of one who <u>knows</u> herself capable of <u>feeling</u>—but regrets her total inability to make thee sensible of the <u>fervor</u> of those feelings by <u>any</u> expressions—the <u>simple</u> assurance of my grateful sense of obligation is <u>all</u> I can offer—may this be accepted?—"Had it not been for his kindness" says my father, in his letter "I could not have sent Anna & Mary to weston School"— I <u>feel</u> the obligation particularly—oh! that I could suitably acknowledge it; but now let me again assure thee, on the behalf of a large family and myself, that if our prayers to Him who is able to bestow every blessing on the deserving, and which will be prefered in the sincerity of our hearts, if they are heard and granted—the happiness of Thomas Jefferson will be so great in this life as to be capable of <u>little</u> addition in that which is to come.

I would ask thee to excuse my freedom of style—but that I believe one, <u>more</u> studied, would be <u>less</u> acceptable—I know that freedom & friendship are synonymous, and where I feel the latter I cannot divest myself of the former.—

With sentiments of the most respectful esteem and high consideration,—I shall ever be thy friend   MARY B BRIGGS

RC (MHi); endorsed by TJ as received 9 Apr. 1816 and so recorded in SJL.

Mary Brooke Briggs (Brooke) (1798–1875), the second child of Isaac Briggs and Hannah Brooke, married her cousin Richard Brooke in 1824. The couple settled at Falling Green, a Brooke family plantation in Sandy Spring, Montgomery County, Maryland (Anna Briggs Bentley, *American Grit: A Woman's Letters from the Ohio Frontier*, ed. Emily Foster

[2002], 6, 16, 315; MdU: Brooke Family Papers).

ANNA Briggs Bentley was the eldest of the Briggs children (Bentley, *American Grit*). Westtown (WESTON) School was established in 1799 as a boarding school for Quaker boys and girls. It is located in West Chester, Pennsylvania (Watson W. Dewees and Sarah B. Dewees, *Centennial History of Westtown Boarding School, 1799–1899* [1899]).

To Patrick Gibson

DEAR SIR   Monticello Mar. 8. 16.

Being uneasy at the delay of my tob° in Bedford, I lately sent an express there to be ascertained as to it's departure. mr Yancey informs me by that, that it is all at Lynchburg, that he has contracted with Dr Cabell to send the whole on the return of his boats which were then down, and makes himself responsible it shall leave Lynchburg by the 10th this being the season to which most of my engagements are referred for payment, I have procured delays to the last of this month, at which time I shall be obliged to draw to the amount of 1000.D. at least: so that it will be necessary for you to sell the tob° as soon as it arrives. in November Yancey supposed it would be from 12. to 14,000 weight. I have no later opinion from him as to that. as the season will not wait for us, & that for using plaiste[r] of Paris is now arrived, I have desired Capt Peyton to send me 8. tons, which I am told can be had at Rocket's at 9.D. and to send it up immediately by the Milton boats, and I have stated that you will be so good as to pay it's cost.   will you be so kind also as to procure and send me a box of about a dozen bottles of <u>good</u> sweet oil. a little more or less, as the box may be, will make no odds

accept the assurance of my friendly respects.　Th: Jefferson

PoC (ViHi); on verso of a reused ad-　　　ROCKET'S was a section of Richmond
dress cover from James L. Jefferson to　fronting on the James River.
TJ; torn at seal, with some words rewrit-
ten by TJ; one word faint; at foot of text:
"Mr Gibson"; endorsed by TJ.

From Christopher Hudson

Dear Sir—　　　　　　　　　Mount Air March 8th 1816

I have received the mulberry lims by your Boy & in turn send the Peach lims & kernals promised you. I also send a few lims of a very valuable Plumb which is well worth cultivating. may you long live & enjoy every comfort of this life is the

ardent wish of your Friend　　　Christopher Hudson

RC (MHi); addressed: "Thos Jefferson Esqre Monticello"; endorsed by TJ as received 8 Mar. 1816 and so recorded in SJL.

To Bernard Peyton

[De]ar Sir　　　　　　　　　Montic[ell]o Mar. 8. 16.

According to your kind permission I am beginning to be trouble-some to you. I have occasion for 8 tons of plaister of Paris, and mr Randolph informs me it is to be had at Rockets's for 9.D. and he names a mr Mordecai who has a large quantity there. will you be so good as to procure me that quantity & engage the Milton boats to go down to Rocket's for it, which I am told they will do for a dollar extra. mr Gibson will furnish the money.　　　being afraid to trust to in-different corks for weak liquors I engaged Capt Miller to procure me some at Norfolk. he writes me he has forwarded to mr Gibsons some very fine, which I presume are arrived there by this time. as every day now presses for bottling cyder & beer,[1] a circumstance which may not occur to them at mr Gibson's you will oblige me by availing me of the first passage by boat or stage which occurs. if by the stage which would be quickest & therefore most desirable, experience has taught me it cannot be trusted unless some one sees the parcel actually put on board. our family are well and remember you affectionately in which I join them with sincerity.　　　Th: Jefferson

PoC (MHi); on verso of reused address cover of Dabney C. Terrell to TJ, 16 Feb. 1816; salutation and dateline faint; at foot of text: "Captn Peyton"; endorsed by TJ.

[1] TJ here canceled "I fear."

To Thomas Ritchie

DEAR SIR   Monticello Mar. 8. 16.

About 18. months ago (Sep. 1814) I proposed to you a work on political economy by mr Tracy of Paris, for translation & publication, the original MS. being in my hands unpublished. you could not undertake it till the then ensuing spring, and I thought I ought not to wait so long. after trusting to Duane, and being continually put off, he at length informed me he had got it translated, but had not the means of publishing it. I then desired he would return me the original. he sent me that & the translation and drew on me for the cost of the latter (60.D) which, altho' without any sort of obligation, I shall pay him. I found the translation wretched, and have set in to correct it myself. I have labored on it a month for 3, 4. or 5 hours a day, and am half thro'. another month of such drudgery will finish it. it is unquestionably the ablest work ever written on the subject [a]nd brings the whole into the compass of 400. 8vo pages, of suc[h] a [...] [t]ype as of the Boston edn of Stewart's philosophy of the mind. for perspicuity, precision, and demonstrative logic, we have had nothing to equal it, and we have in it the benefits of the advancement of the science since Smith's and even Say's works. nothing is so much wanting in this country as the diffusion of this science, and I cannot but believe that when brought into the compass of a single 8vo it will be generally bought and read. it's publication will do honour to any press. will you undertake it? I gladly sacrifice the price paid for the translation, & the drudgery of amending it, which I would not have undertaken for ten times the sum. the groundwork forbids it to be an unexceptionable translation in point of style, but it will be faithful, & tolerable in style. if you will undertake it, I will send you the first half by return of mail, and the rest as it is ready. pray do it, and let me hear from you as soon as possible. I salute you with friendship and[1] respect   TH: JEFFERSON

PoC (DLC); on verso of a reused address cover from John Barnes to TJ; torn at seal, with some words rewritten by TJ; at foot of text: "Mr Ritchie"; endorsed by TJ.

For TJ's letter of ABOUT 18. MONTHS AGO, see TJ to Ritchie, 27 Sept. 1814, and note.

[1] TJ here canceled "esteem."

Receipt from John F. Watson

Germantown

Received March 8. 1816 from Thomas Jefferson Esqre ℔ mail Thirteen dollars being full pay fr the 4th to 8 vol^s inclusive of the Edin^g Reviews forwarded to him, and exceeding my debt 50^{cts}—which I am to have allowed to him out of any subsequent Vol^s which he may receive from me or from E Earle   JOHN F WATSON

MS (DLC); in Watson's hand; addressed: "Thomas Jefferson Esqre Monticello V^a," with "℔ mail" added in an unidentified hand; franked; postmarked Philadelphia, 9 Mar.; endorsed by TJ: "Watson John F."

From George Watterston

DEAR SIR,   City of Washington March 8th 1816.

So far from considering your requests troublesome, I feel no little gratification in having it in my power to comply with them. I wish you to beleive that I esteem & respect you too much to regard any little service I can render the man, who has been so instrumental in ameleorating the condition of mankind & contributing to the happiness of his country, as troublesome or unpleasant—

I send you the epitaph you desire & beg you to accept the assurances of my respect.   GEO. WATTERSTON

P.S. I have received the two vol^s of the Virginia laws & am happy to state that I was under a mistake in relation to Morris'[1] Accounts—

                                        G.W.

RC (DLC); adjacent to full signature: "T. Jefferson Esq^e"; endorsed by TJ as received 13 Mar. 1816 and so recorded in SJL.

For the enclosed EPITAPH, see PTJ, 27:673–5; Dabney Carr to TJ, 1 Dec. 1815, and note.

[1] Closing double quotation mark editorially altered to apostrophe.

From Isaac A. Coles

DEAR SIR,—   Enniscorthy Mar: 9th 1816.

Permit me to return you my best thanks for the Paper Mulberry; which you were kind enough to send me. They have proven more acceptable to my friends than to my self,[1] Mrs Randolph having been good enough to let me have a dozen or fifteen, which my servant brought me during your last visit to Bedford—

My Brother Mr Walter Coles sends eight Lemon Peaches, which will prove a great treasure if they can be defended against the attacks of the Worms.

Tomorrow morning I go to Richd to sell my crop of Tobacco, and as soon as I return I hope to have the pleasure of seeing you at Monticello—I fear I am some weeks too late in getting my crop to market—with sincere & devoted attachment, I Am Dr Sir, ever yrs

I. A. COLES

RC (DLC); at foot of text: "Thos Jefferson"; endorsed by TJ as received 9 Mar. 1816 and so recorded in SJL.

[1] Manuscript: "sely."

From John Tayloe Lomax

DEAR SIR,   Menokin, near Richmond Ct House March 11th 1816.

I have been induced to believe that my fathers family have an interest in some lots in Richmond & Manchester well worth investigation—In the progress of my enquiry I ascertain from an a/c. which I presume is in Mr Wayles's hand writing—that in the year 1768—he sold my grandfather—Lunsford Lomax—6 Tickets in Birds' lottery for £30—In the record of a suit in the Chancery Court of Richmond between speaker Robinsons admrs & Birds & Carters heirs an account is filed of the Tickets sold in Bird's lottery—by whom—to whom—& at what price—It is taken I understand from an old book in Mrs Bird's possession & kept either by Bird—his agent— or the agent of his Trustees—Under the letter L. there is substantially this Entry—"To Lunsford Lomax from J. Wayles 6 Tickets nos 3807 to 3812 inclusive £30." Upon reference to the prise book it is ascertained that 3807 & 3811—drew prises viz two $\frac{1}{2}$ acre lots no: 30 in Manchester and no: 465 in Richmond—both of which are represented as very valuable—I have searched in vain for the Tickets—I think it probable from the connection which subsisted between my grandfather & Mr Wayles—that they were permitted to remain with the latter and it is possible that they may yet be found among his papers—or some information relative to them may be derived from that Source—It is suggested to me that you are in possession of Mr Wayles's papers—I am very much at a loss in what way I shall obtrude upon you a request that you will be So good as to aid me with such information as those papers may impart upon a subject of very great interest to my father's family—

I beg sir you will excuse the Liberty I have taken—and accept the assurances of my most respectfull consideration.

JNO TAYLOE LOMAX

RC (MHi); endorsed by TJ as received 27 Mar. 1816 and so recorded in SJL. RC (DLC); address cover only; with PoC of TJ to Thomas Eston Randolph, 3 June 1816, on verso; addressed: "Thomas Jefferson Esqr Monticello"; stamped; postmarked Port Royal, 11 Mar., and Charlottesville, 27 Mar.

John Tayloe Lomax (1781–1862), attorney, educator, and judge, was the son of TJ's friend Thomas Lomax. The younger Lomax graduated in 1797 from Saint John's College, Annapolis, studied the following year at the College of William and Mary, and practiced law in Fredericksburg thereafter. In April 1826 he became the first professor of law at the University of Virginia. Lomax left the faculty early in 1830. The Virginia General Assembly elected him associate judge of the Superior Court of Law and Chancery the following year, and he continued his teaching career thereafter by conducting a private law school in Fredericksburg. He was the author of a *Digest of the Laws respecting Real Property*, 3 vols. (1839), and *A Treatise on the Law of Executors and Administrators . . . and adapted more particularly to the Practice of Virginia*, 2 vols. (1841). Lomax was awarded an honorary degree from Har-

vard University in 1847. He retired from the bench in 1857 and died in Fredericksburg (*DAB*; Lunsford Lomax Lewis, "Judge John Tayloe Lomax," *Virginia Law Register* 2 [1896]: 1–3; Edward Lloyd Lomax, *Genealogy of the Virginia Family of Lomax* [1913], 20; Elizabeth W. P. Lomax, "John Tayloe Lomax," *Green Bag* 9 [1897]: 373–8; *Commemoration of the One Hundredth Anniversary of St. John's College* [1890], 104; *A Catalogue of the College of William and Mary in Virginia* [1859], 48; Bruce, *University*, 2:31–2, 102–5, 169; TJ to Lomax, 12 Apr. 1826; *JSV* [1830–31 sess.], 272 [18 Apr. 1831]; *Harvard Quinquennial Catalogue of the Officers and Graduates 1636–1925* [1925], 965; *Washington Daily National Intelligencer*, 10 Oct. 1862).

In 1768 William Byrd (1728–77) held a lottery to dispose of a portion of his real estate that included LOTS IN RICHMOND & MANCHESTER in an effort to relieve his own debts and additional obligations to the estate of John Robinson, the late speaker and treasurer of the House of Burgesses (Washington, *Papers, Colonial Ser.*, 8:192, 194n; Donald Jackson and Dorothy Twohig, eds., *The Diaries of George Washington* [1976–79], 2:106–7).

From Thomas M. Randolph & Company

DEAR SIR   Shadwell Mill 12th March 1816

Inclosed you will receive a statement of all the Flour deliver'd to you, by comparing it with the accounts furnish'd you, we believe you will find it correct—

The mistake made with respect to 67 barrels sent down in May last, and which are still in Messrs Warwicks Lumber house, shall be arranged to your satisfaction so soon as either of us go to Richmond which will be in few days—We are with great respect

Your mo: Obdt Serv^ts

THO^s M. RANDOLPH & Co

RC (MHi); in Thomas Eston Randolph's hand; dateline at foot of text; addressed: "Thomas Jefferson Esqre"; with TJ's Analysis of Flour Shipments by Thomas Eston Randolph (on behalf of Thomas M. Randolph & Company), [ca. 12 Mar. 1816], on verso (see note at enclosure printed below); endorsed by TJ as a letter from Thomas Eston Randolph received 12 Mar. 1816 and so recorded in SJL.

Thomas M. Randolph & Company was formed when Thomas Eston Randolph and Thomas Mann Randolph became joint tenants at the Shadwell mills in 1814. Two years later Thomas Eston Randolph became sole tenant (*MB*, 2:1273, 1310; TJ's Agreement with Thomas Eston Randolph & Company, 19 Sept. 1816, with Note by TJ, 18 Oct. 1816).

ENCLOSURE

Account of Flour Shipped by Thomas M. Randolph & Company

[ca. 12 Mar. 1816]

flour sent by Col^o T. M. Randolph & T. E. Randolph to mr Gibson on account of Th:J.

			Barrels		
1814.	Oct.	30.	24.	by	T. E. Randolph's boat.
1815.	Jan.	18.	50.		Wm Johnson's
	Feb.	18.	52.		T. E. Randolph's
		27.	60.		Wm Johnson's
	Mar.	8.	15.		Shifflet's
		10.	56.		Wm Johnson's
	May.[1]	10.	66.		Col^o T. M. Randolph's
		26.	60.		John Pierce's
	June	2.	20.		Col^o T. M. Randolph's
			403.		
	Aug.[2]				
1816	Jan.	6.	20.	by	Gilmer's boat.
		8.	5.		d^o
		9.	15.		d^o
		17.	62.		T. E. R. & Wm Johnson's
		18.	60.		Carver's
	Feb.	20.	52.		T. E. R. & Wm Johnson's
			214.		

67. sent the last year & now to be delivered
684

Tr (DLC: TJ Papers, ser. 10); entirely in TJ's hand; undated; on recto of reused address cover of Wilson Cary Nicholas to TJ, 16 Feb. 1816; with PoC of TJ to Patrick Gibson, 18 Mar. 1816, on verso, and probably also enclosed with the latter letter.

In preparing an 18 Mar. 1816 letter to Patrick Gibson, TJ created an Analysis of Flour Shipments by Thomas Eston Randolph (on behalf of Thomas M. Randolph & Company), [ca. 12 Mar. 1816] (MS in MHi; entirely in TJ's hand; on verso of RC of Thomas M. Randolph & Company to TJ, 12 Mar. 1816). Repeating all but the last column of the information provided in the document above, TJ added a column of dates and quantities of barrels that Gibson had acknowledged receiving. As of 14 Dec. 1814, 24 barrels of flour had reached Gibson. Two more shipments of 215 and 18 barrels had arrived by 8 May 1815. He received another 110 by 15 June, an additional 16 by 24 June, another 20 barrels by 13 July, and by 14 Feb. 1816 Gibson had accounted for a final 162 barrels, for a total of 565

barrels shipped [misentered by TJ as "569"]. At the foot of the text, TJ drew up a table, possibly to aid himself in drafting his 11 Apr. 1816 letter written to Thomas Eston Randolph as proxy for Thomas M. Randolph & Company:

		B	℔	
1814. 15.	crop flour	275 – 123		
"1814. 15.	crop flour	275 – 123		
	rent	213 – 65	488–188
1815. 16	crop —	202 – 15	
	rent "		

[1] A check mark in an unidentified hand is penciled in the margin to the left of this line.

[2] Here is canceled a date of which the first digit is "1."

"A" (Thomas Jefferson) to the Washington *Daily National Intelligencer*

Mar. 13. 1816.

A writer in the National Intelligencer of Feb. 24., who signs himself **B**, is endeavoring to shelter under the cloak of Gen[l] Washington, the present enterprise of the Senate to wrest from the H. of Representatives the power, given them by the constitution, of participating with the Senate in the establishment & continuance of laws on specified subjects. their aim is, by associating an Indian chief, or foreign government in form of a treaty to possess themselves of the power of repealing laws become obnoxious to them, without the assent of the 3[d] branch, altho' that assent was necessary to make it a law. we are then to depend for the secure possession of our laws, not on our immediate representatives chosen by ourselves, and amenable to ourselves[1] every other year, but on Senators chosen by the legislatures, amenable to them only, & that but at intervals of 6. years, which is nearly the common estimate of a term for life. but no act of that sainted worthy, no thought of Gen[l] Washington ever countenanced a change of our constitution so vital as would be the rendering insignificant the popular, and giving to the aristocratical, branch of our government the power of depriving us of our laws.

The case for which Gen[l] W. is quoted is that of his treaty with the Creeks, wherein was a stipulation that their supplies of goods should continue to be imported duty-free. the writer of this article was then a member of the legislature, as he was of that which afterwards discussed the British treaty, and recollects the facts of the day, and the ideas which were afloat. the goods for the supplies of the Creeks were always imported into the Spanish ports of St Augustine, Pensacola, Mobile, New Orleans E^{t}c (the US. not owning then one foot of coast on the gulf of Mexico, or South of St Mary's) and from these ports they were carried directly into the Creek country, without ever entering the jurisdiction of the US. in that country their laws pretended to no more force than in Florida or Canada. no officer of their customs could go to levy duties in the Spanish or Creek countries, out of which these goods never came. G^l Washington's stipulation in that treaty therefore was nothing more than that our laws should not levy duties where we have no right to levy them, that is, in foreign ports, or foreign countries. these transactions took place while the Creek deputation was in New York in the month of July 1790. and in March preceding we had passed a law[2] delineating specifically the line between their country and ours. the only subject of curiosity is how so nugatory a stipulation should have been placed in a treaty? it was from the fears of McGillivray, who was the head of the deputation, who possessed from the Creeks themselves the exclusive right to supply them with goods, and to whom this monopoly was the principal source of income.

The same writer quotes from a note in Marshal's history an opinion of mr Jefferson, given to G^l Washington on the same occasion of the Creek treaty. two or three little lines only of that opinion are given us, which do indeed express the doctrine in broad and general terms. yet we know how often a few words withdrawn from their place may seem to bear a general meaning, when their context would shew that their meaning must have been limited to the subject with respect to which they were used. if we could see the whole opinion, it might probably appear that it's foundation was the peculiar circumstances of the Creek nation. we may say too, on this opinion, as on that of a judge whose positions beyond the limits of the case before him are considered as obiter sayings, never to be relied on as authority.

In July 90. moreover the government was but just getting under way. the duty law was not passed until the succeeding month of August. this question of the effect of a treaty was then of the first impression; and none of us, I suppose, will pretend that on our first reading of the constitution, we saw at once all it's intentions, all the bearings of every word of it, as fully & as correctly as we have since understood them, after they have become subjects of public

investigation and discussion: and I well remember the fact that, altho'
mr Jefferson had retired from office before mr Jay's mission, and the
question on the British treaty yet during it's discussion we were well
assured of his entire concurrence in opinion with mr Madison & others who maintained the rights of the H. of R. so that, if on a primâ
facie view of the question, his opinion had been too general, on stricter
investigation, and more mature consideration, his ultimate opinion
was with those who thought that the subjects which were confided to
the H. of R. in conjunction with the President & Senate, were exceptions to the general treaty[3] power given to the President and Senate
alone; (according to the general rule that an instrument is to be so
construed as to reconcile and give meaning & effect to all it's parts:)
that whenever a treaty stipulation interferes with a law of the 3.
branches, the consent of the 3^d branch is necessary to give it effect;
and that there is to this but the single exception of the question of war
and peace. there the constitution expressly requires the concurrence
of the three branches to commit us to the state of war, but permits
two of them, the President & Senate, to change it to that of peace, for
reasons as obvious as they are wise. I think then I may affirm, in con-
tradiction to **B.** that the present attempt of the Senate is not sanctioned by the opinion either of G^l Washington or mr Jefferson.

I meant to confine myself to the case of the Creek treaty and not
to go into the general reasoning: for after the logical and demonstrative arguments of mr Wilde of Georgia, & others on the floor of Congress, if any man remains unconvinced I pretend not to the powers of
convincing him.   **A.**

Dft (DLC); with wide margins typical
of TJ's drafts; unrelated opening of an
unaddressed letter in TJ's hand on verso
of last page, dated Monticello, 29 Feb.
1816, and stating only "Your favor of the
16th." Recorded in SJL at 13 Mar. 1816,
in the column of letters by TJ, simply as
"A." Printed without dateline in Washington *Daily National Intelligencer*, 18
Mar. 1816.

The WRITER IN THE NATIONAL IN-
TELLIGENCER OF FEB. 24 (actually 23
Feb. 1816), who SIGNS HIMSELF B, stated that "Your paper has been usefully employed for some weeks past, in publishing
to the nation the arguments delivered in
Congress on the interesting question as to
the effect of a treaty on existing laws interfering therewith. The speakers on each
side of this question seemed sensible of
the aid to be derived from precedent, and
therefore recurred to the practice of the
government in similar cases. But I confess
I was not a little surprised, that the gentlemen who maintained the doctrine that
a treaty did repeal an opposing law, and
therefore, that legislation was unnecessary, should have omitted to urge in their
favor, the most decisive case which has
occurred since the foundation of the government. The one to which I allude happened in 1790.—See Marshall's life of
Washington, 5th vol. note 2d, at the end
of the vol. President Washington negotiated a treaty with the Creek nation; in one
of the articles of which, it is said to have
been stipulated, that the supplies which
had formerly passed through the Spanish
territory to their Chief, McGilvary, who

had a monopoly of their trade, should, in future, be carried through the United States, free of imposts. The precise question, namely, whether a treaty repealed or suspended the effect of a law imposing duties, or whether such a result should be produced by legislative provision, occurred then. President Washington, with his usual caution and circumspection, submitted the subject to the consideration of his cabinet, Mr. Jefferson being at that time Secretary of State. The historian above alluded to, states that Mr. Jefferson delivered the following opinion:—'A treaty made by the President, with the concurrence of two thirds of the Senate, was a law of the land, and a law of superior order, because it not only repeals past laws, but cannot itself be repealed by future ones. The treaty then will legally control the duty act, and the act for licensing traders in this particular.' From this opinion, says Mr. Marshall, there is no reason to suppose that any member of the cabinet dissented. Such was the interpretation then given to the constitution, and in which, President Washington concurred. When we reflect on the time when, and the characters by whom this precedent was established, it becomes entitled to great respect.—It is submitted to your readers without comment."

The PRESENT ENTERPRISE OF THE SENATE was a lengthy constitutional discussion provoked by the 1815 commercial treaty with Great Britain (Miller, *Treaties*, 2:595–600). On 6 Jan. 1816 the Washington *Daily National Intelligencer* reported that an "amicable discussion has commenced in the House of Representatives on the bill to regulate our commerce in conformity to the convention of commerce recently concluded with Great Britain. The debate turns not so much on the merits of the Treaty, as on the necessity of Legislation to carry its provisions into effect. Thus one of the questions so much agitated in the year 1795, in regard to Jay's Treaty, is revived; the two political parties appearing, though the government has since changed hands, to maintain the same doctrines on the subject of treaty stipulations, which they then declared and supported."

According to "An Act concerning the convention to regulate the commerce between the territories of the United States and his Britannic Majesty," approved 1 Mar. 1816, "so much of any act as imposes a higher duty of tonnage, or of impost on vessels and articles imported in vessels of Great Britain, than on vessels and articles imported in vessels of the United States, contrary to the provisions of the convention between the United States and his Britannic majesty, the ratifications whereof were mutually exchanged the twenty-second day of December, one thousand eight hundred and fifteen, be, from and after the date of ratification of the said convention, and during the continuance thereof, deemed and taken to be of no force or effect" (*U.S. Statutes at Large*, 3:255).

The Senate received George Washington's request for a STIPULATION regarding commerce with the Creek nation in the form of a secret treaty article on 4 Aug. 1790 and gave its advice and consent the same day (Linda Grant De Pauw and others, eds., *Documentary History of the First Federal Congress* [1972–], 11:86–7). For the 1790 Creek Treaty with a provision DELINEATING SPECIFICALLY THE LINE BETWEEN THEIR COUNTRY AND OURS, see *U.S. Statutes at Large*, 7:35–8. The 29 July 1790 OPINION OF MR JEFFERSON, GIVEN TO Gᴸ WASHINGTON and partially quoted in John Marshall's *Life of George Washington* (Philadelphia, 1804–07; Sowerby, no. 496; Poor, *Jefferson's Library*, 4 [no. 133]), vol. 5, 2d endnote, p. 3, is printed and discussed in *PTJ*, 17:288–91.

In congressional debate on 12 Jan. 1816, Representative Richard Henry WILDE cited an example from the Louisiana Purchase treaty when congressional enabling legislation was passed; remarked that this took place during TJ's administration, which Wilde remembered as "a period of what he had been accustomed to consider as correct principles"; observed that the example was "stronger, because Mr. Jefferson, when Secretary of State, is said to have maintained the opinion now supported by the gentlemen on the opposite side of the House"; argued that "If a treaty could repeal one law, it can repeal another; if it could repeal some, it can repeal all"; and insisted rather that the President and Senate lacked any such authority to use the treaty-making power to expand their authority beyond constitutional limits (*Annals*, 14th Cong., 1st sess., 623–31).

[1] Preceding four words not in *Daily National Intelligencer*.

[2] Reworked from "a law had passed."

[3] *Daily National Intelligencer* here adds "-making."

From Patrick Gibson

SIR   Richmond 13th March 1816

I have received your favor of the 8th Ins[t] in which you make no mention of the receipt of my letter of the 14th Ult[o]. I presume however that it reached you, and that you are aware of the dull and depressed state of our flour market, it is now if possible worse and altho the millers still ask 8½$, I have offer'd 100 bls: ground at your mill at 7½$ without meeting with a purchaser, in conformity with your instructions I have yet done nothing with yours—

Seven hhd[s] of your Tob[o] have come down and will be inspected tomorrow, when I shall dispose of them—I shall send you the box of Oil by the first boat—Inclosed is a note for your signature to renew the one in Bank due 19/22[d] Ins[t]. you will therefore be pleased to return[1] it immediately—With great respect—

Your ob[t] Serv[t]   PATRICK GIBSON

RC (ViU: TJP-ER); at head of text: "Thomas Jefferson Esq[re]"; endorsed by TJ as received 15 Mar. 1816 and so recorded in SJL; with TJ's notes for his 18 Mar. 1816 reply on verso: "acc[t] of flour. sell it tob[o] Yancey's draught 170. taxes e[t]c— Duane 65.D." Enclosure not found.

For Gibson's LETTER OF THE 14[TH] ULT[O], see note to TJ to Joel Yancey, 20 Feb. 1816.

[1] Word interlined in place of "forward."

From John Vaughan

D SIR   Philad. 13 March 1816

I have parted with T[y] Notes proceeds   73.63
rem[d] to N York—   54.24 recd from M Short   34.34
Balle in your fav   53.73 $107.97
                     $107.97

when I receive[1] your Duplicates for M Appleton I shall forward them—M Correa is well—

I remain sincerely[2] yours   JN VAUGHAN

RC (MHi); endorsed by TJ as received 25 Mar. 1816 and so recorded in SJL. RC (DLC); address cover only; with PoC of TJ to Nicolas G. Dufief, 17 May 1816, on verso; addressed: "Thomas Jefferson Monticello"; franked; postmarked Philadelphia, 13 Mar.

T[Y]: "Treasury." REM[D]: "remitted."

[1] Manuscript: "recive."
[2] Manuscript: "sincerly."

To John Barnes

DEAR SIR   Monticello Mar. 14. 16

Having occasion to make a remittance to my grandaughter Ellen W. Randolph now at the President's I take the liberty of putting it under cover to you, because I think it will go safer in that way. I therefore inclose a bill of 100.D. of the bank of Virginia which I understand will be worth more than par in the bills of the District. be so good as to pay it out to the order of my grandaughter, and I will go further, and, on the footing of antient friendship will pray you to answer her calls to any extent she may have occasion to make them, on the assurance that the replacement shall be made by the return of the mail which brings me notice of them. her discretion is so perfect that no confidence in it can be too great.—I am always anxious to hear of your health wishing with great sincerity for as many years of it as you wish yourself.   TH: JEFFERSON

PoC (Mrs. Henry Howe Richards, Groton, Mass., 1947); on verso of reused address cover of George P. Stevenson to TJ, 12 Feb. 1816; at foot of text: "M[r] Barnes"; endorsed by TJ.

To Ellen W. Randolph (Coolidge)

Monticello Mar. 14. 16.

I have been, my dear Ellen, without subject for a letter to you until one has been furnished by the sale of my tobacco. in this you also will feel somewhat of interest, inasmuch as it enables me to replenish your moyens de jouissance, by remitting to mr Barnes 100.D. for you. I do this by the present mail, and have chosen his cover because I thought it would go safer in that way; and because also it has given me an opportunity of requesting that he would furnish your wants beyond that to any extent you may call for, with an assurance of immediate replacement. you have only therefore to draw on him for the present &

any further sums, as you may want them; and I assure you, my dear Ellen, you cannot give me so great a proof of your affection and confidence as by a free use of the opportunity now furnished me of doing what may be acceptable to you.   Your Mama & the girls, I expect, anticipate [m]e in all the small news of the neighborhood; perhaps even in [wh]at we [h]ave heard but this morning, the death of an aunt, & birth of a [ne]ice. we had scarcely wished Jefferson joy of his daughter when we recieved the news of the death of mrs Judy Randolph. have they told you that our neighbor mr Sthreshly has sold out to Capt Meriwether thus giving us a double[1] subject of regret?   I thought you were to have given me occasionel if not regular reports of Congressional incidents & tracasseries, not omitting entirely the babble of the coteries of the place. do not write me studied letters but ramble as you please.[2] whatever books you want, desire Millegan to furnish them and to put them into my account. by the bye do you know any thing of him? by the impossibility of my getting answers from him I begin to suspect something is the matter.   When are you coming home? I shall be in Bedford all April. the void you have left at our fire side is sensibly felt by us all, and by none more than Your's with most[3] affectionate love

TH: JEFFERSON

P.S. my friendly respects to the President, and homage to mrs Madison & mrs Cutts

PoC (MHi); on verso of reused address cover of Joshua Norvell to TJ, 15 Jan. 1816; torn at seal; endorsed by TJ.

MOYENS DE JOUISSANCE: "means of enjoyment." The AUNT was Judith (Judy) Randolph, a sister of TJ's son-in-law Thomas Mann Randolph. She died in Richmond on 10 Mar. 1816 (gravestone inscription in Tuckahoe plantation cemetery, Goochland Co.; Georgetown *Federal Republican*, 15 Mar. 1816). Thomas Jefferson Randolph welcomed the birth of a DAUGHTER, Margaret Smith Randolph, on 7 Mar. 1816 (Shackelford, *Descendants*, 1:255).

Robert B. STHRESHLY sold his Albemarle County land to William D. Meriwether and moved to Kentucky. TJ recorded the purchase of a "guitar" from Sthreshly and his wife on 4 Mar. 1816.

This was probably the instrument (illustrated elsewhere in this volume) that, according to family tradition, TJ presented to his granddaughter Virginia J. Randolph (Trist) (Albemarle Co. Deed Book, 20:122–3; *MB*, 2:1319–20; Stein, *Worlds*, 422–3). Later this month Virginia's sister Ellen reported to their mother from Washington that "I cannot procure a book of instructions for the guitar in this city but I shall probably be more successfull in Baltimore" (Ellen W. Randolph [Coolidge] to Martha Jefferson Randolph, [ca. 26 Mar. 1816], RC in ViU: Coolidge Correspondence).

TRACASSERIES: "bickerings."

[1] Manuscript: "doublee."
[2] TJ here canceled "if."
[3] Word interlined.

From William F. Gray

RESPECTED SIR,   Fredericksburg March 14th 1816
   I this day forward to you, by the Mail Cart, a small bundle of
Books, sent to my care by M[r] Milligan of George Town.
   Wishing them safe to hand
   I remain
   Your Obt. Svt.—   W[M] F. GRAY

RC (DLC); at foot of text: "Tho[s]   For the SMALL BUNDLE OF BOOKS, see
Jefferson Esq. Monticello"; endorsed by   Joseph Milligan to TJ, 6 Mar. 1816.
TJ as received 15 Mar. 1816 and so
recorded in SJL.

From William Annesley

SIR   [received 15 Mar. 1816]
   At the suggestion of M[r] H. G. Spafford I enclose the drawings of a
new System in boat and Ship building. It is 6 years since I conceiv'd
the plan. I have built 2 Vessels on it, one has been running this 3
years from which[1] these few facts are stated. I purpose going to
Washington to lay it before the commissioners of the Navy. On the
Arguments reasoning & Facts which Sir I take the Liberty to present
to you I respectfully solicit Your Judgment.
   The drawing has been executed as this Vessel was built that is bottom upwards. Vessels of a larger Size I build as usual.
   The advantages in this System are in Expence. Room. Duration.
Strength. Sailing. Tightness. Buoyancy and safety,
Expence[2]   In viewing the drawing it is percev'd my first tier of
planking is in place of Ceiling, my cross planking in place of Timbers, It may be admitted my Mould can be got out & my Vessel cross
plank'd ere the Timbers of such a Vessel could be got out & set up,
My Mould is also gained and will do for others the same size. In the
Iron for bolts & 'there is a great saving' It is computed on the Hull is
saved 20 P[r] Cent at least, Room is gained by the difference of space
required for Timbers a fifteenth or 7 P[r] Cent. Duration. my Plank
being immers'd in water and Steam'd alters or extracts the pernicious
Sap and being secured with Tarred paper prevents its being alternate
wet & dry. It is well known Ship Timber best assorted will have a
partial decay and the whole is frequently condemn'd for a part. In this
it will be uniform. Strength in this method is gained from the com-
paritive weight of the materials and considering seasoned plank to be

used will not probably be more than half the weight employ'd with Timbers from the Texture of this Vessel She is Strong but principally from her form, being a complete Arch, Her decks on the same principle a self supporting Arch that does not bear on the abutments but is relieved by caulking. I cannot readily conceive the Violence that would destroy a well built vessel on this principle or what would first give way as the entire capacity of resistance in Her whole frame is brought in opposition to every partial shock. Her Keel would sustain great violence ere it would seperate and even its loss would not essentially hurt the Vessel. Sailing. It is plain the vessel that removes least water and that nighest the Surface with the easiest entrance and freest delivery with the same Quantity of sail will go the fastest thr'o the water and that She holds the best wind that shews most Opposition to leeward, On this supposition I have formed my Model which may be proved by this Experiment

Take it and one after the most approved Pilot boat let a cord be attached to Stem and Stern of each and seined at equal distances to a cord passing over a pully having the same weight suspended and place them in a trough of water it may be proved which takes the longest time to move the same Distance and consequntly the most tedieus holds the best wind. It is Allowed that vessels built expressly for sailing are generally wet and not lively having such a depth immers'd and such a Quantity of Ballast to carry are apt to bury and sail heavy before the wind with a Strong breeze. It is evident this model is a good sea boat and well calculated to sail before the wind. All Vessels in this System will steer easily. Buoyancy. I have not Sufficient data to make an exact calculation between the weight of Timbers and seasoned plank secured by tarred paper from being ever water soaked . . . Tightness Vessels on this construction may be made water proof so as to exclude damp and will keep so. It is well known that all Vessels on the ordinary plan will Strain and make water in a severe gale of wind. from this Vessels form & texture a Strain must equally bear on all parts and would remove every Trundle bolt or rivet in her which I cannot believe probable I might say possible. It may be readily suggested the advantage of this system to particular description of Vessels—for Life boats the inner Tier might be made alternate corkwood and may be formed to live in any surf nor be liable to be stove against a wreck—

They would be particularly serviceable in descending Rapids, for Ferrys and navigating Rivers or Barharbors as Vessels of 80 Tons might be built to hold a good wind and not draw more than 5 or $5\frac{1}{2}$ ftt water

Safety and Healthiness of the crew in not being subject to the putry-fying damps & effluvia of rotting wood & bilge water. The safety of Life & goods as foundering at Sea would be a rare misfortune and in few Places could such a Vessel be wreck'd without [o]pportunity of escape to the Crew ere she would beat to pieces. Vessels of War in this system will not suffer from firing heavy ordinance and working their guns. they may in fact be riddled but not sunk as the Shot holes could be plugg'd from the inside without the imminent danger incurred in the present way—Nor will splinters fly which has been found so destructive to Life. Vessels on discovery or long and hazardous Voyages might take boards & plank sufficient to build a Boat to carry their Crew without a forge and each person be able to assist, the construction being so simple—

I would not solicit the Nation to build a Vessel if my circumstances permitted me it would only be the result of the following experiments I would lay before the Commissioners—To build a Vessel of 60 or 100 Tons. ere she was launch'd to strain a line from Stem to Taffrail with an upright mark'd and plac'd in the Centre then to permit her entire weight to bear on the Centre block to shew what variation— (if any) on the upright measure—That an accurate Account of the expence be kept that a Just estimate may be made. That the vessel be sailed in extremity of Weather by able Seamen and reported of that Weight be placed on her Decks to prove the Strength of them. that heavy ordinance be fired to prove the Shock would not injure. that She be loaded with heavy Articles to prove her superior Tonnage and in this condition to be grounded to Shew She will not Strain—That Targets be built [...] to shew that Splinters will not fly and pr[ove] its greater resistance to solid wood—. I profess to be practically acquainted with every part of the work and will engage to build a Vessel that will on Tryal support the Character fully that is here laid down—

Some Facts. The Nonsuch is a small sloop of Ten Tons built on this plan Her inside Tier is inch white pine boards Her cross planking $\frac{5}{8}$'s inch white wood the last course White Pine of $\frac{7}{8}$'s thick. She was built by a House Carpenter when I was necessarily engag'd about my other business and could not pay that attention necessary to have her well done Under all those desadvantages and being the 1st experiment The following is took from Her performance. The Nonsuch lay aground for 2 Tides deeply laden with Clams on Rockaway bar with a heavy sea and inblowing wind with out Injury or straining; The owners of other Vessels observing at the same time were they in the same situation they would have went to pieces. At Tarlers point

She got on some rocks and beat off[3] her hanging Keel without any further Injury. About the 4th Dec[r] last coming up within 2 miles of Albany got fast in the Ice a large sloop of 70 Tons or upwards heavy laden came right on to windward on her waist crushing her, thro the Ice several rod when 1½ In thick[4] That Willis Post and Partner who then sail'd Her thought she must inevetibly sink and beleive it would have crushed any other boat of Her size. The model of the Nonsuch is inferiour to the model I intend to present to the Commissioners after which I built a smaller called the Nautilus last summer from which I state nothing but superior sailing. After the Nonsuch lost her hanging Keel to the surprize of every one She held as good a Wind as the most of the sloops in the River owing to having a clear and per-pendicular run, When down in the Water and blowing fresh on a Wind few sloops that sail the Hudson will go to Windward of Her and none of her size will Keep up for a sea boat & making good Weather She is not su[r]pass'd perhaps not equall'd The above Ac-count is subscrib'd to and if necessary would be attested by all Who has saild Her and from Whom the facts is taken and, tis their belief that every advantage here imputed to the System is Just. Sir if you will please to give this subject your consideration and favor me with an Answer address'd to W[m] Annesley of Albany to be left at Wash-ington Post Office I hope its future Importance will Justify me in giving You this Trouble   I am Sir with the greatest

Respect & Esteem for Your Character Y[r] Obed[t] Serv[t]

W[M] ANNESLEY

RC (DLC: TJ Papers, 206:36743–5); undated; edge damaged; ellipsis in origi-nal; endorsed by TJ as received 15 Mar. 1816 and so recorded in SJL.

William Annesley (ca. 1767–1848), naval architect, was working in Albany by 1803 as a carver and gilder. On 12 Sept. 1816 he received a United States patent for his method of ship construction, and he received a similar patent in Great Britain in 1818. Annesley made further improvements to his method and was granted a new American patent in 1830, along with an additional patent for a new mode of uniting timber for architectural uses (*Albany Register*, 5 Apr. 1803; *List of Patents*, 169; London *Repertory of Arts, Manufactures, and Agriculture*, 2d ser., 34 [1819]: 18–30; Annesley, *A New*

System of Naval Architecture [London, 1822; Poor, *Jefferson's Library*, 5 (no. 216)]; Franklin Institute, *Journal* 7 [1831]: 175–81; Nathan Reingold, Marc Rothenberg, and others, eds., *Papers of Joseph Henry* [1972–2008], 5:115–6; *Albany Annual Register* [1849]: 180).

The enclosed DRAWINGS OF A NEW SYSTEM IN BOAT AND SHIP BUILDING, not found, were probably similar to the plate and its explanation subsequently in-cluded in Annesley's pamphlet, *Descrip-tion of William Annesley's New System of Boat and Ship Building; Patented in the United States* (Albany, 1816), 2–3.

[1] Manuscript: "whih."
[2] Manuscript: "Expenc," with the word in the left margin.
[3] Manuscript: "of."

4 *Description of William Annesley's New System*: "a sloop of seventy tons or upwards came right on to windward on her waist with such violence as forced her several rods through the ice, then 1 1-2 inch thick" (p. 10).

From George Ticknor

DEAR SIR,   Göttingen March 15. 1816.—

I have already in my letters from London, and in the letters I have written you from here Oct. 14. Oct. 30. and Novem. 25. told you of so many changes in my plans, that, if I were not sure that you will appreciate my reasons, I should be almost ashamed to write you now to tell you of another. The truth, however is, that I find Göttingen so entirely suited to my purposes—the opportunities and means and inducements to pursue those studies to which I mean to devote my life are so admirable here,—that I have determined to protract my stay in Europe in order to enjoy them one year longer. To this resolution I came on the 27. Jan. in consequence of letters received the day before from home, and as I, of course at the same time determined to defer my visit to France a year longer, I immediately made arrangements for the purchase of your Books in Paris. I could have easily effected this by a literary[1] friend of mine there, but as I knew Mr. Warden's personal respect for you and as you had told me that he is "an excellent bibliograph," I wrote to him on the same 27th of Jany desiring him to procure them. A few days since I received his answer of Feb. 12. in which he very willingly promised to undertake it. To day, I have received your favour of Jan. 14. and have instantly written to him and given him your supplement to your catalogue. I hope these arrangements will meet your approbation, and I think they will, as they are the best I could make, though I should much have preferred to purchase them myself, because it is the only opportunity I may ever have of returning you the many obligations you have conferred on me. This I could have done to great advantage in Holland, where the general poverty and the[2] failing spirit of literature has made the classicks disgracefully cheap; but, then your list was not received or even made out. In Germany, I have thought it best to do nothing, for the strong spirit of recovered independence, tho' not freedom, and the perpetual literary labour of the learned make those old editions of the classicks which you desire very rare, and from 120 to 150 per cent. higher than in Holland and probably 50 or 60 higher than in Paris.—If, however, you should like to have any of the recent editions, which have given a new and more philosophical and acute character to the study of antiquity, Germany and Göttingen will best afford them, or if a year hence you should need anything from France or Italy, I shall eagerly seize the opportunity to procure it, and can safely forward it to you, as I am continually sending books to America.—

The letters, however, which your kindness gave me have embarassed me much more than the commission for the books. I have already told you that immediately on my arrival here, I sent the one for the Baron de Moll directly to him by one of the professors and since then, I have returned you the one for Mons. de Nemours, as he is already in the U.S. I could easily send the others to France, but La Fayette and Kosciuzko are no longer there and I can neither procure Mons. Say's addresse or even ascertain in what quarter of the world he is. They, therefore, still remain with me waiting for favourable circumstances.

The longer I have continued here, the better I have been satisfied with my situation, and the more reasons and inducements I have found to protract my residence. The state of society is, indeed, poor; but the means and opportunities for pursuing the study of the languages particularly the ancient, are, I am persuaded, entirely unrivalled. As I have already written you in my long letter on German literature, I was told even in England and by Dr Parr, England's best and perhaps, vainest classical scholar, that Germany was farther advanced in the study of antiquity than any other nation. This I find to be true. The men of letters here bring a philosophical spirit to the labour of exposition which is wanting in the same class in all other countries. The consequence is that the study of the classicks has taken a new and more free turn within the last forty years and Germany now leaves England at least twenty years behind in the course where before it always stood first. This has been chiefly effected by the constitution of their Universities, where the professors are kept perpetually in a grinding state of excitement and emulation, and by the constitution of their literary society generally, which admits no man to its honours, who has not written a good book. The consequence, to be sure, is, that ye professors are more envious and jealous of each other than can be well imagined by one who has not been actually within the atmosphere of their spleen, and that more bad and indifferent books are printed than in any country in the world, but then the converse of both is true; and they have more learned professors and authors at this moment, than England & France put together.

I would gladly hope, that the favour of your correspondence may be continued to me from time to time even after the commission for your books has been executed. If you feel any interest in the state of literature in Germany, which has sprung forth in the last thirty years as unbidden and as perfect as the miraculous harvest of Jason, I can be able to give you occasionally-pleasant information—and when I reach France, I shall be able to write to you from the midst of your old friends and from a place associated in your imagination with very many interesting though, perhaps, not always pleasant recollections.—If these slight inducements are sufficient with your own kindness to procure me the favour of an occasional letter, I shall feel myself under new obligations to you.—I shall, also, feel it as a great favour, if you will give me your opinion on the prospects of learning in the U. S. and the best means of promoting it—a subject which now occupies much of my attention.—

I pray you to remember me very respectfully and gratefully to your family.—

Your obliged & obed^t ser^t GEO: TICKNOR

Letters to me, I believe, will continue to come more safely and quickly through the hands of my father.

RC (DLC); postscript written perpendicularly along left margin of last page; endorsed by TJ as received 11 Aug. 1816 and so recorded in SJL. PrC (MHi). Enclosed in Ticknor to TJ, 23 Apr. 1816.

Ticknor stated in his letter to David Bailie Warden, written from Göttingen ON THE SAME 27TH OF JAN^Y, that "Your friend Mr. Jefferson, when I left America proposed to send out to me a catalogue of books, which I was to purchase for him in Paris. This catalogue reached me in October last, and, as it was then my intention to visit Paris early in the spring, I have kept it in my hands ever since. To day, however, I have changed my determination, and concluded to remain at this University another year, and as I should extremely regret, that Mr. Jefferson should be so long deprived of the use of his books, upon which I know he has calculated as the amusement of his age and retirement, I take the liberty to address myself to you, to know, whether you will undertake to procure or cause them to be procured immediately, and sent out to America by some early vessel in the spring.—I do this, with the greater assurance of success, as I know your long ac-

quaintance with Mr. Jefferson, & attachment to his person, and as he did me the honour to give me a letter of introduction to you, which I yet hope to deliver. If you will inquire of our publick functionaries in Paris, you will probably find a copy of the letter and catalogue—addressed to me and the original of a letter of credit on Messrs. Perregaux Laffitte & Co. for $350, both of which I pray you to open and consider as addressed to yourself. If you should not find these letters, I pray you to notify me and I will forward you the copies, which I have here."

In a second letter to Warden, dated Göttingen, 15 Mar. 1816, Ticknor sent TJ's SUPPLEMENT to his catalogue; noted that "Mr. Jefferson in his letter to me speaks on one subject, on which it may be interesting to you as an American and perhaps as one having friends in America to know his opinion. He thinks that the people, the state legislatures, and the general government are likely to commit great extravagancies in banking, from which he foresees consequences hardly less unfortunate than those which followed the South-sea scheme in England and the assignats in France, to those who may hold the depreciating currency. This was written in the middle of January, and what has happened since I know not"; and added that "I have for you from Mr. Jefferson a copy of the second edition of his 'Manual for the use of the Senate,' which I shall send to you if any opportunity offers, if I find none I shall bring it, in the course of the next winter" (RCs in MdHi: Warden Papers).

The letters YOUR KINDNESS GAVE ME included TJ to Baron Karl von Moll, 31 July 1814; TJ to Lafayette, 14 Feb. 1815; TJ to Pierre Samuel Du Pont de Nemours, 28 Feb. 1815; TJ to Jean Bap-

tiste Say, 2 Mar. 1815; and probably TJ to Tadeusz Kosciuszko, 3 July 1815, which was enclosed, along with TJ's letter to Ticknor of 4 July 1815, in TJ to James Monroe, 15 July 1815. Ticknor's LONG LETTER ON GERMAN LITERATURE was dated 14 Oct. 1815. Jason, leader of the mythological Argonauts, reaped a MIRACULOUS HARVEST of armed soldiers after sowing dragon's teeth (*OCD*, 154).

[1] Word interlined.
[2] Word interlined in place of "increasing."

To Joel Yancey

DEAR SIR   Monticello Mar. 15. 16.

Your's of the 4th was recieved the day before yesterday consequently the very day the Collector of the US. taxes was to call on you. as the law allows 20. days from that date for payment, this will reach you in time. you did not say what is the amount of the tax; but my grandson Th: J. Randolph has happened to be at Lynchburg where he was told by mr Robertson it was about 170.D. I therefore inclose you an order on Richmond for that sum, which I presume will suit the Collector as he deposits his money in one of the banks there. I was to have paid mr Robertson two sums of £20–16–1 and 78. D 35 c the 1st inst. but must beg indulgence till the sale of the tob° gone down. you seem to doubt if advisable to send the stemmed hhd of tob° to Richmond, but I believe it to be a certainty that the difference of market is always more than the cost of carriage. I approve of the exchange of flour for breadstuff as you propose. we shall lose by the Lynchbg price of flour, but the difference is not worth the operations of selling, buying, carrying & delay. I shall be with you the 1st or 2[d] week of April. with respect to my horses they will require a provision of about 40. bushels of oats, which I imagine can be bought. Lovilo reminded us by the last messenger, that he had not recieved his last year's clothes. be so good as to furnish them from homespun if ready, if not, from the store. I send by the cart a boar & sow pig, Guinea, for the plantation, being the breed I wish to get into there as soon as possible. they take little more than half the corn to fatten them & breed much faster than the common hog. he carries some articles for my use there. the box should be put into one of the rooms of the house, the barrels into the cellar, as they require to be in a cool place, also some plants which I pray you to have set out immediately in the Nursery behind the old stable, in a rich part.

I salute you with great esteem and respect.   TH: JEFFERSON

P. S. I promised mr Clarke a clover box which now goes by the bearer, be so good as to send it to him.

The branches of plants without roots are to be cut into lengths of 5. or 6. buds each and stuck in the ground 2 or 3 buds deep to take root.

if the Eastern fence of the garden is run, the strawberries had better be set out in the middle of it that they may spread themselves. they are the famous Hudson strawberry which I got from Philadelphia.

PoC (MHi); on verso of reused address cover of Yancey to TJ, 24 Feb. 1816; first postscript added perpendicularly along left margin; second postscript on verso; at foot of first page: "Mr Yancey"; endorsed by TJ. Enclosure not found.

Yancey's letter OF THE 4TH, not found, is recorded in SJL as received 12 Mar. 1816 from Lynchburg. His 21 Mar. response to the above letter, also missing, is recorded in SJL as received 23 Mar. 1816 from Bedford.

From James Barbour

SIR   Washn March–16th 16—

Presuming that you take no slight interest in the ensuing Presidential election, and that it would be agreeable to you to learn, on whom that distinguished appointment is likely to devolve, I have seized the earliest moment to communicate to you the result of a meeting of the Republicans, this moment adjourned—The ballot was as follows Monroe—65. Crawford—54—For V. P—Tompkins 85—Snyder 30—The utmost harmony and concord prevailed in our deliberations and the minority declared their cheerful acquiescence in the decision and that they would give it their undivided Support.

most respectfully yours &c   JAS BARBOUR

RC (DLC); endorsed by TJ as received 25 Mar. 1816 and so recorded in SJL.

The results of the 16 Mar. 1816 Republican congressional BALLOT for the nomination of presidential and vice-presidential candidates appeared in the Washington *Daily National Intelligencer*, 18 Mar. 1816.

From Benjamin J. Campbell

HONOURED SIR,   Washington March 16 1816

I have understood that you were in want of a number of looms of the most approved construction; Wherefore I take the liberty to inform you that I am now about obtaining a patent[1] for one, not before in use; the outlines of which you will permit me to describe

1st It Superceeds the necessity of warping in the web, for it takes the warp from spools, or bobbins, deposited in the rear of the loom, upon a triangular frame, and So arranged as to admit a person to take off those which become empty, and put on spools which are full.

2d From thence the warp is gathered into a reed suited to the fineness of the cloth, and passes through 4 pairs of rollers, having Screws at each end, that they can be Screwed together So as to press the warp in such a manner as to keep every thread in due order; Passing through an other reed of the Same fineness of the first, the warp goes into the loom.

3d The warp is then put into the harness, or heddles, which pass by each other by means of a shaft at the bottom of the loom, having 4 cranks, and as many[2] Sweeps, or pitmen, attached to the harness frames, one at each end of each frame.

4 The warp is then put through an other reed, fixed into a lathe (which reed is of the same fineness of the two others) going by means of an other Shaft, having two cranks, and going with double the velocity of the first shaft. This last Shaft is connected to the other by a strap.

5 To the last shaft is attached the machinery, which flings the shuttle.

6 Two rollers are placed in front of the loom, which deliver the cloth as fast as it is wove, in such a manner that it can be cut at pleasure without stopping the loom

The expense of building the loom may be 100 dolls

I have a model here which maks cloth eight inches wide—too heavy, however, to be very easily carried to your factory, as it must necessarily be transported by land.

If you are yet unsupplied with looms, it would be to me a great pleasure and advantage to superintend the building of one for you upon this plan, which I will warrant to do business I say <u>superintend</u> because I am not workman enough to do the labour myself. You are no doubt aware, Sir, that it would be of great advantage to me to be able to offer a loom to manufacturers recommended by you, rather than by any other man in the community. There can be no doubt that you have both good tools, and good workmen; These are some of the considerations which induce me to make this proposition. If I go home, I have neither shop, tools nor workmen.—It would cost me to build a loom there, much more, as I must labour under these disadvantages, than at your factory. I think, Sir, that with a skillful carpenter and Smith, I could build you a loom in 8 or 10 days.

Although in a strange land, I should be able, probably, to procure[3] satisfactory recommendations.

As I am confident my loom will do business better than any hitherto introduced; As I am confident you will approve the plan of it (as every gentleman has done who has yet seen it) As your liberality is known to extend to the young and enterprising; In fine as you are a philosopher and philanthropist; I assure you, Sir, that I look with confidence for your patronage

I wish you would have the goodness, Sir, to make me acquainted with your wishes as soon as convenient, for I shall be here on expense for no other purpose, than to hear from you.

I am, with the highest respect, Sir, your hum[l] Ser[t]

BENJ[A] J. CAMPBELL

RC (DLC); at foot of text: "Thomas Jefferson Esqr"; endorsed by TJ as received 24 Mar. 1816, but recorded in SJL as received a day later. RC (ViU: TJP); address cover only; with Dft of Draft Conveyance of Henderson Lands by John T. and Lucy Wood, [ca. May 1816], on verso; addressed: "Thomas Jefferson Esqr Charlottesville (Va.)"; stamp canceled; franked; postmarked Washington City, 17 Mar.

[1] Manuscript: "obtaing a paten."
[2] Manuscript: "may."
[3] Manuscript: "probly, to proceree."

Account with James Leitch

Thomas Jefferson

Bot of James Leitch

2	y[d] Mixed Cloth	$8	⎱	16–
$\frac{1}{4}$	" Drab Cloth	"1–25	⎰	–31
9	Skanes Silk	9[d]		1–12
1	Double Stick twist	1/6		–25
$1\frac{2}{12}$	Doz Best plated Buttons	4/6		–87$\frac{1}{2}$
1	" Common Do	2/		–33
$\frac{8}{12}$	" Vest Do	3/		–34
$4\frac{1}{2}$	y[d] Bro Holland	3/9		2–81
$2\frac{1}{2}$	" Bennetts Cord	21/		8–75

1	Vest pattern Toilenett	10/6	1–75
3½	y^d Shirting Cambrick	3/9	2–17
3	Skanes fine thread	4^d	–16
1	fine Hatt	$7–50	7–50
			$42–26[1]

E Ex

Charlottesville }
March 16th 16 }

JAMES LEITCH
CHARLES STEWART

MS (MHi); entirely in Stewart's hand; endorsed by TJ: "Leitch James."

Charles Stewart (ca. 1791–1835) was the son of William Stewart, who had worked as a blacksmith and run the nailery at Monticello from 1801 until his dismissal for drunkenness in 1807. Late in 1817 the younger Stewart was selected by TJ, Leitch, and Alexander Garrett to be apprenticed to a group of Swiss stocking weavers whom William Lee had brought to Washington, D.C., with the intention of Stewart engaging in that trade in Charlottesville. TJ then described him as "deformed by sickness" in his youth but "intelligent, correct in his habits and entirely worthy." Stewart's poverty induced Leitch to support him in this new endeavor. A series of misunderstandings regarding the length and cost of Stewart's train-ing and board, however, culminated in his early return to Charlottesville. In 1830 James Dinsmore bequeathed the interest on $500 to the "trusty & well beloved Charles Stewart in consideration of his fidelity and helpless situation" (*MB*, 2:1052, 1341; *PTJ*, 34:104; Lee to TJ, 16 June 1817; TJ to Lee, 12 Nov. 1817; Leitch to TJ, 12 Nov., 25 Dec. 1817; Jonas Keller to TJ, 14 Dec. 1817; TJ to Keller, 24 Jan. 1818; Albemarle Co. Will Book, 10:109; Fay V. Early and Constance C. Harris, eds., *Record of Cemeteries in Albemarle County, Virginia, including Charlottesville* [1971–ca. 1982], 3:152).

Brown Holland (BRO HOLLAND) is an unbleached linen fabric (*OED*). E EX: "Errors excepted."

[1] The correct sum is $42.36½.

From John Wood

SIR   Petersburg 16 March 1816

I take the liberty of soliciting your interest with the Executive in my favour, for the purpose of being appointed to survey the exterior boundaries of the Commonwealth according to the 7th section of the act passed by the last Legislature, which orders the Executive to employ a Surveyor or Surveyors upon this business to ensure greater accuracy in the contemplated Map of Virginia. The many years practice which I have had not only in Surveying; but in the drawing of Perspective plans and Landscapes; combined with the time I have devoted to mathematical pursuits; I hope will be an apology for coming forward on the present occasion.

I have suffered so much in my health, the last three years by a residence in this town; that I am extremely anxious to procure a situation, which may be suitable to my qualifications and beneficial to my constitution. I have always felt the greatest reluctance to make any application for public offices; and I should not have been a candidate for the present surveyorship; if I did not flatter myself, that my services will be equal to the compensation I shall receive. Requesting you will excuse the freedom I have taken in addressing you on this subj[ect.]

I have the honour to be Sir with great respect your obedient Servant   JOHN WOOD

RC (DLC); edge chipped; adjacent to closing: "To Thomas Jefferson Esqʳ"; endorsed by TJ as received 22 Mar. 1816 and so recorded in SJL.

For the ACT PASSED BY THE LAST LEGISLATURE, see Wilson Cary Nicholas to TJ, 22 Mar. 1816, and note.

From Frank Carr

DEAR SIR,   [received 18 Mar. 1816]

I was called on this Evening to set a broken leg of your man Moses. He is at Farley's. It would be painful, & would derange what has been done, to move him. He will [be][1] taken care of & attended to where he is—The accident happened in a trial of strength in a wrestle with one of his fellows:

I am respectfully yʳ S &c   FRANK CARR

RC (ViU: TJP-CC); undated; addressed (ink stained): "Thomas Jefferson Esqᵉ Monticello By [...]"; endorsed by TJ as received 18 Mar. 1816 and so recorded in SJL.

On 19 June 1816 TJ recorded payment of $10 to Betsy Farley for "a month's board" of MOSES (*MB*, 2:1324).

[1] Omitted word editorially supplied.

To Patrick Gibson

DEAR SIR   Monticello Mar. 18. 16.

Your favors of Feb. 14. and Mar. 13. were duly recieved. the last came to hand so as to allow time merely to reinclose my renewed note by return of the mail.

The inexactitude of my mill-tenants has sometimes led me into erroneous information to you as to flour sent down on my account. I have lately obtained from mr T. E. Randolph a statement of all sent from Oct. 17.[1] 1814. to Feb. 21. 1816. of which I send you a copy, and pray you to have it compared with your books; that, if any part of it has not been delivered to you, I may have it rectified. their statement amounts to 403. Barrels for 1814. 15. and 214. for 1815. 16. besides these there were 67. barrels for the former period, which had been sent to their agent but not delivered by him to you for want of their instructions. I am promised that these shall be instantly delivered so as to make the whole 684. Barrels for the two periods. this has no connection with any from Bedford. I have always considered March & April as the best months for selling flour[2] altho' it is likely to turn out otherwise this year. I will therefore pray you to sell whatever you have of mine on hand, as soon as you think it best, and for whatever price may be going at the time, without awaiting further advice. M[r] Yancey wrote me that 3. hhds of tob° more would immediately follow the 7. already sent, but that one of them was light, stemmed, & of in-different[3] quality. I shall be glad to hear that the whole is sold, be-cause in addition to the draught which in mine of the 8th I mentioned I should be obliged to make the last of this month, the US. Collectors are calling for their taxes which are very heavy. I have consequently given to Joel Yancey an order on you for 170.D. for the Collector of Bedford, to which I shall have to add those for this county. I must also ask the favor of you to remit 65.D. for me to Gen[l] William Duane. I shall go to Bedford in a fortnight or 3. weeks, before which I hope to hear what my tob° turns out.   Your's with friendship & esteem.   TH: JEFFERSON

PoC (DLC: TJ Papers, ser. 10); on reused address cover of Wilson Cary Nicholas to TJ, 16 Feb. 1816; at foot of text: "M[r] Gibson"; endorsed by TJ.

For Gibson's letter OF FEB. 14., see note to TJ to Joel Yancey, 20 Feb. 1816.

On the other side of the PoC of this letter is the enclosure to Thomas M. Randolph & Company to TJ, 12 Mar. 1816, a copy of which was probably the STATE-MENT enclosed here.

On this date TJ recorded the disposi-tion of the 65.D. FOR ME TO GEN[L] WILLIAM DUANE: "to wit 5.D. for the Au-rora to May 1. 1816. and 60.D. for a trans-lation of Tracy's Pol. economy, on account of Joseph Milligan to whom I am to charge it" (*MB*, 2:1320). This payment was not in fact made at this time (Duane to TJ, 9 Jan. 1817; TJ to Duane, 24 Jan. 1817).

[1] Reworked from "12."
[2] Word interlined.
[3] Manuscript: "indiffent."

From Patrick Gibson

SIR   Richmond 18th March 1816

I received this morning your favor inclosing a note for $2000. I have had your seven hhd[s] Tobacco inspected, and am sorry to inform you, they turn out wretchedly three were refused and four passed, but not without hesitation—I set them up to the highest bidder—the refused brought $15. 1 passed $16 and 3—$16⁵⁵/. as p^r Statement at foot—This article is on the decline—

As to flour I know not where it will stop, it is offering at $7 on 4 mos credit

With great respect Your ob^t Servt PATRICK GIBSON

ales of Seven Hhds tob° made on a/c of Thomas Jefferson Esqr

March 15th	To P. F. Smith	Shockoe	1660. 152. 1290		
			1661. 150. 1328		
			1662. 156. 1170	3788 at 16⁵⁵	$626.91
"	to Jn° M Warwick		1709. 142. 1100	16	176.—
"	to Wm Gilliat	refused	224. 169. 1235		
			225. 170. 1130		
			231. 154. 1220	3585 15	537.75
			8473 8473		1340.66¹

RC (ViU: TJP-ER); in Gibson's hand, with subjoined statement in James Ligon's hand and a final notation by TJ as indicated below; between dateline and salutation in Gibson's hand: "Thomas Jefferson Esqre"; endorsed by TJ as received 22 Mar. 1816 and so recorded in SJL. RC (DLC); address cover only; with PoC of TJ to David Bailie Warden, 17 May 1816, on verso; addressed in James Ligon's hand: "Thomas Jefferson Esqr Monticello"; postmarked Richmond, 20 Mar.

TJ's FAVOR, written immediately after he received Gibson's letter of 13 Mar. 1816 on 15 Mar., is not recorded in SJL, and neither it nor its enclosed NOTE FOR $2000 has been found.

¹ TJ added this line and the rules immediately above it.

From Stephen Cathalan

MY DEAR &

MOST RESPECTED SIR!   Marseilles the 19th March 1816

I have the honor of Confirming you my last Respects of the 15th Ult° by the Brig Pilot of Philad^a Alex^{er} Dixon Master beared of one Case Cont^{ing} 50 Bottles White hermitage wine & one Box Maccaroni to be Consigned to the Collector of the District of that City, as p^r Invoice amounting to F 248.02—and p^r Bill of Loading;—herein Inclosed, I Remit you the Invoice of 4 Boxes or Cases Containing each 50 B^{tls} old Red Wine of Bellet (Nice) which I have at Last Received from the Successors of Sasserno of nice, amounting to F 346—which as p^r Bill of Loading, Inclosed in my Letter to the Collector of the district of Alexandria, virginia, by the Brig Agenoria of Warren, Cyril Martin

Master, bearer of this, I have Shipped on the Said Brig, Bound for alex^a to be Consigned to the Said Collector, to be forwarded by him to you.

I have recommended to Said Collector to Return me the Aquit a Caution of this Customhouse duly Discharged by the Consul of France in that district, as in order to Save the heavy duties of Import of this now a foreign wine for France, I entered it in to Real enterpot of the Customs, & for Reéxportation a Broad, & this instrument is my Bond to prove it has been Landed in to forreign Country, & I would Incur the Penalties & fine, therein mentioned, Should I not be enabled to Return it to this custom house Regularly Discharged; for tho' Marseilles appears to be enjoying of a Free Port & it's territory,[1] it is only Called So, the only advantage, is, that the Foreign (& of Course the American) vessels are, Since it's Reéstoration Exempted of Paying in this Port the Tonage Duty, while they Continue to Pay it, as before, in all the Ports of France F 4. 12 e^{ach} /—p^r Ton; The Permits from the Customhouse to Land & to Ship Goods, Provisions &^{ca} which Costed f 1–10:/– Each are now delivered Gratis; The whole together which amounted high enough, is a good Economy, for forcing vessels & their inward & outwards Cargoes;—I Reffer you to the Inclosed Pamphlet Just Published; on the question of the Free Port & Territory of Marseilles;

I hoped I could have Sent you by this Same opportunity the wine of Roussillon, but Since my Last, I have not heard from Mr F^{ois} Durand of Perpignan about it; I hope however it will Soon Reach me; I beg your Refference to the herein Inclosed Copy of the Letter that Mr Spreafico has wrote me, in Sending me the Invoice of the wine, about the U.s. Consulate at nice, in favor of the Son of Sasserno; he adds that he hopes that you will be Satisfied of the quality of the wine of Nice, which, at my Request, he has charged at the Same Price of the Parcel I Sent you in october 1807—Tho' on account of the Great demand for England & a Broad, & the Late Bad Crops it has much Risen, in Price—

as Soon as I was Informed that our mutual Friend James Monroe Esqr had been appointed Secretary of State; I wrote him on the 21st October 1811 a Letter of Congratulation &^{ca} &^{ca} & Since Several others on the Pending affairs of this U.s. Consulate all thro' our Ministers or chargé d'affaires at Paris, with Copies Thro' the American Consul at Bordeaux, but owing, no Doubt, to Wars & more Important affairs, I have not been honored, hitherto, with a Line from him, as it had been the Case with his Predecessor R^{bt} R. Smith;—

however, as he directed in the year 1814, our Minister Plen^y at Paris to Pay me the old Balance of my advances towards the Govern^t of the U.s. out of which he had Rejected the Interests, with Several other Items of Little Consequence but however due to me, & Lawfully charged in my Statments, which had been Reimbursed to me in all my anterior ones by his Predecessors;

This Prompted me to write him Fully on the 25th Sep^{ber} 1814, Informing him that I was at Same time adressing Separately my Just claims to the President, on that & other Subjects, the whole under Cover of his Exc^y W^{am} H. Crawford our Minister Plen^y at Paris, & Copies Thro' Bordeaux; which were dispatched after the Peace of Ghantz with their own Dispatchs;—herewith is the Copy of my Said adress to the President, in which you will observe that I made use in my Behalf of Some Expressions, of your own, in Your Letter to me of the 29th June 1807—; hopping that you will excuse my Such Liberty;—

Tho' I have not yet Received, as yet, any advice that those objects Rejected have been Redressed, I hope however, that the New Minister Plen^y of the U. States, Soon Expected at Paris, will be Soon Instructed by the Executive to pay them to me, as well as my further advances, tho' Small, with the Interests, as Since h. E. W. H. Crawford Left Paris, M^r h^{ry} Jackson, he Left as chargé d'affaires of the U.s. at Paris, Informed me that—he was not Instructed to Pay any Consular Expences, Except the annual Salary of D 2000—to the Consul of the united states at Paris,—which as I wrote him, in answer, I Think Rather high, Since he has not any more American Prises to deffend before the Council of Prises at Paris, he not being Consul G^{nl} to whom the other Consuls in France are to Resort, or to Render accounts, while the U. states's Legation in Paris appears, now, to me, Sufficient, & he having, as we have, his Casual Fees, on his Consular Seal & Signatures besides;

The Fact is, my Dear sir, as it is Stated in my Letters & vouchers to the Secr^{ry} of State, James Monroe, that I have not only used of the Greatest Economy in my Supplies towards, the Distressed Seamen during the orders in Council & Decrees of Berlin & Milan in force, but that, I was Even Reimbursed for Part of my Said advances towards Some of Said Seamen, by the Govern^t of Bonaparte & his Privateers, which Sums I have Passed on the Credit of the Gov^{nt} of the U. States, on the Days I was Paid, I bonifying the Interests on So much Recovered;—but is it Just they Should not allow me the Interest's Balance, Resulting from Six years upwards on my own advances? & this in a Period that the Casual Fees of my Consulate <u>could not</u> amount all together to one hundred Dollars p^r annum, & While I was however, much Busied on account of these Distressed Seamen, Employing a Secretary at Three hundred Dollars p^r annum Salary, the whole time, writing with me, Claiming, recurring about, to attend to Said Seamen & to the affairs Pending in this Consulate, Even Borowing money to go on, I having Lost great deal in these Circumstances, instead of waining, while my landed Properties in great Part unrented, did not Render Enough to pay the Taxes Imposed upon, or to keep them in Repairs,! I Could then, I Think State with Propriety in my adress, that <u>I am Poorer than before</u>,! as I could not nor cannot, now, with Decency Lessen too much my Expences nor hospitality, towards the Americans, <u>for their Credit</u>, as Cap^n Greene of the Sch^{er} <u>Grace Ann</u>, Greene of New York, Cap^n John Holman of the Brig <u>Star</u> of <u>Talun</u> (whose names & vessels have been mentioned in the notes of James Monroe to the British Minister at washington), have experienced in the year 1810 & 11 & Can be witnesses as Some others & Lately Mr C. D. Coxe late Consul at Tunis, while in this Place & in my Consular house.

Should then it be the case against my Expectation, that when this will Reach, Redress Should not have been Granted to me, I beg Leave to Rely on your kind assistance, Interference & Protection, near the President & the Secr^y of State, to cause them to be Settled in a fair Just & Generous Way.—as you are So kind as to take Interest on me & my Family, I must Inform you that in october 1808 my Daughter & Son in Law found Proper to Part from my house, my mother & me in taking an other for themselves, we were happier & more Peaceably! but unfortunately on the 21st January 1810—I Lost my mother at 88 years age, and as I could not Remain alone in my house I followed her previous advice, in Contracting a Second marriage, to which they opposed So far as to abuse of the authority of the Duke of otrante Fouché minister of the Police Generale at Paris against my then future wife; I Started for Paris & Soon took away all the opposition, & married;—everything was forgiven from our Part, & at the Sollicitation of my wife I visited Several times my Daughter but She has always Refused obstinately to See her & to Come to my house; of Course we Are rather Cold together;—her husband Dead of a Pulmony the 23^d D^{ber} Last, leaving a Daughter & a Boy with an handsome fortune for this city. I have not any children from my Second Wife 40 years age, but we Live happy and as Comfortably as Possible.—you will thus observe that my Family is but Short & that you are happier & better Rewarded by yours Larger in number than mine & more Gratefull!

Wishing you a Continuation of Good health & enjoyment.

I have the honor to be with Great Respect my Dear Sir   your most obed^t and affectionate Servant   STEPHEN CATHALAN,

RC (DLC); endorsed by TJ as received 4 June 1816 and so recorded in SJL. Enclosed invoice not found. The enclosed pamphlet may be the second enclosure described at Cathalan to TJ, 15 Feb. 1816. Other enclosures printed below.

John Steele was the federal customs collector at Philadelphia, and Charles Simms was COLLECTOR OF THE DISTRICT OF ALEXANDRIA. An "acquit à caution" (AQUIT A CAUTION) is a customhouse bond. On 14 Oct. 1807 Cathalan advised TJ that he had shipped him one hundred bottles of wine from Victor SASSERNO (DLC).

A copy of Cathalan's 21 Oct. 1811 LETTER OF CONGRATULATION to James Monroe on his appointment as secretary of state is in DNA: RG 59, CD, Marseilles. William Lee was the AMERICAN CONSUL AT BORDEAUX.

The PEACE OF GHANTZ was the Treaty of Ghent. The NEW MINISTER PLEN^y OF THE U. STATES to France was Albert Gallatin. BONIFYING: "doing or making good; benefitting" (OED).

[1] Manuscript: "territory."

ENCLOSURES

I

Amant Spreafico to Stephen Cathalan

Nice 23 fevrier 1816

Monsieur le Consul, par votre honnorêe lettre du 13ᵉ je vois que vous avez eu l'extrême bonté d'écrire à M^r jefferson, encien president des Etats Unis, pour l'engager à vouloir bien m'accorder Sa protection afin d'obtenir le consulat de Nice; je Serais certainement très flatté, dêtre honnoré de cet emploi, que je cederai très volontier au fils de feu mon ami Victor Sasserno; ce jeune homme qui est actuelement à Paris, ainsi que j'ai eu l'honneur de vous le dire, par ma precedente, Suivant ce que m'a écrit Son oncle, viendra Se fixer à Nice vers la fin de cette année; daprês ce je vous prierais, Monsieur le consul, de vouloir bien Solliciter cette honnorable place pour ce jeune homme, qui je peux vous l'assurer, Sera digne de la remplir: d'ailleurs il Sait la langue anglaise, ce qui est on ne peut plus essentiel.

J'ose esperer de votre complaisance, Monsieur le Consul, que vous voudrez bien vous interesser en faveur de ce jeune homme en écrivant a M^r jefferson et en le recommandant d'une maniere particuliére;

J'ai l'honneur d'être avec la consideration la plus distinguée, Monsieur Le Consul

Votre très humble et très obeissant Serviteur

(Signé) AMANT[1] SPREAFICO

EDITORS' TRANSLATION

Nice 23 February 1816

Mister Consul, I see by your honorable letter of the 13th that you had the utmost kindness of writing to Mr. Jefferson, former president of the United States, to encourage him to help me obtain the consulship at Nice. I certainly would be very flattered to be honored with this position, which I shall very willingly cede to the son of my late friend Victor Sasserno. This young man is currently in Paris, as I had the honor of telling you in my preceding letter, and, according to what his uncle wrote me, will be coming to settle in Nice toward the end of this year. Based on this, Mister Consul, please solicit this honorable position for this young man, whom, I can assure you, will be worthy of it. Besides, he knows the English language, which could not be more essential.

I dare hope, Mister Consul, that you will kindly be willing to intercede in favor of this young man by writing to Mr. Jefferson and recommending him personally;

I have the honor to be, with the most considerate regards, Mister Consul

Your very humble and very obedient servant

(Signed) AMANT SPREAFICO

Tr (MHi); at head of text: "Copy"; at foot of text, in Cathalan's hand: "a Monsr Et^{nne} Cathalan &^{a} &^{a} Marseille p^r Copy Marseilles the 19th March 1816. Stephen Cathalan." Translation by Dr. Genevieve Moene.

The FILS DE FEU MON AMI VICTOR SASSERNO was Victor Adolphus Sasserno, and the ONCLE was a Mr. Arson.

[1] Manuscript: "Amand."

II

Stephen Cathalan to James Madison

SIR

Marseilles 25 Sepr 1814.

I beg leave to reffer you to the contents of the letter, I addressed on this day to the Secretary of States, James Monroe Esqr in which I request him to Lay it before you;

You will be pleased to observe that I claim against the unprecedented exceptions he has instructed H Ex^y Will. H Crawford to reject from my Statment of disbursment & acc^t Current with the U.S. in reimbursing me of my advances for the public Service, Viz:

1° the interest I charged on my advances, tho' I had bonnified the interest on the money I encashed for the acc^t of the U.S. from the days of its recovery;

2^d The loss on the exchange, the brokerage & the Stamp paper on my drafts for my reimbursment on Paris;[1]

3^d The postages for the public Service of the United States, as per detailed Statment annexed to the Said account.

I was far from expecting Such deductions after upwards five years of Silence undeserved from my part of the Secretaries of State R. R. Smith your Successor & James Monroe Esqr & not a Single line from both in answer to my repeated letters to them!

It was not So when I had the honor of corresponding with you, when Secretary of State & with your predecessors Th^y Pickering & Th^s Jefferson.— There is an Instance however when no interests nor commission was allowed to me on my disbursments & advances; it was my Statment for the americans redeemed by late Joel Barlow consul of the U.S. at Algiers, who arrived here with the pleague on the 20th July 1796, & Sailed from this port on the 6th Nov^{ber} D^{tto}, but why? because I volontarily charged nothing on the said acc^{ts}, the motive was that I embraced that opportunity to Ship Gratis of passage the late duke of Montpensier & comte de Beaujolais Sons of the duke of Orleans, for whom I volontarily answered personally, to the late Directoire of France, that I would have them Sent from Prison to the United States with thr[ee] individuals of their Suite, the dangers of the Sea excepted; I thought I was doing honor to my office of american Consul in that respect & that the amount of interest and commission (about f4500) which I did not charge, was a kind of compensation for their passage on board the Swedish Ship Jupiter, I frieghted for that voyage; I received a thankfull letter from the Sec^y of State on his arrival at Philadelphia for my disinterested exertions & good care towards these american redeemed Seamen & those unfortuned french Princes.

This reject I am experiencing leads me to represent you humbly my deceased father & my own past services;

In July 1775 Cornelius Vanhorn of New-york was dispatched with a circular from the Secret committee of congress directed to merchant[s] in the european ports, to purchase Gun-powder ammunitions &c—being unable to fulfill his mission in Portugal & Spain, he arrived here in Novr 1775; he Showed me, that letter directed to S. Cathalan my father; but after he was Convinced we were Zealous friends to the american cause against Great Britain; but the great difficulty to execute this mission was to obtain the permission of buying them from the king's arsenals, with their free exportation & above all Secrecy!

I prompted my father to Start for Paris, & he Succeeded in obtaining, from the Cabinet of Versailles, that free exportation, not only for himself, but from all ports of France; we dispatched the first cargo with the Said Van horne on board in Jany 1776, but the most important object was the insinuations of my father near that cabinet; & the information he transmitted to the Secret committee, who on receipt Sent Sylas Deane as their Secret Envoy near that cabinet. these facts can be verified in the archives of the Government of the united States.

Then resulted the act of Independency of the United States, on the 4 July 1776, the auxiliary assistance of Louis the Sixteenth, the war of France against England, the War in 1778 &^{2} glorious peace of 1783^3—but after! the french revolution of 1789 which became So fatal & cruel to that worthy and unfortunate monark, his family & the whole french nation!!!

While the United States by it's consequences & the war between France, England & other European maritim power, which took place in 1792 have from that epoqua to 1809 increased in population, industry, wealth, navigation and commerce all over the world, to such a prosperous degrée, that they could not expect to attain in a period of 50 years, without such causes, tho' from time to time unjustly molested in their trades either by one or other belligerant powers.

It is during that period & ever Since I was honored with the appointment of Consul of the U.S. at Marseilles Toulon &ᵃ, tho' I am not a native nor an american citizen, that by my exertions, using according to circomstances, & the Sundry cases that occured in my Department, & the character of the Several french authorities which Succeeded one an other, imploying moderation, or energy, but above all patience & perseverance in the Justice of my claims for the protections of the american citizens, their property & vessels, & with a disinterested zeal, I have hitherto So well Succeeded in their behalf; the detail of which would be too long: but I beg your referrence to my correspondance with the Secretaries of States & the ministers plenipᵃˢ of the U.S. at Paris for the particulars. on the 9ᵗʰ Febʸ 1796, I informed Thoˢ Jefferson then Secʸ of State that I had money lodged in the hands of John Mason Esqʳ of Georgetown, not only as a Security for my consular bond,[4] but further to be employed Either in the Loans of the Goverᵗ or in bank Shares of the U.S., or in Land property, as I wished to pay taxes into the U.S. because by the french constitution, then existing, Since the abolition of royalty, the foreign consuls natives of France, had lost their rights of french citizenship (& I was not Sorry of it) but as I wanted to belong to Some country, being long ere commissioned at the Service of the U.S., I considered them as my adoptive country. in Short I begg'd him to ask & obtain from the proper authorities, letters of naturalisation for me, as citizen of the U.S. as my residence: in the consulate of the U. States in Marseilles, ought to be considered as a real residence within the U. States, and this as a reward for my & my father's past Services;

By the advice of my old respectable friend Thˢ Jefferson, Mʳ John Mason employed my funds in bank Shares of the U.S. as Per certificate of the 1ˢᵗ July 1796 of the Said bank Nᵒ 3776. but as to my naturalisation, a previous residence within the U.S. was absolutely deemed necessary & my residence in my consulate not Sufficient; however an application made by the President to congress in my behalf, to be naturalized a citizen of the City of Washington, Stating my Services & Situation, might probably have caused an act of exception to be issued in my favor, while I have been by fact a bastard of country! I took great care to conceal to the french authorities at Paris & here, that I was So poorly Situated & I found it was even better for the interest of the U.S. to make them believe I was a citizen of the U.S., the proof is the Exequatur of the first consul Buonaparte of the 3ᵈ Thermidor year 11ᵗʰ on my commissio[n] of the 15ᵗʰ July 1805. which is Similar to the other for american native consuls; whereas in my Exequatur Signed by his most christian Majesty Louis the Sixteenth on the 24ᵗʰ Novemᵇʳ 1790 on my first commission, (which I have now under my eyes—having never parted with it) it is mentioned, "& as Said Stepⁿ Cathalan[5] is a french of nation & Subject of H. Majesty, he expects that in letting him exercise without hinderance the Said employment of consul for the navigation, Seamen and merchants of the U.S., he cannot on that little forsake himself in any thing whatever in his person or properties to the justice or Souvereignty of H. Majesty, whereof he must[6] stick to as well as the other citizens or Subjects of France"—I then hope, that, Since the Royal dinasty of the Bourbons is, at last, restaured in France, I have of course, recovered also my country & french rights! & I continue at Same time, with the same zeal & assiduity, to exercise the office of consul of the U.S. as before the french revolution & Since;[7]

Be pleased now, Sir, to allow me to make use for myself & behalf, of part of the paragraph of the confidential letter that Th[s] Jefferson, wrote me, on the 29th June 1807 informing me that—at the Close of his 2[d] presidency—he Should retire to the bosom of his eight grand-children & to the enjoyment of his farms, books &c &c he then adds "I have another great consolation, that after 40 years Services to my country" (I must[8] Say to the United States!) "I retire poorer than when I entered it, not that I have any thing to reproach them with; they have always allowed me as much as I thought I deserved my-self, but I have believed it my duty to Spend for their credit whatever they al-lowed me, & Something more; no servant ever retired better satisfied with his employers,"[9] &c &c.—all what is underlined I may apply to my self, with the difference, that Th[s] Jefferson is a native citizen of the US. & I am not; that in his eminent office of President, he had an adequate salary &c[a] &c while Since 40 years that I am Serving the U. States, the consulat fees are but mere casuelties in Marseilles & have not been Sufficient to defray me of the Salaries to my Secretary, stationaries & to do honor to my office; finding myself after all—a great deal poorer than when I entered in it.—

I have vainly claim'd since 1809 an annual indemnification for such expences, not exceeding $500 P[r] annum & that, in my humble opinion, it Should be just that I (as well as the other american consuls) should have by an act of the congress a prospect, after Such a long exercise & when disabled to receive an annuity during their old days, not exceeding $500. to[10] one thousand Dollars, as a due reward for their satisfactory & disinterested Services.

Such an honorable Retreat is granted by most all the other maritim pow-ers to their old Consuls.

I will further observe that tho' I am the eldest appointed american consul, being born on the 10th June 1757, thank god, I am Still in a good state of health & Spirit & I hope I will be able for some years Still to continue in the active Service, as long as I will be agreable to the President & the Senate; but during my long exercise I have heard that a good number of native amer-ican consuls have been dismissed; some by bad conduct or Superseded on calomnious denonciations; that others did ask for their dismission, by dis-gust or for want of Such proper encouragment as I am asking. & I must[11] own it to you candidly, that it is as honorable to the american executive, as it is to me, that I am continuing So long Still Standing in office & not dis-satisfied one of the other; but I fully rely on you for the Support of the jus-tice of my claims & that tho' the moment of Laying them by a message from you before congress, may not be opportune on account of the war So unjustly & So cruelly carried on by the british against the united States, you will be So kind as to do it, as soon as possible; wishing Sincerely for a Speedy & an honorable peace & prosperity to the united States.

I have the honor to be with great respect
Sir your most obedient and devoted servant   STEPHEN CATHALAN.

Tr (DLC); in a clerk's hand, signed by Cathalan, with his corrections and emen-dations, only the most significant of which are noted below; first page written on printed letterhead with depiction of Unit-ed States seal encircled by "Commer[al] Agency of the United States of America and of the Navy at Marseilles"; edge trimmed and chipped; at head of text in Cathalan's hand: "Copy"; at foot of first page in Cathalan's hand: "The Honble James Madison President of the united States, Washington." FC (FrM); in French.

For the letter ADDRESSED ON THIS DAY TO THE SECRETARY OF STATES, JAMES MONROE, see note to covering letter. Bonified (BONNIFIED): "made good; benefitted" (*OED*). The LATE DUKE OF MONTPENSIER (Antoine Philippe d'Orléans) and the COMTE DE BEAUJOLAIS (Louis Charles d'Orléans) sought refuge in the United States in 1796, after their father, Louis Philippe d'Orléans, was guillotined in 1793 (*PTJ*, 29:312–3, 369; Guy Antonetti, *Louis-Philippe* [1994], 291–308). The THANKFULL LETTER FROM THE SEC[y] OF STATE was Timothy Pickering to Cathalan, 7 Dec. 1796 (MHi: Pickering Papers). For Cathalan's letter to TJ of 9TH FEB[y] 1796, see *PTJ*, 29:369n. 3[D] THERMIDOR YEAR 11TH: 22

July 1803. TJ's letter of 29TH JUNE 1807 is in DLC.

[1] Preceding two words, added by Cathalan, are not in FC.
[2] Preceding four words, interlined by Cathalan, are not in FC.
[3] FC: "1789."
[4] Manuscript: "bound."
[5] Remainder of quotation not in FC.
[6] Manuscript: "most."
[7] Preceding two words, interlined by Cathalan, are not in FC.
[8] Manuscript: "most."
[9] Omitted closing quotation mark editorially supplied.
[10] Preceding two words, interlined by Cathalan, are not in FC.
[11] Manuscript: "most."

From Ellen W. Randolph (Coolidge)

MY DEAR GRANDPAPA · Washington March 19th 1816

Your letter of the 14th reached me yesterday and I hasten to return you thanks for this new proof of your affection. the remittance made to M[r] Barnes will indeed add considerably to my moyens de jouissance, & I need not tell you how gratefull I am for your kindness. I have no idea that my wants will exceed the 100.D. but if they should I will apply as you have directed.

If I have not written to you hitherto it has been because I found myself unable to perform my promise of giving you the little news of Congress. I do not hear subjects of the kind much spoken of either at home or abroad. I have very little acquaintance with the members, who are not in the habit of visiting familiarly in the family; some of them attend the drawing rooms regularly, but these parties are always crouded, and the conversation consists of compliments, & common place observations made 'en passant.' I did not know untill I came here, how much more amusement may sometimes be found in the solitude of one's own chamber, than in a gay circle. The Election of the next President is a subject so interesting to every body, that even the most idle and indifferent think and talk a good deal about it. the merits of the candidates are discussed, & even the ladies of their families come in for their full share of praise or blame. M[rs] Monroe has made herself very unpopular, by taking no pains to conceal her aversion to society, & her unwillingness to be intruded on by visitors. The English Minister and his lady M^r & Mrs Bagot arrived in town last evening. she is niece to the Duke of Wellington and said to be a great <u>dasher</u>, if the word is well applied, she will not make a good model for our city ladies, who are generally willing to fashion themselves after any thing foreign, & particularly English.

There was a report in circulation some short time ago that Milligan had broken, but I believe it was without foundation, for Mr Barnes tells me he is doing very well.—I heard of the death of my Aunt & the birth of Jefferson's daughter immediately after they took place.

I have so little interesting to write about my dearest Grandpapa, that I cannot flatter myself, my letters will give you pleasure, except as they are proofs of my affection. with 'congressional incidents & tracasseries' I am unacquainted, because those with whom I associate, either take no interest in, or forbear to speak of them; and the babble of the coteries of the place I can never remember an hour.   I wish very much to visit Baltimore this spring, I have a curiosity to see the place, & shall probably never again have so good an opportunity; this wish gratified, I shall have no other but to return to the bosom of my family, where alone I can expect to find <u>real</u> happiness.

Adieu my dearest Grandpapa, I remain most affectionately yours

E. W. RANDOLPH.

P. S. Mrs Madison & Mrs Todd desire to be particularly remembered to you. Mrs Cutts I have not seen since I recieved your letter.

RC (MHi); endorsed by TJ as received 22 Mar. 1816 and so recorded in SJL.

MOYENS DE JOUISSANCE: "means of enjoyment." MY AUNT: Judith Randolph. Thomas Jefferson Randolph's DAUGHTER was Margaret Smith Randolph.

In describing to her mother her plans to VISIT BALTIMORE and Philadelphia, Ellen noted that "I feel secure of Grand Papa's approbation. but for him I could never have thought of it, for I should have had <u>no</u> means to execute the plan. he wrote to me to say that the sale of his tobacco afforded him an opportunity for encreasing my 'moyens de jouissance' and God knows how much they are increased. my stock was reduced very low, the money I brought with me frittered away I know not how. circumstances seem to have combined to make my trip expensive" (Ellen W. Randolph [Coolidge] to Martha Jefferson Randolph, [ca. 26 Mar. 1816] [RC in ViU: Coolidge Correspondence]).

From LeRoy, Bayard & McEvers

SIR   Newyork the 19 March 1816.

Our friends Mess. N. & J. & R Van Staphorst of Amsterdam have requested us to wait upon you with the enclosed account and to receive from you the amount thereof $6249:60 together with interest from the first day of the present year untill discharge.

May we therefore make free to ask in what manner it will be agreeable to you to Settle this matter So that we may meet your wishes as far as lays in our Power.   The three Bonds alluded to are in our possession and will in course be at your order—

We have the honor to Subscribe with the utmost respect[1]

Sir Your very obed^t & h^{ble} Servants

LEROY BAYARD & M^{c}EVERS

RC (DLC); in an unidentified hand; at foot of text: "The Honorable Thomas Jefferson Monticello, Virg^a"; endorsed by TJ as a letter from "Leroy, Bryam & McCorn" received 27 Mar. 1816 and so recorded in SJL. Dupl (DLC); on verso of address cover of LeRoy, Bayard & McEvers to TJ, 10 Apr. 1816; in an unidentified hand; unsigned; endorsed by TJ as received 3 May 1816; enclosed in LeRoy, Bayard & McEvers to TJ, 10 Apr. 1816.

LeRoy, Bayard & McEvers, a mercantile firm in New York City, began business as LeRoy and Bayard by 1787. The founding partners were William Bayard (1761–1826) and Herman LeRoy (ca. 1758–1841). The firm was known as LeRoy, Bayard & McEvers from about 1796 until the retirement in 1816 of James McEvers (d. 1817). It continued to operate as LeRoy, Bayard & Company in New York City until at least 1827, providing both mercantile and banking services. TJ transacted business with the partnership beginning in 1790 (NN: Bayard-Campbell-Pearsall Collection; David C. Franks, *The New-York Directory* [New York, 1787], 24; *MB*; *PTJ*, 16:296; *Longworth's New York Directory* [1796]: 231; [1827]: 303; *New-York Courier*, 4 July 1816; *New-York Herald*, 21 June 1817; Henry Wysham Lanier, *A Century of Banking in New York, 1822–1922* [1922], 94, 118, 121).

[1] Dupl: "regard."

ENCLOSURE

Account with N. & J. & R. van Staphorst

The Honble Thos Jefferson Esq^e Debet. to N & J. & R. van Staphorst

1797 March	26	To your Bond in our favour		$1000.—
	"	Ditto		"1000.—
November 25	"	Ditto of *f*2800.— a 50 St: p^r D^r		"1120.—
				$3120.—

Intrest on $1000.— from 1st October 1796 to 31st
Decemb^r 1815, 19 Years and 3 months a 6% $1155.—

Ditto on $1000.— from 1st November 1796 to
31st December 1815, 19 Years and
2 Months a 6%   "1150.—

Ditto on *f*2800.— a 50 St p^r D^r $1120.— from
25 December 1797 to 31st December 1815
18 Years and 6 Days a 6%   "1210.72.
                                                      $3515.72.

Deduct
For Cash paid by you to Messrs Danl Ludlow & Co
$186.12
" Ditto "200.—
─────────
"386.12.
─────────
"3129.60
$6249.60
─────────
E.E.
Amsterdam the 31st Decembr 1815.—
N. & J. & R. VAN STAPHORST.

MS (DLC); in an unidentified hand.

N. & J. & R. van Staphorst was a powerful Dutch banking house. The brothers Nicolaas and Jacob van Staphorst were the founding partners. Their firm was part of a consortium of Dutch investors collectively known as Willink, van Staphorst & Hubbard, which issued major loans to the United States beginning in 1782. While serving as minister to France and secretary of state, TJ dealt with the van Staphorst partnership in an official capacity as a representative of the American government, and he also employed it for his private accounts. In 1801 Roelof van Staphorst, a nephew of Nicolaas and Jacob, joined the firm, but he retired the following year. From 1802 forward the house retained the van Staphorst name, but no family members were actively involved. The firm was dissolved in 1824 (Lyman H. Butterfield and others, eds., *Diary and Autobiography of John Adams* [1961], 2:444–5; Robert J. Taylor, Richard Alan Ryerson, C. James Taylor, and others, eds., *Papers of John Adams* [1977–], 13:18–9; *PTJ*; *MB*, esp. 1:681, 2:945–6, 1406; Pieter J. van Winter, *American Finance and Dutch Investment, 1780–1805: With an Epilogue to 1840* [1977], 2:662, 684, 772, 811).

On 7 Feb. 1799 and 11 Apr. 1800 TJ recorded interest payments to the van Staphorst agent in New York, DANL LUDLOW & CO (*MB*, 2:997, 1016). E.E.: "errors excepted."

From Bernard Peyton

DEAR SIR, Richd 19th March 1816

Your favor of the 8th: Inst. came safe to hand and its contents noted—I lost no time after its rect in waiting on Mr Mordecai of whom you speak and found he had no Plaister of Parris on hand, those gentleman who have it aprehend a rise in the Article and hold theirs now at a much higher price than you seem to expect—it was not offerd to me either at Rockets or in Town at less than 12 and some as high as fourteen dollars, except the parcel I purchased which belongd to a House that has lately fail'd here and was compell'd to dispose of it—this I got at $11.50 immediately on the Basin; with respect to the quality I can say nothing as I am entirely unacquainted with the Article it has the appearance tho' of Plaister generally—least it should not be of the description you wish I hav[e] reserved the right of taking any portion of the 8 Tons I may please,

I have exerted myself for the last eight days to procure a conveyance for at least a part of it, and have found it impracticable to forward more than one Ton as yet altho' there has been several Boats from Milton, their reluctance is so great to handle this article that they will not take it if they can possibly get any other Load—I succeeded yesterday in dispatching one Ton by a Mr Beck after much persuasion, beside paying him $4 in advance on a/c of the Freight which alone would induce him—

You may rest assured Sir this Plaister has been procured at the very lowest possible price, to be convinced of this I examin'd every Vessel at Rockets and found there was none on Board and very litle on the Wharfs, & that held at the prices stated above—Should you be pleased with what I have sent be so good as to write me and the balance shall be forwarded as soon as it is possible, if not I will be govern^d by your future directions—it costs a dollar per Ton to bring it from Rocket[s] to the Basin by the Drays, and the Boats will not go down—no other purchase can be made at up therre from $12\frac{1}{2}$ to $13 per Ton on the Basin—

I have waited on Mr Gibson two or three times with the hope of hearing of the arrival of your Corks from Norfolk but have been disappointed—they could not have been shp^d so soon as you expected; so soon as they arrive I'll see them myself put in the first stage

I beg you will not consider the little offices I can perform for you here as troublesome, I assure you it affords me the utmost pleasure to have it in my power to be useful to you, when I can I pray you to command me fuly, I only regret I have not the ability at all times to execute your orders to your satisfaction—I can only renew the assurance of my best exertions—   for the friendly recollections of you and your esteem^d family please accept my thanks with an assurance that it is reciprocated on my part to its utmost extent—   I am very respectfully Sir

Your Obd: Hub: Servt: BERNARD PEYTON

N.B. Since writing the above I have prevail^d on Mr Ruby to take a
    Ton of your Plaister which I presume will reach you as soon as
    this   B.P.

RC (MHi); edge trimmed; endorsed by TJ as received 22 Mar. 1816 and so recorded in SJL.

On 9 May 1816 TJ recorded payment to Thomas BECK of $4.33 for "bringing up plaister" (*MB*, 2:1323).

From Thomas Appleton

SIR   Leghorn 20th march 1816.

The departure of a vessel for the U: States, in the course of an hour, allows me only the time to say, that I have just return'd from paying the last tribute of affection, to my inestimable friend, m[r] mazzei, who died yesterday in Pisa—The first symptoms of his disorder, appear'd about a week since, by an erisipola on his legs, which it seems, his physicians were unable to prevent extending to the more noble parts; for little aided by nature, this morbid humour gain'd rapidly his breast, and baffled every effort of art.—as in health, the continual subjects of his conversation, were his "Cara patria adottiva," and his unbounded affection for your virtues, so likewise, were they the unceasing themes on which he dwelt, until life expir'd.—In the course of a fort'night a vessel will depart for New York, by which time, I shall be enabled to inform you the State of his pecuniary concerns; as I shall then forward to you, the legal attestations of his decease, together with the dispositions of his executors, relating to the money arising from the Sale of his house & lot in Rich[d]

Accept, Sir; the expressions of my highest respect & esteem.

TH: APPLETON

Dupl (DLC); at foot of text: "Thomas Jefferson, esq."; between dateline and salutation: "duplicate"; with RC of Appleton to TJ, 15 Apr. 1816, subjoined; endorsed by TJ as received 20 June 1816 and so recorded in SJL. RC (DLC); lacking text of 15 Apr. 1816 letter; endorsed by TJ as a "Duplicate" received 10 July 1816 and so recorded in SJL. RC (DLC); address cover only; with PoC of TJ to William Clark, 8 Sept. 1816, on verso; addressed: "Thomas Jefferson esquire Virginia United States of America ℗ Brig Clarissa Ann Capt: Blanchard via Philadelphia"; stamped "SHIP"; second stamp canceled; franked; postmarked Philadelphia, 22 June.

ERISIPOLA: erysipelas. CARA PATRIA ADOTTIVA: "beloved adopted country."

The last letter from Philip Mazzei to TJ, dated 16 Feb. 1816, is recorded in SJL as received 14 Aug. 1816 from Pisa, but has not been found.

From Christopher Clark

DEAR SIR,   Grove 20 march 16

The arrival of James this moment with the box to sow clover seed affords me much pleasure mingled with a little regret for fear this act of your kind attention may have given you too much trouble It has come in excellent time as we are deeply engaged in the Clover and Plaister System having laid in twenty five bushels of the seed of the former and three Ton of the latter about one half of which has been scattered in the common way using the box for the balance will afford a just standard to test the respective merit of the two different modes

I hope to have the pleasure of seeing you at the Forest during the next month untill which you will be pleasd to accept my best wishes for your health[1] and happiness   CHRISTOPHER CLARK

RC (MHi); addressed: "Thomas Jefferson esquire Monticello" by a "Servant"; endorsed by TJ as received 23 Mar. 1816 and so recorded in SJL.

[1] Manuscript: "heath."

From Gideon Fitz

SIR,   Opelousas Louisiana, March 20th 1816

Permit me to lay before you a copy of my letter lately transmitted to the President of the United States, with a copy of its enclosure, on a subject which has greatly interested my feelings, and which I fear may have injured my reputation.

I hope it may not be thought amiss[1] that I should feel desirous of affording you, to whose kindness I am indebted for my present promotion in life, a brief explanation of circumstances which have given rise to the Presidents dissatisfaction alluded to in the enclosed Copy of my letter. On the 12th July 1811 the Board of Commissioners at Opelousas received a communication from Mr Gallatin expressive of the Presidents disapprobation of their proceedings, and concluding with the following remarks. "I can only add the subject in itself and in its consequences is viewed by the President as of such vital importance that a conviction of the purity of your motives, the great confidence placed in you and a sense of your usefullness in other respects, have alone prevented a more efficient prevention of the evil."—

I am sorry it was thought necessary by some person in New Orleans, who by means unknown to the Board, became possessed of a copy of this communication of Mr Gallatins soon after its arrival, to publish it in the Orleans Gazette.—The slightest intimation from the President would have promply attended to by the Board in conforming their decisions to his construction of the laws, and to correspond with the decisions made by the Orleans Board, untill the necessary explanations of the difference in the nature of some of the claims in the two districts should have been made known at the seat of government. The general principals on which the Board had decided to act in confirming claims were transmitted to the Treasury

Department in December 1810 with a view of their being investigated, and if objectionable, that those objections should be made known to the Board before they should enter fully on the business of issuing certificates of confirmation. Many of the uninformed inhabitants of the country at that time were apprehensive that their claims held under the lower grades of title and even Orders of Survey from the Spanish government, though in all respects fair & equitable in their nature, would be disallowed by the American government, and therefore, as is believed, were disposed to transfer them to speculating Americans for a small consideration and would have thereby deprived themselves and their posterity of property which might become valuable to them. To prevent this occurrence which would tend in a short time to excite animosity between the ancient inhabitants and new[2] settlers in the country, the commissioners permitted their principals of decision on the claims to be made known in the District,—and if, as I have stated in my letter to the President, we have "in our zeal to serve the government by quieting the apprehensions of the inhabitants of an extensive District of country lately transfered from a Despotic government to one of whose liberal principals they had began to evince doubts by their murmurs at their title papers being so long witheld from them, without their being able to perceive any object for it, we shall be thought to have confirmed a few claims not strictly within the contemplation of the acts of congress, and which it may not have been intended by the government should be immediately confirmed, it will be a matter of lasting regret to me."—I will only add Sir, and I feel persuaded you will believe me, that if in any thing relating to my office I have erred, they have not been errors of the heart.—I should be happy if circumstances would permit it, to see & pay my respects to you in your enviable retirement at Monticello, where I could more satisfactorily afford you explanations of my conduct in the performance of official duties entrusted to my charge.—

I have the honor to be, Sir, With great respect your Ob[t] Serv[t]

GIDEON FITZ

RC (DLC); endorsed by TJ as received 8 May 1816 and so recorded in SJL. RC (DLC); address cover only; with PoC of TJ to Nicolas G. Dufief, 9 June 1816, on verso; addressed: "Thomas Jefferson Late President U. States Monticello Albemarl C[y] Virginia" and "Recommended to the care of Th[s] M Randolph Esq[r] near Milton V[a]"; franked; postmarked Opelousas, 21 Mar. 1816. Enclosures: (1) Fitz to James Madison, Opelousas, 26 Feb. 1816, explaining his circumstances and expressing concern over a 24 May 1811 letter from Albert Gallatin, received 12 July 1811 (printed in *Terr. Papers*, 9:934–6), in which Gallatin reported the "Presidents disapprobation of the construction of the Act of Congress of the 3rd March 1807 and the principals on which the Board of

Commissioners had decided to act in ascertaining and adjusting the land claims of this District"; stating that Fitz had shared with land office register Levin Wailes enclosure no. 2 as well as "the Communication refered to in Mr Gallatins letter in which (it will not have escaped your recollection) I gave it as my decided opinion that it would be good policy in the government to quiet the apprehensions of claimants in this District with the least possible delay by confirming their claims very generally, as it was not believed there were many of a fraudulent nature then entered in the land office, and that great discrimination ought to be made in favor of claims supported by written evidence of title emanating from the former government of Louisiana, as there was a probability of some having witheld title papers for the purpose of taking the advantage of the provisions of the Acts of Congress by claiming a larger quantity of land under settlement than they could have obtained under their written titles"; asserting that Wailes agreed with his opinion that Gallatin's 11 May 1810 letter should be viewed as approval of Fitz's suggestions both by the secretary of the treasury and the president; indicating that William Garrard of the board of commissioners had agreed with Fitz's methods for deciding land claims; noting that the "next steps were to promulgate them throughout our District to prevent as much as possible speculation, and to communicate them to the Honorable Secretary of the Treasury, in order, if objectionable, that such objections might be made known to us"; attributing any confirmation of claims "not strictly within the contemplation of the Acts of Congress, and which it may not have been intended by the government should be immediately confirmed," to his zeal to serve the United States government and quiet the apprehensions of territorial residents; confirming that "no improper motives can be attributed to the commissioners"; and concluding with his opinion that it is "greatly to be regretted that such facility has been afforded by law to claimants in establishing their claims entirely by oral evidence, and it has been

remarked by the former inhabitants of the Country holding under the lower grades of written titles, tho in all respects fair and regular in their nature, that new commers settling on the best pieces of vacant land without any written evidence to establish the fairness of their claims, have obtained their confirmation, while those of the ancient inhabitants have been rejected" (Tr in DLC, entirely in Fitz's hand, at head of text: "(Copy)," at foot of text: "James Madison President of the United States"; RC in DNA: RG 59, MLR). (2) Gallatin to Fitz, Treasury Department, 11 May 1810, acknowledging receipt of Fitz's letter to TJ regarding unsettled land claims in the western district of Orleans Territory and informing Fitz of his appointment as a commissioner for land claims; naming the remaining board members, Wailes and Garrard; enclosing a letter from Gallatin to Wailes of 5 May 1810 indicating that "congress did not at their last session provide any compensation, and that the commissioners must trust for remuneration to such provision as may hereafter be made by law"; explaining that the compensation would likely be proportional to the number of claims decided on in order that "no improper suspicion will attach that the business is unnecessarily protracted"; asserting that "it seems that there can be but very little difficulty in deciding on those claims not exceeding one league square of which the Commissioners are made the final and absolute judges.—For it is generally understood that there are but few if any fraudulent or doubtfull claims of that size in the District: those which are considered of a doubtfull nature being the large provincial grants to Bastrop, Maison rouge, the parish of Attakapas &c. And perhaps some purchases of Indian Villages and Vacheries" [enclosures for cattle]; and concluding with the hope that Fitz and his fellow commissioners will decide the outstanding claims within the year and "transmit their transcript in time for the next session of Congress which will enable them to open the land office and will in every respect be attended with beneficial effects" (Tr in DLC, entirely in Fitz's hand, at head of text: "Private," at foot of text: "Gideon Fitz Esqʳ Principal Deputy Surveyor &c. Opelousas"; printed in *Terr. Papers*, 9:882–3).

In a letter dated 16 Dec. 1810 (not found), the commissioners explained the GENERAL PRINCIPALS they had been using (*Terr. Papers*, 9:930–1).

¹ Manuscript: "a miss."
² Word interlined.

From John Barnes

Dear Sir— George Town 21ᵗ March 1816—

On receipt of your Esteemed favr 14ᵗʰ received 19ᵗʰ Evenᵍ I had yesterday the Honor of presenting the inclosed $100 Bank of Richmond to the Amiable Miss Randolph. to whom I beg'd permission to be Considered, as her Banker for the Accomodation of her Supplies while in washington, and having exchanged said note, into small change, I shall dispose of it, a the Currᵗ ex—from 6 a 7 ⅌Ct advance and repay the differance—

Reflecting on the State of the good Generals—Certificates for $4.500 & Int thereon to 21ˢᵗ Aprˡ a 5⅔ say $243.—and how, to dispose of them, as no Int. wᵈ be allowed from that date—was, the Question I had to determine—I availed myself of the advice of Mʳ Jos: Nourse—who inform—there was no Governent Stock, I could invest them in, Except the 6 per Cents, now much above par, that the Markets both to the Eastwᵈ and Sᵒward—were equally unfavorable. and in his Opinion, I could not do better than to invest the Amoᵗ in any Approved, Chartered Bank stock in this Dist. where¹ the paper would be recd—in its expressed Currʸ—I informed him, of your wish & express directions for its investmᵗ in Govermᵗ Stock— to this objection he Answered that as my Anxious Object, was, to secure an immediate Interest, I might, without risque, purchase Bank Stock, if done immediately and thereby secure at least 3 ⅌Ct. and in Course of the 6 Mᵒˢ dividᵈ if not Approvable—the diffᵗ exchanges might become more favorable for a Sale and purchase, of Govermᵗ Stock, And on this, my immediate inquiries convinced me of its Correctness, in point of immediate Int—the Bank of Columbia was my first object and the Critical day, 20ᵗʰ Insᵗ could I conclude a Sale of the Certificates and purchase of Columbia Bank Stock, no time would be lost in the gain of Interest—On application to my friend Mʳ C. Smith, Cashʳ of the Farmers and Mechanic's Bank, and by whose assistance I have, I trust, happily succeeded—and when Maturely considered—you will I persuade my self, Excuse the Liberty I have taken in doing that, which in former situation—you so much Opposed—the remedy (if not approved.) can be Corrected without loss—but I am rather inclined—the increase of Int—(the most desirable,) may induce you to aquies[ce?] in this Arrangement, done purely, for the Sake of the proprietor, whose situation, I fear is not so affluent, as to suffer any dimunition of Int if it could possibly be Avoided—the next and pointed Circumstance I have to provide for him—a Bill of Ex: to eliviate his wants,—it is realy grevious—to Announce the pres^t Ex on London a 20 per Cent above par, on Amsterdam equally disadvantagous $20,000 have been given by one House here at this Annexd Rate Balt° Phila^a & N York tho proportionably less becomes Nearly Equal in the different exchanges in paper,—whether or not, by waiting a M° or two, Circumstances might fav^r the purchase is very Uncertain it cannot I presume—increase this Extra premum—at all Events—I shall Endeavour to purchase a sett of ex—at Sight—will be the means of Relief equal to the Usual a 60 days

most Respectfully—and with great Sincerily Dear Sir Your very Obed^t serv^t   JOHN BARNES,

PS. in the course of a few days, I shall be able to detail to you the particulars of my Sale & purchase

RC (ViU: TJP-ER); one word illegible; addressed: "Thomas Jefferson, Esquire Monticello—Virginia"; franked; postmarked; endorsed by TJ as received 30 Mar. 1816 and so recorded in SJL.

The GOOD general was Tadeusz Kosciuszko.

[1] Manuscript: "were."

Account with George Cabell

[ca. 21 Mar. 1816]

Thos Jefferson Esqr
1816   To Geo Cabell   D^r
March 4. To Cash ℔ J Hallcombe

for 60 lbs Bacon @ 20 C^ts		$12
2 Bushels Corn		2.50
To Carriage 7 Hh^ds Tob° 9763 @ 3/–		48.81
21. To Carriage of 3 Hh^ds 4119. @ 2/–		13.73
26 lbs Bacon		5.20
1. Bushel Corn		1.25
		83.49

MS (ViU: TJP-ER); written in Cabell's hand on a scrap; undated; endorsed by TJ: "Cabell Dr George"; with an unrelated 1812 account in Cabell's hand on verso.

George Cabell (1766–1823), physician and surgeon, attended Hampden-Sydney College and in 1790 received a medical degree from the University of the State of Pennsylvania (later the University of Pennsylvania). He established a medical practice in the vicinity of Lynchburg and cared for Patrick Henry during the latter's final illness. Cabell also maintained a fleet of bateaux that he employed in transporting tobacco on the James River. In 1805 the Virginia General Assembly authorized him to construct a public tobacco warehouse, known as Blackwater, on his property at the junction of the Blackwater and James rivers in Campbell County, near Lynchburg. Cabell's business venture prospered and enabled him to construct a mansion he named Point of Honor (Alexander Brown, *The Cabells and their Kin*, 2d ed., rev. [1939; repr. 1994], 262–4; *Catalogue of the Medical Graduates of the University of Pennsylvania* [1839], 15; Chambers, *Poplar Forest*, 99, 100; William Wirt Henry, *Patrick Henry: Life, Correspondence and Speeches* [1891], 2:624–6; *Acts of Assembly* [1805–06 sess.], 7–8; Lynchburg Hustings and Corporation Court Will Book, A:36–7).

J HALLCOMBE: John Holcombe, of Campbell County.

From Emmor Kimber

ESTEEMED FRIEND
THOMAS JEFFERSON   Philadelphia 3 mo 22nd 1816

At a very great expense, and by the industry and labour of several years, I have at length produced a large and elegant Map of the United States—The draftsman employed to effect this was Samuel Lewis, and the engravers William and Samuel Harrison—A few copies of the first attempts at finishing them, have been deposited in the publick offices at Washington, and which I hope thou hast seen—

I am now prepared to publish the Map, and my agent Solomon Humphreys, who is to supply subscribers with it, will leave this City in about two weeks, on a journey through the Southern States, who will have in charge a copy to offer for thy acceptance—What reception he may meet with from the publick, or to what extent I shall be remunerated for my labour, is to be proved—but I have beleived, if thou approves of the attempt to produce from the best information practicable, such an extensive Map, and was free to communicate thy approbation to me, by a letter that thou would be willing I should print annexed to the enclosed review, it would be of extensive benefit to me, and of great advantage to my agent in disposing of them

from thy friend   EMMOR KIMBER

RC (MWA: Thomas Jefferson Papers); endorsed by TJ as received 27 Mar. 1816 and so recorded in SJL. RC (MHi); address cover only; with PoC of TJ to Charles Simms, 5 June 1816, on verso; addressed: "Thomas Jefferson Monticello Virginia"; franked; postmarked Philadelphia, 22 Mar.

Emmor Kimber (1775–1850), educator, publisher, and Quaker minister, was a teacher in Philadelphia by 1799 and later wrote an arithmetic textbook. He established a printing and stationery partnership with Solomon White Conrad by 1806. Kimber opened a boarding school for girls by 1818 at French Creek farm in Chester County, Pennsylvania. In 1831 he received a patent for a "Carriage, locomotive, and rails adapted thereto." Kimber's varied philanthropic activities included providing aid to runaway slaves (Sidney A. Kimber, *The Descendants of Richard Kimber* [1894], 38; Emmor Kimber, *Arithmetic Made Easy to Children*, 2d ed. [Philadelphia, 1805]; Kimber & Conrad to TJ, 7 June 1809; James Robinson, *Robinson's Philadelphia Register and City Directory, for 1799* [Philadelphia, 1799]; Robinson, *The Philadelphia Directory for 1806* [Philadelphia, 1806]; West Chester, Pa., *Village Record, or Chester and Delaware Federalist*, 14 Jan. 1818, 15 Nov. 1820; *List of Patents*, 488–9; Franklin Institute, *Journal* 8 [1831]: 22–3; Robert C. Smedley, *History of the Underground Railroad* [1883], 194; Philadelphia *North Ameri-*

can and United States Gazette, 2 Sept. 1850).

The ENCLOSED REVIEW praised the accuracy and execution of the map; noted its utility both for "foreigners" and "*natives* of the soil"; asserted that "there are among us but few individuals, not excepting those of the most respectable acquirements, who are not better acquainted with the geography of Europe, and even of some parts of Africa, than they are with that of the United States"; claimed that "Were a map of this description hung up in the hall of every family of our country, able to afford it, the children of the people of the United States would become geographers by instinct"; observed that "Kimber's map being, in the true sense of the word, a national work, creditable to the country, and finished after six years of labour and trouble, and at an expense that must have been seriously felt by the resources of an individual, it is hoped that it will be received under national patronage"; and concluded that, although not "free from errors and defects," those faults "are so few and inconsiderable that a detailed notice of them might justly be deemed hypercritical and superfluous" (*A New and Correct Map of the United States, published by Emmor Kimber, Philadelphia, price 22 dollars* [Philadelphia, 1816, copy in MWA]; reprinted from *Port Folio*, 3d ser., 6 [1815]: 304–8).

From Wilson Cary Nicholas

MY DEAR SIR   Richmond March 22d 1816

With the most anxious desire to serve my country I fear my ability will not be commensurate with my wishes. The last assembly, had as little mercy in the labour they assigned me, as they showed discernment in the selection of an agent. There are some of the duties I have to perform, that, I feel myself entirely incompetent to and shou'd be quite in despair, but for the hope of obtaining your aid and instruction. There are two subjects upon which I am particularly anxious to have that advantage, before I move a step. The map of the state & the report that is called for from the president & directors of the literary fund on the subject of a system of education. The last admits of delay, but the first requires dispatch, because if we precede the county

courts, in our part of the work it will be better done and at less expence. The original design was to have made the county charts a
county expence, but this caused the bill to be rejected, the money was
then directed to be taken from the fund for internal improvement &
the power suffered to remain in the courts. If they commence the
work the boundaries of most of the counties will be run twice and
many of them three times, as the rivers & mountains that are directed
to be surveyed under the direction of the executive are in so many instances the lines of the counties. my wish is to have the boundaries &
the great divisions of the commonwealth, by the mountains & rivers
surveyed first, to controul & lessen the Expence of the county charts
by furnishing the county surveyors with as much of the gen^l surveys
as will apply to their respective counties. I enclose the Law and beg
the favour of you to suggest your opinion of its execution, particularly
the duties to be performed under the 7th & 8th sections. Who shall we
employ to take the astronomical observations to fix the latitude and
longitude of such "remarkable points" as shall effectually serve to
correct any geometrical errors in the principle surveys? What points
shall be selected? Who (that can be employed) is qualified to furnish
the geological description required?

I have endeavoured to obtain the cooperation of Pennsylvania,
Maryland, Ohio, & north Carolina in our efforts to procure an effectual defence of the Chesapeake bay. We ask for a defence of the entrance of the Bay if practicable. If that cannot be effected that the
place lowest down the Bay or contiguous to it, that affords a good
harbour, that is of easy access from the sea, from the upper parts of
the bay & from our rivers shou'd be strongly fortified on the land as
well as the water side. Will you urge this subject upon the President?
such works can only be executed in time of peace & require to be well
seasoned to give them strength. My daughter Jane was remarkably
well for the first eight days after her confinement, from change of
weather or some other cause she then had a fever for two days. It
is with infinite pleasure I inform you she is now and has been for several days very well. Our grand child is uncommonly good and is said
to be very pretty. Be pleased to present me respectfully to the family
at Monticello & believe me to be with the

 greatest respect & regard your hum. Serv. W. C. NICHOLAS

RC (DLC); endorsed by TJ as a letter
of 22 Mar. received 26 Mar. 1816, but
mistakenly recorded in SJL as a letter of
26 Mar. received on that date; with additional notation at foot of endorsement
page in TJ's hand: "Goudon. mineralo-
gist." RC (DLC); address cover only;
with PoC of TJ to Joseph Delaplaine, 20
May 1816, on verso; addressed: "Thomas
Jefferson Esqr Monticello milton"; stamp

canceled; franked; postmarked Richmond, 23 Mar.

For the 24 Feb. 1816 joint resolution of the Virginia General Assembly calling for a REPORT on public education from the president and directors of the Literary Fund, see Joseph C. Cabell to TJ, 26 Feb. 1816. The enclosed LAW of 27 Feb. 1816 was "An Act to provide an accurate chart of each county and a general map of the territory of this Commonwealth." The 7TH section instructed the governor to have surveys made of the boundaries and geographical divisions of the Commonwealth, including a provision for taking ASTRONOMICAL OBSERVATIONS. The 8TH section authorized him to appoint one or more mineralogists to accompany the surveyor and FURNISH THE GEOLOGICAL DESCRIPTION (*Acts of Assembly* [1815–16 sess.], 39–42). OUR GRAND CHILD: Nicholas's granddaughter and TJ's great-granddaughter Margaret Smith Randolph.

From William Thornton

DEAR SIR   City of Washington 22nd March 1816—

I expected long before now to have returned the fine painting of Stewart & the Drawing of West that you were so obliging as to send to me and for which I am very much obliged, but I have been disappointed in getting the Head modelled, which I wished to have got done by an Italian artist who promised to do it, but has since expressed a wish to do after the original: his name is Valaperta. He is now engaged in the Public works.—I was at different times disappointed also in making the Copies, by sickness by numerous public Duties, by confinement to my Bed, by an accident in consequence of the falling of my Horse; & among other dire complaints by laziness— all these put together will apologize I hope for my keeping them a little longer, under a promise of better behaviour. In the mean time, they are kept with the greatest care, & never exposed, but when while shewn to my Friends.—

I have been always mindful of your request to have a Copy of the List of Patents, but while I was laying confined, they were neglected, and not sent to my office, which occasioned a difficulty in getting them, and I never got a Copy till this Day.—

Your charming Grand-daughter is well, and very much admired— I am dear Sir with the highest respect & consideration Y^{rs} &c

WILLIAM THORNTON—

A beautiful Invention of a Saw has been lately presented for a Patent by Adam Stewart of Baltimore—It is a Circular Saw, that passes round two (three-feet) drums, the teeth on one edge—so that one log is sawed up, while the other is sawed down; & the Saw goes continually round, not by intermission as in the common way; thus one Saw must saw four times as much in the same time, but requiring double force—The circular Saw is composed of several, dovetailed together, in a very simple & effectual manner—

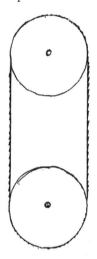

RC (DLC); with drawing on verso of blank page with TJ's endorsement; between signature and postscript: "Hon: Thomas Jefferson"; endorsed by TJ as received 27 Mar. 1816 and so recorded in SJL. RC (DLC); part of address cover only; with PoC of TJ to William D. Meriwether, 3 June 1816, on verso; addressed: "Honorable T[…]"; postmarked Washington City, 23 Mar. Enclosure: *Letter from the Secretary of State, transmitting A List of the Names of Persons to whom Patents have been Granted, for the Invention of Any New or Useful Art, or Machine, Manufacture, or Composition of Matter, or Improvement Thereon, from the 1st of January, 1815, to the 1st of January, 1816* (Washington, 1816; Poor, *Jefferson's Library*, 6 [no. 224]).

For the FINE PAINTING OF STEWART & THE DRAWING OF WEST, see Thornton to TJ, 11 Dec. 1814. TJ's CHARMING GRAND-DAUGHTER was Ellen W. Randolph (Coolidge). On 5 July 1817 ADAM STEWART received patents for a "Belt or band saw," a machine for sawing and veneering, and a "Horizontal or verticle radial saw" (*List of Patents*, 180).

To Patrick Gibson

DEAR SIR   Monticello Mar. 24. 16.

Your favor of the 18th is recieved, and informs me how much the quality of my tobᵒ falls short of what I had been given to expect. this afflicts me not merely as to the first loss, but also as it injures the reputation of that tob° which has heretofore commanded high prices. the present loss too is sensibly felt.[1] short as my crops both of flour & tob° turned out the last year, I had still confided that they would not only enable me to meet my contracts of this spring, but also to lessen my note in bank. the last however seems[2] now impracticable, and my remaining anxiety is to make them replace your advances, and clear off my existing demands. the 3. last hhds of tob° left Lynchburg in D[r] Cabell's boat on the 21st as Yancey informs me, and will be with you I suppose about the time of your recieving this. My former letters had advised you that I should be obliged to draw on you about the close of the month for about[3] 1000.D. I accordingly[4] now give a draught to Th: J. Randolph for that sum to which I must shortly add one in favor of Archibald Robertson for 167.10 D and another in favor of Doct[r] Fernandez for one or two quarter casks of wine.[5] I have drawn on you, as before advised for my Congressional taxes in Bedford. those in this county about 300.D. can lie over, I am told, a month or two longer, which gives more time for the sale of some of the flour if you think delay in it's sale of any advantage. some neighborhood debts will be deferred with the same view.[6]   this miserable turn out of the last year will barely carry me thro' the present one, extra-burthened as it has been with between 900 & 1000.D. State and Congressional taxes. I believe however it will do it, and I willingly look forward to the pleasanter assurances of my new managers that from 800. bushels of wheat now in the ground, I shall have at least 800. Barrels of flour for the next[7] winter market, and about 30. or 40[8] M of tob° from Bedford. we are prone[9] to believe what we wish, and to the wish I add that for your health and happiness.

Th: Jefferson

Dft (DLC: TJ Papers, ser. 10); at foot of text: "M[r] Gibson"; endorsed by TJ.

[1] Preceding two words interlined in place of "very inopportune."

[2] Word interlined in place of "is."

[3] Word interlined in place of "upwards of."

[4] Preceding two words interlined in place of "to which were still to be added the demands for my Congressional taxes.

for those in Bedford I have drawn on you as before advised. at this place they amount to   and are included in a draught I."

[5] TJ here canceled "and some time hence for some neighborhood debts."

[6] Preceding three sentences interlined.

[7] Word interlined.

[8] Preceding two words interlined.

[9] Word interlined in place of "apt."

From Francis Adrian Van der Kemp

SIR!   Olden barneveld 24 March 1816.

The manÿ condescending proofs, which I received from your po-
liteness, imbue me with the confidence to Sollicit another favour from
your kindness. I know too well, I can have no claims, but that, which
originates in your indulgence—and in your ardent wish to promote
the indagation of truth. About three years past I Spend a few days
with my old respected friend at Quincÿ, whom you, perhaps, know,
that continues to favour me with his affectionate esteem. Various topics of literature were then freely discussed—and—as I enjoy'd his full
confidence—Some of a more Serious cast. He had then lately received
from you a Syllabus, exhibiting your view on a most momentous Subject—Developing it in part, he favoured me at last with its perusal
for a few moments: I was Surprised with this new point of view and
deemed it deserving a more full consideration. I requested a copÿ:
this was peremtorly refused, as He was not at liberty to keep one for
himself, and was resolved not to violate this Sacred truth.[1] Its memory was nearly erased from my mind, at least its traces were So faint,
that recollection was not powerful enough, to call up again its Sum-
marÿ. This Spring I received—with a parcel of Books—among whom
The Month: Repos. of Theol: and Gen: Literat: which by its candour
would entertain you in a moment of leisure, Belsham's Mem. of my
late friend Th. Lindseÿ—in which Pag. 539 I once more did See your
Views of Christianity—Some what in a cloud—I wrote on the blank
page at P. 539 "I have Seen this view with Surprise and delight, and
regret, that I was not permitted to copy it. It Showeth an unpreju-
diced Inquirer, and a Sincere lover of truth."

Actuated by the Same motives, which impelled you to that communication, I now Sollicit, to grant me the favour of the Same Sight,
with which you honoured my friend—under what restrictions—you
maÿ please to command I will engage to adhere faithfully to these—
even—if required—to return it uncopied—I request in Such a case
only the permission, of extracting its leading features. But could you
look at it as So much interesting, as I consider it, then you would
allow me its copying, with the Liberty to Send it to mÿ correspondents in England—for insertion in the Month. Rev. when it shall
open the waÿ for its more full and impartial discussion. I would forbear to hint even at your name, till you Self Should have given leave.
I doubt not or it must do good.

Having in view, if my days are prolonged, to draw up a historÿ of
J. C. it would be of great use to me, to contemplate the whole in this

[595]

new point. If after all prudence dictates to decline my demand, I Shall not be hurted by it—but then yet I Should not regret my application, if by it you was induced to communicate this plan for discussion, to one of your European friends—and then Great-Brittain again must be the Spot where it Shall appear.

I was yesterday gratified with a few lines of my old respected friend—His Strength[2] fails—his Ladÿ is on the decline, and Shall, I apprehend, Sink under this Severe attack of illness—and He would not Survive Her long—She is indeed an accomplished woman! So my old friends go awaÿ—Pensionary de Gyzelaer—my oldest friend Dr. Toulmin—at the time, he intended—as his legacÿ—to publish my corrected Sketch on the Achaic Republic—Both gone! and if these Worthies follow—I am nearly left alone.

I expect, ere long, the criticisms of de Witt Clinton upon my <u>Philosophical Researches</u> which you have Seen in embryo—and which my young friend C. Eliot, after the correction of the Idiom, intended to publish, had he not been prevented by death—Now theÿ remain with the rest of my lucubrations here—to be burned in the tomb of the capulets.

I am informed by my correspondents in Europe, that my Sketch on the moral and Physical causes—which I corrected and enlarged by the hints with which you honoured me, begins to attract Some notice. I Should rejoyce, if Such a momentous work was undertaken; then I Should reap a large and honourable recompence.

I dare not encroach longer on your precious time, but confide, that you will not misinterpret the Liberty, which I have taken. Permit me without anÿ further apologÿ to assure you, that I remain with unabated respect and the highest consideration

Sir! Your most obed: humble Servant

FR. ADR. VAN DER KEMP

RC (DLC); dateline adjacent to signature; endorsed by TJ as received 9 Apr. 1816 and so recorded in SJL. RC (MHi); address cover only; with PoC of TJ to Peter Cottom, 7 May 1816, on verso; addressed: "Thomas Jefferson L.L.D. Monticello Virginia"; franked; postmarked Trenton, N.Y., 26 Mar.

John Adams was the FRIEND AT QUINCŸ. TJ first lent his SYLLABUS to Adams in a letter dated 22 Aug. 1813 and sent him a copy to keep on 12 Oct. 1813. TJ's VIEWS OF CHRISTIANITY, specifically his 9 Apr. 1803 letter to Joseph Priestley (DLC), were published in Thomas Belsham, *Memoirs of the Late Reverend Theophilus Lindsey, M.A.* (London, 1812), 538–9. J. C.: Jesus Christ. In his FEW LINES of 2 Mar. 1816, Adams informed Van der Kemp that he had read his "travels in the wilderness" and was sending the manuscript to Alexander Bryant Johnson, of Utica, and he reported that Abigail Adams had been "sick all winter, and is still very weak though we hope somewhat better" (Lb in MHi: Adams Papers). Cornelis DE GYZELAER (1751–1815) was the pensionary of the Dutch commune of Dordrecht (Dort),

1779–87 (Helen Lincklaen Fairchild, ed., *Francis Adrian Van der Kemp, 1752–1829: An Autobiography, Together with Extracts from his Correspondence* [1903], 24). The CAPULETS are the family of the tragic heroine in William Shakespeare's *Romeo and Juliet*. For MY SKETCH ON THE MORAL AND PHYSICAL CAUSES, see Van der Kemp to TJ, 18 Feb. 1812, and

enclosure. For the HINTS WITH WHICH YOU HONOURED ME, see TJ to Van der Kemp, 22 Mar. 1812, and Van der Kemp to TJ, 14 Apr. 1812.

[1] Thus in manuscript. Van der Kemp may have intended "trust."
[2] Manuscript: "Strenght."

From Joseph Fox

RESPECTED FRIEND   Phila: March 25, 1816—323 Spruce St.—

I received your kind favour of Feb[y] 1816.—and thank you for your attention and subscription—since—the subscription goes on extremely well in every direction of the country—But true it is—I find the expence is somewhat above my present means of resource—the work is retarded for the want of nine reams of paper, otherways my arangements are attained to my satisfaction—Having it through, would yield an immediate sum, adequate to all my demands—But at present, I am under the necessity of waiting till some kind ray shall appear to carry me through—

Accept, D[r] Sir, my best wishes for Your health and happiness—
                                                JOSEPH FOX—

RC (MHi); at foot of text: "Tho[s] Jefferson, Esq[r]"; endorsed by TJ as received 9 Apr. 1816 and so recorded in SJL.

Account with James Leitch

Charlottesville march 25 1816
Thos. Jefferson
                    Bot of Ja[s] Leitch
16½ y[ds] Linnen Shirting [d] 9/6 ⎱ $25–33
   8 Skanes thread   3[d] ⎰   –33
                    E E $25–66
                                    CHARLES STEWART

MS (ViU: TJP); entirely in Stewart's hand.   E E: "errors excepted."

From Richard Peters

DEAR SIR   Belmont March 25th 1816.

I was gratified by the Receipt of your polite Letter of the 6th instant
which only came to hand a few Days ago. Amidst the Storms which
have long agitated our Country, & rendered our Citizens more hostile
to each other, when political opinions were adverse, than public Enemies; Recollections of old Attachments are doubly pleasant. I have
preserved a Tranquillity on such Subjects which has contributed, in
no small Degree, both to my Health & Comfort; although I have not
been without keen Feelings & unavoidable Anxieties. Indeed I have
continued in my judicial Employment to avoid political Turmoil,
more than for any Gratification its Pursuits or its Emolument (very
inadequate to its Duties) afford. My Agricultural Propensities I have
indulged, because they were necessary for my Support; & gratified
my Desire to be useful to others. In answer to your Inquiry as to <u>my
Activity</u> in those Pursuits, that I have, for a long time past, intermit-
ted my personal Attention to them, on any great Scale. I let my Farms
on Shares; & pay as much Attention to them as I can, consistently
with other Engagements. I keep in my own Hands, a large Garden
& about 30as of Land, which give me the Opportunities of trying
Experiments, & setting as good an Example as I can to my Neighbours—some of whom benefit by it more than I do myself. <u>Time,</u>
most assuredly, has "commenced its Inroads on me;" but I think he
treads lightly. My "bodily faculties" are less impaired than most Men
of my Age (approaching 72) experience. I use much Exercise, & generally on Horse back; & avoid all Intemperance, being a Water
Drinker; & although not abstemious, live on plain Food. I have not
tasted Wine for 12 Years past. Save an annual Attack of a vertiginous
Complaint in my Head (which is encreased by all stimulating Food
or Liquors) I am generally in good Health. I find myself capable,
without Injury, of severe Attention to sedentary Employment. But
what a Gil Blas would say of my Homilies, I know not. I think, however, I would not be so petulant under his warning Censure, as was
the old Arch bishop, who discharged him for his impolitic Candour.
I was never indolent; but ever relished Disengagement from Pressure of Business or law. Of both I have had enough; but my Mind,
when the Weight is even temporarily removed, recovers its constitutional but innocent Playfulness, & sometimes to a Degree, of which
rigid & impenetrable Gravity would say—non deceat Senectutem. I
call it <u>innocent</u>, because it is not affected by Bile on my Stomach, or

Gass in my System, either mental or corporeal. You have brought on yourself this egotistical History, by the Interest your polite Good will seemed to take in it.

I am obliged by your Information relative to Col Randolph's Farming, & his Adaptation of it to local Circumstances. This is the Perfection of Good Sense; without which all theoretical Knowledge is learned Folly. Europeans generally fail here; because they bring over with them Practices & Systems entirely unsuitable to our Situation. They often give themselves, too, more Credit than they merit, even for Intelligence in their own Practices & Systems. I have found many of them haughtily vain, & not a few intolerably ignorant. Some Exceptions there are; but generally they do not succeed. There are certain inviolable Principles in Husbandry, applicable to all Situations. But Hill farming, in its mechanical Branches, is as different from the Husbandry appropriate to Vales or flat Country, as if it did not belong to the same Art. The Mode of Aration pursued by Col R is, for the most Part, like that of the Swiss & Germans, in their Hill Countries; tho' his personal Attention to it has, no Doubt, improved their Practice. They lay their Furrows always down-hill, with an awkward Plough with one, & sometimes two Wheels. They shift the Mould board at every Bout, on the one Side or the other, to suit the Direction of the Plough & turning the Furrow. I have an old Hessian Soldier who has lived with me 30 odd Years, & being accustomed to Hill-ploughing with a shifting Mould board, & always down Hill, he could not plough with our common Instruments, in our accustomed Way. I taught him the use of our Ploughs; & he is now a complete Ploughman. He says, they lay their Furrows in general horizontally, but sometimes they plough them somewhat diagonally, & sometimes with Curvatures convex up-hill; which, he says, resist, like an Arch, the Torrents, & carry off the Water without gullying. They mark out their Lands, at first, according as they intend they shall lie; but most commonly the old Lands direct succeeding Operations. I wish Col R. would favour me with a Model or Draft of his Plough, & any Account of his Practice he pleases; & I will deposit it among our agricultural Collections. I do not recollect ever to have heard, before, of his Plough. Peale performs his Work with a common Plough; but much in Mr R's Mode. He has again resumed his Brush & Pallette.

I long ago told some of my english Correspondents, that our Ploughs were more simple & better than theirs. But they laughed at my Nationality. One of them was, however, daring enough to venture at a comparative Experiment. At his Request, I had made for & sent to him since the Peace,[1] 3 Ploughs, according to my own Ideas, combining the best Parts of our American Swing Ploughs. 1. A 3 horsed Plough, for breaking up $2\frac{1}{2}$ Acres per Day, at any Depth not exceeding 9 Inches. 2. A 2 horsed Plough for common Purposes. 3. A one horsed Plough. He writes to me, that he has had 2 complete Trials of N°s 1. & 2, against the best english Ploughs. Once with 4 Horses, & a Driver, in the English Plough; & at no time with more than 2 Horses in my Ploughs, & a Man with Lines. His Work in both equalled, & in one Instance exceeded, the english Ploughs. I saw an Account of the Ploughing Match, in an english Paper. They eulogize the American Plough, for its Simplicity & Neatness of Work; & allow it to be equal to the best english Plough. But say it will not do in stony & heavy Soils, as well as the english Plough. I am sure they are mistaken; & will have it put to the Test. I fear my Friend has put only two Horses in the 3 horsed Plough; which, with 3 Horses abreast, will turn & clear the heaviest Furrow in England. It is a great Point, that they allow an Equality in Work with their <u>crack</u> plough; & they agree that it is superior in Simplicity, & Facility of Management. If <u>they</u> talk of a drawn Battle, it looks like a Defeat.

I sent to you the hasty Discourse (not well printed or correctly punctuated) I delivered before our Society, not only as a Token of Remembrance (& am obliged by your polite Reception of it) but in Hopes you would help me to get the Subject engrafted in the proposed Plan of a national Seminary, if such Plan takes Effect. It will elevate the Art in the public Mind, render it an Object of[2] Emulation, & rescue it from the low Estimation in which many have held it, who believe that any Clodhopper may be a Farmer.

I reciprocate your Kindness with my best Wishes & respectful Regards. Christina, Queen of Sweden, used to say, that Health was Youth, & Sickness old Age. But I believe both you & I would prefer Youth & Health; tho' we may be grateful that any Portion of the latter, is the inestimable Companion of declining Years.

truly yours   RICHARD PETERS

RC (DLC); addressed: "Thomas Jefferson Esqr Monticello Virginia"; franked; postmarked Philadelphia, 29 Mar.; endorsed by TJ as received 9 Apr. 1816 and so recorded in SJL.

The fictional character GIL BLAS promises the ARCH BISHOP that he will critique the prelate's homilies for signs of senility, but after initially delivering posi-tive reviews, Blas's frank assessment of a sermon results in his being DISCHARGED (Alain René Le Sage, *Histoire de Gil Blas de Santillane* [Paris, 1715–35, and later French and English eds.; Sowerby, no. 4346]). NON DECEAT SENECTUTEM: "may it not benefit old age." HEALTH . . . OLD AGE was a maxim of Queen Christina of Sweden (*The Works of Christina Queen of Sweden. containing*

Maxims and Sentences . . . Now first translated from the Original French [London, 1753], 53).

¹ Preceding seven words interlined in place of "him."
² Word interlined in an unidentified hand.

To William Annesley

SIR   Monticello Mar. 26. 16.

I am duly sensible of the mark of consideration you ha[ve] been so kind as to shew me in consulting me on the subject of your new system in ship and boat building; but neither my occupations nor habits permit me any longer to indulge myself in speculations of that kind: and at no time of my life should I have been a competent judge of this. born and educated among the mountains, I am quite a stranger to Nautical subjects. as far as I see, your method is plausible, and especially promises strength of construction. I return you the drawing, which possibly may be useful to you, and pray you to accept the assurance of my respect.   TH: JEFFERSON

PoC (MHi); on verso of a reused address cover from Thomas Eston Randolph to TJ; one word faint; at foot of text: "Mr William Annesley"; endorsed by TJ. Enclosure not found.

To Benjamin J. Campbell

SIR   Monticello Mar. 26. 16.

I recieved the last night your favor of the 16th and hasten to acknolege it. I had before remarked in the newspapers an account of your new invented loom, which appeared to promise considerab[le] advantages. but manufacturing with me is on too small a scale to make it an object, making only coarse cloths for my family and people. two common looms with flying shuttles do this. I had at one time thought of trying one of Janes's looms, but his patentee for this state asked double it's price in the other states, and I percieve in fact that it has not been adopted in practice. another circumstance would have put it out of my power of being useful to you which is that I set out within 10. days on a visit to a possession 90. miles distant Southwardly, and shall not return till 6. weeks hence. under these circumstances I can only contribute my good wishes for the success of your loom [and add?] to them the assurances of my respect.

                                       TH: JEFFERSON

PoC (DLC); on verso of reused address cover of Garrit Storm to TJ, 23 Feb. 1816; edge trimmed, mutilated at seal; at foot of text: "Mr Benjamin J. Campbell"; endorsed by TJ.

An ACCOUNT of Campbell's NEW INVENTED LOOM appeared in the Washington *Daily National Intelligencer*, 18 Mar. 1816: "A young man, whose name is Campbell, is now in this city, for the purpose of procuring a patent for a loom of the most singular construction we have yet seen. It does away the necessity of warping; and when once in operation can be kept so for any length of time, that is, a web may be wove of any desired length, as the cloth is rolled out in such a manner as it can be cut off at any time without stopping the loom. The machinery is very simple, and put in operation merely by turning a crank, and requires but a moment's inspection to be fully understood. The warp is taken from bobbins or spools There can be no doubt but this new combination of machinery will greatly reduce the expense of fabricating cloth; and will therefore be of much use to our country." Walter Janes's PATENTEE for Virginia was Francis C. Clopper.

To John F. Oliveira Fernandes

DEAR SIR   Monticello Mar. 26. 16.

I have been in the daily expectation that you would be so good as to forward to me a note of the amount of the cask of Teneriffe, that I might forward you a draught for it. the Port you were so kind as to send me is indeed excellent. I certainly would not wish to be indulged a second time from your private stock, but if you have, among that which is for sale, any of as good quality, I should be much gratified with another quarter cask to be forwarded as before. in that case be pleased to add it's cost to that of the Teneriffe, and in the instant of knowing the amount I will forward you a draught for it. I salute you with great esteem and respect.   TH: JEFFERSON

PoC (DLC); on verso of reused address cover to TJ; at foot of text: "Dr Fernandes"; endorsed by TJ.

From Bernard Peyton

DEAR SIR   Richmond 27th March 1816

From my not having heard forther from you on the subject of the Plaister sent, I have concluded its quality suited and have forwarded the balance of the eight Tons, two on Monday last by a Boat belonging to Mr Thomas E. Randolph and the balance (four Tons) to-day by Mr Gilmore—the tolage on the former load by Mr Randolph's Boat has been paid by me—

I regret to say your Corks have not yet arrived from Norfolk, I have, and shall continue to make frequent enquiry for them, and see myself that they have the first conveyance by the stage to Charlottesville after they are to hand—

On the inner side of this sheat you will find a statement of the Bill for the Plaister &C:—which agreeable to your request we shall call on Mr Gibson for.

Very respectfully Sir
Your Obd: Hub: Servt: Bernard Peyton

Thomas Jefferson Esqr

	To Green & Peyton	D^r
For Cash paid for 8 Tons Plaister Parris at $11.50		$92.
" " " part of Freight & Tolage		4.34
		$96.34

RC (MHi); account on verso of attached address leaf; addressed: "Thomas Jefferson Esqr Monticello near Milton" by "Mail"; stamp canceled; franked; postmarked Richmond, 27 Mar.; endorsed by TJ as received 30 Mar. 1816 and so recorded in SJL.

From Thomas Ritchie

Dr Sir   March 27. 1816.

I have been apprehensive that I could not undertake the work you propose. The Curtailments of Bank, and the general severity of the times, almost forbid the idea of vesting money in any fund, the returns from which are not instantaneous.

I am disposed, however, to believe that M. Tracy's Treatise will sell—and I have very little doubt of it if you will give it the Sanction of your name, and the aid of your intellectual resources.

Will you, Sir, annex the name of the Author?

Will you, moreover, subjoin, that the translation is revised by yourself, and annex such an Introduction, or Notes, or an Appendix, as are best calculated in your own opinion to display the present state of the Science?—The Introduction need not be written immediately; it may be forwarded to the Printer, after M. Tracy has been disposed of.

I mean no Compliment, Sir—but, I state it, as a dry matter of calculation, that without the sanction of your name, (and may I not add, in some form, of your own abilities and resources,) the work would be too uncertain in its profits to induce me to undertake it.

I can commence it, so as to bring out by the month of November.—In about 3 weeks, a portion of the M. S. will be wanted.

Will you do me the favor, Sir, to acknowledge the Rec^t of this letter, with your answer, as early as possible.

With the sincerest respects, I am, Sir,

Yours,   THOMAS RITCHIE.

RC (MHi); endorsed by TJ as received 2 Apr. 1816 from Richmond and so recorded in SJL.

To Archibald Robertson

DEAR SIR   Monticello Mar. 28. 16.

I now inclose you an order which you ought to have recieved at the beginning of the month, but my tob° was later getting down than had been counted on, and I was unwilling to draw till I knew of it's actual sale. the draught is for 167. D 10 C to wit

an advance for leather £20–16–1	69–35
my assumpsit for Goodman	78–35
balance of order for 170.D. for taxes	19–40
	167–10

my tob° which was all I had for market from Bedford sold very poor[ly.] you know that the wretched management there the last year oblige[d] me to turn away two overseers, and I had to remove two here for the same cause. add to this that my State and Congressional taxes ther[e] and here have taken between 900. & 1000.D. so that I am almost withou[t] the means of current expences. in this state of my affairs, I shall be unab[le,] my dear Sir, to do any thing towards my debt to you till the crop of the present year comes in. 800 bushels of wheat in the ground there & here[,] a good crop of tob° aimed at there and a small one here, under better management, will I hope place me at ease; but until then I must ask your indulgence. I shall be at Poplar Forest the 2^d week of April, and shall always be happy to see you there when your convenience admits such a ride. Accept the assurance of my great esteem and respect   TH: JEFFERSON

PoC (MHi); on verso of a reused address cover from John Adlum to TJ; edge trimmed; at foot of text: "Mr Robertson"; endorsed by TJ. Enclosure not found.

For the TWO OVERSEERS TJ turned away at Poplar Forest, see Sackville King to TJ, 17 May 1815, and note. William Ballard's service as an overseer at Tufton ended in 1815 (TJ to Joel Yancey, 18 July 1815). Elijah Ham was overseer at Lego, 1812–16 (*MB*, 2:1313).

From José Corrêa da Serra

DEAR SIR   Philadelphia 29 March. 1816
At Last Mrs Barton has sent me a Little morocco bound volume, part
of Capt. Lewis journal containing his observations from April 9 of
1805 to February 17 1806, and the meteorológical observ. for July
August September. 1805, together with the drawing of a quadruped
which he calls the Fisher. As the chaos of His Library begins to clear,
by the separation of printed books which are sold to the hospital i
doubt not the remaining papers of Capt. Lewis may be found, but
you could help me much by sending me a description of their external appearance, and their probable volume, because Mrs Barton who
acts in all this very honestly (but does not permit any body to search
the papers of her husband, but by what i understand only herself
and her brother who is also a very honest person) will be much
helped in finding them. In the mean time i expect your directions
about what i am to do with the volume i have got, and the others that
may appear.

I hope you have enjoyed perfect health, and your winter probably
has not been so capricious as in Pennsylvania, where after very pleasant weather, we have felt two rather severe snow storms since the
middle of the month.

Marshall Grouchy has been here a few days in the same hotel with
Mr Short whose acquaintance he is. I have spoken with him, and he
did not seem to me very sanguine in his expectations about what is
going in Europe. From his account Bonaparte's talents did not shine
in the Last years of his political existence.

I remain with the highest respect and esteem
Most sincerely Yours   J. CORRÈA DE SERRA

RC (DLC); endorsed by TJ as received
9 Apr. 1816 and so recorded in SJL.
RC (MHi); address cover only; with PoC
of TJ to Levin Gale, 7 May 1816, on
verso; addressed: "Thomas Jefferson
Esqr Monticello Albemarle C^ty Virginia";
franked; postmarked Philadelphia, 29
Mar.

For the LITTLE MOROCCO BOUND VOL-
UME, see Moulton, *Journals of Lewis
& Clark*, 2:534–5. The DRAWING OF A

QUADRUPED WHICH HE CALLS THE
FISHER was created by Charles Willson
Peale based on a specimen brought back
by Meriwether Lewis and William Clark
(PPAmP: Lewis and Clark Journals, vol.
7). Benjamin Smith Barton's books were
sold to the Pennsylvania HOSPITAL (*Catalogue of the Medical Library of the Pennsylvania Hospital* [1829], ix). Mary Pennington Barton's BROTHER was Edward
Pennington.

[605]

From Isaac Briggs

My dear Friend, Washington City, 3 mo 30[1]—1816

Thy kind letter of 27 Ultimo, I received on the 2 instant. It was like a healing balm to my wounded mind. I immediately called on the Secretary of the Treasury—He shewed me thy communication to him—on perusing it, his presence was scarcely a restraint sufficient to prevent my tears, the warm effusions of gratitude.

On the 4, I wrote to my wife and children, now in Wilmington, a narrative of my proceedings and thy goodness. I received, in answer, from my second Daughter, Mary (my eldest daughter, Anna, is married and is the mother of two fine sons) a letter from which permit me, like a fond and partial father, to transcribe one paragraph—"I have attempted to write to T.J. I send thee the _attempt_. I fear it will not do—and that thou wilt smile as thou layest it aside, and say, 'Ah! Mary, my dream is realized, it is _ridiculous_!'—though I deny having made any efforts at the _sublime_; thou knowest, dear father, to that I make no pretensions. I fear too thou wilt think some parts extravagant—do not, my father, for it is not _half_ I feel—I cannot think of him with moderation. Great and excellent man! mayest thou have the promised reward for such deeds as thine!—happy thou _must_ be, for thou art good!"

Could she be honored with an answer from thyself, she would, I know, esteem it as a thing most precious—but however great would be her gratification, if it be not entirely convenient, do not consider this as a request.

My petition for relief was presented to the Senate by William H. Wells, Senator from Delaware, who in his youth at school was one of _my_ pupils. It was committed to William H. Wells, Chairman, Dudley Chace of Vermont, a firm[2] and generous republican, and Nathaniel Macon, of North Carolina. From the _last_ I expected opposition, but I hoped to soften it by my candor—From the Chairman I _expected_, that the recollections of his youthful days would produce a warm and friendly feeling in my favor; but I have _found_ an apparent indisposition to act, to me unaccountable, united with a cold, repulsive hauteur in his manner—But in Dudley Chace, with whom I had no acquaintance previous to the present occasion, I have found an union of estimable qualities—generous and magnanimous feelings for a private individual, with the soundest principles of public justice. The day before yesterday, after many unavailing efforts to procure a meeting of the Committee, it met, and the Chairman requested _me_ to have drawn a bill for my relief, in conformity with certain notes which he gave me—I drew a bill and handed it to him—It is this day reported to the Senate.

Some years past, I had the pleasure to see, in the hands of William Canby of Brandywine, the copy of a letter he had written to thee, and thy excellent answer—I afterwards saw the latter published in a newspaper in Baltimore. I saw this publication with great regret, <u>because I had no doubt it would be unpleasant to thee</u>. When I had removed to Wilmington, I enquired of William Canby how the thing happened—he said he knew not, but supposed that some friend, to whom he had lent the letter for perusal, had, without his permission and contrary to his wish, taken a copy and caused it to be published. William Canby's mind is a lovely personification of Innocence and Simplicity—Severe to himself alone, liberal and benevolent to all others. He regrets deeply, and blames himself much for, not having been more careful to prevent so unwarranted, and so indiscrete an act, as the publication of a private letter, without permission of the author. No suspicion entered his innocent mind that any person would thus act—he was therefore off his guard. I mention this subject at his request, for he highly values thy esteem.

With friendship, love, and gratitude, I salute thee.

Isaac Briggs.

RC (DLC); addressed: "Thomas Jefferson, Monticello, Virginia"; endorsed by TJ as received 9 Apr. 1816 and so recorded in SJL. FC (MdHi: Briggs-Stabler Papers); entirely in Briggs's hand; at head of text: "(Copy.)."

TJ's letters to SECRETARY OF THE TREASURY Alexander J. Dallas and WILLIAM CANBY were dated 26 Feb. 1816 and 18 Sept. 1813, respectively. Canby's letter to TJ of 27 Aug. 1813 and TJ's response (misdated 15 Sept. 1813) appeared in the *Baltimore Patriot & Evening Advertiser*, 16 Jan. 1815.

[1] Reworked in FC from "29."
[2] Word interlined in FC in place of "noble."

To John Wayles Eppes

Dear Sir   Monticello Apr. [Mar.][1] 30. 16.

Francis returns as much improved, I am in hopes, as you will have expected. he reads French with so much ease as to read it for amusement, has not much occasion for his dictionary, pronounces generally well, the few defects remaining being such as will be easily corrected hereafter. being kept almost entirely at French, he could afford only the time before breakfast for keeping up his Latin. yet he has done more than that, being very sensibly improved in his knolege of the construction of the language. he will probably require at least two years more to perfect him in that, and to get so far advanced into the Greek as to be able to pursue it alone afterwards.   I suppose you are well satisfied of the qualifications of the tutor in N. Carolina, to whom you propose to send him. our own to be sure are bad enough; yet I should not readily have believed they were before us there. at the New London academy there is a teacher (mr Mitchell I think is his name) about equal to mr Halcomb, a young man very anxious to do what is best, and open to advice. I am sure he would pursue any plan I should recommend to him; and should your mind not be made up for N. Carolina, I believe he would carry Francis on very competently. his situation there would have the advantages of being within 10. or 12. hours ride of you, and under my eye 3. months in the year for I pass that much at Poplar Forest in the 3. or 4. visits I make there in the course of the year. he would be more in the way too of being always furnished with the best books, and could take some future occasion of passing two or three months here again and of learning Spanish. Ellen has the true pronuntiation more perfectly than myself. it is a language which will be very important to an American; as we shall have great intercourse with Spanish America within his day. I confess too I contemplate with pleasure his early familiarisation with that part of the country, having the wish to make him a comfortable future home there. after acquiring the languages, a course of a couple of years at W^m & Mary for Mathematics E^{t}c. would be very necessary.

I am almost afraid to propose to you to yield to me the expence and direction of his education. yet I think I could have it conducted to his advantage. certainly no expence which could be useful to him, and no attention on my part would be spared; and he could visit you at such times as you should wish. if you say Yea to this proposition, he might come on to me at Poplar Forest for which place I shall set out about the 6th of April, and shall be there to about the 21st and could I hear from you soon after my arrival there, I could be taking preparatory steps for his reception and course to be pursued. all this is submitted to your good pleasure. Patsy, supposing mrs Eppes to have an attachment to flowers, sends her a collection of seeds. your servant asks for the large Lima bean we got from Wm Hylton from Jamaica. it has dwindled down to a very poor one, not worth sending if we had it to spare, which we have not. she thinks there may be some at Edgehill and is now sending to see. if there are any they are of the genuine sort & will be sent. all here join with me in affectionate esteem and respect to mrs Eppes & yourself.

Th: Jefferson

RC (PPAmP: Thomas Jefferson Papers); misdated; at foot of first page: "J. W. Eppes esq." PoC (DLC); endorsed by TJ as a letter of 30 Mar. 1816 and so recorded in SJL.

Patsy: Martha Jefferson Randolph.

[1] Month corrected by TJ on PoC.

From Levin Gale

Dear Sir   Chesapeake M[d] March 30th 1816

I received some time ago a letter from Major John Adlum near George Town D.C. requesting me to forward you some cuttings of a particular grape which we origanally got from him. The same day this goes by the mail there will be put in the stage a box containing 150 cuttings of the kind mentioned Directed to you to the Care of M[r] W[m] F Gray Fredrecksburgh Virginia—I have to apologise for not complying sooner with his request but being from home at the time his letter reached this together with other circumstances prevented attending to his request with the alacrity I could have wished—Should you wish more cuttings next year shall be happy to forward them and regret that our vines from neglect furnished so few.

I am Sir respectfully your obt. Ser[t]   Levin Gale

RC (MHi); endorsed by TJ as received 9 Apr. 1816 and so recorded in SJL. RC (DLC); address cover only; with PoC of TJ to John F. Dumoulin, 7 May 1816, on verso; addressed: "Thomas Jefferson Esquire late President—U.S. Monticello _____ County Virginia" by "Mail"; stamped; franked; postmarked Chesapeake, 3 Apr., and Washington, 5 Apr.

Levin Gale (1784–1834), attorney and public official, served in the Maryland state senate, 1816–21, and he represented Cecil, Harford, and Kent counties in the United States House of Representatives, 1827–29. In the latter year he was appointed a director of the Chesapeake and Delaware Canal Company, and in 1834 he joined a committee charged with superintending the interests of creditors of the Bank of Maryland. He died at his home near Elkton in Cecil County (Biog. Dir. Cong.; Papenfuse, Maryland Public Officials, 1:40, 354; Baltimore Patriot & Mercantile Advertiser, 5 Oct. 1826, 31 Oct. 1829, 2 Apr., 23 Aug. 1834).

From Susan Maria Bruff

RESPECTED SIR,   Washington City 31st March 1816.

I flatter myself that the generosity of your heart will induce you to excuse the seeming presumption of a stranger. But truely I have been no stranger to those condescending manners which helped to endear you so much to my dear Father.—My beloved Father, as you, Sir, well know, possessed an uncommon active genius—was engaged in many Inventions; particularly one for making Shot & Ball; and for which I beleive Sir, you had the goodness to recommend him to Mr Madison. But he was not so fortunate as to be patronized—repeated disappointment was his lot in life. At the blowing up of the Navy Yard & Fort he lost two very valuable machines, which had been the toil and labour of several years. His losses at that time he estimated at not less than ten thousand dollars. He petitioned Congress, at the last session, for <u>some</u> compensation: it was merely read, and then laid by.—These misfortunes depressed his spirits, and began visibly to undermine his Health. About 6 months ago, he was induced by the almost certain prospect of making a brilliant fortune, to visit N. York. Indeed, it was not ambition that allured my pious Father: but to acquire a competency for his children. in this he failed.—and last week, when we were just looking forward with painful anxiety for his return to a beloved family, Alas! the heart-rending intelligence arrived that he was no more—   Oh Sir, picture to yourself our agony—our distraction—deprived of our staff—my Mamma left in a state of ill Health,[1] with 5 children to support and educate, without the means.   Pardon me, honoured Sir, It is not my wish to intrude my griefs—you will excuse a young female who has been raised with the tenderest care, and from Infancy taught to beleive that she should one day be independant of the <u>unfeeling</u> world: but in one Sad hour, bereft of a precious, tender Father; and with him vanished all the golden dreams—the bright Illusions that dazzled in anticipation.

You, dear Sir, were among the few that evinced a friendly disposition toward my Father—How often, and sweetly have I heard your name sounded from those lips that are now mouldering in the silent dust. Yes: I beleive, Sir, that had you continued in that important Station which you were So emminently calculated to fill—my everlamented Father would have Shared a better fate; and in all probabillity would now have been here to rejoice our weeping Eyes.

It is not Sir for myself that I have presumed [to] appeal to your humanity—but in behalf of my three little helpless brothers, who seem to have inherited somewhat the genius of their father, as it is developed in a considerable talent for drawing and painting.   My disconsolate Mother joins her prayers to mine, that every blessing may attend you.

Yours, with the highest respect   SUSAN MARIA BRUFF.

RC (DLC); edge chipped; endorsed by TJ as a letter of 30 Mar. 1816 received 9 Apr. 1816 and so recorded in SJL.

Susan Maria Bruff (ca. 1799–1822) married Georgetown newspaper publisher William A. Rind in 1818 (Brigham, *American Newspapers*, 1:92, 93; Washington *Daily National Intelligencer*, 24 Nov. 1818, 26 Apr. 1822).

For TJ's recommendation of Bruff's father, Thomas Bruff, to President James MADISON, see TJ to Madison, 6 June 1812, and TJ to Thomas Bruff, 7 June

1812. The elder Bruff PETITIONED CONGRESS on 17 Oct. 1814, but no further action was taken after the appeal was referred to the secretary of war on 23 Nov. of that year. His widow, Mary Bruff, had a similar petition introduced on 30 Dec. 1816, but on 2 Feb. 1820 the House Committee on Pensions and Revolutionary Claims gave it an unfavorable report, and it was tabled (*JHR*, 9:478, 542, 10:116, 13:189).

[1] Manuscript: "Heath."

From Pierre Samuel Du Pont de Nemours

EXCELLENT AMI,   Eleutherian 31 mars 1816.

J'ai l'honneur de vous renvoyer mon petit Evangile à l'usage des Républiques espagnoles, que je vous avais porté il y a quatre mois.

J'ai eu dieu merci, et j'aurai encore plusieurs exemplaires à en donner: et je n'ai qu'un Seul Secrétaire. de plus, j'ai un grand défaut: pressé par l'âge et par les circonstances, je m'engage à plusieurs travaux à la fois. Je Sais que ce n'est point une bonne méthode: ce n'en est pas une du tout.

Mais dans les orages du monde, la vie n'est pas une occupation qu'on ait le tems de régler. Elle est un état de guerre et d'inondation, où il faut courir du côté que Se présentent le flot, le besoin, l'ennemi.

Ce travail Sur les Républiques naissantes, ou à naitre, ou à restaurer, est un de mes écrits pour lequel je désirerais le plus votre Suffrage et votre bénédiction.

Je voudrais trouver un bon Ecrivain qui le traduisit en Espagnol.

Je n'ai pas cru devoir le faire imprimer en francais avant d'avoir donné ma démission de la place de Conseiller d'Etat. Et j'ai reculé cette démission parceque j'ai à Paris ma Femme blessée depuis Seize mois d'une chute dont elle demeurera estropiée, n'ayant pas encore pu quitter Sa Chambre, ni presque Son lit.—Mon 13eme Chapitre pourrait attirer Sur elle une persécution, ou au moins exposer une centaine de cartons qui contiennent le Travail de ma vie à être menés par mesure de Sureté chez le ministre de la Police, lequel les ferait jetter au feu, ou mettre au pilon.

Je voudrais que la pauvre dame pût m'envoyer Successivement les plus importans de ces cartons, que j'aime mieux laisser après moi en Amérique qu'en Europe. Quelqu'un de mes Petits-Fils en tirera un jour parti.

Je ne Suis pas Sûr de ne point retourner dans cette triste Europe dont je regarde la Subversion totale comme inévitable. Les gages du travail manquant, et la France ayant à payer, tant au dehors qu'aux pillards étrangers du dedans, le double de ce qu'elle peut, il est à peu près impossible que le désespoir de l'intérieur n'amene par des tentatives contre les troupes, le renversement du Gouvernement, le partage du Pays peut-être; le pillage général avec certitude, et le gaspillage de presque tout ce qui restera de Capitaux.—Ce desordre ne pourra pas avoir lieu en France Sans apprendre aux dernieres classes du Peuple de la Prusse, des petits Royaumes d'Allemagne et ensuite de l'Autriche, au quel on a fait quitter les travaux utiles pour la <u>Landwer</u> digne Sœur de la conscription et encore plus cruelle que rien n'est refusable à la multitude qui veut prendre. Elle prendra: et les Soldats Se mettront à Sa tête.[1] l'incendie gagnera l'Italie, et même l'Angleterre qui dans Sa folie a ruiné Ses meilleures pratiques

C'est la Seule chose qui pourra vous préserver de la guerre, car Si la catastrophe retarde plus de deux ans, il n'y a point de doute que les Anglais enverront Soixante dix mille Hommes vous aguerrir, vous réunir, vous affranchir, et vous faire payer fort cher cet utile <u>improvement</u>.

Il y aura aussi en définitif de l'improvement en Europe, acheté encore plus cher qu'il n'aura valu, acheté au prix de la moitié de Ses habitans, des trois quarts de Ses richesses, et de la dispersion du dernier quart qui demeurera plusieurs années presque impuissant pour remettre les Travaux en activité.—les nouveaux Gouvernemens ne seront pas des Monarchies.[2]
Mais Vous jugez quel Sera pour un Philosophe non encore réduit à la derniere misere le malheur d'être témoin et vraisemblablement victime de ces Tragédies tant qu'elles dureront.

Si je ne puis éviter d'y aller, j'y périrai peut-être en prison, peut-être fusillé; peut-être massacré à domicile, et certainement calomnié par tous les Partis.

Je demande à ma Femme de Se faire porter en chaise longue et par des Hommes de Paris au Havre, et là hisser Sur un Vaisseau; d'en redescendre à Philadelphie, ou a New Castle comme elle y Sera montée; et nous la ferons apporter ici de la même maniere qu'elle aura voyagé en France.—Mais, Si elle ne le peut physiquement pas, car moralement Son courage est au dessus de tout, Je ne peux pas davantage lui écrire: reste et meurs; je mourrai de mon coté. nous voila Séparés pour jamais. Il faut donc que je revienne la consoler un pêu, l'assister, et mourir auprès d'elle.—Comment aurait-on la prétension d'être bon au monde, Si l'on ne commençait pas par être bon, très bon, dans l'intérieur de Son ménage?—C'est dans l'intérieur qu'est le devoir réel et positif. le reste est toujours Souillé d'un peu de vanité.

La vieillesse donne du courage contre la mort.—demandez à Solon—

La bonté de dieu, les Lumieres des Génies qui approchent de lui plus que nous ne pouvons le faire pauvres Humains, l'estime de ceux qui dans les Animaux de notre espèce ont le plus de rapports de cœur et de tête avec ces Etres Supérieurs, en donnent contre la calomnie.— On ne vous persuadera jamais que je fasse cas des titres au dessus desquels j'ai tâché de me mettre, ni de l'argent que j'ai toujours dédaigné et que d'ailleurs on ne me donnerait point ni que, même pour la gloire, Si elle pouvait y être, je fasse ou dise en aucun cas rien contre ma conscience, que mes illustres Amis, parmi lesquels vous tenez une Si belle place, ont Suffisamment éclaireé.

J'ajoute à ce paquet, Sur la question de vos manufactures, une petite note, que j'ai cru devoir écrire parceque l'on allegue mon autorité, comme on faisait la vôtre, contre[3] notre propre conseil.

Mais autre chose est d'administrer l'Europe, où Colbert et les Anglais, Séduits par le Luxe, ont comprimé l'Agriculture pour avoir des mendians dont on fît des Ouvriers à bas prix, et où le Parlement Britannique a poussé cette folie jusqu'à mettre en danger la Subsistance d'un Septieme de la Population de Ses trois Royaumes et au contraire de porter en avant les destins de l'Amérique, qui marche avec Ses capitaux imaginaires de confiance, de crédit réciproque, et de papiers devenus aussi puissans que s'ils étaient réels parceque les travaux qu'ils font exécuter ont une valeur effective qui à la fin paye tout. Votre Agriculture pour S'étendre jusqu'à la Californie, n'a besoin que de consommateurs à Sa portée qui payent Ses récoltes en Services utiles.

Je présente mes respects à Madame Randolph, et à toutes Ses, vos belles dames et demoiselles, Miss Septimia comprise comme il est juste.

Et je vous embrasse avec tendresse et vénération

DuPont (de Nemours)

EXCELLENT FRIEND,   Eleutherian 31 March 1816.

I have the honor of sending you again my little gospel for the use of the Spanish republics, which I brought to you four months ago.

Thank God I have had and will still have several copies of it to give away, as I have only one secretary. Furthermore, I have one big shortcoming: pressed by age and circumstances, I commit myself to several projects at the same time. I know it is not a good method; it is not a method at all.

But in the the storms of the world, life is not an occupation that one has time to control. It is a state of war and flood, in which one has to confront the flood, the need, and the enemy.

This book on republics, newly born, to be born, or to be restored, is one of my writings for which I most desire your approval and blessing.

I would like to find a good writer to translate it into Spanish.

I did not deem it necessary to have it printed in French before submitting my resignation from the Council of State. And I have postponed the decision to resign, because I have in Paris a wife who, for sixteen months, has been suffering from an injury caused by a fall and from which she will remain crippled. She has not yet been able to leave her room and hardly even her bed.— My thirteenth chapter might lead to her persecution, or at least expose a hundred or so boxes that contain my life's work to being taken as a security measure to the office of the minister of police, who would have them thrown into the fire or pulped.

I would like the unfortunate lady to be able to send me, one at a time, the most important of these boxes, which after my death I would rather leave in America than Europe. One of my grandsons will someday make use of them.

I may yet return to this sad Europe, whose total subversion I regard as inevitable. Because working wages are lacking, and because France has had to pay foreign looters, from outside as well as inside, double what she is able to pay, internal despair will almost certainly lead to attempts against the troops, the overthrow of the government, perhaps the partition of the country; general looting for sure, and the squandering of almost all the remaining capital.—This disorder in France cannot fail to teach the lower classes in Prussia, the small kingdoms in Germany, and Austria who were made to leave useful jobs for the national militia (a worthy sister of conscription and even crueler) that nothing can be refused to a multitude determined to take. It will take: and the soldiers will lead it. The conflagration will spread to Italy and even to England, who in her folly has ruined her best practices.

Only such an outcome can keep you from war because, if the disaster is delayed for more than two years, the English will certainly send seventy thousand men to harden, unite, and free you, and they will make you pay a steep price for this useful improvement.

In the end, Europe will see improvement too, bought at a price even higher than it is worth, costing half its inhabitants, three-quarters of its wealth, and the dispersion of the last quarter, which will for several years be almost powerless to get work going again.—The new governments will not be monarchies.

But you can imagine what a misfortune it will be for a philosopher not yet reduced to the worst state of misery to be a witness and probably a victim of these tragedies as long as they last.

If I cannot avoid going there, I will perhaps perish in prison, I may be executed or massacred at home, and certainly I will be slandered by all parties.

I am asking my wife to have men transport her in a chaise longue from Paris to Le Havre, to be lifted onto a ship, and to get off in Philadelphia or New Castle in the same way she embarked. We will have her brought here just as she traveled in France.—But, if she is unable to make the trip physically, her moral courage being indomitable, I can no longer write her: stay and die; I will die over here; we are separated forever. Under these circumstances I must go back and console her a little, help her, and die by her side.—How could one pretend to be good to the world, if one cannot start by being good, very good, within one's marriage?—It is within this union that the real and positive duty lies. The rest is always sullied with a little vanity.

Old age gives courage against death.—Ask Solon—

God's kindness, the lights of the geniuses who come closest to him, nearer than we poor humans can, the esteem of those who, among animals of our own species, are the most closely connected through their hearts and minds with these superior beings, give courage against slander.—You will never be persuaded that I value titles, above which I have always striven to rise, nor money, which I have always disdained, and which in any case I would not be given, nor that, even for glory, if it could be had, I would do or say under any circumstances anything against my conscience, which has been sufficiently enlightened by my illustrious friends, among whom you hold such a prominent place.

I add to this package a little note regarding your manufactures, which I felt I had to write because my authority is invoked, as yours used to be, against our own advice.

But it is another thing to govern Europe, where Colbert and the English, seduced by luxury, have reduced agriculture in order to create beggars who become poorly paid workers. Europe, where the British parliament pushed this folly far enough to endanger the subsistence of a seventh of the population in its three kingdoms and, on the contrary, to advance the destinies of America, which moves forward with its imaginary capital based on trust, reciprocal credit, and paper, which has become as powerful as if it were real, because the work it enables has an effective value that pays for everything in the end. Your agriculture, in order to spread all the way to California, needs only nearby consumers, who can pay for its crops with useful services.

I send my regards to Madame Randolph and to all of her and your beautiful ladies, Miss Septimia included of course.

And I embrace you with tenderness and veneration

DuPont (de Nemours)

RC (DLC); at head of text: "a Monsieur Jefferson"; endorsed by TJ as received 9 Apr. 1816 and so recorded in SJL. FC (DeGH: Pierre Samuel Du Pont de Nemours Papers, Winterthur Manuscripts). Tr (DeGH: Sophie M. Du Pont Papers; Longwood Manuscripts); posthumous copy by Sophie M. Du Pont, possibly based on a missing Dft; with significant omissions and some variations in wording. Translation by Dr. Genevieve Moene.

For the PETIT EVANGILE À L'USAGE

DES RÉPUBLIQUES ESPAGNOLES, see Du Pont to TJ, 26 May 1815, and note. In February 1816 Du Pont enclosed to his wife a letter to King Louis XVIII resigning his PLACE DE CONSEILLER D'ETAT, but she never forwarded the correspondence (Ambrose Saricks, *Pierre Samuel Du Pont de Nemours* [1965], 354). The Athenian lawgiver SOLON was said to have attributed his courageous stance against the tyrant Peisistratus to his old age (Plutarch, *Solon*, book 31, in *Plutarch's Lives, with an English Translation*, trans. Bernadotte Perrin, Loeb Classical Library [1914–26; undated reprint], 1:492–5).

[1] Sentence interlined.
[2] Sentence interlined.
[3] Word interlined in place of "pour" ("for").

ENCLOSURE

Pierre Samuel Du Pont de Nemours's Notes on the Encouragement of American Manufactures

[ca. 31 Mar. 1816]

Observations Sommaires
Sur l'utilité des Encouragemens à donner
aux Manufactures Américaines

Pour juger quels sont les intérêts que l'on recommande au Congrès, en l'exhortant à donner un grand appui aux Manufactures Américaines, il faut s'être occupé de la Science des Valeurs, et considérer de quoi elles sont composées.

La Valeur des Marchandises manufacturées est formée de l'Addition de plusieurs Valeurs.

1° Celle de la Matière première.—Pour les deux principales Manufactures de l'Amérique, celle des Etoffes de laine et celle des Etoffes de Coton, la Matière première est en totalité Américaine: tout ce qui en sera employé le sera au profit de l'Agriculture des Etats unis; et l'Education des Bêtes à laine peut donner des gains immenses aux Etats de l'ouest.

2° la Valeur des gages ou Salaires des Ouvriers.—C'est la plus considérable de toutes les dépenses de Manufactures. Elle est payée tous les jours; et tous les jours les ouvriers en consomment le prix en pain, Viande, beurre, œufs, lait, fromages, dindons, poulets, légumes et boissons. Toutes ces choses sont vendues par les Fermiers; et toutes ces dépenses au profit de l'Agriculture sont payées comptant, sans frais de Commission ni de transport, sans dangers de Mer, ni de Corsaires.

3° Le Surplus consiste dans l'Intérêt des Capitaux et les gains ou Salaires dûs aux peines et au travail des Entrepreneurs. Ces deux derniers Articles se confondent ordinairement. Ils passent rarement quinze pour cent du prix de la Marchandise, et sont souvent bornés à dix. D'ici à long-tems, ils ne s'élèveront même pas à ce taux, la concurrence Anglaise est trop puissante.

Il résulte de cet examen du prix des Etoffes Américaines qu'il y en a quatre-Vingt dix ou au moins quatre-vingt cinq pour cent en encouragement direct donné à l'Agriculture.

Et dix à quinze pour cent au plus constituant le profit ou les Salaires—du travail des Entrepreneurs Manufacturiers, et comprenant l'intérêt de leurs avances.

La question pour les Législateurs se réduit donc à dire: "Voulez-Vous donner à l'Industrie Nationale en général un Encouragement qui se partagera, Savoir: quatre-Vingt dix ou au moins quatre-Vingt cinq sur cent, en faveur de l'Agriculture; et seulement dix ou au plus quinze au profit des hommes Industrieux?"

Ces hommes industrieux font de la partie qui leur revient dans le prix de leurs Etoffes, d'abord[1] des consommations qu'ils achètent aussi à l'Agriculture, et ensuite[2] des improvemens des Améliorations, des extensions à ce genre d'entreprises dont le produit se partagera toujours dans la même proportion, quatre-Vingt dix ou quatre-Vingt cinq pour les Cultivateurs; dix ou quinze pour les Manufacturiers.[3] Et dans les improvemens même il y a toujours une grande depense en Salaires d'ouvriers qui passe tout de Suite en consommations au profit divers de l'Agriculture.[4]

Cette marche peut continuer[5] jusqu'à ce que l'Amérique soit partout, complettement et de tous points, parfaitement cultiveé. Il y en a au moins pour Six cents ans; et plus vraisemblablement le Règne de la prospérité et de la Population croissante dans les Etats unis sera le Règne de Mille ans.

Les heureuses mœurs de cette sage Nation font qu'aucune Entreprise n'y a lieu comme en Europe, au détriment des autres; bien au contraire, toutes S'y entr'aident. L'ingénieuse invention des Banques fait que les Capitaux ne manquent pas, et qu'ils y profitent même avant d'être créés. On est convenu tacitement de se faire au moyen des Banques un crédit mutuel, jusqu'à ce que la chose à mettre en activité y soit parvenue, et qu'elle ait donné les moyens de Se payer elle-même. Il y a peu de pertes, et l'on ne doit les envisager que comme une légère prime d'assurance pour un si grand bien.

Ces Considérations ne regardent que les Richesses, l'abondance, et la prospérité intérieures.

Mais le noble intérêt de l'Indépendance Nationale, celui de ne pas donner à l'Agriculture et à l'Industrie d'une autre Nation ambitieuse, Tyrannique, et jalouse, les moyens d'envoyer et d'entretenir des Armées de Mercenaires dans nos Campagnes, pour les dévaster, dans nos Villes pour les brûler, chez nos Femmes pour les insulter, est d'une bien plus haute importance pour des hommes fiers et libres, pour des Républicains.

MS (DLC: TJ Papers, 200:35609–10); in a clerk's hand, with emendations by Du Pont; undated. MS (DeGH: Pierre S. du Pont Papers, Longwood Manuscripts); entirely in Du Pont's hand; undated, but enclosed in a letter to Robert M. Patterson dated 28 Mar. 1816; lacking emendations described in note 4. 1st FC (DeGH: Pierre S. du Pont Papers, Longwood Manuscripts); entirely in same clerk's hand as DLC MS; undated; text corresponding to version sent to Patterson. 2d FC (DeGH: Pierre Samuel Du Pont de Nemours Papers, Winterthur Manuscripts); entirely in same clerk's hand; undated; text corresponding to version sent to Patterson. 3d FC (Pierre Samuel Du Pont de Nemours Papers, Winterthur Manuscripts); in same clerk's hand, with minor emendations by Du Pont and paragraph added in Du Pont's hand corresponding to the second addition described in note 4; undated. Tr (ViU: FWG); in same clerk's hand, with addition described in note 4 cleanly incorporated; undated; endorsed by Francis W. Gilmer: "By Mr. duPont (de Nemours.) 1816."

Writing from Eleutherian Mills on 28 Mar. 1816, Du Pont enclosed a copy of this document to Robert M. Patterson, explaining that "j'ai l'honneur de vous envoyer un petit Mémoire que je crois de quelque importance pour votre Pays. J'en avais fait Sur le même Sujet un plus étendu, moins bon, moins décisif, que j'avais envoyé à M^r duane, qu'il avait reçu avec indulgence, et m'avait promis de traduire, d'inserer dans Sa Feuille. Il n'en a pas eu le tems: ce qui est heureux, puis qu'il en est résulté que je l'ai réduit des trois quarts et rendu infiniment plus clair. Vous m'obligeriez beaucoup de mettre une demie heure à le traduire. Il ne vous couterait pas davantage: et de vous entendre avec M^r duane, pour qu'il le publiât" ("I have the honor to send you a short treatise that I think of some importance for your country. I had written a more extensive one, not as well executed and less decisive. I sent it to Mr. Duane, who received it with indulgence and promised me to translate it and insert it in his paper. He has not had the time, which is fortunate, since in the meantime I have reduced it by three-quarters and made it infinitely clearer. You would oblige me greatly by taking half an hour and translating it. It would not take you longer than that: and if you would do so, arrange with Mr. Duane so that he will publish it") (RC in DeGH: Pierre S. du Pont Papers, Longwood Manuscripts; at head of text: "au docteur Patterson le Fils"; dateline at foot of text; endorsed by Patterson on last page of enclosure).

The MS in Gilmer's papers at ViU may not have been enclosed in Du Pont's letter to him of 4 Apr. 1816. Early in that letter Du Pont states that "Je vous envoie à ce sujet une Observation qui montre comment les Manufactures qui Servent aux besoins du Pays donnent à Son Agriculture quatrevingt dix ou au moins quatrevingt cinq pour cent du prix des choses qu'elles Fabriquent" ("I send you on this subject an Observation which shows how manufactures serve the needs of the country and give its agriculture ninety or at least eighty-five percent of the cost of what they produce"). However, along the left margin of the final page he adds that "Je reçois en ce moment dans l'Aurora du 3 avril, la traduction très bien faite par le Docteur Patterson, des Observations Sommaires dont je vous parlais au commencement de cette lettre; il est donc inutile que je les joigne ici en Français Vous les lirez avec plus de plaisir dans votre langue" ("I receive just now in the Aurora of 3 April the very able translation by Doctor Patterson of the Summary Observations that I mentioned at the beginning of this letter; hence it is unnecessary for me to enclose them here in French. You will read them with more pleasure in your own language") (RC in ViU: FWG; postmarked Wilmington, 5 Apr.; endorsed by Gilmer as received 10 Apr. 1816). Writing from Eleutherian Mills on 18 Jan. 1816, Du Pont sent President James Madison a more complete version of this essay (RC and enclosure in DLC: Madison Papers; both printed in Gilbert Chinard, *The Correspondence of Jefferson and Du Pont de Nemours* [1931; repr. 1979], 239–50).

[1] Word interlined by Du Pont in place of "ou" ("or"). All other texts retain original wording.

[2] Preceding two words interlined by Du Pont in place of "ou" ("or"). All other texts retain original wording.

[3] MS in DeGH and 1st and 2d FCs end paragraph here.

[4] Sentence interlined by Du Pont. In place of this sentence, in 3d FC Du Pont here keyed a note written along the left margin: "La dépense même des improvemens et des extensions Se fait presque entièrement en constructions de bâtimens et de machines; c'est-à-dire en Salaires d'ouvriers qui les traduisent journellement en consommations, tellement que ce qui parait d'abord avoir été donné le plus Specialement a l'industrie repasse de Suite à l'agriculture, et continuera de le faire tant que la nation ne Sera pas réduite à tirer de l'étranger des Subsistances et les matieres de son travail" ("The expenditure even for improvements and augmentations is devoted almost entirely to the construction of buildings and machines, that is to say in salaries for workers who turn these daily into consumption. Hence, even that which appears at first to have been given most particularly to industry passes eventually to agriculture, and will continue to do so as long as the nation is not obliged to import her provisions and work materials"). Text cleanly incorporated in ViU MS.

⁵ In place of this word, in 3d FC Du
Pont interlined: "Se prolonger avec des
avantages toujours nouveaux" ("continue

always with new benefits"). Revision
cleanly incorporated in ViU MS.

CONTEMPORARY TRANSLATION

SUMMARY OBSERVATIONS,
ON THE ADVANTAGES OF GIVING ENCOURAGEMENT TO
AMERICAN MANUFACTURES.

In order to judge what are the interests which we recommend to congress, when we beg them to afford an effectua[l] support to American manufactures, it is necessary to have studied the *science of* VALUES, and to consider of what these are composed.

The value of manufactured goods is made up of several distinct values.

1st. *That of the raw material.*—For the two principal manufactures of the United States, those of wool and of cotton, the raw material is entirely American; and whatever is employed, is *to the profit of the agriculture* of the country. The raising of sheep may produce an immense gain to the Western States.

2dly. *The value of the wages of the workmen.* This is the most considerable part of the expense of manufacturing. It is paid from day to day, and is consumed by the workmen in bread and meat and vegetables and other necessaries of life,[1] all of which are sold by the farmers, and *for the profit of agriculture.* The payments, moreover, are made in cash, without the expense of commission or of transport, and without danger from storms or from pirates.

3dly. *The surplus consists of the interest of the capital required, and in the gain or profit accruing to the employers, for their trouble and labor.*—These two last articles are commonly confounded. They rarely exceed *fifteen per cent.* of the price of the goods, and are often confined to *ten.* For a long time hence, they will not even reach to this rate, the English competition being too powerful.

From this examination of the price of American manufactures, it results that *ninety,* or at least *eighty-five* per cent. of this price is a direct encouragement given *to agriculture;* and *ten,* or at most *fifteen* per cent. constitutes the profit or salary of the employers, comprehending the interest of their capitals.

The[2] question for the legislators is reduced then[3] to this:—are you willing to give to the national industry in general an encouragement to be divided thus:—*ninety,* or at least *eighty-five* per cent in favor of AGRICULTURE; and *ten,* or at most *fifteen* per cent. to the profit of *industrious men.*

These industrious employers spend the par[t] which comes to them, in the price of the goods, [e]ither in articles of consumption derived from agriculture, or in improvements, meliorations, and extensions of their establishments, the produce of which will still be divided in the same proportion;—*ninety or eighty-five* per cent. for the former, *ten or fifteen* for the manufacturer.[4]

This course may continue until America shall be, throughout, and at all points, completely and perfectly cultivated. This will be at least for six hundred years; and more probably, the reign of the increasing prosperity and population of the United States will be a true *millenium*.

The happy manners of this prudent nation, prevent any enterprize from being established, as in Europe, to the detriment of others; on the contrary, they mutually support each other. The ingenious invention of banks prevents the want of funds, and gives the advantage of capitals even before they are created. It is tacitly agreed, by the medium of banks, to establish a mutual credit until the proposed enterprise shall be brought into activity, and shall afford the means of defraying its own cost. There are but few losses, and these should be regarded only as a light premium of insurance for so great a benefit.

These considerations have respect only to the interior riches, abundance, and prosperity of the country. But the noble interest of the national independence, that of not giving to the agriculture and the industry of any[5] jealous foreign nation, the means of sending and supporting among us mercenary armies, to lay waste our fields, burn our cities, and insult our women, is an object of much higher importance to freemen, to republicans.

Printed translation by Robert M. Patterson in Philadelphia *Aurora General Advertiser*, 3 Apr. 1816; undated; some characters obscured by fold or printer's error in copy at PPAmP supplied from version in Philadelphia *Weekly Aurora*, 9 Apr. 1816; at head of text: "FOR THE AURORA"; at foot of text: "D P. D. N."

[1] *Aurora* here condenses from "pain, Viande, beurre, œufs, lait, fromages, dindons, poulets, légumes et boissons" ("bread, meat, butter, eggs, milk, cheese, turkeys, chickens, vegetables, and beverages").

[2] Extraneous opening double quotation mark in front of this word editorially omitted.

[3] *Aurora*: "them."

[4] *Aurora* here omits "Et dans les improvemens même il y a toujours une grande depense en Salaires d'ouvriers qui passe tout de Suite en consommations au profit divers de l'Agriculture" ("And even these same improvements always carry with them a great expenditure on worker's salaries, which, through consumption, immediately profit agriculture").

[5] *Aurora* here omits "ambitieuse, Tyrannique, et" ("ambitious, tyrannical, and").

From Albert Gallatin

DEAR SIR   Washington April 1st 1816

I have much regretted that a detention in my journey to this place prevented my arriving at Baltimore till after your nephew's departure. I had brought with me letters for Geneva which I have sent after him. Mr Erving[1] takes duplicates, and I will send triplicates on my arrival at Paris; so that I hope that he will experience no disappointment on that account. I found the institutions and Professors as good at Geneva as when I had left it 35 years before.

After what I had written to you, you could hardly have expected that I would have accepted the French mission. It was again offered to me in so friendly manner and from so friendly motives that I was induced to accept. Nor will I conceal that I did not feel yet old enough, or had I philosophy enough to go into retirement and abstract myself altogether from public affairs. I have no expectation however that in the present state of France I can be of any utility there, and hope that I will not make a long stay in that country. The late events must have dispersed a great number of your acquaintances there. If you have yet any correspondents to which you wish any letters to be safely transmitted, such as you will send by me will be delivered in their own hands. I presume that I will sail the latter end of this month from New York, for which place I will set off to morrow. In every country and at all times I never can cease to feel gratitude, respect and attachment for you. With every wish for your happiness I remain sincerely & respectfully

Your's   ALBERT GALLATIN

RC (DLC); endorsed by TJ as received 9 Apr. 1816 and so recorded in SJL. RC (DLC: TJ Papers, ser. 10); address cover only; with PoC of TJ to Patrick Gibson, 8 June 1816, on verso; addressed: "Thomas Jefferson Esqre Monticello near Milton Virginia"; franked; postmarked Washington City, 2 Apr. Tr (NHi: Gallatin Papers); posthumous copy.

YOUR NEPHEW'S DEPARTURE was that of Dabney C. Terrell. Gallatin informed Secretary of State James Monroe on 2 Feb. 1816 that he ACCEPTED THE FRENCH MISSION (NN: Monroe Papers).

[1] Manuscript: "Erwing."

To John Wood

SIR   Monticello. Apr. 1. 16.

I have duly recieved your favor of the 16th Ult. expressing your wish to be employed in the survey of the exterior boundaries of the state, under the 7th section of the act providing for a general map of the state, and I shall very conscientiously espouse your wish with the Executive from a conviction of your superior qualifications for that service. I have the fitter occasion of doing it, as I now have under consideration a letter from the Governor consulting me on the execution of the act. this act presents very extensive views, which will require much developement. the first member of the 7th section which you wish to undertake calls for two very distinct operations. that on the tidewaters must be aided by nautical means, the soundings being required, as well as the courses of the rivers. that above the tidewaters is what I presume you wish to undertake. the following is a general view of what is to be done.

Mountains.   1. a continued survey along their ridges.

2. a notation of their gaps.

3. their elevation.

4. the breadth of their bases.

Rivers.   5. their courses.

6. their breadths?

7. their fall?

General.   8. Latitudes and Longitudes?

Instruments.—for the 1st 2^d 5th & 6th operations will a Theodolite with telescopes be too troublesome of management? and will a Circumferentor with a graduated rim, a fixed, and a moveable Index to take angles independant of the needle, and cross-spirit levels on the face of the plate, be sufficient?

3^d the uncertainty of finding good baselines seems to render the geometrical admeasurement of heights less practicable than the barometrical, which the latter theories have brought to quite a sufficient correctness.

7th would the barometrical variations be sufficient for this? I doubt it; & if not I know no other method but what would make the undertaking more troublesome than useful: altho it would really be both curious & desirable, as would also be the velocity of the general current, if obtainable.

8. I presume a good Hadley's sextant best for these operations.

I have distinguished by a ? the operations not expressly called for by the act, but which ought not to be left out of so great a work.

I should be very glad if you would take these several articles into consideration, and favor me with your views on them, adding any others omitted by me, and which may appear to you important. in hopes you will do me this kindness with as little delay as your convenience admits, I will withold for a while my answer to the Governor on this branch of the subject.

I do not know whether you have paid so particular an attention to mineralogy, and especially to the late geological systems, as to enable you to unite this object of the act with the other. it would be a convenient, as well as economical association. Accept the assurance of my esteem & respect.   TH: JEFFERSON

PoC (DLC); at foot of first page: "Mr John Wood."

A CIRCUMFERENTOR is a surveying "instrument consisting of a flat brass bar with sights at the ends and a circular brass box in the middle, containing a magnetic needle, which plays over a graduated circle; the whole being supported on a staff or tripod" (*OED*). A photograph of one of these devices is reproduced elsewhere in this volume.

To Wilson Cary Nicholas

Dear Sir   Monticello Apr. 2. 16.

Your favor of Mar. 22. has been recieved. it finds me more labori-
ously, and imperiously engaged than almost on any occasion of my
life. it is not therefore in my power to take into immediate consideration all the subjects it proposes. they cover a broad surface, & will
require some developement. they respect
I. Defence.
II. Education.
III. the Map of the state. this last will comprise
      1. an Astronomical survey, to wit Longitudes and Latitudes.
      2. a Geometrical survey of the external boundaries, the
         mountains & rivers.
      3. a Topographical survey of the counties.
      4. a Mineralogical survey.
each of these heads require distinct consideration. I will take them up
one at a time & communicate my ideas as leisure will permit.

I. on the subject of Defence, I will state to you what has been
heretofore contemplated & proposed. some time before I retired from
office when the clouds between England & the US. thickened so as
to threaten war at hand, and while we were fortifying various assail-
able points on our seaboard, the defence of the Chesapeak became,
as it ought to have been, a subject of serious consideration, and the
problem occurred, whether it could be defended at it's mouth? it's
effectual defence in detail being obviously impossible. my idea was
that we should find or prepare a station near it's mouth for a very
great force of vessels of annoyance of such a character as to assail,
when the weather & position of an enemy suited, and keep or withdraw themselves into their station when adverse. these means of annoyance were to consist of gun boats, row boats floating batteries,
bombketches, fireships, rafts, turtles, torpedoes, rockets & whatever
else could be devised to destroy a ship becalmed, to which could now
be added Fulton scows. I thought it possible that a station might be
made on the Middle grounds, (which are always shallow, and have
been known to be uncovered by water,) by a circumvallation of stones
dropped loosely on one another, so as to take their own bevil, & raised
sufficiently high to protect the vessels within them from waves and
boat attacks. it is by such a wall the harbor of Cherburg has been
made. the Middle grounds have a firm bottom, and lie 2. or 3. miles
from the ship channel on either side, and so near the Cape as to be at
hand for any enemy moored or becalmed within them. a survey of

them was desired, and some officer of the navy recieved orders on the subject, who being opposed to our possessing any thing below a frigate or line of battle ship, either visited, or did not visit them, & verbally expressed his opinion of impracticability. I state these things from memory and may err in small circumstances, but not in the general impression.

A second station offering itself was the mouth of Lynhaven river,[1] which having but 4. or 5. feet water, the vessels would be to be adapted to that, or it's entrance deepened. but there it would be requisite to have 1. a fort protecting the vessels within it, and strong enough to hold out until a competent force of militia could be collected for it's relief. and 2. a Canal uniting the tidewaters of Lynhaven river and the Eastern branch, 3. or 4. miles apart only of low level country. this would afford to the vessels a retreat for their own safety, and a communication with Norfolk & Albemarle sound, so as to give succour to these places if attacked, or recieve it from them for a special enterprise. it was believed that such a canal would then have cost about 30,000.D.

This being a case of personal as well as public interest, I thought a private application not improper, and indeed preferable to a more general one, with an Executive needing no stimulus to do what is right; & therefore in May & June 1813. I took the liberty of writing to them on this subject, the defence of the Chesapeak; and to what is before stated I added some observations on the importance and pressure of the case. a view of the Map of the US. shews that the Chesapeak recieves either the whole, or important waters of five of the most producing of the Atlantic states, to wit, N. Carolina (for the Dismal canal makes Albemarle Sound a water of the Chesapeak, and Norfolk it's port of exportation) Virginia, Maryland, Pennsylvania and New York. we know that the waters of the Chesapeak from the Genesee to the Sawra towns and Albemarle Sound, comprehend $\frac{2}{5}$ of the population of the Atlantic states, and furnish probably more than half their exported produce, that the loss of James river alone, in that year, was estimated at 200,000. barrels of flour, fed away to horses, or sold at half price, which was a levy of a million of Dollars on a single one of these numerous waters, and that levy to be repeated every year during the war; that this important country can all be shut up by two or three ships of the enemy, lying at the mouth of the bay; that an injury so vast to us, and so cheap to the enemy, must for ever be resorted to by them; & maintained constantly thro' every war; that this was a hard trial of the spirit of the middle states, a trial which, backed by impossible taxes, might produce a demand for peace on any terms;

that when it was considered that the Union had already expended 4. millions of Dollars for the defence of the single city of N.York, and the waters of a single river, the Hudson, (which we entirely approved, and now we might probably add 4. more since expended on the same spot) we thought it very moderate for so great a portion of the country; the population, the wealth, and contributing industry, & strength of the Atlantic states, to ask a few hundred thousand Dollars, to save the harrasment of their militia,[2] conflagrations of their towns & houses, devastations of their farms, & annihilation of all the annual fruits of their labor.   The idea of defending the bay at it's mouth was approved; but the necessary works were deemed inexecutable during a war; and an answer more cogent was furnished by the fact that our treasury and credit were both exhausted.   Since the war I have learned (I cannot say how) that the Executive has taken up the subject & sent on an Engineer to examine & report the localities; and that this Engineer thought favorably of the Middle grounds. but my recollection is too indistinct, but to suggest enquiry to you. after having once taken the liberty of solliciting the Executive on this subject, I do not think it would be respectful for me to do it a second time; nor can it be necessary with persons who need only suggestions of what is right, & not importunities to do it. if the subject is brought before them, they can readily recall or recur to my letters if worth it. but would it not be advisable in the first place to have surveys made of the Middle grounds, and the grounds between the tide-waters of Lynhaven & the Eastern branch, that your representations may be made on known facts? these would be parts only of the surveys you are authorised to make, and might, for so good a reason, be anticipated & executed before the general work can be done

Perhaps however the[3] view is directed to a defence by frigates or ships of the line, stationed at York or elsewhere. against this, in my opinion, both reason and experience reclaim. had we half a dozen 74[s] stationed at York, the enemy would place a dozen at the Capes. this great force called there would enable them to make large detachments against Norfolk when it suited them, to harass and devastate the bay-coasts incessantly, and would oblige us to keep large armies of militia, at York to defend the ships, and at Norfolk to defend that. the experience of New London proves how certain and destructive this blockade would be; for New London owed it's blockade & the depredations on it's coasts to the presence of a frigate sent there for it's defence: and did the frigate at Norfolk bring us defence or assault?[4]

II. Education. the President and Directors of the literary fund are desired to digest and report a system of public education comprehending the establishment of an University, additional Colleges or Academies and Schools. the resolution does not define the portions of science to be taught in each of these institutions: but the first and last admit no doubt. the University must be intended for all useful sciences; and the Schools mean Elementary ones, for the instruction of the people, answering to our present English schools. the middle term, Colleges or Academies may be more conjectural. but we must understand from it some middle grade of education. now, when we advert that the antient classical languages are considered as the foundation preparatory for all the sciences, that we have always had schools scattered over the country for teaching these languages, which often were the ultimate term of education; that these languages are entered on at the age of 9. or 10. years, at which age parents would be unwilling to send their children from every part of the state to a Central & distant University and when we observe that the resolution supposes there are to be a plurality of them, we may well conclude that the Greek & Latin are the objects of these Colleges. it is probable also that the legislature might have under their eye the Bill for the more general diffusion of knolege, printed in the Revised code of 1779. which proposed these 3. grades of institution, to wit an University, district Colleges, or Grammar schools, & County, or Ward schools. I think therefore we may say that the object of these Colleges is the classical languages, and that they are intended as the Portico of entry to the University. as to their numbers, I know no better rule to be assumed, than to place one within a day's ride of every man's door, in consideration of the infancy of the pledges he has at it. this would require one for every 80. miles square.

Supposing this the object of the Colleges, the Report will have to present the plan of an University, analysing the sciences, selecting those which are useful, grouping them into professorships commensurate each with the time and faculties of one man, and prescribing the regimen and all other necessary details.　　　on this subject I can offer nothing new. a letter of mine to Peter Carr, which was published during the last session of assembly is a digest of all the information I possess on the subject, from which the board will judge whether they can extract any thing useful; the professorships of the classical languages being of course to be expunged, as more effectually supplied by the establishment of the colleges.

As the buildings to be erected will also enter into their report I would strongly recommend to their consideration, instead of one immense building, to have a small one for every professorship, arranged at proper distances around a square, or rather three sides of a square, to admit extension, connected by a piazza so that they may go dry from one school to another. this village form is preferable to a single great building for many reasons, particularly on account of fire, health, economy, peace & quiet. such a plan had been approved in the case of the Albemarle college, which was the subject of the letter abovementioned; and should the idea be approved by the board more may be said hereafter on the opportunity these small buildings will afford, of exhibiting models in Architecture of the purest forms of antiquity, furnishing to the Student examples of the precepts he will be taught in that art.

The Elementary or Ward schools is the last branch of this subject. on this too my ideas have been long deposited in the Bill for the diffusion of knolege, beforementioned, and time & reflection have continued to strengthen them as to the general principle, that of a division of every county into wards, with a school in each ward. the details of the bill will of course be varied as the difference of present circumstances from those of that day will require.

My partiality for that division is not founded in views of education solely, but infinitely more as the means of a better administration of our government and the eternal preservation of it's republican principles. the example of this most admirable of all human contrivances in government is to be seen in our Eastern states; and it's powerful effect in the order and economy of their internal affairs, and the momentum it gives them as a nation, is the single circumstance which distinguishes them so remarkably from every other national association. in a letter to mr Adam[s] a few years ago I had occasion to explain to him the structure of our scheme of education as proposed in the bill for the diffusion of knolege, & the views of this particular section of it; and in another lately to mr Cabell on the occasion of the bill for the Albemarle College, I also took a view of the political effects of the proposed division into wards, which being more easily copied than thrown into new form here, I take the liberty of inclosing extracts from them. should the board of Directors approve of the plan, and make Ward divisions the substratum of their elementary schools, their report may furnish a happy occasion of introducing them, leaving all their other uses to be adopted from time to time hereafter as occasions shall occur.[5]

With these subjects I should close the present letter, but that it may be necessary to anticipate on the next one so far as respects proper persons for carrying into execution the Astronomical and

Geometrical surveys. I know no one in the state equal to the first who could be engaged in it; but my acquaintance in the state is very limited. there is a person near Washington possessing every quality which could be desired, among our first mathematicians and Astronomers, of good bodily activity, used to rough living, of great experience in field operations, and of the most perfect integrity. I speak of Isaac Briggs who was Surveyor general South of Ohio, and who was employed to trace the route from Washington to New Orleans, below the mountains, which he did with great accuracy by observations of Longitude and latitude only, on a journey thither. I do not know that he would undertake the present work—but I have learnt that he is at this time disengaged; I know he is poor, & was always moderate in his views. this is the most important of all the surveys, and if done by him, I will answer for this part of your work standing the test of time and criticism. if you should desire it, I could write and press him to undertake it: but it would be necessary to say something about compensation.

John Wood of the Petersburg academy has written to me that he would be willing to undertake the Geometrical survey of the external boundaries, and internal divisions. we have certainly no abler Mathematician, and he informs me he has had good experience in the works of the field. he is a great walker, and is therefore probably equal to the bodily fatigue, which is a material qualification. but he is so much better known where you are that I need only mention his readiness to undertake, and your own personal knolege or enquiries will best determine what should be done. it is the part of the work above the tide waters which he would undertake; that below, where soundings are to be taken requiring Nautical apparatus and practice.

Whether he is a mineralogist or not, I do not know. it would be a convenient and economical association with that of the Geometrical survey.

I am obliged to postpone for some days the consideration of the remaining subjects of your letter. Accept the assurance of my great esteem and high consideration   TH: JEFFERSON

PoC (DLC); edge trimmed; at foot of first page: "Govr Nicholas." Tr (ViU: TJP); posthumous extract by Nicholas P. Trist. Enclosures: (1) Extract from TJ to John Adams, 28 Oct. 1813. (2) Extract from TJ to Joseph C. Cabell, 2 Feb. 1816. (3) TJ's Notes on Popular Election of Juries, [ca. 2 Apr. 1816].

BOMBKETCHES are small, ketch-rigged vessels armed with one or two mortars (*OED*). TURTLES refers to David Bushnell's innovative but unsuccessful Revolutionary War submarine, the *Turtle* (note to George Hargraves to TJ, 4 Aug. 1814). FULTON SCOWS: during the War of 1812 Robert Fulton developed a steam-powered warship, but it did not see battle (*ANB*). Beginning in 1783 the French port of Cherbourg (CHERBURG) was enclosed by dikes to enhance its defensibility (*Le Petit Neptune Français; or, French Coasting Pilot* [London, 1793], 143–7).

In describing his ideas for the creation of artificial harbors on the MIDDLE GROUNDS, TJ called for a SURVEY OF THEM (TJ to Henry Dearborn, 31 Aug., 17 Oct. 1807 [DLC]). TJ's letters of MAY & JUNE 1813 were addressed to President James Madison on 21 May and 21 June 1813. SAWRA TOWNS: Saura Towns. 74ˢ were warships carrying seventy-four guns (*OED*). TJ's letter TO PETER CARR was dated 7 Sept. 1814.

[1] Preceding five words reworked from "Lynhaven bay."
[2] TJ here canceled "burnings of."
[3] TJ here canceled "idea is."
[4] Page 4 ends short at this point.
[5] Tr consists solely of this paragraph.

Notes on Popular Election of Juries

[ca. 2 Apr. 1816]

to the preceding Extracts I will add an observation. our republic is founded on the principle that the people are the source of all powers, & the safest depository of such as they are competent to exercise. their competency is principally restrained to the election of those who are to exercise powers over them. hence, in the Executive department, they chuse the Chief magistrate, indirectly. in the Legislature they chuse both branches directly. in the Judiciary, they are not competent to the appointment of judges of law, but they are of the judges of fact, that is, of Jurors. that every ward then should elect from among themselves, either for the year or pro hâc vice, a juror to serve in whatever court he may be allotted to, would be in exact analogy with this first principle of our government, and would perfect it's application, by carrying into the Judiciary department the same fundamental safeguard against systematic abuses of power or principle, as now exists in the Executive & Legislative authorities. in that branch too it is the more important as the Judges are found, practicably, irremovable. our Jurors, under both governments, are at present named by an officer holding at the will of the Executive, which certainly does not secure to the citizen as independant a jury as the choice of the people would.

PoC (DLC: TJ Papers, 199:35493); entirely in TJ's hand; undated; subjoined to PoCs of Trs of portions of TJ to John Adams, 28 Oct. 1813, and TJ to Joseph C. Cabell, 2 Feb. 1816, and enclosed with those extracts in TJ to Wilson Cary Nicholas, 2 Apr. 1816.

BOTH BRANCHES of the Virginia legislature were chosen by popular vote, which suggests that TJ wrote primarily with his own state in mind, although his subsequent reference to BOTH GOVERNMENTS also encompassed jurors at the federal level.

From Archibald Robertson

DEAR SIR   Lynchburg 3ʳᵈ April 1816

Your favor of the 28ᵗʰ ultᵒ enclosing a dft on Messʳˢ Gibson & Jefferson for $167–10. I received by last mail, the delay in receiving which has been no inconvenience and will answer our purposes as well as if it had been[1] received at the time appointed—

After the statement you have made of your present situation in money matters, nothing but necessity shall induce us to call on you before your next crop can be in market, which I hope will not be necessary

It will at all times give me pleasure to see you, and during your stay in the Forest will certainly call on you—I remain

Very Respectfully Your ob Sᵗ   A. ROBERTSON.

RC (MHi); endorsed by TJ as received 9 Apr. 1816 and so recorded in SJL. RC (MoSHi: TJC-BC); address cover only; with PoC of TJ to William Wingate, 4 May 1816, on verso; addressed: "Thomas Jefferson Esquire Monticello"; stamp canceled; franked; postmarked Lynchburg, 3 Apr.

[1] Manuscript: "been been."

Title and Prospectus for Destutt de Tracy's
Treatise on Political Economy

[ca. 6 Apr. 1816]

Title. 'A Treatise on Political Economy by the Count Destutt-Tracy, member of the Senate and Institute of France, and of the American Philosophical society, to which is prefixed a Supplement to a preceding work on the Understanding, or Elements of Ideology, by the same author, with an Analytical table, and an Introduction on the faculty of the will, translated from the unpublished French original.'

Prospectus.

Political economy, in modern times, assumed the form of a regular science first in the hands of the political sect in France called the Economists. they made it a branch only of a comprehensive system on the Natural order of societies. Quesnai first, Gournay, Le Trosne, Turgot, and Dupont de Nemours, the enlightened, philanthropic, and venerable citizen now of the United states, led the way in these developements, and gave to our enquiries the direction they have since observed. many sound and valuable principles, established by

[630]

them, have recieved the sanction of general approbation. some, as in the infancy of a science might be expected, have been brought into question, and have furnished occasion for much discussion. their opinions on Production, and on the proper subjects of Taxation have been particularly controverted: and whatever may be the merit of their principles of taxation it is not wonderful they have not prevailed; not on the questioned score of correctness, but because not acceptable to the people, whose will must be the supreme law. taxation is in fact the most difficult function of government, and that against which their citizens are most apt to be refractory. the general aim is therefore to adopt the mode most consonant with the circumstances and sentiments of the country.

Adam Smith, first in England, published a rational and systematic work on Political economy, adopting generally the ground of the Economists, but differing on the subjects before specified. the system being novel, much argument and detail seemed then necessary to establish principles which now are assented to as soon as proposed. hence his book, admitted to be able, and of the first degree of merit, has yet been considered as prolix & tedious.

In France, John Baptist Say has the merit of producing a very superior work on the subject of Political economy. his arrangement is luminous, ideas clear, style perspicuous, and the whole subject brought within half the volume of Smith's work. add to this considerable advances in correctness and extension of principles.

The work of Senator Tracy, now announced, comes forward with all the lights of his predecessors in the science, and with the advantages of further experience, more discussion, and greater maturity of subject. it is certainly distinguished by important traits; a cogency of logic which has never been exceeded in any work, a rigorous enchainment of ideas, and constant recurrence to it to keep it in the reader's view, a fearless pursuit of truth whithersoever it leads, and a diction so correct that not a word can be changed but for the worse; and, as happens in other cases, that the more a subject is understood, the more briefly it may be explained, he has reduced, not indeed all the details, but all the elements and the system of principles, within the compass of an 8vo of about 400. pages. indeed we might say within two thirds of that space, the one third being taken up with some[1] preliminary pieces now to be noticed.

Mr Tracy is the author of a treatise on the elements of Ideology, justly considered as a production of the first order in the science of our thinking faculty, or of the Understanding. considering the present work but as a second section to those Elements, under the titles of Analytical table Supplement, and Introduction, he gives, in these preliminary pieces a supplement to the Elements, shews how the present work stands on that as it's basis, presents a summary view of it, and, before entering on the formation, distribution, and employment of property, he investigates the question of the origin of the rights of property and personality, a question, not new indeed, yet one which has not hitherto been satisfactorily settled. these investigations are very metaphysical, profound and demonstrative, & will give satisfaction to minds in the habit of abstract speculation. readers however, not disposed to enter into them, after reading the summary view, entitled 'on our actions' will probably pass on at once to the commencement of the main subject of the work, which is treated of under the following heads;

Of Society.
of Production, or the formation of our riches.
of Value, or the measure of utility.
of Change of form, or Fabrication.
of Change of place, or Commerce.
of Money.
of the Distribution of our riches.
of Population.
of the Employment of our riches, or Consumption.
of Public revenue, Expences and Debts.

altho' the work now offered is but a translation, it may be considered in some degree as the original, that having never been published in the country in which it was written. the author would there have been submitted to the unpleasant alternative either of mutilating his sentiments, where they were either free or doubtful, or of risking himself under the unsettled regimen of their press. a manuscript copy communicated to a friend here has enabled him to give it to a country which is afraid to read nothing, and which may be trusted with any thing, so long as it's reason remains unfettered by law.

In the translation, fidelity has been chiefly consulted. a more correct style would sometimes have given a shade of sentiment which was not the author's, and which, in a work standing in the place of the original, would have been unjust towards him. some Gallicisms have therefore been admitted, where a single word gives an idea which would require a whole phrase of Dictionary-English. indeed the horrors of Neologism, which startle the purist, have given no alarm to the translator. where brevity, perspicuity, & even euphony can be promoted by the introduction of a new word, it is an improvement of the language. it is thus the English language has been brought to what it is; one half of it having been innovations, made at different times, from the Greek, Latin, French, & other languages. and is it the worse for these? had the preposterous idea of fixing the language been adopted in the time of our Saxon ancestors, of Pierce Plowman,[2] of Chaucer, of Spencer, the progress of ideas must have stopped with that of the progress of the language. on the contrary nothing is more evident than that as we advance in the knolege of new things, and of new combinations of old ones, we must have new words to express them. were Van-Helmont, Stahl, Scheele, to rise from the dead at this time, they would scarcely[3] understand one word of their own science. would it have been better then to have abandoned the science of Chemistry rather than admit innovations in it's terms?[4] what a wonderful accession of copiousness and force has the French language attained by the innovations of the last 30. years! and what do we not owe to Shakespear for the enrichment of the language by his free and magical creation of words? in giving a loose to neologism indeed, uncouth words will sometimes be offered: but the public will judge them, and recieve or reject, as sense or sound shall suggest, & authors will be approved or condemned according to the use they make of this licence, as they now are from their use of the present vocabulary. the claim of the present translation however is limited to it's duties of fidelity & justice to the sense of it's original; adopting the author's own word only where no term of our own language would convey his meaning.

FC (DLC: TJ Papers, 206:36786–7); entirely in TJ's hand; undated. Printed with variations in spelling, capitalization, and punctuation in Destutt de Tracy, *Treatise on Political Economy*, iii–vii. Enclosed in TJ to Joseph Milligan, 6 Apr. 1816.

The Vision of Piers Plowman (PIERCE PLOWMAN) was a fourteenth-century poem by the English author William Langland (*ODNB*).

[1] Word not in printed *Treatise*.
[2] Printed *Treatise* incorrectly inserts a comma between preceeding two words.
[3] Word interlined in place of "not."
[4] Word interlined in place of "style."

Note for Destutt de Tracy's
Treatise on Political Economy

[ca. 6 Apr. 1816]

A Note communicated to the Editor. Our author's classification of taxes being taken from those practised in France, will scarcely be intelligible to an American reader, to whom the nature as well as names of some of them must be unknown. the taxes with which we are familiar class themselves readily according to the bases on which they rest. 1. Capital. 2. Income. 3. Consumption. these may be considered as commensurate; Consumption being generally equal to Income; and Income the annual profit of Capital. a government may select either of these bases for the establishment of it's system of taxation, and so frame it as to reach the faculties of every member of the society, and to draw from him his equal proportion of the public contributions. and if this be correctly obtained, it is the perfection of the function of taxation but when once a government has assumed it's basis, to select and tax special articles from either of the other classes is double taxation. for example, if the system be established on the basis of Income, and his just proportion on that scale has been already drawn from every one, to step into the field of consumption, and tax special articles in that, as broadcloth or homespun, wine or whiskey, a coach or a waggon, is doubly taxing the same article. for that portion of Income, with which these articles are purchased, having already paid it's tax as Income, to pay another tax on the thing it purchased, is paying twice for the same thing. it is an aggrievance on the citizens who use these articles in exoneration of those who do not, contrary to the most sacred of the duties of a government, to do equal & impartial justice to all it's citizens.

How far it may be the interest and the duty of all to submit to this sacrifice on other grounds, for instance, to pay for a time an impost on the importation of certain articles, in order to encourage their manufacture at home, or an Excise on others injurious to the morals or health of the citizens, will depend on a series of[1] considerations of another order, and beyond the proper limits of this note. the reader, in deciding which basis of taxation is most eligible for the local circumstances of his country, will of course avail himself of the weighty observations of our author.

FC (DLC: TJ Papers, 206:36788); entirely in TJ's hand; undated; with FC of TJ's Addition to his Note for Destutt de Tracy's *Treatise on Political Economy*, [ca. 18 May 1816], on verso. Printed with variations in spelling, capitalization, and punctuation in Destutt de Tracy, *Treatise on Political Economy*, 202. Enclosed in TJ to Joseph Milligan, 6 Apr. 1816.

[1] Manuscript: "of of."

From William McIlhenney

Sir   Philad[a] April 6. 1816

I take the liberty of submitting to your consideration some remarks on perception, which altho' they throw no light on that mysterious faculty may tend to shew the errors which arise from the use of indefinite terms. I particularly[1] allude to the use of the word image in explaining vision.

I shall remark that our knowledge of each of the senses is alike limited, and when rigidly examined will be found to consist of but a few facts derived from sensation and experience. The first conclusion formed by the human mind appears to be that every change must proceed from some cause. whenever we perceive a change we are excited to the discovery of the cause (as each new sensation must necessarily interest a sensitive being) and to the cause when discovered (or beleived so to be) we give a name; and in common language we say[2] we perceive the object, when in fact we are only conscious of a new[3] perception or change, which we from reason or experience conclude is occasioned by a certain object.   Thus when absolute stillness is interrupted, we say we hear something; more correctly we have a perception of the ear which we conclude must proceed from some cause—if upon examination we can find that this effect is connected with a tremulous[4] body of a certain form, we give that body a name, and then say I hear a Bell—when in fact we are only conscious of a perception—

When a change is produced in the appearance of the æther or surrounding medium, we have a new sensation which we call colour, accompanied by outline, we seek in like manner for the cause, and discovering reflecting bodies by touch[5] we distinguish them by names and then say, I see a man, or a tree, or something; when in fact we have only a perception of change by the eye, which we have learned to proceed from rays of light reflected by surfaces capable of reflection—

When we attempt to move the hand and experience resistance, we have a new sensation and discovering the resisting body give it a name, and then say I feel a ball or spoon, when in fact we have only a sensation which we have learned proceeds from a body of a certain form. The same in taste.

M[r] Hume understanding the expression "I see a table" literally has shewn its absurdity by proving the change of apparent magnitude, whereas if he had considered it as used figuratively (the cause for the

effect) he would have perceived that by the laws of light those variations of <u>apparent</u> magnitude were the necessary result of reflection
from the <u>same</u> real magnitude in different angles. He has therefore
substituted the word <u>image</u> or <u>picture</u> as the cause of perception, and
endeavours to weaken the belief of real existences, and introduce
Phantoms in their place.   I shall now shew that the words
<u>image</u> and <u>picture</u> are without meaning, <u>and like the Nymph Echo</u>,
have but a <u>nominal</u> existence—we shall be obliged therefore to return
to the old theory of external objects being the causes of our perceptions, and, without explaining[6] the modus operandi, be content to say
the Author of nature has <u>so willed</u> it.

"It is a law of our nature, says Dr Ried, established by the will of
the Supreme Being, that we perceive no external object, but by
means of the organs given us for that purpose. We know how the eye
forms a <u>picture</u> of the visible object on the <u>retina</u>; but how this <u>pic-
ture</u> makes us see the object we know not—" "we <u>know</u> that in vision
an <u>image</u> of the visible object is formed in the bottom of the eye by the
rays of light." It is unnecessary for me to make further quotations
from this author to shew that by <u>image</u> or <u>picture</u> he understood
something different from the <u>object</u> and the <u>perception</u>—many other
authors have expressly stated this as their conception, for they have
enquired how it is that we see an object single when an image is
formed in <u>each</u> eye, or erect[7] when the <u>images</u> are inverted. When
they thus speak of <u>two images</u> and <u>inverted</u>, while they admit that the
object is both really and by perception single and erect, they must of
necessity speak of some thing intervening between the <u>object</u> and
<u>perception</u>; and this they call an <u>image</u> or <u>picture</u>.

Is it true, as asserted by these authors, that in vision an <u>image</u> of
the visible object is (in any sense) formed in the bottom of the eye.
We are not conscious of the existence of such an object. But it may be
said it has been proved by the following experiment. "Take a bullock's eye while it is fresh, and having cut off the three coats from the
back part, quite to the vitreous humour put a piece of white paper
over that part and hold it to any coloured object, you will see an <u>in-
verted picture</u> of the object <u>upon the paper</u>"[8]—Is there in <u>fact</u> any
thing upon the <u>paper</u>?—does the paper do any more than receive and
transmit rays of light from the coloured object, and these rays being
converged and <u>crossed</u> before passing to the eye, must they not of necessity, from the laws of vision, change the apparent <u>position</u> of the
body? When we look at an object thro' a convex glass the apparent
magnitude[9] is changed, yet we say we see the object, and not a picture of it. But when we see an object in a reflecting mirror we then

fancy we see a picture, altho nothing exists on the surface of the mirror, and the only difference[10] is that by reflecting the rays from the opposed body, the apparent position is changed.

The question why impressions on two eyes, or two ears, or many nerves of sensation, produce single perceptions, may be answered when we discover how our perceptions and sensations are connected, and the mode of communication between mind and body— This will I believe allways remain among the arcana of nature—Philosophers having fancied they had discovered the cause of complete perception in each eye, thought it necessary to account for the single effect resulting from two causes—Take away the doctrine of images altogether, and you save the time and ingenuity wasted on a frivolous question.

It will follow from this analysis that we do not, strictly[11] speaking, perceive external objects by any of the senses, and that their existence is a conclusion of the understanding from sensations—It will of course remain a question of innocent speculation whether Berkly's theory be true or false—It is not difficult to determine whether his Guess has more of probability than the common sense of mankind.

I shall be much indebted to you for your opinion on this subject; and if you should find any thing new, I trust in your hands it may become of importance. you will not be surprised that the word image has been so long suffered to impose on the world, when the word idea has from the time of Aristotle until Dr Ried been used to express a real existence—

I am respectfully Your obt ser^t WM M^{c}ILHENNEY J^R

It is my particular request that whether you consider this letter worthy of notice or not, you would do me the favour of destroying it immediately on perusing it. Were I not an entire stranger to you and sure of remaining so, I should not [have][12] the confidence to submit my Crude thoughts to your notice.

RC (MHi); dateline between signature and postscript; addressed: "Thomas Jefferson Esquire Montecello Virginia"; franked; postmarked Philadelphia, 6 Apr.; endorsed by TJ as received 3 May 1816 and so recorded in SJL.

William McIlhenney (ca. 1779–1854), attorney and diplomat, received an A.B. from the University of Pennsylvania in 1797. In 1820 he became the librarian of the Athenæum of Philadelphia, and in 1823 he was chosen as its secretary, holding both positions for the rest of his life. For at least a decade starting in 1839, McIlhenney was consul for Venezuela at Philadelphia (*University of Pennsylvania: Biographical Catalogue of the Matriculates of the College, 1749–1893* [1894], 39; *The Charter, By-Laws, and Seventy-Fifth Annual Report of the Athenæum of Philadelphia, to which is prefixed A Sketch of its History* [1890], 61; *A. M'Elroy's Philadelphia Directory for 1839* [1839], 324; *McElroy's Philadelphia Directory for 1849* [1849], 238).

David HUME explored ideas of space, time, and perception in the section "of the understanding" that constituted the first volume of his work, *A Treatise of Human Nature: being An Attempt to introduce the experimental Method of Reasoning into Moral Subjects*, 3 vols. (London, 1739). The NYMPH ECHO was said to have refused the attentions of the god Pan, who caused her death by sending mad shepherds to attack her. The earth absorbed her body, but her voice lingered (*OCD*, 502). McIlhenney quotes from Thomas Reid (RIED), *Essays on the Intellectual Powers of Man* (Edinburgh, 1785), 103, 104. The experiment using a BULLOCK's EYE appeared in numerous scientific works, including James Ferguson, *Lectures on Select Subjects in Mechanics, Hydrostatics, Pneumatics, and Optics* (London, 1760; Sowerby, no. 3735), 223. George Berkeley's (BERKLY'S) work, *An Essay Towards a New Theory of Vision* (Dublin, 1709), examined the psychology of perception.

[1] Manuscript: "particulary."
[2] Preceding two words interlined.
[3] Word interlined.
[4] Word interlined.
[5] Preceding two words interlined.
[6] Word interlined.
[7] Manuscript: "errect."
[8] Omitted closing quotation mark editorially supplied.
[9] Manuscript: "magnitudes."
[10] Word interlined in place of "effect."
[11] Manuscript: "strickly."
[12] Omitted word editorially supplied.

To Joseph Milligan

SIR   Monticello Apr. 6. 16.

Your favor of Mar. 6. did not come to hand until the 15th. I then expected I should finish revising the translation of Tracy's book within a week, and could send the whole together. I got thro' it, but on further consideration thought I ought to read it over again, lest any errors should have been left in it. it was fortunate I did so, for I found several little errors. the whole is now done and forwarded by this mail, with a Title, and something I have written which may serve for a Prospectus, and indeed for a Preface also with a little alteration. you will see by the face of the work what a horrible job I have had in the revisal. it is so defaced that it is absolutely necessary you should have a fair copy taken, and by a person of good understanding. for that will be necessary to decypher the erasures, interlineations E[t]c of the translation. the translator's orthography too will need great correction, as you will find a multitude of words shamefully mispelt, and he seems to have had no idea of the use of stops. he uses the comma very commonly for a full stop, and as often the full stop, followed by a capital letter for a comma. your copyist will therefore have to stop it properly quite thro' the work. still there will be places where it cannot be stopped correctly without reference to the original. for I observed many instances where a member of a sentence might be given either to the preceding or following one, grammatically, which would yet make the sense very different, and could therefore be rectified only by the original. I have therefore thought it would be better for you to send me the proof sheets as they come out of the press. we have two mails a week which leave this Wednesdays & Saturdays and you should always recieve it by return of the first mail. only observe that I set out for Bedford in 5. or 6. days and shall not be back till the first week in May.

The original construction of the style of the translation was so bungling that altho' I have made it render the author's sense faithfully, yet it was impossible to change the structure of the sentences[1] to any thing good. I have endeavored to apologise for it in the prospectus; as also to prepare the reader for the dry, and to most of them, uninteresting character of the preliminary tracts, advising him to pass at once to the beginning of the main work, where also you will see I have recommended the beginning the principal series of pages. in this I have departed from the order of pages adopted by the author.

My name must in no wise appear connected with the work. I have no objection to your naming me, in conversation, but not in print, as the person to whom the original was communicated. altho' the author puts his name to the work, yet, if called to account for it by his government he means to disavow it, which it's publication at such a distance will enable him to do. but he would not think himself at liberty to do this if avowedly sanctioned by me here. the best open mark of approbation I can give is to subscribe for a dozen copies; or if you would prefer it, you may place on your subscription paper a letter in these words. 'Sir, I subscribe with pleasure for a dozen copies of the invaluable book you are about to publish on Political economy. I should be happy to see it in the hands of every American citizen. Th Jefferson.'

The Ainsworth, Ovid, Cornelius Nepos & Virgil came safely. I shall be glad of another copy of the same edition of Virgil as also of the 2. books below mentioned, & formerly written for. I fear I shall not get the Ovid and Nepos I sent to be bound, in time for the pocket in my Bedford trip. Accept my best wishes and respects.

TH: JEFFERSON

Moore's greek grammar translated by Ewen.
Mair's Tyro's dictionary.

PoC (DLC); on reused address cover to TJ; at foot of first page: "Mr Joseph Milligan." Enclosures: (1) TJ's Title and Prospectus for Destutt de Tracy's *Treatise on Political Economy*, [ca. 6 Apr. 1816]. (2) TJ's Note for Destutt de Tracy's *Treatise on Political Economy*, [ca. 6 Apr. 1816].

The revised translation FORWARDED BY THIS MAIL has not been found. For background on this French-language manuscript and TJ's role in its subsequent publication as Destutt de Tracy, *Treatise on Political Economy*, see Destutt de Tracy to TJ, 15 Nov. 1811, and note. Although TJ here specified that MY NAME MUST IN NO WISE APPEAR CONNECTED WITH THE WORK, he later agreed to public acknowledgement of his involvement with the translation and publication (TJ to Milligan, 25 Oct. 1818, first and second letters).

[1] Reworked from "senses."

To Thomas Ritchie

DEAR SIR   Monticello Apr. 6. 16.

I have really placed myself in a very mortifying situation before you with respect to Tracy's book. I shall state the case. when I recieved information from mr Duane that he could not print it, mr Millegan of Georgetown happened to be here. I proposed to him to undertake it, and promised, if he would, that I would revise the translation. he agreed to it, and the more readily as he said Duane had before proposed it to him. he promised to write for the translation, & to forward it to me. he did not however do it; and on my writing to Duane for the original, he sent me both that and the translation. some months elapsed before I could enter on the revisal. after I had got one fourth through, I wrote to Millegan that, if he was ready, I would send that part to him and be sure to forward [the remainder?] as fast as he could print, and I pressed for an answer by return of mail. I did this because he had not, in the first instance, asked the translation from Duane, and for 6. months before that I had been writing letters to him as a bookseller[1] on other matters of business, and had never got an answer. I began to give credit to suggestions I had heard of his faultering in business from embarrasments & ill habits, and I concluded he had abandoned the design altogether. I then wrote to you my letter of Mar. 8. and took his abandonment so much for granted that I did not even mention the transaction to you in that letter. there was my fault; of which I became sensible on recieving a letter from him a week after, pressing me to forward the translation immediately; that his types were in readiness, and would be kept unemployed until he should recieve it. I was really mortified at the situation my incaution had led me into; and altho' his tardiness and silence were the cause, yet considering his right of contract, I thought my self bound to send him the work. I regretted it the more, as I had infinitely rather you should have edited it because, in the mutilated state of the translation, it will require more than common abilities to publish it correctly. to yourself perhaps it will be of less disappointment, as I could not have had my name in any way connected with the publication, which you seemed to expect. this would have defeated the author's resort to a disavowal of the work in the event of his being called to account for it by his own government, which he wrote me was his purpose. besides, after every thing I could do with the translation, the original structure of it was so abominable, that altho' I have made it faithful, it was impossible to make it passable in point of style. I hope you will see in this business only a want of caution on my part, in not apprising you of a previous claim which I too hastily supposed relinquished, and that all circumstances considered, your regret will be less than mine that the work does not go from your press. with this apology for my fault accept the assurance of my constant esteem and respect.   TH: JEFFERSON

PoC (DLC); on reused address cover to TJ; damaged at crease; at foot of first page: "Mr Thomas Ritchie"; endorsed by TJ.

[1] Preceding three words interlined.

From Jesse Torrey

DEAR SIR,   Washington April 6, 1816.

In compliance with an intention* which I have many years entertained, and also with the advice of one of the Editors† of the National Intelligencer, I now use the freedom of presenting for your consideration, my proposed scheme of a universal and economical system for the general dissemination of knowledge and moral improvement in the United States, through the medium of <u>free</u> Libraries.

The expression of your sentiments, when convenient, on the suggestions[1] relative to this subject, contained in the accompanying publication, would be received as a particular favor, by your most obedient servant and friend,   JESSE TORREY JN^R

*The object of carrying this intention into effect, by communicating with you personally on the subject, formed a great share of the inducements which led me to visit your residence at Monticello, in August last. But from your having declined an investigation of the physiological problems, which I proposed to suggest, and from your being under an engagement to ride from home soon, I conceived it to be improper to introduce the subject at that moment, or to obtrude a proposal for a second call; and therefore concluded to defer the execution of my purpose to a future period.
†Mr Seaton.

RC (MHi); at foot of text: "Thomas Jefferson Esqr"; endorsed by TJ as received 3 May 1816 and so recorded in SJL. RC (Mrs. T. Wilber Chelf, Mrs. Virginius Dabney, and Mrs. Alexander W. Parker, Richmond, 1944; photocopy in ViU: TJP); address cover only; with PoC of TJ to Patrick Gibson, 15 May 1816, on verso; addressed: "Thomas Jefferson Esqr Monticello Virg—."

The enclosed work, written by Torrey under the pseudonym "Discipulus Libertatis atque Humanitatis (Pupil of Liberty and Humanity.)," was *The Intellectual Flambeau, demonstrating that National Happiness, Virtue & Temperance exist, in a Collateral Ratio, with the Dissemination of Philosophy, Science & Intelligence, with* *an Appendix, containing several Splendid Poems on the Advantages of Mental Improvement, and on Charity* (Washington, 1816; Poor, *Jefferson's Library*, 9 [no. 489]). It argued that a public system of Lancasterian schools and FREE LIBRARIES should be underwritten by taxes on strong alcoholic beverages, thereby *"extracting the greatest Good from the worst Evil"* (p. 100).

[1] Word interlined in place of "propositions."

From John Wood

SIR   Richmond 6th April 1816

I received your favour of the 1st instant yesterday in Petersburg; and I beg leave to return my sincere thanks for the favourable opinion you are pleased to express of my qualifications. Having had occasion to come to Richmond to day, I waited upon the Governor in order to receive some information in regard to the contemplated survey of Virginia.

The Governor informed me, that it is the intention of the Executive to have the river and coast line surveyed, with those portions of the other external Boundaries which have not been yet accurately ascertained. With regard to the operations above Tide water, the Governor seems to be of opinion that the Legislature only contemplated having a survey executed of the principal ranges of Mountains, and not those of an insulated nature or of an inferior description

With respect to the method which ought to be adopted in order to accomplish the survey above Tide water; I am of opinion that the geometrical admeasurement will in some instances be found preferable, and the barometrical in others. Where good base lines can be found I would use the geometrical, and when the summits of mountains are accessible without much difficulty; I should prefer the barometrical. M[r] de Luc of Geneva who has the merit of bringing the barometrical measurements to perfection, made a survey of the principal mountains of Savoy and Switzerland both with the Theodolite and the Barometer. The use of the later instrument he seems in most cases to prefer. General Roy the celebrated British Engineer as also Sir George Shuckburg give also the preference to the Barometer as a more expeditious instrument, although in their time it was not brought to its present correctness.

As to the instruments to be used above Tide water; besides Barometers, a Theodolite, Hadleys Sextant, and surveying chain will be sufficient. The Theodolite to be used for the Terrestrial observations and the Hadley's sextant for the Latitudes and Longitudes. A Hadley's Sextant alone will answer in many instances on land; for when the objects are at a considerable distance; the error which the Glasses occasion in the measurement of angles is trifling. A circumferentor would answer the purpose of horizontal angles; but as the Theodolite is calculate to measure both horizontal and vertical Angles, I think it is the most convenient instrument.—

To accomplish the survey of the River and Sea coast line I am of opinion that a good Surveyor's Compass, a Gunters Chain and a Hadleys Sextant will be the only necessary instruments The distances & courses can easily be obtained by the Compass & Chain— The Latitudes & Longitudes of the principal points on the sea coast will be discovered by the sextant. The fewer instruments that are used provided they will effect the purpose will render the survey much easier in its execution and less expensive to the state.

In addition to those operations which you have mentioned; I beg leave to suggest the propriety of adding perspective representations of the principal ridges of mountains, the most remarkable insulated mountains & views of the windings of the several rivers and other natural objects of importance in the state. Engravings of these might be annexed at each end of the map. They would be interesting to many persons who are satisfied with having a representation of the general appearance of a country without investigating the particulars.—

The Governor thinks that it will be necessary to employ four principal surveyors to execute the several objects which the act of the Legislature contemplates. For my own I should be desirous of being employed either in the operations which regard the mountains; or in the survey of the River and sea coast line as may seem to be the wish of the Executive I shall esteem it[1] a favour therefore if you would inform the Governor that I shall be happy to give my services to accomplish either of these objects and that I am desirous that the work should be commenced, as soon as he may deem expedient. for in Surveys of this description the earlier in the season they are begun the more favourable to those who are engaged in them.

I request you will accept my most grateful thanks for the desire you have expressed to espouse my cause with the Executive and believe me to be

Sir with esteem & respect your most obedient Servant

JOHN WOOD—

N. B. I have no farther knowledge of mineralogy than what I acquired by attending the Classes of Chemistry & Natural History in the University of Edinburg, and the opportunities[2] which my pedestrian journies among the Alps of Switzerland & Savoy afforded me.

RC (DLC); between signature and postscript: "Thomas Jefferson Esqr"; endorsed by TJ as received 9 Apr. 1816 and so recorded in SJL.

[1] Manuscript: "I shall it esteem it."
[2] Manuscript: "opportunies."

From Giovanni Carmignani

CHIARISSIMO SIGNORE   Pisa 7. Aple 1816

Filippo Mazzei che si onorava dell'amicizia Sua ha cessato di vivere nel 19. del decorso mese di marzo. Egli ha lasciata una figlia ed una moglie superstiti. Ha conferita a quest'ultima la tutela dla figlia attualmente costituita in età minore, ed a me la curatela dla tutrica

Uno degli assegnamenti di qualche rilievo di questa famiglia è il credito di resto di prezzo di una tenuta che Ella, chiarissimo Signore, vendè costì ℔ conto ed interesse del defonto Mazzei. Questa famiglia raccomanda all'ottimo suo cuore, ed all'amicizia che Ella nutriva per il defonto, il Sollecito incasso di questo prezzo, e la trasmissione di esso per sicuro canale a Livorno.

Debto ad una circostanza dolorosa[1] ed infausta la occasione e l'onore di rivolgermi ad un'uomo il di cui nome è citato con venerazione ℔ tutto ove la dignità della natura umana è Sentita.

Raccomandando alla pietà Sua uno dè più forti interessi d'una desolata famiglia io ho l'onore di essere con alta, e invariabile Stima

Di Lei chiariss. Sig^e

Umiliss. Divotiss. Obb. Servitore   GIOVANNI CARMIGNANI

EDITORS' TRANSLATION

DEAR SIR   Pisa 7. April 1816

Philip Mazzei, who was honored by your friendship, died on the nineteenth of this past month of March. He is survived by his daughter and wife. He has conferred on the latter the guardianship of the daughter, currently a minor, and to me the care of the guardian.

One of the sizable assets of this family is the net income from the sale of a holding that you, dear Sir, sold on behalf and in the interest of the deceased Mazzei. Relying on your benevolence and the friendship that you nourished for the deceased, this family requests a quick collection of this sum and its transmission via a secure channel to Leghorn.

I owe to a painful and unfortunate circumstance the occasion and honor of turning to a man whose name is cited with veneration wherever human dignity is appreciated.

Recommending to your mercy one of the most important assets of a desolated family, I have the honor to be with high and unwavering esteem
Dear Sir
Your very humble devoted obliging servant

GIOVANNI CARMIGNANI

RC (MoSHi: TJC-BC); dateline beneath closing, with "Thomas Jefferson esquire" below that; with attestation on verso, dated 16 Apr. 1816, in an unidentified hand, signed by Giuseppe Maria Pazienza, auditor for the governor of Pisa, and Francesco Furiosi, chancellor; followed by Governor Niccolo Viviani's 16 Apr. 1816 attestation of Pazienza's and Furiosi's signatures; with attestation of Viviani's signature by Thomas Appleton, dated 15 Apr. 1816, on a separate sheet; with additional notes by TJ on verso of Appleton's attestation: "Professor of Law in the Imperial University of Pisa, and Advocate in the courts of Florence"; endorsed by TJ as received 20 June 1816 and so recorded in SJL. Dupl (DLC); at foot of text: "Sig: Tommaso Jefferson"; with attestations identical to those on RC, except that Appleton's is dated 20 Apr. 1816; endorsed by TJ as received 29 Aug. 1816 and so recorded in SJL. Translation by Dr. Jonathan T. Hine. Enclosed in Appleton to TJ, 15 Apr., 15 May 1816.

Giovanni Carmignani (1768–1847), attorney, educator, and writer, was born near Pisa, graduated with a law degree from the University of Pisa in 1790 and established a practice in Florence. Although he published an essay defending the death penalty in 1795, he later retracted that position, even refusing a judgeship in 1808 because of his opposition to capital punishment. Carmignani became a professor of public law at the University of Pisa, taught criminal law for much of his career, and in 1840 assumed a new professorship in legal philosophy at Pisa. He published journal essays and works on criminal law, legal history, and literature. Carmignani wrote Philip Mazzei's epitaph (*Cause Celebri Discusse dal Cav. Commendatoré Giovanni Carmignani Professore dell' I. e R. Università di Pisa Socio di Più Accademie Italiane e Straniere* [1843]; *Dizionario Biografico degli Italiani* [1960–], 20:415–21; Mazzei, *Writings*, 3:471–2).

[1] RC: "circostanza e dolorosa." Dupl: "circostanza dolorosa."

To Nicolas G. Dufief

DEAR SIR   Monticello April 7. 16.

I have too long neglected to remit you the amount of your account, which I believe is 24. D 68 c the reason has been that I wished to have made up a little catalogue of wants in the same way which has not yet been done; and being about setting out on a journey of a month's absence, I must defer my catalogue, but in the mean time inclose you an order on mr Vaughan for the above sum. Accept the assurance of my great esteem and respect   TH: JEFFERSON

RC (NNPM); at foot of text: "M. Dufief." PoC (DLC); endorsed by TJ. Enclosure not found.

In an account dated 30 Aug. 1815 (MS in DLC: TJ Papers, 204:36419; written in Dufief's and TJ's hands on a small scrap; endorsed by TJ: "Dufief. N. G.") Dufief noted TJ's purchase of "Ovidii Opera" for $2.75. Beneath this amount TJ wrote the sum of $21.93 to settle an account Dufief had enclosed to him on 25 Aug. 1815. TJ added the two figures to arrive at the total of 24. D 68 C that he owed Dufief, and he concluded with a notation at foot of text: "1816. Apr. 7. gave order for 24.68 on John Vaughan."

In his financial records TJ indicated that the order on Vaughan in favor of Dufief covered the "balance due him for books" (*MB*, 2:1321).

To LeRoy, Bayard & McEvers

GENTLEMEN   Monticello Apr. 7. 16.

I recieved, by our last mail only, your favor of Mar. 19. reminding me of a very ancient and very just debt to Messrs Van Staphorsts, and which I ought certainly long ago to have replaced to them, unasked. but, engaged constantly in offices of more expence than compensation, our means are ever absorbed as soon as recieved by the needy who press, while the indulgent lie over for a moment of greater convenience. yet ancient and just as is this debt, it presents itself at a moment when I am not prepared to meet it. I am a land holder, and depend on the income of my farms. three years of war & close blockade of the Chesapeak compleatly sunk the produce of those three years, and the year of peace which has followed has barely met arrearages and taxes. commerce and free markets being now restored to us, we may count on the future with more certainty. I shall be able to pay off one of my bonds at the date of a year from this time, and one other each year after until the three are discharged. I hope that this arrangement will be acceptable to Messrs Van Staphorsts, and that their indulgence will not be withdrawn suddenly and all at once. with the forbearance I ask, I shall replace their money from annual income which I can spare, and be saved the regret of injuriously mutilating my landed property.   it will give me great pleasure to learn that the measure of kindness hitherto shewn, will be filled up by so much further forbearance, as will make it in the end, as it was in the beginning, a[1] salutary accomodation. Accept the assurance of my great esteem & respect   TH: JEFFERSON

PoC (DLC); on verso of reused address cover of David Gelston to TJ, 8 Jan. 1816; mutilated at seal, with several words rewritten by TJ; at foot of text: "Messrs Leroy & co."; endorsed by TJ.

[1] Manuscript: "a a."

To John Tayloe Lomax

[Dea]r Sir   Monticello Apr. 7. 16
Your favor of Mar. 11. is just now [re]cieved.[1] on the death of mr
Wayles, I sorted and arranged the whole of his papers, but the revolutionary troubles commencing immediately after, I was called off,
and the whole papers were kept by mr Eppes, and the entire settlement of the affairs of the estate left to him. I think it very certain,
from recollection, that there was not a single lottery ticket among mr
Wayles's papers; however those papers are all [in] the possession of
mr Archibald Thweatt, son in law of mr Eppes. [...] [re]siding at mr
Eppes's seat, Eppington, to whom if you will [be so go]od as to address the enquiry, it can be answered with more certainty. do me the
favor to present me respectfully to mrs Lomax your mother and family, and to accept the assurance of my great esteem and respect.
                                                    Th: Jefferson

PoC (MHi); on verso of reused address   [1] Word faint.
cover to TJ; edge trimmed; torn at seal;
at foot of text: "John Tayloe Lomax esq.";
endorsed by TJ.

To Josiah Meigs

                                        Monticello April 7. 16.
    I have referred asking the favor of you to return my thanks to D[r]
Drake for the copy of his account of the state of Ohio which he has
been so kind as to send me until I could ha[ve] time to peruse it. I
have done this with great pleasure and may now express my gratification on this able additio[n] to the knolege we possess of our different states; and I may say with truth that were all of them as well
delineated as that which is the subject of this volume, we should be
mor[e] accurately and scientifically known to the rest of the world[.]
with my thanks for this mark of attention be pleased to accept the
assurance of my great esteem & respect.   Th: Jefferso[n]

PoC (DLC); several line endings cut off due to polygraph malfunction; at foot of
text: "Josiah Meigs esq."; endorsed by TJ.

To William Short

DEAR SIR   Monticello Apr. 7. 16.

I have to acknolege your favor of Mar. 14. and will answer it's several enquiries. le mot de l'enigme as to the boundary of the land is that Monroe's land lies North of yours. you must recollect on being reminded that your land adjoined Blenheim, Monroe's joined Colle and my lands. mr Carter not being considered as a party direct, and having formerly shewn no disposition to attend personally, but rather to acquiesce in any impartial decision, was not notified to attend. he is a man of perfect candor; and will himself recollect & admit all the facts of the case; that he had previously sold to Monroe by a particular boundary, that that boundary was unknown to us, that he attended the survey, and went before the Surveyor, shewing the boundary himself, and according to the quantity found within that line by the Surveyor, recieved 23/6 an acre for it. the last payment was made by a draught on John Barnes in Philadelphia June 6. 1795. which of course being the overpayment, the interest must run from the reciept of that. I have no doubt that on your writing to mr Carter & giving him some time, suppose 9. or 12. months, which will admit the sale of his growing crop, he will send you his bond. when that becomes due you had better inclose it for collection to John W. Green at Fredericksbg[1] a respectable attorney who attends Culpeper court, and a most excellent man, and he will recieve and remit you the money without trouble or delay. I paid your share of the costs of survey & witnesses 5.D. which you can put into the hands of mr Vaughan who is kind enough to recieve & pay my little concerns in Philadelphia.   I wrote urgently to Monroe on behalf of La Motte. he answers me in terms of the strongest friendship to La Motte but observes that a mr Barnett has been long the incumbent, and may perhaps chuse to return to it; and that there are very numerous applications for all these places from officers of the army and navy of great merit, and the current of disposition entirely in their favor. I am therefore apprehensive that between Barnet & the military competitors La Motte's chance is weak.   I set out in 3. or 4. days for Bedford to be absent a month. accept the assurance of my constant affection & respect.   TH: JEFFERSON

RC (ViW: TJP); at foot of first page: "Mr Short"; endorsed by Short as received 15 Apr.

Only the address cover of Short's

FAVOR OF MAR. 14. has been found (RC in MHi; with PoC of TJ to William Thornton, 20 May 1816, on verso; addressed: "Thomas Jefferson Monticello Mail to Milton Va"; franked; postmarked

Philadelphia, 14 Mar.; recorded in SJL as received 25 Mar. 1816 from Philadelphia).

LE MOT DE L'ENIGME: "the answer to the riddle." For the DRAUGHT ON JOHN BARNES, see *PTJ*, 28:381, 383.

TJ probably enclosed here a receipt showing his payment of Short's SHARE OF THE COSTS OF SURVEY & WITNESSES,

dated 4 Mar. 1816: "Received of Thomas Jefferson Esqʳ Five dollars in full for Surveying the land in dispute between Colᵒ Jaˢ Monroe & Wᵐ Short Esqʳⁿ" (MS in ViW: TJP; written on a scrap in William Woods's hand and signed by him).

¹ Preceding two words interlined.

To John Vaughan

[DE]AR SIR   Monticello Apr. 7. 16.

Your favor of Mar. 13. has been duly recieved. I forwarded to mr Appleton a duplicate of the letter I inclosed to you by a gentleman going direct to Paris, from whence he would forward it to Leghorn.   owing to mr Dufief a balance of 24. D 68 c I have taken the liberty of inclosing him a draught on you for that sum.   you will perhaps have seen that our late legislature has taken up the subject of public improvement with great spirit, and I hope they will pursue it. an University for the sciences, district colleges for classical education, and elementary schools in every county, Astronomical, geometrical, topographical, & mineralogical surveys of the state, with roads [and] canals are provided for. all this undertaken while [...] paying five times higher taxes than ever were paid in the st[ate] before, shews that the spirit of the state is roused, and taking an excellent direction. ever & affectionately your's

TH: JEFFERSON

PoC (MHi); on verso of reused address cover of Joseph Miller to TJ, 29 Feb. 1816; salutation faint; mutilated at seal; at foot of text: "John Vaughan esq."; endorsed by TJ.

The GENTLEMAN GOING DIRECT TO PARIS was Dabney C. Terrell.

To John Adams

DEAR SIR   Monticello Apr. 8. 16.

I have to acknolege your two favors of Feb. 16. & Mar. 2. and to join sincerely in the sentiment of mrs Adams, and regret that distance separates us so widely. an hour of conversation would be worth a volume of letters. but we must take things as they come.

You ask if I would agree to live my 70. or rather 73. years over again? to which I say Yea. I think with you that it is a good world on the whole, that it has been framed on a principle of benevolence, and more pleasure than pain dealt out to us. there are indeed (who might say Nay)[1] gloomy & hypocondriac minds, inhabitants of diseased bodies, disgusted with the present, & despairing of the future; always counting that the worst will happen, because it may happen. to these I say How much pain have cost us the evils which have never happened! my temperament is sanguine. I steer my bark with Hope in the head, leaving Fear astern. my hopes indeed sometimes fail; but not oftener than the forebodings of the gloomy. there are, I acknolege, even in the happiest life, some terrible convulsions, heavy set-offs against the opposite page of the account. I have often wondered for what good end the sensations of Grief could be intended. all our other passions, within proper bounds, have an useful object. and the perfection of the moral character is, not in a Stoical apathy, so hypocritically vaunted, and so untruly too, because impossible, but in a just equilibrium of all the passions. I wish the pathologists then would tell us what is the use of grief in the economy, and of what good it is the cause, proximate or remote.

Did I know Baron Grimm while at Paris? yes, most intimately. he was the pleasantest, and most conversible member of the diplomatic corps while I was there: a man of good fancy, acuteness, irony, cunning, & egoism: no heart, not much of any science, yet enough of every one to speak it's language. his forte[2] was Belles-lettres, painting & sculpture. in these he was the oracle of the society, and as such was the empress Catharine's private correspondent and factor in all things not diplomatic. it was thro' him I got her permission for poor Ledyard to go to Kamschatka, and cross over thence to the Western coast of America, in order to penetrate across our continent in the opposite direction to that afterwards adopted for Lewis and Clarke: which permission she withdrew after he had got within 200. miles of Kamchatka,[3] had him siesed, brought back and set down in Poland. altho' I never heard Grimm express the opinion, directly, yet I always supposed him to be of the school of Diderot, D'Alembert, D'Holbach. the first of whom committed their system of atheism to writing in 'Le bon sens,' and the last in his 'Systeme de la Nature.' it was a numerous school in the Catholic countries, while the infidelity of the Protestant took generally the form of Theism. the former always insisted that it was a mere question of definition between them, the hypostasis of which on both sides was 'Nature' or 'the Universe': that both agreed in the order of the existing system, but the one supposed it from eternity, the other as having begun in time. and when the athe-

ist descanted on the unceasing motion and circulation of matter thro'
the animal vegetable and mineral kingdoms, never resting, never annihilated, always changing form, and under all forms gifted with the
power of reproduction; the Theist pointing 'to the heavens above,
and to the earth beneath, and to the waters under the earth,' asked if
these did not proclaim a first cause, possessing intelligence and
power; power in the production, & intelligence in the design & constant preservation of the system; urged the palpable existence of final
causes, that the eye was made to see, and the ear to hear, and not that
we see because we have eyes, and hear because we have ears; an answer obvious to the sense's, as that of walking across the room was to
the philosopher demonstrating the non-existence of motion. it was in
D'Holbach's conventicles that Rousseau imagined all the machina-
tions against him were contrived; and he left, in his Confessions the
most biting anecdotes of Grimm. these appeared after I left France;
but I have heard that poor Grimm was so much afflicted by them,
that he kept his bed several weeks. I have never seen these Memoirs
of Grimm. their volume has kept them out of our market.

I have been lately amusing myself with Levi's book in answer to D^r
Priestley. it is a curious and tough work. his style is inelegant and incorrect, harsh and petulant to his adversary, and his reasoning flim-
sey enough. some of his doctrines were new to me, particularly that
of his two resurrections: the first a particular one of all the dead, in
body as well as soul, who are to live over again, the Jews in a state of
perfect obedience to god, the other nations in a state of corporeal
punishment for the sufferings they have inflicted on the Jews. and he
explains this resurrection of bodies to be only of the original stamen
of Leibnitz, or the homunculus in semine masculino, considering that
as a mathematical point, insusceptible of separation, or division. the
second resurrection a general one of souls and bodies, eternally to
enjoy divine glory in the presence of the supreme being.   he
alledges that the Jews alone preserve the doctrine of the unity of god.
yet their god would be deemed a very indifferent man with us: and it
was to correct their Anamorphosis of the deity that Jesus preached,
as well as to establish the doctrine of a future state. however Levi in-
sists that that was taught in the old testament, and even by Moses
himself & the prophets. he agrees that an anointed prince was
prophecied & promised: but denies that the character and history of
Jesus has any analogy with that of the person promised. he must be
fearfully embarrassing to the Hierophants of fabricated Christianity;
because it is their own armour in which he clothes himself for the attack. for example, he takes passages of Scripture from their context

(which would give them a very different meaning) strings them together, and makes them point towards what object he pleases; he in-
terprets them figuratively, typically, analogically, hyperbolically; he
calls in the aid of emendation, transposition, ellipsis, metonymy, and
every other figure of rhetoric; the name of one man is taken for another, one place for another, days and weeks for months and years;
and finally avails himself of all his advantage over his adversaries by
his superior knolege of the Hebrew, speaking in the very language
of the divine communication, while they can only fumble on with
conflicting and disputed translations. such is this war of giants. and
how can such pigmies as you and I decide between them? for myself
I confess that my head is not formed tantas componere lites. and as
you began your Mar. 2. with a declaration that you were about to
write me the most frivolous letter I had ever read, so I will close mine
by saying I have written you a full match for it, and by adding my
affectionate respects to mrs Adams, and the assurance of my constant
attachment and consideration for yourself.   TH: JEFFERSON

RC (MHi: Adams Papers); endorsed by Adams as answered 3 and 6 May 1816; docketed by Charles Francis Adams. PoC (DLC); at foot of first page: "John Adams."

Instead of FEB. 16., Adams's letter was dated 2 Feb. 1816. HOW MUCH PAIN . . . NEVER HAPPENED: for other occasions when TJ used this expression, see TJ to William Short, 28 Nov. 1814, and note. Paul Henri Dietrich, Baron d'Holbach, was the author of both of the works that COMMITTED THEIR SYSTEM OF ATHE-ISM TO WRITING. The first was Le Bon-Sens, ou Idées Naturelles Opposées aux Idées Surnaturelles (London [i.e., Amsterdam], 1772; Sowerby, no. 1292; possibly Poor, Jefferson's Library, 9 [no. 471]). The second was originally published in French under the name of Jean Baptiste de Mirabaud as Système de la Nature. Ou Des Loix du Monde Physique & du Monde Moral, 2 vols. (London [i.e., Amsterdam], 1770; possibly Poor, Jefferson's Library, 9 [no. 472]). The first English edition printed in America, System of Nature; or, The Laws of the Moral and Phys-

ical World, 2 vols. (Philadelphia, 1808; Sowerby, no. 1260), also credited it to Mirabaud. TO THE HEAVENS ABOVE . . . UNDER THE EARTH quotes the Bible, Exodus 20.4.

Jean Jacques Rousseau's Confessions, containing the ANECDOTES OF GRIMM, seems not to have been in TJ's library. He was reading David LEVI'S BOOK IN AN-SWER TO DR PRIESTLEY, Dissertations on the Prophecies of the Old Testament, 3 vols. (London, [1793]–1800). Joseph Priestley's Letters to The Jews; inviting them to an Amicable Discussion of the Evidences of Christianity (Birmingham, 1786) provoked a printed dialogue between the two men, the culmination of which for Levi was this extensive work (Richard H. Popkin, "David Levi, Anglo-Jewish Theologian," Jewish Quarterly Review 87 [1996]: 79–101). SEMINE MASCULINO: "male seed." TANTAS COMPONERE LITES: "to settle such great disputes."

[1] Parenthetical phrase interlined.
[2] Manuscript: "fort."
[3] Manuscript: "Kamschatska."

From William Wingate

DEAR SIR,   Portsmouth New Hampshire April 8. 1816,

The candor and Integrity of Your Heart, Manifested in Your Letter to me, has induced me for to communicate to You the enclosed volume, for Your perusal, Sincerely wishing that it may prove usefull to you, but if you Should find that it contains Sentiments different from your own, I am confident that your candor and charity will induce You for to impute my error to a fault in the Head and not in my Heart, I now appeal to God and my own conscience, my Innocence of any known fault—

As I have not reserved any copy of it, I now request you for to return it safe to me, perhaps within a fortnight from the time you receive it, you can take Such minutes from it as you may See fit, But remember for to keep them Secret, if you Should See Joseph Buonaparte I have no objection to your either Shewing him this volume, or conversing with him on this Subject—I will thank you when you peruse it and compare it with Holy writ, for to minute down all the errors you find I have made, and forward them to me, also write to me the result of your Judgment on the whole Subject, That I may also be enlightened by you, not doubting but that you will do me Strict Justice, Shall add no more on this Subject—

Sir, I wrote to m^r Madison last year, and Solicited Him for to appoint me Inspector at Newburyport, in the room of m^r Swett who now holds that office, I Stated to m^r Madison that I personally knew that m^r Swett had been a violent malicious Enemy to the Republican cause, and that m^r Swett Secretly remained So, That m^r Swett married a daughter of General Varnums, and that his wife was dead, and m^r Swett had married again—That General Varnum well knew m^r Swetts Political Principles before He obtained the office for him, which was a very dishonorable act in m^r Varnum, That no young man that is a violent enemy to the General Goverment, ought never to hold any office under the Goverment he is Seeking for to overthro, that all offices belonged to Such Men only as had merrited Them, &c.

As m^r Madison had not noticed my letter—I wrote a letter to m^r Meigs and Solicited Him for to appoint me Postmaster at Haverhill my Former office, expecting that the Postmaster would at that time died, but then recovered contrary to the expectation of the Physician—The Emolument[1] of this last office is only from one hundred to one hundred and fifty dollars a year—Sir, As I am extreme poor and destitute of any imploy, I Should feel my Self very much obliged, if you would assist me at this time in procuring one of Those offices or any other, By writing to m^r Madison or to m^r Meigs and Solicit the office for me, as it cannot be obtained in no other way, I wish you for to do it—The Sooner it is done the better it will be for me—

Sir, you will please for to let me know the result of your mind on this Subject—

I remain as always with wishes for Your welfare Yours Sincerely

W^M WINGATE

RC (MoSHi: TJC-BC); at foot of text: "Honorable Thomas Jefferson Esquire"; endorsed by TJ as received 3 May 1816 and so recorded in SJL. Enclosure not found.

In 1797 Daniel Swett married Mehitable "Hitty" Varnum (1773–1814),

the DAUGHTER of Joseph Bradley Varnum (Arthur Meredyth Burke, ed., *The Prominent Families of the United States of America* [1908; repr. 2008], 150; Haverhill, Mass., *Merrimack Intelligencer*, 31 Dec. 1814).

[1] Manuscript: "Emomulent."

From François Gard

SIR.   Bordeaux, 9th April 1816.

You will perhaps be Surprized at the Liberty I take in addressing you, but being governed by motives of humanity & encouraged in my design by Some military gentlemen and merchants of the united States now in this place, I Beg leave to claim your attention for a moment, on the Situation of the unhappy persons in your country who have the misfortune to be deaf & dumb. afflicted myself with these infirmities & feeling with great Sensibility for all these in the Same Situation I have enquired of the american gentlemen who have visited our Institution in Bordeaux, for the Instruction of deaf and dumb, whether there existed any Similar establishment in the united States. Being informed that no Such School had been established with you & Learning that among your deaf and dumb all those who had not the means of coming to Europe were deprived of Instruction I feel an ardent desire to devote my Labours and existence to procure for them the inestimable blessing of the education of which their organisation is Susceptible & which is So indispensable both for their own happiness & to render them useful members of Society.

I was educated myself in the Institution of the deaf & dumb in this city & having acquired by long application a Perfect Knowledge of the most approved method of Instructing this unfortunate Portion of society I have for these eight years exercized the Function of Teacher & have also acquired a tolerable Knowledge of the English Language. If The american Government or Benevolent Individuals of your Country are disposed [to] Form an Institution in the united States I would Willingly go there for that purpose. I can procure Satisfactory testimonial of my moral character and my Capacity for Teaching the deaf & dumb from american Consul & Several respectable military & Commercial Gentlemen of the united States who honour me with Their friendship & Esteem—I will entirely depend on the wisdom & judgment of the american Government or of the individuals who undertake to assist me in the proposed establishment, to fix the mode & plan of its organisation.

Our Institution here is calculated for 60 Poors Students at the expence of the Government which pays for each 600 francs P^r annum & 24000. for Professors & Sundry others charges to which is to be added the expence of a Suitable building, Beds, Linen &^{c} Making the agregate expence about 1000 fr. annually for each individual. the rich pay the expence of their children & if as I have been Told a considerable portion of the deaf & dumb in the united States have the means of paying for their instruction the Expence to the Government or a private Society would be inconsiderable for myself I do not claim great emoluments my desire & object, is to Serve an afflicted portion of humanity I have a Wife & Soon expect to be a father, my only ambition, is to procure a comfortable existence for my wife & family

If you think your Government Cannot from its formation establish Such an Institution, Will you inform me what probability there is of any one of States Governments undertaking to create Such [an] Establishment, or whether in your Opinion Individual Subscription could be raised for its formation. Your worthy consul, m^r Lee. has given me great encouragement, but I wish to feel Secure of a competency before I undertake a Voyage, as it would not be prudent in me to let go a certainty for an uncertainty having from the Institution here a Salary of 1800 francs besides other Emoluments

I Should be highly flattered by your honouring me with a reply to this, on which Permit me to say, I calculate from the Knowledg[e] I have from m^r Lee of your Patriotism & useful Labours.

I have the honour to be with high respect, Sir, your humble Servant

F^s Gard
Professeur à L'Institution royale des
sourds muets à Bordeaux.

RC (DLC); torn at crease and edge trimmed; addressed: "Thomas Jefferson Monticello in Virginia"; endorsed by TJ as received 10 July 1816 and so recorded in SJL. Enclosed in William Lee to TJ, 11 May 1816.

François Gard (d. 1838), educator of the deaf and mute in France, became deaf himself at the age of seven. After studying under the direction of Jean Saint-Sernin at the National Institution for the Deaf-Mute in Bordeaux, Gard became a teacher there. He was educated in Latin and Greek, taught himself English, and employed teaching methods that encouraged deaf students to communicate using the grammar and structure of spoken language. Gard taught in Bordeaux for his entire career (Adrien Cornié, *Étude sur l'Institution Nationale des Sourdes-Muettes de Bordeaux, 1786–1889* [1889], 25, 36, 43; *Quarterly Journal of Foreign Medicine and Surgery; and of the sciences connected with them* 1 [1819]: 322, 327–9; Harlan Lane, *When the Mind Hears: A History of the Deaf* [1984], 32, 214–5, 221; National Institution, for the Education of Deaf and Dumb Children of the Poor, in Ireland, *Eleventh Report [viz. for 1826]* [1827]: 76–7).

A SIMILAR ESTABLISHMENT for the education of the deaf and mute was established in 1815 by William Bolling and the British educator John Braidwood. The institution, located at Cobbs, Virginia, near Petersburg, was financially unsuccessful and closed in mid-1816. Concurrently with Gard's proposal, Thomas Hopkins Gallaudet and Laurent Clerc were leading an effort that culminated in the chartering later in 1816 of the Connecticut Asylum for the Education and Instruction of Deaf and Dumb Persons, which opened in Hartford the following year (Alexander Graham Bell, "Historical Notes Concerning the Teaching of Speech to the Deaf," in American Association to Promote the Teaching of Speech to the Deaf, *Association Review* 2 [1900]: 385–401; *ANB*, 8:645–6).

William LEE returned to the United States from his consular post at Bordeaux in 1816, carrying a circular letter from Gard to American philanthropists. Consisting nearly verbatim of the first three paragraphs of the above letter, Gard's circular was published in the New York *National Advocate*, 16 July 1816, and reprinted elsewhere. In response, New York physician Samuel L. Mitchill formed a committee to study the possibilities for deaf education. Gard was not employed, but a New York Institution for the Deaf and Dumb was chartered in 1817 (Lane, *When the Mind Hears*, 215, 221–2; Bell, "Historical Notes," *Association Review* 4 [1902]: 19–23).

From James Leitch

SIR   Charlottesville April 9th 16

Under Cover you have 3\frac{25}{100}$ having Overpaid Chas Stewart that sum to day for Butter. I had taken a part of the Butter for my Own Use which he was not apprised of

Yours   JA^s LEITCH

RC (MHi); dateline beneath signature; addressed: "Thos Jefferson Esqre Monticello"; endorsed by TJ as received 9 Apr. 1816 and so recorded in SJL.

From Louis Philippe Gallot de Lormerie

                                                        a Paris ce 9. avril 1816—

MONSIEUR L'EX PRÉSIDENT,   Plaçe roÿale N° 10

Je saisis avec Empressement une Occasion favorable, celle de Monsieur hide de Neuville nouvellement Ambassadeur de france près

Votre Gouvernement, pour Vous renouveller les assurances de mon respect, de mon ancien Attachement, et de toute ma gratitude—Je vous ai dit et n'oublierai jamais L avantâge que vous m'avés procuré de revenir dans ma Patrie avec S: E. Monsieur Crawford et Mr Jackson aujourdhuy chargé des affaires des E: u: qui j'ai Lhonneur de Voir Souvent a Paris. il a la Bonté de remettre Lui même a M^r De neuville que je n'ai pas l'avantâge de Connoître ma Lettre que je vous supplie Monsieur d agréer comme un témoignâge des sentimens que je vous ai voüés pour toujours

mes vœux sont pour votre santé & votre Bonheur. Je joüis graces a dieu de L'une & de L'autre a L'âge de près de 71 ans dans une Aisance honnête (a good competency) et je dis avec action de graces au tout puissant

Saltem, remoto, das Pater angulo
horas Senectæ duçere Liberas.

Daignés agréer Monsieur L'ex President, Lhommage de mon Respect et de ma très haute Considération   DE LORMERIE

Paris 9. April 1816—
MR. EX-PRESIDENT,   Place Royale Number 10

I eagerly seize a favorable occasion, that of Mr. Hyde de Neuville's recent appointment as France's ambassador to your government, to renew to you the assurances of my respect, my old affection, and all my gratitude. I have told you before and I will never forget the advantage you procured me in allowing me to come back to my country with his excellency Mr. Crawford and Mr. Jackson, now chargé d'affaires of the United States, whom I have the honor of seeing often in Paris. He is kind enough to hand my letter to Mr. de Neuville, whom I do not have the honor of knowing. I beg you Sir to receive this letter as a testimony of the feelings I will always dedicate to you

I wish you good health and happiness. Thank God I enjoy the one and the other at the age of almost 71, in moderate prosperity (a good competency), and I offer this thanksgiving to the all powerful

Saltem remoto, das Pater angulo
horas Senectæ ducere Liberas.

Please accept, Mr. Ex-President, my respectful regards and very high consideration   DE LORMERIE

RC (DLC); dateline at foot of text; endorsed by TJ as received 10 July 1816 and so recorded in SJL. Translation by Dr. Genevieve Moene.

SALTEM REMOTO . . . LIBERAS: "Seats, like These, thou guardian Pow'r, Bless my Day's declining hour!" comes from an ode composed by Thomas Gray in 1741 (Roger Lonsdale, ed., *The Poems of Thomas Gray, William Collins, Oliver Goldsmith* [1969], 317–8; Edward Greene Burnaby, *The Latin Odes of Mr Gray, in English Verse, with An Ode on the Death of a favorite Spaniel* [London, 1775], 8).

To James Monroe

DEAR SIR Monticello Apr. 9. 16.

It had escaped my recollection till this moment that you had desired me to send you the copy of La Harpe's journal. you will find bound up with it some Extracts from it which I had made because bearing immediately on the question of right, and a duplicate copy of the letters of Cevallos Salcedo & Herrera. if your office possesses the original, as I am sure it does, I will be glad to have this returned, that I may deposit it with the A. Philosophical society where it will be safe and more open than it would be in your office for the use of writers on that subject. but indeed you should have it printed, that being the only certain way of preserving any thing. you will see that this was meditated by a calculation in my hand at the foot of the 1st page, from which it appears that 300. copies sold @ 1.D 10 C. would repay the whole expence of printing them.

Affectionately yours TH: JEFFERSON

RC (NN: Monroe Papers); between closing and signature: "James Monroe esq."; endorsed by Monroe, with his additional notation: "memoir on Louisiana." PoC (DLC); on verso of reused address cover to TJ; endorsed by TJ.

The enclosed manuscript of Benard de LA HARPE'S "Journal historique Concernant l'Etablissement des françois à la Louisianne tiré des memoires de Mrs D.Iberville et de Bienville Commandants pour le Roy au dit Paix, et sur les decouvertes et recherches de Mr Benard de la harpe, nommé au commandements de la Baye s^t Benard" ("Historical journal concerning the settlement of the French in Louisiana drawn from the reports of Messrs. d'Iberville and de Bienville commanders for the king in the said country, and on the discoveries and investigations of Mr. Benard de la Harpe, appointed to the command of Saint Benard Bay") (DNA: RG 59, HFL) was found among the papers of Athanaze de Mézières. It came to the attention of John Sibley who, through the agency of William C. C. Claiborne, forwarded a version of it in 1805 to James Madison, then the secretary of state. Before sending it to Washington, Sibley had copies made, including one for TJ (Sibley to TJ, 9 Aug. 1805, and to

Madison, 10 Aug. 1805 [both in DLC]). On the copy now enclosed, TJ noted at the foot of the first numbered page: "[...] [l]eaves of 370. words each. = 20 sheets of print @ 16.D. for 300. copies = 320.D." Also bound with this copy is a sheet folded to form four pages consisting of notes in TJ's hand. The DUPLICATE letters also bound with this copy are Trs of Pedro CEVALLOS to Charles Pinckney and Monroe, Aranjuez, 13 Apr. 1805 (printed in ASP, Foreign Relations, 2:660–2), Nemesio SALCEDO to Claiborne, Chihuahua, 18 Sept. 1806 (extract printed in ASP, Military Affairs, 1:205–6), and Antonio Cordero to James Wilkinson, Camp of Nacogdoches, 11 Oct. 1806 (printed in ASP, Military Affairs, 1:205). The location of the manuscript Sibley sent to Madison is unknown. After Monroe received TJ's enclosure, another copy was made. This second copy in DNA: RG 59, HFL, in an unidentified hand, includes TJ's notes on the cost of printing in the same hand as the rest of the MS. Despite TJ's effort to retain a copy so that he could give it to the American Philosophical Society, both texts are now in the National Archives (TJ to Peter S. Du Ponceau, 30 Dec. 1817; Du Ponceau to TJ, 6 Jan. 1818; TJ to Josiah S. Johnston, 13 Feb. 1825). However, an additional copy of the La Harpe manuscript was deposited at the American Philosophical Society in 1816 by William Darby. The text was published in French in 1831 by A. L. Boimare as *Journal Historique de l'Établissement des Français a la Louisiane* and in 1851 in English translation by Benjamin F. French in *Historical Collections of Louisiana*, pt. 3. The history and provenance of this work are discussed fully in Mildred Mott Wedel, "The Benard de La Harpe Historiography on French Colonial Louisiana," *Louisiana Studies* 13 (1974): 9–67.

From John F. Oliveira Fernandes

DEAR SIR   New york 9ᵗʰ April 1816

Desirous to See some of my Philadelphia and New york friends, I Left Norfolk on the 24ᵗʰ ulto Your favour dated 26ᵗʰ dᵒ was recieved here on the 6ᵗʰ instant— Immediatly after the reception of yours of the 24ᵗʰ January—I wrote to Messʳˢ Gibson and Jefferson, requesting them, to examen the Tenerife wine; and (if approved of) to Send up to you a quart Cask, well precautioned, against the boat's Men's villany— The two pp of wine, were Shipped on board the Brig Jane Couts, bound to Richmond—where Capᵗ did not like to have them landed in Norfolk— Mʳ Richardson, my Correspondent in that City, had them entered, and landed; but, notwitstanding my repeated requests has not informed me, as yett, of the ammt—of Duties; freght; any other Small charges—All this, when Known to Me, will be communicated to you—it being my intention, to charge you, with what Costs me.

By the Letter of my Tenerife Friend hereby enclosed—(which you will be so Kind as to return) you will See its first Cost at Tenerife— $345—for the 2 pp—that is $43–12½/—every quart Cask—besids the other charges, which will bring each Cask to $62–64. at furthest— of this I will inform you, as Soon as I—return home— within 4 to 5 weeks—

As for the Porto-wine; I Know it is of—the best quality: If you permit me to refer you to my Letter of the 6ᵗʰ January; you will observe, that, that quart Cask, was the only one I had; requested by, and Sent to me, for my own private use, while, the Sole desire to oblige you, could Compell me to part with. However, as, immidiatly, after my forwarding it to you, I ordered Some more for me; I will take the liberty, to inform you of its arrival; Sincerely willing to Share with you, some of it; if Still, in need of—

With great respect and regard

I remain Dʳ Sir Your mo: ob: Servant

JOHN F. OLIVEIRA FERNANDES

RC (DLC); addressed: "Th^as Jefferson Esquire Monticello Milton Virginia— Sch: Siminghton"; franked; postmarked Norfolk, 11 Apr.; endorsed by TJ as received 3 May 1816 and so recorded in SJL.

pp: "pipes," with one pipe equaling two hogsheads, or 126 gallons.

E N C L O S U R E

Joseph de Monteverde to John F. Oliveira Fernandes

Muy Est^do S^or mio: Sta Cruz de Ten^e 2 de Dic^e a 1815
Correspondo á la favorecida de U^d 20 de Ag^to ult° acompañandole la adjunta Carta de D^n Domingo Madan en resp^ta á la q^e U. le escrivió á dho S^or, por la q^e quedará U. enterado de la aplicacion que hizo de los $109.37, q^e yo le satisfice, y U. reclamará de la persona q^e cita.

Hizo U. muy bien de no remesar el Cargam^to de articulos q^e señale á U. en la mia de 25 de Junio ult° med^te á q^e llegó á Sus manos atrasada, p^q en efecto despues de la paz, no cesan de venir buques Cargados, de forma q^e estamos surtidos de todos los artículos que proceden de esa, que nos faltavan—

He mandado llenar del vino mas particular de mis bodegas las dos medias pp. y quatro quart^s q^e se Sirve encargarme, q^e no dudo sea de Su gusto: su precio á 38£. Est. pipa imp^ta $342, y con tres de costos de embarque son $345: q^e he adevitado á U. en/c: nabegan en el Berg^n Jane Coutes, Capn, Guillermo B[. . .], consignados á dho Reardon p^a entregrar á U. de q^e acompaño Conocimiento.

Esta Suma he de merecer á U. me remese empleado en 1er barco, la mitad en Duelas de Pipa, y la otra mitad p^r partes iguales, tambien en duelas de media Pipa, y quarterola

No da lugar p^a mas el Buque: agradezco á U. Sus finas ofertas, y desea corresponderle con iguales veras Su af° Leg Serv^or QSMB.

JOSEPH DE MONTEVERDE

E D I T O R S ' T R A N S L A T I O N

My Very Dear Sir: Santa Cruz de Tenerife 2 December 1815
I am answering your favor of this past 20 August and enclosing the letter from Mr. Domingo Madan in response to the one you wrote him. This letter will inform you how I applied and settled the $109.37, which you may claim from the above-mentioned person.

You were right not to ship the articles I mentioned to you in my letter of this past 25 June, which reached you late, because, since the peace, loaded ships have arrived continuously, so that we now have an assortment of all the goods we previously lacked.

I have filled the two half-pipes and four quarters that you ordered with the best wine from my cellars, which I do not doubt will please you. Their price, at £38 sterling per pipe, comes to $342, which with three dollars for customs comes to $345. I herewith charge that amount to you and inform you that the pipes sail on the Brig Jane Couts, Captain William Burrows, and that we have arranged with Reardon to deliver them to you.

This sum should seem fair to you. I am sending half of the shipment in wooden pipes with the first boat and the other half, in equal parts, in wooden half-pipes and quarter pipes.

The ship has no more room. I appreciate your kind offers and wish to reciprocate similarly. Your affectionate loyal servant, who kisses your hand.

JOSEPH DE MONTEVERDE

RC (DLC); one word illegible; addressed: "A Dⁿ Juan Fran^co de Olivera Fernandez Norfolk"; postmarked Tenerife, 15 Jan. 1816, with additional notation: "By Mr. Mast. Reardon." Translation by Dr. Jennifer McCune and Dr. David T. Gies.

Joseph de Monteverde y Molina (ca. 1756–1831) was born in Garachico on the island of Tenerife. He was given a lifetime appointment as governor of the Castillo de San Cristóbal in Santa Cruz de Tenerife in 1783. In 1797 Monteverde helped defend Santa Cruz against invading British forces, for which he was promoted to lieutenant colonel. The following year he published an account of the battle. Monteverde died in La Laguna, Tenerife (Juan Carlos Cardell Cristellys, *Héroes y Testigos de la Derrota de Nelson en Tenerife* [2004], 261–2; Madrid *Almanak Mercantil ó Guia de Comerciantes* [1804]: 459; [1807]: 497).

The brig *Jane Couts* (JANE COUTES), under the command of William Burrows, reached Norfolk on 17 Jan. 1816 (Norfolk *American Beacon and Commercial Diary*, 17 Jan. 1816).

To William Short

Monticello Apr. 9. 16.

Th:J. to W. Short.

The inclosed was omitted by accident to be forwarded to you in my last. it is a necessary document for you in your settlement with mr Carter. I salute you ever and affectionately.

P. S. I send also mr Carter's letter shewing he had agreed to pay what he recieved & interest.

RC (ViW: TJP); dateline adjacent to postscript; endorsed by Short as received 15 Apr. Enclosure: William Champe Carter to TJ, 22 Dec. 1813. Other enclosure printed below.

William Woods's Survey of Land in Dispute
between James Monroe and William Short

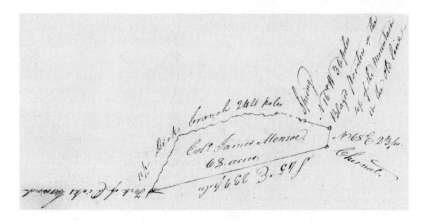

This is a Plat of 68 acres of land lying in the County of Albemarle on the South side of Carters Mountain, & on the east side of Dick's branch, being the land in controversy between Col° James Monroe & Wm Short Esqr which has been determined by arbitration to belong to Col° Monroe.
Surveyed February 21st 1816.   W^M Woods. S.A.C.

MS (ViW: TJP); written on a scrap in an unidentified hand; endorsed in same hand on verso: "Col° James Monroe 68 acres Albemarle."

William Woods (ca. 1777–1849) was the surveyor of Albemarle County, 1796–1828. He became a county magistrate in 1816, served as a colonel in the militia in 1817, and was sheriff in 1837. Woods was a founding member of the Agricultural Society of Albemarle in 1817 and received

several awards for his skill in animal husbandry. At the time of his death he owned land worth $4,800 as well as fifty-one slaves and other personal property (Woods, *Albemarle*, 356, 375, 379; Rodney H. True, "Minute Book of the Agricultural Society of Albemarle," *Annual Report of the American Historical Association for the Year 1918* [1921], 1:269, 314, 315, 330, 345; Albemarle Co. Will Book, 19:347–50, 360–2; *Richmond Whig and Public Advertiser*, 8 Jan. 1850).

From LeRoy, Bayard & McEvers

SIR   Newyork the 10 April 1816
    Apprehending that our respect of the 19th ult° may have miscarried we beg to wait upon you with a Copy thereof and craving your

Kind attention to the Same we have the honor to Subscribe with great consideration

Sir   Your obed^t h^l Servants

LeRoy Bayard & McEvers

RC (DLC); in an unidentified hand. RC (DLC); address cover only; with Dupl of LeRoy, Bayard & McEvers to TJ, 19 Mar. 1816, on verso; addressed: "The Honble Thos Jefferson Monticello V^a"; stamp canceled; franked; postmarked New York, 10 Apr.; endorsed by TJ as a letter of 11 Apr. from "Leroy & co." received 3 May 1816 and so recorded in SJL. Enclosure: LeRoy, Bayard & McEvers to TJ, 19 Mar. 1816.

To Albert Gallatin

Dear Sir   Monticello Apr. 11. 16.

Your last favor is recieved just as I am setting out for a possession 90. miles Southwardly, from whence I shall not return until the first week of the ensuing month. I hasten therefore to drop you a line of Adieu. I sincerely rejoice that you are going to France. I do not think with you that nothing can be done there. Louis XVIII is a fool, & a bigot, but bating a little duplicity he is honest, and means well. he cannot but feel the heavy hand of his masters, and that it is England which presses it, and vaunts the having had the glory of effecting their humiliation. his ministers too, altho' ultra-royalists must feel as Frenchmen. altho our government is an eyesore to them, the pride and pressure of England is more present to their feelings, and they must be sensible that having a common enemy, an intimate connection with us must be of value to them. England hates us, dreads us, and yet is silly enough to keep us under constant irritation instead of making us her friends. she will use all her sway over the French government to obstruct our commerce with them, and it is exactly there you can act with effect by keeping that government informed of the truth, in opposition to the lies of England.   I thank you for your attention to my request as to mr Terril. you judge rightly that I have no acquaintances left in France. some were guillotined, some fled, some died, some are exiled, and I know of nobody left but La Fayette. I correspond with his connection M. Destutt Tracy, the ablest writer in France in the moral line. your acquaintance with M. de la Fayette will of course bring you to that of M. Tracy. will you permit me to tell you a long story, and to vindicate me in conversation to both those friends, before whom it is impossible but that I must stand in need of it. M. Tracy has written the best work on Political economy which has ever appeared. he has established it's principles more demonstratively than has been done before, & in the compass of one third[1] of even M. Say's work. he feared to print it in France, and sent it to me to have it translated & printed here. I immediately proposed it to Duane who engaged to have it done. after putting me off from 6. months to 6. months he at length (after 2 or 3 years delay) wrote me that he had had it translated, but was not able to print it. I got from him the original and the translation, and proposed the publishing of it to Millegan of George town promising to revise the translation if he would undertake it. he agreed to it. when I came to look into the translation, it had been done by one who understood neither French nor English, and I then rejoiced that Duane had not published it. it would have been horrid. I worked on it 4. or 5 hours a day for 3. months, comparing word by word with the original, and altho' I have made it a strictly faithful translation yet it is without style. le premier jet was such as to render that impossible. I sent the whole to Millegan about 10. days ago, & he had informed me his types & every thing was ready to begin it. I have not the courage to write to mr Tracy until I can send him a copy of the book; and were I to write to M. La Fayette & be silent on this subject, they would conclude I had abandoned it: but in truth I have never ceased to urge it. indeed I take great interest in it's publication. it's brevity will recommend it to our countrymen, & it's logic set their minds to rights as to principle; & you know there is no science on which they are so little informed.—now can you remember all this? and will you be so good as to place me erect again before my friends, by a verbal explanation? God bless you and give you a safe & pleasant voyage, and a safe return to us in the fulness of time.   TH: JEFFERSON

I trouble you with 2. letters to mr Terril to be forwarded to Geneva

RC (NHi: Gallatin Papers); addressed: "Albert Gallatin esq. New York"; endorsed by Gallatin. PoC (DLC); on a reused address cover from Josiah Meigs to TJ; endorsed by TJ. Enclosures not found.

Lafayette's son George Washington Lafayette had married DESTUTT de Tracy's daughter Émilie in 1802 (Jason Lane, *General and Madame de Lafayette: Partners in Liberty's Cause in the American and French Revolutions* [2003], 257). LE PREMIER JET: "the first attempt."

[1] Preceding three words interlined.

Promissory Note to John Neilson

On a settlement with John Nelson on the 16ᵗʰ of April 1809. there was then due to him from me four hundred and thirty five Dollars 75 cents with interest from that date till paid, the certificate of which then given him being said to be lost, I now give him this duplicate under my hand this 11ᵗʰ of April 1816.   TH: JEFFERSON

PoC (MHi). Not recorded in SJL.

In 1820 TJ brought the SETTLEMENT of his 1809 note with Neilson up to date by sending him "a new one for principal & interest 843.50" (TJ to Neilson, 31 May 1820; *MB*, 2:1245, 1365).

To Thomas Eston Randolph

DEAR SIR   Monticello Apr. 11. 16.
From the account you were so good as to furnish me I make out the inclosed statement for the last & present year. the first year is of flour specifically, both the crop and rent consisting of flour only. the balance 67. Barrels. the 2ᵈ year's account being for flour as to the crop, and money as to the rent, I carry on the balance of 67. Barrels to the flour accᵗ of the 2ᵈ year which leaves only 41 B.–57 ℔ due to me; an order for that much therefore will discharge that without regard to it's money value.   The account of the 2ᵈ year's rent is stated in money, so as to keep the money balance clear [of?] that for flour. I send it for your consideration & correction—being to set out for Bedford tomorrow morning, you can inform me on my return if it is right. but in the mean time if the flour balance is right I should be glad that that should be delivered to mr Gibson as my letters have given him reason to expect.
Affectionately yours   TH: JEFFERSON

PoC (MHi); on verso of reused address cover to TJ; damaged at seal; at foot of text: "Thoˢ E. Randolph esq."; endorsed by TJ. Enclosure not found.

From John F. Dumoulin

SIR   Pennsylvania Avenue Washington City April the 12ᵗʰ 1816
Permit me the honor of presenting you with the copy of an Essay on Naturalization and Allegiance which perhaps I have been too hazardous in publishing. Conscious of the many errors and faults which crowd in the Press and composition of its pages, I feel however some

satisfaction in reflecting that leading principles I contend for, have had your approbation. With this impression I have occasionally taken a liberty with your name, and invoked it in the behalf of the assertion of human rights. Devoted as your life has been to liberty and philanthropy, your name has become too consecrated to humanity not to be recalled whenever it becomes the theme of discussion. You are now too well accustomed to this familiarity with your name and the freedom which the vanity of writers indulge themselves with, in presenting you with copies of crude and coarse productions, to be displeased at the liberties they take. May I therefore Sir request you will receive the acccompanying copy of my very imperfect Essay on Naturalization and Allegiance as a small token of the highest respect and of the most lively feelings of gratitude for your kind attentions and hospitality to me in the visit which I had the honor of making to Monticello in October. Be pleased also to present the other copy which attends this, to your Son Mr Randolph—I was happy to hear from Miss Randolph who was sometime since at the Presidents of your being in perfect health as also Mrs Randolph—May I beg you to present my respects to Mrs Randolph and Mr Jefferson Randolph and with many apologies for thus trespassing on you. I have the honor to remain Sir

with the greatest respect your humble and Obedient Servt

J: F: DUMOULIN

RC (DLC); at foot of text: "Thos Jefferson Esqr"; endorsed by TJ as received 3 May 1816 and so recorded in SJL. Enclosure: Dumoulin, *An Essay on Naturalization & Allegiance* (Washington, 1816; Poor, *Jefferson's Library*, 11 [no. 633]).

In the enclosure Dumoulin took A LIBERTY with TJ's name by praising him as "the best and purest statesman of the age, the man whose virtuous life is a model of rigid republicanism . . . . the philosophic JEFFERSON, devised a measure of magnanimous, but secure policy, for his country" (p. 11; ellipsis in original). Dumoulin also quoted TJ's views on the revisal of naturalization laws as expressed in his First Annual Message to Congress: "'Shall we,' said the virtuous Jefferson, in one of those enlightened addresses which, while President, he made to the legislature, 'refuse to the unhappy fugitives from distress, that hospitality which the savages of the wilderness extended to our fathers arriving in this land? Shall oppressed humanity find no asylum on this Globe?' These were the words of Jefferson; of that illustrious man whose character fulfils every precept of the most rigid virtue, whose policy was peace, whose practice is virtue, whose words are wisdom, and whose heart is benevolence" (Dumoulin, p. 126; *PTJ*, 35:612–7, 620, 648–9).

From Charles P. De Lasteyrie

MONSIEUR   Paris ce 14 Avril 1816.

je prend la liberté de vous adrésser Monsieur Geo. flower Agriculteur Anglais qui veut aller exercer son activité et ses talents Sur une terre où l'industrie est Sûre de ne point trouver d'obstacles, et où l'homme peut retirer une juste récompense de ses travaux.

M^r flower que j'ai eu occasion de connoître particuliérement en france est doué d'un dégré de Sagesse et de raison qu'on trouve rarement dans un âge même avancé parmi les habitans corrompus de notre vieux continent. je félicite votre patrie de faire de pareilles conquêtes. Elle vous Seront plus utiles que celles que nous faisons et que nous apprécions tant en Europe. je voudrois être moi même plus jeune, et j'irois vous demander L'hospitalité. je compte asses sur votre amitié pour moi, et sur votre philantropie éclairé, pour espérer que vous serés utile à M^r flower en ce qui dependra de vous.

Mr Lafayette habite Sa campagne, où il vit éloigné des affaires, entièrement adonné aux travaux des champs.

je viens de former à Paris un établissement Lithographique. c'est un art qui rendra de grand services aux arts et aux sciences; et quoique dans son enfance, il est déja très utile, mais il le deviendra bien davantage lorsqu'il sera perfectionné. c'est à quoi je travaille, et j'espere que je parviendrai à le rendre d'un usage plus facile et plus économique. il seroit bien a désirer qu'il s'introduisit en Amérique, ou il vous seroit encore plus utile qu'en Europe. Vous manqués de graveurs, et ceux que vous avés ne sont pas aussi habiles que les notres. La Lithographie vous donneroit autant de graveurs que vous avés de déssinateurs, et vous trouveriés ainsi un moyen de propager dans votre patrie Les choses utiles. s'il venoit dans la tête de quelqu'un de vos compatriotes de vouloir former un établissement lithographique ils n'auroient qu'à m'envoyer un échantillon grand comme la main des pierres d'amérique. j'esserai ces pierres pour Savoir si elles Sont bonnes. Ces pierres doivent être calcaire et Argileuses, prendre a peu de chose près le polis du Marbre, être sans trous ni cavités, et d'un grain fin. La Cassure en est concoide. c'est l'espèce de pierre que Werner nomme <u>Schiste calcaire.</u> je pourrai vous en envoyer un échantillon si vous le désirés. Vous me permettrés de vous envoyer quelques échantillons qui sortiront de mes presses.

j'espere que vous jouissés toujours d'une heureuse santé. je vous en désire bien Sincérement la continuation, et je vous prie de croire aux Sentiment d'estime et d'attachement que j'ai et que j'aurai toujours pour vous.   C. P. DE LASTEYRIE

EDITORS' TRANSLATION

SIR   Paris 14 April 1816.

I take the liberty of recommending to you Mr. George Flower, an English farmer, who wants to go and practice his occupation and his talents in a land where industry is certain to find no obstacles and a man can get a just reward for his labor.

Mr. Flower, whom I got to know particularly well in France, is gifted with a degree of wisdom and reason that is rarely found, even in persons of an advanced age, among the corrupt inhabitants of our old continent. I congratulate your country on its conquests. They will be more useful to you than those that we are making and appreciate so much in Europe. I myself would like to be younger, in which case I would go and ask for your hospitality. I am counting on your friendship and enlightened philanthropy, and I hope that you will be useful to Mr. Flower to the extent of your ability.

Mr. Lafayette lives on his estate, away from public affairs, entirely devoted to farming.

I have just created in Paris a lithographic establishment. This art will render great services to the arts and sciences. Even though in its infancy, it is already very useful, but it will become much more so when it is perfected. This is what I am working on, and I hope to be able to make it easier and cheaper to use. Its introduction is much to be desired in America, where it would offer even greater advantages than in Europe. You lack engravers, and the ones you have are not as skilled as ours. Lithography would provide you with as many engravers as you have sketchers, and you would thus find a way to publicize useful things in your country. If it occurred to one of your fellow citizens to form a lithographic establishment, they need only send me a sample of American stones the size of a hand. I will test them to see if they are any good. These stones must be calcareous and clayey, able to acquire almost the polish of marble, free of holes or cavities, and showing a fine grain. The fracture should be conchoidal. It is the kind of stone that Werner calls calcareous schist. I could send you a specimen if you wish. You will allow me to send you a few samples of the work produced by my presses.

I hope that you are still enjoying good health. I sincerely wish for its continuation. Please accept my sincere regards and the attachment I have and will always have for you.   C. P. DE LASTEYRIE

RC (MoSHi: TJC-BC); at foot of first page: "a M^r jefferson"; endorsed by TJ as received 25 Nov. 1816 and so recorded in SJL. Translation by Dr. Genevieve Moene.

George Flower (ca. 1788–1862) was a native of Hertford, England, who helped establish a British community in Illinois. Before his departure from the United Kingdom, he traveled through France with Morris Birkbeck, an accomplished sheep farmer. Both men were disappointed with what they learned about opportunities for immigration to that country, and they turned their attention to the United States, with Flower arriving in 1816 and Birkbeck following the next year. As a part of his western exploration, Flower visited TJ at Poplar Forest and Monticello, accounts of which were included in his posthumously published *History of the English Settlement in Edwards County, Illinois* (1882). Flower and Birkbeck joined in founding a community in southeastern Illinois. In 1817 Flower briefly returned to England, where he recruited additional settlers and arranged for the publication of Birkbeck's book promoting the venture. When Flower returned to the settlement in 1818, however, he and Birkbeck had a falling out. The planned establishment then split into two communities, Flower's in Albion and Birkbeck's in Wanborough. Flower opposed slavery adamantly and fought against its introduction into Illinois. He also contributed to the science of prairie management by publishing *The Western Shepherd* (1841), a pamphlet reissued the following year in a series of newspaper articles. Flower moved in 1849 from Albion to New Harmony, Indiana. He died on a visit to his daughter in Grayville, White County, Illinois (*ANB*; *DAB*; Flower's Accounts of Visits to Poplar Forest, [25–28 Nov. 1816], and to Monticello 12–16 [Dec. 1816]; *Chicago Tribune*, 22 Mar. 1862).

From Thomas Appleton

Leghorn 15ᵗʰ April 1816.

The preceding, Sir, is a copy of my letter written to you, the day following the death of mʳ mazzei.—I now inclose you, the legal attestation of his decease; an attested Copy of his will; together with a letter from the guardian of his daughter, as to the disposal of the property in your hands.—all these acts I have confirm'd in my official capacity, and which I presume, are the only requisites necessary for your guidance.—although our friend, Sir, had arriv'd at an age to which few attain, yet it was in some degree premature, as his end was undoubtedly hasten'd, by the undisguis'd manner, in which his family evinc'd thier weariness of exercising towards him, those attentions which his age requir'd; and as he frequently told me, his single desire was, that they might soon be gratified, and thus liberate himself from the continual pains of being depriv'd of many indispensable comforts of life, and the still greater torment of witnessing thier ingratitude, and criminal eagerness to grasp, uncontroul'd, his little estate.— about two years ago, he finish'd a work, which I suppose, if printed, might fill about 2000 pages in 8ᵛᵒ and which contains many events of his life; together with numerous letters from the last King of Poland—from what I have read of this work, he seems to have spun out some parts of it, beyond what the subject requir'd; and I am inclin'd to think, he has totally omitted others—he admir'd the concision of Tacitus, but it does not appear to me that he has succeeded in the imitation of his style, while many of the anecdotes he relates as having occur'd during his residence in france, I am of opinion, from having been myself present at those periods in Paris, that they are deficient of that sort of evidence, which events of a political nature require.— he seems on too slight foundations to have establish'd, what he gives as facts; and in relation to himself, he is frequently diffuse on puerilities which little interest the reader.—This work he gave to his friend the advocate Carmigniani of Pisa, but there is no probability that it will ever be printed; for in Italy, reading is by no means so general, as in many other countries of Europe; and the studious, are commonly of that cast of men, who attach little worth, to writings of the nature of m^r mazzei's.—as I have formerly mention'd to you in my letters, that he had much reduc'd his estate, so from what I can now discover, it will not exceed 25,000. dollars, including the sum you have in your hands; tho' it certainly did surpass 50,000 ten years ago.—A few days since, I reciev'd, Sir, your letter to me, in date of the 14th of January, which came by land from Gibraltar.—The letter you mention having written to m^r mazzei, two months before the reciept of my first letter, never reach'd his hands.—I very greatly regret, Sir, that the talents of m^r Bartolini, are not likely to find in the U: States, a corresponding encouragement; and it is unfortunate that he will be unable to obtain from m^r Andreis the sculptor, who lately came from America, that information he is desirous of procuring; for from the very narrow views of the latter, he indulges the most improper jealousy for every one who might cause his own talents to be less esteem'd; and as he has, I presume, been consulted in the choice of those who have been sent, they will certainly not rise above the level of his own extreme mediocrity.—the truth is, I oppos'd m^r mazzei at the time, in the choice he made of this workman, but he consulted me when he had already contracted with them, and there was no remedy for the error he had committed, as they were both consider'd as very inferior workmen.—

You will at once perceive,[1] Sir, that nothing could be more useless than the presence, and return of m. andreis to carrara, for it must have been evident, he would oppose the choice of any one of superior merit to himself; and as to the capitals to be made at Carrara, nothing more was requisite than to designate the orders of the architecture, and the dimensions of the columns. whereas by the mode adopted, the frigate J. Adams has been employ'd a considerable time to convey the family of m^r Andreis to Italy: exclusive of the great expence which will accrue to the government, from the salary, & travelling charges of the latter during, at least, one year. on reading over my letter, I find I have omitted mentioning, what is perhaps necessary to the understanding of the 4th line of this page; to wit, "that I presume m^r andreis has been consulted in the choice &^{c}"—the truth is, that m^r m^{c}Call Consul of Barcelona, & agent of the squadron in the mediterranean, it appears was authoris'd by the commissioners for the rebuilding of Washington, to procure the Sculptors to be sent to the U: States, and direct the work of the capitals for the columns— He therefore proceeded to this place, in company with m^r Andreis, for the objects I have stated; as he was likewise instructed by the Commissioners, to invest the money necessary for these purposes, in the hands of m^r Samuel Purviance, late partner of his brother William, who a few years since acted as navy-agent here under m^r Smith, and in his bankruptcy involv'd the U: States for about 100.000 Dollars: not a cent of which, to this hour, has been recover'd.—I feel persuaded, Sir, from what I have now written, you are already convinced, that the mode adopted by the Commissioners, has neither been the most eligible, for obtaining the best workmen, or to prevent an useless expenditure of the public money.—In my former letters, when I mention'd that I possess the original bust in gesso of Cerrachi, it was merely with the view, to offer the intire use of it to the government, should they determine to erect a monument to General Washington; or simply to place his Statue in some public edifice at the federal-City; as I have understood something of this kind was thier intention: either of which, could be work'd in Italy, in a far superior style, I presume, and certainly, for about one half the price, it would cost in the U: States.—I have not, Sir, the material time requisite, as the vessel will sail in a day, or two, to know from Carrara the precise sum that a bust in gesso would cost for your own use, but it will be very inconsiderable; in marble, it would cost from the workman's hands, about Sixty dollars.—previous to recieving your letter, I had written to montepulciano, for samples of the last growth of wine; but generally the vintage of the last year, has been greatly inferior to preceeding ones; and in a particular manner, I found it so with that of montepulciano, which induced me intirely to relinquish the intention I had, to purchase of that kind for my own use.—we have, however, many other wines equally light, and very nearly as well flavour'd, at about one half the price: for the former is transported in flasks, nearly 150 miles over land, before it arrives at Florence.—not willing, therefore, to send you a quality; inferior to that formerly sent, I shall defer complying with your order; until the next vintage, which, however, is not drawn from the lees, until January; but should you prefer some of the other qualities, I shall be able to send it much earlier.—Since the return of the, legitimate Sovereigns of Italy, innumerable are the applications to me of every description of men, to find conveyances to the U: States; for the truth is, they are sorely disappointed in the hopes they had indulg'd, that a change of government, would restore them to the enjoyments of the least painful period of thier history; but they now percieve, that they are reliev'd from none of the burthens impos'd by the french, while in some cases, they are even augmented.—The clergy, you will readily believe, Sir, as a class of men, were the most clamorous, tho' not an acre of church-ground had been sold in all Tuscany, during the government of Napoleon: but since the return of the Grand-Duke, the finest of thier lands are Sold, or are for Sale; even with the approbation of His Holiness the Pope.—no one of the princes of Italy, not excepting His Holiness, has return'd to his former possessions, but under such enormous pecuniary conditions; impos'd by the chiefs of the allied Sovereigns, as must reduce the countries they govern, in the space of a few years, to the utmost state of depression.—The fate of the little republic of Lucca is yet undecided; in the meantime, they are govern'd by an Austrian military force.—The genoese having lost thier liberties, are now given over to the Sardinians; between whom, for ages there has existed the most irreconcilable hatred and animosity.—In short Sir, if the vexations of the people of Italy, during the government of the french, had excited a general discontent, this feeling under thier present masters, is now universal—excessive taxes, are collected with excessive rigour; while the hospitals are neglected, and the clamours of the public pensioners, produce no alleviation to thier misery.—Justice is procrastinated beyond all example, and the enormous fees of the tribunals, leave no alternative to the honest man, but to be legally despoil'd by the government, or accept the fraudulent Conditions of his debtor.—Mendicants & thieves have increas'd to so alarming a degree, that the government believe, if we may judge by thier total inattention, that the evil has no remedy.—In addition to these, & innumerable other miseries, the last harvest not having suffis'd for quite five months we have been compell'd to seek for Corn from asia & africa, which has drawn from the little state of Tuscany alone, at least ten millions of dollars; but the hand of Government has not bestow'd a Cent to relieve thier wretched State, while every art of the avaricious speculator, to increase the price of grain, has been permitted with impunity; and during the last three months, the peasants have intirely subsisted on the horse-beans of Egypt.—from this faint picture, of the present state of Italy, you will readily believe, Sir, that even anarchy itself is regretted: as it may likewise tend, to correct the exagerated eulogiums, which the corrupt editors of gazettes so lavishly bestow, on the virtues & wisdom of the legitimate sovereigns of europe.

Accept, Sir, the Sincere expressions of my unalterable esteem and respect—   TH: APPLETON

RC (DLC); subjoined to Dupl of Appleton to TJ, 20 Mar. 1816; endorsed by TJ as received 20 June 1816 and so recorded in SJL. Enclosures: (1) Death record for Philip Mazzei, Pisa, 26 Mar. 1816, giving time and date of death as

7:30 a.m., 19 Mar. 1816 (MS in DLC: TJ Papers, 206:36815–6; in the hand of Natale Squanci, prior of the church of San Martino, Pisa; in Italian; attested by Giovanni Battista Tortolini, chancellor of the archbishop of Pisa; with Niccolo Viviani's attestation of Tortolini's signature, followed by Appleton's attestation of Viviani's signature). (2) Giovanni Carmignani to TJ, 7 Apr. 1816. Other enclosure printed below.

Before his death Mazzei completed an autobiographical work containing MANY EVENTS OF HIS LIFE, but it remained unpublished until 1845–46, when the Italian historian Gino Capponi issued a two-volume edition, *Memorie della Vita e delle*

Peregrinazioni del fiorentino Filippo Mazzei. The first unabridged English translation appeared in 1980 (Margherita Marchione, ed., and S. Eugene Scalia, trans., *Philip Mazzei: My Life and Wanderings* [1980], 13–6). The LAST KING OF POLAND was Stanislaw II. Samuel and William Young PURVIANCE, navy agents in Leghorn, were partners in the failed firm of Degen, Purviance & Company. The American government had been its main creditor (Madison, *Papers, Pres. Ser.*, 1:68–9, 75–6). The GRAND-DUKE of Tuscany was Ferdinand III, and HIS HOLINESS THE POPE was Pius VII.

[1] Manuscript: "perieve."

ENCLOSURE

Will of Philip Mazzei

Estratto dalle Minute degli Atti ricevuti dal Dottor Giovanni Bonci Notaro Pubblico residente in Pisa

Al Nome di Dio Amen. L'anno del Nostro Signor Gesù Cristo mille ottocento quattordici, Indizione Romana Seconda, e questo di tre del Mese di Decembre, sotto il Pontificato di Sua Santità Pio Settimo, e Sua Altezza Imperiale, e Reale il Serenissimo Ferdinando Terzo Principe Reale d'Ungheria, e di Boemia, Arci-Duca di Austria, e Gran-Duca di Toscana, Nostro amatissimo Sovrano felicemente dominante

Di Avanti di Me infrascritto Dottor Giovanni Bonci, Notaro pubblico residente nellà Città di Pisa dalla parte del Nord in Via Lung'Arno al Numero Settecento tre Dipartimento del Mediterraneo, ed alla presenza dei Signori Molto Reverendo Sacerdote Signor Don Gaspero del fù Signor Anton Francesco Forti domiciliato in Pisa, in via di San Martino al Numero cinque cento novanta quattro, Luigi del fù Signor Giuseppe Del Seppia Dottore in Legge, e possidente domiciliato in Pisa in via, e Numero antedetto, Gaetano figlio del Signor Bartolommeo Gagliardi di professione Giovine di Studio domicilato in Pisa in via Sant'Antonio al numero cento sessanta nové, Giovan Battista del fù Signor Francesco Acconci di condizione possidente domiciliato in Pisa in Via del Montino al numero mille cento quaranta, il Molto Reverendo Sacerdote Signor Don Niccolò del fù Signor Vincenzo Niccolai domiciliato in Pisa in Via del Carmine nel Locale del Soppresso Convento di detto nome testimoni aventi i requisiti richiesti dalla Legge è comparso il Signor Filippo del fù Signor Domenico Mazzei Oriundo del Poggo a Cajano, Cittadino degli Stati uniti di America, Ciamberlano, e Consigliere Intimo del fù Stanislao Augusto, ultimo Re di Pollonia, attualmente domiciliato in Pisa in Via Cariola al numero cinque cento sessanta sei, a Me Notaro, e testimoni suddetti benissimo cognito, il quale essendo sano di mente come è apparso a Me Notaro suddetto, ed infrascritto, ed ai testimoni antedetti ha fatto, e fà il presente suo Nuncupativo testamento col quale delle sostanze, e beni suoi ha disposto, e dispone nel modo, che appresso cioè

Per validità della presente sua Disposizione lasciò, e lascia per una sola volta all'Opera di Santa Maria Del Fiore della Città di Firenze la tassa di lire tre, e soldi dieci; che nell'atto presente, ed alla presenza dei testimoni suddetti ha consegnate nelle mani di Me Notaro infrascritto per rimettersi all'Archivio dei Pubblici Contratti di Firenze unitamente alla Mandata del presente testamento—Per Ragione di Legato lasciò, e lascia alla Signora Carolina Volpe, Moglie del Dottor Sorini di Pescia la mensual Prestazione di scudi sei, sua vita natural durante e non più oltre

Per l'istessa ragione di Legato lasciò, e lascia Venti quattro Monete di dieci Paoli l'una per una volta soltanto a Fortunato Guerrucci suo Parrucchiere. Venti scudi per una volta soltanto ad ogni persona senza distinzione di sesso, che alla sua Morte sarà al suo Servizio, e avrà servito quattro anni Compiti. Quindici scudi a chi vi sarà, ed avrà servito tre intieri Anni: Dieci scudi a chi vi sarà, e avrà servito due anni intieri: A ragione di lire tre per mese per il tempo del prestato Servizio a chi attualmente vi sarà, e non avrà servito due intieri Anni: Cento scudi per una volta soltanto a Maddalena Stefanini, che fù circa dodici anni al suo servizio, che ora è Moglie di Bartolommeo Guidi, ed ordina, e vuole, che il detto Bartolommeo Guidi, che ora è al suo Servizio, possa continuandovi fino alla sua Morte, continuare ad abitar gratis colla sua famiglia nella Casetta contigua alla stalla della Casa di attuale Abitazione di detto Signor Testatore per lo spazio di due Anni da computarsi dal di della Morte del medesimo Signor Testatore, e che gli sia pagato una somma a ragione di scudi quattro all'anno computabile per il tempo, che sarà stato al suo servizio, incominciando a contare da questo presente soprascritto giorno fino a quello della Morte di esso Signor testatore, e ciò oltre gli scudi venti lasciati come sopra, a Chi avrà a detta Epoca servito per anni quattro

Per l'istessa Ragione di Legato lasciò, e lascia alla Signora Antonia Antoni, ne, Mazzei sua dilettissima sposa, e Consorte, oltre i mille scudi, che le assegnò prima di sposarla, la metà della netta Rendita dell'intiero suo Patrimonio, L'uso del primo, o del secondo Piano a sua scelta della Casa di attuale abitazione di esso Signore testatore con quella mobilia, che dagli infrascritti suoi Esecutori testamentarj sarà creduta necessario per fornirlo decentemente; la Metà dell'Argenteria, e Biancheria di tutta la Casa in piena proprietà, siccome il suo Vestiario, e Gioje: L'uso, ed i Comodi del Pian terreno per tenervi le cose di Necessario uso, come Olio, Vino, legna, Carbone Il libero uso dell'acqua di Asciano della Fonte, e dei Pozzi a comune coll'infrascritta sua Erede: La Metà del prodotto dell'orto, coll'onere di contribuire per detta metà alla Coltivazione del medesimo, il libero uso di uno dei due fienili, di una parte della stalla, e rimessa, e di uno dei suoi legni con libertà di variare, e ciò finchè detta Sua Signora Consorte naturalmente viverà, e condurrà vita Vedovile, ad eccezione però del vestiario, e delle Gioje, le quali legò, e lega alla medesima assolutamente, dichiarando a correzione di quanto sopra, che relativamente alla Metà dell'Argenteria, e della Biancheria, detta metà si intende concessa per semplice Uso alla condizione, che sopra—In tutti gli altri anzi ordina, e vuole il detto Testatore, che il giorno della sua Morte, o il seguente siano dati quaranta scudi per Elemosina repartibili egualmente alle famiglie povere nella Parrocchia di San Martino, e per quel riguarda la Deposizione del Cadavere, ed altre funzioni Funebri, di qualsiasi[1] condizione si voglia considerare, intende, e vuole, che non si mettano più di sei Ceri al Corpo, e che non oltrepassino il peso di libbre tre per ciascuno: Che non si mettano più di sei Candele di libbra, e quattro di mezza libbra all'Altar Maggiore, e due di mezza libbra ad ògni altro altare della Chiesa: Che, la distribuzione dei moccoli si faccia, come si crede necessaria: Che le Messe, di Requie siano trenta coll'elemosina di lire due per ciascheduna, oltre la doppia per la Messa Cantata: Che sia esclusa ogni sorte di Musica, e finalmente, che il suo Corpo sia sepolto nel Campo Santo fuori delle Mura, e per l'Adempimento della sua volontà nella forma da lui prescritta si rimette intieramente all'Onore dei suoi Esecutori Testamentarj; In tutti gli altri suoi beni Mobili, Immobili, Semoventi, Diritti, Azioni, e generalmente in tutto quello, e quanto detto Signor Testatore si troverà avere, e possedere all'Epoca della sua Morte, sua Erede universale istituì, e istituisce, e di sua propria boccà nominò, e nomina la Signora Elisabetta Mazzei sua dilettissima figlia e qualora la detta sua figlia non volesse, o non potesse adire la di lui Eredità, sostituì, e sostituisce, volgarmente, e pupillarmente alla medesima la prenominata Signora Antonia Mazzei sua Consorte, e nel caso, che neppur questa volesse, o potesse adire la detta Eredità, sostituì, e sostituisce volgarmente alla medesimà i Poveri di questa Città di Pisa con onere agli infrascritti Signori Esecutori testamentarj di chiedere in questo ultimo Caso autorizzazione al Real Governo, se occorra.

A detta Signora Antonia Mazzei sua Consorte, tutrice per disposto di legge dell'indicata sua Erede Universale, detto Signor testatore nominò e nomina in Curatore il Signore Avvocato Giovanni, del fù Signor Giovanni Antonio Carmignani, Professore nell'Imperiale, e Reale Università di Pisa. Il medesimo Signor Testatore ha eletto, ed elegge per Esecutori del presente suo testamento il Signor Cavalier Giovan Battista Ruschi, il Signor Conte Francesco Del Testa Del Tignoso, e il ridetto Signore Avvocato Giovanni Carmignani, e nel caso che detti Signori, o alcuno di essi non potesse, o non volesse accettare l'incarico, sostitui, e sostituisce detto Signor Testatore il Signore Avvocato Filippo Montemerli, i Signori Antonio, e Andrea fratelli Pini, il Signor Cavalier Ranieri Pesciolini, il Signor Cavaliere Ranieri Lorenzani Ghettini, il Signore Avvocato Bartolommeo Lazzerini, e i Signori Giacomo, e Cesare fratelli Lucchesini, Gentiluomini Lucchesi, bramando, che la sostituzione seguiti l'ordine della nomina, e che gli Esecutori non siano mai, nè più, nè meno di tre—Dichiarò, e dichiarà espressamente il detto Signor Testatore, che il presente suo testamento, qualora venisse invalidato rapporto all'Istituzione dell'Erede, deva valere, e sostenersi in quanto ai Legati, e a tutte le altre Disposizioni in esso contenute: E questo detto Signor Testatore disse, ed asserì essere, e voler che sia la sua ultima volontà, e Testamento Nuncupativo col quale esso Signor Testatore ha pronunziato alla presenza di Me Notaro, e testimonj suddetti con voce chiara, ed intelligibile l'Istituzione, e nome dell'Erede, non meno che i Legati, e le altre Disposizioni che vi si contengono, con essere stato da Me Notaro il detto Testamento contestualmente, <u>ridotto in scritto, e letto di parola</u> anzi, e senza diversione ad altri atti, ridotto in scritto, e letto di parola in parola alla presenza dell'istesso Signor Testatore, e testimoni suddetti—Fatto, è rogato in Pisa, e precisamente nella Casa di Abitazione del detto Signor Testatore, come sopra indicata l'anno, e il giorno soprascritto a ore quattro Pomeridiane avendo detto Signor Testatore alla presenza dei testimoni sopra nominati firmato insieme con Me Notaro il presente suo Testamento

FILIPPO MAZZEI

DOTTOR GIOVANNI BONCI Notaro pubblico residente in Pisa

E D I T O R S '   T R A N S L A T I O N

Extract of the brief of the proceedings received by Doctor Giovanni Bonci, notary public residing in Pisa

In the name of God amen. In the year of our Lord Jesus Christ one thousand eight hundred and fourteen, second Roman indiction, and this third day of the month of December, under the pontificate of His Holiness Pius the Seventh, and his imperial and royal highness the Most Serene Ferdinand the Third, royal prince of Hungary and Bohemia, archduke of Austria, and grand duke of Tuscany, our most beloved sovereign happily ruling,

Before me, the undersigned Doctor Giovanni Bonci, notary public residing in the city of Pisa, north district, Lung'Arno Street, number seven hundred and three, District of the Mediterraneo, and in the presence of the following witnesses, who meet the conditions required by law, the Most Reverend Don Gaspero, son of the late Mr. Anton Francesco Forti living in Pisa on San Martino Street number five hundred and ninety-four, Luigi, son of the late Mr. Giuseppe del Seppia, doctor in law and landowner residing in Pisa at the above-mentioned street and number, Gaetano, son of the late Mr. Bartolommeo Gagliardi, clerk, residing in Pisa on Sant'Antonio Street number one hundred and sixty-nine, Giovan Battista, son of the late Mr. Francesco Acconci, landowner, living in Pisa on Montino Street number one thousand one hundred and forty, the Most Reverend Father Don Niccolò, son of the late Mr. Vincenzo Niccolai, living in Pisa on Carmine Street, where the old convent of the same name used to be, has appeared Mr. Filippo, son of the late Mr. Domenico Mazzei, native of Poggio a Caiano, citizen of the United States of America, chamberlain and private counselor to the late Stanislaw II, last king of Poland, currently residing in Pisa on Cariola Street number five hundred and sixty-six, well known to the above-mentioned witnesses, being of sound mind as he appeared to me, the notary above and herein mentioned and to the aforesaid witnesses, and has made and makes the present nuncupative will, with which he has disposed and disposes his property and assets as follows:

As validated by this, his disposition, he bequeathed and bequeaths to the charity of Santa Maria del Fiore in the city of Florence the one-time payment of three lire and ten soldi, which in accordance with the present document and in the presence of the witnesses mentioned above, he delivered to me, the undersigned notary, to be remitted to the archive of public contracts of Florence together with the warrant of the present testament. By the terms of this legacy he bequeathed and bequeaths to Mrs. Carolina Volpe, wife of Doctor Sorini, of Pescia, the monthly allowance of six scudi, not to extend beyond the duration of her natural life.

By the same terms of this legacy he bequeathed and bequeaths a one-time payment of twenty-four coins of ten paolis each to his hairdresser Fortunato

Guerrucci; a one-time payment of twenty scudi to each person, regardless of sex, who is in his service at the time of his death, and has served four years in full; fifteen scudi to anyone who has been or will be in his service for three complete years; ten scudi to those who have served or will serve two complete years; three lire per month for the length of service performed, to those who are in his service and have not served two complete years; one hundred scudi in a one-time-only payment to Maddalena Stefanini, who has been in his service for approximately twelve years, and presently is the wife of Bartolommeo Guidi. He orders and desires that the said Bartolommeo Guidi, currently in his service, and continuing in such fashion until his death, be allowed to continue to live free of payment with his family in the cottage contiguous to the stable belonging to the present house of the said testator, for the period of two years beginning on the day of the said testator's death. He shall be paid a sum of four scudi per year, for the time he shall have been in his service, to be computed from the day indicated above, until the day of the testator's death. This is in addition to the twenty scudi bequeathed as indicated above to all those who by that time will have served for four years.

By the same terms of this legacy he bequeathed and bequeaths to Mrs. Antonia Antoni Mazzei, his beloved wife and consort, in addition to the thousand scudi that he awarded her before their marriage, half of the net income of his entire estate; the use of the first or second floor, as she chooses, of the testator's current domicile, with all the furniture that the undersigned executors believe necessary for furnishing it decently; the full possession of half of the silver and all the household linens, as well as her clothing and jewelry; the use of the ground floor and its amenities in order to store items of necessity, such as oil, wine, firewood and coal; the free use of the Asciano water from the fountain and wells, jointly with the heir of the undersigned; half of the garden produce, with the obligation of contributing half the cost of its cultivation; the free use of one of the barns, of part of the stable and storehouse, and of one of his carriages, whichever she chooses. All of this for as long as said spouse shall remain a widow, with the exception however of her clothing and jewelry, which the testator has bequeathed and bequeaths absolutely to her. By way of correction to what is decreed above relative to half of the silver and the household linens, the said half is conceded for simple use in accordance with the conditions indicated above. Regarding everything else, said testator orders and wishes that on the day of his death or the following day, forty scudi be given as alms, divided equally among the poor families of the parish of San Martino. As regards the disposition of the corpse, and other funeral services, the testator wills and desires that, under any conditions, no more than six candles be placed by the body, each candle to weigh no more than three pounds; that no more than six candles of one pound each, and four of a half-pound each, be placed on the main altar; and that two half-pound candles be placed on all other church altars. The candle ends shall be distributed as deemed necessary. There shall be thirty memorial masses, with alms at a cost of two lire each, and in addition there will be a chanted mass at double the cost. Every sort of music shall be excluded, and finally, his body shall be buried in the cemetery outside the city walls. For the fulfilment of his wishes in accordance with his will he relies entirely on the honor of his testamentary executors. As regards all of his other assets, personal property, real estate, vehicles, royalties, stocks, and generally everything else the testator will be found to have and possess at the time of his death, he has named and names, and has appointed and appoints from his own mouth, Miss Elisabetta Mazzei, his beloved daughter, to be his sole heir. In the event said daughter does not wish to, or cannot take possession of his inheritance, in her place he has substituted and substitutes, as vulgar and pupillary heir, the previously named Mrs. Antonia Mazzei, his spouse. In the event that she also does not wish to, or cannot accept said inheritance, in her place he has substituted and substitutes as vulgar heirs the poor of this city of Pisa, on the condition that the undersigned executors request the royal government's authorization, if necessary.

For the said Mrs. Antonia Mazzei his spouse, the lawful guardian of the above-designated sole heir, the said testator has appointed and appoints as administrator the attorney-at-law Giovanni, son of the late Mr. Giovanni Antonio Carmignani, professor at the imperial and royal University of Pisa. The same testator has selected and selects as executors of the present testament the Chevalier Giovan Battista Ruschi, the Count Francesco del Testa del Tignoso, and the above-mentioned attorney-at-law Giovanni Carmignani. In the event that these gentlemen, or any of them, are unable or do not wish to accept the charge, the said testator has substituted and substitutes the attorney-at-law Filippo Montemerli, the brothers Antonio and Andrea Pini, the Chevalier Ranieri Pesciolini, the Chevalier Ranieri Lorenzani Ghettini, the attorney-at-law Bartolommeo Lazzerini, and the brothers Giacomo and Cesare Lucchesini, gentlemen of Lucca, wishing that the substitution follow the order in which they are named and that the number of executors never be more nor less than three.—The said testator has declared, and expressly declares, that should his testament be at any time invalidated as regards the appointment of the heir, it must still be valid and upheld with regard to the bequests and all other dispositions included herein. The said testator stated and desired this testament to be his last nuncupative will and testament, whereby he has declared, in a clear and intelligible voice, in my presence and that of the above-mentioned witnesses, the appointment and name of his heir, as well as his legacies and other dispositions contained herein. The said testament has been concomitantly put into writing and read word-by-word by the undersigned; in the absence of any other contracts it has been put into writing and read word-by-word in the presence of the said testator, and the above-mentioned witnesses. The testament having been drafted and drawn up in Pisa, specifically in the said testator's house, on the year and day indicated above, at four o'clock in the afternoon, the said testator has signed with me, his notary, in the presence of the above-named witnesses, this, his testament.

FILIPPO MAZZEI

DOCTOR GIOVANNI BONCI notary public residing in Pisa

Tr (DLC: TJ Papers, 206:36807–15); in an unidentified hand; with a 3 Apr. 1816 attestation at foot of text in the hand of Bonci, with his signature and seal, followed by a 3 Apr. 1816 attestation of Bonci's signature in the hand of Pisa governor Niccolo Viviani, with his signature and seal, and with a 15 Apr. 1816 attestation of Viviani's signature at head of text in the hand of Thomas Appleton, the United States consul at Leghorn, with his signature and seal. Translation by Dr. Adrienne Ward. Also enclosed in Appleton to TJ, 15 May 1816.

The spring at ASCIANO was described as located "Two miles and a half east of the Pisa baths, passing by a pleasant road at the mountain's foot, through the valley of Asciano, and near the great aqueduct of the town, you come to a prolongation of the mountain Colle, which, advancing into the plain, takes the name of Monticello; at its extremity arises the acidulous spring of Asciano" (John Nott, *A Chemical Dissertation on the Thermal Waters of Pisa, and on the neighbouring Acidulous Spring of Asciano* [London,

1793], 59). VOLGARMENTE, E PUPILLARMENTE ("vulgar and pupillary"): a vulgar substitution is the "nomination of a person to take the place of a previously named heir who has refused or failed to accept an inheritance" (*Black's Law Dictionary*), while a pupillary substitution is the "nomination of a substitute to take the place of someone who dies before inheriting" (*OED*).

[1] Manuscript: "qualsisia."

From Lafayette

MY DEAR FRIEND — La Grange April 16[h] 1816

This Letter Will Be delivered By Mr Geo. Flower Who is Going over With an intention to Settle in America. I know Him to Be one of the Most desirable Acquisitions the U.S. Can Make. His departure from England is Suspended Untill a Line of introduction from me to You Can Reach Him. While it Shows the proper Sense He Has of Your Acquaintance, I find in it a Very pleasing Gratification, as Mr Flower, in my Opinion, Unites Every thing that is Respectable and Amiable. I Have Been Very Happy to Receive Him at La Grange With His fellow traveller mr Birkbeck Whose Account of their Agricultural tour, Both Being Capital farmers, Has Been published. He Was a friend to Whitbread. His political Sentiments are Congenial With Yours and Mine—But I Shall only Request in His Behalf Your kind Welcome and Good Advices, and present You With the Best Wishes and Most Affectionate Regard of

Your old friend — LAFAYETTE

RC (DLC); endorsed by TJ as received 25 Nov. 1816 and so recorded in SJL.

From LeRoy, Bayard & McEvers

SIR — Newyork the 16 April 1816.

We will communicate to Mess[r] Van Staphorst what you have done us the honor of writing to us under date of the 7[t] ins[t] and 'till we can receive their further directions we think we may Say that these friends will not object to the further extension you desire while they must be assured, as we ourselves fully are, that at the expiration of the Several terms, which you are pleased to fix, you will punctually provide for the reimbursement of the bonds. —

We have the honor to be with the highest regard Sir   Your obed^t h^l S^t LeRoy Bayard & McEvers

RC (DLC); at foot of text: "The Honble Thomas Jefferson"; endorsed by TJ as a letter from "Leroy & co." received 3 May 1816 and so recorded in SJL.

To Isaac Briggs

Dear Sir   Poplar Forest near Lynchburg. Apr. 17. 16

Your favor of Mar. 30. was recieved just as I was setting out for this place, 90. miles S.W from Monticello. I inclose an answer to the acceptable letter of your daughter. the sensibility expressed in hers for services so moderate shews a heart of great susceptibility, and which under your careful instruction promises to make happy parents and friends.

I am glad you have explained what I had considered as a breach of confidence in mr Canby, but which seems to have been a want of caution only in trusting my letter to a person capable of copying and publishing it without leave. this has so repeatedly happened to me that I have at times been near coming to a resolution never to answer a letter from any one whom I did not personally know and confide in. a similar abuse has been lately committed against mr Adams and myself by a person's publishing our answers to a letter written by himself.

Our legislature has past a law for having an accurate map made of the whole state, by actual surveys of the roads, rivers, mountains E^{t}c. to be corrected by astronomical observations. this last will be a distinct work. in the execution of it, I suppose, the person employed will travel with his assistant & instruments a gigg and strong horse, short journies of half a day at a time, from county to county, taking the Longitudes & Latitudes of the mouths of water courses, remarkable mountains, towns, Courthouses E^{t}c. employing the intervening days of rain, or of cloudy noons or evenings in making his calculations. as in a former letter you stated to me that you had quitted the business at Baltimore, presuming you might be as yet disengaged, I proposed to our Governor the inviting you to undertake this work, provided they would give such compensation as would make it worth your while. on this point I have fears. I mentioned that a prime Hadley's circle of Borda's construction would be necessary and perhaps an

Equatorial. should you undertake it, I would wish you to consider again the idea I had when Capt Lewis was about to undertake his Western journey, of relieving him from a dependance on any portable instrument of time, liable in such a journey to so many accidents, by substituting the use of a meridian, which, with an Equatorial, after ascertaining your latitude, can always be found, at land. I then explained this idea to you, and will here recall it to your recollection. the method I proposed was 'to observe the moon's distance from the meridian of the place at any moment and take by observation her right ascenscion at that moment. find from the tables her distance from the meridian of Greenwich at the moment she had that right ascenscion. if she was between the two meridians, add the two distances, if she was East or West of both, subtract one from the other, and you have the distance between the two meridians. in this way the appulse of the moon with a star, or the instant when she is in the same vertical with a star, may be advantageously taken for the moment of observation.' that the meridian of the place of observation has never been resorted to in Europe as an element in taking the lunar distances, does not deter me from supposing it may be used to advantage because there they have no occasion for them, having every where observatories, with good timepieces and telescopes, with which they can practise the method by Jupiter's satellites; and at sea they can have no meridian. but in our perambulations by land for the purpose of fixing our geography, where we can have no apparatus but what we can carry with us, I do not see why we should not avail ourselves of this important element of the meridian of the place of observation, it being so obvious that it's distance from the moon, and her's, at the same moment from the meridian at Greenwich give the difference of meridians. I am but a theorist, very little practised in these operations. but I wish you to turn your mind to it, and if it appears practicable, and to offer any advantages, tell me so, and whether you would undertake this business, and I will propose the providing an Equatorial. I suppose this operation will employ you a year at least, as we have about 100 counties in every one of which several points should be fixed: indeed I think the distances of our observations should not exceed 20. miles. I salute you with friendship and respect.   Th: Jefferson

PoC (DLC); ink stained, with some text rewritten by TJ; at foot of first page: "Mr Isaac Briggs"; endorsed by TJ. Enclosure: TJ to Mary B. Briggs, 17 Apr. 1816.

The similar abuse alluded to by TJ was the publication of replies by him and John Adams to letters from Noah Worcester in which Worcester enclosed and invited reactions to several pamphlets

(Worcester to TJ, 18 Oct. 1815). Worcester's letter to Adams of 23 Jan. 1816 noted that he had sent "Similar copies to Mr Jefferson, and intend soon to send to Mr Jay." Worcester hoped to "obtain a testimony from three able and aged statesmen, before they shall leave the world" (MHi: Adams Papers). TJ's letter to Worcester of 29 Jan. 1816 and Adams's written from Quincy, 6 Feb. 1816, were published in Worcester, *The Friend of Peace, No. IV. reasons for believing that efforts for the abolition of war will not be in vain* (Cambridge, Mass., [1816]; Poor, *Jefferson's Library*, 9 [no. 488]), 22–4, 25–6.

To Mary B. Briggs

April 17. 16

I thank you, my excellent young friend, for your kind letter of Mar. 7. the heart must be of uncommon sensibility which feels so strongly slight degrees of merit in others. if I have ever been useful to your father, it was by doing what was much more useful to the public for whom I acted, by availing them of the services of a faithful and able citizen. it is not then to me, you are indebted, but to his worth and science which marked him for notice. mine was but an act of duty, which like the payment of a debt, has no merit to claim; and I feel my self fully remunerated by it's having been the means of introducing to me the knolege of an amiable daughter, inheriting the kind heart of her father, copying, in the age of the passions, the virtues of a model tested by time, and[1] experience. go on then, my worthy friend, in this career of excellence, and be strong in the assurance given by an inspired pen, 'I have been young, and now I am old; and yet never saw I the righteous forsaken, or his seed begging their bread': and if the prayers of an old man can be of any avail, you shall ever have mine most ardently. accept my friendly salutations   TH: JEFFERSON

PoC (MHi); on verso of reused address cover to TJ; at foot of text: "Miss Mary B. Briggs"; endorsed by TJ. Enclosed in TJ to Isaac Briggs, 17 Apr. 1816.

'I HAVE BEEN YOUNG . . . BEGGING THEIR BREAD': Psalms 37.25.

[1] TJ here canceled what appears to be "ripened by."

To Susan Maria Bruff

April 17. 16.

I sincerely condole with you, Madam, on the loss of your worthy father, of which your letter gives me the first information. to the public he bade fair to be very useful by his inexhaustible ingenuity; and to his family he must have been inestimable. these afflictions are our common lot; and they come from a hand to which we must bow with resignation. the example of virtue and industry he exhibited will be useful to all; and honorable to his family. to them I know that no words can carry consolation. time & silence are the only medecines, which can abate their sorrows: and under this persuasion, I think it a duty not to awaken painful recollections by dwelling on them further than by assuring you of my sympathy, and my high respect and best wishes for his family and for yourself.   TH: JEFFERSON

RC (DLC); addressed: "Miss Susan Maria Bluff Georgetown." PoC (DLC); on verso of a reused address cover from William F. Gray to TJ; mutilated at seal, with missing words rewritten by TJ; at foot of text: "Miss Susan Maria Bruff"; endorsed by TJ. Enclosed in TJ to James Monroe, 17 Apr. 1816.

To James Monroe

DEAR SIR   Poplar Forest Apr. 17. 16.

The inclosed letter is for a daughter of the late Dr Bruff, who wrote me a pathetic letter on the death of her father. altho I considered him as an ingenious and virtuous man, and always shewed him that I wished his success, yet there never was any particular acquaintance between us beyond the drawing of a tooth or two. I do not therefore exactly see the scope of the letter. but whatever it be I have given it the go-by by a few commonplace expressions of condolance. unwilling to excite curiosity by sending a letter with her address and my frank to the post office,[1] I was sure you would permit me to pass it to her under your cover, and that you would have it delivered by one of your messengers without going thro' the post office. ever and affectionately yours   TH: JEFFERSON

RC (NjP: Andre deCoppet Collection); addressed: "James Monroe esq. Secretary of State Washington"; franked; postmarked Lynchburg, 20 Apr.; endorsed by Monroe. PoC (MHi); on recto of a portion of a reused address cover to TJ; endorsed by TJ. Enclosure: TJ to Susan Maria Bruff, 17 Apr. 1816.

[1] Preceding four words interlined.

From James L. Jefferson

DR UNCLE   Warren April 19 1815 [1816]

There has been no court on the account of the judge not comeing down he sent a mesenger to the court house on monday stating that he was very ill but that he would try and be down on wednesday but yesterday Mr Booker received a letter from him stating that he was quite Disabled and could not attend but that he would have a call court to try my fathers will we were ready to come to a trial every esential witness on our side was at the court house but I beleive the widow was not

    I am Sir affectionate nephew   JAMES L JEFFERSON

RC (ViU: TJP-CC); misdated; between closing and signature: "Mr Thomas Jefferson"; endorsed by TJ as received 24 Apr., without year of composition or receipt, but recorded in SJL as received 24 Apr. 1816.

Randolph Jefferson's WILL was being contested by his sons in the Buckingham County Court. THE WIDOW was Mitchie B. Pryor Jefferson.

To Wilson Cary Nicholas

DEAR SIR   Poplar Forest Apr. 19. 16.

    In my letter of the 2^d inst. I stated, according to your request what occurred to me on the subjects of Defence and Education; and I will now proceed to do the same on the remaining subject of your's of Mar. 22. the construction of a general map of the state. for this the legislature directs that there shall be

I.   a topographical survey of each county.

II.   a General survey of the Outlines of the state, and it's leading features of rivers and mountains.

III. an Astronomical survey for the correction & collocation of the others, and

IV. a Mineralogical survey.

    I. altho' the topographical survey of each county is referred to it's court in the first instance, yet such a controul is given to the Executive as places it effectively under his direction. that this controul must be freely and generally exercised I have no doubt. nobody expects that the justices of the peace in every county are so familiar with the astronomical and geometrical principles to be employed in the execution of this work as to be competent to decide what candidate possesses them in the highest degree, or in any degree: and indeed I think it would be reasonable, considering how much the other[1] affairs of the state must engross of the time of the Governor & Council, for them to make it a prerequisite for every candidate to undergo an examination by the Mathematical professor of W^m & Mary college, or some other professional character, and to ask for a special and confidential report of the grade of qualification of each candidate examined. if one, competently qualified, can be found for every half dozen counties, it will be as much perhaps as can be expected.

Their office will be to survey the Rivers, Roads, Mountains and Boundaries of each county.

1. a proper division of the surveys of the **Rivers** between them and the General surveyor might be to ascribe to the latter so much as is navigable, and to the former the parts not navigable, but yet sufficient for working machinery, which the law requires. on these they should note confluences, other natural & remarkable objects, towns, mills or other machines, ferries, bridges, crossings of roads, passages thro' mountains, mines, quarries E^{t}c.

2. in surveying the **Roads**, the same objects should be noted, and every permanent stream crossing them, and these streams should be laid down according to the best information they can obtain, to their confluence with the main stream.

3. the **Mountains**, other than those ascribed to the General surveyor should be laid down by their names and bases which last will be generally designated by the circumscription of water courses and roads on both sides, without a special survey around them. their gaps are also required to be noted.

4. on the **Boundaries** the same objects should be noted. where a boundary falls within the operations of the General surveyor, it's survey by them should be dispensed with, and where it is common to two counties, it might be ascribed wholly to one, or divided between the surveyors respectively. all these surveys should be delineated on the same scale, which the law directs, I believe, (for I have omitted to bring the copy of it with me to this place.) if it has not fixed the scale, I think about half an inch to the mile would be a convenient one, because it would generally bring the map of a county within the compass of a sheet of paper. and here I will suggest what would be a great desideratum for the public, to wit, that a single sheet map, of each county separately, on a scale of half an inch to the mile be engraved and struck off. there are few housekeepers who would not wish to possess a map of their own county, many would purchase those of their circumjacent counties, and many would take one of every county, & form them into an Atlas, so that I question if as many copies of each particular map would not be sold as of the general one. but these should not be made until they recieve the astronomical corrections, without which they can never be brought together and joined into larger maps, at the will of the purchaser.

Their instrument should be a Circumferentor with cross spirit levels on it's face, a graduated rim, and a double Index, the one fixed, the other moveable, with a Nonius on it. the needle should never be depended on for an angle.

II. the General survey divides itself into two distinct operations; the one on the tide waters, the other above them.

On the tide-waters the State will have little to do. some time before the war, Congress authorised the Executive to have an accurate survey made of the whole sea-coast of the US. comprehending, as well as I remember, the principal bays and harbors. a mr Hassler, a mathematician of the first order from Geneva, was engaged in the execution and was sent to England to procure proper instruments. he has lately returned with such a set as never before crossed the Atlantic, and is scarcely possessed by any nation on the continent of Europe. we shall be furnished then by the General government with a better survey than we can make, of our sea-coast, Chesapeak bay, probably the Potomak to the Navy yard at Washington, and possibly of James river to Norfolk, and York river to York town. I am not however able to say that these, or what other are the precise limits of their intentions. the Secretary of the Treasury would probably inform us. above these limits, whatever they are, the surveys & soundings will belong to the present undertaking of the state: and if mr Hassler has time, before he commences his general work, to execute this for us, with the use of the instruments of the US. it is impossible[2] we can put it into any train of execution equally good: and any compensation he may require, will be less than it would cost to purchase instruments of our own, and have the work imperfectly done by a less able hand. if we are to do it ourselves, I acknolege myself too little familiar with the methods of surveying a coast and taking soundings, to offer any thing on the subject approved by practice. I will pass on therefore to

the General Survey of the **Rivers** above the tide waters, the **Mountains**, and external **Boundaries.**

1. **Rivers.** I have already proposed that the General survey shall comprehend these from the tide-waters as far as they are navigable only. and here we shall find one half of the work already done, and as ably as we may expect to do it. in the great controversy between the Lords Baltimore & Fairfax, between whose territories the Potomak from it's mouth to it's source was the chartered boundary, the question was which branch, from Harper's ferry upwards, was to be considered as the Potomak? two able mathematicians therefore were brought over from England at the expence of the parties, and under sanction of the sentence pronounced between them, to survey the two branches, and ascertain which was to be considered as the Main

stream. Ld Fairfax took advantage of their being here to get a correct survey by them of his whole territory, which was bounded by the Potomak, the Rappahanoc, and a line uniting their two[3] sources. the work was executed, as was believed in the most accurate manner, their survey was doubtless filed and recorded in Ld Fairfax's office, and I presume it still exists among his land papers. he furnished a copy of that survey to Col° Fry and my father, who entered it on a reduced scale into their map. as far as latitudes, and admeasurement accurately horizontal could produce exactness, I expect this survey is to be relied on. but it is lawful to doubt whether it's longitudes may not need verification; because at that day, the corrections had not been made in the lunar tables, which have since introduced the method of ascertaining the longitude by the lunar distances; & that by Jupiter's satellites was impracticable in an ambulatory survey. the most we can count on is that they may have employed some sufficient means to ascertain the longitude of the first source of the Potomak, the meridian of which was to be Ld Baltimore's boundary. the longitudes therefore should be verified and corrected, if necessary; and this will belong to the Astronomical survey.

The other rivers only then, from their tidewaters up as far as navigable, remain for this Operator, and on them the same objects should be noted as proposed in the county surveys; and, in addition, their breadth at remarkable parts, such as the confluence of other streams, falls, and ferries, the soundings of their main channels, bars, rapids, and principal sluices thro' their falls, their current at various places, and, if it can be done without more cost than advantage, their fall between certain stations.

2. **Mountains.** I suppose the law contemplates, in the general survey, only the principal continued ridges, and such insulated mountains as being correctly ascertained in their position, and visible from many and distant places, may, by their bearings, be useful correctives for all the surveys, and especially those of the counties.   of the continued ridges, the Alleganey, North mountain & Blue ridge are principal. ridges of partial lengths may be left to designation in the county surveys. of insulated mountains there are the Peaks of Otter in Bedford, which I believe may be seen from about 20 counties, Willis's mountains in Buckingham, which from their detached situation, and so far below all other mountains, may be seen over a great space of country, Peter's mountain in Albemarle, which, from it's eminence above all others of the South West ridge, may be seen to a great distance, probably to Willis's mountain, and with that and

the Peaks of Otter furnishes a very extensive triangle; and doubtless there are many unknown to me, which being truly located, offer valuable indications and correctives for the county surveys.   for example. the sharp peak of Otter being precisely fixed in position by it's longitude and latitude, a simple observation of latitude, taken at any place from which that peak is visible, and an observation of the angle it makes with the meridian of the place, furnish a right angled spherical triangle, of which the portion of meridian intercepted between the latitudes of the place, and peak, will be one side. with this and the given angles, the other side, constituting the difference of longitude, may be calculated, and thus by a correct position of these commanding points, that of every place from which any one of them is visible, may, by observations of latitude and bearing, be ascertained in longitude also. if two such objects be visible from the same place, it will afford, by another triangle, a double correction.

The gaps in the continued ridges, ascribed to the General surveyor, are required by the law to be noted; and so also are their heights. this must certainly be understood with some limitation, as the height of every knob in these ridges could never be desired. probably the law contemplated only the eminent mountains in each ridge, such as would be conspicuous objects of observation to the country at great distances, and would offer the same advantages as the insulated mountains. such eminences in the Blue ridge will be more extensively useful than those of the more Western ridges. the height of gaps also, over which roads pass, were probably in view.

But how are these heights to be taken, & from what base? I suppose from the plain on which they stand. but it is difficult to ascertain the precise horisontal line of that plain, or to say where the ascent above the general face of the country begins. where there is a river or other considerable stream, or extensive meadow plains near the foot of a mountain, which is much the case in the vallies dividing the Western ridges, I suppose that may be fairly considered in the level of it's base, in the intendment of the law. where there is no such term of commencement, the Surveyor must judge, as well as he can from his view, what point is in the general level of the adjacent country.   How are these heights to be taken, and with what instrument? where a good base can be found, the geometrical admeasurement is the most satisfactory. for this a theodolite must be provided of the most perfect construction, by Ramsden or Troughton if possible; and for horizontal angles it will be the better of two telescopes. but such bases are rarely to be found. when none such, the height may still be measured geometrically, by ascending or descending the mountain with the theodolite, measuring it's face from station to station, noting it's inclination between these stations, and the hypothenusal difference of that inclination, as indicated on the vertical ark of the theodolite. the sum of the perpendiculars corresponding with the hypothenusal measures, is the height of the mountain.   but a barometrical admeasurement is preferable to this. since the late improvements in the theory they are to be depended on nearly as much as the geometrical, and are much more convenient and expeditious. the barometer should have a sliding Nonius and a thermometer annexed, with a screw at the bottom to force up the column of mercury solidly. without this precaution they cannot be transported at all; and even with it, they are in danger from every severe jolt. they go more safely on a baggage horse than in a carriage. the heights should be measured on both sides to shew the rise of the country at every ridge.

Observations of longitude and latitude should be taken by the surveyor at all confluences of considerable streams, and on all mountains of which he measures the heights, whether insulated, or in ridges. for this purpose he should be furnished with a good Hadley's circle of Borda's construction, with three limbs & Nonius indexes. if not to be had, a sextant of brass, and of the best construction may do; and a Chronometer. to these is to be added a Gunter's chain, with some appendix for plumbing the chain.

3. the External Boundaries of the state. to wit, Northern, Eastern, Southern and Western. the Northern boundary consists of 1. the Potomak. 2. a Meridian from it's source to Mason & Dixon's line. 3. a continuation of that line to the meridian of the North Western corner of Pensylvania, and 4. of that meridian to it's intersection with the Ohio. 1. the Potomak is supposed, as beforementioned to be surveyed to our hand. 2. the Meridian from it's source to Mason and Dixon's line was, I believe surveyed by them when they run the dividing line between Ld Baltimore & Penn. I presume it can be had from either Annapolis or Philadelphia, and I think there is a copy of it, which I got from Dr Smith, in an Atlas of the library of Congress. nothing better can be done by us. 3. the continuation of Mason & Dixon's line and the meridian from it's termination to the Ohio was done by mr Rittenhouse & others, and copies of their work are doubtless in our offices as well as in those of Pensylvania. what has been done by Rittenhouse can be better done by no one.

The **Eastern** boundary being the sea coast we have before presumed will be surveyed by the general government.

The **Southern** boundary. this has been extended and marked in different parts in the chartered latitude of 36.° 30.′ by three different sets of Commissioners. the Eastern part by Dr Byrd and other Commissioners from Virginia & N. Carolina: the middle by Fry & Jefferson from Virginia, & Churton & others from N. Carolina: and the Western by Dr Walker and Daniel Smith now of Tennissee. whether Byrd's survey now exists, I do not know. his journal is still in possession of some one of the Westover family, and it would be well to seek for it in order to judge of that portion of the line. Fry and Jefferson's journal was burnt in the Shadwell house about 50. years ago, with all the materials of their map. Walker & Smith's survey is probably in our offices. there is a copy of it in the Atlas beforementioned. but that survey was made on the spur of a particular occasion, and with a view to a particular object only. during the revolutionary war we were informed that a treaty of peace was on the carpet in Europe on the principle of Uti possidetis: and we dispatched those gentlemen immediately to ascertain the intersection of our Southern boundary with the Missisipi, and ordered Col^o Clarke to erect a hasty fort on the first bluff above the line, which was done as an act of possession. the intermediate line between that & the termination of Fry & Jefferson's line was provisory only, and not made with any particular care. that then needs to be resurveyed as far as the Cumberland mountain. but the Eastern & Middle surveys will only need, I suppose, to have their longitudes rectified by the Astronomical surveyor.

The **Western** boundary, consisting of the Ohio, Big Sandy & Cumberland mountain, having been established while I was out of the country, I have never had occasion to enquire whether they were actually surveyed and with what degree of accuracy. but this fact being well known to yourself particularly, and to others who have been constantly present in the state, you will be more competent to decide what is to be done in that quarter. I presume indeed that this boundary will constitute the principal, and most difficult part of the operations of the General surveyor.

The injunctions of the act to note the magnetic variations merit diligent attention. the law of those variations is not yet sufficiently known to satisfy us that sensible changes do not sometimes take place at small intervals of time and place. to render these observations of the variations easy, and to encourage their frequency, a copy of a table of amplitudes should be furnished to every surveyor, by which, wherever he has a good Eastern horison, he may, in a few seconds, at sunrise, ascertain the variation. this table is to be found in the book called the Mariner's compass rectified; but more exactly in the Connaissance des tems for 1778. and 1788. all of which are in the library of

Congress. it may perhaps be found in other books more easily procured, and will need to be extracted only from $36\frac{1}{2}$.° to 40.° degrees
of latitude.

III. The Astronomical survey. this is the most important of all the
operations. it is from this alone we are to expect real truth. measures
and rhumbs taken on the spherical surface of the earth, cannot be
represented on a plain surface of paper without astronomical corrections: and, paradoxical as it may seem, it is nevertheless true that
we cannot know the relative position of two places on the earth, but
by interrogating the sun, moon, and stars. the Observer must therefore correctly fix, in longitude and latitude, all remarkable points
from distance to distance. those to be selected of preference are
the confluences, rapids, falls and ferries of water courses, summits of
mountains, towns, courthouses, and angles of counties. and where
these points are more than a third, or half a degree distant, they
should be supplied by observations of other points, such as mills,
bridges, passes thro' mountains E^tc. for in our latitudes, half a degree
makes a difference of three eighths of a mile in the length of the degree of Longitude. these points first laid down, the intermediate
delineations to be transferred from the particular surveys to the general map, are adapted to them by contractions or dilatations. the Observer will need a best Hadley's circle of Borda's construction, by
Troughton if possible (for they are since Ramsden's time) and a best
chronometer.

Very possibly an Equatorial may be needed. this instrument set to
the observed latitude, gives the meridian of the place. in the lunar
observations <u>at sea</u> this element cannot be had, and in Europe <u>by
land</u>, these observations are not resorted to for longitudes, because at
their numerous fixed Observatories they are prepared for the better
method of Jupiter's satellites. but here where our geography is still to
be fixed by a portable apparatus only, we are obliged to resort, as at
sea, to the lunar observations; with the advantage however of a fixed
meridian. and altho' the use of a meridian in these observations is a
novelty yet, placed under new circumstances, we must countervail
their disadvantages by what ever new resources they offer. it is obvious, that the observed distance of the Moon from the meridian of the
place, and her calculated distance from that of Greenwich at the same
instant, give the difference of meridians, without dependance on any
measure of time; by addition of the observations, if the moon be between the two meridians, by subtraction if East or West of both. the
association therefore of this instrument with the Circular one, by introducing another element, another process, and another instrument,

furnishes a test of the observations with the Hadley, adds to their certainty, and, by it's corroborations, dispenses with that multiplication of observations which is necessary with the Hadley when used alone. this idea however is suggested by theory only; and it must be left to the judgment of the Observer, who will be employed, whether it would be practicable and useful. to him, when known, I shall be glad to give further explanations. the cost of the Equatorial is about the same with that of the Circle, when of equal workmanship.

Both the Surveyor and Astronomer should journalise their proceedings daily, and send copies of their journals monthly to the Executive, as well to prevent loss by accident, as to make known their progress.

IV. Mineralogical survey. I have never known in the US. but one eminent mineralogist, who could have been engaged on hire. this was a mr Goudon from France who came over to Philadelphia 6. or 7. years ago. being zealously devoted to the science, he proposed to explore the new field which this country offered: but being scanty in means, as I understood, he meant to give lectures in winter which might enable him to pass the summer in mineralogical rambles. it is long since I have heard his name mentioned, and therefore do not know whether he is still at Philadelphia, or even among the living. the literary gentlemen of that place can give the information, or perhaps point out some other equal to the undertaking.

I believe I have now, Sir, gone over all the subjects of your letter. which I have done with less reserve to multiply the chances of offering here and there something which might be useful. it's greatest merit however will be that of evidencing my respect for your commands and of adding to the proofs of my great consideration & esteem.

TH: JEFFERSON

RC (MHi). PoC (DLC: TJ Papers, 207:36822–3, 36825, 36824, 36826–7); at foot of first page: "Govʳ Nicholas."

English-born professionals who were chosen to SURVEY THE TWO BRANCHES of the Potomac River, 1736–37, included William Mayo and Robert Brooke (Sarah S. Hughes, *Surveyors and Statesmen: Land Measuring in Colonial Virginia* [1979], 85–6, 144–9; Robert A. Brock and Virgil A. Lewis, *Virginia and Virginians* [1888], 1:88). UTI POSSIDETIS is the "doctrine that old administrative boundaries will become international boundaries when a political subdivision achieves independence" (*Black's Law Dictionary*). For TJ's instructions to George Rogers Clark, Thomas Walker, and Daniel Smith regarding the survey of the INTERSECTION OF OUR SOUTHERN BOUNDARY WITH THE MISSISIPI and the establishment of a fort at the mouth of the Ohio River, see *PTJ*, 3:273–9. MR GOUDON: Silvain Godon.

[1] Word interlined.
[2] Manuscript: "impospossible."
[3] Word interlined.

From William Short

Dear Sir   Philadelphia Ap: 23—16

Your two favors of the 7th & 9th have come to my hands & I return you many thanks for them. I calculated from your letter that you would be absent until the early part of May, & therefore did not acknowlege its reciept immediately. This will be anterior to your return & will wait for you at Monticello, where I hope you will arrive at the time expected & in good health. You will find there also one from Mr Vaughan which will inform you that I paid to him the 5. doll. Accept my thanks for having thus settled this trifle—I was considering how I should be able to discharge this part of the sum allotted, & had intended to have diminished so much on the draught a^{ct} Mr Higginb^m has authorized me to make on Richmond for the balance of his last payment—& for which I am only waiting to learn from Mr Gibson that he has recieved it—The mode of paying to Mr Vaughan is more convenient.

I have written to Mr Carter to inform him of the decision—but I was not able to tell him the sum he owed me, because I did not know how to calculate the interest on account of the law of the state regulating that matter. I do not know when the law was passed, nor do I know certainly whether contracts anterior to that law are to change the rate of interest from that epoch, or to go on at the old rate of 5. p^{ct}—Would you be so good as to complete all your other favors on this head by calculating the interest on Mr Carters debt for me, & letting me know the sum to which I am now entitled. I will wait for your letter in order to ascertain this point—& I shall then be able to proceed on sure ground.

I regret extremely the prospect of the honest old servant[1] la Motte. I think Monroe might have strained a point in his favor—but probably he thought that all that could be given to foreigners had been exhausted in placing a Minister of that description at Paris—& I take for granted that M. in his present state of probation is obliged to be particularly on his guard—It is like a woman before securing the husband, but with every prospect of doing so. She is obliged to take heed to her steps. He has had a hard apprenticeship, & it would be still harder if he were to fail now; of which however I should suppose there were no probability. I am sorry for the issue of La Motte's application, because acts of injustice are always painful, & most so when growing out of the commission or omission of a friend.

I cannot tell you the pleasure I have had in the unexpected treat of seeing one of your family here, & of tracing in her the likeness of your family. How much it would have added to this pleasure if I had had a house with a Lady in it, in which I could have received & entertained & lodged Miss R. It would seem so natural to me that any & every part of your family should be received by me in this City, that I have not been able to keep out of my mind the pleasure such a circumstance would afford me. It is doubtful whether I shall ever possess such an house, & therefore I regret it the more. I have had few opportunities of seeing Miss R. as I have long renounced going to those parties where the beaux & belles of Philadelphia assemble—but I have had great pleasure in the few moments of conversation I have had with her, & she has had a general success here. Although I have given up such parties I am not the less in society, passing all my evenings in the coteries of those families with which I am intimate.

The late revolution in France has as you probably know brought some of its actors amongst us—The ex-king of Spain, & Marechal Grouchy (whom you may perhaps remember as the brother of M^{de} de Condorcet) are the most remarkable—The former passed the last winter at N. York—but there declined altogether going into society— He has lately come here, says he prefers the appearances of things in this quarter, & gives a proof of it by renting a house in the neighborhood where he means to take up his residence—He appears disposed also here to partake of society—I have dined once in company with him, & am to meet him again in the same way to-morrow. As he does not speak English I of course have a great deal of his conversation in company. He converses sensibly & with a great deal of philosophy— affects to be much pleased with the manners, ou plutôt la maniere d'être, of this country—He has written for his wife to join him & hopes she will come—I took the liberty of suggesting some reasons which I thought would prevent her, & he had no good objections to make to them; so that I do not believe she will come or that he will stay amongst us finally.

Some very remarkable men of another description have also been thrown on our coast from France, & who will more probably stay amongst us. They belonged to the conservatory of Music at Paris, an establishment created or perfectionned by the revolutionary Goverments of France. It seems now to be abolished—And its members are dispersed in various ways—Many have gone to Rio Janeiro—Three have come here—A performer & composer on the Piano, one on the Violoncello & another on the Hautboy—Performers of equal distinction have certainly never been heard in this country. They give public concerts & I hope will improve the taste & the talents of the country in this department. They purpose visiting our various Cities—&

should they exhibit at Richmond, I really think it would be worth your while to go & hear them. I suppose however that your time is so completely filled by regular occupation that you will hardly subtract any portion for such a purpose.

There is one thing that I have long wished to know whether, as I hoped, it made a part of your occupation. I mean the writing of your memoirs. It seems to me that when a man has passed a great part of his life in public & important situations, & retires like the gladiator alluded to by Horace, it is clapping the climax, to employ himself for the advantage of his country, during his retirement, to trace over & leave behind him a map of his navigation as a guide to future explorers. It is thus that human knowlege becomes advanced. You have I know a most valuable collection of papers—& I do not doubt that they will be left in good hands—But be assured that no one can utilize them in the manner that you can. Independently of this mode of employing your usefulness, there is one of another kind which I have long wished for—And that is that you would use the influence of your counsel to perfection our political institutions at present. We may safely assume I suppose that they are not perfect, as nothing perfect comes from the hand of man—We may assume also that no person on earth has had as good an opportunity as you have had of perceiving their defects, & judging of the proper remedies—You have unquestionably more influence, if you would use it, than any other individual with the efficient part of the community—And your situation is peculiarly favorable for using it—Many defects must be obvious to you besides those which are seen by the vulgar herd—and all of us I think see now the defect of the re-eligibility of the President—You saw it I think, from your first inspection of the constitution. Would it not be worthy of you to endeavour to have this evil remedied—I do not think you would find it difficult—And it certainly would be a benefit conferred on your country that would be worthy of your best exertions—Let the term be for seven years or more & no re-election—And let the incumbent after his term be incapable of any other office but endowed for his life with the allowance that may[2] be made to the Vice-president.   Other alterations present themselves to me but wch may not be so obvious to others & wch would encounter the prejudice of the great number—If your opinion should be established & known, it would perhaps remove the prejudices of others, & the more prejudices which are removed, the better—I would allow the President to take his Ministers in Congress if he chose it—And if not I would allow them <u>ex officio</u> to have seats on the floor of Congress, so as to debate, but not to vote—This would form a better connexion between the Executive & Legislative departments than now exists—And they would understand each other better— As to the fear of danger to liberty from executive influence I take that to be a prejudice—It is not warranted by history, which teaches us, as far as we will be taught by experience, that in Republics, danger originates much more often & much more naturally from the democratic principle.

I fear your numerous correspondents take up so much of your time, as to leave you not enough for the occupations in which it is my most anxious & ardent wish to see you engaged—And I have much to reproach myself with on this score—I will therefore end this letter, assuring you at the same time of the invariable sentiments of respect & attachment, with which I am, my dear Sir;

ever & truly your[s]   W Short

RC (DLC); endorsed by TJ as received 3 May 1816 and so recorded in SJL.

The LAW OF THE STATE limiting the collection of interest in Virginia to an annual maximum of 6 percent passed the General Assembly on 23 Nov. 1796 and took effect on 1 May 1797 (*Acts of Assembly* [1796 sess.], 16–7). Albert Gallatin was the foreign-born American MINISTER plenipotentiary to France. MISS R.: Ellen W. Randolph (Coolidge). The EX-KING OF SPAIN was Joseph Bonaparte, and his wife was Julie Clary Bonaparte. Emmanuel GROUCHY's sister was Sophie de Grouchy, marquise de Condorcet. OU PLUTÔT LA MANIERE D'ÊTRE: "or rather the manner of being" (the behavior).

The VERY REMARKABLE MEN OF ANOTHER DESCRIPTION were the pianist Denis Germain Étienne, the oboist Peter Gilles, and the latter's namesake son, a

cellist. After the trio arrived in New York late in 1815, they began giving concerts in New York, Philadelphia, Boston, and Baltimore. All three settled in the United States (Vera Brodsky Lawrence, *Strong on Music: The New York Music Scene in the Days of George Templeton Strong* [1988], 1:xl; New York *Columbian*, 9 Dec. 1815; *Boston Gazette*, 2 Sept. 1816). Horace's GLADIATOR, Veianius, "hangs up his arms at Hercules' door, then lies hidden in the country, that he may not have to plead with the crowd again and again from the arena's edge" (*Epistles*, 1.1.4–6, in Fairclough, *Horace: Satires, Epistles and Ars Poetica*, 250–1). For TJ's early opposition to the RE-ELIGIBILITY OF THE PRESIDENT, see *PTJ*, 12:440–1.

[1] Manuscript: "sevant."
[2] Manuscript: "is may."

From George Ticknor

DEAR SIR,   Göttingen April. 23. 1816.—

Four days ago, I received your favor of Feb. 8. from which I am led to hope that I may soon receive from you another letter which you wrote Jan. 31. and which as it comes through France must probably be somewhat longer on the way. My own letters to you as well as to my friends generally have not been fortunate, and as my last contained some facts, which it may be important for you to know, I send the copy of it with this for fear of accidents.

The books you have desired to be procured are all, except Lœsner's Hesiod, to be had in Göttingen as reasonably as in any part of Europe. I shall, therefore, purchase them immediately and send them out with some books, which I shall ship to my father from Hamburg, and he will give you immediate notice of their arrival and send them to any Southern port you may have directed on the receipt of this. I think you will find none of them high, except Coray's éditions and I imagine you will be satisfied even with these as they are really learned, and curious as well as beautiful and an interesting monument of the exertions that have been made and are still making for the restoration of Greece to the comforts of civilization, which whether successful or not must always be respected.

Perhaps, when you have received these specimens of German editions you will be induced to permit me to send you some others. The longer I remain here, the more I learn to value the German modes of study and the enlarged and liberal spirit of German scholarship and, for the same reason I think the more you see of German editions of the classicks, the more you will be disposed to admit them into your library. Within forty years the scholars of this country, I am persuaded, have done more towards the final understanding of the classicks, than all Europe had done during the century that preceded, not by imitating the minute and tedious accuracy of the Dutch commentators, but by reducing the whole study of antiquity to a philosophical system, in which one part assists to explain the other and all together form a harmonious and happy whole. They have, in fact, done for the ancients what Blackstone did for the English law and though I cannot say that their digest, like his, is to be found in a single treatise, yet no man is now considered a scholar here, who is not master of it. The effect of this has been particularly favourable in the investigations it has occasioned into the Spirit of Grecian philosophy and the different characters it assumed in different ages—in the fine histories of Grecian arts and policy it has produced—and the new and more liberal direction it has given to the study [of][1] Greek literature and manners generally. They have, in fact, already done for all the ages of Greece, what all Barthelemy's learning, for want of a philosophical spirit to direct it, has not been able to do for one. To say nothing of the numberless editions, which are offered at every Leipzig fair, of the classical authors, the practise of bringing all learning into the form of philosophical histories & treatises is

[697]

gaining ground very fast and really doing wonders. In these respects, Winkelmann's History of ancient art—Heeren's tho'ts on the Policy and commerce of the Ancients—Tiedemann's History of Greek philosophy—Creuzer's mythology of the Ancients—&c &c are works which have no parallell in other languages, & which, except ye first, are so recent, yt. yy. are yet hardly known beyond the limits of Germany. The great difference between a German scholar and those of England & Holland, is, that, with even more minute, verbal learning than they, <u>he</u> treats the study of antiquity as a liberal science, while <u>they</u> treat it as a mechanical art. This change has been effected by the schools of Heyne and Wolf, who, by turning their immense learning to its appropriate objects have made a revolution in the study of antiquity, which is alrea[dy] felt in England in defiance of the difference of language and their inveterate prejudice against every thing foreign & continental—and which, I am persuaded, in thirty years more will make it toto cælo a different affair to be a scholar there from what it is now.—

I am exceedingly anxious to have this spirit of pursuing all literary studies philosophically—of making scholarship as little of drudgery & mechanism as possible transplanted into the U. States, in whose free and liberal soil I think it would, at once, find congenial nourishment: It is a spirit, which in Germany now goes through everything— through Theology, history, modern literature &c It surprized me, I assure you, to find an admirable philosophical history of English literature, written by a man who was never even in England, and yet compared [with]² which Warton's fragment is but a clumsy piece of pedantry. A remark of similar import was made to me in relation to his own country a few days since by a very learned Portuguese and the same thing might be said by a Spaniard & Italian tho' I believe not by a Frenchman.—But, I suspect, it is better for me to stop; and yet I know of nobody who will more readily credit my accounts than you will, or who would more rejoice at the state & spirit of learning in Germany.—

Remember me, I pray you, respectfully & gratefully to all your family. I have been for some time trying to ascertain whether Mr. Gilmer is in Europe, for I wish to write to him & do not know where to direct my letters.

Your's very respectfully,   GEO: TICKNOR.

RC (DLC); mutilated at seal; at head of text: "No. VI."; addressed: "His Excellency Thomas Jefferson Monticello, Albermarle County Virginia U.S."; stamp canceled; franked; postmarked Baltimore, 3 Aug.; with additional notations in an unidentified hand: "☙ Captⁿ Churchill" and "Rᵈ 6 May & forᵈ by P. [...] 1816"; endorsed by TJ as received 11 Aug. 1816 and so recorded in SJL. Enclosure: Ticknor to TJ, 15 Mar. 1816.

ᴠᴛ. ʏʏ.: "that they."

[1] Omitted word editorially supplied.
[2] Omitted word editorially supplied.

To Pierre Samuel Du Pont de Nemours

Poplar Forest Apr. 24. 16.

I recieved, my dear friend, your letter covering the Constitution for your Equinoctial republics, just as I was setting out for this place. I brought it with me, and have read it with great satisfaction. I suppose it well formed for those for whom it is intended, and the excellence of every government is it's adaptation to the state of those to be governed by it. for us, it would not do. distinguishing between the structure of the government and the moral principles on which you prescribe it's administration, with the latter we concur cordially, with the former we should not. we of the United States, you know are constitutionally & conscientiously Democrats. we consider society as one of the natural wants with which man has been created; that he has been endowed with faculties and qualities to effect it's satisfaction by concurrence of others having the same want; that when, by the exercise of these faculties, he has procured a state of society, it is one of his acquisitions which he has a right to regulate and controul, jointly indeed with all those who have concured in the procurement, whom he cannot exclude from it's use or direction more than they him. we think experience has proved it safer, for the mass of individuals composing the society, to reserve to themselves personally the exercise of all rightful powers to which they are competent, and to delegate those to which they are not competent to deputies named, and removable for unfaithful conduct, by themselves immediately. hence, with us, the people (by which is meant the mass of individuals composing the society) being competent to judge of the facts occurring in ordinary life, they have retained the functions of judges of facts, under the name of jurors: but being unqualified for the management of affairs requiring intelligence above the common level, yet competent judges of human character, they chuse, for their management, representatives, some by themselves immediately, others by electors chosen by themselves. thus our President is chosen by ourselves, directly in

<u>practice</u>, for we vote for **A.** as elector only on the condition he will vote for **B.** our representatives by ourselves immediately, our Senate and judges of law through electors chosen by ourselves. and we believe that this proximate choice and power of removal is the best security which experience has sanctioned for ensuring an honest conduct in the functionaries of the society. your three or four alembications have indeed a seducing appearance. we should concieve, primâ facie, that the last extract would be the pure alcohol of the substance, three or four times rectified. but in proportion as they are more and more sublimated, they are also farther & farther removed from the controul of the society; and the human character, we believe, requires in general constant and immediate controul, to prevent it's being biassed from right by the seductions of self love. your process produces therefore a structure of government from which the fundamental principle of ours is excluded. you first set down as zeros all individuals not having lands, which are the greater number in every society of long standing. those holding lands are permitted to manage in person the small affairs of their commune or corporation, and to elect a deputy for the canton; in which election too every one's vote is to be an unit, a plurality, or a fraction, in proportion to his landed possessions. the assemblies of Cantons then elect for the Districts; those of Districts for Circles; and those of Circles for the National assemblies. some of these highest councils too are in a considerable degree self-elected, the regency partially, the Judiciary entirely, and some are for life. whenever therefore an esprit de corps, or of party, gets possession of them, which experience shews to be inevitable, there are no means of breaking it up; for they will never elect but those of their own spirit. juries are allowed in criminal cases only. I acknolege myself strong in affection to our own form, yet both of us act and think from the same motive. we both consider the people as our children, & love them with parental affection. but you love them as infants whom you are afraid to trust without nurses; and I as adults whom I freely leave to self government. and you are right in the case referred to you; my criticism being built on a state of society not under your contemplation. it is in fact like a critique on Homer by the laws of the Drama.

But when we come to the moral principles on which the government is to be administered, we come to what is proper for all conditions of society. I meet you there in all the benevolence & rectitude of your native character; and I love myself always most where I concur most with you. liberty, truth, probity, honor, are declared to be the four cardinal principles of your society. I believe with you that moral-

ity, compassion generosity are innate elements of the human construction; that there exists a right independant of force; that a right to
property is founded[1] in our natural wants, in the means with which
we are endowed to satisfy these wants, and the right to what we acquire by those means without violating the similar rights of other sensible beings; that no one has a right to obstruct another, exercising his
faculties innocently for the relief of sensibilities made a part of his nature; that justice is the fundamental law of society; that the majority,
oppressing an individual is guilty of a crime, abuses it's strength, and
by acting on the law of the strongest breaks up the foundations of society; that action by the citizens in person, in affairs within their reach
and competence, and in all others by representatives, chosen immediately, & removable, by themselves, constitutes the essence of a republic; that all governments are more or less republican in proportion as
this principle enters more or less into their composition; and that a
government by representation is capable of extension over a greater
surface of country than one of any other form. these, my friend, are the
essentials in which you & I agree; however, in our zeal for their maintenance, we may be perplexed & divaricate, as to the structure of society most likely to secure them.

In the constitution of Spain, as proposed by the late Cortes there
was a principle entirely new to me, and not noticed in yours, that no
person, born after that day, should ever acquire the rights of citizenship until he could read and write. it is impossible sufficiently to estimate the wisdom of this provision. of all those which have been
thought of for securing fidelity in the administration of the government, constant ralliance to the principles of the constitution, and progressive amendments with the progressive advances of the human
mind, or changes in human affairs, it is the most effectual. enlighten
the people generally, and tyranny and oppressions of body & mind
will vanish like evil spirits at the dawn of day. altho' I do not, with
some enthusiasts, believe that the human condition will ever advance
to such a state of perfection as that there shall no longer be pain or
vice in the world, yet I believe it susceptible of much improvement,
and, most of all, in matters of government and religion; and that the
diffusion of knolege among the people is to be the instrument by
which it is to be effected. the constitution of the Cortes had defects
enough; but when I saw in it this amendatory provision, I was
satisfied all would come right in time, under it's salutary operation.
no people have more need of a similar provision than those for whom
you have felt so much interest. no mortal wishes them more success
than I do. but if what I have heard of the ignorance & bigotry of the

mass, be true, I doubt their capacity to understand and to support a free government; and fear that their emancipation from the foreign tyranny of Spain, will result in a military despotism at home. Palacios may be great; others may be great; but it is the multitude which possesses force; and wisdom must yield to that. for such a condition of society, the constitution you have devised is probably the best imaginable. it is certainly calculated to elicit the best talents; altho' perhaps not well guarded against the egoism of it's functionaries. but that egoism will be light in comparison with the pressure of a military despot, and his army of Janissaries. like Solon, to the Athenians, you have given to your Columbians, not the best possible government, but the best they can bear.   by the bye, I wish you had called them the Columbian republics, to distinguish them from our American republics. theirs would be the most honorable name, and they best entitled to it: for Columbus discovered their continent, but never saw ours.

To them liberty and happiness; to you the meed of wisdom & goodness in teaching them how to attain them, with the affectionate respect & friendship of   TH: JEFFERSON

RC (DeGH: Pierre Samuel Du Pont de Nemours Papers, Winterthur Manuscripts). PoC (DLC); at foot of first page: "M. Dupont de Nemours."

ALEMBICATIONS are refinements, distillations, or overly subtle expressions (OED). On p. 7 of the *Constitution of the Spanish Monarchy. Promulgated at Cadiz on the 19th of March, 1812* (Philadelphia, 1814; Sowerby, no. 2424; enclosed in

Luis de Onís to TJ, 13 Apr. 1814), article 25 relating to Spanish CITIZENSHIP stipulated that, "from and after the year 1830," rights would be forfeited by those "unable to read and write." RALLIANCE: "rallying" (OED). For the reference to SOLON, see Du Pont de Nemours to TJ, 14 Apr. 1812, and note.

[1] RC: "found-." PoC corrected by TJ to "founded."

To Charles Clay

TH:J. TO MR CLAY   Poplar Forest Apr. 25. 16.

I return the 10. first volumes and will be glad of the next 10. I found several sheets of the 7th missing, but some of them were stuck into other volumes which I restored to their proper place in the 7th but I have not examined it since to see if it is now perfect. Asparagus acceptable as usual. shall I not see you again? I shall be returning about the middle of the ensuing week. friendly salutations.

RC (VtMiM); dateline at foot of text; addressed: "M[r] Clay." Not recorded in SJL. Enclosure not identified.

To Francis Adrian Van der Kemp

Your favor of Mar. 24. was handed to me just as I was setting out on a journey of time and distance, which will explain the date of this both as to time and place.   the Syllabus, which is the subject of your letter, was addressed to a friend to whom I had promised a more detailed view. but finding I should never have time for that, I sent him what I thought should be the Outlines of such a work.   the same subject entering sometimes into the correspondence between mr Adams and myself, I sent him a copy of it. the friend to whom it had been first addressed dying soon after, I asked from his family the return of the original, as a confidential communication, which they kindly sent me. so that no copy of it, but that in possession of mr Adams, now exists out of my own hands. I have used this caution, lest it should get out in connection with my name; and I was unwilling to draw on myself a swarm of insects, whose buz is more disquieting than their bite.   as an abstract thing, and without any intimation from what quarter derived, I can have no objection to it's being committed to the consideration of the world. I believe it may even do good by producing discussion, and finally a true view of the merits of this great reformer. pursuing the same ideas after writing the Syllabus, I made, for my own satisfaction, an Extract from the Evangelists of the texts of his morals, selecting those only whose style and spirit proved them genuine, and his own: and they are as distinguishable from the matter in which they are imbedded as diamonds in dunghills. a more precious morsel of ethics was never seen. it was too hastily done however, being the work of one or two evenings only, while I lived at Washington, overwhelmed with other business: and it is my intention to go over it again at more leisure. this shall be the work of the ensuing winter. I gave it the title of 'the Philosophy of Jesus extracted from the text of the Evangelists.'   to this Syllabus and Extract, if a history of his life can be added, written with the same view of the subject, the world will see, after the fogs shall be dispelled, in which for 14. centuries he has been inveloped by Jugglers to make money of him, when the genuine character shall be exhibited, which they have dressed up in the rags of an Impostor, the world, I say, will at length see the immortal merit of this first of human Sages. I rejoice that you think of undertaking this work. it is one I have long wished to see[1] written on the scale of a Laertius or a Nepos. nor can it be a work of labor, or of volume. for his journeyings from Judaea to Samaria, and Samaria to Galilee, do not cover much country; and the incidents of his life require little research. they are all at hand, and need only to be put into human dress; noticing such only as are within the physical laws of nature, and offending none by a denial, or even a mention, of what is not. if the Syllabus and Extract (which is short) either in substance, or at large, are worth a place under the same cover with your biography, they are at your service. I ask one only condition, that no possibility shall be admitted of my name being even intimated with the publication. if done in England, as you seem to contemplate, there will be the less likelihood of my being thought of. I shall be much gratified to learn that you pursue your intention of writing the life of Jesus, and pray to accept the assurances of my great respect and esteem.

Th: Jefferson

RC (NBuHi: Van der Kemp Papers). PoC (DLC); at foot of first page: "M^r Fr. Adr. Vanderkemp." Not recorded in SJL. Enclosures: enclosures 1–2 to Richard Rush to TJ, 12 Aug. 1813. Enclosed in a covering note from TJ to Theodorus Bailey, [ca. 25 Apr. 1816], not recorded in SJL and not found (see Bailey to TJ, 10 May 1816).

TJ had FIRST ADDRESSED the enclosures to Benjamin Rush. His EXTRACT FROM THE EVANGELISTS is printed in EG, 55–122.

[1] TJ here canceled "executed."

To José Corrêa da Serra

Dear Sir   Poplar Forest April 26. 16.

Your favor of Mar. 29. was recieved just as I was setting out for this place. I brought it with me to be answered hence. since you are so kind as to interest yourself for Capt Lewis's papers, I will give you a full statement of them.

1. ten or twelve such pocket volumes, Marocco bound, as that you describe, in which, in his own hand writing, he had journalised all occurrences, day by day, as he travelled. they were small 8^{vos} and opened at the end for more convenient writing. every one had been put into a separate tin case, cemented to prevent injury from wet. but on his return the cases, I presume, had been taken from them, as he delivered me the books uncased. there were in them the figures of some animals drawn with the pen while on his journey. the gentlemen who published his travels must have had these MS. volumes, and perhaps now have them, or can give some account of them.

2. Descriptions of animals and plants. I do not recollect whether there was such a book or collection of papers, distinct from his jour-

nal; altho' I am inclined to think there was one: because his travels as published, do not contain all the new animals of which he had either descriptions or specimens. mr Peale, I think, must know something of this, as he drew figures of some of the animals for engraving, and some were actually engraved. perhaps Conrad, his bookseller, who was to have published the work, can give an account of these.

3. Vocabularies. I had myself made a collection of about 40. vocabularies of the Indians on this side the Missisipi, and Capt Lewis was instructed to take those of every tribe beyond, which he possibly could. the intention was to publish the whole, and leave the world to search for affinities between these and the languages of Europe and Asia. he was furnished with a number of printed vocabularies of the same words and form I had used, with blank spaces for the Indian words. he was very attentive to this instruction, never missing an opportunity of taking a vocabulary. after his return, he asked me if I should have any objection to the printing his separately, as mine were not yet arranged as I intended. I assured him I had not the least; and I am certain he contemplated their publication. but whether he had put the papers out of his own hand or not, I do not know. I imagine he had not: and it is probable that Doct^r Barton, who was particularly curious on this subject, and published on it occasionally, would willingly recieve and take care of these papers after Capt Lewis's death, and that they are now among his papers.

4. his observations of longitude and latitude. he was instructed to send these to the war-office, that measures might be taken to have the calculations made. whether he delivered them to the war-office, or to Dr Patterson, I do not know; but I think he communicated with Dr Patterson concerning them. these are all-important: because altho', having with him the Nautical almanacs, he could & did calculate some of his latitudes, yet the longitudes were taken merely from estimates by the log-line, time and course. so that it is only as to latitudes that his map may be considered as tolerably correct; not as to it's longitudes.

5. his Map. this was drawn on sheets of paper, not put together, but so marked that they could be joined together with the utmost accuracy; not as one great square map, but ramifying with the courses of the rivers. the scale was very large, and the sheets numerous, but in perfect preservation. this was to await publication, until corrected by the calculations of longitude and latitude. I examined these sheets myself minutely, as spread on a floor, and the originals must be in existence, as the Map published with his travels must have been taken from them.

These constitute the whole. they are the property of the government, the fruits of the expedition undertaken at such expence of money and risk of valuable lives. they contain exactly the whole of the information which it was our object to obtain for the benefit of our own country and of the world. but we were willing to give to Lewis and Clarke whatever pecuniary benefits might be derived from the publication, and therefore left the papers in their hands, taking for granted that their interests would produce a speedy publication, which would be better if done under their direction. but the death of Capt Lewis, the distance and occupations[1] of General Clarke, and the bankruptcy of their bookseller, have retarded the publication, and rendered necessary that the government should attend to the reclamation & security of the papers. their recovery is now become an imperious duty. their safest deposit as fast as they can be collected, will be the Philosophical society, who no doubt will be so kind as to recieve and preserve them, subject to the orders of government; and their publication, once effected in any way, the originals will probably be left in the same deposit. as soon as I can learn their present situation, I will lay the matter before the government to take such order as they think proper.   as to any claims of individuals to these papers, it is to be observed that, as being the property of the public, we are certain neither Lewis nor Clarke would undertake to convey away the right to them, and that they could not convey them, had they been capable of intending it. yet no interest of that kind is meant to be disturbed, if the individual can give satisfactory assurance that he will promptly & properly publish them. otherwise they must be restored to the government; & the claimant left to settle with those on whom he has any claim.   my interference will, I trust, be excused, not only from the portion which every citizen has in whatever is public, but from the peculiar part I have had in the design and execution of this expedition.

To you, my friend, apology is due for involving you in the trouble of this enquiry. it must be found in the interest you take in whatever belongs to science, and in your own kind offers to me of aid in this research. be assured always of my affectionate friendship and respect.

TH: JEFFERSON

RC (PPAmP: Thomas Jefferson Papers); at foot of first page: "M. Correa de Serra." PoC (DLC).

For the provenance of CAP^T LEWIS'S PAPERS, the journals of the Lewis and Clark Expedition, see Moulton, *Journals* of *Lewis & Clark*, 2:530–48. Paul Allen and Nicholas Biddle were THE GENTLEMEN WHO PUBLISHED HIS TRAVELS (Biddle, *Lewis and Clark Expedition*; TJ to Paul Allen, 18 Aug. 1813, Document I in a group of documents on the Biography of Meriwether Lewis, printed above under that date). For the role of Charles Willson PEALE in the creation of drawings based on journal sketches and specimens gathered during Lewis and Clark's exploration, see Donald Jackson, ed., *Letters of the Lewis and Clark Expedition with Related Documents, 1783–1854*, 2d ed. (1978), 2:410–1.

[1] Preceding two words interlined.

From Eusebio Valli

MIO SIGNORE   Trenton–N.–j. 26 Aprile 1816

Il Sig.r Botta mio compatriotta, ed amico, volendo procurarmi L'avvantaggio della di Lei preziosa conoscenza mi diede a quest'oggetto una Lettera per VS: che é quella, cui mi permetto di trasmetter le— Avrei desiderato grandemente d'esserne io stesso il portatore, ma mi trovo forzato a rimanere quá sino alla stagione della febbre gialla, per portarmi in allora su quei punti, ov'essa si presenterà—Doppo aver fatte Le mie ricerche su questa terribile malattia avró L'onore di presentar Le in persona i miei rispetti—

Sono intanto con la piu profonda e sentita stima Di VS:
Umilissimo Servitore   VALLI

E D I T O R S '   T R A N S L A T I O N

SIR   Trenton–N.J. 26 April 1816

My compatriot and friend Mr. Botta, wanting to procure for me the advantage of your inestimable acquaintance, gave me for this purpose a letter to you, which I permit myself to pass on to you—I greatly desired to deliver it, but I find myself forced to remain here until the yellow fever season, in order to travel then to those places where it will present itself—After I complete my research on this terrible disease I will pay my respects to you in person—

Meanwhile, I remain with the deepest and most sincere esteem your
Most Humble Servant   VALLI

RC (DLC); endorsed by TJ as received 3 May 1816 and so recorded in SJL. Translation by Dr. Christina Ball. RC (DLC: TJ Papers, ser. 10); address cover only; with PoC of TJ to Patrick Gibson, 6 Aug. 1816, on verso; addressed: "Thomas Jefferson Esq.re Monticello Virg.a"; stamp canceled; franked; postmarked Trenton, 26 Apr. Enclosure: Carlo Botta to TJ, 29 Nov. 1815.

From James Ligon
(for Patrick Gibson),
with Thomas Jefferson's Notes

Sir   Richmond 27th April 1816

I omitted to inform you of a Sale I made on the 8th Ins^t of 138 Bbls of your Superfine flour to W^m H Hubbard at 6$ on 60 days time—I have since then disposed of the remainder of it say 81 Bbls Superfine & 36 Fine to Smith & Riddle on the Same time at $6\frac{1}{4}$$—in this last sale is included 41 Bbls Superfine delivered me by mr Warwick by direction of Colo^l Randolph—I was induced to close the Sales of your flour by the advanced State of the Season & the anxiety shewn by the holders of it here to accept of present prices—at which our Millers have made considerable Sales upon long credit—

respectfully yr ob^t Servt   Patrick Gibson
                                         p Ja^s Ligon

[*in TJ's hand at lower left:*]

	B		D
S.F.	138 @ 6.D.	=	828
d^o	40.		
F.	36		
S.F.	41	= 117 @ $6\frac{1}{4}$ =	731.25
	255		1559.25

RC (ViU: TJP-ER); in Ligon's hand, with TJ's subjoined notes; endorsed by TJ as a letter from Gibson received 3 May 1816 and so recorded in SJL. RC (MHi); address cover only; with PoC of TJ to Charles Simms, 2 June 1816, on verso; addressed: "Thomas Jefferson Esqr Monticello"; franked; postmarked.

From George Logan

Dear Sir   Stenton April 27th 1816

your venerable friend Charles Thompson, resides on his farm about eight miles from Stenton. I visit him three or four times every year, at which times, I derive instruction and amusement, from his lively and interesting conversation. I dined with him a few days since, when I found him highly gratified by your last Letter to him; in which you inform him, of your having been engaged in collecting a code of ethics from the Holy[1] scriptures, highly satisfactory to yourself. Pray give it to your country: it will remove slanders respecting your unbelief in the Christian religion; and will promote virtue and[2] morality in the rising generation.

The more I read of history—the more I contemplate the character of man; the more I am convinced of the necessity of introducing the spiritual doctrines of Christ into governments;[3] in order to render nations happy and[4] prosperous

I this morning received two packets from my valuable friend Sir John Sinclair. I send you one of the inclosed papers, which will give you a partial view of his present humane and patriotic engagements.

I also inclose part of a Letter from my worthy ancestor James Logan, to his friend in Ireland on the nature[5] of religion—How consoling such opinions to posterity, when compared with the miserable sophistry of such characters[6] as Voltaire: of whom the great Frederic says in a Letter to Dalembert dated Potsdam 1753. "Voltaire is the most malignant lunatic I ever was acquainted with—He is excellent only in his writings. It is impossible you should imagine all the duplicity and infamous knavery of which he has here been guilty." Dalembert in a Letter to the King of Prussia dated Paris June 30th 1778. giving him an account of the death of Voltaire, says, "the image of this great man dying, excited emotions so strong, and fixed itself so powerfully on my imagination, that it never can be effaced. It gave birth to the most maloncholy reflections, on the non entity of life and fame, and the misery of man."[7]

My Wife unites with me in respects to yourself and amiable family,[8] Accept assurances of my friendship   GEO: LOGAN

RC (DLC); at foot of text: "Tho⁵ Jefferson Esq⁽ʳ⁾"; endorsed by TJ as received 8 May 1816 and so recorded in SJL, with TJ's additional notation beneath endorsement: "C. Thompson   S⁽ʳ⁾ J. Sinclair." Dft (PHi: Logan Papers); endorsed by Logan. First enclosure not found.

JAMES LOGAN, colonial statesman and scholar, was Logan's grandfather (ANB; DAB). A letter from the elder Logan TO HIS FRIEND IN IRELAND appeared in the Philadelphia Poulson's American Daily Advertiser on 17 Apr. 1816. Dated Philadelphia, 15 Mar. 1729, and headed "Part of a letter from the honorable James Logan to a Gentleman in Ireland," the extract argues that "To know the operation of God in the Soul, is the only Religion that can subsist on a solid foundation, and . . . is the only end for which a man

was formed"; that "the force of reason and truth will gradually prevail over all prejudices"; but that Logan fears that "darkness and delusion must yet be exalted and raised to a mighty power" in order "that all who see it may forever hold it in utter abhorrence."

The letter DATED POTSDAM, April 1753, from Frederick II, king of Prussia, was written to Jean Baptiste de Boyer, marquis d'Argens. For this letter and that of JUNE 30TH 1778 from Jean Le Rond d'Alembert, see Thomas Holcroft, trans., Posthumous Works of Frederic II. King of Prussia (London, 1789), 12:130–52, 456–7.

[1] Word interlined in Dft.
[2] Logan here canceled "religion."
[3] Dft: "government."
[4] Dft: "or."

⁵ Logan here canceled "and character"
in RC and Dft.
⁶ Word interlined in Dft in place of
"miserable sophists."

⁷ Dft: "men."
⁸ Preceding twelve words not in Dft.

From James Monroe

DEAR SIR   washington april 28. 1816

The enclosed may gave you some amusement. I have read neither, and cannot therefore speak of their merits. one is attributed to armstrong & the other to winder.

The book which you were so kind as to send me respecting Louisiana will be taken advantage of, in the contemplated discussion with the Spanish gov^t. It shall be restord afterwards.

your letter to Miss Bruff was sent to her as soon as receiv'd.

Congress will adjourn on tuesday, after which I shall be at liberty, and intend visiting albemarle, when I shall have the pleasure of seeing[1] you, I hope in good health.

very respectfully and affecty. your friend   JA^S MONROE

RC (DLC); endorsed by TJ as received 3 May 1816 and so recorded in SJL. RC (DLC); address cover only; with PoC of TJ to George Watterston, 20 June 1816, on verso; addressed (trimmed): "Thomas […]"; postmarked Washington City, 28 Apr.

The enclosed pamphlets vindicated the conduct of Secretary of War John Armstrong and General William H. Winder, respectively, during the War of 1812. The work by "Spectator," which was ATTRIBUTED TO ARMSTRONG, was *An Enquiry respecting the Capture of Washington by* *the British, on the 24th August, 1814; with an Examination of the Report of the Committee of Investigation Appointed by Congress* (Washington, 1816; Poor, *Jefferson's Library*, 5 [no. 163]). The response on behalf of WINDER, thought to have been authored by Rider H. Winder, was *Remarks on a Pamphlet, entitled "An Enquiry respecting the Capture of Washington by the British, on the 24th of August, 1814, with, &c. &c. by Spectator"* (Baltimore, 1816; Poor, *Jefferson's Library*, 5 [no. 163]).

[1] Manuscript: "seing."

To Elizabeth Trist

Poplar Forest Apr. 28. 16.

I am here, my dear Madam alive and well, and notwithstanding the murderous histories of the winter, I have not had an hour's sickness for a twelvemonth past. I feel myself indebted to the fable however for the friendly concern expressed in your letter, which I recieved in good health, by my fireside at Monticello. these stories will come true one of these days, and poor printer Davies need only reserve a while the chapter of comminations he had the labor to compose, and the mortification to recall after striking off some sheets announcing to his readers the happy riddance. but, all joking apart, I am well, and left all well a fortnight ago at Monticello, to which I shall return in two or three days. Ellen past the winter at Washington, with mrs Madison, and has taken a flight to Philadelphia, with mr Dallas's family. I hope however her return to Monticello nearly as soon as my own. Jefferson is gone to Richmond to bring home my new great grandaughter. your friends mr & mrs Divers are habitually in poor health; well enough only to recieve visits, but not to return them. and this, I think, is all our small news which can interest you.   On the general scale of Nations, the greatest wonder is Bonaparte in St Helena. and yet it is where it would have been well for the lives and happiness of millions and millions, had he been deposited twenty years ago. France would now have had a free government, unstained by the enormities she has enabled him to commit on the rest of the world, and unprostrated by the vindictive hand, human or divine, now so heavily bearing on her. she deserved much punishment; and her successes and reverses will be a wholsome lesson to the world hereafter. but she has now had enough, and we may lawfully pray for her resurrection; and I am confident the day is not distant. no one who knows that people, and the elasticity of their character, can believe they will long remain crouched on the earth as at present. they will rise, by acclamation, and woe to their riders! what havoc are we not yet to see! but these sufferings of all Europe will not be lost. a sense of the rights of man is gone forth, and all Europe will, ere long, have representative governments, more or less free. mother-England indeed seems moving in the opposite direction: the wretchedness of her people however under the oppressions of her taxes and national debt, will relieve her also by a revolution, & more purified government.—we are better employed in establishing universities, colleges, canals, roads, maps E^{t}c. what do you say to all this? who could have believed the old dominion would have roused from her supineness, and taken such a scope at her first flight? my only fear is that an hour of repentance may come, and nip in the bud the execution of conceptions so magnanimous. with my friendly respects to mr & mrs Gilmer, accept the assurance of my constant attachment and respect.   TH: JEFFERSON

PoC (MHi); at foot of first page: "Mrs Trist"; endorsed by TJ.

Augustine Davis (DAVIES) was the printer of a Federalist newspaper, the

Richmond *Virginia Patriot* (Brigham, *American Newspapers*, 2:1152–3). ELLEN: Ellen W. Randolph (Coolidge). Thomas JEFFERSON Randolph's daughter was Margaret Smith Randolph.

To John Wayles Eppes

DEAR SIR   Poplar Forest. Apr. 30. 16

Yours of the 8th was recieved here on the 19th inst. the information you have had as to the schools at Staunton and Lexington is correct. the latter has been at all times under the direction of an infuriated Presbyterian bigot and tory, better fitted to fanaticise than to instruct youth in useful knolege. when I was last here, I heard of their expelling two or three youths for the heinous sin of dancing. I have seen, since I came here a well informed gentleman from the neighborhood of chapel hill, who assures me it has latterly declined in it's reputation. however without any reference to that, my enquiries here have given me entire satisfaction as to the mr Mitchell of the New London academy whom I mentioned to you. no moral character can stand higher, and his diligence and undivided attention to his school is equally attested. some disapprove of his having renounced the ancient coarse discipline of the rod, which he supplies by moral substitutes. I asked him to dine with me two days ago, and had a full conversation with him as to his method. it is more solid than mr Halcomb's was, and he attends particularly to what the other entirely neglected, the reading the language according to quantity. I found both Francis and Baker horribly barbarous in this. he is sensible, modest anxious to improve himself, and will conform to any desire I shall express to him. to this is to be added another important circumstance. every one with whom I have spoken on the subject concurs in the highest praises and esteem for old mr & mrs DeHaven, who keep the boarding house of the academy. all assure me it is impossible even for parental care to attend more anxiously to the boys, both in sickness and in health than they do. they have no children of their own, and seem to adopt, in affection those who live with them. there are about 20. at the school, which is about 3. miles hence, along a good road, on a dead level. they have two vacations a year, to wit the months of May & November, which Francis can pass with you, and their sessions as they are called, are each of the five intervening months. they have their public examination I believe this day, to separate for a month and recommence on Monday the 3d of June, by which day Francis should be here. he will be put into Virgil and

Cicero's orations. the former I gave him, and I believe the latter also. he will begin the Greek grammar as soon as he has got thro' his prosody: and if you could hear him a lesson or two in that every day while at home, he would be ready for the Greek grammar on his arrival here.

I am sensible, my dear Sir, of the delicacy of your sentiments on the subject of expence. I am indeed an unskilful manager of my farms, and sensible of this from it's effects, I have now committed them to better hands, of whose care and skill I have satisfactory knolege, and to whom I have ceded the entire direction. this is all that is necessary to make them adequate to all my wants, & to place me at entire ease. and for whom should I spare in preference to Francis in sentiments either of duty or affection? I consider all my grandchildren as if they were my children, & want nothing but for them. it is impossible that I could reconcile it to my feelings that he alone of them should be a stranger to my cares & contributions. you must then permit me to come in for my share, and to do something which may give me somewhat of the parental character with him; not to the diminution of what he feels and owes to you, or of your authority; but yet to be something affectionate in his eyes. we will both then do what falls in our way. I have accordingly advanced to mr Mitchell, the ensuing session, for so they divide the year. and it is all but nothing; being no more than I paid to mr Maury for my own education 55 years ago. their terms are 10£ board and 10.D. tuition for each session, and something additional for a bed and washing which mr Mitchell could not specify. there is no doubt but that the plantations here will furnish them every year necessaries to a greater amount than their demand.—if you come with Francis you had better make this your headquarters. you will get a better bed & breakfast here than at the tavern in New London. I will not answer for the dinner, beyond bacon & chicken.[1] the only inconvenience will be the waiting the sending a mile for the keys. the woman Hanah (Francis's acquaintance) at the head of the spinning house will do this and take care of you. if your serv^t comes ahead it will shorten the delay. present me respectfully to mrs Eppes & accept my affections for yourself & Francis

TH: JEFFERSON

P.S. Monticello. May 7. 16. I lodged the letter of which this is a duplicate in Maj^r Flood's post office on Thursday the 2^d inst. but mr Chisolm now telling me you were to set out for N. Carolina, on Saturday the 4th and fearing the letter may not have got to your hands, I have concluded to send a duplicate by mail to Halifax.

PoC (CSmH: JF); on reused address cover to TJ; at foot of first page: "John W. Eppes esq"; postscript written perpendicularly along left margin of last page; endorsed by TJ.

Eppes's letter OF THE 8ᵀᴴ, not found, is recorded in SJL as received 19 Apr. 1816 from Mill Brook. The school at LEXINGTON was Washington College (later Washington and Lee University). From 1799 to 1829 this institution was headed by George A. Baxter, an educator and Presbyterian minister (*DVB*). The University of North Carolina at CHAPEL HILL was chartered in 1789 and began instruction six years later (Robert D. W. Connor, *A Documentary History of the University of North Carolina, 1776–1799*, 2 vols. [1953]). On this date TJ gave an order on Archibald Robertson for $53.33 payable to Abraham DEHAVEN, consisting of $33.33 "for himself board of Francis Eppes 6. mo.," $10 for "bed and washing," and $10 "for Mr. Mitchell for tuition from June 1." (*MB*, 2:1322).

¹ Sentence interlined.

From Tadeusz Kosciuszko

MON CHER ET TRES RESPECTABLE AMI   Soleure Avril 1816.

Votre lettre datée le 3 Juliet 1815 m'a fait un tres grand plaisir. Je tois a Paris lorsque lAngleterre envoya ses trouppes en Amerique et j'ai dis aux Diplomates Anglais qu'au Commencement leurs Armées seront victorieuses à cause du manque d'Officiers en Amerique mais que bientot elles seront chassèes ignominieusement et je leur en donnois ma Parole d'honneur. Vous ne connoissez dis je leur bravoure si bien comme moi—Vous voyez bien mon Cher Ami que j'ai prevu davance la defaite des Anglais, tellement j'ai eté sur d'un Character noble, et d'une bravoure Nationale de vos Concitoyens. Mais en Europe tout le monde à été surpri et éttoné, aussi votre réputation s'est accrue considerablement et les Noms Madison¹ et Jefferson sont répétés Mille fois par toutes les bouches.—C'est sans doute quelque chose que le Nom <u>La Pologne</u> et nous avons une réconnoissance éternele à l'Empereur Aléxandre mais il ne fait pas une Nation, Comme la Grandeur du Pays avec un nombre considerable d'habitants. l'Empereur Alexandre m'a promit d'agrandir le Duché de Varsovie jusqu'à la Dzwina et Dnieper a nos anciens limites; mais à ses intentions généreuses et Magnanimes, son Gabinet d'execution n'a pas répondu, et il se trouve malheureusement, que Le Royaume de Pologne a present est moindre d'un bon tiers que le Duché de Varsovie; J'ai fais un Voyage exprès à Vienne pour savoir au juste, et je ne voulois pas rétourner en Pologne à l'invitation de l'Empereur lui même, que lorsque je serais persuadé de l'exécution réele, et n'ayant pas l'assurance satisfaisante de son Ministre, J'ai ecris à l'Empereur le supliant de m'assurer par un écrit ce qu'il ma promit verbalement et que je tiendrai cela un secret jusqu'à l'execution; Mais je n'ai pas eu le bonheur de récevoir la réponse; alors je suis revenu en Suisse pour ne pas abuser de la Confiance de mes Concitoyens². — Oui Mon Cher Ami jai pensé aux bonnes Lois, l'Empereur Alexandre m'a promit un Gouvernement Constitutionel, Libéral, Independant. même l'affranchissement de nos Paysans malheureux et les rendre Proprietaires des terres qu'ils possedent. par cela seul il s'immortaliseroit; mais mais S'est evanui en fumée. — Je suis maintenant dans la Ville de Soleure en Suisse regardant Les Puissances Allieés manquant de bonne fois, faisant des Injustices aux autres petits États et agissant avec Leur Peuple, Comme des Loups avec les Moutons — Vous voiez mon Cher Ami dans qu'elle position je me trouve a present;³ Si Vous croyez qu'il serat plus avantageux pour moi de tirrer les intérets anuelle de mon fond, que de me l'envoyer en Éurope faites le, mais je Vous prie du grace que mes interets soyent regulierement envoyés car jen ai grand besoin, et que mon fond soit dans la Banque Sous mon Nom mais non pas sous le votre. Si au contraire il y à une petite perte à essuyer en transportant mon fond en Europe j'aurois preferé sans doute, j'ai ma Confiance toute entiere en Vous faites comme Vous jugez Le mieux pour Moi.⁴ — C'est Vous que l'Angleterre considère le plus et Vous craint aussi, mais non pas Les Puissances Alliees les Ministres de quelles sont tous Corompus; Les nouvelles possesions d'Angleterre en Europe; Mettent des grands entraves au Comerce partout, et La France bientot perdra toutes ses manufactures par sa protection particuliere.

Agreez Mon Cher Ami L'assurance de ma Consideration La plus Distinguee et La plus Affectionée   T Kosciuszko

My dear and very Respectable Friend   Soleure April 1816.
Your letter dated 3 July 1815 pleased me greatly. I was in Paris when England sent her troops to America, and I told the English diplomats that initially their armies would be victorious because of the lack of officers in America, but that before long they would be driven off ignominiously; and I backed this with my word of honor. I told them that they do not know your bravery as well as I do — You see clearly, my dear friend, that I have predicted the defeat of the English, because I was so sure of the noble character and national bravery of your fellow citizens. But in Europe everybody was surprised and astonished, so that your reputation increased considerably and everyone repeated the names of Madison and Jefferson thousands of times. — The name Poland is certainly something, and we feel an everlasting gratitude to the Emperor Alexander, but this alone does not make a nation, as would a large country with numerous inhabitants. Emperor Alexander promised me that he would enlarge the Duchy of Warsaw to our former borders, all the

way up to the Dvina and the Dnieper, but his executive cabinet did not support his generous and magnanimous intentions, and unfortunately the Kingdom of Poland is at present a third smaller than the Duchy of Warsaw. I took a special trip to Vienna to find out for sure, and I did not want to return to Poland, even at the invitation of the emperor himself, until I had been persuaded of the actual execution of Alexander's promise. Lacking a satisfactory guarantee from his minister, I wrote to the emperor, begging him to assure me in writing what he had promised me verbally, and telling him that I would keep it secret until the pledge was honored, but I did not have the pleasure of a reply. Therefore I returned to Switzerland rather than abuse the trust of my fellow citizens.—Yes, my dear friend, I thought about good laws. Emperor Alexander promised me a liberal, independent, constitutional government, even the emancipation of our miserable peasants and making them owners of the lands they occupy. For this alone he would become immortal, but it all vanished in smoke.—I am now in the city of Soleure in Switzerland watching the allied powers, who lack good faith, commit injustices toward the other small states, and act toward their people like wolves among sheep— You see my dear friend in what position I find myself at present. If you believe that it will be more advantageous for me to draw the annual interest on my capital than to send it to Europe, do it, but I beg you to have my interest sent regularly, as I have great need of it, and make sure that my capital is in the bank under my name, not yours. If on the other hand only a little loss would result from transporting my capital to Europe, I would certainly prefer that. You have my complete trust; act on my behalf as you think best.— England both respects and fears you the most, but does not think the same of the allied powers, whose ministers are all corrupt. The new possessions of England in Europe place great obstacles in the way of commerce everywhere, and France will soon lose all of her manufactures because of her special protection.

Please accept, dear friend, the assurance of my most distinguished and affectionate consideration   T Kosciuszko

RC (MHi); partially dated; dateline at foot of text; with penciled mark by TJ; endorsed by TJ as a letter of 16 Apr. 1816 received 24 July 1816 and so recorded in SJL. Dft (PlKMN); undated. Translation by Dr. Genevieve Moene. Enclosed in TJ to John Barnes, 12 Oct. 1816 (first letter), and Barnes to TJ, 7 Jan. 1817.

The DUCHÉ DE VARSOVIE was a Napoleonic satellite state created in 1807 and composed of Prussian (and later Austrian) Polish lands. Having been occupied by allied forces early in 1813, the duchy was partitioned at the Congress of Vienna, with Russia receiving the largest share, a quasi-independent ROYAUME DE POLOGNE over which Czar Alexander I reigned as king (Connelly, *Napoleonic France*, 487, 499–502).

[1] RC and Dft: "Addison."
[2] RC: "Concytoyens." Dft: "Concitoyens."
[3] Dft here adds "je Vous laisse juger Vous même" ("I leave you to judge for yourself").
[4] TJ marked the section from "Vous voiez" to this point for the attention of John Barnes (TJ to Barnes, 12 Oct. 1816).

List of Slave Vaccinations

1816.   Vaccinations.

April ⎱ Edy's   James
May ⎰   Maria

                     Patsy ⎰ Betsy
                            ⎱ Peter

Fanny's   Ellen.

                  Jenny
Sally's   Madison
                  Eston.

                 ⎧ Mary
Moses's ⎨ William
                 ⎩ Davy

                  Celia
                  Tucker.
                  Zacharias
                  Patsy.

Ursula's   Joe.

                  Anne.
                  Cornelius ⎰ Thomas
Cretia's   John
                  Randal.
                  Henry
                  Milly
                  Lilburn
                  Matilda.
                  James.

Ned's   Moses
                  Sucky

Jerry's   Jupiter.
                  Isaiah
                  Jerry.

Minerva's   Willis
                  Archy
                  Jordan.

Virginia's   Robert
                  Amanda

Esther's   Lindsay.
Mary's   Washington.

Rachael's   Eliza.
             Ellen.
   Lilly's   Lucy
             Stannard
     Bedford Billy.

MS (MHi); entirely in TJ's hand; on same sheet as lists of inoculations of 7 Aug.–17 Sept. 1801 (*PTJ*, 35:34–5), 10–26 May 1802 (*PTJ*, 37:442–3), and 17 Mar. 1826.

This list continues TJ's documentation of the VACCINATIONS for smallpox he began in 1801 as a result of his correspondence and collaboration with Benjamin Waterhouse (*PTJ*, 32:264–5, 35:34–5, 277–8, 572–3, 37:442–3). Except for the final name, the slaves on this list were all at Monticello and Tufton.

Appendix

Supplemental List of Documents Not Found

JEFFERSON'S epistolary record and other sources describe a number of documents for which no text is known to survive. The Editors generally account for such material at documents that mention them or at other relevant places. Exceptions are accounted for below.

From Samuel Leitch, undated. Recorded in SJL as received 17 Jan. 1816.

From Joseph Léonard Poirey, 17 Apr. 1816. Recorded in SJL as received from Paris on 11 Dec. 1816.

INDEX

Adams, John (*cont.*)
J. Morse, 256, 257n; letters from,
174–6, 431–4, 526–9; letters to,
345–7, 649–52; mentioned, 250n;
opinion of sought, 680–2; political
creed of, 174; on publication of correspondence, 175–6, 433; reflects on his
life, 526–7, 649–50; on religion, 256,
431–2, 433, 527–9, 649–52; and TJ's
syllabus on Jesus's doctrines, 595,
596n, 703
Adams, John Quincy: on France, 256–7;
negotiates convention with Great
Britain, 45–6; as peace negotiator, 485
Adams, Samuel: and Mass. Committee
of Correspondence, 369n
Addison, Joseph: *Cato: A Tragedy*, 247,
249n
*An Address to the Clergy of Massachu-
setts* (W. Cobbett), 4–6, 78, 79n
Adeline (brig), 114, 116, 118n
Adkinson, Mr. *See* Atkinson, Michael
Adlum, John: and grape cuttings, 348,
348–9, 514–5, 609; identified, 1:587n;
letter from, 514–5; letter to, 348;
moves to Georgetown, 514; and wine,
288, 311, 348, 348–9
Adrain, Robert: experiments of, 204
Aeneid (Virgil), 59
*Aeschyli Tragoediae Quae Supersunt ac
Deperditarum Fragmenta* (Aeschylus;
ed. C. G. Schütz), 196, 455
Aeschylus: *Aeschyli Tragoediae Quae Supersunt ac Deperditarum Fragmenta*
(ed. C. G. Schütz), 196, 455; authenticity of works of, 87; mentioned, 456
Aesop's Fables: referenced by TJ, 90,
91n
Africa: corn from, 672
African Americans: living at Milton,
444. *See also* slavery; slaves
Agenoria (brig), 569–70
Aggy (TJ's slave; b. *1789*; daughter of
Dinah): family of, 40, 215–6
aging: P. S. Du Pont de Nemours on,
613, 616n; R. Peters on, 598–9,
600–1; TJ on his own, 341
Agiorgitiko (St. George) (wine), 513n
agriculture: contour plowing, 538–40,
599; "Essays on the Natural History
and Origin of Peat" (R. Rennie),
75–6; European methods of,
599–600; fences, 282; government
subsidies to, 616–7; hemp brake,
303–4, 461–2, 463; implements of,

539, 540n, 583–4; and insects, 545;
and manufacturing interests, 334–6,
534–7, 616–8, 620n; study of, 600;
surplus products of, 476n; TJ on, 515;
tree cultivation, 542; use of gypsum
in, 66, 493–4, 538, 541, 583. *See also*
crops; Philadelphia Society for Promoting Agriculture; plows
Ainsworth, Robert: *An Abridgement
of Ainsworth's Dictionary* (ed.
T. Morell), 274, 464, 538, 639
Albemarle Academy: lottery for, 93n,
361, 498n; petition of, 47–8, 92–3,
329, 331; requests Literary Fund divi-
dend, 360; and sale of glebe lands,
496; TJ's Estimate and Plans for
Albemarle Academy/Central College,
626–7; TJ's proposed curriculum
for, 396. *See also* Central College
(Charlottesville)
Albemarle County, Va.: Hardware River,
99n; mail service in, 317; map of,
xxxix (*illus.*); petitions to General Assembly, 287, 328–9, 498n; schools in,
396–7, 713; Statement of TJ's Taxable Property in Albemarle County,
430–1; surveyor of, 362, 363n, 488,
519, 519–20, 648, 649n, 662; taxation
of property in, 99, 133. *See also* Central College (Charlottesville)
albinism, 12
Alcidamas (Greek rhetorician): TJ on,
456
alcohol: abuse of, 131–2; beer, 4, 29,
30n, 329, 371, 542; bottles and jugs
for, 371, 512; brandy made from
porter, 3; cider, 124, 151, 262, 267,
269, 270n, 371, 512, 542; shared purchase of, 20, 21n; taxation of, 642n;
temperance, 598; whiskey, 329, 483,
512. *See also* wine
Alembert, Jean Le Rond d': J. Adams
on, 527, 528; philosophy of, 650; and
religion, 527; on Voltaire, 709
Alexander I, emperor of Russia: criti-
cized, 217–8; mentioned, 347; and
Polish territories, 714–6; political
views of, 110–1; TJ on, 90; and
U.S., 9
Alexander, James, 348
Algiers: *1815* U.S. treaty with, 17, 18n
alidades: for U.S. Coast Survey, 222
Allegheny Mountains: altitude of, 10,
172n, 193; and map of Va., 687
Allen, Paul: and N. Biddle's history of

INDEX

Baltimore, Md.: cotton factories in, 534–7; newspapers, 607n

Baltimore Patriot & Evening Advertiser (newspaper), 607n

Bancroft, Edward: correspondence with TJ, 8n, 283; identified, 7n; introduces P. I. Barziza to TJ, 6–7, 394; letter from, 6–8

Bankhead, Ann (Anne) Cary Randolph (TJ's granddaughter; Charles Lewis Bankhead's wife): identified, 2:104n; mistreatment by husband, 131; visits Monticello, 131

Bankhead, Charles Lewis (Ann Cary Randolph Bankhead's husband): alcohol abuse by, 131–2; Carlton estate of, 131–2; identified, 3:188n; mistreats wife, 131; visits Monticello, 131

Bankhead, John: identified, 8:278n; letter to, 131–2; relationship with C. L. Bankhead, 131–2; visits Monticello, 132

Bankhead, Mary Warner Lewis (John Bankhead's wife): TJ sends greetings to, 132

Bank of Columbia, 587–8

Bank of Germantown (Pa.): cashier of, 447

Bank of Richmond. *See* Bank of Virginia (Richmond)

Bank of the United States: opposition to, 407

Bank of the United States, Second, 354–5

Bank of Virginia (Richmond): and C. Bellini estate, 123, 136, 291, 490, 492, 530; bills from, 443, 447, 522, 525, 553, 587; TJ's loan from, 37, 51, 62, 99, 106, 124, 133, 273, 312, 313, 552, 567, 568, 593–4

banks: currency issued by, 44–5, 95–7, 202–3; P. S. Du Pont de Nemours on, 617; stock issued by, 587–8; TJ on, 95–6, 329–30, 353–4, 358, 407, 562n; in Va., 286–7, 332, 365, 401, 496; in Washington, D.C., 587–8; works on, 61, 90

Baptists: in Va., 380, 382

Barber, Mr. *See* Barbour, James

Barbour, James: identified, 4:415–6n; letters from, 532, 563; letter to, 532–3; on Republican presidential nominations, 563; seeks plants, 532, 532–3

Barbour, Lucy Johnson (James Barbour's wife): seeds for, 533

Barboursville (J. Barbour's Orange Co. plantation), 532

Barclay, John D.: certifies Treasury Department warrants, 495n

Bargellini, Giovanni Santi: merchant, 293

Baring Brothers & Company: identified, 7:440n; letter from, to John Barnes, 182–3; and remittances to T. Kosciuszko, 181, 182, 367, 448, 465

Barlow, Joel: identified, 1:589–90n; as minister to Algiers, 575

Barnes, John: account with T. Kosciuszko, 465; handles financial transactions, 130, 131n, 553, 648, 649n; identified, 1:32n; introduced to G. W. Campbell by TJ, 14; and T. Kosciuszko's American investments, 181–2, 182, 367, 448, 465, 500, 587–8; letters from, 181–2, 367, 465, 500, 587–8; letters to, 448, 553; letter to, from T. Kosciuszko, 465; manages funds for TJ's granddaughter, 553, 553–4, 578, 579, 587

Barnet, Isaac Cox: as claims commissioner, 388; as consul, 388, 648; identified, 5:463–4n

barometers: altitude calculated with, 9–10, 11, 12n, 71–2, 187, 188–92, 193, 313–7; and meteorological observations, 239–43; mountain, 224, 225n; for surveying, 642–3, 689

The Baronage of England (W. Dugdale), 109

Barraud, Ann B.: and Bremo (J. H. Cocke's Fluvanna Co. estate), 502n

Barrett, Jean Jacques de: translates Cicero, 354, 420

Barsac (wine), 209, 513n

Barthélemy, Jean Jacques: scholarship of, 697

Bartolini, Lorenzo: Italian sculptor, 127–8, 350, 387, 670

Barton, Benjamin Smith: death of, 309, 310n; identified, 1:521n; and journals of M. Lewis, 309, 310n, 467, 605; library of, 467, 605

Barton, Mary Pennington (Benjamin Smith Barton's wife): and M. Lewis's journals, 467, 605

Barton, William: identified, 5:371–2n; *Memoirs of the Life of David Rittenhouse*, 204

Barziza, Antonio, Count: family of, 6, 230

INDEX

Dearborn, Henry Alexander Scammell: and gypsum for TJ, 226; identified, 4:197n; and seeds for TJ, 262–3

Dearborn, Sarah Bowdoin (James Bowdoin's widow; Henry Dearborn's third wife): conveys correspondence and publications to TJ, 4, 75, 78; identified, 5:165n; invites TJ to Boston, 263; letter from, 262–3; letter to, 404; plans to visit TJ, 46–7; sends greetings to TJ, 227; sends letter to M. J. Randolph, 263; sends seeds to TJ, 262–3, 404; visits Monticello, 76, 404

debt, public: A. Gallatin on, 202–3; TJ on, 88–9, 329–30

Déclaration de la Chambre des Représentants (*1815*), 69n

Déclaration des droits des Français et des principes fondamentaux de leur constitution (*1815*), 69n

Declaration of Independence: medal commemorating, 54, 91

Degen & Purviance (Leghorn mercantile firm), 671, 673n

Dehaven, Mrs. (Abraham Dehaven's wife): operates boardinghouse, 712

Dehaven, Abraham: operates boardinghouse, 712, 714n

De l'Allemagne (Staël Holstein), 84, 88n

Delamotte, Mr.: seeks consulship at Le Havre, 319–20, 358, 362–3, 388, 446, 648, 693; as vice-consul at Le Havre, 319, 362–3

Delaplaine, Joseph: *Delaplaine's Repository*, 270, 405, 459, 460–1; identified, 3:51n; letters from, 270, 351–2, 405, 460–1; letter to, 459; and portraits of TJ by G. Stuart, 351–2; proposal for printing *Delaplaine's Repository*, 270, 351, 352n, 405n; sends artwork to TJ, 405

Delaware: manufacturers in address Congress, 476, 515; militia of, 236

Delessert, Jules Paul Benjamin: and letters for Madame de Staël Holstein, 326

Delphin edition: TJ orders, 274, 464, 538, 639

Deluc, Jean André: and barometric calculation of altitude, 314, 317n, 642

Democratic Press (Philadelphia newspaper), 478, 480n

Demosthenes: J. Adams on, 528; *Oratorum Graecorum, quorum princeps est Demosthenes* (ed. J. J. Reiske), 196; TJ on, 456

dental care: T. Bruff as dentist, 683

Depriest, John: and building supplies for Poplar Forest, 505; sells horse to TJ, 58n

Derham, William: and barometric calculation of altitude, 314, 316n

Derieux, Maria Margherita Martin (Peter Derieux's wife): sends greetings to TJ, 252; stepdaughter of P. Mazzei, 114–5, 119n

Derieux, Peter (Justin Pierre Plumard): financial situation of, 114–5, 119n, 251–2, 399–400, 451–2; identified, 3:395–6n; letters from, 251–3, 451–3; letter to, 399–400; and P. Mazzei, 118n, 119n, 251–2, 399–400, 451–2; money sent to by French relatives, 252, 253n; requests assistance from TJ, 252, 399–400, 451–2

Descotils, Hippolyte Victor Collet: and *Nouveau Bulletin des Sciences*, 325, 326n

Description of some of the Medals, Struck in relation to Important Events in North America (J. Mease), 55n

Description of William Annesley's New System of Boat and Ship Building; Patented in the United States (W. Annesley), 558n, 559n

Desmarais. *See* Regnier-Desmarais, François Seraphin

Destutt de Tracy, Antoine Louis Claude: and American Philosophical Society, 485; *Commentary and Review of Montesquieu's Spirit of Laws*, 377, 435–6, 441–2, 485, 486n, 517; and V. Destutt de Tracy, 485; *Élémens d'Idéologie*, 441–2; *Élémens d'Idéologie: Idéologie proprement dite*, 485; *Grammaire*, 485; health of, 69, 377, 442, 484; identified, 1:262n; and Lafayette, 484; letter from, 441–3; letter from, to P. S. Du Pont de Nemours, 484–6; *Logique*, 441–2, 485; *Observations sur le Système Actuel d'Instruction Publique*, 442, 443n; sends manuscript to TJ, 485; TJ on *Treatise*, 639; *Traité de la volonté et de ses effets*, 441–3, 485, 486n, 493; *A Treatise on Political Economy*, 131, 439, 441, 463–4, 485, 537–8, 543, 568n, 603–4, 630–3, 633–4, 638–9, 640–1, 663–4

Destutt de Tracy, Victor: military service of, 485

Dexter, Aaron: agricultural writings of, 75–6

INDEX

"Essays on the Natural History and Origin of Peat" (R. Rennie), 75–6
An Essay Towards a New Theory of Vision (G. Berkeley), 637, 638n
Essex Junto, 4, 5, 256, 457
Estes, Triplett T.: and Albemarle Academy, 93n, 361, 496–8
Esther (TJ's slave; b. *1795*): and smallpox vaccination, 717
Estienne, Henri (Stepani; Stephani): edits *Opera Omnia Graece et Latine* (Dionysius of Halicarnassus), 109
Eston (TJ's slave; b. *1808*). *See* Hemings, Eston (TJ's slave and probable son; b. *1808*)
Étienne, Denis Germain: pianist, 694–6
Euclid: *Elements*, 394
Euripides: authenticity of works of, 87
Europe: allied powers of as threat to U.S., 89, 90–1; intellectual freedom in, 85–7; relations with U.S., 109–11; TJ on freedom in, 515, 711
Everett, Edward: books sold by, 186, 276, 277n; identified, 8:49–50n; travels to Europe, 186, 464
Ewen, Mr. *See* Ewing, Greville
Ewing, Greville: *Elements of the Greek Language . . . Being a Translation of Dr. Moor's Celebrated Greek Grammar*, 464, 538, 639
eyeglasses, 341

Fabbroni, Giovanni Valentino Maria: on TJ's letter to P. Mazzei, 113
Faial (Fayal) (wine), 513
Fairfax, Thomas, 6th Baron Fairfax of Cameron: lands of surveyed, 686–7
Fairman, Gideon: engraver, 352n; identified, 4:357n
Fancelli, Giovanni Battista: and C. Bellini estate, 113, 290, 291–2, 292–4, 297, 492, 530; power of attorney from, 290, 292–7, 530
Fancelli, Pietro: family of, 292
Fanny (TJ's slave; b. *1788*). *See* Hern, Fanny Gillette (TJ's slave; b. *1788*; wife of David Hern [b. *1784*])
Farley, Betsy: boards TJ's slave, 567
Farmers and Mechanics' Bank (Georgetown), 587
Fayal. *See* Faial (Fayal) (wine)
The Federalist (A. Hamilton, J. Madison, J. Jay), 436
Federalist party: in Congress, 42n; in New England, 4–6, 90–1. *See also*

Essex Junto; Hartford, Conn.: Federalist convention at
fences: wire, 282
Fenwick, Joseph: conveys letters, 323
Ferdinand, Duke of Parma: family of, 478, 480n
Ferdinand VII, king of Spain: U.S. diplomatic relations with, 388–9, 391
Ferdinand III, Duke of Tuscany, 114, 115, 673n, 673
Ferguson, Findlay: executor of T. Reed's estate, 258
Ferguson, James: *Lectures on Select Subjects in Mechanics, Hydrostatics, Pneumatics, and Optics*, 638n
Ferrall, Patrick: Treasury Department clerk, 495n
Fessenden, Thomas: translates Latin verse, 265, 267
fevers: treatment for, 237. *See also* yellow fever
Fidler, Robert: scientific-instrument maker, 225
La Figure de la Terre (P. Bouguer), 314, 317n
files (tools), 223
first meridian. *See* prime meridian
fish: anchovies, 371, 371–2, 418
fisher (animal), 605
Fitch, Gideon. *See* Fitz, Gideon
Fitch, William D.: account with TJ, 482–4; identified, 483n; TJ's Notes for a Settlement with, 482–4
Fitz, Gideon: identified, 1:215n; and La. land claims, 584–5; letter from, 584–7; surveying work of, 474–5
Fitzwhylsonn & Potter (Richmond firm): agent for J. Delaplaine's *Repository*, 352n; identified, 3:599n
Fitzwilliam, Richard: as boundary commissioner, 178
flax: TJ on, 303
Fleischer, Guillaume: *Annuaire de La Librairie*, 354, 355n, 420
Fleming, George: Description of a Steam Engine, 141–3; Drawing of a Steam Engine, 140; identified, 139n; letters from, 138–9, 461–3; letter to, 302–4; as miller, 139; and steam engines, 138–9, 140, 141–3, 302–3, 462–3; and TJ's hemp-brake design, 303–4, 461–2, 463
Fleury, François Louis Teissèdre de: medal commemorating Revolutionary War service of, 54, 55n, 91
Flood, Henry: Buckingham Co. tavern-

[740]

keeper, 19–20; identified, 4:515n; and
letters for J. W. Eppes, 713
Flood's ordinary (Buckingham Co.; proprietor Henry Flood), 19–20
Flora Americæ Septentrionalis (F.
Pursh), 339n
Florence, Italy: wine of, 359
Florida: boundaries of, 479. *See also*
East Florida; West Florida
Floridablanca, Conde de. *See* Moñino y
Redondo, José, Conde de Floridablanca
flour: in Lynchburg market, 562; from
Poplar Forest, 133, 254, 313, 370,
493, 505, 593–4; price of, 124, 133,
273, 406, 500, 552, 569, 624, 708; as
rent, 665; at Richmond, 498–9, 569,
708; sale of, 254, 567–8, 708; shipment of, 547–8; transported to Richmond, 99, 133, 272–3, 312–3, 370,
498–9, 546–7. *See also* Monticello
(TJ's estate): flour from
Flower, George: identified, 668–9n; introduced to TJ, 667, 679; U.S. tour of,
667, 679
flowers: M. J. Randolph sends seeds
to M. B. J. Eppes, 608. *See also*
plants
food: anchovies, 371, 371–2, 418; apples,
533; asparagus, 702; bacon, 588, 713;
bon-bons, 317–8; bread, 505, 616,
620n; butter, 616, 620n, 656; cheese,
616, 620n; cherries, 533; chicken,
616, 620n, 713; cocoa, 426; eggs, 616,
620n; haricots, 532–3; hickory nuts,
348n; horse beans, 672; kale, sprout,
532; lima beans, 608–9; macaroni,
323, 421, 470, 569; milk, 616, 620n;
olive oil, 198; tavern charges for, 19,
20, 21n, 21; turkey, 616, 620n. *See
also* alcohol; coffee; corn; currants;
flour; oil; rice; spices; sugar; tea;
wine
Formigli, Giuseppe: archivist in Florence, 291n
Forti, Anton Francesco: family of, 673
Forti, Gaspero: witnesses will, 673
Fortin, Jean Nicolas: scientific-
instrument maker, 223
Fossett, Betsy-Ann (Betsy) (TJ's slave;
b. *1812*): on smallpox vaccination list,
717
Fossett, James (TJ's slave; b. *1805*): on
smallpox vaccination list, 717
Fossett, Maria (TJ's slave; b. *1807*): on
smallpox vaccination list, 717

Fossett, Patsy (TJ's slave; b. *1810*): on
smallpox vaccination list, 717
Fossett, Peter (TJ's slave; b. *1815*): on
smallpox vaccination list, 717
Foster, Augustus John: British minister
to U.S., 572
Fouché, Joseph, duc d'Otrante, 317,
318n, 376, 572
Fourth of July: orations, 4, 6n, 41–2, 78
Fox, Joseph: dedicates work to TJ, 355,
448; identified, 355–6n; letters from,
355–6, 597; letter to, 447–8; proposed
work on dyeing, 355, 447–8, 597
Fox & Richardson (Richmond firm):
and wine for TJ, 499. *See also*
Richardson, Thomas
fractures, bone, 567
France: allies invade, 211; Berlin and
Milan decrees, 210–1, 571; Bourbon
dynasty restored, 9, 45, 108, 202, 210,
211, 247, 304–5, 309–10, 353, 359,
360n, 376–7, 432, 458, 576; Chambre
des Pairs, 376–7, 391–3; Chambre des
Représentants, 68, 69n, 376–7; commerce of, 570; and conscription, 74–5;
Constituent Assembly, 377; constitutional monarchy of, 68; Constitution
of *1791*, 346; Directory, 74, 75n, 575;
economy of, 329, 331n, 354, 407,
561n, 715; education of deaf and mute
in, 654–5; and Great Britain, 516,
663; and Lafayette, 484; laws of, 317,
391, 393n; medal commemorating
U.S. alliance with, 91–2; military
power of, 9; musicians from, 694–6;
newspapers of, 390–1, 393n; oppression in, 333–4, 458, 711; and partition
of Poland, 345; political situation in,
388, 390–2; relations with Austria,
347; revolutionary calendar, 576,
578n; Saint Bartholomew's Day massacre, 175, 257; Senate, 630; social
conditions in, 9; TJ on, 108, 304,
305, 333–4, 346–7, 353, 403, 421–2.
See also Crawford, William Harris:
minister plenipotentiary to France;
Gallatin, Albert: minister plenipotentiary to France; Institut de France;
Napoleon I, emperor of France
franking privilege: of TJ, 270
Franklin, Benjamin: as American commissioner in France, 362–3, 446; and
medal about Franco-American
alliance, 91–2; mentioned, 327
Franzoni, Giuseppe Antonio: sculptor at
U.S. Capitol, 350, 351n

INDEX

History of the Expedition under the command of Captains Lewis and Clark (N. Biddle), 704, 705, 707n

The History of the Late War between the United States and Great Britain (G. J. Hunt), 414n, 522

The History of the Rebellion and Civil Wars in England, Begun in the Year 1641 (E. Clarendon), 109

The History of Virginia (J. D. Burk, S. Jones, and L. H. Girardin): mentioned, 137, 369n, 407; sources for, 108, 109n; TJ's role in the preparation of, 367

Hock (wine), 513

hogs: at Poplar Forest, 562; transportation of, 562

Holbach, Paul Henri Dietrich, Baron d': *Le Bon-Sens, ou Idées Naturelles Opposées aux Idées Surnaturelles*, 650, 652n; philosphy of, 650; *Système de la Nature. Ou Des Loix du Monde Physique & du Monde Moral*, 650, 652n; *System of Nature; or, The Laws of the Moral and Physical World*, 652n; TJ on, 651

Holcombe, John: payment to, 588, 589n

Holcombe, Thomas Anderson: and festivities for A. Jackson, 145, 147n; identified, 6:451–2n; letter from, 145–7; tutor to F. W. Eppes, 608, 712

Holcroft, Thomas: translates *Posthumous Works of Frederic II. King of Prussia* (Frederick II, king of Prussia), 709n

Holland. *See* The Netherlands

holland (textile), 565, 566n

Holland, James: TJ writes to, on behalf of I. Briggs, 509, 510n, 515

Hollis, Thomas Brand: and J. and A. Adams, 176n

Holman, John: ship captain, 572

Holmes, John: identified, 8:649n; letter to, 41–2; *An Oration, Pronounced at Alfred, on the 4th of July, 1815*, 4, 6n, 41–2, 78

home manufacturing. *See* manufacturing, household

Homer: authenticity of works of, 86–7; A. Coray edition of, 195, 455; G. G. Heyne edition of *The Iliad*, 196, 455; Ὁμήρου Ἰλιὰς καὶ εἰς Αὐτὴν Σχόλια τῶν Παλαιῶν. *Homeri Ilias, et Veterum in Eam Scholia* (ed. Didymus Chalcenterus), 196, 455; TJ on, 700; works of translated by J. H. Voss, 84

Hopkins, Arthur Francis: identified, 43n; introduced to TJ, 42

Hopkins, Judith Jefferson (TJ's cousin; Field Jefferson's daughter): family of, 42, 43n

Horace: allusions to, 695, 696n; quoted by J. Adams, 432, 434n; quoted by J. Corrêa da Serra, 467, 469n; TJ quotes, 374–5

horizon. *See* artificial horizon

Horrors of Slavery: or, The American Tars in Tripoli (W. Ray), 237, 531

horses: disabled, 269; fodder for, 562, 624; and hemp brakes, 303–4; and plows, 599–600; tavern charges for, 19, 20, 21; taxes on, 430; TJ purchases, 52n, 58n, 255n

Horsley, John: *Britannia Romana: or the Roman Antiquities of Britain*, 109

Houdon, Jean Antoine: bust of J. Necker, 328n; bust of G. Washington, 352n; statue of G. Washington for Va. state capitol, 385–7

household articles: blankets, 76, 147; bottles, 371, 371–2, 418, 512; buttons, 565; cloth, 565; corks, 371, 371–2, 418, 523, 542, 582, 602–3; shot, 301; thread, 565, 566, 597. *See also* building materials; clocks; clothing; furniture; tools

House of Representatives, U.S.: Claims Committee, 508–9; and implementation of treaties, 548–51, 551n, 552n; and purchase of TJ's library, 409–10; Roads and Canals Committee, 338–9; and taxes, 513n; Ways and Means Committee, 510n. *See also* Congress, U.S.

Howard, John Eager: medal commemorating Revolutionary War service of, 54

Hoyle, Charles: identified, 21n; Lynchburg innkeeper, 20–1

Hubbard, William H.: purchases TJ's flour, 708

Hudson, Christopher: exchanges tree cuttings with TJ, 542; identified, 8:653n; letter from, 542

Hudson River, 558

Hudson strawberry, 563

Hughes, Anne (TJ's slave; b. *1807*): on smallpox vaccination list, 717

Hughes, Cornelius (TJ's slave; b. *1811*): on smallpox vaccination list, 717

Hughes, Joe (TJ's slave; b. *1805*): on smallpox vaccination list, 717

INDEX

JEFFERSON, THOMAS (*cont.*)
75–6, 97, 104, 105n, 107, 143, 144n,
149, 194, 217, 218n, 249, 297–8,
307–8, 343, 344, 365n, 377, 414,
476, 502, 503n, 526, 555, 592, 653,
665–6, 710 (*See also* Library of
Congress)

Business & Financial Affairs
account with W. Ballard, 105–6; ac-
count with S. Cathalan, 470, 471n;
account with C. & A. Conrad &
Company, 130; account with M.
Dawson, 301; account with W.
Duane, 130, 439, 552n, 568; ac-
count with N. G. Dufief, 130, 447n,
645, 646n; account with W. D.
Fitch, 482–4; account with Green
& Peyton, 603; account with J.
Leitch, 565–6, 597, 656; account
with J. Milligan, 59–60, 130, 131n,
133, 463, 537; account with A.
Robertson, 50, 51, 52, 562, 594,
604, 630, 714n; account with W.
Steptoe, 40; account with J.
Vaughan, 514, 552, 645, 646n, 649;
Auditor's Report on the Purchase of
TJ's Library, 494–5; and C. Bellini
estate, 113, 122–3, 123, 136, 290–2,
292–7, 297, 490, 491–2, 530; bill
from R. Douthat, 21–2; bill from H.
Flood, 19–20; bill from Guerrant &
Staples, 19; bill from C. Hoyle,
20–1; bill from R. Hunter, 20; bill
from Liberty, Va., tavern, 21; buys
and sells slaves, 215–6; debt to T.
Kosciuszko, 715; debt to P. Mazzei,
583, 644, 673–8; debt to W. Short,
320, 322n, 357; debt to N. & J. &
R. van Staphorst, 579–80, 580–1,
644, 662–3, 679–80; dispute with
D. Michie, 52–4, 63, 443–4; exchanges Treasury notes, 360n, 514,
552; and Highland–Indian Camp
boundary dispute, 289–90, 319,
357, 362, 388, 488, 519, 519–20,
648, 649n, 661, 662, 693; and R.
Jefferson's will, 30–3, 488, 489,
683–4; and T. Kosciuszko's American investments, 181–2, 367, 448,
465, 500, 587–8; and lease of Natural Bridge, 402, 449, 450; and lease
of Shadwell mills, 133, 498–9,
546–7, 547; lines of credit in Europe, 82, 152, 153n, 196, 209, 353,
492–3, 561n; loan from Bank of

Virginia, 37, 51, 62, 99, 106, 124,
133, 273, 312, 313, 552, 567, 568,
593–4; loan from T. J. Randolph,
133; and P. Mazzei's property, 114,
118n, 119n, 120n, 126, 350, 583,
644, 670, 673–8; orders wine from
T. Appleton, 350–1, 359, 416, 671;
orders wine from S. Cathalan, 186,
209–10, 212n, 276, 323, 420–1,
470, 471–2, 569–70; orders wine
from J. F. Oliveira Fernandes, 263,
313, 324–5, 366, 370, 401–2, 449,
499, 594, 602, 659, 660; orders
wine from H. Sheaff, 77, 98, 130;
payments by J. Harvie, 449; payments to T. J. Randolph, 406; pays
taxes, 50, 52n, 62, 99, 106, 133,
313, 430, 562, 568, 594, 604;
Promissory Note to Edmund Bacon,
301; Promissory Note to Charles
Clay, 58; Promissory Note to John
Neilson, 665; sells flour, 133; sells
tobacco, 133; and W. Short's property, 519, 519–20, 661, 662 (*See
also* Barnes, John; Gibson & Jefferson [Richmond firm]; Henderson
case)

Correspondence
anonymous letters to, 533–7; anonymous publications by, 378, 380–1,
381–3, 548–52; European, 417,
429; fatiguing to, 299, 306, 341,
357, 398, 459; franking privilege,
270; letter of condolence, 682–3;
letters of application and recommendation from, 412–3, 419, 446,
511, 521–2, 627–8; letters of application and recommendation to, 102,
126–8, 183–4, 194, 220–1, 235–7,
337–9, 408, 653–4; letters of introduction from, 26–7, 38–9, 39, 413,
431; letters of introduction to, 6–8,
13–4, 42–3, 55–7, 125, 134–5,
180–1, 207–8, 267–8, 300–1,
667–9, 679; publication of papers,
175, 176n, 403, 457–8, 595–6,
680–2, 703–4; return of confidential letters to, 515; threatening letter,
100–1

Family & Friends
friendship with Bankheads, 131–2;
friendship with J. Corrêa da Serra,
310; friendship with J. Miller, 278,
279; friendship with J. and L. L.
Paradise, 283, 285n; relations with

INDEX

INDEX

INDEX

National Institute of France. *See* Institut de France

National Intelligencer (Washington newspaper): advertisements in, 274, 275n, 503–4; editors of, 641n, 641; prints letter from "A" (Thomas Jefferson), 548–52; prints political results, 563n; prints TJ's correspondence, 411n

National Utility, in opposition to Political Controversy: Addressed to the Friends of American Manufactures, 249n, 336n

Natural and Statistical View, or Picture of Cincinnati and the Miami Country (D. Drake), 526, 647

Natural Bridge, Va.: calculations of latitude, 26n, 36; lease of, 402, 449, 450; route to from Poplar Forest, 35, 450; TJ visits, 21–2, 26, 108, 122, 308, 309; visitors to, 18, 26, 26–7, 108, 122, 308

natural history: study of, 529, 644

The Natural History of Carolina, Florida, and the Bahama Islands (M. Catesby), 108

naturalization: An Act to establish an uniform rule of Naturalization, and to repeal the acts heretofore passed on that subject (*1802*), 259, 261n; S. Cathalan desires, 576; J. F. Dumoulin on, 665–6; TJ on, 666n

natural philosophy: study of, 529

The Nautical Almanac and Astronomical Ephemeris (E. M. Blunt): TJ orders, 60

The Nautical Almanac and Astronomical Ephemeris (J. Garnett): TJ orders, 60, 274

Nautilus (boat), 558

Navy Department, U.S.: applications to, 408, 412–3, 415, 482; appointments to, 458, 498; and floating batteries, 623; gunboats of, 623; war craft of, 555, 557, 623, 629n

Necker, Jacques: bust of, 326, 328n; family of, 327

Ned (TJ's slave; b. *1760*). *See* Gillette, Ned (TJ's slave; b. *1760*)

Neilson (Nelson), John: identified, 5:299–300n; TJ's promissory note to, 665

Nelson, Mr. *See* Neilson (Nelson), John

Nelson, Matthew: and *Jefferson v. Michie*, 52

Nepos, Cornelius: TJ references, 703; works of, 274, 464, 538, 639; works of bound for TJ, 274, 464, 538, 639

Nestor (mythological character): J. Adams compared to, 374, 375n

The Netherlands: book prices in, 196, 559; government of, 516; scholarship in, 83, 697–8

Nettleton, Thomas: and barometric calculation of altitude, 314, 317n

Neue Erdbeschreibung (A. F. Büsching), 137, 138n

Newburyport, Mass.: revenue inspector at, 653–4

Newcomen, Thomas: steam engine of, 302

New England: clergy of, 4–6, 78–9, 255–6, 378–9, 380–1, 381–3; colleges in, 331; Federalists in, 90–1; politics in, 4–6, 41; TJ's essay on religious intolerance in, 378–9, 380–1, 381–3

New Granada (Spanish viceroyalty), 271, 272n

New Hampshire: mountains in, 9–10, 11, 12n, 71, 187

A New Introduction to the English Grammar (J. Ware), 525n

New Jersey: mountains in, 12n

New London, Va.: academy at, 608, 712–4

New Orleans: and land claims in Orleans Territory, 584. *See also* Lafayette, Marie Joseph Paul Yves Roch Gilbert du Motier, marquis de: land of, in La.

newspapers: *Baltimore Patriot & Evening Advertiser*, 607n; Boston *Independent Chronicle*, 403; French, 390–1; London *Times*, 218; *Lynchburg Press*, 173, 174n; Philadelphia *Aurora*, 439, 618n, 619–20; Philadelphia *Democratic Press*, 478, 480n; Philadelphia *Poulson's American Daily Advertiser*, 709n; politics of, 202, 203; Richmond *Virginia Argus*, 480n, 487–8, 516, 518; Richmond *Virginia Patriot*, 710–2; W. Short on, 321; subscriptions to, by TJ, 108, 439, 568n; TJ on, 41, 381, 444, 457. *See also* Enquirer (Richmond newspaper); National Intelligencer (Washington newspaper)

A New System of Banking (P. S. Chazotte), 61, 90

Newton, Sir Isaac: J. Adams on, 434; and barometric calculation of altitude,

263, 325; and wine for TJ, 263, 313, 324–5, 366, 370, 401–2, 449, 499, 594, 602, 659, 660
olives: trees, 198–9
Olivet, Pierre Joseph Thoulier d': translates Cicero, 354, 420
Ὁμήρου Ἰλιὰς καὶ εἰς Αὐτὴν Σχόλια τῶν Παλαιῶν. *Homeri Ilias, et Veterum in Eam Scholia* (Homer; ed. Didymus Chalcenterus), 196, 455
Onís y González Vara López y Gómez, Luis de: identified, 1:602n; minister plenipotentiary of Spain, 388–90, 516, 517n; negotiations with U.S. government, 388–9, 478–80, 516
On the Geological Formation of the Natural Bridge of Virginia (F. W. Gilmer), 26n
On the Importance of Assisting Young Men of Piety and Talents in Obtaining an Education for the Gospel Ministry (L. Beecher), 255–7, 378–9, 381, 381–2, 383
Opelousas District, Orleans Territory, 584–7
Opera. Interpretatione et Notis (Virgil, Delphin edition; ed. C. de La Rue), 274, 464, 538, 639
Opera Omnia Graece et Latine (Dionysius of Halicarnassus; eds. H. Estienne, J. J. Reiske, and others), 109
Opere di Platone (Plato; trans. D. Bembo), 394
Opinion de M. de Broglie Sur la Loi d'amnistie portée par les Ministres de Sa Majesté à la Chambre des Pairs le 9 janvier 1816 (Broglie), 377
opium: used in medicine, 44
Oram, James: identified, 525n; letter to, 525; payment to, 414n; sends prospectus to TJ, 525
An Oration, Pronounced at Alfred, on the 4th of July, 1815 (J. Holmes), 4, 6n, 41–2, 78
An Oration, Pronounced at Lexington, Mass. (J. T. Austin), 4, 6n, 78
Oratio Pro M. Marcello (Cicero; ed. F. A. Wolf), 87
Oratorum Graecorum, quorum princeps est Demosthenes (Demosthenes; J. J. Reiske), 196, 456
Orders in Council. *See* Great Britain: Orders in Council
Ordinances Passed at a General Convention of Delegates and Representatives, From the several Counties and Corpo-

rations of Virginia, Held at the Capitol, in the City of Williamsburg, on Monday the 6th of May, Anno Dom: 1776, 405, 406n
Orléans, Louis Charles d'. *See* Beaujolais, Louis Charles d'Orléans
Orléans, Louis Philippe. *See* Montpensier, Antoine Philippe d'Orléans
Orléans, Louis Philippe Joseph, duc d': guillotined, 575, 578n
Orleans Territory: land claims in, 584–7; land commissioners in, 584–7. *See also* Claiborne, William Charles Coles; Louisiana (Spanish and French colony); Louisiana Territory
Osgood, David: mentioned, 79, 381, 383
Osnaburg (Oznabrig): fabric, 301
Otis, Harrison Gray: federalist legislator, 217
Ould, Robert: educator, 502–3, 529–30; identified, 503n; letter from, 502–3; letter to, 529–30; sends book to TJ, 502, 503n, 529
overseers: depart, 99; hiring of, 34; at Lego, 604n; TJ on, 604; TJ's accounts with, 105; TJ's instructions to, 147; at Tufton, 604n. *See also* Bacon, Edmund; Goodman, Jeremiah Augustus; Yancey, Joel (d. *1833*)
Ovid: *Metamorphoses*, 274, 464; *Minellius Anglicanus, sive Publii Ovidii Nasonis Metamorphoseon* (ed. N. Bailey), 464, 538, 639; *P. Ovidii Nasonis Opera* (ed. P. Burman), 646n; *Pub. Ouidii Nasonis Metamorphoseon* (ed. J. Pontanus), 274, 275n, 464, 538, 639; works of bound for TJ, 464, 538, 639
oxen: blood of, 466, 468n

Pacharetti. *See* Pajarete (wine)
Page, John: correspondence of, 108, 109n
paintings, 592
Pajarete (wine): TJ on, 513
Palacio Fajardo, Manuel: South American patriot, 271, 702
Palladio, Andrea: TJ on, 500; works of, owned by TJ, 502n
Pallas, Peter Simon: edits *Linguarum Totius Orbis Vocabularia comparativa*, 373n
Palus (wine), 513
paper: for printing, 597
Paradise, John: family of, 6–7, 230; identified, 284–5n; marriage

INDEX

nership formed, 301; payments made for TJ, 111, 112n

Watt, James: steam mill of, 302–4

Watterston, George: *Catalogue of the Library of the United States*, xliv–xlv, 70, 80, 237, 238n, 318, 344 (*illus.*), 396n, 409–10, 435, 438n, 469, 531–2; and catalogue of TJ's library, 409–10; identified, 8:445n; letters from, 79–80, 237–8, 409–10, 544; letters to, 69–70, 107–8, 318, 531–2; librarian of Congress, 69–70, 79–80, 107, 318, 544

Watts, Edward: as Va. state senator, 361

Wayles, John (TJ's father-in-law): identified, 5:162–3n; and lottery for W. Byrd (*1728–77*), 545–6, 647; papers at Eppington, 545–6, 647; TJ as executor for, 647

The Wealth of Nations (A. Smith), 631

weather: cold, 147, 341; effect on crops, 51, 254; effect on health, 456–7; hurricanes, 51, 94–7, 404; ice, 370; rain, 112; snow, 357, 443, 605; TJ on climate, 310; in Va., 122, 144, 443. *See also* meteorological observations

weaving. *See* textiles

Webster, Noah: writings of, 300n

Weightman, Roger Chew: conveys manuscript to J. Milligan, 537–8; identified, 4:193n

weights, measures, and coinage: standard measures of, 223

Weiske, Benjamin: *Commentarius Perpetuus et Plenus in Orationem M. Tullii Ciceronis pro M. Marcello*, 87, 88n

Weld, Isaac: and steamboat *Thames*, 134, 135n

Wellington, Arthur Wellesley, 1st Duke of (formerly Viscount): converses with Madame de Staël Holstein, 326, 328n; family of, 579; and M. Ney's clemency plea, 393n

Wells, William Hill: as U.S. senator, 477n, 606–7

Werner, Abraham Gottlob: mineralogical theories of, 667

West, Benjamin: *The Fright of Astyanax*, 592, 593n; portrait of R. Fulton by, 405n

West Florida: Spain demands U.S. surrender of, 388–9; and War of *1812*, 103, 128–9. *See also* Florida

Westtown School (West Chester, Pa.):

coeducational Quaker institution, 540, 541n

wheat: as cash crop, 594; in Italy, 470; at Monticello, 313, 594, 604; as payment for debts, 40; at Poplar Forest, 51, 313, 505, 594, 604

Wheeler, Guy C.: ship captain, 57, 269, 272

whiskey: negative effects of, 329, 512; TJ orders, 483

Whitbread, Samuel: friend of G. Flower, 679

White House. *See* President's House

whites: taxes on, 430

Wickham, Mr.: provides legal counsel, 93

Wickham, John: identified, 2:395–6n; and *Livingston v. Jefferson*, 450n

Wickham, William: and P. I. Barziza, 230, 282

Wickliff, John. *See* Wycliffe, John

Wieland, Christoph Martin: on authenticity of Homer's works, 86; edits *Der Teutsche Merkur*, 86, 88n; popularity of, 84

Wilde, Richard Henry: as U.S. congressman, 550–2

William (TJ's slave; b. *1801*). *See* Hern, William (TJ's slave; b. *1801*)

William and Mary, College of: faculty of, 684; president of, 396n, 435–6; riots at, 397, 398n; slaves at, 490; textbooks of, 396; TJ on, 397, 398n, 608

Williams, David (of New York): medal commemorating Revolutionary War service of, 91, 92n

Williams, Francis: and G. Ticknor's correspondence, 196

Williams, Jonathan: and altitude calculations, 10, 71–2, 172n, 187, 193–4, 313; and American Philosophical Society, 12n; identified, 3:94–5n; and United States Military Philosophical Society, 192n

Williamsburg, Va.: meeting at Raleigh Tavern, 367–8

Williamson, Hugh: *The History of North Carolina*, 178, 179n; identified, 8:603–4n

Willis (TJ's slave; b. *1806*): on smallpox vaccination list, 717

Willis's Mountain: and altitude of Peaks of Otter, 156; surveying of, 687

Wilson, Alexander: *American Ornithology*, 59–60, 130

INDEX

Wilson, Peter: identified, 373n; letter from accounted for, 373n; letter to, 372–3; linguistic studies of, 372–3
Winckelmann, Johann Joachim: art scholar, 84, 88n; *Geschichte der Kunst des Alterthums*, 698
Winder, Rider Henry: *Remarks on a Pamphlet, entitled "An Enquiry respecting the Capture of Washington by the British, on the 24th of August, 1814, with, &c. &c. by Spectator,"* 710
Winder, William Henry: brother's pamphlet defending, 710; and defense of Washington, D.C., 710
wine: Barsac, 209, 513n; Beaumes, 513n; Bellet, 471–2, 569; Blanquefort, 513n; Bordeaux, 288; burgundy, 288, 348, 513; Calon, 513n; Cantenac, 513n; Cape, 513; Carbonnieux, 513n; champagne, 209, 288, 513; cisterns for storage of, 466, 468n; claret, 512, 513; Condrieu, 513; Côte-Rôtie, 513; currant, 348; of Faial (Fayal), 513; of Florence, 359; friendship compared to, 76; Graves, 513; Haut-Brion, Château, 513n; Hermitage, 209–10, 212n, 323, 421, 470, 513, 569; Hock, 513; Lafite, Château, 513n; Langon, 513n; Latour, Château, 513n; Léoville, 513n; Madeira, 263, 288, 421, 513; of Málaga, 513; Malmsey, 513; Margaux, 513n; Médoc, 513; Montepulciano, 350–1, 416, 671; Moselle, 513; of Nice, 210, 323, 421, 470, 569, 570, 573n; Pajarete (Pacharetti), 513; Palus, 513; Podensac (Podenac), 513n; port, 263, 313, 324, 325, 366, 402, 474, 602, 659; Portuguese, 77, 98, 133, 313, 324, 325n, 513; Preignac, 513n; production of, 198, 311; of Rivesaltes, 421; of Roussillon, 323, 421, 470, 570; St. Bris, 513n; St. George (Agiorgitiko), 513n; Sanlúcar, 513; Sauternes, 209, 513n; sent to TJ, 348, 366, 401–2, 573n, 602, 659, 660; sherry, 77, 98, 313, 324, 513; of Sicily, 513; Spanish, 513; straw, 209, 212n; subsidy for production of, 426; tariff on, 512–3; tavern charges for, 19; of Tenerife, 324, 366, 401–2, 499, 513, 602, 659, 660; Termo, 263; TJ arranges delivery of, 313, 351, 370, 402, 416, 449, 499, 659; TJ orders from T. Appleton, 350–1, 359, 416; TJ orders from S. Cathalan, 186,

209–10, 212n, 276, 323, 420–1, 470, 471–2, 569–70; TJ orders from J. F. Oliveira Fernandes, 263, 313, 324–5, 366, 370, 401–2, 449, 499, 594, 602, 659, 660; TJ orders from H. Sheaff, 77, 98, 130; TJ's notes on consumption of, 474; Tokay, 513. *See also* grapes; Monticello (TJ's estate): viticulture at; viticulture
Wingate, William: identified, 8:392n; letters from, 653–4; seeks federal appointment, 653–4; sends book to TJ, 653
Winn, John: as agent for C. Massie, 269; identified, 2:201n
Winston, Samuel L.: clerk to I. Briggs, 474–5
Wirt, William: identified, 1:341–2n; *Sketches of the Life and Character of Patrick Henry,* 219–20, 407; and Theological Seminary of Virginia, 379n
Wistar, Caspar: and J. Corrêa da Serra, 66, 67; health of, 66–7; and Historical and Literary Committee of the American Philosophical Society, 180n; identified, 1:101n; on Indians, 64–6, 121; letter from, 64–7; letter to, 121–2; mentioned, 282; proposed visit to Monticello of, 66–7, 122; and T. J. Randolph, 122; *A System of Anatomy for the Use of Students of Medicine,* 67
Wolf, Friedrich August: *Briefe an Hernn Hofrath Heyne von Professor Wolf,* 88n; classical scholar, 698; edits *Oratio Pro M. Marcello* (Cicero), 87; *Prolegomena ad Homerum,* 86–7
women: letters from: M. B. Andrews, 93–4; M. B. Briggs, 540–1; S. M. Bruff, 610–1; E. W. Randolph (Coolidge), 578–9; S. B. Dearborn, 262–3; V. Murray, 213–5; Madame de Staël Holstein, 326–8; E. Trist, 456–7; letters sent under cover to, 683; letters to: M. B. Andrews, 27–9; F. W. Brand, 262; M. B. Briggs, 682; S. M. Bruff, 682–3; E. W. Randolph (Coolidge), 553–4; S. B. Dearborn, 404; M. J. Randolph, 147–8; E. Trist, 710–2; spousal mistreatment of, 131
wood: firewood, 482, 483–4. *See also* building materials
Wood, James (of Albemarle Co.): clerk for Watson & Dawson, 111, 112n
Wood, John (ca. *1775–1822*): identified, 2:96n; letters from, 566–7, 642–4;

THE PAPERS OF THOMAS JEFFERSON are composed in Monticello, a font based on the "Pica No. 1" created in the early 1800s by Binny & Ronaldson, the first successful typefounding company in America. The face is considered historically appropriate for The Papers of Thomas Jefferson because it was used extensively in American printing during the last quarter-century of Jefferson's life, and because Jefferson himself expressed cordial approval of Binny & Ronaldson types. It was revived and rechristened Monticello in the late 1940s by the Mergenthaler Linotype Company, under the direction of C. H. Griffith and in close consultation with P. J. Conkwright, specifically for the publication of the Jefferson Papers. The font suffered some losses in its first translation to digital format in the 1980s to accommodate computerized typesetting. Matthew Carter's reinterpretation in 2002 restores the spirit and style of Binny & Ronaldson's original design of two centuries earlier.

✧

DOMINICAN UNIVERSITY LIBRARY

3 3645 00149482 5

E 302 . J442 2004 v.9
The papers of Thomas Jefferson